ALASKA

DON PITCHER

ARCTIC

Barrow

ALASKA

North

Chukchi Sea

RUSSIA

*Noatak
National
Preserve*

*Cape Krusenstern
National
Monument*

Kotzebue

*Kobuk Valley
National Park*

*Selawik
National Wildlife
Refuge*

*Bering
Land Bridge
National
Preserve*

*Koyukuk
National
Wildlife
Refuge*

Bering

Strait

Nome

Galena

*Innoko

National

Wildlife

Refuge*

RUSSIA

UNITED STATES

St. Lawrence
Island

*Bering
Strait*

Yukon

Holy
Cross

*Bering
Sea*

*Yukon Delta
National Wildlife
Refuge*

St. Matthew
Island

Bethel

Nunivak
Island

*Togiak

National Wildlife

Refuge*

Dillingham

*Katmai
National Park
and
Preserve*

St. Paul
Island

King Salmon

Pribilof
Islands

St. George
Island

*Becharof
National Wildlife
Refuge*

*Aniakchak
National
Monument
and
Preserve*

Alaska Peninsula

*Izembek
National Wildlife
Refuge*

*Alaska
Peninsula
National Wildlife
Refuge*

*Alaska Maritime
National Wildlife
Refuge*

Unalaska

The Aleutian Islands

0   100 mi

0   100 km

OCEAN

Beaufort Sea

NORTHWEST
TERRITORIES

Prudhoe
Bay

Slope

Inuvik

Arctic
National
Wildlife
Refuge

**Vuntut
National Park**

Arctic   Circle

**Gates of the Arctic
National Park
and
Preserve**

River

Mackenzie

CANADA

UNITED STATES

Porcupine

River

DEMPSTER HWY.

**Kanuti
National
Wildlife
Refuge**

**Yukon Flats
National Wildlife
Refuge**

Circle

YUKON
TERRITORY

White Mts.
Nat. Rec.
Area

Yukon

TOP OF THE
WORLD
HWY.

Fairbanks

**Yukon-Charley
Rivers
National
Preserve**

Dawson
City

River

**Nowitna
National
Wildlife
Refuge**

(2)

Delta
Junction

(2)

(5)

(6)

(4)

Tok

River

KLONDIKE HWY.

**Denali
National
Park
and
Preserve**

DENALI HWY.

(8)

(2)

TOK CUTOFF

(2)

Beaver
Creek

(4)

(6)

(3)

Talkeetna

(1)

ALASKA HWY.

Whitehorse

(4)

Watson
Lake

Glennallen

McCarthy

Haines
Jct.

(1)

Valdez

**Wrangell-St. Elias
National Park
and Preserve**

**Kluane
National Park**

(1)

**Lake Clark
National Park
and
Preserve**

Anchorage

**Kenai
National
Wildlife
Refuge**

**Chugash
National
Forest**

Cordova

(3)

(?)

Skagway

BRITISH
COLUMBIA

CASSIAR HWY.

Seward

(1)

Haines

Homer

Yakutat

Kenai Peninsula

Cook Inlet

**Kenai Fjords
National Park**

**Glacier Bay
National Park
and
Preserve**

Juneau

Gulf of Alaska

Chichagof
Island

Petersburg

Kodiak

**Admiralty
Island
National
Monument**

Sitka

**Tongass
National
Forest**

Wrangell

Hyder

Kodiak Island
**Kodiak
National Wildlife
Refuge**

Baronof
Island

**Misty
Fiords
National
Monument**

Stewart

Ketchikan

Prince of Wales
Island

PACIFIC   OCEAN

Prince Rupert

Queen
Charlotte
Islands

© AVALON TRAVEL PUBLISHING, INC.

DISCOVER ALASKA

There is something about Alaska that has always stirred the imagination. From the first migrants who crossed the Bering land bridge during the ice ages, to today's travelers escaping the madness of city life, Alaska draws people from the world over to see its wonders: dramatic mountains and immense glaciers, rivers thick with migrating salmon, lush forested islands draped in mist and mystery, northern lights dancing across a velvety winter sky. Here you can still find Native peoples following their subsistence way of life and view wildlife that is truly wild – foraging grizzlies, herds of caribou filling a valley, or walruses jousting for elbow room on a rocky shoreline. This is still a place where crabbers risk their lives in wild Bering Sea storms; where you can encounter dog teams on remote winter trails, fly by floatplane to places unchanged since primeval times, kayak in pristine inlets with eagles and breaching whales as your companions, hike in the footsteps of Klondike gold-rush miners, or hear the cry of a wolf as dusk falls.

A totem stands guard in the rain forest at Sitka National Historic Park.

Alaska is a place apart – both physically and culturally – from the rest of the United States. In Alaska, the term *wilderness* does not refer to a small enclave of the natural world surrounded by shopping malls, traffic jams, and suburban sprawl. The Great Land is so huge, so wild, so underpopulated, that it's almost incomprehensible: It falls right off the edge of your imagination. Here, like nowhere else on earth, human developments will always be dwarfed by the vastness of the land.

One aspect of Alaska that comes as a surprise to first-time visitors is its diversity. It isn't just the high mountains and forested valleys of Interior Alaska, but also vast rainforests carpeting the islands of the Inside Passage, the wildlife-rich tundra that reaches to the horizon on the Yukon Delta, the volcanic Aleutian Islands where earthquakes are an almost daily occurrence, and even a surfing beach that extends 70 miles along the Gulf of Alaska. You could spend an evening in Anchorage dining on king crab and sampling

Trees become ice sculptures in the mountains near Juneau.

French wines, and the next day take a one-hour floatplane ride to a cabin where the only sounds are singing loons and droning mosquitoes.

Alaska has not just the continent's tallest mountain (20,320-foot Mt. McKinley), but entire ranges where unnamed peaks rim the valleys. One of the most spectacular areas – Wrangell–St. Elias National Park – covers an astounding 13 million acres, with three mountain ranges, many active volcanoes, a glacier larger than Rhode Island, massive rivers, and nine of the 16 highest mountains in North America. Admiralty Island in Southeast Alaska has the highest brown bear density of any place on earth, with thick spruce forests, gorgeous alpine country, graceful bays, and one tiny Native village on the southwestern shore. Located above the Arctic Circle, Kobuk Valley National Park has sand dunes topping 250 feet in height and covering 25 square miles, but the park is so remote that only a handful of people ever visit.

I first came to Alaska more than 25 years ago to visit a friend working as a cook at a geology exploration camp. When I stepped off

young brown bears at play on Kodiak Island

© DON PITCHER

the plane in Juneau, I was awestruck by the panorama of glaciers, mountains, and rainforest. A week later, I took the ferry back south, watching the fishing and logging towns slip past, feeling the mist on my face, and wondering about a single light coming from a quiet cove where someone's waterside cabin stood – surrounded by wilderness. I knew I would be back.

In the intervening years I have stood in the fog on St. Paul Island and watched as hundreds of murres, auklets, puffins, and cormorants nested on cliffs that plunged 200 feet to the Bering Sea. I have paddled canoes across remote lakes, surprised a tiny spotted fawn on Kodiak Island, watched hundreds of eagles dotting snow-covered trees along the Chilkat River, marveled as enormous pieces of ice crashed from Childs Glacier into the Copper River, and dip-netted salmon with my children at China Poot Creek.

In *Travels in Alaska,* John Muir wrote of his 1880 discovery of Glacier Bay: "At length the clouds lifted a little, and beneath their gray fringes I saw the berg-filled expanse of the bay, and the feet of the mountains that stand about it, and the imposing fronts of five

commercial fishing boats in a busy Alaskan harbor

huge glaciers, the nearest being immediately beneath me. This was my first general view of Glacier Bay, a solitude of ice and snow and newborn rocks, dim, dreary, mysterious. I held the ground I had so dearly won for an hour or two, sheltering myself from the blast as best I could, while with benumbed fingers I sketched what I could see of the landscape, and wrote a few lines in my notebook. Then, breasting the snow again, crossing the shifting avalanche slopes and torrents, I reached camp about dark, wet and weary and glad."

It's been more than 125 years since those words were written, but visitors to Alaska can still experience incredible places where the natural world remains. There really is something magical about Alaska, something that gets in your soul and won't let go. If you haven't been to the Great Land before, you're in for a treat. If you have, you will almost certainly want to return.

Mountain goats scramble up a cliff in Glacier Bay National Park.

Contents

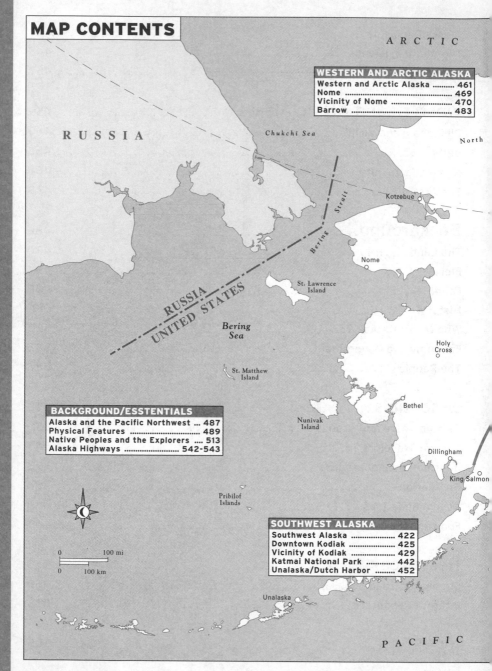

MAP CONTENTS

A R C T I C

RUSSIA

Chukchi Sea

North

Kotzebue

Bering Strait

RUSSIA
UNITED STATES

Nome

St. Lawrence
Island

Bering
Sea

Holy
Cross

St. Matthew
Island

Bethel

Nunivak
Island

Dillingham

King Salmon

Pribilof
Islands

0   100 mi

0   100 km

Unalaska

P A C I F I C

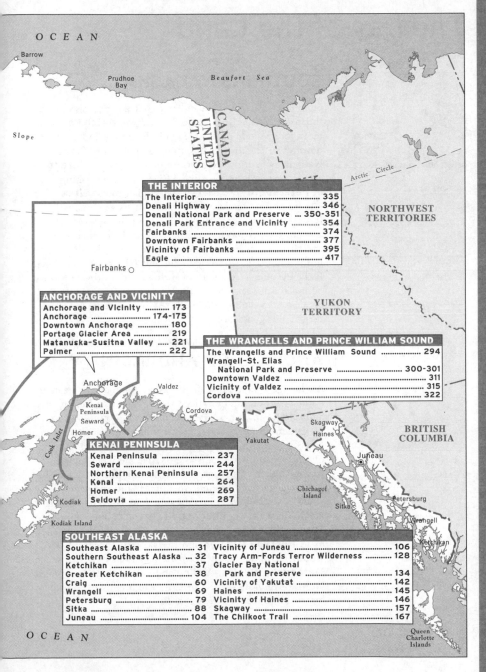

13

O C E A N

Barrow

Prudhoe Bay

Beaufort Sea

CANADA
UNITED STATES

Slope

Arctic Circle

NORTHWEST TERRITORIES

Fairbanks

YUKON TERRITORY

Anchorage   Valdez

Kenai Peninsula
Seward
Homer
Cook Inlet

Cordova

Skagway
Haines
Yakutat

BRITISH COLUMBIA

Juneau

Chichagof Island
Sitka
Petersburg
Wrangell

Kodiak
Kodiak Island

Ketchikan

Queen Charlotte Islands

O C E A N

The Lay of the Land

SOUTHEAST ALASKA

Southeast is Alaska's "Panhandle," a coastal region dissected by the Inside Passage. The southernmost town, **Ketchikan,** is famous for its totem poles, steep hillside setting, and old-timey downtown. The town is a jumping-off point for Misty Fiords National Monument and Prince of Wales Island. **Wrangell** acts as a gateway for the Stikine River, while the fishing town of **Petersburg** shows off its Norwegian roots. **Sitka** has a remote setting on Baronof Island, but its attractions make it worth the detour. **Juneau** is both the state capital and a major destination for travelers, with Mendenhall Glacier, the Mt. Roberts tram, and other adventures. Nearby are the fjords and glaciers of Tracy Arm and Glacier Bay National Park. The quiet settlements of **Haines** and nearby **Skagway** occupy the northern end of the Inside Passage. Along the Gulf of Alaska lies the town of **Yakutat,** with fishing lodges and surprisingly good surfing.

ANCHORAGE AND VICINITY

Anchorage is home to half the state's population, an international airport, and a variety of lodging places, restaurants, and cultural amenities. Hanging baskets of flowers and colorful gardens decorate Town Square in front of the Performing Arts Center. A few blocks away is the Anchorage Museum of History and Art. The Alaska Native Heritage Center, the Alaska Heritage Museum, and Alaska Aviation Heritage Museum are scattered around Anchorage, and the paved Tony Knowles Coastal Trail skirts the shoreline. Great day-hiking is a short drive away in **Chugach State Park,** or head south to **Turnagain Arm** with its enormous tides and beluga whales, or to **Portage Glacier** and the ski resort town of **Girdwood.** The booming towns of Wasilla and Palmer occupy the **Matanuska-Susitna Valley** an hour north of Anchorage. North of the valley, the Talkeetna Mountains rise abruptly, bisected by a road over Hatcher Pass.

KENAI PENINSULA

The Kenai Peninsula is perfect for quick escapes into the wild. Two primary roads—the 125-mile Seward Highway and the 140-mile Sterling Highway—cross the peninsula, which is dominated by Chugach National Forest, Kenai National Wildlife Refuge, and Kenai Fjords National Park. The last of these is based in **Seward,** where you can join boat or kayak trips to view park glaciers, whales, and seabird colonies, hike to Exit Glacier, or visit the fun and educational Alaska SeaLife Center. The off-the-beaten-path settlement of **Hope** has a picture-perfect collection of gold rush–era buildings along Turnagain Arm. The towns of **Kenai** and **Soldotna** are bases for sports fishing on the Kenai and Russian Rivers, both of which attract hundreds of anglers when the salmon are running. The Sterling Highway ends at the hip little town of **Homer,** with its spectacular vistas across Kachemak Bay, fine lodging and restaurants, and abundant art galleries.

THE WRANGELLS AND PRINCE WILLIAM SOUND

This section of Alaska encompasses the **Copper River Valley** and Wrangell Mountains, along with Prince William Sound. The Glenn Highway crosses the northern edge, passing Matanuska Glacier and Eureka Summit before dropping to the town of **Glennallen.** The Richardson Highway heads north to Tok and south through Thompson Pass before plunging into Keystone Canyon. The road ends at **Valdez,** terminus of the Trans-Alaska Pipeline. America's largest park, Wrangell–St. Elias National Park is considered by many Alaskans more interesting (and less crowded) than Denali. The rough McCarthy Road leads 50 miles into the heart of the park, where the tiny town of **McCarthy** and the old mining buildings of **Kennicott** provide a mix of history, food, lodging, and wilderness access. Ferries cross Prince William Sound, providing access to the fishing town of **Cordova.** Ferries also connect Cordova with **Whittier,** and a 2.5-mile tunnel provides a road and rail link to Anchorage.

THE INTERIOR

Interior Alaska is capped by Mt. McKinley, along with the rest of the towering Alaska Range and hundreds of miles of hilly and forested country. **Talkeetna** is a base for McKinley flightseeing trips and mountaineering expeditions. Farther north is the Denali Highway and **Denali National State Park,** the main attraction for visitors. The city of **Fairbanks** is home to two large military bases and the University of Alaska. Don't miss the University of Alaska Museum of the North, Pioneer Park, the ice museum at Chena Hot Springs, Gold Dredge No. 8, and a riverboat tour down the Chena and Tanana Rivers. The Dalton Highway heads north across the Arctic Circle, paralleling the Trans-Alaska Pipeline all the way to Prudhoe Bay. Southeast of Fairbanks are **Delta Junction** and **Tok,** while the gold-rush town of **Eagle** is accessible via an arduous road off the Alaska Highway.

SOUTHWEST ALASKA

Southwest Alaska includes **Kodiak Island,** the **Alaska Peninsula,** the **Aleutian Islands,** and the **Pribilof Islands.** It's ruggedly beautiful, but the weather is a mix of rain, fog, and wind. Kodiak Island has forests on the northeast end that give way to tundra. The fishing town of **Kodiak** features the Baranov Museum, an old Russian Orthodox church, and hiking trails through Fort Abercrombie State Park. Country roads head south to remote beaches and wandering bison. Bear-viewing is a major attraction in the region, with day trips from the town of Kodiak, along with lodging and camping at Brooks Camp within Katmai National Park. The Aleutian Island fishing town of **Unalaska** has two outstanding historical museums, a Russian Orthodox church, and various World War II sites. Even more remote are the Pribilof Islands, consisting primarily of **St. George Island** and **St. Paul Island,** where wildlife attracts birders and photographers.

WESTERN AND ARCTIC ALASKA

This is true bush Alaska, where the marshy tundra, powerful rivers, and high mountains are almost untouched by human developments. **Dillingham** serves as a commercial fishing center for the Bristol Bay region and as a jumping off point for Wood–Tikchik State Park. West of here, **Round Island** is the best spot to see walruses. **Bethel** sits at the mouth of the wide Kuskokwim River, with the Yukon Delta National Wildlife Refuge on all sides. Farther north, the Seward Peninsula juts into the Bering Sea, positioning the old gold-mining town of **Nome** just 190 miles from Siberia. The Arctic region occupies an enormous expanse of country dotted with modest towns at **Kotzebue** and **Barrow,** along with **Prudhoe Bay.** Barrow draws visitors to its Inupiat Heritage Center and the chance to dip toes in the Arctic Ocean. Intrepid adventurers hike in spectacular Gates of the Arctic National Park, or float rivers within Arctic National Wildlife Refuge.

Planning Your Trip

For many tourists, planning an Alaskan adventure entails going to a travel agent or website and booking an all-inclusive voyage on the HMS *Geezer*, where everything is packaged neatly for mass-market vacationers. Cruises *do* provide an introduction to the state, but people who really want to see Alaska need to get off the mega-ships and away from the canned bus tours, shops selling made-in-China totems, and "eco-adventures" where you paddle a kayak around the harbor. Independent travelers have a slightly more difficult time arranging a trip to Alaska, but they will be rewarded a hundredfold with a more authentic experience. With the right planning, an Alaskan adventure can be the trip of a lifetime.

The type of travel you arrange depends, of course, upon your interests, budget, and how much time you have. Retirees driving the Alaska Highway have very different needs from families riding the ferry to Juneau or mountaineers heading out on a grand wilderness adventure. Sit down with this book and see what works for you.

Getting around such a vast state forces visitors to put transportation at the core of planning, especially when ferry and train travel are involved. Don't schedule your trip too tightly since weather delays or mechanical problems may appear at the most inopportune moment. Leave some time to relax in your schedule, even if you have just a week. Those with specific must-see destinations such as bear-viewing flights, bus tours into Denali National Park, or three-day sea kayaking trips should be sure to make reservations well ahead of time. Lodging places in such prime spots as Brooks Camp within Katmai National Park may fill a year ahead of the peak summer season.

A good starting point when planning a trip to Alaska is the Alaska State Vacation Planner, distributed by the Alaska Travel Industry Association (907/929-2200 or 800/862-5275); find the same information online at www.travelalaska.com. Other contacts are listed throughout this book, and you can visit the author's websites (www.donpitcher.com and www.explorealaska.info) for links to hundreds of Alaska websites.

WHEN TO GO

Alaska is primarily a summer destination, and the vast majority of the 1.5 million annual visitors travel mid-May to mid-September, with the peak in July and August. The advantages of summer travel are obvious: long days, warmer weather, all the attractions are operating, and children are out of school. Not to mention the return of salmon and the emergence of bears and other wildlife. Because of Alaska's northern location, spring arrives late and much of the state does not green up until mid-May. The road into Denali National Park is closed by snow until late May, and the landscape can be rather bleak before leaves emerge. Farther north in the Arctic, summer doesn't really arrive until July, while Alaska's mild Panhandle can have daffodils and green grass in April. The month of June sees fewer tourists and the weather (especially in Southeast Alaska) is generally drier. Summer has its drawbacks too, including mosquitoes and other insectoid annoyances, high lodging prices, and crowded venues across the state.

Fall comes early across much of Alaska, and it isn't uncommon to see snow creeping down the Alaska Range in late August. Autumn colors (primarily yellows on the aspen, birch, and willows, with reds and oranges in alpine areas) typically peak in early September across Interior Alaska, and a couple of weeks later for Southcentral Alaska.

Days shorten dramatically by October—en route to the December 21 winter solstice—but longer nights also make Alaska's famous northern lights visible in the sky. Winter visitors come to view them (best time is in March when temperatures have moderated), to watch such events as the Iditarod, Yukon Quest, and World Ice Art Championships. Cross-country and downhill skiing, snowmobiling, and skating are popular with both locals and winter visitors. Mid-winter temperatures in northern and Interior Alaska can be bitterly cold, but Anchorage and points south are typically milder, especially by mid-February.

Spring (especially April) is the ugly season, at least until the trees leaf out. Most winter activities are closed and the summer fun hasn't cranked up, so do what Alaskans do and head to Hawaii instead.

WHAT TO TAKE

Wearing your clothing in layers allows you to add or remove items, depending on the temperature or your level of exertion. Start out with a T-shirt, thermal, or polypropylene top (and bottom). Summer visitors will want to bring a light, waterproof jacket (Gore-Tex works well) and rain pants, plus a sweater or polypro pullover for warmth. Hiking boots are recommended if you plan to spend any time away from town, but good running shoes are fine for many purposes. Hikers in Southeast Alaska will need rubber boots (wait to buy them there to find the right kind) and heavy-duty raingear (Helly Hansen or Grundens recommended). Bring a warm cap and gloves. A hooded parka comes in handy, though a poncho is adequate and light and can double as a ground cloth or awning. Very few restaurants expect dressy attire, so leave it at home unless you're trying to impress the bears and moose.

Winter visitors should be prepared for the cold, especially anyone planning a trip to Fairbanks, where temperatures are often well below zero, sometimes plummeting to -40°F or lower. Recommended winter wear for these extreme conditions includes parkas, heavy winter boots, snow pants, mittens, and warm headgear. Local stores have the appropriate winter wear. Southcentral winters are milder, with Anchorage temperatures often in the teens or single digits in January. Travelers to Southeast Alaska should expect a mix of snow, rain, sleet, freezing rain, wind, and occasional sun. There's a reason so few tourists visit Juneau in the off-season!

Technology has changed the definition of "travel essentials," and most Alaskan tourists—and locals—wouldn't think of a trip without their cell phone, though coverage varies and can be nonexistent in remote areas. Travelers are also increasingly carrying laptop computers to check email, store and show off digital photos, and keep up on the latest news. They're especially useful when set up for wireless Internet, which is becoming the norm in hotels, coffee shops, and other businesses. Global positioning system (GPS) units are popular with backcountry hikers and sea kayakers, but are still rather spendy.

Bug dope and headnets are essential for hikers and campers, especially in Interior and northern Alaska. Campers should also be sure to carry waterproof matches, a sleeping pad, synthetic-fiber sleeping bag, high-quality tent, bear spray, and other camping essentials. Practice putting up your tent, cooking on your camp stove, and so on, before you set out. Categorize and separate all your things in plastic bags or stuff sacks; pack it that way for convenient access and protection from moisture.

Explore Alaska

BEST OF ALASKA

This trip is perfect if you only have a week and want a taste of Alaska. It uses Anchorage as a base, while mixing travel by train, bus, car, boat, and air.

Day 1

Fly into Anchorage, settle into your hotel, and then cruise downtown to check out the flowers, gift shops, and visitor center. Enjoy a fine seafood dinner at Simon & Seaforts, where you can sip an 11 P.M. cocktail as the sun arcs across the summer sky over Cook Inlet.

Day 2

Hop on the 8 A.M. **Alaska Railroad** northbound train, arriving in Denali National Park eight hours later. (The luxurious GoldStar railcars cost more, but have open-air viewing platforms to take in the grand scenery along the way.) Stay at one of the hotels just outside the park entrance; Denali Bluffs Hotel or Denali Crow's Nest are good choices.

Day 3

Join an all-day bus tour into **Denali National Park.** It's eight hours round-trip to the visitor center at Eielson (fine views of Mt. McKinley when it's out), or 11 hours if you want to go all the way out to Wonder Lake and back. This tour is the highlight of many Alaskan visitors' trips, and you're likely to see grizzlies, moose, caribou, Dall sheep, and the occasional wolf along the way.

Day 4

After a morning visit to the Denali Visitor Center and a short hike, take the noon train back south, getting to Anchorage that evening. It won't get dark, so you might as well take a stroll out the scenic Tony Knowles Coastal Trail.

Day 5

Rent a car and drive 225 miles down the Kenai Peninsula to the town of **Homer.** There's plenty to see and do, from sea kayaking and strolling the beach to shopping and fine dining at Homestead Restaurant or Café Cups. If you're looking for a spectacular bay vista, stay at the appropriately named Majestic View B&B.

Day 6

This is a day that could go in three completely different directions. If you have the cash, hop on one of the all-day bear-viewing flights to **Katmai National Park.** Sea kayaking is a less expensive option, and True North Adventures has an all-day trip that includes a water taxi to Yukon Island, where you join a guided kayak adventure. The third option is to hop on an early morning halibut fishing charter boat. You're almost certain of getting your limit, and fish over 200 pounds are occasionally pulled in. Coal Point Seafood will process, freeze, and ship your catch.

Days 7-8

Head out early and drive back north to Whit- tier. (It is 191 miles from Homer to Whittier; allow at least four hours travel time plus any tunnel delays.) In Whittier, take a leisurely five-hour glacier tour to Blackstone Bay. Seals lounge on the icebergs, and several active glaciers are visible at once. Spend the night in Girdwood and then continue on to Anchorage the next morning, or return to Anchorage late and fly out the next day. You'll want more time for your next Alaskan adventure!

ALASKA'S HEARTLAND

This trip provides the chance to see the highlights of Southcentral and Interior Alaska, and could easily be extended to three weeks or shortened to one week. It is especially popular with families, since flights into Anchorage are relatively cheap with lots of car rental or RV rental options available.

Day 1

Fly into **Anchorage,** get a rental car, then find your hotel and settle in. (If you haven't already, make reservations for your trip to Denali on Day 4.) If you have time, you may want to get oriented by heading to the downtown visitor center. Or if the weather cooperates, take a stroll along the Coastal Trail; it offers great vistas across Cook Inlet and is readily accessible from downtown.

Day 2

Head to New Sagaya's for an espresso, croissant, and sack lunch. Spend the day exploring the Anchorage Museum of History and Art and the Alaska Native Heritage Center, or heading out for a short hike in Chugach State Park. Overnight in Anchorage again.

Day 3

Get an early start since this is a long day. Drive north on the Parks Highway, stopping in **Talkeetna** (115 miles) for lunch. If you want to add a one-hour flightseeing trip over the park (recommended), you should probably spend the night in Talkeetna, adding another day to your trip. Otherwise, continue north to the Denali Park area (150 miles from Anchorage) where a range of lodging and camping options are available.

Day 4

This is your day to explore **Denali National Park** by tour bus, but advance reservations are absolutely necessary for this all-day adventure (many people book several months ahead of time to be sure of space). Many buses turn around near Eielson, where you'll get a fine view of Mt. McKinley (if it isn't obscured by clouds), but you could also ride to Wonder Lake and back (11 long hours) or take a shorter wildlife-focused tour. Return to your hotel or campsite for a second night.

Day 5

Drive north on the the Parks Highway, stopping in Nenana for a quick visit before rolling into **Fairbanks** for the night (125 miles). Head over to Pioneer Park to see the historical buildings, ride the kiddie train, do a bit of shopping, or take in a musical comedy show, but be sure to stick around for dinner at Alaska's best salmon bake.

Day 6

Set aside a couple of hours to see the University of Alaska Museum of the North and other nearby sights, including the Large Animal Research Station (musk ox and caribou) and Creamer's Field (great birding). Two fun—though touristy—options are an afternoon Riverboat Discovery tour and a visit to Gold Dredge No. 8.

Day 7

Check out of your hotel and get an early start. Drive to **Chena Hot Springs** for a soak in the wonderful outdoor pool and a tour of the Ice Museum (don't miss this), before turning south on the Richardson Highway. Make a short stop at Santa Claus House in the town of **North Pole,** and bed down in **Delta Junction,** home to historic Rika's Roadhouse.

Day 8

Head south on the Richardson Highway through beautiful country around Summit Lake (several nice day hikes in this area) and on to **Glennallen** for a gas-and-groceries stop before ending the day in quiet **Copper Center** (165 miles). Stay at the historic Copper Center Lodge and head to the **Wrangell-St. Elias National Park** Visitor Center for an introduction to this part of Alaska.

Day 9

Drive to the little town of **Chitina** (50 miles) with its century-old buildings, dirt streets, and fish wheels before continuing out a scenic 60-mile dirt road to **McCarthy** in the heart of Wrangell–St. Elias. (Many rental car companies prohibit driving on this road, but a shuttle service is available.) Food and lodging can be found in McCarthy and nearby **Kennicott,** where you can tour the old copper mine buildings or take a glacier hike.

Day 10

Drive back out to the main (Richardson) highway and head south to **Valdez,** with short stops at Worthington Glacier and Keystone Canyon en route. Valdez is only 180 miles, but plan to take at least six hours. Take the fast ferry to **Cordova,** an out-of-the-way fishing town, and bed down for the night. A good place is The Reluctant Fisherman.

Day 11

Drive the 50-mile Copper River Highway (gravel) to the Million Dollar Bridge and Childs Glacier, where you could spend several hours just watching enormous chunks of ice calving into the Copper River. Excellent hiking is available, along with lovely campsites if you don't want to spend the night back in Cordova.

Day 12

Take the morning ferry to **Whittier** and drive through the tunnel to Portage and then south to **Seward** (90 miles) where you can visit the Alaska SeaLife Center and enjoy dinner at Yoly's Bistro or Christo's Palace. Hotels and in-town campsites are both available.

Day 13

Take a half-day boat tour into Resurrection Bay

or a hike to Exit Glacier, and then head north in the afternoon to **Soldotna** (150 miles). Bring your fishing pole if you want to join the throngs of anglers catching red salmon on the Kenai and Russian Rivers. The Aspen Hotel and the Kenai River Lodge both offer riverside accommodations in Soldotna.

Day 14

Turning south, the Sterling Highway ends in **Homer,** where the Homer Spit, Islands and Ocean Center, Pratt Museum, and art galleries are all big draws. You'll find lots of fine restaurants and lodging places, or you can pitch a tent on the Spit (but make sure it's anchored well against the wind).

Day 15

Take a Kachemak Bay tour to Gull Island and **Halibut Cove** or a day trip to **Seldovia,** returning to Homer for the evening. Other options include halibut charter fishing or the budget option: try your luck in the Fishing Hole.

Day 16

It's a five-plus-hour drive to **Anchorage,** but if you get going early enough you could still have fun along the way or in the big city on those long summer days. If you have kids along, take them to H2Oasis Indoor Waterpark as a treat. Couples should head to Marx Bros. Café for the ultimate Alaskan dining experience.

KODIAK ADVENTURE

This trip begins in Anchorage, where you rent a car for a voyage that includes the Kenai Peninsula, but focuses on Kodiak Island. It could easily be extended a couple of days with additional time in Kodiak or Homer. The schedule is entirely dependent upon the ferry (it doesn't run every day), so make those arrangements before you set up other travel plans.

Day 1

It's a five-hour drive from Anchorage to **Homer,** where you can camp out on the Homer Spit or stay in a hotel, cabin, or B&B. Eat dinner at Fat Olives or Café Cups, and check out the local sights that include Islands and Ocean Center, Pratt Museum, and shopping.

Day 2

Take the state ferry to **Kodiak.** This 10-hour sailing is often an overnight run, and if so, you can either take a berth or spread out a sleeping bag in the solarium. The Fish & Wildlife Service naturalist onboard will point out birds and whales along the way, especially around the remote Barren Islands. (Be sure to take medicine for seasickness.) In Kodiak, stay at a local hotel or camp out at Ft. Abercrombie State Park, a great place to hike in the moss-draped rainforest or to explore rocky shoreline for nesting puffins.

Day 3

Start the day at Mill Bay Coffee and Pastry for authentically French treats, and then take the Chiniak Highway south of town to Pasagshak Bay (good salmon fishing), past a rocket launch complex and grazing bison, to **Fossil Beach** with its fossilized shells and sandy shoreline. Return the same way, but take a detour out Chiniak Road to sample the fruit wines at Kodiak Island Winery. Back in Kodiak, hop onboard a Galley Gourmet dinner and wildlife cruise to Long Island for a relaxing meal in a beautiful setting, or stay on land for fresh sushi at The Old Power House Restaurant.

Day 4

Time to see the **brown bears** for which Kodiak is so famous. A number of air taxis offer half-day floatplane trips (around $450) to salmon streams on Kodiak or the coast of Katmai National Park; one of the best is Rolan Ruoss of Sea Hawk Air. A cheaper alternative would be a hike on one of the many trails around Kodiak, including ones up Pyramid Peak or Barometer Mountain.

Day 5

This is a day to relax and explore places you have missed. Check out the Baranov Museum with its remarkable gift shop selling fine Russian china and nesting dolls, the old Russian Orthodox Church, the Alutiiq Museum, and the Kodiak National Wildlife Refuge Visitor Center in town, or join a sea kayaking day trip from Orcas Unlimited or Alaskan Wilderness Adventures.

Days 6-7

Spend the day on a halibut charter fishing boat or along one of the road-accessible creeks when the salmon are running. Take the ferry overnight from Kodiak to **Whittier** and drive back to Anchorage, where you began your adventure.

NORTHERN EXPOSURE

This trip begins and ends in Fairbanks, with long day trips launching out to adventures in all directions, including the Dalton Highway all the way to Prudhoe Bay. Several airlines have flights into Fairbanks, or you can start from Anchorage and take the train or a rental car north.

Days 1-2

Fairbanks is a good base for day trips into surrounding areas, and has an abundance of lodging and dining options. Stay at the budget-priced Golden North Motel, or find more upscale accommodations at Sophie Station Hotel or Westmark Hotel. Fans of Thai food will enjoy a visit to Lemongrass Thai Cuisine, and Lavelle's Bistro serves gourmet meals in a classy setting. While in Fairbanks, be sure to see the University of Alaska Museum of the North, Pioneer Park, Large Animal Research Station, and Creamer's Field (great birding).

Day 3

It's an easy 1.5-hour drive to **Chena Hot Springs,** where indoor and outdoor pools are available, along with a year-round Ice Museum that houses amazingly intricate carved pieces by a world-renowned ice sculptor. Several streams offer good fishing in the area, and the resort has lodging, food, and campsites.

Day 4

Today's long day trip goes out the paved-and-gravel **Steese Highway** to Circle, 161 miles each way from Fairbanks. Heading north, you may want to stop in the settlement of Fox to

Day 5

Take a break from travel to spend time in Fairbanks, shopping downtown, enjoying a canoe float down the Chena River, or visiting the Tanana Valley Farmers Market (held Wednesdays and Saturdays) for local arts and crafts, baked goods, and other treats.

Day 6

Another long trip into the country, this time on the 150-mile **Elliott Highway** northwest of Fairbanks. The main attractions here are access to hiking trails in the White Mountains and Manley Hot Springs at the end of the road, the last 80 miles of which are gravel. The historic Manley Roadhouse—here since 1906—has rustic accommodations and homemade food.

Days 7-8

Time to head north, way north up the **Dalton Highway,** where flat tires and broken windshields are common occurrences. Don't try this in a standard rental car; Arctic Outfitters has vehicles set up specifically for travel on the "Haul Road," which parallels the Trans-Alaska Pipeline to the oilfields at Prudhoe Bay. A less stressful trip is to join one of the bus tours—some combine bus travel up with a flight back—from Fairbanks to the Arctic Circle (200 miles) or Prudhoe Bay/Deadhorse (500 miles). Lodging is available in Fairbanks and Coldfoot (where most buses stop for the night).

take a tour of historic Gold Dredge No. 8 and to see the Trans-Alaska Pipeline. The road climbs over scenic Cleary Summit, down to the old gold settlement of Chatanika (interesting mining artifacts), to Davidson Ditch Historical Site (good for gold panning), over Twelvemile Summit (nice alpine hike), and finally to the Yukon River town of Circle. There are no accommodations in Circle, so consider camping at Upper Chatanika or Cripple Creek for the night. Hikers can just take the road to Twelvemile Summit for a fun day hike and then return to Fairbanks (170 miles round-trip) for an easier day.

FERRYING THROUGH THE INSIDE PASSAGE

Alaska's Inside Passage consists of thousands of islands spread in a long "Panhandle" hanging from the rest of the state. Most towns here are off the road system, with access by air or sea. Cruise ships are the most popular way to visit Southeast, but the Alaska Marine Highway ferry system is a wonderful alternative for independent travelers. There are all sorts of possible routes, and your options depend upon how much time you have, the ferry schedule, and, of course, money. The routing below begins and ends in Seattle.

Alaska-bound ferries depart from Bellingham, Washington, and passengers flying into Seattle will need to take a shuttle bus from Sea-Tac Airport. The ferries run daily during summer and have comfortable cabins, reasonably priced dining, and a Forest Service naturalist onboard, but budget travelers can spread out their sleeping bags in the solarium. (The trip below could be extended by a day or two by taking the Inter-Island Ferry from Ketchikan to Prince of Wales, where you can drive north up this large island and catch a second ferry to Wrangell.)

Days 1-2

It's a 36-hour ferry ride from Bellingham to the first Alaska stop, **Ketchikan,** famous for its rainforests, totem poles, and picturesque waterside setting. The town has good bus service, but a rental car makes it easy to get around in the rain, especially if you're heading out the road or camping at Ward Lake. Local attractions include historic Creek Street, famous for its buildings on pilings that once housed the local red light district, a fine Forest Service visitor center, and gorgeous collections of totem poles at Saxman, Totem Heritage Center, and Totem Bight State Historical Park.

Day 3

Take a day trip to spectacular **Misty Fiords National Monument,** accessible by boat tours, floatplane trips, or a combination of the two.

Days 4-5

Hop back on the ferry for the five-hour ride to **Wrangell** with its cozy harbor centered around Chief Shakes Island. The big attraction here is the Stikine River, and several companies have half-day jetboat trips up the river to an active glacier and a relaxing riverside hot springs. Also popular are trips to see black bears at Anan Creek.

Days 6-7

Next up is the ferry ride though scenic Wrangell Narrows to **Petersburg,** where snow-capped mountains create a backdrop for this pretty town known for its Norwegian heritage. Day trips to LeConte Glacier are popular.

Days 8-9

Take the ferry north and west to remote **Sitka,**

located on the Pacific Ocean side of Baranof Island. The town hosts the Alaska Raptor Center, Sitka National Historical Park (totem poles, Native arts, and the old Russian Bishop's house), and other interesting sights, but also has fun hiking trails, good fishing, and one of the finest restaurants in Southeast, Ludvig's Bistro.

Days 10-11

The fast ferry *Fairweather* provides frequent service connecting Sitka with the next stop, **Juneau,** considered by many the nation's loveliest state capital. The city is home to the Alaska State Museum, a fun tramway up Mt. Roberts, an interesting salmon hatchery, and easily accessible Mendenhall Glacier. One could easily spend several days here checking out the sights, hiking a couple of trails, taking a day trip by floatplane to Taku Glacier Lodge or a helicopter flight onto Juneau Icefield, or just enjoying the fine dining, funky bars, rainforest ziplines, and other adventures. There are enough roads and out-of-the-way places in Juneau to justify renting a car.

Day 12

Take an all-day boat tour to **Tracy Arm** onboard the Adventure Bound boat to see an active glacier up close and personal, or tack on a couple of days for a side trip to **Glacier Bay National Park**. The latter requires a flight from Juneau to Gustavus, followed by an all-day boat tour into this spectacular bay. Lodging and food are available (Gustavus Inn is especially nice), or you could pitch a tent at the Park Service campground.

Day 13

Haines is the next ferry stop, with the old white clapboard buildings of Fort Seward as a focal point. The Chilkat River is popular for summertime floats and wintertime eagle viewing. Stay at Hotel Halsingland—in one of the old fort buildings—and walk down the hill to Fireweed Restaurant for meals.

Day 14

A private ferry service provides fast connections between Haines and **Skagway,** an amazingly busy town packed with thousands of cruise ship passengers all summer. The town's downtown contains more than a dozen buildings within Klondike Gold Rush National Historical Park, and the narrow-gauge trains from the White Pass & Yukon Route Railroad take visitors on an incredible ride to the summit of the pass at the Canadian border. The town is the starting point for the difficult Chilkoot Trail, a four-day trudge up the route traversed by the miners more than a century ago. Skagway has several fine restaurants (try Alaskan Gourmet Café) and comfortable B&Bs.

Day 15

It's the end of the line, so turn back south to Juneau on the ferry (or hop on one of the frequent flights from Skagway). You could return by ferry all the way to Bellingham, but an Alaska Air flight from Juneau gets you home quicker.

SOUTHEAST ALASKA

For many people, the name Alaska conjures up images of bitterly cold winters and sunshine-packed summers, of great rivers, enormous snowcapped mountains, and open tundra reaching to the horizon. If that's your vision of the state, you've missed its Garden of Eden, the Southeast. Almost entirely boxed in by British Columbia, Southeast Alaska's "Panhandle" or Inside Passage stretches 500 miles along the North American coast. Everything about this beautiful, lush country is water-based: the rain that falls on the land, the glaciers that drop from giant icefields, and the ocean that surrounds it all. Gray-blue clouds play a constant game of hide-and-seek with the verdant islands; deep fjords drive up between snow-covered summits; waterfalls plummet hundreds of feet through the evergreen forests to feed rivers rich in salmon; brown bears prowl the creeks in search of fish; bald eagles perch on treetops beside the rugged, rocky coastline; and great blue glaciers press down toward the sea.

ORIENTATION
The Land

Nearly 95 percent of the Southeast is federal property, most of it within Tongass National Forest and Glacier Bay National Park. The Panhandle is composed of a mountainous mainland and hundreds of islands, varying from rocky reefs that barely jut out of the sea at low tide to some of the largest islands in North America. Collectively, these islands are called the Alexander Archipelago. This ragged shoreline stretches for more than 11,000 miles and

HIGHLIGHTS

◖ Totem Bight State Historical Park:
Ketchikan is home to several notable totem pole collections, but Totem Bight takes the prize with a gorgeous waterside setting, historic clan house, and lush forests (page 41).

◖ Misty Fiords National Monument:
Almost always encased in clouds, this wilderness has spectacular cliffs that plummet into deep fiords. Tours by air and boat are offered from Ketchikan (page 52).

◖ The Stikine River: Jetboat trips from Wrangell are the main attraction for visitors to this mighty river with its hidden glaciers and relaxing hot springs (page 76).

◖ Sitka National Historical Park: This gem of a park encompasses Sitka's rich Tlingit and Russian heritage with historic buildings, totems bordering a wooded trail, and the chance to watch Native artisans at work (page 91).

◖ Mendenhall Glacier: Southeast's best-known drive-up glacier, Mendenhall has fine hiking trails and a fascinating visitor center. It's just a few miles north of Juneau (page 110).

◖ Tracy Arm – Fords Terror Wilderness:
Almost unknown outside Alaska, this wilderness area is a popular destination for day tours by boat from Juneau. It's a great place to watch ice calving from the glacier or to see seals resting atop icebergs (page 126).

◖ Visiting Glacier Bay: Made famous by John Muir, this national park has towering mountains, thundering glaciers, abundant wildlife, fun day trips, and memorable sea kayaking adventures (page 133).

◖ Fort Seward: Looking more like a New England village than a fort, this picture-perfect collection of historic Haines buildings now houses a variety of artistic, commercial, and cultural endeavors (page 147).

◖ Klondike Gold Rush National Historical Park: The town of Skagway's gold rush heritage is preserved in a dozen classic –

LOOK FOR ◖ TO FIND RECOMMENDED SIGHTS, ACTIVITIES, DINING, AND LODGING.

and immaculately restored – downtown buildings that now hum with tourism all summer (page 159).

◖ White Pass & Yukon Route Railroad:
Originally built to haul miners into the Klondike and gold back out, this narrow-gage railroad now fills with travelers and hikers. It may be the most scenic train ride in America (page 159).

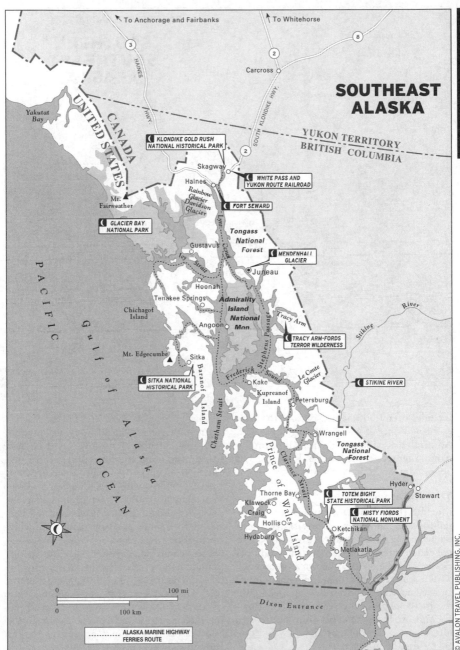

To Anchorage and Fairbanks

To Whitehorse

③

②

⑧

Carcross

Yakutat Bay

HAINES HWY.

SOUTH KLONDIKE HWY.

SOUTHEAST ALASKA

CANADA

UNITED STATES

YUKON TERRITORY
BRITISH COLUMBIA

KLONDIKE GOLD RUSH
NATIONAL HISTORICAL PARK

②

Skagway

WHITE PASS AND
YUKON ROUTE RAILROAD

Haines

Rainbow
Glacier
Davidson
Glacier

Mt.
Fairweather

FORT SEWARD

GLACIER BAY
NATIONAL PARK

Tongass
National
Forest

Lynn Canal

Gustavus

MENDENHALL
GLACIER

P A C I F I C

Icy Strait

Juneau

Hoonah

Tenakee Springs

Admirality
Island
National
Mon.

G u l f

Chichagof
Island

Angoon

Tracy Arm

Stephens Passage

Stikine   River

Mt. Edgecumbe

Sitka

Baranof Island

Chatham Strait

Frederick

Sound

TRACY ARM-FORDS
TERROR WILDERNESS

Le Conte
Glacier

STIKINE RIVER

SITKA NATIONAL
HISTORICAL PARK

o f

Kake

Kupreanof
Island

Petersburg

A l a s k a

Wrangell

Tongass
National
Forest

O C E A N

Prince

Clarence Strait

of

Hyder

Thorne Bay

Stewart

Klawock

TOTEM BIGHT
STATE HISTORICAL PARK

Craig

Wales Island

Hollis

MISTY FIORDS
NATIONAL MONUMENT

Hydaburg

Ketchikan

Metlakatla

0   100 mi

0   100 km

Dixon Entrance

ALASKA MARINE HIGHWAY
FERRIES ROUTE

© AVALON TRAVEL PUBLISHING, INC.

includes over 1,000 named islands, the largest being Prince of Wales, Chichagof, Baranof, Admiralty, Revillagigedo, and Kupreanof—names that reflect the English, Russians, and Spaniards who explored the area.

The Rainforest

Much of the Southeast is covered with dense rainforests of Sitka spruce (the state tree), western hemlock, Alaska yellow cedar, and western red cedar. Interspersed through these rainforests are open boggy areas known as "muskegs," with a scattering of stunted lodgepole pines and cedars. Above the tree line (approx. 2,500 ft.) are rocky peaks covered with fragile flowers and other alpine vegetation. Shorelines often sport a fringe of grass dotted with flowers during the summer.

The rainforests here are choked with a dense understory of huckleberry, devil's club, and other shrubs. Berry lovers will enjoy a feast in late summer as the salmonberries, red and blue huckleberries, and thimbleberries all ripen. If you're planning a hike, learn to recognize **devil's club,** a lovely, abundant plant with large maple-shaped leaves and red berries. Barbed spines cover the plants, and when touched they feel like a bee sting. The spines become embedded in your fingers and are difficult to remove, often leaving a nasty sting for several days. If you're planning a cross-country hike, wear leather gloves to protect your hands. Surprisingly, mosquitoes and other biting insects are not nearly as abundant in the Southeast as they are in, for example, Alaska's Interior. They can, however, make your life

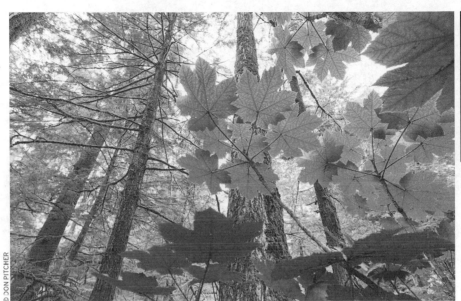

© DON PITCHER

devil's club in rainforest near Ward Lake, Tongass National Forest

miserable some of the time, especially during no-see-um season.

Climate

Tourist brochures invariably show happy folks cavorting around gleaming glaciers under a brilliant blue sky. Photographers might wait weeks to capture all three elements: Southeast Alaska is rain country! Expect rain or mist at least half of the time. In much of the region, blue-sky days come once a week, if that. The cool maritime climate brings rain in summer, and rain and snow in winter. Most towns in the Southeast get 80 inches or more of precipitation, and of the major towns, Ketchikan takes top honors with 162 inches per year. The tiny fishing settlement of Port Alexander on the south end of Baranof Island drowns in 220 inches per year!

Weather patterns vary greatly in the Southeast; Skagway gets just 22 inches a year, but only a few miles away, precipitation tops 160 inches annually on the peaks bordering Canada. Fortunately, the driest months are generally June–August.

Residents learn to tolerate the rain, which they call "liquid sunshine." You won't see many umbrellas, but heavy raingear and red rubber boots are appropriate dress for almost any occasion. If you ask, locals will admit to a grudging appreciation for the rain; it not only creates the lush, green countryside and provides ample streamflow for the vital salmon runs, it also keeps the region safe from overcrowding by the drier-minded set.

The People

Southeast Alaska has only 70,000 people. Nearly half live in Juneau, with the rest spread over nearly two dozen isolated towns and settlements strung along the Inside Passage. Much of the economy is based upon fishing, logging, governing, and tourism. The towns are dependent upon the sea for their survival, not only for the fish it provides, but also as a way to transport huge log rafts to the mills. Fully 95 percent of the goods brought to the Southeast arrive by barge or ship, and most of the visitors arrive aboard cruise ships or state ferries.

The Southeast corresponds almost exactly to the ancestral homeland of the Tlingit (KLINK-it) Indians, and signs of their culture—both authentic and visitor-oriented—are common. Almost every town has at least one totem pole, and some have a dozen or more. Tlingit artwork generally includes carvings, beadwork, sealskin moccasins, and silver jewelry. It *doesn't* include the *ulus,* Eskimo dolls, and other paraphernalia frequently sold in local tourist shops.

PLANNING YOUR TIME

All the major Inside Passage towns are separated by water or mountainous coastlines, with planes, state ferries, and cruise ships providing the connections. This limitation is a blessing in disguise: a long ferry ride north allows time to soak up the scenery and plan adventures in the next port. Anyone traveling with a vehicle is limited to ferry travel, while others can mix and match ferries or plane flights with local car rentals when needed. Cruise ships, of course, offer the leave-the-driving-to-us version. Plan on at least a week in Southeast Alaska—and preferably more—unless you are simply taking the Alaska Air jet to Sitka (or another town) and stopping for a few days of exploration.

Rain-soaked Ketchikan is the southernmost port, and a very popular destination for travelers of all ages and incomes. Downtown's Creek Street forms a picturesque stop, while totem poles and Tlingit (KLINK-it) culture are the big draws at Saxman and **Totem Bight State Historical Park.** Day trips by air or sea to **Misty Fiords National Monument** provide a great introduction to a dramatic wilderness of high cliffs and deep inlets.

Nearby Metlakatla and Prince of Wales Island are off-the-beaten-path destinations, and to the north lie the fishing towns of Wrangell and Petersburg, with the mighty **Stikine River** (popular for jetboat trips) heading into the mountains of British Columbia. Stop in the old Native and Russian town of Sitka with its gemlike setting, **Sitka National Historical Park,** and the Alaska Raptor Center. Juneau is not just the state capital and third largest city, but

also home to a fun tramway up Mt. Roberts, the Alaska State Museum, and famous **Mendenhall Glacier.** Boat tours to the deep fjords and calving glaciers of **Tracy Arm** are popular day trips from Juneau, as are boat tours (and kayaking trips) into magnificent **Glacier Bay.** The quiet town of Haines is home to **Fort Seward,** where century-old homes surround the old parade grounds. The touristy town of Skagway has a gold-rush aura courtesy of the many buildings preserved within **Klondike Gold Rush National Historical Park.** Especially popular here are narrow-gauge train rides aboard the **White Pass & Yukon Route Railroad.**

GETTING THERE

Visitors come to the Southeast by three primary means: cruise ship, jet, and ferry (the Alaska Marine Highway). Cruise ships are easily the most popular method—more than 900,000 people travel this way each year—but also the most expensive and the least personal. See the *Essentials* chapter for various cruise options, including the more expensive small-ship voyages that take you to less-traveled spots.

The second option, air, is more popular with independent travelers. **Alaska Airlines** (800/426-0333, www.alaskaair.com) has daily flights from Seattle, with service to Juneau, Ketchikan, Wrangell, Petersburg, Sitka, Gustavus, and other Alaskan cities. Floatplanes connect these towns to smaller places and provide access to even the most remote corners of the Inside Passage, such as Elfin Cove, Tokeen, and Port Alexander.

The Ferry System

Only three Southeast towns (Haines, Skagway, and Hyder) are connected by road to the rest of the continent. All the others, including Juneau, the state capital, are accessible only by boat or plane. This lack of roads—hopefully they will never be built—has led to an efficient public ferry system, the best in the Western Hemisphere and the longest in the world. Most ferries sail between Prince Rupert, B.C., and Skagway, stopping along the way in the major towns. There is also weekly service from Bellingham, Washington, all the way to Skagway, a three-day voyage. In the larger towns, summer service is almost daily, but in the smallest settlements, ferries may be up to two weeks apart. Get schedules and make reservations from the **Alaska Marine Highway** (907/465-3941 or 800/642-0066, www.ferryalaska.com). Since most travel in the Southeast centers around the ferry schedules, it's wise to check the ferry schedule before making any solid travel plans. Reservations for the summer can be made as early as December, and travelers taking a vehicle should book as early as possible to be sure of space.

The **Inter-Island Ferry Authority** (907/826-4848 or 866/308-4848, www.interislandferry.com) serves Prince of Wales Island, with service connecting the island with Ketchikan, Wrangell, and Mitkof Island (Petersburg). Travelers can use their ferries to create a side trip to Prince of Wales without backtracking. For example, you can take the state ferry to Ketchikan, then transfer to an Inter-Island ferry to Hollis on POW Island, drive up the island, and then catch another ferry to Wrangell and Mitkof Island, where you can continue north on the state ferry system.

Ketchikan

After the 36-hour ferry ride up from Bellingham, Ketchikan is many first-timers' introduction to Alaska. Along the way they've heard tales from sourdoughs (and those who claim to be), talked to Forest Service naturalists, and watched the logging towns and lush, green islands of British Columbia float past. As the ferry pulls into busy Tongass Narrows, an air of expectancy grows among the newcomers who are about to take their first steps in Alaska.

The state's fourth-largest city (pop. 8,000, plus another 6,000 in nearby areas), Ketchikan bills itself as "Alaska's First City," and even its zip code, 99901, seems to bear this out. Quite a few ferry passengers don't bother to stop here, instead hurrying on toward Juneau and points north. Because downtown is two miles away, they only have time for a superficial bus tour or a walk to the grocery store for provisions. But with its great scenery, fine local trails, the world's largest collection of totem poles, a bustling downtown, and the famous Misty Fiords nearby, Ketchikan certainly deserves a longer stay.

The Setting
Located 90 miles north of Prince Rupert, Ketchikan clings to a steep slope along Tongass Narrows, on Revillagigedo (ruh-VEE-ya-he-HAY-do) Island; locals shorten the name to

"Revilla." Fortunately, it doesn't bear the onetime viceroy of Mexico's full name: Don Juan Vicente de Guemes Pacheco de Pedilla y Horcasitas, Count of Revilla Gigedo! Locals call the town "three miles long and three blocks wide." It forms a continuous strip of development along the waterfront from the ferry terminal to beyond Thomas Basin. Because of this, Tongass Avenue—the only through street—has long been one of the busiest in the entire state. A hilltop bypass opened a few years back, but traffic is still very heavy on Tongass Avenue.

Much of Ketchikan is built on fill, on pilings over the water, or on hillsides with steep, winding ramps for streets. Fishing boats jam the three boat harbors (there are almost as many boats as cars in Ketchikan), and the canneries and cold-storage plants run at full throttle during the summer. Floatplanes are constantly taking off from the narrows, cruise ships crowd the docks, and tourists explore the downtown shops and attractions.

Ketchikan is one of the rainiest places in Alaska, getting upward of 13 feet a year, or an average of half an inch per day. Luckily, May–August are the driest months, but expect to get wet nevertheless. Locals adapt with "Ketchikan sneakers" (red rubber boots) and Helly Hansen raingear; umbrellas are the mark of a tourist. Residents pride themselves on almost never

Ketchikan

© DON PITCHER

canceling baseball games, and enjoy weekend picnics at Ward Lake in a downpour. Weather predicting is easy in Ketchikan: If you can't see the top of Deer Mountain, it's raining; if you can, it's *going* to rain. For an only-in-Ketchikan sight, check out the Valley Park Grade School on Schoenbar Road. This unique school was built atop its own playground, creating an escape from the rain.

History

The name Ketchikan comes from *Kitcxan,* a Tlingit word meaning "where the eagles' wings are," a reference to the shape of a sandspit at the creek mouth. The sandspit was dredged in the 1930s to create Thomas Basin Boat Harbor. Rumor has it that several bodies were found then, and suspicious fingers were pointed toward the denizens of nearby Creek Street, the local red-light district.

One of Southeast Alaska's youngest major towns, Ketchikan began when the first of many salmon canneries at the mouth of Ketchikan

Creek opened in 1885. By the 1930s it had become the "Salmon Capital of the World" (13 canneries), and Alaska's largest town. Overfishing caused salmon populations to crash in the 1940s, and the fishing industry was supplanted in the 1950s by a new pulp mill that turned the town into a major logging center.

For several decades Ketchikan's pulp mill was the biggest employer in Southeast Alaska, processing spruce and hemlock for the production of rayon and cellophane. The pulp mill closed in 1997, just as Ketchikan's economy shifted full-bore into tourism.

The big story today for Ketchikan—as in Juneau and Skagway—is cruise ships. More than 900,000 cruise ship travelers step onto Ketchikan's docks annually, with four or five ships tied up along Tongass Narrows most summer days. The rough old downtown with its sawmill, flophouses, and bars has been transformed into rows of jewelry stores (63 at last count!) staffed by employees from the Caribbean, and trinket shops selling plastic totem

To Ward Cove and
Totem Bight
State Historical Park

AIRPORT FERRY
TERMINAL

Carlanna Creek

HENEGHAN ST

ALASKAN & PROUD MARKET
POST OFFICE
FERRY TERMINAL

HECKMAN ST
BRYANT ST
BEST WESTERN
LANDING

DALE ST

Hoadly Creek

BARANOF ST

TONGASS AVE

FOREST SERVICE
DISTRICT OFFICE

BAR HARBOR RESTAURANT ▼

HIGHLINER
LAUNDROMAT ▼

Bar
Harbor

JACKSON ST
MONROE ST
MADISON ST
2ND AVE
ADAMS
AUSTIN
WASHINGTON ST
1ST AVE
WATER ST
BYPASS RD

Tongass Narrows

VIEWPOINT

TONGASS AVE
WATER ST

SCHOENBAR RD
STATE JAIL

FOREST AVE

TUNNEL
YOUTH HOSTEL
GILMORE HOTEL

FRONT ST
MAIN ST
GRANT ST
BAWDEN ST

SEE DETAIL

DOCK ST
MILL ST
PARK AVE
CREEK ST
STEDMAN ST

Ketchikan Creek

DEER
MOUNTAIN
HATCHERY AND
EAGLE CENTER

CRUISE
SHIP
DOCK

Thomas
Basin

WOODLAND AVE

★

★

POTLATCH BAR ▼
DEEPMOUNT ST

TOTEM
HERITAGE
CENTER

TATSUDA'S IGA

To Saxman

To Deer Mtn
Trailhead

0 ———— 0.5 mi
0 ———— 0.5 km

KETCHIKAN

FRONT ST
MAIN ST
DOCK ST
BAWDEN ST

FISH
LADDER

KETCHIKAN
VISITORS
BUREAU

MISSION ST
LIBRARY AND TONGASS
HISTORICAL MUSEUM ★

Ketchikan Creek
CREEK ST

CAPE FOX
● LODGE

MILL ST

SPRUCE
MILL MALL

SOUTHEAST
★ ALASKA DISCOVERY
CENTER

DOLLY'S
■ HOUSE
MUSEUM

SALMON LANDING
MARKET

LUMBERJACK
SHOW

NEW YORK
■ HOTEL AND CAFE

CRUISE
SHIP
DOCK

Thomas Basin

poles and stuffed animals made in China. Crossing guards at the intersections, horse-drawn wagon rides, amphibious "duck" tours, a pseudo-logging show, and thousands of befuddled cruise shippies add to what Edward Abbey labeled "industrial tourism." Sad, but it makes the cash registers ring, at least those businesses willing to accept kickback deals with the cruise lines in exchange for promotion onboard the ships. Fortunately, the cruise ships generally depart by early evening, allowing locals and overnight visitors to rediscover this fascinating town.

SIGHTS

Outside the library/museum is **Raven Stealing the Sun Totem,** and not far away stands the **Chief Johnson Pole** (an older version is inside the Totem Heritage Center). Tiny Whale Park occupies the intersection across from the Forest Service office and is home to the **Chief Kyan Totem,** raised in 1993 to replace an older version. The older one was reputed to reward those who touched it by bringing money within a day. It's worth a try on the new one, but don't head immediately to Las Vegas on the basis of this claim.

Check out some of Ketchikan's many long aerobic **stairways** up to hillside homes and outstanding vistas. The best ones start from the tunnel at Front and Grant streets, and from the intersection of Main and Pine streets. If you have a bike (or better yet, a skateboard), you may want to test your mettle on Schoenbar Road, the route blasted out of a steep hillside behind town. By the way, the Front Street **tunnel** is said to be the only one in the world that you can drive through, around, and over! Or so claims the *Guinness Book of World Records.*

Picturesque **Thomas Basin Boat Harbor** is just across the bridge over Creek Street. Walk out Thomas Street, past the Potlatch Bar (good for a game of pool or a beer with local fishermen), and out the jetty for a fine view back towards town.

Visitor Center

The **Ketchikan Visitors Bureau** (131 Front St., 907/225-6166 or 800/770-3300, www .visit-ketchikan.com) is right on the downtown dock. It's open whenever cruise ships are docked, which means daily 6:30 A.M.–6 P.M. most days May–September, and Monday–Friday 8 A.M.–5 P.M. the rest of the year. Pick up their free map that includes a walking tour of local sites. The building also houses booths for local tour companies.

Southeast Alaska Discovery Center

A great place to start your exploration of Ketchikan is the Southeast Alaska Discovery Center (50 Main St., 907/228-6220, www.fs.fed. us/r10, open Mon.–Sat. 8 A.M.–5 P.M. and Sun. 8 A.M.–4 P.M. May–Sept., and Tues.–Sat. 10 A.M.–4:30 P.M. the rest of the year, $5 adults, kids under 15 free). Operated by the U.S. Forest Service, it's filled with impressive exhibits—including a full-scale rainforest—that offer an educational portrait of the land and people of the Southeast. The 13-minute multimedia show "Mystical Southeast Alaska" is a must-see. Look through the spotting scope for mountain goats on Deer Mountain or

check out the video feed from the fish cam in Ketchikan Creek. The staff will help you with information on the outdoors, and the big gift shop features books, trail guides, and maps.

Logging Show

Located on Mill Street next to the cruise ship dock, the **Spruce Mill Complex** is the tourist shopping center for downtown Ketchikan, with retail stores, souvenir shops, galleries, and restaurants. Ketchikan's old spruce mill stood on this site for many years, so it is perhaps fitting to also find **The Great Alaskan Lumberjack Show** (907/225-9050 or 888/320-9049, www.lumberjackshows.com, three shows daily—rain or shine—May–Sept., $32 adults, $16 kids) here. This cornball 90-minute exhibition of old-time logging skills features ax throwing, bucksawing, springboard chopping, logrolling, and a speedy 50-foot tree climb. Covered grandstands protect the audience from the inevitable rain. If you're looking for a cheesy, Disneyfied imitation of old-time logging, this may be your ticket.

Tongass Historical Museum

The cramped Tongass Historical Museum (629 Dock St., 907/225-5600, www.city .ketchikan.ak.us, $2) shares the library building, and is open daily 8 A.M.–5 P.M. early May–September; and Wednesday–Friday 1–5 P.M., Saturday 10 A.M.–4 P.M., and Sunday 1–4 P.M. the rest of the year. The museum contains local historical items with changing exhibits that include examples of Native culture and commercial fishing. Look around for the model of a clan house, the 200-year-old Chilkat blanket, the dance paddle inlaid with abalone shell, the bentwood boxes, and the amusing totem pole with President Truman's features.

Creek Street

Ketchikan's best-known and most-photographed section features wooden houses on pilings along Ketchikan Creek. A boardwalk connects the buildings and affords views of salmon and steelhead in the creek. Now a collection of tourist shops, Creek Street once

SOUTHEAST ALASKA

Dolly's House Museum on Creek Street

© DON PITCHER

housed the red-light district; during Prohibition it was the only place to buy booze. Jokesters call it "the only place where both salmon and men came up from the sea to spawn." By 1946 more than 30 "female boardinghouses" operated here. Prostitution on Creek Street was stopped in 1954, and the house of Dolly Arthur was eventually turned into the **Dolly's House Museum** (907/225-2279, open daily all summer, $4). Inside are antiques, liquor caches, and risqué photos. Born in 1888, Dolly moved to Ketchikan in 1919, and worked at the world's oldest profession for many decades. When she died in 1975, her obituary was featured in newspapers across the West. Dolly's is fun to tour with grandmothers who would never otherwise step foot in such a place, and the fascinating collection of memorabilia makes it well worth a visit.

A **funicular car** ($2; free if you hike up and ride down) connects Creek Street with Cape Fox Lodge, where you'll discover impressive vistas over Ketchikan and Tongass Narrows.

Totem Heritage Center

One of the highlights of the Ketchikan area, the Totem Heritage Center (907/225-5900, www.city.ketchikan.ak.us, daily 8 A.M.–5 P.M. May–Sept., Mon.–Fri. 1–5 P.M. the rest of the year, $5 adults, kids under 12 free) is a quarter-mile walk up Deermount Street. The center was established in 1976 to preserve a collection of 33 original totem poles and house posts retrieved from abandoned village sites. Unlike other totems in the area, these works are not brightly painted copies or restorations, but were carved more than a century ago to record Tlingit and Haida events and legends. Guides answer your questions and put on a short video about the totem recovery program. Surrounding the building is a short trail with signs identifying local plants. Out front is the Fog-Woman pole by noted carver Nathan Jackson.

Deer Mountain Hatchery and Eagle Center

This small hatchery along Ketchikan Creek is just across a footbridge from the Totem Heritage

Center. Signboards illustrate the process of breeding and rearing king and coho salmon, and visitors can feed the young fish. The hatchery is run by the **Ketchikan Indian Council** (907/225-5158, www.kictribe.org, daily 8 A.M.–4:30 P.M. May–Sept., $9), with educational tours and a video on the life cycle of salmon. A large enclosure houses two eagles with permanent injuries—you might even see them catching salmon.

King salmon arrive from the Pacific Ocean to spawn at the hatchery late in the summer; look for them in the creek. A **fish ladder** to help them get past the falls is visible from the Park Avenue bridge. If too many fish return to spawn, the state opens Ketchikan Creek to dipnet fishing by locals, creating an astounding scene. Thousands of pink (humpback, or "humpies") salmon also spawn in the creek each summer. Another good place to see spawning humpies is **Hoadly Creek,** a half-mile south of the ferry terminal.

◖ Totem Bight State Historical Park

Located eight miles northwest of the ferry terminal, Totem Bight (907/247-8574, www.alaskastateparks.org, free) has 15 Haida and Tlingit totems and a realistic replica of a clan house, complete with a brightly painted facade and cedar-scented interior. Be sure to pick up the brochure describing the poles and their meanings. The totems, carved 1938–1941, are modeled after older poles. They are surrounded by a stand of young hemlock trees and a gorgeous view across Tongass Narrows. Drop by the gift shop for details on the poles or the informative weekly tours. Don't miss free performances by the **Haida Descendant Dancers** here the second Friday of each month at 6:30 P.M. Access to Totem Bight is easy and cheap: city buses stop at Totem Bight hourly on weekdays.

Saxman

This Native village (ironically named for a white schoolteacher) is a 2.5-mile walk via a paved path, a $2 city bus ride, or a $12 taxi ride south of Ketchikan. Saxman (pop. 400)

is crowded with the largest collection of standing totem poles in the world—more than two dozen. Most were brought from their original sites in the 1930s and restored by Native Civilian Conservation Corps (CCC) workers; others came from a second restoration project in 1982. The oddest pole is topped with a figure of Abraham Lincoln, and commemorates the settlement of a war begun by the U.S. revenue cutter *Lincoln.* Probably the most photographed is the Rock Oyster Pole, which tells the story of a man who drowned after his hand became caught in a large oyster. Behind the poles is a cedar **Beaver Clan House,** open most days.

Adjacent to the totem park is a **carving shed** (free admission) where you'll find local artisans completing totems, masks, and other pieces. You're welcome to drop in whenever a carver is at work, which is most weekdays in the summer. Renowned carver Nathan Jackson can often be found working here. Interested in having a pole carved? Expect to pay at least $2,000 per linear foot.

Cape Fox Tours (907/225-4846, www.capefoxtours.com, $35) guides 1.5-hour tours that include a visit to the carving shed, a video on Tlingit culture, and a performance by the Cape Fox Dancers. Get tickets at the Ketchikan Visitor Center or the **Saxman Village Store** (907/225-4421), which sells a mix of wares, including some locally made totems, masks, carved pieces. Two blocks downhill is the **Saxman Arts Co-op** (907/225-4166), with historic photos and local pieces.

Ziplines

Eight miles south of town at Herring Cove is **Alaska Rainforest Sanctuary** (907/225-5503, www.alaskarainfroest.com), where a former lumber mill serves as headquarters for a series of seven high ziplines (longest is 850 ft.) and three suspension bridges through the treetops. Three-hour guided tours cost $149 per person, or $160 with round-trip transportation from town. A gift shop and a half-dozen reindeer (!) are at the old mill site, and a boardwalk leads along the creek—a good place to watch black bears fishing for salmon most summer evenings.

TOTEM POLES

These largest of all wooden sculptures were carved in cedar by the Tlingit, Haida, Tsimshian, Kwakiutl, and Bella Bella peoples of the Pacific Northwest. Their history is not completely known, but early explorers found poles in villages throughout Southeast Alaska. Apparently, totem-pole carving reached its heyday in the late 19th century with the arrival of metal woodworking tools. The animals, birds, fish, and marine mammals on the poles were totems that represented a clan, and in combination, conveyed a message.

Totem poles were very expensive and time-consuming to produce; a clan's status could be determined in part by the size and elaborateness of its poles. In a society without written words to commemorate people or events, the poles served a variety of purposes. Some totem poles told a family's history, others told local legends, and still others served to ridicule an enemy or debtor. In addition, totems were used to commemorate the dead, with a special niche at the back to hold the ashes of a revered ancestor.

Totem poles were never associated with religion, yet early missionaries destroyed many, and as recently as 1922, the Canadian government outlawed the art in an attempt to make the Natives more submissive. Realizing that a rich heritage was being lost because of neglect, skilled Native carvers worked with the Civilian Conservation Corps during the 1930s to restore older totems and create new ones. Today, active carving and restoration programs are taking place in Saxman, Ketchikan, Sitka, and Haines. Other good places to find totems include the Southeast towns of Hydaburg, Klawock, Kasaan, Juneau, Wrangell, and Kake.

Saxman Village is one of the best places to see totem poles.

© DON PITCHER

ENTERTAINMENT AND EVENTS

A local theater group, First City Players (1716 Totem Way, 907/225-4792), puts on the light-hearted melodrama, *Fish Pirate's Daughter* Friday evenings in July. The show has been going on since 1966, and tickets cost $40 with an all-you-can eat crab dinner. Catch a movie downtown at the **Coliseum Twin Theater** (405 Mission St., 907/225-2294).

Ketchikan's live music scene changes each year, but something is always happening downtown; just follow your ears. **First City Saloon** (830 Water St., 907/225-1494) tends to bring in the better bands, and is the main dance spot in town. More rock at the **Arctic Bar** (907/225-4709), near the Front Street tunnel, where a pleasant patio hangs over Tongass Narrows. Shock your friends back home with one of its risqué baseball caps. If Dave Rubin and his rockin' Potlatch Band are playing at the **Potlatch Bar** (907/225-4855), next to Thomas Basin, make tracks in that direction. You won't regret it. The finest bar views are from **Cape Fox Lodge,** overlooking town above Creek Street. It's a nice place to get romantic.

Ketchikan's fun **4th of July** celebration includes the usual parade and fireworks, plus a **Timber Carnival** with ax throwing, pole climbing, and a variety of chainsaw contests, ending with a dramatic pole-felling event. In the first week of August, check out the **Blueberry Arts Festival,** complete with slug races, pie-eating contests, a fun run, arts and crafts exhibitions, and folk music. Ketchikan also has king and silver salmon fishing derbies and a halibut derby each summer. The **Winter Arts Faire** on the weekend after Thanksgiving is a good time to buy local arts and crafts. **Festival of the North** arrives in February, complete with music, art shows (including edible art!), and various workshops for the entire month.

SHOPPING

The **Spruce Mill Mall** is the primary focal point for shopping in downtown Ketchikan. Cruise ships dock directly in front, disgorging their passengers to feed the hungry cash registers of such places as Caribbean Gems or Tanzanite International. Needless to say, locals would never step foot in these jewelry stores owned and staffed by Outsiders cashing in on the tourists. Fortunately, many of the other downtown shops—including a number of places in Salmon Landing Marketplace—are locally owned and worth a visit.

Locals do much of their shopping at **Plaza Mall,** centering around Safeway and McDonald's, and the **Wal-Mart** (907/247-2156) five miles north of town. There's even a free summertime shuttle from downtown to Wal-Mart; it's mainly for cruise ship workers, but is also popular with cheapskate travelers

Arts and Crafts

A surprisingly creative town, Ketchikan is home to a number of fine artists. The center of Ketchikan's art action is the historic 5-Star building on Creek Street, where the artist Ray Troll holds down the fort at **Soho Coho** (907/225-5954 or 800/888-4070, www.trollart.cosm), with his weird and fishy T-shirts and prints. Other artists—including the wonderfully prolific printmaker Evon Zerbetz—also display their works here. The same building houses **Alaska Eagle Arts** (907/225-8365 or 800/308-2787, www.marvinoliver.com), with colorful T-shirts, jewelry, and prints, along with samples of the stunning Native designs by world-famous sculptor and printmaker Marvin Oliver.

Herring Cove Originals Studio and Gallery (229 Stedman St., 907/247-2693, www.sharronhuffman.com), has fish-print T-shirts and distinctive linocuts and block prints. Other downtown galleries worth a visit include **Exploration Gallery** (633 Mission St., 907/225-4278, www.explorationgallery.com), **Blue Heron Gallery** (123 Stedman St., 907/225-1982, www.blueheronalaska.com), **Eagle Spirit Gallery** (310 Mission St., 907/225-6626 or 866/867-0976, www.eaglespirit alaska.com), **Scanlon Gallery** (318 Mission St., 907/247-4730 or 888/228-4730, www .scanlongallery.com), **Crazy Wolf Studio** (607 Mission St., 907/225-9653 or 888/331-9653, www.crazywolfstudio.com), and **Dockside**

Gallery (907/225-2858, www.alaskanart.net) inside Salmon Landing.

For additional artwork, visit the **Mainstay Gallery** at the Ketchikan Area Arts & Humanities Council (716 Totem Way, 907/225-2211, www.ketchikanarts.org) near Creek Street. Exhibits change monthly, and they produce the *Ketchikan Arts Guide* with brief bios of local artists, plus descriptions of galleries, museums, and other places to find creative works. In the winter, their Monthly Grind brings fun events to the Saxman Tribal House.

RECREATION

The Ketchikan area is blessed with an abundance of hiking trails and remote wilderness cabins maintained by the U.S. Forest Service. If you arrive in Ketchikan unprepared for a cabin stay, **Alaskan Wilderness Outfitting** (907/225-7335, www.latitude56.com) rents outboard motors, coolers, stoves, and dishes (but not sleeping bags). It even has a "cabin outfit" set up with the supplies you'll need at a Forest Service cabin.

Take in a **panoramic view of Ketchikan** from the short trail that climbs from the high-point along Bypass Road (Forest Ave.). The road takes off from Schoenbar Road on the south end.

Deer Mountain

The best hike from Ketchikan is up to the 3,000-foot summit of Deer Mountain (6 miles round-trip). Begin by heading a half-mile uphill from Deermount and Fair streets. Take the first left—the road to Ketchikan Lakes, source of the city's drinking water—and then an immediate right to the trailhead. The trail climbs along an excellent but strenuous path through dense Sitka spruce and western hemlock forests. There's an incredible view in all directions from the top of Deer Mountain, but right into July you'll have to cross snowbanks to reach the summit. (Rain gear works fine for sledding down again.)

Just before the final climb to the peak, a trail to the left leads around the north slope and on to tiny **Blue Lake** and **John Mountain** (3,238 ft.). Entirely above the tree line, this portion

Ketchikan, with Deer Mountain in the background

© DON PITCHER

can be hazardous for inexperienced hikers. Carry a map and compass since it's easy to become disoriented if the clouds drop down. Ambitious hikers can do a 12-mile trek over the top, ending at Beaver Falls powerhouse, at the end of South Tongass Highway. Free **shelter cabins** (no reservations) are atop Deer Mountain and at Blue Lake; get current trail info at the Discovery Center.

Ward Lake Area

Several good trails are near the Forest Service campground at Ward Lake, eight miles north of downtown via Revilla Road. The 1.3-mile **Ward Lake Nature Trail** is an easy loop with interpretive signs and good summertime fishing for steelhead and salmon. **Ward Creek Trail** starts across from the day-use area and follows the creek 2.5 miles to Last Chance Campground. It's built for wheelchairs, with a couple of short spur paths leading to platforms over this beautiful creek.

Perseverance Trail climbs two miles to Perseverance Lake following a "stairway-to-heaven" boardwalk, passing through several muskegs along the way. Beyond this, you can take the **Minerva Mountain Trail** all the way to Carlanna Lake. Contact the Forest Service for details on the latter since this is a newly built trail.

Settler's Cove State Recreation Site, 16 miles north of Ketchikan, has a one-mile trail through the rainforest, with a pretty waterfall and spawning pink salmon in mid-summer.

Nearby Cabins

The Naha River watershed, 20 miles north of Ketchikan, contains one of the finest trail and cabin systems in the Southeast. The river once supported astounding runs of sockeye salmon and is still a popular salmon, steelhead, and trout fishing area for locals. At one time the town of **Loring** (established 1888) at its mouth had the world's largest fish cannery and was the main point of entry into Alaska. Today, it's a tiny settlement of retirees and vacation homes. **Heckman Lake,** six miles upriver, supported the world's largest and most costly

salmon hatchery at the turn of the century. The hatchery failed, however, and all that remains are the overgrown ruins.

The pleasant six-mile **Naha River Trail** begins at Naha Bay, follows the shore of Roosevelt Lagoon, then climbs gently up to Jordon and Heckman Lakes. At the mouth of Roosevelt Lagoon is an interesting salt chuck where the direction of water flow changes with the tides. Covered picnic tables are nearby. More picnic tables are two miles up the trail at a small waterfall—a good place to watch black bears catching salmon late in the summer. There's a Forest Service cabin on Jordan Lake and two cabins on Heckman Lake (one wheelchair accessible); all three have rowboats and cost $35. Reservations can be made at 518/885-3639 or 877/444-6777, or online at www.reserveusa.com. Access to the Naha area is by sea kayak, floatplane, or skiff. Contact **Knudsen Cove Marina** (907/225-8500 or 800/528-2486; www.knudsoncovemarina.com) for skiff rentals or dropoffs.

Lake Shelokum, 40 miles north of Ketchikan, has a free three-sided shelter near a hot springs. A two-mile trail stretches from the shelter to Bailey Bay, passing the scenic lake and an impressive waterfall. Other cabins well worth visiting include **Lake McDonald, Reflection Lake, Helm Creek,** and **Blind Pass.** Get details at the Discovery Center in Ketchikan.

Sea Kayaking and Canoeing

The Discovery Center has detailed information on sea kayaking in the waters near Ketchikan, including Misty Fiords and a circumnavigation of Revilla Island. **Southeast Sea Kayaks** (907/225-1258 or 800/287-1607, www.kayakketchikan.com) leads a variety of kayak trips, starting with a 2.5-hour paddle along Tongass Narrows ($79), and a four-hour trip ($149) that includes a boat ride to a cove on Gravina Island and the chance to explore this quiet area by kayak. An all-day trip to Misty Fjords ($389) includes the boat ride over and back, lunch, and four hours of paddling.

Southeast Exposure (515 Water St.,

907/225-8829, www.southeastexposure.com) has easy paddles for the cruise ship crowd, including a 2.5-hour waterfront tour ($50), and a 4-hour trip to Tatoosh Islands ($76) by bus, boat, and kayak. Both companies also offer multi-day trips to Misty Fiords and kayak rentals.

Ketchikan Parks and Recreation Department (2721 7th Ave., 907/225-9579) rents canoes and sports equipment, as well as skis and snowshoes in the winter.

Fishing, Boating, and Diving

Many Ketchikan companies offer charter fishing trips in search of salmon or halibut; see the visitors bureau for a complete listing. Rent skiffs and fishing gear to head out on your own from **Knudsen Cove Marina** (13 miles north of town, 907/247-8500 or 800/528-2486, www.knudsoncovemarina.com) If you're just looking to try your luck with all the locals who fish from the Creek Street bridge, rent a pole a block away from the little stand across from the Federal Building. **Mountain Point,** 5.5 miles south of Ketchikan, is a good spot to try your luck at salmon fishing from the shore.

The **Ketchikan Yacht Club** (907/225-3262, www.ketchikanyachtclub.org) sponsors low-key races on Wednesdays at 5:30 P.M. in the summer, and the skippers are always looking for volunteer crew. It's a fun way to sail with the locals for free.

ACCOMMODATIONS

For an up-to-date listing of local lodging places, browse over to the Ketchikan Visitors Bureau website (www.visit-ketchikan.com).

Hostel

The **Ketchikan Youth Hostel** (907/225-3319, June–Aug.), downtown in the basement of the Methodist church at Grant and Main, costs $15. It's open 6 P.M.–9 A.M., and the doors are locked at 11 P.M. If your ferry gets in after that, call the hostel promptly upon arrival and they'll open for you. The hostel isn't fancy— we're talking simple cots—but is friendly and clean, with kitchen facilities and showers. It's

a good place to meet other budget travelers. There's a four-night maximum stay.

Hotels and Motels

Built in the 1930s and now on the National Register of Historic Places, the centrally located **Gilmore Hotel** (326 Front St., 907/225-9423 or 800/275-9423, www.gilmorehotel.com), ex-udes an old-fashioned ambience, but has been updated with modern furnishings. Rates are reasonable: $120 d for cramped rooms, $130 d for larger rooms with two beds and a harbor view, or $140 d for the suites. Amenities include courtesy van service, a light breakfast, free Wi-Fi, and parking. Rooms over the bar may get noisy at night.

Cozy ◖ **New York Hotel** (207 Stedman St., 907/225-0246 or 866/225-0246, www .thenewyorkhotel.com) has been painstakingly restored to its Roaring '20s heyday. It's a great location—facing the harbor and just a few steps off Creek Street—and the downstairs café is one of the best in town. Free airport and ferry shuttles, too. The eight rooms in the historic main building are small but nicely furnished: $109 s or $119 d with private baths and queen beds. Also available are four luxury suites with covered waterside decks along Creek Street for $179 d (plus $15 for each additional guest). The latter units feature lofts with spiral stairs, full kitchens, and jetted tubs. Book early for the popular suites.

The Narrows Inn (907/247-2600 or 888/686-2600, www.narrowsinn.com, $130–145 d) sits four miles north of Ketchikan along Tongass Narrows. Rooms are small, but modern, bright, and nicely appointed. Free Wi-Fi and continental breakfast too. Waterside rooms (ask for room 1209) have small balconies where you can watch the parade of boats and planes, and three larger suites are available. A steak and seafood restaurant is also on the premises, and the staff is very accommodating.

Ketchikan's largest lodging place, **Best Western Landing** (3434 Tongass Ave., 907/225-5166 or 800/428-8304, www.landing hotel.com) sits right across from the ferry terminal. The 107 rooms are newly refurbished and include microwaves and fridges; $180 s or $190 d in standard rooms, $210 s or $220 d for suites. Also on the premises are two restaurants, a fitness center, courtesy van, and free Wi-Fi.

At the top end of Ketchikan's lodging spectrum is the elaborate **Cape Fox Lodge** (800 Venetia Way, 907/225-8001 or 866/225-8001, www.capefoxlodge.com, $200 d, $251 d for a two-room suite). This attractive hilltop hotel overlooks Tongass Narrows, and has spacious, modern rooms. A funicular car takes guests to the Cape Fox from Creek Street.

Fishing Lodges

Many fishing lodges can be found in the Ketchikan area, particularly on nearby Prince of Wales Island; see www.visit-ketchikan.com for a complete listing.

Located 17 miles north of Ketchikan, **Salmon Falls Resort** (907/225-2752 or 800/247-9059, www.salmonfallsresort.net, open mid-May–mid-Sept.), has modern rooms and a dramatic shoreside setting. Fishing packages start at $1,100 per person for three nights, or $1,550 with a guide.

Yes Bay Lodge (907/225-7906 or 800/999-0784, www.yesbay.com) is a remote fishing lodge near Lake McDonald on the Cleveland Peninsula north of Ketchikan. The setting is wonderful, and the fishing is great, most notably a famous steelhead stream adjacent to the property. Rates start at $6,000 d for a four-night all-inclusive package.

Also check out **Naha Bay Outdoor Adventures** (907/247-4453, www.nahabay outdooradventures.com), a 20-minute boat ride from Knudson Cove Marina. Good fishing, hiking, sea kayaking, and more, starting at $1,800 d for three nights.

B&Bs and Vacation Rentals

You'll find links to Ketchikan B&Bs at www.visit-ketchikan.com, or contact **Ketchikan Reservation Service** (907/247-5337 or 800/987-5337, www.ketchikan-lodging.com) or **Alaska Travelers** (907/247-7117 or 800/928-3308, www.alaskatravelers.com) for assistance in booking a room, cabin, or guest house.

Captain's Quarters B&B (325 Lund St., 907/225-4912, www.ptialaska.net/~captbnb, $100–110 d) has three rooms with private baths, harbor views, and continental breakfasts; no kids.

Two miles north of the ferry terminal, **Black Bear Inn B&B** (907/225-4343, www.stayinalaska.com, $150 d) is an elegant, newly built four-bedroom house with an outdoor hot tub, plenty of privacy, and tall windows facing Tongass Narrows. A separate apartment ($200 d) on the top floor has its own entrance and porch. A make-it-yourself breakfast is provided.

Lundberg's South Shore Inn (907/225-0909, $125 d with continental breakfast), has a private two-bedroom apartment with kitchenette, woodstove, large deck, and private beach. The very comfortable home is seven miles southeast of town near Mountain Point.

Located four miles south of town, and right on the water, **Anchor Inn by the Sea** (907/247-7117 or 800/928-3308, www.alaskatravelers.com, $125–135 d) is a fine option for families, with three large suites with kitchenettes. All of these feature private baths and entrances. A five-night minimum stay is required.

Located close to downtown, **Madame's Manor** (324 Cedar St., 907/247-2774 or 877/531-8159, ext. 2484, www.madamesmanor.com, $149–169 d) is a hillside B&B with three lavish Victorian-style suites with private baths. The deck overlooks the harbor and Tongass Narrows, making this a delightful spot to sip your tea or enjoy a filling gourmet breakfast. Also available are two downstairs apartments ($115–125 d, $25 for additional guests) that are popular with families; breakfast not included. A two-night minimum is required.

Located along picturesque George Inlet eight miles south of Ketchikan, **Waypoint Inn at Herring Bay** (907/225-8605, www.waypointinn.com, $175 d) is a studio apartment with a big deck for relaxing and a full kitchen. There is a minimum four-night stay.

Alaska's Hidden Cove Vacation Rentals (907/225-7934, www.akhiddencove.com) has two lovely places north of town: a three-bedroom home ($210 d; 4-night minimum) and a one-bedroom suite ($125 d; 3-night minimum).

CAMPING

There are no campsites in town, but the Forest Service operates two summer-only campgrounds ($10) in the scenic Ward Lake area—a world away from the craziness of downtown Ketchikan when the cruise ships are in port. Get there by heading five miles north from the ferry terminal and turning right up Revilla Road. Ward Cove is a good place to see eagles, so stop for a look before heading to the lake. The most popular camping area is scenic **Signal Creek Campground,** along Ward Lake. Another mile and a half north is **Last Chance Campground.** Both campgrounds have running water, and can be reserved (518/885-3639 or 877/444-6777, www.reserveusa.com, $9 extra).

Settler's Cove State Recreation Site (16 miles north of the ferry, $10) has campsites beneath the trees. The beach is a popular spot for summer picnics, and a trail takes you through the rainforest to a small waterfall.

Clover Pass Resort (907/247-2234 or 800/410-2234, www.cloverpassresort.com, open mid-May–Sept.), 15 miles north of Ketchikan, has RV hookups for $29–31, plus a restaurant on the premises.

FOOD
Breakfast and Lunch

Housed within the historic New York Hotel, the bizarrely named **That One Place Cafe/ The Other Place Lounge** (207 Stedman St., 907/225-8646) has big windows facing Thomas Basin Harbor. Lunchtime salads, soups, and sandwiches give way to a $5-per-plate tapas menu in the evening, including chicken satay, gorgonzola fries, coconut prawns, and tempura vegetables to name a few.

Dockside Diner (1287 Tongass Ave., 907/247-7787) is a hometown place with burgers, halibut and chips, hot beef sandwiches, liver and onions, and fried chicken, plus a big

selection of pies. Breakfast is available all day, and the covered deck provides a view of busy Tongass Narrows and escape from the thick cigarette smoke inside.

Located right across from the ferry terminal, **The Landing Restaurant** (3434 Tongass Ave., 907/225-5166), fills with locals and travelers in search of a filling breakfast.

A fine little fish and chips stand called **Alaskan Surf** attracts tourists and locals to its shipside location on the downtown dock. An order of halibut and fries is $11. It's owned by the folks from Bar Harbor Restaurant, so you know the fish is fresh and tasty. Find the best local chicken sandwiches, salmon burgers, and hamburgers at the tiny **Burger Queen** (907/225-6060) just north of the Front Street tunnel. **McDonald's** is in the Plaza Mall 0.75 mile south of the ferry, and the local **Subway** (415 Dock St.) is downtown.

Coffee and Sweets

Several places serve espresso downtown, but the best is probably **Ketchikan Coffee Company** right on the dock. If you just want to relax and enjoy looking over busy Tongass Narrows, stop by **Coffee Connections** (521 Water St., 907/247-0521) for a cup of espresso or a pastry. **KetchiCandies** (315 Mission St., 907/225-0900 or 800/225-0970, www.ketchicandies.com) makes hand-dipped chocolates, and will ship your purchases.

Dinner

Upstairs in the Spruce Mill Mall, **Steamers** (907/225-1600, $15–40) is a large and noisy tourist restaurant where you'll find fresh seafood, pasta, and steaks, along with 31 brews (half of these Alaskan beers) on draft. The featured attraction is crab (all you can eat for $30), but all the seafood is good, and servings are ample. Try the po' boy oyster sandwich, chicken pasta, or seafood tacos. Make reservations for a window seat facing Tongass Narrows, though the view is usually blocked by one of those honking cruise ships.

Ocean View Restaurant (1831 Tongass Ave., 907/225-7566, $11–20) is a favorite of locals, and with good reason. The food is varied and nicely prepared, the atmosphere is classy, prices are reasonable, and delivery is free. The menu encompasses pasta (including halibut fettuccine), steaks, seafood, burgers, and best-in-town pizzas, but Mexican dishes are the real attraction, and all meals come with chips and a dose of Mexican tunes over the speakers.

Next to the footbridge on the north end of Creek Street, **Good Fortune Chinese Restaurant** (907/225-1818) has upstairs seating overlooking the water. It's authentically Chinese, but also reasonable, including a $7 lunch of sweet and sour pork or spicy Kung Pao chicken. A la carte dinners are $12–14. Service is quick and friendly, but the setting is unpretentious. Not far away—and also overlooking the creek—**On's Thai House** (127 Stedman St., 907/225-8424)—serves Thai and Chinese dishes.

Fine Dining

With its 1920s-style decor, **Annabelle's Keg and Chowder House** (326 Front St., 907/225-6009, www.gilmorehotel.com) wins the "best atmosphere" prize among Ketchikan restaurants. The menu features seafood (including four kinds of chowders), steaks, salads, and sandwiches, along with prime rib on weekends. There are daily specials, plus cocktails, espresso, and a jukebox. Located in the historic Gilmore Hotel, this is a good place to impress a friend.

Bar Harbor Restaurant (2813 Tongass Ave., 907/225-2813, www.barharbor ketchikan.com, $16–25) fills a tiny building south of the ferry terminal, and the back deck provides outdoor dining with a view of this busy harbor if it isn't raining too hard. The food is dependably good, and includes such specialties as clams a la Karl, bleu steak salad, crab cakes, and weekend prime rib. Free Wi-Fi too. Open Monday–Saturday for dinner only; reservations recommended.

Héen Kahídi Restaurant and Lounge (800 Venetia Way, 907/225-8001, www.cape foxlodge.com, $20–40) inside Cape Fox Lodge, serves seafood and steak dinners—try the pepper steak or halibut Olympia—in a quiet and romantic setting. Reserve ahead to get a window seat for an evening sunset over town.

Located 17 miles north of Ketchikan, **Salmon Falls Resort** (907/225-2752 or 800/247-9059, www.salmonfallsresort.net, dinners May–Sept. only) is a large octagonal restaurant specializing in steaks and seafood, with blackened halibut, king crab, steaks, lobster, and other filling fare for $22–36. The building vaults 40 feet overhead, with an impressive waterfall and views across Clover Passage.

Groceries

The closest grocery store to the ferry is **Alaskan & Proud Market** (907/225-1279 or 800/770-8258) right across the road, while **Safeway,** 0.75 mile south of the ferry, has a salad bar and the biggest selection of groceries. **Tatsuda's IGA** (633 Stedman, 907/225-4125) is on the south edge of town.

Salmon Etc. (907/225-6008 or 800/354-7256 outside Alaska, www.salmonetc.com), has two locations: on Creek Street, and down town at 322 Mission Street. It sells high-quality canned, smoked, or frozen salmon, halibut, crab, clams, and other sea critters.

INFORMATION AND SERVICES

The two primary information centers are the Ketchikan Visitors Bureau and the Southeast Alaska Discovery Center, described in *Sights*. Forest Service offices for **Ketchikan and Misty Fiords** ranger districts (3031 Tongass Ave., 907/225-2148, www.fs.fed.us/r10/tongass) are a half-mile south of the ferry terminal.

Showers are available at **Highliner Laundromat** (2703 Tongass Ave.) and **Thomas Wash Basin** (989 Stedman St.). A better option is to head up Madison Street to the **high school swimming pool** (2610 4th Ave., 907/225-2010), where a swim, sauna, and shower cost $5.

Get fast cash from ATMs at First Bank and Wells Fargo downtown, and at the Safeway and A&P grocery stores.

The main post office is next to the ferry terminal on the north end of town, and a branch post office is downtown in the Great Alaskan Clothing Company (422 Mission St.).

Ketchikan General Hospital (3100 Tongass Ave., 907/225-5171, www.peacehealth.org) is the largest in southern Southeast Alaska. **Ketchikan Medical Clinic** (3612 Tongass Ave., 907/225-5144) is out near the ferry terminal.

Books and Internet Access

Ketchikan's woefully small **public library** (629 Dock St., 907/225-3331, www.firstcitylibraries. org) is a great place to relax, with big windows overlooking Ketchikan Creek. Unfortunately, this may be the only Alaskan library where the computer terminals are off-limits to non-residents.

A book-lover's bookstore, **Parnassus Bookstore** (907/225-7690) is upstairs above Soho Coho on Creek Street. Sit down and talk with the friendly owner, Lillian Ference, about the latest Ketchikan news. Parnassus stocks an especially impressive collection of women's books. The other bookstore in town is **Waldenbooks** (907/225-8120) in Plaza Mall.

Surf the web for a fee at **Seaport CyberStation** (Salmon Landing Mall, 907/247-4615 or 888/295-0965, www.seaport cyber.com) or **The Crows Nest** (308 Grant St., 907/225-6119) next to the tunnel. Quite a few places have free Wi-Fi; try Annabelle's Restaurant, The Edge (Salmon Landing Mall), Thomas Basin Harbor, plus the airport and the ferry terminal.

GETTING THERE
Ferry

Ketchikan's ferry terminal is two miles north-west of downtown, and is open Monday–Friday 9 A.M.–4:30 P.M. and when ships are in port. Call 907/225-6182 or 907/225-6181 for recorded arrival and departure times. During the summer, ferries provide almost-daily runs to Prince Rupert, Metlakatla, Wrangell, and points north. Ferry service to Bellingham is once a week. Contact the **Alaska Marine Highway** (907/465-3941 or 800/642-0066, www.ferryalaska.com) for the current schedule and prices.

The **Inter-Island Ferry Authority** (907/826-4848 or 866/308-4848, www .interislandferry.com) operates from the same building, with daily service to Hollis on Prince of Wales Island.

Air

Ketchikan Airport is on Gravina Island, directly across Tongass Narrows from the ferry terminal. In 2005, Ketchikan became a national laughingstock when Alaska's congressional delegation rammed through a bill that included funding for a pair of bridges to the otherwise-uninhabited island. The notorious "bridge to nowhere" became a national symbol of pork barrel politics before the funding was hurriedly cut off. There really isn't a need for bridges since an **airport ferry** (907/225-6800, $4 one-way plus $6 for vehicles) operates every half-hour daily 6:15 A.M.–9:30 P.M. Several companies provide van service from the airport to downtown for around $20 (including ferry fare). If you're heading downtown and don't have a rental car, a better option is the **Tongass Water Taxi** (907/225-8294); Rich Schuerger takes you directly from the airport to Thomas Basin in the heart of Ketchikan for $18 s or $25 d. He meets most flights and can be found next to the baggage claim.

Alaska Airlines (800/426-0333, www .alaskaair.com) has flights from Ketchikan to Juneau, Petersburg, Sitka, Wrangell, and other cities in Alaska and the Lower 48.

Three air taxi operators, **ProMech Air** (907/225-3845 or 800/860-3845, www .promechair.com), **Pacific Airways** (907/225-3500 or 877/360-3500, www.fly pacificairways.com), and **Taquan Air** (907/225-8800 or 800/770-8800, www.taquanair.com), have daily service to Prince of Wales Island and Metlakatla, while **L.A.B. Flying Service** (907/772-4300, www.labflying.com) flies from Ketchikan airport to Klawock.

ProMech, Pacific Airways, and Taquan also do flightseeing trips around Ketchikan. Other air taxi operators include **Carlin Air** (907/225-3036 or 888/594-3036, www.carlinair.com), **Family Air Tours** (907/247-1305 or 800/380-1305, www.familyairtours.com), **Island Wings Air Service** (907/225-2444 or 888/854-2444, www.islandwings.com), **Misty Fjords Air and Outfitting** (1285 Tongass Ave., 907/225-5155 or 877/228-4656, www.mistyfjordsair.com), **Alaska Seaplane Tours** (907/225-1974 or 866/858-2327, www.alaskaseaplanetours.com), **Seawind Aviation** (907/225-1206 or 877/225-1203, www.seawindaviation.com), and **Southeast Aviation** (907/225-2900 or 888/359-6478, www.southeastaviation.com). Especially popular is a two-hour flightseeing trip to Misty Fiords National Monument that includes a landing on a lake for around $220. Some of these companies include a half-hour on land as part of the tour, providing a good chance to stretch your legs and take in the wild country.

GETTING AROUND

The Bus (907/225-8726, www.borough.ketchikan.ak.us, $2 each direction) runs throughout Ketchikan, south to Saxman, and north to Totem Bight approximately every hour daily 7 A.M.–7 P.M. Schedules are available at the visitors bureau and ferry terminal, or find a bus stop and wait.

The local taxi companies are **Alaska Cab Co.** (907/225-2133), **Sourdough Cab** (907/225-5544, www.ketchikantaxicabtours.com), and

Yellow Taxi (907/225-5555). They charge about $11 from the ferry to downtown, $12 from downtown to Saxman, or $75 an hour for tours (up to six people).

Tours

The downtown visitors bureau houses booths from companies promoting their trips, including two-hour city tours for $30. Most of these—including an embarrassing "Duck Tour"—are for cruise ship travelers. Also popular are two-hour waterfront cruises offered by **Alaska Cruises** (907/225-6044 or 800/228-1905, www.mistyfjord.net, $50 adults, $25 kids) and visits to Saxman village from **Cape Fox Tours** (907/225-4846, www.capefoxtours.com, $35).

Car Rentals

Because Ketchikan's sights are so spread out, renting a car is a good idea. Rental rates (with unlimited miles) are around $60 from **Alaska Car Rental** (2828 N. Tongass Ave., 907/225-5000 or 800/662-0007, www.akcarrental.com) and **Budget** (4950 N. Tongass Ave., 907/225-6004 or 800/478-2438, www.budget.com). Both companies have cars at the airport and on the Ketchikan side of Tongass Narrows; it's a $6 ferry ride each way to transport a vehicle.

SOUTHEAST ALASKA

Vicinity of Ketchikan

◖ MISTY FIORDS NATIONAL MONUMENT

The 2.2-million-acre Misty Fiords National Monument is the largest national forest wilderness in the United States, covering the east side of Revillagigedo Island, the adjacent mainland all the way to the Canadian border, and the long narrow Behm Canal that separates island and mainland. Misty contains a diversity of gorgeous scenery—glaciers, rainforests, narrow fjords, and rugged mountains—but is best known for the spectacular cliffs that rise as much as 3,000 feet from the ocean. Almost unknown until its establishment in 1978, Misty Fiords is today one of the highlights of an Alaskan trip for many visitors. Be forewarned, however, it's an expensive highlight.

The name "Misty" comes from the wet and cloudy conditions that predominate throughout the summer. Rainfall averages almost 160 inches per year, so be sure to bring rubber boots and raingear. Because of all this rain the land exhibits a verdant beauty, even when clouds drape the mountain slopes.

Flightseeing and Boat Tours

On any given summer day, flightseeing planes constantly take off from Tongass Narrows for trips over the monument. One-hour-and-fifteen-minute flightseeing trips cost around $220 (including a water landing) and are offered by all the local air taxis listed in *Getting Around.*

Another excellent way to see Misty is by boat from either **Alaska Cruises** (907/225-6044 or 800/228-1905, www.mistyfjord. net, 6.5 hrs., $130 adults, $80 kids) or **Allen Marine Tours** (907/225-8100 or 877/686-8100, www.allenmarinetours.com, 4 hrs., $149 adults, $99 kids). Both companies oper-

floatplane and cruise ship, Tongass Narrows

© DON PITCHER

ate catamaran cruises into Misty Fiords in the summer. Along the way, the boats pass towering cliffs, peaceful coves, and dramatic New Eddystone Rock, which juts straight out of the water from a tiny island in the midst of Behm Canal. The tours turn around in Rudyerd Bay before returning to Ketchikan. A delicious and filling lunch is included, and the onboard naturalist is exceptionally knowledgeable. When the weather cooperates, this is one of the best side trips you can take anywhere in Alaska. Alaska Cruises also offers a faster 3.5-hour trip—most folks choose this version—that includes a flightseeing return to Ketchikan (or vice versa) for $260 adults or $220 kids.

Sea Kayaking Tours

The best way to see Misty Fiords is from a kayak. You can paddle there from Ketchikan, but only if you're experienced and adequately prepared. Two Ketchikan companies offer guided, multi-day sea kayaking trips in Misty Fiords: **Southeast Sea Kayaks** (907/225-1258 or 800/287-1067, www.kayakketchikan.com) and **Southeast Exposure** (907/225-8829, www.southeastexposure.com). Both companies also rent kayaks and set up transportation into Misty for those who prefer to paddle independently. Kayakers should be warned that flightseeing planes and cruise ships may impact your wilderness experience in Rudyerd Bay, but other areas get far less use.

Hiking and Cabins

Misty Fiords National Monument has 14 recreation cabins (518/885-3639 or 877/444-6777, www.reserveusa.com, $35). Those near magnificent **Rudyerd Bay** are very popular, and reservations must be made months in advance. There are also 10 trails that take you from saltwater to scenic lakes, most with cabins or free three-sided shelters. Two of the best trails lead up to shelters at Punchbowl and Nooya Lakes. The three-quarter-mile **Punchbowl Lake Trail** switchbacks up from Rudyerd Bay, passing spectacular Punchbowl Creek Waterfall on the way. Punchbowl is one of the finest short hikes in Southeast Alaska, and there's a canoe and

skiff at the lake. Both brown and black bears may be encountered on any of these trails, so be certain to make plenty of noise and to hang all food.

Before heading out on any overnight trips into Misty, talk with staff at the District Office (1817 Tongass, 907/225-2148, www.fs.fed.us/r10/tongass). They can provide information on trail conditions, campsites, and what to expect. Be sure to request a copy of their Misty Fiords map.

METLAKATLA

Twelve miles southwest of Ketchikan on the western shore of Annette Island is the community of Metlakatla (pop. 1,500). Metlakatla (it means "saltwater channel" in Tsimshian) is Alaska's only Indian reservation, a status that was reaffirmed in 1971 when its residents refused to join other Native groups under the Alaska Native Claims Settlement Act. This quiet, conservative town—the only predominantly Tsimshian settlement in Alaska—has a strong religious heritage and the air of a pioneer village. Large frame houses occupy big corner lots, while vacant lots yield abundant berry crops. There seems to be a church on every corner—eight in all, none of them Catholic. Metlakatla boasts a flourishing cannery, cold-storage facility, fish hatchery, rock quarry, and a sawmill. Most of Annette Island is wooded, mountainous terrain reaching up to 3,500 feet, but the town of Metlakatla spreads out across a large, relatively flat portion of the island that contains many muskegs and lakes. Although Metlakatla is only a dozen miles away from Ketchikan, it gets 118 inches of precipitation per year, 44 inches less than Ketchikan.

History

In 1887, a Tsimshian Indian group left Canada in search of religious freedom in Alaska. They discovered an abandoned Tlingit settlement on Annette Island offering a sheltered bay, gently sloping beaches, and a beautiful nearby waterfall. Under the direction of Anglican missionary William Duncan (who established a similar community in Metlakatla, Canada), 823 Tsimshian

© DON PITCHER

Yellow Hill on Annette Island, near Metlakatla

followers began clearing a town site. The converts took new Christian names, dressed in suits, and abandoned much of their cultural heritage. At Metlakatla, Alaska, the settlers established a sawmill to produce lumber for the construction of houses and the first cannery.

The most ambitious building erected was a 1,000-seat church, "The Westminster Abbey of Alaska." It burned in 1948 but was replaced by a replica six years later. In 1891, the U.S. Congress granted the Tsimshians the entire 86,000-acre island as a reservation, a right they jealously guard to this day. Duncan maintained his hold over most aspects of life here until 1913 when a government school opened. (Duncan's paternalism extended in other directions, too: Rumors persist that the bachelor fathered many Metlakatla children.) He opposed the school, preferring that education remain in the hands of his church. The ensuing conflict led to intervention by the U.S. Department of the Interior in 1915, which seized the sawmill, cannery, and other facilities that had been under his personal control. Duncan died

three years later, but his memory is still revered by many, and his influence can still be seen in the healthy little Indian settlement of today. For a fascinating account of Father Duncan and the two Metlakatlas, read Peter Murray's *The Devil and Mr. Duncan* (Sono Nis Press, Victoria, B.C.).

During World War II, the U.S. Army constructed a major military base seven miles from Metlakatla on Annette Island. The base included observation towers (to search for Japanese subs), a large airfield, hangars, communications towers, shore batteries, and housing for 10,000 men. At the time the airport was built, it was the most expensive one ever constructed by the government—everything kept sinking out of sight into the muskeg. Until construction of an airport on Gravina Island in 1973, this airfield was used for jet service to Ketchikan, forcing passengers to land on Annette and fly by floatplane to Ketchikan. With the area's notorious weather, delays were common; many times it took longer to get the last dozen miles to Ketchikan than the 600 miles from

Seattle to Annette Island. Today, the Air Force is slowly constructing a 14-mile road across the northern end of the island to what will eventually (possibly by 2010) become a new dock for the ferry to Ketchikan.

Sights and Events

Father Duncan's Cottage (907/886-8687)—where the missionary lived from 1894 until his death in 1918—is open as a museum when cruise ships are in port or by appointment. The old photographs of Metlakatla and the fascinating assortment of personal items owned by Duncan make a stop here a must. Unique items housed within these walls include old glass fire extinguishers, an 1890 flag with 38 stars, and the second Edison phonograph ever made. Operated by a sewing machine treadle, it was given to Duncan by Edison. Duncan's tiny bed (he stood just over five ft. tall), old medical books, and medicines line the wall. The rather run-down **William Duncan Memorial Church** (built in 1954) stands at the corner of 4th Avenue and Church Street. Duncan's grave is on the left side.

A traditional **longhouse** (open Mon.–Fri. afternoons in summer) has been erected on the waterfront to stimulate local arts and crafts and to help recover the cultural traditions lost because of Duncan's missionary zeal. The back of the building has three totem poles, and the front is decorated with Tsimshian designs. Native dance performances take place when cruise ships are in port. Inside is a small library and a model of one of the floating fish traps that were used on the island for many years. An adjacent **Artists' Village** has booths selling locally made crafts, and is open when cruise ships are in port.

Metlakatla Tours (907/886-8687, www.metlakatlatours.net) leads tours that include the Duncan house, artist village, and a dance performance at the longhouse. These often fill with cruise ship folks, but space may be available if you call ahead.

Locals celebrate the establishment of Metlakatla each year on **Founder's Day,** August 7. As with most other American towns, Metlakatla also has a parade and other events on the 4th of July.

Recreation

Unlike almost everywhere else in Alaska, there are no bears on Annette Island, a relief to those who fear encounters with bruins. A short hiking trail runs from the corner of Milton Street and Airport Road on the southeast edge of town along **Skaters Lake,** a large pond where native plants and ducks can be observed. **Yellow Hill,** a 540-foot-tall fragment of 150 million-year-old sandstone, is unique in Southeast Alaska. The rock is rich in iron and magnesium, giving it a lovely desert-like yellow color set off by gnarled old lodgepole pines. An easy boardwalk trail (20 min. each way) leads up to its summit where you catch panoramic vistas of the western side of Annette, along with the snowcapped peaks of nearby Prince of Wales Island. Get there by walking or hitching 1.5 miles south from town on Airport Road to the signed trailhead on the right side. Some people claim to see George Washington's profile in a nearby mountain visible from Yellow Hill.

Two trails access alpine lakes in the mountains east of Metlakatla. The **Chester Lake Trail** starts at the end of the road, 0.25 mile beyond the ferry terminal. From the trail you get views over the impressive **Chester Lake Falls,** which first attracted Duncan's flock to Annette Island. The trail climbs steeply up steps and a slippery path along a waterline used for power generation. Plan on 45 minutes to reach beautiful Chester Lake, where there's a small dam. From this point, the country is above the tree line and it's possible to climb along several nearby ridges for even better views. Good camping sites are available, but be careful coming up the steep, slippery path with a pack.

Farther afield and not quite as scenic is the **Purple Lake Trail.** Take Airport Road four miles south of town and turn left near the Quonset huts at the unmarked Purple Mountain Road. Follow it two miles to the power plant. The unmarked trail heads directly up a steep jeep road. After a 30-minute climb, you reach a saddle and from there you can head up adjacent ridges into the alpine or drop down to Purple Lake (10 min.). Another place worth a look is the aptly named **Sand Dollar Beach** on the southwest end of the island. Ask locally for directions.

The flat country around Metlakatla contains a labyrinth of dirt roads built during World War II, and if you have a mountain bike or car, they're well worth exploring. You'll find abandoned structures of all types: huge communications towers, strangely quiet empty hangars, old gun emplacements, and a major airport with no planes. From the south end of the road network are excellent views of Prince of Wales and Duke Islands, as well as the open sea beyond Dixon Entrance. This is the southernmost road in Alaska.

Accommodations and Food
Metlakatla Hotel and Suites (3rd Ave. and Lower Milton St., 907/886-3456, www.metlakatlainn.com, $98 s or d) has standard motel rooms with microwaves, fridges, and a guest computer. Meals and car rentals are available.

Tuck'em Inn B&B (907/886-6611, www.alaskanow.com/tuckem-inn, $75 s or $85 d) has six comfortable and well-kept bedrooms in two houses on the same street. A continental breakfast is included.

Get huge portions of burgers, fish and chips, and other greasy fare at the **Mini Mart.** No wonder half the local population seems obese! There's a little espresso stand near the floatplane dock, or head to **Leask's Market** for groceries. Check the bulletin board here for such items as hand-carved fossil ivory or fresh Ooligan grease (if you don't know what it is, you probably won't like it). Metlakatla is a dry town, so alcoholic beverages are not allowed.

Services
Drop by the **municipal building** (907/886-4868), for local information. Camping is discouraged, and visitors who want to stay on Annette Island more than five days must obtain a special permit from the city. A local sponsor is required, and fishing is not allowed. The **Lepquinum Wellness Center,** next to the high school, houses an Olympic-size swimming pool, plus a weight room, racquetball, sauna, and showers. Out front is **Raven and the Tide Woman Totem,** with a descriptive plaque.

Getting There
The ferry *Lituya* provides daily runs between Metlakatla and Ketchikan, stopping at the **ferry terminal** (907/465-3941 or 800/642-0066, www.alaska.gov/ferry) a mile east of town.

ProMech Air (907/225-3845 or 800/860-3845, www.promechair.com) and **Taquan Air** (907/225-8800 or 800/770-8800, www.taquanair.com) have daily floatplane service between Ketchikan and Metlakatla for $80 round-trip.

HYDER AND STEWART
The twin towns of Hyder, Alaska, and Stewart, British Columbia, lie at the head of the long, narrow Portland Canal that separates Canada and the United States. The area's remoteness has kept it one of the relatively undiscovered gems of the entire Pacific Northwest coast. Most people arrive via the stunning 41-mile drive down Highway 37A from Meziadin Junction into Stewart, passing beautiful lakes, majestic glaciers, high waterfalls, spectacular mountain peaks, the narrow Bear River Canyon, and finally the mountain-rimmed, water-trimmed towns.

The town of Stewart (pop. 800) lies at the mouth of the Bear River, while tiny Hyder (pop. 90) is two miles down the road next to the mouth of the Salmon River. They are as different as two towns could possibly be. Stewart is the "real" town, with a hospital, churches, schools, a museum, a pharmacy, a bank, and the other necessities of life; it bills itself as Canada's northernmost ice-free port. In contrast, Hyder, "the friendliest ghost town in Alaska," makes the most of its flaky reputation. Between the two settlements lies an international boundary that seems of little importance; border checks are only made when re-entering Canada. Residents send their kids to school in British Columbia. Everyone uses Canadian currency and the Canadian phone system (area code 250). You can, however, mail letters from a post office in either country, saving postage and the hassles of shipping parcels internationally. Hyder is officially on Alaska Time, but everyone except the postmaster sets their watches one hour later, to Pacific Standard Time.

History

In 1793, Captain George Vancouver, searching for the fabled Northwest Passage, turned into Portland Canal. For days his men worked their boats up the narrow fjord, but when they reached its end after so many miles he was "mortified with having devoted so much time to so little purpose." Over a century later the area finally began to develop. In 1896, Captain David Gilliard of the Army Corps of Engineers (for whom Gilliard Cut in the Panama Canal was later named) explored the region and left behind four stone storehouses, Alaska's first masonry buildings. Prospectors soon arrived and found an incredible wealth of gold, silver, and other minerals in the nearby mountains. Stewart received its name from two of its earliest settlers, Robert and John Stewart. The adjacent Alaskan town was initially named Portland City, but postal authorities, wary of yet another Portland, vetoed it. Instead, the town was named after Frederick B. Hyder, a Canadian mining engineer.

Gold fever and the prospect of a transcontinental Canadian railway terminus attracted more than 10,000 newcomers to the area. The steep, mountainous terrain was difficult to build on; much of Hyder was constructed on pilings driven into the mudflats. The planned railroad made it only a few miles out of town, but in 1919 prospectors struck it rich. The Premier Gold and Silver Mine was, until its 1948 closure, the largest gold mine in North America. After it shut down, the local population dwindled to less than a thousand until development of the Granduc copper mine in the 1960s. To reach the rich Leduc ore vein, workers dug the longest tunnel ever built from one end—10 miles. A devastating avalanche in 1965 buried 40 men in a tunnel entrance, killing 27 of them. The mine operated until 1984 when it was closed down and dismantled, and the site was restored to a relatively natural condition.

The spectacular Stewart/Hyder area has served as the location for several Hollywood movies: *Insomnia, Bear Island, The Thing, Iceman,* and *Leaving Normal.* Recent years have also seen sporadic promises of new gold, silver, coal, or asbestos mines, but times have been hard of late. As one local told me, "The Moose Park Graveyard is full of people still waiting for Hyder to boom."

Sights

Housed in a Fire Hall from 1910, **Stewart Historical Society Museum** (Columbia and 6th Sts., 250/636-2568, www.stewartmuseum. homestead.com, daily July and Aug., C$5) has wildlife specimens on the first floor as well as numerous historical items both upstairs and out front.

On the U.S. side of the international border stands a tiny **stone storehouse** built in 1896 by Captain Gilliard. The building looks like an old jail and once served that purpose, but for much of its life it was a shoe repair shop. On the mudflats in front of Hyder are hundreds of old pilings, remnants of what was once a town of 1,000 people. The straight row of pilings in front of Stewart is all that remains of the aborted transcontinental railroad.

About eight kilometers (5 miles) out of Hyder (turn right at the end of the main drag) is **Fish Creek Wildlife Viewing Area.** From late July to mid-September the creek is filled with pink salmon, along with some of the world's largest chum salmon—some weighing as much as 35 pounds. A viewing platform here provides an excellent vantage point for watching the black and brown bears that feast on the salmon. Forest Service (250/636-2367) staff are on hand to ensure the safety of bear-watchers and to answer questions; see bear photos at www.fishcreek.org.

The road beyond Fish Creek is well worth driving, but before heading out, be sure to ask about road conditions and snow levels; travel by RV is not recommended. Just a quarter-mile beyond Fish Creek are remains of an old brothel operated by Dolly, Ketchikan's best-known madam. Continuing north, the road

FISH TRAPS

The floating fish trap was developed in 1907 and quickly proved an amazingly efficient way to catch salmon. The traps were constructed with heavy wire netting that directed migrating salmon into progressively smaller enclosures. All one had to do was wait. The traps were hated by most Alaskans because they were owned by "outsiders" who could afford the high construction and maintenance costs, and because their efficiency took jobs from local fishermen. Their efficiency also robbed many streams of needed brood stock.

For many years these traps brought in over half of Southeast Alaska's salmon catch. Locals got even by stealing fish from the traps, and those who did often became folk heroes. As a territory, Alaska had no say in its own affairs, but when statehood came in 1959, the first act of the state legislature was to outlaw all fish traps. Only the Annette Island Reservation (which manages all waters within 3,000 feet of the island, and sets its own fish and game regulations) was allowed to continue operating the floating fish traps after statehood, but the last of these was closed in the 1990s.

follows the Salmon River, passes the remains of a covered bridge that once provided access to a remote mine, then begins a torturous climb, re-entering Canada along the way. The first glimpses of stunning **Salmon Glacier** come into view 17 miles from Hyder, but the views improve as the ever-narrowing road climbs above the tree line to a lookout point 23 miles from town. Beyond the glacier is **Tide Lake,** site of the world's greatest yearly snowfall: 88 feet in 1971.

Gorgeous **Bear Glacier,** 20 miles east of Stewart on Highway 37A, should not be missed. Like its more famous cousin, Juneau's Mendenhall, it is a "drive-up glacier" with the highway passing close to its base. The small lake in front is often filled with icebergs.

Accommodations

Ripley Creek Inn (on 5th Ave., 250/636-2344, www.ripleycreekinn.homestead.com, C$110–120 d) in Stewart is the finest local lodging choice, with a dozen large and nicely furnished rooms, including access to the sauna and exercise room. The lobby houses **Toastworks Museum,** an offbeat collection of some 600 antique kitchen appliances. The owners also run Bayview Hotel, with simple but clean rooms for C$45–60 d.

A new home in the center of Hyder, **Kathy's Korner B&B** (250/636-2393, summers only, $60–75 s or d) has four rooms, shared or private baths, continental breakfasts, and a large deck. Other options include **King Edward Hotel/Motel** (250/636-9160 or 800/663-3126, www.kingedwardhotel.com, C$79–99 s or C$89–109 d) in Stewart, and two seasonal Hyder places: **Grandview Inn** (250/636-9174, www.grandviewinn.net, $60 s or $65 d) and **Sealaska Inn** (250/636-9006 or 888/393-1199, www.sealaskainn.com, C$58 s or C$64 d).

Stewart's city-run **Rainey Creek Campground** (250/636-2537 or 888/366-5999, open May–Sept.) is quietly situated on the edge of town and has a cookhouse, firewood, and pay showers. Park RVs at **Camp Run-A-Muck** (250/636-9006 or 888/393-1199, www.sealaskainn.com, C$20 RVs, C$12 tents) in Hyder, or **Bear River RV Park** (250/636-9205, www.stewartbc.com/rvpark, C$21 RVs, C$12 tents) in Stewart.

Food and Drink

Several places serve meals in Stewart, but your best bet is **Bitter Creek Café** (5th Ave., 250/636-2166, May–Sept., www.bittercreek.homestead.com) with gourmet pizzas, pasta, seafood, Mexican, burgers, and homemade breads and desserts, along with espresso and nightly specials. An outside deck is a good place for a beer on a summer day. Inside, a 1930 Pontiac is the centerpiece for an eccentric collection of antiques.

Hyder has three bars for fewer than a hundred inhabitants, and getting "Hyderized" at the **Glacier Inn** (250/636-9248) is an experience that attracts folks from all over the world. It's cheap and lasts a lifetime (you even get an official card), but could also prove expensive if you fail the test. Warning: It involves Everclear. The walls of the Glacier Inn are papered with thousands of dollars in signed bills left by drinkers, creating the "world's most expensive wallpaper." The tradition began when prospectors would tack up a dollar bill on the wall, in case they were broke next trip into town.

Information and Services

Stewart/Hyder International Chamber of Commerce operates the **Stewart Visitor Information Centre** (250/636-9224 or 888/366-5999, www.stewart-hyder.com, daily 9 A.M.–6 P.M. mid-May–Sept.) in Stewart, at the west end of 5th Avenue.

The U.S. Forest Service has a summertime office/information center in Hyder; stop here for details on bear-viewing up the road. For swimming, showers, and a weight room, head to **Stewart High School pool** on 9th Avenue.

The public library is also at the high school. There are no U.S. banks in the area, but Stewart has a branch of the Canadian Imperial Bank of Commerce with an ATM.

Canada Day (July 1) and the American Independence Day (July 4) provide the opportunity for a four-day party in Stewart and Hyder. **International Days,** as it's called, features a parade of pets, daily pancake breakfasts, and culminates in a fireworks display in Hyder as darkness falls on the fourth.

Getting There and Around

There is no ferry service to Hyder. **Taquan Air Service** (250/636-9150 or 907/225-8800, www.taquanair.com) flies every Monday and Thursday between Ketchikan and Hyder. This is also the only time mail goes in or out of the Hyder post office.

Seaport Limousine (250/636-2622, www.seaportnorthwest.com) has vans between Terrace and Stewart, as well as guided tours of the area, including to Fish Creek and Salmon Glacier.

Prince of Wales Island

With more miles of roads than the rest of Southeast Alaska combined, a beautifully wild coastline, deep U-shaped valleys, rugged snow-topped mountains, hidden caves, and a wealth of wildlife, you might expect America's third-largest island (after Kodiak and Hawaii) to be a major tourist attraction. But Prince of Wales Island (POW) has thus far remained off the tourist path for a number of reasons, the primary one being logging. Much of the land has been heavily logged, with huge clear-cuts gouged out of the hillsides, particularly along the extensive road network. Logging has slowed markedly in recent years as the Forest Service shifts to a more diverse land-management policy, and as the Native corporations run out of trees to cut.

Actually, POW's notoriety is its saving grace as well: The towns are authentically Alaskan, with no pretext of civility for the tourists. The

7,000 or so people who live here are friendly, and the roads offer good opportunities for a variety of recreation—including mountain biking—not available elsewhere in the Southeast. The island is very popular with hunters, and the roads provide easy access to many bays for fishing. Black bears and deer are common sights, and wolves are occasionally seen. As logging has declined on POW, tourism—especially from those looking to catch halibut and salmon—has increased. Most of the main roads are now paved, and a ferry provides daily service between Ketchikan and Hollis.

Prince of Wales Island's largest settlement is Craig, on the west coast, but Klawock, Thorne Bay, and Hydaburg each have several hundred people. Rainfall on POW ranges 60–200 inches per year, depending upon local topographic conditions. As an aside, this is one of four Prince of Wales Islands on the planet. The others are in Canada's Northwest Territories, in Australia, and in Malaysia.

Located in Klawock, the **Prince of Wales Chamber of Commerce** (907/826-3870, www.princeofwalescoc.org, Tues.–Fri. 10 A.M.– 3 P.M. year-round) is a good source for local info, and their website features links to many island lodging places and fishing resorts.

CRAIG

Just across a short bridge from the western shore of POW Island, the town of Craig (pop. 1,500) overflows Craig Island. Named for Craig Miller—founder of an early fish cannery here—it was originally even more prosaically called "Fish Egg," for the herring eggs that are considered a Tlingit delicacy. Fishing and logging are the mainstays of Craig's econ-

omy, giving it a likable feeling. The town has two fish-processing plants and a number of sportfishing lodges. No real "sights" in town, but as you enter Craig you pass the **Healing Heart Totem Pole.** Black bears and bald eagles are often seen at the dump, a mile north of town.

Hidden in the J. T. Brown Industrial Park a mile north of town, is **Stone Arts of Alaska** (907/826-3571, www.stoneartsofalaska.com), an unpretentious stone yard and gallery space where you can watch Gary McWilliams as he works on one-of-a-kind pieces—all created from stones he collected in Southeast Alaska. The gallery/stone yard is open daily in the summer, and includes both functional pieces (tables, benches, bowls, and garden art) and fine art—the finest of which sell for upwards of $40,000.

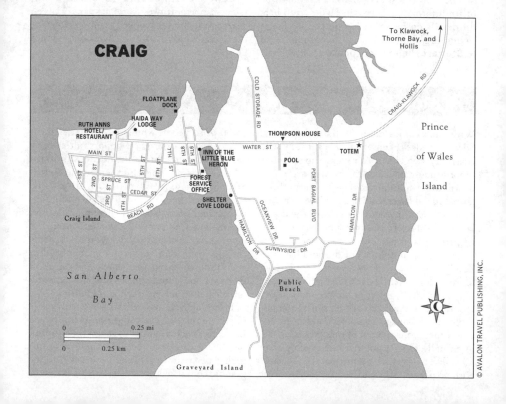

Accommodations

Find quaint, cozy rooms (some with kitchenettes) at **Ruth Anns Hotel** (907/826-3378, $95–115 d), and a suite that includes a private hot tub $(127 d). Nearby is **Haida Way Lodge** (907/826-3268), which charges $110 s or $125 d for standard rooms, or $135 d for rooms with whirlpool tubs. Wi-Fi is available.

Facing the south boat harbor, **Inn of the Little Blue Heron** (907/826-3608, www.little blueheroninn.com) has four rooms with private baths and fridges. The back deck overlooks the boat harbor, and a continental breakfast is served. One room contains two twin beds ($79 s or $89 d), and the other rooms ($99–115 d) have double beds. Also available is a new two-bedroom waterfront home ($155 d or $295 for up to six guests).

Located above Voyageur Bookstore, **Water Street Apartments** (907/826-2333, www.slcntzrcntals.com, $125 for up to six) consists of two efficiency units with small kitchens and Wi-Fi.

Dreamcatcher B&B (1405 Hamilton Dr., 907/826-2238, www.dreamcatcherbed andbreakfast.com, $105 d) is a modern home with three attractive rooms, all with private baths. A continental breakfast is served in the morning, and Wi-Fi is free.

If you have the money and like to fish, **Waterfall Resort** (907/225-9461 or 800/544-5125, www.waterfallresort.com), will put you in seventh heaven. Located on the south end of POW in a beautifully refurbished fish cannery, Waterfall is extremely popular with the elite crowd. Pampered guests stay in tiny Cape Cod–style cottages along a remote stretch of coast, and are treated to great fishing with a personal fishing guide, plus three sumptuous meals daily. It's not cheap: two people should be ready to drop $7,000 for three nights, but this does include floatplane fare from Ketchikan and all expenses.

Right in Craig, **Shelter Cove Lodge** (907/826-2939 or 888/826-3474, www.shelter covelodge.com) has package lodging-and-fishing trips from a modern and comfortable lodge.

RainCountry RV Park (907/826-3632) is on JS Drive.

Food and Services

Meal prices are high on POW; your best bet may be to stock up in Ketchikan or at the grocery store in Craig, **Thompson House** (907/826-3394), which has a deli. The historic **J. T. Brown's General Store** (907/826-3290) is a classic heart-of-town place with groceries, fishing gear, and other supplies. Right next door in another historic structure is **Ruth Anns Restaurant** (907/826-3377, $20–32), a classy place with an old-time atmosphere. You'll find good food three meals a day with a front-row view of the harbor from the dining room. The diverse menu includes seafood, chicken, and steaks for dinner, plus burgers, salads, halibut, fish and chips, and sandwiches for lunch. Dinner reservations are advised if you want a window seat. The building also houses a popular but minuscule bar.

Also downtown is **Dockside Café,** with reasonable breakfasts—available all day—plus tasty lunches and great pies. It's extremely popular with chain-smoking locals, so be ready to gag on the smoke. The $11 fish and chips are the most expensive item on the menu.

Craig's fine-dining experience, **Shelter Cove Lodge** (703 Hamilton Dr., 907/826-2939 or 888/826-3474, www.sheltercovelodge.com, daily June–Aug., $22–30 entrées) has tall windows facing the boat harbor, and a dinner-only menu of fine seafood, steaks, ribs, pasta, and nightly specials.

Very good pizzas—including a pesto and artichoke version—can be had at **Papa's Pizza** (907/826-2244), which also serves chicken and lasagna.

For fresh-roasted coffees, espresso, and pastries—plus books, gifts, CDs, computer rentals, and free Wi-Fi—head to **Voyageur Bookstore** (907/826-2333), across from the grocery store on Cold Storage Road. This is a fine spot to hang out.

Located along the south boat harbor, the Forest Service's **Craig District Office** (907/826-3271, www.fs.fed.us/r10/tongass) has maps and

© DON PITCHER

Ruth Anns Restaurant in Craig

recreational information, including a listing of more charter fishing operators. ATMs can be found at the Wells Fargo and First Bank offices in Craig, and at the Thompson House grocery store.

Craig has an indoor **swimming pool** (907/826-2794) complete with water slide, hot tub, sauna, and weight room. **Log Cabin Sporting Goods** (1 Easy St., 907/826-2205 or 888/265-0375) sells outdoor gear.

KLAWOCK

Six miles from Craig is the Tlingit village of Klawock (pop. 700), home to the oldest cannery in Alaska (1878), along with a bustling sawmill, state fish hatchery, and POW's only airport; all other POW settlements have floatplane service. Klawock is best known for its 21-pole **Totem Park,** which dominates the center of town. These brightly painted poles—all originals—were moved from the old abandoned village of Tuxekan (20 miles north) in the 1930s and restored. The **Prince of Wales**

Hatchery (907/755-2231, www.powhasalmon. org) in Klawock raises coho and sockeye salmon, and has a 250-gallon aquarium filled with coho fry. Free tours are offered Monday–Saturday 1–5 P.M. in the summer. **Stan Snider Park** is a pleasant picnic spot beneath the trees.

Practicalities

Log Cabin Resort and RV Park (907/755-2205 or 800/544-2205, www.logcabinresort andrvpark.com) has a variety of lodging options, starting with basic cabins that share a bathhouse for $70 d. Three suites with kitchenettes in the modern main lodge are $120 d, and a separate log house with a full kitchen is $120 d or $150 for five guests. RV sites ($25) are also available, along with canoe and skiff rentals, and charter fishing.

Although primarily geared to weekly fishing packages, **Southeast Retreat Lodge** (907/755-2994, www.southeastretreat.com) has a furnished apartment with full kitchen for

$250 for up to four, including use of a 4WD vehicle. The lodge sits along Salt Lake.

Fireweed Lodge (907/755-2930, www.fire weedlodge.com), is a full-service fishing lodge in Klawock. Other lodging options include **Klawock Bay Inn** (907/755-2929, www.klawockbayinn.com) and **Changing Tides Inn** (907/755-2305, www.changing tidesinn.com).

Dave's Diner (907/755-2986) serves breakfasts, subs, soups, and sandwiches, or buy groceries and baked goods from **Klawock IGA** (907/755-2722). Next door is **Alaska Kustom Kayaking** (907/209-7082, www .alaskakustomkayaks.com) with guided tours and kayak rentals.

OTHER TOWNS
Thorne Bay
The settlement of Thorne Bay (pop. 600) was for many years the world's largest logging camp, and there's still a bit of logging going on, but the focus has shifted to fishing and tourism.

Thorne Bay isn't the most beautiful place, but it does have all the basics, including a grocery store, gas, lodging, a large and underpopulated high school, and a Forest Service district office (907/828-3304, www.fs.fed.us/r10/tongass).

McFarland's Floatel B&B (907/828-3335 or 888/828-3335, www.mcfarlandsfloatel.com) has modern two-bedroom log cabins that sleep four for $260. No TVs or phones, but the units do have full kitchens, baths, and Wi-Fi. Car and skiff rentals are also available.

Right in town, **Welcome Inn B&B** (907/828-3940 or 888/828-3940, www.lodginginn alaska.com, $75 s or $95 d) has three rooms. A full breakfast is included. Two businesses offer packages that include lodging, a vehicle, and your own skiff: **Adventure Alaska Southeast** (907/828-3907 or 877/499-3474, www.fishorhunt.com) and **The Landing at Otter Cove** (907/247-3528 or 888/424-5445, www.otterinlet.com).

Boardwalk Lodge (907/828-3918 or 800/764-3918, www.boardwalklodge.com)

Thorne River, near Thorne Bay

© DON PITCHER

is a luxurious fishing lodge near Thorne Bay, with access by boat or air.

Ten miles north of town on Forest Highway 30 is **Sandy Beach Picnic Area,** an attractive sandy beach (rare in the Southeast) where you can pitch a tent. The road is narrow and slippery after a rain.

Get very good pizzas from **Dale's Pizza** (907/828-8222), groceries from **Thorne Bay Market** (907/828-3306), and booze from **Riptide Bar** (907/828-3353). **Some Place to Go** has burgers and other fast food.

Thorne Bay's **Prince of Wales Island Logging Show and Fair** takes place the last weekend of July, with fun logging contests, a fair, and vendor booths. Even though logging is becoming less and less important on the island, this is still the island's biggest annual event.

Hydaburg

Hydaburg (pop. 400), 42 miles south of Craig, is the largest Haida settlement in Alaska. The Haida Indians are relative newcomers to the state, arriving in this Tlingit land around 1700. Originally from Canada's Queen Charlotte Islands, the Haida were given parts of POW in compensation for the accidental killing of a Haida chief by the Tlingits. Hydaburg was established in 1911 when three nearby Haida villages combined into one. Hydaburg has the prettiest setting on POW, situated along scenic Sukkwan Strait. Most of the houses, however, are very plain BIA-style boxes. The newly paved road to Hydaburg was only completed in 1983, opening the town to the outside world. In town is a nice row of totems restored by the CCC in the 1930s, along with a newer one erected in 1991. For food, head to **Do Drop In Groceries** (907/285-3311). Ask locally for rooms to rent.

Kasaan

The Tlingit village of Kasaan (pop. 50) is a rough 16-mile drive off the main road between Klawock and Thorne Bay. This is a wonderful out-of-the-way settlement, and just a 15-minute walk from the community hall are a beautiful **clan house** and a number of totem poles set in the woods. The poles were mostly carved in the 1930s and '40s, and the clan house belonged to Chief Son-i-hat, who is buried nearby. (Try to ignore the logging that has been allowed almost right up to the graves.) Older totems are in the abandoned village of Old Kasaan, accessible only by boat.

Logging and Fishing Villages

Several tiny communities (mostly former logging camps) are along the road network on the north end of POW Island.

The little settlement of **Coffman Cove** (pop. 200) is 53 miles north of Klawock. Visitors will find a restaurant and a general store (The Riggin Shack) with groceries, gas, and other essentials. Coffman Cove boasts several lodging options, all on the Web at www.coffmancove. org. They include **Coffman Cove Bunkhouse** (907/329-2219), **Coffman Cove Cabins** (907/329-2251), and **Oceanview RV Park/ Campground** (907/329-2226), which has beach-front campsites, a coin laundry, and showers. The InterIsland Ferry Authority (see the *Getting There* section) has summer-only service four days a week connecting Coffman Cove with the town of Wrangell.

Sixty-five miles north of Klawock is **Whale Pass** (pop. 60), with a general store and gas. Find lodging at **Northend Cabin** (907/846-5315) and **Bear Valley Lodge** (907/247-8512 or 800/936-9600, www.bearvalleylodgealaska.com).

On the far northern end of POW are a couple of minuscule fishing/retirement villages. A long boardwalk connects the homes of **Port Protection** (pop. 50), where **Wooden Wheel Cove Lodge** (907/489-2288 or 888/489-9288, www.woodenwheellodge.com) has fishing-lodge accommodations by the day or week. **Point Baker** (pop. 50) has a small general store and the nation's only floating post office.

RECREATION
Hiking, Camping, and Cabins

There are only a few trails on POW. One of the best and most accessible is the 1.5-mile **One Duck Trail** southwest of Hollis. The trailhead is on the east side of the Hydaburg Road, two miles south of the junction with the Craig–Hollis Road. The path climbs sharply to an Adirondack shelter (free) on the edge of the alpine where the scenery is grand and the hiking is easy. Be sure to wear rubber boots since the trail can be mucky.

The **Soda Lake Trail** (marked) begins approximately 14 miles south of the junction along the Hydaburg Road. This 2.5-mile trail leads to a pungent collection of bubbling soda springs covering several acres. There are colorful tufa deposits (calcium carbonate, primarily) similar to those in Yellowstone, but on a vastly smaller scale. **Control Lake,** at the junction of the Thorne Bay and Big Salt Lake Roads, has a nice cabin ($45) with a rowboat. There are 20 other Forest Service cabins (reservations: 518/885-3639 or 877/444-6777, www.reserveusa.com) scattered around POW, most accessible only by floatplane or boat.

For world-class steelhead and salmon fishing, reserve one of the four cabins in the Karta River area north of Hollis. The five-mile-long **Karta River Trail** connects Karta Bay to the **Salmon Lake Cabin** ($35) and provides panoramic views of surrounding mountains. This is part of the 40,000-acre **Karta Wilderness.**

You can camp almost anywhere on POW's National Forest land, but avoid trespassing on Native lands (these are generally quite easy to identify since the trees have been scalped for miles in all directions). **Eagle's Nest Campground** ($8) is just east of the intersection of the Klawock–Thorne Bay Road and Coffman Cove Road. Also here is a pleasant pair of lakes (Balls Lakes—named for, well, you figure it out) with a short path down to tent platforms overlooking the water. This is a good place for canoeing. **Harris River Campground** ($8) is 19 miles west of Hollis on the road to Klawock. Eagle's Nest and Harris River campground sites can be reserved (518/885-3639 or 877/444-6777, www.reserveusa.com, $9 extra).

Spelunking

Prince of Wales Island has the best-known and probably the most extensive system of caves in Alaska, and spelunkers keep discovering more.

In **El Capitan Cave** explorers found a treasure trove of bones from black bears, brown bears, river otters, and other mammals, the oldest dating back more than 12,000 years. The cave is located on the north end of the island at Mile 51 near Whale Pass. Free Forest Service tours (907/828-3304, www.fs.fed.us/r10/tongass) are offered three times a day in the summer. Bring flashlights, warm clothing, and hiking boots; hard hats are provided. Reservations are required at least two days in advance; no kids under seven.

Three miles south of El Capitan is another underground wonder. A stream flows out of Cavern Lake, and then underground for a few hundred feet before emerging from **Cavern Lake Cave.** You can wade up the waters into the cave for 150 feet or so.

Canoeing

The **Sarkar Canoe Trail** is an easy 15-mile loop route with boardwalk portages connecting seven lakes. The trailhead is at the south end of Sarkar Lake, on the northwest side of Prince of Wales, off Forest Road 20.

A more strenuous route is the 34-mile-long **Honker Divide Canoe Route.** This paddle-and-portage route begins near Coffman Cove at the bridge over Hatchery Creek on Forest Road 30, and works up Hatchery Creek to Honker Lake, which has a Forest Service cabin ($25). You may need to pull the canoe up shallow sections of the creek. The route then continues over Honker Divide on a mile-long portage to the upper Thorne River before heading downstream all the way to Thorne Bay. There is a two-mile portage to avoid dangerous rapids and falls. The route is strenuous and should only be attempted by experienced canoeists. For more information on either of these routes, contact the Thorne Bay Ranger District (907/828-3304, www.fs.fed.us/r10/tongass).

Sea Kayaking

With its hundreds of miles of rugged coastline, and numerous small islands, inlets, and bays, POW offers tremendous opportunities for sea kayakers. One of the wildest areas is

TONGASS NATIONAL FOREST

Three times larger than any other national forest in the country, Southeast Alaska's Tongass National Forest is America's rainforest masterpiece. Within these 17 million acres are magnificent coastal forests, dozens of glaciers, snowcapped peaks, an abundance of wildlife, hundreds of verdant islands, and a wild beauty that has long since been lost elsewhere.

Originally named Alexander Archipelago Forest Reserve in 1902, the area became Tongass National Forest in 1907 by proclamation of President Theodore Roosevelt. It was later enlarged to include most of the Panhandle. For more information, visit the Forest Service Tongass website (www.fs.fed.us/r10/tongass) or contact the Southeast Alaska Discovery Center (907/228-6220) in Ketchikan.

RECREATION

The Tongass is a paradise for those who love the outdoors. It has dozens of scenic hiking trails and over 1,000 miles of logging roads accessible by mountain bike (if you don't mind the clear-cuts and can avoid the logging trucks and flying gravel). The islands contain hundreds of crystal-clear lakes, many with Forest Service cabins on them. Fishing enthusiasts will enjoy catching salmon, cutthroat trout, and other fish from these lakes, the ocean, and the thousands of streams that empty into bays.

The Inside Passage is composed of a wonderful maze of semiprotected waterways, a sea kayaker's dream come true. Particularly popular with kayakers are Misty Fiords National Monument, Admiralty Island National Monument, Glacier Bay National Park, and the waters around Sitka and Juneau, but outstanding sea kayaking opportunities can be found throughout the Southeast. If you have a sea kayak, access is easy, since they can be carried on the ferries (extra charge). Ask the Forest Service recreation staff in the local district offices for information on nearby routes and conditions.

WILDERNESS AREAS

Less than 5 percent of the Tongass has been logged or otherwise developed, so it isn't necessary to visit an official wilderness area to see truly wild country. However, 21 wilderness areas total well over five million acres in the national forest, offering outstanding recreational opportunities. The largest are **Misty Fiords National Monument** (2.1 million acres) near Ketchikan and **Admiralty Island National Monument** (956,000 acres) near Juneau. Other major wildernesses include **Tracy Arm-Fords Terror** (653,000 acres) south of Juneau, **Stikine-LeConte** (449,000 acres) near Wrangell, **Russell Fiord** (349,000 acres) near Yakutat, **South Baranof** (320,000 acres) south of Sitka, and **West Chichagof-Yakobi** (265,000 acres) near Pelican.

Several wilderness areas, such as the remote

---

the 98,000-acre **South Prince of Wales Wilderness,** but access is difficult and much of the area is exposed to fierce ocean storms. Nearby **Dall Island** has exploring possibilities, but parts of it have been logged. On beaches exposed to the open sea, you'll occasionally find beautiful Japanese glass fishing floats that have washed ashore.

Three other wilderness areas along POW's outer coast—**Maurelle Islands, Warren Island,** and **Coronation Island**—offer remote and rarely visited places to see whales, sea otters, and nesting colonies of seabirds. You're likely to see a few fishermen, but nobody else.

GETTING THERE
Ferry

The **Inter-Island Ferry Authority** (907/826-4848 or 866/308-4848, www.inter islandferry.com) operates two vehicle and passenger ferries connecting POW with other parts of Southeast Alaska. The M/V *Prince of Wales* provides daily connections between Ketchikan and the tiny spot called Hollis (no services other than phones and toilets). It's 25 miles from Hollis to Klawock, the nearest town. Reservations for vehicles on this ferry are highly recommended. The M/V *Stikine* connects Coffman Cove on the north end of Prince of Wales with islands off the west coast of Prince of Wales (Coronation, Maurelle, and Warren Islands) are exposed to the open ocean and are inaccessible for much of the year, even by floatplane. Others, such as the Stikine-LeConte, Admiralty Island, Russell Fiord, and Petersburg Creek-Duncan Salt Chuck wilderness areas are relatively accessible. There are developed trails or canoe/kayak routes within the Misty Fiords, Admiralty Island, Stikine-LeConte, Tebenkof Bay, and Petersburg Creek-Duncan Salt Chuck wilderness areas.

FOREST SERVICE CABINS

Tongass National Forest has 150 public recreation cabins scattered throughout Southeast, providing a wonderful way to see the *real* Alaska. Most cabins are rustic, one-room Pan-Adobe log structures 12 by 14 feet in size, with bunk space for 4-6 people. They generally have a woodstove with cut firewood (some have oil stoves), an outhouse, and rowboats at cabins along lakes. You'll need to bring your own bedding, cookstove, cooking and eating utensils, Leatherman or Swiss army knife, food, playing cards, candles, flashlight, matches, and mousetraps. (Some of this will probably be there, but it's better to be sure by bringing your own.) No cell phone coverage, so you're generally on your own when it comes to emergencies.

Many Forest Service cabins can only be reached by floatplane. These flights can be very expensive, but even those on a tight budget should plan to spend some time at one of these cabins. A few can be reached by hiking from towns (Ketchikan, Petersburg, Juneau, and Skagway), cutting out the expensive flight. If you're considering a flight-seeing trip anyway, make it to one of these remote cabins where you get to see what the country is really like. This is one splurge you won't regret!

CABIN RESERVATIONS

The Forest Service charges $35-45 a night for these cabins, with all fees going toward their maintenance. Reservations are on a first-come, first-served basis up to six months in advance; some of the most popular cabins are even chosen by lottery. The Forest Service publishes brochures describing recreation facilities, and can also supply Tongass National Forest maps showing cabin locations. Both the **Forest Service Information Center** (907/586-8751) at Centennial Hall in Juneau and the **Southeast Alaska Discovery Center** (907/228-6220) in Ketchikan, can provide cabin information, as can the ranger district offices scattered around the Southeast. All cabin rentals are made through **Reserve USA** (518/885-3639 or 877/444-6777, www.reserveusa.com.) There is no extra charge for cabin reservations.

Wrangell and the south end of Mitkof Island (home to the town of Petersburg), with service Thursday–Sunday late May to mid-September; no winter service on this route.

Prince of Wales Transportation (907/957-2224) provides shuttle vans from the ferry in Hollis to Craig ($25 per person) and from Craig to the ferry in Coffman Cove ($75 per person). Call a day ahead for reservations.

Air

On a rainy midsummer day when the clouds were almost to the water, I sat in Craig waiting to fly back to Ketchikan. The weather looked marginal to me, but when I asked at the air taxi counter if they were flying, the woman glanced outside and nonchalantly responded, "Oh sure, it looks pretty good today." We flew. Three air taxi operators, **ProMech Air** (907/225-3845 or 800/860-3845, www.promechair.com), **Pacific Airways** (907/225-3500 or 877/360-3500, www.flypacificairways.com), and **Taquan Air** (907/225-8800 or 800/770-8800, www.taquanair.com) have daily floatplane service from Ketchikan to Craig, Hollis, and Thorne Bay. Taquan also flies to smaller settlements scattered across the island. **L.A.B. Flying Service** (907/826-5220, www.labflying.com) flies between Ketchikan airport and Klawock.

GETTING AROUND

For a good road map, pick up the *Prince of Wales Road Guide* at Forest Service offices in Ketchikan, Craig, or Thorne Bay. In the last few years the roads have improved dramatically, and the most-used sections are now paved and in good condition, including roads connecting Hollis, Craig, Klawock, Thorne Bay, and Coffman Cove. Some 1,500 miles of rough gravel roads, most built for logging operations, remain on POW, providing lots of interesting mountain bike rides—if you don't mind the old clearcuts and soggy weather.

Rent cars in Craig from **Wilderness Car Rental** (907/755-2691 or 800/949-2205, www.wildernesscarrental.com) or **Shaub-Ellison Tire & Fuel** (907/826-3450).

Wrangell

Quiet, friendly, and conservative, the settlement of Wrangell (pop. 2,000) sits on an island near the mouth of the Stikine River. The streets are full of folks in pickup trucks, with their dogs hanging out the back and country tunes on the radio. Wrangell is quite unlike its neighbor, prim and proper Petersburg. Wrangell's inner harbor resonates with salmon- and shrimp-processing plants, fishing boats, and seaplanes, while totem poles guard historic Chief Shakes Island. Surrounding the harbor are old buildings on piles, wooded hillsides, and snowcapped mountains. Wrangell is compact enough that visitors can hoof it around to the most interesting sites in an hour or two and still have time to buy beer for the ferry. To see the area right, however, you should spend a couple of days, or longer if you're interested in exploring the mighty Stikine River.

HISTORY
Redoubt St. Dionysius

Third-oldest community in Alaska, Wrangell is the only one to have been governed by four nations: Tlingit, Russia, Britain, and America. Tlingit legends tell of an ancient time when advancing glaciers forced them to abandon their coastal life and move to what is now British Columbia. As the ice retreated after the last ice age, the Stikine River was their entryway back to the newly reborn land. When the Tlingits discovered that the river suddenly disappeared under a glacier, they sent old women to explore, expecting never to see them again. One can only imagine their astonishment when the women returned to lead canoes full of people out to the coast.

For many centuries the Tlingits lived in the Stikine River area, paddling canoes upstream to catch salmon and trade with interior tribes. Similarly, the river figured strongly in Wrangell's founding. Russians began trading with Stikine Indians in 1811; by 1834 the British were trying to move in on their lucrative fur-trading monopoly. To prevent this, Lieutenant Dionysius Zarembo and a band of men left New Archangel (present-day Sitka) to establish a Russian fort near the Stikine River mouth. The settlement, later to become Wrangell, was originally named Redoubt St. Dionysius. When the British ship *Dryad* anchored near the river, the Russians boarded the vessel and refused to allow access to the Stikine. The *Dryad* was forced to return south, but a wedge had been driven in Russia's Alaskan empire. Five years later, the Hudson's Bay Company acquired a long-term lease to the coastline from the Russian government. Redoubt St. Dionysius became Fort Stikine, and the Union Jack flew from town flagpoles.

Gold Fever

The discovery of gold on Stikine River gravel bars in 1861 brought a boom to Fort Stikine. Hundreds of gold-seekers arrived, but the deposit proved relatively small and most

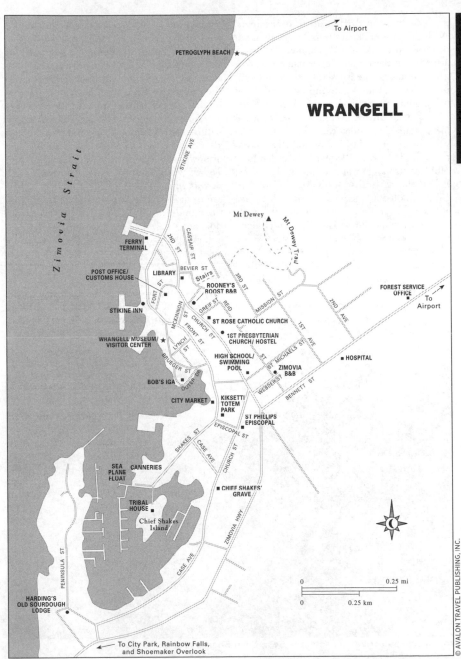

WRANGELL

To Airport

PETROGLYPH BEACH ★

Zimovia Strait

Mt Dewey ▲

Mt Dewey Trail

FERRY TERMINAL

STIKINE AVE

2ND ST

CASSAIP ST

BEVIER ST

POST OFFICE/ CUSTOMS HOUSE

LIBRARY

Stairs

3RD ST

FORT ST

GREIF ST

REID

ROONEY'S ROOST B&B

MISSION ST

2ND AVE

FOREST SERVICE OFFICE

To Airport

STIKINE INN

MCKINNON ST

CHURCH ST

FRONT ST

ST ROSE CATHOLIC CHURCH

1ST PRESBYTERIAN CHURCH/ HOSTEL

1ST AVE

WHANGELL MUSEUM/ VISITOR CENTER ★

LYNCH ST

BRUEGER ST

OUTER DR

HIGH SCHOOL/ SWIMMING POOL

ST MICHAELS ST

HOSPITAL

ZIMOVIA B&B

BOB'S IGA

WEBBER ST

BENNETT ST

CITY MARKET

KIKSETTI TOTEM PARK

ST PHILLIPS EPISCOPAL

SHAKES ST

CASE AVE

EPISCOPAL ST

CHURCH ST

SEA PLANE FLOAT

CANNERIES

CHIEF SHAKES' GRAVE

TRIBAL HOUSE

Chief Shakes Island

ZIMOVIA HWY

PENINSULA ST

CASE AVE

HARDING'S OLD SOURDOUGH LODGE

To City Park, Rainbow Falls, and Shoemaker Overlook

0   0.25 mi

0   0.25 km

prospectors soon drifted on to other areas. With the transfer of Alaska to American hands in 1867, Fort Stikine was renamed Wrangell, after Baron Ferdinand Petrovich von Wrangel, governor of the Russian-American Company. Its population dwindled until 1872 when gold was again discovered in the Cassiar region of British Columbia. Thousands of miners quickly flooded the area, traveling on steamboats up the Stikine. Wrangell achieved notoriety as a town filled with hard-drinking rabble-rousers, gamblers, and shady ladies. When the naturalist John Muir visited in 1879 he called it "the most inhospitable place at first sight I had ever seen… a lawless draggle of wooden huts and houses, built in crooked lines, wrangling around the boggy shore of the island for a mile or so in the general form of the letter *S,* without the slightest subordination to the points of the compass or to building laws of any kind."

By the late 1880s, the second gold rush had subsided and lumbering and fishing were get-

ting started as local industries. The Klondike gold rush of the late 1890s brought another short-lived boom to Wrangell as the Stikine was again tapped for access to interior Canada, but Skagway's Chilkoot Trail became the preferred route. With its rowdy days behind, Wrangell settled into the 20th century as a home to logging and fishing operations, still mainstays of the local economy. Rebuilt after destructive fires in 1906 and 1952, much of downtown is now on rock-fill and pilings. Today, Wrangell is searching for a more prosperous future—and tourism is right at the forefront of that quest—while getting by on the remaining industries: fishing, construction, and small timber operations. It's an easygoing, slow-paced, and friendly town, and a good place to unwind.

SIGHTS

Wrangell is home to the oldest Protestant church building in Alaska, the **First Presbyterian Church,** as well as the oldest

totem pole and Tribal House of the Bear, Chief Shakes Island

© DON PITCHER

Roman Catholic parish, **St. Rose of Lima Catholic Church.** Appropriately located on Church Street, both were founded in 1879. The large, red neon cross atop the Presbyterian church is one of only two in the world used as a navigational aid (the other is in Rio).

Keep your eyes open for local kids selling **garnets** for $0.25 to $10 depending upon the size. They put up tables at the museum and on the cruise ship dock when ships are in port. These imperfect but attractive stones come from a garnet ledge along the Stikine River, deeded to the Boy Scouts in 1962 by a former mayor. At one time the mine was owned by the Alaska Garnet Mining and Manufacturing Company, the world's first women-only corporation.

Chief Shakes Island

This is the centerpiece of picturesque Wrangell harbor. A footbridge at the bottom of Front Street near Wrangell's cannery and cold-storage plant gives access to the island. Here you'll find the **Tribal House of the Bear** (907/874-2023, $2), a Native log house built in 1939–1940 by the CCC. Inside are various artifacts, including beautifully carved houseposts that date from 1835. The house is only open when cruise ships are in port or by appointment. Surrounding the house are seven totems, reproductions of older poles from the area. Shakes Island is especially beautiful at night, surrounded by the town and harbor.

The Shakes lineage was established more than three centuries ago, after the Stikine Tlingits defeated Niska invaders and then forced the vanquished chief, We-Shakes, to give away his name in exchange for peace. **Chief Shakes V's gravesite** is on Case Avenue opposite the Hansen Boat Shop. A white fence surrounds it, and two carved killer whales watch silently. (Surprisingly, Chief Shakes isn't really buried in this grave.)

Several impressive totem poles, carved by the CCC, stand in front of the Library on 2nd Street. Wrangell's small **Kiksetti Totem Park,** next to the City Market along Front Street, has four poles that were carved without the aid of power tools.

Wrangell Museum and Visitor Center

Given the size of Wrangell, its museum (296 Outer Dr., 907/874-3770) is a delightful surprise. Housed in the spacious and modern Nolan Center, it's open Tuesday–Saturday 10 A.M.–5 P.M. May–September, and when cruise ships are in port. The rest of the year, hours are Tuesday–Saturday 1–5 P.M. Admission is $5 adults, $3 seniors, $2 ages 6–12, free for younger children, and $12 for families. Professional exhibits take you through Wrangell's rich past with an in-depth look at the Tlingit, Russian, English, and American peoples who all called this place home. Petroglyphs, Native baskets, old photographs, and local relics are crowded into this provocative museum. Of particular interest are the original houseposts from the Chief Shakes house. Carved in the 1740s—before contact with whites—they are the oldest Tlingit houseposts in existence. The gift shop has a fine selection of books.

Also within the Nolan Center is the **Wrangell Visitor Center** (907/874-3901 or 800/367-9745, www.wrangell.com), staffed Monday–Friday 9 A.M.–3 P.M., and whenever cruise ships are in port. Winter hours are Tuesday–Friday 9 A.M.–3 P.M. You can pick up brochures here if the museum is open, and a computer is available to check your email (fee).

Petroglyphs

Hundreds of ancient petroglyphs (rock carvings) are found on Wrangell Island, but precisely who carved them or when is uncertain. They may date back more than 8,000 years. The best nearby carvings are only a 20-minute walk from town. To get there, turn left (north) from the ferry terminal and walk two-thirds of a mile to a small parking area on the left. A newly built boardwalk provides access to the beach, where you will find a dozen petroglyph rocks along upper parts of the beach, especially those on the right side (facing the water). One of the best, a killer whale, lies on the edge of a grassy lawn to the right of the path. Most petroglyphs face seaward and are near the high-tide line. They may be covered by water if the tide is over

THE PETROGLYPH MYSTERY

Petroglyphs (ancient rock carvings) are found along the coast from Kodiak to the Columbia River, although the greatest concentration is between Sitka and Puget Sound. The coastal type is very different from the petroglyphs of the interior plateau and central Oregon, but has similarities to carvings in the Amur River region of Siberia. Although a single style can be followed down the coast, no one knows who carved the petroglyphs, when they were carved, or why. Contemporary Natives have no knowledge of them. Many petro-glyphs – such as those in Wrangell – face west and were carved on rocks below the high-tide mark. Were they territorial boundary signs? Greetings to returning salmon? Sacred places? As with Stonehenge, we can only speculate. Some have posited that the petroglyphs were just the idle doodles of some ancient graffiti artist. This is unlikely not only from a cultural perspective, but also because of the difficulty of pecking out a design in these hard, fine-grained rocks using only stone tools.

© DON PITCHER

Petroglyph Beach in Wrangell

10 feet. To protect the originals, the state has set up several stone reproductions of the petroglyphs along the boardwalk for those who want to make rubbings. Rubbings are made by placing rice paper—available in local stores—over the copies and rubbing the surface with crayons, ferns, or charcoal. Other petroglyphs are in the Wrangell Museum and in front of the library. Do not make rubbings of the originals.

Mt. Dewey

An excellent half-mile boardwalk/trail winds up Mt. Dewey (actually more of a hill) from 3rd Street behind the high school. It's a steep 15-minute climb up to the top where a platform provides a vantage point over Wrangell. You could probably find a place to camp up here in a pinch. On a wild stormy night in 1879, John Muir did just that. He, however, also decided to build a huge bonfire atop the hill, its flames dancing off the clouds. Muir later wrote, "Of all the thousands of camp-fires I have elsewhere built none was just like this one, rejoicing in triumphant strength and beauty in the heart of the rain-laden gale." To the Native people below, however, the fire ig-nited fears of evil spirits, and as Muir's partner noted, "the Tlingits ever afterward eyed Muir askance, as a mysterious being whose ways and motives were beyond all conjecture."

ANAN CREEK WILDLIFE VIEWING SITE

Anan Creek, 30 miles south of Wrangell on the mainland, is a fine place to watch black and brown bears catching salmon and steelhead. A half-mile boardwalk leads from saltwater to an observation platform above the creek, and a three-sided blind sits closer to the falls where most of the action takes place. The best time to visit is the peak of the pink salmon run, mid-July–mid-August. Forest Service personnel are at the trailhead and observation area to provide information. No food is allowed along these trails, and flash photography is discouraged. The creek is shaded by tall trees and it's often raining, making photography a challenge.

Because of Anan Creek's popularity, permits ($10) are required, and a maximum of 60 visitors are allowed per day in July and August. If you're traveling on your own, get the permit from the Forest Service office in Wrangell (907/874-2323, www.fs.fed.us/r10/tongass). If you're in a guided group, the guide already has your permit.

The Forest Service's **Anan Bay Cabin** (518/885-3639 or 877/444-6777, www .reserveusa.com, $35) is just a mile away on a good trail, but is often booked months in ad-vance; reserve early.

Many visitors to Anan Creek arrive on flights by **Sunrise Aviation** (907/874-2319 or 800/874-2311, www.sunriseflights.com) in Wrangell or **Taquan Air** (907/225-8800 or 800/770-8800, www.taquanair.com) from Ketchikan.

A number of companies offer guided boat trips to Anan Creek, including **Alaska Vistas** (907/874-3006 or 866/874-3006,

www.alaskavistas.com), **Alaska Waters** (907/874-2378 or 800/347-4462, www.alaska waters.com), **Alaska Charters and Adventures** (907/874-4157 or 888/993-2750, www.alaska upclose.com), and **Breakaway Adventures** (907/874-2488 or 888/385-2488, www.break awayadventures.com). Expect to pay $200 per person for a trip that includes four hours on the ground at Anan.

Those with a sea kayak may want to paddle along the east side of Wrangell Island to Anan Bay. En route, be sure to visit scenic **Berg Bay,** an area rich in moose, mountain goats, grizzlies, deer, geese, and other wildlife. A Forest Service cabin ($35) is available here, and a trail leads from the cabin along Berg Creek for several miles into a cirque basin with old mine ruins.

EVENTS

Wrangell's **Stikine River Garnet Festival** in late April celebrates the arrival of spring with natural history presentations, eagle-watching tours, live music, and even garnet bingo. From mid-May to mid-June, pull out your fishing pole for the **King Salmon Derby**—top prize is $6,000. The main summer event is the town's **July 4th** celebration, with a parade, logging show, log rolling contests, tug of war, tugboat races, street dance, and fireworks. All this is funded by a handful of teenagers and their fam-ilies who run downtown food booths in June.

RECREATION

Rain Walker Expeditions (907/874-2549, www.rainwalkerexpeditions.com) rents bikes, canoes, and kayaks, plus a floating cabin near Anan Creek, from its office across from Sti-kine Inn. Owner Marie Oboczky leads infor-mative nature hikes and bus tours, from two hours to all day. They're fun and geared to your area of interest, whether it's petroglyphs or rainforests.

A paved **walking/biking path** runs from Wrangell for six miles to the trailhead for Rainbow Falls at Shoemaker Bay.

Alaska Vistas (907/874-3006 or 866/874-3006, www.alaskavistas.com) guides sea kaya-king day trips and multi-day adventures in the

Wrangell area. **Klondike Bike** (502 Wrangell Ave., 907/874-2453, www.klondikebike.com) has quality mountain bikes for rent.

Muskeg Meadows Golf Course (907/874-4653, www.wrangellalaskagolf.com) is an attractive nine-hole course with putting greens, a pro shop, and driving range.

Wrangell's **swimming pool** (907/874-2444) is at the high school. Fishing and sightseeing **charters** are available through a number of local outfits; get brochures from the visitor center.

Boat Tours

Wrangell is the primary starting point for fun and fast jetboat tours to watch bears at Anan Creek (see the *Anan Creek Wildlife Viewing Site* section) or to motor up the mighty Stikine River (see *The Stikine River* section). Three companies also offer excellent all-day jetboat trips to LeConte Glacier and Petersburg: **Breakaway Adventures** (907/874-3455 or 888/385-2488; www.breakaway adventures.com), **Alaska Waters** (907/874-2378 or 800/347-4462, www.alaskawaters .com), **Alaska Vistas** (907/874-3006 or 866/874-3006, www.alaskavistas.com).

Hiking

Scenic **Rainbow Falls Trail,** a moderately steep 0.75-mile hike (710 stairsteps!), begins across the road from Shoemaker Bay Campground, five miles south of town. More ambitious bodies can continue three miles up the trail to **Shoemaker Overlook** (1,500 ft.). The trail accesses large, ridge-top muskeg areas and ends at a three-sided Adirondack-style shelter offering a panoramic vista of Zimovia Strait. The trail and shelter provide an excellent opportunity for an overnight camping trip. The trail is steep and often muddy, but has boardwalk in places.

Logging roads crisscross most of Wrangell Island, providing cycling opportunities for mountain bike enthusiasts—if you enjoy seeing cut-over land. Those with wheels may want to visit several areas on the island. **Long Lake Trail,** 28 miles southeast of Wrangell along Forest Road 6271, is a half-mile boardwalk

that ends at an Adirondack shelter complete with a rowboat, fire grill, and outhouse. In the same vicinity is a 300-foot path to **Highbrush Lake,** where you'll find a small boat in which to practice your rowing skills. Individuals with disabilities may want to try fishing at **Salamander Creek,** 23 miles south of town on Forest Road 6265, where ramps lead right up to a pad along the creek. Good fishing for king salmon here, along with three campsites. For information on cabins and other trails around Wrangell, visit the Forest Service's **Wrangell Ranger District Office** (525 Bennett St., 907/874-2323, www.fs.fed.us/r10/tongass).

Cabins

There are 21 different Forest Service cabins (info: 907/874-2323; reservations: 518/885-3639 or 877/444-6777, www.reserveusa.com; $35) near Wrangell, including several described in the *Stikine River* section. The closest is at **Virginia Lake,** accessible by floatplane—and another nearby cabin is at **Kunk Lake,** across Zimovia Strait from the south end of the Wrangell Island road system. Access is by kayak, or skiff if you can get someone to run you across. A 1.5-mile trail climbs to a three-sided shelter at the lake. From here, it's a relatively easy climb into high-elevation muskeg and alpine areas that cross Etolin Island.

ACCOMMODATIONS

Housed within the Presbyterian church, Wrangell's **Youth Hostel** (220 Church St., 907/874-3534, $18 per person) is open late May–early June. It's clean and well-managed, but nothing fancy, with air mattresses for sleeping, along with kitchen and shower facilities. A private room ($40 s or d) is also available if you call ahead, along with a family room ($18 per person). The hostel is open all day, so you don't need to be out during the day.

New owners brought major improvements to the centrally located **Stikine Inn** (107 Stikine Ave., 907/874-3388 or 888/874-3388, www .stikineinn.com). Standard rooms cost $95–105 s, $105–115 d, and suites with kitchenettes cost $120 d. Be sure to request a remodeled room.

Zimovia B&B (319 Webber St., 907/874-2626 or 866/946-6842, www.zimoviabnb.com, $85 d) has a quiet, edge-of-the-woods location in a cedar-shingled home just a few blocks from downtown. The two guest rooms each have private baths and entrances, and one includes a sauna. The light breakfast includes home baked goods. Free Wi-Fi and van transport around town.

Rooney's Roost B&B (206 McKinnon, 907/874-2026, www.rooneysroost.com) has five comfortable guest rooms for just $80 d with shared bath, or $100 d with private baths. The attractive home contains avian collectibles, and a gourmet breakfast is included. Friendly owners, too.

Located two miles south of town, Grand View B&B (907/874-3225, www.grandviewbnb.com, $95–105 d) is a nice hillside home facing Zimovia Straits. The three guest rooms have private baths and the breakfast is filling.

Wrangell's most unique lodging option is ⟨ Rain Haven Houseboat (907/874-2549, www.rainwalkerexpeditions.com), a surprisingly cozy little place with room for five, plus cooking and bath facilities. During July and August it's located in remote and beautiful Bradfield Canal, southwest of Wrangell. Take the canoe to nearby Berg Bay for a hike, or it's an hour paddle to the bears at Anan Creek. Three-day stays are $575 d, including transportation from Wrangell and a Stikine River jetboat trip; add $100/day for use of a skiff. The rest of the year the houseboat is docked at Shoemaker Bay, five miles south of Wrangell, where it rents for $85 d, including transportation from town and a bike to explore nearby trails.

CAMPING

Free tent camping is allowed (no RVs) at City Park just beyond the ball field, two miles south of the ferry on the water side of Zimovia Highway. The official limit is 24 hours, but this is not strictly enforced. Showers are available at a coin laundry near Chief Shakes Island, and at the high school swimming pool.

You'll find additional camping at the city-run Shoemaker Bay RV Park (907/874-2444, RVs $25), five miles south of town and right alongside the highway. Open all year. Guests get a pass to the city pool for showers and a free swim, and the area is near trails to Rainbow Falls and Shoemaker Overlook. The Forest Service's free Nemo Campground is 14 miles south of town and up Forest Roads 16 and 6267; impressive views across Zimovia Strait.

Alaska Waters RV Park (241 Berger St., 907/874-2378 or 800/347-4462, www.alaskawaters.com, RVs $25) is on the south side of the harbor.

FOOD

Wrangell eating places deliver old-fashioned American meals without pretense. The Garnet Room inside Stikine Inn (107 Stikine Ave., 907/874-3388) has Zimovia Strait views from the dining room, with three meals a day; try the tender New York steak.

Get espresso—and use the free Wi-Fi—at the seasonally open Java Junkie next to the downtown dock. Nearby is Memories, a little trailer where you'll find tasty fish and chips and fresh oysters.

Zak's Café (316 Front St., 907/874-3355) offers a good variety of food: pasta, stir-fries, and steaks for dinner ($15–20), and lunchtime salads, sandwiches, and wraps. The setting is simple and clean, with fast service.

The Elks Club (9126 Front St., 907/874-3716) is open to the public for reasonably priced dinners most nights, including Saturday-night steak specials.

Bob's IGA (on Outer Dr., 907/874-2341) has a deli with inexpensive sandwiches. City Market (on Front St., 907/874-3336) is Wrangell's other grocery store. Both are closed on Sundays.

Locals hang out in Marine Lounge (274 Shakes St., 907/874-3005)—a.k.a. the Hungry Beaver—which has the best pizzas in town. The Totem Bar (116 Front St., 907/874-3533) also serves burgers and other pub fare; these smoke-filled bars are the only places serving meals after 8 P.M.

SERVICES

The Forest Service's **Wrangell Ranger District Office** (525 Bennett St., 907/874-2323, www.fs.fed.us/r10/tongass) is three-quarters of a mile from town on the left side of the road. It has information on local hiking trails, the Stikine River, and nearby recreation cabins.

Adjacent to the Stikine Inn is **River's Edge Fine Arts and Gifts** (907/874-3508, www.marineartist.com), selling locally made clothing, carved wooden bowls, pottery, and jewelry, plus the distinctive marine art of owner Brenda Schwartz.

The **library** (124 2nd Ave., 907/674-3535) has a good collection of books about Alaska and a couple of petroglyphs out front, along with computers for Internet access. Head to the Nolan Center theater for weekend movies.

Located out Airport Road, the **Wrangell Medical Center** (907/874-3356, www.wrangell medicalcenter.com) has physicians on staff.

GETTING THERE AND AROUND

Wrangell's **ferry terminal** (907/874-2021; 907/874-3711 for departure times) is right in town. **Alaska Marine Highway** (907/465-3941 or 800/642-0066, www.ferryalaska.com) ferries head both north and south almost daily during the summer, but the terminal is open only for vessel arrivals and departures.

The **Inter-Island Ferry Authority's** (907/826-4848 or 866/308-4848, www.inter islandferry.com) M/V *Stikine* connects Coffman Cove on the north end of Prince of Wales with Wrangell, and continues northward to the south end of Mitkof Island, where a good gravel road continues to the town of Petersburg. This ferry operates Thursday–Sunday late May–mid-September; no winter service.

The airport is 1.5 miles from town on Bennett Street. **Alaska Airlines** (800/426-0333, www.alaskaair.com) has daily flights from Wrangell to Juneau, Ketchikan, Petersburg, and Sitka. **Sunrise Aviation** (907/874-2319 or 800/874-2311, www.sunriseflights.com) provides flightseeing trips and charter flights to nearby Forest Service cabins and Anan Creek.

They often have seat fare rates if someone else has already set up a charter; this can be a fast and reasonable way to fly to Petersburg or Prince of Wales.

Rent cars at the airport from **Practical Rent-A-Car** (907/874-3975) for $50 a day. Both **Northern Lights Taxi** (907/874-4646) and **Star Cab** (907/874-3622) charge $5 from the airport to town.

◖ THE STIKINE RIVER

Seven miles north of Wrangell is the Stikine River, one of the top 10 wild rivers of Canada, and the fastest navigable river in North America. The river begins its 330-mile journey to the sea high inside British Columbia's Spatsizi Wilderness Park. The 55-mile-long **Grand Canyon of the Stikine,** just above Telegraph Creek, B.C., has thousand-foot walls enclosing fierce white water. River travel is easier below Telegraph Creek all the way to Wrangell, between high peaks of the coast range, past glaciers and forested hills. At one spot on the river, 21 different glaciers are visible! These glaciers dump tons of silt into the river, coloring it a milky gray; at the mouth of the Stikine, the sea takes on this color for miles in all directions. So much for the advertisements about glacially pure water.

Each spring, upward of 1,500 bald eagles flock to the river mouth to eat "hooligan" (eulachon), an oily fish that spawns here from late March to early May. The fish also attract hundreds of thousands of gulls and kittiwakes, plus harbor seals, Steller sea lions, and even killer whales.

River Tours

Several Wrangell charter boat operators provide fun jetboat trips up the Stikine River with a lunch break at Shakes Glacier and fast runs up the back sloughs. Three of the larger operators are **Breakaway Adventures** (907/874-3455 or 888/385-2488; www.breakawayadventures .com), **Alaska Waters** (907/874-2378 or 800/347-4462, www.alaskawaters.com), and **Alaska Vistas** (907/874-3006 or 866/874-3006, www.alaskavistas.com). All of these do a great job of showing the sights, but the Break-

© DON PITCHER

Stikine River, near Wrangell

away and Alaska Vistas trips are cheaper ($150 versus $179 for a 6-hour trip) and also include a soak at Chief Shakes Hot Springs.

Running the River

The Stikine River is a popular destination for kayakers, canoeists, and river rafters. (It's even more popular with local jetboaters, so don't expect peace and quiet in the lower reaches.) Most folks choose to float down the river, after being transported up from Wrangell by boat or plane. You will need to go through customs (907/874-3415) at the Wrangell airport if you cross the border. In addition, a Canadian agent is frequently stationed along the river just across the border. The Forest Service publishes a helpful guide to canoeing or kayaking the Stikine River; it's available from the Wrangell Ranger District (907/874-2323, www.fs.fed .us/r10/tongass).

Stikine Riversong Lodge (250/235-3196, www.stikineriversong.com) in Telegraph

Creek 160 miles upriver from Wrangell, has lodging, supplies, and a pleasant café. The owners also offer river tours, canoe and kayak rentals, and will help you set up trips down the Stikine.

In Wrangell, rent kayaks and canoes from **Rain Walker Expeditions** (907/874-2549, www.rainwalkerexpeditions.com) or **Alaska Waters** (907/874-2378 or 800/347-4462, www.alaskawaters.com); they can also set up jetboat transportation to Telegraph Creek. **Alaska Vistas** (907/874-3006 or 866/874-3006, www.alaskavistas.com), leads nine-day raft trips down the Stikine River.

Camping and Cabins

The lower Stikine is a multi-channeled, silt-laden river nearly a mile wide in places. The route is spectacular, wildlife crowds the banks, campsites are numerous, and 13 Forest Service cabins (reservations: 518/885-3639 or 877/444-6777, www.reservcusa.com, $35) are available. One of the finest is the **Mount Rynda Cabin** along crystal-clear Andrew Creek, a spawning area for king salmon. You may also want to stay in one of the two extremely popular cabins near **Chief Shakes Hot Springs.** At the springs you'll discover beautifully maintained wooden hot tubs (one enclosed to protect you from the mosquitoes); these are great places to soak those aching muscles. The area gets mighty busy on summer weekends, so you probably won't have it to yourself, and things can get rowdy after the locals pop a few beers. Escape the crowds at the main hot springs by finding your own undeveloped springs nearby.

The upper portion of the Stikine is a vastly different river, with less noise and development than on the U.S. side of the border and a drier, colder climate. The vegetation reflects this. The historic settlement of **Telegraph Creek** is accessible by road from the rest of British Columbia, or you can charter a small plane or jetboat from Wrangell. The upper river above here is some of the wildest white water anywhere; canoeists and kayakers intent on running the river would do best to begin at Telegraph Creek.

Petersburg

Southeast Alaska's picture-postcard town, Petersburg (pop. 3,200) sits at the northern tip of Mitkof Island along Wrangell Narrows. Great white walls of snow and ice serve as a dramatic backdrop for the town. "Peter's Burg" was named after Peter Buschmann, who built a sawmill here in 1897, followed by a cannery three years later. With ample supplies of fish, timber, and glacial ice, the cannery proved an immediate success—32,750 cases of salmon were shipped that first season. Unlike boom-and-bust Wrangell, the planned community of Petersburg has kept pace with its expanding fishing base. A number of the present inhabitants are descended from Norwegian fishermen, who found that the place reminded them of their native land. The language is still occasionally heard on Petersburg's streets, and Norwegian *rosemaling* (floral painting) can be found on shutters of the older homes.

Petersburg is a prosperous and squeaky-clean town with green lawns, tidy homes, and a hardworking heritage that may appear a bit cliquish to outsiders. The country around Petersburg is filled with opportunities for exploration by those who love the outdoors, but this off-the-beaten-path community still views tourism with a degree of skepticism. Although Petersburg has a lumber mill, fishing remains the main activity, with salmon, halibut, herring, crab, and shrimp all landed. The odor of fish hangs in the air, and bumper stickers proclaim "Friends don't let friends eat farmed salmon." Petersburg has the most canneries in Southeast Alaska (four) and is home to a large halibut fleet.

Wrangell Narrows

Between Wrangell and Petersburg the ferry passes through tortuous Wrangell Narrows, a 46-turn nautical obstacle course that resembles a pinball game played by ship. This is one of

humpback whale sign, Petersburg

© DON PITCHER

the highlights of the Inside Passage trip and is even more exciting at night when the zigzag course is lit up like a Christmas tree. Be up front to see it. The larger cruise ships are too big to negotiate these shallow waters between Kupreanof and Mitkof Islands, thus sparing Petersburg from the tourist blitz and glitz that most other Southeast towns endure.

SIGHTS
In Town

Petersburg's main attraction is its gorgeous harbor and spectacular setting. The sharply pointed peak visible behind Petersburg is **Devil's Thumb,** a 9,077-foot mountain 30 miles away on the U.S.–Canadian border. Built in 1912, the large **Sons of Norway Hall** (907/772-4575) stands on pilings over scenic Hammer Slough, and is adorned with traditional Norwegian *rosemaling* designs. Next to Sons of Norway is the surprisingly small *Valhalla,* a replica of the original Viking boat. It was built in 1976 and sailed in the parade of ships bicentennial celebration in New York Harbor. A memorial to fishermen lost at sea stands next to the Sons of Norway Hall. Walk up the wooden street along **Hammer Slough** to see old homes hanging over this tidal creek.

© DON PITCHER

Valhalla, replica of a Viking boat, in front of Sons of Norway Hall

The boat harbors usually have several Steller sea lions cruising around.

Clausen Memorial Museum (2nd and Fram Sts., 907/772-3598, www.clausenmuseum .alaska.net, $3, free for kids under 13) is open Monday–Saturday 10 A.M.–5 P.M. May–early September; call for winter hours. Inside are exhibits on commercial fishing—including the world's largest king salmon (a 126-pound monster) and chum salmon (36 pounds)—plus the Cape Decision lighthouse lens, a 200-year-old Tlingit dugout canoe, bentwood box, and other historical exhibits. Outside is *The Fisk,* a fishy sculpture and fountain by Carson Boysen.

Nearby

A good place to watch for America's national bird is **Eagle's Roost Park,** north of the Petersburg Fisheries cannery. Upward of 30 eagles can be seen along here when the tide is low. Whales, seals, and sea lions are frequent sights in Frederick Sound near **Sandy Beach Park**

north of town. Covered picnic tables and a playground add to the allure, and by late summer, pink salmon spawn in the tiny creek that flows through the park. Hike to the west side of Sandy Beach Park to discover ancient petroglyphs on the rocks. Icebergs from LeConte Glacier are common along the north side of Frederick Sound and sometimes drift across to Petersburg, especially in winter.

Heading out the Road

South of town, the main road is paved for 18 miles, with a gravel road continuing another 16 miles to the southeast end of Mitkof Island. From this point you have excellent views of the nearby Stikine River mouth and the white-capped peaks of the Coast Range. Canoeists or kayakers (with transportation) may want to start their trip up the Stikine from here rather than at Wrangell.

Approximately eight miles out is a small turnoff to **Falls Creek,** a pleasant picnic spot. Stop here to look at the fish ladder (built in 1959) used by coho and pink salmon, as well as steelhead.

Located 15 miles south of town, the **Blind River Rapids Trail** is an easy half-mile boardwalk that leads through the muskeg to a three-sided shelter overlooking the saltwater rapids. Bring your fishing pole. The trail loops back through the muskeg for a total distance of nearly a mile.

A **trumpeter swan observatory** is set up on Blind Slough 16 miles south of Petersburg. A dozen or so of these majestic birds overwinter here, and other waterfowl abound during spring and fall migrations. The state-run **Crystal Lake Fish Hatchery** (907/772-4772), 18 miles south of Petersburg, produces king and coho salmon. The kings return in June and July, while the coho come back to spawn from mid-August through September. Blind Slough flows away from the hatchery and is a great place to explore by canoe or kayak. The water gets swimmably warm by mid-summer, and picnic tables sit in the trees. The Forest Service's Ohmer Creek Campground is three miles farther down the road.

LECONTE GLACIER

LeConte Glacier, the southernmost tidewater glacier in North America, dips into LeConte Bay on the mainland, 25 miles east of Petersburg. Part of the vast Stikine Icefield, its glacial ice was once used by local fishermen to keep their catches cold on the way to market in Seattle. Today, locals use it to cool their drinks. LeConte Bay is home to 2,000 harbor seals. The entire area is included within the 448,841-acre **Stikine-LeConte Wilderness.**

There are no Forest Service cabins in LeConte Bay, but an excellent one is on **Mallard Slough** (reservations: 518/885-3639 or 877/444-6777, www.reserveusa.com, $35), near its entrance. A 1.5-mile trail connects the cabin and Le Conte Bay, where you're likely to find icebergs high and dry at low tide. A fine trip for experienced sea kayakers is to head up the Stikine River from Wrangell and then into LeConte Bay, 10 miles north, before crossing Frederick Sound and continuing on to Petersburg. Total distance is approximately 50 miles (longer if you explore the Stikine River or LeConte Bay).

Getting There

The visitor center has a complete listing of boat charters for glacier sightseeing, whale-watching, and fishing. Good companies include **Kaleidoscope Cruises** (907/772-3736 or 800/868-4373, www.petersburglodgingandtours.com), **Hook & Eye Adventures** (907/772-3400, www.alaska.net/~hookeye), and **Whale Song Cruises** (907/772-9393, www.whalesongcruises.com).

Kupreanof Flying Service (907/772-3396, www.kupreanof.com), **Nordic Air** (907/772-3535), **Pacific Wing** (907/772-4258, www.pacificwing.com), and **Temsco Helicopters** (907/772-4780 or 877/789-9501, www.temscoair.com) all offer flightseeing tours over the glacier.

ENTERTAINMENT AND EVENTS

Petersburg's **Little Norway Festival,** held each year on the weekend nearest Norwegian Independence Day (May 17), is the town's biggest event. The three-day festivities include a parade, crafts, pageant, and a big seafood feast. The **American Independence Day** (July 4) is another time for fun and games, and the annual king salmon derby in late May is always popular with locals.

The **Petersburg Canned Salmon Classic** is a contest to guess the number of cans of salmon packed by local canneries each year; $2,000 goes to the person who comes closest. It's awarded in mid-August.

Live music, booze, cigarette smoke, and a clientele of local toughs make for good fights in **Kito's Kave** (on Sing Lee Alley, 907/772-3207). The nautically themed **Harbor Bar** (on Nordic Dr., 907/772-4526) is a good place to meet local fishermen over a beer.

RECREATION

Contact **Tongass Kayak Adventures** (907/772-4600, www.tongasskayak.com) for sea kayaking around the harbor and up Petersburg Creek. Four-hour trips with guide are $70. The company also runs multi-day kayaking tours to LeConte Glacier, the Stikine River, and Tebenkof Bay, and rents kayaks for do-it-yourselfers.

Stop by the **Forest Service district office** (reservations: 518/885-3639 or 877/444-6777, www.reserveusa.com, $35) at Nordic and Haugen for detailed maps of local hiking trails and 25 nearby cabins. A pleasant walk takes off from Nordic Drive, three miles from town and just beyond Sandy Beach, and continues down a mile-long boardwalk to **Frederick Point.** Along the way, you get a taste of muskeg, rainforest, and a creek that's packed with salmon in August. You can return to town along the beach.

A short in-town boardwalk leads through the muskeg from the top of Excel Street to the senior center on 12th Street. The center is crowded with flowers outside, along with a menagerie of ducks, rabbits, geese, turkeys, and chickens. Right across the street is the Forest Service's area office. In addition, the half-mile **Hungry Point Trail** traverses the muskeg from Hungry Point to the ball field.

SOUTHEAST ALASKA

Ravens Roost Cabin

Petersburg has one of the few Forest Service cabins in Southeast Alaska that can be reached by hiking from town. The Ravens Roost cabin lies 1,600 feet above sea level at the end of a four-mile trail that starts near the airport. The trail crosses muskeg for the first mile and becomes very steep (and often mucky) for the next mile through the forest before breaking into open muskeg again along a ridge. Here the trail is in better condition and you are treated to grand views of Devil's Thumb and the surrounding country. The path ends at a two-level Forest Service cabin with space for up to eight people. Allow three hours for the hike up and be sure to make advance reservations for the cabin through the Forest Service.

Three Lakes Recreation Area

Very popular with locals for picnicking, fishing, and berry picking is the beautiful Three Lakes Recreation Area along Forest Service Road 6235, 22 miles southeast of town. You can hitch there, but it's a long hike back to town if your thumb is numb. Each lake has a rowboat and picnic table and you may want to camp nearby at the old three-sided shelter built by the CCC along tiny **Shelter Lake.** An easy three-mile boardwalk loop trail connects the lakes, and a boardwalk trail continues from Sand Lake to nearby Ideal Cove, a mile and a half away. The three main lakes (Sand, Hill, and Crane) are named after the sandhill cranes that announce each spring.

Kupreanof Trails and Cabins

On nearby Kupreanof Island, the Petersburg Mountain and Petersburg Lake trails provide good hiking and great views. Both paths begin at Bayou Point directly across Wrangell Narrows. Contact **Petersburg Creek Charters** (907/772-2425, www.alaska.net/~psgcreek) for a water taxi from town. A number of Forest Service cabins are available on Kupreanof.

For **Petersburg Mountain Trail,** walk north (right) up the road 1.5 miles to the trail marker. Be prepared for a very steep, muddy, and brushy path, rising 3,000 feet in a distance

of only 2.5 miles. From the top, however, you'll be rewarded with outstanding views of the entire Petersburg area.

Petersburg Lake Trail provides an easy 6.5-mile hike to a Forest Service cabin on Petersburg Lake within the 46,777-acre **Petersburg Creek-Duncan Salt Chuck Wilderness.** Check with the Forest Service for current conditions on both of these trails. From Petersburg Lake it's possible to continue another 10.5 miles along a primitive trail to the Forest Service's Salt Chuck East Cabin. The trail is nearly level the entire distance and offers spectacular views of Portage Mountain.

On the south end of Kupreanof Island is **Kah Sheets Lake,** where the Forest Service has a very popular A-frame cabin. It's a 30-minute flight from Petersburg. A three-mile trail leads from the lake to Kah Sheets Bay, where you can fish for coho and sockeye salmon. A second Forest Service cabin sits along the bay.

West Point Cabin, in Portage Bay on the north end of Kupreanof Island, is a great spot to watch for whales, and the beach makes for good hiking.

Thomas Bay Area

Several of the most popular local Forest Service cabins are in the country around Thomas Bay, on the mainland approximately 20 miles from Petersburg. Spectacular Baird and Patterson Glaciers feed into this bay. Reserve months ahead to ensure a spot. **Cascade Creek Cabin** is on the saltwater and is accessible by either air or charter boat. Backpackers will love **Cascade Creek Trail,** one of the best (and steepest) paths in the Southeast. This three-mile path climbs 3,000 feet from the cabin to Falls Lake, passing cascading water much of the way. A three-sided shelter (free) sits along the shore of Falls Lake, and there's good fishing for rainbow trout. Hikers can continue two more miles up the trail beyond Falls Lake to Swan Lake. **Swan Lake Cabin** is on the opposite end of the lake from the trailhead and offers great views of the rocky mountain country. Contact the Petersburg Forest Service office for details on trail conditions and access.

ACCOMMODATIONS

For a complete list of local lodging choices, see the Petersburg Chamber of Commerce website (www.petersburg.org) or try www.petersburgalaska.com. The best deal in town is **Alaska Island Hostel** (805 Gjoa St., 907/772-3632 or 877/772-3632, www.alaskaislandhostel.com, $25 per person) where Ryn Schneider makes everyone welcome. There are separate men's and women's dorms (four bunks per room), along with a kitchen, laundry, and free Internet access. No children under six, and check-in is 5–8 P.M. Reservations required for winter stays.

Petersburg's largest lodging place, **Tides Inn** (307 N. 1st., 907/772-4288 or 800/665-8433, www.tidesinnalaska.com, $90 s, $105 d) has clean and well-maintained rooms, Wi-Fi, a guest computer, and very friendly owners. Some rooms include fridges and microwaves.

Scandia House (110 Nordic Dr., 907/772-4281 or 800/722-5006, www.scandiahousehotel.com) is a modern building with 33 brightly furnished rooms. Standard rooms (some with kitchenettes) go for $90–110 s or $100–110 d. Full suites with in-room hot tubs and king beds cost $185 d. A courtesy van and Wi-Fi are available.

The Lucky Loon (907/772-2345, www.theluckyloon.com) is a private beach house three miles south of town. It sleeps up to five for $190 a day with a three-day minimum.

A number of fishing lodges line the Wrangell Narrows, offering multi-night stays, but the nicest is **Rocky Point Resort** (907/772-4420, www.rockyptresort.com), midway along the channel.

Bed-and-Breakfasts

Water's Edge B&B (705 Sandy Beach Rd., 907/772-3736 or 800/868-4373, www.petersburglodgingandtours.com, $100–110 d) is a fine place if you want peace and quiet, with a beachfront room facing Frederick Sound. The two guest rooms have private baths, and a light breakfast is served. Bikes, free Wi-Fi, and courtesy transport are available for guests,

and the owners (30-year residents) also run Kaleidoscope Cruises.

One of Petersburg's older homes (built in the 1920s), **Broom Hus B&B** (411 S. Nordic, 907/772-3459, www.broomhus.com, closed Feb.–April, $90 d) has a downstairs apartment and a kitchen stocked for a make-it-yourself breakfast.

Das Hagedorn Haus—The Hawthorne House (400 2nd St., 907/772-3775 http://home.gci.net/~dhh, $90 d)—is similar, with an attractive basement apartment. The owners prepare a full breakfast and provide a guest computer and free Wi-Fi.

Nordic House B&B (1106 Nordic Dr., 907/772-3620, www.nordichouse.net, $75–95 s, $85–95 d) is a comfortable and attractive home with a glassed-in deck overlooking the harbor. Six guest rooms have private or shared baths, and a light breakfast is served. A separate apartment costs $115.

Waterfront B&B (1004 S. Nordic Dr., 907/772-9300, www.waterfrontbedandbreakfast.com, $95–115 d) stands on pilings along the shore just north of the ferry terminal. Five guest rooms have private baths and share a sitting room and large waterside deck; full breakfast and free Wi-Fi included.

Other places to check out include **Feathered Nest B&B** (907/772-3090, www.featherednestbandb.com), **Heather & Rose Guest Hus** (907/772-4675, www.alaska.net/~hrosehus), and **A Lille Hus B&B** (907/772-4810).

CAMPING

Those with a vehicle or willing to try hitching should head south 22 miles to the Forest Service's **Ohmer Creek Campground** ($6). This is a quiet place in a flower-filled meadow along Blind Slough, with tap water available. Not far away is the quarter-mile-long, wheelchair-accessible Ohmer Creek Trail, complete with interpretive signs. This is a beautiful old-growth rainforest walk, with steelhead fishing in the spring.

Le Conte RV Park (4th and Haugen, 907/772-4680) has tent and RV spaces in town. Out-of-town options are **Twin Creek**

RV Park (7 miles south, 907/772-3244, www.twincreekrv.com, $25 RVs, $10 tents), and **The Trees RV Park** (10 miles south, 907/772-2502, $30 RVs).

FOOD

Open seasonally, **Tina's Kitchen** (907/772-2090) occupies a little downtown stand next to Scandia House with chicken teriyaki, halibut tacos, burritos, and even Philly steak sandwiches for $7–9. The local latte joint, **Java Hus** (907/772-2626) is next door. Get sandwiches, soups, and salads, plus ice cream and shakes from **Helse Café** (13 Sing Lee Alley, 907/772-3444).

Given the importance of fishing in the local economy, it comes as no surprise that Petersburg has a number of places offering fresh seafood. **Coastal Cold Storage Fish Market** (306 N. Nordic Dr., 907/772-4177) serves tasty halibut beer bits, shrimp baskets, reubens, wraps, and other lunch fare, plus Ole and Lena omelets for a Norwegian breakfast. You can also buy fresh fish, scallops, crab (cooked if you like), and other seafood—including, of course, lutefisk.

Tonka Seafoods (907/772-3662 or 888/560-3662, www.tonkaseafoods.com) specializes in premium smoked, canned, or fresh salmon, rockfish, and halibut. The retail store, across from the Sons of Norway Hall on Sing Lee Alley, is open weekdays, with hour-long tours ($5) at 1:30 P.M.

A small shop across from the ferry terminal, **Papa Bear's Pizzeria** (907/772-3727) serves pizzas (whole or by the slice), sandwiches, wraps, and ice cream.

Open three meals a day, **Rooney's Northern Lights Restaurant** (203 Sing Lee Alley, 907/772-2900) has windows facing the harbor and dependably good meals. Located inside Kito's Kave on Sing Lee Alley, **La Fonda** (907/772-3207) is worth a visit for fast Mexican lunches.

Prices for food and other items are higher in Petersburg than in other Southeast towns. Two local grocers have all the supplies: **Hammer & Wikan** (1300 Howkan Dr., 907/772-4246, www.hammerandwikan.com), with a full deli

rockfish at Tonka Seafoods

© DON PITCHER

and bakery, and the downtown **Trading Union** (907/772-3881).

INFORMATION AND SERVICES

The **Petersburg Visitors Information Center** (corner of 1st and Fram Sts., 907/772-4636 or 866/484-4700 message only, www.petersburg .org) has travel brochures. Hours are Sunday noon–4 P.M., Monday–Saturday 9 A.M.–5 P.M., May–September; and Monday–Friday 10 A.M.– 2 P.M. the rest of the year.

The Forest Service (907/772-3871) publishes a map of the Petersburg area, *Mitkof Island Road Guide,* available from the visitor center or its office on Main Street. The map is a must if you're planning to ride a mountain bike around the island.

Get cash 24 hours a day from ATMs at First Bank and Wells Fargo. The post office (907/772-3121) is out near the airport on Haugen Drive, and the **Petersburg Library** (907/772-3349, www.ci.petersburg.ak.us) is upstairs in the municipal building on Nordic Drive. Stop by here to check your email. For additional Internet access, plug into **System Overload** (110 Harbor Way, 907/772-2343).

Coin-op showers are downtown at the harbormaster's office, and at **Glacier Laundry** on Nordic Drive. For a better deal, paddle over to the Petersburg High School swimming pool (907/772-3304). A fine community gym is nearby, complete with weight room and racquetball courts. **Petersburg Medical Center** (on 2nd and Fram Sts., 907/772-4299) is the local hospital.

Shopping

Sing Lee Alley Books (907/772-4440), next to the Sons of Norway Hall, has an excellent collection of Alaskan books and other choice reading material. **CubbyHole** (102 S. 2nd St., 907/772-2717) sells Norwegian-style handicrafts decorated with *rosemaling* designs.

Petersburg has two notable galleries: **The Framers Loft Gallery** (on Sing Lee Alley, 907/772-2471) and **Seaport Gallery & Gifts** (on Main St., 907/772-3015). Get beautiful Norwegian and Icelandic sweaters at **Lee's Clothing** (207 Nordic Dr., 907/772-4229).

GETTING THERE AND AROUND

Petersburg is strung out along Wrangell Narrows, with the **ferry terminal** (907/772-3855) a mile south of the town center. During the summer, ferries run almost daily both northbound and southbound from Petersburg. They usually stop for an hour or two, long enough to walk into town or at least check out the nearby harbor. The ferry terminal opens two hours before ship arrivals and generally stays open a half-hour after it departs. For reservations and schedules, contact the **Alaska Marine Highway** (907/465-3941 or 800/642-0066, www.ferryalaska.com).

Metro Cab (907/772-2700) and **Midnight Rides** (907/772-2222) charge $5 for transport from the state ferry to town.

The **Inter-Island Ferry Authority's** (907/826-4848 or 866/308-4848, www.interislandferry.com) M/V *Stikine* provides summer-only service Thursday–Sunday between the south end of Mitkof Island and Wrangell, continuing south to Prince of Wales Island. The ferry dock is 28 miles south of Petersburg. If you have a vehicle, this is the fastest way to travel between Wrangell and Petersburg since the *Stikine* takes just two hours for the shorter route, versus four hours for the state ferry. Of course, this route requires a 45-minute paved-and-gravel drive to Petersburg, and the ferry doesn't go through scenic Wrangell Narrows. **Viking Travel** (907/772-3818 or 800/327-2571, www.alaskaferry.com) has a shuttle van to Petersburg for $23 one-way, but call ahead for reservations.

Rent cars from **Allstar Rent-A-Car** (907/772-4281 or 800/722-5006, www.scandiahousehotel.com) at Scandia House or **Avis** (907/772-4716 or 800/331-1212, www.tidesinnalaska.com) in Tides Inn.

Petersburg Airport is a mile southeast of town on Haugen Drive. **Alaska Airlines** (907/772-4255 or 800/426-0333, www.alaskaair.com), has daily service to other Southeast towns and the Lower 48. **Pacific Wing** (907/772-9258, www.pacificwing.com), **Kupreanof Flying Service** (907/772-3396, www.kupreanof.com), and **Nordic Air** (907/772-3535) all provide air charter service to Forest Service cabins. **Temsco Helicopters** (907/772-4780 or 877/789-9501, www.temscoair.com) offers helicopter flightseeing. **Sunrise Aviation** (907/874-2319 or 800/874-2311, www.sunriseflights.com) often has seat fares to Wrangell.

KAKE

The small Tlingit village of Kake (pop. 700) lies along the northwest shore of Kupreanof Island, halfway between Petersburg and Sitka. Kake's claim to fame is the **world's tallest totem pole,** exhibited at the 1970 World's Fair in Osaka, Japan. This 132-foot pole is unique in that it contains figures representing all the Tlingit clans on a single pole. Kake is also the starting point for sea kayak trips into two large wilderness areas on nearby Kuiu Island. Also of interest is the quaint **Kake Presbyterian Church.** Built in 1929, it is the oldest public building in town.

History

During the 1800s the Kake tribe had a reputation as one of the fiercest in the Southeast. Richard Meade recorded the following incident: "In 1855 a party of Kakes, on a visit south to Puget Sound, became involved in some trouble there, which caused a United States vessel to open fire on them, and during the affair one of the Kake chiefs was killed. This took place over 800 miles from the Kake settlements on Kupreanof Island. The very next year the tribe sent a canoe-load of fighting men all the way from Clarence Straits in Russian America to Whidby's Island in Washington Territory, and attacked and beheaded an ex-collector—not of internal revenue, for that might have been pardonable—but of customs, and returned safely with his skull and scalp to their villages. Such people are, therefore, not to be despised, and are quite capable of giving much trouble in the future unless wisely and firmly governed." John Muir later described a visit to a Kake village where human bones were scattered all over the ground, reminders of previous battles: "Chief Yana Taowk seemed to take pleasure in kicking the Sitka bones that lay in his way, and neither old nor young showed the slightest trace of superstitious fear of the dead at any time." Needless to say, the people of Kake treat outsiders in a friendlier manner today.

Practicalities

Keex' Kwaan Lodge (907/785-3434, www.kakealaska.com, $85 s or $98 d) is a comfortable and modern lodge with a full-service restaurant and free Wi-Fi. If you're in search of a budget place where the basic older rooms have a down-the-hall bath, try **Nugget Inn** (907/785-6469, $40 d).

Get groceries from **SOS Value-Mart** (907/785-6444), a quarter-mile from the ferry. Kake has a java joint and liquor store, but no bank. Get local information from the **City of Kake** (907/785-3804).

Camping facilities are not available and much of the land around Kake is privately owned, but camping is permitted on Forest Service land, two miles south of town. Kake is one of the drier towns in the Southeast, with only 50 inches per year of precipitation. The town has a fish hatchery and cold-storage plant but no Forest Service office. Ask at the Forest Service office in Petersburg about the Cathedral Falls, Goose Lake, and Hamilton River Trails. **Big John Cabin** on Big John Bay is accessible via the road network from Kake.

The **Alaska Marine Highway** (800/642-0066, www.ferryalaska.com) ferry *LeConte* visits Kake twice a week, heading both east to Petersburg and west to Sitka. It docks a mile and a half from the center of town. There is a covered shelter area, but no phone. The ferry usually stops just long enough to load and unload cars (a half-hour or so).

L.A.B. Flying Service (907/785-6435, www.labflying.com) has daily service from Kake to Petersburg and Juneau.

Kuiu Island

If you have the time, equipment, and skill, nearby Kuiu Island (pronounced Q-U) provides excellent kayaking and canoeing opportunities. Two wilderness areas encompass the south and west sides of Kuiu Island; other parts have been heavily logged. Dozens of interesting islands, islets, and coves crowd the west side of Kuiu in the 67,000-acre **Tebenkof Bay Wilderness,** while the south end includes the 60,000-acre **Kuiu Wilderness.** The Forest Service publishes a detailed map of Kuiu Island, with descriptions of all portages and routes. Get a copy of *Kuiu Island/Tebenkof Bay Canoe/Kayak Routes* from Petersburg Ranger District (907/772-3871, www.fs.fed.us/r10/tongass).

Experienced kayakers will enjoy the paddle between Kake and Petersburg around the south end of Kupreanof Island. There is open water in places, but a good portion of the route is protected and the state ferry makes it easy to get between Kake and Petersburg. Contact Tongass Kayak Adventures (907/772-4600, www.tongasskayak.com) for sea kayak tours within Tebenkof Bay Wilderness.

Sitka

With its gemlike, island-dotted setting, Sitka (pop. 9,000) is everybody's favorite Southeast Alaska town. On a typical summer day you'll see fishing boats heading out to sea from the four harbors around Sitka Sound, and cruise ships steaming by, their decks crowded with tourists as they pass Mt. Edgecumbe, the Fuji-like snowcapped volcano that adorns Sitka's outer waters. Back in town, other visitors glance inside the Russian church that dominates Sitka's center, wander along totem-pole-lined paths in peaceful Sitka National Historical Park, and climb the sharply rising wooded peaks behind town. The people who make this their home are similarly diverse, ranging from beer-guzzling fishermen barely making ends meet, to wealthy retirees from California who are pushing housing prices into the stratosphere. The gorgeous setting makes Sitka a detour well worth the effort. Be fore-

warned, however, to expect rain—the town soaks in 94 inches a year. By the way, Sitka lays claim to being the "biggest city in America"; its boundaries encircle Baranof Island, fully 4,710 square miles! (New York City covers only 301 square miles.)

Peril Strait

Located on the western shore of Baranof Island, "Sitka-by-the-Sea" is Southeast Alaska's most remote ferry stop, and the only major Inside Passage town to front on the Pacific Ocean. Getting to Sitka by ferry requires a long detour through the scenic but treacherous Peril Strait that separates Baranof and Chichagof Islands—a great place to watch for eagles perched on trees along the shore. During larger tides, fierce currents prevent ferries from going through, and the ships must time their passage to coincide with a high or low slack tide. The

© DON PITCHER

Sitka

SITKA

Baranof Island

To Indian River Trail

To Sawmill Creek Campground

ALASKA RAPTOR REHABILITATION CENTER

Indian River

SITKA NATIONAL HISTORICAL PARK

INDIAN RIVER RD

VISITOR & CULTURAL CENTER

SHELDON JACKSON MUSEUM

SHELDON JACKSON COLLEGE

SITKA NATIONAL CEMETERY

SHELDON JACKSON HATCHERY

JEFF DAVIS ST

SITKA HOSTEL

Crescent Harbor

PARK ST

ETOLIN ST

LINCOLN ST

SAWMILL CREEK BLVD

BIORKA ST

DEGROFF ST

SAWMILL ST

Gavan Hill Trail

BARANOF ST

MONASTERY ST

LAKE ST

Crescent Bay

SEE DETAIL

VERSTOVIA ST

LAKE ST

Swan Lake

LAKE ST

LAKEVIEW DR

POINT RD

SEWARD ST

MARINE ST

ERLER ST

HARBOR DR

LINCOLN ST

KOGWANTAN ST

KATLIAN ST

O'CONNELL BRIDGE

LAKESIDE GROCERIES

JUNIOR HIGH SWIMMING POOL

HALIBUT

NEWARCHANGEL ST

OSPREY ST

PETERSON AVE

ERGECUMBE DR

KIMSHAM ST

KATLIAN ST

FRESH FISH CO

FOREST SERVICE REGIONAL OFFICE

Thomsen Harbor

Sitka Channel

SEWARD AVE

Turning Island

To Ferry Terminal and Starrigen Campground

TONGASS ST

Japonski Island

HARBOR DR

AIRPORT TERMINAL

AIRPORT

Whiting Harbor

Detail

RUSSIAN BISHOP'S HOUSE

MONASTERY ST

Crescent Harbor

WESTMARK LODGE

CENTENNIAL HALL/ ISABEL MILLER MUSEUM

LAKE ST

SEWARD ST

HARBOR DR

LIBRARY

Crescent Bay

SITKA CONVENTION & VISITORS BUREAU

OBSERVA-TORY ST

AMERICAN ST

ST MICHAEL'S CATHEDRAL

RUSSIAN GRAVES

BARRACKS

OLD HARBOR BOOKS

Castle Hill

MARINE ST

LINCOLN ST

BLOCKHOUSE

PIONEERS HOME

SITKA HOTEL

O'CONNELL BRIDGE

KOGWANTAN ST

NAA KAHIDI COMMUNITY HOUSE

SHEE ATIKA INN

KATLIAN ST

0.25 mi

0.25 km

0

passage narrows to only 300 feet in one spot (24 ft. deep). When the tide is really cooking, the buoys are often bent far over by the wild currents. This has one side benefit: The ferry is forced to stay for three hours or so in Sitka, long enough for you to get a taste of this fascinating town. But to see this pretty place better, be sure to stay awhile.

HISTORY
Russian America
First established as a base for collecting sea otter pelts, Sitka has a long and compelling history. In 1799, Alexander Baranov—head of the Russian American Company—founded the settlement under a charter from the czar. Baranov (also spelled Baranof) built his original fort, Redoubt St. Michael, near the present Alaska ferry terminal, only to see it destroyed by a Tlingit attack in 1802. (There is evidence that the British, long enemies of the Russians, assisted the Tlingits in the fort's destruction.) Two years later, Baranov returned with 120 soldiers and 800 Aleuts in 300 *baidarkas*, defeating the Tlingits in what was to become the last major resistance by any Northwest Coast Indians. The Russians rebuilt the town, then called New Archangel, on the present site and constructed a stockade enclosing what is now downtown Sitka. New Archangel soon became the capital of Russian America and a vital center for the sea otter and fur seal trade with China. Although the Tlingits were invited back in 1821 (Native leaders say the Russians begged them to return), the groups coexisted uneasily. Tlingits built their houses just outside the stockade, facing a battery of eight Russian cannons.

Once labeled the "Paris of the North Pacific," New Archangel quickly became the Northwest's most cosmopolitan port. By 1840, it was already home to a library of several thousand volumes, a museum, a meteorological observatory, two schools, a hospital, an armory, two orphanages, and dozens of other buildings. The wealthier citizens lived in elaborate homes filled with crystal and fine lace, but as in czarist Russia itself, the opulence of Sitka did not extend beyond a select few. Slavelike working and living conditions were forced upon the Aleut sea otter hunters.

America Takes Over
An emotional ceremony at Sitka in 1867 marked the passage of Alaska from Russian to American hands, and most of the Russians returned to their motherland, including many third-generation Sitkans. Even today, there are locals who speak Russian. Although the town served as Alaska's first capital city for three decades, its importance declined rapidly under the Americans, and it was almost a ghost town by the turn of the century. The territorial government was moved to the then-booming mining town of Juneau in 1900.

During World War II, Sitka became a major link in the defense of Alaska against Japan. Hangars remain from the large amphibious air base just across the bridge on Japonski Island (Fort Ray), and the barracks that once housed 3,500 soldiers were turned into Mt. Edgecumbe High School, Alaska's only boarding high school for Natives. The boarding school is now fully integrated.

Sitka's largest employer until 1993 was a Japanese-owned pulp mill five miles east of town. The mill closed mainly because of the high cost of production and competition from mills elsewhere. Before it closed, the mill gained national attention for dumping large quantities of cancer-causing dioxin into nearby Silver Bay, and for being one of the primary forces behind the clear-cut logging of Tongass National Forest. Many Sitkans still work in the fishing and tourism industries, or for the government. The mill's closure did not have nearly the devastating effect the prophets of doom had predicted; in fact Sitka seems to be doing just fine, fueled by tourism and the arrival of retirees. Large cruise ships are in port most summer days, but things aren't nearly as bad (yet) as in Juneau, Ketchikan, or Skagway.

SIGHTS
One of the finest views of Sitka is from the walkway along the distinctive cable-stayed, girder-span bridge that connects Sitka with

Japonski Island. On a clear day, you'll have a hard time deciding which direction to look: The mountains of Baranof Island rise up behind the town, while the perfect volcanic cone of **Mt. Edgecumbe** (3,000 ft.) on Kruzof Island dominates the opposite vista. Beside the old post office on Lincoln Street a stairway leads up to **Castle Hill,** a tiny state park commemorating the spot where the ceremony transferring Alaska to the United States was held on October 18, 1867. The Kiksadi Indians inhabited this hill for many generations before the Russians' arrival. After defeating the Kiksadi, Alexander Baranov built his castlelike house here, but the building burned in 1894. The splendid view makes Castle Hill a must.

The most prominent downtown feature is the large yellow **Alaska Pioneers Home** (built in 1934), housing elderly Alaskans with 15 or more years of state residence. The *Prospector* statue out front was based upon William "Skagway Bill" Fonda, an Alaskan pioneer. Across the road is a **totem pole** bearing the Russian coat of arms, three old English anchors, and a couple of Indian petroglyphs. Adjacent to the Pioneers Home is **Sheet'Ka Kwaan Naa Kahidi Community House,** based upon traditional longhouse designs, offering Native dance performances in summer. Two tall housescreens dominate the interior.

Atop a small hill just west of the Pioneer Home stands a reconstructed **Russian blockhouse** from the stockade that kept the Indians restricted to the area along Katlian Street. It's open Sunday afternoons during the summer. **Kogwantan and Katlian streets,** directly below the blockhouse, are a picturesque mixture of docks, fish canneries, shops, and old houses, one with its exterior entirely covered in Tlingit designs. The main **Finnish Lutheran Cemetery** (400 graves dating from 1848) is behind the blockhouse at the end of Princess Street. The grave of the Russian **Princess Maksoutoff** is here, and nearby are more Russian graves, including that of Iahov Netsvetov, a Russian Orthodox saint. Cemetery buffs might also be interested in the small **Sitka National Cemetery,** accessible via Jeff Davis Street beside Sheldon Jackson College. It's the oldest national cemetery west of the Mississippi. Built in 1900, the **Geodetic Survey House** (210 Seward St., Tues.–Thurs. 9 A.M.–4 P.M.) houses displays on Mt. Edgecumbe and Tongass National Forest.

St. Michael's Cathedral

The most striking symbol of Russian influence in Sitka is St. Michael's Cathedral (907/747-8120), right in the center of town. Built in 1848, the building burned in 1966 but was replaced by a replica a decade later. The original Russian artifacts and icons, including the Sitka Madonna (purportedly a miraculous healer), were saved from the fire and have been returned to their original setting in this, the mother church for all of Alaska's 20,000 Russian Orthodox. During the summer, the church ($2) is open Monday–Friday 9 A.M.–4 P.M., or whenever a large cruise ship is in port. It's open by appointment at other times, but is not open to tourists during religious services.

Isabel Miller Museum

This small museum (330 Harbor Dr., 907/747-6455, www.sitkahistory.org, donation) is tucked away inside Centennial Hall. It's open daily 8 A.M.–5 P.M. in summer; Tuesday–Friday 11 A.M.–5 P.M. and Saturday 10 A.M.–4 P.M. in winter. The museum houses local artifacts and an interesting scale-model of Sitka in 1867 (the year Alaska became a U.S. territory). Out front is a 50-foot carved and painted replica of a **Tlingit war canoe.**

Russian Bishop's House

Administered by the National Park Service, the Russian Bishop's House (907/747-6281, www.nps.gov/sitk, daily 9 A.M.–5 P.M. in summer, by reservation the rest of the year) is Sitka's oldest building and one of just four Russian structures still standing in North America. Built in 1842, it was home to Ivan Veniaminov, bishop of Alaska and later head of the entire Russian Orthodox church hierarchy in Moscow. The first floor houses exhibits describing the building and its occupants, as well as the exploits of Russia's American colony. The second floor has been fully restored to its 1853 appearance and is filled with original furnishings and artifacts. Access to the second floor is part of a half-hour tour ($4) led by park interpreters.

Sheldon Jackson Museum

Farther along the waterfront is **Sheldon Jackson College,** with its distinctive brown and white buildings. Established in 1878 as a place to train Alaska's Natives, this is the oldest educational institution in the state. The outstanding Sheldon Jackson Museum (907/747-8981, www.museums.state.ak.us, daily 9 A.M.–5 P.M. mid-May–mid-Sept., Tues.–Sat. 10 A.M.–4 P.M. rest of year; $4, free for students) is the state's oldest museum. Dr. Sheldon Jackson (1834–1909) worked as both a Presbyterian missionary and as the first General Agent for Education in Alaska. His extensive travels throughout the territory between 1888 and 1898 allowed him to acquire thousands of Eskimo, Athabascan, Tlingit, Haida, and Aleut artifacts. To protect this priceless collection, a fireproof museum (the first concrete structure in Alaska) was built here in 1895. The museum houses a remarkable selection of kayaks, hunting tools, dogsleds, baskets, bentwood boxes, Eskimo masks, and other artifacts. Be sure to check out the drawers of artifacts beneath the display cases. Also here is a small gift shop selling quality Alaskan jewelry, crafts, and note cards. Native artisans are often at work inside the museum during the summer. Across the street is the **Sheldon Jackson College Aquarium and Hatchery** (907/747-5254, free) with an 800-gallon saltwater aquarium and three touch tanks to get up close to tidepool creatures.

(Sitka National Historical Park

For many, the highlight of a visit to Sitka is Sitka National Historical Park, at the mouth of Indian River where the Tlingits and Russians fought their final battle in 1804. The Indians kept the invaders at bay for a week, but with their ammunition exhausted and resup-

Chilkat blanket weaving, Sitka National Historical Park

© DON PITCHER

ply efforts thwarted, they abandoned the fortress and silently withdrew to Peril Strait. The visitors and Native cultural center (907/747-6281, www.nps.gov/sitk, daily 8 A.M.–5 P.M. in summer, and Mon.–Fri. 8 A.M.–5 P.M. the rest of the year, $4) includes an informative small museum of Tlingit culture. In summertime, Native craft workers can be seen producing bead blankets, jewelry, and woodcarving in the workshop. The 10-minute historical video, "Battle of Sitka," is very informative, and rangers offer daily historical walks in the summer.

Quite a few historical totems are housed in one large room, and outside are 15 more totems, most of which were carved for the 1904 St. Louis World's Fair. The totems line a one-mile trail through the lush second-growth spruce forest, with outstanding views of Sitka Sound along the way. You'll find spawning pink salmon in Indian River (near the 1804 battleground) late in the summer. The park is a peaceful place where mysterious in-the-trees totems, the strident calls of ravens and eagles, and the lapping of waves combine to enhance the beauty.

Alaska Raptor Center

Located off Sawmill Creek Road, this impressive facility (907/747-8662 or 800/643-9425, www.alaskaraptor.org, $12 adults, $6 kids under 12) has two dozen or so bald eagles and other birds of prey—including owls, hawks, falcons, and ravens—at any given time. Most are recovering from gunshots, car accidents, or encounters with power lines. Of the birds brought in, a third recover sufficiently to be released back into the wild. Most of the others end up in captive breeding or educational programs in the Lower 48. Get to the center by walking out of town along Sawmill Creek Road a couple hundred feet beyond the Indian River bridge. The access road takes off to your left a short distance beyond this. A more scenic route is to follow the trails through Sitka National Historical Park or along the Indian River behind Sheldon Jackson College. It's an easy 10-minute walk from Sitka National Historical Park, or 20 minutes from the center of town. The Community Ride Bus ($2) takes you within two blocks of the center.

A focal point is the 20,000-square-foot flight-training center that replicates the rainforest environment outside; visitors watch the eagles through one-way glass. Staff use the enclosure to teach eagles survival skills prior to their release. Out back is a deck overlooking a large enclosure (mew) where eagles unable to survive in the wild are kept. Additional mews with hawks, owls, and other birds are along a rain forest path. The gift shop sells all sorts of eagle paraphernalia.

Visitors get the chance to meet one of the birds up close, and are given a half-hour tour and video. The center is open daily 8 A.M.–4 P.M. May–September, and there's always someone on hand whenever a cruise ship is in town. No winter tours.

Whale Park

Six miles out Sawmill Creek Road is Whale Park, consisting of a roadside turnout with interpretive signs and a boardwalk to an overlook where there's a good chance of seeing whales during the fall and winter months. Offshore hydrophones broadcast the sounds of passing whales (if they are around).

ENTERTAINMENT AND EVENTS
Cultural Performances

When cruise ships are in town, Herrigan Centennial Hall auditorium comes alive with half-hour performances of traditional Russian, Ukrainian, Armenian, and Moldavian dance by the 35-member, all-female **New Archangel Dancers** (907/747-5516, www.newarchangeldancers.com, $8). The troupe has toured extensively, including visits to Japan, Russia, Canada, and Mexico.

For a very different form of dance, the **Sheet'Ka Kwaan Naa Kahidi Dancers** (907/747-7290, $7 adults, $5 kids) give Tlingit performances in full regalia through the summer months. These excellent half-hour productions are offered when cruise ships are in port. Most folks see them as part of a bus tour given by Tribal Tours. Performances take place in the imposing Sheet'Ka Kwaan Naa Kahidi Community House, next to the Pioneers Home on Katlian Street.

Nightlife

Fishermen and would-be crew members hang out at the sometimes-rowdy **Pioneer Bar** (on Katlian St., 907/747-3456). The P-Bar's walls are crowded with hundreds of photos of local fishing boats, and the blackboard often has "crew wanted" ads. Don't miss the **Sunday afternoon jam sessions** at Backdoor Café; it's an authentic taste of life in small-town Alaska.

Inside the Sitka Hotel, **Victoria's Pourhouse** (907/747-9301) has a gigantic TV, beer on draught, a smoke-free setting, and free Wi-Fi. **Ernie's Old Time Saloon** (907/747-3334) has live music most weekends and a couple of offbeat stuffed animals, including a "sidehill" salmon.

Events

For three weeks in June, the renowned **Sitka Summer Music Festival** (907/747-6774, www.sitkamusicfestival.org) attracts musicians from all over the world. Chamber music concerts are given several evenings a week in Centennial Hall, but the most fun is the annual BoatParty

Concert (reserve early). Concert tickets may be hard to come by, but you can always visit rehearsals for free. Another cultural event, the **Sitka Symposium** (http://home.gci.net/ ~island) in mid-July, attracts nationally known poets and writers.

In late May, visitors can join locals in the **Sitka Salmon Derby**, where the top fish is often a 60-pound-plus king salmon. **July 4th** features a parade, races, softball tournament, live music, dancing, and fireworks. On Labor Day weekend, the **Mudball Classic Softball Tournament** attracts teams from around the nation for fun in the muck.

As the town where Alaska was officially transferred from Russian to American hands, Sitka is also the place to be on **Alaska Day**. A celebration of "Seward's Folly" is held each October 18 with dances (including a remarkable performance by the New Archangel Dancers), traditional Russian costumes, a parade, and a reenactment of the brief transfer ceremony.

In early November, the **Sitka Whalefest** (907/747-7964, www.sitkawhalefest.org) attracts biologists and those who love whales and other marine mammals to a series of scientific seminars, whale-watching tours, concerts, crafts, and exhibits.

RECREATION

Sitka is a popular destination for **sportsfishing;** drop by the Sitka CVB office (www.sitka.org) for a handout listing more than 30 charter boats.

The protected waters near Sitka provide excellent kayak access to many Forest Service cabins and trails. **Sitka Sound Ocean Adventures** (907/747-6375, www.ssoceanadventures.com) guides kayak day trips (starting at $63 for 2 hrs.) and rents kayaks. **Esther G Sea Taxi** (907/747-6481, www.puffinsandwhales.com) provides kayaker and hiker drop-offs if you're heading out. **Island Fever Diving and Sports** (805 Halibut Point Rd., 907/747-7871, www .islandfeverdiving.com) sets up snorkeling excursions using dry suits.

Rent quality mountain bikes from **Yellow Jersey Cycle Shop** (329 Harbor Dr., 907/747-6317) downtown. Jeff Budd of **Sitka**

Bike & Hike (907/747-4821 or 877/292-5325, www.sitkaadventures.com) leads biking and hiking tours, including trips to the summit Mt. Edgecumbe.

The Forest Service's **Sitka Ranger District Office** (204 Siginaka Way, 907/747-4220, www.fs.fed.us/r10/tongass) has up-to-date information on the more than 40 miles of local trails, ranging from gentle nature walks to treks that take you high up onto nearby peaks. Contact **Sitka Bike & Hike** (907/747-4821 or 877/292-5325, www.sitkaadventures.com) for guided treks.

Indian River Trail

One of the finest of Sitka's trails, this is an easy valley hike within walking distance of town. The route follows a clear salmon stream through the rainforest, with a chance to see brown bear and deer. Begin by heading out Sawmill Creek Road and turning left onto Indian River Road. Continue past the gate about a half-mile to the city water pumphouse. The gentle trail leads from here up along the Indian River and a tributary to the right as far as a lovely 80-foot waterfall in a V-shaped valley. The last mile of the trail is not well maintained. Allow six hours round-trip to cover the 5.5-mile trail.

Gavan Hill Trail

This "stairway to heaven" walkway starts at the end of Baranof Street and climbs three miles to the top of 2,650-foot Gavan Hill. (Bear right at the junction with Cross Trail just under a mile up.) Gavan Hill Trail then switchbacks to a long ridge that opens onto subalpine meadows before a steep final climb up the last 200 feet of elevation. From here, it's relatively easy to follow rock cairns on through the alpine, connecting to the Harbor Mountain Trail. This makes an outstanding loop hike with impressive vistas of Sitka Sound.

Harbor Mountain Trail

One of the easiest and most scenic ways to get into the alpine is via Harbor Mountain Trail. Built by the Army during World War II, the road originally provided access to a lookout post for invading Japanese ships and submarines (none were ever seen, though a whale was once mistakenly bombed). Head four miles out Halibut Point Road and turn right onto Harbor Mountain Road. The gravel road climbs five miles up the mountain to an elevation of 2,000 feet. Snow blocks the road until June, but you can park at the gate and walk up if you don't mind hiking atop snow. On sunny days the view over Sitka Sound is breathtaking. Those without a car or mountain bike should be able to hitch a ride up with locals.

A trail begins at the parking area on top and switchbacks up a side hill before leveling out in the subalpine meadows. A spur trail heads to an overlook here, but the main trail turns right and continues past the ruins of wartime lookout buildings. Beyond this, rock cairns follow the ridge, and the path eventually connects with the Gavan Hill Trail back to town. A small hut provides a camping place approximately three miles in.

Mt. Verstovia Trail

On a clear day get spectacular views of Sitka Sound and Mt. Edgecumbe from the Mt. Verstovia Trail, a strenuous climb to this pointy peak overlooking Sitka. The steep 2.5-mile trail begins on the west side of the Kiksadi Club, two miles east of town on Sawmill Creek Road. The trail is brushy and poorly maintained, and inexperienced hikers have gotten lost. You'll pass some old Russian charcoal pits (signposted) only a quarter-mile from the trailhead. The route switchbacks to a ridge, which you follow to the shoulder of Mt. Verstovia. The true summit is farther northeast along the ridge. Allow four hours for the return trip as far as the "shoulder" (2,000 ft.), six hours round-trip to the top (2,550 ft.).

Beaver Lake Trail

This family friendly mile-long trail begins at the bridge in Sawmill Creek Campground seven miles east of town. The path gains 250 feet in elevation as it climbs through the forest

Sitka Sound and Mt. Edgecumbe

© DON PITCHER

and out onto a boardwalk over the muskeg to Beaver Lake. The lake has been stocked with grayling and is one of the only places to catch these fish in the Southeast. There are fishing platforms along the lakeshore.

Mt. Edgecumbe

Mt. Edgecumbe, a 3,000-foot volcanic cone that looks like Mt. Fuji, can be climbed via a 6.5-mile trail that starts on the southeast shore of Kruzof Island. The last mile is above tree line through red volcanic ash. The island is 10 miles west of Sitka and can be reached by kayak (beware of ocean swells) or by arranging for a skiff drop-off. Stay in Fred's Creek Cabin at the trailhead or in the free three-sided shelter halfway up. Panoramic views can be had from atop this dormant volcano.

Cabins

The Forest Service has 24 cabins (reservations: 518/885-3639 or 877/444-6777, www.reserveusa.com, $35) in the Sitka area, most accessed by floatplane or water taxi from Sitka.

Redoubt Lake Cabin is at the end of a six-mile trail that starts in Silver Bay (10 miles southeast of Sitka). The cabin is also accessible by sea kayak from town, and a short portage takes you to Redoubt Lake.

The wheelchair-accessible **Lake Eva Cabin** is 27 miles northeast of Sitka on Baranof Island. **Plotnikof Lake Cabin** sits in the heart of the spectacularly rugged South Baranof Wilderness Area, a 45-minute flight from Sitka.

Baranof Lake Cabin looks across this blue-green lake to a waterfall. A trail at the end of the lake leads a half-mile to the little settlement of **Baranof Warm Springs**, where privately owned hot springs are available.

Brent's Beach Cabin is on the eastern shore of Kruzof Island, 15 miles northwest of Sitka. There's a white-sand beach out front (rare in the Southeast), and interesting caves and lava domes just up the shore.

The **Allan Point Cabin**, 16 miles north of Sitka, is an impressive, two-story log cabin that commands a fine view across Nakwasina Sound from its location on the northeast end of

Halleck Island. The equally spacious **Samsing Cove Cabin** sleeps 10 folks comfortably and is just six miles south of Sitka.

ACCOMMODATIONS

The Sitka Convention & Visitors Bureau produces a pamphlet and website that detail hotels, motels, B&Bs, fishing lodges, wilderness lodges, private apartments, and houses.

Hostel

After many years of operating out of a church basement, the **Sitka Youth Hostel** (109 Jeff Davis Rd., 907/747-8661, open June–Aug., $24 per person) moved into a historic building next to Sheldon Jackson College in 2007. Inside are two dorms, a kitchen, and commons area. The hostel is open 6 P.M.–9:30 A.M., with an 11 P.M. curfew. If you're arriving by ferry, the shuttle bus will drop you at the door, but call ahead for reservations.

Hotels and Motels

Built in 1939, **Sitka Hotel** (118 Lincoln St., 907/747-3288, www.sitkahotel.com) has been restored to a Victorian splendor that it probably never had before. Rooms with private baths are a reasonable $85 s or $90 d, and most of these have small fridges. Those with a bath down the hall are a bargain: $65 s or $70 d, but these are small rooms with basic furnishings. The hotel isn't to everyone's liking, but is fine if you are looking for authenticity, with free Wi-Fi.

Cascade Inn (2035 Halibut Point Rd., 907/747-6804 or 800/532-0908, www.cascadeinnsitka.com) has standard rooms for $115–125 d, and kitchenettes for $140 d. The building is two miles out of town, and all rooms include private balconies facing the water. Guests also have access to a sauna. A convenience store is downstairs.

Westmark Lodge (330 Seward St., 907/747-6241 or 800/544-0970, www.westmarkhotels.com, $159 d, $199–249 for suites) is Sitka's largest lodging place, with a big lobby accented by a Tlingit screen, a lounge and restaurant, plus free Wi-Fi.

The newly renovated **Shee Atika Totem**

Square Inn (201 Katlian St., 907/747-3693 or 866/300-1343, www.totemsquare.com, $139–149 d) features a harborside setting, continental breakfast, exercise room, and Wi-Fi.

Sitka's most distinctive lodging option is (**Rockwell Lighthouse** (907/747-3056), a three-bedroom home built in the shape of a lighthouse on an island less than a mile from town. Access is by skiff (transport provided). With its nautical decor, curving interior staircase up into the lighthouse, and picture-perfect setting, you'll be signing up for lighthouse duty after a night or two here. The entire house rents for $150 d or $200 for four people. This place fills up fast in the summer, so call a year ahead for reservations in mid-summer. No credit cards, and a two-night minimum is required (but you will want more time).

Bed-and-Breakfasts

The Sitka Convention and Visitors Bureau website (www.sitka.org) has links to local B&Bs.

Ann's Gavan Hill B&B (415 Arrowhead St., 907/747-8023, www.annsgavanhill.com, $75 s, $85 d) features six guest rooms with shared baths, a hot tub on the covered side deck, filling homemade breakfasts, and a relaxed Alaskan atmosphere. One room is handicap accessible.

Helga's B&B (www.sitkaalaskalodging.com, 907/747-5497, $100–130 d) is a large beachside home three miles out Halibut Point Road. The four guest rooms have private baths, and a continental breakfast is available. The pricier rooms face the water, and a two-bedroom unit sleeps four for $190.

Alaska Ocean View B&B (1101 Edgecumbe Dr., 907/747-8310 or 888/811-6870, www.sitka-alaska-lodging.com, $109–189 s, $129–209 d) is a lovely home with fabulous Sitka Sound vistas. Two guest rooms and a suite have private baths, and include a big breakfast. Other amenities include in-room fireplaces, free Wi-Fi, and a hot tub on the patio.

Other B&Bs worth a look include **Annahootz B&B** (907/747-6498 or 800/746-6498, www.sitka.org/annahootz, $110 d), **Baranof Island B&B** (907/747-8306, www.baranofislandbandb.com, $85 d), **Biorka**

B&B (907/747-3111, $65–85 d), **Finn Alley B&B** (907/747-3655, www.finnalleybedandbreakfast.com, $115 d), and **Sitka Woodside Lodging** (907/747-8287, http://home.gci.net/~sdenherder, $85–100 d).

Vacation Rentals and Lodges

Sitka has a number of homes, apartments, and cabins that are rented out to travelers, including **An Abode** (407 Degroff St., 907/747-4932, $85–150 d), **Frank & Gloria's Place** (907/747-8711, www.sitkadream.com, $125 d), **Chocolate Moose** (907/747-5159, $90–125), and **Baranov's Rest** (907/747-8368, www.baranovsrest.com, $250). Visit www.sitka.org for links to other rentals.

A number of Sitka-area lodges provide all-inclusive fishing, meals, and lodging packages. These include **Baranof Wilderness Lodge** (530/579-3394 or 800/613-6551, www.flyfishalaska.com), **Dove Island Lodge** (907/747-5660 or 888/318-3474, www.aksitkasportfishing.com), **Quest Alaska Lodges** (605/229-8685, www.questalaskalodges.com), and **Wild Strawberry Lodge** (907/747-8883 or 800/770-2628, www.wildstrawberrylodge.com).

Sitka Sound Ocean Adventures (907/747-6375, www.ssoceanadventures.com) has a floathouse ($175 for up to six) at Coogan Bay south of Sitka that makes a good base for soft-adventure kayaking or fishing. It sleeps six for $175, and includes a kayak. Access is by skiff (rentals available), and a two-night minimum is required.

CAMPING

No campgrounds are near downtown Sitka, but the Forest Service provides camping at each end of the road. The outstanding **Starrigavan Campground** ($12–30, reservations $9 extra) is seven miles northwest of town and three-quarters of a mile beyond the ferry terminal. Open all year, but no services October–April. All sites are wheelchair accessible. Campsites to the left of the road face onto a rocky beach, while those to the right border Starrigavan Creek, where you can watch spawning coho salmon in late summer. Starrigavan fills up with RVs in

July and August, but there are six walk-in sites on the ocean side of the campground. Starrigavan also has an **artesian well** with wonderfully fresh spring water. Sitkans often drive out to fill big bottles for themselves.

The 0.25-mile boardwalk **Estuary Life Trail** (wheelchair accessible) leads along the edge of the marsh from the campground, and connects with a 0.75-mile **Forest and Muskeg Trail.** Placards describe points along this easy trail. On the road between the ferry and campground are interpretive display signs marking the site of **Old Sitka**—burned by the Tlingits in 1802.

The quiet and little-used **Sawmill Creek Campground** (free, but no water) is up Blue Lake Road, six miles east of town. The campground is a bit remote, making it hard to reach on foot, and the rough road is not recommended for RVs.

Park RVs at the city-run **Sealing Cove RV Park** (907/747-3439, $21, open April–Sept.) on Japonski Island, with hookups. **Sitka Sportsman's RV Park** (907/747-6033, $20 RVs) is adjacent to the ferry terminal.

FOOD
Breakfast and Lunch
A delightful place to spend time is **Backdoor Café** (907/747-8856), an espresso shop behind Old Harbor Books on Lincoln Street. The Backdoor is the literary/greenie hangout, and also serves tasty bagels, soups, calzones, and pastries. This is the definitive Sitka meeting place.

Victoria's (118 Lincoln St., 907/747-9301), in the Sitka Hotel, is a decent breakfast and lunch spot but also serves a full dinner menu. Pop open your laptop for free Wi-Fi. A few doors up the street is a pharmacy that houses **Harry's Soda Shop** (907/747-8006) for malts, shakes, and banana splits and homemade ice cream.

All-American
Popular with tourists and families, **Bayview Restaurant** (407 Lincoln St., 907/747-5440), upstairs in Bayview Trading, is open 5 A.M.– 8 P.M. daily with every possible type of burger (16 at last count), plus Wednesday- and Friday-night prime rib. Big windows provide a view of the harbor.

Get burgers, milk shakes, and other fast food—plus hearty breakfasts—at **Lane 7 Snack Bar** (236 Katlian St., 907/747-6310). **Subway** probably has the cheapest meal-deal in town; it's behind the Westmark on Seward Street. Of course, there's always the **McDonald's** a mile out on Halibut Point Road for industrial-strength junk food. With the harbor-and-mountains view, this McD's certainly has one of the most impressive vistas in the entire corporate chain.

While waiting for your flight, stop by the airport's **Nugget Restaurant** (907/966-2480) for a slice of their locally famous pies.

International
Pizza Express (236 Lincoln St., 907/966-2428) serves surprisingly authentic Mexican food and decent pizzas. They're directly across from the Russian Orthodox church.

If you like Japanese food in an unpretentious setting, **Little Tokyo** (907/747-5699) is one of the best deals in town. In addition to fresh sushi, they offer a filling bento box dinner (miso soup, potstickers, sushi, salad, and teriyaki chicken) for just $11.

Fine Dining
Van Winkle & Sons (205 Harbor Dr., 907/747-7652), near the bridge, has seafood, pasta, prime rib, and pizzas, but is best known for halibut fish and chips. This is the real thing, Alaskan style. The upstairs setting is quiet and romantic.

Sitka's culinary gem, **Ludvig's Bistro** (256 Katlian St., 907/966-3663, www.ludvigsbistro.com, closed Sun. and Mon.), ranks among the top cafés in Alaska. It's stylish and noisy, with a new Mediterranean-inspired menu every week. You'll always find Caesar salads, daily chowders, fresh seafood specials, and pasta. Ludvig's is two blocks down Katlian, which, fortunately, is too far for most of the cruise ship folks to walk. Dinner reservations are advised, but singles will usually find space at the wine bar. Entrées run $21–32, or you can choose a selection of small tapas dishes for

$15 each. The restaurant also has a soup cart on Lincoln Street in the summer if you're just looking for quick eats.

Groceries

Sea Mart (907/747-6266, www.seamart.com) two miles from town along Halibut Point Road, has a salad bar, deli, bakery, food court, and Sitka's most complete selection of groceries. Closer to town is **Lakeside Grocery** (705 Halibut Point Rd., 907/747-3317).

The **Fresh Fish Company** (907/747-5565 or 888/747-5565, www.sitkahookandline.com), behind Murray Pacific on Katlian Street, sells fresh local salmon, halibut, shrimp, snapper, and smoked salmon. They'll also smoke fish that you bring in.

INFORMATION AND SERVICES

The Centennial Building houses a small information desk and brochure rack, or stop by the **Sitka Convention & Visitors Bureau** (upstairs at 303 Lincoln St., 907/747-5940, www.sitka.org, Mon.–Fri. 8 A.M.–5 P.M.).

The Forest Service office (907/747-6671 or 907/747-6685 for recorded info) is in the orange-red building at 204 Siginaka Way.

Get showers at **Baranof Laundromat** (1211 Sawmill Creek Rd.) and **Sitka Laundry Center,** across from McDonald's on Halibut Point Road. A better deal is the public **swimming pool** (601 Halibut Point Rd., 907/747-8670) in Blatchley Middle School, where you can swim, sauna, and shower. The pool at Sheldon Jackson College is also open to the public daily.

Sitka's main post office is on Sawmill Creek Road, 1.5 miles south of town, but a substation is downtown at 338 Lincoln Street. For medical emergencies, head to **Sitka Community Hospital** (209 Moller Ave., 907/747-3241, www.sitkahospital.org).

Shopping

Sitka's specialty is Russian art, especially the colorful nesting eggs, painted icons, and other traditional works. Several shops sell Russian crafts downtown; walk around until you find something you like. More noteworthy is **Sitka**

Rose Gallery (907/747-3030 or 888/236-1536, www.sitkarosegallery.com) in a historic century-old home next to the Russian Bishop's House on Lincoln Street. Inside, find a mix of quality Native art and Alaskan paintings, sculpture, and jewelry. The same building houses **WinterSong Soap Company** (907/747-8949 or 888/819-8949, www.wintersongsoap.com), where colorful scented soaps are handcrafted on the premises.

Located five miles east of town, **Theobroma Chocolate Company** (907/966-2349 or 888/985-2345, www.theobromachocolate.com) manufactures gourmet chocolates in a building next to the old pulp mill. You can watch them creating and packaging the chocolates, or sample unusual varieties—try the Dark Midnight Espresso or one of the salmon and halibut-shaped chocolates.

Fairweather Gallery & Gifts (209 Lincoln St., 907/747-8677, www.fairweatherprints.com) is a good place to buy "wearable art" in the form of exquisite hand-painted dresses, tops, and scarves. It has the most unique T-shirts in town, plus a backroom art gallery. The Sheldon Jackson Museum sells Native crafts.

Books

Old Harbor Books (201 Lincoln St., 907/747-8808, www.oldharborbooks.com) has an outstanding collection of books on Alaska (and beyond), along with a pleasant coffee shop in the back.

The **Sitka public library** (907/747-8708, www.cityofsitka.com), next to Centennial Hall downtown, has a free paperback exchange with plenty of titles, plus a phone for free local calls. Check your email on the computers here, or borrow the binoculars to watch whales, seals, and porpoises from the library windows that overlook the bay. The curved benches out back make a pleasant lunch spot when it isn't raining.

GETTING THERE
Ferry
Alaska Marine Highway (907/465-3941 or 800/642-0066, www.ferryalaska.com) ferries reach Sitka several times a week during the

summer, but the schedule is confusing with various ships plying different routes. When it's operational—and this can be frustratingly uncommon—the high speed *Fairweather* makes a quick 4.5-hour connection between Juneau and Sitka, but be sure to confirm the ferry departure time so you don't end up sitting in the ferry terminal. The terminal (907/747-8737) is open two hours before ship arrivals, and is seven miles north of town. **Sitka Tours shuttle buses** (907/747-8443) are available for $6 each way or $8 round-trip, and a taxi runs around $19 each way. Other options include tours and hitching—easy and often faster than the buses, both into and out of town.

Air
The airport is on Japonski Island, just under a mile from town by road. **Alaska Airlines** (907/966-2926 or 800/426-0333, www.alaskaair.com) flies to Juneau twice a day, plus non-stop to Seattle in the summer. Note that these flights can be canceled or delayed when the weather gets particularly adverse, a common winter experience. **Harris Aircraft Services** (907/966-3050 or 877/966-3050, www.harrisaircraft.com) has service several times a week to Angoon, Kake, Klawock, and Port Alexander, plus flightseeing and charters. **Hunter Air** (907/738-8098, www.hunterairak.com) also has flightseeing trips, and the plane features unusual windows that photographers love.

For transit into town, **Airport shuttles** (907/747-8443, $8 round trip) meet Alaska Airlines flights, or get a ride (around $9 one-way) with **Hank's Taxi & Tours** (907/747-8888) or **Sitka Cab** (907/747-5001).

GETTING AROUND
The city's **Community Ride Bus** (907/747-7103), has hourly service on weekdays, taking you from downtown out Halibut Point Road and Sawmill Creek Road for $2 one-way or $4 round-trip. **Transit Shuttle** (907/747-7290, $10 day pass) buses cruise around Sitka, stopping at all the major sightseeing destinations. The bus operates weekdays and when cruise ships are in port.

Rent cars (starting at $60/day) at the airport from **North Star Rent-A-Car** (907/966-2552 or 800/722-6927) or **Avis** (907/966-2404 or 800/478-2847). Book ahead for the busy summer months.

Tours
The ferry terminal is seven miles from town, but despite the distance you'll have time for a quick "ferry stopover tour," even if you don't stay. Many folks ride the **Sitka Tours** buses (907/747-8443, round-trip $12 adults, $6 kids) that meet the ferries and stop at the cathedral and Sitka National Historical Park. They also offer guided historic and nature walks, but these are geared to cruise ship travelers.

Tribal Tours (907/747-3770 or 888/270-8687, www.sitkatours.com, $44 adults, $34 children), offers a Tlingit slant to tours of Sitka's sights. The 2.5-hour bus tours include a traditional dance performance at the Tribal Community House, plus visits to most local sights.

St. Lazaria Islands National Wildlife Refuge is a great place to see tufted puffins, storm petrels, auklets, whales, seals, and Steller sea lions. **Sitka's Secrets** (907/747-5089, www.sitkasecret.com) has three-hour cruises to the refuge and to other parts of Sitka Sound for $100 per person.

Allen Marine Tours (907/747-8100 or 888/289-0081, www.allenmarinetours.com) offers a two-hour "Wildlife Quest" ($59 adults, $39 children) Tuesday and Thursday evenings, plus three-hour tours ($79 adults, $49 kids) on Saturday and Sunday mornings. If sea conditions aren't too rough, these include time at St. Lazaria Island and Salisbury Sound. A naturalist is onboard.

For something completely different, **Sea Life Discovery Tours** (907/966-2301 or 877/966-2301, www.sealifediscoverytours.com, May–Sept., $84 adults, $63 kids) operates the only semi-submersible vessel in Alaska, with large underwater windows plus a camera for close-up views on the monitor as a diver heads to deeper water. This is a fun way to view kelp forests, fish, crab, sea urchins, anemones, starfish, and other creatures without getting wet.

Chichagof Island

HOONAH

The largest Tlingit village in the Southeast, Hoonah (pop. 900) nestles in Port Frederick, 20 miles south of Glacier Bay. Port Frederick has served as a home for the Tlingits since the last ice age drove them out of Glacier Bay and across Icy Strait to the north coast of Chichagof Island. There they found a protected bay they called Huna, meaning "place where the north wind doesn't blow." The Northwest Trading Company opened a store here in 1880 and missionaries added a church and school the following year. A cannery opened in 1912, operating until 1953. The attractively restored old cannery still stands a mile north of town on the entrance to Port Frederick, but the old village and many priceless Tlingit cultural items were destroyed by a fire in 1944. The people rebuilt their village on the ashes.

Today Hoonah is far from being the prettiest town in Alaska. The weathered clapboard houses are unpainted, and junk cars pile up in the yards. It's the sort of town where the eagle calls blend with the sounds of motorboats and mufflerless dump trucks. There are dogs in almost every house and children playing on every porch. Life in Hoonah follows a slow pace: Residents half-complain that they are unable to go anywhere without meeting someone who wants to talk the hours away. Hoonah's economy is a blend of commercial fishing, a bit of logging, and traditional activities such as deer hunting, fishing, and berry picking.

The impressive cliff faces of **Elephant Mountain** (2,775 ft.) guard the southern flank of Hoonah. Unfortunately, two Native corporations, Huna Totem and Sealaska, have logged much of their land near town, selling off their centuries-old heritage for short-term gain. Hoonah is now surrounded by a spider web of logging roads on both Native and Forest Service land, making this a good place to explore by mountain bike if you're ready for clearcuts.

In the last few years Hoonah has plunged into cruise ship tourism in a big way. The picturesque cannery building at Port Frederick (Icy Strait Point) has been restored, and cruise ship passengers get a look at the way canneries operated in the 1930s, along with cultural presentations, a salmon bake, Native crafts, whale- and bear-watching excursions, charter fishing, mountain biking, and other "soft" adventures. These are really for cruise passengers, but contact Huna Totem (907/789-8018, www.icystraitpoint.com) for access by independent travelers.

Recreation

The Hoonah area offers little in the way of developed trails or other recreation facilities for independent travelers. If you have a car, the quarter-mile **Bear Paw Lake Trail,** 18 miles south of town on Road 8508, leads to a good lake where you can catch trout or coho salmon. Kayakers and canoeists may want to paddle the 40 miles from Hoonah to Tenakee Springs. The route goes to the head of Port Frederick, where there is a 100-yard portage into Tenakee Inlet. Neka Estuary in Port Frederick is a good place to see bears. A Forest Service cabin is available at nearby **Salt Lake Bay,** but a considerable amount of logging has beaten you there. Ask at the **Forest Service Hoonah District Office** (907/945-3631, www.fs.fed.us/r10/tongass) for details on these and other possible kayak trips in the area, including to **Neka Hot Spring,** 16 miles west of Hoonah.

Accommodations and Food

Icy Strait Lodge (907/945-3636, www.icystraitlodge.com, $85 s or $95 d) is the main place in town, with 23 rooms, plus a full-service restaurant and bar. **Wind'N Sea Inn** (907/945-3438 or 877/945-3438, $75 s or $85 d) is a fine lodging choice, with seven guest rooms that share two baths and two kitchens, and include a self-serve breakfast.

Information and Services

The **Hoonah Cultural Center** (907/945-3545) has a few local artifacts. Hoonah has two small grocery stores, and a coin laundry with coin-operated showers. Showers are also available in the harbor building or at the **swimming pool** (907/945-9911) next to the high school. In addition, Hoonah has a bank, tavern, variety store, and liquor store. A few miles southwest of town is the only agricultural commune in Southeast, Mt. Bether Bible Center.

Getting There

Hoonah's **ferry terminal** (907/945-3293) is a half-mile from town. Across from the ferry terminal is a tiny but interesting old cemetery. Ferries arrive six days a week, stopping for approximately an hour, long enough for a quick jog into town and back. Make reservations through Alaska Marine Highway (907/465-3941 or 800/642-0066, www.ferryalaska.com).

Wings of Alaska (907/789-0790, www.wingsofalaska.com), **L.A.B. Flying Service** (907/945-3661, www.labflying.com), **Air Excursions** (907/697-2375 or 800/354-2479, www.airexcursions.com) all have frequent flights between Juneau and Hoonah.

PELICAN AND VICINITY

If you're looking for a place to get away from it all, it's hard to get more remote than the tiny, picturesque fishing village of Pelican (pop. 150) inside narrow Lisianski Inlet on the western shore of Chichagof Island. During the summer, Pelican's population doubles with the arrival of fishermen and cold-storage workers. The town received its name from *The Pelican,* a fishing boat owned by the town's founder; there are no pelicans in Alaska.

Locals drive 4-wheelers down the boardwalk connecting Pelican's restaurants, bars, general store, coin laundry, and cold-storage plant. Showers are available at the coin laundry, or try the steam baths at the liquor store (no joke). The **Pelican Visitors Association** (907/735-2460, www.pelican.net) has info on local businesses.

Tiny Pelican has achieved notoriety as a party town, particularly when festivities reach their peak at the **Boardwalk Boogie**

(www.boardwalkboogie.com) in late May, with two days of live music (including a filthy-song contest) and some major-league partying. Lodging is in dorms at the old cannery, and Allen Marine makes a special boat run from Juneau for the event.

Practicalities

Situated in the heart of town, **Highliner Lodge** (907/735-2476, www.highlinerlodge.com) has a variety of lodging options, including simple sleeping rooms ($95 s or $120 d), and three large, nicely furnished units for $225–250 d, all with Wi-Fi and access to the sauna. Kayak and skiff rentals are available, along with fishing charters, kayak drop-offs, and meals at **Highliner Restaurant.**

Lisianski Inlet Lodge (907/735-2266 or 800/962-8441, www.pelicanalaskafishing.com, May–mid-Sept.), two miles west of Pelican, offers a pricey but idyllic setting for a splurge. Package trips are $2,350 per person for four nights, including lodging, meals, fishing, and guide service. Other lodging options include **Wheelwatch Lodge** (907/735-2252, www.wheelwatch.net) and **Salmon Way Inn** (907/735-2485).

Infamous **Rosie's Bar and Grill** (907/735-2288, www.rosesbarandgrill.com) is a good place for drinking and pub grub, including burgers, chicken dinners, oysters, and BLTs. The ceiling is plastered with signed dollar bills, but you may get a surprise when you put yours up.

Lisianski Inlet Café (907/735-2282) is open for delicious breakfasts and lunches in the summer, with big omelets, sandwiches, and a killer borscht. The bar is a hopping place.

Several local folks run fishing and sightseeing boat charters, and will be happy to run you and your kayak out to such local destinations as White Sulfur Springs.

Getting There

Ferry service to Pelican arrives only once or twice a month. The *LeConte* usually stays for two hours and then turns around for the return trip to Juneau. Get details from

Alaska Marine Highway (800/642-0066, www.ferryalaska.com).

Alaska Seaplane Service (907/735-2244 or 800/478-3360, www.akseaplanes.com) has daily flights to Pelican from Juneau.

West Chichagof-Yakobi Wilderness

On the northwestern shore of Chichagof Island is the wildly rugged 264,747-acre West Chichagof–Yakobi Wilderness. Brown bears, marten, and deer are common, with sea otters and Steller sea lions in the waters. The coast is deeply indented with many small bays, lagoons, and inlets. It also supports areas of distinctive open spruce forest with grassy glades. Except for White Sulfur Springs, this wilderness gets little recreational use because of its remoteness and the storms that frequently make it a dangerous place for small boats and kayaks.

One of the most popular Forest Service cabins in Southeast (make reservations well in advance) is at **White Sulfur Springs,** accessible by boat, sea kayak, helicopter, or floatplane. The springs are a 20-mile kayak trip from Pelican. Much of the trip is through the protected waters of Lisianski Inlet and Strait, but the last five miles are exposed to the open ocean and require great care. The cabin has a wonderful hot springs bathhouse overlooking Bertha Bay just 50 feet away. Note, however, that the springs are free and open to the public, so fishermen, kayakers, and others from nearby Pelican will probably disturb your solitude.

Elfin Cove

This tiny fishing settlement (pop. 50 year-round, but 200 in the summer) tops the north end of Chichagof Island and is considered one of Alaska's prettiest towns. The setting is hard to beat: right on the edge of the wild waters of Cross Sound, yet protected within a narrow harbor. Elfin Cove has two general stores, lodging facilities, plus showers and a sauna during the summer.

The waters of Cross Sound and Icy Strait separate Chichagof Island from Glacier Bay National Park. This is one of the best areas to see whales

in Southeast Alaska, especially near Point Adolphus. Charter boats offer day trips from Glacier Bay to Elfin Cove during the summer months. Also nearby is the 23,000-acre **Pleasant-Lemesurier-Inian Islands Wilderness.**

It's pretty easy to see what makes the village tick, with 10 fishing lodges in such a small place, including **Tanaku Lodge** (www.tanaku.com), **Elfin Cove Lodge** (www.elfincove.com), **Inner Harbor Lodge** (www.innerharborlodge.com), **The Cove Lodge** (www.covelodge.com), and **Eagle Charters & Lodge** (www.elfincoveeaglecharters.com). The last of these operates the only gift shop in town.

No state ferry service, but small cruise ships visit Elfin Cove several times a week in the summer, and **Alaska Seaplane Service** (907/789-3331 or 800/478-3360, www.akseaplanes.com) has scheduled flights from Juneau.

TENAKEE SPRINGS

Residents of the tiny hamlet of Tenakee Springs (pop. 100) include retirees, counterculture devotees, and a handful of fishermen. Many Juneau folks have second homes here. Tenakee's houses stand on stilts along the shoreline; some have "long-drop" outhouses over the water. The town has only one street, a dirt path barely wide enough for Tenakee's three vehicles (its oil truck, fire truck, and dump truck). Everyone else walks or uses four-wheelers and bicycles.

Tenakee is best known for its hot (106°F) **mineral springs,** housed in a building right beside the dock. The springs feed a small concrete pool with an adjacent changing room. There are separate hours for men (2–6 P.M. and 10 P.M.–9 A.M.) and women (6–10 P.M. and 9 A.M.–2 P.M.), but after midnight the rules tend to relax a bit. If the ferry is in town for more than a half-hour, be sure to take a quick dip in the pool.

Practicalities

You can pitch your tent two miles east of town along Indian River, but be sure to hang your food, since brown bears are sometimes a problem. Trails extend out of town for several miles in both directions along the shore. The trail south of town reaches eight miles to an old cannery and a homestead at Coffee Cove.

Beside the dock is **Snyder Mercantile Co.** (907/736-2205), a classic bush Alaska store with groceries, supplies, and the latest gossip. Great folks. The other main feature of town is the Shamrock building, which houses **Rosie's Blue Moon Café,** serving lunch and dinner daily: cheeseburgers (with freshly cut fries), chicken, and steaks, plus the **Artist Co-op,** displaying pieces by local artists. A coin laundry is in the back, and next door is **The Bakery** (907/736-2262) for pastries, coffee, light breakfasts, and lunches. There are local fishing charter boats, a small library, a grade school, and two bars, but only one place to stay: **Tenakee Hot Springs Lodge** (907/736-2400 or 9097/364-3640, $90 s or $150 d) on the edge of town. Five guest rooms share three baths.

Getting There

Tenakee is a popular weekend vacation spot for both Juneauites and travelers. The ferry *LeConte* arrives in Tenakee four times a week with a schedule that makes it possible to stop over for a Friday night before returning to Juneau the following evening. There is no ferry terminal and cars cannot be off-loaded. The ferry usually stays in town briefly, sometimes not even long enough to get off the boat for a walk around. Get details from Alaska Marine Highway (800/642-0066, www.ferryalaska.com).

Both **Wings of Alaska** (907/789-0790, www.wingsofalaska.com) and **Alaska Seaplane Service** (907/789-3331 or 800/478-3360, www.akseaplanes.com) have flights most days between Tenakee Springs and Juneau.

Juneau

America's most beautiful state capital, Juneau (pop. 30,000) is a thriving slice of civilization surrounded by rugged Inside Passage scenery. The city perches on a thin strip of land at the mouth of Gold Creek, and behind it rise the precipitous summits of Mt. Juneau and Mt. Roberts. Out front, Gastineau Channel separates it from Douglas Island and the town of Douglas. The city abounds with cultural and artistic attractions, and the adjacent wild country provides a broad sampling of Southeast Alaska, from glacially capped mountains to protected coves where sea kayakers relax.

Juneau is the only state capital with no roads leading in or out. A government town, nearly half the local jobs are at state, federal, or city agencies. Tourism provides another mainstay for the local economy, fed by an annual influx of more than 700,000 visitors, primarily aboard luxury cruise ships. On summer days, up to five different ships tie up simultaneously, disgorging thousands of passengers. (To avoid the worst of the rush, get here before July or after August.) Juneau has a small fishing fleet and provides workers for a silver mine on nearby Admiralty Island.

Juneau may be small in population, but its boundaries extend to the Canadian border, covering 3,100 square miles. Less than half of Juneau's population actually lives downtown. The rest are spread into Douglas (across the channel), Mendenhall Valley (10 miles northwest), and other surrounding areas. As might be expected, these areas exhibit diverse personalities. Even the weather varies, with an average of 92 inches of rain each year downtown, but only 55 inches in Mendenhall Valley.

Downtown Juneau is marked by a mix of modern government offices and older wooden structures, many dating from the early 1900s. Across the bridge is Douglas Island and its bedroom community of Douglas. The town now consists of a few shops, but at its peak in 1915, when the Treadwell Gold Mine was operating, Douglas housed 15,000 miners. The road north from downtown Juneau is the Southeast's only divided highway. Heading north, you first reach Mendenhall Valley, Juneau's version of

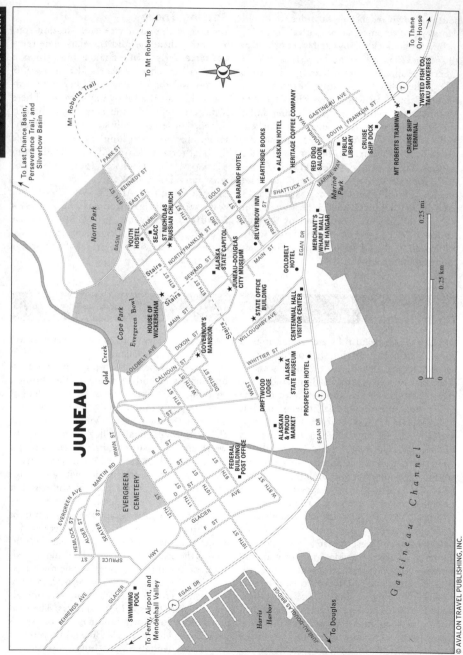

JUNEAU

To Last Chance Basin,
Perseverance Trail, and
Silverbow Basin

To Mt Roberts

To Mt Roberts

To Thane
Ore House

Mt Roberts Trail

PARK ST

North Park

Cope Park

Evergreen Bowl

Gold Creek

EVERGREEN
CEMETERY

EVERGREEN AVE

HEMLOCK ST
ALDER ST
SEATER ST
SPRUCE ST

BEHRENDS AVE

GLACIER

SWIMMING
POOL

To Ferry, Airport, and
Mendenhall Valley

Harris
Harbor

JUNEAU-DOUGLAS BRIDGE

To Douglas

EGAN DR

HWY

MARTIN RD
IRWIN ST

A ST
B ST
C ST
D ST
GLACIER AVE
F ST

W 12TH ST
11TH ST
10TH ST

9TH ST
W 8TH ST

FEDERAL
BUILDING/
POST OFFICE

ALASKAN
& PROUD
MARKET

EGAN DR

BASIN RD

6TH ST
KENNEDY ST
EAST ST
HARRIS

PARK ST

GOLDBELT AVE

DISTIN ST
CALHOUN ST
DIXON ST

MAIN ST
5TH ST
6TH ST
7TH ST

WEST

WHITTIER ST

WILLOUGHBY AVE

YOUTH
HOSTEL

SEACC

HOUSE OF
WICKERSHAM

Stairs
Stairs
Stairs

Stairs

GOVERNOR'S
MANSION

ST NICHOLAS
RUSSIAN CHURCH

SEWARD ST
NORTH FRANKLIN ST

4TH ST
3RD ST
2ND ST

GOLD ST

ALASKA
STATE CAPITOL

JUNEAU-DOUGLAS
CITY MUSEUM

STATE OFFICE
BUILDING

ALASKA
STATE MUSEUM

DRIFTWOOD
LODGE

PROSPECTOR HOTEL

CENTENNIAL HALL
VISITOR CENTER

SHATTUCK ST

FRONT ST
MAIN ST

EGAN DR

BARANOF HOTEL

SILVERBOW INN

HEARTHSIDE BOOKS

ALASKAN HOTEL

HERITAGE COFFEE COMPANY

GOLDBELT
HOTEL

GASTINEAU AVE
ADMIRALTY WAY

RED DOG
SALOON

MERCHANT'S
WHARF MALL/
THE HANGAR

MARINE WAY

Marine
Park

SOUTH FRANKLIN ST

PUBLIC
LIBRARY

CRUISE
SHIP DOCK

MT ROBERTS TRAMWAY

CRUISE SHIP
TERMINAL

TWISTED FISH CO/
TAKU SMOKERIES

Gastineau Channel

0   0.25 mi
0   0.25 km

© AVALON TRAVEL PUBLISHING, INC.

suburbia: three shopping malls, a slew of fast fooderies, and hundreds of pseudo-rustic, split-level homes and condos. But you can also see something most suburbs don't have: a drive-up glacier spilling out from the massive Juneau Icefield. The road continues north from Mendenhall Valley for another 30 miles, passing Auke Lake, the ferry terminal, and scattered homes along the way, ending at scenic Echo Cove.

HISTORY
Gold in the Hills

In October 1880, two prospectors—Joe Juneau and Richard Harris—arrived at what would later be called Gold Creek. Along its banks was a small Tlingit fishing camp of the Auke tribe. Chief Kowee showed the prospectors gold flakes in the creek, and the resulting discovery turned out to be one of the largest gold deposits ever found. Harris and Juneau quickly staked a 160-acre town site. The first boatloads of prospectors arrived the next month, and almost overnight a town sprouted along the shores of Gastineau Channel. Three giant hard-rock gold mines were developed in the area, eventually producing some seven million ounces of gold, worth *$4 billion* at today's prices! Compare that to the $7.2 million the United States paid Russia for Alaska only 13 years before the discovery.

The **Alaska Juneau (AJ) Mine** proved the most successful, operating for more than 50 years. Built in Last Chance Basin behind Juneau, its three tunnels connected the ore source to the crushing and recovery mill site on Gastineau Channel. Inside the mine itself was a maze of tunnels that eventually reached over 100 miles in length. Because the ore was low grade—it could take 28 tons of ore to yield one ounce of gold—enormous quantities of rock had to be removed. At its peak, the mill (still visible just south of town) employed 1,000 men to process 12,000 tons of ore a day. Tailings from the mill were used as the fill upon which much of downtown Juneau was constructed. (Franklin St. was originally built on pilings along the shore.) The AJ closed down in 1944 because of wartime labor shortages and never reopened.

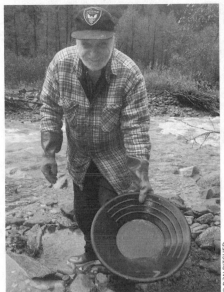

gold panning on Gold Creek

© DON PITCHER

The **Perseverance Mine** operated between 1885 and 1921, with a two-mile tunnel carrying ore from Gold Creek to the mill four miles south of Juneau. It eventually ran into low-grade ore and was forced to close.

The best known Juneau-area mine was the **Treadwell,** on Douglas Island. The Treadwell Complex consisted of four mines and five stamping mills to process the ore. It employed some 2,000 men who were paid $100 a month, some of the highest wages anywhere in the world at the time. The men enjoyed such amenities as a swimming pool, Turkish baths, tennis courts, bowling alley, gymnasium, and 15,000-volume library. The giant Treadwell stamping mills where the ore was pulverized made so much noise that people in downtown Douglas had to shout to be heard. Everything changed on April 21, 1917, when the ground atop the mines suddenly began to collapse, swallowing first the gymnasium and swimming pool, then the fire hall. Sea water rushed in, filling the tunnels as the miners ran for their lives. Amazingly, all apparently escaped alive. (The

VICINITY OF JUNEAU

Echo Cove

Point Bridge State Park

Lynn Canal

Tongass National Forest

Benjamin Island

Sentinel I

Lincoln Island

VETERANS MEMORIAL HWY

CABIN

EAGLE BEACH STATE RECREATION AREA

CABIN ● Windfall Lake

SHRINE OF ST THERESE

Shelter Island

Favorite Channel

GLACIER HWY

Eagle Glacier

Herbert Glacier

Montana Creek Tr

Peterson Lake

CABIN ●

Spaulding Tr

JOHN MUIR CABIN

Auke Nu Tr

Mt McGinnis ▲

West Glacier Tr

MENDENHALL GLACIER

Amherst Peak ▲

Mendenhall Lake

Bullard Mtn ▲

Nugget Mtn ▲

Nugget Creek Tr

VISITOR CENTER

AUKE BAY CAMPGROUND

FERRY TERMINAL

Auke Bay

Auke Lake

SEE DETAIL

Heintzleman Ridge Route

Coghlan Island

Portland Island

Spuhn I

Fritz Cove

NORTH DOUGLAS HWY

Lemon Creek Tr

COSTCO

Salmon Creek Res

Tongass National Forest

ALASKA BREWING COMPANY

HOSPITAL

▲ Mt Juneau

Perserverance Tr

Juneau

▲ Mt Roberts

Sheep Creek Tr

Douglas Island

Treadwell Ditch Tr

EAGLECREST RD

EGAN DR

THANE RD

Gastineau Channel

EAGLECREST SKI AREA

Douglas

SANDY BEACH PARK

THANE ORE HOUSE SALMON BAKE

DAN MOLLER CABIN

SAVIKKO PARK RV CAMPING

Treadwell Mine Tr

Mansfield Peninsula

Stephens Passage

0   5 mi
0   5 km

Admiralty Island

© AVALON TRAVEL PUBLISHING, INC.

Inset: Detail map

UNIVERSITY OF ALASKA JUNEAU

MENDENHALL LAKE CAMPGROUND

SPRUCE MEADOW RV PARK

AUKE BAY RV PARK

DEHART'S STORE

Mendenhall R

Auke Lake

MENDENHALL LOOP RD

MARINE LAB

FRITZ COVE RD

GLACIER

MENDENHALL MALL/SAFEWAY

Auke Bay

HWY

JORDAN CREEK MALL

FRED MEYER

GLACIER GARDENS

NUGGET MALL

AIRPORT

FOREST SERVICE DISTRICT OFFICE

MENDENHALL GLACIER

only missing miner was reportedly later seen in a nearby tavern before he skipped town.) Only one of the four mines was not destroyed in the collapse, and that one closed five years later.

Later Years

Juneau became the capital of Alaska in 1906 as a result of its rapid growth and the simultaneous decline of Sitka. Several attempts have been made to move the capital closer to the state's present power center, Anchorage. In 1976, Alaskan voters approved a new site just north of Anchorage, but six years later, when expectations for petro-billions had subsided into reality, voters thought better of the move and refused to fund it. Juneauites breathed a sigh of relief and went on a building spree that only ended with the sudden drop in state oil revenue from the 1986 oil-price plummet. Recent years have seen ever-increasing cruise ship tourism. Locals are starting to tire of the influx and its impact on the town; in 1999 they slapped a head tax on every cruise passenger who steps off in Juneau. By the way, Fridays are usually a light day for cruise ship traffic, so time your downtown visits accordingly.

SIGHTS

Juneau is jam-packed with things to see and do, from glaciers to salmon bakes and tram rides. It's the sort of place that travelers love. Many interesting places are right downtown—including two museums, numerous historic buildings, unusual shops, and even a library-with-a-view. Farther afield are dozens of hiking trails, several easily accessible glaciers, and such attractions as an informative fish hatchery, a brewery, old mining buildings, a stone church, and much more. Even on a rainy day, you'll find something fun in Juneau.

Alaska State Museum

Anyone new to town should not miss the Alaska State Museum (395 Whittier St., 907/465-2901, www.museums.state.ak.us, $3, free for under 18). Inside, you'll find an impressive collection of Native artifacts (including wildly creative Yup'ik Eskimo spirit masks) and exhibits relating to the Russian-American period and other aspects of Alaskan history. The museum also houses a gallery of contemporary fine arts, and brings in special exhibits each summer. But the highlight is the circular stairwell, which houses a full-size bald eagle nest and other Alaskan wildlife. The museum is open daily 8:30 A.M.–5:30 P.M. mid-May–late September, and Tuesday–Saturday 10 A.M.–4 P.M. the rest of the year.

Juneau-Douglas City Museum

The fine Juneau–Douglas City Museum (4th and Main Sts., 907/586-3572, www.juneau.org/parksrec/museum, $4) houses an interesting collection of maps, artifacts, photos, and videos from Juneau's rich gold-mining history. Be sure to check out the three-dimensional model of Perseverance Mine with its intricate maze of tunnels. Other features include a 19th-century store, a hands-on history room that's popular with kids, and a small gift shop, as well as brochures describing **walking tours** of historic Juneau—60 remaining downtown buildings were built before 1904! The museum is open Monday–Friday 9 A.M.–5 P.M. and Saturday–Sunday 10 A.M.–5 P.M. mid-May–late September; Thursday–Saturday noon–4 P.M. the rest of the year.

Mt. Roberts Tramway

The Mt. Roberts Tramway (907/463-3412 or 888/461-8726, www.goldbelttours.com, daily 9 A.M.–9 P.M., May–Sept.) provides a fast way into the high country above Juneau. The tram starts at the cruise ship dock on the south end of town and climbs 1,800 feet up the mountain, providing panoramic views of the surrounding land and water. The six-minute ride ends at an observation deck surrounded by tall Sitka spruce trees. Facilities here include a nature center, restaurant, gift shops, and theater where you can watch an award-wining 20-minute film about Tlingit culture. The tram costs $24 adults, $13 for kids ages 7–12, and is free for children under seven. If you hike up (see *Climbing Mt. Roberts*), the ride down is only $5. Tickets are good all day, but the lines can

SOUTHEAST ALASKA

© DON PITCHER

Mt. Roberts Tramway, with Juneau and Gastineau Channel in the background

get very long in late afternoon as cruise ship passengers rush back down to avoid missing their ship departures.

Gastineau Guiding (907/586-2666, www.stepintoalaska.com) leads easy "tram and trek" hikes that include a short bus tour of town, a tram ride up Mt. Roberts, and a one-hour hike for $59 ($32 kids). Or you can save your cash and simply strike out on your own along scenic alpine trails. Be sure to look for several live spruce trees carved with traditional Tlingit designs.

State Office Building

Enter the State Office Building (SOB) from Willoughby Avenue and take the elevator up to the 8th floor. Here you'll discover a 1928 Kimball organ, a lovingly preserved totem pole from the 1880s, the Alaska State Library, and an incredible panoramic view from the big **observation deck** (great for bag lunches). The airy lobby is also a pleasant place to stay dry on a rainy day; Friday at noon you'll enjoy the added bonus of an organ recital.

Governor's Mansion

Just up Calhoun Avenue from the SOB is the large, white Governor's Mansion. Built in 1912 in the New England Colonial style, it overlooks much of Juneau from its hilltop location. The mansion is not open to the public. Out front is a **totem pole** carved in 1939–1940. Near its base are the figures of a mosquito and a man, representing the Tlingit tale of the cannibalistic giant, Guteel, and his capture by hunters in a pit. The hunters built a fire to kill him, but just before he died he warned, "Even though you kill me, I'll continue to bite you." His ashes swirled into the air, becoming the mosquitoes that fulfill Guteel's promise.

More than 20 other totems are scattered around downtown. Most are recent carvings, but some date to the 19th century. Pick up the "Totem Pole Walking Tour" brochure from the Juneau–Douglas City Museum to find them all.

State Capitol

Back on 4th Street is the marble Alaska State Capitol. Completed in 1931, it was originally the federal office building and post office. The building is not at all like a traditional state capitol, and from the outside it could easily be mistaken for an aging Midwestern bank, complete with wide steps and marble columns. Free tours (907/465-2479 for reservations) of the bank—oops, Capitol are every half-hour Monday–Friday 9 A.M.–4:30 P.M. and Saturday noon–4:30 P.M. June–mid-September. Historical photos line the 2nd floor. You may sit in on the legislature when it's in session January–May. The antics of the legislature are always a hoot, especially after the FBI raided their offices in 2006 and found T-shirts brazenly labeled "Corrupt Bastard's Club." Makes me proud to be an Alaskan.

Last Chance Mining Museum

Behind town, Basin Road climbs 1.5 miles to the old AJ Gold Mine. The former compressor building here has been turned into the Last Chance Mining Museum (907/586-5338, daily 9:30 A.M.–12:30 P.M. and 3:30–6:30 P.M. mid-

May–late Sept., $4, free for kids), which houses mining paraphernalia and a 3-D map of the ore body.

Historic Downtown

Dozens of historic buildings fill the heart of downtown Juneau. Get a brochure describing them from the Juneau–Douglas City Museum. One of Juneau's most photographed sights is the onion-domed **St. Nicholas Russian Orthodox Church** (5th and Gold Sts., 907/586-6790, Mon.–Fri. 9 A.M.–5 P.M. mid-May–Sept., $2), built in 1894. Inside are icons and artwork, some dating from the 1700s. For a more evocative experience, attend a service (Sat. 6 P.M., Sun. 10 A.M.).

Marine Park, along Shattuck Way, with its lively mix of people and picturesque views, is a good place to relax after your tour of downtown. Directly across the street a bright mural depicts the Haida creation legend.

Evergreen Cemetery, between 12th and Seater streets on the north side of town, has the graves of Juneau's founders, Joe Juneau and Richard Harris, along with a marker near the spot where Chief Kowee was cremated.

House of Wickersham

Built in 1889, the House of Wickersham (213 7th St., 907/586-9001, www.alaskastateparks. org, open daily except Wed. 10 A.M.–noon and 1–5 P.M. mid-May–Sept., $2) offers a good view of Juneau and the surrounding country, and visitors are provided a fine tour. This was the home of Judge James Wickersham (1857–1939), a man who had a major impact upon Alaskan history. As Alaska's longtime delegate to Congress he introduced the first statehood bill in 1916—43 years before it passed—and was instrumental in the establishment of the territorial legislature, McKinley National Park, the University of Alaska, and the Alaska Railroad. Be sure to take a gander at the Native ivory carvings that Judge Wickersham collected from around the state.

Macaulay Salmon Hatchery

The impressive Douglas Island Pink and Chum

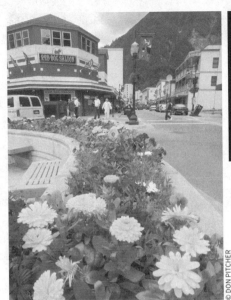

Franklin Street in downtown Juneau

© DON PITCHER

(DIPAC) salmon hatchery (2697 Channel Dr., 907/463-4810 or 877/463-2486, www.dipac. net, $3.25 adults, $1.75 kids under 13) is three miles north of town. Here you can learn about salmon spawning and commercial fishing, watch fish moving up one of the state's largest fish ladders, and check out the saltwater aquariums and underwater viewing windows. The facility includes shops and a visitor center where tours are offered. It's a fascinating place, and well worth the entrance fee. Open Monday–Friday 10 A.M.–6 P.M. and Saturday–Sunday 10–5 P.M. May–September, or by appointment the rest of the year. The king, coho, and chum salmon return mid-June–September, and during that time you can try your hand at fishing out front.

Glacier Gardens

This unique private botanical garden (7600 Glacier Hwy., 907/790-3377, www .glaciergardens.com, daily 9 A.M.–6 P.M. May–Sept., $20 adults, $17 ages 6–12, under 6 free) is eight miles north of downtown Juneau. The gardens are spread over 50 acres of hillside forest and include hiking trails, waterfalls, ponds, and "flower tower" cascades of blooms from upside down trees. Motorized carts (some set up to carry wheelchairs) transport visitors along four miles of paved paths to an overlook 500 feet up the mountainside, with views across the Mendenhall Wetlands. The city bus stops out front.

Alaskan Brewing Company

For something completely different, take the city bus to Anka Street in Lemon Creek and walk two blocks to Shaune Drive. Follow it a block to the Alaskan Brewing Company building (907/780-5866, www.alaskanbeer.com, tours every half-hour Mon.–Sat. 11 A.M.–4:30 P.M. May–Sept., free). You're given a sample of various beers at the end of the tour. The brewery has developed into one of America's finest, with its beers winning top prizes at national and international festivals. The brewery gift shop sells T-shirts, hats, and other items.

◖ Mendenhall Glacier

The Southeast's best-known drive-up ice cube, Mendenhall Glacier is without a doubt Juneau's most impressive sight. This moving river of ice pushes down from the 1,500-square-mile **Juneau Icefield** (fifth largest in North America) and is 12 miles long and up to 1.5 miles wide. Since 1750, the glacier has been receding, and is now several miles farther up Mendenhall Valley. It is retreating at about 150 feet each year, but still calving icebergs into Mendenhall Lake.

The **Mendenhall Glacier Visitor Center** (907/789-6640, www.fs.fed.us/r10/tongass, $3, free for kids) provides panoramic views of the glacier from the floor-to-ceiling windows. Use the spotting scopes to check the slopes of nearby Bullard Mountain for mountain goats. Walk through the interpretive exhibits, slip into the theater for an excellent 11-minute film on the glacier, or buy a couple of glacier postcards in the bookstore. The center is open daily 8 A.M.–7:30 P.M. May–mid-September, and Thursday–Sunday 10 A.M.–4 P.M. the rest of the year. Forest Service naturalists lead walks

on nearby trails and can answer your questions. Walk up at least one of these excellent paths if you want to come away with a deeper appreciation of Mendenhall Glacier.

Although it's 13 miles northwest of town, the glacier is easily accessible by city bus. Have the driver let you off when the bus turns left a mile up Mendenhall Loop Road. It's a one-mile walk up the road from here to the glacier. Buses run both directions around Mendenhall Loop Road. On the way back you can catch a bus heading either direction since both eventually drop you off downtown.

Mighty Great Trips (907/789-5460, www.mightygreattrips.com) provides transportation from downtown to the glacier for $12 round trip, and offers a 2.5-hour tour that includes time at the glacier for $22. Most other tour companies also offer tours to Mendenhall (see *Getting Around* for details).

University and Auke Lake

The campus of the University of Alaska Southeast (2,600 students) is a dozen miles northwest of Juneau on beautiful Auke Lake. The view across the lake to Mendenhall Glacier makes it one of the most attractive campuses anywhere. Also here is **Chapel by the Lake,** a popular place for weddings, with a dramatic backdrop of mountains and the Mendenhall Glacier. Across the highway, **Auke Bay Fisheries Lab** (Mon.–Fri. 8 A.M.–4:30 P.M.) has a small saltwater aquarium and fisheries displays.

Glacier Highway

If you have a vehicle, the 40-mile drive north from Juneau provides a wonderful escape. Twenty-three miles out is a quaint Catholic chapel built in 1939, the **Shrine of St. Therese** (907/780-6112, www.shrineofsainttherese .org). The cobblestone chapel is hidden away on a small, bucolic, wooded island connected to the mainland by a 400-foot causeway. Named for Alaska's patron saint, St. Therese of Lisieux, the chapel is open all the time, with Sunday service at 1 P.M. This is a nice, quiet place to soak up the scenery or to try your hand at fishing for salmon from the shore. The trail to Peterson Lake is nearby, and cabins are available for rent.

Eagle Beach (at Mile 28, $5 parking) is a popular day-use area with picnic tables and panoramic vistas of the snowcapped Chilkat Range. Pull out your binoculars to look for whales in Lynn Canal. Stop at **Point Bridget State Park** (Mile 38) for a pleasant hike. The road ends at scenic **Echo Cove,** a launching point for boats and kayaks.

Taku Glacier Lodge

Historic Taku Glacier Lodge (907/586-6275, www.takuglacierlodge.com, early May–Sept.) sits just across Taku Inlet from the glacier of the same name. This classic log structure (no overnight visits) was built in 1923, and short nature trails lead into the surrounding country. Black bears and eagles are frequent visitors (the bears were Juneau garbage bears that would have been shot if they had not been brought here). Visits to the lodge cost $225 for adults

or $185 for kids, and include a half-hour scenic flight over Taku Glacier, along with two hours at the lodge and a filling salmon lunch or dinner. Flights depart the Juneau waterfront up to five times a day between 9 A.M. and 5 P.M. The lodge is oriented to the cruise-ship crowd, so expect to see lots of other folks if you go on a day when several ships are docked.

ENTERTAINMENT AND EVENTS

Nightlife

Juneau has an active night life, with plenty of live music almost every evening. The famous **Red Dog Saloon** (on South Franklin St., 907/463-3658, www.reddogsaloon.cc) has sawdust on the floor and honky-tonk music in the air every day and night during the summer, starting at 2 P.M. Be sure to look for Wyatt Earp's gun; he checked it in when passing through on June 17, 1900, but his ship left for Nome before the Marshall's office reopened, so

© DON PITCHER

Red Dog Saloon

it remained unclaimed in Juneau. This is where cruise ship tourists and crewmembers drink.

A block up the street, inside the Alaskan Hotel, is the **Alaskan Bar** (167 S. Franklin, 907/586-1000), a quieter place with blues or folk music on weekends, and Thursday night jam sessions. It's always packed with locals, who head here in summer to escape the Red Dog crowds. The Alaskan has a Victorian decor and you can hear lawyers and lobbyists talk shop from any seat in the place during the legislative session.

Billiards aficionados fill the half-dozen tables upstairs at the **Viking Lounge** (218 Front St., 907/586-2159). Downstairs in the back is a classy disco with occasional live music and the best dance floor in Juneau. Across the street is **Imperial Bar** (907/586-1960), popular with the young crowd on weekends, when live bands perform. More music around the corner at the **Rendezvous** (184 S. Franklin, 907/586-1270); very loud rock and a lowlife crowd.

The Hangar (2 Marine Way, 907/586-5018, www.hangaronthewharf.com), on the wharf, has music to make you kick up your rain boots on Friday and Saturday nights, and is especially popular with state government workers on weeknights, with over 100 brews on tap or in bottles. Get here early for the window seats facing the water. **The Island Pub** (1102 2nd St., 907/364-1595, www.theislandpub.com) is a classy smoke-free bar in Douglas with live bands most Friday and Saturday nights.

Out near the airport, **The Sandbar** (2525 Industrial Blvd., 907/789-3411) has a large dance floor and rock or country music on weekends. Also out in Mendenhall Valley is **Marlintini's Lounge** (9121 Glacier Hwy., 907/789-0799), which mixes karaoke on weeknights with rock bands Thursday–Saturday nights.

Performing Arts and Music

On Friday evenings 7–8:30 P.M. in the summer, Marine Park in downtown Juneau comes alive with free **Concerts in the Park** (907/586-2787), ranging from classical to Middle Eastern folk. The **Juneau Symphony** (907/586-4676, www.juneausymphony.org) has monthly concerts October–April at various local venues. **Perseverance Theatre** (907/364-2421, www.perseverancetheatre.org) is a respected Douglas-based group that puts on plays September–May.

Movies

Local movie houses are the **20th Century Twin Theatre** (222 Front St., 907/586-4055) downtown and **Glacier Cinemas** (9091 Cinema Dr., 907/789-9191) in Mendenhall Valley. **Silverbow Inn** (120 2nd St., 907/586-9866 or 800/586-4146, www.silverbowinn.com) screens free classic flicks Monday–Wednesday in the back room, or head to **Goldtown Nickelodeon** (174 S. Franklin St., 907/586-2875) for indy and art-house films.

Events

Call 907/586-5866 for a recording of upcoming events and activities in Juneau. If you're around in April, don't miss the free weeklong **Alaska Folk Festival** (907/463-3316, www.juneau.com/aff), which attracts musicians from Alaska and the Northwest. You can attend workshops and dance to some of the hottest folk and bluegrass bands. Lots of fun, and completely authentic.

In late May, culture comes to town with the **Juneau Jazz and Classics** (907/463-3378, www.jazzandclassics.org), a 10-day series of performances and workshops by local musicians and nationally acclaimed guest artists.

During even-numbered years (2008 and 2010) Juneau is home to a colorful **Native Celebration** (907/463-4844) that attracts hundreds of participants from throughout the state. This is primarily a conference, but there are also performances, crafts, and a grand procession. The celebration takes place on the first weekend of June.

As in most every Alaskan town, June 21, the **summer solstice** is a time for celebration in Juneau; there's always some sort of party that long day and short night. **July 4th** is Juneau's day to play. Parades and a big fireworks show (see them from Douglas Island for the most impressive backdrop) are joined by dog Frisbee-catching and watermelon-eating contests, along with a sand castle contest at Sandy Beach Park.

Those who like to fish should throw in their lines at the annual **Golden North Salmon Derby** in early August. A top prize of $15,000 in cash makes it *the* big summer event for locals.

SHOPPING

Most locals do their shopping out the road at Nugget Mall in Mendenhall Valley, Fred Meyer (near the airport), or at either Costco or Wal-Mart in Lemon Creek. **Foggy Mountain Shop** (134 N. Franklin St., 907/586-6780, www.foggymountainshop.com) sells camping gear, topographic maps, and sports equipment. It also rents skis and inline skates. The best place for rugged raingear, boots, and outdoor clothes is **Nugget Alaskan Outfitter** (Nugget Mall, 907/789-9785 or 800/478-0770, www.outdoorhq.com). While there, check out the mall's nine-foot-tall stuffed brown bear.

Galleries

If you happen to be in town, be sure to check out the **First Friday Art Walk** the first Friday of each month, with art openings and snacks at local galleries. **Wm. Spear Designs** (174 S. Franklin St. upstairs, 907/586-2209, www.wmspear.com) has the complete collection of colorful enameled pins by this local artisan with an international reputation. A former lawyer, Spear's work covers the spectrum from UFOs to dinosaurs. Definitely worth a stop.

Rie Muñoz Gallery (2101 Jordan Ave., 907/789-7411, www.riemunoz.com), near the airport, features works by several of Alaska's best-known artists. Muñoz's works are famous for their bold colors and fanciful designs of Alaskans at work and play.

The cooperatively run **Juneau Artists Gallery** (175 S. Franklin St., 907/586-9891, www.juneauartistsgallery.com) features a wide range of artwork, including paintings, pottery, jewelry, and photography.

Annie Kaill's Fine Art and Craft Gallery (244 Front St., 907/586-2880, www.annieandcojuneau.com) is packed with whimsical gifts, pottery, jewelry, and fine art.

For Native and other fine Alaskan art—plus changing exhibits in the back rooms—visit **Alaska State Museum Gift Shop** (124 Seward St., 907/523-8431).

Native Arts

Juneau is a good place to purchase Native Alaskan artwork, and one of the best is downstairs at the airport: **Hummingbird Hollow Gift Shop** (907/789-4672, www.hummingbirdhollow.net). Fair prices and authentic Alaskan work, with a big choice of Tlingit, Haida, Yup'ik, and Eskimo pieces. **Raven's Journey** (439 S. Franklin St., 907/463-4686), across from the tram, is another reputable shop with authentic Native Alaskan and Canadian art.

Scads of other galleries and gift shops sell artwork and trinkets. The quality varies widely, but much of it is overpriced, particularly anything by a Native artisan. Unfortunately, the romanticized paintings, carvings, and sculpture depicting these original Alaskans hunting seals in kayaks or carving totem poles meets head-on a much sadder picture of inebriated Natives leaning against the windows of downtown Juneau bars.

The Literary Scene

Juneauites enjoy several fine public libraries. The award-winning **Juneau Main Library** (907/586-5249, www.juneau.lib.ak.us/library), is on the top floor of the parking garage on South Franklin Street. There's a wonderful view of all the activity in Gastineau Channel from the outside walkway. Visitors may want to stop by the freebie shelves near the entrance for a trashy novel to read. Located on the 8th floor of the State Office Building, the **Alaska State Library** (907/465-2921, www.library.state.ak.us), is a good place to track down historical documents and photos.

Hearthside Books (254 Front St., 907/586-1760 or 800/478-1000, www.hearthsidebooks.com) is a packed downtown bookshop; it also has a larger store (907/789-2750) in the Nugget Mall near the airport. **The Observatory** (235 2nd St., 907/586-9676, www.observatorybooks.com) sells used books—including the largest collection of out-of-print Alaskana—plus first editions and antiquarian maps. Also worthy of a visit is **Rainy Day Books** (113 Seward St., 907/463-2665, www.juneaubooks.com), with over 10,000 used and rare titles.

HIKING AND CABINS

The Juneau area has an amazing wealth of hiking paths leading into the surrounding mountains. For a complete listing, pick up a copy of *Juneau Trails* from the Centennial Hall Visitor Center (101 Egan Dr., 907/586-8751). This is also the place to go for hiking and cabin information in Juneau. Rubber boots are recommended for all these trails, though you could get by with leather boots on some of the paths when the weather is dry.

Guided Hikes

The **City Parks and Recreation Department** (907/586-5226 or 24-hour line 907/586-0428, www.juneau.lib.ak.us/parksrec) offers guided free day hikes into areas around Juneau every Wednesday (adults only) and Saturday all summer.

Gastineau Guiding (907/586-2666, www.stepintoalaska.com) leads hikes in the Juneau area, including a three-hour rainforest nature walk on Douglas Island ($64 adults, $39 kids), and a considerably more challenging four-hour "guide's choice" hike ($79 adults, $49 kids). Or you can join the blue-haired throngs for an easy "tram and trek" ($59 adults, $32 kids) that includes a 20-minute bus tour, a tram ride up Mt. Roberts, and a one-hour hike. The half-day "whales and trails" trip ($179 adults, $129 kids) combines a whale-watching boat tour and a Mendenhall Glacier hike, or join a photo safari ($169) for tips from a professional photographer on land and sea.

Mendenhall Glacier Trails

The Mendenhall area is laced with trails, including a couple of paved interpretive paths that swarm with visitors all summer. The relatively easy **East Glacier Loop Trail** (3.5 miles), also begins near the center and provides good views of the glacier. A more challenging hike splits off from this trail and follows Nugget

Creek uphill to an Adirondack shelter. Vegetation along the East Glacier Trail consists of brush and trees established since the glacier's recent retreat, while trees along the Nugget Creek Trail are much older.

My favorite Mendenhall trail is the **West Glacier Trail** (7 miles round-trip), which begins from the end of Montana Creek Road, just beyond the Mendenhall Lake Campground: incredible views of the glacier and icefalls en route. Experienced ice-climbers use the path to access the glacier itself. Finally, for the really ambitious there's a primitive route up 3,228-foot **Mt. McGinnis** from the end of the West Glacier Trail, an additional four miles (6 hrs.) round-trip. This trail is generally covered with snow until late summer, but offers panoramic vistas of the entire Juneau area—on clear days.

Up Gold Creek

Some of the finest hiking around Juneau is found in the old gold mining areas up beyond the end of Basin Road, a pleasant half-hour walk from town. The area is amazingly quiet and scenic, particularly given the proximity to hectic downtown Juneau. You'll hear birds singing, see waterfalls, and feel the land enveloping you. One could easily spend several days exploring this scenic area. In Last Chance Basin, 1.5 miles up Basin Road, are the fascinating remains of the **AJ Mine.** A number of paths lead around the compressor building (which houses the Last Chance Mining Museum), a locomotive repair shop, and a variety of remains from the heyday of gold mining. For more details of the area, pick up the "Last Chance Basin Walking Tour" brochure from the Juneau–Douglas City Museum.

Perseverance Trail leads past Last Chance Basin to Silverbow Basin, site of the Perseverance Mine, three miles away. The **Mt. Juneau Trail** branches off from Perseverance Trail a half-mile up. It's very steep and only suitable for experienced hikers, but offers unparalleled vistas across Gastineau Channel. Plan on seven hours round-trip. Directly across from the Mt. Juneau trailhead is a short path down to Ebner

Falls. Continue another mile out Perseverance Trail to the **Granite Creek Trail** (1.5 miles each way), which follows the creek up past several waterfalls into the alpine. Just before Silverbow Basin yet another side trail leads right to the Glory Hole, which is connected to the AJ Mine by a tunnel. Old mining ruins are at the end of the trail, but signs warn of potential hazards from toxic tailings at the mine site.

Douglas

The remains of the **Treadwell Mine**, destroyed by the collapse and flood of 1917, offer a fascinating peek into the past. Pick up the "Treadwell Mine Historic Trail" brochure from the Juneau–Douglas City Museum for a description of the area. The trail starts from the south end of St. Ann's Avenue in Douglas and passes the crumbling remains of old buildings. Get there by catching the hourly Douglas bus ($1.50) in Juneau and riding it to the end of the line at Sandy Beach. Keep right on the main trail to reach the **Treadwell Glory Hole,** once the entrance to a network of shafts under Gastineau Channel, but now full of water and wrecked cars. A waterfall drops into the hole. Return to the fork in the trail and continue down to the shore to see remains of more buildings and pieces of old mining machinery. Mine tailings dumped into Gastineau Channel created an attractive sandy beach along the shore here (Sandy Beach Park). Just to the south is a steep-sided pit where the mine collapsed in 1917. Walk back along the beach and past the Small Boat Harbor to Douglas Post Office, where you can catch a bus back to Juneau.

Climbing Mt. Roberts

The most convenient way to get a panoramic view of Juneau and Gastineau Channel is by taking the tram ($24 round-trip) to the summit of Mt. Roberts, directly behind town. A more aerobic way is to take the 2.5-mile rainforest trail that begins at the east end of 6th Street. This enjoyable climb attracts many locals, especially on summer weekends, when you'll even encounter ironman-type joggers.

After a strenuous hike you're suddenly surrounded by hundreds of folks—some barely ambulatory—who have ridden the tram from their cruise ships to commune with nature in the gift shop, restaurant, espresso stand, and theater. It's a bit disconcerting, but that's the new *Alaskan Wilderness Experience,* made easy for everyone. Beyond the tram station, well-maintained trails climb uphill past Native-carved trees to spectacular viewpoints and a large wooden cross just above the tree line at 2,030 feet. There may be snow above this point until late July.

Once you get beyond the cross, the crowds quickly thin and then virtually disappear. The trail continues up to 3,666-foot **Gastineau Peak,** six miles from town, then on along the ridge to the summit of **Roberts Peak** (3,819 ft.), nine miles from your starting point. Experienced hikers with a map and compass may want to continue along the ridge, eventually connecting up with other trails in the area. Weather conditions change rapidly on these ridge tops, so be aware of incoming clouds and never hike into fog.

Point Bridget State Park

Point Bridget is a delightful park along the edge of Lynn Canal, 38 miles north of Juneau, and near Echo Cove. It's a great place to hike if you have the wheels to get there. Several paths lace this 2,850-acre park, including the **Point Bridget Trail** (7 miles round-trip) which takes hikers out to a fine vantage point across Lynn Canal to the Chilkat Mountains. Sea lions, harbor seals, and humpback whales are often seen from here. Before heading out, pick up a park map from the Department of Natural Resources (400 Willoughby Ave., 907/465-4563, www.alaskastateparks.org). Three cozy public-use cabins ($45) each sleep eight.

Cabins

The Juneau area has four popular Forest Service cabins that can be reached by hiking trails or on skis in winter. Some of these book up six months in advance. For more details on all Forest Service cabins in the area, contact the

Forest Service Information Center downtown or the district office near Nugget Mall.

Located on a scenic alpine ridge, the **John Muir Cabin** overlooks Auke Bay and the surrounding islands. Get there by following the **Spaulding Trail** a half-mile, turning left onto the **Auk Nu Trail,** and continuing another 2.5 miles to the cabin. The trail starts from a parking area on the right side of the road 12 miles northwest of town and just beyond the Auke Bay Post Office.

The **Peterson Lake Cabin** lies at the end of a 4.5-mile trail. Although it's mostly boardwalk, rubber boots are highly recommended. The trailhead is on the right, 24 miles northwest of town, and just beyond the Shrine of St. Therese. Experienced hikers or cross-country skiers with a map and compass may want to cross the alpine ridges from Peterson Lake to the John Muir Cabin (2.5 miles away), where they can head back along the Auke Nu and Spaulding Trails.

The **Dan Moller Cabin** on Douglas Island lies at the end of a three-mile trail. Get there by taking the Douglas bus to West Juneau. Get off the bus on Cordova Street and hike three blocks up the street. Turn left onto Pioneer Avenue; the trail begins from a small parking lot next to 3185 Pioneer Avenue. One of the most popular wintertime skiing trails in the area, it leads up to the beautiful alpine country of central Douglas Island.

Eagle Glacier Cabin faces this magnificent glacier, and is accessed via the **Amalga (Eagle Glacier) Trail** that begins 28 miles north of town. The path is relatively easy to hike, passes the cabin at the 5.5-mile point, and ends at the Eagle Glacier, 7.5 miles from the trailhead. The cabin faces across a lake to the glacier, offering some of the most dramatic vistas anywhere. Wear rubber boots for the oft-muddy trail.

Windfall Lake Cabin is a modern cabin with a gorgeous setting on this lake north of Juneau. It's accessible via a three-mile trail from Herbert River Road.

Two trail-accessible cabins (reservations: 907/465-4563, www.alaskastateparks.org, $45) are in Point Bridget State Park, at Mile 39 of Glacier Highway. The 12-person **Cowee Meadows Cabin,** is a three-mile hike (or wintertime ski) from the road, and the **Blue Mussel Beach Cabin** is four miles with a wonderful bay vista.

In addition to these hike-in cabins, there are five other Forest Service cabins on the mainland around Juneau, plus another 15 on nearby Admiralty Island. Access to these cabins is by floatplane or sometimes by sea kayak. The **Berners Bay Cabin** is just eight kayak miles from the north end of Glacier Highway. The location is grand, with fine vistas across the bay, good fishing, a beautiful waterfall, and lots to explore on the two-mile-wide river delta just north of here. But book early for this cabin.

Two close and extremely popular cabins (they fill up several months in advance) are on **Turner Lake,** 20 miles east of Juneau. Great fishing for cutthroat trout and incredible waterfall-draped rock faces on all sides. The flight in takes you near the enormous Taku Glacier, an added bonus.

RECREATION

Rent mountain bikes from **Driftwood Lodge** (435 W. Willoughby Ave., 907/586-2280 or 800/544-2239, www.driftwoodalaska.com). **Cycle Alaska** (907/780-2253, www.cycleak.com) leads fun "bike & brew" tours through Mendenhall Valley, with a van ride to the Alaskan Brewing Co. for some sampling afterwards. Owner John McConnochie is one of the most experienced cyclists in the area.

The **Augustus Brown Swimming Pool** (1619 Glacier Ave., 907/586-5325) at the high school has a pool, co-ed sauna, and workout equipment.

Rock climbers will enjoy a visit to the **Rock Dump** (1310 Eastaugh Way, 907/586-4982, www.rockdump.com, $10 day pass), an indoor climbing facility south of Juneau off Thane Road.

Juneau Racquet Club/Alaska Club (2841 Riverside Dr., 907/789-2181, www.thealaskaclub.com) features exercise equipment, indoor racquetball and tennis courts, a sauna, and a hot tub. A second downtown location (641 W. Willoughby Ave., 907/586-5773) has more limited facilities. Non-members pay $10 per day.

Golfers should head to **Mendenhall Golf Course** (907/789-1221), a nine-hole course near the airport, where $25 gets you the full package. Not quite up to Arizona standards, but where else would you have a glacier backdrop?

Sea Kayaking

For an adventurous intro to sea kayaking, join **Above & Beyond Alaska's** (907/364-2333, www.beyondak.com, $185 adults, $165 kids) five-hour trip that includes a bus to Auke Bay and two hours of kayaking followed by a boat-based whale-watching trip. The company also provides water taxi drop-offs for kayakers at local bays and cabins. **Alaska Travel Adventures** (907/789-0052 or 800/478-0052, www.alaskaadventures.com, $85) has kayak three-hour trips from the north end of Douglas Island, but these are mainly for the cruise ship crowd.

Rent kayaks from **Alaska Boat & Kayak Rental** (907/789-6886, www.juneaukayak .com) at Auke Bay boat harbor 12 miles north of Juneau. Guided trips and water taxi services are also available. **Auke Bay Landing Craft** (907/790-4591, www.aukebay landingcraft.com), operates a helpful kayak drop-off service to Oliver's Inlet and other points in the Juneau area, and **Adventure Bound Alaska** (907/463-2509 or 800/228-3875, www.adventureboundalaska.com) provides kayak drop-offs in Tracy Arm.

Floating Mendenhall River

Experienced rafters and canoeists sometimes float the Mendenhall River, but be sure to ask the Forest Service for the details. The river is not particularly treacherous, but a number of people have died in independent boating accidents. For a guided float, join the cruise ship folks on a raft from **Goldbelt Tours** (907/586-8687 or 800/820-2628, www.goldbelttours.com, $99 adults, $66 kids) or **Alaska Travel Adventures** (907/789-0052 or 800/478-

0052, www.alaskaadventures.com, $85 adults, $57 kids). These four-hour floats include lunch and transportation from downtown.

Fishing and Whale-Watching

The visitor center offers a listing of Juneau's many **charter boat** operators. All sorts of options are available, from half-day fishing and whale-watching ventures to two-week cruises around Southeast. If you want to do it on your own, rent a skiff and fishing gear from Alaska Boat & Kayak Rental at Auke Bay.

A half-dozen companies specialize in whale-watching day trips out of Juneau, including **Orca Enterprises** (907/789-6801 or 888/733-6722, www.alaskawhalewatching.com), **Dolphin Whale Watch Tours** (907/463-3422 or 800/719-3422, www.dolphintours.com), **Four Seasons Marine** (907/790-6671 or 877/774-8687, www.4seasonsmarine.com) and **Juneau Sportfishing & Sightseeing** (907/586-1887, www.juneausportfishing.com).

Skiing and Snowboarding

Come wintertime, the **Eaglecrest Ski Area** (907/790-2000, www.skijuneau.com, Thurs.–Mon. early Dec.–March) on Douglas Island provides excellent skiing opportunities—when the weather cooperates. Thirty ski trails are available, with a vertical drop of 1,400 feet. Adult lift tickets cost $34, and cross-country skiers can get a special two-ride pass for $10 that takes them into the alpine meadows, or you can play on the tubing hill for $10. Call 907/586-5330 for current snow conditions. A bus provides weekend-only transport to Eaglecrest for $5 each way. Just downhill from the ski area are 5 kilometers of groomed cross-country trails (free).

The City Parks and Recreation Department (907/586-5226, www.juneau.lib.ak.us/parksrec) leads **guided cross-country ski tours** in the winter if there's enough snow. These take place every Wednesday (adults only) and Saturday.

Flightseeing and Glacier Landings

Flightseeing and charter flights are available from **Ward Air** (907/789-9150 or 800/478-9150, www.wardair.com), a long-established company with a good safety record. Glacier Bay flightseeing can also be booked, but they're expensive due to the distance. Wait until you visit Haines, Skagway, or Gustavus where the cost and flying time to the park are less.

Several companies offer helicopter glacier tours to the spectacular Juneau Icefield, with landings on crevasse-free portions of the glaciers. These flights remain controversial in Juneau, primarily because of the constant din they create in Mendenhall Valley. Flights operate May–September, but trips that include dogsledding start later and end earlier due to snow conditions. All prices are per person.

Era Helicopters (907/586-2030 or 800/843-1947, www.flightseeingtours.com) lands on Norris or Taku Glacier. A one-hour trip with a 15-minute walk is $244. It also offers a longer two-hour trip ($425) that includes a dogsled ride.

Temsco Helicopters (907/789-9501 or 877/789-9501, www.temscoair.com) has a one-hour flight ($199) that spends 25 minutes on Mendenhall Glacier. Other flight options include a "pilot's choice" 90-minute flight ($339) with two glacier landings, and a 1.5-hour trip ($419) that includes a 25-minute dogsled ride.

Coastal Helicopters (907/789-5600 or 800/789-5610, www.coastalhelicopters.com) charges $192 for a 60-minute trip, or $315 for a 90-minute trip; both include 15 minutes on a glacier. Also popular are dogsled tours on Herbert Glacier. These include an hour on the ice with the dogs and 30 minutes of flying time for $395.

Northstar Trekking (907/790-4530, www.glaciertrekking.com) specializes in Mendenhall Glacier hikes of varying lengths, starting with a flight plus one-hour hike for $295, up to a trek that includes more technical climbing and four hours on the ice for $459. Clients are fully outfitted with mountaineering gear and crampons for these adventures.

All four of these companies include transportation from downtown to their landing pads and also provide chartered flights to the glaciers for heli-hiking or skiing. Warning: Helicopters can be dangerous, and a number of fatal crashes have taken place around Juneau. Be sure to ask about safety procedures before stepping onboard.

Glacier Hikes

Travelers looking for something more challenging than a helicopter glacier tour should check out **Above & Beyond Alaska** (907/364-2333, www.beyondak.com). Their six-hour Mendenhall Glacier trek ($185) involves a hike to the west side of the glacier and time on the ice exploring its features, including the ice caves; crampons, helmet, and ice axe are provided. Another trek ($185) teaches basic ice climbing skills. Recommended, but you need to be in good physical condition.

Ziplines

Juneau is home to two high-adventure (literally) ziplines. The locally owned **Alaska Zipline Adventures** (907/790-2547, www.alaskazip.com) operates at Eaglecrest Ski Area on north Douglas Island, with access via a road to a high suspension skybridge and seven ziplines that drop through the forest and along a beautiful creek. The cost is $115 for a fun three-hour adventure. They also have a "zip and feast" trip that includes the zipline and a cooking demonstration.

A second company, **Alaska Canopy Adventures** (907/523-2920, www.alaska canopyadventures.com), operates on the site of the old Treadwell Gold Mine on Douglas Island. Participants take a short boat ride over from Juneau and then hop on an off-road vehicle to climb to the starting point in a platform high up a tree. A series of nine ziplines (one 800 ft. long) take you through the forest and eventually over the "glory hole" 200 feet below. Two suspension bridges link other sections, providing treetop views of the rainforest. The cost is $169 per person for a three-hour tour.

ACCOMMODATIONS

A full range of options is available to travelers staying in Juneau, but you should make reservations well in advance for arrivals in July and

August, when everything in town is sometimes booked. See the Juneau Convention and Visitors Bureau website (www.traveljuneau.com) for links to many local hotels, motels, B&Bs, lodges, and resorts. If you aren't bringing a vehicle up on the ferry, be sure to ask about if your lodging place offers a free pickup; it could save you the $30 taxi fare.

Hostel

Alaska's finest hostel, **Juneau International Hostel** (614 Harris St., 907/586-9559, www.juneauhostel.org) is in a lovely old home just a few blocks uphill from downtown. In addition to dorm space for 46 people, the hostel has a comfortable community room with guest computer, kitchen facilities, washer, and dryer. It does not have a TV. The hostel is open year-round, but is closed daily 9 A.M.–5 P.M. The doors are locked at midnight, putting a damper on your nightlife. Lodging costs just $10, with a maximum stay of three nights. Rooms are clean and the managers are friendly, but things are often crowded. Reserve ahead in summer, or get here early to be certain of a place.

Hotels and Motels

In-Town: The **Alaskan Hotel** (167 S. Franklin St., 907/586-1000 or 800/327-9347, www.thealaskanhotel.com) has reasonably priced downtown Juneau lodging in a historic setting. Built in 1913, this is Juneau's oldest lodging place, with 45 small, but surprisingly charming rooms. Bare-bones units with a shared bath and no TV cost $60 s or d; nicer ones with private baths and TVs are $80 s or d, and some of these include fridges and microwaves. Larger kitchenette units sleep four for $90. Try to get a room away from the bar and not on the second floor since these can get noisy when bands are playing. During the Folk Festival each April the Alaskan is the heart of the music scene, with impromptu jams in the halls and downstairs at all hours. The Alaskan is a classic—and rustic—place, so it may not please people expecting the latest in accouterments. Wi-Fi is available in the lobby and bar.

Driftwood Lodge (435 W. Willoughby Ave., 907/586-2280 or 800/544-2239, www.driftwoodalaska.com), is convenient to town, with dated rooms (some with kitchenettes) for $94 d; one-bedroom units with kitchens for $102 d, and two-bedroom units that sleep four for $125. The Driftwood provides a courtesy van to the airport or ferry terminal, and a guest computer.

Prospector Hotel (375 Whittier St., 907/586-3737 or 800/331-2711, www.prospector hotel.com), has spacious in-town rooms, most of which contain kitchenettes. Rates are $159 d in standard rooms, up to $179 d in two-room kitchenette suites. Amenities include a restaurant, courtesy van to the airport or ferry terminal, and Wi-Fi.

Baranof Hotel (127 N. Franklin St., 907/586-2660 or 800/544-0970, www.westmarkhotels.com) is a nine-story downtown classic with a dark lobby and a romantic restaurant. It's a favorite haunt of state legislators and lobbyists in the winter, and 20 of the rooms have kitchenettes ($209 d). Several smaller and older rooms have twin beds for just $109 d, but nicer rooms (ask for a remodeled unit) are $169–194 d, and suites run $209–259 d. The lobby has Wi-Fi and a guest computer. The higher levels offer the best views and least street noise.

The seven-story **Goldbelt Hotel Juneau** (51 W. Egan Dr., 907/586-6900 or 888/478-6909, www.goldbelttours.com, $169–179 d) has a convenient downtown location, modern rooms, Wi-Fi, a restaurant (The Zen), and a free airport shuttle. Ask for a room facing the water.

Mendenhall Valley/Airport: Most of Juneau's newest hotels are clustered around the airport in Mendenhall Valley. These lack the charm of the historic downtown places, and you will probably want a rental car to get around. Of course, they are also close to Mendenhall Glacier, and offer the predictability of corporate lodging.

Super 8 Motel (2295 Trout St., 907/789-4858 or 800/800-8000, www.super8.com, $111–120 s or d) has reasonable rates. Amenities include a continental breakfast, Wi-Fi, and courtesy shuttle. Some rooms have fridges and microwaves.

A good family place is **Frontier Suites Airport Hotel** (9400 Glacier Hwy., 907/790-6600 or 800/544-2250, www.frontiersuites.com, $130–160 d). It has a wide variety of rooms, all with full kitchens (including dishes), and some with jetted tubs. Three family units contain bunks. Free shuttle to the airport and ferry.

Also near the airport is **Grandma's Feather Bed** (2358 Mendenhall Loop Rd., 907/789-5566 or 888/781-5005, www.grandmasfeatherbed.com, $160 d) a 14-unit motel with spacious rooms, whirlpool tubs, and a hot breakfast. Nearby (same owners) is **Best Western Country Lane Inn** (9300 Glacier Hwy., 907/789-5005 or 888/781-5005, www.countrylaneinn.com, $130–140 d) with standard motel rooms and a continental breakfast. Both places have guest computers, Wi-Fi, and a courtesy shuttle to downtown, the ferry, or the airport.

Extended Stay Deluxe (1800 Shell Simmons Dr., 907/790-6435 or 888/559-9846, www.extendedstaydeluxe.com)—just a block away from the airport and nine miles from downtown—has all the amenities travelers have come to expect, including an indoor swimming pool, hot tub, exercise room, kitchenettes in all rooms, continental breakfast, Wi-Fi, guest computers, and free shuttle service to town and the ferry. Most rooms go for $159 d and have either two queens or a king bed, but a few rooms ($179 d) also feature private whirlpool tubs.

Lighthouses and Cabins

For something really different, spend a night or two at **Sentinel Island Lighthouse** (907/586-5338, $50 per person) a few miles north of Juneau. Built in 1935, the art deco tower has bunks (bring sleeping bags), and guests can also stay in the keeper's house which contains a kitchen. Get to Sentinel Island by kayak, skiff, or helicopter. The island has two active eagle nests and sits right across from a Steller sea lion haulout.

Two other lighthouses currently being restored may be open to the public in the next few years: **Point Retreat Lighthouse** (907/364-2410, www.aklighthouse.org), on the northern tip of Admiralty Island west of Juneau, and **Five Fingers Lighthouse** (907/364-3632, www.5fingerlighthouse.com), 75 miles south of Juneau.

Located 23 miles north of Juneau, the **Shrine of St. Therese** (907/780-6112, www.shrineofsainttherese.org) has a delightful collection of cabins for rent. A rustic cabin with wood stove is just $20 s or $25 d; no kitchen, and you'll need to use the nearby bathrooms. A historic 1938 log cabin has two bedrooms, plus a kitchenette and private bath for $35 s or $45 d. Three larger places are available, including a lodge that can sleep 22 guests! You don't have to attend Catholic mass, but guests must abide by the contemplative spirit of this unique and peaceful place.

Bed-and-Breakfasts

Couples may want to spend the extra money to stay at one of more than 40 Juneau B&Bs. Accommodations run the gamut from old miner's cabins to gorgeous log hillside homes. Pick up the *Juneau Visitors Guide* brochure at the visitor center for a listing of local places, or check its rack for flyers from many B&Bs. Two good Web resources for Juneau B&Bs are the Juneau Convention and Visitors Bureau (www.traveljuneau.com) and the B&B Association of Alaska INNside Passage Chapter (www.accommodations-alaska.com).

Downtown B&Bs: Gold Street Inn B&B (907/586-9863, www.juneauinn.com, open May–mid-Sept.) has unpretentious but clean accommodations in a historic downtown rooming house. The four rooms ($95–125 d) have private entrances and baths, and include a continental breakfast and Wi-Fi. A two-bedroom suite ($155 for four) has a kitchenette.

Best known for its bagels and other baked goods, **Silverbow Inn** (120 2nd St., 907/586-4146 or 800/586-4146, www.silverbowinn.com, $100–175 d) also has 11 bright guest rooms, each with private bath, phone, TV, and Wi-Fi. The least expensive rooms are small, while two more spacious new units have Jacuzzi tubs. Add $20 to access the rooftop deck with a hot tub, sauna, and fine views. Guests are served a tasty breakfast each morning, along with evening cheese and wine. A two-night minimum is required in mid-summer.

Built in 1906, and beautifully restored to its foursquare glory, **⟨ Alaska's Capital Inn** (113 W. 5th St., 907/586-6507 or 888/588-6507, www.alaskacapitalinn.com) offers sumptuous heart-of-Juneau lodging with commanding views of the city. Four guest rooms ($179–239 d) are filled with period antiques—including an 1879 pump organ and maplewood floors from a 1920s YMCA—and the entire top level has been transformed into a very private suite ($275 d) with a gas fireplace, jetted tub, and king-size sleigh bed. Two smaller gardenside rooms ($149–179 d) are more contemporary, with private entrances—making them popular with families. All rooms have private baths, and most also feature clawfoot tubs. Amenities include a flower-filled yard with a gazebo-enclosed hot tub, free Wi-Fi and guest computer, a wonderful Alaskan breakfast, plus evening wine and treats. Two-night minimum in the summer.

Farther Afield B&Bs: Located on a cove near Auke Bay, **Serenity Inn** (907/789-2330 or 800/877-5369, www.alaskaserenityinn.com, $189 d, $239 for four) has an apartment suite that features a full kitchen (make-your-own breakfast fixings included), hot tub on the deck, and extraordinary views across Lynn Canal from the deck. Two-night minimum.

Pearson's Pond Luxury Inn and Garden Spa (907/789-3772 or 888/658-6328, www.pearsonspond.com, $249–349 s, $299–399 d) is a comfortable home with two hot tubs, a three-level deck, five guest rooms, guest computers, Wi-Fi, and Mendenhall Glacier vistas. The premium rooms include large spa tubs and canopy beds. Borrow a bike to ride around, paddle a kayak around the small pond, or just enjoy the beautiful gardens. Breakfast is a make-it-yourself affair. Two-night minimum.

On the north end of Douglas Island, six miles from Juneau and close to the Eaglecrest Ski Area, **Fireweed House B&B** (907/586-3885 or 800/586-3885, www.fireweedhouse.com) has a scenic and very peaceful setting. Accommo-

dations (all with private baths and jetted tubs) include two rooms in the main house ($189 d) and an apartment with kitchen ($229 d). A separate two-bedroom guesthouse ($399 for four; three-night minimum) sits on a quiet two-acre site away from the other buildings, and has its own hot tub. Delicious breakfasts are a real attraction, and kids are welcome. Wi-fi and guest computers are available.

A lovely waterside home on Douglas Island, **Gill's Horizon** (907/586-2829, www.gillshorizon.com) is eight miles from Juneau. Guests stay in the apartment suite ($169 d), and will appreciate the waterside hot tub, private beach, lush grounds, driving range, and even a pair of nesting eagles. Three-night minimum stay.

Auke Lake B&B (11595 Mendenhall Loop Rd., 907/790-3253, www.admiraltytours.com) occupies a prime piece of shoreline on this picturesque lake. The 5,000-square-foot home has a deck with a hot tub for relaxing, two suites ($145–165 d), and a rather small guest room ($125 d), all with private baths, fridges, and a light breakfast. Borrow the kayak for a paddle around the lake.

CAMPING

The Forest Service maintains two campgrounds (reservations: www.reserveusa.com) in the Juneau area, but neither is close to town, and both are only open in the summer. **Mendenhall Lake Campground** hugs the shore of Mendenhall Lake, with glacier views and access to several hiking trails. Here you will find backpacker units and vehicle sites ($10), along with RV sites with full hookups ($28). From the ferry terminal, turn right and go two miles to De Hart's Store, then left onto Loop Road. Follow it three miles to Montana Creek Road, then another three-quarters of a mile to the campground. From Juneau by foot, take the city bus to where Montana Creek Road intersects Mendenhall Loop Road. Walk up Montana Creek Road, bear right at the Y after a half-mile, then continue another half-mile to the campground (well marked).

Auke Village Campground ($8) is 16 miles north on Glacier Highway and another two miles out Point Louisa. The area is secluded, with a nice beach and views of nearby islands. If you lack a vehicle, the nearest city bus stop is four miles away.

Eagle Beach State Recreation Area (Mile 28, 907/465-4563, mid-May–mid-Sept., $10) has rustic campsites (no water). Nearby is a picnic area with all-encompassing views of the Chilkat Range.

RV Campgrounds
The city of Juneau has four RV spaces at **Savikko Park** (907/586-5255) on Douglas Island. Free, but no hookups, no tents, and stays are limited to three days.

Auke Bay RV Park (907/789-9467, open year-round, $24 with full hookups, no tent camping) is a mile and a half southeast of the ferry terminal. Reservations are recommended here.

Spruce Meadow RV Park (10200 Back Loop Rd., 907/789-1990, www.juneaurv.com, $27 RVs or $20 tents) is four miles from the ferry terminal. In addition, RVs can generally overnight at Nugget Mall near the airport for free, but no facilities, of course.

FOOD
Breakfast and Lunch
No other Alaskan restaurant is even remotely like **C Costa's Diner,** located in Merchant's Mall downtown. Owner, chef, and general rabble-rouser Costa Collette runs this free-form place where the board lists today's specials ($5–8), typically crepes, pancakes, and egg dishes. Write your order on a sticky note, pour your own coffee, dig out the dishes and silverware, open the fridge for condiments and salsa, and sit back to take in the chaos. Payment is on the honor system: just put your money in the bucket, along with a tip. Ask a local if you can't figure out the system at Costa's. At lunch, Costa's spot becomes **The Soup Queen,** with homemade soups for under $6.

Rainbow Foods (224 4th St., 907/586-6476, www.rainbow-foods.org) is the local natural foods market, but also has a buffet

($6.50/pound) with healthy hot meals to go; it's great for a fast lunch without a lot of fat.

For a Mendenhall Valley lunch, head to **Heritage Glacier Café** (9112 Mendenhall Mall Rd., 907/789-0692) where favorites include fajitas, burgers, and portobello wraps. Or just get today's soup with focaccia for $4. Well off the tourist path, and worth the side trip. They also have a breakfast menu and free Wi-Fi.

Coffee Shops and Bakeries
Three local spots are popular for coffee and light meals, and all three provide free Wi-Fi for customers. **Heritage Coffee** (174 S. Franklin St., 907/586-1087 or 800/478-5282, www.heritagecoffee.com) is easily the most popular and crowded Juneau espresso-and-pastries shop, and remains open until 11 most summer nights. It's a great place to meet tie-and-sportcoated politicians, ring-nosed teens, plaid-shirted fishermen, and Gore-Texed vacationers. Walk down the halls of this building to view over-sized historic photos of Juneau.

Valentine's Coffee House & Bakery (111 Seward, 907/463-5144, www.valentines coffeehouse.com) is smaller and away from the action, with a lunch menu of focaccia sandwiches, salads, and calzones.

Alaska's oldest bakery, **Silverbow Inn Bakery** (120 2nd St., 907/586-4146, www.silverbowinn.com) is great for a hot bagel (try one with cream cheese and lox), soup, or latte. The atmosphere is homespun and funky, and the side-street location keeps the crowds at bay. They're open till 8 P.M.

Get an ice cream to go at **Chilkat Cone Kitchen** (inside the Merchant's Wharf on Marine Way, 907/463-2663), where the waffle cones are decorated with traditional Native designs.

Local Favorites
The Hangar (2 Marine Way in Merchant's Wharf, 907/586-5018, www.hangaronthe wharf.com, $11–30) is an extremely popular waterfront pub with seafood, steaks, pasta, burgers, sandwiches, and salads, but I usually keep it simple with halibut fish and chips and a local beer. Historic photos line the

walls, and you can head upstairs for a game of pool. It's a great place to watch the sun go down while enjoying one of its 24 brews on draught. Loud, energetic, and fun are the operative terms.

Farther afield is **Hot Bite** (907/790-2483) at Auke Bay Harbor. The menu includes charbroiled burgers (best in town), halibut and chips, grilled portobello mushroom sandwiches, milk shakes, and other tasty bites. Service can be slow since it's all made to order.

Pizza and Italian

Juneau's best-known pizza joint is **Bullwinkle's** (907/586-2400, www.bullwinklespizza.com), directly across from the State Office Building on Willoughby Avenue and also in Mendenhall Valley next to Super Bear Market. Daily lunch pizza specials start at $6, and the popcorn is always free. Good salad bar, too. You'll get better and more authentic pizza—including by the slice—from **Pizzeria Roma** (Merchant's Wharf, 907/463-5020).

Over in Douglas, **The Island Pub** (1102 2nd St., 907/364-1595, www.theislandpub.com) serves pizzas, sandwiches, and wraps in a great smoke-free setting with big windows facing Juneau.

International

In business since 1974, **Olivia's de Mexico** (222 Seward St. downstairs, 907/586-6870) serves traditional Mexican food, with fair prices and big portions.

Located across from the Auke Bay boat harbor, **(Chan's Thai Kitchen** (907/789-9777, lunch and dinner until 8:30 P.M., closed Sun. and Mon.) is popular with locals looking for a little spice in their lives. The food is dependably fine, but the place gets packed most nights so be ready to wait. The spring rolls, chicken coconut soup, and any of the curries are recommended. Delicious Thai ice tea too.

For surprisingly good Japanese sushi and Chinese head to the Korean-American owned **Seong's Sushi Bar** (740 W. 9th St., 907/586-4778, $7–9) across from the Federal Building. Lunches are the real attraction, with big plates of chicken sukiyaki, broccoli beef, or shrimp with veggies.

Another locals' favorite is **Dragon Inn** (5000 Glacier Hwy., 907/780-4616), three miles out in Lemon Creek, serving dim sum appetizers, seafood with pan-fried noodles, sautéed eggplant in garlic sauce, and more. Downtown, head to **Wild Spice Restaurant** (140 Seward St., 907/523-0344, www.thewildspice.com) for Mongolian BBQ–style meals; you select a bowl full of ingredients and spices, and watch the chefs do their wonders.

Out near the airport, **Sweet Dream** (8585 Old Dairy Rd., 907/789-4401, www.sweetdreamteas.com) is certainly the most unexpected Juneau establishment. The shop rents Japanese anime videos (and screens them on Saturday nights), and serves bubble tea—an iced Asian tea smoothie with tapioca balls—along with pho or udon soups. It's also a Wi-Fi hotspot.

Pel' Meni (on Marine Way in Merchant's Wharf, 907/463-2630) is a tiny Russian eatery, where the house specialty is dumplings made with sirloin steak and topped with a spicy curry and cilantro sauce. This late-night hangout is popular with teens.

Seafood

Juneau has two excellent salmon bakes with all-you-can-eat dinners and free bus transport from town. Both are open May–September. Housed in a rustic waterside building four miles south of town, **(Thane Ore House Salmon Bake** (907/586-3442, www.thaneorehouse.com), charges adults $22 and kids $11 for a big dinner of king or sockeye salmon, beer-battered halibut, BBQ ribs, baked beans, cornbread, and unusual salads. Outside tables are perfect for those rare sunny days.

Gold Creek Salmon Bake (907/789-0052 or 800/323-5757, www.alaskaadventures.com, $32 adults, $21 kids) has a similar menu north of town near the hospital.

Get high-quality, freshly smoked salmon at **Taku Smokeries** (550 S. Franklin St., 907/463-3474 or 800/582-5122, www.takusmokeries.com), a few blocks south of town.

Drop by for a sample or to watch through the windows as they process the fish.

On the water side of the Taku Smokeries building is **Twisted Fish Co.** (907/463-5033, May–Sept., $16–26), where the decor is playful and the food is contemporary. Big windows face Gastineau Channel, where floatplanes and cruise ships create a busy scene all summer. Watch the crew in the open kitchen as they prepare grilled halibut burgers, halibut tacos, eight-inch pizzas, cedar plank salmon, and a tasty clam chowder. It's a noisy and fun spot. (The owners also operate the equally popular Hangar.)

Groceries

You'll find no-frills grocery shopping at the big **Fred Meyer** (907/789-6503), nine miles northwest of town along Glacier Highway. Other grocers out in Mendenhall Valley are **Safeway** (3033 Vintage Blvd., 907/790-5500) and **Super Bear Supermarket** (in Mendenhall Mall, 907/789-0173).

In town, head to friendly **Alaskan & Proud Market** (615 Willoughby Ave., 907/586-3101 or 800/478-2118)—better known as A&P, but not to be confused with the East Coast chain—for a complete selection of fresh produce and meats. Safeway, A&P, and Fred Meyer are all open 24 hours a day. You might also try the somewhat-downsized **Costco** (5225 Commercial Way, 907/780-6740) in Lemon Creek, though most visitors won't find much need for cases of tuna fish or 50-pound bags of charcoal.

The local natural foods market downtown, **Rainbow Foods** (224 4th St., 907/586-6476, www.rainbow-foods.org) has a healthy and tasty lunchtime buffet with salads, veggie dishes, and pizza slices.

INFORMATION AND SERVICES

Juneau's info spot is the **Centennial Hall Visitor Center** (101 Egan Dr., 907/586-2201 or 888/581-2201, www.traveljuneau.com). Hours are Monday–Friday 8:30 A.M.–5 P.M. and Saturday–Sunday 9 A.M.–5 P.M. May–September, Monday–Friday 9 A.M.–4 P.M. the

rest of the year. Ask for the "Juneau Walking Tour" map on a nice day, or pick out a video for a rainy-day diversion. You can make ferry reservations here, and there's usually a Forest Service volunteer available to answer your questions.

Three other information kiosks in Juneau have brochures and may be staffed in the summer. Find them at Marine Park, the airport, and the Cruise Ship Terminal on South Franklin Street. Other useful online info sources for Juneau include www.juneaualaska.com, www.juneau.com, and the city site www.juneau.org.

Services

The main post office is in the downtown Federal Building at 9th Street and Willoughby Avenue, and a branch post office at 225 Front Street. **Bartlett Regional Hospital** (907/796-8900, www.bartletthospital.org), halfway between Juneau and Mendenhall Valley, is the largest medical facility in Southeast Alaska. For non-emergencies, contact **Juneau Urgent Care** (8505 Old Dairy Rd., 907/790-4111, www.juneauurgentcare.com).

A number of local places have computers where you can check your email. The Juneau Public Library has free computers and wireless Internet, or pay to view downtown at **Seaport Cyber Station** (170 S. Franklin St., 907/586-8676, www.seaportcyber.com).

Coin-operated showers can be found at **Harbor Washboard** (1114 Glacier Ave., 907/586-1133), **Zach Gordon Youth Center** (396 Whittier St., 907/586-2635), the **Alaskan Hotel** (167 S. Franklin St., 907/586-1000), and out of town at **Auke Bay Boat Harbor** (907/789-0819). A better deal is the high school **swimming pool** (1619 Glacier Ave., 907/586-5325), where your entrance buys access to a shower, pool, sauna, and weight-lifting equipment. Plus, you get to check out the pallid-skinned Juneauites. Coin laundries include Harbor Wash Board, along with **The Dungeon** (4th and Franklin Sts., 907/586-2805) and **Mendenhall Laundromat** (Mendenhall Mall, 907/789-9781).

SEACC

The Southeast Alaska Conservation Council, or SEACC (419 6th St., 907/586-6942, www.seacc.org), has material on regional environmental issues, plus activist T-shirts. This is the primary environmental group in the Southeast and has a reputation as a highly effective organization both locally and in Washington, D.C. Members receive a quarterly newsletter and periodic notices of important environmental issues. You can join for $25 per year.

GETTING THERE
Ferry

Juncau's Alaska Marine Highway **ferry terminal** (907/465-3940) is 14 miles northwest of town at Auke Bay. Ferries arrive and depart daily during the summer, headed north to both Haines and Skagway, southwest to Sitka, and south to other Alaskan towns. Arrivals are sometimes very late at night, so be ready to stumble off in a daze. Ferries generally stay one to two hours in Auke Bay. The *Fairweather* is a high-speed passenger and vehicle ferry with frequent service from Juneau to Sitka, Haines, and Skagway. Unfortunately, the ferry suffers from frequent breakdowns, so check ahead to make sure it's on schedule. The other state ferries are larger and slower. Several covered picnic tables are behind the terminal where you can crash if you have an early-morning departure. Make ferry reservations through Alaska Marine Highway (907/465-3941 or 800/642-0066, www.ferryalaska.com).

A cab ride to town will set you back $30, but hitching to town is relatively easy during the day. You can also walk the two miles from the ferry terminal to De Hart's Store, where hourly city buses will pick you up Monday–Saturday 7 A.M.–11:30 P.M.

Air

Juneau airport is nine miles northwest of downtown. Express **city buses** ($1.50) arrive hourly in front of the airport between 8 A.M.–5 P.M. On weekends or later hours (until 11:15 P.M.) you can catch the regular city bus behind Nug-

get Mall, a half-mile away. Taxis cost $20 to downtown.

Inside the terminal, take a look at the glass cases with various stuffed critters, including a huge polar bear (upstairs). The upstairs Glacier Restaurant offers impressive vistas out across Mendenhall Glacier, along with surprisingly good and reasonable meals; locals actually come here to eat!

A good place to see waterfowl and eagles is the **Mendenhall Wetlands** that surround the airport. An overlook provides a view from Egan Highway on the way into Juneau.

Alaska Airlines (800/426-0333, www.alaskaair.com) has daily flights into Juneau from Seattle, and on to Anchorage. Alaska's jets also connect Juneau with other Southeast towns and points south all the way to Mexico.

Options abound for small-plane service to communities around Juneau. **Wings of Alaska** (907/789-0790, www.wingsofalaska.com) has daily flights to Angoon, Gustavus, Haines, Hoonah, Skagway, and Tenakee Springs. **Alaska Seaplane Service** (907/789-3331 or 800/478-3360, www.akseaplanes.com) offers daily service to Angoon, Elfin Cove, Pelican, and Tenakee. **Skagway Air** (907/789-2006, www.skagwayair.com) flies to Haines and Skagway daily. **L.A.B. Flying Service** (907/789-9160, www.labflying.com) has daily service to Gustavus, Haines, Hoonah, Kake, and Skagway. **Air Excursions** (907/697-2375 or 800/354-2479, www.airexcursions.com) offers the cheapest flights to Gustavus from Juneau. Flightseeing and charter flights are also available from these companies.

GETTING AROUND
Tours

Mighty Great Trips (907/789-5460, www.mightygreattrips.com) runs 2.5-hour summertime tours that include Juneau and Mendenhall Glacier for $22. Other bus tour companies include **Gray Line of Alaska** (907/586-3773 or 800/544-2206, www.graylineofalaska.com), **Last Frontier Tours** (907/789-0742 or 888/396-8687, www.lastfrontiertours.com), and **Princess Tours** (907/463-3900 or

800/774-6237, www.princess.com). Princess operates excellent three-hour trips ($65 adults, $35 kids) to the historic AJ Mine south of town, with detailed tours inside the mine, plenty of historical info, and the chance to pan for gold.

For something different, hop onboard the **Juneau Steamboat Co.** (907/723-0372, www.juneausteamboat.com), a little wood-fired boat modeled after ones used a century ago. One-hour tours of Gastineau Channel depart the downtown dock and cost $30.

City Buses

Capital Transit buses (907/789-6901, www.juneau.org/capitaltransit, $1.50) operate daily, connecting Juneau, Douglas, and Mendenhall Valley. Buses to and from Mendenhall Valley run every half-hour 7 A.M.–10:30 P.M. (9 A.M.–5:30 P.M. on Sun.), with both regular and express service (weekdays only). Bus service to Douglas is hourly. Pick up route maps and schedules from the various visitor centers or at the ferry terminal or airport.

Trolley

The **Juneau Trolley Car Company** (907/586-7433, www.juneautrolley.com, daily May–Sept. 8 A.M.–6 P.M., day pass $19, $9 kids) covers most of downtown. This red trolley features a 30-minute narrated tour, and you can get on and off at various points along the way.

Taxis

The local taxi companies are **Alaska Taxi & Tours** (907/780-6400), **Capital Cab** (907/586-2772), **Juneau Taxi & Tours** (907/790-4511), and **Evergreen Taxi** (907/586-2121). From the airport to downtown the charge is typically around $20. A cab ride from downtown to the ferry terminal (14 miles) will cost upward of $30–35, but might be worth it if you get several people together. Taxi tours are $55 per hour.

Car Rentals

With nearly 100 miles of roads in the Juneau area, renting a car is a smart idea. Be sure to call two or three weeks ahead of mid-summer arrivals, or you may find every car already rented. Three national chains have offices at the airport: **Avis** (907/789-9450 or 800/478-2847), **Budget** (907/790-1086), **Hertz** (907/789-9494 or 800/654-3131), **Kipco Auto Rental** (907/796-2880, www.kipcoak.com), and **National** (907/789-9814 or 800/478-2847). The other companies are all within a few blocks, and will pick you up during business hours: **Rent-A-Wreck** (907/789-4111, www.juneaualaska.com/rent-a-wreck), **Mendenhall Auto Center** (907/789-1386 or 800/478-1386, www.mendenhallauto center.com; closed weekends), and **Evergreen Ford** (907/789-9386, www.evergreenmotors juneau.com). The best rates are typically with Mendenhall Auto or Kipco Auto Rental, starting around $50 per day for a compact. The Kipco and Rent-a-Wreck cars are older vehicles, so you might want to check them out first.

◖ TRACY ARM–FORDS TERROR WILDERNESS

Located 50 miles southeast of Juneau, the 653,000-acre Tracy Arm–Fords Terror Wilderness contains country that rivals Glacier Bay National Park, but costs half as much to reach. The wilderness consists of a broad bay that splits into two long glacially carved arms—Tracy Arm and Endicott Arm. (Fords Terror splits off as a separate channel halfway up Endicott Arm.) Within Tracy Arm, steep-walled granite canyons plummet 2,000 feet into incredibly deep and narrow fjords. We're talking rocks-to-the-waterline here. The fjords wind past waterfalls to massive glaciers, their icebergs dotted with hundreds of harbor seals. Humpback whales are a common sight, as are killer whales. Look closely on the mountain slopes and you're bound to see mountain goats, especially near North Sawyer Glacier. John Muir noted that the fjord was "shut in by sublime Yosemite cliffs, nobly sculptured, and adorned with waterfalls and fringes of trees, bushes, and patches of flowers, but amid so crowded a display of

© DCN PITCHER

harbor seal on ice, Tracy Arm–Fords Terror Wilderness

novel beauty it was not easy to concentrate the attention long enough on any portion of it without giving more days and years than our lives can afford." Modern-day visitors come away equally impressed.

Two glaciers—Sawyer and South Sawyer—cap the end of Tracy Arm. Sawyer Glacier is retreating up-bay at 85 feet per year, while South Sawyer is losing over 300 feet per year. South Sawyer is larger and more interesting, but ice often blocks access. Other treats include get-wet visits to waterfalls and the chance to view seals lounging on the ice. Contact the Forest Service Information Center in Juneau (907/586-8751, www.fs.fed.us/r10/tongass) for details on Tracy Arm.

Boat Trips

Visitors to Tracy Arm have two all-day boat tour options. **Adventure Bound Alaska** (907/463-2509 or 800/228-3875; www.adventureboundalaska.com) is the original and best tour into Tracy Arm. Owner Steve

Weber has been doing this for many years and knows the best places to see mountain goats, seals, and whales. The boat typically spends at least an hour at the face of one of the glaciers, providing a great opportunity to witness the calving of icebergs. All-day cruises on the 56-foot boat are offered every summer day for $120 adults or $80 kids. Fresh sandwiches, drinks, and snacks are available onboard for a few bucks more, and kayak drop-offs are available. Highly recommended.

Goldbelt Tours (907/586-8687 or 800/820-2628, www.goldbelttours.com, $148 adults, $103 kids) offers a speedy 87-catamaran, and the higher price includes a light lunch. These run three days a week in the summer. No kayaker drop-offs, and the boat cannot approach the glaciers as closely as Adventure Bound trips. Goldbelt also makes occasional trips to Fords Terror and Dawes Glacier.

On Your Own

There are no trails in the Tracy Arm–Fords Terror

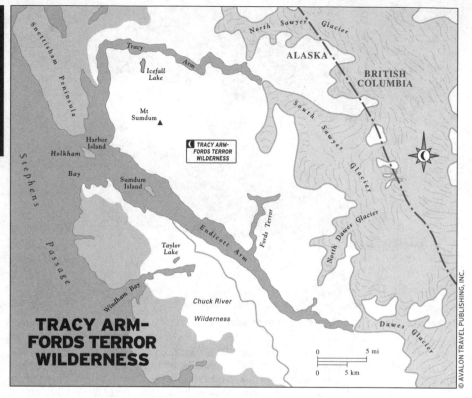

© AVALON TRAVEL PUBLISHING, INC.

Wilderness, but experienced sea kayakers discover spectacular country to explore. Unfortunately, kayakers in Tracy Arm should be prepared for a constant parade of giant cruise ships, leaving large wakes and plenty of engine noise to contend with. (Sound travels a long way over the water. Wilderness rangers report being startled to suddenly hear loudspeakers announcing, "Margaritas will be served at 1630 in the aft lounge.") You can, however, escape the boats by hiking up the ravines into the high country, or by heading into the less-congested waters of Endicott Arm where the big cruise ships and powerboats rarely stray. Adventure Bound Alaska provides kayaker drop-offs.

If you plan to go into Tracy Arm in a kayak, check ahead with the Forest Service's Juneau Ranger District for the good campsites. As you

approach the glaciers at the upper end of Tracy, these become harder to find. Many boaters anchor in No Name Cove near the entrance to Tracy Arm. Kayakers will probably prefer to head to the middle part of the fjord and away from the motorboats. Ambitious folks (with a topo map) may want to try the steep half-mile cross-country climb up to **Icefall Lake** (1,469 ft. above sea level).

Massive **Dawes Glacier** jams the top of Endicott Arm with thousands of bergs of all sizes and shapes, making it tough to get close to the face of the glacier. **Fords Terror** is a turbulent but spectacular inlet that angles away from Endicott Arm. Tidal changes create wild water conditions near the entrance, so kayakers and boaters need to take special precautions. Only run the narrows at slack tides, when the water

© DON PITCHER

iceberg, Tracy Arm-Fords Terror Wilderness

is relatively calm. (The narrows are named for the terror felt by H.R. Ford, who rowed into the inlet one day in 1889 when the water was calm, but nearly died while fighting the currents, whirlpools, and icebergs on the way back out.) Fords Terror has no tidewater glaciers, but numerous hanging glaciers and craggy peaks are visible.

Chuck River Wilderness

Twelve miles south of Tracy Arm is **Windham Bay,** entrance to the Chuck River Wilderness. This small wild area receives very little use, but offers good fishing for salmon and a chance to explore the ruins of the Southeast's oldest mining community, Windham Bay. You can hike up the mile-long **Taylor Creek Trail** from Windham Bay to Taylor Lake.

Endicott River Wilderness

Although it encompasses 94,000 acres, this is one of the least-visited wilderness areas in America. Located some 60 miles northwest of Juneau, the wilderness borders on Glacier Bay National Park and includes the Endicott River watershed along the eastern slope of the Chilkat Range. The country is spruce and hemlock forests, mixed with alders. Trails are nonexistent, and access from Lynn Canal is virtually impossible. Visit the Forest Service's Juneau Ranger District office for more on this decidedly off-the-beaten-track area.

Admiralty Island

Just 20 miles west of Juneau lies the northern end of **Admiralty Island National Monument** (907/586-8800, www.fs.fed.us/r10/tongass) and the massive Kootznahoo Wilderness. At nearly a million acres, the wilderness covers 90 percent of Admiralty, making it the only large island in the Southeast that has not been extensively logged or developed. The Tlingit name for Admiralty is Kootznahoo (Bear Fortress). The island is aptly named: It has perhaps 1,500 brown bears, giving it one of the highest bear densities anywhere on earth. Eagles are extraordinarily abundant along the shoreline, and the cries of loons haunt Admiralty's lakes. This is truly one of the gemstones of Southeast Alaska.

ANGOON

Located along Admiralty's southwestern shore, the Tlingit village of Angoon (pop. 600) is the island's lone settlement. It sits astride a peninsula guarding the entrance to Kootznahoo Inlet, an incredible wonderland of small islands and saltwater passages. Locals have cable TVs and microwave ovens, but smokehouses sit in front of many homes and you'll hear older people speaking Tlingit. Angoon weather generally lives up to its reputation as Southeast Alaska's "Banana Belt"; yearly rainfall averages only 38 inches, compared to three times that in Sitka, only 40 miles away. By the way, the word *hootch* originated from the potent whiskey distilled by the "Hoosenoo" Indians of Admiralty in the 19th century. Today, Angoon is a dry town with a reputation as a place where traditional ways are encouraged.

History

The village of Angoon still commemorates an infamous incident that took place more than a century ago. While working for the Northwest Trading Company, a local shaman was killed in a seal-hunting accident. The villagers demanded 200 blankets as compensation and two days off to honor and bury the dead man. To ensure payment, they seized two hostages. Unaware of Tlingit traditions, the company manager fled to Sitka and persuaded a U.S. Navy boat to "punish them severely." On October 26, 1882, the town was shelled, destroying most of the houses. All the villagers' canoes were smashed and sunk, and all their winter supplies burned. Six children died from the smoke and the people nearly starved that winter. In a U.S. Congressional investigation two years later, the shelling was called "the greatest outrage ever committed in the United States upon any Indian tribe." Finally, in 1973, the government paid $90,000 in compensation for the shelling, but the Navy has never formally apologized.

Sights

Even if you don't stay overnight in Angoon, get off the ferry and walk across the road and down to the beach. From there you can look up to a small **cemetery** with old gravestones and fenced-in graves. Another interesting cemetery is near the end of the peninsula a half-mile behind the **Russian Orthodox church** in town. A number of rustic old houses line the shore, one with killer whales painted on the front. A hundred feet uphill from the post office are five memorial **totems** topped by representations of different local clans. Near Angoon Trading you get a great view of the narrow passage leading into **Kootznahoo Inlet,** where tides create dangerous rapids.

Accommodations and Food

Built in 1937, **Favorite Bay Inn B&B** (907/788-3123 or 800/423-3123, www.whalers covelodge.com, all year, $139 s, $209 d) is on the edge of town near the boat harbor. Five guest rooms share three baths; full breakfast included. The owners also run **Whaler's Cove Sportfishing Lodge** (open June–Sept.) with multi-day packages for anglers in search of salmon and halibut. Guests of Favorite Bay Inn can also eat other meals at Whaler's Cove, and canoe and skiff rentals may be available.

Angoon Trading (907/788-3111) sells a limited and rather expensive selection of groceries and supplies. Both Whaler's Cove Sportfishing Lodge and Favorite Bay Sportfishing Lodge serve meals during the summer, but you'll need to make reservations if you aren't a guest.

Getting There

The state ferry *LeConte* (800/642-0066, www.ferryalaska.com) visits Angoon six times a week, staying just long enough to unload and load vehicles. The dock (no ferry terminal) is 2.5 miles out of town, so you won't see Angoon up close unless you disembark, but "taxis" will run visitors into town.

Wings of Alaska (907/789-0790, www.wingsofalaska.com) and **Alaska Seaplane Service** (907/789-3331 or 800/478-3360, www.akseaplanes.com) have floatplane service between Angoon and Juneau.

PACK CREEK

Located a short flight from Juneau along the west side of Seymour Canal, Pack Creek is one of Alaska's premier brown bear–viewing areas. The creek fills with spawning humpback and chum salmon during July and August, and they attract the bears, which in turn attract the people. Most visitors arrive on day trips from Juneau on the local air taxis. Others come aboard kayaks and boats, or with commercially guided groups. Pack Creek is jointly managed and staffed by the U.S. Forest Service and the Alaska Department of Fish and Game. Special regulations apply to travel and camping in the area, and it's only open for visitation 9 A.M.–9 P.M.

Bear-Watching

The number of bears varies greatly through the summer, but most visitors see at least one bear, and often several. Plan to spend a full day—or longer—to increase your odds and to soak in the beauty of the area. Binoculars or a spotting scope are helpful, and photographers should be sure to bring plenty of film and long lenses. Rubber boots and raingear are highly recommended for anyone visiting Pack Creek. Food and drinks must be stowed in a special

bear-resistant box, and neither is allowed in the viewing areas.

There are two primary bear-viewing areas along Pack Creek. The most accessible is a sandy spit of land right at the mouth of the creek and a short beach hike from where floatplanes land and boats tie up. A bit more challenging is a beautiful one-mile trail that leads through an old-growth rainforest to a viewing tower. The tower has room for eight people, and is an excellent place to watch bears as they pass directly below you.

Forest Service or Fish and Game rangers at Pack Creek will be happy to answer your questions, so it isn't necessary to come with a guide (unless you can't get in otherwise). They will not, however, accompany you to the observation tower.

Rules and Regulations

If you travel independently, you will need to obtain a permit and set up a charter with a local air taxi. Guided visitors are provided with transportation and permits, but the fee is much higher. Because of its popularity with both bears and people—and the potential for conflicts between the two—Pack Creek has stringent and rather confusing rules. Permits are required June 1–September 10, and only 24 people per day are allowed during the peak of the bear-viewing season (July 5–Aug. 25).

Reservations cost $50, and can be postmarked as early as February 20 for the following summer. Apply early to be sure of getting a permit for the peak season. Of the 24 permits, 4 are held for late arrivals, and are available three days in advance of your visit. These are in high demand, however, and are chosen by lottery from the applicants who show up. An unlimited number of shoulder-season permits (June 1–July 4 and August 26–September 10, $20) are available, but bear activity is lower. Get additional details from the Forest Service in Juneau (907/586-8800, www.fs.fed.us/r10/tongass).

Getting to Pack Creek

Most visitors to Pack Creek arrive by

floatplane on day trips from Juneau, landing next to the south sandspit. The following companies fly to Pack Creek: **Alaska Fly'N Fish Charters** (907/790-2120, www.alaskabyair.com), **Alaska Seaplane Service** (907/789-3331 or 800/478-3360, www.akseaplanes.com), **Ward Air** (907/789-9150, www.wardair.com), and **Wings of Alaska** (907/789-0790, www.wingsofalaska.com). The costs vary depending upon how many people are on the flight, but with three or more people in a group the price drops to around $155 per person round-trip (but you'll need to get your own permit).

Guided Trips

Several guide companies offer trips to Pack Creek, and are likely to have space available at the last minute. They're a good option if you can't get a permit—and if you have the cash. **Alaska Discovery** (510/594-6000 or 800/586-1911, www.akdiscovery.com) has $600 day trips to Pack Creek that include charter air service, an experienced guide, lunch, rubber boots, and raingear. They also have all-inclusive three-day kayak trips from Anchorage to Pack Creek for $1,090.

Alaska Fly'N Fish Charters (907/790-2120, www.alaskabyair.com) offers guided day trips to Pack Creek; $500 for a five-hour tour includes air transport from Juneau. Two companies have multi-day boat trips that include a day at Pack Creek: **All Aboard Yacht Charters** (360/898-7300 or 800/767-1024, www.alaskacharters.com) and **Dolphin Charters** (510/527-9622 or 800/472-9942, www.dolphincharters.com).

Camping

Camping is not allowed on Admiralty Island near the mouth of Pack Creek, but is permitted on Windfall Island, where you're far less likely to have encounters with the bears. The island is a quarter-mile from Pack Creek. Independent travelers can rent a sea kayak on Windfall from Alaska Discovery (advance reservation required) to reach Pack Creek or to explore the area.

Seymour Canal

The bear-viewing area along Pack Creek is only a tiny portion of Seymour Canal. This is a wonderful place to explore by sea kayak, with beautiful country, relatively protected waters, and the chance to see eagles, brown bears, and other wildlife. Many kayakers head south from Juneau, crossing the often-rough Stephens Passage and entering Oliver Inlet. **Auke Bay Landing Craft** (907/790-4591, www.aukebaylandingcraft.com) can deliver you to Oliver's Inlet, where an ingenious boat tramway makes it easy to bring kayaks across to upper Seymour Canal, a mile away. Alaska State Parks maintains the **Oliver Inlet Cabin** ($35) at the northern tip of Seymour Canal.

In Seymour you'll find many coves and islands to explore, and have a chance to observe bears that are protected from hunting. If you're adventurous, take a climb up the nearby peaks for fantastic views of the entire area. A three-sided shelter (free) is available in **Windfall Harbor**. Bears can be a real problem in Seymour Canal so be sure to select your camping spots very carefully (preferably on a small island) and hang all food.

Cross-Admiralty Canoe Route

Admiralty Island is ideally suited for people who enjoy canoeing or sea kayaking. Kootznahoo Inlet reaches back behind Angoon through a labyrinth of islands and narrow passages, before opening into expansive Mitchell Bay. From there you can continue to Salt Lake or Kanalku Bay, or begin the Cross-Admiralty Canoe Route—a chain of scenic lakes connected by portages, one of which is over three miles long. Using this 42-mile route you should reach Seymour Canal in four to six days (the record is 12 hours). Along the way are six Forest Service cabins ($35) and six Adirondack shelters (free), so you won't have to sleep out in the rain all the time. For more specific canoe-route information, contact the office of **Admiralty Island National Monument** (907/586-8790, www.fs.fed.us/r10/tongass) in Juneau.

Glacier Bay National Park and Preserve

America's national parks are this country's version of Mecca, places where hordes of pilgrims are drawn in search of a fulfillment that seems to come from experiencing these shrines of the natural world. Since Glacier Bay's discovery by John Muir in 1879, the spectacles of stark rocky walls, deep fjords, and giant rivers of ice calving massive icebergs into the sea have never ceased to inspire and humble visitors.

Established as a national park in 1925, Glacier Bay received major additions in the Alaska National Interest Lands Conservation Act of 1980. The park and preserve now cover more than 3.3 million acres and contain half a dozen glaciers that reach the ocean, making this one of the largest concentrations of tidewater glaciers on earth. These glaciers originate in the massive snowcapped Fairweather Range, sliding down the slopes and carving out giant troughs that become fjords when the glaciers retreat. **Mt. Fairweather,** rising 15,320 feet, is Southeast Alaska's tallest peak. On a clear day, it is prominently visible from park headquarters, 72 miles away. The vegetation of Glacier Bay varies from a 200-year-old spruce and hemlock forest at Bartlett Cove to freshly exposed moraine where tenacious plant life is just starting to take hold. Wildlife is abundant in the park: Humpback whales, harbor porpoises, harbor seals, and bird rookeries can be seen from the excursion boats and kayaks. Black bears are fairly common.

HISTORY

Glacier Bay has not always looked as it does today. When Captain George Vancouver sailed through Icy Strait in 1794, he found a wall of ice more than 4,000 feet thick and 20 miles wide. Less than 100 years later (1879) when Hoonah Indian guides led John Muir into the area, he discovered that the glaciers had retreated nearly 50 miles, creating a new land and a giant bay splitting into two deep fjords on its upper end. The bay was shrouded by low clouds, but Muir, anxious to see farther into the country, climbed a peak on its western shore:

> All the landscape was smothered in clouds and I began to fear that as far as wide views were concerned I had climbed in vain. But at length the clouds lifted a little, and beneath their gray fringes I saw the berg-filled expanse of the bay, and the feet of the mountains that stand about it, and the imposing fronts of five huge glaciers, the nearest being immediately beneath me. This was my first general view of Glacier Bay, a solitude of ice and snow and newborn rocks, dim, dreary, mysterious. I held the ground I had so dearly won for an hour or two, sheltering myself from the blast as best I could, while with benumbed fingers I sketched what I could see of the landscape, and wrote a few lines in my notebook. Then, breasting the snow again, crossing the shifting avalanche slopes and torrents, I reached camp about dark, wet and weary and glad.

Today's traveler is less likely to take such pains to see this grand place.

The rapid retreat of the glaciers over the last 200 years has caused the land to rebound, much like a sponge that has been squeezed and then re-forms. The process is astoundingly rapid by geological standards; around Bartlett Cove it is rising nearly two inches a year and even faster farther up the bay. Ask the park rangers to point out some of the changes in vegetation because of this rebound effect.

◀ VISITING GLACIER BAY

The vast majority of the over 350,000 visitors who come to Glacier Bay each year arrive aboard cruise ships, two of which are allowed in each day; they're given a talk by a Park Service naturalist as the ship heads up the west arm of the bay and never set foot on the land itself. Most other visitors stay

GLACIER BAY NATIONAL PARK AND PRESERVE

Lynn Canal

To Haines

Chilkat Range

Excursion River   Excursion Inlet

Excursion Ridge

Icy Passage

Gustavus

Bartlett L

SEE DETAIL

Pleasant Island

Icy Strait

Tongass National Forest

Casement Glacier

McBride Glacier

Takhinsha Mountains

Beartrack River

Beartrack Mtns

Bartlett River

Bartlett Cove

Gustavus Point

Lemesurier Island

Chichagof Island

Riggs Glacier

Muir Glacier

Adams Inlet

Muir Point

S Marble Island

Beardslee Islands

North Passage

Inian Islands

South Passage

Muir Inlet

N Marble Island

Cushing Glacier

Wachusetts Inlet

Sandy Cove

Elfin Cove

Tlingit Point

Drake Island

Willoughby Island

ALASKA

Glacier Bay

Dundas Bay

Carroll Glacier

Queen Inlet

Geikie Inlet

Dundas River

Taylor Bay

Cross Sound

Rendu Glacier

Rendu Inlet

Cape Spencer

Reid Glacier

Abyss Lake

Brady Glacier

Tarr Inlet

Lamplugh Glacier

GLACIER BAY NATIONAL PARK

Brady Icefield

Palma Bay

Hopkins Inlet

Mt Abbe

Johns Hopkins Glacier

Mt Crillon

Lituya Glacier

Icy Point

CANADA

UNITED STATES

BRITISH COLUMBIA

Grand Pacific Glacier

Ferris Glacier

Margerie Glacier

Fairweather Range

Crillon Lake

Lituya Glacier

Lituya Bay

Mt Quincy Adams

Mt Fairweather

Fairweather Glacier

Mt Root

St Elias Mtns

Grand Plateau Glacier

Alsek Glacier

Gulf Of Alaska

Cape Fairweather

Dry Bay

DRY BAY RANGER STATION

Glacier Bay National Preserve

10 mi

10 km

GLACIER BAY NATIONAL PARK AND PRESERVE

N

DETAIL INSET

BEAR TRACK INN

AIRFIELD

POST OFFICE

BEAR TRACK MERCANTILE

Icy Passage

ALASKA DISCOVERY INN

BEAR'S NEST B&B

LIBRARY

GUSTAVUS INN

ANNIE MAE LODGE

Gustavus

DOCK

Goode River

GLACIER BAY COUNTRY INN

GOOD RIVER BED & BREAKFAST

Glacier Bay National Park

Bartlett River Trail

VISITOR INFORMATION CENTER/ GLACIER BAY LODGE

NATIONAL PARK SERVICE HEADQUARTERS

Bartlett Cove

DOCK

Forest Loop Trail

BARTLETT COVE CAMPGROUND

Glacier Bay

Gustavus Point

0.2 mi

200 m

© DON PITCHER

Steller sea lions on South Marble Island

in Glacier Bay Lodge at Bartlett Cove or in nearby luxury lodges in the town of Gustavus, venturing out only to cruise past the glaciers on a tour boat. The tiny percentage who come to actually see and touch their national park—rather than view it in a naturalist's slide show—are often prevented from doing so by prohibitive costs. It is somewhat ironic that the park is most accessible to those who would rather look out on its glaciers from their stateroom windows.

The nearest tidewater glacier is 40 miles from park headquarters in Bartlett Cove. To see these glaciers, expect to spend at least $400 from Juneau for a fast two-day trip. A visit to Glacier Bay is a wonderful experience, but there are few options for the budget traveler, and you should probably make other plans if you're pinched for cash. (Consider a day trip from Juneau to Tracy Arm instead.)

The park concessionaire, **Glacier Bay Lodge & Tours/Aramark** (907/264-4600 or 888/229-8687, www.visitglacierbay.com) oper-

ates the *Baranof Wind* which heads up the west arm of Glacier Bay daily in the summer, departing at 7:30 A.M. and returning at 3:30 P.M. Tours on this high-speed catamaran cost $170 for adults or $85 for kids under 13. A light lunch is served, and a Park Service naturalist is on board to provide information on wildlife, geology, and cultural history along the route. The boat typically visits Margerie and Grand Pacific Glaciers before July, and heads up to Johns Hopkins Glacier later in the summer. Another *Baranof Wind* option is to pay $300 per person for a day-long trip that includes a flight from Juneau to Gustavus followed by a trip up the bay and another flight back to Juneau that evening.

Park Information

The Park Service maintains a visitor center upstairs in the Glacier Bay Lodge at Bartlett Cove, open daily 12:30–9 P.M. in the summer. A small museum here contains natural history and geology exhibits. Naturalists lead interpretive walks every day, and also put on evening talks and slide shows in the auditorium. The park's **backcountry office** is near the boat dock, a short hike from the lodge, and is open daily 8 A.M.–7 P.M. during the summer. Stop here before heading into the park on an overnight trip. For additional details, contact Glacier Bay National Park (907/697-2230, www.nps.gov/glba).

HIKING

There are several enjoyable walks in the Bartlett Cove area. The mile-long **Forest Loop Trail** connects the lodge, boat dock, and campground, providing an excellent introduction to the area. **Bartlett River Trail** (4 miles round-trip) leads from park headquarters to the mouth of the river, with opportunities to observe wildlife. Salmon can be seen moving up the river in August. For a satisfying beach walk, head south along the shore from the campground. If you're ambitious, it is possible to walk to **Point Gustavus** (six miles) or on to **Goode River** (13 miles). Follow the river upstream a mile to Gustavus, where you can walk or hitch back along the road. Beach walking is easiest at low tide; the backcountry office has tide charts. Note that none of these trails goes anywhere near the tidewater glaciers for which the park is famous, and there are no developed trails anywhere in the park's backcountry.

SEA KAYAKING
Guided Trips

Alaska Discovery (510/594-6000 or 800/586-1911, www.akdiscovery.com) has all-day ($130) and half-day ($90) guided kayak trips from the Bartlett Cove dock in the summer. These are a good way to learn the basics of sea kayaking, and include kayak and gear, guide, food, and boots. Alaska Discovery also offers several excellent but pricey longer trips into Glacier Bay National Park. Kayak trips up the bay cost $2,200 for a five-day trip, plus airfare from Juneau. The company also has nine-day trips to beautiful Icy Bay for $2,100. These trips are based out of Yakutat.

Spirit Walker Expeditions (907/697-2266

or 800/478-9255, www.seakayakalaska.com) runs excellent sea kayak tours, including overnight trips to nearby Pleasant Island. All sorts of longer voyages are available, all the way up to eight-day trips to remote islands off Chichagof Island. It does not tour within Glacier Bay National Park itself.

On Your Own

An increasingly popular way to visit Glacier Bay is by sea kayak. Some folks bring their own folding kayaks on the plane, but most people rent them from the friendly proprietors of **Glacier Bay Sea Kayaks** (907/697-2257, www.glacierbayseakayaks.com) in Bartlett Cove. Kayak rentals include a two-person boat, paddles, life vests, spray skirts, flotation bags, and a brief lesson. Reservations are a must during mid-summer. They also rent raingear and rubber boots, and will help set up your trip, including making the all-important boat reservations. In addition, you can rent kayaks in Gustavus from **Sea Otter Kayak** (907/697-3007, www.he.net/~seaotter).

Several focal points attract kayakers within Glacier Bay. The **Beardslee Islands,** in relatively protected waters near Bartlett Cove, make an excellent two- or three-day kayak trip and do not require any additional expenses. Beyond the Beardslees, Glacier Bay becomes much less protected and you should plan on spending at least a week up-bay if you paddle there. (It is 50 miles or more to the glaciers.) Rather than attempting to cross this open water, most kayakers opt for a drop-off. The locations change periodically, so ask at the backcountry office in Bartlett Cove for specifics.

Muir Inlet (the east arm of Glacier Bay) is preferred by many kayakers because it is a bit more protected and is not used by the cruise ships or most tour boats. The **West Arm** is more spectacular—especially iceberg-filled Johns Hopkins Inlet—but you'll have to put up with a constant stream of large and small cruise ships. If the boat operators have their way, even more ships can be expected in future years.

The *Baranof Wind* does camper and sea kayaker drop-offs in Glacier Bay ($190 round

© CON PITCHER

kayakers in Glacier Bay National Park

trip). For details, contact Glacier Bay Lodge & Tours (907/264-4600 or 888/229-8687, www.visitglacierbay.com).

Talk with Park Service personnel in Bartlett Cove before heading out on any hiking or kayaking trip. You'll need to be in Gustavus airport by 3 P.M. the day before to go through all the hoops (getting to Bartlett Cove, renting the kayak, going through the Park Service camping and bear safety session, and getting your kayak onboard the *Baranof Wind*). This means you cannot take the evening Alaska flight; it arrives too late in the day.

CAMPING

An excellent free campground at Bartlett Cove comes complete with bear-proof food storage caches, outhouses, and a three-sided shelter with a woodstove (great for drying your gear after a kayak trip up the bay). The campground is only a half-mile from Glacier Bay Lodge and usually has space. Running water is available next to the backcountry office. All cooking must be done below the high-tide line (where the odors

are washed away every six hours) to reduce the chance of bear problems. You can store things for free in the shed next to the backcountry office.

Backcountry Camping

No trails exist anywhere in Glacier Bay's backcountry, but Park Service rangers can provide details on hiking and camping up the bay. Camping is allowed in most park areas. Exceptions are the Marble Islands—closed because of their importance for nesting seabirds—and a few other areas closed because of the potential for bear incidents. A gas stove is a necessity for camping, since wood is often unavailable.

Free permits (available at the backcountry office) are recommended before you head out. Park naturalists provide camper orientations each evening, including information on how and where to go, bear safety, and minimum-impact camping procedures. Bears have killed two people within the park in the past decade or so, and to lessen the chance of this happening, free bear-proof containers are loaned to all kayakers and hikers. A small storage shed beside the backcountry office is a good place to store unneeded gear while you're up the bay. Firearms are not allowed in Glacier Bay.

TATSHENSHINI AND ALSEK RIVERS

Along the western edge of Glacier Bay National Park flows the Tatshenshini River, considered one of the world's premier wilderness-rafting routes. Bears, moose, mountain goats, and Dall sheep are all visible along the way. The river rolls through Class III white water and spectacular canyons along its way to the juncture with the Alsek River. **Alaska Discovery/ Mountain Travel** (510/594-6000 or 800/586-1911, www.akdiscovery.com) has several trips each summer down this spectacular route, as well as down the more remote Alsek. A 12-day river-rafting trip isn't cheap at $3,700, but the price includes a van ride from Haines to the put-in point at Dalton Post in the Yukon, and a spectacular helicopter portage around the Class VI rapids of Turnback Canyon. One of the real treats of this trip is paddling past the seven-mile-wide Alsek Glacier. The trip begins in Haines and ends in Yakutat.

Other good companies offering Alsek and Tatshenshini trips include **Chilkat Guides** (907/766-2491 or 888/292-7789, www.raftalaska.com) and **Canadian River Expeditions** (867/668-3180 or 800/297-6927, www.canriver.com). Contact the park (907/697-2230, www.nps.gov/glba) for details on running the rivers.

GUSTAVUS AND VICINITY

There are two basic centers for visitors to Glacier Bay. **Bartlett Cove,** inside the park, has Park Service Headquarters, a campground, Glacier Bay Lodge (with bar, restaurant, and park service visitor center), and boat dock. Ten miles away (a $10 shuttle bus ride) and outside the park boundaries is the community of **Gustavus** (pop. 370). Here you will find the airport, main boat dock, a general store, B&Bs, and luxury lodges.

The town of Gustavus consists of equal parts park employees, fishermen, and folks

dependent upon the tourism trade. It's one of the only places in Southeast Alaska that has enough flat country to raise cows, and the only Southeast town of any size without service from the state ferry system. Be sure to check out the historic—and still working—gas pumps decorated with the old Mobil flying horse at **Gustavus Dray** (907/697-2481), which also sells antiques and gifts. **Smokehouse Gallery** (907/697-2336) is a seasonal cooperative gallery along the river, with paintings, woodwork, drawings, watercolors, and pottery by local artisans. Gustavus is also home to the nine-hole **Mt. Fairweather Golf Course** (907/697-3080, www.gustavus.com/gdf.html).

The **Gustavus Visitors Association** (907/697-2454, www.gustavusak.com) has information and links to local lodging and other businesses; also try www.gustavus.com for info. Based in Gustavus, **Glacier Bay Travel Cruises and Tours** (907/697-2475, www.glacierbaytravel.com) can help you find local lodging and book trips into the park.

Fishing and Whale-Watching

Fishing, primarily for halibut and salmon, is a big attraction for many visitors, and most of the lodges offer package deals for anglers. Get a list of charter boat operators from the Park Service or at www.gustavusalaska.org. Most of these companies also run whale-watching trips, and some can carry sea kayaks onboard.

Flightseeing

Air Excursions (907/697-2375 or 800/354-2479, www.airexcursions.com) and **L.A.B. Flying Service** 907/789-9160, www.lab flying.com) both provide flightseeing trips over the park. Flightseeing over Glacier Bay are also available from Juneau, Haines, and Skagway, but prices are generally higher since you'll need to fly farther.

Accommodations

Located within Glacier Bay National Park is **Glacier Bay Lodge** (907/264-4600 or 888/229-8687, www.visitglacierbay.com, open late May–early Sept., $187–207 d). The shoreside lodge is surrounded by tall trees at Bartlett Cove (park headquarters), and has a restaurant, informal deck dining, a pleasant bar, plus a big stone fireplace that makes a cozy place to sit on a rainy evening—even if you're not a guest. Guests stay in plain-vanilla units with double or twin beds. Laundry facilities, coin-operated showers, and gear storage are available. The lodge rents a few mountain bikes and fishing poles. Many guests opt for a package that includes a night's lodging, an all-day tour of Glacier Bay, three meals, and transportation to and from Gustavus for $400 per person.

Glacier Bay Lodge provides the only in-park accommodations, but far nicer options are available in nearby Gustavus. Most of these provide free transport to and from the Gustavus airport or boat dock, along with clunker bikes to ride on the roads. All of these will also help set up tours, fishing, sea kayaking, and other activities within the park.

Honeymooners or others looking to splurge will love a visit to ❰ Gustavus Inn (907/697-2254 or 800/649-5220, www.gustavusinn.com, open mid-May–mid-Sept.), the most famous local lodging place. Built in 1928 as the centerpiece for a homestead, the farmhouse was transformed into Gustavus Inn in 1965. Owners David and Jo Ann Lesh have created a delightful country place with a picturesque garden that provides fresh vegetables all summer. Gourmet meals are served family style. Lodging and meals cost $370 d per day, with private baths and Wi-Fi (a rarity in Gustavus).

Modern **Bear Track Inn** (907/697-3017 or 888/697-2284, www.beartrackinn.com, open mid-May–mid-Sept.) occupies a 57-acre spread six miles from Gustavus. This luxuriously furnished 15,000-square-foot log inn has a central lobby with fireplace, large windows fronting on Icy Strait, a big deck and grassy front lawn, plus 14 spacious guest rooms. A number of packages are available for stays of one ($990 d) to seven nights ($4,420 d), including transportation from Juneau, lodging, and sumptuous meals; activities are extra.

Glacier Bay Country Inn (907/697-2288 or 800/628-0912, www.glacierbayalaska.com,

open mid-May–mid-Sept.) combines a rambling log structure with modern amenities. Guests stay in five well-appointed cabins ($430 d) or the main lodge ($370 d) and are treated to three gourmet meals a day. Same owners for **Whalesong Lodge** (www.whalesonglodge.com, $75 s, $100 d) with five small and simple rooms, all with private bath. It's in "downtown" Gustavus. No phones, TVs, or meals, but you can eat dinners at the inn for $35.

Annie Mae Lodge (907/697-2346 or 800/478-2346, www.anniemae.com) is a quiet two-story lodge in a meadow-and-forest setting along the Goode River. The 11 guest rooms cost $80 s or $90 d with shared bath, and $90–100 s or $120–140 d with private bath, including three big meals and round-trip transportation from Juneau.

Bear's Nest B&B (907/697-2440, www.gustavus.com/bearsnest, $120–150 d) has a distinctive round cedar cabin, a cozy room over the café, and a simple A-frame cabin, all with private baths and full breakfasts. Package deals with three meals a day are also offered.

Good River Bed & Breakfast (907/697-2241, www.glacier-bay.us, open June–late Aug., $95–105 d) has four guest rooms (shared baths) in an attractive three-story log home, plus a private but rustic log cabin with outhouse. A full breakfast and free bikes are included.

Alaska Discovery Inn (907/780-6505 or 800/586-1911, www.akdiscovery.com, open June–Aug.) has five rooms for $125 d with a private bath. A full breakfast is served. They're often filled up by Alaska Discovery clients.

Food and Groceries
Bear's Nest Café (907/697-2440, www.gustavus.com/bearsnest) serves lunch and dinner in the summer, specializing in locally caught salmon, halibut, and crab, along with salads and daily specials. Save room for a slice of their rhubarb-strawberry pie. Saturday night brings a fun open-mic jam session with talented local musicians. The café is open daily in the summer.

Located six miles from town, **Bear Track Inn** (907/697-3017 or 888/697-2284, www.beartrackinn.com) has one of the finest local chefs; delicious four-course dinners are $40. Another outstanding dinner option is **Gustavus Inn** (907/697-2255 or 800/649-5220, www.gustavusinn.com, $35), where a few spots are held for those who aren't overnighting. Reservations required.

Glacier Bay Lodge (907/697-4000, $19–29 dinner entrées) in Bartlett Cove serves so-so meals; try the Dungeness crab or the sweet potato fries. A lighter bar menu is also available, and the outside deck is open for casual dining.

Open daily in the summer, the small grocery store at Gustavus, **Beartrack Mercantile** (907/697-2358), has a deli and sells essentials for a price, but it's cheaper to bring all your own food from Juneau. **Pep's Packing** (907/697-2295) sells locally caught salmon if you have access to a BBQ. Nobody in Gustavus sells alcohol, but Glacier Bay Lodge has a full bar, and Bear's Nest serves beer and wine.

Getting There

There is no ferry service to either Glacier Bay or Gustavus, and residents receive most of their supplies by barge every two weeks.

Many visitors fly by jet from Juneau to Gustavus on **Alaska Airlines** (800/426-0333, www.alaskaair.com); but book ahead to be sure of getting on these popular afternoon flights. The trip takes only 15 minutes in the air, so the flight attendants don't even have time to throw bags of pretzels at you.

More rewarding are flights by **Skagway Air** (907/789-2006, www.skagwayair.com), **Wings of Alaska** (907/789-0790, www.wingsofalaska.com), and **L.A.B. Flying Service** (907/789-9160, www.labflying.com). They offer more personal service and the small

planes fly lower, providing excellent on-the-way sightseeing for around $165 round-trip. **Air Excursions** (907/697-2375 or 800/354-2479, www.airexcursions.com) doesn't have scheduled service, but usually fly to Juneau several times a day. L.A.B. also connects Gustavus with Skagway and Haines.

Note that it's illegal to transport white gas and other potentially explosive fuels in any commercial aircraft, so be sure your gas stove and fuel bottles are empty before you reach the airport. You can buy white gas in Bartlett Cove next to the visitor center or in Gustavus at Beartrack Mercantile. Also, you can't carry "bear mace" on the jets, though the floatplanes will sometimes carry it in their floats.

Getting Around

The airport in Gustavus is 10 miles from Bartlett Cove/Park Headquarters. A **shuttle bus** meets all Alaska Airlines flights, transporting you to Bartlett Cove for $10 each direction (free if you have a room reservation for Glacier Bay Lodge). Hitching eliminates this, but traffic can be downright scarce in tiny Gustavus. **TLC Taxi** (907/697-2239), provides passenger and kayak transport in the Gustavus area, and meets Alaska Airlines jets, air taxis.

Bud's Rent-A-Car (907/697-2403) has a dozen beater rental cars for $60 per day, and you don't even need to fill up the tank at the end. Of course, it's also pretty hard to put many miles on around here! Check out his nonexistent license plates; in their place it simply says "Bud's Rent-A-Car" in big red letters. Apparently the state doesn't require license plates in Gustavus because it's so difficult to get in or out of here. Most local lodging places have loaner bikes, and Glacier Bay Lodge in Bartlett Cove rents bikes.

Yakutat

The friendly town of Yakutat (pop. 800) is in a protected harbor on Yakutat Bay—halfway between Juneau and Cordova along the Gulf of Alaska. The name of this out-of-the-way settlement was derived from the Eyak name *Yak-tat* (lagoon behind the breakers). Behind Yakutat soars the pyramidal 18,008-foot summit of **Mt. St. Elias,** second-tallest in the United States. Across the bay is **Malaspina Glacier,** the largest piedmont glacier on the continent (it's bigger than Rhode Island). Both of these lie within mighty Wrangell–St. Elias National Park.

Yakutat is a famous fishing destination, particularly for steelhead on the Situk River, but also for king, silver, and sockeye salmon, plus halibut. But it isn't just fish that attracts visitors; in recent years Yakutat has drawn cold-water surfers who come to ride the big ones on the 70 miles of sandy beaches that stretch southeast from town. These beaches are also great places for bird-watching, beachcombing, or simply relaxing. Head out to **Ocean Cape** (just west of town) on a clear day for spectacular views of Mt. St. Elias and the Gulf of Alaska.

The weather in Yakutat can be summed up on one word: wet. Summers are rainy and winters are snowy. The town gets over 130 inches of precipitation annually, so visitors can plan on seeing their share of that. All this precipitation feeds the enormous glaciers and productive salmon and trout streams for which the area is famous.

HISTORY

The area around Yakutat served for centuries as a winter village for the Eyaks, a people with links to both the Tlingits to the east and Athabascans to the north. In 1805, the Russian-American Company built a fort at Yakutat, using it as a base for the harvesting of sea otters. The post was later destroyed by the Eyaks. Gold seekers came to the area in the 1860s, mining the black-sand beaches, followed by missionaries, loggers, and fishermen. During World War II, Yakutat was home to an aviation base, and the long paved runway that was developed now serves as the local airport. Quite a few military bunkers and other signs of the war are still visible. Today, commercial and sportfishing provide most of the local jobs. More than half of the people who live in Yakutat are Native Alaskans.

SIGHTS
Surfing Safari

Yakutat is Alaska's surfing capital, with mile after mile of sandy beaches, virtually no competition for waves, and great swells rolling off the Gulf of Alaska. On a warm summer day you might see as many as 15 surfers—typically a mix of locals and wandering California beach bums—riding the waves at **Cannon Beach** (named for a World War II cannon here) and other spots. Because of all the rainfall, the ocean around Yakutat is less saline than in California or Hawaii, so the boards need to be thicker and more buoyant to keep surfers from sinking. Owned by local surfer Jack Endicott, **Icy Waves Surf Shop** (907/784-3253, www.icywaves.com) sells surfboards (the big ones), wetsuits, booties, hoods, and other gear, along with very popular T-shirts. No rentals, but you may be able to lease gear.

Russell Fiord Wilderness

This beautiful 348,701-acre wilderness is 15 miles northeast of Yakutat. It centers around Russell and Nanatak Fiords, where hanging glaciers fill the rugged mountains and valley glaciers pour icebergs into the water. The area made headlines in 1986 when the advancing **Hubbard Glacier** (the largest tidewater glacier in North America) temporarily dammed Russell Fiord, trapping sea mammals and threatening to change river courses as the water level rose 75 feet behind the ice dam. The ice gave way six months later, freeing the animals and reconnecting the fjord to the

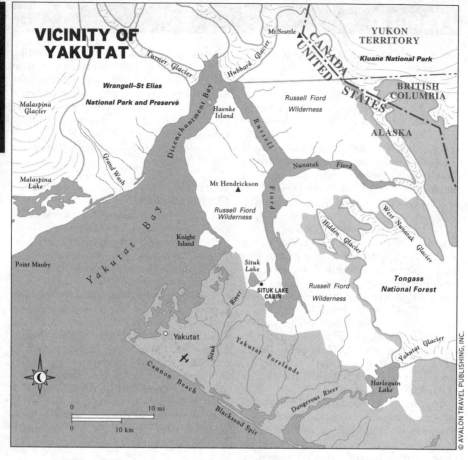

VICINITY OF
YAKUTAT

Mt Seattle

YUKON
TERRITORY

Kluane National Park

Turner Glacier

Hubbard Glacier

CANADA
UNITED
STATES

BRITISH
COLUMBIA

Wrangell–St Elias
National Park and Preserve

Malaspina
Glacier

Haenke
Island

Russell Fiord
Wilderness

ALASKA

Disenchantment Bay

Russell

Grand Wash

Malaspina
Lake

Mt Hendrickson

Nunatak   Fiord

Fiord

West Nunatak Glacier

Russell Fiord
Wilderness

Hidden Glacier

Knight
Island

Yakutat   Bay

Point Manby

Situk
Lake

SITUK LAKE
CABIN

River

Russell Fiord
Wilderness

Tongass
National Forest

Yakutat

Situk

Yakutat Forelands

Yakutat Glacier

Cannon Beach

Harlequin
Lake

Blacksand Spit

Dangerous River

0   10 mi

0   10 km

ocean. Because of all the icebergs from this glacier, access into Russell Fiord is difficult by boat, though floatplanes or wheeled planes fly into the area from Yakutat. The Hubbard Glacier is still an amazing sight, 6 miles wide by 70 miles long, and rising 400 feet out of the water at its snout. It is a prime stopping point for cruise ships heading between Southeast Alaska and Seward. Visit the U.S. Geological Survey website (http://ak.water.usgs.gov) for more on the Hubbard.

On the southeastern edge of the wilderness is the five-mile-long **Harlequin Lake,** dotted with ice from the enormous Yakutat Glacier. A 26-mile gravel road leads from Yakutat to just across the "bridge to nowhere" over the Dangerous River (which drains from the lake). A 0.75-mile trail leads to Harlequin Lake from here, and charter boats are available for trips to the face of the glacier.

The Forest Service's **Situk Lake Cabin** ($35) is inside the wilderness, and accessible by trail (often flooded) or floatplane. Eleven other cabins are scattered along the **Yakutat Forelands,** the relatively flat and forested area that stretches for 50 miles east of town. Especially popular with anglers are three cabins along the Situk River ($35).

ACCOMMODATIONS AND CAMPING

Leonard's Landing Lodge (907/784-3245 or 877/925-3474, www.leonardslanding.com, $165–175 s, $270–290 d) is a large fishing lodge with a seasonal restaurant. Package rates with meals and a fishing guide are available, along with boat rentals. **Yakutat Lodge** (907/784-3232 or 800/925-8828, www.yakutat-lodge.com) has a variety of all-inclusive fishing packages.

Mooring Lodge (907/784-3300 or 888/551-2836, www.mooringlodge.com, open all year) rents out six two-bedroom apartment units that can sleep six, with full kitchens, a sauna, and views across Monti Bay to the St. Elias Mountains. Rates are $350 for up to four people.

Red Roof B&B (907/784-3297, www.yakutatlodging.com, $85 s or $170 d) has three comfortable guest rooms with a full breakfast and private baths. **Blue Heron Inn B&B** (907/784-3287, www.johnlatham.com, $180 d) provides a hunting and fishing decor and two guest rooms, both with private entrances and baths. The home overlooks the bay, and rooms come with a full breakfast.

Camping

A couple of simple campsites are along Cannon Beach. In addition, much of the land surrounding Yakutat is within Tongass National Forest, and is open to camping. Above the tide line on Cannon Beach is a fun (but exposed) place to pitch a tent.

FOOD

Several places serve meals in Yakutat, but **Leonard's Landing Lodge** is your best bet, with good food three meals a day and a waterfront setting.

Get groceries and supplies from **Mallott's General Store** (907/784-3355). **Raven's Table Smokery** (907/784-3497 or 888/784-3497) sells freshly smoked fish. Yakutat's **Glass Door Bar** (907/784-3331) has a pool table and big-screen television for sports.

INFORMATION AND SERVICES

The **Yakutat Chamber of Commerce** (907/784-3933, www.yakutatalaska.com) will send you a brochure on the area, or call the **City of Yakutat** (907/784-3323, www.yakutatak.govoffice2.com) for additional information. The best local Internet site is www.yakutat.net, with links to local businesses. Alaska Pacific Bank has an ATM. A number of local folks run fishing charters; contact any of the lodging places for recommendations.

Wrangell-St. Elias National Park and Preserve has a district office (907/784-3295, www.nps.gov/wrst) in Yakutat, where you can get information on Malaspina Glacier and other incredible sights northeast of Yakutat. The office also exhibits Native artifacts, and the staff leads interpretive programs in the summer.

Stop by Tongass National Forest's **Yakutat Ranger District** (907/784-3359, www.fs.fed.us/r10/tongass) for details on the Russell Fiord Wilderness, public-use cabins, and other recreation opportunities. Looking for wildlife? Head out to the dump, where the brown bears often forage.

Fairweather Days each August at Cannon Beach is a good time to camp out and party with the surfers. There's live music, food, and local crafts.

GETTING THERE

Yakutat is the smallest community in the world served by year-round commercial jet service. **Alaska Airlines** (800/426-0333, www.alaskaair.com) connects Yakutat with the outside world, with two flights daily: one northbound flight to Cordova and Anchorage, and the other southbound to Juneau. **Yakutat Coastal Airlines** (907/784-3831, www.flyyca.com) provides air charters. **Leo's Vehicles** (907/784-3909) has pickups and Suburbans for $75/day.

The **Alaska Marine Highway** (907/465-3941 or 800/642-0066, www.ferryalaska.com) ferry *Kennicott* stops in Yakutat on its twice-a-month summertime sailings between Juneau and Whittier.

SOUTHEAST ALASKA

Haines

The pleasant and friendly town of Haines (pop. 1,400) provides a transition point between the lush greenery of the Southeast and the more rugged beauty of the Yukon and Alaska's Interior. As the ferry sails north to Haines on the Lynn Canal—at 1,600 feet deep it's the longest and deepest fjord in North America—the Inside Passage gets narrower, and you sense that this unique waterway, and your passage on it, are coming to an end. To the east, waterfalls tumble off the mountainsides, while to the west, glaciers lumber down from the icefields of the Chilkat Range. The long river of ice you see 40 minutes before Haines is **Davidson Glacier. Rainbow Glacier,** also on the left, hangs from a cliff just beyond. Both originate from the same icefield that forms part of Glacier Bay National Park.

Haines lies 90 miles north of Juneau, straddling a narrow peninsula between Chilkoot and Chilkat Inlets. Its mountain-ringed setting seems to define the word *spectacular:* From the ferry you catch a glimpse of the white Victorian buildings of Fort Seward in front of the 6,500-foot Cathedral Peaks. Haines has a wealth of outdoor experiences, almost as many for those without cash as for those with. Plenty of hiking trails run up surrounding peaks, camping is right next to town, and travelers will discover a pleasant mixture of working stiffs, fishermen, and artisans. It could serve as the poster child for what most folks expect in an Alaskan town: cozy, homespun, and earthy—the kind of place where the local radio station broadcasts birthday wishes, road updates for drivers heading over the pass, and bush messages for folks without a phone.

Unlike nearby Skagway where a tidal wave of tourists inundates the town daily, Haines only sees a few large cruise ships. Most Haines visitors arrive by ferry and head on up the highway (or vice versa), but Haines is also becoming a popular weekend getaway for Canadians from Whitehorse. With "only" 60 inches of precipitation a year, the weather here is decidedly drier than points farther south.

HISTORY

Long before the arrival of whites to the Haines area, the Tlingit people of the Chilkoot and Chilkat tribes established villages nearby. Fish were plentiful, as were game animals and berries. The area's "mother village" was Klukwan, 20 miles up the Chilkat River, but another large Chilkoot village nestled near Chilkoot Lake, and a summer camp squatted just northwest of present-day Haines. The Chilkat people were renowned for their beautiful blankets woven from mountain-goat wool and dyed with an inventive mixture of copper nuggets, urine, lichen, and spruce roots. The blankets were (and are) worn during dance ceremonies. Today they are also exceedingly valuable.

In 1879, the naturalist John Muir and the Presbyterian minister Samuel Hall Young reached the end of Lynn Canal. The Reverend Dr. Young was looking for potential mission sites to convert the Natives to Christianity. Muir was along for the canoe ride, wanting a

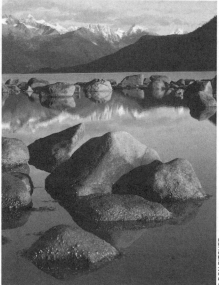

© DON PITCHER

Portage Cove and the Coast Mountains

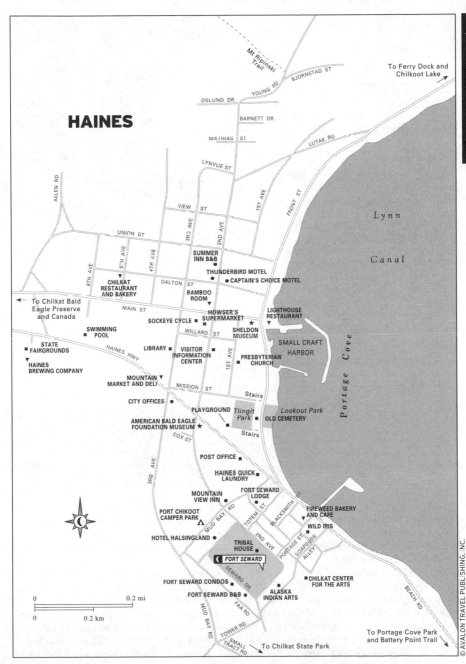

HAINES

To Ferry Dock and
Chilkoot Lake

Mt. Ripinski Trail

BJORNSTAD ST

YOUNG RD

OSLUND DR

BARNETT DR

MATHIAS ST

LUTAK RD

LYNVUE ST

ALLEN RD

VIEW ST

1ST AVE

FRONT ST

Lynn

UNION ST

3RD AVE

2ND AVE

Canal

5TH AVE

4TH AVE

SUMMER
INN B&B

6TH AVE

CHILKAT
RESTAURANT
AND BAKERY

DALTON ST

THUNDERBIRD MOTEL

CAPTAIN'S CHOICE MOTEL

To Chilkat Bald
Eagle Preserve
and Canada

MAIN ST

BAMBOO
ROOM

HOWSER'S
SUPERMARKET

SOCKEYE CYCLE

LIGHTHOUSE
RESTAURANT

SWIMMING
POOL

WILLARD ST

SHELDON
MUSEUM

SMALL CRAFT
HARBOR

Portage Cove

STATE
FAIRGROUNDS

HAINES HWY

LIBRARY

VISITOR
INFORMATION
CENTER

1ST AVE

PRESBYTERIAN
CHURCH

HAINES
BREWING COMPANY

MOUNTAIN
MARKET AND DELI

MISSION ST

CITY OFFICES

Stairs

PLAYGROUND

*Tlingit
Park*

Lookout Park

AMERICAN BALD EAGLE
FOUNDATION MUSEUM

OLD CEMETERY

COX ST

Stairs

3RD AVE

POST OFFICE

HAINES QUICK
LAUNDRY

MOUNTAIN
VIEW INN

FORT SEWARD
LODGE

TOTEM ST

FIREWEED BAKERY
AND CAFE

PORT CHIKOOT
CAMPER PARK

MUD BAY RD

BLACKSMITH

WILD IRIS

HOTEL HALSINGLAND

2ND AVE

PORTAGE ST

SOAPSUDS
ALLEY

TRIBAL
HOUSE

FORT SEWARD

FORT SEWARD CONDOS

SEWARD DR

CHILKAT CENTER
FOR THE ARTS

FORT SEWARD B&B

ALASKA
INDIAN ARTS

FAA RD

BEACH RD

0   0.2 mi

0   0.2 km

MUD BAY RD

TOWER RD

SMALL
TRACT RD

To Chilkat State Park

To Portage Cove Park
and Battery Point Trail

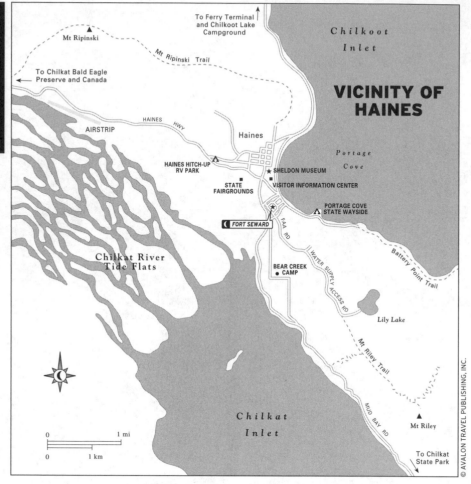

VICINITY OF HAINES

To Ferry Terminal and Chilkoot Lake Campground

Mt Ripinski

Mt Ripinski Trail

Chilkoot Inlet

To Chilkat Bald Eagle Preserve and Canada

HAINES HWY

AIRSTRIP

Haines

HAINES HITCH-UP RV PARK

SHELDON MUSEUM

Portage Cove

STATE FAIRGROUNDS

VISITOR INFORMATION CENTER

FORT SEWARD

PORTAGE COVE STATE WAYSIDE

FAA RD

Battery Point Trail

Chilkat River Tide Flats

BEAR CREEK CAMP

WATER SUPPLY ACCESS RD

Lily Lake

Mt Riley Trail

MUD BAY RD

Mt Riley

Chilkat Inlet

To Chilkat State Park

0   1 mi

0   1 km

© AVALON TRAVEL PUBLISHING, INC.

chance to explore this remote territory. While there, they met with members of the Chilkat tribe at a settlement called Yendestakyeh. Both men gave speeches before the people, but the Chilkats were considerably more interested in Muir's "brotherhood of man" message than Dr. Young's proselytizing. Muir wrote: "Later, when the sending of a missionary and teacher was being considered, the chief said they wanted me, and, as an inducement, promised that if I would come to them they would always do as I directed, follow my councils, give me as many

wives as I liked, build a church and school, and pick all the stones out of the paths and make them smooth for my feet." Two years later the mission was established by two Presbyterian missionaries (Muir had other plans) and the village was renamed Haines, in honor of Mrs. F. E. H. Haines of the Presbyterian Home Missions Board. She never visited her namesake.

During the Klondike gold rush, an adventurer and shrewd businessman named Jack Dalton developed a 305-mile toll road that began across the river from Haines and followed an old Indian trade route into the Yukon. He charged miners $150 each to use his Dalton Trail; armed men never failed to collect. To maintain order among the thousands of miners, the U.S. Army established Fort William H. Seward at Haines. Named for Alaska's "patron saint," it was built between 1900 and 1904 on 100 acres of land deeded to the government by the Haines mission. Renamed Chilkoot Barracks in 1923 (in commemoration of Chilkoot Pass), it was the only military base in all of Alaska until 1940.

In 1942–1943 the Army built the 150-mile Haines Highway from Haines to Haines Junction as an emergency evacuation route from Alaska in case of invasion by the Japanese. After World War II, the post was declared excess government property and sold to a veterans' group that hoped to form a business cooperative. The venture failed, but many stayed on, making homes in the stately old officers' quarters. The site became a National Historic Landmark in 1978 and its name was changed back to Fort Seward.

Today the town of Haines has a diversified economy that includes fishing (no canneries, however), tourism, and government jobs. Haines has also recently become something of a center for the arts, attracting artists and crafts workers of all types, from creators of stained glass to weavers of Chilkat blankets.

SIGHTS

Lookout Park (next to the harbor) is a great place to watch the fishing boats, eagles, and scenery. Bring a lunch. Behind it is a small cemetery with Tlingit graves dating from the 1880s. An old building, all that remains of **Yendestakyeh,** is just beyond the airport, 3.5 miles from town. The mission bell (1880) that once called the Tlingit people to worship now sits out front of the Presbyterian church on 2nd Avenue.

Tsirku Canning Company (5th and Main Sts., 907/766-3474, www.cannerytour.com, open mid-May–mid-Sept.) has re-created an old salmon-canning line with reconditioned antique equipment. The 45-minute tours, with

a video, are $10, free for kids under 12. No fish guts here; for that you'll need to get a job at a salmon cannery to see how it's done today.

Walt Disney's *White Fang* was filmed next to Haines in 1990, and the **Dalton City** gold rush town created for the movie is at the Southeast Alaska State Fairgrounds. Wander around the buildings or poke your head inside Alaska's smallest brewery, **Haines Brewing Company** (907/766-3823), for a sample of Paul Wheeler's Lookout Stout, Eldred Rock Red, IPA, and seasonal beers. Haines bars have them on draught. Locals especially rave about the stout—at least until they taste the Bigger Hammer Barley Wine.

Museums

Located on Main Street in the center of town, the **Sheldon Museum** (907/766-2366, www.sheldonmuseum.org, $3 adults, under 13 free) houses a fine collection of items from the gold rush, such as Jack Dalton's sawed-off shotgun, and Tlingit artifacts—including Chilkat blankets, a gorgeous carved ceremonial hat from the Murrelet clan, and a model of a tribal house. Upstairs, you can watch the excellent Audubon Society video about the Chilkat Bald Eagle Preserve, or see a slide show about local history. The museum is open Monday–Friday 10 A.M.–5 P.M. and Saturday Sunday 1–4 P.M. mid-May–mid-September, and whenever cruise ships are in port. Winter hours are Monday–Friday 1–4 P.M.

The strangest sight in Haines has to be the **Hammer Museum** (108 Main St., 907/766-2374, www.hammermuseum.org, Mon.–Fri. 10 A.M.–5 P.M. mid-May–mid-Sept., $3, under 13 free). Collector—and hammer expert—Dave Pahl displays some 1,500 types of hammers here, from cobbler's hammers to ones used by 19th-century bankers. The little museum is enough to make you break out in song: "If I had a hammer . . . ."

◖ Fort Seward

Circled around a grassy parade ground, the graceful buildings of historic Fort Seward are backdropped by snow-capped mountains.

Along the top of the hill is **"Officers' Row,"** the white century-old homes that once housed captains, lieutenants, and their families. Today, the buildings are used as private residences, bed and breakfasts, and the Hotel Halsingland.

A reconstructed **Tlingit tribal house**—decorated inside and out with colorful carvings—sits within the parade grounds, and the nonprofit **Alaska Indian Arts** (907/766-2160, www.alaskaindianarts.com, Monday–Friday 9 A.M.–5 P.M. year-round) operates from the old hospital building on the southeast side of Fort Seward. Inside you'll find master woodcarvers, silversmiths, blanket weavers, and other crafts workers, plus a gallery.

Stop by the Haines visitor bureau for a free, detailed historical guide and walking tour of Fort Seward.

American Bald Eagle Foundation

The Bald Eagle Foundation (907/766-3094, www.baldeagles.org, $3 adults, $1 ages 8–12, free for younger kids) sits at the intersection of Haines Highway and 2nd Avenue. Inside, you'll find a collection of stuffed animals and a video about eagles. Outside is a mew containing live bald eagles that could not survive in the wild. Don't miss talks by founder Dave Olerud, who provides an introduction to eagles and their role in the web of life. The facility is open Monday–Friday 9 A.M.–6 P.M., Saturday–Sunday 10 A.M.–4 P.M. May–August, with shortened hours the rest of September and during the Eagle Festival in early November; closed the rest of the year.

CHILKAT BALD EAGLE PRESERVE

Each fall, the Chilkat River north of Haines becomes home to the largest eagle gathering on earth. Throughout the summer, water flows into a massive underground reservoir created by gravel deposits at the confluence of the Tsirku, Klehini, and Chilkat Rivers north of Haines. When fall arrives this water percolates upward, keeping river temperatures above freezing. These warm waters attract an unusual late run of spawning chum

© DON PITCHER

Fort Seward and the Chilkat Range

and silver salmon. The dying salmon attract bears, wolves, gulls, magpies, ravens, and up to 3,500 bald eagles along a four-mile stretch of river just below the Tlingit village of **Klukwan** (pop. 140). Covering 48,000 acres, the Chilkat Bald Eagle Preserve (907/766-2292, www.dnr.state.ak.us) protects this unique gathering of eagles.

During the peak of the salmon run (Nov.–Jan.), black cottonwoods along the river are filled with hundreds of birds, and many more line the braided riverbanks. The area is very popular with photographers, but be sure to stay off the flats to avoid disturbing these majestic birds. During the summer, local eagle populations are much lower, but with 80 active nests and up to 400 resident eagles on the river, you're guaranteed to see some eagles.

A state campground ($10) is at **Mosquito Lake,** five miles north of Klukwan and three miles off the highway. Tours by van or boat go through the bald eagle preserve, and the Alaska

Bald Eagle Festival in mid-November brings more tours and educational workshops.

ENTERTAINMENT AND EVENTS
Entertainment
Chilkat Dancers' Storytelling Theater (907/766-2540, www.tresham.com/show, Mon.–Fri. 4:30 P.M., $12 adults, $6 kids) brings four ancient Tlingit legends to life with theatrical performances, magnificent costumes, and masks. Hour-long shows take place in the tribal house at Fort Seward throughout the summer.

If you hit the bar at **Fort Seward Lodge** (907/766-2009), be sure to ask for a Roadkill, the flaming house drink that's guaranteed to set your innards on fire. Fishermen school up at two Front Street bars: **Harbor Bar** (907/766-2444) with occasional live bands and **Fogcutter Bar** (907/766-2555).

Events
The **Great Alaska Craftbeer & Homebrew Festival** in mid-May is a fine opportunity to taste regional microbrews.

Around the summer solstice in June, the **Kluane to Chilkat International Bike Relay** (www.kcibr.org) attracts more than 1,100 cyclists for an exciting 160-mile relay race that ends in Haines. Other solstice events include live music and dancing at the fairgrounds.

July 4th brings a parade, barbecue, pie-eating contest, soapbox derby races, a race up Mt. Ripinski, and other fun events.

Every year during the last week of July thousands of visitors from all over Alaska and the Yukon flock to Haines for the five-day-long **Southeast Alaska State Fair** (www.seakfair.org). Events include a logging show, farmers' market, parade, pig races, dog show, exhibits, and evening concerts by nationally known artists. Don't miss this one!

The **Alaska Bald Eagle Festival** (www.baldeaglefest.org) in early November—peak time for eagle viewing on the Chilkat Preserve—features scientific talks, workshops, and evening entertainment. The highlight comes with the dramatic release of formerly injured eagles back into the wild.

SHOPPING
Haines is an excellent place to buy arts and crafts. (For more about Alaska Indian Arts, see the *Fort Seward* section.) The best local gallery is **Wild Iris Shop** (on Portage St., 907/766-2300), run by Fred and Madeleine Shields, who act as a comedy tag-team. Fred (the mayor of Haines) will be happy to give you a dose of his "retail therapy," complete with a German accent stolen from old TV shows. Oh yes, the gallery is great too, with jewelry, trade beads, carved ivory, and photos. Find it a block up from the Port Chilkoot Dock and just down from the fort. The garden out front overflows with flowers all summer.

Extreme Dreams (907/766-2097, www.extremedreams.com) has the unusual watercolors, block prints, and textiles of John and Sharon Svenson, in a gorgeous setting, seven miles out Mud Bay Road. Another interesting Mud Bay Road gallery is nearby, **Catotti & Goldberg Studio** (907/766-2707, www.artstudioalaska.com), where you can see the paintings of Donna Catotti and Rob Goldberg. Although he isn't Native, Tresham Gregg makes distinctive woodcarvings and prints using Tlingit-inspired designs. Find them in his **Sea Wolf Gallery** (907/766-2540, www.tresham.com) near the center of Ft. Seward.

For quality outdoor gear, head to **Backcountry Outfitters** (210 Main St. upstairs, 907/766-2876, www.alaskanaturetours.net). Get Alaskan and other books from **The Babbling Book** (907/766-3356), on Main Street next to Howser's.

Haines is home to one of several birch syrup producers in Alaska—**Birch Boy Products** (907/767-5660, www.birchboy.com). The syrup is sold locally in gift shops. Don't expect the smoothness of maple syrup; birch syrup has a bit of a bite to it, but is quite good on ice cream and when blended with sugar syrup.

RECREATION

The Haines area has a number of excellent hikes, ranging from the easy (Battery Point) to the strenuous (Mt. Ripinski). For more details, pick up the *Haines is for Hikers* pamphlet from the visitor center.

Mt. Riley

Three trails lead to the top of 1,760-foot Mt. Riley, from which you get a panoramic view of Lynn Canal, Davidson and Rainbow Glaciers, the Chilkat River, Taiya Inlet, and 360 degrees of snowcapped peaks. The shortest and steepest route (2 miles) starts three miles southeast of Haines on Mud Bay Road. A small parking area is opposite the trailhead. You can also follow FAA Road from behind Fort Seward to another trail. This one is four miles long and follows the city water supply route for two miles before splitting off to join the more direct trail.

Battery Point

An easy and relatively level four-mile path starts from the end of the road at Portage Cove and follows the shore to a campsite at Kelgaya Point and across pebbly beaches to Battery Point.

Mt. Ripinski

The full-day hike up and down Mt. Ripinski (3,610 ft.) offers unparalleled views of mountains and inland waterways, but it's strenuous and long (10 miles round-trip). You may want to camp in the alpine country and make this a two-day hike. From Haines, take Young Road north until it intersects with a jeep road that follows a buried pipeline around the mountain. The trail begins about a mile along this dirt road and climbs through a spruce/hemlock forest to muskeg and finally alpine at 2,500 feet. You can continue along the ridge to the north summit (3,160 ft.), or on to the main peak. Return the same way, or via a steep path that takes you down to a saddle and then to the Haines Highway, seven miles northwest of Haines. Mt. Ripinski is covered with snow until mid-summer, so be prepared. Don't go in bad weather and do stay on the trail in the alpine areas.

Seduction Point

For a gentle, long, and very scenic beach walk, head to Chilkat State Park campground, seven miles southeast of Haines on Mud Bay Road. Seduction Point is on the end of the peninsula separating Chilkoot and Chilkat Inlets, a five-mile hike from the campground. The trail alternates between the forest and the beach, and it's a good idea to check the tides to make sure that you're able to hike the last beach stretch at low tide. This hike also makes a fine overnight camping trip.

ACCOMMODATIONS

The Haines Convention and Visitors Bureau website (www.haines.ak.us) has detailed info and links to local lodging places.

Hostel

The youth hostel in Haines, **Bear Creek Cabins and Hostel** (907/766-2259, www.bearcreek cabinsalaska.com, open May–mid-Nov.), is a mile and a half south of town on Small Tract Road. Dorm spaces are $18 and the six private cabins run $48 d. Bear Creek has kitchen facilities. The hostel is a clean and friendly place to stay, but reservations are advised in the summer. If it's full, pitch a tent out back for $12.

Hotels and Motels

◀ **Hotel Halsingland** (907/766-2000 or 800/542-6363, www.hotelhalsingland.com, open April–mid-Nov.) is a beautiful old Victorian hotel that originally served as the commanding officer's quarters at Fort Seward. In addition to the standard rooms ($109 d), it has a few small but inexpensive shared-bath rooms ($69 s or d). All rooms have been updated, but retain the original charm; it's like a step back in time to a quieter, more gracious era. Wi-fi is available in the lobby, and the restaurant is one of the nicest in town.

Fort Seward Lodge (907/766-2009 or 800/478-7772, www.ftsewardlodge.com, open May–early Oct.) is located in another of the Fort Seward structures: This one once housed the fort's PX, bowling alley, and gym. Rooms are simple but clean; none have phones. Those with

© DON PITCHER

Hotel Halsingland in Fort Seward

private baths are $70 s or $80 d. Tiny rooms with a bath down the hall and no television cost $50 s or $60 d. Also available are a couple of rooms with kitchenettes for $85 s or $95 d.

Head a mile out of town on Beach Road to **Beach Roadhouse** (907/766-3060 or 866/736-3060, www.beachroadhouse.com, $125 d), with a mix of kitchenette rooms (85 d) and small cabins ($125 d or $145 for four) with full kitchens and Lynn Canal vistas. A guest computer and Wi-Fi are available.

Mountain View Inn (Mud Bay Rd. near Ft. Seward, 907/766-2900 or 800/478-2902, www .mtviewinn.net, $78 s or $88 d) has nine large rooms, most with kitchenettes. Free Wi-Fi too.

Thunderbird Motel (216 Dalton St., 907/766-2131 or 800/327-2556, www.thunder bird-motel.com), has standard rooms with fridges and microwaves ($80 s or $90 d) and full kitchenettes ($118 for up to four).

On Haines Highway as you head out of town, **Eagle's Nest Motel** (907/766-2891 or 800/354-6009, www.alaskaeagletours.com, $79 s or $89–99 d) offers comfortable rooms and reasonable prices. Pets are $10 extra.

Housed within a historic officer's row building, **Fort Seward Condos** (907/766-2425, www.fortsewardcondos.com, $125–145 d) are one- and two-bedroom units with full kitchens; two-night minimum stay.

The nicest local motel, **Captain's Choice Motel** (108 2nd St., 907/766-3111 or 800/478-2345, www.capchoice.com) has standard rooms for $107–132 d, and suites (these sleep six comfortably) for $155. All rooms contain small fridges, and a courtesy van is available.

Bed-and-Breakfasts

Fort Seward B&B (907/766-2856 or 800/615-6676, www.fortsewardbnb.com, $89–135 d) is a beautifully maintained historic home that once housed the fort's chief surgeon. Four of the seven guest rooms have private baths, and two can be combined into a family suite for $239. Guests are served a filling sourdough pancake breakfast. Free Wi-Fi.

Built in 1912 by a member of Soapy Smith's gang, **Summer Inn B&B** (2nd and Main Sts., 907/766-2970, www.summerinnbnb.com, $75 s or $90 d) is a cozy five-bedroom home near the center of town. The five guest rooms share three baths, and a big breakfast is served each morning.

Other options include **Bear Lodge B&B** (907/957-1035, www.hainesbearlodge.com), **Chilkat Eagle B&B** (907/766-2763, www.eagle-bb.com), **A Sheltered Harbor B&B** (907/766-2741, www.geocities.com/asheltered), and **Tanani Bay B&B** (907/766-3936, www.tananibaybnb.com).

CAMPING

The best campsite near Haines is at **Portage Cove State Wayside** ($5), just three-quarters of a mile from town. Water and outhouses are available, but there is no overnight parking; the site is for hikers and cyclists only. The location is quiet and attractive, and eagles hang around nearby.

If you have a vehicle, stay at one of the two other excellent state-run campgrounds, both with drinking water, toilets, and picnic shelters. **Chilkat State Park** ($10), seven miles southeast of Haines, has a fine hiking trail to Seduction Point; and **Chilkoot Lake State Recreation Site** ($10), five miles northwest of the ferry, has good fishing and a lovely view over this turquoise-blue lake. More camping is at **Mosquito Lake State Park** ($10), 27 miles north of Haines.

RV Parks

Most local RV parks are open May–September. Located behind Hotel Halsingland, **Port Chilkoot Camper Park** (907/766-2000 or 800/542-6363, www.hotelhalsingland.com, $10–16 tents, $23 full hookups) has attractively wooded campsites, showers, and a coin laundry. **Salmon Run Adventures RV Campground** (907/766-3240, www.salmonrunadventures.com, $14 for RVs or tents, no hookups), seven miles out Lutak Road, also offers showers for $2. **Haines Hitch-Up RV Park** (851 Main St., 907/766-2882, www.hitchuprv.com) is $27–32 with full hookups; no tents. RVers also park at the gravel lot on Main Street named **Oceanside RV Park** (907/766-2437). **Swan's Rest RV Park** (907/767-5662, May 30–Sept.

snow-covered cache near Haines

© DON PITCHER

15, $20 full hookups, $7 tents) is near Mosquito Lake, 27 miles north of Haines.

FOOD

For a town of this size, Haines has surprisingly good food, and the prices won't ruin your credit rating. Get filling meals, friendly service, and an unpretentious setting at the **Bamboo Room** (on 2nd Ave., 907/766-2800, www.bamboopioneer.net). Breakfasts are a standout, but the Bamboo also fills up at lunch and dinner when the menu features burgers, fried chicken, halibut fish and chips, and other greasy fare. Be sure to check the board for today's specials.

Chilkat Restaurant and Bakery (5th and Dalton Sts., 907/766-3653) bakes pastries, bagels, and croissants daily, and serves up tasty breakfasts and lunches (including homemade soups, burgers, and sandwiches) in a relaxing setting. The new owners are from Thailand, and they've added spicy Thai meals for lunch on Thursday and Saturday. The restaurant is open for breakfast and lunch most days, plus dinners (Thai and American food for $10–18) on Friday and Saturday nights.

When I'm in Haines on a chilly winter morning I bee-line it to the perpetually busy **Mountain Market & Deli** (3rd St. and Haines Hwy., 907/766-3340) for a steaming mocha and a scrambled egg croissant. Fresh baked goods fill the displays, and the lunch menu encompasses turkey club wraps, falafels, deli sandwiches, and smoothies. A natural foods market here sells organic produce and "Beware of the Crows" T-shirts.

New owners have transformed **Lighthouse Restaurant** (101 Front St., 907/766-2442) into an East-meets-West spot for harborside dining. They're open for dinner daily; try the ginger Alaskan sable fish with coconut wasabi sauce, the baked oyster appetizers, or the locally famous buttermilk pie.

Get groceries from **Howser's IGA Supermarket** (on Main St., 907/766-2040). Ask around the boat harbor to see who's selling fresh fish, crab, or prawns if you want to cook your own. A summertime **Farmers Market** takes place at the fairgrounds every other Saturday 9 A.M.–1 P.M.

Fort Seward Eateries

Housed in one of Fort Seward's historic buildings, (**Fireweed Restaurant** (on Blacksmith Rd., 907/766-3838, $9–19, open May–mid-Nov. for dinner only; closed Sun. and Mon.) serves delicious meals in a classy setting. There's a wrap-around deck with a couple of tables outside, plus an earthy interior where the scents of freshly baked bread and the daily specials fill the air. The bar features local brews, and the menu encompasses salads, halibut burgers, eggplant parmesan heros, portabello mushroom ravioli alfredo, Caesar salads, pizzas with homemade sauce, and more. Highly recommended, but don't come here in a hurry. This is slow food that's worth the wait.

The restaurant at **Hotel Halsingland** (907/766-2000 or 800/542-6363, www.hotel halsingland.com, $19–28 entrées) is a pleasant place for an evening out, with a fine-dining menu that stars Caesar salads, braised lamb shank, pan-roasted duck, and butternut squash ravioli. The bar menu serves simpler meals.

Dejon Delights Smokery (on Portage Rd., 907/766-2505 or 800/539-3608, www .alaskasmokery.com) at Fort Seward has freshly smoked salmon for sale or will smoke fish that you catch.

Just downhill is **Local Catch** (907/766-3557, $4–9), a little hole-in-the-wall with a couple of tables out front and a morning menu (open weekdays 8 A.M.–3 P.M.) of breakfast burritos, eggwiches, fish tacos, curry spinach quesadillas, and lattes.

INFORMATION AND SERVICES

The **Haines Visitors Information Center** (907/766-2234 or 800/458-3579 message only, www.haines.ak.us) is on 2nd Avenue near Willard Street. Mid-May–mid-September, it's open Monday–Friday 8 A.M.–6 P.M., Saturday–Sunday 9 A.M.–6 P.M. The rest of the year, hours are Monday–Friday 8 A.M.– 5 P.M. Packs can generally be left here while you walk around town. Stop here for a listing of local charter fishing boats if you want to catch salmon or halibut.

Check your email at **Northern Lights Internet Lounge** (715 Main St., 907/766-2337), or for free at the modern **Haines Public Library** (111 3rd Ave., 907/766-2545, www .haineslibrary.org). The post office is on Haines Highway near Fort Seward. Get cash from ATMs inside Howser's Supermarket and the First National Bank of Alaska. Buy topographic maps from **Chilkoot Gardens** (2nd Ave. and Main St.).

Showers are available at **Port Chilkoot Camper Park,** behind Hotel Halsingland, and **Haines Quick Laundry,** across from Fort Seward Lodge. Another option is the fine **swimming pool** (907/766-2666), next to the high school, where the entrance fee gets you a shower and swim.

The unique **Valley of the Eagles Golf Links** (907/766-2401, www.hainesgolf.com) is a mile north of town on tidelands that are occasionally covered by larger tides. The setting is dramatic, and you might even see the occasional moose or bear.

GETTING THERE
Ferry
The Haines **ferry terminal** (907/766-2111) is 3.5 miles north of town on Lutak Highway. Ferries arrive in Haines almost every day during the summer, heading both north to Skagway and south to Juneau. They generally stop for an hour and a half. Call Alaska Marine Highway for information (907/465-3941 or 800/642-0066, www.ferryalaska.com).

Alaska Fjordlines (907/766-3395 or 800/320-0146, www.alaskafjordlines.com) operates a high-speed catamaran with daily summertime runs from Skagway to Haines and then on to Auke Bay in Juneau. The boat leaves Haines at 9 A.M., arrives in Juneau at 11:30 A.M., and then heads back at 5 P.M., returning to Haines at 7:30 P.M. The cost is $139 round trip, including a bus to downtown Juneau. A light breakfast and dinner are included, and the skipper stops for wildlife and photo opportunities. One-way trips and overnight stays in Juneau are sometimes allowed; reservations recommended.

Chilkat Cruises (907/766-2100 or 888/766-2103, www.chilkatcruises.com, mid-May–mid-Sept., $51 round-trip, $25 kids) offers high-speed catamaran service between Skagway and Haines, with several departures a day. There is no bus service out of Haines.

Air
The airport is 3.5 miles west of town on the Haines Highway. The flight between Juneau and Haines is pretty spectacular; on clear days you'll be treated to views of glaciers along both sides of Lynn Canal. Several companies have scheduled daily service to Juneau and Skagway: **Wings of Alaska** (907/789-0790, www.wingsofalaska.com), **Skagway Air** (907/789-3233, www.skagwayair.com), and **L.A.B. Flying Service** (907/766-2222, www.labflying.com).

Mountain Flying Service (907/766-3007 or 800/766-4007, www.flyglacierbay.com), a few doors up from the visitor center, is a good company that offers charters and flightseeing trips over Glacier Bay starting at $139 per person for one hour. A longer trip ($279) includes two hours in the air and a beach landing within the park that gives you the chance to see bears and other wildlife. **Fly Drake** (907/723-9475, www.flydrake.com) and L.A.B. also offers Glacier Bay flightseeing trips and beach landings.

GETTING AROUND
Tours
The visitor center has a complete listing of local guide companies and charter boat operators. **Alaska Nature Tours** (210 Main St., 907/766-2876, www.alaskanaturetours.net) leads very educational three-hour bus-and-hiking trips to the eagle-viewing area along the Chilkat River and Chilkoot Lake for $65 ($50 kids). A four-hour tour with lunch is $77 ($62 kids); same price for a four-hour rainforest hike with lunch. Wintertime ski trips are also available, and their outdoor shop (Backcountry Outfitter) rents skis, snowboards, and snowshoes.

Keet Gooshi Tours (907/766-2168 or 877/776-2168, www.keetgooshi.com, $60) is a Native-owned company with 2.5-hour van tours that take in the Bald Eagle Preserve and the village of Klukwan, including an introduction to traditional culture.

Chilkat Cruises (907/766-2100 or 888/766-2103, www.chilkatcruises.com) leads half-day bus tours ($105) to a wildlife preserve run by well-known cinematographer Steve Kroschel (www.kroschelfilms.com). You'll see wolves, foxes, reindeer, wolverines, and more. Chilkat Cruises also offers sea kayak day trips and kayak rentals.

River Trips
Chilkat Guides (907/766-2491 or 888/292-7789, www.raftalaska.com, $79 adults, $62 kids) guides an excellent four-hour float trip down the Chilkat River. This is a leisurely raft trip (no white water) with good views of the Chilkat Mountains, glaciers, and roosting eagles. They also guide multi-night adventures around Alaska. **River**

Adventures (907/766-2050 or 800/478-9827, www.jetboatalaska.com) runs half-day jetboat tours up the Chilkat, and **Chilkoot Lake Tours** (907/766-2891, www.alaskaeagletours.com) has two-hour pontoon boat tours of this turquoise lake.

Glacier Valley Wilderness Adventures (907/767-5522, www.glaciervalleyadventures. net) offers a variety of trips that include a flight into a gold mine camp at the base of DeBlondeau Glacier followed by a rafting or jetboat trip down the Tsirku River, and then past the Chilkat Bald Eagle Preserve to Haines; $253 per person. Overnight accommodations are also available in a cabin or tent at the basecamp, and the company also has airboat trips and rafting floats.

Taxi and Car Rentals
Haines Shuttle & Tours (907/766-3138) charges a gut-wrenching $20 per person (!) to town from the ferry terminal or airport.

Rent cars from **Captain's Choice Motel** (907/766-3111 or 800/478-2345, www.cap choice.com), **Eagle's Nest Car Rental** (907/766-2891 or 800/354-6009, www.alaskaeagle tours.com), or **Hotel Halsingland** (907/766-2000 or 800/542-6363, www.hotelhalsing land.com). Eagle's Nest has the cheapest rates, starting at $50 per day with 100 free miles.

Rent mountain bikes from **Sockeye Cycle** (907/766-2869, www.cyclealaska.com) at Fort Seward. A variety of bike tours are also offered.

Heading North
The paved highway north from Haines is the most direct route to Fairbanks (665 miles) and Anchorage (775 miles). For cyclists it's much easier than the Klondike Highway out of Skagway. If you're thinking of driving to Skagway from Haines, think again. It's only 15 water or air miles away, but 359 road miles. Take the ferry! There is no scheduled bus service from Haines.

Crossing the Border
The Canadian border is 42 miles north of Haines. Both Canadian and U.S. Customs are open 7 A.M.–11 P.M. Alaska Time (8 A.M.– midnight Pacific Time). Be prepared for lots of questions if you're traveling on the cheap. No handguns are allowed across the Canadian border.

Skagway

Occupying a narrow plain along the mouth of the Skagway River at the head of Lynn Canal, Skagway (year-round pop. 800; twice that in the summer) is a triangle-shaped town that seems to drive a wedge into the sheer slopes that lead to White Pass. The name of this northern terminus of the Inside Passage is derived from an Indian word meaning "home of the North Wind." During the Klondike gold rush, the town was the gateway to both the Chilkoot and White Pass Trails, a funnel through which thousands of frenzied fortune-seekers passed. Today, the boardwalks, frontier storefronts, restored interiors, gift shops, historic films and slide shows, and old-time cars and costumes all in the six-block town center give it the flavor for which it has been famous for nearly a century. Skagway survives on the thousands of visitors and adventurers who come each summer to continue on the trail that led to gold. This is the most popular cruise port in Alaska, and the Skagwegians are inundated with over 7,000 cruise ship visitors on a typical mid-summer day; up to five ships can dock at once. Today, 900,000 travelers spend time in Skagway each year, the vast majority stepping off these mega-ships.

Independent travelers often leave Skagway with mixed feelings, and some regard it as a schmaltzy shadow of its former self. To some extent this is true, but the town also has genuine charm, and when the cruise ships sail away each night, the locals come out to play. Skagway is compact enough to walk around easily, and is filled with all sorts of characters. Besides, if the downtown scene isn't to your taste, it's easy to escape into the surrounding mountains or to head up the Chilkoot Trail where only the hardy stray. One way to avoid most of the crowds is to get here before mid-May or after mid-September. Come in the winter and you'll have it almost to yourself!

Skagway's weather is considerably drier than other parts of the Southeast. It gets only 27 inches of precipitation a year, and alder, willow, and cottonwood carpet the adjacent hillsides. It is especially colorful in mid-September when the leaves are turning. The driest time is before July; after that rain is more likely.

HISTORY
Klondike Gold

An enormous amount of Alaskan history was compressed into the final decade of the 19th century at Skagway. In August 1896, on the day that George Carmack struck it rich on Bonanza Creek, Skagway consisted of a single cabin, constructed eight years previously by Captain William Moore, but only occupied sporadically by the transient pioneer. News of the Klondike strike hit Seattle in July 1897; within a month 4,000 people huddled in a haphazard tent city surrounding Moore's lone cabin, and "craft of every description, from ocean-going steamers to little more than floating coffins, were dumping into the makeshift village a crazily mixed mass of humanity." Almost immediately, Frank Reid surveyed and plotted the town site, and the stampeders grabbed 1,000 lots, many within Moore's homestead. There was no law to back up either claims or counterclaims, and reports from the time describe Skagway as "the most outrageously lawless quarter" on the globe.

Into this breach stepped Jefferson Randall "Soapy" Smith, Alaska's great bad man. A notorious con artist from Colorado, Soapy Smith oversaw a mind-bogglingly extensive system of fraud, theft, armed robbery, prostitution, gambling, and even murder. He had his own spy network, secret police, and army to enforce the strong-arm tactics. Finally, a vigilance committee held a meeting to oppose Soapy. Frank Reid, the surveyor, stood guard. Soapy approached. Guns blazed. Smith, shot in the chest, died instantly, at age 38. Of Soapy, the newspaper reported, "At 9:30 o'clock Friday night the checkered career of 'Soapy' Smith was brought to a sudden end by a 38 caliber bullet from a revolver in the unerring right

SOUTHEAST ALASKA

SKAGWAY

To Carcross and Whitehorse, Yukon

0   0.2 mi

0   0.2 km

To Gold Rush
Cemetery and
Lower Reid Falls

YOU SAY
TOMATO GROCERY

SCENIC
VISTA

ALASKA ST
22ND AVE
21ST AVE
20TH AVE
18TH AVE
18TH AVE
17TH AVE
15TH AVE
14TH AVE
13TH AVE
MAIN ST
STATE ST

DYEA RD

River

AIRSTRIP

GARDEN CITY
RV PARK

RECREATION
CENTER

SKAGWAY MT
VIEW RV PARK

ALASKA ST

Skagway

To Dyea and
Chilkoot Trailhead

Skagway

11TH AVE
10TH AVE
STATE ST
12TH AVE
BROADWAY

MILE ZERO
B&B

9TH AVE

HAVEN CAFE

WHITE PASS
AND YUKON
ROUTE RAILWAY

THE WHITE
HOUSE INN

6TH AVE
MAIN ST
2ND ST
7TH AVE
8TH AVE
SPRING ST

LIBRARY

5TH
AVE

SGT
PRESTON'S
LODGE

SKAGWAY
INN B&B

4TH AVE

CORNER
CAFE

BANK/
POST
OFFICE

Molly
Walsh
Park

SCULPTURE
GARDEN

3RD
AVE

FAIRWAY
MARKET

CITY HALL/ TRAIL
OF '98 MUSEUM

SKAGWAY
HOME
HOSTEL

WILLIAM MOORE CABIN

AIRPORT
TERMINAL

1ST AVE

SOAPY
SMITH'S
PARLOR

GOLDEN
NORTH HOTEL

SKAGWAY AIR

Yakutana
Point Trail

SITE OF
GUNBATTLE

RED
ONION

WESTMARK
INN

ARCTIC BROTHERHOOD HALL/
SKAGWAY VISITORS CENTER

WP&YR RR DEPOT

CHILKOOT TRAIL CENTER

2ND AVE

PARK SERVICE
VISITOR CENTER

To Icy Lake

Pullen
Pond

PULLEN CREEK
RV PARK

ORE CRUISE
SHIP DOCK

Taiya Inlet

BROADWAY
CRUISE SHIP
DOCK

ALASKA
FERRY
TERMINAL

SMALL BOAT
HARBOR

STOWAWAY CAFE

SKAGWAY
FISH COMPANY

RAILROAD CRUISE
SHIP DOCK

CONGRESS WAY

To Lower
Dewey Lake

MAP AREA (inset)

To Dyea   To Carcross

CHILKOOT TRAILHEAD

Nahku Bay

A B Mountain Trail

JEWELL
GARDENS

Skagway

River

Lower
Reid Falls

Upper
Reid Falls

GOLD RUSH
CEMETERY

Dyea
Point

Icy
Lake

Yakutania
Point

MAP AREA

Skagway

Taiya Inlet

Lower
Dewey
Lake

Upper
Dewey
Lake

Snyder Creek

Devil's
Punchbowl

Sturgill's
Landing

0   0.5 mi

0   0.5 km

© AVALON TRAVEL PUBLISHING, INC.

hand of City surveyor Frank H. Reid . . . ." Reid was shot in the groin, and died in agony a week later. His gravestone reads, "He gave his life for the honor of Skagway." More recent evidence has been less kind to Frank Reid's reputation. It turns out that he had been a prime suspect in an Oregon murder, and as a surveyor for the railroad was deeply involved in the theft of William Moore's homestead lands. Some locals say both men got what they deserved.

Over the Top

Skagway was the jumping-off point for **White Pass,** which crossed the Coastal Range to Lake Bennett and the Yukon headwaters. This trail, billed as the "horse route," was the choice of prosperous prospectors who could afford pack animals to carry the requisite "ton of goods." But it was false advertising at best, and death-defying at worst. The mountains were so precipitous, the trail so narrow and rough, and the weather so wild, that the men turned merciless; all 3,000 horses and mules that stepped onto the trail in 1897–1898 were doomed to a proverbial fate worse than death. Indeed, men swore that horses leaped off the cliffs on purpose, committing suicide on the "Dead Horse Trail."

The famous **Chilkoot Trail,** which started in Dyea (die-EE), 15 miles from Skagway, was the "poor-man's route." Stampeders had to backpack their year's worth of supplies 33 miles to Lake Lindeman, which included 40 trips up and down the 45-degree "Golden Stairs" to the 3,550-foot pass. This scene, recorded in black and white, is one of the most dramatic and enduring photographs of the Days of 1898. At Lindeman, the men built wooden boats for the sometimes-treacherous journey to the gold fields at Dawson.

Building the Railroad

The late 19th century was a time when the railroad was king, and the sudden rush of men to the gold fields attracted entrepreneurs intent upon figuring a way to build a railroad from Skagway over White Pass. Into this breach stepped Michael J. Heney, an Irish-Canadian

contractor with a genius for vision, fund-raising, management, and commanding the loyalty of his workers. Heney punched through the 110-mile narrow-gauge White Pass & Yukon Route Railway to Lake Bennett by July of 1899, and then on to Whitehorse a year later. The route, so treacherous to pack animals, was no less malevolent to railroaders. They worked suspended from the steep slopes by ropes, often in 50-below temperatures and raging Arctic blizzards, for $3 a day. Completion of the railroad ensured the constant flow of passengers and freight to the gold fields—as well as Skagway's survival. For the next four decades, the railroad was virtually the only way into the Yukon.

During World War II, the White Pass & Yukon Route hauled much of the construction equipment and personnel to build the Alaska Highway. In the 1970s, the railroad shifted to hauling lead, zinc, and silver ore concentrate from a big mine in the Yukon. The concentrate was shipped from Skagway for processing in Asia. When metal prices plummeted in 1982, the mine closed and train traffic halted. (One legacy of this mine is the presence of lead and other toxins in the waters off Skagway.) But just as mining was ending, Alaska's current gold rush arrived in the form of cruise ships. The WP&YR reopened for excursion travel in 1988, and it is once again not only Skagway's favorite attraction, but one of the only operating narrow-gauge railroads in North America. Today, over 300,000 passengers ride the train each summer.

SIGHTS

Downtown Skagway is made up of seven blocks on Broadway, along which are most of the sights. The ferry terminal is at the bottom of Broadway: A three-minute hike and you're in the heart of beautiful downtown Skagway.

Corrington's Museum of Alaskan History (5th Ave. and Broadway, 907/983-2637 or 800/943-2637) is a combination gift shop and free scrimshaw museum. The collection includes 40 or so exquisitely carved pieces that tell the history of Alaska on walrus ivory. It's well worth a visit. The building is flanked by a colorful flower garden.

Be sure to poke your head into **Skagway Hardware Company** (Broadway at 4th Ave., 907/983-2233, www.skagwayhardware.com), one of the few old-time hardware stores left in Alaska. The wooden floors creak, and items of all types (even washers and dryers) are crammed into the shelves. A block away is the distinctive gold-colored cupola of the **Golden North Hotel.** Built in 1898, the hotel closed in 2002.

Skagway Sculpture Garden (8th Ave. at Spring St., 907/983-3311, www.skagway sculpturegarden.com, $7.50) features a flower garden filled with 37 bronze pieces by Austin Deuel, Sandy Scott, and other well-known artisans.

Broadway has more than its share of soak-the-tourists gift shops staffed by folks whose only connection to Skagway is a paycheck. The most egregious examples are the Caribbean, Colombian, British, and Swiss jewelry shops that barely make an effort to sell anything remotely connected with Alaska. Despite this, do step inside the Little Switzerland Store (Broadway and 5th Ave.), where you'll discover both the world's largest and smallest gold nugget watch chains. Local people do run many of the other shops in town.

Klondike Gold Rush National Historical Park

More than a dozen historic downtown buildings are owned and managed by the National Park Service as Klondike Gold Rush National Historical Park in commemoration of the 1898 stampede of miners to Canada's Yukon. Most of the restored structures are leased to private businesses. (The park is actually split into two pieces, with one visitor center in Skagway, and another in Seattle, where nearly all the miners began their journey.)

The old White Pass & Yukon administration building houses the **Klondike Gold Rush National Historical Park Visitor Center** (907/983-2921, www.nps.gov/klgo). It's open daily 8 A.M.–6 P.M. early May–late September;

closed the rest of the year. Don't miss *Days of Adventure, Dreams of Gold,* a 30-minute film shown hourly. Ranger talks typically take place at 10 A.M. and 3 P.M., and 45-minute walking tours of old Skagway are offered five times a day—sign up early in the day to be sure of a space. Additional programs and daily tours to Dyea are also offered; see the event schedule for details. There's no charge for any of these talks. Personnel behind the desk have the latest weather and transportation information, and can probably answer that burning question you've been carrying around all day.

Across Broadway and next to the tracks, the historic Martin Itjen House contains the **Chilkoot Trail Center,** where rangers can provide details on hiking in the footsteps of the miners. This 32-mile trail starts from the old Dyea town site, nine miles from Skagway, and climbs over Chilkoot Pass (3,535 ft.) before dropping down to Bennett, British Columbia. (See *Chilkoot Trail* later in this chapter for the full story.)

Just up 2nd Street is **Soapy Smith's Parlor,** the saloon from which the infamous blackguard supervised his various nefarious offenses. The building is not open to the public.

The original **Captain William Moore cabin** (5th Ave. and Spring St., daily 10 A.M.–5 P.M., free), which was moved under pressure from the early stampeders to its present location, has been completely refurbished by the Park Service. Its interior walls are papered with newspapers from the 1880s.

Be sure to step inside another Park Service building, the old **Mascot Saloon** (3rd Ave. and Broadway, open daily in summer, free) with exhibits depicting the saloon and life in the days of '98.

White Pass & Yukon Route Railroad

Adjacent to the Park Visitor Center is the **White Pass & Yukon Route Depot** (on 2nd St. 907/983-2217 or 800/343-7373, www.white passrailroad.com) built in the 1990s to closely resemble the town's many historic structures. Narrow gauge WP&YR trains depart from the depot several times a day from early May until late September; there is no winter service.

White Pass Summit Excursion trains leave Skagway at 8:15 A.M. and 1 P.M. and at 4:30 P.M. Monday through Thursday. These go to the summit of White Pass and back, a round-trip of 40 miles that takes three hours. The tracks follow along the east side of the Skagway River, with vistas that get better and better as the train climbs. Tour guides point out the sights and explain the railroad's history. Be sure to sit on the left side from Skagway (right side returning) for the best views. The diesel smoke is less toward the rear of the train. These excursions cost $98 for adults, $49 for ages 3–12, and are free for tots.

The WP&YR has two photogenic old **steam engines**—one built in 1920, the other from 1947—that huff and puff out of town most days, with video cameras rolling in all directions. For most runs the steam engine is replaced by a diesel engine on the edge of town to save it from wear and tear on the strenuous climb.

The railroad's special four-hour **Fraser Meadows Steam Excursions** ($125 adults, $63 kids) is a real treat for train lovers. Pulled by a steam engine, these trains leave at noon Saturday and Sunday and stop in the mountains just beyond the White Pass Summit to let passengers out for a chance to photograph as the engine rolls by with steam billowing before returning back down the mountain to Skagway at 4 P.M.

Also available is a **Skagway-Whitehorse rail-and-bus connection** that costs $106 for adults, $53 for kids, each way. Trains depart Skagway daily at 8 A.M., with passengers transferring to buses at Fraser, British Columbia, before continuing on to Whitehorse, arriving at noon. The buses leave Whitehorse daily at 12:30 P.M., connect with the train in Fraser, and reach Skagway at 4:30 P.M. You can also take the train one-way from Skagway to Fraser for $72 adults, $36 kids; several bus companies use this as part of a train-up, bus-back trip. Also available is a once-daily train service between Skagway and Carcross for $150 one-

way. Trains stop for a hot lunch (included) at Lake Bennett.

The **Chilkoot Trail Hikers Service** provides a shuttle Friday, Saturday, and Monday from late May to mid-September from Lake Bennett (the end of the trail) to Fraser ($50) or Skagway ($90).

Arctic Brotherhood Hall

You can't miss Arctic Brotherhood (AB) Hall between 2nd and 3rd streets—the only example of turn-of-the-century Alaska driftwood stick architecture, and probably the most-photographed building in Alaska. Thousands of pieces of wood—8,841 to be exact—decorate the exterior. The brotherhood was organized aboard the vessel *City of Seattle,* which waited out the winter of 1899 in Skagway Harbor. The order spread, and local chapters were established in most Alaskan towns, with dues paid solely in nuggets.

The AB Hall now houses the **Skagway Visitors Information Center** (907/983-2854 or 888/762-1898 message, www.skagway.com).

historic Arctic Brotherhood Hall

© DON PITCHER

It's open daily 8 A.M.–6 P.M. mid-May–mid-September, and Monday–Friday 8 A.M.–5 P.M. the rest of the year. It has the standard brochures, plus helpful walking tour and hiking maps. Stop in and take Buckwheat out to lunch, but be sure to ask about his travels with Martha Stewart. Tell him I sent you.

Skagway Museum
This excellent collection is housed in the beautifully restored City Hall (700 Spring St., 907/983-2420), a block off Broadway. It's open Monday–Friday 9 A.M.–5 P.M., Saturday 10 A.M.–5 P.M., and Sunday 10 A.M.–4 P.M. in the summer, with variable off-season hours. Check out the old gambling equipment, the "Moorish queen" from the Chicago World's Fair of 1893, the Native artifacts (including a 19th-century Tlingit canoe and an amazing seal-gut parka), the colorful duck-neck feather quilt, and Soapy Smith's derringer. Several videos are available if you want to know more about the characters in Skagway's past. Entrance costs $2 for adults, $1 for students, and free for under age 13.

North of Town
The historic Gold Rush Cemetery sits right beside the railroad tracks two miles north of town. The largest monument is Frank Reid's, while Soapy Smith only rates a wooden plank. While you're here, be sure to follow the short trail above the cemetery to scenic **Lower Reid Falls.** City-run SMART buses will take you as far as 23rd Avenue for $1.50 each way; from there it's an almost-level stroll to the cemetery.

Continue out the Klondike Highway and cross the bridge over Skagway River. On the left is **Jewell Gardens** (907/983-2111, www.jewellgardens.com, open early May–Sept.), with a very impressive collection of flowers and vegetables plus a garden railroad for model train enthusiasts. Tours cost $14, including round-trip transportation from downtown, or pay $9 for adults, $4 for kids, to just walk around on your own. The café serves nasturtium cucumber tea sandwiches and other garden treats.

Dyea
Located nine miles northwest of Skagway, the ghost town of Dyea is the starting point for the famed Chilkoot Trail. The old town site sits at the head of Taiya Inlet. During the Klondike gold rush of 1898, Dyea was where miners began the long trek into the Yukon Territory, and at its peak, the town provided a temporary home to some 10,000 people. Two factors caused Dyea to disappear: a devastating avalanche on Chilkoot Pass in April of 1898, and the completion of the White Pass & Yukon Route Railroad in 1899. Just four years later, only a half-dozen people lived in Dyea.

Little remains to be seen at Dyea except for the **Slide Cemetery,** where 45 men and women who died in the Palm Sunday avalanche of 1898 are buried. Walk through the forests that now cover old Dyea to find a few crumbling buildings and wharf pilings extending into the bay. Hard to imagine that this was once Alaska's largest city! The town site is now part of Klondike Gold Rush National Historical Park, and not far from old Dyea is the trailhead for the Chilkoot Trail and the free **Dyea Campground.**

The Park Service leads free 1.5-hour **walking tours** (907/983-2921) of the old Dyea town site Wednesday–Sunday at 2 P.M. in the summer, but you'll need to find your own transportation from Skagway.

ENTERTAINMENT AND EVENTS
Entertainment
Skagway's best-known boozing establishment, the **Red Onion** (2nd Ave. and Broadway, 907/983-2222), delivers live tunes most summer afternoons courtesy of musicians off the cruise ships. The bar, mirrors, and stove are from the time it served as both a saloon and brothel. But don't believe any tall tales about ghosts; they're all made up for the tourists. The Red Onion is now entirely non-smoking. If you want to get down and dirty and start drinking with the locals at 10 A.M., head across the street and up the block to **Moe's Frontier Bar. Bonanza Bar & Grill** (3rd Ave.

and Broadway, 907/983-6214) has pool tables, microbrews, and sports on the TVs—if you can tolerate the pall of smoke.

The most fun thing to do at night is to attend the **Days of '98 Show** (6th Ave. and Broadway, 907/983-2545, www.alaskan.com/daysof98) in the Fraternal Order of Eagles building. The great-granddaddy of them all, this production is the oldest running theater in Alaska—over 80 years! Matinees are offered most summer days at 10:30 A.M. and 2:30 P.M., and full evening performances start at 7 P.M. Warm-up gambling with "Soapy money" comes first, then the show goes on at 8. The cost is $16 for adults, $8 for kids under 16. Splurge on this one—it's worth the cash.

"Buckwheat" Donahue, a memorable local character (and head of the Skagway Convention and Visitors Bureau), occasionally recites "The Cremation of Sam McGee," "The Shooting of Dan McGrew," and other Robert Service ballads at the Park Service building on Broadway. It's a first-rate show, and Buckwheat always knows how to make people laugh. Free, and worth every penny.

Events

Skagway's first July 4th in 1898 was celebrated with the outlaw Soapy Smith leading the parade on a white horse; he was dead four days later. **July 4th** is still a big day, with a huge parade (locals call it the best in Alaska) and other events. **Soapy Smith's Wake** on July 8 toasts the conman's life and death at the Eagles Hall. The less savory aspects of the wake have been (officially at least) deleted from the program, but certain individuals may still join in after massive consumption of cheap champagne.

The **Klondike Trail of '98 International Road Relay** (www.sportyukon.com) takes place in early September, with more than a 150 teams composed of 10 runners each competing over a grueling 110-mile course from Skagway to Whitehorse.

The main winter event is the **Buckwheat Ski Classic,** a cross-country ski race that attracts both serious competitors and rank amateurs (including the "lazy and infirm") each March.

RECREATION

Rent a quality mountain bike from **Sockeye Cycle** (5th Ave. near Broadway, 907/983-2851, www.cyclealaska.com), which also offers a speedy ride down White Pass: Sockeye drives you up and you roll back down on the bikes for $75. Another popular option includes a train ride up to Fraser, followed by a downhill ride to town for $175. A 2.5-hour Dyea bike tour is $75. **Sourdough Car Rental** (6th Ave. and Broadway, 907/983-2523) also rents bikes, including tandems.

Chilkoot Horseback Adventures (907/983-3990, www.chilkoothorseback.com) has 3.5-hour horseback rides up historic Dyea Valley for $155. The same folks (www.alaskasleddog.com) also offer sleddog cart rides at Dyea for $109.

Nearby Hiking

A network of well-marked trails on the slopes just east of town offers excellent day hikes and a place to warm up for the Chilkoot Trail. Cross the small footbridge and railroad tracks beyond the end of 3rd and 4th Avenues, then follow the pipeline up the hill. **Lower Dewey Lake** is a 20-minute climb that gains 500 feet in elevation. A trail right around the lake branches at the south end off to **Sturgill's Landing** (3.5 miles) on Taiya Inlet. **Upper Dewey Lake** and the **Devil's Punchbowl** are a steep 2.5-mile climb from the north end of the lower lake. Icy Lake is a relatively level two miles from the lower lake, but the trail to **Upper Reid Falls** is steep and hard to follow. A number of clearings with picnic tables surround the lower lake where camping is possible; more are at the other lakes and Sturgill's Landing.

At 2nd Avenue and Alaska Street, go around the airport and take the footbridge over Skagway River. A short hike goes left to beautiful **Yakutania Point,** with views down Taiya Inlet. Go right and head steeply up to the Dyea Road; you'll see the trailhead in a mile for **A.B. Mountain,** named for the Arctic Brotherhood—the letters *AB* are supposedly visible in snow patches each spring. This five-mile hike is steep and strenuous; the summit is 5,100 feet above your starting point (sea level).

The Forest Service maintains a refurbished rail car as the **Denver Caboose Cabin** ($35). This attractive old caboose is six miles north of Skagway near where the railroad crosses the East Fork of the Skagway River. Access is by foot, or the WP&YR train will drop you off for $60 round-trip. Take your binoculars to scan nearby slopes for mountain goats. The **Denver Glacier Trail** begins right beside the caboose, and climbs five miles and 1,200 feet to Denver Glacier. It's a beautiful hike through subalpine fir, paper birch, cottonwood, spruce, and other trees.

Another excellent hiking option begins at Glacier Station (14 miles north of Skagway). Have the WP&YR train drop you off here, and then hike up the easy two-mile trail that leads to a Forest Service cabin near **Laughton Glacier** ($35). Flag down the train to return. Make cabin reservations for either the caboose or cabin at 518/885-3639 or 877/444-6777, www.reserveusa.com.

Located at the Mountain Shop in Skagway, **Packer Expeditions** (907/983-2544, www.packerexpeditions.com) leads guided hikes in the Skagway area, including day trips, and multi-day hikes over Chilkoot Pass. Its most popular trip combines a helicopter flight over the Juneau Icefield with a four-mile hike to Laughton Glacier, followed by a train ride back to town. The cost is $300 for this 5.5-hour trip that is mainly for cruise shippies.

On the Water

A number of companies offer charter fishing out of Skagway; get their brochures in the downtown visitor center or find them at www.skagway.com.

Skagway Float Tours (907/983-3688, www.skagwayfloat.com) has easy three-hour float trips down the Taiya River for $75 ($55 kids). A combination trip that includes a one-hour hike up the first part of the Chilkoot Trail followed by a float down the river is $85 for adults, $65 for kids. The company also has a variety of other hiking, floating, and tour options.

Flightseeing

Skagway Air (907/983-2218, www.skagway

air.com) does 90-minute Glacier Bay flightseeing trips for $150 per person, and 45-minute gold rush tours to Lake Bennett for $100. **Temsco Helicopter** (907/983-2900 or 866/683-2900, www.temscoair.com) offers 80-minute "glacier discovery" flights ($250) that include a guided 40-minute glacier hike, and a tour that includes an hour on the Denver Glacier where you get to practice dogsledding ($420).

ACCOMMODATIONS

If you're heading here in midsummer, try to make reservations at least two weeks ahead of time to be sure of a room. Visit www.skagway.com for links to local lodging places.

Hostel

The delightful **Skagway Home Hostel** (3rd Ave. and Main St., 907/983-2131, www.skagwayhostel.com) is right in town. Built more than a century ago, the home was once owned by the marshall who arrested the Soapy Smith gang after the shoot-out. An 11 P.M. curfew may put a crimp in your social life, but the owners are very friendly and the hostel is open year-round. There's space for only 12, so reserve ahead. Registration is 5–9 P.M., but late ferry arrivals are accommodated. The hostel has a kitchen, commons area, showers, laundry, bag storage, and free guest computer. Bunks are $15–20, and a couple's room costs $50 d. The owners offer family-style, shared lunches, and mostly vegetarian dinners ($5). Reservations highly advised.

Hotels

Sgt. Preston's Lodge (6th Ave. and State St., 907/983-2521 or 866/983-2521, www.sgtprestonslodgeskagway.com) is a tidy 35-room motel right in town, with clean, nicely remodeled rooms, and free Wi-Fi. Budget units are $80 s or $90 d, and moderately priced spacious rooms cost $95–108 s or $105–115 d. Families appreciate the two-bedroom apartment units ($150 for up to five) with full kitchens.

You might also check out the new units at **4th St. Hotel** (444 4th St., 907/983-3200, www.skagwaypizzastation.com, $75–120 d), located over Pizza Station Restaurant. No TVs or phones, except in the suite ($200 d).

Skagway's largest lodging place is the seasonally open **Westmark Inn** (3rd Ave. and Broadway, 907/983-2291 or 800/544-0970, www .westmarkhotels.com, $119 d) with all the charm of a retirement home; you might feel you were in one, given the cruise ship folks. Grossly overpriced.

Bed-and-Breakfasts

Hosted by longtime Alaskan Tara Mallory, **Mile Zero B&B** (9th Ave. at Main St., 907/983-3045, www.mile-zero.com, $135 d) is a modern seven-room B&B with six large rooms, private entrances and baths, covered porches, a cozy parlor, continental breakfast, and Wi-Fi.

Located within one of the town's oldest buildings, **Skagway Inn B&B** (7th Ave. and Broadway, 907/983-2289 or 888/752-4929, www.skagwayinn.com, open mid-May–mid-Sept.) served through the years as a bordello, a residence, a boarding house, and now as a delightful inn. Six guest rooms ($149–189 d) have private baths, and the others (99–$119 d) share three baths. A full hot breakfast is served downstairs.

Built in 1902 and completely rebuilt after a fire, **The White House Inn** (8th Ave. and Main St., 907/983-9000, www.atthewhitehouse.com, $120–145 d) is a large plantation-style home with 10 guest rooms, one of which is wheelchair accessible. All rooms feature a country Victorian decor, with private baths and continental breakfasts.

Chilkoot Trail Outpost (907/983-3799, www.chilkoottrailoutpost.com) is a modern lodge eight miles out Dyea Road. Eight cabins are available, all with private baths and kitchenettes; $138 d in duplex cabins, or $165 d for deluxe units with queen beds. A full buffet breakfast is included, along with evening campfires, but you'll need to find your own transport from town. Guests can use the screened-in gazebo cooking area for other meals, or pay $25 for a tasty picnic dinner. Because of its location, this lodge is popular with hikers setting out for the Chilkoot Trail; the trailhead is just a half-mile away. Free Wi-Fi too.

Cabins

Two miles from downtown Skagway, **Cindy's Place** (907/983-2674 or 800/831-8095, www .alaska.net/~croland, open May–Sept.) includes two modern cabins with private baths, microwave, and mini-fridge for $120 d. Also available is a tiny cabin with a toilet (but no shower) for $35 s or $49 d; it will look like luxury if you just got off the Chilkoot Trail. Breakfast fixin's are provided, along with a courtesy shuttle to town, and access to the hot tub.

Another place with cabins on the way to Dyea is **Skagway Bungalows** (907/983-2986, www.aptalaska.net/~saldi, open March–Oct., $125 d). It's a mile from town, and the two in-the-woods cabins have private baths, fridges, and microwaves.

CAMPING

The Park Service maintains a peaceful campground ($6) at **Dyea,** northeast of Skagway. It is especially popular with hikers along the Chilkoot Trail. You'll need to bring water or filter it from the river. For those without wheels, hitching is possible, or contact one of the local taxi companies for a ride. Showers are available from local RV parks or at the small boat harbor.

Skagway's three private campgrounds are all priced around $16 for tents and $29 for RVs, and are open seasonally. **Skagway Mountain View RV Park** (14th Ave. and Broadway, 907/983-3333 or 888/778-7700, www.alaskarv.com) is the in-town tenters' campground, with wooded sites, toilets, showers, and Wi-Fi. The narrow-gauge tracks border the grounds, making this a good place for photo opportunities. **Pullen Creek RV Park** (907/983-2768 or 800/936-3731, www.pullencreekrv.com) is next to the harbor and cruise ship dock. This is great if you like being in the heart of the action, with steam engines, cruise ships, and shopping, but not so great if you're looking for a quieter, more natural setting. **Garden City RV Park** (16th Ave. and State St., 907/983-2378 or 866/983-

2378, www.gardencityrv.com) is little more than a parking lot with bathhouse.

FOOD

With so many visitors flashing the cash, Skagway's high meal prices should come as no surprise. But at least the variety and quality are considerably higher than what you'll find in Wrangell!

Breakfast and Lunch

Corner Café (4th Ave. and State St., 907/983-2155) is the local greasy spoon, with burgers and pizzas, plus reasonable breakfasts and fast service—if you don't mind all the cigarette smoke. A better bet (smoke-free) is **Sweet Tooth Café** (3rd Ave. and Broadway, 907/983-2405, daily 6 A.M.–3 P.M.), with good all-American breakfasts and lunches. Both Corner Café and the Sweet Tooth stay open year-round; most other eateries close when the cruise ships flee to the Caribbean.

At **C** **Alaska Gourmet Café** (361 5th Ave., 907/983-2448, www.akgourmet.com, $7–11) owner Lara Cavanelli serves up an eclectic world of flavors: enormous bowls of kosher sockeye salmon chowder, Indian samosas with chutney, Aussie meat pies, smoked turkey sandwiches on homemade bread, fair-trade espresso (best in town), and even fresh sushi. Great breakfasts, too. Locals know about this place, so it gets packed for lunch.

Haven Café (9th Ave. and State St., 907/983-3554, www.haven-cafe.com, open year-round, $7–10) is far enough off the tourist path to be mainly for locals, and they like it that way. It's a great place for homemade granola, breakfast sandwiches, paninis, salads, soups, espresso, and even Wi-Fi (fee). Come back Sunday evenings for live music.

Other places worth a visit include **Glacial Smoothies & Espresso** (336 3rd Ave., 907/983-3223) and **Skagway Pizza Station** (444 4th Ave., 907/983-2220, www.pizzastation .eskagway.com). Both are open year-round.

Dinner

Skagway Fish Company (907/983-3474, daily May–Sept.) is the tent-like structure near the cruise ship dock and facing the small boat harbor. The menu includes T-bone steaks, pork chops, BBQ ribs, oysters, and fresh salmon or halibut, but I recommend the halibut fish and chips ($13). The fish is locally caught, and it comes with a pile of fries and homemade coleslaw. Good strawberry cheesecake too.

Skagway Inn (7th Ave. at Broadway, 907/983-2289 or 888/752-4929, www.skagwayinn.com) puts on a three-hour **Alaska Garden and Gourmet Tour** for $60 where you can watch chef and owner Karl Klupar prepare a delicious three-course seafood meal. **Red Onion Saloon** (2nd Ave. and Broadway, 907/983-2222) serves surprisingly good pizzas, chili, and sandwiches in a historic setting.

Stowaway Café (907/983-3463, $16–27 entrées) is where locals (and tourists) go for good food in a harborside setting. There's even a big deck for sunny days. The café specializes in seafood of all types, and the wasabi salmon is always great, but also serves everything from smoked ribs to steaks. Be sure to ask about the daily specials. Reservations advised for dinner.

Starfire Grill (4th Ave. and Spring St., 907/983-3663, $11–13) serves excellent Thai lunches, chicken satay, curries, potstickers, soups, and pad Thai. The express menu is great if you're in a hurry. Starfire closes at 4 P.M.

Groceries

Fairway Market (4th Ave. and State St., 907/983-2220) is Skagway's grocery store. Fresh produce arrives on Tuesdays, and may be wiped out by the weekend.

You Say Tomato (2075 State St., 907/983-2784) is a little natural-foods market with freshly baked breads and locally grown produce for reasonable prices.

INFORMATION AND SERVICES

Both the Park Service Visitor Center and the Skagway Visitors Information Center are described in *Sights*. The small **town library** (8th Ave. and State St., 907/983-2665) offers free reading material on the paperback racks inside, and you can check your email on its computers. Rent computer time at **Glacial Smoothies** (336 3rd Ave., 907/983-3223) or **Ports of Call** (363 2nd Ave., 907/983-2411). Both places also serve light meals.

Mountain Shop (4th Ave. between Broadway and State St., 907/983-2544, www.packer expeditions.com) is the outfitter in town, and also sells supplies for the trail. Books are available from **Skaguay News Depot** (Broadway, 907/983-3354, www.skagwaybooks.com).

One of Alaska's oldest bank buildings, **Wells Fargo** (6th Ave. and Broadway), changes green dollars into multicolored Canadian dollars, and has an ATM.

The **Skagway Recreation Center** (13th and Main Sts., 907/983-2679, www.skagway recreation.org, $5/day) is a surprisingly impressive place in such a small town, with a gym, weight room, cardio room, climbing wall, skate park, and various classes.

For medical emergencies, **Skagway Medical Clinic** (11th Ave. and Broadway, 907/983-2255) has a physician's assistant on staff.

GETTING THERE
On the Water
Skagway is the northern terminus of the Alaska Marine Highway ferry system (907/465-3941 or 800/642-0066, www.ferryalaska.com), and ferries arrive daily during the summer, stopping at the **ferry terminal** (907/983-2941), just a block from downtown.

Alaska Fjordlines (907/766-3395 or 800/320-0146, www.alaskafjordlines.com) operates the *Fjord Express,* a large and stable high-speed catamaran with daily summertime runs from Skagway to Haines and then on to Auke Bay in Juneau. The boat leaves Skagway at 8 A.M., arrives in Juneau at 11:30 A.M., and then heads back at 5 P.M., returning to Skagway at 8:15 P.M. The cost is $139 round trip, including a bus to downtown Juneau. A light breakfast and dinner are included, and the boat stops for wildlife and photo opportunities. This passenger-only ferry is very popular with RVers who want to see Juneau in a day. One-way trips and overnight stays in Juneau

are allowed; reservations recommended. This is an efficiently run and friendly operation.

Chilkat Cruises (907/766-2100 or 888/766-2103, www.chilkatcruises.com) offers high-speed catamaran service between Haines and Skagway, with several departures a day mid-May–mid-September. The cost is $51 round-trip ($25 for kids). The boat does not stop on any of these trips for wildlife viewing or photos, but does have a few snacks on board.

Air
Three companies have daily flights connecting Skagway with Juneau and Haines: **Skagway Air** (907/983-2218, www.skagway air.com), **Wings of Alaska** (907/983-2442, www.wingsofalaska.com), and **L.A.B. Flying Service** (907/983-2471, www.labflying.com).

Long-Distance Buses
Yukon Alaska Tourist Tours (867/668-5947 in Whitehorse or 866/626-7383, www.yatt.ca) has a daily bus to Whitehorse ($65), along with a mix of bus/train combo tours. In Whitehorse, catch the **Alaska Direct Bus Line** (867/668-4833 in Whitehorse or 800/770-6652, www.alaskadirectbusline.com) for service north to Anchorage or Fairbanks.

GETTING AROUND
City-run **SMART** (Skagway Municipal and Regional Transit) buses (907/983-2743, www.skagwaytransit.com) run daily, shuttling from the cruise dock into town out to 23rd Avenue (access to the gold rush cemetery). The one-way cost is $1.50. Buses run continuously 7:30 A.M.–9 P.M. May–September.

Several local tour outfits offer drop-off services for hikers heading up the Chilkoot Trail and for campers staying at Dyea: **Dyea Dave's** (907/209-5031), **Frontier Excursions** (907/983-2512 or 877/983-2512, www.frontierexcursions.com), and **Klondike Taxi** (907/983-2400).

Rent new cars from **Avis** (2nd Ave. and Spring St., 907/983-2247 or 800/331-1212), or used vehicles from **Sourdough Car Rental** (6th Ave. and Broadway, 907/983-2523). If you're driving to Whitehorse, stick with Avis since Sourdough hits you with $0.25 per mile after 100 miles. **Skagway Classic Cars** (907/983-2886, www.skagwayclassiccars.com) has immaculate cars from the 1950s and '60s, with chaufered trips around town for $33 per hour.

Tours

Given the influx of tourists to Skagway, it's no surprise to find a multitude of tour options. The most unique local tours are aboard the canary-yellow 1920s vintage White Motor Company cars run by **Skagway Street Car Company** (907/983-2908, www.skagwaystreetcar.com). The complete two-hour trip costs $40 ($20 kids), but most seats are pre-sold to cruise ship passengers. To be sure of a spot, book a week in advance. This is one of the few Alaskan guided tours that I'd actually recommend.

A number of other companies also offer van tours around the area; get their brochures at the visitor center. These typically cost $25 for a 2.5-hour trip that includes the town of Skagway and White Pass Summit; some take an alternate route to the Chilkoot Trailhead and Dyea, or a longer trip into the Yukon.

Skagway Carriage Company (907/723-3117) provides a completely different sort of tour: horse-drawn carriage rides around town. Just look for the carriages on Broadway.

CHILKOOT TRAIL

One of the best reasons for coming to Skagway is the historic and surprisingly scenic 33-mile Chilkoot Trail. During the gold rush of 1897–1898, what had once been an Indian route from the tidewater at Dyea to the headwaters of the Yukon River became a trail for thousands of men and women. Today, the trail is hiked by several thousand hardy souls each summer, along with a few insane wintertime trekkers. The western portion of this route lies within **Klondike Gold Rush National Historical Park,** while the eastern half is managed by Parks Canada as **Chilkoot Trail National Historic Park.** All hikers crossing the border must clear Canadian Customs, so an official ID (preferably a passport) is needed.

THE CHILKOOT TRAIL

A minimum of three days and nights (but preferably four or five) is needed to hike from Dyea to Bennett over 3,246-foot-high Chilkoot Pass. This is no easy Sunday outing: You must be fit and well prepared. It is best to hike north from Dyea rather than south from Bennett since this is the historic route, and a descent down the "Golden Stairs" can be dangerous.

You will be above the tree line and totally exposed to the elements during the 11 miles from Sheep Camp to Deep Lake (the hardest stretch). Weather conditions can change quickly along the trail, and hikers need to be prepared for strong winds, cold, low fog, rain, and snow, even in mid-summer. Because of the rain-shadow effect, the Canadian side is considerably drier than the Alaskan side. Mosquitoes and other insects are an annoyance, and snowfields linger between Sheep Camp and Happy Camp well into the summer. Despite these challenges, for scenery and historical value the Chilkoot Trail is unsurpassed in Alaska and western Canada.

Flora and Fauna

The vegetation changes from coastal rainforest up the Taiya Valley to alpine tundra as you approach the pass and rise above the 2,700-foot level. On the drier Canadian side you'll find an open boreal forest of alpine fir and lodgepole pine. Although black bears are often seen along the trail, there has never been an attack on a hiker. Help keep it this way by storing food and garbage properly.

History

It took each would-be miner an average of three months and dozens of trips back and forth from cache to cache to pack his required ton of supplies into Canada. By the spring of 1898, three aerial tramways were operating on the Chilkoot. The thousands of stampeders stopped at Lindeman and Bennett, built boats and rafts, and waited for spring break-up, which would allow them to sail the 900 kilometers to Dawson City along a series of lakes and rivers. When the ice broke up in May 1898, some 7,124 boats and rafts sailed

from the shores of Lakes Lindeman and Bennett. Mounted Police records show 28,000 people traveling from Bennett to Dawson in 1898. Ironically, by the time they got to Dawson every claim in the Klondike was already staked. By 1900, the railway had opened from Skagway to Whitehorse, and Dyea and the Chilkoot Trail became ghost towns.

The Route

The Chilkoot Trail begins just before the bridge over the Taiya River at Dyea, nine miles northwest of Skagway. The first section of the trail traverses lush rainforests along the Taiya River. Artifacts from the gold rush litter parts of the path here, including bits of clothing, rusting stoves, pulleys, cables, and old wagons. At **Canyon City,** 7.5 miles from the trailhead, a short side trail and a suspension bridge across the Taiya River provide access to the remains of one of the settlements that sprang up during the rush to the Klondike. You'll find a number of artifacts here, including a boiler that powered tramways to haul supplies over the summit. Beyond this, the trail climbs steeply to another long-abandoned settlement, **Sheep Camp** (Mile 13), where a ranger is in residence nearby all summer.

Beyond Sheep Camp, the trek becomes far more challenging as the route takes hikers through a narrow valley before heading above tree line. Artifacts—including metal telegraph poles and pieces from an old tramway used to haul goods up the mountain—become more common as you climb past "The Scales" (Mile 16), where packers reweighed their loads and increased their fee for the difficult final climb. Modern-day hikers start to wonder about their sanity at this point, since the infamous "Golden Stairs" lie ahead; the name came from the steps carved in the ice and the snow by the miners. During the winter of 1897–1898 thousands of prospectors carried their heavy loads to the 3,535-foot summit of **Chilkoot Pass.** Photos of men going up here in single file are still the best-known images of the gold rush. Today, hikers struggle up this 45-degree slope with full backpacks. Snow generally covers the pass until mid-July, and can be waist-deep early in the summer.

Avalanches can occur before early July, and avalanche transceivers are recommended. Ask at the Trail Center for current snow conditions and other hazards. A warming hut provides protection from the weather once you cross into British Columbia; Parks Canada wardens here check to make sure you have a permit.

After the challenging summit climb, hikers are rewarded with easier hiking and spectacular vistas (when weather permits), but it's still a long distance to the end of the trail. Many hikers camp at **Deep Lake** (Mile 23), while others continue on to **Lindeman Lake** (Mile 26) for the night. A Canada Parks warden station and warming huts are at Lindeman. During the stampede, thousands of miners halted along the shores of this lake, quickly forming the town of Lindeman City. Here they built boats for the journey down the Yukon River to the Klondike gold fields. Reminders of the gold rush can be found in the countryside here, and a small cemetery marks the final stop for those who never made it to the Klondike.

Beyond Lindeman, the trail climbs a ridge overlooking the lake and then splits, with one path turning south to meet the Klondike Highway at **Log Cabin,** where you can catch a bus back to Skagway or Whitehorse. Those who continue straight at the junction will reach a pretty place called **Bennett** on the shores of Lake Bennett. Only one family lives here today, but hikers will enjoy exploring the log church built by the miners and a grand White Pass & Yukon Route Railroad depot. Most hikers end their trip here, catching the train back to Skagway.

Hiking Permits

Backcountry permits are required of hikers on the Chilkoot, and the number of hikers is limited. The U.S. permit is C$20, and permits for the Canadian side cost an additional C$35. For trail information, maps (including an excellent *Hiker's Guide to the Chilkoot Trail*), a helpful listing of transportation options, and backcountry permits, contact the Park Service's **Chilkoot Trail Center** (907/983-9234, www.nps.gov/klgo, daily late May–early Sept.

8 A.M.–5 P.M.) in the historic Martin Itjen house in Skagway. You can also buy trail permits through Parks Canada in Whitehorse (867/667-3910 or 800/661-0486, www.pc.gc.ca/chilkoot).

Most permits are reserved months ahead of time (C$12 extra), but eight permits are reserved for walk-ins each day at 1 P.M. In July and August, folks without permits start lining up at the Trail Center by 11 A.M. to be sure of a spot. At other times you won't have a problem getting onto the trail even at the last minute, but call the Trail Center for the latest situation.

Practicalities

Official campgrounds—most with tent platforms, outhouses, cooking shelters, and bear-proof food storage—are at nine sites along the Chilkoot Trail in addition to the one at the Dyea Trailhead; most popular are those at Canyon City (Mile 7.5), Sheep Camp (Mile 12), Happy Camp (Mile 21), Lindeman City (Mile 26), and Bennett (Mile 33). Campfires are permitted only at Canyon City and Sheep Camp. There are shelters with woodstoves at Canyon City, Sheep Camp, and Lindeman, but these are for drying out only (not overnighting). Everything along the trail dating from the gold rush (even a rusty old tin can) is protected by law, and there are severe penalties for those who damage or remove items.

Everyone entering Canada must clear Canadian Customs. If you come in along the Chilkoot Trail and do not speak to an official at either Whitehorse or Fraser, you should report at the first opportunity to either the RCMP in Carcross or the Immigration Office (open Mon.–Fri.) at the Federal Building in Whitehorse.

Getting There

Several Skagway companies offer drop-off services ($10) from town for hikers heading up the Chilkoot Trail. Best known is **Dyea Dave's** (907/209-5031), but similar services are available from **Frontier Excursions** (907/983-2512 or 877/983-2512, www.frontierexcursions.com) and **Klondike Taxi** 9907/983-2400).

The WP&YR's **Chilkoot Trail Hikers Service** (907/983-2217 or 800/343-7373, www.whitepassrailroad.com) provides a shuttle train on Fridays, Sundays, and Mondays from Bennett to Fraser ($50) or Skagway ($90). Make advance reservations since space is limited. Meals are available at the Bennett station.

Although most hikers choose the train, some prefer (or have no option because the rail bus is full or the timing doesn't work out) to hike out along the railroad tracks from the Lindeman area to Log Cabin, where they catch a **Yukon Alaska Tourist Tours** (867/668-5947 in Whitehorse or 866/626-7383, www.yatt.ca) bus, or get a ride with Dyea Dave, Frontier Excursions, or Klondike Taxi for around $25; advance reservations essential. A final option is to fly by floatplane from Lake Bennett to Whitehorse via **Alpine Aviation** (867/668-7725, www.alpineaviationyukon.com).

THE KLONDIKE HIGHWAY

This 98-mile road from Skagway to the Alaska Highway 21 miles south of Whitehorse closely follows the White Pass & Yukon Route rail line built at the turn of the century. The 65-mile stretch north to Carcross was opened in 1981, completing the route started by the U.S. Army in 1942 from the Alaska Highway south to Carcross. The road ascends quickly from sea level at Skagway to White Pass at 3,290 feet in 14 miles. Many turnouts provide views across the canyon of the narrow-gauge White Pass & Yukon Route track, waterfalls, gorges, and long dropoffs—if you're lucky and the weather cooperates. At the summit, **Canadian Customs** welcomes you to British Columbia, and is open 24 hours a day in the summer, and 8 A.M.–midnight at other times; set your watch ahead an hour to Pacific Time on the Canadian side. U.S. Customs is open 24 hours a day year-round.

ANCHORAGE AND VICINITY

Texas always seemed so big, but you know you're in the largest State in the Union when you're anchored down in Anchorage ....

– from "Anchored Down in Anchorage"
by Michelle Shocked

It's hard to arrive in Anchorage (pop. 277,000) without some strong preconceived notions of what to expect—especially if you've been traveling around the state for a while. Generally, Alaskans either love or hate Anchorage, and their degree of affection or distaste is usually revealed by their chosen proximity to the city. You'll certainly have heard of Anchorage's urban sprawl, its traffic jams, sprouting apartment buildings and condos, corporate skyscrapers, mall mania, fast-food frenzy, and crime; in other words, that it's the antithesis of every virtue and value that God-fearing, law-abiding, and patriotic Alaskans hold sacred. And you've probably also heard the old joke about being "able to see Alaska from Anchorage." You might also have been told that Anchorage has nothing to offer travelers, and that if you're looking for a true *Alaskan* experience, you should avoid the city altogether. Don't believe everything you hear; Anchorage is an attraction of its own and definitely worth some time.

Anchorage can be an eminently enjoyable *and* affordable place in which to hang out. It certainly has one of the most flower-filled downtowns of any American city; visitors are always impressed with the summertime bounty of blooms. You can easily fill a whole day touring downtown, or just lying around a park for the one day in four that the sun

© DON PITCHER

HIGHLIGHTS

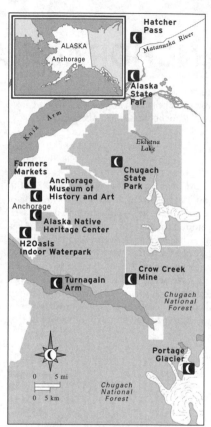

◖ Anchorage Museum of History and Art: One of Alaska's top museums, and it's right downtown. Fascinating exhibits and a fine lunchtime café too (page 178).

◖ Alaska Native Heritage Center: Learn about the state's Native peoples through exhibits, demonstrations, and cultural presentations. Free shuttle from the downtown visitor center (page 183).

◖ H2Oasis Indoor Waterpark: Older kids love the Master Blaster ride, but there's something for all ages in this surprisingly large year-round funhouse (page 191).

◖ Farmers Markets: Now covering Saturdays and Sundays all summer, this downtown gathering is packed with Alaskan arts and crafts, great finger-food, and live music. Don't miss it (page 205).

◖ Chugach State Park: Who would imagine that you could get into the wilderness so quickly from Anchorage? Lots of wonderful hiking trails here, especially the climb up Flattop Mountain (page 211).

◖ Turnagain Arm: South from Anchorage, the highway skirts the shore of this long inlet where you can watch for beluga whales and bore tides or turn around to see Dall sheep on the cliffs behind. Nearby Potter Marsh is great for birding (page 213).

◖ Crow Creek Mine: Just a few miles from Alyeska Ski Resort in Girdwood are picture-perfect log cabins from this authentic old mine where your might find flakes of gold – or nuggets – in the creek (page 215).

◖ Portage Glacier: Fifty miles south of Anchorage, this is one of the state's most-visited glaciers. A boat tour across Portage Lake leaves hourly from the visitor center (page 218).

◖ Alaska State Fair: Where else can you find a demolition derby, supersized turkey legs, enormous peonies, and 90-pound cabbages?

LOOK FOR ◖ TO FIND RECOMMENDED SIGHTS, ACTIVITIES, DINING, AND LODGING.

Take the special Alaska Railroad trains to avoid the traffic jams (page 223).

◖ Hatcher Pass: This beautiful area of the Mat-Su Valley region is perfect for hiking in the summer or cross-country skiing when the snow flies. Take time to explore the weathered old buildings of Independence Mine State Historical Park (page 231).

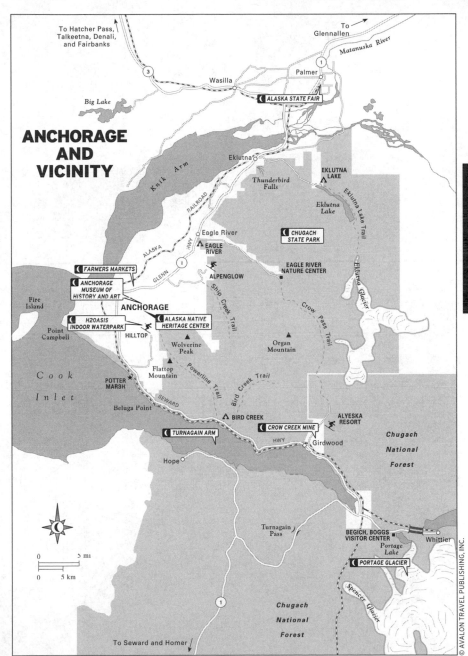

ANCHORAGE AND VICINITY

To Hatcher Pass, Talkeetna, Denali, and Fairbanks

To Glennallen

Matanuska River

Big Lake

Wasilla

Palmer

ALASKA STATE FAIR

Knik Arm

Eklutna

Thunderbird Falls

EKLUTNA LAKE

Eklutna Lake

Eklutna Lake Trail

RAILROAD

ALASKA HWY

Eagle River

EAGLE RIVER

ALPENGLOW

CHUGACH STATE PARK

EAGLE RIVER NATURE CENTER

Eklutna Glacier

GLENN

FARMERS MARKETS

ANCHORAGE MUSEUM OF HISTORY AND ART

Fire Island

ANCHORAGE

H2OASIS INDOOR WATERPARK

ALASKA NATIVE HERITAGE CENTER

Point Campbell

HILLTOP

Ship Creek Trail

Crow Pass Trail

Wolverine Peak

Organ Mountain

Cook Inlet

Flattop Mountain

Powerline Trail

Bird Creek Trail

POTTER MARSH

SEWARD

Beluga Point

BIRD CREEK

CROW CREEK MINE

ALYESKA RESORT

Chugach National Forest

TURNAGAIN ARM

HWY

Girdwood

Hope

Turnagain Pass

BEGICH, BOGGS VISITOR CENTER

Portage Lake

Whittier

PORTAGE GLACIER

Spencer Glacier

0   5 mi

0   5 km

1

Chugach National Forest

To Seward and Homer

© AVALON TRAVEL PUBLISHING, INC.

ANCHORAGE AND VICINITY

ANCHORAGE AND VICINITY

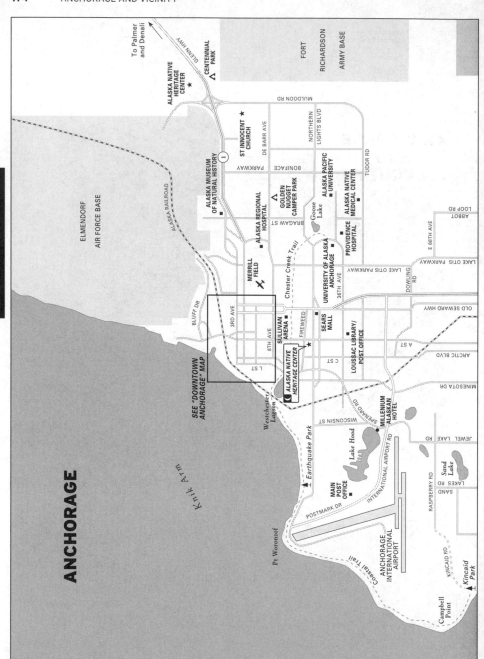

ANCHORAGE

To Palmer and Denali

GLENN HWY

ALASKA NATIVE HERITAGE CENTER

CENTENNIAL PARK

FORT RICHARDSON ARMY BASE

MULDOON RD

ST INNOCENT CHURCH

DE BARR AVE

NORTHERN LIGHTS BLVD

ALASKA MUSEUM OF NATURAL HISTORY

PARKWAY

BONIFACE PARKWAY

ALASKA PACIFIC UNIVERSITY

TUDOR RD

ELMENDORF AIR FORCE BASE

ALASKA RAILROAD

ALASKA REGIONAL HOSPITAL

GOLDEN NUGGET CAMPER PARK

ALASKA NATIVE MEDICAL CENTER

BRAGAW ST

Goose Lake

ABBOT LOOP RD

PROVIDENCE HOSPITAL

E 88TH AVE

Chester Creek Trail

MERRILL FIELD

UNIVERSITY OF ALASKA ANCHORAGE

LAKE OTIS PARKWAY

DOWLING RD

BLUFF DR

3RD AVE

36TH AVE

OLD SEWARD HWY

8TH AVE

SULLIVAN ARENA

FIREWEED

SEARS MALL

A ST

SEE "DOWNTOWN ANCHORAGE" MAP

L ST

LOUSSAC LIBRARY/ POST OFFICE

C ST

ARCTIC BLVD

Westchester Lagoon

ALASKA NATIVE HERITAGE CENTER

MINESOTA DR

Knik Arm

Earthquake Park

SEWARD RD

WISCONSIN ST

MILLENIUM ALASKAN HOTEL

JEWEL LAKE RD

Lake Hood

INTERNATIONAL AIRPORT RD

Sand Lake

Pt Woronzof

MAIN POST OFFICE

POSTMARK DR

RASPBERRY RD

LAKES RD

SAND

Coastal Trail

ANCHORAGE INTERNATIONAL AIRPORT

KINCAID RD

Kincaid Park

Campbell Point

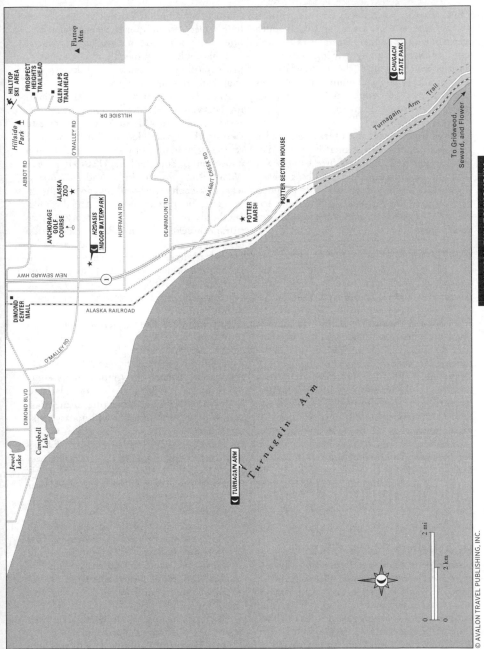

ANCHORAGE AND VICINITY

Flattop Mtn

CHUGACH STATE PARK

HILLTOP SKI AREA
PROSPECT HEIGHTS TRAILHEAD
GLEN ALPS TRAILHEAD

Turnagain Arm Trail

Hillside Park

HILLSIDE DR

O'MALLEY RD

ABBOT RD

RABBIT CREEK RD

To Girdwood, Seward, and Flower

ALASKA ZOO

H2OASIS INDOOR WATERPARK

POTTER SECTION HOUSE

ANCHORAGE GOLF COURSE

HUFFMAN RD

DEARMOUN RD

POTTER MARSH

NEW SEWARD HWY

1

DIMOND CENTER MALL

ALASKA RAILROAD

O'MALLEY RD

DIMOND BLVD

Campbell Lake

Jewel Lake

TURNAGAIN ARM

Turnagain Arm

2 mi

2 km

0

0

© AVALON TRAVEL PUBLISHING, INC.

shines. Explore Anchorage's far-flung corners such as the resort town of Girdwood south of Anchorage (popular for winter skiing and summer hiking), rapidly growing Matanuska-Susitna Valley (home to the towns of Palmer and Wasilla), and grand mountain country at Hatcher Pass. Or spend a day researching the many places to go from Anchorage and the best ways to get there.

Of course, if you can't overcome the idea that "Alaska population center" is a contradiction in terms, you can simply breeze into town, make your connection, and quickly "get back to Alaska." But if you want a fully rounded experience of the 49th state, get to know Anchorage, *urban* Alaska, and come to your own conclusions.

CLIMATE

Two of the deciding factors in choosing Anchorage as a main construction camp for the Alaska Railroad were mild winters and comparatively low precipitation. The towering Alaska Range shelters Cook Inlet Basin from the frigid winter breath of the Arctic northerlies; the Kenai and Chugach Mountains cast a rain shadow over the basin, allowing only 15–20 percent of the annual precipitation in communities on the windward side of the ranges. Anchorage receives around 20 inches of annual precipitation (10–12 in. of rain, 60–70 in. of snow), while Whittier, 40 miles away on the Gulf side of the Chugach, gets 175 inches. Anchorage's winter temperatures rarely drop much below 0°F, with only an occasional cold streak, compared with Fairbanks's frequent -40°F; its summer temperatures rarely rise above 65°F, compared with Fairbanks's 80s and 90s.

PLANNING YOUR TIME

Anchorage is an outstanding base for travelers to Alaska's heartland, with Denali National Park, the Kenai Peninsula, and a multitude of other attractions within a day's drive. The state's largest airport provides flights to all regions of the globe, and the Alaska Railroad has daily trains north to Denali and Fairbanks or south to Seward and Whittier. The city has long served as a hub for travelers, but it also offers many attractions not available elsewhere, and one could easily spend two or three days just exploring local museums, hiking trails, shops, and restaurants.

Anchorage's highlights include its outstanding **Museum of History and Art** (one of the state's best), the **Alaska Native Heritage Center,** the Alaska Heritage Museum, along with an abundance of good restaurants, hip coffeehouses, hopping bars, **H2Oasis Indoor Water Park** for the kids, and two minor league baseball teams—all that you might expect from the state's largest city. And don't forget the always-packed **Farmers Market** every summer weekend, with locally made crafts, tasty finger food, live music, and even a bit of fresh produce from the farmers. But with the natural beauty of Mt. McKinley and the Alaska Range visible beyond the city skyline on clear days, it's hard to forget that you're in Alaska.

And there are also attractions you would only find in an Alaskan city: a wonderful coastal trail that starts right downtown, great day-hiking in nearby **Chugach State Park,** fascinating **Turnagain Arm** with its enormous tides and beluga whales, and places to outfit yourself for any adventure in the Alaskan outdoors. Anchorage is within easy striking distance of some of the most exciting and extensive hiking, climbing, fishing, kayaking, river rafting, flightseeing, and wilderness areas. Budget travelers will enjoy reasonable food prices, inexpensive flights to the Lower 48, several hostels, and a good bus system.

Nearby to the south, the town of Girdwood is home to Alyeska Resort—Alaska's only significant ski area—and funky **Crow Creek Mine** where you still might find a gold nugget in your pan. A bit farther south is the much-photographed **Portage Glacier,** accessed by a tour boat from the Forest Service visitor center.

North of Anchorage the Glenn Highway passes a tiny Tanaina Native village where Eklutna Historical Park houses a picturesque graveyard filled with spirit houses before emerging in the Matanuska-Susitna Valley (Mat-Su, for short), where the pastures and farms of the past are giving way to homes and strip malls for folks fleeing Anchorage housing prices and crowding. The valley's two main towns are booming Wasilla and semi-rural Palmer, home to a fun musk ox farm and the **Alaska State Fair,** a 12-day blast in late August and early September. North of the valley, the Talkeetna Mountains rise abruptly, bisected by a road over Hatcher Pass, where **Independence Mine State Historical Park** provides a base for day hikes or wintertime skis.

Sights

It doesn't take long to get the hang of downtown Anchorage. The blocks are square, with the lettered streets (A through L) going north–south and the numbered avenues (starting at 2nd Ave. just up the hill from the tracks) running east–west. Once you get east of the lettered streets they start over again using alphabetized names (Barrow, Cordova, Denali, Eagle, Fairbanks).

Beyond downtown, the city of Anchorage sprawls across the Anchorage Bowl, with hillside homes peering down on the masses below. A number of neighborhoods are scattered around Anchorage, but most travelers are likely to spend their time in downtown and **Midtown.** The latter is a nondescript Anytown, USA, collection of malls, shopping centers, supermarkets, fast food joints, bars, movie theaters, discount stores, gas stations, and other businesses just a 20-minute walk or a 10-minute bus ride south of downtown. Midtown is encompassed by Northern Lights and Benson Boulevards between Minnesota Drive and Old Seward Highway. It isn't exactly a tourist attraction, but this, along with shopping malls on the south and east end of town, is where locals—and others looking to save money—spend their cash. Another large shopping district is along Dimond Boulevard in South Anchorage; here are all the stalwarts: Best Buy, Wal-Mart, Costco, Borders, CompUSA, and more.

DOWNTOWN
Visitor Center
Start your tour of downtown at the **Anchorage Convention and Visitors Bureau** (ACVB), a sod-roofed log cabin on the corner of 4th Avenue and F Street. The cabin isn't actually the main place for information; go out the back door to a more spacious visitor center, where you'll find a plethora of brochures from around the state and a helpful staff. Be sure to pick up a copy of the fat *Anchorage Visitors Guide* which includes a downtown walking tour and an Anchorage-area driving tour, plus details on sights, attractions, activities, lodging, restaurants, and more.

The ACVB office is open daily 7:30 A.M.–7 P.M. June–August; daily 8 A.M.–6 P.M. in May and September; and daily 9 A.M.–4 P.M. the rest of the year. Details at 907/274-3531, www.anchorage.net; the website is packed with information on the city and links to local businesses. Call 907/276-3200 for a recording of forthcoming events.

Free city buses (907/343-6543, www.peoplemover.org) run around downtown daily if you get tired of walking. They stop right in front of the ACVB. For a quick one-hour introduction to the city, hop on one of the red **Anchorage City Trolley Tours** (612 W. 4th Ave., 907/276-5603, www.alaskatrolley.com, $10) with daily departures on the hour 9 A.M.–6 P.M. all summer.

Public Lands Center
Kitty-corner from the ACVB is the old Federal Building, which now houses the **Alaska Public Lands Information Center** (907/271-2737 or 866/869-6887; www.nps.gov/aplic, daily 9 A.M.–5 P.M. mid-May–early Sept., Mon.–Fri. 10 A.M.–5 P.M. the rest of the year). This is a great starting point to learn about federal lands in Alaska, including national parks and forests, wildlife refuges, and Bureau of Land

ANCHORAGE AND VICINITY

ANCHORAGE HISTORY

In June 1778, Captain James Cook sailed up what's now Turnagain Arm in Cook Inlet, reaching another dead end on his amazing search for the Northwest Passage. But he did dispatch William Bligh (of HMS *Bounty* fame) to explore, and he saw some Tanaina Indians in rich otter skins. George Vancouver, who'd also been on Cook's ship, returned in 1794 and noted Russian settlers in the area. A century later, prospectors began landing in the area and heading north to Southcentral Alaska's gold country, and in 1902 Alfred Brooks began mapping the Cook Inlet for the U.S. Geological Survey. In 1913, five settlers occupied Ship Creek, the point on the inlet where Anchorage now stands.

A year later, Congress passed the Alaska Railroad Act and in April 1915, the route for the federally financed railroad from Seward to Fairbanks was made official: It would pass through Ship Creek, where a major staging area for workers and supplies would be located. This news traveled fast, and within a month a ramshackle tent city of nearly 2,000 railroad job seekers had sprung up. Things developed so quickly that in July, the U.S. Land

Office auctioned off 650 parcels at the new town site. The settlement, renamed Anchorage, grew quickly, with water, telephone and power lines, sidewalks, and schools in place within a year.

SLUMPS AND SPURTS

Railroad laborers, earning 37 cents an hour (low for Alaska), struck in 1916, after which the minimum wage was raised to 45 cents an hour. The population continued to boom, topping out at around 7,000 in 1917. With World War I and completion of the southern portion of the railroad, the number of people dropped below 2,000 in 1920, when the town incorporated, electing its first mayor and city council. Through the 1930s, Anchorage held steady at 3,000–4,000 people, but World War II changed that in a hurry. The town's strategic location led to a huge influx of military personnel, when the Army's Fort Richardson and Air Force's Elmendorf Field were constructed outside of town. By 1950, Anchorage was a prosperous small city of over 11,000. In the following decade Anchorage also experienced the postwar boom, with the

Management areas. Displays introduce you to Alaska's wildlife and wild places, daily historical walks are offered throughout the summer, the bookstore has a good selection of Alaskan titles, and the auditorium is used for nature videos and talks.

A few blocks away is the **Department of Natural Resources Public Information Center** (550 W. 7th Ave., 907/269-8400, www.alaskastateparks.org, open weekdays). Located on the 12th floor, the information center has a helpful staff, and details on state parks, public-use cabins, where to pan for gold, state land sales, and much more.

◖ Anchorage Museum of History and Art

This museum (7th Ave. at A St., 907/343-6173, www.anchoragemuseum.org, $8 adults, $7 seniors, free for kids under 18) is a downtown

Anchorage highlight. Plan to linger awhile in the permanent wing downstairs; the Cook Inlet collection is outstanding. The historical art section is fascinating, especially the paintings by Sydney Laurence, one of Alaska's most famous and prolific artists; his 6- by 10-foot oil of Mt. McKinley is the centerpiece. Upstairs is the extraordinary Alaska Gallery, with Alaska-size dioramas chronicling a spectacular journey from prehistoric archaeology all the way up to the present. Informative documentary films and 45-minute tours are offered several times a day throughout the summer, and the library houses thousands of historical photographs. The museum is open daily 9 A.M.–6 P.M. (Thurs. until 9 P.M.) mid-May–mid-September; Tuesday–Saturday 10 A.M.–6 P.M. and Sunday noon–5 P.M. the rest of the year.

Also inside is **Marx Bros. Café at the Museum** (907/343-6190, www.marxcafe.com), attending shortages of housing and modern conveniences, which created its own construction miniboom. In 1957, when Richfield Oil discovered black gold on the Kenai Peninsula, the oil companies started opening office buildings in the city, and the economy stabilized.

SINCE STATEHOOD

Much of Anchorage collapsed in the incredible **Good Friday earthquake** of March 27, 1964, which lasted an interminable five minutes, registering 9.2 on the Richter Scale. The north side of 4th Avenue wound up 8-10 feet lower than the south side of the street. A very rich residential section on the bluff overlooking Knik Arm was destroyed. Nine people were killed and upward of $300 million in damages were recorded. Anchorage was rebuilt, and because only a few large buildings survived the quake, nearly everything in the city was put up after 1964.

Though the pipeline doesn't come within 300 miles of Anchorage, oil money towers over the city in the form of tall office buildings scattered around town. The military still plays an important role in the local economy, with Elmendorf Air Force Base and Fort Richardson right on the margins of town, and military jets and surveillance planes a common presence in the sky. Tourism also affects Anchorage enormously, especially in the summer months when the city is a way point for many travelers. Anchorage fancies itself quite the cosmopolitan city, boasting dozens of arts organizations, a modern performing arts center, a 16-theater cinema with stadium seating, plus many fancy hotels, restaurants, cafés, and bars catering to the thousands of suits who fill the skyscrapers that gleam in the light of the midnight sun. Indeed, if Juneau is bureaucratic Alaska, and Fairbanks is rank-and-file Alaska, then Anchorage is corporate and commercial Alaska.

If you can't find it at an Anchorage store, it probably isn't sold anywhere in the state. And if you find it elsewhere, you'll probably pay more. For bush dwellers, Anchorage is a shopping trip disguised as a city. Put people from Bethel, Nome, or Homer in Anchorage for a day and they're likely to spend most of their time at Costco and Wal-Mart!

with delicious light lunches; it's worth a visit even if you don't plan to explore the museum! A major museum expansion is in the works, but it isn't scheduled to be completed until 2010.

Kids' Play

The **Imaginarium** (5th Ave. and G St., 907/276-3179, www.imaginarium.org, Mon.–Sat. 10 A.M.–6 P.M., and Sun. noon–5 P.M., $5.50 adults, $5 ages 2–12 and seniors, free for tots) is a fun place if you've got young ones in tow. Learn all about northern lights in the planetarium, hold a starfish, stand inside a mega-bubble, or see the world through the eyes of a grasshopper at Alaska's only science discovery center. Exhibits change all the time, and the Imaginarium is open all year.

Performing Arts Center

Anchorage's central focal point is the **Alaska Center for the Performing Arts** (907/563-9171, www.alaskapac.org)—better known as "the PAC," short for Performing Arts Center—an unusual brick and glass building with colorful Olympic-like rings of light around the top. Find it at 5th Avenue and G Street. Inside are three auditoriums with wonderful acoustics and horrific carpeting; wags say it looks like a pepperoni pizza. Hold the anchovies! Free tours of the center are offered Wednesdays at 1 P.M., and two IMAX films are also screened throughout the summer: one on wolves and the other on the Great Land. The latter is narrated by Charlton Heston, so check your NRA pistols at the door. In addition, the center has an interesting slide show on the northern lights.

The spacious front lawn of the Performing Arts Center comprises **Town Square,** a fine, flower-filled field of fecundity. It's a wonderful place to meet up with friends or just relax on a

ANCHORAGE AND VICINITY

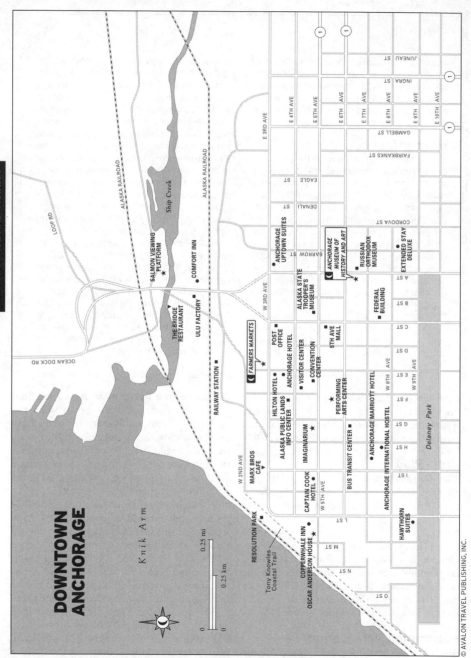

DOWNTOWN ANCHORAGE

Knik Arm

Tony Knowles
Coastal Trail

Ocean Dock Rd

Loop Rd

ALASKA RAILROAD

Ship Creek

ALASKA RAILROAD

SALMON VIEWING PLATFORM

COMFORT INN

THE BRIDGE RESTAURANT

ULU FACTORY

RAILWAY STATION

FARMERS MARKETS

POST OFFICE

ANCHORAGE UPTOWN SUITES

ANCHORAGE HOTEL

VISITOR CENTER

CONVENTION CENTER

ANCHORAGE MUSEUM OF HISTORY AND ART

RUSSIAN ORTHODOX MUSEUM

EXTENDED STAY DELUXE

ALASKA STATE TROOPER'S MUSEUM

FEDERAL BUILDING

5TH AVE MALL

PERFORMING ARTS CENTER

HILTON HOTEL

ALASKA PUBLIC LANDS INFO CENTER

IMAGINARIUM

MARX BROS CAFE

BUS TRANSIT CENTER

ANCHORAGE MARRIOTT HOTEL

ANCHORAGE INTERNATIONAL HOSTEL

CAPTAIN COOK HOTEL

Delaney Park

COPPERWHALE INN

OSCAR ANDERSON HOUSE

HAWTHORN SUITES

RESOLUTION PARK

E 3RD AVE
E 4TH AVE
E 5TH AVE
E 6TH AVE
E 7TH AVE
E 8TH AVE
E 9TH AVE
E 10TH AVE
E 6TH AVE

JUNEAU ST
INGRA ST
GAMBELL ST
FAIRBANKS ST
EAGLE ST
DENALI ST
CORDOVA ST
BARROW ST
A ST
B ST
C ST
D ST
E ST

W 3RD AVE
W 2ND AVE
W 5TH AVE
W 8TH AVE
W 9TH AVE

F ST
G ST
H ST
I ST
L ST
M ST
N ST
O ST

0.25 mi
0.25 km
0

© AVALON TRAVEL PUBLISHING, INC.

sunny summer day. **Egan Civic & Convention Center** is right across 5th Avenue.

Museums and Historic Buildings

Anchorage is pretty short on historical buildings since much of the city was destroyed in the 1964 quake and most of the city's development and growth has taken place since the 1970s. The neighborhood around 2nd Avenue at F Street includes several of the original town site homes constructed in the early 1900s, and historical panels describe the city's early days.

A few other structures survive from quieter times, including the **Oscar Anderson House Museum** (420 M St., 907/274-2336, $3 adults, $1 kids) open for 45-minute tours Monday–Friday 1:30–5:30 P.M. June–mid-September. This refurbished little bungalow—built in 1915 by Anchorage's first butcher—is the oldest frame residence in this young city. It reopens during the first two weekends of December, when it is festooned with traditional Swedish Christmas decorations. The Tony Knowles Coastal Trail passes right in front of the Oscar Anderson House, and adjacent is tiny **Elderberry Park,** a pleasant place to relax on a sunny afternoon, with picnic and playground facilities.

Across the street from the Museum of History and Art, the **Russian Orthodox Museum** (605 A St., 907/276-7257, Mon.–Fri. 10 A.M.–6 P.M. and Sat. 1–5 P.M., free) houses relics, icons, the kayak frame of St. Innocent, and other artifacts from Alaska's Orthodox tradition, with a gift shop selling nesting dolls and Russian crafts. Russian Orthodoxy is not just history, but a living, breathing, dynamic religious organization, with over 90 parishes and roughly 20,000 members in Alaska. Based in Sitka, the Alaskan Orthodox Church is the mother diocese of the church in the Western Hemisphere. Anchorage's **St. Innocent Russian Orthodox Church** (6724 E. 4th Ave.) is one of the most dramatic in Alaska. Check out the 12 onion-shaped domes, or attend a Sunday service to view the interior.

The **Alaska State Trooper Museum** (245 W. 5th Ave., 907/279-5050 or 877/770-5050, www.alaskatroopermuseum.com, Mon.–Fri. 10 A.M.–4 P.M. and Sat. noon–4 P.M.) is

Alaska Center for the Performing Arts

worth visiting to check out the gleaming 1952 Hudson Hornet patrol car.

A block from the Museum of History and Art, is **Wolf Song of Alaska** (corner of 6th Ave. and C St., 907/274-9653, www.wolfsongalaska .org), a nonprofit organization dedicated to educating the public about wolves. It houses a small museum with exhibits and a gift shop.

Across the street from the old Federal Building is the **4th Avenue Theater,** built in 1947, and one of the few structures to survive the 1964 earthquake. Up the street and right next to the log cabin visitor center is **Old City Hall,** housing the offices of the ACVB. Step inside the lobby to view a few exhibits and historic photos from early Anchorage.

Ship Creek Area

Immediately north of downtown on West 1st Avenue is the **Alaska Railroad Depot,** where you can book train travel or check out the 1907 train engine out front. Behind it is **Ship Creek,** a favorite place to cast for king or silver salmon all summer long—it's probably the only place where you can catch kings within sight of office high-rises. But watch out for the quicksand-like mud at the mouth of the creek; it can trap unwary anglers.

The **Elmendorf State Fish Hatchery** (Reeve Blvd. and Post Rd., 907/274-0065), has a salmon viewing area where you'll see king salmon late May–July and silver salmon August to mid-September.

Delaney Park

Enjoyable Delaney Park runs between 9th and 10th Avenues from L Street to Barrow. Known as the "park strip," early in Anchorage's history it marked the boundary where the town stopped and the wilderness started, and in 1923 the strip where the park is today was cleared as a firebreak. Since then it has served as a golf course, an airstrip, and now hosts half a dozen softball games every night of summer, tennis and basketball courts, and large grassy sections for Frisbee, hackey sack, tai chi, sunbathing, or people-watching. Right next to the park on the corner of 10th and I is a cage housing **Star, the pet reindeer.** The owners have had a succession of reindeer here since 1962; this is number six.

Resolution Park

A very popular stop for tour buses, visitors on foot, and the occasional (probably drunk) local is Resolution Park, on the west end of 3rd Avenue at L Street. This tiny city park consists of a viewing platform centered around a statue of Captain James Cook, who discovered what is now called Cook Inlet in 1778. The park is named for his ship, the *Resolution*. On clear days you'll delight to the mountainscape vistas. **Mt. McKinley** (many locals call it Denali) rises 125 miles to the north, and the low mountain just northwest across Cook Inlet is aptly named **Sleeping Lady** (the maps call it Mt. Susitna). Behind it, and just a bit south, stands a chain of active volcanoes that dump ash on Anchorage every few years, including **Mt. Spurr** and **Mt. Redoubt.** If you have eagle eyes and crystalline weather, you might pick out a third volcano, **Mt. Iliamna,** far to the southwest. Out of sight is yet a fourth volcano, **Mt. Augustine,** which last spewed ash in 1986.

Tony Knowles Coastal Trail

This is one of Anchorage's highlights, a wonderful 11-mile asphalt track that wends its way along the shore from downtown past the airport to Kincaid Park at Point Campbell, where the Knik and Turnagain Arms meet. From downtown, the trail is accessible from the west ends of 2nd, 5th, and 9th Avenues, with additional access at Westchester Lagoon, Earthquake Park, Point Woronzof, and Kincaid. Stroll the trail a ways, at least through the tunnel, beyond which you leave downtown behind and emerge into a new world: the grand sweep of the Arm, tidal flats, railroad tracks, and a residential neighborhood. On warm summer evenings this trail is more like a freeway, with people on every kind of wheels imaginable: bike riders, inline skaters, skateboarders, and babies in carriages. In winter, they trade the wheels for skis. The Coastal Trail gets especially crowded around duck-filled **Westchester Lagoon,** a mile south of downtown, and the city's favorite wintertime ice skating rink.

A second paved path intersects the Coastal Trail at Westchester Lagoon, the **Chester Creek Trail,** which creates another greenbelt across Anchorage. This one heads east along the creek, continuing for five miles to the University of Alaska at Anchorage campus.

BEYOND DOWNTOWN

Earthquake Park, out West Northern Lights Boulevard near the airport, has interpretive signs about the Big One on Good Friday 1964, and a view of the skyline and the Chugach Mountains. But the views are even more dramatic from **Point Woronzof,** another mile or so out. Tony Knowles Coastal Trail parallels the coast along Earthquake Park and Point Woronzof; it continues from downtown all the way south to **Kincaid Park.** And speaking of Kincaid, the trails here are a destination for hikers and mountain bikers all summer, and cross-country skiers when the snow flies.

Covering 11 acres of land at Campbell Airstrip

feeding ducks at Westchester Lagoon

Road off Tudor Road, the **Alaska Botanical Garden** (907/770-3692, www.alaskabg.org, daily year-round, $5 adults, $3 kids and seniors) is home to more than 1,100 varieties of plants. An information kiosk is at the entrance, and a pleasant one-mile nature trail leads through the perennial, rock, wildflower, and herb gardens. Take a guided tour of the garden Wednesday or Saturday June–August at 1 P.M.

◖ Alaska Native Heritage Center

Located on a 26-acre site facing the Chugach Mountains, the Alaska Native Heritage Center (907/330-8000 or 800/315-6608, www.alaskanative.net) provides an excellent introduction to Native culture in the state. The central "Welcome House" has a variety of exhibits and is used for concerts and demonstrations. Outside, five traditional village settings have been recreated around a small lake, and Native guides explain Alaska's various cultures. The center is open daily 9 A.M.–6 P.M. mid-May–mid-September, and admission costs $24 adults, $21 seniors, $16 ages 7–16, and free for kids

under 7. The remainder of the year, the main building (but not the village settings around the lake) is open Saturdays only, 10 A.M.–5 P.M. and costs $10 adults, $7 kids. The Heritage Center is east of downtown near the intersection of the Glenn Highway and Muldoon Road. Get there on the free summertime shuttle from the visitor center downtown.

Heritage Museum

Housed in the lobby of the Wells Fargo bank in Midtown, and officially called the **Alaska Heritage Museum at Wells Fargo** (Northern Lights Blvd. and C St., 907/265-2834, www.wellsfargohistory.com/museums, Mon.–Fri. noon–5 P.M. late May–early Sept., Mon.–Fri. noon–4 P.M. the rest of the year, free) is one of the state's largest privately owned collections of Alaskan artifacts and books. It will keep you spellbound for hours, if you have the time. Be sure to check out the 3.2-pound (!) gold nugget found in 1963 near Ruby, Alaska. Only a handful of the other highlights—many Native baskets, parkas made from bird skins and walrus intestines, Sydney Laurence's paintings, Nome and Fairbanks newspapers from the early 1900s, and bookcases filled with rare books and maps. This little gem of a museum is not to be missed.

Natural History Museum

Located off Mountain View Drive on the northeast end of town, the **Alaska Museum of Natural History** (201 N. Bragaw, 907/274-2400, www.alaskamuseum.org, $5 adults, $3 ages 6–12, free for younger children) houses exhibits on dinosaurs, wildlife, rocks, and minerals. Hours are Monday–Saturday 9 A.M.–5 P.M. and Sunday noon–5 P.M. in summer, and Wednesday–Saturday 10 A.M.–5 P.M. and Noon–4 P.M. the rest of the year.

Up in the Air

The **Alaska Aviation Heritage Museum** (4721 Aircraft Dr., 907/248-5325, www.alaska airmuseum.com, $10 adults, $8 seniors, $6 ages 5–12, free for younger kids) is off the Lake Hood exit from International Airport Road. It's open daily 9 A.M.–5 P.M. mid-May–mid-September, and Wednesday–Sunday 9 A.M.–5 P.M. the rest of the year. This unusual museum displays 25 vintage aircraft in three connected hangars—including a 1928 Stearman and a 1944—as well as Japanese artifacts from the World War II Aleutian Island battles

and historical photos. The theater shows videos on early Alaskan aviation, and the museum fronts on **Lake Hood,** the world's largest seaplane base, where floatplanes take off and land almost constantly in the summer.

One of the nation's busiest airfields is **Merrill Field,** on the east side of town along the Glenn Highway. There are more than 230,000 takeoffs and landings each year here; overall, Alaska has 16 times as many aircraft per capita as the Lower 48 states! (But it also has a far higher airplane accident rate.)

Alaska Zoo

Located two miles east of New Seward Highway, the zoo (4731 O'Malley Rd., 907/346-3242, www.alaskazoo.com, daily 9 A.M.–6 P.M. year-round, until 9 P.M. Tues. and Fri. in summer, $9 adults, $8 seniors, $5 ages 12–17, $4 ages 3–11, free for tots) is connected by a special hourly shuttle bus from the Transit Center. The zoo has nice grounds, enjoyable shady paths, and all the Alaskan animals, plus a number of more exotic critters (including, inexplicably, an elephant named Maggie). If you have kids, they'll enjoy it, especially the star attractions: Ahpun and Lyutvik the polar bears. You can watch the bears' underwater antics through the glass of their swimming pool, or check out the polar bear cam on the zoo's website.

Entertainment and Events

PERFORMING ARTS

Anchorage's active cultural scene centers on the **Alaska Center for the Performing Arts** (907/263-2900, www.alaskapac.org), downtown at 5th Avenue and G Street. There are events throughout the year, including modern dance, ballet, Broadway musicals, comedy troupes, opera, and concerts by nationally known artists, along with winter performances by the **Anchorage Concert Association** (www.anchorageconcerts.org), **Anchorage Symphony Orchestra** (907/274-8668 or 800/478-7328, www.anchoragesymphony.org), the **Anchorage Concert Chorus** (907/274-7464, www.anchorageconcertchorus.org), and the **Anchorage Opera** (907/279-2557, www.anchorageopera.org).

Call 907/566-2787 for a recording of upcoming events at the PAC and elsewhere. Tickets are available at the PAC box office, in all Carrs stores, and at 800/478-7328 or www.tickets.com. Check Friday's Play section of the *Anchorage Daily News* (www.adn.com/play) for upcoming events.

Anchorage is a city that showers appreciation on traveling musicians who come out of their way to visit the city, particularly those with a folk-rock or Celtic bent. Many of Anchorage's best folksy performances arrive courtesy of **Whistling Swan Productions** (www.whistlingswan.net); visit their website for upcoming shows.

For live performance, check out productions by **Cyrano's Off Center Playhouse** (413 D St., 907/274-2599, www.cyranos.org), **Out North Contemporary Art House** (3800 DeBarr Rd., 907/279-3800, www.outnorth.org), and **Anchorage Community Theatre** (1133 E. 70th Ave., 907/344-4713, www.actalaska.org).

DRINKING AND DANCING

The best source for Anchortown action is the Friday **Play** section of the *Anchorage Daily News* (www.adn.com/play). With dozens of listings from coffeehouse folk guitarists to the Young at Heart big band that livens up the senior center on Friday nights, there's something to satiate even the most bored visitor. The newspaper's pithy descriptions of Anchorage's nightclubs and coffeehouses are a big help in making your evening plans.

The *Anchorage Press* (www.anchoragepress.com) is a free weekly newspaper available in racks all over town. There's always some sort of muckraking article here, and its coverage of the night life scene is strong.

In 2007, Anchorage joined many other American cities by **banning smoking in bars** and virtually all other indoor places. If you smoke, this should be one more incentive to quit.

Neighborhood Bars

Anchorage is a *Cheers*-type town, with lots of corner bars and local pubs tucked away. Downtown, a popular place is **F Street Station** (4th and F Sts.), which also serves good-value lunches and dinners. **Darwin's Theory** (426 G St., 907/277-5322), attracts a fun after-work crowd. Free hot pepper schnapps—if you can stomach it—when the bartender rings the bell (quite often some evenings).

Popular Anchorage sports bars include **Peanut Farm** (5227 Old Seward Hwy., 907/563-3283), **Crossroads Lounge** (1402 Gambell, 907/276-9014), and **Eddie's Sports Bar** (6300 Old Seward Hwy., 907/563-3970).

Rockin' Out

Anchorage's favorite downtown bar is **Humpy's Great Alaskan Alehouse** (610 W. 6th Ave., 907/276-2337, www.humpys.com). Drop by on any night of the week to rub shoulders (arms, legs, and other body parts—it gets mighty crowded) with a hip, raucous, and youthful crowd. The bar has dozens of microbrews on tap, the kitchen cranks out pub fare, and bands play nightly. Humpy's is a must-see place if you're staying downtown, especially if you're single.

Chilkoot Charlie's (2435 Spenard Rd. at Fireweed, 907/279-1692, www.koots.com) is a ramshackle building where you can do some serious jumping up and down to real rock 'n' roll and generally have a night of good raunchy fun—so long as you don't ask the wrong guy's girl (or the wrong girl's guy) to dance. There are three separate dance floors and eight (!) bars inside. It's big enough to get lost in. The main stage has loud and very live rock, while the other two dance floors are filled with folks dancing to DJ Top 40 or swing tunes. 'Koots is a love-it or hate-it sort of place; if you aren't into the bar cruisin' and pick up scene, try elsewhere. The motto should give you fair warning, "We cheat the *other* guy and pass the savings on to *you!*" But you should at least go here to say you didn't miss the most famous place in town. 'Koots gets extremely crowded on weekend nights, so you may have to wait quite a while to get in if you come after 10 P.M. There's a cover charge on weekends. You can't miss Chilkoot's, just look for the tall, lighted windmill.

Chef's Inn (825 W. Northern Lights Blvd., 907/272-1341, www.bluescentral.biz) is Anchorage's "Blues Central," with live bluesy bands nightly. The bar attracts leather-clad bikers and others. Good food (especially the French dip) and great blues tunes.

Downtown's **Rumrunners** (415 E St., 907/278-4493, www.rumrunnersak.com) is a spacious no-cover DJ and live music club.

Club Soraya (333 W. 4th Ave., 907/276-0670) is a fun downtown place where Latin dance bands fill the air with salsa and merengue on weekends. Latin dance lessons are offered on Saturday nights.

Snow City Café (1034 W. 4th Ave., 907/272-2489, www.snowcitycafe.com) has Wednesday-night Irish music sessions until 11 P.M.

Gay and Lesbian

If your boyfriend or girlfriend happens to be of the same sex as you, pop into **Mad Myrna's** (530 E. 5th Ave., 907/276-9762, www.alaska. net/~madmyrna) or **The Raven** (708 E. 4th Ave., 907/276-9672). Myrna's has drag shows on Fridays, karaoke Thursdays, and DJ tunes on Fridays and Saturdays; Raven is a pool-shootin'

joint. **PrideFest** (www.anchoragepride.com) in mid-June is Alaska's big coming-out party, so to speak.

Date Bars

Several Anchorage bars offer a quiet and romantic atmosphere. If you luck into a clear evening, have packed something a little dressy, and don't mind blowing two days' budget on a beer, head up to the **Crow's Nest** (4th Ave. and K St., 907/276-6000) atop the Captain Cook Hotel—the view is worth the effort. The **Millennium Hotel** (4800 Spenard Rd., 907/243-2300 or 800/544-0553) has an upscale bar with outdoor seating overlooking Lake Hood.

MOVIES

Free documentary flicks are shown several times a day at the **Public Lands Information Center** and the **Museum of History and Art.** For something more dramatic, the downtown **Alaska Center for the Performing Arts** (907/263-2900, www.alaskapac.org) offers summer-only slide shows on the **northern lights,** offered daily on the hour 9 A.M.–9 P.M. all summer. The **Alaska Experience Theatre** (705 W. 6th Avenue, 907/276-3730 or 877/276-3730, www.alaskaexperiencetheatre.com), has a wraparound visual show and earthquake shaker for the tourists.

Bear Tooth Theatrepub (1230 W. 27th Ave., 907/276-4200, www.beartooththeatre. net) has a winning combination: inexpensive second-run and art-house movies ($3), tasty light meals (including tacos, nachos, salads, burritos, and pizzas), plus brewery-fresh draught beer. It's a great place with a family atmosphere, and is run by the same geniuses who created Moose's Tooth Pub & Pizzeria. You can eat downstairs and drink while watching the movie; upstairs is reserved for underage kids. It also has a restaurant area (very noisy) in the lobby for those who just want a meal in a family setting, and the adjacent **Bear Tooth Grill** with a big menu of burgers, Mexican platters, pasta, and seafood.

See what's showing at all local theaters by visiting www.anchoragemovies.com. Anchorage's main theater action is the **Century 16** (36th Ave. and A St., 907/929-3456), where all 16 theaters have stadium seating and reclining chairs. Other Anchorage multiplexes include **Totem 8** (3131 Muldoon Rd., 907/566-3329), **Fireweed 7** (Fireweed and New Seward, 907/566-3328), and **Dimond Center 9** (in Dimond Mall at Dimond and Old Seward, 907/566-3327).

EVENTS

Winter is the time for Anchorage's best-known events (the Iditarod and Fur Rendezvous), but the city is certainly full of life in the summer. Check the Anchorage Convention and Visitors Bureau website (www.anchorage.net) for a complete listing of events.

Summer

Anchorage's most popular ongoing event is the **Saturday and Sunday Markets** (907/272-5634, www.anchoragemarkets.com), which takes place at the parking lot on 3rd Avenue and E Street on Saturdays and Sundays 10 A.M.–6 P.M. mid-May–mid-September. It features over 300 vendors selling fresh produce, quality arts and crafts, and great food. Don't miss it! A smaller market takes place Wednesday afternoons at Northway Mall.

Every Wednesday and Friday at noon, head downtown to 4th Avenue and E Street for free **Music in the Park** (907/279-5650, www.anchoragedowntown.org) next to the visitor center. Other events take place here most other weekday afternoons in the summer.

Anchorage has not just one, but two different semi-pro baseball teams—the **Anchorage Bucs** (907/561-2827, www.anchoragebucs.com) and the **Anchorage Glacier Pilots** (907/274-3627, www.glacierpilots.com)—so there's usually a game worth watching between June and early August. Past players have included such pro stars as Reggie Jackson, Dave Winfield, Mark McGuire, and Randy Johnson. Games take place at Mulcahy Stadium at East 16th and Cordova.

The **Arctic Thunder Air Show** (907/552-7469, www.elmendorf.af.mil) at Elmendorf

Air Force Base comes around each June, and includes a stunning performance by the Air Force's Thunderbirds.

Three Barons Renaissance Faire (907/868-8012, www.3barons.org) takes place in early June at Hilltop Ski Area, and the crowd gets into the act by pelting rotten acting with rotten tomatoes. The **Spenard Solstice Street Party** brings an offbeat parade, live music, and food booths to Spenard, while the serious athletes race in the big **Mayor's Midnight Sun Marathon** (www.mayorsmarathon.com).

Held at Kincaid Park in June, **Blues on the Green** (907/272-1341, www.bluescentral.biz) attracts such acclaimed artists as Otis Rush and Bo Diddley. There's a **4th of July** parade downtown, but when the fireworks show starts at midnight the sky still isn't very dark!

Also in early July, the **Bear Paw Festival** (907/694-4702, www.cer.org) comes to nearby Eagle River, with a classic car show, races, a chili cook-off, carnival rides, and the state's biggest parade.

Several of the biggest "local" events—the State Fair in Palmer, the Girdwood Forest Fair, the Talkeetna Bluegrass Festival, the Mountain Marathon in Seward, and the KBBI Concert on the Lawn in Homer—are not in Anchorage. But, if you're around when any of these are happening, get out of town to where the fun really is!

Winter

In recent years, tourism to Alaska has increased in the winter months as visitors discover what Alaskans already know—that winter opens up a panoply of outdoor options. Several companies specialize in winter tours and activities; see the visitor center for brochures.

The **Anchorage Folk Festival** (907/566-2334, www.anchoragefolkfestival.org) is a major winter diversion, with free concerts that fill two consecutive weekends in late January. Concerts take place on the campus of the University of Alaska Anchorage.

In mid-February, the **Fur Rendezvous** (907/274-1177, www.furrondy.net) is one the city's biggest annual events, with all sorts of fun activities during this 10-day-long festival. A carnival packs a downtown lot, and there are car races, fireworks, snow sculpture and ice carving contests, dress balls, concerts, ski races, dog-pulling contests, and—most exciting of all—the world championship sled dog race.

The one Alaskan event that always attracts national attention is the **Iditarod Trail Sled Dog Race** (907/376-5155 or 800/545-6874, www.iditarod.com) from Anchorage to Nome. The start is in downtown Anchorage in early March.

Another very popular event is the **Great Alaska Shootout** (907/786-1250, www.gosea wolves.com/shootout) basketball tournament that takes place in Sullivan Arena each November, and features seven top college teams and the lowly University of Alaska Seawolves. This one gets national media attention because it's so early in the year.

The **Nordic Skiing Association of Anchorage** (907/276-7609, www.anchorage nordicski.com) keeps dozens of miles of local trails groomed, and puts on such events as the **Tour of Anchorage** (www.tourof anchorage.com) in early March. The **Ski for Women** (907/279-9581, www.alaskaskifor women.org) in early February is the largest North American ski event for women, attracting more than 1,500 participants.

Spring Carnival and Slush Cup, in mid-April, is a wet and wild event for skiers as they try to cross a slushy pond at Alyeska Resort (907/754-1111, www.alyeskaresort.com).

Shopping

Although big-city folks sometimes complain that Anchorage doesn't have the fancy boutiques they're accustomed to finding, it *does* have just about every other sort of place—from Sam's Club to Nordstrom. The city is a car haven, so many of these stores are scattered in the various shopping malls that help give Anchorage its "charming" urban sprawl.

Downtown Anchorage's **5th Avenue Mall** includes two big stores—JCPenny and Nordstrom—along with several dozen storefronts on four levels. The city's largest mall is **Dimond Center** on the south side at Dimond Boulevard and Old Seward Highway. Other malls include **The Mall at Sears** (Northern Lights and Seward Highway) and **Northway Mall** (Airport Heights and Glenn Hwy.). Anchorage has all the mega-stores, including Wal-Mart, Fred Meyer, Costco, Home Depot, Toys 'R' Us, Barnes & Noble, ad nauseam.

GIFTS AND NATIVE ART

Much of downtown is given over to shops selling tourist doo-dads, particularly along 3rd and 4th Avenues, where you'll find everything from $2 made-in-China trinkets to $20,000 sculptures.

One People (425 D St., 907/274-4063) has a fine selection of Native Alaskan art in a convenient downtown location. One of the best places to buy Native crafts is the out-of-the-way **Alaska Native Medical Center Gift Shop** (4315 Diplomacy Dr. off East Tudor Rd., 907/729-1122, www.anmc.org). Excellent grass baskets, dolls, masks, yo-yos, and more are sold on consignment here. Another recommended place is the gift shop at the **Alaska Native Heritage Center** (Glenn Hwy. and Muldoon Rd., 907/330-8000 or 800/315-6608, www.alaskanative.net, open Mon.–Fri. 10 A.M.–2 P.M.).

Anyone looking for a traditional Alaskan parka should stop by Downtown Co-Op in the 5th Avenue Mall for **Laura Wright's Alaskan Parkys** (907/274-4215; www.alaskan.com/ parkys).

An unusual (and very expensive) purchase to consider is *qiviut:* caps, scarves, shawls, sweaters, or baby booties, hand-knitted by Natives from the wool of domestic musk ox (the musk ox farm is outside of Palmer). Many times warmer and lighter than wool, these fine knits can be seen and salivated over at **Oomingmak**

Co-op (609 H St., 907/272-9225 or 888/360-9665; www.qiviut.com).

GALLERIES

On the **First Friday** of each month Anchorage's art scene comes alive with openings, hors d'oeuvres, and the chance to meet regional artists at a dozen or so galleries. Check the Friday *Anchorage Daily News* or the weekly *Anchorage Press* for details.

Anchorage's premier gallery is the **International Gallery of Contemporary Art** (427 D St., 907/279-1116, www.igcaalaska.org, Wed.–Sun. noon–4 P.M. and Tues. 5:30–8 P.M.), with something new each month from top regional artists.

Three good places to buy original artwork in Anchorage are **Artique, Ltd.** (314 G St., 907/277-1663, www.artiqueltd.com), **Arctic Rose Gallery** (420 L St., 907/279-3911, www.arcticrosegallery.com), and the jam-packed **Aurora Fine Arts Gallery** (737 W. 5th Ave., 907/274-0234). A fun shop for wearable art is **Tracy Anna Bader Design Studio & Gallery** (416 G St., 907/278-9327).

A fun option is the **Saturday and Sunday Markets** (907/272-5634, www.anchoragemarkets.com) held at the parking lot on 3rd Avenue and E Street every summer Saturday. The market has works by Alaskan painters, photographers, potters, and others.

OUTDOOR OUTFITTERS

Anchorage is an excellent place to stock up on outdoor gear before heading into the bush. The biggest place to shop—and one of the best—is **REI** (907/272-4565, www.rei.com) on the corner of Northern Lights and Spenard Road. "REI" stands for Recreation Equipment Inc. This Seattle-based cooperative where members get an end-of-the-year dividend on their purchases has a knowledgeable staff who offer free clinics and talks throughout the year. You can also rent canoes, kayaks, tents, backpacks, skis, snowshoes, and other outdoor equipment from REI.

Another excellent outdoor store with a technically adept staff is **Alaska Mountaineering &**

Hiking (2633 Spenard Rd., 907/272-1811, www.alaskamountaineering.com)—better known as AMH—just a block away from REI. Though much smaller, AMH often has equipment unavailable elsewhere. This is where the hard-core climbers and backcountry skiers go.

Check the bulletin boards at AMH and REI for used gear and travel partners. Or cross the street to **Play it Again Sports** (907/278-7529, www.playitagainsports.com), where used equipment of all sorts is available, from backpacks and tents to baseball gloves and fishing poles. They also buy used equipment if you need a little cash on your way out of town.

Downtown shoppers head to the **Army Navy Store** (320 W. 4th Ave., 907/279-2401) for more traditional Alaskan outdoor clothing and boots. **B&J Commercial** (2749 C St., 907/274-6113) has a downstairs packed with sport and commercial fishing supplies. This is where you'll find the really heavy-duty clothing and equipment at fair prices.

BOOKS AND MUSIC

Alaska's largest independent bookstore is **Title Wave Books** (1360 W. Northern Lights Blvd., next to REI, 907/278-9283 or 888/598-9283, www.wavebooks.com). Offering a fine choice of new and used titles, this is a great hangout spot, with a literate crowd and an adjacent Kaladi Brothers espresso shop to sip coffee and surf the Web.

Also in Midtown is **Metro Music and Books** (530 E. Benson Blvd., 907/279-8622), with a huge selection of CDs, any of which you can listen to before deciding to buy.

A fine downtown bookstore, **Cook Inlet Book Company** (415 W. 5th Ave., 907/258-4544 or 800/240-4148, www.cookinlet.com) specializes in Alaskan titles. **Borders Books & Music** (1100 E. Dimond Blvd., 907/344-4099) features books and CDs, plus an espresso café. Even bigger (and more centrally located) is **Barnes & Noble Bookseller** (200 E. Northern Lights Blvd., 907/279-7323 or 888/279-7323). In addition to books and CDs, you'll find an impressive magazine selection, plus a Starbucks.

Recreation

SUMMER
Hiking and Horseback Rides

One of the most popular hiking trails in Alaska is the 1.5-mile path to the summit of **Flattop Mountain** within Chugach State Park. The trailhead is on the southeastern edge of Anchorage, so you'll need a car to get there. (For a description of this and other hiking trails around Anchorage, see *Chugach State Park*.)

The **Alaska Mountaineering Club** (907/272-1811, www.mcak.org) holds meetings at 7:30 P.M. on the third Wednesday of each month at the First United Methodist Church (9th Ave. and G St.). Visitors are welcome to enjoy the presentations, and it only costs $15 to join the club and go along on any of their frequent outings.

Alaska Outback Guide Service (907/744-7054, www.akoutbackonline.com) guides day-hikes into the Chugach Mountains. **Horseback Alaska** (907/336-4077, www.horsebackalaska.net) and **Horse Trekkin Alaska** (907/868-3728, www.horsetrekkinalaska.com) both offer horseback rides in Anchorage parks.

Biking

Anchorage has 200 miles of urban cycling/jogging trails; pick up bike trail maps at the downtown visitor center. A delightfully easy ride—it's all paved—goes 11 miles from the west end of 2nd Avenue along the Tony Knowles Coastal Trail, past Westchester Lagoon, Earthquake Park, and Point Woronzof, and then all the way to Kincaid Park at Point Campbell, out on the western tip of the city. The Chester Creek Trail meets the Coastal Trail at Westchester Lagoon and takes you almost five miles to Goose Lake, where you can take a dip if you're hot. Or just bomb around to wherever the wind blows you. Note, however, that the major Anchorage arteries are not especially bike-friendly, so you may want to stick to the side streets to avoid contending with exhaust fumes and speeding pickup trucks. Dirt biking/hiking trails abound within Kincaid Park, Hillside Park, and Far

North Bicentennial Park, or you can head up Powerline Pass Trail inside Chugach State Park, Eklutna Lake (bike rentals available onsite), or out the 40-mile Resurrection Pass from the town of Hope.

Based in Anchorage, the **Arctic Bicycle Club** (907/566-0177, www.arcticbike.org) organizes races and tours, and has a very helpful website. **Alaska Backcountry Bike Tours** (907/746-5018 or 866/354-2453, www.mountainbikealaska.com) guides all-day cycling trips into backcountry areas around Anchorage.

For mountain bike rentals, head to **Downtown Bicycle Rental** (333 W. 4th Ave., 907/279-3334, www.alaska-bike-rentals.com) or **Pablo's Bicycle Rentals** (440 L St., 907/250-2871, www.pablosbicyclerentals.com); both are close to the Coastal Trail. In Midtown, rent them from **Sunshine Sports** (1231 W. Northern Lights Blvd., 907/272-6444).

Glacier Tours

Several companies have downtown Anchorage offices promoting boat day-tours to glaciers in Prince William Sound (via Whittier) or Resurrection Bay (via Seward). These include Prince William Sound tours from **Phillips Tours and Cruises** (www.26glaciers.com), **Prince William Sound Cruises and Tours** (www.princewilliamsound.com), and **Major Marine Tours** (www.majormarine.com), plus Resurrection Bay trips from **Kenai Fjords Tours** (www.kenaifjords.com), **Major Marine Tours** (www.majormarine.com), and **Renown Charters and Tours** (www.renowncharters.com). (Whittier-based tours are detailed in the *Wrangells and Prince William Sound* chapter, while Seward-based cruises are in the *Kenai Peninsula* chapter.) The companies can arrange bus transport to the starting points in Seward or Whittier, or you can ride the Alaska Railroad. Also popular are the day trips from Anchorage to Portage Glacier operated by **Gray Line of Alaska** (www.graylineofalaska.com).

Flightseeing

The best way to get a bird's-eye view of the Anchorage area is from a bird's-eye vantage point: in an airplane. Anchorage has a large number of companies offering flightseeing; see the Yellow Pages under "Aircraft Charter" for the full list, or visit the flightseeing links on www.anchorage.net. Two respected Lake Hood operations have been around for many years: **Rust's Flying Service** (907/243-1595 or 800/544-2299, www.flyrusts .com) and **Regal Air** (907/243-8535, www.regal-air.com). The following long-established companies fly out of Merrill Field: **Jayhawk Air** (907/276-4404), **Spernak Airways** (907/272-9475), and **VernAir** (907/258-7822, www.alaskavernair.com). **Era Helicopters** (907/266-8351 or 800/843-1947, www.flight seeingtours.com) is based at the airport.

Typical flights include a 90-minute flight over the Chugach Mountains and Knik Glacier for $120 per person; a three-hour flight over Prince William Sound and Columbia Glacier for $280 (including a remote water landing); and a three-hour flight over Mt. McKinley for $390 (including a glacier landing). The air taxis also feature fly-in fishing trips, primarily to the Susitna River area, where Rust's has rental cabins available. Also popular are bear-viewing day trips out of Anchorage; these generally start around $500 per person. Charter service may be the way to go if you have a group of four or more people and a specific destination, such as a public cabin in Chugach National Forest.

Rock-Climbing

Alaska Rock Gym (4840 Fairbanks St., 907/562-7265, www.alaskarockgym.com) has climbing walls, classes, a pro shop, locker rooms, and a weight room. For the real thing, most folks head south to Turnagain Arm, which is also popular with ice-climbers in the winter. Talk to folks at AMH or REI for details on other climbing options.

Bird-Watching

Anchorage is home to a surprising diversity of bird species in the summer. The **Anchorage Audubon Society** (907/276-7034, www .anchorageaudubon.org) offers bird-watching field trips and a bird hotline (907/338-2473) with the latest unusual sightings.

Fishing and Rafting

Although Anchorage sits along Cook Inlet, wild tides and strong winds create notoriously treacherous conditions. As a result, there are no charter boat fishing operations out of Anchorage. A popular salmon-fishing stream, **Ship Creek,** flows right through downtown, and has good runs of king salmon (late May–July) and silver salmon (August–mid-Sept.). You can also rub shoulders with fellow anglers in mid-summer at **Bird Creek,** 25 miles south of town on the Seward Highway.

The downtown visitor center has brochures for many sportfishing options on the Kenai Peninsula, just a couple of hours by car from Anchorage. To figure out where the fish are running, or what the local regulations are, call Fish and Game (907/344-0541, recorded message 907/349-4687) or visit the Public Lands Information Center downtown for a copy of the fishing regulations. Both the *Anchorage Daily News* (www.adn.com/outdoors) and the *Anchorage Press* publish weekly fishing reports for the Anchorage area.

Increasingly popular are fly-in fishing trips. All the local air-taxi services offer guided or unguided trips to nearby rivers and lakes for world-class salmon fishing.

Two companies lead white-water trips down the wild Six Mile Creek near Hope: **Chugach Outdoor Center** (907/277-7238 or 866/277-7238, www.chugachoutdoorcenter.com) and **Nova Riverrunners** (907/745-5753 or 800/746-5753, www.novalaska.com); see the *Kenai Peninsula* chapter for details.

(H2Oasis Indoor Waterpark

If you have children, don't miss H2Oasis Indoor Waterpark (1520 O'Malley Rd., 907/522-4420 or 888/426-2747, www.h2oasiswaterpark.com, open daily 10 A.M.–9 P.M. all summer, reduced school-year hours), a cavernous indoor water park near the intersection with New Seward

SAFETY IN AVALANCHE COUNTRY

Skiing and snowmobiling are becoming increasingly popular in Alaska's limitless backcountry. Unfortunately, many of these winter outdoor enthusiasts fail to take necessary precautions before heading out. Given the heavy snowfalls that occur, the steep slopes the snow piles up on, and the high winds that accompany many storms, it should come as no surprise that avalanches are a real danger in Alaska. Nearly all avalanches are triggered by the victims. This is particularly true for snowmobilers who often attempt such dangerous practices as "high-marking" – riding as high as they can up steep slopes – and are killed in avalanches that result.

If you really want to avoid avalanches, ski only on groomed trails or "bombproof" slopes that, because of aspect, shape, and slope angle, never seem to slide. Unfortunately, this isn't always possible, so backcountry skiers and snowmobilers need to understand the conditions that lead to avalanches. The best way to learn is from a class such as the avalanche safety programs taught by the **Alaska Mountain Safety Center** (907/345-3566, www.alaskaavalanche.com) in Anchorage, or Juneau's **Southeast Alaska Avalanche Center** (907/586-5699, www.avalanche .org/~seaac). Learn more at www.avalanche .org, including information on avalanches and course offerings around the nation.

HEADING OUT

An avalanche safety course is extremely valuable, but you can also help protect yourself by following these precautions when you head into the backcountry:

- Before leaving, get up-to-date avalanche information. The **Chugach National Forest Avalanche Information Center** (907/754-2369, www.fs.fed.us/r10/chugach/glacier/snow.html) has current snow conditions for the Kenai Peninsula; it's updated several times a week in the winter.

- Be sure to carry extra warm clothes, water, high-energy snacks, a cell phone, a dual-frequency avalanche transceiver (make sure it's turned on and that you know how to use it!), a lightweight snow shovel (for digging snow pits or emergency snow shelters, or for excavating avalanche victims), first-aid supplies, a Leatherman knife, topographic map, extra plastic ski tip, flashlight, matches, and compass. Many skiers also carry that cure-all, duct tape, wrapped around a ski pole. Let someone know exactly where you are going and when you expect to return. It's also a wise idea to carry special ski poles that extend into probes in case of an avalanche.

- Check the angle of an area before you ski through it; slopes of 30–45 degrees are the most dangerous, while lesser slopes do not slide as frequently.

- Watch the weather; winds over 15 mph can pile snow much more deeply on lee slopes, causing dangerous loading on the snowpack. Especially avoid skiing on or below cornices.

- Avoid skiing on the leeward side (the side facing into the wind) of ridges, where snow loading can be greatest.

- Be aware of gullies and bowls; they're more likely to slip than flat open slopes or ridgetops. Stay out of gullies at the bottom of wide bowls; these are natural avalanche chutes.

- Look out for cracks in the snow, and listen for hollow snow underfoot. These are strong signs of dangerous conditions.

- Look at the trees. Smaller trees may indicate that avalanches rip through an area frequently, knocking over the larger trees. Avalanches can, however, also run through forested areas.

- Know how much new snow has fallen recently. Heavy new snow over older, weak snow layers is a sure sign of extreme danger on potential avalanche slopes. Most avalanches slip during or immediately after a storm.

- Learn how to dig a snow pit and how to read the various snow layers. Particularly important are the very weak layers of depth hoar or surface hoar that have been buried under heavy new snow.

Highway on the south end of Anchorage. On busy weekends half the kids in town seem to be here, splashing in the wave pool, shooting jets of water at each other from the pirate ship, gliding down the lazy river, zipping through the body slide, and riding the roller coaster—like Master Blaster water ride. Hot tubs are reserved for the over-16 set. Entrance is $22 for ages 13 and up, $17 for ages 3–12, and free for tots with a paying adult. Towel and swimsuit rentals are available, and the food court sells greasy snacks.

Swimming

If you're lucky enough to be in Anchorage during a hot spell and want to cool off under the bright blue sky, head out to **Lake Spenard/ Lake Hood** (the two are actually one connected lake) down Spenard Road toward the airport, then right on Lakeshore Drive. **Jewel Lake** also has swimming on Dimond Boulevard between Jewel Lake and Sand Lake Roads in the southwest corner of the city. The most developed outdoor swimming is at **Goose Lake,** out Northern Lights between Lake Otis and Bragaw near the University of Alaska Anchorage, on the bike trail, with basketball courts, changing room and toilets, and a snack bar.

If you're in the mood for a swim anytime, Anchorage is a good place to experience Alaska's love affair with Olympic-size indoor pools. There are seven to choose from-five at the various high schools; call 907/343-4474 for locations and times. Other pools are at Alaska Pacific University (APU) and the University of Alaska Anchorage (UAA). With its high ceiling, taut diving boards, and hard-body swimmers, the **UAA pool** (907/786-1231), is easily the finest in Alaska, and your entrance fee also provides access to the other facilities here, including a fine ice rink, weight room, saunas, racquetball courts, and gym.

Golf

There are four Anchorage-area public golf courses: **Anchorage Golf Course** (907/522-3363, www.alyeskaresort.com; 18 holes) on lower hillside in South Anchorage, **Russian**

Jack Springs Course (5200 DeBarr Rd., 907/343-6992; 9 holes), **Tanglewood Lakes Golf Club** (11701 Brayton Dr., 907/345-4600; 9 holes), and **Moose Run** (27000 Arctic Valley Rd., 907/428-0056, www.moose rungolfcourse.com; 36 holes).

WINTER

Contrary to popular belief, Alaska—and Anchorage in particular—does not go into hibernation for the long months of winter. Instead, many locals look forward to the cold and snow because of the wonderful outdoor activities they bring. Anchorage is a national center for cross-country skiing, dogsledding, skijoring (skiing behind a dog), hockey, and all sorts of other winter fun.

Visitors soon discover what the residents already know—the city is blessed with excellent facilities for all of these. There are dogsled race tracks; dozens of miles of free, groomed ski trails; several excellent ice rinks; and three downhill ski areas, including the state's best resort—Alyeska. Add in such events as the Iditarod and Fur Rendezvous, the college and semipro hockey games, and it's easy to see why more and more visitors are coming to Anchorage in the winter.

Downhill Skiing

Alpine skiers and snowboarders head 37 miles south of Anchorage to **Alyeska Resort** (907/754-1111 or 800/880-3880; www.alyeska resort.com) for the finest skiing to be found, and some of the deepest snow at any American resort. (See the *Girdwood* section of this chapter for details.)

Hilltop Ski Area (907/346-1446, www .hilltopskiarea.org) is right on the edge of town at Abbott Road near Hillside Drive, and consists of a small chairlift and two rope tows. It has lights for night skiing, plus a modern lodge with rentals and a snack bar, and is a favorite place to learn skiing or to play around without having to suffer the 45-minute drive to Alyeska. Tickets cost $26 for weekends ($28 with night skiing) for adults, $2 less for students, or free for kids under eight skiing with an adult.

The rope tow is free if you just want to play around on the bunny slope. Call 907/346-2167 for the ski hotline.

A bit farther afield is **Alpenglow at Arctic Valley** (907/428-1208; www.skialpenglow.com). All-day rates are $28 adults, $20 students and seniors, and free for kids under seven. There are two chairlifts and a T-bar, providing a wide range of slopes and conditions. Arctic Valley is only open weekends and holidays, generally early November–mid-April. Downhill skis and snowboards can be rented from several places in Anchorage, including REI and the ski areas.

Sledders of all ages play on the steep powerline slope that cuts along the road up to Arctic Valley, with parents taking kids back uphill in their cars. Another great sledding hill (600-ft. run) is in Centennial Park. Popular short sledding hills are at Kincaid Park and Service High School.

Cross-Country Skiing

Any Anchorageite over the age of four seems to be involved in cross-country skiing in one form or another. The city is laced with trails that serve as summertime cycling and jogging paths and wintertime ski routes. Most of these are groomed, with set tracks for traditional cross-country skiers and a wider surface for the skate-skiing crowd. Skate-skiing is getting more popular each year, and skijorers are also often seen on the Coastal Trail in this dog-happy town (dogs aren't allowed on most ski trails).

The **Nordic Skiing Association of Anchorage** (907/276-7609, www.anchoragenordicski.com) is Alaska's largest cross-country association, and its website has all sorts of information on the sport. Pick up *The Alaska Nordic Skier* at local ski shops and newsstands; it's published October–April each year.

The best-known cross-country area is **Kincaid Park,** where a convoluted maze of paths cover the rolling terrain, offering fun for all levels of ability. Kincaid is considered one of the top three competitive ski venues in America. You can warm up inside the Kincaid chalet and enjoy the vistas of Sleeping Lady and Mt. McKinley.

Russian Jack Springs Park, near Debarr Road and Boniface Parkway, has many more groomed ski trails, as well as a small rope tow and a warming house. Several more miles of groomed trails await at **Hillside Park** off Abbot Road next to Hilltop Ski Area; watch out for the moose here. All these trails are groomed for both traditional cross-country and the faster skate skis, which are becoming increasingly popular. Rent cross-country skis from REI or AMH.

Backcountry Skiing

If you're more ambitious—and have the wheels to get there—you'll find incredible backcountry skiing all around Anchorage. The Chugach Mountains offer an endless choice of skiing options that last from mid-October all the way into late June in some places. Note, however, that these areas are *not* for novices, so don't head out without knowing about and being prepared for such dangers as avalanches and hypothermia. Quite a number of skiers (and more snowmobilers) have died in the mountain avalanches near Anchorage. Even such favorites as the nearby summit of Flattop Mountain have taken a high human toll over the years.

The best-known backcountry areas are in Chugach State Park and at Turnagain Pass and Hatcher Pass. Access to **Chugach State Park** is the same as in the summer; pick up a winter routes map from the state park office. **Turnagain Pass** is 60 miles southwest of Anchorage on the way to Seward. The west side of the road is open to snowmachiners, but teleskiers avoid them by heading to the east side. There's a big parking lot, and from here you can continue into the open meadows or high into the mountains for deep, untracked powder.

Located 70 miles northeast of Anchorage, **Hatcher Pass** is a favorite backcountry area, and serves as a training area for the U.S. National Cross-Country Ski Team. The road can sometimes be a bit treacherous if you don't have studded tires, so be sure to call the park for road conditions (907/745-2827). REI in Anchorage offers cross-country and telemark clinics.

Ice-Skating

Anchorage is wild about ice-skating and hockey. The **UAA Seawolves** (907/786-1293, www.uaa.alaska.edu) and the semi-pro **Alaska Aces** (907/258-2237, www.alaskaaces.com) attract crowds all season, and the area has five indoor rinks. All are open year-round and offer skate rentals as well as instruction: **Ben Boeke Ice Arena** (334 E. 16th, 907/274-5715, www.benboeke.com) in the Sullivan Arena, **Dempsey Anderson Ice Arena** (1741 W. Northern Lights Blvd., 907/277-7571, www.sullivanarena.com), **UAA Sports Center** (2801 Providence Dr., 907/786-1233), and **Dimond Ice Chalet** (800 E. Dimond, 907/344-1212, www.dimondicechalet.com) in the Dimond Mall. Ben Boeke is an Olympic-size hockey rink.

Accommodations and Camping

As might be expected in a city of more than a quarter-million people, Anchorage has a wide range of lodging options. Unfortunately, most of these also have Alaskan-sized prices. A good one-stop place to begin your search for local lodging is the Anchorage Convention & Visitors Bureau website (www.anchorage.net). Be sure to make Anchorage lodging reservations far ahead for July and August, or try bidding at www.priceline.com for last-minute deals. Add a 12 percent lodging tax to the rates listed below. Anchorage is a spread-out city and many of the places listed below are in Midtown rather than downtown, making a rental car a wise investment. Parking may or may not be available at downtown locations, so ask ahead to be sure.

UNDER $100

Popular with outdoor enthusiasts of all types, **Anchorage Guesthouse** (2001 Hillcrest Dr., 907/274-0408, www.akhouse.com) is off a quiet tree-lined street above Westchester Lagoon and near the Coastal Trail. Inside are two private rooms ($82) that work well for couples and families, and three bunk rooms ($32 per person). All units share three baths. Ingredients for a make-it-yourself breakfast are provided, and guests can use the living room, dining room, kitchen, and sunroom. Bike rentals, Internet access (fee), and free Wi-Fi are available, along with a big garage to store your kayak, camping gear, bikes, and more. The friendly owner, Andy Baker, is an accomplished singer/songwriter.

Another cheap and well-run option is **Spenard Hostel International** (2845 W. 42nd Place, 907/248-5036, www.alaskahostel.org, $22 per person), with 47 dorm spaces. Things are less restrictive than at the youth hostel, and there's no curfew (but no alcohol either). Spenard Hostel has three kitchens, four baths, and laundry facilities. They rent mountain bikes, have space for tents ($19 s or $34 d), and put on potluck dinners most Sunday nights. Sheets and blankets are provided. Call for reservations two to four weeks ahead of your visit if arriving in mid-summer.

Other Midtown hostels are **26th Street International Hostel** (1037 W. 26th Ave., 907/274-1252, www.26streethostel.com, $25 per person) and **Jason's International Youth Hostel** (3324 Eide St., 907/562-0263, $20 per person with breakfast).

The managers at **International Backpackers Hostel** (3601 Peterkin St., Unit A, 907/274-3870), maintain several houses on the northeast side of Anchorage in the Mountain View area. These contain 30 beds in coed or same-sex dorm rooms for $25, including a full kitchen. No curfew, private rooms, or alcohol. Tent spaces are $10 per person, and short-term bag storage is available. The hostel is in good condition and open all day, but Mountain View is the most crime-ridden section of Anchorage so be prepared to hear gunfire in the night.

The **Anchorage International Hostel** (700 H St., 907/276-3635, www.anchorage internationalhostel.org, $20 per person) has deteriorated in recent years, but might do if you're desperate for a downtown bed. Personally, I'd rather sleep in my car. **Qupqugiaq Inn** (640 W. 36th Ave., 907/562-5681, www.qupq.com) occupies the upstairs of a boxy Midtown building, but the interior is filled with distinctively curved walls. Accommodations are cramped and spartan, but everything is well maintained and guests have access to the communal kitchen and two guest computers. This is a good place for couples on a budget, but can be noisy at times. Rooms with shared bath are $59 s or $69 d; add $10 for a private bath in the nicer downstairs rooms. Downstairs is Istanbul Café, serving Turkish food.

$100-200

Creekwood Inn (2150 Gambell St., 907/258-6006 or 800/478-6008, www.creekwoodinn.com) is a no-frills Midtown place with a mix of older budget rooms: $99–109 d for standard units with microwaves and fridges, $129–139 for kitchenette suites.

Merrill Field Inn (420 Sitka St., 907/276-4547 or 800/898-4547, www.merrillfieldinn.com, $110 s or $126 d) has large rooms with continental breakfasts, fridges, microwaves, and a guest computer, plus free airport and downtown transport in the summer. The neighborhood isn't the best.

Motel 6 (5000 A St., 907/677-8640 or 800/466-8656, www.motel6anchorage.com, $130 s or $135 d) is one of the newest Anchorage hotels, with predictable Midtown accommodations, but no microwaves or fridges in the rooms.

Far from the center of town at New Seward Highway and Tudor Street in South Anchorage, **Parkwood Inn** (907/563-3590 or 800/478-3590, www.parkwoodinn.com) is a decent family option. All of the apartment-style rooms include full kitchens with dishes, Wi-Fi, and guest computer. Studio units are $149–159 d, and two-bedroom apartments sleep up to six for $289 d.

Lakeshore Motor Inn (3009 Lakeshore Dr., 907/248-3485 or 800/770-3000, www.lakeshoremotorinn.com) is a quiet and clean motel near the airport with standard rooms for $129 s or $139 d, rooms with kitchenettes for $149 s or d, and one-bedroom suites at $169 for up to six, and two-bedroom suites that sleep eight for $189. Free airport transport and Wi-Fi too. All rooms contain fridges.

One of the better reasonably priced options is **Microtel Inn & Suites** (5205 Northwood Dr., 907/245-5002 or 888/680-4500, www.microtelanchorage.com) near the airport. Rates are $140 d in large rooms, or $150 d in mini-suites with fridges and microwaves, including a continental breakfast, airport shuttle, two indoor whirlpool tubs, and free Wi-Fi.

Long House Alaskan Hotel (4335 Wisconsin St., 907/243-2133 or 888/243-2133, www.longhousehotel.com) is a large log-sided building near the airport where spacious rooms are $149–169 d, and suites go for $179–189 d. Free airport shuttle and continental breakfast, plus Wi-Fi in the lobby. The long and narrow configuration of the rooms is a bit odd; rumor has it the building was once an Army barracks.

It's hard to beat the location for **Copper Whale Inn** (440 L St., 907/258-7999 or 866/258-7999, www.copperwhale.com), right on the edge of downtown with a flower-packed back patio overlooking Cook Inlet. Next door is Simon and Seafort's, one of the city's finest restaurants. This attractively appointed inn has two rooms ($165 d) that share a bath, but the other 13 rooms ($199 d) have private baths. A filling breakfast is included, along with guest computers and Wi-Fi.

Right in the heart of town, the 31-room **Anchorage Grand Hotel** (505 W 2nd Ave., 907/929-8888 or 888/800-0640, www.anchoragegrand.com, $199 d) is a cozy all-suites hotel with reasonable prices, friendly service, and business center. Guests receive a voucher for breakfast at a nearby café.

A family run boutique hotel right downtown, **Voyager Hotel** (501 K St., 907/277-9501 or 800/247-9070, www.voyagerhotel.com, $179 d), offers 40 large, clean rooms with microwaves and fridges, plus Wi-Fi in the lobby.

Another moderately priced option is the

20-unit **Anchorage Uptown Suites** (234 E. 2nd Ave., 907/279-4232 or 800/478-4232, www.anchorageuptownsuites.com) with standard rooms for $129 d, one-bedroom apartments with kitchens for $169 d, and deluxe suites with fireplace, king bed, and whirlpool tub for $199 d. German spoken, and a continental breakfast is provided in the summer.

A couple of blocks downhill from the heart of town, **Comfort Inn Ship Creek** (111 Ship Creek Ave., 907/277-6887 or 800/424-6423, www.comfortinnanchorage.com, $175 d) sits along this urban creek where salmon fishing draws locals and visitors alike. The railroad depot is just up the way, but that also means a fair amount of noise as the trains roll past. The hotel has decent rooms, along with a small pool, workout machines, continental breakfasts, wireless Internet, and free shuttles.

OVER $200

Built in 1953 but lovingly remodeled, **Inlet Tower Suites** (1200 L St., 907/276-0110 or 800/544-0786, www.inlettower.com) is a 14-story tower atop a hill halfway between downtown and Midtown. Rooms are nicely furnished and spacious, and with great views of the mountains or Cook Inlet from higher floors. Rooms with microwaves and fridges are $219 d; two-room suites sleep four for $269. Free airport or railroad transportation is included, along with Wi-Fi in the lobby. A free breakfast is served in the restaurant (Mixx Grill), best known for gourmet dinners.

One of my favorite Anchorage hotels, **Dimond Center Hotel** (700 E Dimond Blvd., 907/770-5000 or 866/770-5002, www.dimondcenterhotel.com, $229–269 d), has a less-than-appealing location, next to Wal-Mart and a big shopping mall on the south side of town. But inside you'll find a gorgeous lobby, custom-designed furnishings, and luxurious rooms with huge TVs. Even the baths are special, with jetted tubs and windows opening into the main room. A light breakfast is included and the hotel contains guest computers and Wi-Fi, plus free airport and train station shuttles.

Anchorage Hotel (330 E St., 907/272-4553 or 800/544-0988, www.historicanchoragehotel.com) is a classy little 26-room hotel built in 1916, and is now on the National Register of Historic Places. Standard rooms (small in size) cost $189 d, and two-room suites are $249 d. A continental breakfast is available in the lobby, and the hotel has Wi-Fi.

Hotel Captain Cook (5th Ave. and K St., 907/276-6000 or 800/843-1950, www.captaincook.com), occupies an entire block, with three towers and three restaurants. The hotel is owned by the family of former governor Wally Hickel, who also served as President Nixon's Secretary of Interior in the 1970s. The hotel's 550 rooms follow a nautical theme (befitting the name), and the building has an old-money feeling with dark woods and lots of suits and power ties. Hotel amenities include concierge service, free Wi-Fi throughout, and a full athletic club with hot tub, sauna, and indoor pool. It does not, however, provide shuttle vans. Rates start at $255 d for a standard room or $270 for junior suites, up to $405 d for a two-bedroom suite.

Millennium Alaskan Hotel (4800 Spenard Rd., 907/243-2300 or 800/544-0553, www.alaskanhotel.com, $280–300 d) sits along Anchorage's floatplane headquarters, Lake Hood, and has comfortable rooms and an Alaskan decor. The lobby is decked out in trophy heads and fish, with a stone fireplace in the center. Ask for a room facing the lake. Amenities include an exercise facility, whirlpool tub, sauna, Wi-Fi in the lobby, and free airport and downtown shuttle. The restaurant has a deck right on the water, and serves a popular Sunday brunch. It's a ways from town, but close to the airport. The Millennium has a cozier feeling than most other large Anchorage hotels, but is rather overpriced for what you get.

ALL-SUITES HOTELS

Anchorage's newest corporate boxes are geared to business travelers and families looking for more space, who don't mind the inevitable this-could-be-Tacoma atmosphere. These places typically have one room with two queen beds and a separate sitting room with pull-out sofa, plus a microwave and fridge. All also include indoor pools, hot tubs, exercise facilities, a breakfast buffet, Wi-Fi, and shuttles to the airport and train station. Summer rates are typically $190–220 d.

Two recommended downtown places are **Extended Stay Deluxe** (108 E. 8th Ave., 907/868-1605 or 866/506-7848, www.extendedstaydeluxe.com) and **Hawthorn Suites** (1110 W. 8th Ave., 907/222-5005 or 888/469-6575, www.hawthorn.com).

Quite a few Midtown places have similar facilities and prices, including the following good ones: **Hilton Garden Inn** (4540 A St., 907/562-7000 or 800/445-8667, www.hiltongardeninn.com), **Fairfield Inn & Suites** (5060 A St., 907/222-9000 or 888/236-2427, www.fairfieldinnanchorage.com), **SpringHill Suites by Marriott** (3401 A St., 907/562-3247 or 888/287-9400, www.springhillsuites.com), **Hampton Inn** (4301 Credit Union Dr., 907/550-7000 or 800/426-7866, www.hamptoninn.com), and **Homewood Suites** (140 W. Tudor Rd., 907/762-7000 or 800/225-5466, www.anchorage.homewoodsuites.com).

B&BS AND GUEST HOUSES

Anchorage had over 175 B&Bs at last count, including luxurious hillside homes with spectacular vistas, cozy older downtown places, and rent-out-the-spare-room suburban houses. An excellent starting point when looking for a local B&B is the **Anchorage Alaska B&B Association** (907/272-5909 or 888/584-5147, www.anchorage-bnb.com). Its website has links to 50 or so B&Bs, with location and price details. See the *Anchorage Visitors Guide* (available from ACVB's Visitors Information Center downtown or on the web at www.anchorage.net) for a fairly complete listing of local B&Bs, or take a look at the blizzard of B&B brochures filling visitor center racks. If the task seems too daunting on your own, contact **Alaska Private Lodgings** (907/235-2148 or 888/235-2148, www.alaskabandb.com) or **Alaska Sourdough B&B Association** (907/563-6244, www.alaskan.com/aksourdoughbba).

Downtown Guest House (1238 G St., 907/279-2359, www.downtownguesthouse.com, $150 for up to four) is an immaculate and peaceful two-bedroom apartment with a full kitchen. It's just a block or so from New Sagaya's (gourmet food, coffees, and deli), and a short walk from downtown.

Built in 1913, **Oscar Gill House B&B** (1355 W 10th Ave., 907/279-1344, www.oscargill.com, $105–135 d) is a historic home facing the downtown Park Strip. Two attractive guest rooms share a bath, while the largest has its own. Guests appreciate the central location, full breakfasts, friendly owners, and grandma's-house atmosphere. Call well ahead since Gill House fills fast.

For top-end lodging, it's hard to compete with ◖ **Sleeping Lady B&B** (548 Coastal Place, 907/258-4455 or 877/705-4455, www.anchsleepingladybnb.com, $179–199 d). The four rooms are elegant and immaculate, breakfasts are memorable, and the deck provides a sunset vista across Cook Inlet to the mountain called Sleeping Lady.

The following are additional recommended B&Bs in the under-$110 d price range: **Anchorage Downtown B&B** (907/278-9275, www.anchoragedowntown.com), **Coastal Trail B&B** (907/243-5809, www.coastaltrail.com), **Donna's B&B** (907/522-6025 or 888/421-6025, www.anchoragedonnasbandb.com), **Earth B&B** (907/279-9907, www.earthbb.com), **Gallery B&B** (907/274-2567), and **Susitna Place B&B** (907/274-3344, www.susitnaplace.com).

Other recommended finer B&Bs (over $120 d) include: **Aawesome B&B Retreat** (907/338-8873 or 877/226-9645, www.aawesomeworld.com), **Anchorage Lakeside Jewel B&B** (907/242-2126 or 866/539-3555, www.anchoragelakesidejewel.com), **Alaskan Frontier Gardens B&B** (907/345-655, www.alaskafrontiergardens.com), **Alaskan Leopard B&B** (907/868-1594 or 877/454-3046, www.alaskanleopard.com), **Arctic Fox Inn** (907/272-4818, www.arcticfoxinn.com), **Camai B&B** (907/333-2219 or 800/659-8763, www.camaibnb.com), **Highland Glenn Lodge** (907/336-2312 or 888/507-2312, www.alaskahighlandglen.com), **Jewel Lake B&B** (907/245-7321 or 877/245-7321, www.jewellakebandb.com), **Lake Hood Inn** (907/258-9321, www.lakehoodinn.com), **Mahogany Manor** (907/278-1111 or 888/777-0346, www.mahoganymanor.com), **North County Castle B&B** (907/345-7296, www.castlealaska.com), **Wandering Moose B&B** (907/522-3780, www.alaskawanderingmoose.com), and **Wildflower Inn** (907/274-1239, www.alaska-wildflower-inn.com).

CAMPING

The city-run **Centennial Park Campground** (907/343-6986, www.ci.anchorage.ak.us/parks, open mid-May through Sept.) has space for both tents and RVs (no hookups), and costs $20, plus $3 for showers. Take Muldoon Road south from the Glenn, hang your first left onto Boundary, then the next left onto the highway frontage road for a half-mile to the campground.

Anchorage RV Park (1200 N. Muldoon Rd., 907/338-7275 or 877/777-4081, www.anchrvpark.com, $16 tents, $32 RVs) is in a quiet, wooded area on the northeast edge of town near the Alaska Native Heritage Center.

Other RV campgrounds include **Anchorage Ship Creek Landings RV Park** (150 N. Ingra St., 907/277-0877 or 888/778-7700, www.alaskarv.com, $16 tents, $32 RVs), **Golden Nugget Camper Park** (4100 DeBarr Rd., 907/333-5311 or 800/449-2012, www.goldennuggetcamperpark.com, $22 tents, $37 RV), and **Creekwood Inn** (2150 Gambell St., 907/258-6006 or 800/478-6008, www.creekwoodinn.com, $30 RVs, no tents). Many travelers also park RVs for free in the Wal-Mart and Fred Meyer parking lots, but check with store managers for any restrictions.

Food

If you can't find a good meal in Anchorage you aren't trying. The city's size and diverse population are mirrored in a wide range of eating places, from grab-a-bite fast-food joints to high-class (and high-priced) gourmet restaurants. To reach many of the best places, you'll need a vehicle or knowledge of the bus schedule, but there are several fine restaurants right downtown. Two useful free dining publications are available from racks around town: *Cuisine Scene* (www.anchoragepressinfo.com) and the *Restaurant and Entertainment Guide.* Both are filled with restaurant ads (often with menus) and brief descriptions. Note: Smoking is banned in Anchorage restaurants; all bars are also entirely smoke-free.

BREAKFAST

Looking for a great downtown breakfast in an unpretentious setting? Join the throngs at the spacious ◖ **Snow City Café** (1034 W. 4th Ave., 907/272-2489, www.snowcitycafe.com, $8–11), where meals are ample, reasonably priced, and dependably good. Breakfast is available until the 4 P.M. closing time; try the Mediterranean scramble, huevos rancheros, or one of the daily specials. But get here early on weekends to avoid a wait. Lunchtime sandwiches bring in the legal staff from nearby offices along "lawyer row." Come back on Wednesday evenings for an Irish music jam session. The café also has free wireless Internet.

An old-time favorite, **Gwennie's Old Alaska Restaurant** (4333 Spenard Rd., 907/243-2090) specializes in breakfast (available all day), especially sourdough pancakes and reindeer sausage. Meals are Alaska-size, so those with small appetites may want to split an order. Memorabilia crowds the walls on this sprawling two-story place, and big tables fill with families filling up.

Decorated with an impressive collection of pig trinkets, **Hogg Bros. Café** (1049 W. Northern Lights Blvd., 907/276-9649) serves gigantic breakfasts and burgers. Not surprisingly, the menu is heavy on the fat, featuring

20 different omelets and other artery-cloggers. It's very noisy and crowded on weekends as Alaskans and tourists pig out.

Two very good places for a Sunday splurge are **Sacks Café** (328 G St., 907/276-3546, www.sackscafe.com) downtown, and **Millennium Hotel** (4800 Spenard Rd., 907/243-2300 or 800/544-0553, www.millennium-hotels.com). The latter has a popular Sunday brunch ($30) with crab legs, create-your-own omelets, and champagne, plus a big deck facing Lake Hood, where you can watch floatplanes take off. Sacks is à la carte.

BAKERIES AND SWEETS

Some of the best Anchorage breads and pastries come from **Europa Bakery** (601 W. 36th, 907/563-5704), where the rustic, thick-crusted artisan breads compare favorably to anything you might find in Europe. Similarly noteworthy breads and sweets can be found at **L'Aroma Bakeries,** inside both New Sagaya stores.

Morty's New York Bagel Deli (901 E. Dimond Blvd., 907/336-1315) makes the city's most authentic bagels and bagel sandwiches. And yes, the owner really is from New York.

Alaska Wild Berry Products (907/562-8858 or 800/280-2927, www.alaskawildberryproducts.com) has a large chocolate factory and gift shop on Juneau Street near the corner of Old Seward Highway and International Airport Road. This is a fun place for chocoholics; there's even a 20-foot melted-chocolate waterfall. Free taste samples, too. Fifteen-minute tours are given throughout the day, and this is a very popular stop on the Anchorage tour-bus circuit. The big gift shop offers all the standard tourist junk (and then some), while the theater shows a unique 30-minute film ($7.50) about Alaska.

A famous Fairbanks ice cream shop, **Hot Licks** (1340 W. Northern Lights Blvd., 907/929-5425, www.hotlicks.net) has finally come to Anchorage, with premium homemade ice cream, including one made with Alaskan blueberries. It's right next to REI and has free Wi-Fi. On the south end of town, **Cold Stone Creamery** (9001 Jewel Lake Rd., 907/248-2644, www.coldstonecreamery.com) serves rich ice cream with "add-in" flavors of all types.

COFFEE AND TEA

Anchorageites love strong coffee, and the town is jam-packed with espresso stands and cafés—including the bland Starbucks versions. Tucked away in a Midtown shopping mall, **Café del Mundo** (341 E. Benson, 907/274-0026, www.cafedelmundo.com) is a favorite of the lawyer/Volvo crowd, and a relaxing place to while away a morning. Also in Midtown, but this time next to REI, **Middle Way Café** (1200 W. Northern Lights Blvd., 907/272-6433, www.middlewaycafe.com) is a surprising little coffeehouse with delicious, mostly vegetarian lunches. Both Café del Mundo and Middle Way provide free Wi-Fi. Downtown's **Side Street Espresso** (412 G St., 907/258-9055) is where the greenie art crowd hangs out.

A personal favorite is the local chain of 10 **Kaladi Brothers** espresso shops (www.kaladi.com), including ones inside the New Sagaya groceries and Titlewave Books. The latter, located in the best Anchorage bookstore—at 1360 W. Northern Lights Boulevard next to REI—includes an Internet café. Many other Alaskan coffee shops buy their espresso beans from Kaladi Brothers, and they've even opened a shop in Seattle—the heart of enemy (Starbucks) territory.

LUNCH AND QUICK MEALS

Just a block from the downtown visitor center, **Sweet Basil Café** (335 E St., 907/274-2434) serves cold or hot sandwiches on freshly baked basil bread, along with juice bar specials, light breakfasts, and lattes. Another recommended lunch spot is Snow City Café.

◖ **Sacks Café** (328 G St., 907/276-3546, www.sackscafe.com, lunch $10–13, dinners $18–34), crafts some of Anchorage's finest lunches and dinners, and is especially popular with the business crowd. You'll find an arty decor, creative cooking, and heady talk. The menu changes frequently, but typically includes fresh halibut or salmon, baked penne pasta, chipotle sirloin burgers, and chicken curry. Great desserts, too. Reservations are essential for dinner, though they aren't taken for the wine bar.

Housed within the Anchorage Museum of History and Art, the **Marx Bros. Café** (121 W. 7th Ave., 907/343-6193, www.marxcafe.com) occupies an open atrium surrounded by works of art. The food is equally notable, with homemade soups, fresh salads, and creative sandwiches.

Don't miss the perpetually crowded **L'Aroma Bakery and Deli** at both New Sagaya stores (in Midtown at 3700 Old Seward Hwy., and close to downtown at 900 W. 13th Ave.; www.laromabakery.com) for panini sandwiches, small pizzas baked in wood-fired ovens, sushi, spring rolls, salads, Chinese specials, and American "comfort food" (mac and cheese, meatloaf, lasagna, and so on), along with freshly baked breads and sweets. You're guaranteed to find something that appeals. Eat here or get it to go. Both New Sagayas also house Kaladi Brothers Coffee shops.

Middle Way Café (1200 W. Northern Lights Blvd., 907/272-6433, www.middleway cafe.com) hides out next to the REI store, but always manages to fill up when lunch arrives. Check out today's specials on the board, order at the counter, and wait for your name to be called. The menu includes vegetarian sandwiches and wraps, soy burgers, salads, fruit smoothies, and daily specials. The lip-ringed barista will make a mocha while you wait, or serve a big piece of carrot cake.

Several vendors have downtown carts in front of the old Federal Building on 4th Avenue in the summer. The best of these—look for the queue—is the vendor of reindeer sausage and grilled onions. On weekends in the summer your best downtown bet is the Saturday and Sunday Farmers Market. For more downtown fast food, head to the **food court** on the 4th level of the 5th Avenue Mall (5th Ave. and C St.), with fast-food eateries of all persuasions, from Thai to frozen yogurt. Other inexpensive places covered elsewhere include **Bear Tooth Theatrepub** (see *Movies*), and **Taco King** (see *Mexican*).

Anchorage's two top burger-and-fries joints are **Arctic Roadrunner** (2477 Arctic Blvd.,

907/279-7311) and **Tommy's Burger Stop** (W. Benson at Spenard Ave., 907/561-5696).

PIZZA AND ITALIAN

Anchorage has all the national pizza chains, and the "Pizza" listing in the Yellow Pages includes some 60 different places. Out of these, **Pizza Olympia** (2809 Spenard Rd., across from REI, 907/561-5264) is a personal favorite. Four generations of the Maroudas family run this place with authentic affection, rolling out such unique offerings as garlic and feta cheese pizzas and all the standard Greek specialties.

Two excellent pizza options are **Moose's Tooth Pub and Pizzeria** (see *Brewpubs*) and **L'Aroma Bakery & Deli** (see *Bakeries and Sweets*). Other good pizza places include **Sorrento's** (610 E. Fireweed, 907/278-3439), with the best southern Italian food in Anchorage, and **Fletcher's** (in Hotel Captain Cook at 5th Ave. and K St., 907/276-6000), where Anchorage waiters and cooks go after work.

For delicious northern Italian dinners with an Alaskan twist, visit the small **CampoBello Bistro** (601 W. 36th Ave., 907/563-2040, $15–23). This is a relaxing and romantic spot for lunch or dinner; try the seafood crepes.

For creative Tuscany-inspired food in the heart of town, you won't go wrong at **Ristorante Orso** (737 W. 5th Ave., www.orsoalaska.com, 907/222-3232, $18–37). This popular restaurant exudes energy, and the menu includes wild mushroom ravioli, osso buco lamb, and cashew-crusted halibut, along with a dessert selection that stars a wonderful molten chocolate cake. Open for lunch and dinner. Reservations recommended.

ASIAN
Chinese and Korean

Many of Anchorage's Chinese restaurants are actually run by Korean-Americans, who make up a surprisingly large ethnic community in the city. The best local Korean option is **Kimchi Korean Restaurant** (3337 Fairbanks St., 907/276-5130). Try any of the barbecue dishes, or the kalbee dolsot bibimbob (beef and veggies served in a sizzling stone pot).

Panda Restaurant (605 E. Northern Lights Blvd., 907/272-3308) has a big Chinese menu and gets high marks from locals; it's open late most nights.

Twin Dragon Mongolian Bar-B-Que (612 E. 15th Ave., 907/276-7535) is a fun place where you fill a plate with veggies and meat and watch the chefs do their show. Great fun, and reasonable too: $9 for the lunch buffet or $13 for dinner.

Golden Pond Restaurant (300 W. 36th, 907/563-5525) has a big all-you-can-eat Chinese buffet for lunch or dinner, as does **Yen King Restaurant** (3501 Old Seward Hwy., 907/563-2627). The latter provides free delivery. **Chinese Kitchen** (2904 Spenard Rd., 907/279-2222) is a tiny family eatery with lunch specials and friendly owners. If you're adventurous, ask about the menu items listed only in Chinese.

A personal favorite is **Fu Du** (2600 E. Tudor Rd., 907/561-6610), where service is efficient and friendly, the setting is cozy, and servings are enormous. Entrées come with soup, Chinese kimchee, rice, eggroll, and tea. Lunch specials are an even better deal, and they offer free delivery.

Thai and South Asian

Anchorage has quite a few Thai restaurants—seven at last count. None of these measures up to what you'd find in Thailand (or Berkeley for that matter), but several are well worth a visit. Hip locals rave about **Thai Kitchen** (3405 E. Tudor, 907/561-0082, www.thaikitchenalaska.com) tucked away in a strip mall on Tudor near Bragaw. With 120 choices on the menu, you're sure to find something to your taste, but favorites include Popeye chicken or any of the spicy soups. The restaurant is open for lunch and dinner on weekdays, but dinners only on weekends. Get there early since it closes at 9 P.M.

Housed within an old Pizza Hut building in Midtown, **Chaing Mai Ultimate Thai** (3637 Old Seward Hwy., 907/563-8900) is a family-friendly spot decorated with Thai linen and portraits of the royalty. Meals are consistently

great, service is super-friendly, and the prices are fair: $10–12 for most items. Everything is made fresh while you wait.

Also recommended is **Thai Orchid Restaurant** (219 E. Dimond Ave., 907/868-5226), with the best pad Thai in town and a diverse and inexpensive menu that includes many vegetarian choices.

Get Vietnamese meals from **Saigon Restaurant** (3561 E. Tudor Rd., 907/563-2515), and Filipino specialties at the misnamed **RJ Pastries & Bread** (9212 E 6th Ave., 907/277-5332).

One of the only Indian restaurants in Alaska, **Bombay Deluxe** (555 W. Northern Lights Blvd., 907/277-1200, www.bombaydeluxe.com) has an ample weekday lunch buffet ($10) and free delivery.

Japanese

Get the finest fresh sushi, tempura, and teriyaki from **Peter's Sushi Spot** (4140 B St., 907/276-5187, www.peterssushispot.com) behind Moose's Tooth, or **Yamato Ya** (3700 Old Seward Hwy. 907/561-2128), next to New Sagaya's.

Kumagoro (533 W. 4th Ave., 907/272-9905) is a plant-bedecked downtown restaurant with house-made udon noodle soups, and an evening-only sushi bar. The restaurant fills up for lunch with the business crowd. Local Carrs/Safeway, Fred Meyer, and New Sagaya supermarkets also have fresh sushi in their delis.

MEDITERRANEAN

Aladdin's (4240 Old Seward Hwy. at Tudor, 907/561-2373, www.aladdinsak.com) serves traditional Mediterranean dishes from North Africa and the Middle East, including mousaka, lamb couscous, seafood kebab, and various vegetarian specialties for $11–15. The restaurant has a big local following.

MEXICAN

A longtime favorite—it's the oldest Mexican restaurant in Alaska—is **La Cabaña** (312 E. 4th Ave., 907/272-0135). This is a good place for lunch, with tasty halibut fajitas. **La Mex** (2552

Spenard Rd., 907/274-7511) is popular for evening nachos and margaritas, or for full meals. Fast service, and the steaks aren't bad, either.

In business since 1972, **Mexico in Alaska** (7305 Old Seward Hwy., 907/349-1528, www.mexicoinalaska.com) is one of the more authentic south-of-the-border spots, but it's a long way out if you don't have a car.

If you're looking for the quick version, **Taco King** (112 W. Northern Lights Blvd., 907/276-7387) serves fat burritos and tacos. Order at the counter and then slather it up with your choice of salsas. You'll never want to go Taco Bell after this!

A great family option for nachos, burritos, and pizzas is **Bear Tooth Theatrepub** (1230 W. 27th Ave., 907/276-4200, www.beartooththeatre.net), where you can take in a $3 movie while you eat.

VEGETARIAN

Organic Oasis (2610 Spenard Rd., 907/277-7882, www.organicoasis.com), in the heart of Spenard, serves tasty organic wraps and sandwiches (even a few with meat), fresh-squeezed juices (including wheatgrass), smoothies, and other lunch and dinner fare. The enjoyable, airy setting is right next to a yoga studio. **Natural Pantry** (3801 Old Seward Hwy., 907/770-1444, www.natural-pantry.com) has groceries, organic smoothies, fresh juices, and light lunches.

All the places listed in the *Lunch* section have vegetarian specials of one sort or another; Middle Way Café is particularly notable. Also try Snow City Café, Aladdin's, and any of the aforementioned Thai restaurants for vegetarian specialties.

SEAFOOD

Countless Anchorage restaurants serve fresh seafood in season, and some of the best are described elsewhere: Sacks Café, Ristorante Orso, Simon & Seaforts, Marx Bros. Café, Jens', and F Street Station.

They don't serve meals, but the best places to find fresh fish, clams, crab, and other Alaskan specialties are **10th & M**

Seafoods (1020 M St., 907/272-6013 or 800/770-2722, www.10thandmseafoods.com) and **New Sagaya** (900 W. 13th Ave., 907/274-6173, www.newsagaya.com). For smoked salmon (and reindeer sausage), drop by **Alaska Sausage & Seafood** (2914 Arctic Blvd., 907/562-3636 or 800/798-3636, www.alaskasausage.com).

STEAK

As you might guess, Anchorage has several of the meat-lover chain restaurants, including Black Angus, Cattle Company, Lone Star Steakhouse, and Outback Steakhouse. More upscale is **Sullivan's** (in 5th Ave. Mall at C St., 907/258-2882, www.sullivansteakhouse.com), where two-inch-thick steaks are seared at high temperatures and cooked to perfection, and the dessert soufflés are to die for.

Just a block away is Anchorage's old-time steakhouse, **Club Paris** (417 W. 5th Ave., 907/277-6332, www.clubparisrestaurant.com), a plain-Jane fixture on the downtown scene since 1957. The atmosphere is dark and one wall is lined with the famous and infamous visitors who've eaten here over the decades. Super-tender filet mignon is the house specialty, $34 and worth it, but other items are somewhat cheaper, including fresh seafood, burgers, and salads.

BREWPUBS

Anchorage's food-and-booze scene is thriving, with several quite-different options from which to choose. Right downtown, ◖ **Glacier BrewHouse** (737 W. 5th Ave., 907/274-2739, www.glacierbrewhouse.com) is a lively and noisy place that overflows most evenings; reservations recommended. Chefs work furiously in the open kitchen, sending out delicious meals of salmon, steak, ribs, and thin-crusted pizzas, while the bar pours beers made in the behind-the-glass brewery. Most dinner entrées run $19–26, though you can get small pizzas for $11.

A few blocks away is **Snow Goose Restaurant** (717 W. 3rd Ave., 907/277-7727, www.alaskabeers.com), featuring king crab, steak, and more downstairs, plus an upstairs pub where the outdoor patio overlooks Cook

Inlet, with the white triangle of Mt. McKinley in the distance. Snow Goose always has a half-dozen homebrews on tap from its Sleeping Lady Brewery (on the premises), along with a substantial wine selection.

Moose's Tooth Pub and Pizzeria (3300 Old Seward Hwy., 907/258-2537, www.moosestooth.net) is *the* Anchorage place for pizza and beer—hands down. The huge parking lot fills with cars most evenings, and you're likely to endure a wait for a table, but the distinctive pizzas (try the "brewhouse favorite" with chorizo sausage, sun-dried tomatoes, red onions, sauce and cheese) are all made from scratch and baked in a stone oven. Medium pizzas cost $12–18. The dozen or so prize-winning beers are great too. Same owners as the equally popular Bear Tooth Theatrepub (see *Movies*).

You won't go wrong with a meal at tiny **F Street Station** (325 F St., 907/272-5196) where there are always reasonably priced, ultra-fresh seafood specials, fast service, and a convivial, white-collar atmosphere. Try the perfectly cooked beer-batter halibut for $11, or the $15 New York steak and fries. Be sure to ask the bartender the story behind the huge hunk of cheddar that's always on the counter. This is a bar, so it's not for kids.

They don't brew their own beers, but **Humpy's Great Alaskan Alehouse** (610 W. 6th Ave., 907/276-2337, www.humpys.com) attracts a 20-something crowd with more than 40 brews on tap and a pub menu of halibut burgers, salads, pastas, nachos, and other crunchy fare. Live bands play nightly in this perpetually packed hangout.

FINE DINING

Several of Anchorage's fine-dining establishments are described elsewhere, including Ristorante Orso, Sacks Café, and Club Paris. Reservations are strongly advised (or required) for all the following places.

Simon & Seaforts (420 L St., 907/274-3502, www.simonandseaforts.com) has an eclectic menu, efficient service, and splendid views. Simon's serves daily fresh fish specials and aged prime rib; wonderful cracked wheat sourdough bread comes with each meal. Expect to pay $30 for dinner, though lunch (try the Cajun chicken fettuccine for $13) is considerably less expensive. If you don't have restaurant dinner reservations, head to the more relaxed dinner bar, where the menu is more limited, but still diverse enough to satisfy. If you're in the bar, check out the collection of single-malt Scotch whiskies, said to be one of the largest in the nation.

A much smaller and quieter place than Simon's, the elegant **Marx Bros. Café** (627 W. 3rd Ave., 907/278-2133, www.marxcafe.com) has been in business since 1979, and is open Tuesday–Saturday. Hors d'oeuvres cost $13–15 and dinner entrées $30–45. The Caesar salad—made at your table—is especially memorable. The menu changes daily, but it's always innovative, and the big wine list and good dessert selection complement the meal. Reservations are essential at this dinner-only café; call well ahead of your visit to be assured of a table.

Crow's Nest (907/343-2217 or 800/478-3100, www.captaincook.com) sits atop the Hotel Captain Cook at 4th Avenue and K Street, 20 floors above masses. Fine dining, with prices (and a view) to match. You can either order off the sky-high menu or choose a five-course tasting menu spectacular for $65 or $95 with matched wines from run the 10,000-bottle wine cellar. Other entrées run $30–48. This is one of the only places in Alaska where you can't eat in Carhartts; not only would you stand out from the rest of the crowd, but there's also a dress code. Reservations required.

Don't let the strip-mall setting for **Jens'** (701 W. 36th Ave., 907/561-5367, www.jensrestaurant.com), throw you off—this is a great European-style bistro with an Alaskan twist. The atmosphere is art-filled, and the food is equally beautiful, from the rockfish filets to the tenderloin of veal. Attentive service, a nice wine list, and delectable desserts complete the picture. Reservations recommended. It's easy to spend well over $100 for two people here, but you'll go away satiated and happy. You can also hang out at the wine bar, which serves appetizers until midnight (and can get noisy).

It's pretty far off the main tourist trails, but **Kincaid Grill** (6700 Jewel Lake Rd., 907/243-0507, www.kincaidgrill.com, $26–46) is well worth the detour. Telegenic owner/chef Al Levinsohn—whom you might recognize from his Food Network appearances—has created a playful setting, with a wine bar and an ever-changing menu. Alaskan seafood is always on the menu, along with filet mignon, shrimp gumbo, and ginger Florentine pineapple upside-down cake.

Befitting its name, **The Bridge Restaurant** (221 W. Ship Creek Ave., 907/677-6771, www.thebridgealaska.com, $19–30) sits astride a footbridge over Ship Creek, a popular fishing spot just north of downtown. House specialties bridge Asian, European, and Alaskan flavors, with grilled filet mignon, Moroccan-seasoned lamb, and sesame crusted ahi, along with crab and mango summer roll appetizers and sourdough bread pudding. Open for lunch and dinner.

GROCERIES

Carrs/Safeway has 10 stores scattered around Anchorage, including one at the Sears Mall in Midtown. Grocery prices are generally a bit lower at the four big **Fred Meyer** stores, including one at Northern Lights and New Seward. Most Carrs/Safeway and Fred Meyer stores have delis, fresh sushi, salad bars, ATMs, and in-store Starbucks outlets.

A distinctive gourmet grocer is **New Sagaya**

(stores at 3700 Old Seward Hwy., 907/561-5173; and 900 W. 13th Ave., 907/274-6173, www.newsagaya.com), where the featured attractions include exotic produce and Asian foods, outstanding delis and L'Aroma Bakeries and Kaladi Coffee, live crab and oysters, and fresh-from-the-sea seafood.

Many Alaskans buy groceries at the two **Costcos** (on Dimond Ave. at C St., and Muldoon at 15th Ave.), where you need to be a member and most things come in sizes meant to feed whole villages (or two rather obese Alaskans). Their pizza-by-the-slice and polish dogs are a fattening bargain, once you've finished your shopping ordeal.

FARMERS MARKETS

Anchorage's finest and freshest produce can be found at the **Anchorage Market & Festival** (907/272-5634, www.anchoragemarkets.com), held at the downtown parking lot on 3rd Avenue and E Street every Saturday and Sunday 10 A.M.–6 P.M. from mid-May to mid-September. More than 300 vendors offer local arts and crafts, a diverse mix of finger food—everything from salmon quesadillas to sweet funnel cakes—and, of course, produce. Live music and entertainment add to the allure. Be sure to stop by **Kahiltna Birchworks** (907/733-1309, www.alaskabirchsyrup.com) where you'll find distinctive and flavorful birch syrups and caramels created from Michael and Dulce East's home in the Alaskan bush. A smaller **Wednesday Market** takes place at Northway Mall mid-June–late August 11 A.M.–5 P.M.

Information and Services

VISITOR CENTERS

One of the best things about Anchorage is how easy it is to collect all the information you could possibly need, not just for the city, but also for much of the state. Two stops near the corner of 4th Avenue and F Street downtown can supply you with a ton of fliers, brochures, booklets, guides, schedules, and maps, plus the synthesizing expertise of the knowledgeable staffs who can help you make sense of it all. The **Anchorage Convention and Visitors Bureau** (ACVB) is the place to go for every possible Anchorage brochure, handout, or free newspaper. Across the intersection is the **Alaska Public Lands Information Center** where you can learn about national parks, forests, wildlife refuges, and much more. Both of these places, and the nearby **Department of Natural Resources Information Center,** are described in detail in the *Sights* section.

The ACVB also maintains two **Airport Visitor Centers:** one near the baggage area in the domestic terminal (907/248-4979) and the other in the international terminal (907/266-2657). Both are staffed daily 9 A.M.–4 P.M. in the summer.

LIBRARIES

The **Z. J. Loussac Library** (36th and Denali, 907/261-2975, http://lexicon.ci.anchorage. ak.us, Mon.–Thurs. 10 A.M.–8 P.M., Fri.–Sat. 10 A.M.–6 P.M.) is a spacious facility out in Midtown. You could easily lose an afternoon just wandering among the stacks, enjoying the cozy sitting room on Level 3, studying the huge relief map of the state, browsing among the paintings hanging on the walls, or picking a book at random from the large Alaskana collection. Getting to the Alaskana section is an adventure in its own right—the architects did everything they could to make it difficult to reach: up two flights of stairs, across a long connecting walkway, and then back down two levels. And it's back out the same way, since

there is no exit here! The library has computers for free Internet access, but you may have to wait awhile.

INTERNET ACCESS

Local libraries all have computers and free wireless Internet access. More and more Anchorage businesses—especially hotels, B&Bs, and coffee shops—now have guest computers and Wi-Fi. Visit www.free-hotspot.com or www.jiwire.com for updated listings, or try one of the following places for free Wi-Fi: Café del Mundo, Hot Licks Ice Cream, Middle Way Café, Organic Oasis, Peanut Farm, Sub Zero, and some Kaladi Brothers (see the *Food* section for addresses). The Anchorage airport has free Wi-Fi, and there is even an experimental program to add it to People Mover buses.

BANKING

As might be expected, ATMs can now be found practically anywhere, including most banks and grocery stores. Wells Fargo (630 E. 5th Ave., 907/267-5700) offices will exchange traveler's checks or bills in Canadian dollars, Japanese yen, Euros, and other currency for greenbacks.

MEDICAL SERVICES

Alaska's three largest hospitals are in Anchorage. Of the first two, **Alaska Regional Hospital** (2801 DeBarr Rd., 907/276-1131, www.alaskaregional.com) and **Providence Alaska Medical Center** (3200 Providence Dr., 907/562-2211, www.providence.org), Providence has a better reputation and is a nonprofit. The modern **Alaska Native Medical Center** (4315 Diplomacy Dr., 907/257-1150, www.anmc.org) is perhaps the finest facility in Alaska, but is only for Native people.

To find a doctor, call the **physician referral services** offered by Providence (907/261-4900) and Alaska Regional (907/264-1722 or 800/265-8624). You'll find a 24-hour pharmacy inside the **Carrs** (907/297-0560) store at West Northern Lights Boulevard and Minnesota Drive.

Several "Doc-in-a-box" offices are scattered around Anchorage, but you're likely to see a physician's assistant rather than a doctor. Try

FirstCare (3710 Woodland Dr., 907/248-1122) or **Urgent Care** (5437 E. Northern Lights Blvd., 907/333-8561). **Primary Care Associates** (3500 LaTouche St., 907/562-1234) is a recommended place to find a real doctor, but you'll need an appointment.

Getting There and Around

AIR

Almost everybody who flies into Alaska from the Lower 48 lands at Anchorage International Airport, even if just to connect to other carriers around the state. While waiting for your luggage, take a look at the collection of stuffed Alaskan animals and fish on the upper level. The city skyline and Chugach Mountains are visible from up here; go out, breathe the air, dig the view, and indulge in a private smile—you finally made it to Alaska. You, and the other five million people (honest) who pass through the airport annually.

Anchorage International Airport (907/266-2525, www.anchorageairport.com) is six miles southwest of downtown. (Officially, it is Ted Stevens Anchorage International Airport, in honor of the U.S. senator who continues to bring home the pork to fund all sorts of Alaskan projects, including the airport.) An information booth (907/248-0373, daily 9 A.M.–5 P.M. in the summer) is near the baggage area; if it's closed, check the racks for free brochures. You can store luggage (even frozen fish) nearby.

The **People Mover** bus 7 (907/343-6543, www.peoplemover.org, $1.75) runs from the lower level into downtown Anchorage almost hourly, seven days a week. Taxi fare is $15–18 to downtown, and there's always a line of cabs waiting out front as you exit the baggage claim area.

The Alaska Railroad has a terminal at the airport that is used by cruise ship companies, with passengers flying into Anchorage and riding the train to Whittier or Seward, where they disembark for their cruise to Southeast Alaska

(or vice versa). In addition to passengers, the airport serves a vital link for air cargo companies. Both Federal Express and UPS have major international terminals, and hundreds of cargo flights land and refuel each week.

Domestic Airlines

Many of the big domestic carriers fly into and out of Anchorage from the Lower 48, including **Alaska Airlines** (800/426-0333, www.alaskaair.com), **American** (800/433-7300, www.aa.com), **Continental** (800/523-3273, www.continental.com), **Delta** (800/221-1212, www.delta.com), **Frontier** (800/432-1359, www.flyfrontier.com), **Northwest** (800/225-2525, www.nwa.com), and **United** (800/241-6522, www.ual.com).

Most of these flights arrive via Seattle, but Alaska also has year-round nonstop flights to Chicago, Denver, Las Vegas, Los Angeles, Portland, Oregon, with connecting service via Seattle to most Western cities and all the way to Boston, Denver, Washington D.C., Miami, Newark, Orlando, and a number of Mexican cities. Northwest has year-round nonstop service to Minneapolis–St. Paul, while Delta flies nonstop year-round to Salt Lake City, and United to San Francisco and Denver. In addition, **Hawaiian Vacations** (907/261-2700 or 800/770-2700, www.hawaiianvacations.com) offers charter flights several times a week between Anchorage and Hawaii, while **Sun Country Airlines** (800/359-6786, www.suncountry.com) has seasonal charters between Anchorage and Minneapolis.

Summer-only nonstop Anchorage flights arrive from Chicago (American and United),

ANCHORAGE AND VICINITY

Cincinnati (Delta), Dallas (American), Denver (Frontier), Detroit (Northwest), and Houston (Continental). In the winter, Northwest flies nonstop to several Hawaiian cities.

International Flights

Anchorage has what may be the best connections to international destinations of any city its size in America. The following companies offer nonstop service into Anchorage: Alaska Air and **Air Canada** (888/247-2262, www.aircanada.com) from Vancouver, **Japan Airlines** (800/525-3663, www.jal.com) from Tokyo, **Korean Air** (800/438-5000, www.koreanair.com) from Seoul, **China Airlines** (800/227-5118, www.china-airlines.com) from Taipei, and **Condor Airlines** (800/524-6975, www.condor.com) from Frankfurt. **Magadan Airlines** (907/248-2994) has weekly summertime service from Anchorage to Petropavlovsk on Russia's Kamchatka Peninsula using old Aeroflot jets.

Regional Airlines

Anchorage's largest regional airlines are **Era Aviation** (907/266-8394 or 800/866-8394, www.flyera.com), with daily flights to Cordova, Homer, Kenai, Kodiak, and Valdez; **PenAir** (907/243-2323 or 800/448-4226, www.penair.com), with flights to Aniak, Cold Bay, Dillingham, Dutch Harbor, Iliamna, King Salmon, McGrath, Pribilof Islands, Sand Point, and Unalakleet. **Frontier Flying Service** (907/450-7200 or 800/478-6779, www.frontierflying.com) flies from Anchorage to Fairbanks, Aniak, Bethel, Dillingham, Togiak, Galena, and **Arctic Circle Air** (907/842-3870 or 888/214-2364, www.arctic-circle-air.com) serves Cordova, Iliamna, King Salmon, and Yakutat. **Grant Aviation** (907/243-3592 or 888/359-4726, www.flygrant.com) connects with Homer and Kenai, and **Hageland Aviation** (907/245-0119 or 866/239-0119, www.hageland.com) flies to Unalakleet.

ALASKA RAILROAD

Anchorage is a major stop for the Alaska Railroad, with service north all the way to Fairbanks, and south to Seward and Whittier.

The Alaska Railroad train depot (411 W. 1st Ave., 907/265-2494 or 800/544-0552, www.akrr.com) is just down the hill from the center of Anchorage. Its daily express to Fairbanks has prices comparable to those of the tour buses but is a much more comfortable, historical, enjoyable, and leisurely ride. The **Denali Star train** departs Anchorage mid-May–mid-September at 8:15 A.M. for Denali (arriving around 4 P.M., $135 one-way) and Fairbanks (arriving 8 P.M., $189 one-way). The train also stops in Wasilla and Talkeetna, where you can hop off, but you're not allowed to check any luggage—only what you can carry on.

A variety of rail/lodging and rail/lodging/boat tour options are listed in Alaska Railroad's brochure or online. Especially popular is the **Spencer Glacier float tour** ($181 round trip from Anchorage), where the train stops in the Kenai Mountains for an easy rafting trip down the Placer River. Day-hikers and backpackers can also take advantage of special whistle-stop service at Spencer Glacier.

Take the **Coastal Classic train** (daily, $65 one-way, $109 round-trip) south to Seward for a fantastic over-the-top voyage across the Kenai Peninsula. The route diverges from the highway near Portage, and then winds steeply into the Kenai Mountains past several glaciers. The Anchorage to Whittier **Glacier Discovery train** ($72 round-trip) departs at 10 A.M., arriving three hours later. Service to both Whittier and Seward is from mid-May to mid-September only. Both of these trains also stop in Girdwood, but only hand-carry baggage is allowed from there.

The Alaska Railroad now offers **GoldStar** double-decker coaches with open-air viewing platforms for an old-fashioned luxury rail experience. Add $85 extra to Denali, $110 extra to Fairbanks. Both **Princess Tours** (206/336-6000 or 800/426-0500, www.princesslodges.com) and **Holland America Tours/Gray Line** (907/277-5581 or 800/544-2206, www.graylinealaska.com) hook their superdome cars to the back of the express for a similar experience. These are mostly for the cruise ship crowd, but they also sell seats to independent travelers. Be ready to plunk down $530 d for an Anchorage–Denali–Anchorage trip that includes two nights at a hotel near the park, or $460 d from Anchorage to Fairbanks for a trip that includes an overnight near Denali.

BUSES

A number of bus companies head out from Anchorage to other parts of the state, and most will carry bikes for an extra charge. Try a city bus for a cheaper option if you're just heading to Palmer or Wasilla from Anchorage.

Alaska/Yukon Trails (907/479-2277 or 800/770-7275, www.alaskashuttle.com) has a daily Anchorage–Talkeetna–Denali–Fairbanks run in the summer, and several times a week the rest of the year.

In the summer **Alaska Direct Bus Line** (907/277-6652 or 800/770-6652, www.alaska directbusline.com) has service three times a week from Anchorage to Tok, continuing to Whitehorse and Fairbanks. Winter service is twice weekly.

Denali Overland Transportation (907/733-2384 or 800/651-5221, www.denali overland.com) offers charter service to Talkeetna and Denali, and often has space for individual travelers. **Alaska Park Connection** (907/245-0200 or 800/266-8625, www.alaskacoach.com) provides summertime bus service connecting Anchorage with Seward, Talkeetna, and Denali. **Anchorage Denali Shuttle** (907/569-0022, www.anchorage denalishuttle.com) has daily summertime runs to Denali National Park and back.

Homer Stage Line (907/883-3914, www .homerstageline.com) has daily summertime service to Seward, Soldotna, Kenai, Cooper Landing, and Homer—plus all points in between. Winter runs are twice a week to Homer and six days a week to Seward. **Seward Bus Lines** (907/563-0800, www.sewardbuslines.net) provides daily year-round bus service to Seward.

GETTING AROUND
City Buses

People Mover (907/343-6543 www.people mover.org), Anchorage's public bus system, covers the entire Anchorage Basin. Weekday service is extensive, with all routes operating 6 A.M.–10 P.M. On Saturday, most lines run 8 A.M.–8 P.M., but Sunday service is only offered on certain routes 9:30 A.M.–6:30 P.M. Visit the **Transit Center** at 6th Avenue and G Street, where you can pick up a *Ride Guide* timetable of all routes. It's open Monday–Friday 7 A.M.–6 P.M. Exact fare ($1.75 adults, $1 for ages 5–18) is required, and transfers are valid only on a different bus traveling in the same direction within two hours of the time of receipt. People Mover buses are free all day in the downtown area; just get on board and ride. A $4 day pass—good for unlimited rides—is sold on all buses.

All People Mover buses can transport wheelchairs, or call the **Anchor Rides** program (907/562-8444) for special transportation needs. You'll need to call at least a day in advance.

Mat-Su Community Transit bus, better known as **MASCOT** (907/376-5000, www.matsutransit.com), has weekday commuter runs from Anchorage to Palmer, Wasilla, and even Big Lake for just $2.50.

Taxis

Taxis are expensive: Most charge $2 per flag drop, plus $2/mile thereafter. The companies include **Alaska Cab** (907/563-5353), **Yellow Cab** (907/272-2422), and **Anchorage Checker Cab** (907/276-1234). There's always a line of waiting cabs outside the airport if you are just arriving and need a way into Anchorage; the fare is $15–18 to downtown. Disabled travelers should contact Alaska Cab; it has wheelchair lifts on some vehicles.

Car Rentals

Anchorage is car-happy, so rental cars can be very hard to come by. Make car reservations as much as two months ahead to be sure of a car in the peak season. All the major companies (Alamo, Avis, Budget, Dollar, Enterprise, Hertz, National, Payless, Rent A Wreck, and Thrifty, and U-Save) operate from the Anchorage airport, offering rates starting around $50/day for an economy car with unlimited mileage. Many of these companies also rent 4WD vehicles and vans. Don't even think of renting a car in Anchorage and leaving it elsewhere in Alaska; the charges are sky-high for this luxury.

Check www.travelocity.com to see who currently has the cheapest Anchorage rentals. The best rates are frequently through **Payless** (907/243-3616 or 800/729-5377), **Budget** (907/243-0150 or 800/248-0150), and **Dollar** (907/248-5338 or 800/800-4000). **Denali Car Rental** (907/276-1230 or 800/757-1230, www.denalicarrentalak.com) has lower rates (starting at $45/day or $270/week plus an 18 percent car rental tax), but its cars are older.

Most car rental companies prohibit driving on the McCarthy Road, Denali Highway, and other rough roads, but many drivers also ignore these. If you're traveling in the winter, ask for a car with studded tires, which are—surprisingly—not on many Anchorage rental cars; Denali Car Rental is one exception.

When making a reservation, be sure to mention if you have a AAA card; you can often save substantially on the rates. Most of the national companies have car rental desks at the airport, but if you rent one there you'll add on an extra 29 percent tax to the rate (versus 18 percent in town). Especially for long rentals, it's usually best to *not* get a rental car from the airport.

RV Rentals

Quite a few places let you rent honkin' Alaska-size RV land yachts—the ones you sit behind for miles as they waddle down the road at 30 mph and four miles to the gallon. Recreational vehicles may be of some value for groups of six or more, but are completely unnecessary for smaller groups.

The following Anchorage companies rent RVs: **Great Alaskan Holidays** (907/248-7777 or 888/225-2752, www.greatalaskan holidays.com; recommended), **Clippership Motorhome Rentals** (907/562-7051 or 800/421-3456, www.clippershiprv.com), **ABC Motorhome Rentals** (907/279-2000 or 800/421-7456, www.abcmotorhome .com), **Alaska Economy RVs** (907/561-7723 or 800/764-4625, www.goalaska.com), and **Alaska Motorhome Rentals** (907/258-7109 or 800/254-9929, www.alaskarv.com). **Alaska Camper Adventures** (907/929-9445 or 888/552-5238, www.alaskacamperadventures.com) rents both RVs and pickup-truck campers.

Tour Buses

At least a half-dozen tour companies are happy to sell you bus tours of Anchorage and the surrounding area; get their brochures from the visitor center. The larger companies—**Gray Line of Alaska** (907/277-5581 or 800/544-2206, www.graylineofalaska.com), **Cruise West** (907/441-9571 or 800/426-7702, www.cruisewest.com), and **Princess Tours** (800/835-8907 or 800/774-6237, www.princess .com)—also offer a wide range of other package trips on land, sea, or air throughout Alaska.

Boat

Although there are no boat tours out of Anchorage, it *is* a good place to check out boat trips across Prince William Sound and out of Seward. Several tour companies offer trips that include a bus from Anchorage to Whittier, boat across the Sound, and flight or bus ride back to Anchorage. Or get to Whittier on your own and hop on one of these tour boats.

The **Alaska Marine Highway** (800/642-0066, www.ferryalaska.com) does not reach Anchorage, but you can connect up with the system in Whittier via the Alaska Railroad or in Homer by bus.

Vicinity of Anchorage

◖ CHUGACH STATE PARK

Alaska's second-largest chunk of state-owned land, Chugach State Park (907/345-5014, www.alaskastateparks.org) encompasses nearly half a million acres—half the size of Delaware. The park covers the entire Chugach Range from Eagle River, 25 miles north of Anchorage, to Girdwood, 35 miles south. It could take a committed hiker years to explore all its trails, ridges, peaks, and passes. From the short but steep 1.5-mile trail up Flattop Mountain in Anchorage, to the 25-mile trek from the Eagle River Nature Center over Crow Pass down to Girdwood, there are a wide range of trails to choose from, each varying in length, elevation, difficulty, access, and congestion.

Pick up hiking brochures at the Alaska Public Lands Information Center in Anchorage, decide on a trail, then dress for rain! The clouds often sit down on these city-surrounding mountaintops and when it's sunny and hot in Anchorage, it could be hailing only a few minutes away on the trails. But don't let that stop you. This whole park is within a few miles of where half of Alaska's population huddles, but up in these mountains it's easy to pretend you're a hundred years behind the crowds, and all the hustle and bustle on the Inlet flats is far in the future.

The Turnagain Arm Trail and several other popular Chugach State Park hiking paths are described in the *Turnagain Arm* section, along with the Potter Section House, where the park headquarters is located. Jenny Zimmerman's *A Naturalist's Guide to Chugach State Park, Alaska* tells the full story on the park.

Camping and Cabins

Developed state park campgrounds are found at **Eklutna Lake** ($10) and **Eagle River** ($15) north of Anchorage, and at **Bird Creek** ($15) to the south. All three have four-day limits, outhouses, and water, and are generally open May–September. Located just off the Hiland Road exit a dozen miles north of Anchorage, the often-full Eagle River Campground can be reserved by calling 907/694-7982 or 800/952-8624.

A wonderful cabin ($50) can be rented on the shore of Eklutna Lake, and two yurts and an eight-person cabin (907/694-2108, www.ernc.org, $65) are available near the Eagle River Nature Center.

Hillside Trails

Two trailheads on the city's southeastern outskirts give access to a network of crisscrossing and connecting trails in the section of the range that hems in Anchorage Bowl. They're all off Hillside Drive, which skirts a suburb of sparkling glass houses and gorgeous views of the skyline, inlet, and Mt. Susitna to the west. City buses do not reach the park in this area, so you'll really need a vehicle to get to the Hillside trailheads. Day-use parking costs $5 per vehicle.

For the **Glen Alps Trailhead** drive south on New Seward Highway, and turn east toward the mountains on O'Malley Road. Follow it to Hillside Drive, where you turn right, then left on Upper Huffman Road. In a half-mile, go right again onto aptly named Toilsome Hill Drive. Toil steeply uphill for 2.5 miles to reach the Glen Alps parking lot ($5 day-use fee). On warm summer weekends every space in the lot fills with cars, so get there early or take the **Flattop Mountain Shuttle** (907/279-3334, www.alaska-bike-rentals.com, $22 round-trip) from downtown. Take a look from the nearby overlook, and then head up the **Flattop Mountain Trail** for even better looks. This extremely popular 1.5-mile trail gains 1,500 feet and is very steep near the top as you scramble through the boulders.

Also from the Glen Alps Trailhead are several moderate and very scenic hikes: **Little O'Malley Peak**, 7.5 miles round-trip; the **Ramp and Wedge**, 11 miles round-trip; and **Williwaw Lakes**, 13 miles round-trip. A great mountain bike route is the 11-mile (one-way) **Powerline Trail** that also takes off from the Glen Alps Trailhead and goes over 3,550-foot

Powerline Pass all the way to the Indian Creek Trailhead on Turnagain Arm.

Continue north on Hillside past Upper Huffman Road and take a right on Upper O'Malley Road. The second left leads to **Prospect Heights Trailhead,** where the **Wolverine Peak Trail** leads to the top of this 4,455-foot mountain (11 miles round-trip). You'll discover great views of the Alaska Range and Anchorage, but go in late summer when the snow has melted.

Eagle River Area

Take the Eagle River exit 13 miles north of Anchorage on the Glenn Highway, then your first right onto Eagle River Road, a dazzling, paved, 11-mile ride right into the heart of Chugach State Park. Rafters and kayakers on the Class II Eagle River can put in at two access points (Miles 7.5 and 9) along this road. The road ends at the **Eagle River Nature Center** (907/694-2108, www.ernc.org), which features a "close-up corner" with furs and a track book, as well as an aurora display, and gift shop. The center is open daily 10 A.M.–5 P.M. (until 7 P.M. Fri. and Sat.) June–August, Tuesday–Sunday 10 A.M.–5 P.M. May and September, plus Friday–Sunday 10 A.M.–5 P.M. the rest of the year. Park rangers lead 1.5-hour hikes on weekdays at 11 A.M. June–August. Parking is $5. The **Rodak Nature Trail** is a wide gravel route, a half-mile round-trip, with informative signs on snow, glaciers, forest, and the sun. It's 15 minutes well spent. For a longer walk, take the seven-mile **River Trail** along the Eagle River.

Eklutna Lake

Twenty-six miles north of Anchorage on the Glenn Highway is the exit for Eklutna Lake, a favorite weekend destination. Narrow and winding Eklutna Road follows the Eklutna River 10 miles to the lake, where you'll find a pleasant, small **campground** ($10) with outhouses and a large picnic area. The 14-mile **Lakeside Trail-Eklutna Glacier Trail** starts nearby, skirting the west side of Eklutna Lake and then climbing to this very scenic glacier. Three side trails lead off the main route to Twin Peaks, Bold Ridge,

and East Fork of Eklutna River. This is an outstanding mountain biking area in summer, and a popular wintertime ski/snowmachine trail. Most of the route is also open to ATVs Sunday–Wednesday, so you may not have peace and quiet. Experienced skiers may want to continue beyond Eklutna Glacier via a multiglacier traverse that takes them 31 miles to Crow Pass. The Alaska Mountaineering Club (907/272-1811, www.mcak.org) has three huts along the way.

Kayak and bike rentals are available near the Eklutna Campground from **Lifetime Adventures** (907/746-4644 or 800/952-8624, www.lifetimeadventures.net), along with a popular paddle-and-peddle option ($75 per person): you kayak across the lake and ride a mountain bike back.

Also from the Eklutna exit, you can follow the access road a mile south to scenic **Thunderbird Falls** (if you're heading north from Anchorage, there's a marked Thunderbird Falls exit before you reach the Eklutna exit). The trail takes you on an easy one-mile hike up Thunderbird Creek. Follow your ears to the falls.

Crow Pass

For one of the longest and most scenic hikes in the park, head out the 25-mile **Crow Pass Trail.** This trail (also known as the Historic Iditarod Trail) provided a turn-of-the-20th century overland route from Seward through the Chugach to the Interior gold mining town of Iditarod. The gradual climb to Crow Pass fords several streams, including Eagle River midway along the trail. It might be wise to camp overnight and cross the river in the morning, when the glacial runoff is lower. Raven Glacier and Crystal Lake are scenic highlights near Crow Pass, where you leave Chugach State Park and continue in immense Chugach National Forest. The Forest Service has a popular A-frame **cabin** (reservations: 518/885-3639 or 877/444-6777, www.reserveusa.com, $35) on the summit that you can rent. From the cabin it's four miles down to the trailhead on rough Crow Creek Road, then another five miles to the Alyeska Ski Resort access road. Experienced skiers sometimes use the Iditarod/Crow Pass Trails for a winter traverse of the mountains, but be aware that avalanche danger can be very high.

NORTH OF ANCHORAGE

Chugach State Park includes several popular destinations north of Anchorage around Eklutna Lake and Eagle River.

Arctic Valley

Six miles north from Anchorage along the Glenn Highway is the exit to Arctic Valley Road, which climbs seven steep miles to the parking lot at the Alpenglow ski area (see *Downhill Skiing* in the *Anchorage* section). A trailhead about a mile before road's end leads to long **Ship Creek Trail,** which with a little cross-country hiking hooks up with Bird Creek and Indian Creek Trails via the passes of the same names. It's 22 miles from Arctic Valley to Indian Creek Trailhead. Plan on two or three days to do this traverse. From the Alpenglow parking lot a two-mile trail goes up to **Rendezvous Peak,** an easy hike with great views of the city, inlet, and even Mt. McKinley if you're lucky.

Eklutna Historical Park

This is one of those surprising discoveries just off the Glenn Highway. Take the Eklutna Road exit (26 miles northeast of Anchorage), and cross back over the highway to Eklutna Village. From this point, at the site of the first Tanaina (a branch of the Athabascans) settlement on the Inlet, down through the western Kenai Peninsula, Kodiak, and the Aleutians, Russian Orthodoxy is strongly overlaid on the Native culture. The ancestors of most of these Indians were converted by Russian missionaries, and **St. Nicholas Russian Orthodox Church**—a miniature log chapel that dates from the 1830s and was reconstructed in the 1970s—is the oldest building in the Anchorage area. Nearby is a newer and larger church. Both are set against a backdrop of 80 or so colorful above-ground **spirit houses** that sit atop Native graves. Informative half-hour tours (907/688-6026, $5 adults, $3 seniors and ages 10–15, free for kids

under 10) are offered Monday–Friday 10 A.M.–5:30 P.M., Saturday 10 A.M.–4:30, and Sunday 1–4 P.M., mid-May–mid-September; the rest of the year you'll have to look in from the picket fence. There's also a small gift shop that sells Native crafts.

(TURNAGAIN ARM

Cook Inlet bends east from Anchorage, becoming Turnagain Arm. The inlet was named by Captain James Cook's master, William Bligh, who later captained the ill-fated HMS *Bounty.* The Seward Highway curves around Turnagain Arm, past the town of Girdwood and the turnoff to Portage Glacier and Whittier, and finally over the Kenai Mountains to Seward, 127 miles away. The Turnagain Arm stretch is exceptionally scenic, but traffic is often heavy, so drive carefully and keep your headlights on at all times. Travelers will find places to watch birds, beluga whales, Dall sheep, and rock climbers along the way, and can stop for hikes or to fish along the way.

Potter Marsh Area

Potter Marsh is on the south edge of Anchorage, with a boardwalk extending into the marsh. This is a good spot to look for waterfowl, including Canada geese, trumpeter swans, and even the flyin'-fool Arctic terns. Bring binoculars and a light jacket for the often-breezy conditions. This marsh was created when the railroad builders installed an embankment to protect the track from Turnagain Arm's giant tides, which dammed the freshwater drainage from the mountains.

A mile south on the other side of the highway is the **Potter Section House** (907/345-5014, Mon.–Fri. 8 A.M.–4:30 P.M. year-round), a small railroad museum of interpretive displays and signs outside, and inside, the restored original "section" house. This is also headquarters for Chugach State Park; get brochures on local trails here. Check out the nine-foot rotary snowplow once used to clear avalanches. A small gift shop sells railroad memorabilia and books.

Turnagain Arm Trail

Across the highway from Potter Section House

is the parking lot for **Potter Creek Trailhead,** the first access to the Turnagain Arm Trail, which parallels the highway for over nine miles, with good opportunities to see Dall sheep, moose, and spruce grouse. The trail began as a turn-of-the-century wagon road built to transport railroad workers and supplies. This is a very popular early-summer path since its south-facing slopes lose the snow early. In three miles is **McHugh Creek,** an always-crowded day-use area and trailhead for the seven-mile hike up to **Rabbit Lake.** You can continue south along the Turnagain Arm Trail past three more trailheads all the way to **Windy Corner Trailhead** nine miles from your starting point, and not far from Beluga Point.

Beluga Point

Twenty miles south of Anchorage is Beluga Point, a good place to see the small white **beluga whales** cavorting in Turnagain Arm in late May and late August; they follow salmon into these shallow waters. Unfortunately, over-hunting by Natives caused the population of belugas to plummet in the 1990s, and they still have not recovered.

Look behind you for the **Dall sheep** that often wander close to the highway in this area. Or just have a picnic and wait for the Cook Inlet's famous **bore tides.** The tides here, at 30 feet, are among the world's highest, and the lead breaker can be up to eight feet high, a half-mile across, and can move at over 10 miles per hour. This is the only bore tide in the U.S., created when a large body of water (Cook Inlet) is forced by strong tidal action into a narrow, shallow one (Turnagain Arm). Look for a series of small swells (2–3 ft. high, larger depending on the wind) that crash against the rocks and send up a mighty spray. You won't soon forget the roar of the bore, which goes by Beluga Point roughly two hours after low tide in Anchorage-check the tide tables in the daily newspapers. One warning: Never go out on the Turnagain Arm mudflats at any time. The mixture of glacial silt and mud creates quicksand; people have drowned after getting their feet stuck in the mud and being inundated by the incoming tide. Don't take a chance!

Indian and Bird Creeks

Twenty-five miles south of Anchorage, and right before Turnagain House Restaurant in Indian, take a left on the gravel road and head 1.5 miles to the **Indian Valley Trailhead.** This trail, which follows Indian Creek over Indian Pass (especially rewarding during Indian summer), is five miles of easy walking on a well-maintained path. You can then continue for several miles of undeveloped hiking until you hook up with the Ship Creek Trail, which runs 22 miles to Arctic Valley north of Anchorage. The Powerline Pass Trail goes 11 miles from the Glenn Alps trailhead to Indian Creek Trail; look for the signed turnoff 100 yards up the Indian Valley Trail. Historic **Indian Valley Mine** (907/653-1120, www.indianvalleymine.com) has summertime gold panning, historic buildings, a little museum, and gift shop.

Two miles down the highway from Indian is the Bird Creek area, where dozens of cars line the roadside on July and August afternoons. They're all here trying to hook a silver salmon in this very productive creek. A half-mile north of the creek is a parking area for **Bird Ridge Trail,** which climbs straight up this 3,500-foot promontory in less than two miles.

Also nearby is the **Bird Creek Campground** ($15), a surprisingly pretty place just off the busy Seward Highway. Campsites are just a few feet from Cook Inlet. This thickly forested campground is often full of anglers working Bird Creek. The **Bird to Gird Bike Trail** runs right through the middle of the campground, continuing north for three miles to Indian and south three miles to Girdwood along the old highway.

GIRDWOOD

The town of Girdwood is officially part of the hectic Anchorage municipality, but feels a world away. Located 37 miles south via the Seward Highway, the original town was leveled by the 1964 earthquake. A cluster of businesses stands along the highway, providing a rest stop for travelers, but new Girdwood and the Alyeska Resort sit at the end of a three-mile access road (Alyeska Highway). This winter resort is a favorite destination for locals, package tourists, unsuspecting travelers, and the occasional backpacker who likes a quick ride to the alpine tundra in the summer.

Girdwood doesn't have a visitor center, but you'll find information on the Web at www .girdwoodalaska.com. In addition to the resort, the town has several restaurants, a grocery store, post office, library, and a coin laundry with showers. Both the library and coin laundry have Internet access.

Sights

The six-mile paved **Bird to Gird Bike Trail** starts from the Alyeska Prince Hotel, and continues north all the way to Bird Creek, following Turnagain Arm much of the way.

Next to the Bake Shop, **Girdwood Center for Visual Arts** (907/783-3209, daily in the summer) is a co-op gallery with pottery, paintings, photography, glasswork, jewelry, and other locally crafted pieces.

The Forest Service's **Glacier Ranger District office** (907/783-3242) is on the left as you drive into town from the Seward Highway, and is open weekdays. It can provide details and maps for hikers, anglers, sea kayakers, and other recreation enthusiasts heading into Chugach National Forest.

Stop off at the **Alaska Candle Factory** (907/783-2354) on the access road a half-mile from Seward Highway. Their candles are not only unique and inexpensive souvenirs or gift items, but they also burn until the cows come home.

◖ Crow Creek Mine

The gravel Crow Creek Road leads from Girdwood three miles to Crow Creek Mine (907/278-8060, www.crowcreekgoldmine.com, daily 9 A.M.–6 P.M. mid-May–Sept., $3 adults, kids free; $8 with gold panning), one of the earliest gold strikes in Alaska (1896) and Southcentral Alaska's richest mine. The area was actively mined until World War II, producing over 45,000 ounces of gold. There's still a lot of gold to be found, and the creek attracts both casual panners looking for a flake of gold and

Crow Creek Mine

those who come with metal detectors and large suction dredges. (When I last visited, a German tourist had just discovered a pea-sized nugget of gold.) Eight of the original mine buildings have been restored by the Toohey family and are filled with all sorts of flotsam and jetsam from the past. There's a little gift shop, panning equipment rental, and overnight campsites ($5). It's a pretty place with a rich history, and a *must* stop in the Girdwood area.

Continue another four miles out Crow Creek Road beyond Crow Creek Mine to the **Crow Pass Trailhead.** It's an invigorating and beautiful 3.5 miles to the pass, with a 2,000-foot elevation gain. The trail is in the alpine much of the route, and passes old mining ruins and a Forest Service cabin ($35, www.reserveusa.com). A half-mile beyond the pass is Raven Glacier, where you enter Chugach State Park.

Events

The big summertime event is **Girdwood Forest Fair** (907/566-3039, www.girdwood forestfair.com) held in early July for more than 30 years. Hundreds of folks show up to buy arts and crafts, graze through the food booths, and listen to bands cranking out the tunes from two separate stages. It's a three-day party that seems to attract every free-spirited hippie left in Alaska. No dogs, politicians, or religious orders allowed.

Skiing and snowboarding events fill the winter calendar at Alyeska Resort (907/754-1111, www.alyeskaresort.com), but the most fun for spectators is the **Spring Carnival and Slush Cup** in late April, when costumed skiers and boarders blast downhill and attempt to make it across a slushy pond. Lots of cold, wet folks on this one!

Summer Recreation

First check out Alyeska Resort, and the impressive lobby of the enormous Alyeska Prince Hotel. Next, fork over $16 to catch a ride 2,300 feet up Mt. Alyeska on the **aerial tramway** (907/754-2275). On top are two restaurants. The two 60-passenger tram cars are entirely wheelchair accessible. Follow the well-marked trail to the alpine overlook onto cute Alyeska Glacier. If you have reservations to dine at Seven Glaciers restaurant, the tram ride is free. A tram-and-lunch special to Glacier Express Café costs $10–12; the tram office has details.

A paved path parallels the road to the Alyeska Prince Hotel, and Crow Creek Road provides an easy dirt road for mountain bikers. Rent bikes from **Girdwood Ski & Cyclery** (907/783-2453, www.girdwood-ski-and-cyclery.com).

The Alyeska Prince Hotel houses an excellent indoor pool, hot tub, and fitness center. If you aren't staying here, plunk down $10 for access—it's a great deal for campers who get all the amenities for the price of a shower. **Alaska Paragliding** (907/301-1215, www.alaskaparagliding.com) takes novices on exciting tandem paragliding rides from the top of the tram.

Guides from **The Ascending Path** (907/783-0505 or 877/783-0505, www.theascending path.com) lead glacier hikes ($139 for three hours), ice climbing classes ($189 for five hours), and hikes ($59 for 2.5 hours) in the Girdwood

area. **Two Legged Tours** (907/317-4813 or 877/252-5344, www.twoleggedtours.com) also guides hikes locally.

Alpine Air (907/783-2360, www.alpineair alaska.com) has helicopter flightseeing, tours of Prince William Sound, and a very popular two-hour dog mushing adventure ($400 per person) that includes a glacier landing and the chance to drive a team of sled dogs.

Winter Recreation

Alyeska Resort (907/754-1111 or 800/880-3880, www.alyeskaresort.com) is Alaska's primary center for downhill skiing, with a complex that encompasses the ski and snowboard area, a large hotel, and several restaurants. The resort covers 500 skiable acres and has 60 trails, a 60-passenger tram, eight chairlifts, two pony lifts, and a tubing park. Most of the ski runs are at the intermediate or advanced level. In addition to abundant natural snowfall (depths generally exceed 10 ft.), there is snowmaking capability on the lower slopes.

Alyeska Resort generally opens for skiing and snowboarding around Thanksgiving and closes the end of April. Hours are daily 10:30 A.M.–5:30 P.M., with night skiing Friday–Saturday until 9:30 P.M.; reduced hours early and late in the season. A shuttle bus connects the main ski area with the Alyeska Prince Hotel (where the tram departs). If you're coming from Anchorage, the resort also has a wintertime ski/snowboard bus on weekends and school holidays for $14 round-trip. It's a good way to let someone else do the driving.

Adult lift tickets cost $55 full day, $30 half-day; on Friday and Saturday there's night skiing for $24 extra. A half-day ticket plus night skiing will run you $55. There are discounts for children, students, families, and multi-day passes. Skis, snowshoes, snowboards, and ice skates (for use on the skating pond) can be rented in the day lodge, where you can also get expensive cafeteria food. More cafeteria fare, along with an elaborate restaurant and lounge, is on top of the mountain. Ski and snowboarding classes at all levels are available.

Traffic between Anchorage and Girdwood can back up on winter weekends, so head out early if you're driving. Call 907/754-7669 or visit www.alyeskaresort.com for a recording of the latest snow conditions.

Accommodations

Heading toward the resort on the access road, go right on Timberline, pass gorgeous ski chalets, then turn right again on Alpina. Around a couple of curves is the **Alyeska Hostel** (907/783-2222, www.alyeskahostel.com). This is a great place, with a coed dorm ($18 per person in bunks), private room ($45 d), and summer-only cabin ($60 d or $80 for four), plus a kitchen and bath, free Wi-Fi, and a wood-burning sauna out back. Reservations recommended in the summer, especially for the private room and cabin. No lockout or curfew.

Alyeska Accommodations (907/783-2000 or 888/783-2001, www.alyeska accommodations.com) is the best source for condo, chalet, and home rentals, representing dozens of places around Girdwood. Two organizations provide descriptions and helpful links to websites for most local B&Bs and guest houses: **Girdwood Bed-and-Breakfast Association** (907/222-4858, www .gbba.org) and the larger **Alyeska/Girdwood Accommodations Association** (907/222-3226, www.agaa.biz).

The luxurious 307-room **Alyeska Prince Hotel** (907/754-1111 or 800/880-3880, www .alyeskaresort.com) is an eight-story, 307-room hotel where nicely appointed rooms include heated towel racks, fridges, ski-boot storage boxes, Wi-Fi ($10 fee), and safes. Other in-hotel amenities include three restaurants, a fitness center, large indoor swimming pool, sauna, and hot tub. There's even a virtual golf course where you can play a round without leaving the room. The tram to the top of Mt. Alyeska is right out the back door; guests get a discounted rate of $15. Room rates vary, with lowest prices ($285 d) for small rooms on levels two and three, up to $379 d for an 8th-floor room. Suites cost $440–2,200. Be sure to ask if they have any discounted rates; these can be substantial at times.

Food and Entertainment

At the intersection of the Girdwood Spur Road and Seward Highway is a little strip mall with a variety of services, including a gas station/convenience store, coin laundry, video store, and restaurant. Travelers heading south to Seward or north to Anchorage stop here before pushing back out on the highway. The **Alpine Diner & Bakery** (907/783-2550) serves breakfast, lunch, and dinner, but is best known for enormous pastries. There's always a queue on winter mornings as the après-ski gang comes in to inject sugar and caffeine into their veins.

In business since 1962, famous **Double Musky Inn** (907/783-2822, www.double muskyinn.com, closed Mondays, entrées $19–35) is a quarter-mile up Crow Creek Road on the left. It's crowded and loud, with long waits, a tacky New Orleans–meets–Alaska decor, and brief visits from your server. No reservations, either. Despite these drawbacks, the food is dependably good, if not stellar. Featured attractions are Cajun shrimp, garlic seafood pasta, rack of lamb, and the house specialty, French Pepper Steak. Save space for the ultra-rich Double Musky pie.

At the Alyeska resort is **The Bake Shop** (907/783-2831, www.thebakeshop.com), a fine spot for lunch or an after-ski warm-up. Homemade sourdough bread, hearty soups, sandwiches, big breakfasts, and pizza fill out the menu. The Bake Shop is open daily until 7 P.M. in the summer, and the front yard is packed with flowers, including some enormous peonies. Get espresso or surf the Web on the computers at **Java Haus** (907/783-2827), a couple of doors away.

Down the hill on Arlberg Street is █ **Jack Sprat Restaurant** (907/783-5225, www .jacksprat.net), with "fat and lean world cuisine" in a relaxed atmosphere. Dinners include everything from halibut burritos ($10) to Parisian tenderloin ($29), plus Indian nirvana ($16) for vegetarians and a decadent crème brulée for dessert. Brunches are available on weekends, featuring eggs Benedict, tofu sauté, and blintzes.

Located next to the post office on Hightower Road, **Chair 5 Restaurant** (907/783-2500, www.chairfive.com) is a townie spot for very good pizzas, halibut curry, rib-eye steaks, and daily specials. The bar has a great choice of single malt scotches and microbrews. For quick burritos, tacos, and platters, migrate over to **Mamacita's Mexican Food** (907/783-0088) in the coin laundry building behind Chair 5. Après-ski partiers head to the **Sitzmark Bar & Grill** at Alyeska Resort for a pitcher of beer and the chance to dance the night away to live bands on winter weekends; closed summers.

On top of the mountain, **Seven Glaciers Restaurant** (907/754-2237, www.alyeskaresort .com) offers excellent food with one of the best views you're ever likely to get while dining. Sitting on a crag at 2,303 feet above sea level, you can see the valley below, across to the Crow Pass area, and up Turnagain Arm. Main courses such as ginger-citrus encrusted halibut, Alaskan king crab, or grilled elk rib eye run $28–53. *Très élégant,* but not at all stuffy or pretentious. The seven-minute tram ride gives you the chance to survey the area, and if you have dinner reservations (required), the tram ride is free.

Getting There

The **Alaska Railroad** (907/265-2494 or 800/544-0552, www.alaskarailroad.com) connects Girdwood with Anchorage daily in the summer, but the trains stop at a small shelter out near the Seward Highway. You'll need to make advance reservations for a pickup in Girdwood, and only carry-on luggage is allowed. Both **Homer Stage Line** (907/883-3914, www.homerstageline.com) and **Seward Bus Lines** (907/563-0800, www.sewardbuslines. net) will stop in Girdwood, but call ahead.

PORTAGE GLACIER

Fifty miles south of Anchorage on the Seward Highway is the turnoff to Portage Glacier and Whittier. A six-mile access road takes you through Portage Valley to Portage Glacier. A town that stood on this corner was destroyed when the 1964 earthquake dropped the land 6–10 feet. Saltwater from Turnagain Arm inundated the area, killing the still-standing trees, and the remaining buildings are gradu-

ally disintegrating. Portage Glacier is one of the more popular tourist attractions in Southcentral Alaska, so be ready to share the ride with busloads of cruise ship travelers.

An info booth along the Seward Highway has details on Whittier, and sells tickets for various tour options, including the Alaska Railroad's scenic trips to Grandview.

Visitor Center

The Forest Service's **Begich, Boggs Visitor Center** (907/783-2326, www.fs.fed.us) is named after Nicholas Begich (U.S. representative from Alaska and father of Anchorage mayor Mark Begich) and Hale Boggs (majority leader of the U.S. Senate and father of journalist Cokie Roberts), whose plane disappeared in the area in 1972. They were never found. The center is open daily 9 A.M.–6 P.M. late May–September, and Saturday–Sunday 10 A.M.–5 P.M. the rest of the year. A large picture window overlooks the narrow outlet of Portage Lake. When the visitor center first opened, the glacier was readily visible, but it is now out of sight around a corner, and in recent years the number of icebergs entering the lake has decreased greatly as it continues to shrink.

The visitor center boasts an amazing array of displays, including an ice cave, a small iceberg hauled in from the lake, an engrossing relief map of local icefields, and everything you ever wanted to know about glaciers, including displays on glacial motion and crevasses. Don't miss the vial of tiny iceworms, which inhabit the surfaces of glaciers, feeding on pollen grains and red algae and surviving within a delicate, near-freezing temperature range. There's also good footage on iceworms in the 20-minute movie, *Voices from the Ice* (shown every hour, $1).

During the summer, Forest Service naturalists lead half-mile nature walks. The **observation platform** near Williwaw Campground is a good place to see spawning red and chum salmon in late summer.

Seeing the Glacier

To see Portage Glacier, you'll need to hop onboard the 200-passenger *Ptarmigan* tour boat; catch it at the dock near the visitor center. Operated by Gray Line of Alaska (907/277-5581 or 800/544-2206, www.graylineofalaska.com), these one-hour cruises across Portage Lake cost $29 and start at 10:30 A.M., with the last tour at 4:30 P.M. This boat tour, plus round-trip bus transportation from Anchorage (includes a stop at Alyeska) costs $68 on Gray Line.

Recreation

Two hikes are within walking distance of the visitor center. The **Moraine Loop Trail**, accessible from the path to the lodge, is a five-minute stroll through typical moraine vegetation; Portage Glacier occupied this ground only 100 years ago. Follow the access road past the visitor center (south) just under a mile. At the back of the parking lot starts the **Byron Glacier Trail**, an easy three-quarter-mile walk along the runoff stream to below this hanging glacier.

Practicalities

Two Forest Service campgrounds near Portage contain woodsy sites: **Black Bear**

Campground ($10) and the larger **Williwaw Campground** ($19). The latter has summertime campfire programs on Saturday evenings and a wheelchair-accessible observation platform where spawning salmon are visible in the summer. Williwaw's sites can be reserved ($9 extra, 518/885-3639 or 877/444-6777, www|.reserveusa.com). **Portage Glacier Lodge** (907/783-3117), across from the visitor center has a cafeteria with reasonable prices; try the cross-cut fries for your crunch craving. Open daily year-round.

Alaska Wildlife Conservation Center

This 140-acre game farm (907/783-2025, www.alaskawildlife.org, $7.50 adults, $5 kids and seniors, maximum $25 per vehicle) sits along Turnagain Arm just across the Seward Highway from the turnoff to Portage Glacier. Open daily, this nonprofit center for orphaned and injured Alaskan animals has grizzly and black bears, bison, moose, elk, moose, musk ox, deer, and caribou.

Mat-Su Valley and Beyond

The Parks Highway heads north from Anchorage to Denali and Fairbanks, but before you're even close to either of these, the road takes you through the heart of the Matanuska-Susitna Valley, named for the two rivers that drain this part of Alaska. Originally established as an agricultural center, the Mat-Su is now primarily a bedroom community for Anchorage, with reasonably priced homes and fast-spreading semi-urban sprawl. Two towns dominate the valley. The old farming settlement of Palmer is along the Glenn Highway 42 miles from Anchorage, while Wasilla rears its ugly face 40 miles north of Anchorage along the Parks Highway.

Visitor Center

The **Matanuska-Susitna Convention and Visitors Bureau** (907/746-5000, www.alaska visit.com, daily 8:30 A.M.–6:30 P.M. mid-May–mid-Sept., closed the rest of the year) has a large visitor center just north of the junction of the Parks and Glenn Highway, and six miles south of Wasilla. Take the Trunk Road Exit and follow the "?" signs. Inside you'll find a plethora of brochures and stuffed critter heads lining the walls, plus free Wi-Fi.

PALMER

For its first 20 years, Palmer (pop. 4,100) was little more than a railway depot for Alaska Railroad's Matanuska branch. Then in May 1935, during the height of both the Depression and a severe drought in the Midwest, the Federal Emergency Relief Administration of President Franklin D. Roosevelt's New Deal selected 200 farming families from the relief rolls of northern Michigan, Minnesota, and Wisconsin, and shipped them here to colonize the Matanuska Valley. Starting out in tent cabins, the colonists cleared the dense virgin forest, built houses and barns, and planted crops pioneered at the University of Alaska's Agricultural Experimental

a Matanuska Valley farm near Palmer

© DON PITCHER

ANCHORAGE AND VICINITY

MATANUSKA-SUSITNA VALLEY

To Glennallen and Valdez

Sutton

To Glennallen and Valdez

Knik River

KNIK RIVER RD

KNIK

Bodenburg Butte (881 ft)

OLD GLENN HWY

BODENBURG LOOP RD

ALASKA STATE FAIR

Palmer

KEPLER-BRADLEY STATE RECREATION AREA

Matanuska

GLENN HWY

River

MUSK OX FARM

PALMER-FISHHOOK RD

HATCHER PASS LODGE

MOTHERLODE LODGE

Independence Mine State Historical Park

WASILLA-FISHHOOK RD

MAT-SU VISITOR CENTER

TRUNK RD

FISHHOOK-WILLOW RD

HATCHER PASS

PARKS HWY

FAIRVIEW LOOP RD

To Anchorage

Knik Arm

HATCHER PASS RD

Willow Creek

Susitna River

SCHROCK RD

Wasilla

IDITAROD TRAIL HEADQUARTERS

LAKE LUCILLE CAMPER PARK

Little

PITTMAN RD

KNIK-GOOSE BAY RD

BIG LAKE RD

Houston

KNIK MUSEUM

To Fairbanks (Interior)

3

Big Lake

DECEPTION CREEK CAMPGROUND

3

Willow

Nancy Lake

SOUTH ROLLY

Nancy Lake State Recreation Area

Susitna River

5 mi

5 km

0
0

© AVALON TRAVEL PUBLISHING, INC.

To Musk Ox Farm, Matanuska
Glacier, and Glennallen

Matanuska
River
Park
(camping)

W ARCTIC AVE

E ARCTIC AVE (OLD GLENN HWY)

HIGH SCHOOL
(SWIMMING POOL)

To Lazy Mountain and Bodenberg Butte
(Scenic Route to Anchorage)

LAUNDROMAT

S COBB ST
S SAILEY ST
S ALASKA ST
S COLONY WAY
S VALLEY WAY

E COTTONWOOD ST

POST
OFFICE

VALLEY
HOTEL

DENALI ST

E DAHLIA ST

VALLEY
HOSPITAL

CARRS
MALL

LIBRARY

COLONY
HOUSE

COLONY INN

PALMER-WASILLA HWY

W EVERGREEN ST

GOLD
MINER'S
HOTEL

INFO
CENTER

CHURCH ★ E ELMWOOD ST
OF 1,000
LOGS

E FIREWEED

E EVERGREEN ST

GLENN HWY

ALASKA RAILROAD

AIRPORT RD

To Wasilla and
Denali (Interior)

ALASKA
STATE FAIR

ALASKA
CHOICE INN

ALASKA STATE

FAIRGROUNDS

PALMER

PARKS HWY

0   0.25 mi

0   0.25 km

To Anchorage

© AVALON TRAVEL PUBLISHING, INC.

Station. These hardy transplanted farmers endured the inevitable first-year hardships, including disease, homesickness, mismanagement, floods, and just plain bad luck. But by the fall of 1936, the misfits had been weeded out, 120 babies had been born in the colony, fertile fields and long summer days were filling barns with crops, and the colonists celebrated with a three-day harvest festival, the forerunner of the big state fair. In a few more years, Palmer had become not only a flourishing town, but also the center of a bucolic and beautiful agricultural valley that was and still remains unique in Alaska.

Driving into Palmer from Wasilla along the Palmer–Wasilla Highway is a lot like driving into Wasilla from the bush on the Parks Highway time warp. The contrast between Palmer, an old farming community, and Wasilla, with its spontaneous combustion of helter-skelter development, is startling. Suffice it to say, Palmer is more conducive to sightseeing. I actually know people whose home is in Wasilla, but who keep a post office box in Palmer for their business to avoid the stigma of being labeled from Wasilla!

Today, downtown Palmer is a blend of the

old and new, with Klondike Mike's Saloon right next to Sisters of Essence Holistic Center. Palmer is also home to the **National Outdoor Leadership School's** Alaska campus (907/745-4047, www.nols.edu). From this base, NOLS offers a range of courses that involve backpacking, sea kayaking, and mountaineering in remote parts of Alaska.

Sights

Start your visit at the **Palmer Visitors Information Center** (723 S. Valley Way, 907/745-2880, www.palmerchamber.org, daily 9 A.M.–6 P.M. May–Sept., Mon.–Fri. 10 A.M.–4 P.M. the rest of the year). Outside is a phone with direct connections to local lodging places, and an adjacent garden with elephantine-size produce by late summer. Inside, load up with brochures, check out the gift shop, and visit the little downstairs museum depicting the colonists' lifestyle.

Colony House (316 E. Elmwood Ave., 907/745-1935, Tues.–Sat. 10 A.M.–4 P.M. summers only, $2 adults, $1 kids) is just up the block from the visitor center. This home was originally built by the Beylund family who moved here in 1935 from Wisconsin. It has been restored and filled with period furnishings to provide a window on life for the Matanuska Colonists.

Continue another block east on East Elmwood to visit the appropriately named **Church of a Thousand Logs,** built by the colonists in 1936–1937 and still in use.

Fairgrounds and Farms

Heading north through downtown, take a right on Arctic Avenue, which turns into the Old Glenn Highway. About a mile south of town down the Glenn Highway is the **Alaska State Fairgrounds.** At the fairgrounds is **Colony Village** (Mon.–Sat. 10 A.M.–4 P.M., free), which preserves some of Palmer's early buildings, including houses (one built in 1917 in Anchorage), several barns, a church, and a post office.

Five miles south of Palmer on the Old Glenn Highway, **Bodenberg Loop Road,** is a five-mile drive through some of the most gorgeous valley farmland, with 6,400-foot **Pioneer Peak** towering behind. To see some of the original colony farms, head three miles north out the Glenn Highway to **Farm Loop Road.** The Valley's best-known crop isn't mentioned in any of the tourism brochures: marijuana. The local version (Matanuska Thunder) has a reputation as big as Alaska and is some of the most potent in the nation. It was formerly grown outside, but today nearly all grow operations are indoors under lights.

Knik River Road splits off the Old Glenn Highway at Mile 9. Turn here and drive four miles to the trailhead for the **Pioneer Ridge-Knik River Trail,** which climbs a staggering 5,100 feet in less than six miles. Beyond this alpine ridge, only experienced rock climbers should consider heading to the twin summits of Pioneer Peak.

Seven miles south of Palmer on the Old Glenn Highway is the **Reindeer Farm** (907/745-4003, www.reindeerfarm.com, $6 adults, $5 seniors, $4 kids), where tours are offered daily in the summer. Children especially love the chance to pet a baby reindeer.

◖ Alaska State Fair

Don't miss Alaska's biggest summertime event, an 12-day party to bring down the curtain on summer that draws 300,000 visitors annually. The state fair (907/745-4827 or 800/850-3247, www.alaskastatefair.org) cranks up the fourth Thursday of August, and continues through Labor Day. On a weekend day it may seem as though half of Anchorage has driven up to the fair. Long lines of cars wait to turn into the open field parking lots around the grounds, and crowds throng the 4-H displays, livestock auctions, horse shows, and carnival rides. There's live music daily, a rodeo, demolition derby, three nights of fireworks, and lots of food and craft booths. Favorites always include the roasted corn on the cob, sickly sweet elephant ears, supersized turkey legs, and finger-lickin' halibut tacos. One big attraction is the gargantuan vegetables, including 125-pound pumpkins, 10-pound onions, and two-pound radishes. The

MUSK OX FARM

While in Palmer, take the opportunity to visit the world's only domestic musk-ox farm (907/745-4151, www.muskoxfarm.org) and see 50 or so of these fascinating prehistoric arctic creatures up close. During the half-hour tour you learn that, among other things, these exotic animals were hunted nearly to extinction in the early 1900s, but have been reestablished in northwestern and arctic Alaska.

The musk ox wool is collected here, shipped back east to be spun, then distributed to Native villages to be woven into *qiviut* wool products. *Qiviut* is eight times warmer than sheep's wool and much softer and finer than even cashmere. Scarves, stoles, caps, and tunics are sold in the showroom; don't miss the display of little squares of *qiviut*, cashmere, alpaca, and wool from sheep, camel, and llama to compare the softness. The farm opens on Mother's Day in May (a great time to see the calves) and remains open daily 10 A.M.-6 P.M. through September. Winter visits are available for groups only. Get there by taking the Glenn Highway north of town to Mile 50 and following the signs. Admission to – and a half-hour tour of – this nonprofit facility is $8.50 adults, $7 seniors, $6 ages 5-12, and free for younger tots.

© DON PITCHER

The Musk Ox Farm in Palmer is a great place to view these unusual animals up close.

cabbage weigh-off makes front-page news in Alaska each year; an American record was set in 2000 when a Wasilla woman grew a 105-pound cabbage! Entrance is $10 adults, $6 seniors and youths, and free for kids under five.

The **Alaska Railroad** (907/265-2494 or 800/544-0552, www.alaskarailroad.com, round-trip $49 adults, $45 seniors, $25 ages 6–12, $20 ages 2–5, free for tots) has direct train service from Anchorage to the fair grounds during the state fair; it's a great way to avoid the traffic jams and parking hassles. Prices include your entrance to the fair grounds—an excellent bargain.

Knik Glacier

This impressive glacier is visible approximately seven miles up the Knik River Road, and several companies offer airboat trips to the face of this unusual riverside glacier. Recommended is **Hunter Creek Adventures** (907/745-1577, www.knikglacier.com), with four-hour trips that include two hours at a camp next to the glacier, with kayaks for those who want to explore on their own. Overnight stays are possible in the fully outfitted camp for $300 d. Two other companies also run shorter trips to the glacier: **Mountain View Boat Tours** (907/745-5747 or 800/264-4582, www.mtviewrvpark.com) and **Knik Glacier Outfitters** (907/746-5133, www.knikglacieradventures.com).

Knik River Lodge (907/745-5002, www.knikriverlodge.com, $165 d) has 15 newly built cabins 11 miles out Knik River Road. All include private baths, decks, microwaves, fridges, Wi-Fi, and continental breakfasts.

Entertainment and Events

The **Palmer Open Air Market** has local produce, food, crafts, and musical entertainment. It takes place across from the downtown visitor center Fridays 11 A.M.–6 P.M. May–August.

Klondike Mike's Dance Hall & Saloon (820 S. Colony Way, 907/745-2676) has live rock 'n' roll most nights in a rustic Alaskan setting. Also check the lineup at **Vagabond Blues** (642 S. Alaska St., 907/745-2233), which comes alive on weekends when folk musicians pack the house.

Colony Days takes place the second weekend of June, and includes a downtown parade, arts and crafts booths, bed races, foot races, and games. The main wintertime event is the **Colony Christmas Celebration,** with a lighted parade held on the second Friday and Saturday of December, along with reindeer sled rides, caroling, arts and crafts, visits with Santa, and fireworks.

Recreation

Two excellent hikes are accessible off the Old Glenn Highway east of Palmer. Heading north from downtown, go right on Arctic Avenue, which becomes the Old Glenn. Just beyond the

bridge across the Matanuska River, go left onto Clark-Wolverine Road, then continue about a mile until the next junction. Take a right on Huntley Road, go about a mile and bear right at the fork, then drive a quarter mile to the trailhead for **Lazy Mountain.** It's a two-mile hike to the summit of this 3,270-foot mountain with views of the Matanuska Valley.

A better view and shorter hike are to the top of **Bodenberg Butte** (881 ft.). Keep going south on the Old Glenn, pass the first right onto the Loop Road, and take the second right. A parking lot ($3) is a quarter-mile up, and a 40-minute huff rewards you with a 360-degree view of the farm-filled valley, Chugach, Talkeetnas, Knik Glacier, and some of the uncleared forest, which graphically illustrates what the colonists confronted in "clearing the land."

Swimming is available at Palmer High School's **indoor pool** (1170 W. Arctic Ave., 907/745-5091). The **Palmer Golf Course** (907/745-4653, www.cityofpalmer.org) is an 18-hole course on Lepak Avenue along the Matanuska River.

The **Mat-Su Miners** (907/745-6401, www.matsuminers.org) play semiprofessional baseball on the Alaska State Fair Grounds throughout the summer. They're part of the Alaska Baseball League.

Accommodations

Lodging is reasonable in Palmer—at least by Alaska standards. Visit the **Mat-Su Bed & Breakfast Association's** website (www.alaskabnbhosts.com) for links to local places, including a daily vacancy listing in the summer. Located downtown, **Valley Hotel** (606 S. Alaska St., 907/745-3330 or 800/478-7666) has been here since 1948. Forty-three remodeled rooms go for $79 d, and a few larger ones with two queen beds for $110. Downstairs you'll find a 24-hour coffee shop, plus a lounge and a liquor store.

The **Colony Inn** (325 E. Elmwood Ave., $110 d) is one of the older buildings in the valley, built in 1935 as a teachers' dormitory for the Matanuska Valley Colony. Today this historic structure has been transformed into a 12-room hotel with a central sitting room containing a fireplace and wingback chairs. Most rooms contain antiques, quilts, and jetted tubs; all are non-smoking. It's managed by the Valley Hotel, where you register.

Gold Miner's Hotel (918 S. Colony Way, 907/745-6160 or 800/725-2752, www.gold minershotel.com, $79–99 d) across from the visitor center downtown, has aging upstairs rooms with fridges and microwaves.

Located a mile west of Palmer, **River Crest Manor B&B** (907/746-6214, www.rivercrest manor.com, $90–100 d) is a quiet, colonial-style bed-and-breakfast with an extraordinary view of Pioneer Peak and the Chugach Mountains; private bath and continental breakfast included.

Set on 15 acres backdropped by Pioneer Peak, **Alaska's Harvest B&B** (907/745-4263 or 877/745-4263, www.alaskasharvest.com) is an exquisite place to relax. Four guest rooms ($95 d) have private or shared baths and kitchenettes, and the 900-square-foot suite ($125 d) includes a king bed, day bed, kitchenette, and private bath. All rooms are stocked with more than enough food for breakfast, and a guest computer and Wi-Fi are available.

Other local places worth a look include **Alaska's Caribou Cabins** (907/746-6881 or 888/408-2246, www.akcariboucabins.com) and **A-Lazy Acres B&B** (907/745-6340), and **Moose Wallow B&B** (907/745-7777, www.moosewallow.com).

Camping

Palmer has one of the most luxurious city campgrounds in Alaska. **Matanuska River Park** (on East Arctic Ave. about 0.5-mile east of town, 907/745-9631, www.co.mat-su.ak.us, late May–early Oct., $10 tents, $15 RVs) occupies a lush site full of big old cottonwoods and wild roses. There's lots of space between the 86 campsites, which are usually uncrowded except at state fair time. Surrounding the campground is a day-use area, complete with picnic tables, softball and volleyball, horseshoe pits, and a nature trail around the ponds. The park also has coin-operated showers, firewood, trails, river access, and an observation deck.

Local RV parks include **Homestead RV Park** (907/745-6005 or 800/478-3570, www.homesteadrvpark.com) and **Fox Run RV Campground** (907/745-6120 or 877/745-6120, www.foxrun.freeservesr.com), both six miles east of Palmer, **Town & Country RV Park** (907/746-6642) near the fairgrounds, **Mountain View RV Park** (907/745-5747 or 800/264-4582, www.mtviewrvpark.com) three miles south of town, and **Travel & Country RV Park** (907/746-6642) a mile south of Palmer.

Food and Groceries

Palmer's **Vagabond Blues** (642 S. Alaska St., 907/745-2233) is a surprise in this bacon-and-eggs town. The espresso and pastries are fine, the atmosphere is heady, and the food is prepared with panache. You won't go wrong ordering a big hunk of freshly baked bread and an enormous bowl of today's soup served in hand-painted pottery.

If you just want a good, down-home halibut sandwich or dinner of chicken, pork, steak, scallop, or pasta, head to **Round House Café** (606 S. Alaska St., 907/745-3330) at the Valley Hotel. It's open 24 hours and is non-smoking. More all-American fare (steaks and BBQ ribs) at **The Gold Miners Restaurant** (918 S. Colony Way, 907/357-9444). Get authentic and reasonably priced Mexican food downtown at **La Fiesta** (132 W. Evergreen, 907/746-3335). Treat your sweet tooth at **Slack's Sugar Shack Bakery** (340 W. Evergreen Ave., 907/745-4777).

Palmer has a 24-hour **Carrs** grocery store (907/745-7505) on the corner of the Glenn Highway and Palmer–Wasilla Highway, and the **Fred Meyer** just up the street.

Information and Services

The **Palmer Library** (655 S. Valley Way, 907/745-4690, www.matsulibraries.org/palmer) has public-use computers. The new **Mat-Su Regional Medical Center** (2500 S. Woodworth Loop, 907/746-8600, www.matsuregional.com) occupies the hilltop just off the Parks Highway at Trunk Road.

Getting There

Mat-Su Community Transit, better known as

MASCOT (907/376-5000, www.matsutransit .com), has weekday service throughout the valley ($2) and commuter runs to Anchorage ($2.50). This is half of what you'd pay for gas to drive the same distance!

WASILLA

In 1977, Wasilla consisted of a landing strip and a grocery store, which advertised the convenience of flying in from the bush, buying Matanuska Valley produce, and flying out again—without the hassles of Anchorage. Then, when the capital looked like it might be moved to Willow, 25 miles up the highway, Anchorageites began to discover Wasilla's quiet, beauty, and affordable land, and contractors took advantage of the town's lax restrictions on development. And develop it did, with a vengeance. During 1980–1982, the town's population of 1,200 doubled, then doubled again in 1982–1984. Stores, malls, and fast-food chains popped up faster than you could say, "We do chicken right." Teeland's General Store was jacked up, moved from the corner it had sat on for over 60 years, and unceremoniously dumped in a parking lot around the block to make way for a 7-Eleven. The original airstrip, which had kept Wasilla on the map for so long, was moved out from the middle of all the hustle and bustle of town.

The unbridled growth continues today, as low real estate prices and good roads make the area a favorite of Anchorage commuters wanting a piece of the suburban lifestyle. In the 1990s, Wasilla's Wal-Mart proved so popular that after just a few years Wal-Mart built a new and much larger version across the highway. Dozens of strip-type buildings line the highway, with more added all the time in this fast-growing part of Alaska. Driving south into and through Wasilla on the Parks Highway is like passing through a space warp and reemerging in any southern California suburb. It's the kind of place where locals give directions in relation to the nearest big-box store: "It's up the road a half-mile beyond Wal-Mart."

Historical Sights

Make sure to visit **Dorothy Page Museum**

and **Historical Park** (907/373-9071, www .cityofwasilla.com/museum, Mon.–Sat, 9 A.M.–5 P.M. April–Sept. only, $3 adults, $2.50 seniors, free for kids under 13) on Main Street just off the Parks Highway. The museum houses historical photos, artifacts from early settlers and the Iditarod, plus interesting downstairs exhibits of the mining era, including a diorama of Independence Mine. The adjacent old town site park settlement contains a schoolhouse, bunkhouse, smokehouse, steam bath, blacksmith shop, and cache.

Right across the street from the Dorothy Page Museum is the historic Teeland's Store, one of the oldest buildings in Alaska. Today the beautifully restored structure houses Valley Bistro.

About four miles north of town (Mile 47), take a left at the sign and head 0.75 mile down to the **Museum of Alaska Transportation and Industry** (907/376-1211, www.museumofalaska.org, Tues.–Sun. 10 A.M.–5 P.M. May–Sept., closed the rest of the year, $8 adults, $5 seniors and youths, free for kids under 3, or $18 for families). This museum houses an extensive collection of antiques relating to Alaskan aviation, railroading, fishing, mining, and road transportation. Take a gander at the "Chitina auto railer" an old car built to run on rail tracks. Outside are wooden boats, farm machinery (much of it still running), ancient snowmobiles, and several rail cars.

Just up from the museum is **Alaska Live Steamers** ($4), a delightful scale model railroad that takes families through the forest, over bridges, and through tunnels on summer weekends. It's a good place to meet men living out their model railroad dreams. Trains run on weekends June–September.

Knik Museum (907/745-4751, Thurs.–Sun. noon–6 P.M. June–Aug., $2) is 14 miles out Knik Road from Wasilla. Housed in a century-old building, it exhibits items from the Knik gold rush of 1897–1917 and the Iditarod Trail.

Other Nearby Sights

Wasilla is the headquarters for the 1,049-mile **Iditarod Trail Sled Dog Race** from Anchorage to Nome. The headquarters (907/376-5155

THE IDITAROD

The most Alaskan of all Alaskan events is the Iditarod Trail Sled Dog Race from Anchorage to Nome. The "Last Great Race" is run each March, attracting 60 or more of the world's best mushers, each with a team of up to 20 dogs. With a top prize of $70,000, and a $500,000 purse for the top 20 teams, the race has become an event with an international following.

Today's Iditarod Trail Sled Dog Race is run on the historic Iditarod Trail, a path that had its origins in the 1908 discovery of gold along a river the Ingalik Natives called *Hidedhod*, meaning "Distant Place." Thousands of miners flooded into the region following the find, and trails were cut from Seward to the new boomtown of Iditarod so that mail and supplies could be brought in and gold shipped out. Once the gold ran out after a few years, the miners gradually gave up and left, and the old town began a long, slow return to quietude. But other events would eventually bring Iditarod back to life in a new form.

During the winter of 1925, a diphtheria epidemic broke out in Nome, and the territorial governor hurriedly dispatched a 20-pound package of life-saving antitoxin serum to halt the disease's spread. Regular boat mail would take 25 days, and the only two airplanes in Alaska were open cockpit biplanes. With temperatures far below zero, and only a few hours of light each day (it was mid-January), that option was impossible. Instead, the package was sent by train from Seward to Nenana, where mushers and their dogs waited to carry the antitoxin on to Nome. What happened next is hard to believe: a Herculean relay effort by 20 different mushers and their dogs brought the vaccine to Nome in just six days. They somehow managed to cover the 674 miles in conditions that included whiteout blizzards, 80 mph winds, and temperatures down to -64°F! The event gained national attention, and President Coolidge thanked the mushers, presenting each with a medal and $0.50 for each mile traveled.

Long after this heroic effort, two more people entered the picture: Dorothy Page ("Mother of the Iditarod") and Joe Redington, Sr. ("Father of the Iditarod"). In 1967, the two organized a commemorative Iditarod race over

or 800/545-6874, www.iditarod.com, daily 8 A.M.–7 P.M. mid-May–mid-Sept., Mon.–Fri. 8 A.M.–5 P.M. the rest of the year) includes a log museum containing race memorabilia, Native artifacts, videos, dog-mushing equipment. Also here is Togo, the stuffed sled dog who led Leonhard Seppala's team during the 1925 serum delivery to Nome. Find Togo and friends two miles out Knik Road. Admission is free, though a fee is charged to go for a ride on a wheeled dogsled. Next door is a gift shop selling products from **Alaska Birch Syrup Company** (907/357-4884, www.birchforests.com). Informative half-hour tours of the birch production facility are $7.

Lakeshore Park at Wasilla Lake right off the highway has swimming (not too cold), picnic tables, and a view of the craggy Chugach Mountains—great place to set up your tripod. A less crowded day-use lake area is at **Kepler-**

Bradley Lakes just beyond the junction of the Parks and Glenn Highways, on the Glenn toward Palmer.

Accommodations

Several motels are strung along the Parks Highway. On the south end of Wasilla is **Windbreak Hotel** (907/376-4209, www.windbreakalaska .com, $70–80 d) with 10 budget rooms.

Alaskan View Motel (2650 E. Parks Hwy., 907/376-6787, www.alaskanviewmotel.com, $95–105 d) is a modern two-story log building across from Nye Ford. It's convenient for shopping and dining, and windows frame the Chugach Range.

Alaska's Select Inn (3451 Palmdale Dr., 907/357-4768 or 888/357-4768, www .alaskaselectinn.com) is a newly built place with spacious rooms ($100 d) and suites ($120 d), all with full kitchens and Wi-Fi.

a small portion of the trail. Six years later they set up a full-blown dog sled race from Anchorage to Nome, a distance that is officially called 1,049 miles. It took winner Dick Wilmarth 20 days, 49 minutes, and 41 seconds to make it under the Nome archway. At the finish line, Wilmarth lost his lead dog, Hot Foot. Fourteen days later the dog wandered into his master's home in Red Devil – 500 miles from Nome.

Over the years the race has become much more professional and far faster. The record run of 9 days, 58 minutes, and 6 seconds was set by Doug Swingley in 2000. And this was even with two mandatory layovers of 10 hours along the way. The Iditarod is certainly one of the most strenuous events in the world. With below-zero temperatures, fierce winds, and all the hazards that go with crossing the most remote parts of Alaska in winter, the race is certainly not for everyone. Despite this, the Iditarod has gained a measure of fame as one where both women and men are winners. Between 1985 and 1993, five of the nine winners were female, and the late Susan Butcher won four of these races.

(After Butcher won the race three consecutive years, T-shirts began appearing in local stores saying "Alaska: Where men are men, and women win the Iditarod.")

The Iditarod has not one, but two actual starts. The official start is from 4th Avenue in downtown Anchorage, where several thousand onlookers cheer each team that leaves the starting line. The mushers and dogs race as far as Eagle River (25 miles), where they're loaded into trucks and driven to the "restart" in Wasilla. (This is to avoid having to sled over the thin snow conditions around Palmer and open water on the Knik River.) At the restart, the fastest teams into Eagle River leave first, creating chaotic conditions when several 20-dog teams are pulling to the start at once. The last stop on the road system is 14 miles away in the town of Knik; from here on, it's a thousand miles of wilderness.

The **Iditarod Trail Committee** has its headquarters on Knik Road in Wasilla (907/376-5155 or 800/545-6874, www.iditarod.com), where they have a museum of race memorabilia and offer wheeled dog sled rides in the summer.

Best Western Lake Lucille Inn (1300 W. Lake Lucille Dr., 907/373-1776 or 800/897-1776, www.bestwestern.com/lakelucilleinn, $149–169 d) has 54 roomy rooms, half with private balconies overlooking the lake. Guests will also appreciate the fitness center, sauna, hot tub, business center, Wi-Fi, continental breakfasts, and outside dining in the restaurant.

Agate Inn (907/373-2290 or 800/770-2290, www.agateinn.com), three miles from Wasilla on the Palmer–Wasilla Highway, has a variety of lodging options scattered over four buildings from motel-type rooms with king beds in the main house ($99 d) to suites with kitchens ($145 d) and a two-bedroom cottage ($225 for four people). A continental breakfast is provided. The six pet reindeer on the grounds are a favorite of guests.

Mat-Su Resort (1850 Bogard Rd., 907/376-3228, www.matsuresort.com) charges $100 d for standard rooms or cabins and $115 d for larger rooms with king beds. The resort sits on the quiet north side of Lake Wasilla and has paddleboats for rent.

Lake Lucille B&B (907/357-0353 or 888/353-0352, www.alaskaslakelucillebnb .com) is a gracious home right on the shore of Lake Lucille, just a short distance from Wasilla. The four guest rooms (shared baths) are a reasonable $89 d; a family suite is $135–155. A light breakfast starts each day.

For something more traditionally Alaskan, stay at **Pioneer Ridge B&B** (1830 E. Parks Hwy., 907/376-7472 or 800/478-7472, www.pioneerridge.net, $99–159 d). This distinctive 10,000-square-foot home sits on a hill in the country south of Wasilla. Six guest rooms with shared or private baths are available. A buffet breakfast is served in the common room, where you can also play a game of pool, watch a video, listen to the player piano, surf the Web, or simply relax. On top of the house is a unique glass-enclosed room with a fireplace and 360-degree views.

A new home, **Country Pleasures B&B** (907/376-9030 or 888/376-9030, www .countrypleasuresbedandbreakfast.com, $95–145 d) offers two comfortable suites with private baths and entrances, continental breakfasts, and kitchenettes. The larger suite includes a balcony and in-room Jacuzzi. A path leads through the woods to little Zak Lake, with a gazebo and dock.

Alaska's Snowed Inn B&B (907/376-7495 or 866/799-5169, www.snowedinn-ak.com, $99 d) provides two suites, each with private baths and balconies. A big family style breakfast is included, and the inn has an old-fashioned front porch and a quiet setting.

Visit the **Mat-Su Bed & Breakfast Association's**, website (www.alaskabnb hosts.com) for links to local B&Bs, including a daily vacancy listing in the summer.

Camping

Lake Lucille Park (907/745-9631, www.co .mat-su.ak.us, $10; no RV hookups) is an 80-acre natural area with trails and campsites two miles south of Wasilla off Knik-Goose Bay Road. There's another public campground ($15) at **Finger Lake State Recreation Site,** six miles east of Wasilla on Bogard Road.

Big Bear RV Park (2010 S. Church St., 907/745-7445) has RV and tent sites. Many RVers park for free in local shopping mall lots.

Food

Perhaps because of all the early-morning commuters to Anchorage, Wasilla seems to have an espresso stand on almost every corner—along with an equal number of gun shops. Sounds like a dangerous combination, especially with all those folks listening to Rush Limbaugh each morning. A better bet for a jolt is the delightfully old fashioned **Valley Bistro** (907/357-5633), with good pastries and espresso to start your day, followed by lunchtime salads, sandwiches, burgers, soups, and smoothies.

Windbreak Café (907/376-4484) is a good choice for home-cooked meals, prime rib, and seafood. Breakfast is served all day.

Alaska Cadillac Café (907/357-5533) serves a mix of tacos, burritos, specialty sandwiches, burgers, gourmet pizzas, and even homemade root beer. Other choices include **Chepo's Fiesta** (731 W. Parks Hwy., 907/373-5656) for Mexican food in a fun setting, and **Mekong Thai Cuisine** (473 W. Parks Hwy., 907/373-7690).

Evangelo's Restaurant (907/376-1212, entrées $15–25.) is surprisingly classy, and locals rave about the food: lasagna, calzones, scampi, pizzas, and an excellent Italian sausage sandwich. It's across from Lowe's.

Great Bear Brewing Co. (238 N. Boundary St., 907/373-4782, www.greatbearbrewing.com, daily until midnight) has fresh beers brewed on the premises and huge portions of pub fare, including seafood, pasta, steaks, and burgers. There are rock bands on weekends, and karaoke Mondays.

Mat-Su Resort (1850 Bogard Rd., 907/376-3228, www.matsuresort.com) has a good lakeside dining room that specializes in angus steaks; open for lunch and dinner daily, and breakfast on weekends.

Shoreline Restaurant (1300 W. Lake Lucille Dr., 907/373-1776, $15–22 entrées)—housed within the Best Western Lake Lucille Inn—has steak and seafood dining plus a soup and salad bar. Great views from the lakeside windows help to soften the blow to your wallet. It also serves a popular Sunday brunch ($18).

Located at Settlers Bay Golf Course eight miles out Knik-Goose Bay Road, **Settlers Bay Lodge** (907/357-5678, www .settlersbaylodge.com, $15–30 entrées) is a destination spot for locals who appreciate the towering windows, deck-with-a-vista dining, and menu of steaks, seafood, and pasta.

Wasilla's **Farmers Market** (907/376-5679, Wed. evenings noon–6 P.M.) takes place mid-June–mid-September at the old Wasilla town site.

Events and Services

Wasilla's big event comes in early March, as the

Iditarod Trail Sled Dog Race slides through town. The race officially begins in Anchorage, but after a 25-mile run to Eagle River, the dogs are trucked north for the "restart" at the Wasilla Airport. Just west of here the teams move completely away from the road system, and are in wilderness all the way to Nome.

Adjacent to the museum, the **Wasilla Public Library** (391 N. Main St., 907/376-5913, www.cityofwasilla.com/library) is a good place to stop and check your email or play on the Web. If you don't want to wait, head to **The Digital Cup** (545 S. Knik-Goose Bay Rd., 907/373-2727, www.digitalcup.net) next to Fred Meyer. **iCafé** (907/357-6622, www.valleymacstore.com) next to the Lowes store, has Internet access, Wi-Fi, and Kaladi coffee. Swim at Wasilla High School's **pool** (701 W. Bogard Rd., 907/376-4222).

Getting There

Mat-Su Community Transit, better known as **MASCOT** (907/376-5000, www.matsu transit.com) has weekday service throughout the valley ($2) and commuter runs to Anchorage ($2.50).

◖ HATCHER PASS

This is one of the most beautiful parts of the Mat-Su Valley region, and a wonderful side trip from either the Parks Highway north of Wasilla, or the Glenn Highway at Palmer. It's a 49-mile drive, starting in Palmer and ending at Mile 71 of the Parks (30 miles north of Wasilla).

Most folks get to Hatcher Pass from the Palmer end. Hatcher Pass Road (also called Fishhook–Willow Rd.) begins in rolling forest-and-farm country and then climbs along the beautiful Little Susitna River—popular with experienced kayakers who enjoy Class V white water. After passing Motherlode Lodge, the road climbs steeply uphill to Independence Mine State Historical Park at Mile 17 (where the pavement ends) before topping out at 3,886-foot Hatcher Pass and Summit Lake in an area of vast vistas, high tundra, excellent hiking, and backcountry camping. Then it's downhill through pretty forests along Willow Creek all the way to the Parks Highway; this route was originally a wagon road built to service the gold mines. The road is paved from Palmer all the way to Independence Mine, and for 10 miles from the Willow side; the rest is gravel. A bike path follows the road along the Little Susitna River section, and campsites can be found at Deception Creek, two miles from the Parks Highway.

Independence Mine State Historical Park

It's hard to imagine a park that better combines the elements of the Alaska experience: scenery, history and lore, and that noble yellow metal, gold. This mine is very different from the panning, sluicing, deep-placer, and dredging operations seen in Interior Alaska. This was "hard-rock" mining, with an intricate 21-mile network of tunnels under Granite Mountain. The miners drilled into the rock, inserted explosives (which they set off at the end of shifts to give the fumes time to dissipate before the next crew went in), then "mucked" the debris out by hand, to be sorted, crushed, amalgamated, and assayed.

Hard-rock or "lode" mining is often preceded by panning and placer mining. Prospectors who first took gold from Grubstake Gulch, a tributary of Willow Creek, in 1897 noticed the gold's rough, unweathered nature, which indicated a possible lode of unexposed gold nearby. In 1906, Robert Lee Hatcher staked the first lode claim, and his Alaska Free Gold Mine operated until 1924. In 1908, the Independence Mine opened on the mountain's east slope, and over the next 25 years it produced several million dollars' worth. In 1937, the two mines merged into the Alaska Pacific Consolidated Mining Company, which operated Independence Mine at peak production through 1942, when World War II shut it down. A series of private sales, and public deals with the Alaska Division of Parks, culminated in 1980, leaving the state with 271 acres, including the whole mining camp, and deeding 1,000 acres to the Coronado Mining Corporation, which has active operations in the area.

A couple of dozen camp buildings are in various stages of ruin and refurbishing. Start at the visitor center in the rehabilitated house of the camp manager. Take some time to enjoy the excellent displays: historic charts, gold-mining overview, "touch tunnel" complete with sound effects, and wage summaries of workers and management. Guided tours ($5 adults, $3 seniors, free for kids under 11) are given daily at 1 and 3 P.M. (plus 4:30 P.M. on weekends) by park personnel. At other times, just wander the site on your own; interpretive signs describe the various buildings. Independence Mine State Historical Park is a must-see on any Alaskan itinerary.

The visitor center (907/745-2827 summer only or 907/745-3975, www.alaskastateparks.org) is open daily 10 A.M.–7 P.M. from late May–early September; closed the rest of the year. Parking is $5.

Accommodations

A number of lodging options are scattered along the southern section of Hatcher Pass Road north of Palmer. **Alaska Gold Rush B&B** (907/745-5312 or 877/745-5312, www.alaskagoldrush.com, $109 d, plus $20 per person for additional guests) has two rooms in the main house and four lovely Alaskan-theme cabins, all with private baths, microwaves, fridges, and Wi-Fi. A big buffet breakfast is served each morning. They're out in the country six miles north of Palmer. Not far away is **Hatcher Pass B&B** (907/745-6788, www.hatcherpassbb.com), which has delightful log cabins, all with kitchenettes and private baths. Small "sourdough" cabins are $89 s or $99 d, and large two-bedroom chalets sleeps two for $135; add $15 per person for additional guests (max eight). Cabins are fully stocked for make-it-yourself breakfasts.

Just downhill from Independence Mine is **Hatcher Pass Lodge** (907/745-5897, www.hatcherpasslodge.com, $10–25 dinner entrées). This A-frame lodge is a great spot for sandwiches, fondues, pizza, steaks, and halibut, with a sunset view to die for. Nine cozy cabins cost $165 d, and three tiny upstairs rooms are $95 d each. Also on the grounds is a creekside sauna (guests only). The lodge is open daily all year. Speaking from personal experience, this is the perfect place for a summer wedding. The lodge also maintains 10 kilometers of groomed ski trails (donation) in the winter, and more adventurous backcountry skiers and snowboarders head up the steep (and avalanche-prone) slopes that rise on three sides. In winter the road isn't plowed beyond Independence Mine State Park but you can park here to play; it's a special favorite of snowmobilers. **Motherlode Lodge** (907/745-6171, www.motherlodelodge.com) occupies a rambling old building along Hatcher Pass Road, but was transitioning to new owners as this was written, so call for the latest.

NORTH TO DENALI

It's a long 195-mile drive from Wasilla (and 237 miles from Anchorage) to Denali National Park on the Parks Highway. After the first few miles, the developments peter out and roadside attractions shift from fast food, gun shops, and video stores to the real Alaska of forests and mountains. The land is a seemingly endless birch and spruce forest, with a smattering of half-finished plywood homesteads covered in blue tarps, their yards piled high with firewood. The road follows a gradual climb toward the magnificent Alaska Range that seems to grow in magnitude the farther north you get. Mile after mile of pink fireweed flowers brighten the roadside in mid-summer.

Big Lake

The Big Lake area is a popular recreation destination, especially on summer weekends when many Anchorageites head to summer homes here. Access is via nine-mile-long Big Lake Road which splits off the Parks Highway at Mile 52 (10 miles north of Wasilla). Don't expect quiet along this large and scenic lake. In summer, Big Lake is jet-ski central 24 hours a day, and when winter arrives the snowmobile crowd comes out for more motorized mayhem. Get local information from the **Big Lake Chamber of Commerce** (907/892-6109, www.biglake-ak.com).

Big Lake was near the center of the 1996 Miller's Reach Fire that blackened 37,500 acres and destroyed over 400 buildings. Three state park campgrounds ($15) are in the area: **Rocky Lake State Recreation Site, Big Lake North State Recreation Site,** and **Big Lake South State Recreation Site.**

Lodging is available at **Big Lake Motel** (907/892-7976). **Sunset View Resort** (907/892-8885, www.sunsetviewbb.com) rents out three expensive lakeside homes with a two-night minimum.

Operated by 2002 Iditarod champion Martin Buser, **Happy Trails Kennels** (Mile 4.5 West Lakes Blvd., 907/892-7899, www.buserdog.com) has kennel tours and demonstrations all summer.

Houston

This podunk gathering of 900 or so souls 58 miles from Anchorage includes the usual lineup of suspects: gas, groceries, café, lodging, RV park, coin laundry, and air taxi operators, but it is best known for its fireworks stands. Four of these giant eyesores—it's especially hard to miss Gorilla Fireworks—sit on the edges of town, pulling families from Anchorage looking for fun on the 4th of July. Fireworks are illegal to shoot off almost anywhere in Alaska. Of course, this is one of those legal niceties that is widely ignored. **Little Susitna River Campground** (www.matsugov.us, $10) is a Mat-Su Borough facility on the south side of Houston.

Plettner Sled Dog Kennels (907/892-6944 or 877/892-6944, www.plettner-kennels.com) is run by Iditarod veteran Lynda Plettner, with summertime kennel tours from her home at Mile 53.

Nancy Lake State Recreation Area

Access to Nancy Lake is from Mile 67 of the Parks Highway, just south of Willow, and 25 miles north of Wasilla. This flat, heavily forested terrain is dotted with over 100 lakes, some interconnected by creeks. As you might imagine, the popular activities here are fish-

ing, boating, and canoeing, plus a comfortable campground and a couple of hiking trails. As you might also suspect, the skeeters here are thick in early summer.

Follow the Nancy Lake Road a little more than a mile to **Nancy Lake State Recreation Site Campground** ($10). A half-mile past the kiosk is the trailhead to several **public-use cabins** (reservations: 907/745-3975, www.alaskastateparks.org). The cost is $45, but reserve well ahead to be sure of getting one of these exceptionally popular cabins. Just under a mile beyond this trailhead is the **Tulik Nature Trail,** an easy walk that takes about an hour. Keep an eye out for loons, beavers, and terns, and watch for that prickly devil's club!

The **Tanaina Lake Canoe Route** begins at Mile 4.5, Nancy Lakes Road. This leisurely, 12-mile, two-day trip hits 14 lakes, between most of which are well-marked portages, some upgraded with boardwalks over the muskeg. Hunker down for the night at any one of 10 primitive campsites (campfires in fireplaces only). Another possibility, though requiring a long portage, is to put into the Little Susitna River at Mile 57 on the Parks Highway and portage to Skeetna Lake, where you connect up to the southern leg of the loop trail. **Tippecanoe** (907/495-6688, www.paddlealaska.com), at South Rolly Campground, rents canoes for the Nancy Lake canoe trails. **Nancy Lake Resort** (Mile 65, 907/495-6284, $50 d) has bring-your-bedding cabins with kitchenettes. There's a separate shower house, plus canoe and rowboat rentals.

Willow

At Mile 69 is Willow (pop. 400), a roadside town that you'll miss if you sneeze, with gas, grocery, hardware, café, and air service. Back in 1980, however, Alaskans voted to move the state capital here. A multibillion-dollar city was planned, and real estate speculation went wild. However, when a second vote was held in 1982 to decide whether to actually *spend* the billions, the plan was soundly defeated.

Stay at **Pioneer Lodge & RV Park** (907/495-1000), right on the creek with rustic motel units

($80 d), newer cabins ($110–150 d) with kitchenettes, camping ($25 for RVs, $12 for tents), and a full-service restaurant with good homemade pizzas. **Willow Creek Resort** (907/495-6343, www.willowcreekresort.com) has RV ($26) and tent spaces ($16) on the opposite bank, plus raft rentals and guided fishing.

Operated by Iditarod veteran Vern Halter, **Dream A Dream Dog Farm** (907/495-1197 or 866/425-6874, www.vernhalter.com) has summertime kennel tours and demonstrations in Willow.

Both **Willow Air Service** (907/495-6370 or 800/478-6370, www.willowwir.com), and **Denali Flying Service** (907/495-5899) offer scenic flights over Knik Glacier, Hatcher Pass, and Mt. McKinley from Willow.

North to Talkeetna
At Mile 71 of the Parks is the turnoff to **Willow Creek State Recreation Area,** four miles down the Susitna River access road. Sites are $10, but don't expect a quiet night's repose in the wilderness here if the salmon are running, which they do for most of the summer. The boat launch attracts fishing parties at all hours of the day and night, as well as lots of RVs with their inevitable generator noise. Still, it's a pretty and handy place to spend the night if it's getting late and you plan to travel over the exceptionally scenic Hatcher Pass to Independence Mine State Historical Park. There is more camping along nearby Deception Creek, two miles up Hatcher Pass Road.

In the 45 miles from Willow to the Talkeetna cutoff are scattered lodging places, restaurants, and gas stations. The most notable place is **Sheep Creek Lodge** (Mile 89, 907/495-6227, www.sheepcreeklodge.com), a classic log Alaskan roadhouse rebuilt after a 1986 fire. Its restaurant serves meals year-round. Modern rooms in the lodge with private baths and Wi-Fi are $125 d. Rustic cabins sleep four for $75, with a bathhouse nearby. There's also RV parking and tent spaces ($15), but no hookups.

Gigglewood Lakeside Inn (907/495-1014 or 800/574-2555, www.gigglewood.com, $100–135 d) is a remote and lovingly designed log home on a small lake several miles off the Parks Highway at Mile 88. The home contains three bedrooms and a separate cottage, all with private entrances and baths. A full breakfast is served in the common room overlooking the lake. You can relax in the sauna or try out the paddleboat and mountain bikes.

Mat-Su Valley RV Park (907/495-6300, www.matsurvpark.com) is at Mile 91.

Big Susitna B&B (Mile 92, 907/495-6324, www.bigsusitnabnb.com, $73 s or $93 d) has two rooms with shared baths and full breakfasts in a comfortable log home. The owners are Iditarod veterans.

The privately run **Montana Creek Campgrounds** (Mile 97, 907/566-5267 or 877/475-2267, www.montanacreekcampground.com) provides wooded sites on both sides of this popular salmon fishing creek.

KENAI PENINSULA

The Kenai Peninsula is like a mini-Alaska, compressing all of the state's features into an area roughly one-thirty-fifth the size of the state. You'll find mountains, icefields and glaciers, fjords and offshore islands, large fish-filled rivers and lakes, swampy plains, varied climate and precipitation, a few scattered port towns and a sprawling population center. The Kenai is a major playground for both Anchorage residents and travelers from Outside, and it's possibly the most popular all-around destination for all Alaskans. The outdoor recreational opportunities are practically inexhaustible, with innumerable choices of every pedestrian, pedaled, paddled, piloted, port-holed, piscatory, predatory, and picaresque particular you could ever ponder—just you and 300,000 other folks from the neighborhood. But don't let the pos-

sibility of crowds deter you. The resources are abundant, well developed, and often isolated. And besides, what's wrong with a little company along the trail or under sail?

ORIENTATION
The Land

At 16,056 square miles, Kenai Peninsula is a little smaller than Vermont and New Hampshire combined. The Kenai Mountains form the peninsula's backbone, with massive Harding Icefield dominating the lower lumbar. The east side, facing Prince William Sound, hosts a spur of the Kenai Mountains, with the glimmering Sargent Icefields; the west side, facing Cook Inlet, is outwash plain, sparkling with low-lying swamp, lakes, and rivers. The icefields, glaciers, and plains are all a result of ice sculpting over

© DON PITCHER

KENAI PENINSULA

HIGHLIGHTS

◖ **Hope:** Now almost a ghost town, this once-booming mining town is the place that time forgot. Several fine hikes head out from here (page 239).

◖ **Alaska SeaLife Center:** Touch tanks, puffins swimming underwater, and fascinating exhibits are great, but seals and sea lions steal the show at this popular Seward marine science center (page 245).

◖ **Exit Glacier:** Easily accessible from Seward, this glacier is part of Kenai Fjords National Park and has camping, hiking trails (including one onto the massive Harding Icefield), and glacier tours (page 253).

◖ **Resurrection Bay Boat Tours:** Several Seward companies offer wildlife and glacier tours by boat. Half-day ones tour the bay; all-day versions (take your Dramamine) make it into Kenai Fjords (page 254).

◖ **Combat Fishing:** The Kenai and Russian Rivers are major destinations for Anchorageites and tourists in search of their bag limit of red salmon. It's an elbow-to-elbow frenzy at the mid-summer peak (page 256).

◖ **The Homer Spit:** Jutting four miles into Kachemak Bay, this narrow sandy peninsula provides a great base for halibut charters, sea kayaking, bird watching, cycling, dining, and shopping (page 268).

◖ **Islands and Ocean Center:** Modern and slick, this free center houses exhibits on the Alaska Maritime National Wildlife Refuge. Don't miss the award-winning film about the refuge and its wildlife (page 270).

◖ **Pratt Museum:** One of the finest small museums in Alaska, the Pratt always has something interesting, including a touch tank with tidepool animals in the back room (page 271).

LOOK FOR ◖ TO FIND RECOMMENDED SIGHTS, ACTIVITIES, DINING, AND LODGING.

◖ **Kachemak Bay Tours and Gull Island:** Gull Island with its thousands of nesting seabirds is a favorite destination for day tours. Also popular are trips to the off-the-road-system villages of Halibut Cove and Seldovia (page 285).

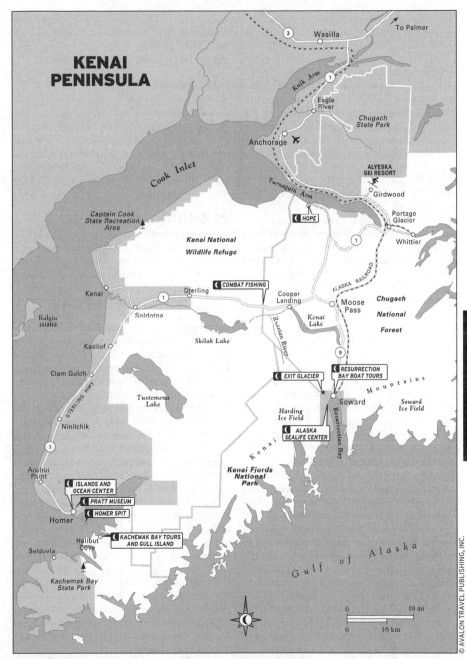

KENAI
PENINSULA

To Palmer

Wasilla

Knik Arm

Eagle River

Chugach State Park

Anchorage

ALYESKA SKI RESORT

Girdwood

Cook Inlet

Turnagain Arm

Captain Cook State Recreation Area

Portage Glacier

HOPE

Whittier

Kenai National Wildlife Refuge

COMBAT FISHING

Cooper Landing

ALASKA RAILROAD

Moose Pass

Chugach National Forest

Kenai

Sterling

Kalgin Island

Soldotna

Kenai Lake

Russian River

Skilak Lake

Kasilof

RESURRECTION BAY BOAT TOURS

Clam Gulch

EXIT GLACIER

Tustemena Lake

Seward

Seward Ice Field

STERLING HWY

Mountains

Ninilchik

Harding Ice Field

ALASKA SEALIFE CENTER

Resurrection Bay

Anchor Point

ISLANDS AND OCEAN CENTER

Kenai

PRATT MUSEUM

HOMER SPIT

Homer

Kenai Fjords National Park

Seldovia

KACHEMAK BAY TOURS AND GULL ISLAND

Halibut Cove

Gulf   of   Alaska

Kachemak Bay State Park

0   10 mi

0   10 km

KENAI PENINSULA

© AVALON TRAVEL PUBLISHING, INC.

the million-year course of the Pleistocene, with its five major glacial periods. During the last, the Wisconsin Period, Portage Glacier filled the entire Turnagain Arm, 50 miles long and a half-mile high. Portage stopped just short—10,000 years ago—of carving a fjord between Prince William Sound and Turnagain Arm; otherwise, Kenai Peninsula would've been Kenai Island. Still, this peninsula is so digitated with pen-insulettes that it has more than 1,000 miles of coastline. The land is almost completely con-trolled by the feds; Chugach National Forest, Kenai National Wildlife Refuge, and Kenai Fjords National Park account for nearly 85 per-cent of the peninsula.

Two roads provide the primary access to the Kenai. The 127-mile **Seward Highway** con-nects Anchorage with Seward on the southwest end of the peninsula, and the 143-mile **Sterling Highway** cuts across the Kenai, leading west and south from Tern Lake (where it meets the Seward Highway) to Soldotna and Homer.

History

You begin to feel the Russian influence strongly in this neck of the woods. Baranov's first ship-yard was somewhere along Resurrection Bay down from present-day Seward. Russians built a stockade near Kasilof in 1786 and a fort at Kenai in 1791. Other than these brief incur-sions, the land belonged to the Kenai Natives: part of the great Athabascan tribe on the north half of the peninsula, while the Alutiiqs occu-pied the southern half.

During the gold rush, color was uncovered around Hope and Sunrise on Turnagain Arm, and at Moose Creek halfway to Seward. First trails ran between the mining communities, then wagon roads, and finally the railroad pushed from Seward through Anchorage to Fairbanks in the early 1920s. The Seward and Sterling Highways were completed in 1952, opening the Kenai's western frontier. When Atlantic Richfield tapped into oil (1957) and gas (1962) off the west coast, the peninsula's economic star began to twinkle. Oil and gas production have dropped steadily since the peak in the 1970s as the reserves are depleted, but new gas deposits are being developed near Ninilchik. Today, the Kenai Peninsula Bor-ough's 50,000 residents are occupied with fish-ing, oil and gas, tourism, and services.

Information

Every Kenai Peninsula town of any size has its own chamber of commerce and website; they're listed under the individual towns. A good overall information source is the **Kenai Peninsula Tourism Marketing Council** (907/283-3850 or 800/535-3624, www.kenai peninsula.org), which produces a detailed an-nual travel publication.

PLANNING YOUR TIME

The Kenai Peninsula is readily accessible by car, bus, plane, or train from Anchorage, making it perfect if you have a few days, but adventurers could easily spend considerably longer exploring backcountry areas or playing in the scenic towns. The off-the-beaten-path settlement of **Hope** has a picture-perfect collection of gold rush–era buildings along Turnagain Arm. A very scenic three-hour drive south from Anchorage, the town of Seward is home to the **Alaska SeaLife Center** (great for kids), along with Kenai Fjords National Park, where visitors can take guided hikes across **Exit Glacier,** join **Resurrection Bay boat tours,** or take longer day (or multi-night) trips into the park. A second highway (The Sterling) heads west across the peninsula through Kenai National Wildlife Refuge, where the Kenai and Russian Rivers are the scene of **"combat fishing"** as hundreds of anglers crowd the banks when the salmon are running.

The Sterling Highway continues west through Soldotna before bending south to the end of the road, Homer. **The Homer Spit,** a sandy strip of land extending four miles into the bay, is the primary visitor attraction here, with charter halibut fishing, sea kayaking, **Kachemak Bay tours** to Gull Island or the remote villages of Halibut Cove and Seldovia, and some of the finest restaurants and lodging in Alaska. Inside attractions well worth a visit include the **Islands and Ocean Center** and the **Pratt Museum.**

Eastern Kenai Peninsula

THE SEWARD HIGHWAY

The 127-mile Seward Highway—a National Scenic Byway—connects Anchorage with Seward on the Kenai Peninsula. Mileposts are numbered from the Seward end; subtract these numbers from 127 for the distance to Anchorage. (See the *Anchorage and Vicinity* chapter for details on the first 48 miles of the road south from Anchorage—including Girdwood and Portage Glacier.) The Seward Highway has passing lanes, wide shoulders, and a 65 mph speed limit much of the way, but take the time to enjoy the scenery. Keep your headlights on at all times, and watch for moose.

Near Portage at Mile 48, the Seward Highway banks sharply to the west along Turnagain Arm before turning again southward as it climbs into the Kenai Mountains. At **Turnagain Pass** (Mile 69, el. 988 ft.), the west side of the road has a big pullout with port-a-potties. Stop and stretch in this pretty alpine area where the snow remains until late June. In the winter the snow is often 10 feet deep. The west side is popular with snowmobilers, while the east side is reserved for those on skis or snowshoes. Turnagain Pass can be deadly at certain times of the winter, and a number of snowmobilers have died in avalanches here while riding on the dangerous upper slopes.

At Mile 64 is the northern trailhead for the **Johnson Pass Trail,** which goes 23 miles over relatively level terrain and emerges at Mile 33 of the Seward Highway. Two in-the-trees Forest Service campgrounds ($11) are nearby: **Bertha Creek Campground** (Mile 65) and **Granite Creek Campground** (Mile 63). The paved **Sixmile Bike Trail** parallels the highway from the Johnson Pass Trailhead south to the junction with the Hope Highway.

Sixmile Creek

At Mile 59 the highway crosses a staging area along Granite Creek for rafters and kayakers down Granite Creek and on to Sixmile Creek. This is one of Alaska's premier white-water

areas. Check out the action from the footbridge that crosses Sixmile Creek, accessible via a short path from the parking area just east of the Canyon Creek bridge. Two companies lead white-water trips here: **Chugach Outdoor Center** (907/277-7238 or 866/277-7238, www.chugachoutdoorcenter.com) and **Nova Riverrunners** (907/745-5753 or 800/746-5753, www.novalaska.com). Three-hour trips ($90–100) arc in Class IV water, while the five-hour trips ($135–145) include some intense Class V sections of the narrowly constricted lower canyon. Nova is the original company on the river, and both have offices near Hope (including a hot tub to warm up in after your adventure at Chugach Outdoor Center). Chugach Outdoor also offers family friendly 2.5-hour Turnagain Pass float trips ($75 per person) on the scenic East Fork of Sixmile Creek.

(HOPE

Now almost a ghost town, Hope is a charming step back into the past, with a quaint cluster of weathered buildings, a little museum, a couple of eateries and lodging places, quiet waterside campsites, and great hiking.

The Hope Highway begins at Mile 56 of the Seward Highway, just west of the towering bridge over Canyon Creek. This sparsely trafficked road follows Sixmile Creek north back up to Turnagain Arm; pan for gold along the first five miles of the crick. The entire 17 miles to Hope is paved.

Gold was discovered on Resurrection Creek in 1888, and by 1896 3,000 people inhabited this boom neighborhood, between Hope and Sunrise on Sixmile Creek. Many came by way of the Passage Canal where Whittier now squats, portaging their watercraft over the Chugach glacial pass to Turnagain Arm, which is how Portage Glacier got its name. Large-scale mining prospered into the 1940s, but then Sunrise was abandoned and left to the ghosts. Hope (www.advenalaska.com/hope) hangs on

CHUGACH NATIONAL FOREST

Much of the eastern Kenai Peninsula lies within Chugach National Forest, the second largest national forest in America after the Tongass. Covering 5.5 million acres – bigger than Massachusetts – the Chugach encompass not just this part of the Kenai, but also continues eastward across all of Prince William Sound, to well beyond the Copper River. Developments and logging are relatively minor on the Chugach, but all this wild country provides incredible opportunities for recreation, with good fishing, hiking, mountain biking, river-rafting, skiing, kayaking, wildlife-watching, glacier-gazing, and a host of other outdoor adventures. Forest headquarters is in Anchorage (3301 C. St., 907/743-9500, www.fs.fed.us/r10/chugach), with district offices in Seward (907/224-3374), Girdwood (907/783-3242), and Cordova (907/424-7661).

CABINS

The Kenai Peninsula has 18 Forest Service public-use cabins available for $35 per night. These are mostly Pan-Abode log structures that sleep four and have wood or oil stoves. Most of these are along hiking trails – including eight cabins on the Resurrection Pass Trail – but a few are accessible only by floatplane. The Chugach website has cabin details, or you can get brochures from the Alaska Public Lands Information Center in Anchorage. Because of their high popularity, it's a wise to reserve cabins well ahead of your visit by contacting **ReserveUSA** (518/885-3639 or 877/444-6777, www.reserveusa.com). Additional public cabins can be found within Kenai Fjords National Park and Kachemak Bay State Park.

CAMPING AND HIKING

Six Forest Service campgrounds are located along the Seward Highway south of Portage, with another four along the Sterling Highway, and two more off the Hope Highway; all are described in this chapter. A number of very popular hiking trails cover the eastern half of the Kenai Peninsula, and it's possible to hike (or mountain bike) all the way from the town of Hope to Exit Glacier near Seward, a distance of 74 miles. Contact the Forest Service for details on various camping and hiking options within the Chugach.

---

today primarily as a place where recreation and tourism support the town's 135 people.

Sights

"Downtown" Hope is marked by a cluster of old buildings, some over a century old. Stop here to walk the dirt street past photogenic **Social Hall**—the original Alaska Commercial Co. store—and down to the tidal flats (caused by the earth sinking seven feet in the 1964 quake); they're dangerous—don't walk on them! Go back and turn left for new Hope, with its post office, its red schoolhouse, and beautiful new and old log cabins. The old one-room school (built in 1938) now serves as a **library.**

Hope & Sunrise Historical and Mining Museum (907/782-3740, summer Fri., Sat., and Mon. noon–4 P.M., Sun. noon–2 P.M., free) is a log museum housing historical photos and artifacts from the Turnagain Arm gold rush of 1894–1899. The grounds contain the original Canyon Creek Mining buildings.

Camping and Hiking

At the end of Hope Highway is the Forest Service's **Porcupine Campground** ($11, www.fs.fed.us/r10/chugach), featuring fine views across Turnagain Arm, and red raspberry hors d'oeuvres in late summer.

Gull Rock Trail begins from the campground and parallels the shoreline of Turnagain Arm. It's a fairly easy stroll out to Gull Rock (5 miles), making this a popular family day hike or overnight camping trip. The **Hope Point Trail** starts at the campground and climbs a steep knob into the alpine. From here you can hike forever along the ridgeline.

Accommodations and Food

Open seasonally, **Seaview Cafe** (907/782-3300)

has tent sites ($10) and RV hookups ($15) along the creek, which is a popular spot to catch pink salmon (humpies) or to pan for gold. The century-old café is open for lunch and dinner, but you're much better off heading to **Discovery Cafe** (907/782-3274, $15–20), serving three meals a day. Dinners include blackened halibut, stir-fry veggies, and daily specials. Homemade pies and soup too.

Clustered around a small pond, **Bowman's Bear Creek Lodge** (Mile 16 of Hope Highway, 907/782-3141, www.bowmansbearcreeklodge .com, $125 d) has five log cabins with woodstoves and a shared bath. The excellent café here serves "rustic cuisine" lunches and dinners ($15–24), with outside dining on summer afternoons.

Discovery Cabins (907/782-3730 or 800/365-7057, www.adventurealaskatours.com, $90 d) has five modern cabins on the edge of Bear Creek in Hope. The cabins share a bathhouse and an outdoor hot tub, and are open summers only. You'll find a grocery, laundry, RV spaces, and motel rooms at **Alaska Dacha** (907/782-3223, www.alaskadacha.com), along the road as you come into town.

Resurrection Pass Trail

A half-mile east of Hope on the Hope Highway is the junction with Palmer Creek Road. Follow it three-quarters of a mile to a fork. Turn left and continue seven long miles to **Coeur D'Alene Campground** with a couple of free spots along a noisy creek. Go right on Resurrection Pass Road four rough miles is the Resurrection Pass trailhead with parking, an information signboard, and a fun bridge across the crick. This popular backpack or mountain bike trip leads 38 miles down to Cooper Landing on the Sterling Highway, or you can cut across on **Devil's Pass Trail** to Mile 39 on the Seward.

SOUTH TO SEWARD

Beyond the Hope Highway junction, the Seward Highway climbs to scenic Summit Lake. At Mile 46 is **Tenderfoot Creek Campground** ($11) in a beautiful area on the shores of this alpine water. Next to it is **Summit Lake Lodge** (907/244-2031, www.summitlakelodge.com, May–mid-

Sept.). Cozy and well placed, it has consistently recommendable food. Breakfast is served until 2 P.M., after which you have your choice of burgers, salads, and other entrées. There's also a small motel ($90 d) and a gift/ice cream/espresso shop. The original lodge was built in 1953, but the big fireplace and chimney are the only parts of the building that survived the '64 quake.

Just after Mile 40 and a mile before the Seward-Sterling junction is **Devil's Pass Trailhead;** this trail leads nine miles to the pass, then another mile to where it joins the Resurrection Pass Trail. An alpine cabin ($35) sits on the pass. Devil's Pass Trailhead is very poorly marked—be prepared.

The **Carter Lake Trail** leaves the highway at Mile 33, climbs 1,000 feet in just over two miles to Carter Lake, and continues another mile around Carter Lake to Crescent Lake. This route gets you into the alpine fast and can be used to loop back to the highway on the Crescent Lake and Crescent Creek Trails. There's a Forest Service cabin ($35) on the south shore of Crescent Lake.

A half-mile beyond the Carter Lake Trailhead is the southern trailhead to **Johnson Pass Trail** (whose northern trailhead is at Mile 64). And just beyond that is **Trail Lakes Fish Hatchery** (8 A.M.–4:30 P.M.), which has a fascinating display about spawning and stocking salmon.

Moose Pass

At Mile 30 you slow down for tiny Moose Pass (pop. 200), where the classic **Estes Brothers Grocery** (907/288-3151), has been updated with a deli and espresso; it's been here since 1928. The main event comes on the **summer solstice** in June, when the town springs to life with music, food, and games. Learn more about Moose Pass on the Web at www.moosepassalaska.com.

Trail Lake Lodge (907/288-3103 or 800/865-0201, www.traillakelodge.com) is the main place to stay at Moose Pass, with comfortable motel rooms ($89 d) and larger lodge units ($105 d). A restaurant and lounge are also here.

An exquisite B&B, **Inn at Tern Lake** (907/288-3667, www.ternlakeinn.com) sits along this picturesque lake six miles north

FOLLOWING THE RESURRECTION PASS TRAIL

The Resurrection Pass Trail covers 38 miles between the towns of Hope and Cooper Landing, with two side routes leading off to trailheads along the Seward Highway. You'll gain and lose 2,000 feet in elevation along the way. A series of Forest Service cabins make this one of the most popular hiking destinations in Southcentral Alaska. The trail winds through spruce forests and tops out in tundra, affording opportunities to see a variety of habitats. Wildlife, wildflowers, and wild fish in the lakes and streams add to the trail's appeal.

The trail begins four rough miles from Hope up Resurrection Pass Road, where a trailhead has parking, an information signboard, and a fun bridge across the creek. Eight cabins along the trail, one of which can only be reached via a floatplane, provide a welcome respite from the often-inclement weather. They're basic, each consisting of wooden bunks, a table and benches, a countertop for cooking, an outhouse, and a heating stove for warmth, but without running water, cooking utensils, or bedding. These very popular cabins cost $35–45 per night, and the farther in advance you can make plans, the more likely you are to secure a reservation. Make reservations through ReserveUSA.

If you can't secure cabins, there are plenty of spots to camp for the night. Be very careful with campfires or, better yet, use a camp stove for cooking. Also filter or boil all drinking water.

Local wildlife includes moose, black and brown bears, wolves, mountain goats, Dall sheep, and even a local caribou herd. The caribou are scattered and often hard to spot in the summer, but if you look up high in the Resurrection Pass and Devil's Pass areas, maybe you'll get lucky. They often like to bed down in snow patches during the heat of the day, so look for dark spots in the snow near ridgelines.

Loop trips are possible, and you can do the Devil's Pass trailhead–Devil's Pass cabin–Cooper Landing trip (27 miles) in three or four days, though hard-core mountain bikers often do it in one day. Hitchhiking to pick up your car is possible, but the Hope trailhead is well off the beaten path for most car traffic.

The high point of the main trail is Resurrection Pass at 2,600 feet. However, even at this comparatively low elevation, the snows of winter can linger well into June. Postholing through thigh-deep snow can dampen the enthusiasm of even the jolliest of hikers. If you're thinking of an early-season hike, check with the Forest Service office in Anchorage (907/271-2500) or the Seward Ranger District (907/224-3374, www.fs.fed.us/r10/chugach) for trail conditions.

At the southern end of the Resurrection Pass Trail at Cooper Landing, you can continue south on the 16-mile **Russian Lakes Trail** which connects with the 16-mile **Resurrection River Trail** all the way to Exit Glacier near Seward. Together, these three trails make it possible to hike 74 miles, a 12-day trek that covers the Peninsula from head to toe.

of Moose Pass. Guests stay in five nicely appointed suites, with access to a hot tub, sauna, kitchen, canoes, kayaks, golf green, and even a private airstrip. A full breakfast is included. The inn is a popular wedding spot.

Other local places include **Alpenglow Cottage** (907/288-3142, www.alpenglowcottage.com), **Cranberry Creek Guest House** (907/288-3150, www.cranberrycreekguesthouse.com), **Jewel of the North B&B** (907/288-3166 or 877/317-7378, www.jewelofthenorth.net), **Midnight Sun Log Cabins** (907/288-3627, www.midnightsunlogcabins.com), **Spruce**

Moose B&B (907/288-3667, www.seward.net/sprucemoose), and **Trail River Gardens B&B** (907/288-3192, www.trailriver.com).

Scenic Mountain Air (907/288-3646 or 800/478-1449, www.scenicmountainair.com) offers one-hour floatplane trips from Trail Lake for $185 per person. If it's a clear day, the views are stunning.

South from Moose Pass
Six miles south of Moose Pass is the turnoff for **Trail River Campground** ($11), a quiet wooded campground just over a mile off the highway,

with some choice sites on the lakeshore loop. Next up on the left at Mile 23 is **Ptarmigan Creek Campground** ($11). Both Trail River and Ptarmigan Creek campgrounds can be reserved through ReserveUSA (877/444-6777, www.reserveusa.com, $9 extra). The **Ptarmigan Creek Trail** climbs from the campground of the same name for 3.5 miles along the creek to Ptarmigan Lake, where there's good fishing for grayling.

Renfro's Lakeside Retreat (907/288-5059 or 877/288-5059, www.seward-alaska.com/renfros, April–Oct.) is eight miles south of Moose Pass along the shore of Kenai Lake. Here you'll find eight cabins, all with private baths and kitchenettes. Five are right on the lake ($145 d) and three are back in the woods ($115–135 d); add $10 per adult for additional guests. RV hookups ($25) are also available, along with paddleboats and a playground. No TVs or phones.

Magnificent **Kenai Lake** comes into view just south of here: huge, beautiful, blue-green, with snowcapped peaks all around. Breathe deeply. Three-mile **Victor Creek Trail** starts at Mile 20; in three miles is the turnoff to the small **Primrose Campground** ($11), a mile from the Seward Highway along Kenai Lake.

Primrose Trail climbs 1,500 feet in eight miles to Lost Lake, where you can hook up to **Lost Lake Trail** and come out at Mile 5 near Seward. This is one of the most popular loop trails in the area. If you planned far enough ahead and made a reservation, you can stay at the Dale Clemens cabin ($45). On clear days, you get a magnificent view of Resurrection Bay and on out to the Gulf of Alaska.

Beautiful **Porcupine Creek Falls** is three miles in on the Primrose Trail and a favorite day hike destination. Above the lake are dramatic alpine views and the chance to explore this high and mighty landscape.

Seward

Seward is a pocket-size (pop. 3,000) port town on a sparkling bay surrounded by snowcapped peaks, and the only large settlement on the east side of the Kenai Peninsula. It's hooked up by bus, ferry, and plane, and has a maritime climate and a seafood industry, just like a half-dozen other places you've visited so far—but with a difference: Seward is right on the doorstep of Kenai Fjords National Park. This park contains some of the most inhospitable visitable country in the state. Harding Icefield—a prehistoric frozen giant with three dozen frigid digits—rivals Glacier Bay for scenery and wildlife but is decidedly less expensive to visit. Combine this with Seward's Alaska SeaLife Center, convenient camping, good food, and excellent access by public transportation, and you've got all the elements for a great time in this old town.

HISTORY

In 1791, Baranov, on a return voyage to Kodiak from around his Alaskan domain, waited out a storm in this bay on Sunday of Resurrection, a Russian holiday. The sheltered waters of Resurrection Bay prompted Baranov to install a small shipyard. In 1903, surveyors for the Alaska Central Railroad laid out the town site for their port. This private enterprise, financed by Seattle businessmen, established Seward, laid 50 miles of track, and went broke. In 1911, Alaska Northern Railroad extended the track almost to present-day Girdwood. In 1912, the U.S. government began financing the completion of this line, which reached Fairbanks, 470 miles north, in 1923. From then, Seward's history parallels Valdez's as one of the two year-round ice-free ports with shipping access to Interior—Seward's by rail, Valdez's by road. And like Valdez, Seward was almost completely destroyed by 1964's Good Friday earthquake.

Today, Seward has a diverse economy supported by tourism, commercial and sport fishing, fish processing, and other activities. The

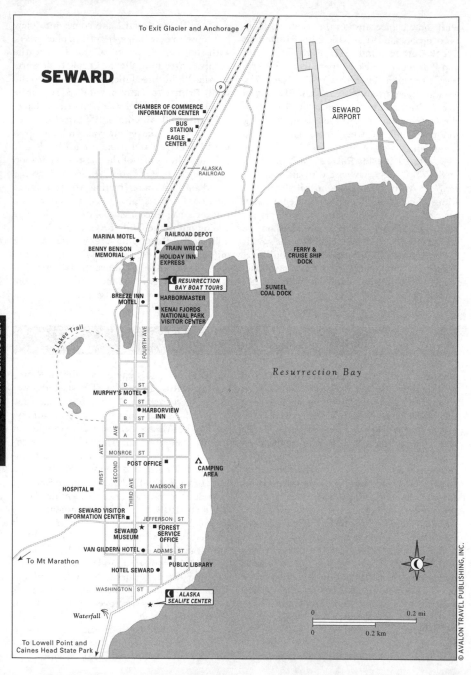

SEWARD

To Exit Glacier and Anchorage

9

CHAMBER OF COMMERCE
INFORMATION CENTER

SEWARD
AIRPORT

BUS
STATION

EAGLE
CENTER

ALASKA
RAILROAD

MARINA MOTEL

RAILROAD DEPOT

BENNY BENSON
MEMORIAL

TRAIN WRECK

HOLIDAY INN
EXPRESS

FERRY &
CRUISE SHIP
DOCK

RESURRECTION
BAY BOAT TOURS

BREEZE INN
MOTEL

HARBORMASTER

SUNEEL
COAL DOCK

KENAI FJORDS
NATIONAL PARK
VISITOR CENTER

2 Lakes Trail

FOURTH AVE

Resurrection Bay

D ST

MURPHY'S MOTEL

C ST

HARBORVIEW
INN

B ST

A ST

AVE

MONROE ST

FIRST AVE

SECOND AVE

POST OFFICE

CAMPING
AREA

THIRD AVE

MADISON ST

HOSPITAL

SEWARD VISITOR
INFORMATION CENTER

JEFFERSON ST

SEWARD
MUSEUM

FOREST
SERVICE
OFFICE

VAN GILDERN HOTEL

ADAMS ST

HOTEL SEWARD

PUBLIC LIBRARY

To Mt Marathon

WASHINGTON ST

ALASKA
SEALIFE CENTER

Waterfall

0   0.2 mi

0   0.2 km

To Lowell Point and
Caines Head State Park

© AVALON TRAVEL PUBLISHING, INC.

Alaska SeaLife Center is the main focal point for travelers, with excellent exhibits. The Alaska Vocational Technical Center trains 1,600 students each year, and a maximum security prison on the east side of Resurrection Bay houses another 450 folks under less academic conditions.

A towering coal-shipping facility dominates the harbor; the Alaska Railroad hauls coal here from the Usibelli Coal Mine in Healy for shipment to Korea. Some cruise ships also dock in Seward, but most companies have shifted their ships to Whittier. Too bad for them, since they miss one of the most enjoyable towns in Southcentral Alaska.

SIGHTS

Seward's main attractions are the Alaska SeaLife Center and **boat tours** of Resurrection Bay and Kenai Fjords National Park (see the *Kenai Fjords National Park* section).

The old-fashioned **Seward Museum** (336 3rd Ave., 907/224-3902, daily 9 A.M.–5 P.M. May–mid-Sept., weekends noon–4 P.M. the rest of the year, $3 adults, 50 cents kids) houses Native baskets and carved ivory, equipment from the original Brown and Hawkins store, the cross-section of a 350-year-old Sitka spruce, and photographs from the 1964 earthquake that dropped parts of this country six feet.

The **Seward Library** (5th and Adams, 907/224-3646), houses the original Alaska flag, designed by a local boy in 1927. The **Benny Benson Memorial** on the north end of the lagoon memorializes this bit of trivia.

Downtown's **Brown & Hawkins Store** (205 4th Ave., 907/224-7313) is Alaska's oldest family-owned business. It's been here since 1900, and still houses the old bank vault and cash register.

Parking is often a problem in Seward, particularly near the harbor, where you'll need to pay $5 per day. (The boat tour companies provide free lots with shuttle buses back to the harbor.)

Alaska SeaLife Center

Seward's most enjoyable attraction, the SeaLife Center (907/224-6300 or 800/224-2525, www.alaskasealife.org, daily late May–early Sept. 8 A.M.–7 P.M., daily 10 A.M.–5 P.M. the rest

harbor seal at the Alaska SeaLife Center

© DON PITCHER

KENAI PENINSULA

of the year, $15 adults, $12 ages 7–12, free for younger children) sits on the south edge of town facing Resurrection Bay. This impressive facility provides visitors with a wonderful way to learn about marine wildlife up-close. There are exhibits, aquariums filled with crabs and octopus, and a fun tidepool touch tank, plus videos, and a gift shop. The main attractions are three gigantic tanks, each with tall windows where visitors can watch puffins and other seabirds, seals, and sea lions swimming. The playful 1,500-pound Steller sea lions come up to check out children next to their windows. For visitors, the SeaLife Center is a place to learn about the marine environment, but this is also an important center for marine research and the rehabilitation of wildlife, including with pigeon guillemots and endangered Steller sea lions. If you want to learn about research here, plunk down an extra $12 for a detailed 1.5-hour behind-the-scenes tour.

ENTERTAINMENT AND EVENTS

The year kicks off in Seward with the **Polar Bear Jump-Off,** a leap of faith into the frigid 39°F water of Resurrection Bay on the third weekend in January. All sorts of goofy-costumed jumpers join the fray.

Every July 4th the **Mt. Marathon Race** attracts more than 800 runners who race up and back down the steep slopes of this 3,022-foot summit that rises behind Seward. Many do it in under an hour, but end up with bruises and bloody knees to show for the torture—the record is 43 minutes and 23 seconds. It has been run annually since 1915. This event is a major Alaskan institution, filling the bars and campgrounds with runners and spectators.

August brings another event that draws the crowds, the **Silver Salmon Derby,** where the top prize is $10,000 and a new truck, and over $100,000 in prizes are available. This is one of Alaska's richest fishing derbies, and it's been going on for over 50 years. Entry costs $11 daily.

Nightlife

If you're looking for nightlife, virtually every other storefront on 4th is a bar. There's the **Yukon, Tony's,** and **DJ's Wheelhouse**—take your pick. Yukon and Tony's both have rock 'n' roll on some weekends; DJ's features an unusual right-angled billiard table that makes for strange bounces. **Liberty Theater** (305 Adams, 907/224-5418) shows movies.

RECREATION
Day Hikes

For an enjoyable one-mile walk on a winding trail through the forest and around the creatively named First Lake and Second Lake, look for the **Two Lakes Trail** behind Alaska Vocational Tech Center at 2nd and C. There's a picnic area at the trailhead.

The high, bare slope hanging over Seward is **Mt. Marathon,** featured attraction for the 4th of July Mountain Marathon Race. It generally takes non-runners at least four hours to get up and back. Follow Jefferson Street due west up Lowell Canyon and look for the trailhead to the right just beyond a pair of large water tanks. You can run all the way back down the mountain on a steep gravel incline if your legs and nerves are good, but beware of slipping on the solid rock face near the bottom. The trail does not actually reach the summit of Mt. Marathon (4,560 ft.), but rather the broad east shoulder (3,022 ft.), which offers a spectacular view of Seward and the entire surrounding country.

Public Lands

Two popular state parks (907/262-5581, www.alaskastateparks.org) are close to Seward on the shores of Resurrection Bay: Caines Head State Recreation Area and Thumb Cove State Marine Park. (See the *Kenai Fjords National Park* and *South to Seward* sections for other local hiking paths.)

Caines Head State Recreation Area was the site of a World War II military base, Fort McGilvray, and the old command post still stands atop a massive 650-foot headland. There are dramatic views of Resurrection Bay and the surrounding country. The 4.5-mile Coastal Trail leads to the old fort from **Lowell Point State Recreation Site,** three miles south of Seward. Parts of the trail follow the shoreline and can only be hiked at low tide; be sure to check the tide charts before heading out. Take a flashlight to explore the maze of underground passages and rooms at Fort McGilvray. Also here are ammunition magazines and firing platforms for the six-inch guns that guarded Seward. This area makes a fine overnight trip, and a walk-in campground complete with three-sided shelter is available at Tonsina Point, a mile in. Caines Head is very popular with sea kayakers who paddle here from Seward to hang out with the sea otters and seals. Also within the park are often-booked hike-in public use cabins ($65) at Derby Cove and Callisto Canyon.

Thumb Cove State Marine Park is on the east side of Resurrection Bay, seven miles from Seward, and accessibly only by boat. The park includes a long sandy beach, forested uplands, and the waters of Thumb Cove. Porcupine Glacier towers behind. Thumb Cove is a favorite stop for recreational boaters, and camping is popular along its beaches. Two cozy cabins are in the park, each sleeping up to eight people for $65 per night. Get there by water taxi from Miller's Landing.

Fishing

Fishing is one of Seward's most popular activities, and in midsummer dozens of boats dot the waters while hundreds of anglers cast from the shore. Salmon are the main attraction, made all the more enticing by a summer-long fishing derby. Your odds of catching one increase if you can get away from the shore, and many charter boats are available. Halibut fishing is another favorite, but you'll need to get quite far out—sometimes all the way to Montague Island in Prince William Sound—to catch one.

Get a complete list of charter operators from the Visitors Information Center, or contact a booking agency. Oldest and largest (it represents 30 or so boats) is **The Fish House** (907/224-3674 or 800/257-7760, www.thefishhouse.net), across from the harbor master's office. Also try **Charter Option** (907/224-2026 or 800/224-2026, www.charteroption.com). If you aren't fishing, drop by the harbor in the late afternoon when charter operators hang today's catch up for photos. It's quite a sight. **Miller's Landing** (907/224-5739 or 866/541-5739, www.millerslandingak.com) rents 16-foot skiffs for do-it-yourselfers.

Sea Kayaking and Rafting

Most Resurrection Bay sea kayaking originates from the scenic Lowell Point area, three miles south of Seward. Three companies—**Sunny Cove Sea Kayaking** (907/224-4426 or 800/770-9119, www.sunnycove.com), **Kayak Adventures** 907/224-3960, www.kayakak.com), and **Liquid Adventures** (907/224-9225 or 888/325-2925, www.liquid-adventures.com)—offer similar paddling trips: a half-day (or sunset) paddle for $65, and an all-day trip for $120. The latter trip typically takes you to Caines Head or up Tonsina River to watch the spawning salmon. In addition, all three companies offer multi-day trips into Kenai Fjords National Park. Another choice includes a boat tour to Aialik Bay within Kenai Fjords National Park, followed by a glacier paddle and return to town for $375. Sunny Cove offers day trips ($149) to Fox Island aboard a Kenai Fjords tour boat followed by a paddle, salmon bake, and wildlife cruise back to town.

Also at Lowell Point, **Miller's Landing** (907/224-5739 or 866/541-5739, www.millerslandingak.com) rents kayaks for experienced do-it-yourselfers, and offers kayaking day trips and instruction, along with water taxi service to transport kayaks into remote parts of Kenai Fjords. Other water taxis are available through **Weather Permitting** (907/224-6595, www.watertaxiak.com) and **Aquetec Water Taxi** (907/362-1291).

Kayakers Cove (907/224-8864) is a unique and well-run operation a dozen miles from Seward. Reasonably priced lodging and kayak rentals are available, with access by water taxi from Millers Landing.

In the summer, **Chugach Outdoor Center** (907/277-7238 or 866/277-7238, www.chugachoutdoorcenter.com) has an easy eight-mile float down the Resurrection River from Exit Glacier. These 2.5-hour floats are $69 adults or $49 ages 5–10.

Sailing

Sailors say Resurrection Bay contains some of the finest sailing waters north of San Francisco Bay, with windy conditions almost every day. Because of this, there are three local yacht clubs and dozens of sailboats berthed in the Small Boat Harbor. In business for more than 30 years, **Sailing, Inc.** (907/224-3160, www.sailinginc.com, May–mid-Sept.) has classes for both novices and experts, but the real attractions are sailing trips onboard a classic 54-foot topsail schooner ($75 adults, $65 kids). Guests can help hoist sails take a turn at the helm, but won't be forced to walk the plank if they mess up. Day trips are also offered by **Alaska Sailing** (907/299-7245, www.alaskasailingtours.com).

Dog Mushing, Horseback Riding, and Biking

Godwin Glacier Dog Sled Tours (907/224-8239 or 888/989-8239, www.alaskadogsled.com, open late May to late August) has the only on-the-snow summertime dog sledding in South-central Alaska. The action begins from Seward

KENAI PENINSULA

KENAI PENINSULA

© DON PITCHER

Beehive Island, Kenai Fjords National Park

Airport, where you climb aboard a helicopter for a 15-minute flight to a world of snow, ice, and rocky peaks on crevice-free Godwin Glacier. The base camp here has 90 dogs and their handlers. Guests are given a tour of the operation, an introduction to mushing, and a fun ride behind a team of 12 dogs. The entire trip lasts an hour and a half, and costs $430 adults, $390 kids. Add just $40 per person for a trip that includes the above tour plus a night in a heated Weatherport tent (sleeping bag on a cot; no showers), dinner, light breakfast, and a snowmobile ride. This is a first-rate operation, and definitely recommended if you have the money.

Veteran musher—and 2004 Iditarod winner—Mitch Seavey operates **IdidaRide Sled Dog Tours** (907/224-8607 or 800/478-3139, www.ididaride.com) from his home off Exit Glacier Road. Summertime visitors are pulled on a wheeled cart along a two-mile route. The cost of these 1.5-hour tours is $59 adults, or $29 kids, including an introduction to the Iditarod and a chance to play with husky puppies.

Bardy's Trail Rides (907/224-7863, www.sewardhorses.com) leads two-hour horseback rides twice daily throughout the summer. This is a fun way to explore the scenic country at the head of Re surrection Bay, with good chances to see bald eagles, moose, and spawning salmon.

You can rent mountain bikes and baby joggers from **Seward Bike Shop** (907/224-2448) in the collection of Alaska railcars at 411 Port Avenue.

ACCOMMODATIONS

Seward has plenty of indoor lodging options, but be sure to book ahead in the summer, especially any weekend in August when the Silver Salmon Derby attracts throngs of visitors and every room for miles around. The city of Seward hits travelers with a 10 percent lodging tax.

A great first stop when looking for lodging is **Alaska's Point of View Reservation Service** (907/224-2323 or 888/227-2424, www.alaskasview.com), where owner Debra Hafemeister makes bookings (no extra charge) for more than 100 local places at a wide range of prices. Recommended.

Hostels

Snow River Hostel (907/440-1907, www.snowriverhostel.org), 16 miles north of Seward, is a quiet place convenient to hikers coming off the

Lost Lake Trail. Inside are dorm rooms with baths, a kitchen, and common room. Bunks are $15 per person, and a private room costs $40 d. Reservations recommended in mid-summer.

Right downtown, **Moby Dick Hostel** (432 3rd Ave., 907/224-7072, www.mobydickhostel.com, mid-April–Sept.) has dorm-style rooms ($19 pp) with kitchen facilities and showers. Basic private rooms cost $55 d, while two nicer rooms with kitchenettes run $65–70 d.

Adventurous travelers should check out **Kayakers Cove** (907/224-8864), on a small bay near Fox Island, 12 water miles from Seward. Rustic hostel-type lodging is $20 per person, or $60 d in a private cabin. No showers and you'll need a sleeping bag, but a kitchen and wood-fired sauna are on the grounds. Kayakers Cove is accessible by water taxi ($58 round trip), and rents kayak ($30/day for doubles).

Hotels and Motels

Located in the center of town and decked out with stuffed critters, the **Hotel Seward** (221 5th Ave., 907/224-2378 or 800/655-8785 www.hotelsewardalaska.com) offers economy rooms for $125 d, and larger ones for $199–224 d.

Just two blocks from the boat harbor, **Murphy's Motel** (909 4th Ave., 907/224-8090 or 800/686-8191, www.murphysmotel.com) provides a mix of older rooms ($109–125 d) and newer units ($159 d), some with balconies. All rooms contain fridges and microwaves.

Situated on the north end of town, **Marina Motel** (1603 Seward Hwy., 907/224-5518, www.sewardmotel.com, $115–135 d) is a comfortable and clean place. All rooms include fridges, and the newer and larger units have microwaves.

Opened in 1916, and now on the National Register of Historical Places, the **Van Gilder Hotel** (308 Adams St., 907/224-3079 or 800/204-6835, www.vangilderhotel.com) gets mixed reviews from guests. Some appreciate this immaculate blast from the past, while other bemoan the lack of an elevator in a three-story structure, small rooms, and steep prices: $149 d, or $199 for two-bedroom suites. A community kitchen is available.

Across the street from the small boat harbor, the clean and comfortable 100-room **Breeze Inn Motel** (1306 3rd Ave., 907/224-5237 or 888/224-5237, www.breezeinn.com) has standard rooms (no view) for $139 d, and newer units with (rather limited) harbor or mountain views for $199 d. Free Wi-Fi too.

Harborview Inn (804 3rd Ave., 907/224-3217 or 888/324-3217, www.sewardhotel.com) has standard units for $144 d, and a king suite for $199 d. The inn is often full throughout the summer, but the name is a misnomer since the harbor views are pretty minimal. It also has beachfront apartments in a separate building for $159–179 d.

It's hard to beat the harborside location of **Holiday Inn Express** (907/224-2550 or 800/465-4329, www.hieseward.com), which also offers a small indoor pool (only one in town), hot tub, breakfast buffet, business center, Wi-Fi, and balconies on some units. The predictable chain-motel rooms cost $189–199 for units facing the mountains, and waterside units cost $249–259.

Across the railroad station, **Whistle Stop Lodging** (411 Port Ave., 907/224-5050, www.whistlestoplodging.biz, $125 d) provides a fun opportunity to overnight in a vintage Alaska Railroad car. Open seasonally.

Bed-and-Breakfasts

Seward has dozens of bed-and-breakfasts. The Visitors Information Center has rack cards from most of these, and its website (www.seward.com) provides links, or give Alaska's Point of View Reservation Service a call to book a good one.

Two Korean-American women own comfortable in-town B&Bs. **Morning Calm B&B** (218 Bluefield Dr., 907/224-3049, www.seward.net/~morningcalm, $70 d) is a great deal for travelers on a budget. Kim Martin's cozy home has two guest rooms that share a bath; a full breakfast is served. Blending Asian and Scandinavian sensibilities, **Soo's B&B** (810 2nd Ave., 907/224-3207 or 888/967-7667, www.sewardbnb.com, $125–145 d) was designed by owner Soo Kang's architect son.

KENAI PENINSULA

Four bright rooms are available, and include a full breakfast, private baths, and Wi-Fi. Centrally located in a quaint 1905 home, **Ballaine House B&B** (437 3rd Ave., 907/224-2362, www.superpage.com/ballaine, mid-May–mid-Sept., $70 s or $97 d) gets rave reviews from guests who appreciate the cozy Grandma's-house setting, reasonable rates, and free Wi-Fi. Friendly owner Marilee Koszewski crafts a made-to-order breakfast each morning. Four guest rooms share two baths.

Located at Lowell Point two miles south of town, **Alaska Saltwater Lodge** (907/224-5271, www.alaskasaltwaterlodge.com, May–Sept.) is right on Resurrection Bay. There are stunning vistas from the common room, and just out the door is a quiet sandy beach. All units have private baths, and guests are served a filling breakfast. Rates run $95 d for small rooms, $129–169 for larger units with windows on the bay, $189–255 for spacious suites with private kitchens, and $189 for a cottage that sleeps six comfortably. The owners also operate a water taxi and whale-watching business.

Also on the beach at Lowell Point is **Ocean Front B&B** (907/224-5699, www.seward.net/~ocean, $159 d), where the single unit has a private entrance and covered deck. A continental breakfast is included.

Six miles north of Seward along Bear Lake, with impressive glacier vistas, **Kim's Forest B&B** (907/224-7632 or 888/512-7632, www.sewardalaskabnb.com) is a luxurious home with six guest rooms ($100–130 d shared baths, $150 d private baths), a very friendly owner, and full breakfasts. Floatplanes take off from the lake on flightseeing trips.

Three miles north of Seward, **Bell-in-the-Woods B&B** (907/224-7271 or 888/729-5655, www.bellinthewoods.net) has four guest rooms ($119–129 d), all with private baths, Wi-Fi, guest computer, and gourmet breakfasts. A kitchenette suite (sleeps four for $159) is stocked for a continental breakfast.

Falls Inn B&B (1103 2nd Ave., 907/224-5790, www.fallsinnalaska.com, $179 d) is a large edge-of-town B&B with a quiet backyard accented by a small waterfall. The home features a comfortable living room, two large suites with private baths, mostly organic continental-plus breakfasts, a computer, and Wi-Fi.

Cabins and Suites

Situated high up the hill behind Seward, the appropriately named **A Cabin on the Cliff** (907/224-2411, www.acabinonthecliff.com, $369 d) provides a unique perspective of Resurrection Bay. Originally a trapper's cabin, this beautiful log cabin has an antique brass bed, fireplace, kitchenette, and a large private deck with a hot tub enclosed by a gazebo.

Located on Fox Island and accessible only by boat, **Kenai Fjords Wilderness Lodge** (907/224-8068 or 877/777-4053, www.kenaifjordslodge.com) sits in the heart of Resurrection Bay. Guests stay in modern private cabins (but no electricity or phones), and enjoy hearty family-style meals at the lodge. Get there onboard a Kenai Fjords Tours boat, and spend a night and two days on the island for $698 for two people, including meals, lodging, and an all-day boat tour into Northwestern Fjord.

Nine miles southeast of town in Humpy Cove, **Orca Island Cabins** (907/224-5846, www.orcaislandcabins.com, May–Sept.) provide a great way to get in touch with your wild side. Three surprisingly comfortable yurts are perched along the shore of this small island, and a floating cabin is adjacent to the dock. All have decks, kitchenettes, private baths (showers and compost toilet in the yurts), and grills. The cost—including round-trip water taxi from Seward—is $300 d, plus $25 per person for additional guests. Rates drop if you stay extra days, and kayak rentals are available.

Other recommended Seward-area suites and cabins include **Alaska's Point of View Suites** (907/224-2323 or 888/227-2424, www.alaskaspointofview.com), **Box Canyon Cabins** (907/224-5046, www.boxcanyoncabin.com), **River Valley Cabins** (907/224-5740, www.rivervalleycabins.com), **Lost Lake Trailhead Lodge** (907/224-3396, www.lostlaketrailheadlodge.com), **Moosewood Guest Cabins** (907/224-8445, www.moosewoodcabin.com), and **Victorian Serenity by the Sea**

(907/224-3635 or 877/239-3637, www.victorian serenity.com).

CAMPING

City officials (907/224-4055, www.cityof seward.net/sprd) provide a long stretch of crowded, year-round camping at **Waterfront Park** along the shore on Ballaine Boulevard, with toilets, showers, picnic shelters, beautiful views, and lots of company (450 sites!). It costs $8 for tents, $12 for RVs ($25 with hookups). You can also camp at the other city campground ($8) at Mile 2 out the Seward Highway—large trees, some highway noise.

Those with wheels can head out to Exit Glacier (13 miles from town) to pitch a tent in the free **Kenai Fjords National Park Campground**. It has only 10 sites and a small parking lot. There's water at the entrance; otherwise, this is minimalist camping on a strange moraine terrain.

RVers who don't mind "camping" in a parking lot can head to **Kenai Fjords RV Park** (907/224-8779) at the Small Boat Harbor. Considerably nicer are **Bear Creek RV Park** (907/224-5725, www.bearcreekrv.com) seven miles north, and **Stoney Creek RV Park** (907/224-4760 or 877/437-6366, www.stoneycreekrvpark.com), five miles north.

FOOD

Get a fast taco, burrito, or quesadilla from **Railway Cantina** (1401 4th Ave., 907/224-8226), directly across from the boat harbor; everything's under $9.

Christo's Palace (133 4th Ave., 907/224-5255, www.christospalace.com, $18–36) offers creative pizzas and pasta, along with Mexican dinners, char-broiled steaks, and a mean tequila honey shrimp. The 150-year-old back bar is particularly impressive, and it's noisy enough that your kids won't even be heard.

Two places serve Chinese food in town, both with $8 lunchtime buffets and Korean-American owners: **Peking Chinese Cuisine** (338 4th Ave., 907/224-5444) and **Oriental Garden** (907/224-7677), right across the street.

Seward's standout dining choice is **◖ Yoly's**

Bistro (220 4th Ave., 907/224-3295), a lively and bright downtown spot where the dinner menu careens in various directions: red curry chicken, wasabi halibut, rib-eye steak, and vermouth scallops are on the dinner menu, while lunch includes tasty burgers and sandwiches, pad Thai, and fish and chips. Dine to musical accompaniment most summer evenings.

Coffee, Bakeries, and Groceries

On summer mornings, the fishing crowd crowds into **Bakery at the Harbor** (907/224-6091) across from the Small Boat Harbor for coffee, fresh-baked pastries, and a $9 breakfast buffet. Good lunch sandwiches and soups, too, but the prices are way too high.

Housed in an old Lutheran church, **Resurrect Art Coffeehouse Gallery** (320 3rd Ave., 907/224-7161), is a wonderful place to hang out over an espresso on a rainy day, play a game of chess, or listen to local musicians most days. It's also one of the best Seward spots to buy Alaskan art, pottery, and jewelry.

Sea Bean Café (225 4th Ave., 907/224-6623) is a pleasant downtown coffeehouse with cushy couches, streetside bay windows, computer rentals, and free Wi-Fi. For espresso (and free Wi-Fi) next to the boat harbor, go to **Alaska Fur Get Me Not** (1412 4th Ave., 907/224-5660, www.shopfurgetmenot.com).

Get groceries and deli sandwiches at **Safeway** (907/224-3698) on the north end of town along the Seward Highway.

Seafood

Ray's Waterfront (907/224-5606, dinner entrées $19–30) at the Small Boat Harbor, is especially convenient for grabbing a bite while you wait for your tour boat (or for a hot toddy when you get back). The walls of Ray's are lined with all sorts of trophy fish, and picture windows look out over the harbor. It also serves big breakfasts. The main problem with Ray's is its popularity. Reservations are not taken, so you'll end up waiting an hour on summer weekends. Winter visitors will be disappointed: It's only open April–September.

Just up the street is **Chinooks Waterfront Grill** (907/224-2207, www.chinookswaterfront.com), with two levels fronting the harbor and a menu of seafood (try the halibut cheek and shrimp stir fry) and steaks.

Out on Exit Glacier Road north of town, **Exit Glacier Salmon Bake** (907/224-2204, www.sewardalaskacabins.com) is popular with locals, offering good salmon, halibut, steaks, and burgers in a wooded setting. The pub specializes in Alaskan microbrews.

INFORMATION AND SERVICES
Visitor Centers
For Seward maps and brochures, start out at the **Seward Chamber of Commerce** (907/224-8051, www.seward.com), located two miles north of town. It's one of the first places you pass as you're driving into Seward from Anchorage. The chamber office is open Monday–Friday 8 A.M.–6 P.M. and Saturday–Sunday 9 A.M.–5 P.M. mid-May–mid-September, and Monday–Friday 9 A.M.–5 P.M. the rest of the year.

The staff at **Chugach National Forest Seward Ranger District** office (334 4th Ave., 907/224-3374, www.fs.fed.us/r10/chugach) can tell you about all the hikes, campgrounds, and cabins.

Shopping and Services
Seward has a number of interesting studios scattered around town, including the **Resurrect Art Coffeehouse Gallery** (described in *Food*). Also worth a look is **Ranting Raven** (224 4th Ave., 907/224-2228) with art and gifts, pastries, and light lunches.

Soap and rinse your entire naked body at the **Harbormaster Building** (907/224-3138), or head to **Seward Laundry** (804 4th Ave., 907/224-5727). Additional showers are in the city campground at the foot of Madison Street. There's a **swimming pool** (907/224-3900) at the high school where they throw in a free swim with your shower; call for hours. The **Seward library** (5th and Adams) houses computers where you can check email.

For medical emergencies, head to **Prov-idence Seward Medical Center** (417 1st Ave., 907/224-5205, www.providence.org).

GETTING THERE
The Alaska Marine Highway ferry no longer stops in Seward; the closest ports are Whittier and Homer.

Train
An Alaska Railroad (907/265-2494 or 800/544-0552, www.akrr.com, $65 one-way, $109 round-trip) **Coastal Classic train** leaves Anchorage daily during the summer at 6:45 A.M. and arrives in Seward at 11 A.M., then returns to Anchorage at 6 P.M., arriving at 10:15 P.M. Passenger service to Seward is only available mid-May–mid-September.

Air
Located six miles north of Seward, **Bear Lake Air** (907/224-5985, or 800/224-5985, www.bearlakeair.com) offers flightseeing trips over the Harding Icefield. **Scenic Mountain Air** (907/224-9152 or 800/478-1449, www.scenicmountainair.com) operates out of the airport.

GETTING AROUND
Seward Bus Lines (907/224-3608 in Seward or 907/563-0800 in Anchorage, www.sewardbuslines.net) has daily year-round bus service to and from Anchorage. **Homer Stage Line** (907/362-3644, www.homerstageline.com) provides daily service all summer (six days a week in the winter) to Anchorage, plus seasonal connections to Cooper Landing, Soldotna, Kenai, and Homer.

Alaska Park Connection (907/245-0200 or 800/266-8625, www.alaskacoach.com) has summertime buses connecting Seward with Anchorage, Talkeetna, and Denali.

Rent a car from **Hertz** (907/224-4378 or 800/654-3131, www.hertz.com) or catch a ride from **PJ's Taxi** (907/224-5555) or **Glacier Taxi** (907/224-5678).

Rent bikes from **Seward Mt. Bike Shop** (411 Port Ave., 907/224-2448), near the north end of the harbor.

Kenai Fjords National Park

Kenai Fjords National Park covers 580,000 acres of ice, rock, and rugged coastline on the southern end of Kenai Peninsula. The centerpiece of this magnificent national park is the Harding Icefield, a massive expanse of ice and snow broken only by "nunataks"—the peaks of high, rocky mountains. The icefield pushes out in all directions in the form of more than 30 named glaciers. Along the coast, eight of these glaciers reach the sea, creating a thundering display of calving icebergs. Kenai Fjords has only been a national park since 1980, but today is one of the most popular attractions in Alaska. Many visitors come to ride the tour boats past teeming bird colonies or up to tidewater glaciers; many others hike to scenic Exit Glacier or up a steep path to the edge of Harding Icefield itself.

Kenai Fjords National Park Information Center (1212 4th Ave., 907/224-2125, www.nps.gov/kefj) is in Seward next to the harbor and is open daily 8.30 A.M.–7 P.M. Memorial Day–Labor Day, Monday–Friday 9 A.M.–5 P.M. in the spring and fall, and closed November–February. Inside are excellent exhibits on Harding Icefield and little-known sights within the park. The center also has videos of the park, along with maps and publications of local interest. (A new multi-agency visitor center for the Park Service and Forest Service is expected to open downtown near the SeaLife Center by 2009.)

☘ EXIT GLACIER

One of Alaska's most accessible glaciers, Exit Glacier has a pretty setting, a mix of hiking trails, nearby campsites, and guided glacier hikes. This is the only part of the park that is accessible by road. Get to Exit Glacier by heading four miles north from Seward and turning left at the sign. The road ends nine miles later at a parking lot.

Exit Glacier Nature Center—the only fuel-cell powered one in Alaska—houses interpretive displays and a natural history bookstore. Rangers give programs and lead one-hour

KENAI PENINSULA

© DON PITCHER

Ragged Island and Aialik Bay, Kenai Fjords National Park

nature walks several times daily, with a longer all-day trip to the icefield on Saturdays in July and August. **Exit Glacier Guides** (907/224-5569, www.exitglacierguides.com) leads five-hour excursions onto the glacier for $125 per person, and also provides a shuttle service ($9 one way) from town.

Hiking

A three-quarter-mile round-trip **nature trail** provides an easy, quiet forest walk. The **Overlook Loop Trail** goes a half-mile, crosses a creek, then climbs a steep quarter-mile up to the 150-foot face of Exit Glacier. The steep and winding **Upper Trail** continues another quarter-mile, offering views across the glacier and of several ice caves (don't go into these).

Harding Icefield Trail, seven miles round-trip, forks off just after the bridge over the creek and climbs to 3,500 feet and the icefield. Plan on at least six hours for this far more difficult hike, and check at the ranger station for current trail conditions since deep snow may block this route until midsummer. Skilled skiers may want to carry cross-country skis and slide around on the relatively crevasse-free icefield. In the winter, the road into Exit Glacier is not plowed but is very popular with skiers and snowmobilers.

The 16-mile **Resurrection River Trail** starts at Mile 8 of the Exit Glacier Road. This is the southern end of the 74-mile, three-trail system from Kenai's top to bottom. Resurrection River Trail leads to the 16-mile Russian Lakes Trail, which hooks up near Cooper Landing to the 38-mile Resurrection Pass Trail to Hope. A Forest Service cabin ($35, reserve at www.reserveusa.com) is six miles from the trailhead. Note that the Resurrection River Trail can become quite a quagmire when it rains, and it may be poorly maintained beyond the cabin; most folks simply hike to the cabin and then turn around. The trail is popular with cross-country skiers in wintertime because of its relatively low avalanche danger.

CAMPING AND CABINS

The **Exit Glacier Campground** (free, no reservations) has a dozen walk-in tent sites just a short distance from the glacier. There's also a bear-proof food locker and cooking shelter.

The Park Service maintains four popular public-use cabins within Kenai Fjords. Three of these are along the coast (June–Labor Day, $50/night), and the fourth is a winter-only cabin at Exit Glacier. Each has its own treat—a pleasant beach walk at **Aialik Bay,** thunderous calving glaciers at **Holgate Arm,** and a little-used one in old-growth rainforest at **North Arm** in remote Nuka Bay. Access to the Aialik Bay and Holgate Arm cabins is primarily by charter boat from Seward, but because of the distance involved, it's cheaper to take a float-plane to North Arm from Homer (the closest town). Contact the Park Service for detailed access info. Be sure to reserve far ahead of time for these extremely popular cabins by contacting the Alaska Public Lands Information Center in Anchorage (907/271-2737). Bookings are available in early January for the summer season, and nearly all the spaces for the Holgate and Aialik cabins fill up by the end of April.

During the winter, the park rents the **Willow Cabin** near Exit Glacier ($35/night). Ski to this cabin the eight easy miles from the highway along unplowed Exit Glacier Road. There is also a second enclosed winter-use structure nearby that is used as a warming shelter. Make reservations for this cabin with the Park Service in Seward (907/224-7500).

◖ RESURRECTION BAY BOAT TOURS

The most exciting thing to do in Seward is to get on a tour boat out into Resurrection Bay or into some nearby fjords. This is *the* cruise for seeing marine wildlife. On a good day, you could see three kinds of whales—including humpbacks and orcas—plus porpoises, seals, sea otters, sea lions, hundreds of puffins, kittiwakes, auklets, and the occasional bald eagle and oystercatcher. A number of tour companies offer cruises with knowledgeable guides. Half-day trips take you around nearby Resurrection Bay and out as far as Rugged Island, while longer voyages include Aialik Bay, Holgate Glacier (calving icebergs), and the Chiswell Islands (a Steller sea lion rookery

© CON PITCHER

killer whale, Kenai Fjords National Park

and nesting seabirds—most notably puffins). The latter is a far more interesting trip and actually goes inside the park rather than to its edge, but the waters are often rough, so take your seasickness pills. Park Service naturalists are onboard for the longer trips. Hot tip: some Seward B&Bs and hostels offer 10 percent discounts on Resurrection Bay tours; ask your lodging place if these are available before booking a trip.

Seward's largest tour company, **Kenai Fjords Tours** (907/224-8068 or 800/478-8068, www.kenaifjords.com) operates large boats that hold up to 150 people. They offer a wide variety of cruises, from a three-hour Resurrection Bay tour ($59) up to a nine-hour sailing to Northwestern Fjord Tour ($159) that includes breakfast and lunch. Their most popular voyage—and my favorite—is an eight-hour trip ($139) to Aialik Bay that includes an hour-long stop on Fox Island for a big salmon dinner at Kenai Fjords Wilderness Lodge. Overnight stays at the lodge are also available. Child rates are half the adult prices.

For a more intimate sailing, book a tour aboard a small 16-passenger boat of **Mariah Tours,** also owned by CIRI, an Anchorage-based Native corporation. "Captain's choice" nine-hour tours ($169) focus on wildlife (particularly birds) and include a light breakfast and lunch. Rates for kids under 12 are half the adult rate.

Major Marine Tours (907/224-8030 or 800/764-7300, www.majormarine.com) offers half-day cruises to Resurrection Bay for $58–67 ($32–37 kids), and all-day trips to Aialik Bay for $135 ($71 kids). Guests are treated to an all-you-can-eat salmon and prime rib buffet for an extra $15 adults, $7 kids. The boat is large and stable, helpful when seas are rough.

For a science-based trip, take a 2.5-hour Resurrection Bay catamaran cruise from **Alaska Coastal Tours** (907/224-2665, www.seward alaskasightseeing.com, $49 adults, $29 kids). These depart from a dock next to the SeaLife Center with a staff member onboard to talk about marine science and natural history in a hands-on way. Eight-hour trips to Aialik Bay are $139 adults, $69 kids, including lunch.

Renown Charters and Tours (907/224-3806 or 888/514-8687, www.renowncharters.com) is a locally owned company. Choose from three-hour Resurrection Bay tours ($69 adults, $35 kids) or six-hour cruises to Aialik or Holgate Glaciers for $129 adults, $65 kids. Basket lunches are included in all trips. Renown also operates gray-whale-watching cruises during their spring migration north (April–mid-May); four hours for $69 adults, $35 kids.

Most of these tour boats operate between mid-May and mid-September only, though Renown Charters runs tours into mid-October, starting up again in April. If you get here early or late in the season, you're likely to find lower prices and fewer people on board. All the tour companies have booths on the dock behind the harbormaster's office on 4th Avenue. Binoculars and telephoto lenses are handy, and a light jacket is wise. This trip is guaranteed to be one of the highlights of your Alaskan visit, but if you get seasick easy, take along medication, especially on the all-day voyages that go into more exposed waters. You may want to wait if the marine weather report predicts rough seas.

KENAI PENINSULA

Northwestern Kenai Peninsula

The northwestern end of the Kenai Peninsula is accessible via the **Sterling Highway** which joins the Seward Highway 37 miles north of Seward and 90 miles south of Anchorage. The mileposts along the Sterling also start counting at 37 from this point. The Sterling Highway heads west through Cooper Landing and Soldotna, then south all the way to Homer, a total of 143 miles.

Between the junction and Cooper Landing (Mile 49) are two USFS campgrounds along Quartz Creek Road. **Quartz Creek Campground** ($14) is in a beautiful setting right on Kenai Lake. Reserve a space at www.reserveusa.com. **Crescent Creek Campground** ($11) is three miles down Quartz Creek Road. A 6.5-mile trail climbs 1,000 feet from the Crescent Creek parking lot to Crescent Lake.

COOPER LANDING

Located a dozen miles west of the junction with the Seward Highway, this is the first of the service centers that cling to both sides of the Sterling Highway. Clumped together in central Cooper Landing (907/595-8888, www.cooperlandingchamber.com) are three motels, a couple of restaurants, a gas station, and tackle shops. A visitor cabin (unstaffed) next to the boat launch on the south side of the Kenai River bridge is open daily in the summer. The little **Cooper Landing Museum** (907/595-3500, www.cooperlandingmuseum.com) at Mile 49 houses the articulated skeleton of a brown bear, historical items, and other items in two old cabins.

◖ Combat Fishing

The Russian River Ferry is a cable-guided, current-powered ferry ($8 adults, $4 kids) that shuttles anglers across the Kenai River to the sockeye-rich opposite bank. Come here in July to learn the true meaning of "combat fishing" as hundreds of folks fight for space, hooking both sockeye salmon and fellow anglers in the process. You'll need hip waders and can only use flies, not lures. Local fishing shops have the correct flies, and often rent poles and boots. Non-fishermen are bemused by the oddity of such crowds, but for anglers it's the salmon fishing that attracts since many folks get their limit despite the hordes. A real fly-fishing angler wouldn't be caught dead here, but this is all about catching fish, not enjoying a wilderness or purist experience! The unusual ferry is an added attraction.

The Resurrection Pass Trail crosses the Sterling Highway just west of Cooper Landing, and is accessible from a trailhead at Mile 53. A half-mile farther is Alaska's most famous salmon-fishing area, near the junction of the Russian and Kenai rivers. The U.S. Fish & Wildlife Service has a big parking lot here ($9 for day use) with a few tent spaces for those who arrive early enough.

Recreation

The main attractions in Cooper Landing are Kenai River fishing and float trips. Several raft companies offer a 14-mile ride to Jim's Landing, which includes some Class II rapids at Schooner Bend. Three-hour float trips cost around $50, and all-day Kenai trips run $125 or so from **Alaska River Adventures** (907/595-2000 or 888/836-9027, www.alaskariveradventures.com), **Alaska Rivers Co.** (907/595-1226 or 888/595-1226, www.alaskariverscompany.com), and **Alaska Wildland Adventures** (907/595-1279 or 800/478-4100, www.alaskarivertrips.com). These and other companies have guided fishing trips aboard drift boats for $250 per person for all day (including lunch), or $150 for a half day.

Alaskan Horsemen Trail Adventures (907/595-1806 or 800/595-1806, www.alaskahorsemen.com) leads trail rides into the scenic country around Cooper Landing. Find them behind Sunrise Inn at Mile 45.

Kenai Lake Sea Kayak Adventures (907/595-3411, www.kenailake.com) offers

NORTHERN KENAI PENINSULA

KENAI PENINSULA

To Whittier

BEGICH, BOGGS VISITOR CENTER

Spencer Glacier

Portage Station

Turnagain Pass

GRANITE CREEK CAMPGROUND

Chugach National Forest

GRANDVIEW

ALASKA RAILROAD

Girdwood

Turnagain Arm

BERTHA CREEK CAMPGROUND

Johnson Pass Trail

Moose Pass

Ptarmigan Lake

To Anchorage

Gull Rock Trail

HOPE

PORCUPINE CAMPGROUND

Trail

TENDERFOOT CREEK CAMPGROUND

Summit Creek Trail

SEWARD HWY

Upper Trail Lake

Crescent Lake

Kenai Lake

Primrose Trail

Lost Lake Trail

Seward

Kenai Fjords National Park

Devil's Pass Trail

Tern Lake

Resurrection River Trail

Exit Glacier

Pass

Resurrection Trail

Cooper Landing

Cooper Lake

Cooper Lakes Trail

Harding Icefield

COMBAT FISHING

HWY

Russian Lake

Russian River

River

STERLING

SKILAK LAKE RD

Skilak Lake

SWANSON RIVER CANOE SYSTEM

SWANSON LAKE CANOE SYSTEM

Kenai National Wildlife Refuge

Sterling

Captain Cook State Recreation Area

Swanson River

SWANSON RIVER RD

FUNNY RIVER RD

Kenai River

Tustumena Lake

Soldotna

KENAI NATIONAL WILDLIFE REFUGE VISITOR CENTER

Nikiski

Kenai

KALIFORNSKY BEACH RD

Kasilof

To Homer

Cook Inlet

5 mi

0

5 km

0

guided sea kayaking on the lake ($65 for three hours) and rents quality mountain bikes for rides up Resurrection Pass Trail.

Accommodations and Food

Cooper Landing spreads out over a seven-mile stretch that centers around Mile 50 of the Sterling Highway. Lodging options are listed from east to west. On the eastern end of Cooper Landing at Mile 45, **Sunrise Inn** (907/595-1222, www.alaskasunriseinn.com) has a full-service restaurant, bar, RV park ($25 with electricity only), gas station, and motel ($100–120 d). The lakeside location is especially pleasant, and they're open all year.

Primarily for cruise passengers, **Kenai Princess Lodge** (907/595-1425 or 800/426-0500, www.princesslodges.com, mid-May–mid-Sept., $239–299 d), near the Kenai River bridge at Mile 48, overlooks the roiling turquoise water of the river, and features a restaurant, lounge, half-mile nature trail, and gift shop. Bungalow-style rooms have naturally finished wood walls, a sitting area, wood-burning stove, TV, phone, and small private deck. Two large hot tubs and saunas add to the appeal.

Just down the road from Kenai Princess Lodge, **Alaskan Sourdough B&B** (907/595-1541, www.alaskansourdoughbb.com, April–Sept., $120 d) has six guest rooms in the main house, along with bunkhouse-style rooms for fishermen. All of these have private baths and access to the Eskimo-style sauna, along with a full breakfast.

TroutFitters Alpine Motel (907/595-1212, www.aktroutfitters.com, May–Oct., $109–129), at Mile 48, has a dozen kitchenette units, and also offer fly-fishing instruction, a fly shop, and rentals of fishing gear and waders. Nearby is **Cooper Landing Grocery** (907/595-1677), and a short distance up the road is **Drifters Lodge** (907/595-5555 or 866/595-5959, www.drifterslodge.com, April–mid-Oct.), with modern chalet-cabins with fridges and microwaves for $269 d, and rooms in the lodge (shared bath) for $139–199 d. Add $20 for each additional guest. A big breakfast is included in these rates.

Located on the western edge of "town" at Mile 52, **Gwin's Lodge** (907/595-1266, www.gwinslodge.com) is a classic Alaskan eatery (since 1952) and a great place to pick up tips from the anglers while enjoying down-home cooking, especially the salmon chowder and carrot cake. The restaurant is open 24 hours a day all summer. Gwin's rents no-frills cabins ($99 d), nicer log cabins with kitchens ($154 d), and new units with lofts ($184 d) and space for six. All of these contain private baths and wireless Internet access. The store sells groceries, sodas, beer, lattes, gifts, and fishing licenses, and you can also buy or rent fishing gear, including poles and hip waders. They book fishing trips, and provide freezer space for your catch. Closed weekdays in the winter.

Upper Kenai River Inn (907/595-3333, www.upperkenairiverinn.com, $150–200 d) is a spacious and modern riverside home with four guest rooms, including a big breakfast.

Alaska Wildland Adventures (www.alaskawildland.com) operates two Kenai Peninsula lodges. Located in Cooper Landing, **Kenai River Sportfishing Lodge** (907/595-1279 or 800/478-4100, www.alaskasportfish.com) has a variety of all-inclusive fishing, food, and lodging packages; a three-night stay is $1,400 per person. More unique is **Kenai Backcountry Lodge** (907/783-2928 or 800/334-8730), hidden away on Skilak Lake and accessible only by boat. Accommodations are comfortably rustic tent cabins and log cabins, with a central bathhouse and lodge. All-inclusive stays—featuring kayaking and hiking—start at $1,025 per person for two nights.

Camping

Just west of Cooper Landing is the Forest Service's **Cooper Creek Campground,** with sites ($16) on both sides of the road. A mile and a half farther is the large **Russian River Campground,** one of the best places in the state to catch sockeye salmon when they're running (generally mid-June and mid-July). Campsites are strung along the two-mile paved road; $14 tents, $22 RVs for one of these large, well-spaced sites. Make campground reservations

KENAI NATIONAL WILDLIFE REFUGE

This large habitat supports so many moose, Dall sheep, bear, salmon, and other wildlife that it was designated a refuge by President Roosevelt in 1941. The Alaska National Interest Lands Act (1980) changed the name from Kenai National Moose Range and expanded the refuge to its present two million acres, managed by the federal Fish & Wildlife Service (907/262-7021, http://kenai.fws.gov). A visitor center is at the refuge headquarters on Ski Hill Road in Soldotna.

An information cabin is at Mile 58, right at the junction of the Sterling and the rough and dusty 19-mile **Skilak Lake Loop Road.** Stop here to pick up a copy of the refuge's annual newspaper, with details on day hikes, wildlife viewing, fishing, canoeing, picnicking, and camping. The big action in this neck of the woods is along the Loop Road, where you'll find five different campgrounds (free–$10); **Hidden Lake Campground** features campfire programs and guided walks on summer weekends. In addition to those along Skilak Lake, three other F&WS campgrounds are on the Sterling Highway between Cooper Landing and Sterling.

Oil was discovered in 1957 in the northern wilderness near the Swanson River, and an 18-mile gravel road built to the oilfields also opened up this lake-studded lowlands. Approximately 13 miles in on Swanson River Road is **Dolly Varden Lake Campground:** free, uncrowded, nice views, right on the lake, with frequent moose visits. For additional information about the campgrounds, more than a dozen trails, and hundreds of miles of boating and fishing waterways, inquire at the USF&WS greeting cabin or their headquarters in Soldotna.

CANOEING

Two canoe routes – Swanson River Route and Swan Lake Route – are accessible by Swanson River Road, a right turn off the Sterling at Mile 84. Both offer a wonderful way to explore the refuge. Pick up the USF&WS brochure *Canoeing in the Kenai National Wildlife Refuge* for detailed information. Mark Weigner of **Weigner's Backcountry Guiding** (907/262-7840, www.alaska.net/~weigner) offers guided canoe trips tailored to your interest and ability. **Alaska Canoe & Campground** (907/262-2331, www.alaskacanoetrips.com) has a similar service. *Kenai Canoe Trails* by Daniel L. Quick is a useful guidebook for anyone heading out on the refuge's lakes.

Located on the northern Kenai Peninsula, **Swan Lake Canoe Route** is the most popular canoeing area within Kenai National Wildlife Refuge. This 60-mile route encompasses 30 lakes that are connected by fairly short portages (longest is under a mile). The entire 60-mile route can be traversed in less than a week. In addition, the route provides access to a 17-mile float down the gentle Moose River. Canoeing on this system offers not only scenic beauty, but also excellent wildlife viewing and good rainbow trout fishing.

The **Swanson River Canoe Route** links 40 small lakes on the northern Kenai Peninsula, and also includes a 46-mile stretch of the Swanson River. The lakes are connected by portages of varying lengths and conditions, but they are more difficult than those on the nearby Swan Lake Canoe Route. Traveling from the Paddle Lake entrance (at Mile 12 on Swan Lake Rd.), trips can stretch from a long weekend to over a week. In remote lake areas of the Swanson River Route east of Pepper Lake, travel is difficult and the routes and portages are often indistinct. This is true wilderness and can be challenging. Bring a compass, an accurate map, a pair of hip waders, and a lot of patience.

for Cooper Creek or Russian River (highly recommended for July) through Reserve-USA (877/444-6777, www.reserveusa.com, $9 extra). Park in the lot if you just want to hike on the 21-mile **Russian Lakes Trail** or take the "fisherman's path" along the river to **Russian River Falls,** where salmon leap. The Russian River runs into the Kenai River near the entrance station.

Located at Kenai Princess Lodge, **Kenai Princess RV Park** (907/595-1425 or 800/426-0500, www.princessalaskalodges.com) charges $35 for full hookups (no tents), and is open mid-May to mid-September. Guests have access to hot tubs at the lodge. **Kenai Riverside Campground and RV Park** (888/536-2478, www.kenairv.com, $28 RVs, $14 tents) is at Mile 50.

Getting There

Homer Stage Line (907/235-2252, www.homer stageline.com) runs to Anchorage, Homer, and Seward. Service is daily to Anchorage in the summer, and twice week in winter. Seward runs are daily, but only in summer.

At Mile 48, **Wildman's** (907/595-1456 or 866/595-1456, www.wildmans.org) has a laundry with showers, and offers a shuttle service. Gwin's Lodge also has a shuttle service for folks floating the river.

STERLING TO SOLDOTNA

The unincorporated settlement of **Sterling** (pop. 6,000) spread over a wide area around Mile 83 is mainly notable for the four-lane highway that cuts across this part of the northern Kenai Peninsula; it seems totally out of place in such a podunk spot. The Sterling Highway crosses the Moose River in Sterling, where it joins the widening Kenai River, and the fish-hook frenzy pervades all your senses. The **Izaak Walton State Recreation Site** (907/262-5581, $10) on the east side of the river is a pretty campground with 38 sites, toilets, and water. Archaeological excavations conducted here indicate that Natives occupied this fish-rich confluence up to 2,000 years ago.

The 13-mile stretch of highway from Ster-

ling to Soldotna bristles with guides and outfitters, fish camps, bait and tackle shops, charters, fish smokeries, boat and canoe rentals, boat engine sales and repairs, and so forth—essential infrastructure in the eternal struggle between sportsmen and salmon.

An excellent local lodging choice is **Alaska Mountain View Cabins** (907/262-4827 or 888/388-4827, www.alaskamountainview.com, $140–215 d). The cabins and guesthouse contain kitchens and private baths; one features an impressive view from the deck. Other local places worth a look are **Angler's Lodge** (907/262-1747 or 888/262-1747, www.anglerslodge.com), **Morgan's Landing Cabin Rentals** (907/262-8343, www.mlcalaska.com), and the inexpensive **Alaska Cozy Cabins** (907/262-2401, www.alaskacozycabins.com).

SOLDOTNA

Soldotna was established in the late 1940s, as World War II veterans filed for homestead lands along Soldotna Creek. Today this town of 4,000 is the seat of the Kenai Borough government, and serves as a busy stopping point for travelers, anglers, and locals. "Slowdotna" has all the charm of Wasilla, another place disparaged by anyone not living there. Fast food joints, strip malls, fishing supply stores, shopping centers, and a jumble of signs greet your arrival in this sprawling suburban burg with no real downtown—unless you count the big Fred Meyer store. Its parking lot also serves as a de facto free RV campground all summer.

Sights

The **Soldotna Visitors Information Center** (907/262-9814; www.soldotnachamber.com, daily 9 A.M.–7 P.M. May–Sept., Mon.–Fri. 9 A.M.–5 P.M. the rest of the year) is on Sterling Highway just south of the bridge over the Kenai River. Stop by to sift through several hundred pamphlets describing B&Bs, fishing charters, RV parks, restaurants, and other businesses. The walls are lined with photos, and be sure to see the 97-pound king salmon that was caught nearby in 1984; it's the largest ever caught by a sport angler. Just out the door, a short path leads to the Kenai River, where the **Kenai River Fish Walk** provides a spot to try your luck at catching an even bigger one.

For the **Kenai National Wildlife Refuge Visitor Center** (907/262-7021, http://kenai. fws.gov), take a left at Kalifornsky (named for a prominent Native family), then an immediate right, and go a mile up Ski Hill Road. The center is open Monday Friday 8 A.M.–5 P.M. and Saturday–Sunday 9 A.M.–6 P.M. June–early September; Monday–Friday 8 A.M.–4:30 P.M. and Saturday–Sunday 10 A.M.–5 P.M. the rest of the year. Buy books and posters, and see the free wildlife videos, stroll the mile-long nature trail, and climb the observation tower.

Soldotna Homestead Museum (Tues.–Sat. 10 A.M.–4 P.M. and Sun. noon–4 P.M. mid-May–mid-Sept., free) is a collection of a half-dozen log cabins on the way into Centennial Park. Inside are the usual settlers' items, stuffed critters, and Native artifacts. The real treat is that this surprisingly quiet spot is just a short distance from the bustling Sterling Highway.

For recreation, try the **Birch Ridge Golf Course** (907/262-5270, www.birchridge golf.com), a nine-hole private course three miles from town.

Accommodations

More than a hundred lodging options crowd the Sterling-Soldotna-Kenai area, from rustic cabins to riverside wilderness lodges. Visitor centers racks are crammed with descriptive flyers, and the chamber's website (www.soldotnachamber.com) has links to most of these. Many local lodges provide freezers for your freshly caught fish.

Aspen Hotel (326 Binkey Circle, 907/260-7736 or 888/308-7848, www.aspen hotelsak.com) is a large, well-managed, and modern place with an indoor pool, whirlpool tub, Wi-Fi, exercise facility, and continental breakfast. Rooms with fridges and microwaves go for $179 d. It's right on the river.

Not far away is another sprawling motel, **Kenai River Lodge** (393 Riverside Dr., 907/262-4292 or 800/977-4292,

www.kenairiverlodge.com, $150–165 d) with rooms facing the river. **Soldotna Inn** (907.262-4305 or 866/262-9169, www.mykels.com) has 28 attractive guest rooms ($129 d) in the main building and apartments ($179–229 for up to six) with full kitchens in the annex. A light breakfast is included, and this is a Wi-Fi hotspot. The area's best restaurant, Mykel's, is downstairs.

Best Western King Salmon Motel (35545 Kenai Spur Hwy., 907/262-5857 or 888/262-5857, www.bestwestern.com, $149–159 d) has large newly remodeled rooms with microwaves. Some also include kitchenettes.

The website of the **Kenai Peninsula B&B Association** (866/436-2266, www .kenaipeninsulabba.com) offers links to a dozen Soldotna B&Bs, or contact Suzanne Richards of **Accommodations on the Kenai** (907/262-2139 or 866/417-3518) for helpful referrals. Recommended places include **Longmere Lake Lodge B&B** (907/262-9799, www .longmerelakelodge.com), **Alaskan Dream B&B** (907/260-3147 or 888/326-3147, www.alaskan dream.net), **Alaskan Serenity B&B** 907/262-6648 or 800/764-6648, www.alaskanserenity bb.com), and **Call of the River B&B** (907/260-6533, www.kenairiver salmon.com).

Fishing Lodges

Fishing is the main attraction for most Soldotna visitors, with many lodges catering to the hip-waders and tackle crowd. Various packages are available at around $1,100 per person for four nights lodging and three days of charter salmon and halibut fishing. Check out **Kenai Riverbend Resort** (907/283-9489 or 800/625-2324, www.kenairiverbend.com), **Soldotna B&B Lodge** (907/262-4779 or 877/262-4779, www.soldotnalodge.com), **King Salmondeaux Lodge** (907/360-3474 or 866/651-3474, www.kingsalmondeauxlodge.com), **Tower Rock Lodge** (907/283-3662 or 800/284-3474, www.towerrocklodge.com), and **Kenai River Raven Lodge** (907/262-5818 or 888/262-5818, www.kenairiverraven.com). **Funny Moose Lodge** (907 or 800/770-3701, www.funnymoose.com) provides the budget version.

Camping

Get to **Centennial Park City Campground** (907/262-5299, www.ci.soldotna.ak.us, $13) by crossing the bridge on the Sterling, taking a right at the light onto Kalifornsky, then another immediate right into the campground. This is a big city park with nice wooded sites (some right on the river), picnic tables, fire pits, water, boardwalks, fishing walkways, and a boat-launching ramp. Identical rates apply at **Swiftwater Campground,** also run by the city of Soldotna, on East Redoubt Street. No reservations at either place.

Local RV parks include **Edgewater RV Park** (907/262-7733) and **River Terrace RV Park** (907/262-5593). **Klondike RV Park & Cabins** (907/262-6035 or 800/980-6035, www.klondikecabins.com) is on Funny River Road close to the Kenai River. Free RV parking in the Fred Meyer parking lot (two-night limit).

Food

When I asked a longtime Soldotna resident for recommendations on local restaurants, I was told something that should perhaps come as a warning: "I'd rather eat at home." Most Soldotna dining comes courtesy of McDonald's, Subway, Dairy Queen, Taco Bell, Burger King, and Arby's, but the town does have a number of reasonably good homegrown options.

Hidden away on a side-street near the Safeway store, **Kaladi Bros. Coffee** (315 S. Kobuk St., 907/262-5890, www.kaladi.com) serves good espresso, and features art on the walls and occasional music. Be sure to check out the unique ceiling tiles.

The Crossing (44789 Sterling Hwy., 907/262-1906, closed Sun., $20–30) is an upscale riverside place near the Kenai River bridge. Specialties include Alaskan seafood (including a sesame-encrusted salmon with peanut sauce), black angus steaks, rack of lamb, and pastas, along with unique drinks—try the chocolate martini. Live acoustic music most nights.

Klondike City is a little shopping center that features a bowling alley and the 24-hour **Sal's Klondike Diner** (907/262-2220), where you can get typical truck-stop food and big pieces of pie. It's *the* place for breakfast in Soldotna, served anytime.

For East Coast–style subs (at Alaska-size prices), stop by **Jersey Subs** (907/260-3343). Best Philly cheese steak in these parts.

Open for lunch and dinner, **Mykel's Restaurant & Lounge** (907/262-4305 or 866/262-9169, www.mykels.com, entrées $19–30) is just up Kenai Spur Highway from the Sterling Highway, and features fresh salads, pasta, seafood, rack of lamb, steaks, and fine wines. Free Wi-Fi too.

Located at the Soldotna Y, **Charlotte's at River City Books and Cafe** (907/260-7722) provides a pleasant escape from the ubiquitous fast-food joints and anglers in hip waders. You'll find both a fair selection of new books and a café serving sandwiches, soups, and espresso.

For fresh veggies and fruits, head to the **Soldotna Farmers' Market** on Saturdays from 10 A.M. to 2 P.M. June–September; it's held at the Soldotna Elementary School parking lot.

Information and Services

Grab a shower at **Alpine Laundromat** on the highway next to Dairy Queen or **Soldotna Wash & Dry** (121 Smith Way, 907/262-8495). **Central Peninsula Hospital** (250 Hospital Place, 907/262-4404, www.cpgh.org) is especially adept at removing fish hooks from all parts of the body; in a typical year they pull out 100 of them! Be sure to wear shatterproof eyewear to protect your eyes while rubbing shoulders with the Kenai River fishing crowds.

Getting There

Air taxis offering charters and flightseeing from the Soldotna Airport include **Talon Air Service** (907/262-8899, www.talonair.com), **Natron Air** (907/262-8440 or 877/520-8440, www.natronair.com), and **High Adventure Air** (907/262-5237, www.highadventureair.com).

Local taxi companies are **Alaska Cab** (907/262-1555) and **Yellow Cab** (907/260-1900). Rent cars from **Wheels 4 Rent** (907/262-6102).

Homer Stage Line (907/235-2252, www .homerstageline.com) runs from Soldotna to Anchorage, Homer, and Seward. Service is daily to Anchorage, Seward, and Homer in the summer, with fewer winter runs.

KENAI

The town of Kenai sits on a bluff above the mouth of the Kenai River overlooking Cook Inlet. With over 7,000 residents, it's the largest town on the Kenai Peninsula. Across the inlet to the southwest rise Redoubt and Iliamna, active volcanoes at the head of the Aleutian Range. The Alaska Range is visible to the northwest. Beluga whales sometimes enter the mouth of the river on the incoming tides to look for fish.

History

Kenai is the second-oldest permanent settlement in Alaska, founded by Russian fur traders who built St. Nicholas Redoubt in 1791. The U.S. Army built its own fort, Kenay, in 1869, two years after the Great Land changed hands. Oil was discovered in 1957 offshore, followed by natural gas two years later, and now Kenai is the largest and most industrialized city on the peninsula. Several of the 15 Cook Inlet platforms are visible from shore. The oil and gas are processed at two petroleum refineries, a liquefied natural gas plant, and a fertilizer plant, all in nearby Nikiski. The rich past has been buried by a rather boring present where town isn't much more than a series of intersections and gas stations.

Sights

Most of the sights of Kenai are in one small area, which you can tour on foot in 90 minutes. Start at the **Kenai Visitors and Cultural Center** (11471 Kenai Spur Rd., 907/283-1991, www.visitkenai.com). The center is open weekdays 9 A.M.–7 P.M., Saturday–Sunday 10 A.M.–6 P.M. Memorial Day–Labor Day, and Monday–Friday 9 A.M.–5 P.M. and Saturday 11 A.M.–4 P.M. the rest of the year. Here you'll find a complete and well-organized selection of brochures and flyers about the area. Its mu-

seum collection ($3 in the summer, free in winter and for kids) is impressive, with gorgeous cultural artifacts from the Native peoples, a permanent exhibit of local historical lore and natural history, and temporary exhibits. Various interpretive programs are taught Monday, Wednesday, and Friday in the summer.

Next, walk down toward the bluff on Overland Avenue to the replica of **Fort Kenay,** built in 1967 for the Alaska Centennial. It isn't open to the public. Next door is **Holy Assumption of the Virgin Mary Orthodox Church,** built in 1895 and the second-oldest Russian Orthodox Church in the state (the oldest is on Kodiak). It's a working church with regular services; tours are available on request, or peek through the windows at the painted altar and brass chandelier. The **Chapel of Saint Nicholas** (1906) nearby, built over the grave of Kenai's first priest, also reflects the traditional Russian Orthodox architectural style. Walk east on Mission Road for two viewpoints over the bluff; from the first, look out over the riverside canneries, with the Kenai Mountains behind and the Aleutian and Alaska Ranges strung out across the inlet. The second has an interpretive sign about beluga whales.

Recreation

My favorite Kenai destination is the wonderful **beach** near the mouth of the Kenai River; it's one of the best, easily accessible beaches in Alaska! Find it at the end of Spruce Street on the north side of the river. A line of low dunes backs the fine sand.

Captain Cook State Recreation Area (907/262-5581, www.alaskastateparks.org) is 25 miles from Kenai at the end of the North Kenai Road. This is a delightful place to camp, hike the rocky shoreline, look for agates, enjoy the views across Cook Inlet, or simply relax. On summer weekends locals come here to swim in the surprisingly warm waters of Stormy Lake.

Families will love spending an afternoon at the North Peninsula Recreation Area's **Nikiski Pool** (907/776-8472, daily), where the featured attractions are 136-foot waterslide, a

© AVALON TRAVEL PUBLISHING, INC.

"rain umbrella," hot tub, and a large pool for lap swimming.

The **Kenai Peninsula Oilers** (907/283-7133, www.oilersbaseball.com) play semiprofessional baseball at Coral Seymour Memorial Park in Kenai. The team has won several National Baseball Congress World Series championships over the years and is always fun to watch. **Kenai Golf Course** (1420 Lawton Dr., 907/283-7500) is an 18-hole public course. In the winter, cross-country ski trails are maintained here; call 907/283-3855 for specifics.

Accommodations

The Kenai Visitors and Cultural Center has a complete listing of local lodging places, along with their brochures. In the middle of Kenai town, **Uptown Motel** (on the Spur Rd., 907/283-3660 or 800/777-3650, www.uptownmotel.com, $149–159 d) has fridges and microwaves in all the rooms, plus a restaurant and lounge. Check out the 100-year-old gold-plated cash register behind the front desk.

Kings Inn (907/283-6060 or 877/883-6060, www.alaskakingsinn.com, $105–140 d) is on the Soldotna side of the Spur Road near the airport. A restaurant is on the premises, and some rooms include fridges and microwaves. You might also try **Kenai Merit Inn** (260 S. Willow St., 907/283-6131 or 800/227-6131, www.kenaimeritinn.com, $120–130 d).

Recommended Kenai B&Bs include **Daniels Lake Lodge B&B** (907/776-5578 or 800/774-5578, www.danielslakelodge.com, $95–250 d) and **Harborside Cottages** (907/283-6162 or

888/283-6162, www.harborsidecottages.com, $125–175 d).

Camping

The nearest public camping places are in Soldotna. Twenty-five miles north of Kenai is quiet **Captain Cook State Recreation Area** (907/262-5581, www.alaskastateparks.org), which contains **Bishop Creek Campground,** a popular tent-only area where you can see spawning salmon in late summer, and **Discovery Campground** with fireside programs on summer weekends. Both campgrounds cost $10.

Beluga Lookout RV Park (929 Mission Ave., 907/283-5999 or 800/745-5999, www .belugalookout.com) has full hookups overlooking Cook Inlet, and **Diamond M Ranch** (907/283-9424, www.diamondmranch.com) has RV sites five miles south of Kenai on Kalifornsky Beach Road.

Food

Cozy **Veronica's** (1506 Tyoyn Way, 907/283-2725) is *the* place in the Kenai-Soldotna area. Hidden in a historic log cabin across the street from the Russian Orthodox Church in Old Kenai, the café serves breakfast quiche specials, fresh salads, soups, sandwiches, espresso, and wonderful desserts. Dinners (around $15) are available Thursdays–Saturdays with acoustic musical accompaniment.

A classy (and pricy) place to eat in Kenai is **Paradisos Restaurant** (907/283-2222) on Kenai Spur Road a block east of the visitor center. They've been serving lunch and dinner to locals and visitors since 1971. The big menu features Italian, Mexican, pizzas (free local delivery), and Greek food.

Getting There

Both **Era Aviation** (907/283-3028 or 800/866-8394, www.flyera.com) and **Grant Aviation** (907/235-2757 or 888/359-4726, www.flygrant.com) offer daily flights between Kenai Airport and Anchorage. Local air taxis include **Mavrik Aire** (907/262-6790 or 888/628-7457, www.mavrikaire.com), and **Alaska West**

Air (907/776-5147, www.alaskawestair.com). Call **Alaska Cab** (907/283-6000) or **Inlet Taxi** (907/283-4711) for rides into town.

A number of companies rent cars and vans at the Kenai Airport: **Avis** (907/283-7900 or 800/331-1212), **Budget** (907/283-4506 or 800/527-0770), **Hertz** (907/283-7979 or 800/478-7980), or **Payless** (907/283-6428 or 800/729-5377).

Homer Stage Line (907/235-2252, www .homerstageline.com) provides summer-only runs to Anchorage, Homer, and Seward.

SOUTH TO HOMER

South of Soldotna, the Sterling Highway hugs the coastline all the way to Homer, a distance of 75 miles. The view across the Cook Inlet is of the Aleutian volcanic crown, **Mt. Redoubt** (10,197 ft.) to the north and **Mt. Iliamna** (10,016 ft.) to the south—both within rhyming Lake Clark National Park. On a very clear day you can also see active **Mt. Augustine,** a solitary volcanic island with a well-defined cone at the bottom of the Inlet; it last erupted in 2006. See www.avo.alaska.edu to check current activity levels.

Travelers will be dismayed to find that nearly all the larger spruce trees in this area have been killed by spruce bark beetles over the last decade, leaving behind the brown skeletons of a once-healthy forest. Many areas of spruce have been logged, but others are simply a mass of standing dead trees. Fortunately, the youngest spruce trees have generally survived the onslaught, and other species, such as birch and alder, are unaffected. The dead spruce forests extend well south of Homer, and across Kachemak Bay through Kachemak Bay State Park. It's a sad sight and one that is not likely to change for decades to come. Unfortunately, the infestation continues to spread to the east across the Kenai Peninsula and all the way to the Wrangell Mountains on the east side of Alaska.

Kasilof and Clam Gulch

From Kenai, backtrack on Kalifornsky over the Kenai River and go right at the fork to the coast; this spur road joins the Sterling at

Mile 109 in Kasilof (ka-SEE-loff), gateway to huge Tustumena Lake, whose turnoff is at Mile 110.

At Mile 117 is the turnoff for **Clam Gulch State Recreation Area,** a two-mile gravel road down to the campground and clamming grounds. Campsites go for $10, and day use is $5 per vehicle. Make sure you have a sport-fishing license (required for clam diggers over age 16), a shovel, a bucket, and gloves before you dig in the cold sand for the razor-sharp clams; best during a low tide in early summer, but possible anytime April–September. Contact the Alaska Department of Fish and Game for regulations.

Clam Gulch Lodge (907/260-3778 or 800/700-9555, www.clamgulch.com, $95 d) is a modern place with a hearty breakfast. Some rooms have shared baths. A variety of fishing packages are available.

Tustumena Lodge (907/262-4216, www.tustumenalodge.com) has lodging, meals, and fishing packages. The exterior is bush-Alaska ugly, but the lodge is famous for its collection of hats that cover every inch of the interior. At over 22,000 it merits the top spot in the *Guinness Book of World Records.* Want more minutiae? The lodge claims to also have the world's largest razor clam on display.

Several B&Bs and cabin rentals dot the Kasilof area. Especially nice is **Ingrid's Inn** (907/262-1510 or 888/422-1510, www.alaskaone.com/ingrids, $115–140 d). Rent cabins from **Kasilof River Cabins** (907/262-6348, www.kasilofriverlodge.com), **Crooked Creek Cabins** (907/262-2729 or 877/302-2729, www.ak-cabins.com), or **Tustumena Ridge Cabins** (907/262-7050, www.trcabins.com).

Park RVs at **Crooked Creek RV Park** (907/262-1299, $25 RVs or $15) or **Kasilof RV Park** (907/262-0418 or 800/264-0418, www.kasilofrvpark.com).

Kasilof Mercantile (907/262-4809) has a café, groceries, and espresso.

Ninilchik

This small town of 700, located where the Ninilchik River empties into the Inlet, has a long history. Settled in the early 1800s by retired Russian-America Company workers who took Native wives, the old village is down a short side road off Sterling Highway. In old downtown are some classic water's-edge houses, a few businesses and weathered structures. Follow the road that parallels the Ninilchik River around toward the "spit"; you wind up on the other side of the river and village on the hardpan inlet beach. A dozen historical buildings and signs are along the way; a short footpath leads up to the beautiful **Russian Orthodox Church,** built on an overlook in 1900. The church is also accessible by road; look for Coal Street on the left side of the highway as you head north from town. Ninilchik hosts the small-town **Kenai Peninsula Fair** the third weekend in August, with games, livestock, and craft booths.

No visitor center, but the **Ninilchik Chamber of Commerce** website (www.ninilchikchamber.com) provides links to local places. Most businesses are strung along the highway above the main town and include Ninilchik General Store (907/567-3378), restaurants, and charter fishing companies. **Boardwalk Cafe** (907/567-3388, summers only) serves clam chowder, along with fresh seafood, espresso, and homemade pies.

Many charter boats put in at nearby Deep Creek State Recreation Area, using large tractors to get the boat trailers out beyond the waves on the beach. It's quite the scene on a summer weekend morning, with the action generally taking place an hour or two before high tide. Trivial celebrity connection enthusiasts may want to stop at Chihuly's Charters (907/567-3374, www.ptialaska.net/~chihuly) to talk with Mike, the cousin of world-renowned glass artist Dale Chihuly. **Deep Creek Custom Packing** (907/567-3395 or 800/764-0078, www.deepcreekcustompacking.com) sells quality fresh and smoked fish, and is open for tours.

Budget travelers should check out **Ninilchik Hostel/The Eagle Watch** (907/567-3905, mid-May–mid-Sept.), with dorm beds for $13 per person. A full kitchen is available, along with two private rooms ($35 d). The hostel is closed 10 A.M.–5 P.M.

Three very popular state campgrounds (907/235-7024, www.alaskastateparks.org, $10) are scattered around town: **Ninilchik River Campground** (big, woodsy, and un-crowded), **Ninilchik View Campground** (atop a high bluff), and **Ninilchik Beach Campground** (undeveloped sites). **Deep Creek State Recreation Area** is just two miles to the south, with undeveloped campsites. Day-use parking is $5.

Park RVs (around $30) at **Heavenly Sights Camping** (907/567-7371 or 800/479-7371, www.heavenlysights.com), **Scenic View RV Park** (907/567-3909, www.scenicviewrv.com), **Alaskan Angler RV Resort** (907/567-3393 or 800/347-4114, www.afishunt.com), **Country Boy Campground** (907/567-3396), and **D&M RV Park** (907/567-4368 or 800/479-7357, www.dnmrvpark.com).

Anchor Point

This small town of 1,100 people is another sportfishing destination, with the Anchor River attracting anglers in pursuit of king salmon, silver salmon, Dolly Varden, and steelhead. Anchor Point is the most westerly highway point in North America (or more precisely, the most westerly town on a road system connected with the Lower 48).

Anchor River Inn (907/235-8531 or 800/435-8531, www.anchorriverinn.com) has aging and tiny "fishermen's special" rooms for $62 d, and standard rooms with fridges and microwaves for $99 d. A better bet is **Sleepy Bear Cabins** (907/235-5625 or 866/235-5630, www.sleepybearalaska.com), where five modern cabins all have microwaves, fridges, and private baths for $110 d or $130 for four people. **Northwood Cabins** (907/235-5142 or 888/972-2246, www.northwoodcabins.com, $100–150 d) has three log cabins, and **Anchor River Lodge** (9097/235-2130, www.anchorriverlodge.com, $85 d) has B&B lodging with comfortable

rooms in a modern log building overlooking the bay and Mt. Iliamna.

Anchor River State Recreation Area covers five campgrounds with campsites ($10) strewn along the Anchor River Beach Road just downhill from town. **Stariski State Recreation Site** ($10) four miles north of Anchor Point, has one of the best views of any state campground. Day-use parking is $5.

The Anchor Point Chamber of Commerce **Visitors Information Center** (907/235-2600, www.anchorpointchamber.org) maintains a museum that houses historical photos and memorabilia. It's open Friday–Monday 10 A.M.–2 P.M. and Tuesday–Thursday 8 A.M.–4 P.M. in the summer, and Monday–Friday 10 A.M.–2 P.M. the rest of the year.

Nikolaevsk

The Russian Old Believer village of Nikolaevsk is nine miles east of Anchor Point via North Fork Road and Nikolaevsk Road. This isolated community is one of several on the Kenai Peninsula where these traditional people live; nearly all speak both Russian and English. There's a picturesque church, and the women and girls wear scarves and ankle-length dresses. But they also have all the modern conveniences, including big pickup trucks, satellite dishes, and computers. Villagers are not particularly accepting of outsiders, so don't go around pointing your camera at folks.

One open local is Nina Fefelov, ultra-friendly owner of the **Samovar Cafe** (907/235-6867, www.russiangiftsnina.com), which serves such traditional dishes as borsch, pelmeni, piroshki, and Russian tea, and sells traditional Russian gifts. Overnight stays at her B&B are just $49–79 d, including a tasty Russian breakfast. Rooms have private baths and kids are welcome. An RV park here has sites for $10 (no hookups, but showers available).

Homer

Homer has a dazzling reputation for some of the finest scenery, the mildest climate, heaviest halibut, biggest bays, longest spits, coolest people, and best quality of life in the state. And the truth is, Homer is one of Alaska's peerless towns. It has an undeniably beautiful setting, with the unruly coastline, lingualate fjords, and cavalcading Kenai Mountains across magnificent Kachemak Bay. The temperatures are generally mild—for Alaska. The halibut sometimes tip the scales at over 200 pounds, and you can try your luck at salmon fishing for the cost of a fishing license. An abundance of fine artists and craftspeople call Homer home, selling their wares at small galleries full of rare and tempting stuff. And some of the state's best fishing, boating, hiking, kayaking, natural history, wildlife, and photo ops revolve around Homer in Kachemak Bay. So the bottom line is: Homer distinctly deserves its reputation. Welcome to Homer, Cosmic Hamlet by the Sea.

sailboat race in Kachemak Bay with Kenai Mountains in the background

HISTORY

The Russians knew of the limitless coal in this area in the early 1800s, and Americans were mining the seams only a decade after the Alaska Purchase. The gold rush began delivering men and supplies to the small port at the end of the sandy spit on their way to the gold fields at Hope and Sunrise up the Inlet in the mid-1890s. One of the most flamboyant prospectors to pass through, Homer Pennock left his name on the settlement. Mining the hundreds of millions of tons of accessible bituminous fuel continued until 1907, when a combination of fire in Homer, federal policy, and falling prices burned out the market. Slowly, the inevitable fishermen and homesteaders began settling in during the 1920s, and they found a lifetime supply of home-heating fuel free for the taking right on the beach; it's still collected by some locals.

Homer remained a small fishing and canning port until the early 1950s, when the Sterling Highway finally connected the town with the rest of the continent. Since then, the population has grown to over 4,000 today, with commercial fishing and tourism the primary economic pillars. Homer has an interesting mix of people. Drop by the docks and you'll encounter both the long-haired rasta crowd and Russian Old Believers whose women wear prim and proper long dresses while the men sport long beards.

SIGHTS
The Homer Spit

This four-mile finger of real estate jutting boldly into Kachemak Bay hosts the Small Boat Harbor, touristy boardwalks, a famous **Fishing Hole,** the infamous Salty Dawg Saloon, Land's End Resort, public camping, charter halibut and salmon fishing, a ferry terminal, and lazy beachcombing with an incomparable view. It is Homer's main attraction, and a wonderfully busy place in mid-summer. You could easily

HOMER

KENAI PENINSULA

KAREN HORNADAY PARK CAMPGROUND

KAREN HORNADAY PARK

SOUTH PENINSULA HOSPITAL

PRATT MUSEUM

HOMER HOSTEL

PIONEER INN

HOMER THEATRE

HERITAGE HOTEL

NOMAR

SAVE-U-MORE

HOMER CHAMBER OF COMMERCE VISITOR CENTER

BUNNELL GALLERY

DRIFTWOOD INN/RV PARK

RING OF FIRE MEADERY

TWO SISTERS BAKERY

OCEAN SHORES MOTEL

WILD BERRY PRODUCTS

PTARMIGAN ARTS

CENTER FOR ALASKAN COASTAL STUDIES

POST OFFICE

LIBRARY

SAFEWAY

ISLANDS AND OCEAN CENTER

HIGH SCHOOL (SWIMMING POOL)

LAKESIDE MALL

HOMER BREWING COMPANY

Beluga Lake

Beluga Slough

Beluga Slough Trail

Bishops Beach

Kachemak Bay

To Kenai

To End of Spit

AIRPORT

SPIT RD

KACHEMAK DR

A ST

OCEAN DR

LAKESHORE DR

STERLING HWY

EAST END RD

LAKE ST

HEATH ST

KACHEMAK WAY

SVEDLUND ST

PIONEER AVE

BAYVIEW

MAIN ST

HOPE ST

BARTLETT AVE

CAMPGROUND RD

SOUNDVIEW AVE

FAIRVIEW AVE

CRITERDON DR

JENNY LN

OLSON LN

BUNNELL ST

KLONDIKE

BONANZA

GRUBSTAKE

0   0.5 mi

0   0.5 km

To Kenai   1

© AVALON TRAVEL PUBLISHING, INC.

Inset map

To Kachemak Selo

SEASIDE FARM HOSTEL

Ohlson Mtn 1,513 ft

OHLSON MTN RD

SKYLINE DR

EAST END RD

EAST HILL RD

WEST HILL RD

STERLING HWY

NORTH FORK RD

DIAMOND RIDGE RD

Diamond Creek Trail

Homestead Trail

BAYCREST SKI TRAILS

ALASKA STATE PARK OFFICE

BAY-VIEW INN

Bishop's Beach

Homer

MAP AREA

ICE RINK

FISHING HOLE

SMALL BOAT HARBOR

LAND'S END RESORT

FERRY TERMINAL

HOMER SPIT

Beluga Lake

Kachemak Bay

Cook Inlet

To Kenai

0   2 mi

0   2 km

KENAI PENINSULA

© DON PITCHER

Homer Spit, Kachemak Bay, and Kenai Mountains

spend several days just exploring the shops, walking the beaches, flying kites, fishing for salmon in the Hole, renting a sea kayak to paddle around, soaking up the mountain vistas, and sitting around a campfire as the mid-summer sun heads down around midnight. No wonder so many folks love Homer! The Pratt Museum's **Historical Harbor Walking Tours** ($5) depart from the Salty Dawg Saloon every Thursday, Friday, and Saturday at 3 P.M. in the summer.

A paved two-mile **bike path** starts at the base of the Spit and continues to the Fishing Hole; it's great for bikes and inline skates, but the traffic is constant and noisy. Come out early in the morning before the cars and wind pick up. Bike rentals are available from Homer Saw and Cycle (1532 Ocean Dr., 907/235-8406, www.homersaw.com) and Lands End Resort (907/235-2500).

In the winter, Homer Spit is home to hundreds of **bald eagles.** Every winter morning octogenarian Jean Keene feeds fish to the eagles from her trailer near the end of the Spit. You can watch, but will need to remain in your vehicle.

The eagles attract photographers from around the globe; most of the close-up, in-flight eagle photos that you see in print were shot here—including those in *National Geographic.*

C Islands and Ocean Center

Located on the edge of Homer, this extraordinary facility provides an introduction to the 4.9 million-acre **Alaska Maritime National Wildlife Refuge,** some 2,500 islands, spires, and coastal headlands scattered from Southeast Alaska to the Arctic. These remote islands provide the largest seabird refuge in America, with millions of them nesting on rugged cliffs. Since opening in 2004, the Alaska Islands and Ocean Visitor Center (95 Sterling Hwy., 907/235-6961, www.islandsandocean. org, daily 9 A.M.–6 P.M. Memorial Day–Labor Day, Tues.–Sat. noon–5 P.M.the rest of the year, free) has quickly become a required stop for Homer visitors and locals. A grand two-story glass lobby faces Kachemak Bay, and visitors can take a stunning voyage to the islands via a 14-minute award-winning film, step into a room that re-creates the sights, sounds, and smells of a bird rookery, and learn about the birds and marine mammals that inhabit these remote places and the researchers that work there through interactive exhibits. During the summer, guided bird-watching and estuary walks are offered. The building also houses the **Kachemak Bay Research Reserve** (907/235-4799, www.kbayrr.org), whose hands-on Discovery Lab is open to the public several times a week.

Bishops Beach

A short trail leads from the Islands and Ocean Center past Beluga Slough to Bishops Beach, which is also accessible by car from Bunnell Avenue; turn right on Beluga Avenue, and follow it to the beach. This is a delightful spot for a low-tide walk, with extraordinary views of mountains, volcanoes, and glaciers lining the bay. Intrepid hikers can follow the beach north seven miles to the Diamond Creek Trail, which heads uphill to the Sterling Highway; leave a car at the trailhead off the highway to make your return easier. You'll need to time this hike with the tides to keep from getting trapped against the cliffs.

The **Diamond Creek Trail** is an easy and fun path, even if you don't do the long beach walk. The trailhead is directly across the Sterling Highway from Diamond Ridge Road. A narrow dirt road—small cars only—takes you a half-mile in, or you could park along the highway and walk in. The trail drops down to the gorgeous, remote beach in a fun and scenic mile.

◖ Pratt Museum

Be sure to visit the Pratt Museum (3779 Bartlett, 907/235-8635, www.prattmuseum. org, daily 10 A.M.–6 P.M. mid-May–mid-Sept., Tues.–Sun. noon–5 P.M. the rest of the year, closed January), just up from Pioneer Avenue. This is one of the finest small museums in Alaska, with interesting historical and cultural pieces, artwork, and wildlife displays. The beaked whale skeleton extends nearly the length of one room; follow the story of how it

was shot and washed up onto a Homer beach, then was taken apart and put back together piece by piece. A gift shop sells Alaskan-made crafts and the museum website features webcams from McNeil River bears and Gull Island. Watch them feed the sea critters Tuesdays and Fridays at 4 P.M. Entrance costs $6 adults, $5.50 seniors, $3 ages 6–18, free for younger kids, and families are $20.

Scenic Drives and Hikes

Head back out the Sterling Highway and take a right on West Hill Road; just after the pavement ends, go right at the fork (a left puts you on Diamond Ridge Rd., which drops you back down to the Sterling) onto **Skyline Drive.** You climb along a high ridge among expensive homes and B&Bs, until you see the famous view of the Spit, the bay, and the march of mountains on the southern coast, all framed by fireweed late in the summer.

Continue on Skyline Drive to the turn-off for **East Skyline Road,** which takes you steeply downhill to Homer, or continue out East Skyline Drive 1.5 miles to **Carl E. Wynn Nature Center** (907/235-6667, www .akcoastalstudies.org). Here you'll find nature trails and a learning center that's open daily 10 A.M.–6 P.M. (Fri. until 8 P.M.) mid-June–Labor Day. Guided walks are $5 adults, $4 seniors, or $3 for anyone under 18.

Keep going out East Skyline, and turn left on remote Ohlson Mountain Road until it ends at **Ohlson Peak** (1,513 ft.). Return to town via East Hill Road, which meets East End Road on—you guessed it—the east side of town.

Pioneer Avenue through town turns into **East End Road,** which also has beautiful homes and great views of the Spit and the bay. Nine miles out are the down-home Fritz Creek General Store and the Homestead Restaurant, along with increasingly jaw-dropping views of the Kachemak Bay and the glaciers. The road ends 20 miles from town, but you can walk down a steep dirt road from here to the shore and past the Russian Old Believer village of **Kachemak Selo** along the beach at the head of Kachemak Bay. Not many folks get this far from Homer, but those who do are well rewarded for the effort. If you don't want to drive all that way, take a hard right onto Kachemak Drive three miles out, and head back down to the Spit.

ENTERTAINMENT AND EVENTS

Homer's old favorite, Alice's Champagne Palace, closed in 2005, leaving a gaping hole in the town's party scene. Several other bars offer music on a relatively regular basis, including **Duggan's Waterfront Pub** (120 W. Bunnell Ave., 907/235-9949) and **The Alibi** (453 E. Pioneer Ave., 907/235-9199).

The **Salty Dawg Saloon** out near the end of the Spit is Homer's most famous landmark. The original building dates from 1897, the second building from 1909, and the tower from mid-'60s. Each building housed different companies in eight different locations before settling down here on the Spit. Open from 11 A.M. until the last patron staggers out the door; have a beer for the experience (if you can stand the cigarette smoke) and leave your business card or signed bra with the thousands of others. The Dawg is closed November–March.

Homer has a high proportion of talent, and some of the performers have gotten together to do **Pier One Theater** (on the Spit, 907/235-7333, www.pieronetheatre.org). Whatever is playing, this is guaranteed to be one of the finest theater experiences in the state. It's typically open on weekends May–August only.

For a different kind of theatrical event, catch a flick at little **Homer Theatre** (Pioneer and Main, 907/235-6728). Get there early to snag one of the comfy couches up front.

Events

The first weekend of May brings the **Kachemak Bay Shorebird Festival** (www.homeralaska.org/shorebird.htm) to Homer, with birdwalks, bay tours, an arts fair, speakers, and other activities, all in celebration of the great northward migration of shorebirds. Memorial Day weekend brings the **Kachemak Kayak Fest** (907/235-7740, www.kachemakkayakfest.com)

Salty Dawg Saloon

© DON PITCHER

with workshops and demonstrations, plus the **Wooden Boat Festival,** a fun chance to see works by local boat builders.

Public radio station KBBI's **Concerts on the Lawn** (907/235-7721, www.kbbi.org) is the biggest summer event, attracting musicians from around the state. It takes place the last weekend of July. This is one of Alaska's best and most eclectic radio stations; find it at 890 AM.

SHOPPING

Alaska Wild Berry Products (528 E. Pioneer Ave., 907/235-8858 or 800/280-2927, www.alaskawildberryproduct.com) specializes in Alaska-made wild berry jams, jellies, chocolates, and sauces, some of which are fashioned on the premises. The counter usually has free samples, but it's hard to resist buying some before you leave.

Downtown near the movie theater, **Nomar** (104 E. Pioneer Ave., 907/235-8363 or 800/478-8364, www.nomaralaska.com) sells high-quality handmade clothing and outdoor gear. Some of its most popular items are specifically designed for commercial fishermen, but Nomar also has warm and windproof outerwear, kids' garb, hats, raingear, purses, duffel bags, and more. Next door is **Main Street Mercantile** (907/235-9102), a beautifully restored 1936 building filled with outdoor gear and home accessories.

Three miles out East End Road is **Kachemak Gear Shed** (907/235-8612 or 800/478-8612), selling quality clothing and outerwear for anyone heading out on the water. It's a great place to check out the commercial fishing supplies too.

The Bookstore (332 E. Pioneer, 907/235-7496) has all of Tom Bodett's books, along with works of other local authors, a big Alaskana section, field guides, and lots more. (Tom Bodett is known to most Americans as the folksy "We'll leave the light on for you" voice in the Motel 6 commercials, but he is also the author of several humor books. Like fellow Homerite celebrity Jewel, Bodett no longer lives in Homer.)

Old Inlet Bookshop (3487 Main St., 907/235-7984, www.oldinletbookshop.com) is a packed used bookstore with a café in the back and lodging upstairs. This beautifully restored (and expanded) log cabin was originally part of a 1905 fox farm on Yukon Island.

Galleries
Homer has a statewide reputation as an arts center, and a few local showcases are must-sees on any Homer itinerary. If you're around on the first Friday of the month, don't miss the aptly named **First Friday,** when new exhibitions open and the hors d'oeuvres come out. A number of galleries are scattered around town, most notably **Bunnell Street Gallery** (106 W. Bunnell Ave., 907/235-2662, www.bunnellstreet gallery.org). This nonprofit gallery is in the old Inlet Trading Post, built in 1937, and just up from Bishop's Beach. Although small, Bunnell attracts nationally known artists, with new exhibitions monthly. In the back are distinctive works for sale in a variety of media.

One of Alaska's oldest cooperative galleries, **Ptarmigan Arts** (471 E. Pioneer Ave., 907 /235-5345) has a diversity of artists, all of whom

also work one day a month. Here you'll find everything from handmade hats to ceramics, beaded jewelry, wildlife and landscape photos (including those of the author), and watercolors. Next door is **Fireweed Gallery** (907/235-3411, www.fireweedgallery.com), and **Picture Alaska** (907/235-2300 or 800/770-2300 www .picturealaska.com) is across the street.

Head out the Spit for several excellent seasonal galleries, including **Sea Lion Gallery** (907/235-3400, www.sealiongallery.com), **High Tide Arts** (907/226-2600), and **Homer Clay Works** (907/235-6118).

RECREATION
Homer High School houses the local **swimming pool** (907/235-7416), open daily for lap swimming. The **Bay Club** (2395 Kachemak Dr., 907/235-2582) is a fine private facility with a small pool, racquetball court, workout equipment, yoga classes, and climbing wall. Entrance costs $12 for visitors, with childcare available while you work out.

Seven miles out East End Road, **Kachemak Bay Lynx Golf Course** (907/235-0606 800/295-5969, www.alaskagolfandfishing.com) is a par-three course with great views of the bay. The little clubhouse rents clubs.

Rent mountain bikes from **Homer Saw and Cycle** (1532 Ocean Dr., 907/235-8406, www .homersaw.com) or on the Spit from **Lands End Resort** (907/235-2500). Local water taxis will transport your bikes across the bay at no extra charge. **Trails End Horse Adventures** (907/235-6393) offers horseback rides in the Fox River area at the head of Kachemak Bay.

If you have kids in tow, drive uphill on Bartlett Avenue, then left on Fairview to **Karen Hornaday Park,** where the playground has all sorts of fun adventures.

See the *Across Kachemak Bay* section below for details on the popular boat trips from Homer to Gull Island, Seldovia, Halibut Cove, and Kachemak Bay State Park.

Sea Kayaking
A number of local companies lead seasonal guided sea kayak trips within Kachemak Bay,

or rent kayaks to do it on your own. Based on protected Yukon Island near Kachemak Bay State Park, **True North Kayak Adventures** (907/235-0708, www.truenorthkayak.com) offers a range of guided trips, from half-day paddles ($90) to multi-night packages. The all-day trip ($140 with lunch) is especially popular. All trips include a round-trip water taxi ride to Yukon Island, sea kayaks, and guide. True North has triple kayaks for families who want to bring the kids along. Kayak rentals ($160 for two people with water taxi) are available for experienced paddlers.

St. Augustine's Kayak & Tours (907/235-6126 or 800/770-6126, www.homerkayaking.com) has a base in Peterson Bay, adjacent to the Center for Alaskan Coastal Studies field station, with half-day ($93) and full-day ($134) trips, plus a combination version that includes morning with naturalists at CACS and an afternoon of paddling for $150. Most people book through the Inlet Charters office on the Spit. All trips include round-trip transportation by water taxi from Homer.

Kachemak Guide Bureau (907/399-4542, www.kgbalaska.com) sets up custom kayak trips of all sorts, including ones that include fly fishing, hiking, of flightseeing. Local water taxis have complete details on their various adventure trips.

Across the Bay Tent & Breakfast Adventure Company (907/235-3633 summer or 907/345-2571 winter, www.tentandbreakfastalaska.com, late May–early Sept.) has a distinctive operation that's perfect for adventurous travelers on a budget. Guests stay in furnished, canvas wall-tents set atop wooden platforms along Kasitsna Bay (8 miles out of Seldovia), with showers, a sauna, and "two of the most beautiful outhouses in Alaska." Tent and all meals are $110 a day per person; tent and breakfast only are $75 a day. You can rent a mountain bike, take a sea kayak tour, or join one of their summertime workshops in art, yoga, or natural history.

Seaside Adventures (907/235-6672, www.seasideadventure.com, May–mid-Oct.) operates out of Little Tutka Bay, a lovely spot surrounded by Kachemak Bay State Park. Tours ($135 all day or $100 half-day) include a water taxi ride from the Spit, knowledgeable guides, and a distinctive lunch that includes "beach soup" made from mussels and clams found along the way.

Local water taxi companies (including Mako's, Smoke Wagon, and Triton) will also book kayak trips through the above companies, and offer rental kayaks. **Alaska Kayak School** (907/235-2090, www.alaskakayakschool.com) offers kayaking lessons year-round.

Charter Fishing

Homer calls itself the halibut fishing capital of the world, with commercial fishermen often landing more halibut here than any other port. Sport fishing attracts droves of enthusiasts every day of the summer, not only for halibut, but also for king and silver salmon. Wear warm, layered clothing topped by raingear, and soft-soled shoes. Binoculars are a definite plus, since seabirds and marine mammals are usually viewable. You can have your catch vacuum-packed, frozen, and shipped home for additional fees, but they add up quickly.

Whatever you do, don't forget to enter the summer-long **Homer Jackpot Halibut Derby** (www.homerhalibutderby.com) if you go fishing. First prize tops $45,000, with additional monthly prizes. Sob stories abound of people who saved $10 by not entering, then caught potential prize-winning sea monsters. Don't let this happen to you!

Homer has dozens of fishing charter boats to help you go out and bag a big halibut. An easy way to find one is through **Central Charter Booking Agency** (907/235-7847 or 800/478-7847, www.centralcharter.com), **Homer Ocean Charters** (907/235-6212 or 800/426-6212, www.homerocean.com), **Inlet Charters** (907/235-6126 or 800/770-6126, www.halibutcharters.com), **Halibut King Charters** (907/235-7303 or 800/770-7303), or **North Country Charters** (907/235-7620 or 800/770-7620, www.northcountycharters.com). In addition to charter fishing, all of these can set up sea kayaking, water taxi

© DON PITCHER

halibut on Homer Spit

service, flightseeing, bear-viewing, and lodging for the area.

Once you do catch a big halibut or salmon, how do you get it back home? **Coal Point Seafood** (907/235-3877 or 800/325-3877, www.welovefish.com) offers processing and flash-freezing, and will FedEx the fish to your home. If you're going to be flying out and can take the fish with you, be sure to get the specially coated cardboard box (sold in grocery stores and at Kachemak Gear Shed) and pack it with blue ice. There are freezers at the Homer and Anchorage airports that charge a daily rental fee.

The Fishing Hole

If you just want to simply drive into town and cast a line in the water, head out to the famous Fishing Hole on the Spit, across from Glacier Drive-In and Sportsman's Supply. The Alaska Department of Fish & Game stocks this little bight with king and silver salmon smolt, and their return draws crowds of anglers all sum-

mer long. It's a classic roadside fishing stop for RVers, kids, lazy locals, and the like. On a busy weekend, you might be able to squeeze in at water's edge.

Get fishing licenses or rent a pole from **Sport Shed** (907/235-5562) across from the Hole or **Sportsman's Supply** (907/235-2617) near the boat launch.

Bear-Viewing and Flightseeing

Homer is a popular base for flightseeing trips and bear-viewing flights to coastal Katmai National Park in the summer, primarily the stretch between Geographic Harbor and Swikshak Lagoon (some trips go to Lake Clark National Park). All-day trips cost $500–600 per person and are offered late May–mid-September.

Pilot Ken Day and his naturalist wife Chris Day operate **Emerald Air Service** (907/235-6993, www.emeraldairservice.com), a long-established company with a great reputation. Operated by lifelong Alaskans Gary and Jeanne Porter, **Bald Mountain Air Service** (907/235-7969 or 800/478-7969, www.baldmountainair.com) is another outstanding choice. Book your mid-summer trip in January or February to be assured of a space with either Emerald Air or Bald Mountain.

Hallo Bay Bear Lodge (907/235-2237, www.hallobay.com) is a unique camp setting in the heart of Katmai National Park; it's described in the *Southwest Alaska* chapter, but is accessed by Homer air taxis.

Smokey Bay Air (907/235-1511 or 888/482-1511, www.smokeybayair.com) takes guests bear-viewing at Homestead Lodge within Lake Clark National Park. **K-Bay Air** (907/235-4818 or 877/522-9247, www.kbayair.com) flies a wheeled plane to the Katmai coast.

Kachemak Bay Flying Service (907/235-8924, www.alaskaseaplanes.com) has a lovingly restored 1929 Travel Air floatplane with one-hour scenic flights; $150 per person with a two-person minimum. This is a truly unique way to see the magnificent glacier country just across Kachemak Bay.

Maritime Helicopters (907/235-7771, www.maritimehelicopters.com) guides eagle-eye tours of the region's glaciers, islands, and mountains on a charter basis.

Birding

Kachemak Bay provides a fine opportunity for birders, especially during the spring migration when thousands of sandpipers and other species fill the tideflats. Call the **Kachemak Bay Bird Alert** (907/235-7337) for a recording of recent bird sightings, or head to www.birdinghomeralaska.org for more information. In early May, the Kachemak Bay Shorebird Festival brings guest speakers and bird experts.

Winter Sports

Homer is just above sea level, and it may even rain in January, but surrounding hills often pile high with snow. **Kachemak Nordic Ski Club** (907/235-6018, www.kachemaknordicskiclub.org) maintains 35 kilometers of groomed cross-country trails near McNeil Canyon (13 miles east of town), at Baycrest (just west of town off Sterling Hwy.), and at Lookout Mountain (out

Ohlson Mountain Rd.). Also popular in the winter are snowmobiling, ice skating on Beluga Lake, and eagle-watching on the Spit. Located half-way out the Spit, the **Homer Ice Arena** (907/235-2647, www.homericearena.com) is open for skaters and hockey players throughout the fall and winter.

ACCOMMODATIONS

The Homer Chamber of Commerce website (www.homeralaska.org) has links to most local lodging places. Many people come to Homer to fish and this typically means very early departures. Because of this you may be subjected to noise at 5 A.M. as folks head out for the one day when you just wanted to sleep in.

Hostels

Homer's old-time favorite is **Seaside Farm Hostel** (907/235-7850, www.xyz.net/~seaside, open May–Sept.), five miles out East End Road. It's a great rural location with horses in the pasture below, beach access, campfire cookouts, and killer views across Kachemak Bay. Beds

sandhill cranes

© DON PITCHER

in the coed dorm cost $20 per person (bring a sleeping bag), including cooking facilities and showers. Private rooms in the lodge and simple cabins are $60–75 d; showers are in the lodge. Scenic tent spaces cost $10 d. (Seaside Farm is owned by Mossy Kilcher, whose internationally known niece is the singer Jewel Kilcher, better known as simply Jewel. Homer's most famous former resident now lives in Texas.)

Housed within the historic Pratt House (built in 1939), the **Homer Hostel** (304 W. Pioneer Avenue, 907/235-1463, www.homerhostel.com, April–Oct.) is a pleasant spot to bed down in the heart of town. Bunks are $22 per person, and three simple private rooms cost $47 s or $59 d. The hostel has a full kitchen, laundry, showers, bike rentals, guest computer and Wi-Fi, outdoor grille, a convenient downtown location, a friendly owner, and no curfew.

Motels and Hotels

Driftwood Inn (907/235-8019 or 800/478-8019, www.thedriftwoodinn.com) is an unexpected gem in the rough. The historic main building has a wonderful common room with stone fireplace, comfortable chairs for relaxing, wireless Internet, and inexpensive breakfast and snack items. Several budget rooms ($65–70 s or $72–77 d)—cute but basic—have shared baths, and a half-dozen "shipsquarters rooms" ($70–75 s or $77–82 d) provide only slightly more space than a ship's bunk, but come with private baths and a charming nautical interior; they're not for anyone with claustrophobia! More standard units with private baths are $113–158 s or $120–165 d. Across the street is the Driftwood Lodge, a gorgeous modern home overlooking Bishops Beach and Kachemak Bay with five guest rooms for $155–175 d. A separate cottage ($275 d) next door is also available.

Popular with fishermen are three units over the **Sport Shed** (907/235-5562, April–Sept.), a fishing shop. These studio units—all with full kitchens and water views—are $95 d, with a two-night minimum, plus $5 each for extra guests. Weekly rates are $495 d. The Sport Shed is right across from the Fishing Hole.

Pioneer Inn (244 W. Pioneer Ave., 907/235-5670 or 800/782-9655, www.pioneer innhomerak.com) is an unpretentious downtown motel with standard rooms for $89 d, and five large apartment-style units with full kitchens for $109 d. The TVs are miniscule, but the rooms are very clean and the owner makes you feel at home.

Ocean House Inn (1065 Krueth Way, 907/235-3294 or 888/353-3294, www.homer oceanhouse.com) sits atop a low cliff facing the Homer Spit, with beach access, private entrances, two hot tubs, Wi-Fi, and a guest computer. Accommodations encompass rooms and suites ($119–139 d) with microwaves and fridges, along with condos ($179–229 d) containing full kitchens.

It's hard to miss the **Heritage Hotel** (147 E. Pioneer Ave., 907/235-7787 or 800/380-7787, www.alaskaheritagehotel.com). Built in 1948, this rambling log hotel has heart-of-town rooms for $119–129 d, and large apartment-style suites for $165 d. This is a love-it or hate-it place; some folks rave about the classic rooms, while others prefer something more modern and complain of thin walls and the older furnishings. Free Wi-Fi.

Spread across four buildings on a gentle slope, **Ocean Shores Motel** (451 Sterling Hwy., 907/235-7775 or 800/770-7775, www.akoceanshores.com) is an old fashioned plain-vanilla place, with prices matching your proximity to the water: $129–189 d. A few $99 rooms are popular with fishermen who don't care much about where they sleep.

Located on the hillside as you drive into Homer, **Bay View Inn** (907/235-8485 or 800/478-8485, www.bayviewalaska.com) has older rooms and kitchenettes ($104–114 d), plus a suite and cottage ($169 d) with full kitchens. The incredible panoramic K-Bay vistas are the real attraction here, and the picnic tables out front are perfect for a summer evening.

Advertised as Alaska's only beachfront hotel, **Land's End Resort** (907/235-0400 or 800/478-0400, www.lands-end-resort.com) occupies the very tip of Homer Spit, with bay-and-mountain views from some rooms, a waterside hot tub, a little exercise pool, and Wi-Fi in the

KENAI PENINSULA

lobby. The 84 rooms range greatly in price and quality, from $125 d for an economy unit facing the parking lot, to $220 d for luxurious two-room suites in the new building. The in-house restaurant features a big back deck on the water. Also available are a number of elaborate condos (Land's End Lodges, www.landsendlodges.com) that line the beach. Downstairs studio apartments are $150 d, and more impressive upstairs apartments cost $300–325 d. These condos are despised by many locals because they block the view from the Spit.

Alaskan Suites (907/235-1972 or 888/239-1972, www.alaskansuites.com, $225 for up to five) consists of five modern cabins on the west side of Homer, each containing two queen beds, a fridge and microwave, private bath, and Wi-Fi. The panoramic views include Kachemak Bay and several volcanoes.

Bed-and-Breakfasts

More than 100(!) Homer bed-and-breakfasts await your visit. A pair of bed-and-breakfast organizations provide one-stop shopping: **Homer's Finest B&B Network** (907/235-4983 or 800/764-3211, www.homeraccommodations.com) and **Homer B&B Association** (907/226-1114 or 877/296-1114, www.homerbedbreakfast.com).

Old Town B&B (106 W. Bunnell St., 907/235-7558, www.oldtownbedandbreakfast.com) is co-owned by artist Asia Freeman who also manages Bunnell Street Gallery, downstairs. The three immaculate rooms have period pieces in this renovated 1936 building with a false-front exterior, and are priced at a remarkable $95 d with shared bath or $115 with a private bath. A full breakfast is served in the parlor.

A block up the hill is **Mermaid B&B** (3487 Main St., 907/235-7984, www.mermaidcafe.net, $185 d), a gorgeous little apartment over Old Inlet Bookshop. It has a hot tub on the deck along with a full kitchen and private bath, and includes $10 off breakfast at the cozy downstairs café. The craftsmanship of builder/chef/bookstore-owner Andy Wills shows in all the little details.

In business for more than two decades, **Magic Canyon Ranch** (907/235-6077, www.magiccanyonranch.com, May–late Sept., $110–125 d) has one of the largest—and quietest—spreads in the area, a 75-acre homestead set against the bluffs at the end a narrow dirt road. The comfortable home contains four guest rooms, private or shared baths, great views, knowledgeable owners, filling country breakfasts, and llamas in the front pasture. There's even a 1915 Model T parked in the barn.

Beach House B&B (1121 Seabreeze Ct., 907/235-3232 or 800/936-7571, www.alaskabeachhouse.com, $125–169 d) is a favorite of travelers, with four guest rooms and a new cottage ($225 d), private entrances and baths, a beach-side hot tub, Wi-Fi, microwaves, fridges, and continental breakfasts brought to your room the evening before.

Whalesong B&B (4002 Kachemak Way, 907/235-7628, www.thewhalesong.com, $109 d with shared bath, $129 d with private bath) is a reasonably priced option just a block from downtown galleries and restaurants. Two rooms have private entrances and guests are served a continental breakfast.

An fine reasonably priced option is **Bay Avenue B&B** (907/235-3757 or 800/371-2095, www.bayavebb.com), with five rooms ($120–130 d) in the main house and two apartment units ($145 d or $185 for six) that are a good deal for anglers and families. The big breakfast features local items, and guests love the hot tub where you can watch the sunset over Kachemak Bay. The marsh below is a good place to spot shorebirds and bald eagles. Free Wi-Fi too.

A Room with a View (840 Rosebud Court, 907/235-3706, www.aroomwithaviewhomer.com, $105 d) is a large hillside home off West Hill Road with two guest rooms, private baths, and filling breakfasts. The owners speak German, and their decades as florists show in the immaculately landscaped grounds. No kids under eight are allowed.

Victorian Heights B&B (61495 Race Rd., 907/235-6357, www.victorianheightsbedandbreakfast.com, $125–145 d) is a hilltop mansion off East Hill Road with four spacious guest rooms, all with private baths. A full breakfast, guest computer, and Wi-Fi are included, and guests love the big deck overlooking the bay. A two-night minimum stay is required.

Just up the road, the aptly named **Majestic View B&B** (907/235-6413 or 888/246-6413, www.majesticviewbb.com) is another very comfortable home with five guest rooms, three with private baths ($130–140 d), and two that share a bath ($95 d). Families are welcome—all rooms contain queen and twin beds—and kids like the downstairs rec room, while adults appreciate the big deck with unobstructed bay vistas, outdoor hot tub, and Wi-Fi. The deluxe room has a whirlpool tub, private balcony, and tall windows. A homemade breakfast is served family style.

Aloha B&B (62209 Glacier View Court, 907-235-0607 or 877/355-0607, www.alohabb.com, $105–120 d) has one of Homer's famous "million-dollar" views—a 180-degree panorama of bay, mountains, and glacier. The owners are natives of Hawaii, and a Hawaiian theme carries through all four guest rooms (two of which share a bath). A continental breakfast and Wi-Fi are included.

Chocolate Drop Inn (907/235-3668 or 800/530-6015, www.chocolatedropinn.com) is six miles out East End Road, and offers views of Grewingk Glacier and a peak locally known as Chocolate Drop. The 8,000-square-foot log home has a hot tub on the back deck, a sauna, private baths and entrances for most of the six guest rooms, plus a filling breakfast. Rates are $125–140 d in the rooms, or $195 d for four guests in the two-bedroom suites. Be sure to ask about the B&B's neighbors; you might know them.

Same owners for another place seven miles out East End Road, **A B&B on the Green** (907/235-0606 or 800/295-5969, www.alaskagolfandfishing.com, May–Sept.) at the site of a par-three golf course. Two rooms over the clubhouse are $115–125 d, or you can rent the adjacent three-bedroom home for $250 d. Rates include private baths, a continental breakfast, and unlimited golf.

A delightful log home six miles out East End Road, **Good Karma Inn** (907/235-4728 or 866/435-2762, www.goodkarmainn.com, $145 d) fits Homer to a T, mixing functionality and comfort, with a fine bay and mountain view and Wi-Fi for good measure. Kindly owner Michael LeMay will fill you in on local attractions and stocks the kitchen with breakfast ingredients. Three guest rooms (private baths) are available; one of which is completely accessible for handicapped travelers.

Popular with families, **Honey's Place B&B** (907/235-8232 or 907/279-5055, www.honeys beachhouse.com, May–Sept., $195 d or $295 for four) is one of the only private homes on Homer Spit. The location is perfect for birdwatchers and folks wanting to be close to the fishing action. Guests get exclusive use of the three-bedroom beachfront home, plus ingredients for a make-it-yourself breakfast.

Three miles east of town, **Bear Creek Winery and Lodging** (907/235-8484 or 888/649-2176, www.bearcreekwinery.com, $225 d) has two lovely log cottages with kitchenettes. Guests are provided a continental breakfast and can unwind in the cedar hot tub or steam bath. A surprisingly good winery here crafts distinctive fruit wines.

Cabins and Guest Houses

Cabins and guest houses provide the perfect option for families looking for a place to call their own, and Homer has dozens of choices; find them on the chamber website, www.homeralaska.org. Start your cabin search at **Homer Cabins & Cottage Network** (907/235-0191 or 888/364-0191, www.cabinsinhomer.com), with two-dozen rental cabins in the Homer area.

Located at the base of the Homer Spit, **Lighthouse Village Cabins** (907/235-7007, www.lighthousecabins.com, $115–169 d) centers around a distinctive two-level apartment housed in a lighthouse-shaped structure; reserve well ahead for this one!. This is an especially good spot for shorebird enthusiasts, with the tideflats right out the door. Cabins

KENAI PENINSULA

include private baths, kitchens, phones, BBQ grills, and Wi-Fi.

Near the end of Homer Spit, **Sea Lion Cove** (907/235-3400 summers or 907/235-8767, www.sealiongallery.com, mid-May–mid-Sept., $120–130 d) is operated by artist Gary Lion, whose gallery is downstairs. The two rooms are right in the heart of the summertime fishing action. Each has a kitchenette, TV, phone, and shared deck delivering full-on bay vistas.

Alaska by the Sea (907/235-2716 or 877/374-2716, www.alaskabythesea.com) rents seven cottages, cabins, and homes, including several near Bishops Beach ($140–175 d), a small in-town place ($95 d), and a large house that sleeps 12 ($350).

A fine shoreside place, **Homer Inn & Spa** (907/235-2501 or 800/294-7823, www.homerinn.com), has a beachside hot tub, day spa facilities (including side-by-side massage), and plush king-size beds. Four mini-suites are $149–189 d, and a separate villa ($219 d) is perfect for families. A hot breakfast is brought to your room each morning.

Situated atop a high bluff on the west side as the highway drops into Homer, **❰ Alaska Adventure Cabins** (907/223-6681, www.alaskaadventurecabins.com, $245 for up to four) has a fun mélange of lodging: three gorgeous cabins, a restored Alaska Railroad caboose, and a landlocked boat called the Double Eagle ($285) that began life as a Gulf Coast shrimper. Each unit contains a full kitchen, private bath, Wi-Fi, and large deck facing the bay. The vista encompasses volcanoes, glaciers, Kachemak Bay, and the Spit.

CAMPING

Camping on the Spit is what most budget travelers, RVers, and backpackers do, though it's no picnic. It's within spitting distance of the noisy road, and it's barren, and often windy. City-maintained camping areas on the Spit cost $8 tents or $15 RVs (no hookups), with bathrooms or port-a-potties close by. Self-register at the sites or pay at the camping fee office (907/235-1583) near the Fishing Hole.

Campsites are open April–October, though a few hardy folks try their luck in winter when the Spit is officially closed to camping. A quieter and more protected seasonal campground is at **Karen Hornaday Park** (907/235-3170, www.ci.homer.ak.us) near the hospital on Fairview; same rates.

In addition to the city campsites, the Spit is home to three RV parks with full hookups. Close to the tip of the Spit, the privately run **Homer Spit Campground** (907/235-8206, May–mid-Sept., $25 tents, $35 RVs) has rustic and crowded sites (electricity only, showers available), some right along the beach. **Sportsman's Supply** (907/235-2617, $30 RVs) has a few spots right across from the boat launch.

With a prime spot next to the Fishing Hole, plus all the latest amenities—including satellite TV and Wi-Fi—**Heritage RV Park** (907/226-4500 or 800/380-7787, www.alaskaheritagervpark.com, May–early Sept., $65–75 RV) commands top dollar; it's easily Alaska's priciest RV park.

Driftwood Inn RV Park (907/235-8019 or 800/478-8019, www.thedriftwoodinn.com, $34–39) is close to Bishops Beach, and **Oceanview RV Park** (907/235-3951, www.oceanview-rv.com, $35 RVs, $18 tents) is a crowded RV lot on the west edge of town.

If you're staying in the city campgrounds, showers ($4) are available at Sportsman's Supply or the Homer Spit Campground. Local coin laundries also have shower facilities; a good bet is **The Washboard** (1204 Ocean Dr., 907/235-6781), where you can even surf the Web for free or get an espresso while watching the clothes spin or after showering. An even better deal is the high school pool, where they throw in a free swim for the cost of a shower.

FOOD

Homer's dining-out options are varied, with several excellent choices. Many of the town's second-tier eateries would be standouts almost anywhere else in Alaska, and the best restaurants really are noteworthy.

Breakfast and Lunch

Mermaid Café (907/235-7649, www.mermaid cafe.net, closed Mon.) fills the back of Old Inlet Bookshop, with delicious breakfasts served all day, along with lunch (try the halibut tacos) and dinner in a cheery setting. A couple of tables on the deck are fun on a summer day.

Duncan House (125 E. Pioneer Ave., 907/235-5344) is a family place with substantial all-American meals three times a day; it's often crowded on weekend mornings.

Open seasonally since 1982 and a real favorite with travelers, **Fresh Sourdough Express Bakery & Café** (1316 Ocean Dr., 907/235-7571, www.freshsourdoughexpress.com, dinner $17–24) is a homey Homer spot serving sourdough hotcakes, scrambles, granola, muffins, and monster pastries for breakfast. Lunch includes sandwiches, buffalo burgers, homemade soups, and salads, while dinners cover the salmon-chicken-and-steak terrain. The menu includes vegetarian meals, but also plenty of carnivorous protein.

Inside historic Old Town B&B building a block away is tiny **Panarelli's** (907/235-1555), with a high-quality deli, along with a chalkboard full of today's sandwiches, soups, and salads.

Coffee

Homer is a coffee-drinkers paradise, with two roasters and several excellent espresso joints. **Captain's Coffee Roasting Co.** (528 E. Pioneer Ave., 907/235-4970, www.captainscoffee.com) has a downtown location and a bright, airy space to relax. Ask owner Ty Gates for tips on surfing in Homer.

A real surprise is ◖ **K Bay Caffé** (907/235-1551, www.kbaycaffe.com), three miles out East End Road next to Kachemak Gear Shed. This one is actually little more than a drive-up window and outside deck, with enough space inside for a few people to read the newspaper and talk politics. Owner Michael McGuire really knows his coffee—he won top prize at a national barista contest a few years back—-and is a connoisseur when it comes to creating the perfect roast.

Just a block from Bishops Beach, **Two Sisters Espresso and Bakery** (907/235-2280, www

.twosistersbakery.net) is a great place to meet the locals any time of year. It's always warm and fragrant with the smell of fresh baked pastries, breads, and savories from the brick oven, along with sandwiches, focaccia, and deep-dish pizza by the slice. Pricey, but highly recommended. A covered deck wraps around the back.

Housed within Lake Street Mall, **Latitude 59°** (3858 Lake St., 235-5574) is a friendly spot for wraps, sandwiches, bagel schemers, salads, and mochas, along with a free computer and Wi-Fi. On the Spit, stop by the seasonal **Coal Towne Coffee** (907/235-9463) with espresso and hot waffles.

Quick Meals on the Spit

Yes, Homer does have McDonald's, Arby's, and Subway, but you're much better off heading out the Spit where two summer-only places vie for your attention. Best-known is the perpetually crowded **Boardwalk Fish and Chips** (907/235-7749), across from the harbormaster and Salty Dawg, with crunchy halibut fish-on-a-stick and chips that will have you smackin' your chops. But there's a new kid on the Spit: **Fresh Catch Café** (907/235-2289), where the fish is lightly breaded and not as greasy. Both are worth a taste and similarly priced ($12 for fish and chips), and the latter also serves a tasty halibut curry, plus rockfish po'boys and wasabi grilled King salmon.

A few doors from Boardwalk is **Finn's Pizza** (907/235-2878), with hot-from-the-oven wood-fired pizzas (whole or slice), along with local beers on draught. Be sure to try the blue pear version, made with D'Anjou pears, gorgonzola cheese, and roasted pine nuts. Climb the side stairs for rustic dining with a beach vista.

Open seasonally, **Spit-Fire Grille** (907/235-9379) occupies a tiny shop just down from El Pescadero Restaurant. The food is amazingly good, with daily fish specials ($10–14), ribs, sandwiches, salads, and fresh shrimp. The emphasis is local and organic, but be sure to sample the homemade ice cream. The walls are decorated with impressive paintings by chef Mike's wife, Margorie Scholl (www.margiescholl.com). Directly across the boardwalk is **Spit Sisters Cafe** (907/235-4921, www.spitsisterscafe.com), serving pastries from Two Sisters, light breakfasts, and grilled panini sandwiches. They open at 5 A.M. to provide box lunches for folks heading out on fishing charters.

Far from the hubbub on the Spit is **☾ Fritz Creek General Store** (907/235-6753), eight miles out East End Road. The store has a small selection of groceries, a little post office, booze, and a great video rack. The real attraction here is the food, including freshly baked bread, hot sandwiches, unusual burritos, pizza by the pie or slice, ribs, sweets, and coffee. Fritz Creek is a delightful place to hang out in an old-time country setting. Homestead Restaurant is right across the road.

Drop by **Frosty Bear** on the Spit and in town (639 E. Pioneer Ave.) for ice cream and hot dogs; the downtown one has a 1943 Wurlitzer jukebox.

International

Downtown's **Cosmic Kitchen** (510 E. Pioneer Ave., 907/235-6355) serves quick Mex food such as cosmic burritos, soft tacos, and steak enchiladas, plus avocado-bacon burgers, chicken tikka with chutney sandwiches, and homemade soups. It's all good and tasty, with a big choice of homemade salsas to spice things up. Cosmic is also open for breakfast. Delicioso.

Get the best local Asian food at **Try My Thai** (177 E. Pioneer Ave., 9097/235-6686), where the $9 lunches are a deal. The two Chinese places in town are forgettable, but have buffets: **Young's** (565 E. Pioneer Ave., 907/235-4002) and **China Grill Restaurant** (3798 Lake St., 907/235-3662). Find fresh sushi and oysters at **The Alibi** (453 E. Pioneer Ave., 907/235-9199), best known as a drinking establishment.

Fine Dining

You can't miss **☾ Café Cups** (162 W. Pioneer Dr., 907/235-8330, www.cafecupshomer.com, $17–21 dinner entrées)—four Alaska-size teacups hang from the front of the converted house. Lunches feature creative sandwiches,

salads, and savories, and dinners encompass everything from Kachemak Bay oysters and chicken coconut curry to baby back ribs and "Dave's twisted fettuccine." I usually opt for the daily specials, especially the fresh seafood. Cups gets crowded and noisy, so make reservations ahead for dinner. A side patio is fun on warm afternoons.

Homer's fine-dining place, **☾ The Homestead Restaurant** (907/235-8723 www.homesteadrestaurant.net, April–Sept., $25–40 entrées) is eight miles out East End Road. The menu specializes—not surprisingly—in fresh Alaskan seafood, but also features rack of lamb, jerked duck, and melt-in-your-mouth prime rib. Homestead is open for dinners only, and is where locals go for a special-event meal. Reservations strongly advised, especially for the window seats.

Another place that gets high marks is **☾ Fat Olives Restaurant** (276 Olson Lane, 907/235-8488, $18–26). The setting evokes a trendy Italian bistro, and the menu stars wood-fired pizzas, calzones, fresh salmon, Kachemak Bay oysters, seafood pasta, and delicious appetizers (including a three-cheese fondue). It's noisy and fun, perfect for kids. Fat Olives is just off the Homer Bypass as you enter town. In a hurry? Get a giant thin-crust pizza slice to go for $3.50–4.50.

At the very tip of the Spit is Land's End Resort where panoramic views and a big beachside deck are the main attractions. The **Chart Room Restaurant** (907/235-0400 or 800/478-0400, www.lands-end-resort.com) at Lands End is open three meals a day, with decent seafood, steaks, prime rib, and daily dinner specials.

Groceries

Open 24 hours, **Safeway** (on Homer Bypass, 907/235-2408) is the main grocery store in town, but locals shop at the warehouse-style **Save-U-More** (907/235-8661), also on Homer Bypass; free Wi-Fi too.

In addition to its reputation as a halibut fishing center, Homer is famous for oysters, and you'll find **Kachemak Bay oysters** in local restaurants and from a small shop on the Spit. Get fresh halibut, crab, scallops, shrimp, and salmon from **Sully's Dockside Fresh Fish** (907/299-3244), just up the road from the Salty Dawg. Get frozen local seafood on the Spit at **Coal Point Trading Company** (907/235-3877; www.welovefish.com), or sidle up to the bar for seafood chowder, steamed crab, and K-Bay oysters on the half shell.

The fun little **Homer Farmers Market** takes place along Ocean Drive on Saturdays 10 A.M.–2 P.M. and Wednesdays 4–6 P.M. mid-June–late September. The booths carry local produce, arts and crafts, food, and games for kids.

Alcohol
Homer is a great place for those who enjoy locally made spirits. A must-see is **Homer Brewing Company** (1411 Lakeshore Dr., 907/235-3626), where you can sample the China Poot Porter, Old Inlet Pale Ale, Red Knot Scottish, and other specialties before buying a half-gallon growler to go. Once a week the brewery also crafts Zen Chai and Alaska Chai teas.

A surprise is **Bear Creek Winery** (907/235-8484 or 888/649-2176, www.bear creekwinery.com), which produces notable wines from local fruits—try their raspberry-rhubarb wine. Even more unexpected is **Ring of Fire Meadery** (178 E. Bunnell Ave., 907/235-2656, www.ringoffiremeadery.com), where you can sample eight different meads crafted from local fruits. The black current and apple cyder meads are especially popular. Both Bear Creek and the Meadery are open daily in the summer.

INFORMATION AND SERVICES
Stop by the Homer Chamber of Commerce **Visitors Information Center** (on the Homer Bypass at Main St., 907/235-7740, www.homeralaska.org), for local details and a plethora of brochures. It's open Monday–Friday 9 A.M.–7 P.M. and Saturday–Sunday 10 A.M.–6 P.M. Memorial Day–Labor Day; Monday–Friday 9 A.M.–5 P.M. and Saturday 10 A.M.–4 P.M. the rest of September, and Monday–Friday 9 A.M.–5 P.M. the rest of the year.

Homer opened a sparkling new library in 2006, with an atrium fireplace for relaxing, tall windows facing Kachemak Bay, a fun kids room, and plenty of computers and free Wi-Fi for Internet users. Find the **Homer Public Library** (500 Hazel Ave., 907/235-3180, http://library.ci.homer.ak.us) a block up Heath Street from the post office. A number of local business provide **free Wi-Fi hotspots,** including The Washboard (1204 Ocean Dr.), The Alibi (453 E. Pioneer Ave.), Amped Café (111 W. Pioneer), and Coal Towne Coffee (on the Spit).

The **post office** (907/235-6129) is nearby on the Homer Bypass, and **South Peninsula Hospital** (4300 Bartlett St., 907/235-8101, www.sphosp.com) is a fully staffed facility.

GETTING THERE
Air
Homer Airport is out East Kachemak Road, which forks off from the Spit Road. **Era Aviation** (907/235-5205 or 800/866-8394, www.flyera.com) and **Grant Aviation** (907/235-2757 or 888/359-4726, www.flygrant.com) both fly between Homer and Anchorage several times a day.

Two local companies have daily flights from the airport to Seldovia ($75 round-trip) and the Native villages of Nanwalek and Port Graham: **Homer Air** (907/235-8591 or 800/478-8591, www.homerair.com) and **Smokey Bay Air** (907/235-1511 or 888/482-1511).

Homer Stage Line (907/235-2252, www.homerstageline.com) runs to Anchorage, Soldotna, Seward, and all points in between. Service is daily in the summer, and twice a week in the winter.

Ferry
The **Alaska Marine Highway** ferry terminal (907/235-8449, www.ferryalaska.com) is out near the end of the Homer Spit. From here, you can catch the *Tustumena* to Seldovia twice a week, and Kodiak three times weekly. Once a month it runs all the way out to Dutch Harbor in the Aleutians. (See the *Across Kachemak Bay* and *Kachemak Bay State Park* sections for other water-travel options in the Homer area.)

KENAI PENINSULA

© DON PITCHER

Alaska state ferry *Tustumena* on Kachemak Bay

GETTING AROUND

Rent cars at the airport from **Hertz** (907/235-0734 or 800/654-3131, www.rentalcarhomeralaska.com), **Polar Car Rental** (907/235-5998 or 800/876-6417, www.polarcarrental.com), or **Jeeps 4 You** (907/235-8640, www.homercarrental.com). **Adventure Alaska Car Rental** (907/235-4022 or 800/882-2808, www.adventurealaskacars.com) has somewhat lower rates for used cars (starting at $50), and will pick you up anywhere in town.

Call **Chux Cab** (907/235-2489), **Kosta's Taxi** (907/399-8008), or **Kache Cab** (907/235-1950) for a taxi ride.

Water Taxis

A small fleet of boats plies the waters of Kachemak Bay all summer, offering wildlife viewing trips to Gull Island, transport for kayakers and hikers heading into the state park, and access to lodges across the bay. You'll find their offices on the Spit. The following are all good operators: **Bay Excursions** (907/235-7525, www.bayexcursions.com), **Mako's Water Taxi** (907/235-9055, www.makoswatertaxi.com), **Smoke Wagon Water Taxi** (907/235-2947 or 888/205-2947, www.homerwatertaxi.com), **Ashore Water Taxi** (907/399-2340), **Red Mountain Marine** (907/235-6384), **Tutka Bay Taxi** (907/399-1723, www.tutkabaytaxi.com), and **Jakolof Ferry Service** (907/235-6384, www.jakolofferryservice.com). Most of these are seasonal, but Mako's operates year-round.

Tours

The Pratt Museum operates excellent one-and-a-half-hour **walking tours of Homer Spit** and the harbor for $5. These depart Thursday–Saturday at 3 P.M. throughout the summer, and include local history and lots of detail on commercial and sport fishing. Get tickets at the Pratt or in the little booth next to the Salty Dawg Saloon on the Spit. Shelly Erickson of **Homer Tours** (907/235-6200, www.ptialaska.net/~ericson) leads custom van tours of the Homer area.

Across Kachemak Bay

◖ KACHEMAK BAY TOURS AND GULL ISLAND

If you have three days in Homer, spend one of them on beautiful Kachemak Bay. A great way to do this is through a **Natural History Tour** (907/235-6667, www.akcoastalstudies.org, late May–early Sept.) with naturalists from the nonprofit Center for Alaskan Coastal Studies. You'll spend time at bird rookeries, tidepools, rainforest trails, and prehistoric sites, and will gain a lifetime appreciation for the marine world. The eight-hour experience costs $100 ($63 for children under 12), a bargain, and includes a visit to Gull Island during your ride across to Peterson Bay. Bring your own lunch, rubber boots, binoculars, and camera. Overnight stays and kayak trips are also available at the Peterson Bay field station. Their office is in a yurt behind Mako's Water Taxi on the Spit.

Local water taxis lead one-hour Gull Island for $35 per person, or $55 for two hours with time at 60-Foot Rock; **Bay Excursions** (907/235-7525, www.bayexcursions.com) is especially good. **Central Charters** (907/235-7847 or 800/478-7847, www.centralcharter.com) books two other boats that spend time at Gull Island: the *Danny J* on its runs to Halibut Cove, and the *Discovery* as it heads to Seldovia. Water taxis are listed below under *Kachemak Bay State Park*. Watch the Gull Island action in real-time through the "birdcam" on the Web at www.prattmuseum.com.

HALIBUT COVE

Even if you only have two days in Homer, spend half of one visiting this enchanted village (pop. 75) across Kachemak Bay on Ismailof Island. At one time Halibut Cove was the center for a thriving herring fishery, with 36 saltries operating. The fishery collapsed in 1928, and today the town is a small center for artists and fishermen. Halibut Cove has long

KENAI PENINSULA

© DON PITCHER

Gull Island, Kachemak Bay

been known for its picturesque harbor ringed by dense green forests; unfortunately, most of the trees were killed by a devastating spruce bark beetle infestation in the 1990s, so the land is in recovery mode now. The town consists of a long boardwalk that connects shorefront businesses and homes. Learn more about the area at www.halibutcove.com.

Sights

Halibut Cove's boardwalks head out in both directions from the boat dock. Straight ahead, stairs climb steeply to the studio of **Diana Tillion** (907/296-2207), known for her subtle octopus-ink watercolors. Head right on the boardwalk past Clem and Diana Tillion's classic Alaskan home (a resident for over 60 years, Clem is jokingly called "the king of Halibut Cove") to a sandy spit of land that leads to the rustic gallery of acclaimed artist **Alex Combs.** When he isn't around you can always do as the sign says and "Leave money, take pottery and paintings."

Head left on the boardwalk for a 20-minute walk to the Saltry Restaurant. Along the way, you pass a tiny visitor center that makes a good place to escape the rain, before continuing past a large boat-building shop to **Halibut Cove Experience Gallery** (907/296-2215), an excellent cooperative. The boardwalk ends near the Saltry; a working pottery studio is directly behind. A hiking path leads from the boardwalk to a hilltop viewpoint over Halibut Cove. Afterwards, be sure to get an espresso from **Nardelli's** floating coffee stand.

Accommodations

At **Cove Country Cabins** (907/296-2257 or 888/353-2683, www.halibutcovealaska.com) stay in attractive timber-frame cabins, each with a kitchenette, running water, and outhouse, plus a central showerhouse. Cabins range from a little unit ($125 d) to a two-story house ($175 d) with a fine view.

Halibut Cove Lodge (907/235-6891, www.halibutcovelodge.com) has four waterside cabins—each with room for four—at the entrance to Halibut Cove Lagoon. These go for $1600 d for a two-night package including

meals. The owners will be happy to book sea kayaking, bear-viewing, fishing charters, and other activities.

Stillpoint in Halibut Cove (907/296-2283, www.centerforcreativerenewal.com) hosts workshops, retreats, and weddings in an architecturally stunning setting.

Quiet Place Lodge (907/296-2212, www.quietplace.com) features three romantic cabins and all-inclusive packages ($2,880 d for three nights).

Food

Halibut Cove's famous **Saltry Restaurant** (907/296-2223, entrées $22–26) serves daily specials featuring daily pasta specials, a wonderful seafood chowder, Kachemak Bay oysters, and buffalo steaks. Everything is homemade, from the plates to the fresh breads, pies, and chocolate cheesecake. There's a waterfront deck for al fresco dining on a sunny afternoon, a full bar, a clamshell-shaped aquarium filled with tidepool creatures, and a blazing fire in the fire pit. The Saltry is open for lunch and dinner; reservations required for dinners.

Getting There

Most visitors arrive onboard the *Danny J,* a classic wooden boat that has been transporting passengers from Homer Spit to Halibut Cove for decades. It does the run twice daily between Memorial Day and Labor Day. The noon sailing costs $48 adults, $43 seniors, or $25 kids, and includes a tour of the Gull Island bird sanctuary, which Alfred Hitchcock should've known about; wear a hat and breathe through your mouth! After three hours onshore in Halibut Cove, the boat returns to Homer. Its second trip ($25) leaves Homer at 5 P.M., and is only for Halibut Cove residents or visitors with dinner or lodging reservations. For details, contact **Central Charters** (907/235-7847 or 800/478-7847, www.centralcharter.com).

SELDOVIA

A sleepy fishing village (pop. 400), Seldovia (from the Russian for herring) was once the bustling metropolis that Homer is now. The road, the earthquake, and fate exchanged their roles. On the same latitude as Oslo, Norway, Seldovia was first settled by Russians in the early 1800s and became an active fur-trading post. Through the years, Seldovia has had many ocean-oriented industries, from the short-lived herring boom to salmon, king crab, and tanner.

Seldovia is a convenient place for really getting away from it all. Catch a ride over from Homer on the state ferry once a week, or on the tour boats; the tour boats give you two hours to visit, just enough time to wander around town and maybe get to the Otterbahn Trailhead.

Sights and Recreation

Start out by strolling along Main Street. Interpretive signs describe Alaska's Russian history, commercial fishing, the earthquake, and more. The picturesque **Russian Orthodox Church** sits atop a small hill overlooking the town like a proud parent. The Seldovia Tribe's

KENAI PENINSULA

Museum and Visitor Center (907/234-7898, daily 10:30 A.M.–4:30 P.M. in the summer) is across from the boat harbor, with a few exhibits and a computer to check your email. Just up the road is Seldovia Slough, where you can walk the last remaining section of original **boardwalk**—the rest was wiped out in the 1964 earthquake. Up the road the other direction is **Alaska Tribal Cache** (907/234-7875 or 800/270-7810, www.alaskatribalcache.com) selling Native-made jams, jellies, and syrups from local berries.

One of the most fun things to do in Seldovia is to pedal out the road to beautiful Outside Beach and Jakalof Bay where you can savor the great views across Kachemak Bay; Main Street Market (907/234-7631) rents mountain bikes. The **Rocky River Road Trail** at the end of Jakalof Bay Road is a locals' favorite. The well-marked **Otterbahn Trail** leads 1.5 miles from the school grounds around the headland to Outside Beach.

For on-the-water fun, rent a kayak or take a guided tour from **Kayak'Atak** (907/234-7425, www.alaska.net/~kayaks); five-hour tours are $120 per person, including a delicious gourmet lunch.

Seldovia's big party comes around on the **4th of July** when the sleepy town comes alive with a parade, canoe jousting, log rolling, an egg toss, foot race, and food booths.

Accommodations

Seldovia has quite a few B&Bs and other lodging choices; visit the Seldovia Chamber of Commerce's website (www.seldovia.com) for links. **Dancing Eagles B&B** (907/234-7627 summer or 907/332-0041 winter, www.dancing eagles.com, Memorial Day–Labor Day, $85 s or $110 d) has perhaps the finest location in Seldovia, with a big deck perched on the water at the entrance to Seldovia Slough. Rooms include a continental breakfast and private baths. A cabin ($175 d; $50 per person for extra guests) sleeps six and includes a kitchen and bath.

Seldovia Seaport Cottages (907/234-7483, www.acsalaska.net/~seaportcottages,

$110–125 d) has three homey cottages along Seldovia Slough, all with kitchens and baths, plus free bikes to tool around town and Wi-Fi to roam the Web. The largest can sleep eight guests.

Seldovia Rowing Club B&B (907/234-7614, www.seldoviarowingclub.com, $110 d) is another fun over-the-water place where the two suites feature a "nautical Victorian" decor, along with private baths and decks. A big breakfast is served.

Seldovia Bayview Suites (907/234-7631 or 800/478-7898, www.alaskaadventure lodge.com) has spacious three-bed suites that sleep six for $119–159, and a four-room apartment with full kitchen and living room that sleeps up to 10 for $275. The rooms are upstairs over the general store.

Boardwalk Hotel (907/234-7816 or 800/238-7862, www.seldoviaboardwalkhotel.com) is right on the boat harbor; the back patio is a great place to hang out. Small rooms with double beds are $129 d, but a better bet are the larger waterside rooms for $139–149 d. A continental breakfast is included.

Just down the street is **Seldovia Harbor Inn** (907/234-1414, www.seldoviaharborinn.com, $130–145 d), with three comfy units, each with a kitchen. Two of these units open onto a deck with a great harbor view.

Open seasonally, **Bridgekeeper's Inn** (907/234-7535, www.thebridgekeepersinn .com, $125–135 d) overlooks the bridge across Seldovia Slough. Two nicely furnished guest rooms have queen beds, private baths, and full breakfasts.

Alaska Treetops Lodge (907/234-6200, www.alaskatreetops.com) is a luxurious hilltop lodge with a mix of activities for guests, from kayaking and fishing to bear-viewing. Open seasonally, with a maximum of 10 guests, most of whom stay five days or longer.

Camping

Pitch a tent for $5 or park RVs for $8 (no hookups) at **Wilderness Park** (907/234-7643) along Outside Beach. It's 1.5 miles out Jakalof Bay Road, and has a water pump and outhouses.

Showers are available in town across from the boat harbor.

Food

Open three meals daily, **Tide Pool Cafe** (907/234-7502, closed Mon.) is a great lunch spot, with sandwiches, wraps, salads, burgers, and fish and chips. Their deck overlooks the boat harbor, and the glass-top tables are inset with playful beach scenes.

For the best local meal, head to **Mad Fish Restaurant** (907/234-7676, May–Sept.) with a menu of local seafood (including Kachemak Bay oysters), steaks, and Caesar salads for dinner ($19–29), plus lunchtime burgers, fish and chips, and sandwiches.

Fenske's High Tide Originals (907/234-7850) sells new and used books—along with coffee—from a tiny building on pilings just up from the bridge. The covered deck is a good spot to watch the tide come in. Get groceries and supplies from **Main Street Market** (907/234-7633).

Getting There

The **State Ferry** (907/235-8449, www.ferry alaska.com, $32 each way) *Tustumena* sails over to Seldovia from Homer four times a week, taking 90 minutes and laying over for several hours before returning to Homer. **Jim's Seldovia Taxi** (907/234-7848) will haul you around town and out to Jackalof Bay.

Two companies offer summertime trips between the Spit and Seldovia. The 75-foot *Discovery* departs at 11 A.M., stopping to watch the puffins and gulls at Gull Island and the sea otters near Sixty Foot Rock. They dock in Seldovia for three hours—perfect for lunch and a walk around town—before heading back across Kachemak Bay. These very informative tours are $48 adults, $43 seniors, or $25 kids. Make reservations at **Central Charters** (907/235-7847 or 800/478-7847, www.centralcharter.com).

The **Rainbow Tours** (907/235-7272, www .rainbowtours.net) shuttle boat leaves Homer at 10 A.M. returning at 5 P.M. No stops along the way, but the round-trip fare is just $35 adults,

$30 seniors, or $25 kids. The boat continues beyond Seldovia for a full day of whale-watching ($125 adults) around Kennedy Entrance before returning to pick up passengers for the ride back to Homer at 5 P.M.

Two Homer **water taxis** (Mako's, 907/235-9055, www.makoswatertaxi.com, and Smoke Wagon, 907/235-2947 or 888/205-2947, www .homerwatertaxi.com) will set up fun combo trips that include a water taxi to Jackalof Bay, a taxi ride into Seldovia, and a return flight back to Homer for $125.

Both **Homer Air** (907/235-8591 or 800/478-8591, www.homerair.com) and **Smokey Bay Air** (907/235-1511 or 888/482-1511, www.smokey bayair.com) fly the 15-minutes from Homer ($75 round-trip), and also to the Native villages of Port Graham and Nanwalek on a daily basis. **Great Northern Airlines** (907/243-1968 or 800/243-1968, www.gnair.com) flies between Anchorage and Seldovia several times a week in the summer.

KACHEMAK BAY STATE PARK

One of the largest coastal parks in the nation, Kachemak Bay State Park reaches for 200 miles along the southwestern edge of the Kenai Peninsula. Within the park's 400,000 acres are glaciers, high mountains, lakes, islands, beaches, and a scenic rocky shoreline. Highlighted by constantly changing weather patterns, the park's outstanding scenery is a backdrop for high quality recreation. Hiking and camping along the shoreline and in the surrounding forests and mountains are excellent. Above tree line, skiers and hikers will find glaciers and snow fields stretching for miles.

Almost three-quarters of the land here is wilderness; it's officially called Kachemak Bay Wilderness State Park. Land mammals include moose, black bear, mountain goats, coyotes and wolves. Kachemak Bay supports a rich diversity of marine life and is famous for its halibut and salmon fishing, plus the chance to view sea otters, seals, porpoise, and whales. Five very popular public-use cabins are available ($65), along with over 80 miles of hiking trails.

KENAI PENINSULA

Unfortunately, a major spruce bark beetle outbreak in the 1990s left massive stretches of dead forest within Kachemak Bay State Park (and in many other parts of the Kenai Peninsula).

The Kachemak Bay State Park office (907/235-7024, www.alaskastateparks.org) is four miles northwest of Homer along the Sterling Highway.

For something different, **Alaskan Yurt Rentals** (907/235-0132, www.nomadshelter.com, May–Sept.) maintains nine cozy yurts ($65) located at trailheads around the park, including China Poot Bay, Glacier Spit, and Tutka Bay. Each includes wood stove, sleeping space for six, foam mattresses, and a camp stove. These can also be booked through local water taxis.

Grewingk Glacier

For an outstanding day (or multi-night) hike, have the water taxi drop you at the Glacier Spit Trailhead, where an easy and very scenic two-mile hike leads to a lake in front of picture-perfect **Grewingk Glacier.** You can camp nearby, and return via the one-mile **Saddle Trail** which takes you over a small ridge to Halibut Cove, where you can get a ride back to Homer. Water taxis cost $60 per person round-trip. A multitude of side trips are available along this route, including ones that take you high into the alpine over the glacier, and a delightful beach walk. Contact the park for many other hiking options.

Guided sea kayak tours to Grewingk are available through **Three Moose Meadow Guide Service** (907/235-0755 or 888/777-0930, www.threemoose.com). These cost $155 per person, including a water taxi from Homer, a hike to the lake, and inflatable kayaks to paddle up to the glacier. Fly-in trips are $255.

Access

In addition to the daily summertime boat tours of Kachemak Bay, local water taxis provide hiker or sea kayaker drop-offs within park waters, for around $65 per person round-trip, or

Grewingk Glacier, near Homer

© DON PITCHER

$95 per person for a sea kayak and transport. No extra charge for kayaks or bikes. Local operators are listed under *Getting Around* in the *Homer* section.

Remote Cabins and Lodges

A number of delightful lodges fill coves surrounding Kachemak Bay State Park. Note, however, that spruce bark beetles have killed the forest in much of this area, so it may not look quite as nice as the Web photos. One exception is Tutka Bay Wilderness Lodge, where the beetles have not (yet at least) wreaked havoc.

For a wonderful escape, **Porter's Alaskan Adventures** (907/235-8060, www .portersak.com) rents three modern cabins on the shore of Hesketh Island near the mouth of Tutka Bay, seven miles from Homer. All cabins contain full kitchens, decks, and waterfront views, but you'll need to bring sleeping bags. There's a sauna on the beach for bathing, and an outhouse in the back. Four people can stay here for $125 on weekdays or $150 on weekends; add $50 per person for the water taxi from Homer. Sea kayak rentals are available.

Sadie Cove Wilderness Lodge (907/235-2350 or 888/283-7234, www.sadiecove.com) is an off-the-grid wilderness retreat in the heart of Kachemak Bay State Park. Guests stay in quaint cabins built by Keith and Randi Iverson, who have lived here since the 1970s. This is a place to escape to a quieter time, so you won't find in-room phones, Wi-Fi, or TVs, though they do have a sauna and creekside bathhouse, communal lounge, and professional chef. Lodging, three meals, and kayaks cost $300 per person/day, plus $90 for the water taxi from Homer. A two-night minimum is required, but most guests book for five nights.

Tutka Bay Wilderness Lodge (907/235-3905 or 800/606-3909, www.tutkabaylodge.com, mid-May–mid-Sept.) occupies the south shore of Kachemak Bay between Halibut Cove and Seldovia, nine water miles from the Spit. The lodge caters to nature lovers, photographers, bird-watchers, and anglers with an appreciation for the finer things in life, and a willingness to pay dearly. Two-night minimum stays will set you back $1,540 for two people, but this does include round-trip transportation from Homer and delicious family-style meals. Activities include boat tours, guided walks, beachcombing, clam digging, wildlife viewing, or just soaking in the hot tub (all included), plus sea kayaking, sportfishing, and bear-viewing (extra fee for these). Accommodations are luxurious; no roughing-it here!

Otter Cove Resort (907/235-7770 or 800/426-6212, www.ottercoveresort.com, late May–early Sept.) sits along Eldred Passage, five miles by boat from the end of Homer Spit. Two duplex cabins provide rustic accommodations with bunk beds, electricity, and showers for a reasonable $80 d, but you'll need to bring sleeping bags (or rent one). Kayak rentals and tours are available and hiking trails lead up to the alpine. The restaurant specializes in seafood and filet mignon, and it is open for lunch and dinner; overnight guests can use the cook shack to prepare their own breakfasts. This is also a popular destination for day-guests who come to dine in the Rookery Restaurant or to enjoy a drink on the waterside deck. Otter Cove is owned by Homer Ocean Charters, which has a variety of day-tour options, including a four-hour trip that include a wildlife boat tour from the Homer Spit and lunch at the restaurant for $55. Transportation to the restaurant for dinner costs just $20 roundtrip; dinner entrées cost $24–31.

Peterson Bay Lodge (907/235-7156 or 866/899-7156, www.petersonbaylodge.com) occupies the head of this remote bay where the owners raise the famous Kachemak Bay oysters. Guests stay in four surprisingly comfortable canvas-walled cabins with screened porches, a sauna, and access to the lodge kitchen to cook meals. Upon arrival, they are given a tour of the oyster farm, along with the chance to sample fresh oysters and mussels. Lodging, kayaks, and a continental breakfast costs $145 per person; a water taxi from Homer is $60 extra.

THE WRANGELLS AND PRINCE WILLIAM SOUND

This sprawling region includes several mountain ranges and gorgeous Prince William Sound. The Wrangell Mountains and St. Elias Mountains form the backbone of massive Wrangell–St. Elias National Park and Preserve, home to the second highest peak in the United States (18,008-ft. Mt. St. Elias), a glacier larger than Rhode Island, towering volcanoes, and country that seems to define the word spectacular. The park is located on the eastern margin of Alaska and is bordered by Canada's Kluane National Park and Tatshenshini-Alsek Park, and Southeast Alaska's Glacier Bay National Park. Together they include more than 24 million acres—the largest protected area on planet earth. The equally impressive Copper River drains much of the Wrangells, reaching the Gulf of Alaska east of Cordova. Given the grandeur of this country, the settlements seem minor in this part of Alaska; largest are Glennallen, Copper Center, and Chitina. Two primary roads cut through this country: the east–west Glenn Highway and the north–south Richardson Highway.

Prince William Sound arcs around the Gulf of Alaska, encompassing a multitude of densely forested islands, dissected bays, and rugged coastlines, with the Chugach Mountains forming a glacier-topped northern border. Virtually all of this wild county lies within Chugach National Forest, the nation's second largest national forest. Within the Sound are three towns: Whittier on the west is connected by tunnel and road to Anchorage, Valdez on the north serves as the terminus of the Alyeska Pipeline, and the fishing town of Cordova on the east provides a gateway to the Copper River.

HIGHLIGHTS

(**Matanuska Glacier:** One hundred miles from Anchorage on the Glenn Highway, this is a good place to get out on the ice – and under it in ice caves (page 295).

(**McCarthy Road:** This 60-mile gravel road cuts into the heart of magnificent Wrangell-St. Elias National Park along an old railroad bed. The Kusulana River bridge is a high point (literally) with the river 400 heart-stopping feet below (page 302).

(**McCarthy:** Think *Northern Exposure* with fewer residents and older buildings; this is a wonderful end-of-the-road settlement from another era. Park your car on the other side of the river and walk the footbridge into town (page 303).

(**Kennicott:** Just five miles up the road from McCarthy are the enormous red buildings from the heyday of copper mining a century ago. The Park Service offers historical tours and concessionaires guide hikes onto Root Glacier (page 303).

(**Thompson Pass:** North of Valdez, the Edgerton Highway climbs over this scenic alpine pass. Stop at Worthington Glacier for a hike, and come back in winter for world-class heli-skiing (page 309).

(**Keystone Canyon:** The Lowe River drops through this narrow canyon where high waterfalls plunge from the cliffs. Located just north of Valdez, this is a popular spot for summertime rafting and winter ice climbing (page 310).

(**Prince William Sound Boat Tours:** Several companies operate day trips from Valdez or Whittier, offering the chance to see glaciers (especially massive Columbia Glacier), sea lions, otters, and the occasional killer whale (page 316).

(**Copper River Highway:** One of Alaska's finest backroads, this 50-mile gravel road leads from Cordova to the Million Dollar Bridge over the Copper River, with opportunities for hiking and wildlife viewing along the way (page 323).

(**Childs Glacier:** Located near the end of the Copper River Highway, this very active glacier dumps enormous chunks of ice into the river on a regular basis. There's nothing like it anywhere in Alaska (page 324).

LOOK FOR (TO FIND RECOMMENDED SIGHTS, ACTIVITIES, DINING, AND LODGING.

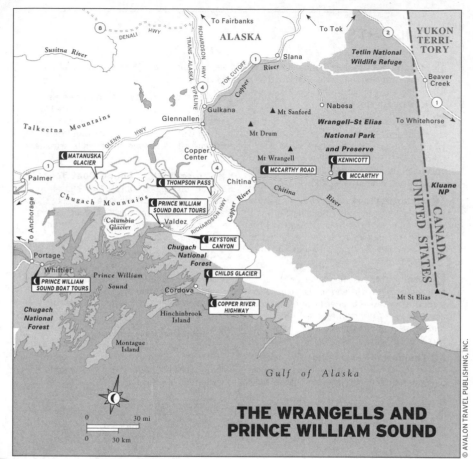

© AVALON TRAVEL PUBLISHING, INC.

PLANNING YOUR TIME

From Anchorage, it is an easy day trip by car or train to the town of Whittier, where state ferries provide connections to the remote town of Cordova as well as Valdez, which is on the road system. A fun one-week loop (it could be done in three days if you saw everything in a blur) would allow time to see Cordova, Valdez, and Wrangell–St. Elias National Park before circling back to Anchorage.

The Glenn Highway connects Anchorage with the town of Glennallen, passing **Matanuska Glacier** (a fun spot for guided glacier hikes) at Mile 102. The mighty Copper River and 13 million-acre Wrangell–St. Elias National Park lie just east of Glennallen. For a wonderful taste of this country, turn east on the Edgerton Highway to the dusty and rusty collection of old buildings called Chitina, then out the gravel **McCarthy Road** for 50 miles to the heart of the Wrangells. The route follows an old railroad bed, with an amazing high bridge and fine vistas en route to the tiny town of **McCarthy,** accessible from a footbridge across the Kennicott River. Vans will shuttle you to **Kennicott,** where colorful old copper mine buildings are wedged between glaciers and mountain peaks.

Back out on the Richardson Highway, the road climbs south through the alpine at **Thompson Pass** and past Worthington Glacier, before dropping through narrow **Keystone Canyon** where high waterfalls plummet off cliffs. The road ends at Valdez, terminus of the Trans-Alaska Pipeline, and a jumping-off point for **touring Prince William**

Sound. The ferry system provides access to the fishing town of Cordova near the mouth of the Copper River. A 50-mile gravel road, the **Copper River Highway** ends near the Million Dollar Bridge. A short distance away is **Childs Glacier,** where icebergs thunder into the river; this may be the most dramatic glacier in Alaska. Ferries also connect Cordova with the little town of Whittier, where a 2.5-mile tunnel cuts through the mountains and the road leads back to Anchorage.

Copper River Valley

GLENN HIGHWAY

Named for Captain Edwin Glenn, an early Army explorer of the area, the **Glenn Highway** (Route 1) stretches 328 miles from downtown Anchorage to Tok, where it joins the Alaska Highway. Most of the Glenn was built during the corridor-construction craze of 1942, first from Tok to Gulkana, where it joins the Richardson Highway, then from Glennallen, where it leaves the Richardson, and finally to Palmer. Palmer was already connected to Anchorage by rail; the final 42 miles of road were completed a few years later.

Twenty miles east of Palmer is the tiny settlement of **Sutton** (pop. 470). Of interest here is the nonprofit **Alpine Historical Park** (907/745-7000, daily 9 A.M.–7 P.M. Memorial Day–Labor Day), with its collection of historical buildings, coal mining relics, and Athabascan Indian artifacts.

At Mile 72 (30 miles from Palmer), **Castle Mountain B&B** (907/745-7818, www .castlemountainb-b.com, $75–125 d) is a bright, modern log home with a large deck facing King Mountain, three guest rooms with shared or private baths, Wi-Fi, and big breakfasts. Friendly owners too. Four miles up the road is **King Mountain State Recreation Area,** a large, beautiful campground with water, outhouses, and choice spots right on the Matanuska River (though the interior loop might be less windy) for $15. The site faces

King Mountain across the river—a perfect triangular peak.

Based in Chickaloon at Mile 77, **Nova Riverrunners** (907/745-5753 or 800/746-5753, www.novalaska.com) guides daily summertime raft trips. Two options are a white-water ride along the Matanuska River past dramatic Lion Head (Class IV) for $90–100 or an easy float trip along lower reaches of the river for $75 adults or $40 kids. The company also does a variety of multi-night trips around Alaska.

A few miles up is **Long Lake State Recreation Area,** Mile 85, where you can stretch your legs. A handful of free campsites are available; no water.

At Mile 98, pull out your binoculars and glass slopes to the north for scattered bunches of white dots—Dall sheep like to congregate here, apparently for a mineral lick on the hillside.

【 Matanuska Glacier

Located at Mile 102 of the Glenn Highway, Matanuska Glacier is a don't-miss highlight. Today, this glacier is 27 miles long and four miles wide; 18,000 years ago it occupied Palmer, but it hasn't done much in the last 400 years. Much of the land in front of the glacier is owned by Jack Kimball, who spent decades developing a road and bridges to a bluff overlooking the ice. Access to **Glacier Park** (907/745-2534 or 888/253-4480, www.matanuskaglacier.com,

May–mid-October) costs $15 adults, $12.50 seniors, $10 students, $5 ages 6–12, and free for younger kids. You can hike on the easier sections with tennis shoes, but will need a guide for the steeper parts of the glacier. Glacier Park also has a snack bar and close-to-the glacier campsites for $15 (plus your admission), but no water. Based just up the road, **MICA Guides** (907/351-7587 or 800/956-6422, www.micaguides.com) leads glacier hiking trips ($40) that often include the chance to explore an ice cave, and ice climbing adventures ($130); entrance to Glacier Park is additional.

Out along the highway is **Matanuska Glacier State Recreation Site** ($15), on a hillside overlooking the ice giant. Nearby is **Long Rifle Lodge** (907/745-5151 or 800/770-5151, www.longriflelodge.com), with homemade meals, a lounge, and motel rooms ($75 d with private bath). However, the real reason to stop here is the view from the dining room of the nearby glacier and valleys—it's hard to keep your eyes on your plate with this mountain panorama in front of you.

Over Eureka Summit

After Long Rifle, it's another 85 miles east to Glennallen and the intersection of the Glenn and Richardson Highways. If you have a chance to make this drive in September, by all means, do it. The acres of aspen trees along this route turn a brilliant gold, and the contrasting dark green spruce, combined with the backdrop of glaciers and snowcapped peaks, make for some extraordinary photo ops. You'll be tempted to pull off at every twist in the road to burn film and take in the surroundings. **Grand View RV Park** (Mile 110, 907/746-4480, www.grandviewrv.com) has RV sites, cottages, and a café.

(**Sheep Mountain Lodge** (907/745-5121 or 877/645-5121, www.sheepmountain.com) at Mile 113 is a rustic summer and winter destination. Its greenhouses and flower gardens add to the gorgeous mountain-backed setting in the summer, and the lodge serves home-cooked meals (summer only). Eleven cabins all have private baths and wonderful views; $135 d for

standard units or $189 d with kitchens. Basic hostel-style dorm rooms with a shared bath are a great bargain: $60 for up to four people. The glassed-in hot tub is a great place to relax after a winter day of skiing on the 10 miles of groomed trails.

Two miles away is **Majestic Valley Wilderness Lodge** (907/746-2930, www.majesticvalley lodge.com), another place with a country setting and grand vistas. Guests stay in motel rooms ($105 s or $115 d), or cabins ($125 s or $135 d) and have access to a wood-heated sauna.

Slide Mountain Cabins (at Mile 135, 907/822-5864, www.rvparkalaska.com) has recently built log cabins: $99 d with private baths, or $75 d for ones that share a shower house. RV spaces are $20, tent sites cost $7.

When you get past **Eureka Summit** (Mile 130), you're in caribou country, so scan the open ground everywhere for members of the Nelchina herd. From Eureka to Glennallen, and then north on the Richardson Highway toward Tok, it's possible to spot caribou almost anywhere. Slow down and keep your eyes open to avoid colliding with one. Lodging, RV spots, and meals are available near the summit at **Eureka Lodge** (907/822-3808, www.eurekalodge.com); $85 d for motel rooms with private baths, $75 d for simple cabins with a shower house. In the winter, this is a vary popular snowmobiling destination. Pitch a tent at **Little Nelchina State Recreation Site** at Mile 138; no charge.

Located 17 miles west of Glennallen at Mile 170 **Tolsona Lake Resort** (907/822-3433 or 800/245-3342, www.tolsonalakeresort.com) is of the Glenn Highway, with a motel ($125 d), suites ($175 for four), plus a restaurant and bar.

Three miles up the road toward Glennallen is **Tolsona Wilderness Campground** (907/822-3865, www.tolsona.com, $32 RVs, $15 tents). A collection of 1920s logging camp artifacts fills the little museum here.

Lake Louise

At Mile 160 of the Glenn Highway (27 miles west of Glennallen), the Lake Louise Road turns north, continuing 19 miles to this popular summer fishing and winter snowmobiling destination. The **Lake Louise State Recreation Area** has campsites ($15) and a swimming area for those who can brave the water.

Stay at **Lake Louise Lodge** (907/822-3311 or 877/878-3311, www.lakelouiselodge.com), where the log building overlooks the lake. Modern rooms cost $90–130 d, including private baths, plus use of canoes. Simple cabins are $59–79 d with shared bath in the lodge. A restaurant and bar are here, and you can also rent motorboats. Open year-round.

The Point Lodge at Lake Louise (907/822-5566 or 800/808-2018, www.the pointlodge.com has comfortable rooms with panoramic views from a wraparound deck. Rates are $89 s or $99–119 d in the lodge (shared bath) or $79 d in cabins (baths in the lodge). Guests in all units get a full breakfast, and can use the sauna, canoe, and paddleboat. Family-style dinners are available.

GLENNALLEN AND VICINITY
At Mile 187 of the Glenn, just before the junction with the Richardson Highway, is this small service town, named for both Edwin Glenn and Henry Allen, leader of the first expedition up the Copper River. Strung along both sides of the road, Glennallen (pop. 900) is the gateway to the big Copper River Valley country and Wrangell–St. Elias National Park.

Glennallen is an odd amalgamation of businesses, including the standard gas stations, motels, and food stops, along with seven churches and three liquor stores. This is the heart of right-wing Christian Alaska, as you will quickly discover with a spin of the radio dial; KCAM 790 AM dominates the air waves with stirring messages of conversion along with its "Caribou Clatters" for those without phone service. The station beams out from the small campus of the Alaska Bible College in Glennallen (www.akbible.edu). Fortunately, the area now also has a repeater for the public radio station out of Valdez, KCHU.

The best thing about Glennallen is its setting. As you approach Glennallen from the west—if the weather's clear—there's a stunning view of the Wrangell Mountains: Mt.

Drum is the beautiful snowcapped peak right in the middle at 12,010 feet elevation, Mt. Sanford is just to the north (left) of it at 16,237 feet, and Mt. Wrangell is to the south at 14,163 feet. It's an incredible backdrop for a very ordinary junction town.

The **Greater Copper River Valley Visitor Center** (907/822-5555, www.travelto alaska.com) occupies the highway junction at the Hub gas station, and is open daily 9 A.M.– 7 P.M. Memorial Day–Labor Day, plus reduced hours in mid-May and early September (closed winters). You'll find exhibits on local attractions and details about every place between Tok and Cordova. The Wells Fargo Bank has an ATM for cash. Warning: the State Troopers have a base in Glennallen, so don't even think about exceeding the speed limit for 50 miles in any direction!

Accommodations
Caribou Hotel (907/822-3302 or 800/478-3302, www.caribouhotel.com) is the largest place in town, but it gets negative reviews from many travelers. Choose from overpriced rooms ($143 d) and suites ($168 for up to six) in the main building, or very basic little rooms with twin beds and communal baths ($69 s or $79 d) in an old Atco unit. Apartments and cabins are also available, and the hotel has a guest computer, Wi-Fi, and a so-so restaurant. Anywhere but Glennallen and this hotel wouldn't survive!

Located 11 miles north of Glennallen, **Bear Creek Cabin** (907/822-5852, $100 d) has a clean and nicely appointed cabin with a full kitchen, continental breakfast, and a spectacular view of the Wrangells.

Historic **Gakona Lodge** (907/822-3482, www.gakonalodge.com) sits along the Gakona and Copper rivers, 18 miles north of Glennallen. Built in the 1920s, the picturesque log building includes a bar, seasonal dinner-only restaurant (steaks, burgers, and chicken), and gift shop with locally made Native crafts. Old-fashioned rooms are $95 d with shared baths.

Three miles up the Tok Cutoff from Gakona Lodge (21 miles north of Glennallen) is

Riverview B&B (907/822-3321, www.alaska. net/~riverv, $90–100 d), with great views across the Copper River to the Wrangell Mountains. Ten guest rooms (seven with private baths and entrances) are available with decks, king or twin beds, and a full breakfast. Next door is laid-back **River Wrangellers** (907/822-3967 or 888/822-3967, www.alaskariverwrangellers.com), offering rafting and fishing trips down nearby rivers.

Other local lodging options include **Little Cabin in the Woods B&B** (907/822-4007), and **Fireweed Hill B&B** (907/822-3627, www.alaska.net/~dmbowler).

Camping
The state's **Dry Creek Campground** ($10) is five miles north of the Glenn-Richardson junction and has pit toilets and too-friendly mosquitoes. **Northern Nights Campground & RV Park** (907/822-3199, www.northern-nights-rv.com, May–Sept., $22 RVs, $12 tents; showers extra) is the nicest local RV park, with a wooded setting, Wi-Fi, room for big rigs, and free desserts on Monday and Friday nights.

Food
Particularly popular with locals is **The Freeze** (907/822-3923), serving fried chicken, burgers, hot dogs, pita wraps, shakes, malts, and ice cream for $5–8. Nothing low-calorie about this place!

Brown Bear Rhodehouse (907/822-3663), three miles west of the junction at Mile 184 of the Glenn Highway, is famous for its hunting lodge atmosphere where dead critters stare from the walls. The filet mignon is great, and they also serve sandwiches, seafood, and roasted chicken. Even if you aren't hungry, stop by to take a gander at the photos or to talk with the locals about those Damn Outside Environmeddlers (unless you are one).

Omni Parks Place (907/822-3334) is a surprisingly large grocery store with a deli, fresh produce, and espresso.

Getting There
Alaska Direct Bus Line (907/277-6652 or 800/770-6652, www.alaskadirectbusline.com) has service to Glennallen, continuing on to Whitehorse, Fairbanks, or Anchorage. Buses run three times a week in the summer, twice weekly in winter.

Glennallen's airport is just north of town, but for some reason it's officially called the Gakona Airport. **Ellis Air Taxi** (907/822-3368 or 800/478-3368, www.ellisair.com) will fly you from Glennallen to McCarthy for $109, or from Anchorage to McCarthy for $299. Other air taxis include **Alaskan AirVentures** (907/822-3905) and **Copper Valley Air Service** (907/822-4200 or 866/570-4200, www.coppervalleyair.com).

Wrangell–St. Elias National Park and Preserve

Though somewhat less accessible than Denali, this park is an excellent alternative to the crowds, clouds, wows, and crying-out-louds. The mountains (Chugach, Wrangells, and St. Elias) are incredible, and Mt. Wrangell—highest volcano in Alaska at 14,163 feet—sometimes puffs away on earth's crustal cigar. In fact, of the 16 tallest mountains in North America, nine are in this park! The icefields are world class, and their glacial tentacles rival any in the state. The Copper River can provide weeks-long raft or canoe rides, with all the fish you can stand. The wildlife is abundant, and this park even has beaches on the Gulf of Alaska. Two roads plunge deep into the park's wildlands, and bus and plane service are available.

This is the largest national park in the country (larger than southern New England), with over 12 million acres; along with Kluane Na-

tional Park across the Canadian border, the whole area was the first designated UN World Heritage Site. Finally, you don't need backcountry permits to traipse around or camp on this federal land—just pick a direction and backpack until you crack. But you will certainly need mosquito repellent and a headnet; the bugs can get downright vicious!

ORIENTATION

The large **Wrangell–St. Elias National Park and Preserve Visitor Center** (907/822-7440, www.nps.gov/wrst, daily 8 A.M.–6 P.M. in the summer, Mon.–Fri. 8 A.M.–4:30 P.M. the rest of the year) is at Mile 107 on the Richardson, seven miles south of Glennallen. Rangers can help with trip planning or sell you books and topographic maps. Talks and guided walks are offered daily, and an acclaimed 20-minute film

© DON PITCHER

a blue pool on Root Glacier

PRINCE WILLIAM SOUND

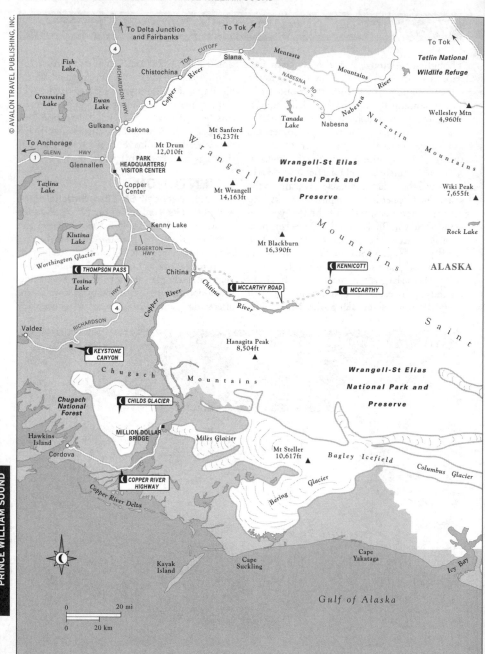

© AVALON TRAVEL PUBLISHING, INC.

PRINCE WILLIAM SOUND

To Delta Junction and Fairbanks

To Tok

Fish Lake

Crosswind Lake

Ewan Lake

TOK CUTOFF

Chistochina

Slana

Mentasta Mountains

Tetlin National Wildlife Refuge

To Tok

NABESNA RD

Nabesna River

RICHARDSON HWY

Copper River

Gulkana

Gakona

Mt Sanford 16,237ft

Tanada Lake

Nabesna

Nutzotin Mountains

Wellesley Mtn 4,960ft

To Anchorage

GLENN HWY

Glennallen

PARK HEADQUARTERS/ VISITOR CENTER

Mt Drum 12,010ft

Wrangell-St Elias National Park and Preserve

Wiki Peak 7,655ft

Tazlina Lake

Copper Center

Mt Wrangell 14,163ft

Wrangell

Klutina Lake

Kenny Lake

Mt Blackburn 16,390ft

Mountains

Rock Lake

ALASKA

Worthington Glacier

EDGERTON HWY

THOMPSON PASS

Chitina

KENNICOTT

Tosina Lake

Chitina River

MCCARTHY ROAD

MCCARTHY

Saint

RICHARDSON HWY

Copper River

Hanagita Peak 8,504ft

Valdez

KEYSTONE CANYON

Chugach Mountains

Wrangell-St Elias National Park and Preserve

Chugach National Forest

CHILDS GLACIER

Hawkins Island

Cordova

MILLION DOLLAR BRIDGE

Miles Glacier

Mt Steller 10,617ft

Bagley Icefield

Columbus Glacier

COPPER RIVER HIGHWAY

Copper River Delta

Bering Glacier

Glacier

Kayak Island

Cape Suckling

Cape Yakataga

Icy Bay

Gulf of Alaska

0   20 mi
0   20 km

WRANGELL-ST ELIAS NATIONAL PARK AND PRESERVE

about the park shows hourly. Outside, an easy trail leads through the forest to a vista point overlooking the Copper River and three of the park's most prominent peaks: Mt. Drum, Mt. Wrangell, and Mt. Blackburn. Seasonal ranger stations are in McCarthy, Kennicott, Chitina, and Yakutat.

Air taxis and charter services can drop you off anywhere inside the park, with most flights departing from Glennallen/Gulkana, Cordova, Chitina, or McCarthy.

Nabesna Road

Ground access to the park is via the Edgerton Highway and McCarthy Road in the center, and the Nabesna Road on the north side. The 42-mile Nabesna Road turns off at Mile 65 of the Tok Cutoff, and leads to the abandoned gold mining town of Nabesna. The Park Service maintains the **Slana Ranger Station** (907/822-5238, daily 8 A.M.–5 P.M. in the summer and weekdays 8 A.M.–4:30 P.M. the rest of the year), just up Nabesna Road from the junction.

Nabesna area lodging and RV options are at **Hart D Ranch** (907/822-3973, www.hartd.com) and a charming log home at **Nabesna House B&B** (907/822-4284, www.nabesnahouse.com).

Located at Mile 4 of the Nabesna Road, **Huck Hobbit's Homestead** (907/822-3196) has three cabins with hostel-type accommodations for a budget price: $20 per person. The setting is quiet, and the owners also offer the full-service version with all meals, guided fishing, and entertainment for $100 per person. This is the real deal in a picturesque setting.

RIVER RUNNING

Cordova-based **Alaska River Expeditions** (907/424-7238 or 800/776-1864, www.alaskarafters.com) leads a variety of rafting trips inside the park, including a five-day float ($1,975) on the powerful Copper River, and 10-day trips ($3,650) that begin in McCarthy and continue all the way to the Million Dollar Bridge near Cordova. All trips start with a scenic floatplane flight into the park.

Operating from McCarthy, in the heart

PRINCE WILLIAM SOUND

of the park, **Copper Oar** (907/554-4453 or 800/523-4453, www.copperoar.com) offers a float-and-fly day trip that includes a float down the Kennicott and Nizina Rivers followed by a flight back to McCarthy for $265. The company also runs a wide variety of longer floats.

Gakona-based **River Wrangellers** (907/822-3967 or 888/822-3967, www.alaska riverwrangellers.com) has Class III trips down the Klutina River ($99 for four hours), and the accessible Tonsina River ($190 for eight hours). They also rent out rafts and other river gear, and provide shuttles for do-it-yourselfers.

St. Elias Guides (907/554-4445 or 888/933-5427, www.steliasguides.com) offers multi-day raft trips in the Wrangells, starting with a three-day trip down the Chitina River for $990.

MCCARTHY AND KENNICOTT

The McCarthy-Kennicott area is a mostly private island surrounded by the vast Wrangell–St. Elias National Park. This was once an incredibly important copper mining area, but today it contains Alaska's most famous almost-ghost towns. Access to the area is via the McCarthy Road, which leads from the town of Chitina to the Kennicott River. Located within Wrangell–St. Elias National Park and Preserve, the historic Kennecott Mine contains picturesque old buildings right alongside Kennicott Glacier, with the pinnacles of snowcapped mountains ringing the horizon.

History

Prospectors discovered rich copper deposits at Kennecott Mine in 1900, and at its peak the mine employed some 600 workers. (Note: Because of a typographic error when the mine was established, the mine, town, and company names are spelled Kennecott, while the glacier, river, and valley are generally spelled Kennicott.) The mines, in their nearly 30 years of operation, extracted $220 million in rich ore, nearly 70 percent copper, with a little silver and gold on the side. The Alaska Syndicate—owned by J. P. Morgan and Daniel Guggenheim—held the controlling interest. They also owned the

CR&NW railroad, which freighted the ore to tidewater, plus the Alaska Steamship Co., which shipped the ore to Tacoma, Washington.

The mines shut down in 1938 when world copper prices dropped and the cost of production became prohibitive. After the mine's closure, the buildings were abandoned and gradually deteriorated. Today, these dark red buildings are in varying states of disrepair. They—and 3,000 acres of surrounding land—were purchased by the Park Service in 1998, and the agency is spending millions of dollars to stabilize and rebuild the buildings. You can walk through the beautifully restored structures, or take a guided tour through ones still being worked on.

◖ McCarthy Road

Cutting into the heart of the Wrangells, this challenging road follows an old railroad route past ragged mountain peaks, picturesque ponds where you'll hear loons (and buzzing mosquitoes), and sweeping vistas of the mighty Copper River. This could be the longest 60-mile road in Alaska—plan on three hours from Chitina, several more if it's clear and you stop for the views of the Wrangells. Despite the old horror stories, the road has been substantially improved in the last few years and is in fairly good shape, but you may have to contend with choking dust if it hasn't rained recently. There are tire repair and towing services in Chitina and McCarthy, along with various lodging options as you approach McCarthy. You may be tempted to speed on the road at times, but try to keep around 30 mph since you never know what's around the next bend. It's also a good idea to have a full-size spare tire.

Note that many car rental and RV companies will not allow their vehicles on the McCarthy Road. Of course this doesn't stop folks from driving the road. As one lodge owner told me, "If everyone obeyed that rule I wouldn't have any guests!"

At Mile 16, get ready for an adrenaline-pumping drive across the **Kuskulana River** on a narrow three-span bridge built in 1910 by the railroad and improved in 1988 (when guardrails were added). The bridge is nearly 600 feet long and sits almost 400 feet above the water—perfect, in other words, for bungee jumping, which does take place here. Another attraction is the abandoned railroad trestle across the Gilahina River at Mile 28. Just before the end of the road is a spectacular overlook of the town of McCarthy, the surrounding mountains, and the Kennicott and Root glaciers.

The road ends on the west side of the Kennicott River, and parking is available ($5/day) on nearby private land. Footbridges cross the river and a smaller tributary. Once across, walk up the road; the right fork takes you a mile to McCarthy, the left fork nearly five miles to Kennicott. Shuttle buses ($5 each way) transport visitors from McCarthy to Kennicott, and mountain bikes are available to rent nearby. Backcountry Connection (see *Transportation*) provides van service to McCarthy from Glennallen or Chitina.

McCarthy

The quaint little settlement of McCarthy (pop. 25) was a boomtown from the early 1900s to 1939, serving the copper workers at Kennicott mines and the railroad workers on the Copper River and Northwestern. At its peak, the town was full of hotels, restaurants, bars, and pool halls, along with the obligatory red light district. Today it's a busy base from which outdoor enthusiasts explore spectacular mountain country and the nearby mine buildings in Kennicott. The tiny **McCarthy-Kennicott Museum** is open daily in the summertime; find it just as you arrive in McCarthy from the footbridge. Inside are interesting photos, maps, and artifacts. A model of the Bonanza mine occupies the adjacent boxcar.

Downtown McCarthy is a fun place to wander about, with dogs lazing on the dirt streets, lots of interesting buildings to explore, and a mix of businesses offering lodging, food, and various adventures. You'll hear the hum of generators behind the log buildings, and the buzz of mosquitoes around your head. McCarthy also has a delightfully old fashioned **4th of July** celebration with a parade and live music.

The old McCarthy Hotel is the primary gathering place, with lodging, meals, and a fine gallery called **Mountain Arts.**

Kennicott

The dark red buildings of the Kennicott Mine are sandwiched between steep mountains and massive glaciers in the semi–ghost town of Kennicott, located five miles from McCarthy on a dirt road. It's a pleasant (but all uphill) mountain bike ride, or pay $5 each way for a ride from two shuttle companies. Vans run back and forth daily in the summer, at half-hour intervals in the peak season.

The Park Service's **Kennicott Visitor Center** (907/554-4417) is open daily 9 A.M.–5:30 P.M. Memorial Day–Labor Day. Rangers offer daily nature and history hikes. Most historic Kennicott Mine buildings are open only for guided tours, but you can visit the restored recreation hall. Visitors are welcome to explore the building exteriors, but watch for nails, glass, and metal scraps underfoot, and don't try to walk on decks or stairs alongside the buildings since the boards may be unsafe.

St. Elias Guides (907/554-4445 or 888/933-5427, www.steliasguides.com) lead educational 3.5-hour historic tours ($25 per person) of Kennicott Mine buildings. The company's specialty is 4–16-day mountaineering expeditions and backcountry hikes in the St. Elias Range, but it also offers glacier day hikes and ice climbing, along with all-day trips to Jumbo Mine or Erie Mine ($95) and various fly-in and rafting adventures.

For a taste of this magnificent place, join **Kennicott Wilderness Guides** (907/554-4444 or 800/664-4537, www.kennicottguides.com) on one of their half-day glacier hikes ($55 per person) or all-day ice climbing treks ($110). These require a 1.5-mile hike to the glacier, where you put on crampons and head out to explore the other-worldly terrain of creeks that abruptly disappear and deep aquamarine pools, all backed by an incredible ring of peaks. The company also leads fly-in backcountry trips and multi-day mountaineering and glacier skills courses. Highly recommended.

An easy and popular hike or mountain bike ride follows the east side of Kennicott Glacier and Root Glacier. When the weather cooperates, hikers are treated to striking views of Mt. Blackburn, Regal Mountain, and Donaho Peak. Take the old road north from Kennecott Mine for a half-mile, turning left when it diverges. The trail follows the Root Glacier, crossing bridges over Bonanza Creek and Jumbo Creek along the way. At approximately 1.25 miles, a side trail leads to primitive campsites near the glacier. An outhouse is nearby, and storage lockers are available to keep food away from the bears that sometimes roam through. The Kennicott Visitor Center has additional details on this and other local hikes.

Fireweed Mountain Arts and Crafts (907/554-4500, late May–mid-Sept.) sells quality works by Alaskan artists and has a wonderful back deck overlooking Kennicott Glacier. They're just downhill from Kennicott Glacier Lodge

Accommodations

In McCarthy, stay at the historic—built in 1916— **McCarthy Lodge** (907/554-4402, www.mccarthylodge.com), the true heart and soul of the area. Friendly owner Neil Darish offers two divergent lodging choices. **Lancaster's Backpacking Hotel** ($48 s or $68 d, mid-May through September) has no-frills private rooms with twin beds, shared baths, and a common area. Considerably more upscale is **Ma Johnson's Hotel** (open year-round, $109 s or $159 d), where the six bedrooms are furnished in period antiques and share three baths. There's even an ATM in the bar.

Located near the end of the McCarthy Road, **Kennicott River Lodge & Hostel** (907/554-4441, www.kennicottriverlodge.com, mid-May–mid-Sept.) has a variety of pleasant lodging choices, all with access to a full kitchen, common area (satellite TV), shower house, and large sauna. Co-ed hostel bunks cost $28 per person (includes bedding), lodge rooms ($35 d or $70–90 d), and private cabins ($100 d plus $25 each for extra guests).

Wrangell St. Elias News B&B (907/554-4454 or 907/590-8753, www.mccarthy-kennicott.com/WSENBB) is two miles before the end of the McCarthy Road. Two basic cabins share a bathhouse ($75–85 d) and are stocked with breakfast fixings.

 Kennicott Glacier Lodge (907/258-2350 or 800/582-5128, www.kennicottlodge.com, mid-May–mid-Sept.) is a sprawling and spotlessly clean modern lodge five miles from McCarthy. The setting is graceful, with a long covered porch facing Root Glacier and the colorful mine buildings. Vacation package rates for rooms—which include three meals, transportation to and from McCarthy, and a tour of the ghost town—are $275–285 d per day in the main lodge (shared baths) or $345 d per day in the newer south wing with private baths. The à la carte rate (rooms, transportation, and a tour only) is $179–189 d in the main lodge or $249 in the south wing. Be sure to request a room facing the glacier.

Kennecott B&B (907/554-4500, May–Sept., $225 for up to four) consists of two new one-bedroom apartments downstairs from Fireweed Mountain Arts and Crafts in Kennecott. Attractive units contain full kitchens, and private baths, plus ingredients for a make-it-yourself breakfast. Step out the door for a panoramic view of Kennicott Glacier.

A half-mile from the end of the McCarthy Road, **McCarthy B&B** (907/554-4433, www.mccarthy-kennicott.com/mccarthybb, May–Sept., $110 d) includes five small cabins with private bath. The rustic screened gazebo is stocked with breakfast items, and guests can also cook meals here.

Currant Ridge Cabins (907/554-4424 or 877/647-2442, www.currantridgecabins.com, $169 d), at Mile 56 on McCarthy Rd., serves up deluxe, newly built cabins with queen beds, full kitchens, and private baths.

Accessible only by air, remote **Ultima Thule Lodge** (907/688-1200, www.ultimathulelodge.com) sits along the Chitina River 50 miles southeast of McCarthy, with seven-day package trips that include a different adventure each day.

For the real Alaskan bush experience, the

Park Service (www.nps.gov/wrst) maintains 13 free public-use **cabins** within Wrangell–St. Elias, most of which are accessible only by air.

Camping

There are no Park Service campsites in Mc-Carthy or Kennicott, but hike-in campsites are located at Root Glacier two miles north of Kennicott. A half-mile from the end of the McCarthy Road, **Glacier View Campground** (907/554-4490, www.glacierviewcampground.com) has tent and RV spaces for $18 and free parking. **Base Camp Root Glacier** (907/746-0606) occupies the end of the road next to the McCarthy footbridge, and has campsites for $20 and parking for $5 a day. Both are open May to mid-September, with showers for a fee if you're camping elsewhere. Kennicott River Lodge & Hostel, provides showers and a sauna for $10.

Food

The restaurant at **◖ Kennicott Glacier Lodge** (907/258-2350 or 800/582-5128, www.kennicottlodge.com, $30–35) serves excellent "wilderness gourmet" meals three times a day, including lunch specials and filling family-style dinners. It is open to both lodge guests and the general public, but dinner reservations are required if you aren't staying here.

McCarthy Lodge (907/554-4402, www.mccarthylodge.com, $26–30) is open three meals a day mid-May–mid-September. Dinners often feature a semolina-encrusted Copper River red salmon and New York steaks. Adjacent is New Golden Saloon, with a lighter bar menu and occasional bands.

The seasonal **Glacier View Campground** (907/554-4490, $9–12) near the end of the McCarthy Road, has a barbecue menu for lunch and dinner, plus half-pound Glacier Burgers.

For tasty and inexpensive meals in downtown McCarthy, **The Potato** (907/554-4432, under $10) is open 11 A.M.–8 P.M. in the summer, with potato and egg burritos, chili dogs, Philly cheese sandwiches, fresh-cut curly fries, and the only espresso in the area.

The **McCarthy Mercantile** (907/554-4506, summer only) has a decent selection of grocer-ies and meats, plus homemade bread (they mill their own wheat), fresh pastries, soups, chili, and ice cream. Get a picnic lunch for $10. Fresh produce arrives Thursday evenings. The **Saturday Market** takes place on their side deck in July and August, with local produce, art, and baked goods.

Information and Services

The Park Service maintains a small **visitor kiosk** 0.75 miles from the McCarthy bridge that is open daily 9:30 A.M.–5:30 P.M. Memorial Day–Labor Day, plus a seasonal visitor center in Kennicott.

Regional visitor centers have a useful free visitor's guide to the area, or find the same information online (www.mccarthy-kennicott.com/vg). Also check out the **Wrangell Mountains Center** (www.wrangells.org), a McCarthy-based organization dedicated to environmental education and research.

McCarthy Lodge has computers and Wi-Fi for **Internet access** (fee). Pay phones are located at the bridge and next to the McCarthy Lodge. Cell phones sometimes work in the McCarthy area, though it depends upon your service provider.

For artwork, visit **Mountain Arts** at McCarthy Lodge or **Fireweed Mountain Arts and Crafts** in Kennicott.

Getting There and Around

It's a rough ride to McCarthy, but you can save wear and tear on your car with a van ride from **Backcountry Connection** (907/822-5292 or 866/582-5292, www.kennicottshuttle.com, daily mid-May–mid-Sept.). The round-trip cost is $99 from Glennallen or $89 from Chitina, but call a month ahead for reservations in July since the vans are often full.

Wrangell Mountain Air (907/554-4411 or 800/478-1160, www.wrangellmountainair.com) has scheduled service several times a day connecting Chitina with McCarthy, plus a variety of flightseeing trips from McCarthy, starting with a $90 half-hour glacier tour.

Ellis Air Taxi (907/822-3368 or 800/478-3368, www.ellisair.com) will fly you from

PRINCE WILLIAM SOUND

Glennallen to McCarthy on Wednesdays and Fridays for $125 one way, or from Anchorage to McCarthy for $300 one way.

A one-man operation run by the affable Gary Green since 1988, **McCarthy Air** (907/554-4440 or 800/245-6909, www .mccarthyair2.com) does flightseeing and backcountry drop-offs; Green is one of the most experienced pilots in the region.

Glacier View Campground (907/554-4490), near the end of the road, has a few beat-up mountain bikes for rent at $25 a day.

CHITINA AND VICINITY

The turnoff for the **Edgerton Highway** is at Mile 82 of the Richardson (18 miles south of Copper Center). This paved 34-mile road leads past the disperse farming community of Kenny Lake and on to the town of Chitina (CHIT-nuh, from the Athabascan *chiti,* "copper," and *na,* "river"). The Chitina Indians used copper tools to hammer copper nuggets into plates, which they traded with the Tlingits; someone who owned five or six plates was considered very rich. Chitina became an important junction in 1909, when the Copper River and Northwest Railroad arrived; a spur road connected the track to the original Richardson wagon trail to Fairbanks. The town began its decline in 1938 when the railroad shut down, and its future was further eroded by the Good Friday earthquake of 1964, which knocked out several bridges on the Copper River Highway. The highway project to link Cordova and Chitina was abandoned at that time.

Home to less than 100 people, Chitina is famous for its dip-netting season in June, when Alaskan residents converge on the confluence of the Copper and Chitina Rivers, "dip" 35-gallon nets on 15-foot-long aluminum poles into the water, and lift out 8-pound reds and 25-pound kings by the score. The dip-net fishery is only open to Alaskans. In addition, a number of **fish wheels** can be seen above the bridge throughout the summer. Chitina also serves as a way station for folks heading out the McCarthy road.

Chitina is decidedly rustic, with aging log cabins in various stages of collapse lining the dusty dirt roads. Poke around a bit more to find antique vehicles, an abandoned railcar, and even an old-fashioned gas pump. The town is also an unbelievably windy spot, with winds funneling through the narrow mountains along the Copper River. Because of the in-the-mountains location, none of the local businesses have TV or radio reception.

Accommodations and Food

Built in 1914, **(Hotel Chitina** (907/823-2244, www.hotelchitina.com, open May–Oct., $150 d) occupies a corner lot as you come into town. This two-store frontier building was restored 90 years later with an Arts and Craft decor in the downstairs restaurant and rustic bar. Guests stay in small rooms ($150 d) with modern furnishings, queen beds, private baths, and Wi-Fi, but no TVs or phones. The restaurant serves three meals a day—try the teriyaki Copper River reds or Cajun-style chicken—and is open until 11 P.M. in the summer. Dinner entrées cost $17–23.

Chitina Trading Post (907/823-2211) has a café and sells food for those who want to cook their own meals. You'll also find everything from videos to dip nets, not to mention gas for your car. **Uncle Tom's Tavern** (907/823-2253) is the local drinking establishment for the "nip and dip" crowd.

Built in 1910 and on the National Historical Register, **Chitina House B&B** (907/823-2298, www.chitinahouse.com, May–mid-Sept., $130 d) is a cute red home that once served as a railroad bunkhouse. Two rooms share a bath, and a continental breakfast is included.

Located in a quiet spot a mile out of town, **Chitina Guest Cabins** (907/823-2266, www .pawandfeathers.com, May–Oct.) rents three recently constructed cabins ($125 d with a light breakfast) that provide an authentic taste of the real Alaska. The cabins are quaint, with outhouses and a wash basin. Hostel-type bunkrooms are $35 per person with your own sleeping bag, or $45 per person with sheets and blankets.

Camp for free along the Copper River just across the bridge a mile east of Chitina at **Copper River State Campground,** with no facilities but lots of sandy land to pitch a tent or park an RV for free. The constant wind keeps mosquitoes away, but can make tenting virtually impossible. **Liberty Falls State Recreation Site** has several $10 sites 10 miles west of Chitina along the Edgerton Highway. It's a beautiful spot.

Practicalities

Housed within an historic cabin, the National Park Service's **Chitina Ranger Station** (907/823-2205, Fri.–Mon. 2–6 P.M. Memorial Day–Labor Day only) has information and videos on the park and the McCarthy Road.

Spirit Mountain Artworks (907/823-2222, open seasonally) sells quality Alaskan art from a classic false-front building in the heart of town.

Local events include a country 4th of July parade and the **Labor Day Cabbage Festival** with giant cabbages, a pig roast, races, and smoked salmon. Learn more about the town from the **Chitina Chamber of Commerce** website (www.chitinachamber.org).

Wrangell Mountain Air (907/554-4411 or 800/478-1160, www.wrangellmountain air.com) provides scheduled flights between Chitina and McCarthy.

Kenny Lake

Kenny Lake Mercantile (907/822-3313, www.kennylake.com) has groceries and gas, a diner with three meals a day, austere lodging, wooded RV park and tent sites, coin laundry, and showers. It's at Mile 7 of the Edgerton Highway, 26 miles west of Chitina.

Find considerably nicer accommodations at **Wellwood Center B&B** (Mile 6, 907/822-3418, www.wellwoodcenter.com, $95 d) with three guest rooms sharing a bath. Make your own breakfast in the stocked kitchen. The home occupies a 95-acre spread with hiking trails leading to mountain vistas.

Golden Spruce Cabins (Mile 10, 907/822-5556, www.goldensprucecabins.com, $69 d) has five comfy cabins with a shared bathhouse, plus an espresso stand and convenience store.

Pippin Lake B&B (907/822-3046, www.pippinlakebnb.com, $125 d, add $10 for additional guests), at Mile 82 Richardson Highway near the Edgerton turnoff has a cozy lakeside cabin that sleeps five. The kitchen is stocked for a make-it-yourself breakfast, and a canoe, kayak, and paddleboat add to the allure.

At **Copper Moose B&B** (Edgerton Hwy. Mile 5.8, 907/822-9244 or 866/922-4244, www.coppermoosebb.com, $125 d) four guest rooms share three baths in a large log home. You can take in the Wrangell Mountains from the deck while surfing the Web (free Wi-Fi).

Richardson Highway South

The 366-mile Richardson Highway provides a north–south connection between Fairbanks and Valdez, passing through the towns of North Pole, Delta Junction, Glennallen, and Copper Center along the way. The 115-mile stretch between Glennallen and Valdez cuts between the rugged Chugach Mountains to the west and the massive Wrangell Mountains to the east. This route—the oldest road in Alaska—was blazed during the stampede of 1898 and has since been used as a footpath, a telegraph right-of-way, a wagon trail, and an auto thoroughfare. The last 25 miles to Valdez is one of the most spectacular drives in Alaska.

COPPER CENTER

Copper Center (pop. 500) is 15 miles south of Glennallen on a side road (the Old Richardson Highway) that splits off at Mile 106 of the Richardson Highway. Settled in 1896, this was the first non-Native town in the interior of Southcentral, opened up by all the explorations on the mighty Copper River. This was also the point where the perilous trail over Valdez Glacier came down from the mountains. When the stampeders arrived, they found a score of tents, several log cabins, a post office, and the Blix Roadhouse, which opened in 1898 for $15,000, with spring beds and a modern bath. Today the settlement has a handful of businesses and a mixed population, including Athabascans in the neighboring village of Kluti Kaah.

Just north of town at Mile 107, the **Wrangell-St. Elias National Park and Preserve Visitor Center** (907/822-7261, www.nps.gov/wrst) is open daily 8 A.M.–6 P.M. in the summer, and Monday–Friday 8 A.M.–4:30 P.M. the rest of the year. Rangers can help with trip planning, sell you books and topographic maps, or show an acclaimed film about the park.

Practicalities

The Blix was replaced in 1932 by beautiful **Copper Center Lodge** (907/822-3245 or 866/330-3245, www.coppercenterlodge.com). Comfortable rooms cost $115 d with shared

Copper Center Lodge, built in 1932

© DON PITCHER

PRINCE WILLIAM SOUND

baths or $125–146 d with private baths. The restaurant serves sourdough pancakes (using a century-old sourdough starter), burgers, sandwiches, shrimp, halibut, and steaks; dinner entrées run $15–24. Great homemade blueberry and rhubarb pies, too. The lodge is open year-round.

Right next door are two small cabins that comprise the **George Ashby Museum** (June–Aug. Sun.–Fri. 10 A.M.–5 P.M. and Sat. 11 A.M.–5 P.M.). Exhibits trace the history of the Copper River Valley, including Athabascan Indian and early-settler artifacts. Gold rush and pioneer days are remembered with photographs, tools used to develop the area, and old Sears catalogs, the only way the local inhabitants could procure many necessary supplies from Outside.

Out on the loop road, **Chapel on the Hill** is the oldest log chapel in the Copper River Basin, was built by Army volunteers in 1943. **Tonsina Native Arts and Crafts** (907/822-3852) at Mile 43 of the Edgerton Highway sells local crafts.

Enjoy a comfortable night at **Sawing Logzz B&B** (907/822-3242, www.sawinglogzz.com, $125 d) where the private suite includes a log bed, TV, and stocked kitchenette for a self-serve breakfast.

Set on a hilltop, the 85-room **Copper River Princess Lodge** (907/822-4000 or 800/426-0500, www.princesslodges.com, $179 d) is at Mile 102 of Richardson Highway. Upscale rooms are large and comfortable, but the view is the real feature, with fine vistas over the Copper River Valley to Mt. Drum and the Wrangells. Most guests are cruise ship passengers, but independent travelers are welcome, and special rates ($100 d) are often available. A restaurant and lounge are on the premises.

Park RVs at two campgrounds on opposite sides of the Klutina River: **Klutina Salmon Charters** (907/822-3991, www.klutinacharters.com) and **Grove's Klutina Charters** (907/822-5822 or 800/770-5822, www.alaskan.com/groves).

🄲 THOMPSON PASS

From the Edgerton Highway junction to Valdez is 82 beautiful miles through green forested hillsides along surging creeks with countless

WORTHINGTON GLACIER

Near Mile 33 of the Edgerton Highway, you come around a bend, unsuspecting, and the Worthington Glacier looms into view, its three fingers creeping out of Girls Mountain like a grotesque hand in a horror movie. In another few miles is the turnoff to this state recreation site, on a short road that leads to the overlook parking lot. There's no established campground here, but a small visitor center is staffed by State Parks folks in the summer. Trails cover the short distance to the glacier, and a one-mile path climbs the lateral moraine for even more dramatic vistas.

Open mid-May to mid-September, **H2O Guides** (907/835-8418 or 800/578-4354, www.h2oguides.com) operates from a little building next to the parking lot. Glacier treks ($95 half-day, $145 all day) and introductory ice climbing classes ($135 half-day or $185 all day) provide a great way to get up close and personal with the glacier. You may even get inside the glacier in an ice tunnel. Also offered is an easy interpretive walk ($35 for 2.5 hours) that stays off the ice. Reservations aren't required, but call ahead for times.

waterfalls emanating from ice patches and small glaciers atop the jagged Chugach. If you're terminally enchanted by this stretch of road and want to linger, two state recreation sites offer camping: **Squirrel Creek** at Mile 79 and **Little Tonsina** at Mile 65. The Tonsina site is a bit noisy, located a half-mile from pipeline pump station number 12, which, run by jet aircraft turbines, sounds like a plane perpetually taking off. Signboards across the highway from the pump station (Mile 65) describe pipeline history, oil spills, communications, the turbines, and the pump station. At Mile 56, the **Tiekel River Lodge** (907/822-3259) has food, gas, rooms, campsites, and a gift shop. (See *Worthington Glacier* for details on one of the Thompson Pass highlights.)

Topping Out

A mere three miles down (or more accurately, *up*) the road from Worthington Glacier is **Thompson Pass** (el. 2,771 ft.). A long row of serrated peaks, like a cosmic cross-cut saw with only a few dull or missing teeth, lines the high horizon. Blueberry and Summit Lakes are accessible by a loop road about a mile on the Valdez side of the pass; the small campground at Blueberry is beautiful—though it's exposed, especially if Thompson Pass is in the process of maintaining its record-setting precipitation levels. Confirming that this is one of the snowiest spots on earth are 15-foot-tall, right-angle, orange poles that show snowplow drivers the edge of the road.

Thompson Pass Mt. Chalet (907/835-4817, www.alaska.net/~chalet, $120 d, $10 each for additional guests) is a rustic cabin at Mile 19 with space for four people, a private bath, kitchenette, and continental breakfast basket. The owners live in a nearby cabin and guide summertime hikes and wintertime backcountry ski adventures.

◖ KEYSTONE CANYON

About seven miles south of Thompson Pass, you drop to Keystone Canyon, one of the most gorgeous sights in Alaska, even in the rain. This four-mile section is steeped in gold rush and copper-frenzy history. At the height of Klondicitis, accounts of the heavy tax and strict regulations that Canadian authorities imposed on the stampeders (which saved countless lives) were passed down the coast, and rumors of an old Indian-Russian trail from Valdez to the Yukon circulated simultaneously. The vague story of an "all-American route" to

the gold sent 4,000 would-be prospectors headlong to Valdez—a measure of the madness that gripped the land. Suicidally unprepared, like lemmings they attempted to cross the brutal Valdez Glacier. Also responding to the rumors, the U.S. Army dispatched Captain William Abercrombie in 1898 to find or blaze a route from Valdez to the Interior. Abercrombie had been on the original American expedition to Copper River country in 1884. He *knew* the land and the conditions; when he crossed Valdez Glacier in 1898, he postponed his trailblazing assignment in order to deal with the horror that he found. Abercrombie returned in 1899 and thoroughly explored and mapped the whole area, locating and naming the Lowe River, Keystone Canyon, and the Thompson Pass route to the Interior.

Then in 1906, during the often-violent race to build a railroad from tidewater to the Kennecott copper mines, two of the competing construction companies clashed over the right-of-way through Keystone Canyon; one man was killed. The ensuing murder trial further fanned the flames, and the "Shoot-out at Keystone Canyon" became a great issue between the opposing sides. All this is highly dramatized in Rex Beach's novel, *The Iron Trail*.

Today, you drive along the raging Lowe River, at the bottom of nearly perpendicular 300-foot cliffs. The entire canyon is a psychedelic green; every crack and crevice in the sheer walls is overgrown with bright lime moss. Waterfalls tumble over the walls to the river below, spraying the road with a fine mist. **Bridal Veil Falls** and **Horsetail Falls** live up to their names. And now you're ready to enter Valdez.

Valdez

At the end of Valdez Arm and completely surrounded by snowcapped peaks, Valdez (val-DEEZ, *never* val-DEZ, pop. 4,000) occupies one of the most picturesque settings in South-central Alaska. The prosperous town has wide streets, and year-round access by land and sea; it's the northernmost ice-free port in America. Because of the latter, Valdez was chosen as the terminus for the 800-mile Trans-Alaska Pipeline. And because of this, the town always seems to prosper.

HISTORY

Captain James Cook sailed into and named Prince William Sound in 1778; Spanish explorer Don Salvador Fidalgo entered "Puerto de Valdez" in 1790, naming it after Spain's Marine Minister. In 1898, Valdez was a tent city of

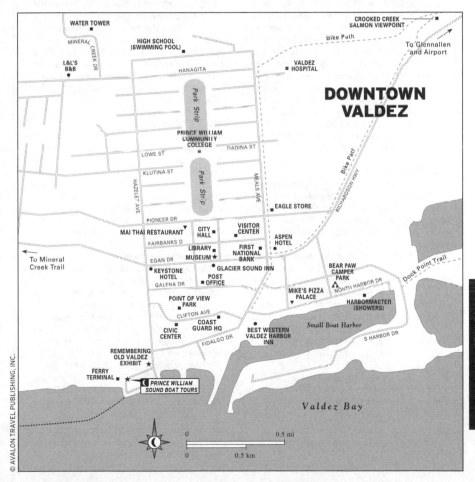

PRINCE WILLIAM SOUND

THE EXXON VALDEZ OIL SPILL

On March 23, 1989 (Good Friday), at 11 P.M., Captain Joseph Hazelwood turned the 987-foot *Exxon Valdez* supertanker, just a few hours after leaving the pipeline terminal loaded with over 20 million barrels of Prudhoe Bay crude, out of the normal shipping lanes of Prince William Sound to avoid icebergs from Columbia Glacier. Through a series of mistakes and misunderstandings, and ignoring standard procedure, at 12:01 A.M. on March 24 the *Valdez* ran up hard aground on Bligh Reef, opening a tractor trailer–size hole in the ship, which began to leak oil at a rapid rate. It took 3 hours for the Coast Guard to be notified, and 12 hours for the spill-response team to arrive at the scene. It was a full 72 hours after the oil began to spill before a containment boom was installed to surround the tanker. But as the rest of the oil was off-loaded onto the *Exxon Baton Rouge*, the fate of more than 1,000 miles of Southcentral coastline had already been sealed. The oil began its inexorable spread.

THE CLEANUP

In the following weeks, the technology available to clean up an environmental disaster of such magnitude proved grossly inadequate. To begin with, Alyeska Pipeline Company's emergency procedures and equipment had atrophied over the years. The use of chemical dispersants, a major part of the plan, was not only ineffective, but controversial as well: Later in the summer workers who'd handled them began to show symptoms of toxic poisoning. Of the few skimmers that could be deployed (a dozen after a week), those that worked were able to clean up 500 gallons of oil an hour – in the face of millions. And then there were no support facilities for unloading the skimmed crude.

Local fishermen mobilized to try to contain the oil with booms, keeping it away from some of the most bountiful fisheries on earth at the peak of their seasons. As the oil washed up on the wildlife-rich shorelines of Prince William Sound, crews were sent to attack the thickening, hardening sludge with shovels, buckets, and plastic bags. As early as the first week in June, 24,000 birds and 1,000 sea otters, killed by the oil, had been counted – some so covered with crude that they were impossible to identify. At the height of the summer clean up, 10,000 workers were engaged in a somewhat futile effort to return the beaches of Prince William Sound, the Kenai and Alaska Peninsulas, Kodiak Island, and all the way down to the Shumagin Islands in the Aleutians to their previously pristine state. Garbage clean up crews were cleaning up after the oil clean up crews. It's estimated that Exxon spent $1.25 billion on the effort.

THE AFTERMATH

Well over a decade after the spill, oil can still be found on some Prince William Sound beaches, particularly under rocks on the worst-hit beaches. Many species of birds and mammals are far below their pre-spill populations, including killer whales, sea otters, loons, cormorants, harbor seals, pigeon guillemots, and harlequin ducks. In addition, research shows that even tiny concentrations of crude oil can harm the eggs of pink salmon and herring. Herring fishermen have been especially hard hit, and the value of commercial salmon fishing permits has plummeted.

Shortly after the spill, Exxon renamed all its ships, replacing the "Exxon" with "Sea River"; if there's ever another Exxon-caused spill its name won't be so indelibly etched in the news accounts. The 1989 spill led to enactment the following year of the Oil Pollution Act which requires double-hulled tankers in Prince William Sound by 2015. Unfortunately, the aging single-hulled tankers are still used today. Many other measures have been taken

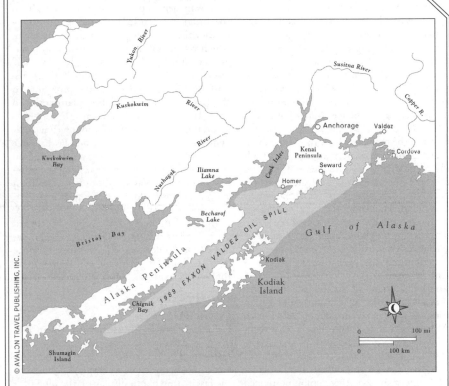

to prevent a repeat, however, including the addition of large ocean-going tugs and response vessels (containing spill equipment) to escort all tankers.

In a 1991 out-of-court settlement, Exxon agreed to a $900 million payout that has been used to buy land, to reimburse cleanup expenses, and to fund environmental research and restoration. More contentious was a 1994 case in which a jury awarded 40,000 commercial fishermen and others damaged by the spill $5 billion in punitive damages. It was one of the biggest damage awards ever. Exxon has been dragging out the appeals process since then, with no end in sight, but if they ever have to pay, it will cost them the $5 billion plus an interest of 5.9 percent, around $2 million more per day! And what of Captain Hazelwood? He was convicted in 1990 of a misdemeanor charge of negligent discharge of oil. After nine years of appeals, Hazelwood was finally sentenced to 1,000 hours of community service, including working in an Anchorage soup kitchen. For the latest on the spill, visit the *Exxon Valdez* Oil Spill Trustee Council website (www.oilspill.state.ak.us).

stampeders similar to Skagway—except for one critical detail: no trail to the Interior. Still, between 4,000 and 6,000 death-defying cheechakos crossed the Valdez Glacier that year. Army Captain William Abercrombie described the foolhardy newcomers as "terrifyingly incompetent... wholly unprepared physically and morally for what they would face." They barely knew how to strap packs on their backs, and few thought to carry the two basic necessities: water and wood. Many were blinded by the sun's reflection off the ice. Many got lost in howling storms, in which it was impossible to see or hear the man ahead. Of those who managed to reach the summit, many lost their loads and lives on slick downhill slides into oblivion. And those who actually got off the glacier intact had to contend with the fast cold waters of the runoff. Many men with heavy packs lost their footing and drowned in knee-deep water. Some attempted to build boats and float down the Klutina River to Copper Center; few made it. And those stuck between the glacier and the river had nothing.

In the final count, all but 300 (and the countless dead) of those who'd set out from Valdez during the spring and summer of '98 returned to Valdez the way they came by fall. Abercrombie found them destitute and broken. Many had gone mad, most had scurvy and frostbitten hands, feet, and faces. Facilities were squalid. And there was no food. Abercrombie postponed his orders to blaze a trail into the Interior for six months to feed, clothe, house, and arrange transportation home for the survivors. Eventually, the army built a road through Keystone Canyon—providing access to the Interior—and a military base across the bay from Valdez called Fort Liscum; it lasted until 1923.

The 20th Century

In the early 1900s a corporate copper rush kicked off a fierce competition among Valdez, Cordova, and a town called Katalla, all vying to be selected as the tidewater terminus of the proposed railway to the copper mines of what's now Kennecott. A dozen projects were conceived, and one was even begun out of Val-

dez, but Cordova won out in the end. For the next 60 years, Valdez was a sleepy fishing and shipping port, competing with Seward, and later Whittier, to provide access for freight to the Interior. Then in 1964 the Good Friday earthquake struck, wiping out the entire town, which was rebuilt four miles inland on property donated by a local. Finally, in 1974, civic leaders sold the virtues of Valdez—its ice-free port, 800-foot-deep harbor, and proximity to the Interior—to the pipeline planners, who chose the town as their terminus.

Everything went along without serious incident until March 29, 1989 (Good Friday once again), when the *Exxon Valdez* ran aground on Bligh Reef a few hours after leaving the pipeline terminal in Valdez, dumping 11 million gallons of North Slope crude into Prince William Sound. The unthinkable had happened. In the mad summer of 1989, Valdez was turned on its head by the "Exxon Economy." The waters of Port Valdez escaped the spill, but Prince William Sound is still a long way from returning to the way it was before the spill.

SIGHTS
Downtown

For its size, **Valdez Museum** (217 Egan Dr., 907/835-2764, www.valdezmuseum.org) right in the middle of town, has an extraordinary amount of comprehensive displays. Check out the fascinating photo display on the pipeline's impact, and the early black-and-whites. Some rare early maps and charts include a Russian one from 1737; look for the beautiful engraving by Webber, Cook's prolific ship's artist. Informative displays illustrate Native, mining, and military history, but two beautifully restored fire pumpers—one from 1886—are the striking centerpieces, along with the lens from Cape Hinchinbrook Lighthouse. There's a small section from the hull of the *Exxon Valdez,* but surprisingly little information on this disaster. From May to mid-September the museum is open daily 9 A.M.–6 P.M., the rest of the year Monday–Saturday 1–5 P.M.

Close to the ferry terminal, the **Remembering Old Valdez Exhibit** (436 S. Hazelet St.,

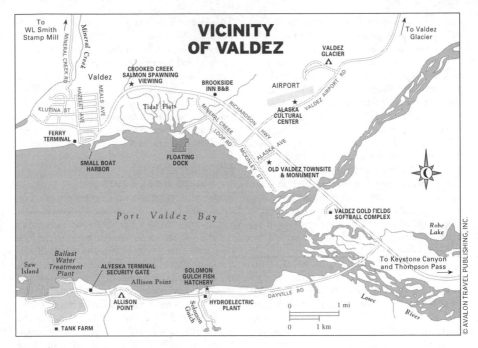

VICINITY OF VALDEZ

To WL Smith Stamp Mill

Mineral Creek

MINERAL CREEK RD

Valdez

HAZELET AVE

MEALS AVE

KLUTINA ST

FERRY TERMINAL

CROOKED CREEK SALMON SPAWNING VIEWING

Tidal Flats

SMALL BOAT HARBOR

FLOATING DOCK

BROOKSIDE INN B&B

MINERAL CREEK LOOP RD

RICHARDSON HWY

McKINLEY ST

ALASKA AVE

AIRPORT

VALDEZ GLACIER

VALDEZ AIRPORT RD

To Valdez Glacier

ALASKA CULTURAL CENTER

OLD VALDEZ TOWNSITE & MONUMENT

Port Valdez Bay

VALDEZ GOLD FIELDS SOFTBALL COMPLEX

Robe Lake

Saw Island

Ballast Water Treatment Plant

ALYESKA TERMINAL SECURITY GATE

Allison Point

ALLISON POINT

SOLOMON GULCH FISH HATCHERY

Solomon Gulch

HYDROELECTRIC PLANT

DAYVILLE RD

To Keystone Canyon and Thompson Pass →

Lowe River

TANK FARM

0   1 mi
0   1 km

© AVALON TRAVEL PUBLISHING, INC.

907/835-5407) houses a warehouse full of earthquake exhibits, including a sprawling 1:20 scale replica of Valdez as it appeared before the big one hit in 1964. You can also watch a video on the quake, check out the 1950 Wurlitzer, and watch the seismograph for more activity. There's even a 1950s Civil Defense Jeep on display. The Annex is open daily 9 A.M.–6 P.M. May–mid-September. One entrance fee ($5 adults, $4.50 seniors, $4 ages 14–18, and free for children) gets you into both the Valdez Museum and the Remembering Old Valdez Exhibit.

Down Meals Avenue by the harbor, bear left onto Clifton and go up past Coast Guard HQ to the **Civic Center,** where a viewing pavilion has an interpretive signboard describing the pipeline terminal across the bay. Climb the steep stairs up to **Point of View Park** for the panorama of town.

Out of Town

The **Whitney Museum** (907/834-1614, www.pwscc.edu, daily 9 A.M.–7 P.M. May–

mid-Sept., by appointment the rest of the year, $5 adults, seniors $4, $3 ages 4–12, or $15 for families) fills a warehouse-type building next to the airport terminal, five miles from town. The location is odd, but the collection is well worth the drive. Housed here are items collected over several decades by Jesse and Maxine Whitney, including trophy big game mounts, an Eskimo kayak and umiak, and a wide range of elaborate Native parkas, baskets, and beautiful, carved ivory pieces. Of particular interest is a large and elaborate model ship built of ivory and baleen; the Smithsonian Museum once attempted to purchase this piece.

The Forest Service's **Crooked Creek Information Site** (907/835-4680, daily 9 A.M.–6 P.M. Memorial Day–Labor Day) is out the Richardson about a mile from town. In late summer, walk out on the boardwalk to see salmon go through the final act of their incredible life cycle. The TV inside the information center is wired to a video camera that provides a live underwater view of the spawning action for salmon voyeurs. A four-mile paved **bike path** leads north from town past Crooked Creek.

Continue out the Richardson about three and a half miles to where a historical sign points to **Old Valdez**. The only thing left of the old town site besides the post office foundation and memorial plaque are the mileposts on the Rich: zero still starts here. In another three miles, turn right onto Dayville Road. In several miles you come to the hydroelectric plant and **Solomon Gulch Hatchery** (907/835-4874). Pause here to see the powerful small falls and to take a self-guided tour around this private pink and coho salmon hatchery. The staff is generally around to answer questions. Black bears sometimes emerge from the nearby forest to catch salmon in late summer.

The **Alyeska Pipeline Terminal** is farther out Dayville Road, but is no longer open to the public due to security concerns. Prince William Sound Community College (303 Lowe St.) shows an interesting 90-minute video about the pipeline, the terminal, double-hull oil tankers, and the Valdez area during the summer. Tickets cost $5 adult, $4 seniors and kids, or $15 families. Showings are daily in the summer at 9:30 and 11:30 A.M. and 1:30 P.M.

TOURING PRINCE WILLIAM SOUND
Columbia Glacier

Prince William Sound has the greatest concentration of tidewater glaciers in Alaska, including Columbia Glacier, the stunning grandfather of glaciers in the Sound. Covering about 440 square miles, Columbia Glacier is 40 miles long and more than three miles wide at its face, which rises up to 250 feet above the water and plunges an incredible 2,000 feet below. Although it's the second largest of its kind in Alaska and still extends 15 miles out into its ancestral fjord, Columbia Glacier is but a minor remnant of the vast glacier that only a few thousand years ago filled Prince William Sound; its face reached a height of 4,000 feet.

Since 1982 the glacier has been in rapid retreat, at a rate averaging a half-mile per year.

This retreat has filled Columbia Bay with icebergs, and tour boats can no longer get within six miles of the face. Ice in the bay has also caused navigational hazards in Prince William Sound, and it was to avoid ice that the *Exxon Valdez* took its fateful shortcut near, and onto, Bligh Reef. Scientists speculate that by the time the glacier stops its current rate of backward movement, a new fjord 25 miles long will be exposed, into which several calving glaciers will flow.

◖ Prince William Sound Boat Tours

The state ferry pauses on its trip between Valdez and Whittier to view the Columbia Glacier, or you can join a private tour. Because of the glacier's recent movement back up the bay, boats can only get to within about six miles of the face. This changes, but does not diminish, the experience, as the boats cruise through and over the fields of drifting ice towering above the deck to see the glacier as more huge chunks shear off and drop into the bay. Beyond the glaciers, the main attraction for Prince William Sound is wildlife, including the chance to see humpback and killer (orca) whales, Dall's porpoises, sea otters, Steller sea lions, and other marine mammals. These animals are most often seen on the southern end of the Sound, an all-day boat ride from Whittier or Valdez.

The *Lu-Lu Belle* (907/835-5141 or 800/411-0090, www.lulubelletours.com) is a comfortable 60-passenger boat with daily Columbia Glacier and wildlife tours in the summer; $85 for five-hours (or longer). A snack bar is on board. This is a fun and personalized tour by owner-operator Fred Rodolf.

A larger company, **Stan Stephens Glacier & Wildlife Cruises** (907/835-4731 or 866/867-1297, www.stanstephenscruises.com) has a 5.5-hour Columbia Glacier tour ($95 adults, $48 kids), and a 12-hour trip that encompasses Columbia and Meares glaciers, plus the sea lions of Glacier Island for $130 adults, $65 kids with lunch.

State Parks

Three state marine parks (www.alaskastateparks.

© DON PITCHER

icebergs from Columbia Glacier

org) offer a variety of recreational opportunities within an hour's boat ride from Valdez. The serene, forest-ringed **Sawmill Bay State Marine Park** has protected anchorage and good camping. For island camping and a fair-weather anchorage, visit **Jack Bay State Marine Park** on the east side of Valdez Narrows. At **Shoup Bay Marine Park** the Shoup Glacier spills into an iceberg-filled saltwater lagoon accessible on most high tides by sea kayaks and small boats. Visitors will enjoy this pretty bay with lots of icebergs and thousands of nesting kittiwakes.

EVENTS

The **Valdez Ice Climbing Festival** in February attracts some of the top climbers to the frozen waterfalls of Keystone Canyon.

Each June, the acclaimed **Edward Albee Theatre Conference** (www.uaa.alaska.edu/pwscc) takes place at the Civic Center. It's a weeklong theatrical event with performances and seminars by nationally known playwrights and actors including, of course, Edward Albee.

Valdez has two popular summertime fishing derbies (907/835-5680, www.valdezfishderbies.com): the **Halibut Derby** all summer

and **Silver Salmon Derby** in August. Each has a $15,000 top prize. Other popular summer events are the **4th of July** celebration and **Valdez Gold Rush Days** in early August. The latter is a weeklong celebration complete with cancan girls, a hoosegow, parade, and fish fry.

RECREATION
Hiking

Get complete details on local hikes from the Forest Service's Crooked Creek visitor center. The easiest local path, the **Dock Point Trail**, starts from Kobuk Drive across from the boat ramp. This three-quarter-mile trail (partially boardwalk) has a grassy meadow and good viewpoints across Valdez Bay. **Mineral Creek Valley** is a beautiful canyon accessible from the north end of town via Mineral Creek Drive. A bumpy gravel road—great for mountain bikes—crosses the creek and then parallels it for the next 5.5 miles, ending at a locked gate. From here it's a one-mile walk to the abandoned W. L. Smith Stamp Mill (1913), which crushed ore from mines up the mountain. A number of beautiful waterfalls crowd the slopes of Mineral Creek Valley, so be sure to bring your camera.

The **Keystone Canyon Pack Trail** (a.k.a. Goat Trail or Trans-Alaska Military Trail) begins from a trailhead at Mile 14 of the Richardson Highway, climbing gradually 2.5 miles. The trail was built in 1899 by the Army to provide an "All-American" route to the gold fields, and this short portion was restored almost a century later.

For an excellent overnight trip, hike the **Shoup Bay Trail,** which begins from the west end of Egan Street. This trail affords views of Valdez and Valdez Bay, and passes a fine camping area along Gold Creek at three miles. It ends at Shoup Bay (across from majestic Shoup Glacier), 10 miles from town.

Sea Kayaking

If you've always wanted to learn how to kayak, or if you know how and want to explore Prince William Sound around Valdez in style, contact Hedy Sarney of **Anadyr Adventures** (225 N. Harbor Dr., 907/835-2814 or 800/865-2925, www.anadyradventures.com). Trips range from a kid-friendly three-hour natural history tour for $55, to customized mother ship multi-night tours. Especially popular are eight-hour Shoup Glacier trips ($159), and 10-hour Columbia Glacier paddles ($199), both of which include an open water crossing by charter boat. Anadyr's most popular multi-night trip is a five-day paddle that encompasses Columbia Glacier, Sawmill Bay, and Shoup Glacier for $845 ($1,075 with meals). Anadyr conducts other excursions of varying lengths, including boat-based and lodge-based trips, along with a remote drop-off and pick-up service. They also rent kayaks, bikes, and camping gear, and the Alaskan arts and crafts sold here make it worth a visit even if you aren't planning a paddle.

Pangaea Adventures (101 N. Harbor Dr., 907/835-8442 or 800/660-9637, www.alaskasummer.com) also leads a wide range of sea kayaking trips. Least expensive ($75) is a three-hour paddle around the duck flats, but more challenging are day trips to Gold Creek ($79), Shoup Glacier ($159), and Columbia Glacier ($199). The last of these lasts 10 hours and includes a water-taxi ride to and from the

Columbia, along with time to explore this magnificent glacier. Longer trips start with an overnight trip to Shoup Glacier, a six-day "mother ship" tour that takes sea kayakers around Prince William Sound aboard a sailboat, and an 11-day trip that combines sea kayaking and backpacking. Kayak rentals are available if you just want to head out on your own.

Rafting

Keystone Raft and Kayak Adventures (907/835-2606 or 800/328-8460, www.alaskawhitewater.com) offers an exciting two-hour raft trip down the Class III Lowe River through Keystone Canyon. Other choices include a half-day trip on the Tsaina River (Class IV) near Thompson Pass and all-day Tonsina River trips (Class III–IV), 80 miles from town. Trips depart from their office at Mile 17 of the Richardson Highway; transport from Valdez is extra. Also ask about longer trips throughout the Copper River Valley.

Fishing and Biking

Valdez has three dozen charter fishing and cruising boats. Contact the visitor center for a listing, or visit their website (www.valdezalaska.org). **Fish Central** (907/835-5090 or 888/835-5002, www.fishcentral.net) books fishing charters, boat rentals, and sightseeing trips. Find them next to the boat harbor. Rent mountain bikes from Anadyr Adventures.

Winter Sports

When winter comes, Keystone Canyon's waterfalls freeze, making them destinations for ice climbers, particularly during the Ice Climbing Festival in February. Valdez itself gets some of the heaviest snowfalls anywhere in Alaska, averaging 25 feet per year; the record came the winter of 1989–1990: 47 feet! It isn't uncommon to arrive in March to find the town buried to the rooftops in snow. More snow falls here than at any other sea-level location in North America. Because of all this snow, the area can be a winter-lovers' paradise, especially since the temperature rarely drops below 20°F. Groomed cross-country ski trails are maintained in Mineral Creek Valley.

Several companies offer heli-sking at Thompson Pass for the ultimate mountain skiing adventure: **Valdez Heli-Ski Guides** (907/835-4528, www.valdezheliskiguides.com), **Valdez Heli-Camps** (907/783-3243, www.valdezhelicamps.com), **Alaska Backcountry Adventures** (530/581-1767 or 888/729-9222, www.swayback.com), and **H2O Guides** (907/835-8418 or 800/578-4354, www.h2oguides.com).

ACCOMMODATIONS

Valdez has a good selection of lodging places, but book a room well ahead for July and August when nearly most rooms get taken early. Visit the Valdez Convention and Visitors Bureau website (www.valdezalaska.org) for links to most local lodging places; their office keeps a list of who has rooms available.

Hotels and Motels

Glacier Sound Inn (210 Egan Dr., 907/835-4485 or 888/835-4485, $100 d) has motel rooms with microwaves, fridges, and free Wi-Fi.

Keystone Hotel (at Hazelet and Egan Drs., 907/835-3851 or 888/835-0665, www.keystonehotel.com, late May–early Sept.) has cramped little rooms with thin walls for $85 s or $95 d, and larger ones with two double beds for $105–115 d. The hotel is well maintained, and a continental breakfast is included. The building was originally constructed as headquarters for the 1989 oil spill cleanup, so may not appeal to everyone.

The **Best Western Valdez Harbor Inn** (100 Fidalgo Dr., 907/835-3434 or 888/222-3440, www.valdezharborinn.com, $139–149 d, suites for $179 d) faces the small boat harbor, and includes a free airport shuttle, workout room, Wi-Fi, and a decent restaurant.

Totem Inn (144 E. Egan Dr., 907/835-4443, www.toteminn.com) has a variety of attractive lodging options, including standard rooms with fridges and microwaves or cabins with kitchenettes ($139 d), and full suites ($179 d). Free Wi-Fi too.

Aspen Hotel (100 Meals Ave., 907/835-4445 or 800/478-4445, www.aspenhotelsak.com,

$159–169 d) is the town's finest hotel with such amenities as indoor pool, hot tub, exercise room, microwaves, small fridges, Wi-Fi, business center, and continental breakfast. A variety of suites ($189 d) with kitchenettes are also available, including ones with king beds and jetted tubs, and others for families.

Bed-and-Breakfasts

Brookside Inn B&B (907/835-9130 or 866/316-9130, www.brooksideinnbb.com) is a quaint home with a long history. Constructed in 1898, it survived the earthquake and was moved to new Valdez. The five guest rooms are $125 d, and the private suite costs $160 d, all with private baths. A full breakfast is served, kids are welcome, and Wi-Fi is available. The front porch and hot tub out back deck are good places to relax.

Located a mile and a half from town, 🄲 **Wild Roses by the Sea B&B** (907/835-2930, www.alaskabythesescabnb.com, $128–165 d) sits atop a bluff with an incredible view across Port Valdez. The home features a mix of Chinese and Alaskan decor, plus a delicious full breakfast. Two guest rooms and a separate apartment are available, all with private baths.

L&L's B&B (533 W. Hanagita St., 907/835-4447, www.lnlalaska.com, $70–80 d) is a large and modern home with five immaculate guest rooms sharing three baths, continental breakfasts, and Wi-Fi.

Also well worth a look are **Anna's Ptarmigan B&B** (907/835-2202, $90–100 d), **Gussie's Lowe Street B&B** (907/835-4448, www.gussiesbb.com), and **Lake House B&B** (907/835-4752, www.lakehousevaldez.net).

CAMPING

The closest official campground is five miles away. Go back out the Richardson Highway, turn left toward the airport, and continue another mile past it to the **Valdez Glacier Campground** (907/835-2282, www.valdezcampgrounds.com, $12). This large and scenic campground has picnic and barbecue areas, outhouses, and water. **Allison Point Campground** (907/835-2282, $12) is on Dayville Road near the Alyeska oil terminal, and has toilets and water. There's good fishing from shore nearby.

Find **public showers** at the harbor master's office, corner of Meals Avenue and Harbor Drive across from the chamber of commerce. Showers are also available from **Like Home Laundromat** on Egan Drive near Meals. A better deal is the **swimming pool** at Valdez High School (907/835-3200), where the showers are free with a swim.

Large RV parks abound right in Valdez: **Bear Paw Camper Park** (907/835-2530, www.bearpawrvpark.com), **Bayside RV Park** (907/835-4425 or 888/835-4425, www.baysiderv.com), **Sea Otter RV Park** (907/835-2787 or 800/831-2787), and **Eagle's Rest RV Park** (907/835-2373 or 800/553-7275, www.eaglesrestrv.com). RV hookups cost $30–38 with full hookups, and tent spaces ($20) may be available. Bear Paw and Sea Otter RV parks are right along the waterfront.

FOOD

Mike's Palace (201 Harbor Dr., 907/835-2365, $12–18) has a harborside location and wide-ranging menu with 12-inch pizzas, burgers, Greek moussaka, pasta, and Mexican meals. Open for lunch and dinner; call for takeout orders. It's almost always packed with locals and visitors.

Ernesto's (326 Egan St., 907/835-2519) serves authentic, reasonable, and tasty Mexican meals. They also operate a little taco stand near the docks. **Fu Kung** (907/835-5255) occupies a Quonset hut at 207 Kobuk. In addition to the expected Chinese favorites, the restaurant also has seafood (try the mu shu shrimp) and lunch specials. Fu Kung is open until 11 P.M. daily. Find Thai meals at **Mai Thai** (310 Pioneer, 907/835-5606).

The **Pipeline Club** (112 Egan Dr., 907/835-4332) is an old-time, smoke-filled place where Captain Hazelwood had a number of drinks before climbing on board the *Exxon Valdez* that fateful night in 1989. It lays claim to the best filet mignon, prime rib, char-broiled steaks, and seafood in town. But don't drink and drive (or boat).

Get groceries at **Eagle** (907/835-2100), the Safeway-owned market near Egan. Several spots sell espresso in town, including **Latte Dah** (130 S. Meals, 907/835-3720), which uses Kaladi Brothers coffees.

INFORMATION AND SERVICES

The **Valdez Visitors Information Center** (200 Fairbanks St., 907/835-4636 or 800/770-5954, www.valdezalaska.org) is across from City Hall. It's open Monday–Friday 8 A.M.–7 P.M. and Sunday 8 A.M.–6 P.M. April–September, and Monday–Friday 8 A.M.–5 P.M. the rest of the year. Out front are phones with direct lines to local businesses, including several B&Bs.

The **Valdez Consortium Library** (Fairbanks St., 907/835-4632, www.ci.valdez.ak.us/library) has computers for checking your email and shows a 30-minute video on Valdez on request. **Anadyr Adventures** (225 N. Harbor Dr., 907/835-2814 or 800/865-2925) also has Web access (as do RV parks and hotels), and their gift shop sells quality Alaskan arts and crafts.

GETTING THERE

Valdez is 366 miles from Fairbanks on the Richardson Highway; from Anchorage it's 189 miles on the Glenn Highway to Glennallen, then another 115 on the Richardson Highway. **Valdez U-Drive** (907/835-4402 or 800/478-4402, www.valdezudrive.com) has rental cars at the airport.

Era Aviation (800/866-8394, www.flyera.com) flies between Valdez and Anchorage several times a day. The airport is four miles outside town; calling a **Yellow Cab** (907/835-2500) will get you a ride into town.

Ferry

The **Alaska Marine Highway** (907/465-3941 or 800/642-0066, www.ferryalaska.com) has daily ferry service connecting Valdez with Whittier and Cordova on both the high-speed *Chenega* and the older (and much slower) *Aurora*. A Forest Service naturalist is on board for summer sailings, and the trip to Whittier includes time among the icebergs near Columbia Glacier.

Cordova

Cordova (pop. 2,200) is noticeably less populated, less prosperous, and less accessible than its big-sister city Valdez—and most people like it that way. Though only a ferry ride away, its setting is its own, its climate is milder and wetter, and its vibration is nothing like Valdez's. Cordova might feel more at home somewhere between Petersburg and Juneau: connected only by boat and plane, with a large commercial fishing fleet, lush forests, small islands, and snowcapped peaks.

But Cordova is more than just the coast; it's also Chugach National Forest, Prince William Sound, and their abundant outdoor recreation; the Copper River and its wild rides and massive delta; spectacular Childs Glacier; railroad history and the Million Dollar Bridge. Amid all of this is a bustling little community bursting at its seams during the summer fishing season, but also glued together by the magic of the fishing lifestyle. Drift over to Cordova and spend a couple of days exploring this special corner of Alaska—you'll be glad you did.

HISTORY

In 1884, Army Captain William Abercrombie surveyed the Copper River delta, which made the area known to a few hardy prospectors. The crazed stampede of 1897–98 opened up the area to settlement. Still, in 1905, Cordova was little more than a couple of canneries processing the pinks and silvers from the Sound. Then Michael J. Heney showed up.

After years of surveying rights-of-way, watching railroad ventures to the rich coal and copper mines nearby start and fold, and failing to convince the Morgan-Guggenheim Alaska Syndicate not to start its road from Katalla, Heney invested his entire savings and in 1907 began laying track from Cordova toward

© DON PITCHER

seafarer's memorial, Cordova

PRINCE WILLIAM SOUND

Kennecott Mines. After the Katalla facilities were destroyed by a storm, the Syndicate bought the Copper River and Northwest line from Heney and completed it in 1911 at a total cost of $23 million; by 1917 it had hauled over $100 million in ore to Cordova for transshipment to smelters. Cordova was a boomtown until the Kennecott Mines closed in 1938.

The 1964 earthquake caused extensive damage to the town, and uplifted the sea floor six feet. Since then the town's economy has re-verted to fishing and canning. The year-round population doubles in the summer, and in good years there's plenty of work. The town's fishing fleet tops 800 vessels at the peak of the sockeye salmon season.

Copper River red and king salmon have attained an almost mythical status. The first major run of Alaska salmon each summer, they're prized for their rich flavor and deep red color, and always garner a high price. Anchorage restaurants often compete to get the first shipment of these salmon, and others are shipped by air directly to markets and restaurants throughout the United States. Find out more at www.crsalmon.org.

SIGHTS

The **Cordova Historical Museum** (622 1st St., 907/424-6665, www.cordovamuseum.org, Tues.–Sat. 10 A.M.–6 P.M. in summer, Tues.–Fri. 10 A.M.–5 P.M. and Sat. 1–5 P.M. the rest of the year, $1) is in the Centennial Building. This museum is small but packed with artifacts, including an old Linotype, an ancient slot machine, a three-seat *baidarka,* and an amusing exhibit on Cordova's famous Iceworm Festival. Look for the aerial views of earthquake damage to the Million Dollar Bridge. The 30-minute *Cordova Story* is shown daily. Next door is the **Cordova Library** (907/424-6667) a good place to read, rest, check your email (free Wi-Fi), and meet fellow travelers.

Many buildings around town were built during Cordova's original construction in 1908, including (all on 1st St.) the Alaskan Hotel and Cordova House, and the Red Dragon, oldest building in town, which served weekdays as a rowdy clubhouse but on Sundays turned into a church when the altar was let down by ropes from the beams. Pick up the historic walking-tour map at the museum for a complete list of the old buildings.

Adjacent to the harbor, the **Ilanka Cultural Center** (110 Nicholoff Way, 907/424-7903, donation) houses a small collection of Eyak Native pieces—both prehistoric and modern—a fine gift shop, and workshop space, but the real attraction is the killer whale skeleton that hangs along the entryway; it's one of just five in the world. Summer hours are Tuesday–Friday 10 A.M.–5 P.M. and Saturday noon–4 P.M., winters are Tuesday–Saturday 9 A.M.–5 P.M. Drop by Wednesdays for demonstrations in basket-making, sewing, beading, carving, or scrimshaw.

Located at the harbor entrance, the **Prince William Sound Science Center** (907/424-5800, www.pwssc.gen.ak.us, Mon.–Fri. 9 A.M.–5 P.M.) is a scientific base for research and education on the regional ecosystem. No exhibits to speak of, but you may want to stop by with questions about the *Exxon Valdez* spill and how it has affected Prince William Sound, or to just enjoy the view from the waterfront deck.

◖ COPPER RIVER HIGHWAY

There aren't enough superlatives in the English language to describe adequately the 50-mile ride out the Copper River Highway from Cordova to the famous Million Dollar Bridge. The scenery—mountains, glaciers, river, and delta—rivals any 50 miles on the continent, let alone the state. The wildlife—thousands of shorebirds and ducks, Canada geese, trumpeter swans, bald eagles, moose, bears, and spawning salmon—gives Denali a run for its money. The history encompasses punching an early-20th-century railroad 200 miles into the Interior and starting a road in the 1960s on its right-of-way, only to be destroyed by the largest earthquake ever recorded in North America. The crowning glory of the trip, as visible in rain or fog as in bright sunshine, built at great expense and great danger in 1910 between the faces of two moving glaciers and left mostly standing by the earthquake, is the Million Dollar Bridge, the vista from which is unsurpassed in a land of unsurpassed vistas.

Just outside of town, the Copper River Highway passes beautiful **Eyak Lake** at the base of Eyak Mountain. Notice how the lake is two colors, deep blue and light green, which don't merge. From around Mile 6 at the bridge over Eyak River to Mile 12 where the pavement ends, keep a sharp eye out for waterfowl and wildlife in the runoff sloughs from nearby Scott Glacier. Take a left at Mile 13 (across from the airport road) and follow a two-mile gravel road up to **Cabin Lake,** with trout fishing, picnic tables, and trails to three other lakes.

At Mile 14, another left and another four miles of gravel bring you to the **Mt. Sheridan** trailhead; hike a mile on the 4WD extension spur and scramble up on the ridge to look out over the two-finger **Sheridan Glacier** flowing down either side of the mountain, and the iceberg-clogged lake at its face. A side road to the right at Mile 17 goes off to **Alaganik Slough;** the three rough miles are excellent for viewing shorebirds. Picnic tables and an information plaque occupy the end of the road, and you can pitch a tent anywhere along here.

The **Haystack Trail** at Mile 19 is a little under a mile, mostly uphill over boardwalks and through second-growth forest. It terminates at a wonderful overlook spot, affording sweeping views of the delta, well worth the short trek. This is a good place to find moose and bears. At Mile 21, the **Pipeline Lakes Trail** leads to the south on a marshy two-mile path. The Forest Service's **McKinley Trail Cabin** is just off the highway at Mile 22. From here, it's an easy two-mile saunter along **McKinley Lake Trail** to McKinley Lake where you can fish for trout or stay in a second cabin.

Across the River

At Mile 27, you cross the first of nearly a dozen bridges and causeways to the other "side" of the Copper River, more than 10 miles distant—it might remind you of the south Florida Keys. Long Island, from Mile 28 to Mile 34, sits smack in the middle of the mighty river delta. Out here you can understand why, out of 196 miles of track from Cordova to Kennicott, 96 miles were built over bridges or trestles.

Finally, at Mile 48, you arrive at **Million Dollar Bridge.** This bridge, which cost a little over a million dollars to build in 1910, was the culmination of Michael Heney's vision, faith, and employee loyalty—not to mention the uncanny abilities of his civil engineers. It had to be built entirely in winter, when the Childs Glacier was dormant. The working conditions were unbearable at best and the danger was extreme, especially as the builders raced to finish the final span even as its supports were being washed away by break-up. The north span collapsed in the 1964 earthquake, but the state eventually repaired the structure.

𝕂 Childs Glacier

On the Million Dollar Bridge, look to your left at the massive face of the Childs Glacier; look right about three miles across Miles Lake to the **Miles Glacier,** which has receded more than two miles since 1910. A short side road on the

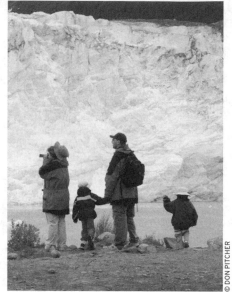

© DON PITCHER

Childs Glacier, Chugach National Forest

left just before the bridge leads to a viewing pavilion set up on a small bluff over the river. From here you can safely view the face of Childs Glacier, under cover from the often-inclement weather. Informative displays give you something to read while you wait for huge chunks of ice to fall into the river. Plan to spend all afternoon here as the glacier creaks, groans, and cracks, dropping calves into the river. Be careful of particularly big calves, whose waves can roll across the river in a few seconds and splash high up the embankment. This is the only road-accessible glacier in Alaska where you will see so much calving action. Don't miss it!

ENTERTAINMENT AND EVENTS

Cordova's **Iceworm Festival** (www.iceworm. org) comes to town the first full week of February. A 140-foot "iceworm" parades through the streets during this offbeat festival. Other events include a fun fair, talent show, crowning of Miss Iceworm, fireworks, and various wacky contests.

The big springtime event is the **Copper River Delta Shorebird Festival** in early May. Held as the first shorebirds appear, it includes workshops, educational seminars, a seafood dinner, and guided field trips to witness the migration of millions of shorebirds.

The arrival of the justly famous Copper River reds (sockeye salmon) is cause for celebration in this fishing town, The **Copper River Wild Salmon Festival** in early June includes a community salmon feed, street dance, and marathon race up the Copper River Highway.

Don't come to Cordova for the night life; other than drinking with the seafood folks, it's strictly make-your-own. The **Alaskan** and **Cordova** bars, next to each other on 1st Avenue, and the **Anchor Bar** on Breakwater Avenue, are hard-core. The Alaskan sometimes has live bands on summer weekends. At the **Powder House** a mile out the Copper River Highway, you can have a drink on the deck along Eyak Lake.

RECREATION
Hiking

Two trails climb **Mt. Eyak**—one through the forest, the other up the ski slope. The unmarked **Tripod Trail** is a little hard to find, but if you cut to the right between a cabin and a driveway near the end of 5th Street, you'll see the trailhead. This is a pretty hike through forest primeval, with salmonberries ripe for the picking in August. Otherwise, head straight up Council Avenue, bear left onto 6th, and follow it around the communications apparatus. You can start right up the mountain from there, and you don't have to go far to get a great view of the town and harbor.

The excellent **Crater Lake Trail** begins opposite Skaters Cabin on Eyak Lake, two miles from town beyond the old cemetery, the seaplane base, and the municipal airstrip. The trail climbs 1,500 feet in two miles through a beautiful forest, with panoramic views near the top of Eyak Lake and the Heney Range. The terrain around Crater Lake is fairly open and it would be easy to scale the surrounding summits, if you have the time and energy. Allow

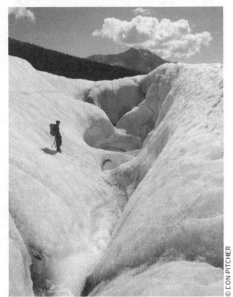

© LON PITCHER

on the surface of Root Glacier, with Porphyry Mountain in the background

a minimum of two hours round-trip from the road to the lake. The trail is solid and very easy to follow; even if a wet wind is blowing, it will be relatively still in the forest, but be careful not to slip. Don't miss this one.

At the end of Power Creek Road, six miles from town, a trail leads about a mile up to Ohman Falls—and when you see it you'll definitely say, "Oh man!" Continue another three miles on **Power Creek Trail** to the Power Creek Cabin.

The Forest Service maintains a number of trails along the Copper River Highway. Pick up a handout on these hikes at the Forest Service office in Cordova (907/424-7661).

Cabins

Ten Forest Service cabins are available for rent ($35, reservations at 877/444-6777, www.reserveusa.com) in the Cordova area; all but three are accessible only by plane or boat. There are cabins at both ends of the McKinley Lake Trail. If you've never seen one, hike for 75 yards up the McKinley Lake Trail (Mile 20)

PRINCE WILLIAM SOUND

and peer in the windows. Staying here is quiet (except for the spawning salmon), secluded, and beautiful. The other foot-accessible cabin (Power Creek Cabin) is four miles north of Cordova via the Power Creek Trail.

On the Water

Alaska River Expeditions (907/424-7238 or 800/776-1864, www.alaskarafters.com) guides fun half-day adventures, including hike and raft trips on the Sheridan River ($85), Sheridan Glacier trekking ($75), and ice climbing classes ($95). Multi-day trips go all the way up to 10-day raft trips ($3,650) from headwaters of the Copper River to the Million Dollar Bridge. Good folks.

The MV *Auklet* (907/424-3428, www.auklet .com) is a classic wooden boat that has been used as a fisheries research vessel. Captain Dave Janka leads overnight or multi-night adventure cruises around Prince William Sound. **Cordova Coastal Outfitters** (907/424-7424 or 800/357-5145, www.cdvcoastal.com) is a one-stop operation with sea kayak day trips and overnight tours, wildlife cruises in Orca Inlet, and shorebird jet boat trips of the Copper River Delta. In addition, they rent gear, including kayaks, canoes, small boats, inflatables, mountain bikes, fishing poles, and camping supplies. They even provide drop-off and pick-ups by van or boat.

Cordova's Olympic-size **swimming pool** (907/424-7282) is on Railroad Avenue.

ACCOMMODATIONS

The Cordova Chamber's website (www .cordovachamber.com) has links to most local lodging places. Add a 12 percent lodging tax to the rates below.

In the heart of town on 1st Street, the **Alaskan Hotel** (907/424-3299), is an old-time place with eight clean and well-maintained rooms over the Alaska Bar. Noise and smoke carry up from below on weekends, but it's inexpensive and authentic. Six simple rooms with no phones or TVs and a bath down the hall are only $44 d; larger rooms with private baths cost $66 d.

Operated by the Salvation Army, **Red Shield Inn** (514 1st St., 907/424-3134, May–Oct., $80 d) is certainly the most unique lodging choice in town. Two furnished studio apartments are available with full kitchens (including dishes and pans) and two double beds; book a month or more ahead for the peak of summer.

The Reluctant Fisherman (407 Railroad Ave., 907/424-3272 or 877/770-3272, www .reluctantfishermaninn.com, $125–145 d) provides recently remodeled accommodations, plus a popular restaurant and lounge. Rooms are large, and many front on the harbor. Free Wi-Fi and guest computers.

Northern Nights Inn (907/424-5356, www.northernnightsinn.com, $75–105 d) has four rooms with private baths and entrances, kitchenettes, and Wi-Fi in a beautiful old downtown home above the harbor.

The **Prince William Motel** (501 2nd St., 907/424-3201 or 888/796-6835, www .pwmotel.com, $100 s, $110 d) has 16 attractive rooms. All include fridges and microwaves; kitchenettes $20 extra.

An old cannery just north of Cordova has been transformed into **Orca Adventure Lodge** (907/424-7249 or 866/424-6722, www.orca adventurelodge.com, $140 d). The rambling buildings sit right on the water, and are decorated with historical items. The old bunkhouse rooms all have private baths and ocean vistas. Meals are available, along with bike and kayak rentals. You can also book a wide range of activities, from white-water rafting to flightseeing.

Bayside B&B (907/424-3675, www.cordova bayside.com, $75 d) is a comfortable home two miles out of town along Orca Inlet. The unit includes two beds, a private bath, and stocked kitchenette to create your own breakfast.

Bear's Den Cabins (907/424-7168, www.bearsdencabins.com, $175–200 d) consists of five delightful cabins (with kitchens and private baths) situated along the Eyak River six miles from town. The largest sleeps eight.

For something unique, **Cordova Rose Lodge** (1315 Whitshed, 907/424-7673, www .cordovarose.com, $150 d) has rooms in a converted landlocked barge filled with nautical antiques and photos. The private lighthouse actually acts as a navigation aid for ships. Rates include a full breakfast and a sauna.

Two comfy places provide private apartments or homes three miles out of town along Eyak Lake: **Bear Country Lodge** (907/424-5901, www.bearcountrylodge.net, $115 d) and **Eyak River Hideaway** (907/424-3922, www.eyakriverhideaway.com, $125 d).

Lighthouses
For something totally out of the ordinary, spend time at **Cape St. Elias Lighthouse** on Kayak Island in the wild Gulf of Alaska 60 air miles southeast of Cordova. This 22-mile long and 2-mile wide island was the first place that Europeans landed on the Northwest coast of North America. Captain Vitus Bering set foot here in 1741, and the island remains virtually unchanged more than two and a half centuries later.

The nonprofit **Cape St. Elias Lightkeepers Association** (907/424-5182) works with the Coast Guard to preserve the lighthouse at the southern end of the island. The old lightkeeper's house still needs work, but you can stay in a comfortable cabin with kitchen, woodstove, and space for 10 people for $70 d. No electricity or running water, and you'll need to hike an hour and a half from where the plane lands on the beach. It costs around $700 round-trip to fly three people from Cordova to Kayak Island. The lighthouse (built in 1916) is of interest, a Steller sea lion haul-out and seabird rookery are nearby, and the beachcombing is some of the best in Alaska (lots of glass balls).

CAMPING
City-run **Odiak Camper Park** (907/424-7282) is a half-mile out Whitshed Road. Camping on this gravel-surfaced area overlooking Orca Inlet is $5 for tents (with showers); RV sites with electricity are $20 (reservations required for these). It's open mid-April through September. Showers are also at the harbormaster's office.

If you've got wheels, head out of town toward the Million Dollar Bridge, and as soon as you pass Mile 17, you're on Forest Service land.

You can theoretically camp anywhere after this point, but the most comfortable places are at the roadside picnic area at Mile 22, or at the parking area of Alaganik Slough.

Out near the airport at Mile 13, **Alaska River Expeditions** (907/424-7238 or 800/776-1864, www.alaskarafters.com, June–mid-Oct., $15) provides a dozen forested campsites.

FOOD
A great place to eat brunch or lunch is the **Killer Whale Cafe** (507 1st Ave., 907/424-7733). The big breakfast menu includes omelets, biscuits and gravy, and waffles, while lunchtime (around $9) features sandwiches, homemade soups, burgers, and salads, along with baked goods and espresso.

The wood-fired oven at **Harborside Pizza** (Nicholoff Way, 907/424-3730) is put to great use baking creative pizzas, available by the pie or slice. They'll deliver to your hotel for $2 extra.

Head two miles out the Copper River Highway to **Powder House Bar and Restaurant** (907/424-3529, $13–29), where a deck overlooks pretty Lake Eyak. (Motto: "I got blasted at the Powder House.") Soups and hoagies are featured, but it also has daily lunch specials, along with steak, shrimp, and salmon dinners on weekends.

OK Restaurant (Main St., 907/424-3433), serves better-than-OK Chinese, Korean, and American dishes, plus fresh sushi.

Alaska Commercial Co. (Nickoloff Rd., 907/424-7141) is Cordova's supermarket. Nearby is **Baja Taco** (907/424-5599, $10 or less), where the friendly staff serves fish tacos, burritos, breakfast burritos, espresso and other fast food all summer, but they wing south to Mexico for the winter months. Order from the kitchen in the funky old red bus and enjoy your meal in the adjacent building with wraparound deck. Free Wi-Fi.

The Reluctant Fisherman (407 Railroad Ave., 907/424-7445 or 877/770-3272, $14–25) is a surf-and-turf restaurant and lounge with a big back deck that to take in the harbor action. Free Wi-Fi.

INFORMATION AND SERVICES

Anything you want to know about Cordova you can find out at the **Cordova Chamber of Commerce** (404 1st St., 907/424-7260, www .cordovachamber.com, Mon.–Fri. 10 A.M.– 4 P.M. all year). Also stop by the Chugach National Forest **Cordova Ranger District office** (2nd Ave., 907/424-7661, www.fs.fed.us/r10/ chugach) for local maps, handouts, and info on cabins and trails. **Cordova Community Medical Center** (Chase Ave., 907/424-8000, www.cdvcmc.com) is the local hospital. Digital cell phones do not work in Cordova, though this could change by the time you visit.

Shopping

Orca Book and Sound (501 1st St., 907/424-5305) is a longtime fixture, with a good choice of regional titles, big art lining the walls, upstairs computer rentals, and free Wi-Fi.

Jenny Parks of **Copper River Fleece** (205 Breakwater Ave., 907/424-4304 or 800/882-1707, www.copperriverfleece.com) crafts handsewn outerwear using wind-stop material and displays them in her downtown shop. The designs are beautiful, warm, and durable. Recommended, but be sure to bring your wallet.

GETTING THERE
Ferry

The **Alaska Marine Highway** (907/465-3941 or 800/642-0066, www.ferryalaska.com) has daily ferry service connecting Cordova with Whittier and Cordova on both the high-speed *Chenega* and the older (and much slower) *Aurora;* a Forest Service naturalist is on board. It's a 20-minute walk from the Cordova ferry terminal to town; take a right at the fork onto Railroad Avenue to avoid the 1st Avenue hill, then walk up Council Avenue.

Air

The airport is 13 miles from town out the Copper River Highway. **Alaska Airlines** (800/426-0333, www.alaskaair.com) provides daily connections to Anchorage, Yakutat, and Juneau. **Era Aviation** (800/866-8394, www .flyera.com) flies turboprops two or three times a day between Cordova and Anchorage. **Cordova Air Service** (907/424-3289) has charter flights throughout the Prince William Sound.

GETTING AROUND

If you want to get out to the glaciers or Million Dollar Bridge, you have two options. You can ferry your own car across from Valdez, but advance reservations are needed. **Chinook Auto Rentals** (907/424-5279 or 877/424-5279, www.chinookautorentals.com) has a variety of cars, SUVs, and vans for $55–95 a day.

Catch a cab to town from the airport ($20 for one person or $36 for two) or within the downtown area ($7) from **Cordova Taxicab** (907/424-5151). Half-hour town tours are $12 per person.

PRINCE WILLIAM SOUND

Whittier

Named for poet John Greenleaf Whittier, this town of 300 friendly people has a picturesque mountains-and-bay setting. Unfortunately, the town itself is anything but poetic, and several other less flattering words come more quickly to mind. Thousands of tourists pass through this settlement every week, but very few choose to spend much time in this strange place where the entire population lives in concrete high-rises and the wind never seems to stop. Ask an Alaskan about Whittier and you're likely to hear the little ditty, "nothing could be shittier than a day in Whittier."

Okay, perhaps I'm too harsh, since Whittier *does* have a gorgeous setting and lots of great outdoorsy things to do in nearby Prince William Sound. So come here for the surrounding land, but don't expect to fall in love with the town, no matter how poetic the name.

HISTORY

While less well known than the Alaska Highway, the construction of the railway to Whittier was one of the great engineering feats of World War II. Two tunnels, one mile and 2.5 miles long, were carved through the Chugach Mountains to link the military bases in Anchorage and Fairbanks to a secret saltwater port. Seward, the main ice-free port in Southcentral Alaska at that time, was considered too vulnerable to Japanese attack, so from 1941 to 1943 the Army blasted through the mountains and laid the tracks that would ensure the flow of supplies for the defense of Alaska. After the defeat of Japan, the military pulled out of Whittier, but a year later they were back as the Cold War began with the Soviet Union. Whittier became a permanent base, and large concrete buildings were built at that time. The 14-story Begich Tower (completed in 1954), an unlikely skyscraper in this small village, is near another anomaly, the "City Under One Roof," which once housed 1,000 men and was the largest building in Alaska. Why build high-rises? To lessen the need for snow removal in a place where the snow sometimes tops 14 feet.

The base was deactivated in 1960 and the buildings were heavily damaged in the 1964 earthquake. One of them is still vacant, but Begich Tower has been restored and converted into condos. A third high-rise, Whittier Manor, was privately built in the 1950s and later turned into more condos. The military presence today is limited to an oil pipeline that supplies military installations in Anchorage. Princess Cruises stops in Whittier, but most of their passengers quickly depart the town.

For nearly half a century the town of Whittier was connected to the road system only via the Alaska Railroad. This changed in 2000, when an $80 million project made it possible for cars to drive in directly from the Seward Highway through two tunnels, one of which is shared with the railroad.

SIGHTS

Most travelers never get farther than the tourist action on the waterfront, where boats of all sizes bob in the picturesque harbor.

Follow the signs for Whittier down past the dry dock, then go left across the tracks onto Whittier Street. Take a right on Glacier Avenue to the **Begich Tower.** In its 198 condos live most of the town's population; the rest reside in the 70 condos at **Whittier Manor.** Many are owned by Anchorageites who use them for weekend and summer getaways, boosting Whittier's summer population to nearly 1,000.

Continue a quarter-mile out Eastern Avenue to quiet, scenic **Smitty's Cove,** where one of Whittier's few private residences sits. You'll get a great view across Passage Canal of waterfalls, a kittiwake rookery, and Billing's Glacier.

C BOAT TOURS

Whittier is a popular departure point for day trips to the glaciers of Prince William Sound in the summer months. **Phillips Tours and**

Cruises (907/276-8023 or 800/544-0529, www.26glaciers.com) operates the 4.5-hour, 26-Glacier Cruise for $129 ($79 kids). The trip aboard its 340-passenger *Klondike Express*— a high-speed, three-deck catamaran—covers a lot of ground but still allows plenty of time to linger at the faces of several glaciers. A hot lunch is included, there's a bar on board, and the lounges provide plenty of room inside should the weather be less than perfect. The schedule is timed so that you can ride the train from Anchorage and back (additional $68 round-trip), or take a bus (additional $45).

Prince William Sound Cruises and Tours (907/835-4731 or 800/992-1297, www .princewilliamsound.com), runs a 6-hour "Wilderness Explorer" tour that includes Barry Arm (Barry and Cox Glaciers) and Esther Passage; $129 adults, $65 kids under 12. Their four-hour trip to Blackstone Glacier is $99 adults, $50 kids. Lunch is included on both of these tours.

Major Marine Tours (907/274-7300 or 800/764-7300, www.majormarine.com, $110 adults, $60 for ages 2–11, free for tots) takes visitors on a leisurely five-hour voyage into stunning Blackstone Bay daily. The cruise includes a filling salmon and prime rib buffet for an extra $15 adults, $7 kids.

In addition to these large operators, a number of locals offer small-boat trips into Prince William Sound. The prices may be a bit higher, but you get a more personal journey. Recommended companies for sightseeing, fishing, water taxis, and kayak drop-offs are **Honey Charters** (907/472-2493 or 888/477-2493, www.honeycharters.com), **Lazy Otter Charters** (907/345-1175 or 800/587-6887, www.lazyotter.com), and **Sound Eco Adventures** (907/472-2312 or 888/471-2312, www.soundecoadventure.com).

RECREATION
Up Portage Pass
The most popular Whittier trail is up to Portage Pass. In the early days when gold was discovered around Hope on the Kenai Peninsula, Hope-bound hopefuls would boat to this harbor, portage their supplies over the glacier pass, and float down Turnagain Arm to their destination. This highly recommended day hike from Whittier affords splendid views of Passage Canal, Portage Glacier, and the Chugach Mountains. On a clear day, the views of the glacier from the Portage Pass area are far superior to those from the Portage Visitor Center.

This trail starts near the oil tanks and tunnel entrance at the foot of Maynard Mountain. Cross the tracks on the dirt road to the left. Take the road to the right and climb southwest along the flank of the mountain up a wide, easy track. If you walk briskly, you can be at Portage Pass (el. 700 ft.) in less than an hour. There are places to camp or picnic beside Divide Lake, but beware of strong winds at the pass. From the lake follow the stream down toward the glacier, then find a way via a tributary on the right up onto one of the bluffs for a view of Portage Lake. Deep crevasses in the blue glacial ice are clearly visible from here. **Portage Glacier** has receded far enough that the gold-rush route is no longer traversable, because of the lake. You must go back the way you came. This hike is highly recommended; allow a minimum of three hours round-trip. Note that there is no clear trail beyond Divide Lake; you must find your own way. Do not attempt to walk on the glacier itself, as the crevasses can be deadly.

Sea Kayaking
A seasonal **Forest Service information station** is housed in the yurt next to the boat harbor; stop by for details on sea kayaking and other outdoor options. Although it is possible to paddle from Whittier to the heart of Prince William Sound, most people prefer to get a boat ride out so they can spend more time near the glaciers and wild country that make this such a special place. A number of local water taxis provide these services, transporting sea kayaks, paddlers, and their gear, and picking them up several days later.

Two companies offer kayak rentals and guided day trips: **Alaska Sea Kayakers** (907/472-2534 or 877/472-2534, www .alaskaseakayakers.com) and **Prince William Sound Kayak Center** (907/472-2452 or

877/472-2452, www.pwskayakcenter.com). An easy three-hour paddle to the kittiwake rookery runs around $80, or take an all-day Blackstone Glacier trip for $300. Multi-night trips are also available.

ACCOMMODATIONS AND CAMPING

June's Whittier B&B (907/472-2396 or 888/472-2396, www.breadnbuttercharters .com) consists of 10 condo suites on the 14th and 15th floors of Begich Tower, starting for $145 d in a one-bedroom apartment, up to $375 for a three-bedroom unit that sleeps six. A continental breakfast is included.

Housed within Whittier Manor, **Soundview Getaway B&B** (907/472-2358 or 800/515-2358, www.soundviewalaska.com, $115 d) features four waterside condo units, including a continental breakfast brought to your door and Wi-Fi.

Anchor Inn (907/472-2354 or 877/870-8787, www.whittierhotel.us) has basic rooms for $88 s or $93–98 d, but noise from the bar can keep you awake. Also here are a restaurant, grocery store, gift shop, and coin laundry.

Camping (907/472-2670, $10) next to Begich Tower is plentiful, with secluded spots for tents and RVs, and a shelter for cooking and socializing in the rain. No hookups or running water, but you can use bathrooms on the first floor of Begich Tower, and showers are available at the harbormaster's office.

FOOD

In addition to grilled halibut, cheese burgers, sandwiches, salads, and espresso, **Cafe Orca** (907/472-2549) has a pleasant waterside deck with picnic tables for sunny mornings.

Swiftwater Seafood Cafe (907/472-2550, www.swiftwaterseafoodcafe.com) is a popular for fish and chips, halibut burgers, and seafood chowder, with smoked prime rib dinners on Friday and Saturday nights.

China Sea Restaurant (907/472-2222) has an all-you-can-eat $10 lunch buffet with soup and salad bar, and **Quigley's Ice Cream Parlor** (907/472-2459) is crowded on those rare sunny days in summer.

INFORMATION AND SERVICES

Get local info from the chamber website (www.whittieralaska.com) or the city site (www.ci.whittier.ak.us). Anchor Inn has a small grocery store, but don't miss the **Harbor Store,** a combination grocery/dry goods/clothing/sporting goods/laundromat/hardware/bait-and-tackle/supermarket/department store—all in an ATCO trailer. The post office is on the first floor of Begich Tower; the library is in the firehall. Get showered at the Harbor Office, next to Hobo Bay.

With an exterior in all sorts of Alaskan memorabilia, **Log Cabin Gifts** (907/472-2501) features arts and crafts items, ivory, and watercolors by the owner, Wilma Buethe Wilcox. You can pet, photograph, and even feed the two pet **reindeer** next door. Also check out at **Sound Ideas** (907/472-2535) for gifts and homemade fudge.

The main Whittier event—other than the rain in summer, snow in winter, and year-round wind—is the **4th of July** celebration featuring a parade, picnic, kid's games, and fireworks.

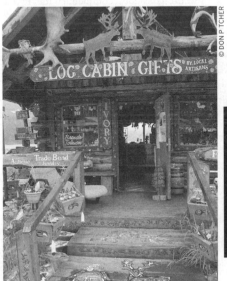
Log Cabin Gifts, Whittier

PRINCE WILLIAM SOUND

GETTING THERE

Whittier is accessible by boat, ferry, train, or car. Drivers get here by turning from Seward Highway at Mile 79 (50 miles south of Anchorage) onto Portage Glacier Highway. The road to Whittier splits off near the Begich, Boggs Visitor Center, heading through a 400-foot tunnel before emerging into Bear Valley. Here you'll find a staging area for access to the 2.5-mile **Anton Anderson Memorial Tunnel** that is shared by both trains and cars. It's the longest auto tunnel in North America, and perhaps the only tunnel in the world where the same roadbed is used by both rail and auto traffic. The tunnel is open to one-way travel throughout the day, but only for 15 minutes out of each hour in each direction (and not at all when trains are transiting the tunnel). Ferry travelers and anyone else on a tight schedule should check the tunnel times in advance to make sure they don't miss their connections. Get a schedule at 907/472-2584 or 877/611-2586, or online at www.tunnel.alaska.gov. The east-bound toll is $12 for autos; no charge heading west.

The tunnel is not recommended for anyone with claustrophobia, and you will be driving on an odd roadbed over the railroad tracks. There are pullouts for emergency use, and enormous fans to clean the air after trains pass through.

Train

The **Alaska Railroad** (907/265-2494 or 800/544-0552, www.akrr.com, $72 round-trip) train connects Whittier with Anchorage daily in the summer, departing Anchorage at 10 A.M. and arriving in Whittier at 12:20 P.M. The northbound train leaves Whittier at 6:45 P.M. and arrives in Anchorage at 9:15 P.M. This makes an excellent day trip from the city. A trivia note: The route to Whittier was used in scenes from the 1986 film *Runaway Train*.

Ferry

The **Alaska Marine Highway** (907/465-3941 or 800/642-0066, www.ferryalaska.com) has daily ferry service connecting Whittier with Valdez and Cordova on both the high-speed *Chenega* and the older (and much slower) *Aurora;* a Forest Service naturalist is on board. Once a week in the summer, the *Kennicott* sails between Whittier and Kodiak.

THE INTERIOR

Interior Alaska is a great tilted plateau between the crests of two long mountain ranges, the Alaska Range and the Brooks Range. The mighty Yukon and Tanana rivers are the main features of this region, but vast expanses of rolling hills are usually in view. Interior Alaska has one fair-sized city, Fairbanks, several small towns, and a number of bush villages, the most interesting along the rivers but some beside the highways. Much of the region is expensive or inaccessible to visit without your own vehicle, but great adventures await on the many wild and scenic rivers, in the wildlife refuges, and in the national parks, especially spectacular Denali National Park.

One of the wonderful aspects of Alaska's Interior is its vastness. A few places—Talkeetna, Fairbanks, and most notably the entrance to Denali National Park—are packed with travelers all summer long, but it's amazingly easy to escape the crowds and find yourself in a land that seems unchanged since time immemorial. Take the time to pull off the highway and fish a bit on one of the creeks or climb a hill for the view. You won't regret it!

This is a place of exceptionally harsh winters, but those long winter nights bring something else, the mysterious northern lights. Winter weather is often clear over Interior Alaska and scientists can now predict the aurora activity level with relative accuracy up to a month in advance. Some lodges around Fairbanks make a special effort to accommodate aurora lovers, and so many Japanese visit that Japan Air even has nonstop flights from Tokyo all winter.

© DON PITCHER

HIGHLIGHTS

◖ **Mt. McKinley Flightseeing:** Talkeetna is the base for several air charter operators with one-hour flights over McKinley that include a bush plane landing on Ruth Glacier (page 339).

◖ **Denali Highway:** This 136-mile mostly gravel road provides dramatic views of the Alaska Range and access to vast stretches of wild country (page 345).

◖ **Denali Shuttle Bus Tours:** This is the only way to reach the heart of Alaska's most famous park. Tours last all day and can be grueling, but grizzlies, moose, wolves, and Dall sheep are commonly seen and you may even get lucky enough to see Mt. McKinley in all its glory (page 355).

◖ **University of Alaska Museum of the North:** This Fairbanks museum is notable not just for its natural history, art, and cultural collections, but also for the monumental building with its high glacier-like entrance (page 379).

◖ **Pioneer Park:** Combining a low-key theme park with a multitude of historical attractions, this city-run facility has everything from an old paddlewheel boat to theatrical productions and carousel rides. Pig out at the salmon bake here; it's the best in Alaska (page 380).

◖ **Riverboat Tours:** Hop onboard a modern day paddlewheeler to cruise the Chena and Tanana Rivers. Although primarily for the package-tour crowd, this is a great way to see the country around Fairbanks (page 381).

◖ **Santa Claus House:** The town of North Pole is home to this kitschy spot with the 40-foot waving Santa out front and all sorts of Christmas paraphernalia inside (page 394).

◖ **Gold Dredge No. 8:** A few miles north of Fairbanks this mechanical monster operated until 1959. It's now open for tours and the chance to practice your gold panning (page 397).

◖ **Chena Hot Springs Resort:** Indoor and outdoor pools are fed by geothermally heated water, and winter guests come for northern lights viewing, but the most unusual feature here is the year-round ice museum filled with intricately carved works of ice art. Chena is an hour's drive east of Fairbanks (page 400).

◖ **Eagle:** Accessible via an arduous 160-mile dead-end road off the Alaska Highway or a fast catamaran from Dawson City, this tiny town displays a multitude of artifacts and historic buildings from the 1890s gold rush (page 416).

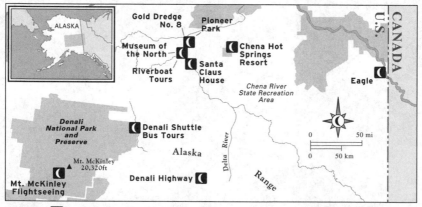

LOOK FOR ◖ TO FIND RECOMMENDED SIGHTS, ACTIVITIES, DINING, AND LODGING.

THE INTERIOR

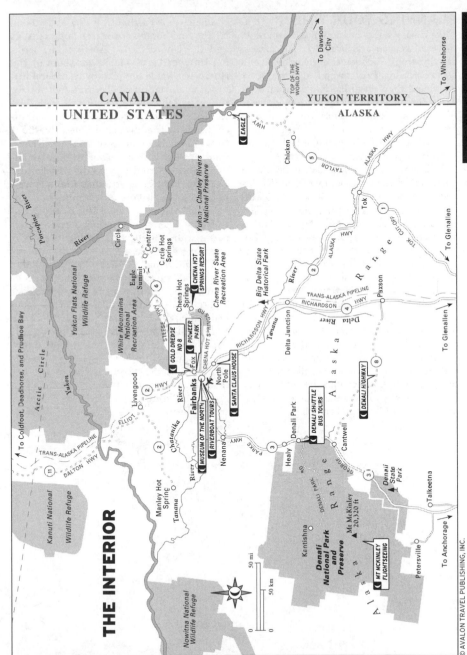

THE INTERIOR

CANADA
UNITED STATES

YUKON TERRITORY
ALASKA

To Dawson City

To Whitehorse

TOP OF THE WORLD HWY

EAGLE

Chicken

ALASKA HWY

Tok

TAYLOR

TOK CUT-OFF

To Glenallen

Yukon – Charley Rivers National Preserve

Porcupine River

River

Circle

Central

Circle Hot Springs

Eagle Summit

CHENA HOT SPRINGS RESORT

Chena Hot Springs

Chena River State Recreation Area

Big Delta State Historical Park

River

ALASKA HWY

Paxson

To Glenallen

TRANS-ALASKA PIPELINE

RICHARDSON HWY

DENALI HIGHWAY

8

Yukon Flats National Wildlife Refuge

White Mountains National Recreation Area

STEESE HWY

6

GOLD DREDGE NO 8

PIONEER PARK

Fox

CHENA HOT SPRINGS RD

SANTA CLAUS HOUSE

North Pole

RICHARDSON HWY

Delta Junction

Tanana

Delta River

A l a s k a   R a n g e

To Coldfoot, Deadhorse, and Prudhoe Bay

Arctic Circle

Yukon

Livengood

2 HWY

Chatanika River

Fairbanks

MUSEUM OF THE NORTH

RIVERBOAT TOURS

ELLIOT HWY

2

TRANS-ALASKA PIPELINE

DALTON HWY

11

Kanuti National Wildlife Refuge

Manley Hot Spring

Tanana

River

Nenana

PARKS HWY

3

Healy

Denali Park

DENALI SHUTTLE BUS TOURS

Cantwell

GEORGE PARKS HWY

DENALI PARK RD

A l a s k a   R a n g e

Denali State Park

3

Denali State Park

Talkeetna

To Anchorage

Petersville

Nowitna National Wildlife Refuge

Kentishna

Denali National Park and Preserve

Mt McKinley 20,320 ft

MT MCKINLEY FLIGHTSEEING

50 mi

50 km

0

0

PLANNING YOUR TIME

The primary sights of Interior Alaska are on the road system and provide ready access. Starting from Anchorage, one could drive to Denali National Park, spend two or three days there, and then on to Fairbanks for another day or two, followed by a return through Delta Junction and Glennallen in another two days. This is, however, a lot of driving for one week (over 1,000 miles), so you might be better off sticking to a few select areas.

Talkeetna is a delightful destination, with outstanding vistas across to Mt. McKinley and a quaint, historic downtown filled with mountaineers and outdoor enthusiasts. Several air taxi operators offer **Mt. McKinley flightseeing** trips that often include a glacier landing. Farther north is the **Denali Highway,** a partly paved, mostly gravel 126-mile route that cuts east to west along the magnificent Alaska Range. **Denali National Park** is always a favorite of travelers and Alaskans. The big draws are 20,320-foot Mt. McKinley (often obscured by clouds), a grand landscape of open tundra and boreal forests, and the chance to watch grizzly bears, moose, wolves, Dall sheep, and caribou. Private cars are not allowed on the road, but **shuttle buses into the park** provide a wonderful way to see the land or to access remote areas for hiking and camping.

The city of Fairbanks is Alaska's second largest, and home to two large military bases and the University of Alaska. The striking **University of Alaska Museum of the North** is notable not just for its natural history, art, and cultural collections, but also for the memorable building with its high, glacier-like entrance. Other local attractions include tourist-friendly paddlewheel **riverboat tours** down the Chena and Tanana Rivers, **Pioneer Park** with its mix of historical buildings, fun-rides, and a great salmon bake, and a visit with St. Nick at **Santa Claus House** in nearby North Pole. A few miles north of Fairbanks is **Gold Dredge No. 8,** which operated until 1959, and is now open for fascinating tours. **Chena Hot Springs Resort** is an hour's drive east of town, with outdoor and indoor pools, wonderful northern lights viewing all winter, and a year-round ice museum filled with intricately carved works of ice art. North of Fairbanks, the challenging Dalton Highway crosses the Arctic Circle and parallels the Trans-Alaska Pipeline all the way to Prudhoe Bay. The town of **Eagle** is accessible via an arduous 160-mile dead-end road off the Alaska Highway, and because of its remoteness many artifacts and historic buildings from the 1890s gold rush are still here.

Talkeetna

The outdoorsy and youthful town of Talkeetna (pop. 360) lies at the end of a 14-mile side road that splits away from the Parks Highway 98 miles north of Anchorage and 111 miles south of Fairbanks. Two closely related phenomena dominate this small bush community: The Mountain, and flying to and climbing on The Mountain. On a clear day, from the overlook a mile out on the Spur Road, Mt. McKinley and the accompanying Alaska Range scrape the sky like a jagged white wall. Though still 60 miles northwest, you actually have to crane your neck to see the summit of the highest peak in North America.

Also on a clear day, local flightseeing and air-taxi companies take off in a continuous parade to circle Mt. McKinley, buzz up long glaciers or even land on them for a champagne lunch, then return to Talkeetna's busy airport to drop off passengers whose wide eyes, broad smiles, and shaky knees attest to the excitement of this once-in-a-lifetime thrill. From late April to early July, these same special "wheel-and-ski" planes might be delivering an American, European, Japanese, or Russian climbing expedition to the Kahiltna Glacier (el. 7,000 ft.), from where—if they're lucky—they inch their way up the popular West Buttress route 13,000 feet to the peak. On a clear day, if you're anywhere within striking distance, make a beeline for Talkeetna and be whisked away to some of the most stunning and alien scenery you'll ever see.

If you visit Talkeetna early in the summer you'll find a peculiar mixing of people: the earthy locals with their beards and rusty pick-ups, the mountaineers—mostly male—decked in color-coordinated Gore-Tex, and the bus-loads of cruise ship passengers who unload on the south side of town and wander through in a dazed blur of gawks and photo-ops.

Talkeetna (Where the Rivers Meet), nesting at the confluence of the Talkeetna, Chulitna, and Susitna Rivers, was originally settled by trappers and prospectors who paddled up the Susitna River to gain access to rich silver, coal, and fur country around the Talkeetna Mountains. The settlement got a boost when the railroad was pushed through in the early 1920s and still remains a popular stop on the route. In 1965 the Spur Road from the Parks Highway to Talkeetna was completed, providing further access to the town.

At the intersection of the Parks Highway and the Talkeetna Spur Road is a helpful visitor center. Covering the area from Willow (south) to Healy (north), the **Talkeetna/ Denali Visitor Center** (907/733-2688 or 800/660-2688, www.alaskan.com/talkeetna denali, daily 10 A.M.–6 P.M. mid-May–mid-Sept.) is staffed by friendly and informative local residents. The rest of the year, the visitor center is above Talkeetna Air Taxi at the airport. The staff (particularly the always-helpful Sheila Keefe) will book flightseeing trips, give you current weather conditions on Denali, set up fishing expeditions or guided hikes, book

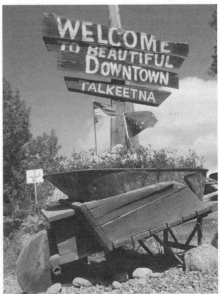

Talkeetna

rooms at hotels and B&Bs, or just supply brochures and information on the area. The Talkeetna Chamber of Commerce (907/733-2330, www.talkeetnachamber.org) has a useful website, and can send out brochures.

SIGHTS

Talkeetna is a wonderful walk-around town, with most of the action within a couple of blocks from Nagley's Store and Fairview Inn. This is one of the few Alaskan towns that still looks the way people imagine Alaskan towns should look, with rustic log buildings lining main street and a local population that encompasses grizzled redneck miners and back-to-the-earth tree-huggers. Local bumper stickers proclaim "Talkeetna, where the road ends and life begins." If you ever saw *Northern Exposure* on TV, this is the place it must have been modeled upon.

For a graphic and detailed look at the history of the town and its connection to The Mountain, check out the excellent **Talkeetna Historical Museum** (907/733-2487, www .talkeetnahistory.org, daily 10 A.M.–6 P.M. mid-May through Sept., and Sat.–Sun. 10 A.M.–5 P.M. the rest of the year, $3 adults, kids under 15 free). Take a left after Nagley's Store, which you can read all about in the museum; the museum is a half-block down the side street on the right in a red schoolhouse built in 1936. Inside are all sorts of local artifacts—including a horsehide coat from the 1890s—but more interesting is the old railroad section house out back which now houses an enormous relief map of Denali surrounded by photos and the stories of climbers, including several famous adventurers who lost their lives on this treacherous peak. Other exhibits show the gear climbers use, such as the required "clean mountain cans" for transporting human waste. Return at 1 P.M. for a Park Service ranger talk on climbing Mt. McKinley.

The Park Service's attractive log **Talkeetna Ranger Station** (B St., 907/733-2231, daily 8 A.M.–6 P.M. mid-April–early Sept., Mon.–Fri. 8 A.M.–4:30 P.M. the rest of the year) is a pleasant place to watch a video or look over the mountaineering books. Park rangers give natural history talks daily in the summer at 7 P.M.

You might also glance inside the **Museum of Northern Adventure** (Main St., 907/733-3999, $2 adults or $1 seniors and kids), a combination gift shop and private collection with 24 north country dioramas.

ENTERTAINMENT AND EVENTS

Talkeetna loves to party. The **Talkeetna Moose Dropping Festival** drops into town the second weekend of July, with a big parade, "mountain mother" contest, foot races, dozens of food and craft booths, and the infamous moose nugget toss and moose nugget dropping contests. If you don't know what moose nuggets are, just ask any Alaskan.

The other big event in these parts is the **Talkeetna Bluegrass Festival** (907/495-6718, www.talkeetnabluegrass.com), held the first weekend of August at Mile 102 of the Parks Highway. Called "Alaska's greatest campout" or "Woodstock Mudhole," this is a great chance to get in touch with your earthy side, hang out with the freaks, and see what mind-altering substances are in fashion. The music rarely strays to bluegrass; more often it's rock, folk, or blues. Great fun, even if it rains.

When winter arrives with a vengeance, **Talkeetna Winterfest** brightens December spirits, especially those of the many local bachelors. The main events are a Wilderness Woman Contest that includes all sorts of wacky activities, followed later that evening by a Bachelor Society Ball during which local bachelors are bid upon by single women, many of whom drive up from Anchorage for the chance. It has all the sexual energy of a male stripper night, except that some of the men are considerably less fit and keep their clothes on (at least during the bidding). This is one of Alaska's most authentic winter events.

The classic **Fairview Inn** (907/733-2423) has live bands nightly in the summer, and is a great place to soak up the atmosphere without the stench; it's finally smoke-free.

© DON PITCHER

Talkeetna Moose Dropping Festival parade

RECREATION
◖ Mt. McKinley Flightseeing

Talkeetna is famous as a launching point for flights over Mt. McKinley, and on a clear summer day a constant parade of planes takes off from the airport on the edge of town. The flight services in town offer a bewildering array of possibilities, including short scenic flights, glacier landings, drop-off hiking or fishing, wildlife viewing, overnight trips, and flights to, around, or over the top of The Mountain. Rates vary according to the type of airplane, length of the flight, and how many people there are in your group. Most outfits will try to match you up with other folks to maximize your flightseeing dollar. Be flexible in your plans, since weather is infinitely variable and is always the most important consideration when it comes to flying you safely. A one-hour flight typically costs $150–165 per person; tack on $70 for a glacier landing. A flight to the summit of Mt. McKinley (good chance to see the climbers) is $220.

Reservations are recommended, but not always necessary. Note that the climbing season on Mt. McKinley runs from early spring until mid or late June, and the flight services are busiest then. As always with bush flying, risks are involved, and fatalities have taken the lives of some of the best local pilots and climbers over the years. Your odds are probably better (not to mention the vistas) if you wait until a clear day to fly.

A number of charter companies provide service to Mt. McKinley. The very knowledgeable staff at the Visitor Center can set up any of these if you don't want to deal with calling each company individually, or you can contact them directly: **Hudson Air Service** (907/733-2321 or 800/478-2321, www.hudsonair.com), **K2 Aviation** (907/733-2291 or 800/764-2291, www.flyk2.com), **Talkeetna Aero Service** (907/733-2899 or 800/660-2688, www.talkeetnaaero.com), **Talkeetna Air Taxi** (907/733-2218 or 800/533-2219, www.talkeetnaair.com), and **Fly Denali** (907/733-7768 or 866/733-7768, www.flydenali.net). Owned by Rust's Flying Service of Anchorage, K2 Aviation is the largest of the five air-taxi operators.

On the Water

Denali View Raft Adventures (907/733-2778 or 877/533-2778, www.denaliviewraft.com) has three-hour Susitna River trips ($95 adults, $65 kids), two-hour Talkeetna River floats ($60 adults, $40 kids), and unique 4.5-hour trip that starts with a train ride upriver followed by a float and lunch on the Susitna River ($155 adults, $105 kids).

Talkeetna River Guides (907/733-2677 or 800/353-2677, www.talkeetnariverguides .com) offers two-hour Talkeetna River floats for $69, and four-hour Chulitna River trips for $115. They primarily book customers from the large hotels.

Mahay's Riverboat Service (907/733-2223 or 800/736-2210, www.mahaysriverboat.com, $55 adults, $28 kids) has a popular two-hour jetboat tour up the Susitna River. Longer trips are also offered.

The fishing in Talkeetna is excellent all summer long; rainbow trout, grayling, Dolly Varden, and all five species of Pacific salmon are there for the catching. Local riverboat services can supply you with a fishing guide or drop you off along the river for the day or overnight. The visitor center has rack cards from most local guides.

Biking and Horseback Riding

A paved bike path parallels the Spur Road all the way to Talkeetna. Turn off onto gravel roads at Miles 3 and 12 for out-of-the-way lakes and camping spots. At Mile 13 is the big turnout with an interpretive sign on the Alaska Range and heart-stopping views—if the clouds are cooperating. **Talkeetna Alaskan Lodge** is on the opposite side of the road; stop in for the Mt. McKinley view from its Great Room even if you aren't overnighting here.

D&S Alaskan Trail Rides (907/733-2205, www.alaskantrailrides.com) has wagon rides and guided horseback rides into the country around Talkeetna. Tour the kennels of Iditarod

musher Jerry Sousa and take a cart ride behind a team of sled dogs at **Sundog Racing Kennel** (907/733-3355 or 800/318-2534, www.sundogkennel.com).

ACCOMMODATIONS

Add a 5 percent lodging tax to the rates listed below.

Hostels

Talkeetna Hostel International (907/733-4678, www.talkeetnahostel.com, mid-April through Sept.) is a fine option for budget travelers. The beds are comfortable, the location—a few blocks east of downtown on I Street—is convenient, and the rate is just $27 per person in a dorm room, $60 s or $75 d for a private room. There are three baths, a full kitchen and laundry, free mountain bikes and Internet access, TV room, and no curfew.

Located in the center of town on Main Street, **House of 7 Trees** (907/733-7733, mid-April–early September) is a cozy little place with hostel bunks for $25 per person, and four private rooms ($70 d) upstairs. Guests have access to the common room with a kitchen and piano. Talkeetna Roadhouse also has bunks.

Hotels

Talkeetna Roadhouse (907/733-1351, www .talkeetnaroadhouse.com, $47 s or $63–89 d) has simple but clean rooms with period antiques and a four-bed co-ed hostel for $21 per bed. All rooms have baths down the hall in this classic Alaskan lodge, constructed in 1917 and in business since 1944.

Latitude 62 Motel (907/733-2262, www .latitude62.com, $60 s or $70 d) is a two-story log building on the south end of town with a 10 clean budget rooms with older furnishings and no phones or TVs.

Above the Wildflower Café, **Main St. Suites** (907/733-2694) consists of a one-bedroom studio ($131 d) and a two-bedroom suite ($163 for up to four), both with private baths and kitchenettes. Open seasonally.

Head across the railroad tracks to **Swiss-**

Alaska Inn (907/733-2424, www.swissalaska .com, $105 s or $130 d) with 20 no-smoking motel rooms with homemade quilts and private baths. No in-room phones or TV reception, but videos are available. German is spoken.

Talkeetna Alaskan Lodge (907/733-9500 or 888/959-9590, www.talkeetnalodge.com, mid-May through Sept.) sits atop a hill a mile south of Talkeetna, with spacious, modern rooms for $259–289 d ($389 d for those that face Mt. McKinley). Luxury suites—most with gas fireplaces and jetted tubs—are $449–549 d. The grand lobby includes a stone fireplace and towering windows framing The Mountain, and a fine-dining restaurant is on the premises. This 200-room Native-owned lodge serves up a million-dollar views for an upscale clientele. It's pretty much the opposite of most Talkeetna lodging places.

Cabins

Paradise Lodge & Cabins (907/733-1471, www .paradiselodge.net, mid-May–mid-September) is aptly named, with a delightful location along Fish Lake five miles south of Talkeetna. Four rustic cabins rent for $100 d with a shared bathhouse, but newer units are being added with private bath. A continental breakfast is served in the lodge.

Right in town **Talkeetna Cabins** (907/733-2227 or 888/733-9933, www.talkeetnacabins.org) has duplex log cabins ($165 d) and a large three-bedroom cabin ($330 for four people), all with full kitchens, private baths, and Wi-Fi.

Susitna River Lodging (907/733-1505 or 866/733-1505, www.susitna-river-lodging.com) has four modern cedar cabins ($229 d) and lodge rooms ($179 d) a half-mile south of Talkeetna. All rooms and cabins have private baths, kitchenettes, and Wi-Fi.

Bed-and-Breakfasts

When it comes to Talkeetna B&Bs the old "location, location, location" saying applies, with several places providing Denali vistas to die for.

Five miles east of town, **Traleika B&B** (907/733-2711, www.traleika.com) has a moun-taintop location facing Denali. The guesthouse rents for $195 d, and a smaller cottage is $165 d; add $20 for extra guests. Both include full baths and kitchens with breakfast supplies.

Not far away—with an equally fine vista— is the reasonably priced **Freedom Hills B&B** (907/733-2455, www.gbfreedomhillsbb.com, $110 d shared bath, $130 d private bath) where five guest rooms are in two adjacent homes. Co-owner and chef Bill Germain creates a de-licious breakfast each morning.

Five miles from Talkeetna, **Denali Overlook Inn** (907/733-3555, www.denali overlook.com, $212 d, mid-June–early August) is a memorable home where the view exceeds your expectations; on a clear day it's impos-sible to miss Mt. McKinley and the rest of the Alaska Range. The five bedrooms have private baths and a continental breakfast is included, along with a guest computer and Wi-Fi. Hon-eymooners will appreciate privacy at the ad-jacent Northern Exposure cabin ($257 d). It doesn't get much better than this!

Built in 1946 and beautifully maintained **Fireweed Station** (907/733-1457 or 888/647-1457, www.fireweedstation.com) is a gorgeous log home off Mile 2 of Talkeetna Spur Road. A spacious suite ($200 d) occupies the entire upstairs, and downstairs are three guest rooms ($150–175 d) with shared or private baths. Also available are a restored 1930s log cabin ($125 d) and a new two-bedroom timber frame home ($300 for four guests). All rates include a full breakfast, and dinners are available upon re-quest.

Another lovely place with fine views of Mt. McKinley is **Talkeetna Chalet B&B** (907/733-4734, www.talkeetnachalet.com, $145–165 d), three miles from town. Three guest rooms have private or shared baths, big breakfasts, and ac-cess to a hot tub on the deck. Guests can use the first two floors of the home, and a guest computer is available.

CAMPING

Find free camping at shady **River Park** at the end of Main Street, but no running water. **Talkeetna Camper Park** (907/733-2693, www.talkeetnacamper.com, April–Oct., $25 RVs) has wooded sites; it's on the right just before you enter town.

Take **showers** ($5 with a towel) and wash your clothes at Washi-Washi or the coin laundry behind Coffee Cabin.

FOOD

Talkeetna has turned into quite the spot for good, inexpensive food, a definite rarity on the Alaska road system.

At **Talkeetna Roadhouse** (907/733-1351, www.talkeetnaroadhouse.com) excellent breakfast starts at 7 A.M. and late risers can still get a delicious filling breakfast until 3 P.M. (when it closes). The giant cinnamon rolls are legendary, and for lunch the Roadhouse cranks out homemade soups, salads, and sandwiches on freshly baked breads. The long tables make for fun family-style dining with crowds of locals and visitors.

Nagley's Store (907/733-3663) opened in the 1920s and is still the main place for groceries in town, but it's also added such staples of 21st-century life as an ATM and espresso.

Behind Nagley's is **West Rib Deli and Pub** (907/733-3663, $8–13), with seafood, sandwiches, salads, burgers, and Alaskan brews on draught. Everyone raves about the caribou chili and cheese fries. Best deal? Meet the locals at the Friday night burger-and-beer for just $6. There's an outside deck for sunny days.

Housed in a modern log building, **Wildflower Café** (907/733-1275, open seasonally) is popular for a cheeseburger and fries, cheese steak sandwich, chicken salad, or veggie burger, but don't miss the crab cake appetizers. Wildflower also has nightly dinner specials.

Mt. High Pizza Pie (907/733-1234, www.mhpp.biz), in the purple log cabin, is a busy spot for pizzas, salads, and subs. They have all the standard pizzas, plus a "mountain high" version, piled high with all the ingredients. The side deck erupts with live music six nights a week in the summer.

You'll find Alaskan favorites such as fresh halibut and salmon dinners at **Swiss-Alaska Inn** (907/733-2424, www.swissalaska.com), along with Swiss-style French toast for breakfast, and other schnitzels at lunch. German is spoken, and the lounge serves cocktails.

One place really stands out in Talkeetna, **Cafe Michele** (907/733-5300, www.cafemichele.com, May–Sept., $19–33 entrées), where the bistro atmosphere is decidedly classy. Chef Michele Camera-Faurot's menu includes such treats as venison flank steak, soy-ginger king salmon, or sun-dried tomato linguine. Open for lunch and dinner, with wonderful desserts, including the bourbon vanilla cheesecake.

INFORMATION AND SERVICES

Several local shops are worth a visit, including two places almost next to each other: **Denali Images Art Gallery** (907/733-2026, www.stevegilroy.com), which displays wildlife and nature photos by Steve Gilroy, and **Wildlife North Art Gallery** (907/733-5811, www.davidtotten.com) with the paintings of David Totten.

Keep in touch with the outside world via the Internet at the **library** on the south side of town. Pop open your laptop for Wi-Fi at Coffee Conscious (free), Coffee Cabin (free), or Talkeetna Travel (fee).

GETTING THERE

The turnoff to Talkeetna is 100 miles north of Anchorage on the George Parks Highway, and the town is another 14 miles out Talkeetna Spur Road.

Buses

Several companies provide van transportation to Talkeetna; one-way rates are around $65 to Anchorage, $52 to Denali, or $85 to Fairbanks. **Alaska/Yukon Trails** (907/479-2277 or 800/770-7275, www.alaskashuttle.com) has a daily Anchorage–Talkeetna–Denali–Fairbanks run in the summer, and several times a week the rest of the year. **Denali Overland Transportation** (907/733-2384 or 800/651-5221, www.denalioverland.com) has charter service connecting Anchorage, Talkeetna, and Denali, and often has space for individual travelers. **Alaska Park Connection** (907/245-0200 or 800/266-8625, www.alaskacoach.com) provides summertime service connecting Talkeetna with Seward, Anchorage, and Denali.

Train

The Alaska Railroad's (907/265-2494 or 800/544-0552, www.akrr.com) Denali Star train costs $82 one-way to Talkeetna. The train leaves Anchorage every morning at 8:15, arrives in Talkeetna at 11:05, and a second train leaves for the return trip at 4:40 P.M. A local flag-stop Hurricane Turn train runs the 50 miles from Talkeetna north to Hurricane and back Thursday–Sunday in the summer. It's a great way to see the countryside with locals for $80 round-trip.

North from Talkeetna

TRAPPER CREEK AND PETERSVILLE ROAD

The minuscule settlement of Trapper Creek (pop. 350) is at Mile 115 of the Parks Highway, and 16 miles north of the junction with Talkeetna Spur Road. Petersville Road splits off at Trapper Creek, providing access to the western end of Denali State Park, and offering some of the finest views of Mt. McKinley. A half-mile out Petersville Road is **Trapper Creek Museum** (907/733-2555), a collection of local historical items and local crafts in a log cabin built in 1959. The museum is on Spruce Lane Farms, which raises miniature horses.

A number of rural subdivisions and homesteads are found along Petersville Road, and this is a popular winter destination for dog mushers and hordes of snowmobilers. The road continues all the way to old mining developments in the Petersville mining camp, 30 miles in, though the last section may not be passable without a high-clearance vehicle. The National Park Service is planning a new visitor center near Petersville, but don't look for it until 2006 or so. By the time it opens, the road will probably be paved the entire distance, and there's even talk of a train or tram to the site. Visit this wonderful area before the crowds get there!

Accommodations

Located at Mile 114 of the Parks Highway, **Trapper Creek Inn & General Store** (907/733-2302, www.trappercreekinn.net) has rooms ($65–75 d), RV sites, groceries, a deli, and coin laundry with showers.

Recently opened, **Alaska's Northland Inn** (907/733-7377, www.alaskasnorthland inn.com, $120 d) has a pair of two-level apartments with private baths and full kitchens. Relax in the great room with a pool table and satellite TV.

Set along two ponds, **Gate Creek Cabins** (907/733-1393, www.gatecreekcabins.com, $130 d, add $40 per person for additional guests) is 11 miles out Trapper Creek Road, and the 10 modern log cabins (the largest has four bedrooms) contain kitchens, private baths, and a community sauna. Guests can borrow a canoe or paddleboat to cruise the ponds or try a bit of fishing. Be sure to ask about the mid-July bear-viewing opportunities. The cabins provide an extremely popular winter base for snowmobilers.

Forks Roadhouse (907/733-1851) 19 miles out, is a classic Alaskan bush roadhouse with a genuine sense of history. Rooms upstairs above the bar are $50 d (bath down the hall), a four-bed hostel-style room there is $25 per person, and basic cabins cost $100 for four people (bath inside the lodge). Breakfast, burgers, and sandwiches are served in the roadhouse, or you can shoot a game of pool and tip a brew in the bar.

If you want remote, check out **Cache Creek Cabins** (907/733-5200, www.cache creekcabins.com), 39 rugged miles out the Petersville Road. Six little cabins ($45 d) share a common bathhouse, and a nicer two-story cabin sleeps eight for $150; it has a private bath. The friendly owners can provide home-cooked meals ($45 pp/day) and gold panning in the creek. It's a pretty setting with wonderful views of Denali on the drive in. High-clearance vehicles are best, but many folks make it here in 4WD Subarus.

DENALI STATE PARK

This 325,240-acre state park (907/745-3975, www.alaskastateparks.org) lies just southeast of Denali National Park and Preserve, and is bisected by the Parks Highway from Mile 132 to Mile 169. Situated between the Talkeetna Mountains to the east and the Alaska Range to the west, the landscape of Denali State Park varies from wide, glaciated valleys to alpine tundra. The Chulitna and Tokositna Rivers flow through western sections of the park, while the eastern half is dominated by Curry Ridge and Kesugi Ridge, a 35 mile-long section of alpine country.

Denali State Park provides an excellent alternative wilderness experience to the crowds and hassles of its federal next-door neighbor. The Mountain is visible from all over the park, bears are abundant, and you won't need to stand in line for a permit to hike or camp while you wait for Mt. McKinley's mighty south face to show itself. Several trails offer a variety of hiking experiences and spectacular views. Trailhead parking is $5 a day.

Sights

Denali State Park is best known for its breathtaking **views of Mt. McKinley** and the Alaska Range from pullouts along the Parks Highway. If The Mountain or even "just" some of the lower peaks of the Alaska Range are out, you won't need to read the next sentence to know what or where the sights are. The best viewpoint along the highway in the park, and the most popular, is at Mile 135, where you will find an interpretive signboard and crowds of fellow travelers on a clear day. Set up your tripod and shoot, shoot, shoot. Other unforgettable viewpoints are at Miles 147, 158, and 162.

The **Alaska Veterans Memorial** at Mile 147 (within walking distance of Byers Lake Campground) consists of five monumental concrete blocks with stars carved out. Turn your back to the monument, and if you're lucky, there's blue-white McKinley, perfectly framed by tall spruce trees.

The western section of Denali State Park lies within the remote Peters Hills, an area known for its pristine Mt. McKinley vistas and open country. This section is accessed via the Petersville Road.

Recreation

Little Coal Creek trailhead is at Mile 164, five miles south of the park's northern boundary. This is the park's gentlest climb to the alpine tundra—five miles east up the trail by Little Coal Creek, then you cut southwest along Kesugi Ridge with amazing views of the Range and glaciers; flags and cairns delineate the trail. Watch for bears! The trail goes 27 miles until it hooks up with Troublesome Creek Trail just up from Byers Lake Campground. About halfway there, **Ermine Lake Trail** cuts back down to the highway, an escape route in case of really foul weather.

Troublesome Creek Trail is so named because of frequent bear encounters; in fact, Troublesome Creek Trail is frequently closed in late summer and early fall because of the abundance of bears. It has two trailheads, one at the northeast tip of Byers Lake (Mile 147), the other at Mile 138. The park brochure describes this 15-mile hike along Troublesome Creek as moderate. It connects with Kesugi Ridge Trail just up from Byers Lake or descends to the easy five-mile **Byers Lake Loop Trail,** which brings you around to both campgrounds. Just down and across the road from the Byers Lake turnoff is a family day hike along Lower Troublesome Creek—a gentle mile.

Based at Byers Lake, **Mountain Light Adventures** (907/733-1237, www.moutainlightadventures.com) guides easy 2.5-hour nature walks ($49 adults, $39 kids), and more interesting 5.5-hour hikes up Kesugi Ridge ($89 adults, $69 kids with lunch and gear). The guides are former national park rangers with years of local experience, and the company also provides a helpful vehicle shuttle service for hikers on the Troublesome Creek Trail.

Denali Southside River Guides (907/733-7238, www.denaliriverguides.com) rents sit-on-top kayaks and canoes at Byers Lake; they're located at the day-use parking lot.

Accommodations

Turn off the highway at Mile 133 for a one-mile side road into **Mt. McKinley Princess Lodge** (907/733-2900 or 800/426-0500, www.princesslodges.com, mid-May–mid-Sept., $179 d). This stylish 334-room retreat is famous for its riverside location and picture-perfect vistas of the Alaska Range and Mt. McKinley. Most rooms are filled with Princess cruise passengers, but anyone can stay or eat here. The lodge itself centers around a "great room" with a stone fireplace, a pianist at the grand piano most evenings, and enormous windows fronting the mountain. Lodging is in smaller buildings scattered around the grounds; ask for one of the new rooms with a king bed. There's also a small fitness center, two outdoor hot tubs, a restaurant, and café.

Located at the southern edge of Denali State Park near Mile 134, **Mary's McKinley View Lodge** (907/733-1555, www.mckinleyviewlodge.com) has a restaurant, great views of The Mountain out the big picture windows, and guest rooms ($100 d) with private baths. This is the home of Mary Carey, one of the most prolific Alaskan authors. You can buy autographed copies of her dozen books, including her best known, *Alaska, Not for a Woman*. The lodge is run by Mary and her daughter, Jean Richardson, who writes children's books.

Cabins and Camping

Byers Lake Campground ($10) has large and uncrowded sites, water, outhouses, interpretive signs, and beautiful Byers Lake a stone's throw down the road. Also at Byers Lake are two popular **public-use cabins** (907/745-3975, www.alaskastateparks.org, $60/night).

Just under two miles along the Loop Trail from the campground or across the lake by boat is **Lakeshore Campground,** with six primitive sites, outhouses, no running water, but unimpeded views of The Mountain and Range from your tent flap. Across the road and a quarter-mile south, **Lower Troublesome Creek Campground** ($10) has 20 sites and all the amenities of Byers Lake.

◖ DENALI HIGHWAY

The Denali Highway, which stretches 136 miles east–west across the waist of mainland Alaska from Cantwell, 30 miles south of Denali Park to Paxson at Mile 122 of the Richardson Highway, may be the best-kept secret in Alaska. Originally, the Denali Highway was the only road into Denali National Park and this beautiful side trip has been largely ignored by visitors since the opening of the George Parks Highway in 1971. Denali Highway is paved for 21 miles on the east end of the road (from Paxson to Tangle Lakes), and for three miles on the western end, but the rest is well-maintained gravel, which has received an undeserved bad rap—usually from folks hoping to set world land-speed records on their Alaska vacation.

The Denali Highway offers a varied selection of outstanding scenery and wildlife-viewing opportunities. Much of the route punches through the foothills of the magnificent Alaska Range. This area is part of the home range of the huge Nelchina caribou herd (30,000 strong). In the fall they begin to group in the greatest numbers—sightings of several hundred caribou are not unusual.

The Denali Highway is closed from October through mid-May, but in the winter it becomes a popular trail for snowmobilers, dog mushers, and cross-country skiers. Die-hard Alaskans also use this trail in the winter for access to unparalleled ice fishing and caribou and ptarmigan hunting.

As always, travelers on the Denali Highway should be prepared for emergencies. Always carry a spare tire and tire-changing tools, water, some snacks, and warm clothing. Towing is available from Paxson, Gracious House,

To Fairbanks
Denali Park

To Delta Junction

DENALI HIGHWAY

Denali NP

GEORGE PARKS HWY

Mount Hess 11,940ft

Mount Deborah 12,339ft

Mount Hayes 13,832ft

Cantwell   Nenana

Lily Creek

BRUSHKANA RIVER CAMPGROUND

To Talkeetna and Anchorage

Seattle Creek
Stixkwan Creek

Brushkana

GRACIOUS HOUSE

◀ DENALI HIGHWAY

Lower Tangle Lake

Maclaren Summit

TANGLE LAKES CAMPGROUND

Long Tangle Lake

Summit Lake

Round Tangle Lake   Paxson

TANGLE RIVER INN

Upper Tangle Lake

Paxson Lake

To Glennallen

0   20 mi
0   20 km

© AVALON TRAVEL PUBLISHING, INC.

and Cantwell. But it ain't cheap, so take your time and be safe.

History

The Denali Highway began as a "cat" track in the early 1950s when a man named Earl Butcher first established a hunting camp at Tangle Lakes. Known for years as Butcher's Camp, it's now the site of Tangle Lakes Lodge. About the same time, Chalmer Johnson established a camp at Round Tangle Lake. Now known as the Tangle River Inn, this lodge is still operated by the Johnson family.

Cantwell

Cantwell is a minuscule settlement (pop. 160) at the junction of the Parks Highway and Denali Highway. The town began as a railroad settlement, and most of the decrepit buildings are along the tracks two miles west of the highway junction. Cantwell is less than 30 miles south of Denali National Park, and a couple of businesses provide the staples: fuel, food, lodging, and booze. Most folks stop to fill up on the expensive gas, get a soda, and tool on up the highway. There aren't a lot of reasons to stay in Cantwell itself, though the surrounding country is grand.

Cantwell Lodge (907/768-2300 or 800/768-5522, www.cantwell-lodge.com) is the main action, though it's little more than a plywood box. Here you'll find motel units for $75 s or $85 d, ancient Atco trailers for $35 per person, a café, bar, liquor store, RV parking ($30), laundry, and showers ($2).

Located a quarter-mile up Denali Highway, **Backwoods Lodge** (907/768-2232 or 800/292-2232, www.backwoodslodge.com, $120–150 d) has modern motel rooms with fridges and microwaves. **Denali Manor B&B** (907/768-2223 or 800/378-5990, www.denalimanor.com) charges $99 d, and provides a full breakfast.

Park RVs at **Cantwell RV Park** (907/768-2210 or 800/940-2210, $23 RVs), an open lot near the junction with the Parks Highway.

Denali Sightseeing Safaris (907/240-0357, www.denalisights.com, June to mid-September) operates from the igloo-on-steroids at Mile 188 of the Parks Highway (22 miles south of Cantwell). These unique tours are in customized big-tired trucks to allow them to cross glacial rivers and take you up old mining roads into the spectacular alpine. Seven-hour treks are $140 adults, $70 kids under 13.

EAST ON DENALI HIGHWAY

About three miles east of the Denali Highway/ Parks Highway junction is a turnout with a view of Cantwell and Mt. McKinley, if it's out. There's another potential view of the mountain at Mile 13, then in another five miles the highway runs parallel to the Nenana River. The headwaters of the Nenana emanate from a western digit of the icefields atop the Alaska Range trio of Peaks: **Mt. Deborah** on the left at 12,339 feet, **Mt. Hess** in the middle at 11,940 feet, and **Mt. Hayes** on the right at 13,832 feet.

Over the next 10 miles the road crosses Lily Creek, Seattle Creek, and Stixkwan Creek; throw in a line and pull up some grayling or Dolly Varden. At Mile 31 you come to the **Brushkana River,** where the Bureau of Land Management (BLM) has a good campground ($6) right on the river, and over the next 10 miles you get some great views of the three prominent peaks, along with the West Fork Glacier. The southern glaciers off Deborah, Hess, and Hayes feed the Susitna River, which travels west (to the Parks Highway), then south, and empties into the Cook Inlet across from Anchorage.

Gracious House Lodge and Beyond

Fifty-four miles east of the junction of the Parks and Denali Highways is Gracious House Lodge (907/259-1111, www.alaskaone.com/ gracious, June–mid-Sept.), with motel rooms ($115 d with private baths, $80 s or $100 d with shower house). RV and tent spaces ($15; no electricity) are also available, along with minor tire and mechanical repairs and towing. The café serves home-style Alaskan meals daily 8 A.M.–8 P.M., and will set up air-taxi and guide services.

Five miles farther you cross the single-lane, 1,000-foot-long Susitna River bridge. Farther south, the Susitna is a popular river to float, but passage between here and there is considered impossible because of the impassable Devil's Canyon just downriver from the bridge.

At Mile 79, the highway crosses Clearwater Creek; there are pit toilets at a rest stop/camping area here. In six miles is a turnout with a view of numerous lakes and ponds that provide a staging area for waterfowl; look for ducks, cranes, geese, trumpeter swans, and migrating shorebirds.

Maclaren

At Mile 93 out of Cantwell, the road crosses the Maclaren River, a tributary of the Susitna, flowing from the southern icefields of mighty Mt. Hayes. From here to the other end of Denali Highway, you get occasional views of the three Alaska Range peaks. A mile west of the bridge is Maclaren River Road, which leads 12 miles north to Maclaren Glacier.

In another seven miles is Maclaren Summit, at 4,080 feet the second-highest road pass in Alaska. It provides breathtaking views of Mt. Hayes and the Maclaren Glacier. Peer through binoculars at the plains below to spot wildlife. Up at the summit you might see rock ptarmigan.

East End

The BLM's **Tangle Lakes Campground** (907/822-3217, www.ak.blm.gov, free) at mile 113 has water pumps, pit toilets, blueberries in season, and a boat launch for extended canoe trips into the "tangle" (or maze) of lakes and ponds and creeks in the neighborhood.

Two miles east of the campground is **Tangle River Inn** (907/895-4022 winter or 907/822-3970 summer, www.tangleriverinn.com, May–Sept.). Jack and Naidine Johnson have owned this place since 1970. The Johnsons sell gas, liquor, and gifts, and offer good home-cooking, a lively bar, lodging ($30 s in the bunkhouse, $70 d with shared bath, or $119 d for new units with full baths), canoe rentals, and fishing gear.

The **Tangle Lakes Archaeological District** begins at Mile 119 and extends back to Crazy Notch at Mile 90. A short hike from the highway to any given promontory along this 30-mile stretch could have you standing at an ancient Athabascan hunting camp where no human footprints have been made for hundreds of years.

At Mile 122, there's a viewpoint from the summit that looks south over a great tundra plain. The three most prominent peaks of the Wrangell Mountains are visible from here: Mt. Sanford on the left, Mt. Drum on the right, and Mt. Wrangell in the middle.

At Mile 125 is a paved turnout with a view of **Ten Mile Lake.** A short trail leads down to the lake, where you can catch grayling and trout. A turnout at Mile 129 affords a spectacular view of the Alaska Range to the north. The Gulkana and Gakona Glaciers can be seen from this point. The Denali Highway joins the Richardson Highway at Paxson.

Paxson and Points North

This tiny settlement at Mile 186 of the Richardson Highway and Mile 136 (from Cantwell) of the Denali Highway has a 3,000-foot airstrip and two lodging options. **Paxson Lodge** (907/822-3330), offers gas, meals, and lodging ($70 s or $80 d). There's a big deck for summertime dining.

Located just north of the highway junction, **Paxson Alpine Tours** (907/822-5972, www .denalihwy.com), guides wildlife float trips on the Gulkana and Delta rivers, birding hikes, and other adventures. Owners Audie Bakewell and Denali Jenny also operate **Denali Highway Cabins,** with peaceful riverside cabins containing private baths for $130–147 d, and rooms in a guesthouse (full kitchen) for $175 d. Rent one of their canoes to paddle the Tangle Lakes.

For one of Alaska's most memorable drives, head north from Paxson along the Richardson Highway. The pipeline parallels the route as it climbs through a grand landscape of tundra, mountains, and rivers. Another 30 miles north is the century-old **Black Rapids Roadhouse,** slowly being restored after years of neglect. Behind this and up the hill is **Black Rapids Lodge** (907/455-6158, www.blackrapids.org), a beautiful timber frame structure with all-inclusive lodging and meals.

The BLM's **Paxson Lake campgrounds** ($6) is at Mile 175 of the Richardson, 10 miles south of the junction with Denali Highway.

Denali National Park and Preserve

Alaska's most famous tourist attraction, Denali National Park (907/683-2294, www.nps. gov/dena) draws over 400,000 visitors during its brief summer season. Most travelers come to see Mt. McKinley, highest peak in North America (20,320 ft.), which towers above the surrounding lowlands and 14,000- to 17,000-foot peaks. Although it's visible only one day in three, and often shrouded for a week or more at a time, those who get lucky and see the mountain experience a thrill equivalent to its majesty and grandeur. Those who don't are usually consoled by lower snowcapped mountains and attending glaciers, high passes and adrenaline-pumping drops off the road, tundra vistas and "drunken forests," and an incredible abundance of wildlife, including caribou, moose, sheep, and bear. But even if the mountain's socked in, the grizzlies are hiding, and the shuttle-bus windows are fogged up, you're still smack in the middle of some of the most spectacular and accessible wilderness in the world. It was the call of the wild that brought you out here in the first place. And all you have to do is step outside and answer.

THE LAND

The Alaska Range is a U-shaped chain that extends roughly 600 miles from the top of the Alaska Peninsula (at the head of the Aleutians) up through the park and down below Tok. It's only a small part, however, of the coastal mountains that include California's Sierra Nevada, the Northwest's Cascades, the Coast Mountains of British Columbia, Yukon's St. Elias Range, and eastern Alaska's Wrangell Range. The Park Road starts out a bit north of the Alaska Range and follows the U 90 miles

COEXISTING WITH BEARS

Bears seem to bring out conflicting emotions in people. The first is an almost gut reaction of fear and trepidation: What if the bear attacks me? But then comes that other urge: What will my friends say when they see these *incredible* bear photos? Both of these reactions can lead to problems in bear country. "Bearanoia" is a justifiable fear, but can easily be taken to such an extreme that one avoids going outdoors at all for fear of running into a bear. The "I want to get close-up shots of that bear and her cubs" attitude can provoke a bear attack. The middle ground incorporates a knowledge of and respect for bears with a sense of caution that keeps you alert for danger without letting fear rule your wilderness travels. Nothing is ever completely safe in this world, but with care you can avoid most of the common pitfalls that lead to bear encounters.

Brown bears occur throughout Alaska, except on islands in southern Southeast Alaska, in the Bering Sea, and out most of the Aleutian Chain. Black bears are found in forested area across most of the state, but not on several islands in northern Southeast Alaska. Old-timers joke that bears are easy to differentiate: a black bear climbs up the tree after you, while a grizzly snaps the tree off at the base. Both grizzlies and black bears pose potential threats to backcountry travelers; polar bears are potentially the most dangerous of the three species, but are almost never encountered by summertime visitors, since they only occur in remote northern and western parts of the state.

Enter bear country with respect but not fear. Bears rarely attack humans; you're a thousand times more likely to be injured in a highway accident than by a bear. In fact, more people in Alaska are hurt each year by moose or dogs than by bears. Contrary to the stories you often hear, bears have good eyesight, but they depend more upon their excellent senses of smell and hearing. A bear can tell who has walked through an area, and how recently, with just a quick sniff of the air. Most bears hear or smell you long before you realize their presence, and hightail it away.

Bears are beautiful, eminently fascinating, and surprisingly intelligent animals. They can be funny, playful and inquisitive, vicious or protective, and unpredictable. The more you watch bears in the wild, the more complex their lives seem, and the more they become individual animals, not simply the big and bad.

southwest toward its heart—Mt. McKinley. One thing that makes the mountain so spectacular is that the surrounding lowlands are so low: The entrance is at 1,700 feet, and the highest point on the road, Thoroughfare Pass, is just under 4,000. The base of Mt. McKinley is at 2,000 feet, and the north face rises at a 60-degree angle straight up to 20,000 feet—the highest vertical rise in the world.

Weather patterns here differ between the south side of the range (wetter and cooler) and the north. During the summer, the prevailing winds come from the south, carrying warm moisture from the Pacific. When they run smack into the icy rock wall of the Alaska Range, they climb, the moisture condenses, and depending on the amount of moisture and altitude, it either rains or snows. A lot. On top of that whole system sits mighty Mt. McKinley—high, cold, and alone. So alone that the mountain has its own relationship to the weather. The combination of wind, wet, cold, and height creates weather extremely localized—and often violent—around Mt. McKinley. Storms can blow in within an hour and last a week or more, dumping 10 feet of snow. Winds scream in at up to 80 mph. The mercury drops below zero in mid-July. Some of the worst weather in the world swirls around up there. But when the mountain emerges bright white against bright blue, and you're craning your neck to see the top, it's an unforgettable sight worth waiting around for—even in the rain.

Flora and Fauna

From sea level to around 2,300 feet is the habitat for the **boreal forest,** in which the black spruce, with its somber foliage and clusters of tawny cones, is the climax tree. Younger white spruce, along with deciduous aspen, birch, and cottonwood, grow near the streams and the road and in recently burned areas.

Climbing out of the forest above 2,300 feet you enter the **taiga,** a Russian word meaning "land of twigs." This transition zone (between the forest below and tundra above) accommodates no deciduous trees; the spruce are thinned out and runty (though they can be over 60 years old), and a green shag carpet of bush, mostly dwarf willow, layers the floor. Sitka spruce is the state tree because of its size, grandeur, and commercial value, but it's the willow that vegetates Alaska. And it has endless uses. Before synthetics like nylon, the bark was stripped, split, and braided and made into rope, bows, wicker baskets, snowshoes, fishnets, and small game and bird snares and traps. The inner bark is sweet; the sap is very sweet. Young buds and shoots are edible and nourishing, and willows are the nearly exclusive staple of the moose diet. The taiga also hosts a variety of berries: blueberries and low bush cranberries by the ton, crowberries, bearberries, soap and salmon berries, and raspberries.

Above 2,500 feet is the **tundra,** its name a Lapp word meaning "vast, rolling, treeless plain." There are two types of tundra: the moist, or Alaskan, tundra is characterized by the taiga's dwarf shrubbery, high grasses, and berries, but no trees; the alpine tundra, the highest zone, has grasses, moss, lichens, and small, hardy wildflowers, including the stunning forget-me-not, Alaska's state flower.

The animal life varies with the vegetation. In the forest, look for moose, porcupine, snowshoe hare, marten, lynx, two kinds of weasels, red or tree squirrels, and several varieties of small rodents. On the taiga—or in both the forest and the tundra—you might see coyote, wolf, fox, grizzly, and ground squirrel. In the tundra, keep an eye out for caribou, wolverine, Dall sheep, marmot, vole, lemming, and shrew.

HISTORY

In 1896, a prospector named Bill Dickey was tramping around interior Alaska looking for

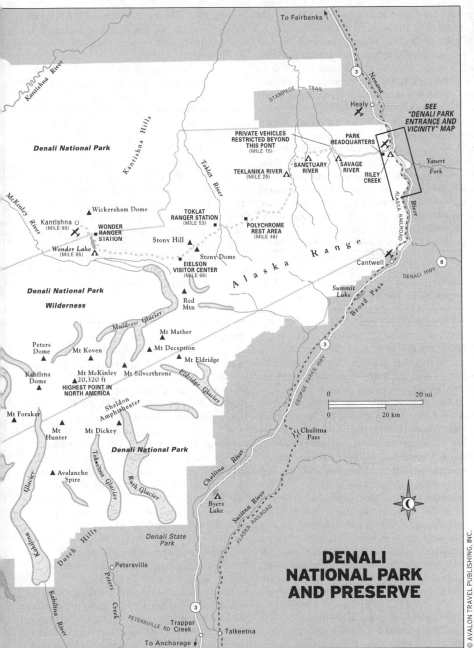

To Fairbanks

3   Nenana

SEE "DENALI PARK ENTRANCE AND VICINITY" MAP

Healy

STAMPEDE TRAIL

Kantishna River

Kantishna Hills

Denali National Park

PRIVATE VEHICLES RESTRICTED BEYOND THIS PONT (MILE 15)

PARK HEADQUARTERS

TEKLANIKA RIVER (MILE 29)

SANCTUARY RIVER

SAVAGE RIVER

RILEY CREEK

Yanert Fork

Toklat River

Wickersham Dome

TOKLAT RANGER STATION (MILE 53)

Kantishna (MILE 90)

WONDER RANGER STATION

Stony Hill

POLYCHROME REST AREA (MILE 46)

ALASKA RAILROAD

River

McKinley River

Wonder Lake (MILE 85)

Stony Dome

EIELSON VISITOR CENTER (MILE 66)

A l a s k a   R a n g e

Cantwell

8

DENALI HWY

Denali National Park Wilderness

Red Mtn

Summit Lake

Muldrow Glacier

Mt Mather

Broad Pass

Peters Dome

Mt Koven

Mt Deception

Mt Eldridge

3

Kahiltna Dome

Mt McKinley ▲20,320 ft HIGHEST POINT IN NORTH AMERICA

Mt Silverthrone

Eldridge Glacier

GEORGE PARKS HWY

Mt Foraker

Sheldon Amphitheater

Mt Hunter

Mt Dickey

Denali National Park

Chulitna Pass

0   20 mi

0   20 km

Kahiltna Glacier

Avalanche Spire

Tokositna Glacier

Ruth Glacier

Chulitna River

Susitna River

ALASKA RAILROAD

Byers Lake

Denali State Park

Dutch Hills

Petersville

DENALI NATIONAL PARK AND PRESERVE

Kahiltna River

Peters Creek

PETERSVILLE RD

Trapper Creek

Talkeetna

3

To Anchorage

gold. Like everyone who sees it, Dickey was captivated by the size and magnificence of the mountain that was then variously known as Tenada, Denali, Densmore's Mountain, Traleika, and Bulshaia. Dickey was from Ohio, William McKinley's home state, and a Princeton graduate in economics. When he came out of the bush and heard that McKinley had been nominated for president, he promptly renamed the mountain "McKinley," wrote numerous articles for stateside magazines, and lobbied in Washington, D.C., in support of adoption of the name, which finally caught on after President McKinley was assassinated in 1901. The name has been something of a sore point with Alaskans ever since, for McKinley had absolutely nothing to do with the mountain, and the more lyrical Native names were completely ignored. Many in Alaska support renaming the peak Denali (The High One), a term used by Natives in the lower Yukon and Kuskokwim rivers. Unfortunately, any move to eliminate "McKinley" from maps is inevitably met by howls of protest from Ohio's congressional delegation.

Creating a Park
Harry Karstens reached the Klondike in 1898 when he was 19, bored by Chicago and attracted by adventure and gold. Within a year he'd crossed over into American territory and wound up at Seventymile, 20 miles south of Eagle. When the local mail carrier lost everything one night in a card game and committed suicide, Karstens took his place. He became proficient in dog mushing and trail blazing and within a few years was delivering mail on a primitive trail between Eagle and Valdez, a 900-mile round-trip every month (the Richardson Highway follows the same route). Later he moved on to Fairbanks and began delivering mail to Kantishna, the mining town on what is now the west end of the Park, growing very fond of and familiar with the north side of the Alaska Range. So when a naturalist from the East Coast, Charles Sheldon, arrived in 1906 to study Dall sheep in the area, Karstens guided him around Mt. McKinley's northern foothills, delineating the habitat of the sheep.

Karstens was also the co-leader of the four-man expedition that was the first party to successfully climb the true peak of Mt. McKinley, the south summit, in 1913.

Meanwhile, Charles Sheldon was back in Washington, lobbying for national-park status for the Dall sheep habitat, and when Mt. McKinley National Park was created in 1917, Karstens was the obvious choice to become the first park superintendent. He held that post from 1921 to 1928, patrolling the park boundaries by dog sled.

Woodrow Wilson signed the bill that created Mt. McKinley National Park, Alaska's first, in 1917. The Park Road, begun five years later, was completed to Kantishna in 1940. In 1980, with the passage of the Alaska National Interest Lands Conservation Act, McKinley Park was renamed Denali National Park and Preserve and expanded to nearly six million acres, roughly the size of Vermont.

Pioneer Climbs
Many pioneers and prospectors had seen the mountain and approached it, but Alfred Brooks, a member of the first U.S. Geological Survey expedition in Alaska (1902), first set foot on it. He approached it from the south and reached an elevation of 7,500 feet before running out of time. He published an article in the January 1903 issue of *National Geographic,* in which he recommended approaching the mountain from the north. Following that suggestion, the next attempt was from the north, led by James Wickersham, U.S. district judge for Alaska. Judge Wickersham was sent from Seattle to bring law and order to Eagle in 1900; he moved to Fairbanks in 1903. That summer, he had a spare couple of months and set out to climb the mountain, traveling more than 100 miles overland and reaching the 7,000-foot level of the north face, later named Wickersham Wall in honor of His Honor.

That same summer, Dr. Frederick Cook, who'd been with Peary's first party to attempt the North Pole (1891) and Amundsen's Antarctic expedition (1897), also attempted to climb the mountain from the north and reached

11,300 feet. In 1906, Cook returned to attempt Mt. McKinley from the south but failed to get near it. His party broke up and went their separate directions, and a month later, Cook sent a telegram to New York claiming he'd reached the peak. This was immediately doubted by the members of his party, who challenged his photographic and cartographic "evidence." But through public lectures and articles, Cook's reputation as the first man to reach the peak grew. Two years later, he claimed to have reached the North Pole several months ahead of another Peary expedition, and Cook began to enjoy a cult status in the public consciousness. Simultaneously, however, his credibility among fellow explorers rapidly declined, and Cook vanished from sight. This further fueled the controversy and led to the Sourdough Expedition of 1910.

Four sourdoughs in Fairbanks simply decided to climb the mountain to validate or eviscerate Cook's published description of his route. They left town in December and climbed to the north peak in early April. Then the three members who'd actually reached the peak stayed in Kantishna to take care of business, while the fourth member, Tom Lloyd, who hadn't reached the peak, returned to Fairbanks and lied that he had. By the time the other three returned to town in June, Lloyd's story had already been published and widely discredited. So nobody believed the other three—*especially* when they claimed they'd climbed up to the north peak and down to their base camp at 11,000 feet in 18 hours, with a thermos of hot chocolate, four doughnuts, and dragging a 14-foot spruce log that they planted up top and claimed was still there! Finally, in 1913, the Hudson Stuck/Harry Karstens expedition reached the true summit, the south peak, and could prove that they'd done so beyond a shadow of a doubt. Only then was the Sourdough Expedition vindicated: All four members of the Stuck party saw the spruce pole still standing on the north peak!

Today more than a thousand mountaineers attempt the summit of Mt. McKinley each year, and approximately half of them actually reach the top. The youngest climbers ever to summit (a girl and a boy) were 12; the oldest man was 71, and the oldest woman 62.

PARK ENTRANCE

Park admission is $10/person or $20/family, or buy a National Park Pass—good for all national parks—for $40 a year. A Golden Age Passport for all national parks is available to anyone over 62 for a one-time fee of $10, and people with disabilities can get a free Golden Access Passport that covers all the parks. Get additional park information at 907/683-2294, www.nps.gov/dena.

Planning Your Time

Denali National Park is open year-round, though most facilities only operate mid-May–mid-September. Plowing of the Park Road generally starts in early May, but only the first 30 miles are open before late May, when the shuttle buses begin running. Those who arrive before this date will not be able to reach the best vantage points for Mt. McKinley.

The wildflowers peak around summer solstice—as do the mosquitoes. The berries, rose hips, and mushrooms are best in mid-August—as are the no-see-ums. The fall colors on the tundra are gorgeous around Labor Day weekend, when the crowds start to thin out and the northern lights start to appear, but it can get very cold. A skeleton winter Park Service crew patrols the park by dog sled. After the first heavy snowfall, the Park Road is plowed only to headquarters.

Visitor Centers

Opened in 2005, the **Denali Visitor Center** (daily 8 A.M.–6 P.M. mid-May–mid-Sept.) is at Mile 1.2 of the Park Road and right across from the railroad depot. Step inside to explore the exhibits, get oriented from the enormous relief map of the park, talk with the rangers, and view an extraordinary 20-minute film, *Heartbeats of Denali.* Pick up a copy of *Denali Alpenglow,* the park newspaper, and check the bulletin board for a schedule of guided walks,

THE INTERIOR

DENALI PARK ENTRANCE AND VICINITY

To Healy and Fairbanks

Nenana

MCKINLEY CHALET

MURIE SCIENCE AND LEARNING CENTER

DENALI RAINBOW VILLAGE RV PARK

DENALI CROW'S NEST

Mt Healy 5,716ft

DENALI PRINCESS LODGE

Horseshoe Lake

Taiga Trail

Mt Healy Overlook Trail

DENALI BLUFFS HOTEL

GRANDE DENALI HOTEL/ALPENGLOW RESTAURANT

Rock Creek Trail

POST OFFICE

WILDERNESS ACCESS CENTER

DENALI VISITOR CENTER

RILEY CREEK CAMPGROUND/STORE AND SHOWERS

Roadside Trail

RR STATION

PARK HEADQUARTERS/ DOG KENNELS

DENALI SHUTTLE BUS TOURS

To Eielson Visitor Center

Denali National Park

River

Yanert Fork

3

DENALI GRIZZLY BEAR CABINS & CAMPGROUND

DENALI RIVER CABINS

MCKINLEY VILLAGE RESORT

ALASKA RAILROAD

GEORGE PARKS HWY

0   2 mi
0   2 km

MCKINLEY CREEKSIDE CABINS

DENALI MOUNTAIN MORNING HOSTEL AND LODGE

DENALI PERCH RESORT / PIZZA PANORAMA

To Talkeetna, Cantwell, and Anchorage

talks, and kids' programs. Adjacent are an Alaska Natural History Association gift shop and Morino Grill, serving sandwiches, burgers, fish and chips, and pizzas.

On the other side of the roundabout, the **Murie Science and Learning Center** (907/683-1269 or 888/688-1269, www.muries lc.org) promotes scientific research and education through youth camps, field seminars, and courses in the summer (daily 9 A.M.–4:30 P.M.). Informative half-day "wildlife tracker" workshops are available all summer for $38 adults, $30 kids. In the off-season—when other facilities are closed—the Murie building becomes the **winter park visitor center** (daily 9 A.M.–4 P.M.).

Get park shuttle bus tickets and campground information at the **Wilderness Access Center** (daily 5 A.M.–8 P.M. mid-May to mid-September), located a half-mile up the Park Road. While here you could also watch an older film about the park or buy snacks. This facility is run by the park concessionaire, Aramark.

Sled Dog Demonstrations

One of the highlights of the park is the sled dog demonstration at the kennels behind headquarters. The dogs are beautiful and accessible (the ones not behind fences are chosen for friendliness and patience with people), and the anxious collective howl they orchestrate when the lucky six dogs are selected to run is something to hear. Naturalists give a talk about the current and historical uses of dogs in the park, their breeding and training, different commands for controlling them, and the challenge of maintaining a working kennel in a national park. Then dogs are hitched up to a wheel sled, and run around a gravel track. The enthusiasm of the dogs to get off the chain and into the harness is an eyebrow-raising glimpse into the consciousness of Alaskan sled dogs—they live to run.

Demonstrations are given daily at 10 A.M. and 2 and 4 P.M. A free shuttle bus leaves the Denali Visitor Center and the Riley Creek bus shelter 30 minutes before the demos. Don't miss this one!

GETTING AROUND DENALI

In 1971, before the George Parks Highway connected McKinley National Park to Fairbanks (125 miles) and Anchorage (245 miles), you had to take the train, or from Fairbanks you had to drive down to Delta Junction, take the Richardson Highway to Paxson, the Denali Highway to Cantwell, then the Parks Highway up to the park entrance, for a grand total of 340 miles. From Anchorage you had to drive to Glennallen, then up the Richardson to Paxson, over to Cantwell and beyond, for 440 miles. That year, nearly 45,000 visitors passed through the park. In 1972, when the George Parks Highway radically reduced driving times from both main urban centers, almost 90,000 visitors came. In anticipation of the huge jump in tourism, the Park Service initiated the shuttle system of school buses running a regularly scheduled service along the Park Road. Today, the park sees well over a million visitors annually.

◖ Denali Shuttle Bus Tours

There's no question that the shuttle system is highly beneficial to the park experience: the road is tricky and dangerous, crowds are much more easily controlled, there's much less impact on the wildlife (which take the buses for granted), and it's much easier to see wildlife when 40 passengers have eyeballs, binoculars, spotting scopes, and telephotos trained on the tundra. The excellent *Denali Road Guide,* available in park bookstores, has detailed information on sights along the road.

Green buses depart from the Wilderness Access Center daily mid-May–mid-September, with some continuing all the way to the Kantishna, an exhausting 89-mile, 13-hour ride round-trip. Most visitors don't go that far (or certainly not in one day), turning around instead at Polychrome Pass, Eielson, Wonder Lake, or other places along the way. Buses for Eielson begin departing from the Wilderness Access Center at 5 A.M. and continue roughly

© DON PITCHER

shuttle bus at Stony Hill

every 30 minutes through 3:30 P.M. Other buses depart during the day for Polychrome/Toklat and Wonder Lake.

You can reserve tickets in advance (907/272-7275 or 800/622-7275, www.reservedenali.com) starting in mid-February over the phone or on December 1 via the Web, and up to the day before you travel. Sixty-five percent of the available tickets go on sale December 1; the other 35 percent are made available just two days ahead of the travel date. Adults pay $19 to Polychrome/Toklat (6 hours round-trip), $24 to Fish Creek/Eielson (8 hours round-trip), $33 to Wonder Lake (11 hours round-trip), and $36 to Kantishna (12 hours round-trip). Kids under 15 ride free, and fares are half-price for ages 15–17. Fares do not include park entrance fees ($10). Wheelchair-accessible shuttle buses are available. Backpackers pay $24 round-trip to anywhere in the park on the special **camper bus.**

It's recommended that you try to get on an early-morning bus into the park: better chance to see wildlife and the mountain in the cool of the morning, and more time to get off the bus and fool around in the backcountry.

Schedules are readily available at the visitor centers and hotels. Take everything you need, as nothing (except books and postcards) is for sale once you get into the park. You can get off the bus and flag it down to get back on (if there's room; the buses leave with a few seats empty to pick up day-hikers in the park) anywhere along the road. Many riders never get off the bus at all and just stay on for the entire, exhausting round-trip.

Local Shuttles

A free **Riley Creek Loop Bus** provides service connecting the Riley Creek Campground, Wilderness Access Center, and train depot every half hour 5:30 A.M.–9:30 P.M. In addition, a free bus connects the Wilderness Access Center with the dog sled demonstrations at park headquarters. The **Savage River Shuttle** also provides a free shuttle service from the visitor center to Savage River Bridge. Private shuttle buses run between the visitor center and Denali Bluffs Hotel, Princess Lodge, and McKinley Village.

Tour Buses

The park's **tan nature tour buses** leave from the Wilderness Access Center throughout the day. For a good introduction, take a five-hour natural history tour ($60 adults or $35 kids) to Primrose Ridge (17 miles each way), or for a better look, join the seven-hour wildlife tour ($91 adults or $51 kids; includes a box lunch) to Toklat (53 miles each way). These wildlife tours are extremely popular and they fill up fast, so you need to make your reservations (907/276-7234 or 800/276-7234, www.reserve denali.com) as far in advance as possible.

Katnishna Wilderness Trails (907/683-8002 or 800/230-7275 www.seedenali.com, $139) provides private all-day bus tours that leave Denali Park hotels at 6:30 A.M. These take you to Kantishna Roadhouse near the end of the road for a lunch, gold panning, and sled dog demonstration, before heading back out, arriving at the hotels by 8 P.M.

Driving

For most of the summer, only the first 15 miles (to Savage River) of the Park Road are open to private vehicles. This portion is paved, and makes for an excellent day trip. From early May (when the road is plowed) to late May (when the shuttle buses start running), it is possible to drive as far as the Teklanika River rest area at Mile 30. The road beyond this doesn't open until late May, so early park arrivals will not be able to see many of the sights for which it is famous.

At the end of summer, the Park Road is opened to auto traffic for four days in mid-September. Only 400 vehicles are allowed per day, and passes are selected by a lottery. In a typical year, you may be competing with 10,000 other entries for these passes! You'll need to apply during July, but contact the Park Service (907/683-2294, www.nps.gov/dena) for details. A handful of professional photographers are allowed vehicular access to the park during the summer, but these slots are highly sought after, and may involve giving up your first-born child and opening your home as a lodging place for all Park Service employees who might be passing through.

HEADING OUT THE PARK ROAD

A few miles beyond headquarters the road climbs out of the boreal forest, levels off, and travels due west through a good example of taiga. The ridgeline to the north (right) of the road is known as the **Outer Range,** foothills of the massive Alaska Range to the south (left). The Outer Range is much older, of different geological origins, and much more rounded and eroded than the jagged Alaska Range. First view of the mountain comes up at Mile 9; look southwest. The day has to be nearly perfectly clear to see Mt. McKinley from here: You're at around 2,400 feet and the mountain is at 20,000 feet, which leaves nearly 18 grand spread over 70-odd miles of potential cloud cover. That's a lot of potential.

Next you pass the **Savage River Campground,** then wind down to the river valley and cross the bridge which marks the end of road access for those in private vehicles. The "Checkpoint Charlie" kiosk at Mile 15 has a park employee to turn back private vehicles; they're prohibited beyond this point. From the bridge, look upriver (left) and notice the broad, U-shaped, glacial valley with large gravel deposits forming braids or channels, then look right to compare the V-shaped valley obviously cut by running water. The Savage Glacier petered out right where the bridge is now around 15,000 years ago during the last ice age. Here you also kiss the pavement good-bye, then start climbing Primrose Ridge, which offers excellent hiking, especially in June and early July when the wildflowers are in full bloom. Turn around and look back at the Savage Bridge; the stark rock outcropping just up from it has a distinct resemblance to an Indian's facial bone structure, which is how the Savage got its politically incorrect name. Just up the road is a pullout—if the mountain's out, the driver should stop for the clear shot.

Savage River to Igloo Canyon

Mt. McKinley disappears behind jagged lower peaks as the road descends into the broad, glacial **Sanctuary River** valley at Mile 23. Watch for moose, caribou, fox, lynx, waterfowl, and eagles along here. Right on the other side of the Sanctuary is a good view down at a "drunken forest," one effect that permafrost has on the vegetation. Notice how many of the trees are leaning at bizarre and precarious angles, with some of them down entirely. As an adaptation to the permafrost, these spruce trees have evolved a root system that spreads horizontally across the surface soil; there's no tap root to speak of. So the taller a tree grows around here, the less support it maintains, and the more susceptible it is to falling over. When the surface soil becomes saturated (because of lack of absorption over the permafrost), it sometimes shifts, either spontaneously or because of slight tremors (a major fault runs through here), taking the trees with it.

Next you descend into the broad **Teklanika River** valley, with a good view across the river of the three vegetation zones on the mountain slopes: forest, taiga, and tundra. You pass a number of small ponds in this area, known as "kettles," usually formed when a retreating glacier drops off a large block of ice, which melts, leaves a depression, and fills with rainwater. The stagnant water is rich in nutrients and provides excellent hatching grounds for Alaska's famous mosquitoes, and as such the ponds are good feeding spots for ducks and shorebirds. Look for mergansers, goldeneyes, sandpipers, buffleheads, and phalaropes in these ponds. And in some of the higher, smaller, more private kettles, look for hikers and park employees with no clothes on... maybe even join them, if you care to brave the skeeters, which have been known to show up on Park Service radar screens.

Cross the river and enter **Igloo Canyon,** where you turn almost due south. The mountain on the right is Igloo (4,800 ft.); the one on the left is Cathedral (4,905 ft.). Igloo is in the Outer Range, Cathedral in the Alaska Range. Closest distance between the two ranges, the canyon is right on the migration route of the Dall sheep and a great place to view the white dots on the slopes. Or climb either mountain to get close.

Sable Pass is next at Mile 38, at 3,900 feet the second-highest point on the road. This area is closed to hiking and photography because of the large grizzly population. Keep your eyes peeled. Also, the next good views of the mountain are from these highlands.

Over Polychrome Pass to Eielson

Once you cross the **East Fork River** at Mile 44 (great hiking out onto the flats from here), you begin your ascent of Polychrome Pass, one of the most spectacular and sphincter-clamping sections of the road. If you're scared of heights or become frightened at the 1,000-foot drop-offs, just do what the driver does—close your eyes. These rocks have a high iron content; the rate of oxidation and the combination of the iron with other minerals determine the different shades of rust, orange, red, and purple. Look and listen for hoary marmots in the nearby rocks, and from here almost the rest of the way to Eielson Visitor Center, watch for caribou and wolves; these are the Murie flats, where wildlife biologist Adolph Murie studied the lifestyle of *Canis lupus.*

Descend to the **Toklat River** at Mile 53, the last and largest you cross before Eielson. This is the terminus of the wildlife tour, but the shuttle buses continue on to Eielson and Wonder Lake. The Toklat's source is the Sunrise Glacier, just around the bend upriver (left). You can see from the size of the river how big the glacier was 20,000 years ago. Great hiking up into the Alaska Range from here. Next you climb up **Stony Hill** and, if the weather is cooperating, when you crest the ridge you're in for the thrill of a lifetime: Denali, The Great One, in all its immense, majestic glory. You can't believe that the mountain is still 40 miles away! But wait, you get another five miles closer, crossing **Thorofare Pass,** highest elevation on the road (3,950 ft.; Mile 62).

Eielson Visitor Center

Located at Mile 66, this is normally the turnaround point for most shuttle buses, but the old visitor center is being replaced by a much-needed new one that is scheduled to open in 2008. As of this writing, shuttle buses (except those heading to Wonder Lake or Kantishna) turn around at **Fish Creek,** Mile 63, which offers a stunning vantage point of Mt. McKinley—if clouds don't obscure the summit.

To Wonder Lake

Beyond Eielson, the road comes within 25 miles of the mountain, passing **Muldrow Glacier,** which is covered by a thick black layer of glacial till and vegetation. From Wonder Lake, the **Wickersham Wall** rises magnificently above the intervening plains, with the whole Alaska Range stretching out on each side. In addition, the reflection from the lake doubles your pleasure and doubles your fun, from which even the mosquitoes here, some of the most savage, bloodthirsty, insatiable beasts of the realm, cannot detract.

HIKING

Note: Guns are not permitted within Denali National Park, but many hikers carry Counter Assault or other pepper-based sprays for protection. There has never been a fatal bear attack in the park, but bears certainly are a potential hazard. Obey all park regulations and follow safety tips from the rangers.

Entrance Area Day Hikes

Several paths take off from the Denali Visitor Center, including two easy ones: the **Spruce Forest Trail** (15 min.) and a longer **Morino Trail** (30 min.). **Horseshoe Lake Trail** (3 miles round trip) starts at the shuttle bus stop and then descends to the lake, where you might see waterfowl and beaver. Ranger-led hikes to the lake are offered daily in the summer; see the visitor center for today's schedule.

Hiking the five-mile round-trip **Mt. Healy Overlook Trail** is a great way to get the lay of the land, see the mountain if it's out, quickly leave the crowds behind, and get your heart pumping. Once at the overlook (a mile in), keep climbing the ridges for another several hours to get to the peak of Mt. Healy (5,200 ft.).

The 2.3-mile **Rock Creek Trail** starts near the post office and climbs to park headquarters,

© DON PITCHER

Wonder Lake and Mt. McKinley

gaining 400 feet along the way. You can then loop back along the road via the 1.8-mile **Roadside Trail. Taiga Trail** is an easy 1.3-mile loop that also begins near the post office.

Backpacking Trips

For details on backcountry hikes and camping, head to the **Backcountry Information Center** (907/683-9510, daily 9 A.M.–6 P.M. May 20–Sept. 20); the office is just across the parking lot from the Wilderness Access Center.

Popular backpacking areas include up the Savage River toward Fang Mountain; down the far side of Cathedral Mountain toward Calico Creek (get off the bus just before the Sable Pass closure); up Tatler Creek a little past Igloo Mountain; anywhere on the East Fork flats below Polychrome toward the Alaska Range; anywhere around Stony Hill; and the circumnavigation of Mt. Eielson (get off five to six miles past the visitor center, cross the hundred braids of the Thorofare River, and walk around the mountain, coming back up to the visitor center). There are backcountry descrip-

tion guides at the backcountry desk, or you can find the same info online, with photos. For additional details and hiking tips, get a copy of *Backcountry Companion* ($9).

On all these hikes, you can get off the outbound bus, explore to your heart's content, then get back on an inbound bus, if space is available. Consult with the driver and study the bus schedule closely; the camper buses usually have space coming back.

Large as it is, it's hard to get lost in Denali—you're either north or south of the road. And since the road travels mostly through open alpine tundra, there aren't any man-made trails to follow—just pick a direction and book. Usually you'll want to make for higher ground in order to: a) get out of the knee- to hip-high dwarf shrubbery of the moist tundra and onto the easy hiking of the alpine, b) get to where the breeze will keep the skeeters at bay, and c) see more. Or walk along the gravel riverbars into the mountains, though depending on the size of the gravel, it can be ankle-twisting. Hiking boots are a must, and carry food,

PROTECTING YOURSELF DURING A BEAR ENCOUNTER

If you do happen to suddenly encounter a bear and it sees you, try to stay calm and not make any sudden moves. Do not run, since you could not possibly outrun a bear; they can exceed 40 mph for short distances. Bear researchers now suggest that quickly climbing a tree is also not a wise way to escape bears, and may actually incite an attack. Instead, make yourself visible by moving into the open so the bear will (hopefully) identify you as a human and not something to eat. Never stare directly at a bear. Sometimes dropping an item such as a hat or jacket will distract the bear, and talking calmly (easier said than done) also seems to have some value in convincing bears that you're a human. If the bear sniffs the air or stands on its hind legs, it is probably trying to identify you. When it does, it will usually run away. If a bear woofs and postures, don't imitate – this is a challenge. Keep retreating. Most bear charges are also bluffs, and the bear will often stop short and amble off.

If a **grizzly bear** actually attacks, hold your ground and freeze. It may well be a bluff charge, with the bear halting at the last second. If the bear does not stop its attack, curl up facedown on the ground in a fetal position with your hands wrapped behind your neck and your elbows tucked over your face. Your backpack may help protect you somewhat. Remain as still as possible even if you are attacked, since sudden movements may incite further attacks. It takes an enormous amount of courage to do this, but often a bear will only sniff or nip you and leave. The injury you might sustain would be far less than if you tried to resist. After the attack, prevent further attacks by staying down on the ground until the grizzly has left the area.

Bear authorities now recommend against dropping to the ground if you are attacked by a **black bear,** since they tend to be more aggressive in such situations and are more likely to prey on humans. If a black bear attacks, fight back with whatever weapons are at hand; large rocks and branches can be surprisingly effective deterrents, as can yelling and shouting. (This, of course, assumes you can tell black bears from brown bears. If you can't, have someone who knows – such as a park ranger – explain the differences before you head into the backcountry.)

Nighttime bear attacks are perhaps the most frightening kind, and could happen to even the most seasoned adventurer. In 1996, one of Alaska's best-known wildlife photographers, Michio Hoshino, was sleeping in his tent on Russia's Kamchatka Peninsula when a brown bear attacked and killed him. In the rare event of a night attack in your tent, defend yourself *very* aggressively. Never play dead under such circumstances, since the bear probably views you as prey, and may give up if you make it a fight. Before you go to bed, try to plan escape routes should you

---

water, compass, binoculars, maps, raingear, and a bear-proof food canister. And keep your eyes and ears wide open for wildlife that you don't want to get close to, sneak up on, or be surprised by.

Backcountry Permits

You need a free permit to spend the night in the backcountry. Permits are issued 24 hours in advance from the Backcountry Information Center, and reservations are not accepted. Check the big maps and look over descriptions of the 43 units, where a limited number of backpackers are allowed. (The same info can be found online at www.nps.gov/dena to help you plan prior to your trip.) Now check the board to find the vacancies in the units. Make sure the unit is open (some are always closed; others periodically close because of overcrowding or bears) and that there are enough vacancies to accommodate your whole party. Watch the 30-minute back-be attacked in the night, and be sure to have a flashlight and pepper spray handy. Keeping your sleeping bag partly unzipped also allows the chance to escape should a bear attempt to drag you away. There are advantages to having multiple tents in case one person is attacked, and if someone is attacked in a tent near you, yelling and throwing rocks or sticks may drive the bear away.

The latest development for campers in bear country is the use of portable **electric fences** made by Electro Bear Guard (907/232-9758, www.electrobearguard.com) to surround your campsite; a backpacker unit runs on two AA batteries, weighs just two pounds, and costs $290.

Many Alaskan guides, government employees, and others working in wild places carry weapons of some sort; 12-gauge shotguns are a common choice. Visitors to Alaska are unlikely to carry such weapons, and even less likely to know when to use them. Don't endanger the lives of bears by heading out into the wilderness with a gun but without an understanding of bear behavior. You have plenty of alternative places to go; the bears do not. Far too many bears die unnecessarily in Alaska following encounters with humans. Guns are not allowed in several Alaskan national parks, including Denali, Katmai, Glacier Bay, Sitka, and Klondike Gold Rush.

Cayenne pepper sprays such as Counter Assault (800/695-3394, www.counteras-sault.com) have proven useful in fending off bear attacks in some situations; they're sold in most Alaskan camping supply stores. These "bear mace" sprays are effective only at close range, particularly in tundra areas, where winds quickly disperse the spray or may blow it back in your own face. Another real problem with bear mace is that you cannot carry it aboard commercial jets, and most air taxis do not allow it inside an aircraft, because of the obvious dangers should a canister explode. Many floatplane pilots will, however, carry it in the storage compartments of the floats. But be sure to let the pilot know that you have it with you on the flight.

If you do carry a pepper spray on a hike, make sure it is readily available by carrying it in a holster on your belt or across your chest. Also be sure to test-fire it to see how the spray carries. Though they *are* better than nothing, pepper sprays are certainly not a cure-all or a replacement for caution in bear country. It's far better to avoid bear confrontations in the first place.

Detailed bear safety brochures are available at Alaska Public Lands Information Centers in Ketchikan, Tok, Anchorage, and Fairbanks, or on the Alaska Department of Fish and Game's website (www.state.ak.us/adfg). Two good bear safety books are *Bear Attacks: Their Causes and Avoidance* by Stephen Herrero and *Bear Aware: Hiking and Camping in Bear Country* by Bill Schneider.

country video that describe bear safety, river crossings, minimum impact camping, emergencies, and other topics, listen to a 10-minute safety talk, and finally get a permit from the ranger. You might have to wait a few days for openings in your chosen area, or have a plan B or C in mind. The park loans out free bear-proof food storage containers; be sure to get one for your hike. Finally, reserve a seat on one of the camper buses ($25) to get you and your gear into the park.

OTHER RECREATION
Mountain Biking

An excellent way to explore Denali at your own pace is by mountain bike. Bikes are allowed on the Park Road, and can be transported aboard the camper shuttle bus, but be sure to mention the bike when you make a reservation. Note that only the camper buses carry bikes and that they only carry two at a time, so it is possible to get far out the Park Road and then find yourself unable to catch a bus back. Be sure to pick

© DON PITCHER

mountain bikers in Denali National Park

up a "rules of the road" handout at the visitor center before heading out.

Denali Outdoor Center (907/683-1925 or 888/303-1925, www.denalioutdoorcenter.com) has mountain bike rentals and tours from its office next to the Denali Riverside RV Park, or you can rent them from **Bike Denali/Aramark** (907/683-2591, www.denalialaska.com) next to the Lynx Creek Store in Denali Park.

Rafting

Three raft companies run the Nenana along the eastern margin of the park, including 2.5-hour Class II–IV whitewater or Class II–III float trips ($70–75): **Denali Outdoor Center** (907/683-1925 or 888/303-1925, www.denalioutdoorcenter.com), **Denali Raft Adventures** (907/683-2234 or 888/683-2234, www.denaliraft.com), and **Nenana Raft Adventures** (907/683-7238 or 800/789-7238, www.alaskaraft.com). All provide raingear, boots, and life jackets, plus transportation to and from local hotels. Denali Raft Adventures and Denali Outdoor Center also offer trips

that combine both segments for a four-hour trip that includes both the rapids and easy sections of the river ($99). Float trips are okay for children, but adults only on the whitewater runs. Denali Outdoor Center would be my first choice, and they also provide inflatable kayak tours for those who want to paddle on their own.

Flightseeing

If the mountain is out and there's room on the plane, this is the time to pull out the credit card. These one-hour flights around Mt. McKinley will leave you flying high for days.

Denali Air (907/683-2261, www.denaliair.com) operates from a private airstrip at Mile 229 of the Parks Highway (8 miles south of the park entrance). Their one-hour trip over the mountain is $285 in a twin-engine plane.

Based in Kantishna at the center of the park, **Kantishna Air Taxi** (907/683-1223, www.katair.com) provides charter air service to end-of-the-road Kantishna lodges, and flightseeing trips within the park. Quite a few other flightseeing companies operate out of Talkeetna and Anchorage.

You can go for a helicopter ride on **Era Helicopters** (907/683-2574 or 800/843-1947, www.flightseeingtours.com), based along the river in Denali Park. Tour options include a 50-minute flight over the park ($284), or a 75-minute trip that includes a glacier landing ($384).

Mountaineering

Mt. McKinley—tallest peak in North America—is a major destination for mountaineers from around the globe. Over a thousand climbers attempt to summit Mt. McKinley each year, with three-quarters of these attempts via the West Buttress. The primary climbing season is May–July. From the south side of Mt. McKinley, the usual approach is by ski plane from Talkeetna to the Southeast Fork of the Kahiltna Glacier or to the Ruth Glacier in the Don Sheldon Amphitheater. From the north, the approach for Denali and other peaks is by foot, ski, or dog sled. Specific route information can be obtained from the Talkeetna Ranger Station. Climbers on Mt. McKinley and Mt. Foraker are charged a special use fee of $200 per climber. Call the ranger in Talkeetna (907/733-2231), or visit the Park Service website (www.nps.gov/dena) for additional mountaineering information.

Six companies are authorized to lead guided mountaineering climbs of Mt. McKinley and other peaks in the Alaska Range; contact the Park Service for specifics. Two of the best are **Alaska Mountaineering School** (907/733-1016, www.climbalaska.org) in Talkeetna and **N.O.L.S.** (907/745-4047, www.nols.edu) in Palmer.

Dog Mushing

Visitors whose appetite is whetted by the daily dog sledding demonstrations at park headquarters may want to return when the snow flies for the real thing. **Earth Song Lodge** (907/683-2863, www.earthsonglodge.com) offers wintertime dogsled adventure tours into Denali National Park. These range from an easy overnight trip to ones lasting 10 days.

Four-time Iditarod winner Jeff King lives with his family at Goose Lake near Denali, and his staff offers summertime tours of his state-of-the-art **Husky Homestead** (907/683-2904, www.huskyhomestead.com) kennels and training area. Two-hour tours and demonstrations ($45 adults, $22 kids) depart from local hotels.

ENTERTAINMENT

All the Denali Park hotels have lounges, but if you want to hang out with the young workerbee crowd head to Denali Salmon Bake. For frivolity, check out **Alaska Cabin Nite Dinner Theater** at the McKinley Chalet Resort or the **Music of Denali Dinner Theater** at the Denali Princess Lodge. Considerably more interesting is **Climb Denali,** a twice-daily program (www.alaska365.com, $6 adults, $3 kids) by mountaineer and photographer Laurent Dick about the experience of climbing Mt. McKinley.

You can also catch the summertime aurora show at **Northern Lights Theatre** (907/683-4000, www.alaskan.com/northernlights, $6.50 adults, $5 kids) in Denali Park.

Park Service rangers give talks, walks, and kids' programs. For specifics, check the bulletin boards at the Denali Visitor Center, or the free park newspaper, *Denali Alpenglow.*

ACCOMMODATIONS

Most of the local lodging action centers around busy Denali Park, though other lodges and B&Bs are a few miles south of the park entrance, or 10 miles north in the town of Healy. Denali area lodging options are expensive, so those on a tight budget will need to either camp or head to the hostel 13 miles south at Carlo Creek.

Denali Park Lodging

If you've been driving the Parks Highway north from Anchorage, soaking up the wild Alaskan wilderness, you're in for a rude awakening when you reach the unincorporated settlement called Denali Park, a.k.a. "Glitter Gulch." Just a mile north of the Denali National Park turnoff, it's impossible to miss: an ugly hodgepodge of giant hotels, restaurants, RV parks, rafting companies, and gift shops crammed between the highway and the Nenana River to the west, and climbing the steep hillside to the east. The area is packed with tour buses, tottering tourists, and rumbling RVs. It's enough to make Wasilla look good.

Most lodging choices start well over $150 a night, but one place offers a less-expensive option: **Denali Salmon Bake Cabins** (907/683-2733, www.denaliparksalmonbake.com, mid-May–early Sept.). For the full-on Alaskan experience, stay in an "economy cabin" ($64 s or $69 d) consisting of insulated tent-like structures with two double beds and a shared bathhouse. Standard cabins with private baths, TVs, and air conditioning are $120 s or $125 d. Not for everyone, but they're right there in the thick of things near the park entrance. Reservations advised.

Denali Crow's Nest (907/683-2723 or 888/917-8130, www.denalicrowsnest.com, $169 d), features 39 cabins perched on a very steep hill. The outdoor hot tub is relaxing after a day of exploring, and they provide a free shuttle for the railroad depot and park visitor center. Parking is limited.

Denali Bluffs Hotel ($219 s or d) is a hillside place where 111 rooms all contain two double beds and fridges. Request one with a private balcony. High atop the bluff is **Grande Denali Lodge,** a modern 154-room hotel accessed by a very steep, switchback road. Guests stay in spacious rooms ($250 d) or family style cabins ($400 d). Both Denali Bluffs and Grande Denali have the same Aramark management and contacts: 907/683-8500 or 866/683-8500, www.denalialaska.com. They provide free shuttles from the rail depot and park visitor center.

Though primarily for cruise ship passengers, the sprawling **Denali Princess Lodge** (907/683-2282 or 800/426-0500, www.princesslodges.com, mid-May–mid-Sept., $239 d) is also open to independent travelers if they don't mind the corporate feeling and constant parade of tour buses. There are so many buildings here that you'll need a map to find your way around. Amenities include outdoor hot tubs overlooking the Nenana River, a fitness center, restaurants and cafes, a dinner theatre, and bar.

Managed by Denali Park Resorts (Aramark), the park concessionaire, **McKinley Chalet Resort** (907/276-7234 or 800/276-7234, www.denaliparkresorts.com, mid-May–mid-Sept., $249 d) is a 345-room hotel along the Nenana River. Most rooms are set aside for Holland America passengers, so call well ahead of your visit.

Carlo Creek Area Lodging

A number of lodging places are in the Carlo Creek area near Mile 224 of the Parks Highway, 14 miles south of the park entrance. Least expensive is the friendly **Denali Mountain Morning Hostel and Lodge** (907/683-7503, www.hostelalaska.com, mid-May–mid-Sept.), with earthy creekside accommodations: bunk cabins ($25 per person), private rooms and cabins ($65–75 d), and family cabins ($100–130 for four). Two-night minimum stay in the private accommodations. A shower house is separate, and guests can use the central kitchen, computers, free Wi-Fi, and lounge. Gear rentals and storage are available, and two good restaurants (Pizza Panorama and McKinley Creekside Café) are right across the highway. The hostel provides a free twice-a-day shuttle to the park visitor center and rail station that's available to anyone.

Denali Perch Resort (907/683-2523 or 888/322-2523, www.denaliperchresort.com) has 20 very small cabins for $85 d with a shared bathhouse, or $125 d with tiny private baths. They're open year-round. Nearby is **Carlo Creek Lodge** (907/683-2576, www.ccldenaliparkalaska.com, late May–early Sept., $85 d with shared bath or $105–130 d with private baths), with a variety of attractive cabins near the creek. Guest computers (fee) are available, along with Wi-Fi. **McKinley Creekside Cabins & Cafe** (907/683-2277 or 888/533-6254, www.mckinleycabins.com, $149–199 d) has cabins, a great café, and espresso.

At Mile 231 (8 miles south of the park turnoff), you'll find **Denali River Cabins** (907/683-8002 or 800/230-7275, www.denalirivercabins.com), in a fine location right on the Nenana River. These Pan-A-bode units include private baths and access to a large riverfront deck with hot tub and sauna. Cabins on the river are $199 d, while those back from the water cost $149 d. Rooms in the newly built Cedars Lodge cost $184 d.

Across the highway is **Denali Grizzly Bear Cabins & Campground** (907/683-2696, www.denaligrizzlybear.com, mid-May–mid-Sept.), with a range of lodging choices sprawling up the hillside. These include simple little cabins ($59–92 d), some of which use a central shower house, and attractive log cabins with private bath and kitchens ($149–248 for up to six). Traffic noise can be an annoyance. Recently added hotel rooms ($179 d) overlook the Nenana River.

McKinley Village Resort (907/276-7234 or 800/276-7234, www.denaliparkresorts.com) is along the Nenana River at Mile 231. Here you'll find 150 comfortable hotel rooms, a café, and lounge. It's run by Denali Park Resorts (Aramark), the park concessionaire.

Kantishna Lodges

The town of Kantishna, 91 miles from the park entrance at the western end of the Park Road, has four roadhouses. The area was first settled in 1905, when several thousand miners rushed to the foothills just north of Mt. McKinley to mine gold, silver, lead, zinc, and antimony. After 1980 and the Alaska National Interest Lands Conservation Act, which expanded Denali National Park's boundaries, Kantishna found itself inside the park, and in 1985, mining was halted by court order. A number of the property owners have moved into the tourism business, and the area is a popular destination for people wanting to escape to the heart of the park. These upscale lodges are definitely not for budget travelers, and it's a long bus ride to Kantishna, so most guests stay at least three nights in this very scenic area. All four of the lodges are open only from early June to mid-September. Private buses transport visitors to the lodges at Kantishna, or you can fly out on Kantishna Air Taxi (907/683-1223, www.katair.com).

At **Kantishna Roadhouse** (907/683-8003 summers or 800/942-7420, www.kantishna roadhouse.com, June–mid-Sept.) the all-inclusive rate of $770 d per day includes lodging in cabins or duplex rooms, meals, bus transportation from the park entrance, dog sled demonstrations, mountain bikes, gold panning, guided hikes, and interpretive programs. A bar and restaurant are on the premises. Two-night minimum required.

Two wonderful Kantishna lodges—Camp Denali and North Face Lodge—have the same management and contacts (907/683-2290, www.campdenali.com, June–mid-Sept.). At both places, the emphasis is on the natural world, with guided hikes, mountain biking, canoeing, fishing, evening programs, and delicious meals. **Camp Denali** has spectacular views of Mt. McKinley, and is operated as a low-key wilderness retreat for a maximum of 40 guests. Special programs are offered throughout the summer, focusing on such topics as bird conservation, nature photography, northern lights, and environmental issues. Lodging is in 18 cozy cabins with woodstoves, propane lights, an outhouse, and shower building. If you can't handle an outhouse, book a room at North Face Lodge instead.

One mile from Camp Denali is **North Face Lodge,** which is operated more like a country inn, with 15 guest rooms, all containing private baths. All-inclusive rates at either Camp Denali or North Face Lodge cost $1,305 adults for three nights ($978 for kids under 12), or $1,740 for four nights ($1,305 kids). The price includes lodging, food, bus transportation to and from Kantishna, lectures, guided hikes, and other activities. Guests must stay at least three nights, with fixed arrival and departure dates. The owners also rent a separate wilderness cabin (Hawk's Nest) nearby that sleeps four and costs $100 per night with a three-night minimum. It's rustic, with a kitchen, wood stove, outhouse, and hand-pumped water. This is the real Alaskan-style deal, but you'll need to book well ahead.

Denali Backcountry Lodge (907/644-9980 or 877/233-6254, www.denalilodge.com) has crowded and overpriced log units ($730 d all-inclusive) with private baths. Add $60 extra for riverside cabins.

CAMPING
Park Campgrounds

Inside Denali National Park are seven campgrounds, four of which have evening nature programs throughout the summer.

Riley Creek Campground ($19 for pull-in sites, $12 for walk-in sites) is the largest and most accessible campground, located just a quarter-mile off the Parks Highway. It's open year-round, but with limited facilities September–May. This campground is very popular with RVers and car campers. Adjacent is **Riley Creek Mercantile** with a few supplies (including firewood), a dump station, and $5 showers.

Savage River, Teklanika River, and **Wonder Lake campgrounds** all have water and flush toilets, and go for $16–18 a night. **Sanctuary River Campground** has chemical toilets, and costs $9. Savage River, Sanctuary River, and Teklanika River campgrounds are open May–September, but Wonder Lake Campground doesn't open until June, and may close early because of snow.

All but the Sanctuary River Campground can be reserved in advance (907/272-7275 or 800/622-7275, www.reservedenali.com, $4 fee) starting in mid-February. You can also reserve campsites for any of these at the visitor center if they aren't already full.

You can drive to Riley Creek, Savage River, and Teklanika River campgrounds, so they fill up fast. There's a three-night minimum stay for vehicular campers at Teklanika River, and only hard-sided campers are allowed. Otherwise, campground access is via the camper buses ($24 per person). The Wonder Lake Campground is also extremely popular for hiking and the potential to see the mountain in all its glory. Reserve well ahead of your trip for campsites there.

RV Parks

Denali Rainbow Village (907/683-7777, www.denalirv.com, mid-May–mid-Sept., $36 RVs, $20 tents) is in the heart of the Denali Park action, with a big lot behind the row of

buildings on the east side of the road. Showers are $2.

Denali Riverside RV Park (907/388-1748 or 866/583-2696, www.denaliriversiderv.com, May–Sept., $35 RVs, $16 tent) is a gravel lot two miles north of the park entrance.

Eight miles south of the park entrance is **Denali Grizzly Bear Resort** (907/683-2696 or 866/583-2696, www.denaligrizzlybear.com, $26 RVs, $20 tents). Showers and laundry are also available. Nearby is **Carlo Creek Lodge** (907/683-2576, www.ccldenaliparkalaska.com, late May–early Sept., $27 RVs, $20 tents), with wooded campsites near the creek. Additional RV parks are in Healy.

FOOD

A number of places offer pricey summertime eats just north of the park entrance at the development called Denali Park; most are shuttered when the tourists flee south. Start your day at **Black Bear Coffee House** (907/683-1656) with eggy breakfasts, bagels, espresso, sandwiches, muffins, and a couple of computers to check your email (fee).

Also along the boardwalk is **Bub's Subs** (907/683-7827), with delicious sandwiches (including Philly cheese steak), soups, salads, and other favorites. Open daily all summer. You'll pay $9–12, but it sure beats the nearby Subway!

Overlook Bar & Grill (907/683-2723, www.denalicrowsnest.com) occupies a hillside location above the frenzy at Denali Park. Big windows a deck face the park, and the menu specializes in burgers (including halibut burgers) and other munchies ($9–13), along with steaks, grilled chicken, and salmon ($21–28). Prime spots are the deck and the bar, which claims Alaska's largest choice of beers.

Located high atop the bluff at Denali Park, **Alpenglow Restaurant** (907/683-8500 or 866/683-8500, www.denalialaska.com, entrées $26–40) has the most impressive vistas in the area. Wraparound windows face Denali National Park and the high ceilings are accented by an open timber-frame design.

One of the better restaurants in the Denali

AVOIDING BEAR HUGS

Surprising a bear – especially a sow with cubs – is the last thing you want to do in the backcountry. Before heading out, check at a local ranger station or visitor center to see whether there have been recent bear problems. If you discover an animal carcass, be extremely alert since a bear may be nearby and might attack anything that appears to threaten its food. Get away from such areas! Do not hike at night or dusk, when bears can be especially active. There's safety in numbers: The more of you hiking together, the more likely a bear is to sense you and stay away.

Be especially wary when traveling through thick brush or high grass, into the wind, or along streams where salmon are spawning. If you're unable to see everything around you for at least 50 yards, warn any hidden animals by talking, singing, clapping your hands, tapping a cup, or rattling a can of pebbles. Some people tie bells to their packs for this purpose, while others regard this as an annoyance to fellow hikers. In general, bells are probably of little value since the sound does not carry far, and it might even attract inquisitive bears.

Don't be shy – make a lot of noise! It might seem a bit foolish, but yelling may prevent an encounter of the furry kind. Unfortunately, it will probably scare off other animals, and other hikers may not appreciate the noise. Personally, I reserve yelling "Hey Bear!" for situations where I'm walking in brushy bear country with low visibility and have to contend with other noises such as a nearby creek.

Hunters and photographers are the main recipients of bear hugs. Never under any circumstances approach a bear, even if it appears to be asleep. Move away if you see cubs, especially if one comes toward you – mom is usually close by. Dogs create dangerous situations by barking and exciting bears – leave yours at home. And, of course, never leave food around for bears. Not only is this illegal, but it also trains the bears to associate people with free food.

Fed bears become garbage bears, and that almost inevitably means that the bear gets killed. Remember, bears are dangerous wild animals. This is *their* country, not a zoo. By going in you accept the risk – and thrill – of meeting a bear.

When choosing a campsite, avoid places like salmon streams, ground-squirrel mounds, berry patches, or game trails. Before camping, take a look around the area to see if there are recent bear tracks, scat, or diggings. Keep your campsite clean! If possible, avoid smelly foods such as fish, fresh meat, cheese, sausage, or bacon; freeze-dried food is light and relatively odorless. Keep food in airtight containers or several layers of plastic bags. Some national parks – including Denali and Glacier Bay – require and provide bear-resistant food containers. Your cooking, eating, and food-storage area should be at least 50 yards away from your tent. Wash up after eating. Burying garbage is useless, as animals soon dig it up. Instead, burn what garbage you can, and wash and flatten tin cans. Store unburnable garbage, and the clothes you were wearing while cooking, in the same place. You may want to also consider using a portable electric fence such as those made by Electro Bear Guard (907/232-9758, www.electrobearguard.com) to surround your campsite.

Put your food, toothpaste, deodorant, and soap in a plastic bag inside a stuff sack and suspend it from a branch or between two trees, at least 12 feet off the ground and four feet from tree trunks; bring 50 feet of rope for this purpose. Tie two cups or pots to it so you will hear if it's moved. In the absence of trees, store food well downwind of your tent.

Researchers have found no evidence that either sexual activity or menstrual odors precipitate bear attacks, despite reports to the contrary. It is, however, wise for menstruating women to use tampons instead of pads and to store soiled tampons in double ziplock bags above the reach of bears.

area is 11 miles south of the park entrance: **McKinley Creekside Cafe** (907/683-2277 or 888/533-6254, www.mckinleycabins.com, entrées $16–24). You'll find great breakfasts, homemade soups, sandwiches, and tacos for lunch, plus filet mignon, pasta, and fresh Alaskan halibut in the evening. The deck out front is perfect for mid-summer dining. Right across the creek is **Panorama Pizza Pub** (907/683-2623), with the excellent pizzas.

Denali Salmon Bake (907/683-2733, www.denaliparksalmonbake.com, mid-May–early Sept. entrées $12–15) gets mixed reviews for the food, but is extremely popular with young seasonal workers. This rustic old building is open three meals a day, including halibut tacos and other seafood on the menu, along with free Wi-Fi and a shuttle to local hotels and campgrounds. At night it turns into a hopping no-smoking bar with live bands, karaoke, or DJs nightly, plus Alaskan beers on tap.

At **C 229 Parks Restaurant** (907/683-2567, www.229parks.com, $22–34) the name is also the location: Mile 229 Parks Highway. Housed within a bright timber frame building nine miles south of Denali Park, the restaurant serves a bistro-style menu that changes frequently. Typical entrée offerings includes tangerine duck salad, rack of elk, chive wrapped scallops, and roasted vegetable Napoleon. Save room for their ice cream sandwich with homemade ice cream between dark chocolate cookies. Organic locally grown vegetables and free-range meats are used whenever possible. Open daily in the summer for dinner, with espresso and pastries for breakfast.

PRACTICALITIES
Services
The Denali Park "Glitter Gulch" area is filled with gift shops, including inside all the large hotels. Two good places for Alaskan art are **Denali Glass Studio** (907/683-4527) behind Princess Lodge, and **Three Bears Gallery** (907/683-3343) on the boardwalk.

The large Denali Park hotels all have ATMs, as does the Lynx Creek Store. A post office is adjacent to the Riley Creek Campground.

For medical help at Denali Park, head to **Urgent Care Canyon Clinic** (907/683-4433), open daily in the summer. The nearest hospital is in Fairbanks.

Getting There
The Alaska Railroad's (907/265-2494 or 800/544-0552, www.akrr.com) *Denali Star* train leaves Fairbanks at 8:15 A.M. and arrives at Denali at noon, $59 each way; it departs Anchorage at 8:15 A.M., arriving Denali at 3:45 P.M., $135. Inside the park depot is a railroad gift shop, storage lockers, and a big rack of brochures.

Several companies have van transportation to Denali, with one-way rates to the park at around $65 from Anchorage, $52 from Talkeetna, or $46 from Fairbanks. **Alaska Park Connection** (907/245-0200 or 800/266-8625, www.alaskacoach.com) provides summertime service connecting Denali with Talkeetna, Seward, and Anchorage. **Denali Overland Transportation** (907/733-2384 or 800/651-5221, www.denalioverland.com) has charter service from Anchorage to Talkeetna and Denali, and often has space for individual travelers. **Anchorage Denali Shuttle** (907/569-0022, www.anchoragedenalishuttle.com) has daily summertime runs between Anchorage and the park.

Alaska/Yukon Trails (907/479-2277 or 888/770-7275, www.alaskashuttle.com) connects Denali with Anchorage or Fairbanks. Van service is daily in the summer, or several times a week in winter. They also provide shuttles to Healy and Cantwell.

Local air taxis include **Denali Air** (907/683-2261, www.denaliair.com), which operates from Mile 229 of the Parks Highway, **Kantishna Air Taxi** (907/683-1223, www.katair.com) from Kantishna, and **Alaska Timberline Aviation** (907/683-2121 or 877/683-2121, www.alaskaflighttours.com) from Healy. (See *Talkeetna* for five other companies with flightseeing and glacier landings.) **Era Helicopters** (907/683-2574 or 800/843-1947, www.flightseeingtours.com) is based along the river in Denali Park.

North to Fairbanks

HEALY AND VICINITY

Located 11 miles north of the turnoff to Denali National Park at Mile 249 of the Parks Highway, the town of Healy (pop. 640) has most of the necessities of life, including gas stations (considerably cheaper than at Denali Park), convenience stores, restaurants, a coin laundry, and medical clinic. Healy has grown up around the coal mining that has operated here since the 1930s. **Usibelli Coal Mine** (907/683-2226, www.usibelli.com) is the largest in Alaska, which isn't saying much, since it's Alaska's *only* commercial coal mine. However, its 1.5 million tons of subbituminous coal mined a year *does* say something: a four million-pound "walking dragline" digs 1,000 cubic yards of overburden every hour, exposing the seams. The coal is shipped to Korea or used at an adjacent power plant that supplies the Tanana Valley and Fairbanks. Healy also benefits greatly from tourism to nearby Denali National Park.

Into the Wild

A few miles north of Healy is the turnoff for the Stampede Road, made famous in the book and movie *Into the Wild.* Access to the old bus where Chris McCandless died is very difficult. Here's what the local chamber tells folks trying to get to there: "This is where you turn off the highway; this is where you park the car; this is where you get eaten to death by mosquitoes; this is where you might drown; this is where the bear mauls you; and this is where you starve to death and die."

Recreation

Iditarod musher **Ramy Brooks** (Mile 264 Parks Hwy., 907/388-7269, www.ramybrooks.com) opens his dog yard for summertime tours and a cart ride behind the dog team; $45 adults, $20 kids. **Denali Saddle Safaris** (907/683-1200, www.denalisaddlesafaris.com) leads horseback rides along the Stampede Trail starting at $59 for a one-hour ride.

Accommodations

Three miles south of Healy is **Denali RV Park and Motel** (907/683-1500 or 800/478-1501, www.denalirvpark.com), where motel rooms with private baths are $84–94 d. Family units with kitchens run $139 for four people. Open late May–early September, with cable TV and Wi-Fi in the office.

Earth Song Lodge (907/683-2863, www.earthsonglodge.com, $135–175 d, add $10 per person for additional guests) rents 12 cozy cabins, all with private baths. It's four miles down Stampede Rd., off the Parks Highway at Mile 251. Earth Song is open all year, with a nightly slide show at the coffeehouse, Wi-Fi in the lodge, winter dogsledding into Denali National Park, and a summertime coffeehouse for breakfast, sack lunches, and light dinners.

White Moose Lodge (907/683-1231 or 800/481-1232, www.whitemooselodge.com, early May–Sept., $95 d) has a dozen reasonably priced motel rooms with a continental breakfast.

Park's Edge Log Cabin Accommodations (907/683-4343, www.parks-edge.com) has simple cabins for $100 d, and a larger one for $125 d or $165 for four people. All include private baths.

Open all year, **Motel Nord Haven** (907/683-4500 or 800/683-4501, www.motelnordhaven.com, $122 s or $132–160 d) is a fine lodging choice with nicely appointed rooms, continental breakfasts, a guest computer, and wireless Internet. Kitchenettes ($160) are also available.

It's hard to miss the geodesic-shaped **Denali Dome Home B&B** (907/683-1239 or 800/683-1239, www.denalidomehome.com, $145 d) has year-round lodging in a unique 7,000-square-foot house with rock fireplaces and seven guest rooms, all with private baths. Guests appreciate two hot tubs, sauna, flower gardens, park-like grounds, extensive art collection, and traditional family-style breakfasts.

Touch of Wilderness B&B (907/683-2459 or

800/683-2459, www.touchofwildernessbb.com, $135–180 d) is another large home in a quiet location five miles north of Healy along Stampede Road. The nine guest rooms have private baths and full breakfasts, and guests appreciate the outdoor hot tub.

Denali Lakeview Inn (907/683-4035, www.denalilakeviewinn.com, $130–175 d) is a large place right on Otto Lake with 20 bright guest rooms and suites. A continental breakfast is brought to your door each morning.

Alaskan Chateau B&B, 907/683-1377, www.alaskachateau.com, $125 d) is an attractive modern log home with seven suites containing private entrances and baths, queen beds, fridges, and microwaves. A light breakfast and Wi-Fi are included, and car rentals are available. Open year-round.

Camping
Three miles south of Healy, **Denali RV Park and Motel** (907/683-1500 or 800/478-1501, www.denalirvpark.com, late May–early Sept.) has RV spaces for $30; showers cost $2 extra.

McKinley RV and Chevron (907/683-2379 or 800/478-2562, www.denaliparkresorts.com, May–Sept., $29 RVs, $18 tents) occupies a somewhat wooded area right next to the gas station. Also here are a convenience store, deli, espresso bar, laundry. Showers are an additional $2.50.

Food
Nothing great on the Healy food scene, but you'll find a lounge and 24-hour restaurant with family fare and pizzas at **Totem Inn** (907/683-2384 or 800/478-2384, www.thetoteminn.com). Try the bacon cheeseburgers from **Rose's Cafe** (907/683-7673). **Henry's Coffeehouse at Earth Song Lodge** has bagels, baked goods, soups, sandwiches, salads, pizzas, and espresso. They're open for breakfast and dinner in the summer. Get fresh produce from **Healy Cool Zone** next to the post office.

Play a round of golf at the nine-hole **Black Diamond Golf Course** (907/683-4653, www.denalihorsetours.com) or take a covered wagon ride two miles south of town on Otto Lake Road. For food, the **Black Diamond Grill** (entrées $20–30) serves a menu of breakfasts, prime rib sandwiches, steaks, and halibut.

Information and Services
The **Greater Healy/Denali Chamber of Commerce** (907/683-4636, www.denalichamber.com) will send you local brochures, and has a log visitor center (Mon.–Fri. 9 A.M.–6 P.M., Sat. 10 A.M.–4 P.M. in the summer). For medical care head to **Interior Community Health Center** (907/683-2211), open Monday–Friday; a physician's assistant and nurse are on call at other times.

Denali Car Rentals (907/683-1377, www.denalicarrental.com) is useful if you arrive in Denali by bus or rail and need wheels to get around.

Clear and Anderson
At Mile 283 of the Parks Highway—45 miles north of Healy and 21 miles south of Nenana—is the turnoff to Clear and Anderson. Clear is a military early-warning station for ballistic missiles, and not surprisingly, entry is prohibited. Six miles down the Clear road is the little settlement of Anderson along the Tanana River. The town is best known for the popular **Anderson Bluegrass Festival,** held the last weekend of July. You'll hear country and bluegrass tunes by musicians from all over Alaska.

Run by the town of Anderson, 600-acre **Riverside Park** (907/582-2500) has tent and RV sites, toilets, and showers along the Nenana River. Gas, groceries, and food are also in town.

At Mile 280 is **Clear Sky Lodge** (907/582-2251), with gas, a steakhouse, and lounge. Four miles south of there is the popular **Tatlanika Trading Company** (Mile 276, 907/582-2341), with a major selection of Alaskan-made arts and crafts. It's worth a stop to browse. They also have RV and tent sites along the Nenana River.

NENANA
Nenana (nee-NA-na; pop. 370) sits at the junction of the Nenana River and Tanana River (TAN-na-naw); a large steel bridge crosses the

⁰

THE INTERIOR

Tanana here. Nenana was an Athabascan village at the confluence of the two rivers (*na* in Athabascan means "river"; Nenana means "Camping Spot at Two Rivers") until it mushroomed into a town of 5,000 in 1916 as a base for construction on the northern leg of the Alaska Railroad. The town is 300 miles north of Anchorage, and 57 miles south of Fairbanks.

At the north end of the 700-foot railroad bridge spanning the Tanana, Warren G. Harding, first president to visit Alaska, drove in the golden spike, marking the completion of the line on July 15, 1923. Harding's visit was the culmination of a long train tour across the country, on which he attempted to rally support for his flagging administration, which was dogged by suspicions of high-level corruption. Before his trip, Harding had supported exploitation of Alaska's resources, but the firsthand experience changed his mind. Returning from Alaska to Seattle, he made a speech calling for more roads and agriculture, and conservation of lumber, fish, and mineral resources. "We must regard life in lovely, wonderful Alaska as an end and not a means, and reject the policy of turning Alaska over to the exploiters." Unfortunately, Harding died a week later, under extremely mysterious circumstances; his new vision was buried with him.

Nenana Ice Classic

© DON PITCHER

Ice Classic

Nenana is famous for its yearly Ice Classic, "Alaska's Biggest Guessing Game" (907/832-5446, www.nenanaiceclassic.com). It all began in 1917, when Alaska Railroad workers started a pool for the exact time the ice on the Tanana River would break up; the payoff was $800. Today, the prize has grown to over $270,000, which is 50 percent of the gross. The rest goes to taxes, salaries, promotion, and the town till. Tens of thousands of Alaskans and Outsiders place $2.50 bets on the day, hour, and minute of the break-up. A four-legged tripod (the town's symbol) is set up on the river ice in February, with a cable running to a clock tower on the river bank. When the ice moves, the cable stops the clock, recording the official time. Earliest break-up was April 20, in 1940; latest was May 20, in 1964. Pick up entry forms

at the visitor center or the Tripod Gift Shop and enter before the April 1 deadline. They're also available at most Carrs stores.

The Ice Classic and the town's active waterfront, where freight and supplies are loaded onto barges for bush towns strung along the Tanana and Yukon Rivers, make Nenana a prosperous, photogenic, and friendly little place—great for a leisurely stroll to break up (sorry) the trip from Fairbanks to Denali.

Sights

Stop off at the log-and-sod **visitor center** at the bottom of the bridge (corner of the Parks Highway and A St., 907/832-5435, daily 8 A.M.–6 P.M. late May–early Sept.). Behind the cabin is the *Taku Chief,* the last commercial wooden tugboat to ply the Yukon and Tanana Rivers, until it was condemned in 1978 in Nenana, where it still sits. Unfortunately, you can't climb on it.

Walk up A Street toward the river. Go right on Front St. and enter the old depot. Inside is the **Alaska State Railroad Museum** (907/832-5500, daily 9:30 A.M.–6 P.M. mid-May–Sept., free). Built in 1922 as a depot, this is a wonderful little museum, full of information, photographs, and artifacts from planning, construction, and maintenance of the Alaska Railroad. Be sure to read the railroad bridge-building history, and flip through the logbooks on the stationmaster's counter. The gift shop inside is worth a few minutes, and sells the fine historical video on the railroad.

Outside there's a monument with a memorial plaque and the once-golden spike. A block over at Front Street and B is **St. Mark's Mission Church,** established in 1904 to educate Native children from around the Interior. The inside of this beautiful log building is equally impressive, with a big stained glass window and an alter covered with Athabascan moosehide beadwork. Keep heading down toward the big single-span bridge, then go left into the heavy-equipment parking lot on the waterfront. Here is the **Ice Classic tower;** next to it is a building with the clock. Information signs about riverboats and railroads stand in the center of the parking lot.

The **Alfred Starr Cultural Center** (907/832-5520, daily 9 A.M.–7 P.M., summers only) houses displays on the Yukon 800 boat race, fish wheels, the Episcopal mission, and dog mushing. Also here is a gift shop with Native crafts. Out front are two old railcars. The **Nenana Public Library** (907/832-5812) has computers you can use to check your email.

The white markers across the river on the hillside are Native headstones in a hillside cemetery. A second graveyard just south of town contains the bodies of those who died during the railroad's construction and in a deadly influenza epidemic in 1920. And on the way out of town, don't miss the oft-photographed log-cabin bank on the left. Fish wheels are visible on both sides of the river.

Five miles north of town is **Woodland Farms** (907/832-5233, www.woodlandfarms alaska.com, $8 adults, $6 kids), a combination tree farm and reindeer ranch that's open for informative tours.

Accommodations and Camping

Bed and Maybe Breakfast (907/832-5272,

mid-May–mid-Sept., $80 d) is upstairs from the Railroad Museum at the depot; this could be the most historic B&B in the state, with hardwood floors, braided rugs, brass beds, and a railroad theme. Four simple rooms share one bath. Request the engineer's room. Breakfast ($7 extra) is served across the street at Two Choice Cafe (same owner), hence the "maybe breakfast" part of the name.

Other Nenana lodging options include **Rough Woods Inn** (2nd and A Sts., 907/832-5299) and **Firehouse 23** (907/832-5239, www.firehouse23.com).

Nenana Valley RV Park (4th and B Sts., 907/832-5230) has tent and RV sites, plus a laundry.

Food

Have a bite at **Two Choice Cafe** (907/832-1010) on Main Street, a classic bush diner. Breakfast is served anytime. (By the way, rumor has it that the two choices are "take it or leave it.") Five miles north of town is **Monderosa Bar & Grill** (907/832-5243), whose "best burger in Alaska" is in fact a great deal—one fills up two. Great fries too.

Coghill's General Store (907/832-5422, Mon.–Sat. 9 A.M.–6 P.M.) has been selling groceries, fresh meat and produce, hardware, guns, and fishing and hunting licenses to Nenanans and travelers since 1917. The building is starting to show its age, as evidenced by the slanting wooden floors. The Coghills are a sixth-generation Alaskan family, well-known throughout the state for their conservative politics.

Getting There

Nenana is 67 miles north of the entrance to Denali National Park, and 54 miles south of Fairbanks. The Alaska Railroad passes through, but it's not a scheduled stop. You can get off there if you want to, but can't check any baggage.

Alaska/Yukon Trails (907/479-2277 or 888/770-7275, www.alaskashuttle.com) has daily bus service connecting Nenana with Fairbanks or Anchorage in the summer, several times a week the rest of the year.

North to Fairbanks

North of Nenana, the highway begins a gradual climb into the wooded Tanana Hills with a multitude of vista points featuring the Alaska Range to the east. Much of this country lies within **Tanana Valley State Forest.**

At Mile 328 you pass the infamous **Skinny Dick's Halfway Inn** (907/388-5770, www .skinnydicksak.com); it *is* halfway between Fairbanks and Nenana, which makes it an even better pun. If it's tasteless, Skinny Dick's has it, including a chef's apron, complete with a small towel covering the "skinny dick."

Fairbanks

Just 150 air miles from the Arctic Circle, Fairbanks sits at 64° 49 minutes north latitude, on par with Reykjavik, Iceland, and considerably north of Helsinki, Stockholm, and Leningrad—not to mention Honolulu. The second-largest city in the state (pop. 31,000) and one of the largest population centers on earth this far north, it's still just one-ninth the size of Anchorage, but with a hospitable homi-ness its big sister has long since forgotten.

Fairbanks has much to offer summer visitors, including a classy new museum, flower-filled downtown, creative restaurants, and an abundance of wild adventures in all directions. Occupying a broad valley surrounded by rounded hills, the city straddles both sides of the Chena River—a major boating playground all summer—with the much larger Tanana River just south of Fairbanks. City streets are convoluted and confusing, partly because of the winding river, so get a map and follow it closely when driving around town.

Fairbanksians take extrovert pride in their toughness surviving the cold, dark winters, but also love to play in the lazy days of summer when the sun is almost always visible. Today, Fairbanks is transitioning from the hard-edged frontier days exemplified by the log cabins that still fill residential neighborhoods, to a present that also mixes in Wal-Marts, in-floor heating, and Wi-Fi.

Climate

Fairbanks has one of the widest temperature ranges of any city in the world. The mercury can plummet to -66°F in January and soar to 99°F in July, for a whopping 165-degree differential. In addition, one day in July could be 90°F and cloudless, while the next day could be 40°F and rainy. But it isn't just the temperatures that change so much. On the summer solstice, Fairbanks days last 21 hours and 50 minutes of glorious daylight, but winter nights get longer and longer. At the winter solstice low point (Dec. 21) the sun creeps above the horizon for just three hours and 42 minutes.

Fairbanks winters are notoriously cold, with temperatures often dropping below zero (though you might also see some times when it's a balmy 20 above Fahrenheit). By 40 or 50 degrees below zero, car tires go hard as a rock and can explode if you drive too fast before they warm up. Fan belts snap in the cold, and vehicles need block heaters or they will never start (electrical outlets are in front of many businesses). Fairbanks folks adapt to the harsh winters, and you'll even find them out skiing, dog sledding, or snowmobiling when the mercury hides out at the bottom of the thermometer. But they also have a comfortable central library with indoor trees where they can pretend it's spring even when it's months away.

HISTORY
E. T. Barnette

In August 1901, E. T. Barnette was traveling up the Tanana River on the *Lavelle Young* with a boatload of supplies bound for Tanacross to set up a trading center on a well-used gold-rush trail. Unable to negotiate some rapids, Captain Charles Adams turned into the Chena River to try to bypass them but got stuck on

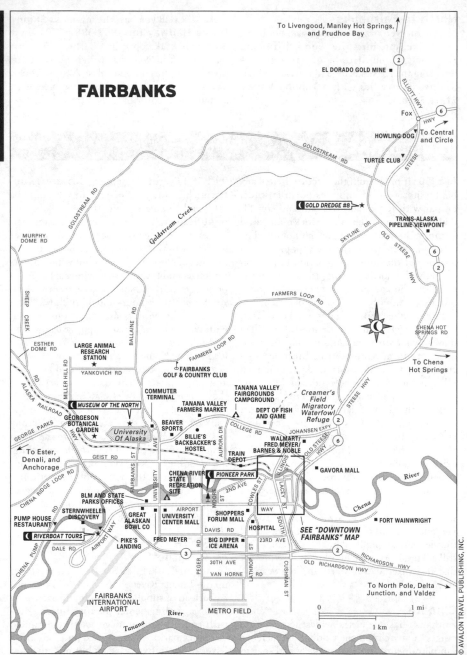

FAIRBANKS

To Livengood, Manley Hot Springs,
and Prudhoe Bay

EL DORADO GOLD MINE ■

2

Fox

HOWLING DOG ▼ To Central
and Circle

6

TURTLE CLUB ■

GOLDSTREAM RD

GOLD DREDGE #8 ★

TRANS-ALASKA
PIPELINE VIEWPOINT ■

MURPHY
DOME RD

Goldstream Creek

GOLDSTREAM RD

SKYLINE DR

OLD STEESE HWY

6

2

SHEEP CREEK

ESTHER
DOME RD

FARMERS LOOP RD

CHENA HOT
SPRINGS RD

LARGE ANIMAL
RESEARCH
STATION ★

BALLAINE RD

FARMERS LOOP RD

To Chena
Hot Springs

MILLER HILL RD

YANKOVICH RD

FAIRBANKS
GOLF & COUNTRY CLUB ★

ALASKA RAILROAD

COMMUTER
TERMINAL

TANANA VALLEY
FAIRGROUNDS
CAMPGROUND ■

Creamer's
Field
Migratory
Waterfowl
Refuge

STEESE HWY

MUSEUM OF THE NORTH ◖

TANANA VALLEY
FARMERS MARKET

DEPT OF FISH
AND GAME ■

2

GEORGE PARKS HWY

GEORGESON
BOTANICAL
GARDEN ★

BEAVER
SPORTS ■

University
Of Alaska

COLLEGE RD

AURORA DR

JOHANSEN EXPY

OLD STEESE HWY

6

To Ester,
Denali, and
Anchorage

GEIST RD

FAIRBANKS ST

BILLIE'S
BACKBACKER'S
HOSTEL ■

TRAIN
DEPOT ■

WALMART/
FRED MEYER/
BARNES & NOBLE ■

GAVORA MALL ■

River

CHENA RIDGE LOOP RD

UNIVERSITY

CHENA RIVER
STATE
RECREATION
SITE ⛺

PIONEER PARK ◖

MOORE ST

2ND AVE

BOWLES ST

ILLINOIS ST

LACEY ST

Chena

BLM AND STATE
PARKS OFFICES ■

WAY

FORT WAINWRIGHT ■

STERNWHEELER
DISCOVERY ▼

AIRPORT
UNIVERSITY
CENTER MALL

SHOPPERS
FORUM MALL ■

DAVIS RD

SOUTH

SEE "DOWNTOWN
FAIRBANKS" MAP

PUMP HOUSE
RESTAURANT ▼

AIRPORT WAY

GREAT
ALASKAN
BOWL CO ■

HOSPITAL ■

RIVERBOAT TOURS ◖

CHENA PUMP RD

DALE RD

PIKE'S
LANDING

FRED MEYER ■

BIG DIPPER
ICE ARENA ■

3

PEGER RD

23RD AVE

LATHROP ST

CUSHMAN ST

OLD RICHARDSON HWY

RICHARDSON HWY

2

To North Pole, Delta
Junction, and Valdez

30TH AVE

VAN HORNE

FAIRBANKS
INTERNATIONAL
AIRPORT

River

METRO FIELD

Tanana

0   1 mi

0   1 km

the Chena's silt-laden sandbars. Adams refused to go any farther, and Barnette refused to turn back, leaving the two men as stuck as the boat.

Peering through field glasses from a distant hill, Felice Pedroni (Felix Pedro, as he's remembered) watched the boat's progress—or lack thereof—by the smoke from its stacks. A mountain man and prospector, Pedro had been looking for gold in the huge wilderness north of the Tanana and Chena Rivers for several years and had found signs of color on some creeks near where he stood watching the steamer. However, running low on provisions, he was facing a several-hundred-mile round-trip to Circle to restock, unless . . . .

Meanwhile, Captain Adams was unceremoniously dumping Barnette, his wife, and their goods on the shore. "We cut some spruce and helped him get his freight off," Adams recalled 30 years later. "We left Barnette furious. His wife was weeping on the bank." They were standing directly in front of the present site of downtown Fairbanks. That's when Pedro showed up, quietly informed Barnette of his prospect, and bought a winter's worth of supplies. Back at his promising creek, Pedro finally hit pay dirt.

News of the strike traveled far and fast. Miners abandoned played-out Klondike and Nome and headed for the tiny outpost on the Chena River, named after Illinois Senator Charles Fairbanks, who soon became vice president under Teddy Roosevelt. Unfortunately, Barnette wasn't content with his good fortune of owning most of the town site of rich little Fairbanks. In 1911, he was tried for embezzling funds from his own Washington-Alaska Bank. Though he was acquitted, he left town with his family, never to return. His wife divorced him in 1920 in San Francisco; where he went from there, and when or how he died, are complete mysteries. Only one clear photograph of his face survives today: Barnette standing in a line with several other early Fairbanks bankers. But when the photo was found, old-timers were hard-pressed to identify which one was the town father. In fact, a discrepancy even

exists over his first name. In *E. T. Barnette*, Terrence Cole calls him "Elbridge," while *The $200 Million Gold Rush Town*, by Jo Anne Wold, remembers him as "Eldridge," and the city fathers commemorated him by naming an elementary school Ebenezer T. Barnette. Whatever his name, possibly no man embodies the boom-bust character of Fairbanks better than its founder, E. T. Barnette.

Gold and Oil Fever

The Fairbanks strike differed markedly from the shiny shores of the Klondike and the golden sands of Nome—this gold was buried under frozen muck anywhere from 8 to 200 feet deep. Fortune hunters quickly became discouraged and left, which rendered Fairbanks's boom much less explosive than Dawson's or Nome's. Even determined miners eventually reached the limits of both their endurance and the primitive placer-mining technology. After fires and floods, by 1913, when the road from Valdez to Fairbanks was completed, the town was in the midst of a serious bust cycle. But in 1923 the Alaska Railroad reached Fairbanks from Seward and Anchorage, which inaugurated the real Golden Age. Major mining corporations freighted up and installed large dredges to uncover the gold, and eventually $200 million worth was pulled from the surrounding area. When the Alaska Highway was pushed through to Delta from Canada in 1942, connecting the Richardson Highway to the outside world, the city's future was assured.

Only one word can really be applied to Fairbanks in the 1970s: boomtown. The Prudhoe Bay oil discovery of 1968 led to a massive influx of pipeline workers and hangers-on. Suddenly demand far exceeded supply, making it a seller's market for everything from canned food to cocaine, from housing to hookers. So many people poured in with dreams of big bucks that officials took out ads in Lower 48 newspapers telling everyone to stay away. Only half the job seekers ever got hired, and the lines at the bank were only exceeded in length by those at the unemployment office.

Fairbanks today is a vastly different place

from the pipeline era, with an economy that prospers on the university and military payroll, the summer tourist season, as a supply center for the bush, construction, and the nearby Fort Knox gold mine.

DOWNTOWN SIGHTS
Visitor Center
Start out at the Log Cabin Visitors Information Center (1st Ave. near Cushman, 907/456-5774 or 800/327-5774 recording, www.explorefairbanks.com, daily 10 A.M.–5 P.M.), a sod-roofed structure along the Chena River. You can access the info line with the day's events at 907/456-4636. While here, load yourself down with a few pounds of publications, including the *Fairbanks Visitors Guide,* a comprehensive listing of local practicalities. Several computers are available to check your email for free.

Just outside the log cabin is **Golden Heart Park,** a flower-packed plaza centered around a large heroic sculpture of *The First Unknown Family,* representing those who first crossed into Alaska over the Bering Land Bridge. Free concerts (907/456-1984) take place Wednesdays at 7 P.M. and Fridays at noon in June and July.

On the opposite side of the visitor center, the Cushman Street Bridge crosses the Chena River. The flags of all 50 states line the bridge. Visit the **Immaculate Conception Church** (1904), just across the river, for its beautiful stained-glass windows.

The **Morris Thompson Cultural and Visitor Center** (www.morristhompsoncenter.org) opens in 2008 at the intersection of Wendell and Dunkel Streets, close to the Chena River and Griffin Park. It will house the Fairbanks Visitor Center, the Alaska Public Lands Information Center, a Tanana Chiefs Cultural Center, an artisans workshop, a theatre with films and presentations, and interpretive exhibit—including a giant 3-D map of Alaska.

Ice Museum
At the corner of 2nd Avenue and Lacey Street in the historic Lacey Street Theatre is the Fairbanks Ice Museum (907/451-8222, www.icemuseum.com, daily 10 A.M.–9 P.M. June–Aug.; $11 adults, $6 ages 6–12, free for younger kids). This is the "coolest show in town," with a 25-minute film about the process of creating ice art at the World Ice Art Championships in Fairbanks each March. There's also glass-walled walk-in freezer that displays intricate pieces of sculpted ice, and you can often watch artisans demonstrate their craft.

Public Lands Information Center
The Alaska Public Lands Information Center (3rd Ave. at Cushman, 907/456-0527, www.nps.gov/aplic) is open daily 9 A.M. to 6 P.M. Memorial Day–Labor Day; Tuesday–Saturday 10 A.M.–6 P.M. the rest of the year. A combination museum and information bureau, this excellent facility represents various state and federal agencies, with interesting aerial and relief maps, videos that provide thumbnail sketches on Alaska; old-time stereoscopic viewers showing three-dimensional views of historic Alaska, scheduled videos in the comfortable theater, plus books, prints, postcards, and topographic maps. (APLIC is scheduled to move into the Morris Thomson Center in 2008.)

Community Museum
The Fairbanks Community Museum (551 2nd Ave., 907/457-3669, daily 10 A.M.–6 P.M. Memorial Day–Labor Day, closed rest of year—except during the Yukon Quest; free admission) is housed within historic City Hall. Inside are displays and photos on dog mushing, the gold rush, and the growth of Fairbanks. My personal favorite is the collection of old bar napkins.

CREAMER'S FIELD
Head north about a mile on Illinois and take a left at College Road. In another mile is the 1,800-acre Creamer's Field Migratory Waterfowl Refuge (907/452-5162, www.creamersfield.org) where you might observe migratory birds and most of the common vegetation of the Interior. Early in the year, the field is plowed and tons of barley are spread around. Sandhill cranes, Canada geese, and many species of ducks stop off at the field in April and May on

THE INTERIOR

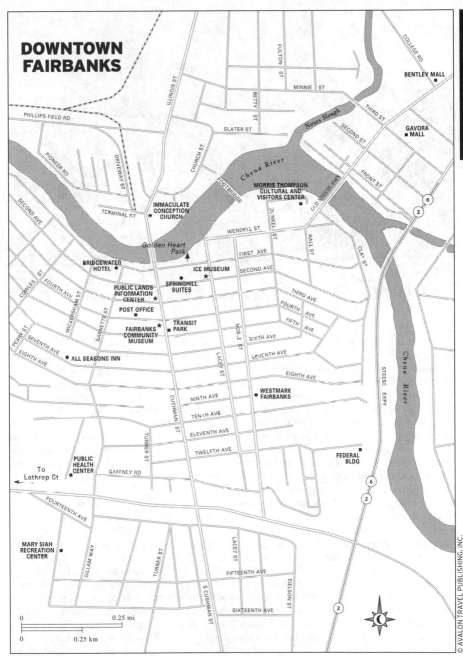

DOWNTOWN FAIRBANKS

COLLEGE RD

BENTLEY MALL

FULTON ST

BETTY ST

MINNIE ST

ILLINOIS ST

THIRD ST

GAVORA MALL

PHILLIPS FIELD RD

SLATER ST

SECOND ST

Noyes Slough

CHURCH ST

DRIVEWAY ST

PIONEER RD

Chena River

FRONT ST

FOOTBRIDGE

MORRIS THOMPSON CULTURAL AND VISITORS CENTER

OLD STEESE HWY

6
2

SECOND AVE

TERMINAL ST

IMMACULATE CONCEPTION CHURCH

DUNKEL ST

WENDELL ST

HALL ST

CLAY ST

Golden Heart Park

FIRST AVE

BRIDGEWATER HOTEL

ICE MUSEUM

SECOND AVE

COWLES ST

FOURTH AVE

PUBLIC LANDS INFORMATION CENTER

SPRINGHILL SUITES

THIRD AVE

WICKERSHAM ST

POST OFFICE

FOURTH AVE

FIFTH AVE

BARNETTE ST

PERRY ST

SEVENTH AVE

FAIRBANKS COMMUNITY MUSEUM

TRANSIT PARK

NOBLE ST

SIXTH AVE

EIGHTH AVE

ALL SEASONS INN

LACEY ST

SEVENTH AVE

EIGHTH AVE

Chena River

WESTMARK FAIRBANKS

STEESE EXPY

CUSHMAN ST

NINTH AVE

TENTH AVE

ELEVENTH AVE

TURNER ST

TWELFTH AVE

FEDERAL BLDG

6
2

To Lathrop St

PUBLIC HEALTH CENTER

GAFFNEY RD

FOURTEENTH AVE

MARY SIAH RECREATION CENTER

GILLAM WAY

TURNER ST

LACEY ST

FIFTEENTH AVE

S CUSHMAN ST

EIELSON ST

SIXTEENTH AVE

2

0   0.25 mi

0   0.25 km

© AVALON TRAVEL PUBLISHING, INC.

sandhill cranes in Creamer's Field Migratory Waterfowl Refuge

© DON PITCHER

their migratory route north—a local herald for the arrival of spring.

Follow the driveway to the old dairy, where you can pick up a free trail guide. The dairy was the first in Alaska (1904) and the northernmost in the Western Hemisphere. Charles Creamer owned it from 1928 to 1966, when he sold it to Fish & Game for use as a migratory-waterfowl refuge. Volunteer-led nature walks (free) depart from the **Farmhouse Visitor Center** on weekdays. It's open daily 10 A.M.– 5 P.M., June–August, and Saturdays only in May and September. The **Sandhill Crane Festival** at Creamer's Field brings nature walks, photography and drawing workshops, music, and talks the last week of August.

At other times, you can head out on the two-mile nature path to explore forest, shrub, muskeg, and riparian areas. The high point of the trail, literally, is a 20-foot observation platform, from which you are supposed to be able to spot wildlife. The trail is mostly boardwalk over swamp, with the predictable insectoid results, so bring your bug dope.

Adjacent to Wedgewood Resort and connected to Creamer's Field by hiking paths, the **Alaska Bird Observatory** (414 Wedgewood Dr., 907/451-7059, www.alaskabird.org) conducts long-term research on Interior Alaska birds and works to protect their habitat. It's the only organization of its kind in the state. Visitors can watch summertime banding demonstrations or join bird walks. Call the **Arctic Audubon Birding Hotline** (907/451-9213, www.arctic audubon.org) for sightings of unusual species.

UNIVERSITY OF ALASKA

Continue west on College Road to the University of Alaska Fairbanks (UAF), Alaska's primary educational facility (Admissions Office 907/474-7500 or 800/478-1823, www.uaf. edu). When it opened in 1922 as Alaska Agricultural College and School of Mines, there were six students and as many faculty; today 9,000 students attend the 2,500-acre campus. This facility is highly regarded for its Arctic research and Alaska Native studies. Smaller University of Alaska campuses are in Anchor-

© DON PITCHER

University of Alaska Museum of the North

age and Juneau. Ask any student to direct you to the **Wood Campus Center,** where you can pick up a free map of the grounds, check the ride board, and grab a cheap breakfast, a slice of pizza, an espresso, a cafeteria lunch, or a beer in the pub. A free shuttle bus runs every 15 minutes around campus.

Free two-hour **walking tours** (907/474-7581) of the campus take place Monday–Friday at 10 A.M. June–August. Led by UAF students, these start from the museum and end at the campus center. No reservations are needed, but the tours may be canceled if it is raining; call to confirm.

University of Alaska Museum of the North

One of Alaska's finest collections or art, human history, and natural history, the University of Alaska Museum of the North (907/474-7505, www.uaf.edu/museum) is now housed within the state's most striking building. A new wing designed by renowned architect Joan Soranno opened in 2005, with a gleaming white exte-

rior that curves and swoops like an enormous piece of glacial ice. The interior is equally interesting, both as a structure and for the contemporary and ancient Alaskan art. Don't miss the door marked "The Place Where You Go to Listen," where the lights and sounds give voice to real-time data from movements of the sun, moon, seismic activity, and auroras.

The second (older) half of the museum houses collections divided according to the state's five geographical areas, and includes hands-on objects, dioramas, and videos. The wildlife and gold exhibits are mind-boggling; the Russian artifacts and the permafrost display are exceptional. So is an exhibit dealing with the incarceration of Japanese-Americans during World War II; read the heartbreaking personal letters from the families pleading for compassion. Other highlights include Blue Babe, a mummified 36,000-year-old steppe bison discovered in 1979 at a placer mine, a 1,250-pound brown bear, a video on whaling, fist-sized gold nuggets, ancient ivory carvings, dinosaur bones from the North Slope, and lots more.

Back in the new wing you'll find a fine gift shop, café, and an auditorium with daily demonstrations by World Eskimo Indian Olympic athletes. On a clear day, Mt. McKinley—across the broad Tanana Valley—can be seen in all its awesome eminence from the museum's tall windows. The museum is open daily 9 A.M.–7 P.M. mid-May–mid-September, and Monday–Friday 9 A.M.–5 P.M., Saturday–Sunday noon–5 P.M. the rest of the year. Admission costs $10 adults, $9 seniors, $5 ages 7–17, and free for younger kids. Add $4 for an audio guide.

Large Animal Research Station

This Arctic biology research center (907/474-7207, www.uaf.edu/lars, late May–early Sept.) houses more than 100 musk ox, caribou, and reindeer, mostly tame animals used for nutritional, physiological, and behavioral studies. Find the 150-acre research station north of the campus on Yankovich Road, 1.5 miles off Ballaine Road. This unique facility is open for guided one-hour tours ($10 adults, $9 seniors, $6 students, and free for kids under 7) daily at 1:30 and 3:30 P.M., and for half-hour tours ($6) six times a day. A free viewing stand area is open at any time.

Georgeson Botanical Garden

This five-acre garden (907/474-7627, daily 7 A.M.–8 P.M. May–September, www.uaf.edu/salrm/gbg, $1) is on the grounds of the Agricultural and Forestry Experimental Station downhill from the museum on the west end of campus. It's the northernmost botanical garden in the Western Hemisphere, and contains flowers, vegetables, fruits, herbs, and perennials that can withstand the northern rigors. Giant cabbages and other veggies are the star attractions, and the gazebo is perfect for a picnic lunch.

Other University Sights

Learn about the northern lights, earthquakes, and more in a tour of the **Geophysical Institute** on Wednesdays at 2:30 P.M. June–August. This building (the tall one with the satellite dishes on top) also houses a Map Office, where you can buy topographic maps. The **International Arctic Research Center** is open for tours on Wednesdays at 4 P.M. June–August; it's adjacent to the Geophysical Institute. Call 907/474-7558 for details on either of these tours. Take a virtual visit to one of the world's fastest supercomputers (yet another example of the largess created by Alaska's powerful congressional delegation) at the Rasmuson Library on the east side of the campus. Tours (907/474-6935) are given June–August on Wednesdays at 1 P.M.

Poker Flat Research Range (907/474-7558, www.pfrr.alaska.edu)—the only university-operated sounding rocket range anywhere—is 33 miles north of Fairbanks on the Steese Highway. Tours are offered some Thursdays in the summer.

◖ PIONEER PARK

This delightful 44-acre theme park (907/459-1087, www.co.fairbanks.ak.us/parks&rec, 11 A.M.–9 P.M., grounds open year-round, shops and rides Memorial Day–Labor Day, no charge)—the only one of its kind in the state—occupies the site of the 1967 state centennial celebration. Many of the original buildings from the early days of Fairbanks and various locations around Alaska have been moved here and assembled into a gold rush–era town. Park headquarters is in one such restored building just inside the entrance off Airport Way between Nome and Peger Roads. Pick up a map of the park and spend a few hours exploring the grounds of this free open-air museum.

The big (227-ft.-long) 1933 sternwheeler riverboat **Nenana** ($3 adults, free for under age 5) has been beautifully restored, and sits just inside the entrance. The second-largest wooden-hull vessel in existence, it now houses an amazingly detailed diorama of towns along the Yukon and Tanana rivers. Be sure to go upstairs for a perspective view of the park.

To your right inside the entrance is the **Harding Car,** a railcar used by Warren G. Harding when he came to Alaska on his ill-fated trip in 1923, just before his death under questionable circumstances.

© DON PITCHER

Pioneer Park, a gold rush-era town

Continue to **Gold Rush Town,** a collection of 29 colorful and historic buildings that includes the interesting home of Alaska's first Territorial Governor, James Wickersham. The **Palace Theatre & Saloon** has a musical-comedy revue nightly ($18 adults, $9 kids), while the **Pioneer Museum** is a free collection of mining and other memorabilia, including a large 1912 map of Alaska. The same building houses **The Big Stampede Show** ($4 adults, $2 kids), a 45-minute look at the lives of early pioneers.

Pioneer Air Museum (907/451-0037, daily 11 A.M.–9 P.M. in the summer, $2) is housed in a dome-shaped building near the center of Pioneer Park. Inside are a number of historic and modern aircraft, from a 1933 Stinson SR-5 to a 1966 Bell UH1 helicopter.

The narrow-gauge **Crooked Creek and Whiskey Island Railroad** ($2 adults, $1 children) circles Pioneer Park throughout the day, and the **Tanana Valley Railroad Museum** houses the oldest operating steam locomotive

in Alaska, built in 1899. Families also love the vintage 1915 carousel ride ($2), dogsled rides ($30 adults, $15 kids), and miniature golf ($4.50 adults, $3 kids). Browse around the replica **Mining Valley** with its antique mining equipment, and the **Native Village** where you will find historic artifacts. Also at Pioneer Park is an excellent **salmon bake** (see the *Food* section).

◖ RIVERBOAT TOURS

The Binkley family, now in its fourth generation of riverboat pilots, runs **Riverboat Discovery Cruises** (907/479-6673 or 866/479-6673, www.riverboatdiscovery.com, $47 adults, $32 for ages 3–12, free for tots). This 3.5-hour, 20-mile cruise on the Chena and Tanana Rivers—a bargain—includes the chance to view an Athabascan-style camp, to watch a floatplane take off, and to see dogs from the late Susan Butcher's team in action (from the boat). The riverboat docks at a re-created

Alaskan bush village with log cabins and giant cabbages. Reservations are necessary. Cruises depart from the dock at the end of Dale Road out by the airport at 8:45 A.M. and 2 P.M. early May–mid-September. A large gift shop awaits if you get there early.

The *Tanana Chief* (907/452-8687 or 866/452-8687, www.greatlandrivertours.com), is a smaller paddlewheel boat with two-hour summertime sightseeing trips ($25), along with prime rib dinner cruises ($50), and Sunday brunch cruises ($37).

RECREATION

Midnight Sun Balloon Tours (907/456-3028, www.alaskaballoontours.com, $175 adults or $125 kids) has one-hour flights over the Tanana Valley, with departures scheduled when wind conditions are mild.

Play a midnight round of summertime golf at **Fairbanks Golf & Country Club** (1735 Farmers Loop Rd., 907/479-6555), where 24-hour tee times are available on the nine-hole course in June and July! **North Star Golf Club** (330 Golf Club Dr., 907/457-4653, www.northstargolf.com), "America's northernmost," is the other local nine-hole club.

Hiking and Biking

For local trails, try Creamer's Field and Chena River Wayside. Farther afield, find hiking and backpacking opportunities in the White Mountains and in the Pinnell Mountains.

Fairbanks has an excellent series of connecting walking or biking paths: from downtown along the river to Pioneer Park; from University and Airport out on Chena Pump Road; and a great up-and-down route on Farmers Loop Road from the Steese Highway to the university. These paved trails connect to all sorts of other trails for more adventurous cyclists. **Alaska Outdoor Rentals & Guides** (907/457-2453, www.akbike.com, $27 for all day) has mountain bike rentals along the river behind Pioneer Park. You can also rent bikes from **GoNorth Adventure Travel Center** (3500 Davis Rd., 907/479-7272 or 866/236-7272, www.gonorthalaska.net).

Swimming

Three indoor pools are open to the public: **Hamme Pool** (Airport and Cowles, 907/456-2969) at Lathrop High School, **Mary Siah Recreation Center** (1025 14th Ave., 907/456-6119), and **Patty Gym Pool** (at UAF, 907/474-7205).

Floating the River

The peaceful Chena River is a favorite destination for canoeists. **Alaska Outdoor Rentals & Guides** (907/457-2453, www.2paddle1.com, late May–mid-Sept.) runs a popular canoe and kayak rental business along the river at Pioneer Park. Put in here and paddle two hours to the Pump House—a great place for a drink or meal while you wait for the van ride back. Half-day rentals cost $33. The company can also provide canoes and transport for longer trips, including overnighters. **GoNorth Adventure Travel Center** (3500 Davis Rd., 907/479-7272 or 866/236-7272, www.paratours.net) has a similar service, with canoe rentals and transportation.

Alaska Fishing & Raft Adventures (907/388-4193, www.aktours.net) takes guests on six-hour raft trips down the upper Chena River. These easy and scenic floats cost $95 per person, including transportation from Fairbanks and a lunch or dinner.

Fishing

A number of local companies provide Chena River fishing trips; get their brochures at the visitor center. Fishing in the Chena for grayling is fair, but better grayling fishing is found at the Chatanika River, between miles 30 and 40 on the Steese Highway toward Circle. Chum, silver, and a few kings run up here from mid-July. Chena Lakes Recreation Area has good rainbow-trout fishing. Fish & Game provides a recorded hot line (907/459-7385) of fishing tips. The *Fairbanks Daily News-Miner* carries fishing updates every Friday.

Dog Mushing

Fairbanks is a major center for dog mushing. Well-known musher and author **Mary**

Shields was the first woman to finish the Iditarod. She offers two-hour summer visits (907/457-1117, www.maryshields.com, $28 adults, or $20 kids) that include time with the dogs at her home. She also leads wintertime sled dog tours.

Other dogsledding tours or rides (depending upon the season) are available from **Paws for Adventure** (907/378-3630, www.pawsforadventure.com), **Chena Dog Sled Adventures** (907/488-5845), **Chena Hot Springs Resort** (907/452-7867 or 800/478-4681, www.chenahotsprings.com), **Northern Sky Lodge** (30 miles south of Fairbanks, 907/388-9954, www.northernskylodge.com), **Sled Dog Adventures** (907/479-5090, www.sleddogadventures.com), and **Sun Dog Express** (907/479-6983, www.mosquitonet.com/~sleddog).

Skiing
Moose Mountain (907/479-4732, www.shredthemoose.com) is 20 minutes north of Fairbanks near Murphy Dome. It has 1,250 feet of vertical drop, and an unusual lift system: a "variable capacity terrestrial tram," more commonly called a bus with ski racks. Ski here for $32 adults, $29 students, and $20 ages 7–12. Get the snow report at 907/459-8132. Fortunately, temperatures are typically 20–30 degrees warmer here than in Fairbanks (because of an inversion). The ski area is open Thursday–Sunday 10 A.M.–5 P.M. in the winter.

Mt. Aurora Skiland (907/389-2314, www.skiland.org, $32 adults, $27 college students, and $22 for younger kids) is 21 miles north of town off the Steese Highway, and is open for downhill skiing and snowboarding December–April. The area has a double chairlift, day lodge, and snack bar, plus ski and snowboard rentals. Call 907/456-7669 for the snow report.

Cross-country skiing is very popular around Fairbanks; the nicest place is **Birch Hill Ski Area**, with a modern Nordic center and 33 kilometers of groomed trails, 6 kilometers of which are lighted. Contact the **Nordic Ski Club of Fairbanks** (907/474-4242,

www.nscfairbanks.org) for details and online maps for these and others, including 15 kilometers next to the university.

Northern Lights Viewing
The Fairbanks area has some of the finest aurora displays anywhere on the planet. The clear winter nights and proximity to the North Pole create ideal viewing conditions (once you get away from the city lights). For predictions of upcoming activity, visit the website for UAF's Geophysical Institute (www.gedds.alaska.edu/auroraforecast). A number of lodges in the Fairbanks area have geared their winter season for people who come to view and photograph the northern lights—notably Chena Hot Springs Resort and Mt. Aurora/Skiland—and many Fairbanks hotels provide aurora wake-up calls upon request.

ENTERTAINMENT
Drinking and Dancing
Visit www.fbxsquare.com for tips and blogs on the Fairbanks bar and music scene. Three miles south on the Parks Highway is **Blue Loon** (907/457-5666, www.theblueloon.com), Fairbanks' party place with hot bands, art house movies, dancing, 15 beers on tap, and good pub meals. Don't miss their Jerry Garcia pig roast each August.

The Hideout Lounge (1288 Sadler Way, 907/456-1830, $5 cover) is another party spot, with two levels indoors, pool and foosball, live bands, plus a sand volleyball court. It's behind the Fred Meyer store.

Other dance-'til-2 places are **The Marlin** (3412 College Rd., 907/479-4646), and **Silverspur Nightclub** (285 Old Richardson Hwy., 907/456-6300).

For a nice riverside drink and hors d'oeuvres in a historic setting, head out to the **Pump House** (1.3 Mile Chena Pump Rd., 907/479-8452, www.pumphouse.com). **College Coffeehouse** (3677 College Rd., 907/374-0468, www.collegecoffeehousefairbanks.com) has folksy music.

Out in Fox, **Silver Gulch Brewery** (907/452-2739, www.silvergulch.com) brews a porter, two lagers, amber ale, and a special reserve barley wine. There are free tours and tastings on Fridays 5–7 P.M. when locals pack the place to refill their kegs. Across the road is the infamous **Howling Dog Saloon** (907/456-4695, www.howlingdogsaloon.com), a great spot for dancing and midnight volleyball.

Movies and Plays

Out on Airport Way at Lathrop, **Regal Cinema** (907/456-5113, www.regalcinemas.com) has comfortable seating and 16 movie screens. The Blue Loon sometimes shows films, too. **Fairbanks Shakespeare Theatre** (907/457-7638, www.fstalaska.org), performs plays behind the University Museum in July and August.

Saloon Theaters

The **Palace Theatre & Saloon** (at Pioneer Park, 907/456-5960, www.akvisit.com) offers a musical-comedy revue nightly mid-May–mid-September. The show, *Golden Heart Revue*, goes on at 8:15 P.M. It's professionally produced, and worth the admission: $18 adults or $9 kids.

The **Malemute Saloon** (10 miles south of Fairbanks, 907/479-2500, www.akvisit.com, $18 adults or $9 kids), in Ester, has been a local institution since 1958, putting on a musical revue and Robert Service recitations nightly at 9 P.M. You sit at plywood and beer-barrel tables; the pitchers keep coming and the peanut shells mingle with the two-inch-deep sawdust.

Baseball

Composed of top college players, the **Alaska Goldpanners** (907/451-0095, www.gold panners.com) plays against teams in the Alaska Baseball League. The games are played at Growden Field (2nd and Wilbur, behind Pioneer Park), starting at 7 P.M. The famous Midnight Sun game, played around the summer solstice, starts at 10:30 P.M. and goes nine innings without using the field's artificial lights. The Goldpanners are composed of college players, dozens of whom have gone on to play in the major leagues, including Dave Winfield, Graig Nettles, and Tom Seaver.

EVENTS
Summer

Locals have roughly 90 days a year to get their fill of outdoor extravaganzas, and they go at it with a vengeance. The first big event of the season is the **Midnight Sun Festival,** held on summer solstice (June 21), with live music (30 bands), food, a car show, and the famous Alaska Goldpanners **Midnight Sun baseball game** that continues past midnight without lights. For details, visit www.downtownfairbanks.com.

Next comes **Golden Days,** between the second and third weekends in July—a week-long party culminating in a fun parade. The whole town turns out, and if you happen to be there, even without your camera, you won't forget it.

After that comes the **World Eskimo-Indian Olympics** (907/452-6646, www.weio .org), featuring Alaska Native athletic games, dance, and art. This three-day mid-July event, includes such unusual competitions as the Ear Pull, Greased Pole Walk, Kneel Jump, Knuckle Hop, Seal Skin, Toe Kick, and Blanket Toss. There's even a Native baby contest. It could be one of the most exotic and memorable events in Alaska. (Note: WEIO takes place in Anchorage during 2007, but will probably return to Fairbanks the following year.)

The **Fairbanks Summer Arts Festival** (907/474-8869, www.fsaf.org) is a two-week-long series of workshops, performances, and concerts, encompassing classical music, opera, dance, theater, figure skating, and visual arts. It takes place from late July to early August, and attracts hundreds of students and instructors.

The big **Tanana Valley State Fair** (907/452-3750, www.tananavalleyfair.org) is at the Fairgrounds on College Road, the second and third weeks of August, with rides, music, food booths, craft booths, and those famous giant cabbages.

YUKON QUEST

The Yukon Quest International Sled Dog Race began in February 1984 with 26 teams in competition. The race has close ties to the past of the Yukon and Interior Alaska, taking place along trails that once carried fur traders and missionaries, gold-hungry pilgrims and determined mail carriers. In the days before airplanes and automobiles, the dog team was often the only method of transportation in the great North. The Yukon Quest has been called the "toughest race on earth." And for good reason.

The race, which takes place in early February, runs from Fairbanks to Whitehorse in even-numbered years and from Whitehorse to Fairbanks in odd-numbered years. It's named for the mighty Yukon River, "the Highway of the North," and travels across some of the wildest and most sparsely populated country in the world. Terrain, trail conditions, and temperatures vary wildly along the trail, from steep hills to miles of flat frozen lake, from hard-packed snow and frozen rivers to rough gravel, from -60 to 30°F.

Although most of the media focus is on the mushers, the real stars of this or any sled dog race are the canine athletes. Since the teams are limited to 14 dogs, the Quest is musher-friendly to those with smaller kennels. And a smaller team ensures better care for individual dogs.

Depending on weather and trail conditions, the race takes 10-14 days. There is a mandatory 36-hour layover in Dawson City, Yukon. This is the only stop where dog handlers can feed and care for the teams while the mushers get some much-needed rest. A large veterinarian tent is set up in the dog camp, which lies across the frozen Yukon River from Dawson.

If a dog exhibits signs of fatigue or illness at a checkpoint, the animal is dropped from the race and turned over to the handlers. If dropped at a remote spot, the dog is transported by one of the many volunteer pilots to a point where it can be met by the handlers.

Unlike other long-distance races, the Quest is easily accessible to onlookers. Race fans may follow the mushers' progress by driving to many of the checkpoints along the way. Photo opportunities are plentiful from start to finish. For further information, contact Quest headquarters (600 3rd St. in Fairbanks, 907/452-7954, www.yukonquest.org).

Winter

The biggest winter event is the **Yukon Quest International Sled Dog Race** (907/452-7954, www.yukonquest.com), held in February. Other sled dog races include the **Limited North American Sled Dog Championships** in early March followed by the **Open North American Championship Sled Dog Races** in mid-March. Details on both are available from the Alaska Dog Mushers Association (907/457-6874, www.sleddog.org).

The **World Ice Art Championships** (907/451-8250, www.icealaska.com) is an early March event that attracts international sculptors who create truly amazing works of art with dramatic and colorful lighting. This isn't your standard fancy restaurant art; some of these pieces may stand 20 feet tall and contain incredibly intricate work. Just getting the 1,500 tons of clear ice is a challenge. The children's ice park here has a super-fast luge for adrenaline junkies.

SHOPPING

On Wednesdays and Saturdays in the summer, the **Tanana Valley Farmers Market** (College Rd., 907/456-3276, www.tvfmarket.com) is *the* place to find locally grown or crafted items, from asparagus and berry pies to Native beadwork and polar fleece booties.

Great Alaskan Bowl Company (4630 Old Airport Rd., 907/474-9663 or 800/770-4222, www.woodbowl.com) sells a variety of nesting birch hardwood bowls, all fashioned from a single split log. This is a good made-in-Alaska product to take home with you. A window overlooks the wood shop; the wood shavings are used for packing material and decoration in the showroom.

Galleries and Gifts

Fairbanks' best and largest art space is **New Horizons Gallery** (519 1st Ave., 907/456-2063 or 866/456-2063, www.newhorizons gallery.com) across from the visitor center. Also of note are **Alaska House Art Gallery** (at 10th and Cushman, 907/456-6449, www.thealaskahouse.com), **Expressions in Glass** (1922 Peger Rd., 907/474-3923 or 888/574-3923, www.expressionsinglass.net), and **The Artworks** (near the university at 3677 College Rd., 907/479-2563).

Gift shops abound downtown; **Arctic Traveler's** (at 201 Cushman, 907/456-7080, www.arctictravelers.com) is the biggest. **The Craft Market** (on the corner of 5th and Noble, 907/452-5495) has a good collection of carved ivory, woven baskets, masks, dolls, and other Native arts and crafts.

Alaska Rag Co. (603 Lacey St., 907/451-4401, www.alaskaragco.com) is a unique shop with hand-woven rag rugs made on the premises, plus jewelry, stained glass, and other gifts. (The rugs are woven from locally recycled cloth, and many of the workers are mentally disabled individuals who could not otherwise find work.) **The Spinning Room** (516 2nd Ave., Studio 220, 907/458-7610, www.spinning-room.com) sells handspun fabrics, including those made from musk ox wool.

Outdoor Gear

Beaver Sports (3480 College Rd., 907/479-2494, www.beaversports.com) is *the* place for outdoor gear of all types in Fairbanks, and has the largest selection of canoes in Alaska. They also rent canoes, mountain bikes, skis, and snowshoes.

Go North (3820 University Ave., 907/479-7272 or 866/236-7272, www.paratours.net) has rental canoes, mountain bikes, tents, sleeping bags, cooking utensils, and all sorts of other gear, including satellite phones! Also check out **Big Rays** (507 2nd St., 907/452-3458,

www.bigrays.com) and **The Prospector** (1512 S. Cushman, 907/457-7312, www.prospector outfitters.com).

Get hand-sewn outdoor creations, along with fast repairs from **Apocalypse Design** (201 Minnie St., 907/451-7555 or 866/451-7555, www.akgear.com).

ACCOMMODATIONS

Fairbanks has the complete lodging spectrum, from backpacker hostel beds to modern hotels with top-end features and amenities. Start your exploration by looking over the descriptions in the Fairbanks Visitors Guide from the CVB, or their online version (www.explorefairbanks.com). The Visitor Center keeps track of daily room availability.

Under $50

Billie's Backpackers Hostel (2895 Mack Rd., 907/479-2034, www.alaskahostel.com) has four-person dorms for $25 per person, or pay $15 per person for a tent space. Private rooms are $50 d, but these go fast. The hostel provides a kitchen, showers, Internet access and Wi-Fi, travel information, and has the added bonus of a sun deck, barbecue and free bikes. Open year-round.

GoNorth Base Camp Hostel (near the airport at 3500 Davis Rd., 907/479-7272 or 866/236-7272, www.paratours.net, mid-May–late Sept.) has beds in cozy tent cabins ($24 per person), along with tent spaces ($12). Kids love the tipi, and other facilities include a kitchen, BBQ, coin-op showers, guest computers (fee), outdoor equipment rentals (from canoes to satellite phones), and trip planning. Staff members are fluent in German and French.

$50-100

Ten miles south of Fairbanks, the **Ester Gold Camp** (907/479-2500 or 800/676-6925, www.akvisit.com, $60 s or $70 d), serves up simple rooms. The historic hotel is adjacent to the Malemute Saloon, famous for nightly music and recitation.

Alaska Motel (1546 Cushman St., 907/456-6393 or 866/374-0476, www.ak-motel.com,

$85 d) is an older motel where many of the rooms contain kitchenettes.

Close to the airport, **Golden North Motel** (4888 Airport Way, 907/479-6201 or 800/447-1910, www.goldennorthmotel.com, $75 s or $79–99 d) has clean and quiet (but small) rooms at reasonable prices. Guests appreciate the continental breakfast, computer, free Wi-Fi, and 24-hour courtesy van.

A good economy choice is **Ranch Motel** (2223 S. Cushman St., 907/452-4783 or 888/452-4783, www.expage.com/ranchmotel, $90–100 s or d), a small family-run motel with clean rooms.

$100-200

The exterior of **Golden Nugget Hotel** (900 Noble St., 907/452-5141, www.golden-nuggethotel.com, $100–130 d) is dated, but the rooms are spacious and have air-conditioning.

Fountainhead Development (907/452-6661 or 800/528-4916, www.fountainheadhotels.com) owns three Fairbanks lodging places: Bridgewater Hotel, Sophie Station Hotel, and Wedgewood Resort. All three include free airport and train depot shuttles, along with guest computers. There is free Wi-Fi throughout Sophie Station, plus in the lobby area and some rooms at Wedgewood and Bridgewater.

Conveniently located just a block from the downtown visitor center, the entirely non-smoking **Bridgewater Hotel** (723 1st Ave., open mid-May–mid-Sept., $134–149 d) has attractive rooms; ask for a corner unit overlooking the river.

Catering to business travelers, **[Sophie Station Hotel** (1717 University Ave., 907/479-3650, $185–235 d) provides large and attractive suites—all with full kitchens. It's also smoke-free, with a fitness center, restaurant, and lounge on the premises.

On the north side of town **Wedgewood Resort** (212 Wedgewood Dr.) offers homey apartment-style units, all with full kitchens, living rooms, and dining rooms. One-bedroom units are $160–185 d or $180–205 for four, and two-bedroom units run $210–235 d

or $230–255 for six people. Also on the resort grounds is the seasonal **Bear Lodge,** with standard hotel rooms for $160–235 d, along with the Alaska Bird Observatory.

Regency Fairbanks (95 10th Ave., 907/452-3200, 800/478-1320, or 800/348-1340 outside Alaska, www.regencyfairbankshotel.com, standard rooms $159 d; with whirlpool tubs $195 d) is a large, centrally located hotel where the well-kept rooms all have full kitchens. The Regency provide free airport and railroad shuttle, plus a business center, workout room, Wi-Fi, and air conditioning.

Extended Stay Deluxe (4580 Old Airport Rd., 907/457-2288 or 888/595-2151, www.extendedstaydeluxe.com, $170 d) has all the amenities travelers have come to expect: indoor pool, jacuzzi, exercise room, business center, in-room fridges, microwaves, Wi-Fi, free airport and train shuttle, and a continental breakfast. Standard rooms, family suites, jacuzzi suites, and suites with full kitchens and king beds are all the same price.

Over $200

River's Edge Resort (4200 Boat St., 907/474-0286 or 800/770-3343, www.riversedge.net) features 90 modern cottages crowded together along the Chena River. Each is charmingly decorated, and includes two queen beds. Weekday rates are $205 d ($230 d for riverside units); Friday–Sunday rates are $149 and $169 respectively. A restaurant and pub are on the premises.

The **Westmark Fairbanks Hotel** (813 Noble St., 907/456-7722 or 800/544-0970, www.westmarkhotels.com) has 400 large and attractively appointed rooms. Standard rooms are $200–210 d (ask for one in the renovated North Tower), and junior suites ($220 d) feature microwaves, fridges, two TVs, and ultra-comfortable beds. Amenities include a fitness center, business center, valet service, free airport and railroad station shuttle, Wi-Fi, restaurants, and lounge.

A modern six-story hotel in the center of Fairbanks, **SpringHill Suites by Marriott** (575 1st Ave., 907/451-6552 or 877/729-0197, www.springhillsuites.com, $204 for up to five) is just across the street from the Chena River. Spacious suites contain two queens or one king bed, and guests appreciate the indoor pool, exercise room, jacuzzi, sauna, mini-fridges, microwaves, buffet breakfast, and free airport shuttle.

Pike's Waterfront Lodge (907/456-4500 or 877/774-2400, www.pikeslodge.com) is one of Fairbanks' newer lodgings. This 180-room motel on Airport Way next to Pike's Landing Restaurant has attractively furnished and air-condiitioned rooms and suites that sleep four people for $217 d, along with cozy modern cabins for $250 d. All guests have access to the fitness center, sauna, steam room, and business center.

Bed-and-Breakfasts

For many travelers, B&Bs are the best deal in Fairbanks, with most places charging around $110–150 d, including a full breakfast. The downtown visitor center has racks of cards from local B&Bs, or find links on their website (www.explorefairbanks.com) or that of the **Fairbanks Association of B&Bs** (www.ptialaska.net/~fabb).

A fine bargain choice, **Ah, Rose Marie B&B** (302 Cowles St., 907/456-2040, www.akpub.com/akbbrv/ahrose.html, $70 s or $80 d) is a small historic home a few blocks from downtown. The four guest rooms have shared or private baths, and the big hot breakfast is always a hit.

All Seasons B&B Inn (downtown at 763 7th Ave., 907/451-6649 or 888/451-6649, www.allseasonsinn.com, $135–175 d) features eight elegant rooms, delicious full breakfasts, friendly owners, Wi-Fi, guest computer, private baths, and air conditioning for those hot summer days.

Owned by a fifth-generation Alaskan family, **Cranberry Ridge B&B** (907/457-4424 or 888/326-4424, www.ptialaska.net/~cranbrry, $180) is an attractive home out in a country setting north of town. Guests stay in a spacious private two-bedroom apartment suite that sleeps five comfortably. A tasty breakfast

is brought to you the night before, and the kitchenette is stocked with food. Ultra-friendly owners also operate a flightseeing service with tours to the Arctic Circle or Mt. McKinley.

A B&B Inn on Minnie Street (345 Minnie St., 907/456-1802 or 888/456-1849, www.minniestreetbandb.com) is a large and modern downtown place with 13 rooms (115–165 d), deluxe suites ($155–175 d) with jetted tubs and full kitchens, and a small private house ($155 d; summer only). All include a big breakfast, outdoor hot tub, guest computer, Wi-Fi, and a surprisingly quiet setting.

A Taste of Alaska Lodge (907/488-7855, www.atasteofalaska.com) is a 7,000-square-foot log home five miles out Chena Hot Springs Road. Located on a 280-acre homestead, the hilltop location faces south towards the Alaska Range making for dramatic wintertime aurora displays. Eight rooms are available in the main lodge ($175–185 d). Also available is a two-bedroom log home ($225 d) with its own hot tub, and a one-bedroom house ($195 d); add $25 for additional guests. Amenities for all accommodations include private baths, an indoor jacuzzi, guest computer, Wi-Fi, and full breakfasts.

Fairbanks' most unique lodging is—without a doubt—**◖ Aurora Express** (907/474-0949 or 800/221-0073, www.fairbanksalaskabedandbreakfast.com, late May–early Sept., $135–150 d). Susan and Mike Wilson have assembled a nostalgic collection of seven Alaska Railroad cars (the oldest dates from 1924) and decorated the interiors with playful themes, including a 19th-century bordello with antiques and crystal chandeliers! Families will love the restored Pullman sleeper with two baths; it sleeps five for $225 (but kids must be over age 12). A big breakfast is served in the dining car each morning. Be sure to ask Susan about her time as the only woman on a pipeline construction crew in the 1970s. Aurora Express is definitely recommended, especially if you're a train enthusiast.

Out in the country five miles north of Fairbanks, **Frog Pond B&B** (131 Frog Pond Circle, 907/457-4006 or 888/457-4006, www.frogpondbb.com) has a two-bedroom apartment ($220 d or $245 for four) with a full kitchen and private entrance. The main house includes two rooms ($115 d), and a full breakfast is included for all guests. Free Wi-Fi and guest computer.

Arctic Oasis B&B (290 Woodland Ave., 907/374-6005, www.arcticoasis.com) is a north-of-town home with a deck facing the Alaska Range, and one feature rarely found in Alaskan B&Bs: a large indoor pool. Other amenities include a hot tub, sauna, pool table, Wi-Fi, and full breakfast. Four guest rooms all have private baths, and range from $75 d for the smallest, to $195 for a four-person room with a fireplace, two queen beds, and a private entrance.

A gorgeous log home along Chena Ridge west of town, the appropriately named **Grand View B&B** (907/479-3388, www.grandview-bb.com, $125 d) overlooks the Tanana River and the Alaska Range. Guests can relax in the big hot tub, warm up in the sauna, or just enjoy the vistas from the back deck. Four guest rooms all have private baths. A filling breakfast is included.

Located atop a knoll near the university, **A Cloudberry Lookout B&B,** 907/479-7334, www.mosquitonet.com/~cloudberry, March–Nov.) is a grand home with a central aurora viewing tower and rooftop walkway that's accessed via a 38-foot-high spiral staircase. The four rooms include a $95 d room with a king bed, up to a $125 d two-room suite; all have private baths and antique furnishings. A full breakfast is served each morning, but the house isn't really kid-friendly.

CAMPING
Public Campgrounds
The **Pioneer Park** parking lot is open to motor homes for $10. No hook-ups or showers, but potable water, restrooms, and a disposal station. Register in the cabin just inside the entrance. Many other folks park RVs for free at several of the larger malls around Fairbanks.

Located within the fairgrounds, **Tanana Valley Campground** (College Rd., 907/456-7956, www.tananavalleyfair.org, mid-May–

mid-Sept., $16 RVs, $10 tents) is close to hiking and biking trails, and not far from Creamer's Field. The setting is woodsy and quiet.

Chena River Wayside (907/452-7275, www.chenawayside.com, $22 RVs, $10 tents) is a state campground on University Avenue just north of Airport Way. It has running water, flush toilets, fireplaces, boat launch, and fishing—a bit high density, but not bad for city camping, if you arrive early enough to get a site; the 11 RV hookup sites go quickly. No showers here, so you'll need to find one at a local coin laundry. Another fine public campground ($10) is **Chena Lakes Recreation Area,** near North Pole.

Private Campgrounds and RV Parks
River's Edge RV Park (on Boat St. off Airport Way near University Ave., 907/474-0286 or 800/770-3343, www.riversedge.net, mid-May–mid-Sept., $30 RVs, $19 tents) is a large handy campground on the banks of the Chena River.

Chena Marina RV Park (1145 Shypoke Dr., 907/479-4653, www.chenarvpark.com, $35–39 RVs) sits next to a floatplane pond out Chena Pump Road. Rates include a continental breakfast, free RV wash, Wi-Fi, and cable TV.

Riverview RV Park (1316 Badger Rd., 907/488-6281 or 888/488-6392, www.alaska one.com/riverview, $25–35 RVs, $18–20 tents) is three miles east of town (near North Pole) and right along the Chena River. Sites include Wi-Fi and cable TV.

FOOD
Fairbanks has a fine diversity of food choices, including not just places with down-home meals (and prices), but also those offering gourmet meals (and prices).

Breakfast and Coffee
The Diner (244 Illinois St., 907/451-0613) serves breakfast anytime—gigantic portions, efficient service, and reasonable prices. It opens daily at 6:30 A.M. Also popular for breakfast is **Sam's Sourdough Cafe** (3702 Cameron St., 907/479-0523).

Popular with families, **The Cookie Jar** (1006 Cadillac Ct., 907/479-8319, www.cookiejar fairbanks.com) offers a full breakfast selection, giant cinnamon rolls, and espresso. Lunch and dinner are also available.

Alaska Coffee Roasting Company (4001 Geist Rd., 907/457-5282, www.alaska coffeeroasting.com) serves the best espresso drinks in town, but their fresh baked breads and pastries (from a wood-fired oven) and friendly setting are the real attractions.

Two Street Station (523 2nd Ave., 907/456-6242) is a popular heart-of-town coffee fix, and **College Coffeehouse** (3677 College Rd., 907/374-0468, www.college coffeehousefairbanks.com) is out by the University. Both of these have computers (fee) and Wi-Fi (free).

Lunch and Quick Meals

Looking for lunch in a hurry? You certainly won't go wrong at **Bun on the Run,** a little trailer parked out front of Beaver Sports at 3480 College Road near the university. Sandwiches are made to order; check the board for today's specials ($7.50) and then wait at one of the cable-spool tables in the parking lot. The Bun is open for lunch Monday–Saturday, May–September.

L'Assiette de Pomegranate (414 2nd Ave., 907/451-7505) is a downtown lunch spot with creative sandwiches, salads, and daily soups, as well as outstanding desserts.

Second Story Cafe (on College Rd. at University Ave., 907/474-9574) is upstairs inside Gulliver's Books. The menu covers the latest trends in wraps, espresso, homemade soups, salads, and other light fare. There is free Internet access, and plenty of books to read.

Satisfy your sweet tooth at **Hot Licks** (3453 College Rd., 907/479-7813, www.hotlicks.net). There's often a line out front on a summer afternoon as folks wait for a scoop of the 20-plus flavors of homemade ice cream, including wild cranberry and Alaska blueberry. Also on the menu are banana splits, Hawaiian shaved ice, and blended coffee drinks.

Long a favorite of locals, **Geraldo's Restaurant**

(701 College Rd., 907/452-2299) gets packed on weekends. Although best known for pizzas (including a garlic-packed version), the restaurant also serves everything from calamari and veal to cheese steak sandwiches.

College Town Pizzeria (3549 College Rd., 907/457-2200) serves pizza by the slice or pie, eggplant parmesan calzones, and "heart attack in a tube" strombolis. Not far away is **Pazzo G's Pizza Joint** (3677 College, 907/456-2604), a little spot where the sauces are homemade, the cheese is freshly grated, and it's just $2 to get your pizza delivered anywhere in town.

Tourists love **Fudge Pot** (515 1st Ave., 907/456-3834, www.thefudgepot.com), just up from the downtown visitor center, where you'll find 30 types of fudge, plus soups, sandwiches, and espresso.

International

If you like Thai food, you could eat in a different place every night for a week. Best known, and always great is **Thai House Restaurant** (412 5th Ave., 907/452-6123, lunch and dinner Mon.–Sat., $12–14 entrées) with big portions spiced to your taste and a casual downtown setting. Try the chicken satay appetizer or the chef's choice: pad-ped sam-sahai (sautéed prawns, squid, and fish with chili sauce, lemon grass, ginger, and crispy basil leaves). There are vegetarian specials too.

Located near Chena Pumphouse. **◖ Lemongrass Thai Cuisine** (388 Old Chena Pump Rd., 907/456-2200) is another family-run Thai restaurant with gracious service and wonderful food, especially the halibut red curry. The extensive menu features produce from Fairbanks whenever possible, and it's perfect for kids.

Osaka Restaurant (402 5th Ave., 907/452-5560) is the best local Japanese restaurant. For Chinese meals, head to Pagoda Restaurant in North Pole.

A tiny downtown stand called **Little Saigon** (527 2nd Ave., 907/452-4399) serves authentic Vietnamese lunches. Or try **Ichiban Noodle Restaurant** (400 College Rd., 900/479-1251) for a fast lunch at a good value.

A number of Mexican-style places are found around Fairbanks; try **Hot Tamale** (112 Turner St., 907/457-8350), with a big lunch and dinner buffet.

Gambardella's Pasta Bella has outstanding Italian meals, but an out-of-town spot, **The Vallata** (2190 Goldstream Rd., 907/455-6600) has many local fans as well, with pasta, pizzas, veal, chicken, steaks, and lobster on the menu.

Salmon Bake

Don't miss the 🄲 **Alaska Salmon Bake** (907/452-7274 or 800/354-7274, www.akvisit .com) at Pioneer Park. For $28 adults or $9 kids, you get all-you-can-eat salmon (flown in fresh daily), halibut, and prime rib, plus a big salad bar and desserts. The owner grew up in Juneau where his father was a commercial angler, so knows his fish. This is the best salmon bake in Alaska. It's open daily 5–9 P.M. mid-May–mid-September, and a salmon bake shuttle bus runs 4–10 P.M., stopping at the major hotels and RV parks around town.

Riverfront Dining

A longtime Fairbanks establishment, **Pike's Landing** (out Airport Rd., 907/479-6500, www.pikeslodge.com, entrées $25–40) is known its huge wooden deck that accommodates hundreds of diners, and for the dock where boaters and Jet Skiers pull up for a meal. The seafood and burger menu isn't especially notable (except for the salmon sandwich with curly fries), but Pike's is all about location, location, location. Inside dining and a sports bar are also available if the engine noise gets too deafening. On the expensive side.

For a more old-time atmosphere on the river, head out to the **Pump House Restaurant & Saloon** (1.3 Mile Chena Pump Rd., 907/479-8452, www.pumphouse.com). A National Historical Monument, the Pump House was built in 1933 to pump water up Chena Ridge to provide pressure for the hydraulic "giants" used in gold dredging. The restaurant/bar has a fascinating interior of mining and pumping artifacts, along with antique Brunswick pool tables. Waterside dining (or drinks) on the big

riverside deck is a draw for locals. Quite good food, too, especially the big lunch buffet (summers only; $13). Dinner entrées cost $19–36, and include the usual Alaskan favorites: steak, chicken, burgers, salmon, pepper steak, and king crab. The Sunday brunch ($19) is justifiably popular.

Chena's Fine Dining (at River's Edge Resort, 4200 Boat St., 907/474-3644, www .riversedge.net) is another pleasant riverside option, with Alaskan halibut and salmon, prime rib, steaks, and pasta, available on the covered veranda or sun deck in the summer, or inside year-round.

Downtown Dinners

Just a block from the downtown visitor center, **Gambardella's Pasta Bella** (706 2nd Ave., 907/457-2992, www.gambardellas.com, $14–22 entrées) is justifiably popular for pasta, homemade Italian bread, the "mother of all lasagnas," gourmet pizzas, calzones, and double chocolate cheesecake. The atmosphere is warm and inviting, service is accommodating, and there's a small upstairs deck. Dinner prices are reasonable.

Hidden away on a back street but just a few blocks from downtown **Café Alex** (310 1st Ave., 907/452-2539, www.cafealexwinebar .com, $8–11) has a playful but relaxed wine-bar atmosphere, with a great choice of tapas that are perfect for sharing with your sweetie. You can get a light gourmet meal without spending a ton of money, and wine is available the glass. Larger dinners and lunchtime sandwiches are also served. This is a great place to avoid the crowds.

A modern and trendy downtown eatery inside Springhill Suites, 🄲 **Lavelle's Bistro** (575 1st Ave., 907/450-0555, www.lavellesbistro.com, $17–33) has a 3,000-bottle wall of wine, an open kitchen where you can watch the chefs at work, and upscale dining. The menu encompasses steaks, pork teenderloin, rack of lamb, Alaskan king crab, and great salads (try the salad Teresa), but locals also rave about the desserts, especially the warm banana wontons with roasted pecans and Meyer's rum.

Groceries and Farmers Market

Fairbanks lacks a downtown grocery store, but you'll find **Safeways** at University Center on Airport Way and in the Bentley Mall on College Road, and two big **Fred Meyer** shopping centers at 3755 Airport Way and on the corner of Johansen Expressway and Old Steese Highway.

Out on College Road at Caribou Way, the **Tanana Valley Farmers Market** (907/456-3276, www.tvfmarket.com) is *the* place to buy locally grown produce, flowers, baked goods, arts, and crafts. The market is open Wednesday 11 A.M.–4 P.M. and Saturday 9 A.M.–4 P.M. mid-May–late September. This is a wonderful place to get a taste of Alaska (literally).

INFORMATION AND SERVICES

In addition to the Fairbanks Visitors Bureau and the Alaska Public Lands Information Center, go to the State of Alaska's **Department of Natural Resources Public Information Center** (3700 Airport Way, 907/451-2705, www.alaskastateparks.org, Mon.–Fri. 9 A.M.–5 P.M.) across the street from Fred Meyer on the west side of town. Stop here to get brochures on state parks and trails, reserve a state park cabin, or to learn about mining claims and state land sales.

Topographical maps of Alaska are sold in Room 126 of the Federal Building (101 12th Ave.) and at the Map Office in UAF's International Arctic Research Center (907/474-6960).

Useful **Fairbanks websites** include the Fairbanks Visitors and Convention Bureau (www.explorefairbanks.com), the *Fairbanks News-Miner* (www.newsminer.com), and the aurora forecast at the Geophysical Institute (www.gedds.alaska.edu/auroraforecast). How cold (or hot) is it in Fairbanks? Visit the National Weather Service (www.arh.noaa.gov).

Books and Internet Access

The **Noel Wien Library** (corner of Airport Way and Cowles, 907/452-5177, http://library.fnsb.lib.ak.us) is a comfortable and complete facility (indoor trees, even). One look inside tells you a lot about Fairbanks's long winters and why the library is such a wonderful escape. You can surf the Web for free in the library, or rent computer time at **College Coffeehouse** (3677 College Rd., 907/374-0468, www.college coffeehousefairbanks.com) or **Two Street Station** (523 2nd Ave., 907/456-6242).

Gulliver's Books (on College Rd. at University Ave., 907/474-9574 or 800/390-8999, www.gullivers-books.com) is a great little two-story place with both new and used titles. A large **Barnes and Noble Booksellers** (421 Mehar Ave., 907/452-6400, www.bn.com) is on the north end of town.

Services

B&C Laundromat (College Rd. at University Ave., 907/479-2696) has showers, or shower and then swim at **Mary Siah Recreation Center** (1025 14th Ave., 907/459-1082). The post office is downtown between 3rd and 4th Avenues.

If you need a doctor, walk in to **Fairbanks Urgent Care** (1867 Airport Way, 907/452-2178) or **1st Care Center** (1101 Noble St., 907/458-2682), and for emergencies, drag yourself to **Fairbanks Memorial Hospital** (1650 Cowles, 907/452-8181, www.fairbanks memorial.com).

GETTING THERE

Air

Fairbanks International Airport is six miles southwest of downtown. The second floor houses a gift shop, snack shop, and lounge. On the first floor are an unstaffed information booth with a bunch of brochures, a few stuffed animals, and the Curtiss JN-4D "Jenny" biplane used by Carl Ben Eielson, one of the earliest and most famous bush pilots from the area.

Alaska Airlines (907/452-1661 or 800/426-0333, www.alaskaair.com) has multiple daily flights between Fairbanks and Anchorage, plus once-a-day nonstop service to Seattle. Both options are available year-round.

Seasonal service includes nonstop flights to Fairbanks from Minneapolis-St. Paul on **Northwest Airlines** (800/225-2525, www.nwa.com), from Salt Lake City on **Delta**

Airlines (800/221-1212, www.delta.com), and from Frankfurt (with a stop in Whitehorse, Yukon) aboard **Condor Air** (800/524-6975, www.condor.com). **Japan Airlines** (800/525-3663, www.japanair.com) has winter-only charter flights between Tokyo and Fairbanks for the legions of Japanese aurora fans.

In business since 1950, **Frontier Flying Service** (907/450-7200 or 800/478-6779, www.frontierflying.com) is the largest regional carrier, with daily flights between Fairbanks and Anchorage, plus scheduled service across most of Interior Alaska. **Warbelow's Air Ventures** (907/474-0518 or 800/478-0812, www.warbelows.com) is another long-established air taxi with extensive connections throughout the Interior. **Larry's Flying Service** (907/474-9169, www.larrysflying.com), **Arctic Circle Air** (907/842-3870 or 888/214-2364, www.arctic-circle-air.com), and **Everts Air Alaska** (907/450-2350, www.evertsair.com), and **Wright Air Service** 9907/474-0502, www.wrightair.net) also have scheduled regional service.

Train

The **Alaska Railroad** (907/265-2494 or 800/544-0552, www.akrr.com) chugs out of Fairbanks from a gorgeous new depot at 1745 Johansen Expressway. Mid-May–mid-September there are daily departures at 8:15 A.M., arriving in Denali National Park at noon ($59), and Anchorage at 8:15 P.M. ($189). Tour-bus fares to Denali and Anchorage are cheaper, but the train is a more comfortable, enjoyable, and historical way to see this part of Alaska. If you want to go in luxury, however, buy a ticket ($85 extra to Denali, $110 extra to Anchorage) on the elaborate double-decker GoldStar coaches, where open-air viewing decks are the main attraction.

Buses

Alaska Direct Bus Line (907/277-6652 or 800/770-6652, www.alaskadirectbusline.com) has service to Tok, continuing on to Whitehorse and Anchorage. Buses run three times a week in the summer, twice weekly in winter. **Alaska/Yukon Trails** (907/479-2277 or 888/770-7275, www.alaskashuttle.com) runs a daily Fairbanks–Denali–Talkeetna–Anchorage van in the summer, and several times a week the rest of the year. In addition, summer-only van tours connect Fairbanks with Delta Junction, Tok, Chicken, Dawson City, and Whitehorse.

GETTING AROUND
City Buses

Fairbanks' public bus system, **Metropolitan Area Commuter Service** (907/459-1011, www.co.fairbanks.ak.us/transportation), known as "MACS," operates Monday–Saturday; pick up timetables at the information center. All routes stop at **Transit Park** on Cushman and Fifth Avenue. The fare is $1.50, or $3 for an all-day pass.

Taxis and Shuttles

There are 20 or so local cab companies; find them in the Yellow Pages. Taxis charge $15–20 to get downtown from the airport. The **Alpenglow Shuttle** (907/479-2277 or 888/770-7275, www.alaskashuttle.com) provides service around town for just $5 per person. They'll pick up and drop off anywhere, but make stops along the way so this only works if you aren't in a big hurry.

Car and RV Rentals

Several companies have reasonable prices, late model cars, and will pick you up at the airport: **Aurora Motors** (907/459-7033 or 800/849-7033, www.auroramotors.com), **National** (907/451-7368 or 800/227-7368), and **U-Save Auto Rental** (907/479-5900 or 877/979-7060).

The following companies all have airport counters: **Alamo** (907/451-0457 or 800/327-9633), **Arctic Rent-A-Car** (907/479-8044 or 800/478-8696, www.arcticrentacar.com), **Avis** (907/474-0900 or 800/831-8000), **Budget** (907/474-0855 or 800/474-0855), **Dollar** (907/451-4360 or 800/800-4000), **Hertz** (907/452-4444 or 800/654-3131), and **Payless** (907/474-0177 or 800/729-5377).

Most rental car companies do not allow their

vehicles north of the Arctic Circle, and other road restrictions are often imposed, but **Arctic Outfitters** (907/474-3530 or 800/474-1986, www.arctic-outfitters.com) rents cars with extra gear for travel on the Dalton Highway.

Rent pickup-truck-based campers from **GoNorth RV Camper Rental** (907/479-7272 or 866/236-7272, www.paratours.net) and gas-guzzling RVs from **Adventures in Alaska RV Rentals** 907/458-7368, www.adventuresakrv.com).

Bus Tours

Gray Line of Alaska (907/451-6835 or 800/544-2206, www.graylineofalaska.com) leads regional bus tours, but you can do all of these on your own for less if you have a vehicle. Several other companies offer less corporate versions: try **River's Edge Resort** (907/474-0286 or 800/770-3343, www.riversedge.net) for $26 historical city tours. (See the *Dalton Highway* section for details on bus tours to the Arctic Circle and Prudhoe Bay.)

Vicinity of Fairbanks

NORTH POLE

In 1949, Con Miller was cleaning out the Fairbanks trading post he'd just bought and found a Santa Claus suit. He liked it so much that he took to wearing it during his trips to the Interior to buy furs and sell supplies. The costume made a big impression on the Native children. A few years later, when he moved 12 miles southeast of Fairbanks near Eielsen Air Force Base, he built a new trading post and called it Santa Claus House. Miller and his neighbors chose the name North Pole for their new town, reportedly to attract a toy manufacturer to the area. It never arrived, but the name stuck.

Today, North Pole (pop. 1,600) is a suburb of Fairbanks, but the business he established has become the town's primary attraction. The town is dotted with more Xmas fever: street names like St. Nicholas and Kris Kringle Drives and Santa Claus and Mistletoe Lanes, business names such as Santaland RV Park, Santa's Pull Tabs, and Elf's Den Diner, along with a 50,000-watt Christian radio station, KJNP (King Jesus of North Pole). There are almost two dozen churches in the area, including, of course, St. Nicholas Church. But, as if to counteract all the religion, there's also Fantasy Video just north of town, where the fantasies certainly aren't about sugarplums.

⬤ Santa Claus House

Santa Claus House (907/488-2200 or 800/588-4078, www.santaclaushouse.com) right along the Richardson Highway, is the largest and tackiest gift shop in the state, and

It's Christmas 365 days a year in North Pole.

© DON PITCHER

VICINITY OF FAIRBANKS

To Deadhorse and Prudhoe Bay

Kanuti National Wildlife Refuge

Yukon Flats National Wildlife Refuge

Yukon River

Arctic Circle

Circle

Circle Hot Springs

Yukon-Charley Rivers National Preserve

Central

Steese National

Eagle Summit

Conservation Area

Pinnell Mtn 14,721ft

Twelvemile Summit 2,982ft

Chena Hot Springs

CHENA HOT SPRINGS RESORT

North Fork

Angel Rocks Trail

Granite Tors Trail

South Fork

Delta Junction

To Valdez, Glennallen, and Whitehorse

DAWSON DITCH

Chena Dome Trail

White Mountains National Recreation Area

NOME CREEK RD

Chatanika Gold Camp

Cleary Summit

GOLD DREDGE NO. 8

Chena River

North Pole

SANTA CLAUS HOUSE

Tanana River

Wickersham Dome 13,207ft

STEESE

Fox

Fairbanks

Livengood

Elliott HWY

Tatalina River

WHITE MTN TRAILHEAD

Ester

To Denali and Anchorage

Sawtooth Mtn 14,494ft

Minto

Tolovana River

DALTON HWY

Wolverine Mtn 14,560ft

Elephant Mtn 13,661ft

Tanana River

Nenana River

Manley Hot Springs

Hot Springs Slough

Yukon River

20 mi

20 km

© AVALON TRAVEL PUBLISHING, INC.

probably the biggest one this side of Las Vegas. Out front stands a 40-foot Santa figure ("the world's tallest"), and inside you'll find Santa in the flesh Wednesday–Sunday 10 A.M.–7 P.M., any day of the year. Outside, two of Santa's reindeer are housed in a pen.

Santa Claus House is open daily 8 A.M.–7 P.M. in the summer, with variable hours the rest of the year. Buy a "holiday message from Santa," mailed in December from North Pole to anyone in the world for $7.50. For an extra $10 they'll send you a deed to one square inch of the Santa Claus subdivision in town. There's even a free summertime shuttle bus to Santa Claus House from hotels and RV parks in Fairbanks.

One of the attractions in town is getting your letters postmarked from "North Pole, Alaska." Mail them at the Santa Claus House or the post office on 5th Avenue. Throughout December, this post office is deluged with letters and cards from people wanting a North Pole postmark—the stacks can be piled 10 feet high. And that's *not* including the estimated 10,000 letters to Santa Claus himself, which are all answered by students at North Pole Middle School.

Not everything is about Christmas here. North Pole is also home to two oil refineries (they tap into the Trans-Alaska Pipeline), along with **Eielson Air Force Base** (12 miles south of town, 907/377-2116, www.eielson.af.mil).

On the Richardson Highway at Mission Road, the North Pole **Visitor Log Cabin** (907/488-2281, www.northpolechamber.com) is open daily 10 A.M.–6 P.M. mid-May–mid-September.

Accommodations and Food

Jolly Acres Motel (907/488-9339, www.jollyacresmotel.com, $80 d) has older but clean suites ($80 d) with full kitchens, plus a couple of smaller rooms ($70 d).

Located on a small private lake, **Beaver Lake Resort Motel** (2555 Mission Rd., 907/488-9600, www.beaverlakeresort.net) has rooms for $120–135 d, and two-bedroom apartments that sleep six for $156. All units include full kitchens and access to the sauna, and most have Wi-Fi.

North Pole Cabins (907/490-6400, www.northpolecabins.com, $115–175 d) rents modern cabins with baths. A continental breakfast is provided.

Santaland RV Park (907/488-9123 or 888/488-9123, www.santalandrv.com, April–Oct., $28–30 RVs, $18 tents) is right next to Santa Claus House. Amenities include cable TV and Wi-Fi.

North Pole is home to the best Chinese dining spots in the Fairbanks area, **Pagoda Restaurant** (North Pole Plaza, 907/488-3338). The setting is fun and the Mandarin, Szechuan, and Cantonese food is ultra-fresh.

Chena Lakes Recreation Area

In August, 1967, it rained seven inches in seven days, and the Chena River overflowed, inundating low-lying Fairbanks under five feet of floodwaters. Half the town's residents were evacuated, and damage neared $200 million. The task of preventing a similar disaster in the future fell to the Army Corps of Engineers, which mucked around for 15 years, building a dam at Moose Creek, a levee and spillway into the Tanana River, and this 2,000-acre park of man-made lakes and recreational facilities. The recreation area contains the nearest beach to Fairbanks, and on hot weekends the exodus is not unlike that of Bostonians fleeing to Cape Cod—you might be able to wedge a dishtowel onto some sand and swim in place.

Most of the season, though, Chena Lakes (907/488-1655, www.co.fairbanks.ak.us) is a delightful place to picnic, stroll (self-guided nature trail), bike (7 miles trail), play volleyball and horseshoes, pick berries, camp, fish, and rent canoes, paddleboats, and sailboats. In the winter, the trails are groomed for cross-country skiing. Camp at either the Lakes campground or the river park. From Fairbanks, go five miles south of North Pole on the Richardson Highway (Mile 347), take a left on Laurance Road, and follow the signs. Fees are $4 for day use, $10 for camping. Canoes, kayaks, and pedal boats are available for rent.

FOX

In 1901, Felice Pedroni (a.k.a. Felix Pedro) found color on what is now Pedro Creek and was credited with the discovery of the Cleary and Goldstream veins, which touched off the rush from the Klondike and Nome to the Fairbanks area. However, the gold here was anything but easy for the taking: This gold-laden bedrock was normally 80–100 feet under gravel, muck, and permafrost. Within 20 years of the find, the rich creeks were worked out, the shallow, low-grade ground was exhausted, and most miners couldn't afford the expense of working the deep claims. In 1923, however, the railroad was finished from Seward to Fairbanks and brought with it the feasibility of large-scale gold production. Hydraulic giants, monster dredges, miles of tailings, and businessmen in three-piece suits replaced the lone prospector with his hammer and bucket. This second—corporate—gold rush to Fairbanks eventually produced almost $200 million worth of the precious heavy metal.

A ride 10 miles up the Steese Highway from Fairbanks to and around Fox clearly reveals the impact of this second boom. Huge cleared fields and stripped hillsides trace the progress of the giants and dredges, and the tailings lie in the snaking mounds they were spit into 50 years ago. Marble, gravel, and sand are for sale along the roadside. Heavy machinery dots the land with the bovine patience of metal and rubber.

Housed within a large warehouse-type metal building, **Silver Gulch Brewery** (907/452-2339, www.silvergulch.com) is a locals' favorite, with tastings of their Copper Creek Amber Ale, Fairbanks Lager, Pick Axe Porter, and Coldfoot Pilsner every Friday 5–7 P.M. A rowdy and popular roadhouse bar, **Howling Dog Saloon** (907/456-4695, www.howlingdogsaloon.com) is right across the road, with live music Wednesday–Saturday nights.

Up the Old Steese a hair (or is it hare?) is the **Turtle Club** (907/457-3883, www.alaskan turtle.com, $20–30), with prime rib (the house specialty), halibut, prawns, lobster, and king crab. It can get somewhat smoky at times.

Check out the turtle collection scattered around the restaurant. Reservations recommended.

Continue another five miles past Fox on the Steese Highway for the monument to **Felice Pedroni,** who started it all rolling in 1902. Across the road is Pedro Creek; try your hand at panning for a little dust, and note the unnatural look of a creek played for gold for most of a century.

Pipe Dreams

Eight miles out the Steese Highway on the way to Fox is a **Trans-Alaska Pipeline Viewpoint,** a favorite pose-for-a-photo stop. Interpretive displays describe the site, and Alyeska Pipeline Services runs a little visitor center here (907/456-9391, daily mid-May–mid-Sept.). The viewing area itself is open year-round.

(Gold Dredge No. 8

Local placer gold derives from ancient quartz veins once exposed in creek beds, now buried up to 100 feet below the surface. To get to it, first you hose off the surface layer down to two feet with hydraulic cannons or "giants," then down another few feet as the exposed frozen gravel thaws on its own. The deeper frozen muck and rock is thawed over a year or so by water pumped through pipes from the surface to bedrock, supplied by monumental aqueducts such as the Davidson Ditch. Once the earth down to bedrock is diggable, a gold dredge is brought in.

The dredge dwarfs even the largest machines in this land of giant machines. It's a true Alaska-size contraption that looks like a cartoon cross between a houseboat and a crane. An endless circular conveyor of up to 100 steel buckets scoops up the gravel, conveys it to the top end of a revolving screen, and dumps it. The screen separates the larger rocks, shunting them off to the tailing piles, from the golden gravel, which is sifted from the screen to riffles, where quicksilver (mercury) gleans the gold, forming an amalgam. The riffles are cleaned every couple of weeks, then the gold is further processed and assayed. In the old days during the height of production, the gold would next be shipped to the mint, where it earned $35 per troy ounce.

THE INTERIOR

© DON PITCHER

Gold Dredge No. 8

Gold Dredge No. 8 (907/457-6058, www.gold dredgeno8.com, daily mid-May–mid-Sept.), the only National Historic Mechanical Engineering Landmark in Alaska, is just a little larger than its official designation. One of Alaska's first steel-hulled bucketline dredges, it was installed in 1928—five stories tall, 250 feet long, weighing over 1,000 tons. The dredge stopped operating in 1959, but it was bought by Holland America in 1996 and completely restored with fascinating exhibits. Tours—including a 20-minute video on gold mining—are offered seven times a day, with the first at 9:30 A.M. and the last at 3:30 P.M. The $25 admission ($19 for kids) also includes a hearty lunch and the chance to pan for gold—and keep what you find. To get there, drive eight miles up the Steese Highway toward Fox, take a left on Goldstream Road and another left on the Old Steese Highway.

El Dorado Gold Mine
Located a mile north of Fox on the Elliott Highway, this active placer mine (907/479-6673 or 866/479-6673, www.eldoradogoldmine.com) is another tourist draw. Here, you climb on-board a small-scale railroad to view the mine, walk into a tunnel in the permafrost, and get a chance to try your hand at panning for a flake or two. Two-hour tours start take place mid-May–mid-September, and cost $30 adults, $20 kids. A $2 shuttle is provided from Fairbanks; reservations recommended. As an aside, the Fort Knox Gold Mine—Alaska's largest active mine—is 25 miles northeast of Fairbanks. It is not open to the public.

ESTER
Like Fox, Ester had a two-boom gold rush: panning and placer mining in the early 1900s, then dredging by the Fairbanks Exploration Co. from the mid-1920s to the late 1950s. Today, Ester, which is 10 miles south of Fairbanks on the Parks Highway, has a few buildings that remain from the once-booming mining days, now housing a hotel, gift shop, gallery, and the famous Malemute Saloon. By car, head down the George Parks Highway toward Denali 10 miles, then follow the signs for Ester and Ester Gold Camp.

Open since 1958, the former Hotel Cripple Creek, now called **Ester Gold Camp** (907/479-2500 or 800/676-6925, www.akvisit.com, late May–early Sept., $60 s or $70 d), has plain but functional rooms (no TVs or phones) with shared bath, plus a campground with tent ($10) and RV sites ($15; no hookups). The restaurant at Ester Gold Camp spreads out an all-you-can-eat **buffet dinner** with broasted chicken, reindeer stew, and cod daily 5–9 P.M., $18. You can also partake of all-you-can-eat Dungeness crab for an extra $10.

Top off the evening with the Robert Service musical extravaganza in the **Malemute Saloon** at 9 P.M. nightly; $18 adults, $9 kids. All the tour companies offer packages with round-trip transportation and the saloon show.

Just up the road in the Firehouse Theater is the **Northern Lights PhotoSymphony** (www.photosymphony.com), a 45-minute musically accompanied slide show with panoramic northern lights photos on a curved screen. The cost is $8 adults, $4 kids, and shows are daily at 6:45 and 7:45 P.M.

Heading out from Fairbanks

The country around Fairbanks offers outstanding opportunities to explore and experience the land and waterways, and then to luxuriate in hot springs that have soothed and refreshed travelers for well over a century. With the Interior's predictable good weather, the long days and low lighting, and the humbling power of this vast humanless wilderness, you'll return from any of these trips knowing a lot more about Alaska, and yourself.

Chena Hot Springs Road boasts three exciting hiking trails, two campgrounds, a cozy public cabin, a choice of canoe routes and fishing spots, and a large pool resort, all within an hour's drive of town on a good paved road. The **Steese Highway** has five campgrounds, abundant canoeing and fishing, a high-country backpack that rivals much of Denali National Park, and the fascinating evidence of gold fever—past and present. The **Elliott Highway** is the longest, roughest, and most primitive ride of the three. Along it is one long trail close to Fairbanks, no campgrounds to speak of, and no facilities of any kind, all of which make the small pool and hot tubs at the road's end in friendly Manley all the more rewarding.

And for a real road adventure, you can head up the **Dalton Highway,** which begins at Mile 73 on the Elliott Highway and continues 414 miles all the way to Deadhorse, a few miles south of Prudhoe Bay.

CHENA HOT SPRINGS ROAD

Depending on whom you believe, either Felix Pedro (1903) or the U.S. Geological Survey (1907) discovered the hot springs off the north fork of the Chena River. Shortly after, the land was homesteaded by George Wilson, who built a lodge and cabins and enclosed the springs in a pool. The 55-mile road from Fairbanks was completed in 1967, only to be wiped out a few weeks later by the great flood. It was finally rebuilt and completely paved by 1983. From Mile 26 to Mile 51 is Chena River Wayside, a well-developed and beautiful playground in Fairbanks's backyard, where numerous trails, river access, picnic areas, and two campgrounds are within an easy hour's drive from town. You could easily fill up three or four days camping, hiking, backpacking, and canoeing (all free), and then satisfy the creature-comfort yearnings you accumulated in the backcountry with a soak in the pool and a drink at the resort at the end of the road. (Note: Don't mix up three confusingly named recreation areas around Fairbanks—the Chena River Wayside along Chena Hot Springs Road, the Chena Lakes Recreation Area near North Pole, and the Chena River State Recreation Site in Fairbanks!)

By car, take the Steese Highway just north of town to the exit to Chena Hot Springs Road. The road starts out somewhat roller-coasterish from frost heaves, but the scenery is pleasing—rolling green hills dotted by small verdant farms.

Nestled along a small lake at Mile 16, **(Two Rivers Lodge** (907/488-6815, www.two riverslodge.com) serves gourmet seafood, pasta, and chicken, but their specialty is all-you-can-eat Dungeness crab prepared in a spicy brine. Expect to pay around $30 per person. The decor is rustically Alaskan. Just up the road a mile, **Earthtone Huskies B&B** (907/488-8074, www.earthtonehuskies.com, $40 s or $50 d) has comfortably rustic log cabins (no running water), including a continental breakfast. Owner Judy Cooper leads dogsled rides in the winter.

Not far away is **Paw Print Bed & Sled** (907/488-5788, www.lara-kesiberians.com, $125 d with breakfast), where three rooms in the post-and-beam lodge share a bath. Iditarod mushers Devan and Judy Currier breed Siberian huskies, and also offer kennel tours and sled dog demonstrations by appointment. A continental breakfast is included.

Chena River Wayside

Covering 254,000 acres, Chena River Wayside boasts luxurious campgrounds, excellent outdoor recreational opportunities, lush greenery, towering trees (for Interior Alaska), rolling hills, the curvy Chena River, and best of all, no crowds. When town becomes oppressive, head a half-hour east to some of the best that Interior has to offer. For the complete story, contact the Alaska Department of Natural Resources in Fairbanks (907/451-2700, www.alaskastateparks.org).

Numerous well-marked pullouts give easy river access and your choice of the length of a canoe trip. A good place to put in is at the Mile 44 bridge—a little faster and more fun than downriver. Watch for sweepers, deadheads, shallows, and especially the many impassable sloughs—stagnant, stinking, and mosquito-ridden. Get details from local canoe rental companies or state park folks before heading out.

Rosehip Campground (Mile 27, $10) right at the entrance to the recreation area, is as big and lush a campground as you could ever want,

only a half-hour from town. The river is never more than a two-minute walk away. There are 25 sites, pit toilets, water pumps, and numerous signboards with information about trails, wildlife, and canoe routes.

The road parallels the river all the way to the hot springs and crosses it four times, at Miles 37, 40, 44, and 49. After heavy rains, the road often floods, especially around Mile 37.

The **Chena River Cabin** ($50) is an easily accessed and attractive log cabin right on the river at Mile 32, with a porch and space for nine people. Make reservations in the Department of Natural Resources Information Center (3700 Airport Way in Fairbanks, 907/451-2705, www.alaskastateparks.org). **Granite Tors** loop trail starts across the road from the campground, and just before the bridge. This well-maintained path is a 15-mile, six-hour round trip. The first mile or so is on boardwalk over muskeg; the first tors (strange granite sculptures thrust near the surface, then exposed when the surrounding earth eroded away) are around six miles from the trailhead on both the north and south forks of the trail.

Angel Rocks trail begins at Mile 49 just beyond a pullout and right before the fourth bridge over the Chena River. It's only three miles or so, though the first couple are uphill. The rock outcroppings in the high country are worth the huff. Allow three to four hours.

For the **Chena Dome Trail,** take the northern trailhead, which starts at Mile 51, a half-mile past Angel Creek on the left side of the road; it's a three-day, 29-mile loop trail mostly along ridgetops marked by cairns—great views. A quarter-mile up the trail is the sign for Chena Dome (9 miles); after a short boardwalk you start to climb and leave the mosquitoes and heat behind. One mile up the trail is a good viewpoint.

(Chena Hot Springs Resort

At Mile 57, the road ends at a sprawling resort (907/451-8104 or 800/478-4681, www.chenahotsprings.com) that seems to always be adding something new. The owner is working to create a completely off-the-grid settlement where everything runs on geothermal energy, from the refrigeration system that cools an ice museum all summer to the greenhouses filled with year-round tomatoes.

Chena's featured attraction is, of course, the hot springs, discovered by Anglos in 1905. The water comes out of the spring at nearly 160°F, and is a little under 110°F in the pools. There's an indoor pool and hot tub, plus a second outdoor hot tub, redwood deck, and large sandy-bottom pond that is best experienced when the stars are obscured by the aurora borealis. It's all first-rate. Resort guests (except campers and RVers) get free access to the springs, but if you aren't staying here a day pass costs $10 adults, $7 ages 5–17, or free for younger children. Towels are $5 extra. The pools are open daily 7 A.M.–11 P.M.

A unique feature at Chena is the **Aurora Ice Museum,** the largest year-round ice environment in the world. Step inside the 30-foot-high arched structure to view intricately carved pieces crafted by famed ice artist Steve Brice, including chandeliers, a giant chess set, life-size jousting knights on horses, and a bar made entirely from ice. Tours of the ice museum are $15 per person, and for another $15 you can enjoy a Stoli apple martini in a goblet carved from ice; you keep the "glass." For the complete experience, spend a night snuggled beneath reindeer hides atop ice beds. The cost is an icy $500 d, but this also includes a room in the main lodge when you get too chilly.

All sorts of activities are available at the 440-acre resort (for an extra fee), including rafting, canoe rentals, fishing, mountain bike rentals, and horseback rides in the summer, along with dogsled rides, a dog mushing school, snowmobiling, horse-drawn sleigh rides, cross-country skiing (8 miles of groomed trails), and ice skating in the winter. And if that isn't enough, the resort has free activities such as volleyball, badminton, hiking, horseshoes, and basketball. In the summer months Chena Hot Springs attracts a mixed American and European crowd, but in winter it's even busier with Japanese travelers who come to experience the spectacular northern lights shows. You'll see aurora displays 90 percent of the winter nights here, and you can even watch in heated comfort at the glass-enclosed aurorium.

Along with the hot springs and ice museum, the resort offers nothing-special hotel rooms and suites ($160–220 d), very rustic cabins ($65 d with outhouses), bring-your-sleeping-bag yurts ($65 d), plus tent and RV sites ($23 with showers). The Victorian-style dining room specializes in steaks, prime rib, chicken, pasta, and seafood.

STEESE HIGHWAY

Gold is the color of this country: The precious metal wrested with brute force from the reluctant earth, the golden-green panoramas of the alpine tundra, and the golden light sparkling through the plumes of dust-fog along the road.

Other than the drive itself and the unlimited fishing and canoeing on the Chatanika River and Birch Creek, the excitement on the Steese can be found at the **Davidson Ditch** and on the challenging **Pinnell Mountain Trail.** The Davidson Ditch was one of the first miracle-of-engineering pipelines in this country and, unlike the oil pipeline, you can play on it! The Pinnell Trail is a three-day stroll along the windswept ridges of the White Mountains, with distant jagged horizons for the long-eyed, and stunning alpine wildflowers for the short.

The Road

Named for Army general James G. Steese, president of the Alaska Road Commission 1920–1927 who oversaw its entire construction, the Steese Highway parallels the original Fairbanks-Circle Trail. Thousands of fortune seekers floated up and down the Yukon to Circle, hit the trail after news of Felix Pedro's strike spread, and helped open up the Interior in the early 20th century. The road was completed in 1928, and is paved for the first 44 miles.

Starting from Fairbanks, the highway immediately climbs into the gold-bearing hills, with a great viewpoint overlooking the Tanana Valley on the left at Hagelbarger Road. On a clear day, turn around to see if the Alaska

Range is "out"—a stunning panorama from Mt. McKinley to the eastern peaks of Deborah, Hess, and Hayes. Just up the road is a pullout to view the **Trans-Alaska Pipeline**—which runs aboveground here—and an informative sign. In a few miles you come to the town of Fox, where you'll note the extensive placer mine tailings from **Gold Dredge No. 8** which operated from 1927 to 1959.

At the junction with the Elliott Highway (Route 2), take a right for the Steese (Route 6). At Mile 16 is a turnout with a plaque mounted on a stone monument to Felix Pedro; walk across the road to Pedro Creek, whose golden sands infected the stampeders with Fairbanks fever.

Cleary Summit

From Pedro Creek the frost-heaved pavement climbs quickly to 2,233-foot Cleary Summit, home to **Mt. Aurora Skiland** (907/389-2314, www.skiland.org). Nearby is **Mt. Aurora Fairbanks Creek Lodge** (907/389-2000, www.mt-aurora.com), a 12-room lodge (shared baths) that was once a bunkhouse for miners. Lodging is $70 per person with breakfast or $135 per person with three meals a day. Most visitation takes place in the winter when this is a prime spot to view and photograph the northern lights.

Fairbanks Exploration Company

Beyond the summit, the road twists and turns down to **Chatanika;** at Mile 28, take a hard right and climb to the site of the Fairbanks Exploration Company Gold Camp. After the completion of the Alaska Railroad in 1923, the U.S. Smelting, Refining, and Mining Co. began acquiring and consolidating many of the placer properties around Fairbanks. By 1938, the subsidiary F. E. Co. had three dredges operating between Chatanika and Ester, had installed the Davidson Ditch (see below), and fueled the entire operation with its own power plant in Fairbanks. In its 30 years of production, F. E. Co. took out nearly $100 million in gold—and that was at no more than $35 per troy ounce. The grounds are covered with vintage equipment and 15 restored buildings

that are still maintained by machinery used during the 1940s. Gold Dredge No. 3 is visible near Mile 29 amid tailings on the north side of the road.

The **Chatanika Old F. E. Gold Camp** resort (907/389-2414, www.fegoldcamp.com) is open year-round, and is chock-full of early Alaska memorabilia and mining artifacts. Rooms in the lodge are $55 s or d with shared baths, or $75 d for two cabins that share a bath containing a jacuzzi tub. Budget travelers will appreciate hostel accommodations in the historic bunkhouse for $25 per person. Tent spaces cost $10. The restaurant ($15–27 entrées) is particularly notable, with gourmet meals including a locally famous halibut Napoleon, plus a great Sunday champagne brunch ($17).

A mile up the road is the **Chatanika Lodge** (907/389-2164, $55 s or $65 d), with a bar, hearty meals, and basic bath-down-the-hall rooms. They host **Chatanika Days Outhouse Races** on the second weekend of March. Five-person outhouse teams race a one-mile course, with four pushing and one riding in the specially built "racing outhouses."

1st Alaska Outdoor School (907/590-5900, www.1stalaskaoutdoorschool.com) is located along the Chatanika River north of Fairbanks. Popular with travelers on a budget, the school has canoeing, kayaking, camping ($15), and hostel accommodations ($25), along with wintertime ski touring, dog mushing, and aurora viewing. The owners are from Germany and Japan, and so are many of the visitors. Access is by a seven-mile hike from Murphy Dome, so this isn't for everyone. Meals are available.

Poker Flat

At **Poker Flat Research Range** (907/474-7558 for times, www.pfrr.alaska.edu), two miles up the Steese from Chatanika, the Geophysical Institute of UAF studies the aurora and upper atmosphere. When it was constructed in the late 1960s, Poker Flat took its name from a Bret Harte short story, "The Outcasts of Poker Flat," about a gambler and a prostitute who were banished from a mythical California gold-rush town in the winter and eventually froze to death. The construction crew building the rocket range for the Geophysical Institute considered themselves similarly outcast. This is the only rocket range owned by a university in the world, and is used for the launching of suborbital rockets. Poker Flats is open some Thursdays in the summer for tours.

Upper Chatanika River Recreation Site

Located at Mile 39, this excellent state campground ($10) has pit toilets, a water pump, and plentiful river access for fishing (grayling) and boating. Head around to the back of the grounds and try for a campsite right on the river. Bring an inner tube and ride from the bridge down to your tent.

Davidson Ditch

The pavement ends at Mile 44; at Mile 57, the U.S. Creek Road leads seven miles to two BLM campgrounds, a recreational gold panning area along Nome Creek, and a put-in point for floating Beaver Creek, all within the White Mountains Recreation Area.

Also at Mile 57 is a highway pullout for a long stretch of pipe, a remnant of the Davidson Ditch, the amazing engineering feat (1925) that slaked the F. E. Co. dredges' enormous thirst for water; the dredges floated on man-made ponds so they could be moved. Starting at a dam on the upper Chatanika River, the 12-foot-wide, 4-foot-deep, 83-mile-long ditch, along with nearly seven miles of 48-inch pipe and a combined mile of tunnels, crossed 90 miles of hilly wilderness, directing 56,000 gallons of water per minute to the gold fields. Notice the expansion or "slip" joint in the middle of the level section of the pipe here, and the wooden saddle below it. The pipe was drained in the winter but the cold still took its toll: Note the bulge in the pipe where it cuts uphill, and the repair job on the joint.

This is one of several views of the ditch in the next 10 miles, standing in mute testimony to the struggle of rugged miners against rugged terrain and harsh elements in the quest for gold. You can't help but be amazed by this project, especially when you consider that the road was barely built, the machinery was primitive, and the land unyielding. F. E. Co.'s contract did not require the removal of the pipe when gold production ceased, so here it still sits—either a blight on the landscape or evidence of the colorful history of this land, depending on your perspective. Whichever it is, watch your footing if you monkey around on the pipe.

Cripple Creek Campground and Beyond

This BLM facility (Mile 60, 907/474-2200, www.ak.blm.gov, $6) consists of an inner loop for cars and RVs and a walk-in section. Either take a site with the RV crowd or park in the walk-in lot by the toilets, head to the back of the campground, and pitch your tent right by the river. The mosquitoes are fierce in mosquito season. A public-use cabin is also nearby.

The road out here gets smoother, wider, and less slippery. From the back of a large pullout at Mile 62 is another view of the pipe disappearing into a tunnel. At Mile 81, natural spring water gushes cold and delicious from an open spigot, about five gallons a minute. While you've got the Davidson Ditch on your mind, multiply the pressure of the water from the spigot by a factor of 10,000 for an idea of the force with which the ditch moved its H20.

Steese National Conservation Area

The BLM's Steese National Conservation Area encompasses 1.2 million acres of land just north of the Steese Highway. This area protects important caribou calving grounds and Dall sheep habitat, and includes the 23-mile **Pinnell Mountain National Recreation Trail.** This trail provides access to alpine tundra, with excellent views of nearby mountain ranges.

The first trailhead for Pinnell Mountain leaves the Steese near Mile 85 at **Twelvemile Summit** (el. 2,982 ft.); the second rejoins the highway near Eagle Summit (Mile 107). A short access road (right) at the first trailhead leads past a signposted section of the Fairbanks-Circle Trail to a small mountain pond—nice spot for a picnic. The Pinnell Mountain Trail follows a boardwalk for the first quarter-mile, then climbs steadily for a long time. Most hikers prefer to start at the second trailhead, 700 feet higher, which has a great signboard full of fascinating information. This beautiful 27-mile, three-day trail through alpine tundra along White Mountain ridgelines is famous for its views of the Alaska and Brooks Ranges and the midnight sun on solstice, plus the incomparable wildflowers (especially the state flower, forget-me-not, with its striking blue dots on the tundra), which also peak in mid-June. Small emergency shelters are at Miles 10 and 18 along the trail. This rolling, treeless high country, with long-distance views in all directions, makes you want to stop, get out, and book all the way to the Edge. But be prepared for wind! Get information and a trail map at the Public Lands Information Center in Fairbanks or the BLM website (www.ak.blm.gov).

Eagle Summit and Beyond

At Mile 94 a road to the right leads to undeveloped camping and the launching point for the popular **Birchcreek Canoe Trail.** Eagle Summit, 13 miles farther out the Steese, is the third of three summits that the highway tops (others are at Cleary and Twelvemile). At 3,624 feet, Eagle Summit is the highest point on the road, and a popular destination for locals and travelers around solstice time to watch the sun skirt the horizon, never setting. If the sun is *shining,* that is. It's been known to snow up here on solstice, or you could be socked in by clouds or fog. In fact, you might wish for a nice blizzard to hold down the skeeters, so thick and ferocious that they've been rumored to pick up men—large men—and carry them off. A mile-long trail leads to the summit, which is carpeted with wildflowers in mid-summer.

Coming down from the summit, there are gorgeous views of the current gold-mining activities on the valley floor, along Mammoth and Mastodon Creeks, so named for the frozen remains of large Alaskan mammals uncovered by strip mining. The tusks on display at the UAF Museum came from here. Make sure to stop at 101 Gas to check out the ancient gas pump, which pumped its last gas(p) in the past. Take a left at Mile 119 and go straight at the fork for Bedrock Creek, a good spot to camp if you can handle the skeeters.

Central

Nine miles farther is Central, whose year-round population of 60 souls triples in the summer because of the influx of miners. **The Circle District Museum** (907/520-1893, daily noo–5 P.M. in the summer, $1) in the log cabin in town has mining and mushing artifacts from the early days and a good wildflower photo display. Walk around back to see the wagon-wheel camper. Eight miles out Hot Springs Road is the historic and Circle Hot Springs Resort, with its buildings from 1905. Unfortunately, it has been closed since 2002.

Circle

Erroneously named by miners who thought the town site was close to the Arctic Circle—it's actually 50 miles north—Circle is a long 34 miles beyond Central. The road is in good condition, just quite winding, particularly the last 11 miles. Gold was discovered on nearby Birch Creek in 1893, and Circle was a boomtown with two dozen saloons, a library, a hospital, and even an opera house, long before anyone had heard of the Klondike. When the miners did hear of the Klondike a few weeks after the strike, Circle immediately lost half its population. The town gradually declined as a supply center for the big Circle Mining District, largest in Alaska, after the Steese Highway hooked up to Fairbanks.

Today, with a population of 75 or so, Circle is typical of end-of-the-road Alaska—a couple of streets, lots of cars (mostly junked). The main attraction is the mighty Yukon. Pitch your tent at the denuded campground (free) on the banks and watch the river flow. **H. C. Company Store** (907/773-1222) sells gas, repairs tires, and has groceries, gold pans, and gifts. Get directions here to the Pioneer Cemetery.

Warbelow's Air Ventures (907/474-0518

or 800/478-0812, www.warbelows.com) flies to Central and Circle. **Circle Air** (907/520-5223 or 866/520-5223, www.circleair.com) has air charters out of Central, and rents rafting equipment.

THE ELLIOTT HIGHWAY
The Elliott Highway, named after Major Malcolm Elliott, president of the Alaska Railroad Commission 1927–1932 (following George Steese), begins at the junction with the Steese Highway in Fox, 11 miles north of Fairbanks. The road is paved to Mile 28 (but watch for frost heaves), then turns into a very wide, occasionally smooth, two-lane gravel road until the junction with the Dalton, when it narrows to a one-and-a-half-lane, rough, hard-dirt ribbon through total wilderness.

Other than the BLM White Mountain Trail at Mile 28, and gorgeous views in several spots on the road (especially Miles 95–96), there's little on the way to Manley Hot Springs, a small town at the end of the highway, 152 long miles from Fox. In fact, there's only one facility between the Hilltop Truck Stop (just outside of Fox, 907/389-7600) and Manley: It's the Arctic Circle Trading Post (907/474-3507) at Mile 49. Most of the road is in the 40–50 mph range, with a few 20–30 mph stretches, totaling four to five hours one-way from Fairbanks.

Between Fox and the Dalton Highway junction, huge supply trucks to and from Prudhoe Bay barrel along, raising blinding clouds of dust; by the time you get back to Fairbanks from Manley, a fine layer of dust will have settled over everything you've got, including your entire respiratory tract. It's essential to have *plenty* of water along for this ride. Also take food, as there's no Denny's at the next exit, since there aren't any exits. And don't forget your bathing suit.

The road climbs quickly out of Fox, with good views of the Interior's rolling hills. One mile north of the abandoned railroad and mining town of **Olnes,** just before the Mile 11 bridge over the Chatanika River, a large gravel road on the left goes a mile in to Chatanika

Pond, part of the **Lower Chatanika River State Recreation Site:** no facilities, but fair fishing and primitive camping. On the other side of the Mile 11 bridge is the rest of the recreation site: free camping, picnicking, pit toilets, and fishing for grayling in the summer and for whitefish in the fall.

White Mountains National Recreation Area
The BLM's White Mountains National Recreation Area covers a million acres of forests, rivers, and mountains approximately 30 miles north of Fairbanks. It is the largest national recreation area in the U.S., and a favorite weekend escape for locals who enjoy the 200 miles of backcountry trails.

At Mile 28 of the Elliott Highway are trailheads for myriad paths through the White Mountains. Read the information board carefully. Most trails are for winter use and are not maintained during the summer for hiking. The **Summit Trail** starts from the trailhead on the left and is designated for summer use. This 21-mile trail (one-way), mostly along alpine ridge tops through the foothills of the White Mountains, ends at Beaver Creek. This trail starts out high up to begin with, and the first mile or so of the Wickersham Creek Trail takes you out of the taiga and onto a ridge top, with a beautiful 300-degree view of the Tanana Valley, Alaska Range, and gigantic sky. Even if you're not hiking all the way, it's worth it to day hike this mile for the view.

During the winter, 12 public-use cabins—each a day's ski apart—are available to rent in the White Mountains. Each cabin has a cookstove and lantern, woodstove, table and benches, bunk beds, and outhouse. In the summer only two of these cabins are readily accessible; the others are difficult to reach because of wet and muddy trail conditions. Cabins rent for $25. Contact the BLM (907/474-2251 or 800/437-7021, www.blm.gov/ak) for details. Also check out **Trailhead Cabins** (907/374-0717, www.trailheadcabins.com, $65), road-accessible three-person cabins on the south side of the mountains.

Bye Bye Pavement

The pavement ends 100 yards north of the White Mountains trailhead. Enjoy this wide gravel stretch while you've got it! Nice views of the oil pipeline here—shining in the sunlight, twisting through the tundra, suddenly disappearing underground and surfacing again. At Mile 49 is **Arctic Circle Trading Post** (907/474-4565)—a.k.a. Wildwood General Store—where you can get snacks, drinks, fresh sandwiches, and Arctic Circle gifts. No gas or lodging, and it's only open mid-May–mid-September.

At Mile 71 is the two-mile access road to **Livengood,** a tiny mining center that flourished briefly as a pipeline construction camp. It now has a population of 30. Two miles farther is Mile 0 of the Dalton Highway. Take a left to stay on the Elliott Highway.

To Manley

A bit past the junction with the Dalton, and right after the bridge over the Tolovana River, is a little pullout (left), a nice spot for a picnic, camping, fishing, or even swimming (no facilities). Here the road narrows considerably, and you follow the two tire-packed stripes down the middle of it, hoping nobody is coming in the other direction. At Mile 96 is a fantastic view overlooking the Minto Flats, the Tanana River, and the foothills of the Alaska Range. If you're very lucky and have charmed cloud karma, you'll get a breathtaking view of Mt. McKinley and the accompanying snowcapped peaks to its right and left, jutting straight up like a big militant fist from the lowlands. Even though the range is more than 100 miles due south, the possibility of seeing it is worth the whole ride—even the dust. From here to Manley are some fun roller-coaster humps and curves; watch for porcupines, foxes, snowshoe hares, squirrels, hawks, and other cars.

Manley Hot Springs

This relaxing and friendly town (pop. 70) is a couple of miles this side of the end of the Elliott at the Tanana River. Like many Interior villages, Manley Hot Springs had its heyday in the early 1900s during the peak activity of nearby mines. The U.S. Army Signal Corps set up a telegraph station here in 1903, and Frank Manley built the town's first resort in 1907. Because of the geothermal activity, Manley boasts agricultural features uncommon for Interior—rich warm soil, a long growing season, even earthworms—and is known for its abundant produce. Manley also has a roadhouse, a popular landing strip, and more ATVs than cars. A lot more. Best of all, the hot springs have no sulfur, so you can enjoy the soak without the stench.

Open since 1906, the **Manley Roadhouse** (907/672-3161, May–Sept.) is a popular meeting place for local miners, trappers, and dog mushers. It has many prehistoric and historic artifacts on display, collected from around the area, along with the usual bar, restaurant with down-home food, friendly atmosphere, and rooms with a bath down the hall for $65 d. Modern motel-type rooms are $90–120 d, and cabins with outhouses cost $100 (shower in the lodge). Showers for campers are $3.

Right on the edge of town are the **Manley Hot Springs** (907/672-3171), on private property belonging to Chuck and Gladys Dart. These long-time Manley residents—the school is named after Gladys—are friendly Alaskan farmers who use the hot springs bubbling up on their property to grow flowers and grapes in greenhouses. Inside the first greenhouse are three concrete soaking tubs with 108° F spring water; a donation is requested.

Keep going toward town and park by the bridge over Hot Springs Slough. Go right just before the bridge and walk a half-mile to the first road to the right. The first part of the trail past the cabins is private property. Then it's three miles to the tower, and two more up to Bean Ridge. Great views and camping up there.

The public campground below the bridge on the other side of **Hot Springs Slough** in the middle of town has toilets, picnic tables, and barbecues for $5.

The Elliott Highway continues past the landing strip and trading post 2.5 miles to the end of the road at the mighty Tanana River.

Here it's scenic and breezy, and you could camp here in a pinch.

DALTON HIGHWAY TO DEADHORSE

Before pipline days, the Elliott Highway ran from just outside of Fairbanks to Livengood, where a 56-mile spur road cut north to the Yukon River. The Dalton Highway began as the "Haul Road" in 1974, constructed to run parallel to the **Trans-Alaska Pipeline** from the Yukon River to Deadhorse, a small oil settlement on Prudhoe Bay. In 1981, the spur road and the Haul Road, a total of 414 miles, were renamed the Dalton Highway after James Dalton, who pioneered early oil exploration efforts on the North Slope. This long road traverses some of the most spectacular and remote land accessible by road in Alaska (and therefore in the country), through taiga and tundra, over the Arctic Circle, past towering snowcapped peaks, through the Brooks Range, and within a mile of Gates of the Arctic National Park. Wildlife is abundant: caribou, Dall sheep, and wolves can be seen if you look closely. For additional information on the Dalton Highway, contact the BLM (907/474-2200 or 800/437-7021, www.blm.gov/ak/dalton) to request—or download—their very helpful publication.

Driving

The Dalton Highway is still primarily a truck-supply route and is fairly wide, but it can become very dusty or slippery depending on recent weather. The road is open all the way to Deadhorse, but make no mistake: this is a somewhat excruciating 7–11 hours on a tire-eating, bone-jarring, teeth-grinding, anus-clenching "highway." A trip up the Dalton is not to be taken lightly!

There are only a few service stations/supply stops along the way: at Yukon River crossing (Mile 56), Coldfoot (Mile 175), Wiseman (Mile 189), and the end of the line in Deadhorse (Mile 414). You'll be maxing out your Visa card if you get towed very far, so extended towing coverage (such as AAA's Plus policy) is highly recommended! Always travel with plenty of water, keep your headlights on, carry two spare tires, and **watch for trucks.** The trucks do not slow down for oncoming traffic, but in most cases you can see them coming thanks to the dust trails they raise. Be prepared for all that dust to come your way, along with a hail of flying gravel that sometimes shatters windshields.

Once you reach Deadhorse, don't expect to simply drive around the oilfields; all access is tightly controlled and only authorized tour operators can pass through the checkpoints. **Arctic Outfitters** (907/474-3530 or 800/474-1986, www.arctic-outfitters.com) in Fairbanks rents cars for travel on the Dalton with two full-size spare tires, a CB radio, first aid kit, and other useful items.

Getting There and Around

Alaska Airlines (800/426-0333, www.alaskaair.com) has daily flights from Anchorage to Prudhoe Bay/Deadhorse or from Fairbanks to Barrow and on to Prudhoe. Two companies offer tours up the Dalton Highway to the Arctic Circle and beyond if you want to save the wear and tear on yourself and your vehicle: **Northern Alaska Tour Company** (907/474-8600 or 800/474-1986, www.northernalaska.com) and **Alaskan Arctic Turtle Tours** (907/457-1798 or 888/456-1798, www.wildalaska.info). Northern Alaska is considerably larger, and the company also owns several businesses along the way, including Coldfoot Camp and Yukon Crossing.

The 13-hour Fairbanks-to-the-Circle-and-back-in-a-day tours cost $149 per person. Arctic Turtle has a two-day butt-bustin' bus tour to Prudhoe Bay and back to Fairbanks for $900 including meals; lodging is extra. Northern Alaska offers many other options, including multi-night trips to Prudhoe Bay or the Brooks Range. One popular choice ($860 s or $1,580 d) includes a flight from Fairbanks to Prudhoe where you tour the oilfield and overnight before taking a bus excursion down the Dalton, stopping in Coldfoot for a night, reaching Fairbanks the third evening. **Dalton Highway Express** (907/452-2031,

THE INTERIOR

www.daltonhighway.com) has scheduled summertime bus service up the Dalton Highway; reservations required. Round-trip fares are $140 to the Arctic Circle, $175 to Coldfoot, and $392 to Prudhoe Bay.

To the Arctic Circle

Mile 0 of the Dalton is 73 miles north of Fairbanks, accessed by the Elliott. From here it's 56 miles to the Yukon River, with sweeping views of the undulating landscape and good glimpses of the pipeline. Only one developed campground is maintained along the Dalton, but the first of many undeveloped areas is at **Hess Creek,** Mile 24.

A 2,290-foot **wooden-deck bridge** crosses the mighty Yukon at Mile 56. On the northern side is **Yukon River Camp** (907/474-3557, www.yukonrivercamp.com), with a mercantile, gas, tire and minor auto repairs, motel rooms ($149–200 d with shared bath) and a restaurant. They're open May–September.

Five miles north is the unpretentious **Hot Spot Café** (907/451-7543) serving surprisingly good meals, a fun gift shop, gas and flat-fixin', and simple rooms.

An interesting pipeline interpretive display is near the bridge, and the BLM's **Yukon Crossing Visitors Station** is open daily 9 A.M.–6 P.M. June–August. Cross the road and drive under the pipeline for an undeveloped camping area.

Isolated granite tors are visible to the northeast at Mile 86, and at Mile 98 are excellent views of the mountains across the tundra before the road descends again to travel along the valley floor. At Mile 115 is the **Arctic Circle:** latitude 66°, 33 minutes. A huge sign proclaims the location, and nearly everyone stops to pose for a photo. A road behind the sign leads a half-mile to camping.

Coldfoot

At Mile 132 are **Gobbler's Knob** and the first views of the Brooks Range on the distant northern horizon. The road winds past Pump Station 5, over numerous rivers and creeks, and by great fishing; at Mile 175 it rolls into Coldfoot. Gold was discovered at Tramway Bar in the upper reaches of the Koyukuk River in 1893, attracting enough prospectors and miners to found the town of Coldfoot. Still, the town reportedly received its sobriquet when most of them got cold feet at the onset of the first winter and left the country. Two of the original mining cabins are still in the bush at the northern end of the airstrip.

It's no wonder the old miners' feet became frosty. In January 1989, Coldfoot recorded a temperature of -82°F, and for 17 days the mercury refused to rise above 62° below. Then, that summer, it got up to 97° above—the 179-degree differential broke all North American records.

The spacious **Arctic Interagency Visitor Center** (907/678-5209, www.blm.gov/ak, daily 10 A.M.–10 P.M. Memorial Day–mid-Sept., closed winters) is staffed by BLM, Park Service, and FWS personnel. Stop here for travel information, wildlife films, natural history publications, and nightly natural history programs.

Coldfoot Camp (907/474-3500 or 866/474-3400, www.coldfootcamp.com, $169 s or d) has an always-open restaurant, plus gas, repairs, RV spaces ($35 with hookups), and rooms in pipeline-era Atco trailers with two twin beds. No TVs or phones in the rooms. Top off your tank here; the next gas is 239 miles away at Deadhorse. The Coldfoot post office and a gift shop are also here.

For flights into the Brooks Range or Arctic National Wildlife Refuge, contact **Coyote Air Service** (907/678-5995 or 800/252-0603, www.flycoyote.com).

Camp at the BLM's beautifully situated **Marion Creek Campground** (five miles north of Coldfoot, June–mid-Sept., $8).

Wiseman

A mining village that dates back to 1910, Wiseman is home to 20 or so folks. The settlement is three miles out a spur road off the Dalton Highway at Mile 185, and 12 miles north of Coldfoot. A number of picturesque log cabins are scattered around, beneath a fantastic mountain setting, including the little Wiseman

JURASSIC PARK ALASKA

Dinosaurs in Alaska? Unlikely as it may sound, dinosaurs did live here during the Triassic, Jurassic, and Cretaceous periods (66 million–248 million years ago). The first discovery of dinosaur bones came in 1961 when a Shell Oil geologist happened upon strange bones along the Colville River. Thinking they were just mammoth bones from the last ice age, the company shelved them for two decades. When government scientists finally took a look, they were stunned to discover that these were instead the bones of dinosaurs. This discovery is now regarded as one of the most important dinosaur finds of the last several decades, and one of the greatest Cretaceous vertebrate deposits anywhere on earth.

Over the last two decades, scientists have come to the Colville site – right along the Arctic Ocean – to discover how the supposedly cold-blooded dinosaurs could survive such a harsh northern climate. Their findings threw several scientific theories into question, and most paleontologists now believe the dinosaurs were warm-blooded and could move fast enough to migrate long distances, much as the caribou do on today's North Slope. In 1998, dinosaur tracks were discovered at more than a dozen sites along the Colville River, providing evidence that these animals were not only present, but actually common 100 million years ago.

TEMPERATE TIMES

The world the dinosaurs inhabited was vastly different from that of northern Alaska today. A warm inland sea ran from the tropics to the polar regions east of Alaska. The Arctic land was covered with dense, fern-filled redwood forests, and winter temperatures rarely dropped below freezing. This moderate climate and abundant food source allowed the dinosaurs to survive for millions of years. The largest animals were the four-ton horned pachyrinosaurs and the three-ton duck-billed hadrosaurs, both of which were vegetarians. They were preyed upon by such meat-eaters as the tyrannosaurs. Why the dinosaurs disappeared is one of the ongoing mysteries in science, though the prevailing theory is that a giant comet slammed into the Earth some 65 million years ago, causing the planet to cool so rapidly that the dinosaurs could not survive.

And what of the possibility of a "Jurassic Park" in Alaska? The dinosaur discoveries along the Colville River are unique in that some of the bones were never mineralized (turned into stone). Some of these are still the original bones, and it is even possible that a bit of the original DNA is present. Don't expect to see mutant dinosaurs roaming around Alaska anytime soon, but the bones could potentially provide information on what the dinosaurs ate and whether or not they were cold-blooded.

Museum (open for Northern Alaska Tour Company buses). Wiseman Trading Company is open sporadically in the summer with a few snacks and some interesting artifacts the Koyukuk River gold rush.

Arctic Getaway B&B (907/678-4456, www.arcticgetaway.com, $90 d or $150 for four) rents out two comfortable log cabins that share a bath. Both have a stove and sink; use the traditional root cellar to keep things cold. A big Alaskan breakfast is included.

At **Boreal Lodging** (907/678-4566, www.boreallodge.com) guests stay in a four-

room lodge ($60 s or $80 d) or a private cabin ($130 for up to four); all include kitchens, phones, TVs, and baths.

To the Slope

North of Wiseman the Dalton Highway parallels the Koyukuk River for 20 miles or so. The edge of Gates of the Arctic National Park is high up on the slopes west of Wiseman (see the *Western and Arctic Alaska* chapter for more on this grand area). At Mile 194 are the first views of 4,000-foot **Sukakpak Mountain.** The road passes along the base of this rugged peak, and a trail at Mile 203 leads a half-mile right to the base. The strange-looking mounds between the road and the mountain are "palsas" formed by ice beneath the soil pushing upward.

Above Disaster Creek at Mile 211, the road climbs quickly up to Chandalar Shelf, a huge basin with a healthy population of grizzlies, then over **Atigun Pass** at Mile 244, the highest highway pass in Alaska (4,800 ft.). The road winds quickly down through the Atigun Valley and onto the North Slope. At Mile 414 is the town of Deadhorse.

Prudhoe Bay/Deadhorse

This is the place that makes Alaska run, home to the massive Prudhoe Bay Oilfield (largest in North America and 18th largest in the world), and starting point for the Trans-Alaska Pipeline that carries oil to Valdez, 800 miles to the south. The oilfield encompasses a 250-square-mile area, though the wells, roads, and facilities actually cover just 2 percent of this land. Keep your eyes open for the caribou that graze amid the small city of buildings, pump stations, and other equipment. Some 3,500 well-paid oilfield and related workers stay around Deadhorse, working on a rotating basis that is typically two weeks on followed by two weeks off. The oil companies fly them home for their days off.

The developed areas are called Deadhorse, but the entire area is commonly called Prud-hoe Bay or even more generically, the North Slope or in local parlance, simply the Slope. It is just a few miles from Deadhorse to Prudhoe Bay on the Beaufort Sea (Arctic Ocean). Are you confused yet? If so, try the Prudhoe website (www.prudhoebay.com). Alaska Airlines has flights to Deadhorse, but the only way to get to the Arctic Ocean or into the oilfields is on a tour.

Artic Caribou Inn (907/659-2368, www.arctic caribouinn.com, open late May–early September) has rooms with two single beds; call for rates. All-you-can-eat buffet meals cost $13 for breakfast, $16 for lunch, and $18 for dinner. They also lead Prudhoe Bay tours that include the Oilfield Visitor Center and a stop at the Arctic Ocean, but reservations are required if you aren't staying at the hotel.

Although primarily for oilfield workers, **Prudhoe Bay Hotel** (907/659-2449, www.prudhoebayhotel.com) is open to the public year-round. Lodging and three meals a day cost a very reasonable $90 s or $150 d for simple rooms with twin beds and a bath down the hall, or $110 s or $180 d for nicer units with double beds, private baths, and TVs.

Prudhoe Bay General Store (907/659-2412) has supplies, a post office, and the Deadhorse Museum (of sorts). Auto and RV parts and repairs are available, and the Tesoro gas station provides free RV parking (but no hookups).

Eastern Interior Alaska

DELTA JUNCTION

This town of 900 people is 100 miles south of Fairbanks on the Richardson Highway at its junction with the Alaska Highway. Delta Junction marks the official ending point for the Alaska Highway, and Milepost 1,422 stands in front of the visitor center. The World War II road designers specifically aimed the Alcan to join at Delta, connecting it to both Interior Alaska and tidewater at Valdez (266 miles to the south).

History

Alaska's first road, the **Richardson Highway** was originally envisioned as an "all-American route" to the Yukon gold fields in the late 1890s, and a trail was constructed in conjunction with the WAMCATS telegraph cable all the way to Eagle. But with the shift of attention to the Fairbanks area in the early 1900s, the trail was redirected there and upgraded to a wagon road in 1907 under the auspices of Wilds P. Richardson, first president of the Alaska Road Commission.

Delta began as one of the numerous roadhouses along the trail, which were spaced a day's journey apart (roughly 30 miles). Bate's Landing was opened in 1906 at the confluence of the Delta and Tanana Rivers, where travelers crossed the Tanana on a government-operated ferry that utilized the current for propulsion.

Delta hit the big time, however, with the construction of the Alcan, and when Allen Army Airbase (later Fort Greely) was established nearby as one of the many military installations along the highway. Delta received another boost when a pipeline-construction camp was located here; the pipe crosses the Tanana right next to the highway—a spectacular first view of it for overland travelers. Today Fort Greely is a major center for the Missile Defense System, a questionably effective system pushed into deployment in 2004.

Delta services the largest agricultural area in the state, including thousands of acres of grain and potato farms and smaller farms. Delta is also home to a herd of nearly 500 bison, a species that once outnumbered caribou in Alaska before being driven into extinction. In 1920, the Delta area was stocked with 23 bison from Montana, and the 70,000-acre Delta Bison Range was created in 1980. Ask locally to find the bison since they are often not visible from the highway. In addition to wild bison, local ranchers raise other bison for meat, along with such exotics as reindeer, elk, and even yak.

Sights

Adjacent to the Delta Junction Visitor Center (see *Practicalities*) is the **Sullivan Roadhouse Historical Museum** (907/895-5068, daily 9 A.M.–4:30 P.M. late May–mid-Sept., free). The oldest roadhouse in Interior Alaska (built in 1905), this log building is packed with memorabilia and old photos from the Valdez–Fairbanks Trail and the roadhouses that operated along its route.

You can take a short loop through Delta's rich **agricultural area** by heading eight miles east down the Alaska Highway; take a left at Sawmill Creek Road, another left on Bailey Way, again a left on Hansen Road, and one more left on Clearwater, which delivers you back to the highway. Good views of the eastern peaks of the Alaska Range from the Clearwater area, if it's clear.

To get the total 360 degrees, though, head to **Donnelly Dome,** 23 miles south of town on the Richardson Highway. Go right on the gravel road at Mile 248, continue for a quarter-mile past the second sharp bend; an obvious though unmarked trailhead is at the car park there. Allow a half-day to the dome and back.

A dozen miles north of town at Mile 278 is **Quartz Lake State Recreation Area,** known for excellent rainbow trout and silver salmon fishing. Several day hiking trails head out from the campgrounds, past a homestead cabin from the 1950s and archaeological sites to hilltop vistas.

Delta's big annual event is **Deltana Fair,** a three-day festival of farming exhibits, a rodeo, carnival, parade, mud bog races, and outhouse races. It takes place the last weekend of July.

Big Delta State Historical Park

If you only do one thing in Delta, take an enjoyable and educational stroll through history at Big Delta State Historical Park (8 miles north of town, daily 8 A.M.–7 P.M.). Set in a scenic spot along the banks of the Tanana just below the pipeline crossing, this lush 10-acre piece of property centers around **Rika's Roadhouse** (www.rikas.com), a longtime travelers' stop on the Richardson Road between Valdez and Fairbanks. Restored and expanded in the mid-1980s, the park now features a museum, barns, poultry pens, flourishing gardens, cabins, signboards, outhouses new and old, and displays on mining, trapping, clothing, and more. Guided tours are given several times a day. The Roadhouse itself now houses a fine gift shop with Alaskan-made items, and you can grab a bite at the **Packhouse Pavillion**

Restaurant (907/895-4201), known for dependably good breakfasts, along with lunchtime sandwiches, homemade soups, salads, and delicious pies and bearclaws. Get here early since the restaurant closes at 5 P.M.

Accommodations

Right in the center of town, **Kelly's Alaska Country Inn** (907/895-4667, www.kellys alaskacountryinn.com, $99 s or $109 d) is probably your best lodging option in Delta Junction. Nothing special, but clean rooms, friendly owners, and some unusual units with curved wooden ceilings.

Other options are **Alaskan Steak House & Motel** (907/895-5175, $70 s or $90 d), **Alaska 7 Motel** (907/895-4848, www.alaska7motel.com, $80 s or d), **M&M's B&B** (907/895-4947), **Diamond Willow Inn** (907/895-4373, www .diamond-willowinn.com, $115–125 d), and **True North B&B** (907/895-4963, $75 s or $85 d). Located six miles north of town, **Bald Eagle Ranch B&B** (907/895-5270 or 877/895-5270, www.baldeagleranchbb.com) has a wide

Rika's Roadhouse at Big Delta State Historical Park

© DON PITCHER

range of lodging, from campsites for cyclists to fully furnished homes.

Camping

You'll find many camping options in the Delta Junction area. Pitch your tent at **Delta State Recreation Site** ($10), just a half-mile west of town near the airport. There's a good view across the flats of the eastern Alaska Range. In the morning, grab a shower at the **Delta Laundry** (907/895-4561), another half-mile west. **Clearwater State Recreation Site** is 11 miles from town on Jack Warren Road, with 16 campsites ($10) and a picnic area along Clearwater Lake. **Big Delta State Historical Park,** eight miles north of town, has parking for RVs ($5; no tents) in its lot. **Quartz Lake State Recreation Area,** 12 miles north of town, has campsites for $10.

Right in town, **Green Acres RV Park** (907/895-4369 or 800/895-4369) has attractive RV and tent spaces. Just east of town along the Alcan is **Bergstad's RV Park** (907/895-4856), open all year.

Food

Serving a big menu three meals a day, **Buffalo Center Drive In** (907/895-5089) gets thumbs up from locals and travelers. Top picks are tasty $8 buffalo burgers made from locally raised bison and crunchy corn fritters. There's a screened gazebo for outside dining.

Across from the visitor center on the Richardson is **Pizza Bella** (907/895-4841), where pizzas, pastas, seafood, steaks, and sandwiches fill the menu. Get steaks and other meaty fare at **Alaskan Steak House & Motel** (907/895-5175). **IGA Food Cache** (907/895-4653) has a deli and decent bakery, or head to the Wednesday and Saturday **Farmers Market** all summer long next to the visitor center.

Information and Services

The **Delta Junction Visitor Center** (907/895-5068 or 877/895-5068, www.deltachamber.org) is right at the junction of the Alaska Highway and Richardson Highway. It's open daily 8 A.M.–7 P.M. Memorial Day–Labor Day, daily

8 A.M.–4 P.M. for the rest of May and through mid-September, but closed the remainder of the year.

Alaska Direct Bus Line (907/277-6652 or 800/770-6652, www.alaskadirectbusline.com) stops in Delta Junction en route to Fairbanks, Anchorage, and Whitehorse.

TOK

The Alaska Highway leads east from Delta Junction toward the border with Canada and then continues south all the way to Dawson Creek, British Columbia. One hundred and eight miles east of Delta Junction—and 96 miles from the border—is the town of Tok (pop. 1,200; rhymes with "joke"). Tok considers itself the "gateway to Alaska" and acts as the service center for several Native villages in the upper Tanana Valley. The Tok Cutoff of the Glenn Highway heads south from Tok, providing connections to Anchorage, 326 miles away.

The town of Tok grew from a mid-1940s highway-construction camp, and is still unincorporated. Where the Tok River empties into the Tanana, the Athabascan tribes once gathered to affirm peace, and Tok is usually translated to mean "Peace Crossing." (Other folks say the name came from "Tokyo Camp"—a term used during construction of the Alcan Highway in 1942. There is, however, no evidence that the town was named by potheads, though more than a few folks have posed next to the town's entrance sign with a joint in hand.)

Much of the land around Tok was burned in a massive 100,000-acre fire in 1990, but the winds abruptly shifted, sparing the town itself.

Sights

The main Tok attractions are restaurants, motels, gas stations, and information centers. The modern Civic Center houses **Tok Mainstreet Visitor Center** (907/883-5775, www.tokinfoalaska.com, daily 8 A.M.–7 P.M. May–mid-Sept., closed rest of year). Next door in the State of Alaska building is the tiny **Alaska Public Lands Information Center** (907/883-5667, www.nps.gov/aplic, 8 A.M.–

7 P.M. mid-May–Sept., Mon.–Fri. 8 A.M.–
4:30 P.M. rest of year).

Mukluk Land (907/883-2571, www.mukluk
land.com, June–Aug.) is a little amusement park
with a kids' igloo for bouncing, skee-ball machines, minigolf, dog sled rides, Alaska's largest
"mosquito," gold panning, gardens, videos, and
a museum of sorts. This peculiar collection of
bush Alaska humor costs $5 adults or $2 kids.

Tetlin National Wildlife Refuge

This 730,000-acre refuge occupies much of the
land east of Tok and south of the Alaska Highway. It borders on Wrangell–St. Elias National
Park and Canada's Kluane National Park. The
refuge gets very little use by travelers, but is an
important home for trumpeter swans, moose,
black and grizzly bears, caribou, wolves, and
other animals. Marshes here contain some of
the highest densities of waterfowl in Alaska,
not to mention mosquitoes. Two refuge campgrounds are accessible from the Alaska Highway. The Tetlin National Wildlife Refuge
Visitor Center (907/883-5312, http://tetlin.
fws.gov, daily 8 A.M.–4:30 P.M. mid-May–mid-
Sept.) is 85 miles east of Tok. The staff offers
nature talks here daily in the summer, plus evening programs at Deadman Lake Campground
(Mile 1249). A three-quarter-mile nature trail
is at the campground.

Accommodations

Tok has a good selection of reasonably priced
places to spend the night. **Young's Motel**
(907/883-4411), right next to Fast Eddy's Restaurant, with clean rooms containing two beds
for $78 s or $83 d. **Snowshoe Motel** (907/883-
4511 or 800/478-4511, www.alaskaone.com/
snowshoe, $78 s or $85 d) features modern
two-room units and a continental breakfast.

Other good options are **Golden Bear Motel**
(907/883-5950 or 888/252-2123, $79–89 s or
$84–94 d), and **Tok Motel** (907/883-2852 or
800/883-3007, www.alaskan.com/toklodge,
$91 s or $95 d).

Burnt Paw Cabins (907/883-4121, www
.burntpawcabins.com, $109–119 d) has seven
modern log cabins with private baths, full

breakfasts, guest computer, and Wi-Fi. They're
next to the post office and open all year. **Cleft
of the Rock B&B** (907/883-4219 or 800/478-
5646, www.cleftoftherock.net, $110 d) has
cabins and guest rooms with private baths and
a full breakfast.

Camping

Pitch your tent at the pleasant **Tok River State
Recreation Site** ($15), five miles east of Tok
on the Alaska Highway. The site is too close
to the highway for a quiet night, but a short
trail follows the river and climbs stairs up the
hillside. Across the river is part of the area that
was burned in the 1990 fires.

Tok offers plenty of parking choices for
RVers at around $25 a night: **Golden Bear
Motel and RV Park** (907/883-2561 or
888/252-2123), **Sourdough Campground**
(907/883-5543 or 800/789-5543, www.sour
doughcampground.com), **Tok RV Village**
(907/883-5877 or 800/478-5878, www.apt
alaska.net/~tokrv), and **Tundra Lodge & RV
Park** (907/883-7875).

Food

Although a number of places serve food in
Tok, you only need to know two: Fast Eddy's and Gateway Salmon Bake. **Fast Eddy's**
(907/883-4411, 6 A.M.–11 P.M. year-round) is
Tok's main restaurant action, a clean and classy
family place with good food, fair prices, and
long hours. The menu covers most standards:
pizzas, halibut burgers, salad bar, sandwiches,
ribs, and steaks.

A fine alternative is the **Gateway Salmon
Bake** (907/883-5555 summer or 907/883-5578
winter, mid-May–early Sept.) with BBQ buffalo or salmon burger, king salmon or halibut slab, ribs, or reindeer sausage. The combo
meal ($18) also includes a big salad bar, salmon
chowder, baked beans, sourdough rolls, and
lemonade. For a lighter option, pig-out at the
chowder and salad bar.

Getting There

Alaska Direct Bus Line (907/277-6652 or
800/770-6652, www.alaskadirectbusline.com)

provides year-round service connecting Tok with Whitehorse, Anchorage, Fairbanks, and Skagway. Service is three times a week in the summer, and twice weekly the rest of the year. Reservations required. **Alaska/Yukon Trails** (907/479-2277 or 888/770-7275, www.alaskashuttle.com) has once-a-week summertime bus tours connecting Tok with Fairbanks, Dawson City, and Whitehorse.

The Alaska Highway crosses into the Yukon Territory 124 miles east of Tok. Both U.S. and Canadian customs are open 24 hours a day, year-round. Be sure to reset your watches since the time is an hour earlier in Alaska.

TAYLOR HIGHWAY

This is the scenic shortcut to Dawson City from Alaska, a 160-mile gravel-and-pavement road through wild and undeveloped country. The road starts at Tetlin Junction (Mile 1302 Alaska Highway), 11 miles east of Tok, and is paved for the first 50 miles. The road is typically open to traffic May–mid-October, but closed the rest of the year by heavy snows. The first portion of the Taylor Highway cuts through the 1.8-million acre **Tanana Valley State Forest**, with periodic hilltop vistas over the rolling green countryside, particularly near the road summit on the slopes of 5,541-foot **Mt. Fairplay.** Keep your eyes open for the Fortymile caribou herd along the highway. Beyond Mt. Fairplay the road descends to the Fortymile River country, reaching the little settlement of Chicken at Mile 66.

Chicken

With barely 20 people, you wouldn't think this wide spot in the road would be worthy of mention, but it is actually a favorite stopping point for travelers. The town was originally named "Ptarmigan," for the chicken-like bird that inhabits the country here. The spelling of "Ptarmigan" proved a problem for the miners who were mucking for gold around here in 1895, so the name was switched to something they could handle: "Chicken." Anyone who's read *Tisha* by Ann Purdy, the story of a young teacher who overcame enormous local resis-

tance to teach in this neck of the tundra, will be interested to know that the author made her home here.

Be sure to stop at **Chicken Mercantile** in "downtown Chicken" for copies of *Tisha*, funny T-shirts, and a taste of Sue Wiren's enormous cinnamon rolls and great pies, along with homemade chicken soup (of course), reindeer bratwurst, sandwiches, a daily salmon bake on summer afternoons, plus a computer and free Wi-Fi. Tenters and RVs can park for free at the Mercantile; or pay to park behind the **Goldpanner,** just up the road, where you can also buy groceries and gas, or try your luck at panning for the yellow stuff.

Behind the Goldpanner is **Gold Dredge No. 4,** in use from 1959 to 1967, and moved here from Pedro Creek. The original town of Chicken, an abandoned mining camp, is now on private property. Hour-long tours are given in the summer; ask at the Goldpanner.

Over on Airport Road, **Chicken Gold Camp & Outpost** (907/235-6396, www.chicken gold.com) has a campground, cabins, gifts, Wi-Fi, a fine little café (paninis and homemade soups), and espresso, plus tours of the 1930s Pedro dredge (on the National Register of Historic Places), kayak rentals, and gold panning.

During the summer, **Alaska/Yukon Trails** (907/479-2277 or 888/770-7275, www.alaskashuttle.com) has bus tours connecting Chicken with Fairbanks and Dawson City several times a week.

To Jack Wade Junction

It's another 30 miles from Chicken to Jack Wade Junction on the Taylor Highway. This section is the most challenging part of the drive: narrow, winding, and often rough as it passes through the forested **Fortymile Country** with its dramatic vistas and tailings from past and present mining operations. Stop for a break at the BLM's **Walker Fork Campground** (Mile 82; $8) to stretch your legs—and maybe soak your feet if it's real hot. The campground is on a beautiful site where the South and Walker Forks of the Fortymile meet. A footbridge across the creek leads to a three-minute trail to the top of the limestone wall—nice view of the valley, one of innumerable similar valleys in the immense Interior of Alaska. Four miles ahead is the gotta-take-a-photo **Jack Wade Dredge No. 1,** abandoned in 1942, and a few miles beyond this are active placer mining operations and the old **Jack Wade** mining camp—take care not to trespass.

To Dawson City

From Jack Wade Junction (Mile 96) the Taylor Highway heads north to Eagle, while the **Top of the World Highway** (the main road) continues east to Dawson, Yukon Territory, 79 miles away. From the junction it is only 13 miles to the U.S.–Canada border, the northernmost border crossing on the continent. The road is wide and well-maintained gravel on the U.S. side, and paved on the Canadian side. The name Top of the World says it all; this is a grand exit from (or entrance into) Alaska, with vistas in all directions on a clear day. The border crossing is at **Poker Creek** on the U.S. side, and Canadian customs are at **Little Gold Creek.** Both American and Canadian Customs operate mid-May–mid-September, 8 A.M.–7 P.M. Alaska Time (9 A.M.–9 P.M. Pacific Time). **Boundary Lodge** on the American side has gas and other emergency supplies—for a price.

To Eagle

From Jack Wade Junction, the Taylor Highway continues north to Eagle, 65 miles away. This stretch is almost more trail than road: very narrow and winding, with steep grades, rough surface, endless hairpin turns, and little traffic—30 mph max. For the same reasons, it's one of the most fun roads in the state. Lots of twists and turns, ups and downs, and not many cars. The scenery is the same Interior hills and spruce trees you've been accustomed to, so it's not a loss to keep your eyes glued to this road at all times; one glance away and you're driving into a ditch or off a 300-foot cliff. Expect to spend at least two hours for these 65 miles, two hours of white-knuckled, bug-eyed, teeth-chattering thrills and chills—hopefully without the spills.

◖ EAGLE

It takes a strong desire and a serious commitment to get to Eagle—more than 160 miles from Tetlin Junction and 145 miles from Dawson. Even if you're on the way from Dawson into Alaska, it's 130 miles, at least five hard hours of driving, from the junction of Top of the World and Taylor Highways to Eagle and back. Is it worth it? Consider this. Eagle is a total history lesson. The small photogenic town of 150 may have more square feet of museum space than anywhere else in the state, and the moving-right-along walking tour can take up to three hours! Add to that a beautiful free campground, great showers, good food, friendly people, and Yukon River scenery, and Eagle is without hesitation worth the extra time, effort, and expense. This is one friendly, peaceful, close-knit community.

History

In 1881, Francis Mercier, a French-Canadian trader, established a trading post at the site of Eagle to compete with Fort Yukon and Fort Reliance, two Hudson's Bay Co. posts along this eastern stretch of the Yukon River. It was a shrewd choice of location. Just inside the American border, stampeders fed up with Canada's heavy-handed laws and taxes organized a supply town here in spring 1898, naming it Eagle for the profusion of the majestic birds in the area. Also, sitting at the southernmost point on the Yukon in eastern Alaska, Eagle occupied a strategic spot for transportation, communication, and supply routes to the Interior from Valdez at tidewater. Within six months, three large trading companies had developed Eagle into a major Yukon port. In 1899, the Army began building Fort Egbert next to the town site. In 1900, Judge James Wickersham arrived to install Interior's first federal court, with jurisdiction over half the state. And by 1902, the WAMCATS telegraph line was completed between Eagle and Valdez, inaugurating the first "all-American" communication system to the Lower 48.

The biggest event in Eagle's history happened in 1905, when a Norwegian Arctic ex-

THE INTERIOR

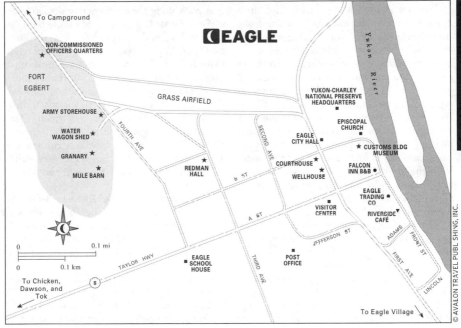

© AVALON TRAVEL PUBLISHING, INC.

plorer appeared out of the icy fog and somehow communicated to the townspeople (he spoke no English) who he was and what he'd done. The man was Roald Amundsen, and he had just navigated the Northwest Passage (for the first time in more than 350 years of attempts) and had crossed over 500 miles of uncharted country by dogsled in the deepest Arctic winter from his ice-locked ship off the north coast of Alaska to announce his feat to the world. The message, going out over the telegraph line, was the news story of the decade.

By then, however, Eagle's star had faded. The stampeders had moved on to Nome and Fairbanks, followed by Judge Wickersham and his court. The importance of Fort Egbert declined, until it was abandoned in 1911. WAM-CATS was replaced, seven years after it was installed, by wireless communication. Eagle's population continually dwindled, to a low of 13 in 1959. Fortunately, the remoteness of the town made it almost impossible to haul out the antiques that had accumulated over the

decades, so they stayed in Eagle where they remain today. Since then, with a small resurgence of gold activity in the area, the establishment of the Yukon–Charley Rivers National Preserve, and increased tourism, Eagle has become a revitalized community, proud of its past and present, and optimistic about its future. The 150 or so residents proudly note that "visiting Eagle is like opening a 100-year-old time capsule."

Sights

In Eagle (907/547-2325, www.eagleak.org), it's almost impossible to find a resident who isn't something of a historian (and a cheerleader) for the area. The Eagle Historical Society is one of, if not the, most successful and well-organized groups in the state. It was founded in 1961 after someone showed up at the old mule barn with a truck and made off with the entire collection of saddles.

The care, devotion, and thoroughness with which they display Eagle's awe-inspiring array of artifacts is something to see. And their guided summertime tours ($5), which leave from Judge Wickersham's courthouse steps at 9 A.M., is really the only way to see it; it's a fun, hands-on outing, during which you're encouraged to operate an old peanut-warming machine or tickle the keys of an ancient pump organ. While waiting in the morning, fill up your water containers at the **wellhouse** next door to the court. The well, dug 60 feet deep by hand in 1910, still pumps cold water—delicious; three out of four residents still haul water from this source. Struggle through the three heavy doors and either fill your bottle at the faucet or stretch the gas-pump-type handle to the jugs in your vehicle.

The tour begins appropriately inside the **courthouse,** built in 1901 by Judge Wickersham for $5,000. All four rooms plus the hallway on the ground floor are covered with displays of the Han Natives, geology and archaeology, early pioneers, the telegraph story, and more. Be sure to check out the front page of the December 7, 1905, issue of *The New York Times,* with Amundsen's story, plus the map of the Northwest Passage in the hallway. (A romantic footnote: The intrepid Suzan Amundsen, Roald's great-granddaughter, continues a family tradition by taking a rest at the popular Eagle checkpoint during the Yukon Quest Sled Dog Race.) Don't miss the amazing Nimrod's false teeth (homemade from caribou and bear teeth) and his remarkably accurate relief map of the vicinity—a newspaper papier-mâché printed with moose blood. Upstairs in Wickersham's courtroom is a small gift shop run by the Historical Society.

Then you mosey down to the **Customs House** on the Yukon waterfront, another two-story museum brimming with history. Study the six dated shots of the freezing of the Yukon River from October 13, 1899, to January 12, 1900, plus the photos upstairs of "wild" animals—Fred Ferwilliger's wolf pups, Mae Collins's pet black bear, and some bewildered-looking moose hitched to wagons and carriages. Sign the original U.S. Customs entry book.

A walk along the town's grassy airstrip leads to **Fort Egbert.** The huge old mule barn, at 150 feet long and 30 feet wide one of the largest restored buildings in Alaska, is full of relics from Eagle's past: tools, weapons, uniforms, wagons and tack, dog sleds, boats, a prototype Sears chain saw, an old outboard motor that looks like a cross between an early sewing machine and a Weedwacker, and much more. Upstairs is the gold-mining exhibit with its own collection of Rube Goldberg equipment. The water wagon shed houses historic vehicles, including a Model A pickup and Model B dump truck.

The **Improved Order of Redmen Building,** a wilderness version of a lodge/benevolent society, was ostensibly dedicated to the preservation of the ways and traditions of the area's Native people. Of course, only white guys were allowed to be members.

For more on the town and its rich history, pick up a copy of *Jewel on the Yukon: Eagle City* by Elva Scott; it's sold in the courthouse.

Out 1st Avenue (take a right coming into town) two and a half miles is **Eagle Village,** a picturesque Native settlement that predates the white settlers. Fish wheels operate just offshore, and racks of salmon dry under the clouds. The residents are friendly, but please respect their privacy.

Accommodations and Services

Follow the signs from town left to the free **campground** just beyond the cemetery (a few old markers; Nimrod's grave is here): big, uncrowded, nice wooded sites, firewood, vault toilets. There's an easy nature walk between the campground and the airstrip.

Eagle Trading Co. (907/547-2220) on the riverfront, has rooms with river views ($60 s or $70 d), groceries, showers, RV hookups ($25), gas, and tire repairs. Next door is the seasonal **Riverside Café.** A couple of gift shops are in Eagle, and locals set up booths selling handicrafts across from the courthouse when the *Yukon Queen II* is in town.

Falcon Inn B&B (907/547-2254, May–mid-Oct.) is an attractive three-story log structure with dormers and a lookout tower right on the Yukon. Rooms are $85 s or $95 d with a full breakfast.

Getting There

The *Yukon Queen II* (206/281-3535 or 800/544-2206 Grayline of Alaska, or 867/993-5599 in Dawson City, www.graylineofalaska.com) is a high-speed, 120-passenger vessel with daily summertime runs between Dawson City in the Yukon and Eagle. Most passengers are part of a Holland America/Gray Line of Alaska trek, but independent travelers can ride for $90 each way, including a meal. No buses run to Eagle, and it's a good four hours by car from Dawson, and at least another five down to Tetlin Junction.

Everts Air Alaska (907/450-2350, www.evertsair.com) and **Arctic Circle Air** (907/474-0112, www.arctic-circle-air.com) offer flights from Fairbanks. This is a real bush-pilot trip, the daily mail and supply run.

YUKON-CHARLEY RIVERS NATIONAL PRESERVE

Eagle itself is pretty far out there, but if you really want to disappear, you can explore Yukon–Charley Rivers National Preserve. This huge, 2.5 million-acre park is primitive, with virtually no facilities or established transportation and only a skeleton Park Service staff. The park protects 115 miles of the Yukon River and the entire Charley River basin.

The park's **Visitor Center** (corner of 1st and Fort Egbert Ave. in Eagle, Mon.–Fri. 8 A.M.–5 P.M., 907/547-2233, www.nps.gov/yuch) has a selection of books and maps on the preserve, and the staff will plug in a video on request and can provide advice for those contemplating a trip.

Most park visitors float the Yukon by raft, kayak, or canoe, starting in Eagle (on the eastern margin) and taking out in Circle (on the western edge of the park). The float takes 5–10 days. Within the park are four public-use cabins available on a first-come, no-cost basis.

You can also charter a bush plane to drop you and a kayak or raft way up around the Charley headwaters and float down to the Yukon. You must be highly experienced, entirely self-sufficient, and have at least a tolerance for, if not a love of, mosquitoes. Check in at headquarters for advice and conditions, and to leave your intended itinerary.

Eagle Canoe Rentals (907/547-2203, www.aptalaska.net/~paddleak) rents canoes to paddle the Yukon from Eagle to Circle City; experienced paddlers only.

SOUTHWEST ALASKA

Southwest Alaska includes Kodiak Island, the Alaska Peninsula, and the barren, windswept Aleutian and Pribilof Islands—all told, an incredible sweep of wild and stormy coastline. This part of the state contains world-famous brown bear-viewing opportunities in Kodiak Island National Wildlife Refuge, Katmai National Park, and McNeil River State Game Sanctuary. In addition, it encompasses less-visited Lake Clark National Park, the remote Aniakchak National Monument, and four national wildlife refuges, one of which reaches all the way out the Aleutian chain. Fur seals, sea otters, walrus, and other marine animals are common around the Aleutians and Pribilofs, and the islands are also a bird-watcher's paradise. Because of climatic conditions there are no forests west of northern Kodiak Island and

the adjacent mainland; most of the Alaska Peninsula and all the Aleutians are open tundra.

The largest settlements in Southwest Alaska are Kodiak and Unalaska/Dutch Harbor, but many smaller fishing towns and Native villages are sprinkled over this remote landscape. Only Kodiak is fairly reasonable to visit; other places will require considerable outlays of cash. A useful regional website is run by the Southwest Alaska Municipal Conference (www.southwestalaska.com).

ORIENTATION
The Land
From Denali National Park the Alaska Range swings southwest to become the Aleutian Range, marching right into the North Pacific as the Alaska Peninsula and Aleutian Islands.

© DON PITCHER

HIGHLIGHTS

◖ Baranov Museum: Occupying the oldest Russian building in North America, this Kodiak museum has an interesting collection of artifacts. The gift shop sells rare samovars, Russian porcelain, and Ukranian Easter eggs (page 428).

◖ Fort Abercrombie State Park: The old World War II fort remains are still visible here, but visitors appreciate the lush rainforest, fun hiking paths, and high cliffs with nesting puffins (page 428).

◖ Exploring Kodiak Roads: Nearly 100 miles of roads fan out from the town of Kodiak. The most interesting leads south to remote beaches where you'll find fossils, perfect surfing waves, a winery, wandering bison, and even a rocket launching complex (page 429).

◖ Bear-Viewing: Floatplanes depart Kodiak for inland parts of the island or the shores of Katmai National Park. These trips are expensive, but unforgettable (page 439).

◖ Valley of Ten Thousand Smokes: Located within Katmai National Park, this still-steaming valley reveals the devastation wrought by the enormous eruption of Novarupta volcano in 1912. A bus takes visitors there from Brooks Camp (page 443).

◖ Brooks Camp: Located along the shore of Naknek Lake, this lodge and campground provide a fine base for exploring Katmai National Park, with bear-viewing and fishing a short hike away. Access is by floatplane from the town of King Salmon (page 443).

◖ Unalaska/Dutch Harbor Historical Sights: Primarily a commercial fishing center, this Aleutian town also has a Russian Orthodox church from the 1820s, two outstanding museums, plus aging bunkers and gun emplacements from World War II (page 453).

◖ St. Paul Island: It's a long flight to this tiny outpost in the middle of the Bering Sea where the weather is almost always wet and chilly, but visitors are rewarded with the chance to find colonies of fur seals and cliffs crowded with puffins, murres, kittiwakes, and other seabirds (page 457).

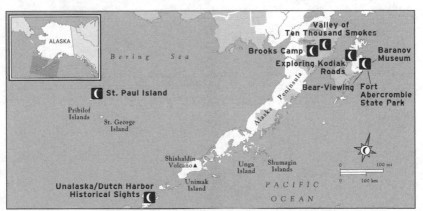

LOOK FOR ◖ TO FIND RECOMMENDED SIGHTS, ACTIVITIES, DINING, AND LODGING.

SOUTHWEST ALASKA

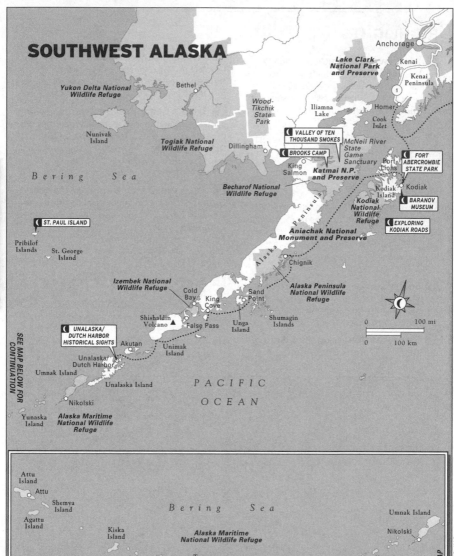

SOUTHWEST ALASKA

Anchorage

Lake Clark National Park and Preserve

Kenai
Kenai Peninsula

Yukon Delta National Wildlife Refuge

Bethel

Wood-Tikchik State Park

Iliamna Lake

Homer

Cook Inlet

Nunivak Island

Togiak National Wildlife Refuge

Dillingham

VALLEY OF TEN THOUSAND SMOKES

McNeil River State Game Sanctuary

FORT ABERCROMBIE STATE PARK

BROOKS CAMP

King Salmon

Katmai N.P. and Preserve

Port Lions

B e r i n g   S e a

Becharof National Wildlife Refuge

Kodiak Island

Kodiak

BARANOV MUSEUM

Kodiak National Wildlife Refuge

EXPLORING KODIAK ROADS

ST. PAUL ISLAND

Aniachak National Monument and Preserve

Pribilof Islands

St. George Island

A l a s k a   P e n i n s u l a

Chignik

Izembek National Wildlife Refuge

Cold Bay

King Cove

Sand Point

Alaska Peninsula National Wildlife Refuge

Shishaldin Volcano

False Pass

Unga Island

Shumagin Islands

0   100 mi
0   100 km

UNALASKA/ DUTCH HARBOR HISTORICAL SIGHTS

Akutan

Unimak Island

Unalaska/ Dutch Harbor

Umnak Island

Unalaska Island

PACIFIC

Nikolski

OCEAN

Yunaska Island

Alaska Maritime National Wildlife Refuge

SEE MAP BELOW FOR CONTINUATION

Attu Island

Attu

Shemya Island

Agattu Island

Kiska Island

B e r i n g   S e a

Umnak Island

Nikolski

Alaska Maritime National Wildlife Refuge

Tanaga Island

Adak

Atka

Atka Island

Seguam Island

Yunaska Island

Amchitka Island

Adak Island

Kanaga Island

PACIFIC   OCEAN

SEE MAIN MAP

This 1,100-mile arc from the northern end of the Alaska Peninsula to the western tip of the Aleutians is an area of extraordinary volcanic and seismic activity, accounting for an amazing 10 percent of the world's recorded earthquakes. Tremors of all sizes—some too small to feel—are a daily occurrence, and three of the four largest earthquakes ever recorded in the United States occurred in the Aleutians; all three had a magnitude of 8.2 or greater. Only the massive Good Friday quake of 1964 that hit Southcentral Alaska was larger.

Kodiak Island sits uneasily on the edge of the Aleutian Trench; Kodiak is nonvolcanic, yet bears the brunt of its fiery neighbors. Great collapsed craters at Katmai and Aniakchak are now administered by the National Park Service, and the 50–60 volcanoes along the archipelago comprise the longest and straightest line of smoke-belchers and ash-spewers anywhere on earth.

The vegetation of Southwest Alaska is a thick, luxurious shag carpet of grass and brush; you can travel for hundreds of miles here without seeing a single tree. The climate, however, is particularly disagreeable—fog, rain, snow, and wind.

PLANNING YOUR TIME

Getting to Southwest Alaska can be a challenge due to both the remoteness of the setting and weather conditions that can shut down flights for days at a stretch. Access is primarily by air, but the state ferry system serves Kodiak several times a week, continuing out the Aleutian Islands twice a month. The second-largest island in the U.S., Kodiak is a fascinating and lush place with forests on the northeast end that give way to tundra across the rest of the island. The small city of Kodiak is home to a big fleet of commercial fishing vessels and a large coastguard base, but also has a rich Russian heritage, as evidenced by the **Baranov Museum.** A few miles north is **Fort Abercrombie State Park** with rainforests and dramatic

rocky cliffs. **Kodiak roads** also lead south to remote beaches where you'll find fossils, perfect surfing waves, a winery, wandering bison, and even a rocket launching complex. Kodiak **bear-viewing** is a major attraction, but many of these floatplane day-trips actually land on the shores of Katmai National Park. The park itself is primarily accessed by jet from Anchorage to the town of King Salmon, followed by a floatplane flight to **Brooks Camp,** home to a comfortable lodge and outstanding opportunities to watch bears or fish. Another favorite park feature is the **Valley of Ten Thousand Smokes,** the remnants from a massive eruption by Novarupta volcano in 1912.

The Aleutians are a volcanic chain of islands that arc west for a thousand miles from the tip of the Alaska Peninsula. Only one of these is readily accessible by air and ferry, Unalaska Island, home to the major fishing town of Unalaska (also called Dutch Harbor). Local **historical sights** include a fine museum, a historic Russian Orthodox church, and various World War II sites. Even more remote are the Pribilof Islands, consisting primarily of St. George Island and **St. Paul Island.** The latter is a very long flight from Anchorage over open water to a dot of a place in the Bering Sea, but the trip is worthwhile for the chance to see colonies of fur seals and cliffs packed with massive numbers of puffins, murres, kittiwakes, and other seabirds.

Getting There

With ferry service from Homer and Seward three times a week, Kodiak is the only easily accessible place in Southwest Alaska. The trusty *Tustumena* sails out as far as Dutch Harbor once a month, but only in summer. Alaska Air flies from Anchorage to Kodiak, Dutch Harbor/Unalaska, and Adak, and PenAir serves King Salmon, Sand Point, Dutch Harbor/Unalaska, and the Pribilofs. Access to remote backcountry areas is by small floatplanes that land on the myriad of lakes and ponds.

Kodiak Island

Kodiak Island is an unlikely land of superlatives. At 60 by 100 miles, it is the largest island in Alaska, and second-largest in the United States (after Hawaii's Big Island). Kodiak has the world's biggest brown bears, Alaska's longest history, and one of the largest fishing fleets, along with the country's largest Coast Guard station and weirdest golf tournament. Besides, what other town has chewing tobacco named for it, and a dump once voted the nation's "most scenic"?

Kodiak Island is home to nearly 14,000 people, 9,000 of whom live in and around the city of Kodiak. Only 250 air miles from Anchorage or 84 nautical miles from Homer, Kodiak is a highly accessible and pleasurable place to visit. The city of Kodiak sits on the island's northeast side along St. Paul Harbor, protected from the wild Gulf of Alaska by wooded islands in Chiniak Bay. Visitors will quickly learn that the town runs on commercial fishing; it's hard to escape not only the sights but also the smell of fish.

THE LAND

The Kodiak Island group, an extension of the Chugach-Kenai Ranges, was once possibly connected to the mainland but is now separated by the "entrances" to Cook Inlet and Shelikof Strait. The group perches on the continental shelf, right on the edge of the Aleutian Trench. This makes it highly susceptible to the after-effects of volcanic and seismic activity, such as the ash of Novarupta and the tsunamis of the 1964 earthquake. However, glaciation, not volcanism, has been the primary agent in the shaping of Kodiak's geologic features. Snow and ice almost completely covered the group during the last ice age, and the alpine is chiseled roughly steep

Fossil Beach, Kodiak

© DON PITCHER

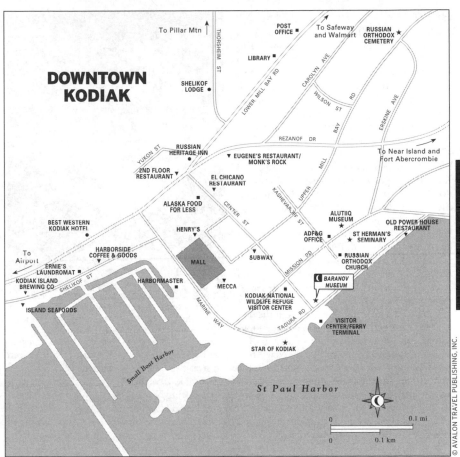

DOWNTOWN KODIAK

To Pillar Mtn

THORSHEIM ST

POST OFFICE ■

To Safeway and Walmart

RUSSIAN ORTHODOX CEMETERY ★

LIBRARY ■

LOWER MILL BAY RD

CAROLYN AVE

WILSON ST

BAY

RD

ERSKINE AVE

SHELIKOF LODGE ●

REZANOF DR

To Near Island and Fort Abercrombie

YUKON ST

RUSSIAN HERITAGE INN ■

▼ EUGENE'S RESTAURANT/ MONK'S ROCK

2ND FLOOR RESTAURANT ▼

EL CHICANO RESTAURANT ▼

KASHEVAROFF ST

UPPER

MILL

ALUTIIQ MUSEUM ★

OLD POWER HOUSE RESTAURANT ■

ALASKA FOOD FOR LESS ■

CENTER ST

ADF&G OFFICE ■

ST HERMAN'S ★ SEMINARY

BEST WESTERN KODIAK HOTEL ●

HENRY'S ▼

MISSION RD

RUSSIAN ORTHODOX CHURCH ■

To Airport

HARBORSIDE COFFEE & GOODS ▼

MALL

SUBWAY ▼

ERNIE'S LAUNDROMAT ■

SHELIKOF ST

HARBORMASTER ■

MECCA ■

🌙 BARANOV MUSEUM

KODIAK ISLAND BREWING CO ■

KODIAK NATIONAL WILDLIFE REFUGE VISITOR CENTER ★

TAGURA RD

ISLAND SEAFOODS ▼

MARINE WAY

VISITOR CENTER/FERRY TERMINAL ■

Small Boat Harbor

STAR OF KODIAK ▼

St Paul Harbor

0   0.1 mi

0   0.1 km

SOUTHWEST ALASKA

© AVALON TRAVEL PUBLISHING, INC.

slopes, short fast runoff streams, and rounded kettles. In addition, Kodiak's coastline is so characterized by long fjords that even with a maximum width of 60 miles, no point on the island is over 20 miles from tidewater.

Dense Sitka spruce forests cover the northwest corner of Kodiak Island, along with nearby Afognak and Shuyak islands. The trees are slowly spreading southward, but most of Kodiak is a open mix of tundra, tall grass, bushes, alder, and other plants that turn florescent green in the too-brief peak of summer. Visit in July to see why they call this "The Emerald Isle."

Climate

Expect cool, wet, and windy weather on Kodiak. The average temperature in August, the "hottest" month, is 54°F. Kodiak's record high is 86°F, but most years only half a dozen summer days even exceed 70. Kodiak receives 75 inches of rain a year, of which 12 inches fall June–September. Locals claim that some sun shines one out of every three days—but it can be clear or partly clear for three glorious days, then soupy for nine in a row! Dress warm, and if you intend to explore the backcountry, bring raingear and rubber boots.

SOUTHWEST ALASKA

HISTORY
Russian America

Russian fur trader Glotoff "discovered" Kodiak in 1763 and told Grigorii Shelikov (also spelled Shelikof) about the abundant sea otters there. The island's second-highest peak (4,450 ft.) was named for Glotoff. Shelikov is remembered as the founder of the Russian America Company and the first European settlement in Alaska, at Three Saints Bay, Kodiak, in 1784. This is the site of present-day Old Harbor and had long been an important Alutiiq (also called Koniag) village. To gain the site, Shelikov ordered his men to massacre hundreds of the Alutiiq on the rock where they had taken refuge. Native leaders refer to the battle as "Wounded Knee of Alaska." This slaughter broke the back of Native resistance to Russian rule.

Alexander Baranov (often spelled Baranof) arrived in 1791 to manage the company and colony; he promptly relocated the whole settlement to St. Paul's Harbor (present-day Kodiak town) after a tsunami nearly wiped out the previous town. The Eskimo-related Alutiiq population wasn't sorry to see the Russians and their Aleut slaves move again, in 1800, to New Archangel (Sitka)—except that the sea otters in the vicinity had been almost completely eradicated and, as happened in the Queen Charlottes, the 20,000 Native inhabitants were decimated to 1,500 in a couple of decades because of war and introduced diseases such as smallpox.

Later Years

Kodiak survived the 19th century by fur trading, whaling, fishing, and even ice-making (Russian die-hards began producing ice in the 1850s to supply California gold rush boom towns; they introduced the first horses and built the first roads in Alaska). Salmon fishing really caught on in the early 1900s, and the living was easy until the awesome explosion of Novarupta on Katmai across the strait in 1912. It showered ash down on the town, blanketing fields and villages, crushing roofs, and changing the green island into a gray-brown desert overnight. After 48 hours of total blackness and gasping for air, 450 residents were evacuated by a U.S. revenue cutter in a daring

This Orthodox church in Karluk is a visible sign of the Russian heritage of the Kodiak villages.

© DON PITCHER

rescue. It took over two years for life to return to normal, and the deep ash layer can still be seen on stream-cut banks around the island.

Kodiak, like the rest of Alaska, was mobilized during World War II, but the fortifications here had a more urgent quality: Forts, gun emplacements, submarine bases, and command centers were installed to protect the island from Japanese invasion and to manage the Aleutian campaign. Thousands of servicemen left a large economic legacy as well. The major economic boom for the island came later, in the form of the famous Kodiak king crab, harvested by the hundreds of millions of pounds in the early 1960s. Then the Good Friday earthquake struck in 1964, quaking the earth for over five minutes, then flooding the town for the next 12 hours with several "waves," that first sucked the tidewater out, exposing the harbor bottom, then swept half the town from its moorings with swells up to 35 feet high. For a gripping description of that terrible night—and a fascinating first-hand look at Kodiak fishing life—read *Highliners* by William B. McCloskeY.

Kodiak Today

Since the earthquake, Kodiak has rebuilt and retooled for the harvesting of salmon, halibut, shrimp, herring, and bottom fish (king crab were nearly fished out by 1983). The bottom-fishing industry—especially for pollock—grew dramatically in the 1990s; these "junk fish" are processed into surimi: imitation crab and shrimp meat. Today, Kodiak consistently ranks near the top of U.S. ports in value of fish landed, and there are eight different canneries around the city.

A 1993 *National Geographic* article noted that "Kodiak's the kind of town where you think the municipal emblem ought to be a red pickup hauling a golden retriever, with the truck shaking to a country tune like 'Achy Breaky Heart.'" Despite this impression, visitors to modern-day Kodiak may be surprised to see how diverse the population actually is. Many of the taxi drivers, cannery workers, and other blue-collar employees are of Filipino, Mexican, or Latin American heritage. You'll hear more Spanish spoken here than almost anywhere else in Alaska. A controversial Korean church has a significant presence in the local economy, and the island even has the only state-owned missile spaceport anywhere.

SIGHTS

Wander along the shore to Kodiak's **Small Boat Harbor,** one of the state's most crowded. When the fleet is in, all the masts, rigging, and fishing equipment make the harbor an almost impenetrable thicket. The danger in a seafarer's life is revealed by the monument in front of the harbormaster's office. The plaque lists the names of more than 150 men and women lost at sea.

A high bridge links Kodiak with nearby Near Island, home to a second boat harbor and floatplane dock. **North End Park** is on your left side just after crossing the bridge. An easy half-mile path leads through the woods to a rocky beach where you're rewarded with a good view of the town. The island is also home to **Kodiak Fisheries Research Center** (907/481-

1800, www.afsc.noaa.gov/kodiak, open weekdays), which houses a small interpretive center, along with a fascinating large aquarium and touch tank. Most of the facility is, of course, devoted to research.

Continue left down Shelikof Street to "cannery row," where **Steller sea lions** are often just off the docks. Additional canneries line the shore on either side of the ferry terminal. Certainly the hardest cannery to miss is the ship-ashore **Star of Kodiak.** Originally christened the *Albert M. Boe,* this was the last Liberty Ship built. It was launched in 1945 as a troop ship, but was towed up from the "mothball" fleet after the 1964 tsunami wiped out other canneries in Kodiak. Today it's owned by Trident Seafoods. One of the other plants—International Seafoods—is owned by the controversial Unification Church (otherwise known as the "Moonies"). They also own several commercial fishing boats, a group house/day care center in town, and a lodge along the Ayakulik River. Reverend Moon himself has come here several summers—along with hundreds of followers—to sportfish for salmon.

Join a van tour of town from **Kodiak Tours** (907/486-3920, www.kodiaktours.com) for an introduction to Kodiak sights and history.

Visitor Centers

The **Visitors Information Center** (907/486-4782 or 800/789-4782, www.kodiak.org) shares the same building with the ferry office on Marine Way and Center Street, and is open daily 8 A.M.–5 P.M. late May–early September, and Monday–Friday 8 A.M.–5 P.M. the rest of the year. Pick up the Kodiak Island map and the excellent visitor's guide.

The **Kodiak National Wildlife Refuge Visitor Center** (Mission at Center Sts., 907/487-2600 or 888/408-3514, http://kodiak.fws.gov) opened a sparkling new downtown Kodiak facility in 2007. Inside are exhibits detailing the refuge and its wildlife, a model of the Karluk River ecosystem, a fine orientation film, and the only intact gray whale skeleton in the nation. A variety of interpretive programs are offered.

SOUTHWEST ALASKA

◖ Baranov Museum

Several downtown buildings are reminders of Kodiak's deep Russian heritage. The Baranov Museum (907/486-5920, www.baranov.us, $3, free for kids under 13), housed in the oldest Russian building in North America, was built around 1808 as a storehouse for sea otter pelts. It's open Monday–Saturday 10 A.M.–4 P.M. and noon–4 P.M. in the summer, and Tuesday–Saturday 10 A.M.–3 P.M. the rest of the year. Closed February.

Displays include an impressive Russian samovar and china collection, along with other artifacts such as a 10-kopek note printed on sealskin; it's from Alexander Baranov's time. Also here are Alutiiq and Aleut items, including a remarkable three-person kayak, an impressive collection of historic grass baskets, and a bear-muzzle carving found in 1956 on Cape Douglas. The photos from the 1964 tsunami are hard to believe: Boats were strewn throughout downtown. The **gift shop**—one of the most unusual in Alaska—sells Lomonosov porcelain china, painted Ukrainian Easter eggs, lacquered boxes, Father Frost carvings, and Russian nesting dolls ($6–800). If you have the money, take a look at the gorgeous antique Russian samovars that start around $600; this is the only place in Alaska where you can buy them. Out front are several large whalebones.

Orthodox Church and Seminary

Just across the green on Mission Road and Kashevaroff Street is Holy Resurrection Orthodox Church, under the distinctive blue onion domes. This is the third church in which Kodiak's Orthodox faithful have worshipped since the parish was founded in 1794. It shelters the earthly remains of St. Herman of Spruce Island, the only Russian Orthodox saint in the Western Hemisphere; he was canonized in 1970. The interior contains colorful icons and religious paraphernalia, with a good view of the room from the balcony. To get inside, either put on clean clothes and attend a service (Thurs. at 7:30 P.M., Sat. at 6:30 P.M., or Sun. at 9:30 A.M.) or take a tour (weekdays

at 1 P.M. in the summer). Call the parish priest (907/486-3854) for details. A small gift shop is adjacent.

Walk up toward the bridge overpass to the **St. Herman's Theological Seminary,** one of three Orthodox seminaries in the United States. The beautiful seminary chapel is open all the time, and is worth a visit.

Alutiiq Museum

The Alutiiq Museum (215 Mission Rd., 907/486-7004, www.alutiiqmuseum.com, $3, free for kids under 13) is open Monday–Friday 9 A.M.–5 P.M. and Saturday 10 A.M.–5 P.M. June–August, and Wednesday–Friday 9 A.M.–5 P.M. and Saturday 10:30 A.M.–4:30 P.M. the rest of the year. This collection features a tiny sampling of the thousands of artifacts found during archaeological digs at the village of Karluk (masks, wooden spoons, stone oil lamps, knives, *ulus,* and more), along with a diorama of a prehistoric village, kayak replicas, and other items such as spruce baskets and seal pokes. The museum store sells Native crafts, or you can watch a video on local archaeology. They organize a summertime archaeological dig at Women's Bay that is open to the public.

OUT-OF-TOWN SIGHTS
◖ Fort Abercrombie State Park

This evocative historical and recreational site (907/486-6339, www.alaskastateparks.org) is five miles northeast of town out East Rezanof Drive. The peninsula supports a lush rainforest of huge Sitka spruce thriving on the volcanic ash from Novarupta. Thick chartreuse moss clings to these stately trees. Check out the gun emplacements on the cliff above the bay-ancient cannons that could never have hit the broad side of any Japanese (floating) barn. From this overlook, watch for whales, puffins (one of the few places in Alaska where they can readily be seen from the shore), sea otters, sea lions, and cormorants. The trails are all well maintained, and one takes you past Lake Gertrude to a beautiful beach. The park also has a campground and some fascinating tidepools.

Rangers guide summertime hikes and provide Saturday evening lectures.

The **Kodiak Military History Museum** (907/486-7015, www.kadiak.org, Fri.–Mon. 1–4 P.M. in summer, $3 adults, free for kids under 12) is within a World War II ammunition bunker at Miller Point. Inside is a 1944 Ford jeep and other items from that era. A self-guided tour takes you past other structures from the war; pick up a free brochure at the museum.

To Monashka Bay

Monashka Bay Road begins at Fort Abercrombie State Park and skirts around this bay north of town, passing the Pillar Creek Hatchery, and a black sand beach at the mouth of Pillar Creek, before terminating 11 miles from Kodiak at Monashka Bay, with its shallow bay and delightful sandy beach. Follow the coast north along the beach, and head into the trees to find a trail that continues three miles to a scenic bluff called **Termination Point.**

Pillar Mountain

A good road climbs right up to the top of Pillar Mountain, from which all the overviews of Kodiak town are photographed. Start out at Thorsheim Street and go as far as Maple, where you turn left and go up Pillar Mountain Road. Hikers can scramble up the front of the mountain from Rezanof Drive (west of town)—steep, but much faster than walking up the road.

◖ Exploring Kodiak Roads

All told, Kodiak Island has nearly 100 miles of fun-to-explore roads, making a rental car a wise investment for visitors. A detailed mileage guide for all the roads is found in the *Kodiak Island Visitors Guide,* but even better is the outstanding *Kodiak Audubon's Hiking & Birding Guide,* a very detailed waterproof map and guide to wild places on the road system. It's available at the visitor center for $12.

The longest road—**Chiniak Road**—heads south from town all the way to Cape Chiniak (43 miles). The drive is worth the time, even if it's

VICINITY OF KODIAK

© DON PITCHER

moss-covered rainforest, Fort Abercrombie State Park

foggy or raining, to see this part of the Emerald Isle. The first 12 miles are paved. Four miles out is the **Kodiak National Wildlife Refuge** visitor center, and **Buskin River State Recreation Site,** with campsites and great fishing in late summer for Dolly Varden and coho.

Another mile down Chiniak Road is the unmarked turnoff to **Anton Larsen Bay,** on the island's northwest tip. This winding 12-mile, mostly-gravel road goes by Coast Guard communications towers, a golf course, trailheads to pointy Pyramid Peak and Cascade Lake, and finally the boat launching area on this scenic and protected fjord.

Back on Chiniak Road, cruise by the airport (Mile 5) and the trail to Barometer Mountain (see the *Hiking* section) to the overlook of the **U.S. Coast Guard Station** at Mile 6. Largest in the nation (21,000 acres), this support center is home to four large cutters and more than 1,100 personnel. Main activities include patrolling the 200-mile fishing zone for illegal fishing (offenders are mostly Japanese and Russian trawlers), as well as search and rescue for commercial fishing boats.

Beyond the Coast Guard Station, the road continues around scenic Women's Bay and on to Kalsin Bay (Mile 30), where you'll find the aging Kalsin Bay Inn—best known for its hat collection. Scan nearby slopes for mountain goats, especially in the spring or fall.

Several pretty beaches are located over the next 10 miles, including **Roslyn Bay Beach** at Mile 37. Not far away is **Kodiak Island Winery** (907/486-4848, www.kodiakwinery.com), where they make berry and rhubarb wines in a spectacular shoreside setting. The wine-tasting room sits on the second floor of a converted barn, and is open daily 1–6 P.M. in the summer. The road ends at Mile 43 near Chiniak Point on the island's eastern tip, and a trail leads to the point itself. The old-timey **Road's End Lounge** (907/486-2885) is open for lunch and dinner if you can tolerate the smoke.

A side route, **Pasagshak Bay Road,** turns south off Chiniak Road in Kalsin Bay and leads nine miles to **Pasagshak River State Recreation Site** with free camping and a great beach. Beyond this, the road continues to Narrow Cape (16 miles from Kalsin Bay) where you're treated to all-encompassing views. Be sure to take the rather steep side road (not for RVs) to **Fossil Beach,** a fascinating and remote place to look for rocks containing fossilized shells. The beach is also a favorite of local surfers. Several of Kodiak's large cattle ranches are visible along the Chiniak and Pasagshak Bay roads, and near Narrow Cape you're likely to see grazing buffalo—part of a herd of 400 that wander freely here. It's a 47-mile drive from Kodiak to the end of the road.

Kodiak Island's unlikeliest surprise is also at Narrow Cape, the **Kodiak Launch Complex** (907/273-1582). The first rocket launch here took place in 1998, and the site will continue to be used to blast military satellites into low polar orbits, and as a base for the testing of "Star Wars" interceptor missiles. See www.akaerospace .com for information on upcoming launches.

Shuyak Island State Park

Shuyak Island is 50 miles and a 40-minute floatplane trip north from Kodiak (or south from Homer); a flight that takes you to another world. This 47,000-acre park contains virgin Sitka spruce forests and a gorgeous coastline pockmarked with small islands and protected waterways. It's perfect for sea kayaking and wildlife watching. Kayak rentals are available within the park from **Mythos Expeditions** (907/486-5536, www.thewildcoast.com), but reserve early.

The state maintains four excellent public-use cabins at Shuyak for $75. Each can sleep up to eight people, and includes a propane cookstove, woodstove, water system, outhouse, and shower. Two of these—**Eagle's Nest Cabin** and **Salmon Cove Cabin**—are within Big Bay, and the other two are **Deer Haven Cabin** in Carry Inlet and **Mulcahy View Cabin** in Neketa Bay. There are only a few hiking trails on Shuyak, and the dense devil's club makes bushwhacking very difficult; it is possible to hike along the shore at low tide if you don't have a kayak.

Request a brochure on Shuyak sea kayaking or make cabin reservations by contacting Alaska State Parks (907/486-6339, www.alaskastateparks.org). The cabins are generally available, but reserve well ahead for the silver salmon run in September.

Afognak Island

This large island lies 30 miles north of Kodiak Island, but is vastly different from its neighbor. Afognak is—or rather was—covered with a luxuriant, dense spruce forest. Unfortunately, much of this spectacular country was logged in the 1990s by the local Native corporation. Much of what remains is within the 49,000-acre **Afognak Island State Park** on the east side of the island, where the land is covered with a mix of forested areas and alpine country. A public use cabin at **Pillar Lake** (907/486-6339, www.alaskastateparks.org, $35) has space for up to six people. The cabin is used as a base for backcountry hiking, fishing, and hunting. A raft or kayak is useful for getting around on Pillar Lake, and you can reach the alpine in approximately an hour of

hiking. When making flight arrangements for the Pillar Lake Cabin, make sure the air taxi service can land on wheels at Izhut Bay beach near the cabin. In addition, the U.S. Fish & Wildlife Service (907/487-2600 or 888/408-3514, http://kodiak.fws.gov, $30) has a wheelchair-accessible cabin in remote **Blue Fox Bay** on Afognak Island.

Another area that managed to escape the chainsaw is the property that surrounds **Afognak Wilderness Lodge** (907/486-6442 or 800/478-6442, www.afognaklodge.com). Anyone willing to part with $700 per person per day (including three meals, guides, and accommodations) will find some of the finest old-time accommodations in Alaska.

Afognak Native Corporation are the folks behind the wholesale clear-cutting of Afognak's forests, but they have four rental cabins ($150) in unlogged sections. Reservations are through **Andrew Airways** (907/487-2566, www.andrewairways.com).

Port Lions

This community of 250 people came into existence after the 1964 earthquake and tsunami destroyed the nearby village of Afognak. It was named to honor the funding and support from the Lions International Club that led to its establishment. The town has a commercial fishing base and also has a handful of lodges, eating places, and stores. The state ferry stops here, and there is air taxi service to the surrounding country.

Contact **Whale Pass Lodge** (907/454-2500 or 800/456-3425, www.whalepasslodge.com) or **Port Lions Lodge** (907/454-2264 or 800/808-8447, www.portlionslodge.com) for fishing packages and whale-watching.

Old Harbor

Located along protected Sitkalidak Straits near the center of Kodiak Island, this village of 250 people has a mixed Native and Russian heritage, and is home to a lovely Russian Orthodox church and an active fishing fleet. Ongoing archaeological digs continue each summer on sites 8,500 years old.

Find accommodations and meals at **Mountain View Guest House** (907/286-2274) or multi-night stays at the fishing lodges: **Kodiak Sportsman's Lodge** (907/286-9246, www.kodiaksportsmanslodge.com) or **Ocean View Lodge** (907/286-2381). There are no cafes, but limited groceries are available. **Servant Air** (907/487-4444 or 866/487-9001, www.servant air.com) has daily flights from Kodiak.

ENTERTAINMENT AND EVENTS

You'd expect a town whose inhabitants live close to the "Edge" to party hearty, and Kodiak definitely won't disappoint. You don't even have to venture any farther than downtown, whose many storefronts are half occupied by bars, big bars. After a big salmon opener, a beer can thrown in any direction would hit a drunk fisherman.

The **Mecca** (907/486-3364) has a popular dance floor; this place competes with the ocean for rockin' and rollin'! For hard drinking with the highliners, sit down at **The Village** or **Tony's**. Tony's advertises itself as the "biggest navigational hazard on Kodiak" and simultaneously "a friendly neighborhood bar with over 3,000,000 drinks spilled." **Tropic Lounge** is a huge bar where some people go bowling. For TV sports, a big choice of draught beers, and good pub grub, head to **Henry's** (512 Marine Way, 907/486-3313), where the decor includes a gorgeous Chilkat robe and other Alaskan pieces of the past. Otherwise, take in a flick at **Orpheum Theater** (on Center St., 907/486-5449).

If you're heading out to Pasagshak Bay, you may want to stop at **Kalsin Bay Inn** (907/486-2659), an old place with an impressive collection of military caps from Navy and Coast Guard ships, signed dollar bills, and big bear photos. It's 30 miles south of Kodiak.

Events

The new year begins with a masquerade ball and celebration of **Russian New Year** in mid-January. Shortly before this is the **Starring ceremony,** during which a choir follows a twirling star to the home of the Russian Orthodox faithful.

The infamous **Pillar Mountain Golf Classic,** on at the end of March, is a deranged, par-70, one-hole tournament up the side of this 1,400-foot mountain behind town. The course, cleared by spotters with machetes, runs all the way to the peak, where a bucket in the snow serves as the hole and lime Jell-O as the green. No power tools allowed, so leave your chainsaw at home.

In mid-April, **Whalefest** celebrates the return of migrating whales with tours, performances, and other productions. The big summertime event on Kodiak is the **Crab Festival,** held on Memorial Day weekend. There's a parade, survival suit races, a foot race, blessing of the fleet, and various concerts. Lots of fun.

The **Kodiak State Fair and Rodeo** comes around on Labor Day weekend, and features everything from craft demonstrations and live music to stock car races and a small-town rodeo with bull riders.

RECREATION

Horseback rides are available from two working cattle ranches south of town near Pasagshak Bay: **Burton's Ranch** (907/486-3705) and **Northland Ranch Resort** (907/486-5578).

Rent a mountain bike from **58° North** (1231 Mill Bay Rd., 907/486-6249). This is also a good place to buy outdoor gear, snowboards, clothes, and even sea kayaks. Just up the street is **Orion's Mountain Sports** (907/486-8380), with more backcountry supplies, including surfboards and wetsuits.

The nine-hole **Bear Valley Golf Course** (907/486-8783) is out Anton Larson Bay Road.

Hiking

Many hikes are available around Kodiak, in addition to those at Pillar Mountain, Fort Abercrombie, and the Termination Point Trail; drop by the visitor center for an outstanding waterproof hiking and birding map ($12) that details 40 popular routes. On summer weekends **Kodiak Audubon** leads free weekend hikes from this office at 9:30 A.M. Call Hans Tshersich (907/486-5648) for details.

Pyramid Peak has two trailheads off Anton

Larsen Bay Road that climb this precipitous, 2,400-foot mountain just west of town. Start near the ski lift 1.5 miles past the golf course. Great vistas from the summit of Kodiak's mountainous interior. **Barometer Mountain Trail** is a steep five-mile hike to the 2,500-foot peak. It starts at an unmarked (but recognizable) trailhead on the first road to the right past the airport runway out Rezanof Drive West. This is one of the most popular local hikes.

Sea Kayaking
Wendy Eskew of **Alaskan Wilderness Adventures** (907/487-2397, www.alaskan wildernessadventures.com) leads half-day kayak trips for $100 per person, and 2.5-hour trip from Kodiak town for $75.

Orcas Unlimited (907/539-1979, www.orcas unlimited.com) offers guided all-day trips at Anton Larson Bay ($180 per person), mother ship day trips to Marmot Bay ($180–220), and five-day all-inclusive mother ship adventures.

Fishing and Boating
Kodiak is world famous as a fishing destination, with remote fishing lodges, charter halibut and salmon fishing boats, and surprisingly good road-accessible fishing. Pick up the informative sport fishing brochure from the visitors information center, which also has a listing of more than 30 charter operators. The same info is online at www.kodiak.org. The **Kodiak Charter Association** (907/486-6363 or 888/972-6363, www.kodiakcharterassn.net) books for a number of these companies, and can also set up bear-viewing and flightseeing trips. Find their booking desk inside Best Western Kodiak Inn.

ACCOMMODATIONS
The Visitor's Bureau website (www.kodiak.org) has links to many local lodging places, and is a good place to start when looking over the lodging options.

Motels
Two modest motels are right in the heart of town. **Shelikof Lodge** (211 Thorsheim Ave., 907/486-4141, www.shelikoflodge.com, $80 s

or $90 d) offers well-maintained rooms (many with fridges and microwaves), Wi-Fi, and a courtesy van to the airport. Nearby is **Russian Heritage Inn** (119 Yukon St., 907/486-5657, www.russianheritageinn.com) with a mix of rooms, all with fridges, microwaves, and Wi-Fi. Standard rooms are $80 d, kitchenettes are $90 d, and two-room suites cost $120 d.

Best Western Kodiak Inn (236 Rezanof W., 907/486-5712 or 888/563-4254, www.kodiak inn.com, $139–149 d, $179–209 d for suites) is one of the nicer local motels, with microwaves and fridges in all rooms, plus a hot tub, Wi-Fi, continental breakfast, and courtesy airport shuttle.

Recently remodeled, **Comfort Inn** (1395 Airport Way, 907/487-2700 or 800/544-2202, www.choicehotels.com) is a 50-room motel close to the airport (5 miles from town). Small rooms (with fridges and microwaves) are $170 d, and suites cost $220–230 d. Free Wi-Fi and continental breakfast. Eagle's Landing Restaurant is also on the premises, with brunch and dinner.

B&Bs and Guest Houses
The Visitor's Bureau website (www.kodiak.org) provides links to more than 50 local B&Bs and vacation rentals. For something simple, **Berry Patch B&B** (1616 Selief Lane, 907/486-6593, www.berrypatchbb.com, $60 s or $70 d) provides accommodations in two guest rooms with a full breakfast.

Beaver Creek Lodge B&B (907/487-4636, www.bclodgekodiak.com) is 11 miles south along the Russian River. The spacious home has a stone hearth, big home-cooked breakfasts, and friendly owners. Anglers appreciate such services as fish processing and rental gear, while honeymooners love the quiet setting and outdoor hot tub.

Right in town, **Kodiak B&B** (308 Cope St., 907/486-5367, http://home.gci.net/~mmonroe, $90 s or $115 d) has two guest rooms sharing a bath, full breakfasts, and a fine harbor view from the deck. In business since 1986, this is the oldest B&B on Kodiak Island.

Emerald Isle B&B (1214 Madsen St., 907/486-4427 or 866/399-4427, www.kodiaklodging

.com, $85 s or $95 d) has five bedrooms with private or shared baths, a patio, Wi-Fi, and a light breakfast. Dinners may also be available.

Eider House B&B (782 Sargent Creek Rd., 907/487-4315, www.eiderhouse.com, $120 d) features four guest rooms with private baths, a full breakfast, Wi-Fi, and a peaceful wooded setting south of town. It's especially popular with fishermen who appreciate the separate room to clean your catch.

Head 35 miles south from Kodiak to **9th Wave B&B** (907/486-0838, www.9thwave bnb.com, $125 d), where the rustic log home faces Kalsiin Bay and Barometer Mountain. Four guest rooms have private baths, and a continental breakfast and guest computer are included.

Other recommended Kodiak B&Bs include **Beachside B&B** (907/486-4941, www.beachsidebandb.com, $80 s or $90 d) on the water just north of town, **A Smiling Bear B&B** (907/481-6390, www.ptialaska.net/~djturner, $100–125 s or $125–150 d) north of town along Monashka Bay, and **Lagoonside B&B** (907/486-5445, www.chiniak.net/lagoonside, $125 d) in a serene spot 35 miles south of Kodiak at Chiniak.

Several guesthouses are available for families or couples looking for their own place to settle into the Kodiak scene. **Parkside Guesthouse** (907/486-9446, www.parksideguesthouse.com, $150 d) is an attractively furnished, new home next to Fort Abercrombie State Park. Also check out two places in the rainforest near Chiniak 37 miles south of town: **Distant Loon Cabin** (907/486-1789, www.chiniak.net/distantloon, $100 d) a nicely appointed cabin, and **Roslyn Ridge Retreat** (907/486-5972, http://home.gci.net/~roslyn, $250 d) a gorgeous two-bedroom home with a hot tub.

Wilderness Lodges

Kodiak is home to more than 30 remote lodges, most focused on fishing, bear-viewing, and hunting, with all-inclusive rates, and access by floatplane. Visit www.kodiak.org, for links to most of these. A few of the more established lodges are **Kodiak Lodge** (907/847-2348 or

888/556-3425, www.kodiaklodge.com), **Larsen Bay Lodge** (907/847-2238 or 800/748-2238, www.larsenbaylodge.com), **Munsey's Bear Camp** (907/847-2203, www.munseysbearcamp.com), **Raspberry Island Remote Camps** (907/486-1781, www.raspberryisland.com), **Spirit of Alaska Wilderness Adventures** (800/677-8641, www.spiritofalaska.com), **Uyak Bay Lodge** (907/847-2350, www.uyakbaylodge.com), and **Zachar Bay Lodge** (907/486-4120 or 800/693-2333, www.zacharbay.com).

Kodiak Treks (907/487-2122, www.kodiak treks.com) offers overnight lodging and meals, bear-viewing hikes, and multi-day hiking trips from the lodge at Uyak Bay on the west side of Kodiak Island.

CAMPING

The closest official campground, **Buskin River State Recreation Site** (campsites $15), is four miles south of town on Buskin Beach Road next to the airport. This is an OK site on the water, with shelters, pit toilets, trails, and runways in your ear. RVers appreciate the flat sites with plenty or room, and fishermen will find plenty of salmon to catch.

A quieter option is **Fort Abercrombie State Park** ($15) on the eastern tip of town, five miles away. It's worth the hitch, bike ride, or extra miles on the rental car—this is a magical place to pass your nights on Kodiak. The sites are beneath tall spruce trees and out of the weather.

Pasagshak River State Recreation Site, 40 miles south of town, also has camping (no charge) at the mouth of this popular salmon-fishing river.

Park RVs year-round at **VFW RV Park** (907/486-5816, $30 with hookups) seven miles north of town out Monashka Bay Road. You may also be able to use the Wal-Mart parking lot.

FOOD
Coffeehouses

Kodiak's favorite hangout is **Harborside Coffee & Goods** (216 Shelikof, 907/486-5862), with lattes, pastries, fresh soups, bagels, and rich espresso shakes. It's a wonderful place to relax on a rainy day.

Monk's Rock Coffee House (202 E. Rezanof Dr., 907/486-0905), is undoubtedly Kodiak's most distinctive gathering place, run by a splinter group of the Russian Orthodox Church. Icons line the walls, and you can check out the books, samovars, and handmade prayer ropes, buy some freshly baked bread, enjoy a sandwich, smoothie, or ice cream. Pick up the brochure about nearby Spruce Island, a fascinating place to learn about the rich Russian Orthodox history, and to meet monks at St. Michael's Skete.

Don't miss Kodiak's legendary **《 Mill Bay Coffee & Pastry** (3833 E. Rezanof Dr., 907/486-4411, www.millbaycoffee.com), where baker Joel Chenet once served as head chef for the president of France! When you taste the chocolate éclairs you'll know why; I've never tasted better anywhere. Delectable pastries and cakes fill the cases, but the café also serves waffles and light breakfasts, quiche, French onion soup, salads, sandwiches, and a locally famous Kodiak salmon burger. The shop is out near Fort Abercrombie, making this a fine lunch stop. Five stars. Most lunch items are around $10, with breakfast waffles for $5 and up. Free Wi-Fi too.

All-American

Locals looking for the best burgers and other dense American grub head to **King's Diner** (beside Lilly Lake at 1941 Mill Bay Rd., 907/486-4100). It's open for breakfast and lunch daily, but closes at 3 P.M. Lots of food for the money: $6 for biscuits, gravy, eggs, and hashbrowns. Noisy, family-friendly, and recommended. They close at 3 P.M.

Get good pub grub at **Henry's Great Alaskan Restaurant** (512 Marine Way, 907/486-8844), where the menu covers the spectrum of pasta, burgers, seafood, fish & chips, along with nightly specials—including a Wednesday crawfish pie. This lively (and somewhat smoky) sports bar is right downtown across from the harbor.

Subway (326 Center, 907/486-7676) is open until 11 P.M. in the summer, and the downtown McDonald's has an indoor playground for kids in need of a rainy-day break.

Big Al's Pizzeria (2161 Mill Bay Rd., 907/486-0044), inside Cost-Savers, makes the best local pizzas, and also sells by the slice.

International

El Chicano (103 Center St., 907/486-6116, $11–15), serves Mexican food in a party atmosphere, with chiles rellenos, homemade tamales, *chorizo con huevos*, and even a little menudo for your hangover. But you might as well start another one; their margaritas go down easy. For the fast version, look for the **Martha's Place** (907/496-0752), a taco truck that can be spotted in various parts of town. This is authentic and tasty.

Several places serve Chinese meals, including **Kodiak Mongolian Barbecue** (1247 Mill Bay Rd., 907/486-2900), an all-you-can-stuff-in place where the chef cooks your spicy meal while you watch.

Eugene's Restaurant (202 E. Rezanof Dr., 907/486-2625) has reasonable prices and a downtown location. Closed Mondays. Across the street is **2nd Floor** (907/486-8555), with a more formal setting and good—but expensive—Japanese food, including tempura and sushi.

Fine Dining

Just a block up the street from the ferry terminal, **《 The Old Power House Restaurant** (516 E. Marine Way, 907/481-1088, $15–25 dinner entrées) has quickly established itself as Kodiak's classiest restaurant. Seafood and steaks occupy important places on the menu, but sushi and sashimi are the real standouts, especially the spicy tuna rolls. Open for lunch and dinner; closed Mondays.

Operated by chef/master gardener/author Marion Owen (www.upbeetcommunications.com) and her harbormaster husband Marty Owen, **《 Galley Gourmet** (907/486-2500 or 800/253-6331, www.kodiak-alaska-dinner-cruises.com) is the perfect way to spend a relaxing evening. Three-hour cruises take place onboard their immaculate 42-foot motor yacht, with time to watch for sea lions, otters, puffins, and whales. The boat anchors in a quiet bay off

Long Island for a sit-down meal of creative appetizers, seafood entrées, organic salads, and desserts. The cost is $120 per person July–September, or $95 in May and June. Various other trips are also available, including all-day hiking adventures or whale-watching.

Groceries

Many visitors to Kodiak buy their groceries at the downtown **Alaska Food for Less** (907/486-5761), but the best selection is at **Safeway** (2 miles out Mill Bay Rd., 907/486-6811). It's said to be the largest Safeway in the western United States, but prices are equally inflated.

Island Seafoods (330 Shelikof Ave., 907/486-8575 or 800/355-8575, www.island seafoods.com), next to the harbor, has a retail shop with salmon, scallops, halibut, shrimp, and king crab; they will process and ship your sport-caught fish.

Alcohol

❰ Kodiak Island Brewing Co. (338 Shelikof Ave., 907/486-2537, www.kodiakbrewery.com, daily 2–7 P.M.) is opposite the harbor. Owner/brewer Ben Millstein typically has a half-dozen brews, most notably the Sweet Georgia Brown and a Liquid Sunshine pale ale. They're available to go in growlers and pigs.

Located 36 miles south of town along beautiful Rosalyn Beach, **Kodiak Island Winery** (907/486-4848, www.kodiakwinery.com, April–Sept.) is best known for their salmonberry wine, but also produces other wines from local fruits, plus a unique rhubarb champagne. A second winery, **Alaskan Wilderness Wines** (907/486-1420, www.alaskawildwine.com), is based in the little settlement of Port Lions. Both company's wines are available in local stores.

SHOPPING AND SERVICES

Budget shoppers head to Kodiak's **Wal-Mart** (907/486-1670); it's three miles north of town on Mill Bay Road.

The too-small **library** (319 Lower Mill Bay Rd., 907/486-8680, www.city.kodiak.ak.us) downtown has books on Alaskan history, plus

computers for surfing the Web. **Fly-By Coffee** on Mill Bay Road at Lily Lake has free Wi-Fi.

The Next Page (3833 E. Rezanof Dr., 907/481-7243) is a fine little bookshop with a good selection of works by local artisans. Mill Bay Coffee & Pastry is adjacent. Also check out **The Treasury** (104 Center St., 907/486-0373) for gifts and Internet access, and **Northern Exposure Gallery** (1314 Mill Bay Rd., 907/486-4956) for prints.

For an indoor shower, head straight to **Dillard's Stop or Drop Laundromat** (907/486-2345), across the street from the Small Boat Harbor on Shelikof.

Providence Kodiak Island Medical Center (1915 E. Rezanof, 907/486-3281, www.providence.org/alaska/kodiak) is the local hospital.

GETTING THERE
On the Water

If you have time and want to save a bundle on transportation, catch the **Alaska Marine Highway's** (800/642-0066, www.ferry alaska.com) trusty *Tustumena* in Homer, arriving in Kodiak 12 hours later (some runs include a stop in Port Lions). This is a great, relaxing way to reach Kodiak, but take seasickness pills upon boarding—you'll need them! A Fish & Wildlife Service naturalist is onboard to help identify whales and birds along the way, especially around the Barren Islands. Twice a month in the summer the *"Tusty"* also heads west out the Aleutians all the way to Dutch Harbor. The larger (and more stable) *Kennicott* has additional summertime sailings from Homer and Whittier. The downtown Kodiak ferry terminal (907/486-3800) is open Monday–Friday 8 A.M.–5 P.M.

Air

Era Aviation (907/266-8394 or 800/866-8394, www.eraaviation.com) and **Alaska Airlines** (800/426-0333, www.alaskaair.com), both have daily flights from Anchorage. If you're a little short on time and don't want to ride the ferry, this is the way to experience Kodiak. On the way down, if you're very lucky the *Tustumena* docked at Kodiak's ferry terminal

© DON PITCHER

and it's clear, sit on the right side of the plane for a view of Mounts McKinley and Foraker, down to Mounts Spurr, Redoubt, Illiamna, and even Augustine—nearly 500 miles of spectacular peaks with just a slight twist of your head. You'll also see enormous swaths of clear-cut Native land on Afognak Island. On the way back, also sit on the right to see the vast Harding Icefield and Kenai Mountains. The airport is five miles from Kodiak town. A cab ride costs $15.

Air Taxis

A number of companies offer flightseeing and floatplane flights to various parts of Kodiak from the dock on Near Island (across the bridge). They include **Sea Hawk Air** (907/486-8282 or 800/770-4295, www.seahawkair.com), **Island Air** (907/486-6196 or 800/478-6196, www.kodiakislandair.com), **Andrew Airways** (907/487-2566, www.andrewairways.com),

Harvey Flying Service (907/487-2621, www.harveyflyingservice.com), **Kingfisher Aviation** (907/486-5155 or 866/486-5155, www.kingfisheraviation.com), and **Bear Quest Aviation** (907/486-2327 or 888/304-2327, www.bearquestaviation.com). Harvey Flying Service uses a classic Grumman Widgeon built in 1943—one of the few still flying in Alaska. If you want to fly with one of the finest pilots in Alaska, ask for Rolan Ruoss at Sea Hawk Air. Most air taxis offer **bear-viewing** flights around Kodiak or to the Alaska Peninsula.

Operating from the airport, **Servant Air** (907/487-4444 or 866/487-9001, www.servant air.com) provides daily wheeled-plane flights to Old Harbor, Ouzinkie, Port Lions, Karluk, Larson Bay, and Akhiok. Island Air has scheduled floatplane service to the same villages.

GETTING AROUND
Car Rentals and Taxis

Avis (907/487-2264 or 800/478-2847) and **Budget** (907/487-2220 or 800/527-0700) both have cars at the airport for around $70 a day with unlimited miles. The Budget folks also run **Rent-A-Heap** (907/486-8550), located downtown, where rates are $37 a day plus 37 cents a mile—good for short jaunts, but not if you plan to really explore Kodiak's wonderful back roads. **A&B Taxicabs** (907/486-4343) charges $12 north to Fort Abercrombie or $15 south to the airport.

KODIAK NATIONAL WILDLIFE REFUGE

Established in 1941 to preserve brown bear habitat on Kodiak, this 1.9 million-acre refuge covers the southwestern two-thirds of the island, along with Uganik Island, Ban Island, and a small portion of Afognak Island. Headquarters (907/487-2600 or 888/408-3514, http://kodiak.fws.gov) are near the Buskin River south of town, and newly opened **Kodiak National Wildlife Refuge Visitor Center** (Mission at Center St., 907/487-2600 or 888/408-3514, http://kodiak.fws.gov) is downtown.

Kodiak National Wildlife Refuge itself begins 25 miles southwest of headquarters and is

BEAR-VIEWING

In the last decade or so a very hopeful trend has begun in Alaska: More and more people come to watch living bears than to kill them for trophies. Bear-viewing is a booming business in some parts of the state, and visitors never forget their first sighting. There are plenty of bears to see in Alaska if you know where to look and are willing to take the time, effort, and money to get there. Most folks, however, choose a package trip to one of the better-known viewing areas where the bears have become habituated to the presence of humans.

See *Avoiding Bear Hugs* and *Protecting Yourself During a Bear Encounter* in the *Interior* chapter for tips on safe travel in bear country. These recommendations especially apply to photographers who sometimes get so distracted that they put themselves in dangerous situations. Long lenses (300 mm or greater) are useful for those full-face shots at McNeil or Brooks Camp, but bring a range of lenses or zooms to get more variety in your photos. A tripod is highly recommended if you're shooting with a telephoto. Be sure to use a fast enough shutter speed to stop the action, generally at least 1/500 second (or faster).

The **Alaska Public Information Center** in Anchorage (907/271-2737, www.nps.gov/aplic) has a free publication on bear-viewing in Alaska. See the appropriate chapters of this book for details on the following bear-viewing areas.

BROWN BEARS

The most famous places to see and photograph brown bears are **Denali National Park** (www.nps.gov/dena) in Interior Alaska, **Brooks Camp** within Katmai National Park and Preserve (www.nps.gov/katm), and at nearby **McNeil River State Game Sanctuary** (www.wc.adfg.state.ak.us/mcneil). Some boats and planes also offer bear-viewing day trips to coastal **Lake Clark National Park** (www.nps.gov/lacl). On Kodiak Island, bear-viewing centers around **Frazer Lake** within the Kodiak National Wildlife Refuge (http://kodiak.fws.gov), but most of the bear-viewing flights out of Kodiak actually head to the Katmai coast. In Southeast Alaska, the most popular area is **Pack Creek** (www.fs.fed.us/r10/tongass) on Admiralty Island, though you will also see brown bears at Anan Creek and Fish Creek.

In addition to the official bear-viewing areas, quite a few air-taxi operators fly out of Anchorage, Homer, Kodiak, Soldotna, and King Salmon on day-long trips in search of brown bears. Most of these head to the outer coast of Katmai National Park and Preserve for $400–600 per person.

BLACK BEARS

The best Alaskan places to see black bears (and some brownies) are **Anan Creek** near Wrangell and **Fish Creek** near Hyder, both within Tongass National Forest (www.fs.fed.us/r10/tongass).

POLAR BEARS

In Alaska, polar bears are most abundant within the Arctic National Wildlife Refuge (http://arctic.fws.gov), but they are occasional visitors to **Barrow** and the village of **Kaktovik**, particularly during the spring and fall whaling seasons when the carcasses attract bears. Local taxis may be able to take visitors to places where the bears are seen, but there is no guarantee of seeing a polar bear. These are powerful and dangerous creatures, and passenger vehicles do not really provide protection from a bear attack.

If you're really looking for polar bears, head to Churchill in Manitoba, Canada, where special tundra buggy vehicles provide safe platforms for viewing and photography.

accessible only by floatplane (unless you have a boat or are willing to do some Olympic-class hiking). Most visitors to the refuge fly to one of the lakes and camp or stay in a Fish & Wildlife Service cabin. Many others stay at one of the expensive wilderness fishing lodges around the island.

Bear-Viewing

Kodiak is world renowned for its enormous brown bears. The largest reach 10 feet tall when standing and approach 1,500 pounds, and most adult males (boars) average 800 pounds, with adult females (sows) averaging 550 pounds. Of the 10 largest brown bears ever killed, 8 were taken on Kodiak Island. There are some 2,500 bears on the island, or an average of one for every 1.5 square miles! Visitors often come to watch or photograph these magnificent animals. Unfortunately, quite a few hunters come to kill them as well. Anyone who has spent time around Kodiak bears quickly gains an appreciation for their beauty, and a respect for their intelligence. Hunting for food is justifiable; how someone could kill such an animal to just mount as a trophy—often in a ludicrously menacing position—may be less so.

Assuming that you're on Kodiak to see—rather than kill—the bears, several local air taxi operators will fly you on four-to-five-hour bear-viewing trips. The price varies depending upon the number of passengers, from around $450 per person for two people, down to $375 each for groups of six. This includes at least an hour on the ground watching the bears. Depending upon the weather and what the bears are doing, these floatplanes land either within Kodiak National Wildlife Refuge (the fishpass at Frazer Lake is a popular destination) or to the west on the coast of Katmai National Park and Preserve. The companies include my favorite (by far) **Sea Hawk Air** (907/486-8282 or 800/770-4295, www.seahawkair.com), along with **Andrew Airways** (907/487-2566, www.andrewairways.com), **Kingfisher Aviation** (907/486-5155 or 866/486-5155, www.kingfisheraviation.com), and **Bear**

Quest Aviation (907/486-2327 or 888/304-2327, www.bearquestaviation.com).

Kodiak Island lodges specializing in bear-viewing include **Kodiak Treks** (907/487-2122, www.kodiaktreks.com), **Munsey's Bear Camp** (907/847-2203, www.munseysbearcamp.com), **Rohrer Bear Camp** (907/486-5835, http://home.gci.net/~sportfishkodiak), and **Zachar Bay Lodge** (907/486-4120 or 800/693-2333, www.zacharbay.com).

These bear-viewing flights and lodges are not, of course, the only way to see brown bears. They are present along all of Kodiak's salmon streams in midsummer (best time is July), especially where there are major runs of sockeye or king salmon. Ask at the visitor center for your best viewing opportunities. In late summer the bears tend to move up to the smaller spawning streams and into berry patches where they are less visible. You aren't likely to see a brown bear from the Kodiak road system; most of the bears were shot long ago, and the rest tend to stay out of sight in the day.

Hiking

The vast Kodiak National Wildlife Refuge is undeveloped country with few trails (other than those created by bears and deer). Despite this, backcountry hiking can be relatively easy since there are almost no trees on the southern three-fourths of the island. The best time is early in summer after the snow is gone and before the grass and brush get too dense; by mid-August hiking can be a real struggle. Besides, it's a bit more risky crawling through bear country when the willow thickets are too dense to see the bears! Be sure to make noise while hiking to alert bears of your presence. Once you get above the brush line (approximately 2,000 ft. in elevation) the hiking gets very easy even in late summer. Much of Kodiak Island is marshy, so rubber boots are highly advised.

Floating Karluk River

The Karluk and Ayakulik rivers are world-famous for their king, sockeye, and silver salmon runs, but also have impressive runs of pink and chum salmon, along with Dolly Varden, steelhead, and rainbow trout. At the turn of the century—before seven local canneries wiped the salmon out and then went out of business—the Karluk River had runs of up to 10 million red salmon! It has taken decades of careful Fish and Game management for the populations to recover, but today this is some of the finest fishing anywhere on the planet.

The most popular time to float the 25-mile-long Karluk River is at peak of the king salmon run in July. Kodiak air taxis can drop you off either at the Karluk Lake outlet or Portage, halfway downriver. Most of these companies also rent rafts. A free **public-use permit** from the F&WS (907/487-2600 or 888/408-3514, http://kodiak.fws.gov) is required for the Karluk River, and just 28 permits are allowed per day during the king salmon season (June 10–July 15). Because of their popularity, these are on a lottery system.

The Karluk River enters the waters of Shelikof Straits near the tiny village of **Karluk** (pop. 30), where you'll find a picturesque old Russian Orthodox church (built in 1888), along with a spectacular cliff-and-ocean backdrop. There is also a small store and a couple of fishing lodges. Daily plane service takes you back to Kodiak.

Cabins

The wildlife refuge maintains rustic public-use cabins ($30) at seven different locations around Kodiak and Afognak islands. These provide a wonderful way to see the wilderness up-close and personal. You will need to bring fuel oil for the heater, plus all the standard camping supplies. And don't forget insect repellent and headnets for the abundant and pesky no-see-ums. Because of their popularity, mail-in lotteries are held for the cabins on the first days of January, April, July, and October. Apply before January for the months of April–June, and before April for the months of July–September. The most popular time is July. Because of cancellations, the cabins sometimes become open; call the refuge at 907/487-2600 or 888/408-3514 if you decide to go at the last minute.

Anyone interested in bear-viewing may want to check out the cabins at **South Frazer Lake** or **Uganik Lake.** It's very helpful to have an inflatable boat or folding kayak to get around these lakes; air-taxi operators have them for rent. It is also possible to camp out anywhere on the refuge without a permit. The abundance of both bears and rain can make this a less enjoyable experience, but experienced backcountry travelers will enjoy the chance to savor an untouched landscape.

Alaska Peninsula

LAKE CLARK NATIONAL PARK

This 3.6 million-acre national park reaches from the western shore of Cook Inlet and across the Chigmit Mountains to enclose 50-mile-long Lake Clark. The park was established in 1980. Although there are a few lodges and cabins, the only developed site within the park is **Port Alsworth** (pop. 60) on the east side Lake Clark. Despite the name, Port Alsworth is *not* a port, since the ocean is 50 miles away.

Because of the park's ocean-to-mountaintop coverage, it includes a diversity of ecosystems, from dense spruce forests along the coast to active volcanoes (Iliamna and Redoubt). The western flank of the Chigmit Mountains is covered with tundra and boreal forests. Just south of the park is huge Iliamna Lake, Alaska's largest lake. The settlement of **Iliamna** (pop. 100) sits on the shore of this lake and has a store selling limited supplies.

Once you get away from the scattering of lodges, Lake Clark National Park is a vast, undeveloped wilderness without roads, trails, or other facilities. Those not staying in the lodges come here to boat and fish on the lake, or to backpack in the mountains. The western foothills have open, dry tundra that's perfect for hiking. Floating down the various rivers that lead westward from the park is another popular activity. Wildlife viewing can be impressive, since you can find caribou, moose, wolves, brown and black bears, and Dall sheep, among other mammals.

Practicalities

Lake Clark National Park headquarters is in Anchorage (4230 University Dr., 907/271-3751, www.nps.gov/lacl). The **Port Alsworth Visitor Center** (907/781-2214) is open weekdays year-round, and offers short hikes, slide shows, and videos. No stores in Port Alsworth, but boats can be rented from local lodges. There's a pretty waterfall on the Tanalian River near town.

Expensive accommodations and bear-viewing are available from more than a dozen fishing lodges on Lake Clark or within the park boundaries along Cook Inlet. These include **Silver Salmon Creek Lodge** (907/252-5504 or 888/872-5666, www.silversalmoncreek.com), **Homestead Lodge** (907/262-1960 or 888/677-9383, www.alaskawildlife.com), **Redoubt Bay Lodge** (907/274-2710, www.withinthewild.com), and **The Farm Lodge** (907/781-2208 or 888/440-2281, www.thefarmlodge.com). Located along Cook Inlet and surrounded by the park, **Lake Clark Bear Camp** (800/544-2261, www.greatalaska.com) is a unique operation with a comfortable Weatherport base camp and lots of nearby bear activity. Guests come on quick day-trips ($400) or multi-night stays ($745 per person for one night and two days) from Anchorage.

Lake Clark Air (907/278-2054, www.lakeclarkair.com) has daily service between Anchorage and Port Alsworth, plus flightseeing trips. Several Kenai and Homer air taxis fly to the Lake Clark shoreline for bear-viewing; contact the Park Service for specifics.

KATMAI NATIONAL PARK

Katmai National Park occupies a large chunk of the northern Alaska Peninsula, over four million acres (roughly the size of Connecticut and Rhode Island), just northwest of Kodiak Island across Shelikof Strait. Several features attract visitors to Katmai: its wild volcanic landscape, outstanding salmon fishing in a world-class setting, and the opportunity to see brown bears up close. The bears are the big attraction nowadays; they're big, they're bad, and they're ubiquitous, thanks to the million or so salmon that run up the Naknek River drainage system from Bristol Bay each year. Dozens of other mammal, bird, and fish species thrive in the park.

The primary starting point for trips into Katmai is the town of King Salmon, which is accessible by jet from Anchorage. From King

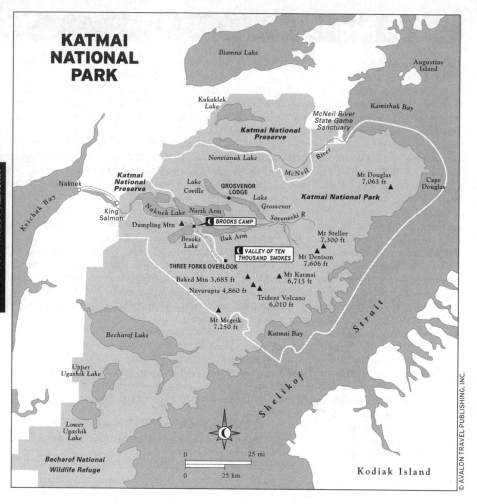

KATMAI NATIONAL PARK

Salmon, most visitors fly into Naknek Lake to either stay at Brooks Lodge or camp at the nearby park campground. The Valley of Ten Thousand Smokes is accessible by a park bus from Brooks Lodge.

Novarupta Erupts

In June 1912, one of the great cataclysms of modern history took place here as Mt. Novarupta blew its top, violently spewing volcanic glass, ash, and sulfurous fumes for three days.

One of the explosions was heard in Ketchikan, 860 miles away. The fallout choked Kodiak, whose 450 inhabitants were evacuated in a daring marine rescue, but nobody is known to have been killed. Hot ash and pumice piled up 700 feet deep over a 40-square-mile area, and acid rain destroyed clothing hanging on clotheslines in Vancouver. Massive amounts of dust cloaked the vicinity in pitch darkness for 60 hours and circulated in the upper atmosphere for two years, changing weather patterns worldwide. Scientists say this was the second largest blast in recorded history, exceeded only by the eruption of Greece's Santorini in 1650 B.C. By way of comparison, the 1883 eruption of Krakatoa in Indonesia was only half as large (though it killed 35,000 people).

It's been more than 90 years since the "Nov-eruption," but volcanologists are still studying this unique phenomenon—a young, intact volcano created by a single event—to determine the hazards from future eruptions. Novarupta, however, is only one of 15 active volcanoes monitored within Katmai National Park. The last to spew was Trident Volcano in 1968, but steam plumes occasionally rise from Megeik and Martin Volcanos as well.

◖ Valley of Ten Thousand Smokes

Robert Griggs, a botanist sent by the National Geographic Society, discovered in 1916 the nearby Valley of Ten Thousand Smokes, where hot gases surfaced through tens of thousands of holes and cracks when the hot ash contacted buried rivers and springs. He reported, "The whole valley as far as the eye could reach was full of hundreds, no thousands—literally, tens of thousands—of smokes curling up from its fissured floor." The area has gradually cooled, and only a few fumaroles remain today. A national monument was created here in 1918; it has since been expanded five times to encompass the large brown bear and salmon habitat. In 1980, under the Alaska National Interest Lands Conservation Act (ANILCA), it was de-clared a national park.

Be sure to take the guided, eight-hour, 46-mile (round-trip) bus tour from Brooks Camp to a viewpoint over the Valley of Ten Thousand Smokes. From Three Forks Overlook, you can join a three-mile hike (round-trip) to the valley floor and back. The bus leaves Brooks Lodge daily 9 A.M. June–mid-September, and costs $96 round-trip, including a sack lunch. Take warm clothing and raingear, along with your binoculars and camera. Advance reservations for the bus are highly recommended in July and August; contact Katmailand (907/243-

5448 or 800/544-0551, www.katmailand.com) a few days in advance of your trip.

Hikers use this bus to access the valley, catch-ing a later bus for the return trip ($51 each way). Two of the most popular hiking destinations are **Megeik Lake** (15 miles away) and **Baked Mountain** (12 miles away). There are no trails across the valley, and the rivers make for haz-ardous crossings, but the barren country is rela-tively easy to hike through. A USGS research cabin at Baked Mountain offers protection from the sometimes harrowing wind conditions that can create fierce dust storms, but check at the visitor center to be sure it is available. Bring ski goggles for your eyes and a bandanna to pro-tect your mouth and nose from the flying ash. Don't let this dissuade you from hiking here, however. This is spectacular country, with a lunar landscape cut through by deep and col-orful canyons. Before heading out, stop by the Park Service visitor center in Brooks Camp for a map, a backcountry permit, and more informa-tion. Jean Bodeau's *Katmai National Park and Preserve* (available at the visitor centers) provides detailed hiking information.

If you can get a bike to Brooks Camp, the 23-mile dirt road to the Valley of Ten Thousand Smokes is a fine place to ride bikes; the views get more dramatic as you go. **Lifetime Adventures** (907/746-4644 or 800/952-8624, www.life timeadventures.net) guides seven-day hike-bike-kayak trips in the park for $3,500 d.

◖ Brooks Camp

Katmai has gained worldwide fame for its brown bears, and is one of the few places where large numbers of visitors can see wild bears through-out the summer. Bear activity centers on the Brooks River, which flows into Naknek Lake just a half-mile from the campground. A float-ing bridge crosses the river to an elevated view-ing platform where you can watch the bears. **Brooks Falls** are a half-mile hike from here. An extremely popular viewing platform at the falls gets crowded during the peak of the season. In fact, it's so popular that park rangers limit use to one hour at a time, and there's often a long wait to get to the Brooks Falls platform.

Added to this is the other reason people come here: fishing. Brooks River is open to sportfishing—mainly for sockeye salmon—and is often lined with anglers. When bears wander by, and this is often, anglers are required to immediately release any fish, and park rangers will even cut your line if you don't act fast enough. Unfortunately, some bears are starting to equate anglers with free fish; sometimes the park has been forced to close the river to fishing to keep the bears from becoming more aggressive toward humans.

The **Dumpling Mountain Trail** leaves from Brooks Camp and climbs four miles to the top of this 2,440-foot peak. You'll discover outstanding panoramic vistas from the summit across the surrounding lake-filled, volcano-crowned country.

Coastal Bear-Viewing

Bear-viewing is becoming increasingly popular on the eastern side of Katmai along Shelikof Strait, where brown bears dig for clams, eat grass and sedges, catch salmon, and scavenge for carcasses that wash ashore. A number of air taxi operators out of Homer, Kodiak, Soldotna, and Anchorage, taking clients on day trips for $450–600 per person. Note that many of these fly-in trips have big groups, and a number of planes can be in one area at once, reducing your wilderness experience. In addition, the day-trips are literally that, while bears are generally more active in early morning or late in the day when most bear-viewing flights have already headed back home.

Hallo Bay Bear Lodge (907/235-2237, www.hallobay.com, late May–early Oct.) is a unique wilderness camp on a wild and beautiful stretch of the Katmai coast. Access is by air from Homer, a one-hour flight. The camp is entirely surrounded by national park land, and includes a half-dozen cabin-like structures (Weatherports) with a central building for dining and relaxing. Bear guides lead hikes to viewing areas around the camp with a maximum of five guests per guide. Extended backpacking trips and professional photography workshops are also offered. Meals are fill-

ing and delicious, and other amenities include hot showers, heated cabins, Internet access, and wind-powered electricity. An all-inclusive three-day, two-night trip is $1,400 per person, and a five-day trip costs $2,400. Bear-viewing day trips from Homer cost $550 for 8 hours.

Located in a private inholding on Kukak Bay, **Katmai Wilderness Lodge** (907/486-8767 or 800/488-8767, www.katmai-wilderness.com) is a modern log-cabin-style lodge on Kukak Bay, where the guest rooms have private baths and hot showers. Guests come here to fish, hike, or watch bears. It's a beautiful spot, but the weather can make it difficult for flights to get in or out. A variety of package trips are offered, starting at three nights for $2,500 d; this includes floatplane travel from Kodiak, lodging, guided bear-viewing, home-style meals, kayaking, and fishing.

Katmai Coastal Bear Tours (907/235-8337 or 800/532-8338, www.katmaibears.com) operates from two boats, the 73-foot wooden tug *The Waters* and the 100-foot *Kittiwake*. The boats serve as floating lodges for photographers, cinematographers, and others who use skiffs to go ashore along the Katmai coast. Meals are great, and the guides are highly knowledgeable naturalists. The boats go where the bears are, providing a mobility lacking in shore-based operations. Most visitors choose a four-day, three-night package for $3,450 per person, including access by floatplane from Kodiak. Skipper/owner John Waters is a respected advocate for bear conservation; the IMAX film *Bears* and many others were filmed from his boats.

Mythos Expeditions (907/486-5536, www.thewildcoast.com) also leads boat-based bear-viewing trips to the Katmai Coast in June and August on the fishing vessel *Mythos*.

Many companies offer bear-viewing day trips ($500–600 per person) to the Katmai coast from Homer, Kodiak, or Anchorage (see the *Anchorage* and *Kenai Penninsula* chapters for details).

Recreation

Savonoski Loop is a favorite backcountry canoe or kayak trip. Boaters start in Brooks

Camp, head up the north arm of Naknek Lake, portage a mile to Lake Grosvenor, float down the Grosvenor and Savonoski Rivers, and paddle across the Iluk Arm of Naknek Lake back to Brooks Camp. Be ready for a 4–10-day trip, and be sure to talk with Park Service rangers for precautions and backcountry permits before heading out. Canoes and kayaks can be rented from Brooks Lake Lodge.

Lifetime Adventures (907/746-4644 or 800/952-8624, www.lifetimeadventures. net) sets up do-it-yourself folding kayak trips around the Savonoski Loop; for $1,800 d, you get airfare from Anchorage to King Salmon, charter flights to and from the park, and folding kayaks. They can also provide camping equipment or folding mountain bikes for an extra charge, and offer guided kayak trips on the Savonski Loop (seven days for $3,500 d).

Several companies offer guided sport fishing, boat tours, and skiff rentals on Naknek Lake; see the King Salmon Visitor Center (907/246-4250) for details.

Park Accommodations

If you want to stay the night at famous █ **Brooks Lodge** (907/243-5448 or 800/544-0551, www.katmailand.com, June–late Sept.), be prepared to shell out wads of cash. During the peak season (June 20–Aug. 10), a package trip that includes round-trip airfare from Anchorage to Brooks Lodge and one night's lodging (far too brief) costs $1,652 d, and a two-night package is $2,238 d. Stuff-yourself buffet meals are extra. If you're willing to arrive sometime other than July, your overall cost will be somewhat lower. Brooks Lodge fills up quickly, so *make reservations a full year ahead* to be assured of a place in July!

A tiny gift shop at the lodge sells snacks, film, and tourist trinkets, and rents canoes, kayaks, fishing poles, and hip waders. Two other fishing lodges are on other lakes within the park. They're even more expensive than Brooks Lodge, but are far from the hubbub. With space for just six people, **Grosvenor Lodge** charges $4,700 d for three nights lodging, meals, fishing guide, and airfare; **Kulik Lodge** charges $4,850

d for the same. Brooks, Kulik, and Grosvenor lodges are all owned by Katmailand, and share the same contact information. Note that the three lodges, along with services such as the bus tours, operate only June–late September. Before or after that, you're on your own.

King Salmon Accommodations

The town of King Salmon is the main gateway to Katmai National Park. Travelers who are unable to get a lodge or campground space at Brooks Camp often stay here and make day trips by floatplane into the park. The village of Naknek, 15 miles west of King Salmon by road, is an important commercial fishing port. Both towns have food and lodging, and taxi service connects the two. The towns represent an odd clash between the upscale tourists out to see Katmai bears and grubby commercial fishermen out to make a buck (or several thousand bucks). Add a 10 percent lodging tax to the rates below. The largest lodging place in town, **Quinnat Landing Hotel** (907/246-3000 or 800/770-3474, www.quinnat.com) burned

gillnet fishermen at the mouth of Naknek River

MCNEIL RIVER STATE GAME SANCTUARY

Wedged above the northeast corner of Katmai and 100 air miles west of Homer, this state sanctuary is where many of the famous photographs of brown bears were taken. At the peak of the season (late July-early Aug.), visitors may see 40 or more bruins as they catch chum salmon at McNeil River falls. More brown bears congregate here than in any other single site on earth; up to 130 have been counted in a single day! The sanctuary is managed by the Alaska Department of Fish and Game (ADF&G), which allows only 10 people per day into the viewing area. Because of all these bears, the department has stringent rules, and visitors must remain within small viewing areas throughout the 6-8 hour day. A permit system and user fees are required of all visitors.

National Geographic photographer Cecil Rhode first published frames of McNeil River – without identifying it – in 1954, after which the federal government closed the area to hunters. It became a state game sanctuary in 1967, and the limited permit system was installed in 1973. And in 1979, the river was completely closed to sportfishing. Since ADF&G instituted these restrictive use policies, there have been no casualties to either humans or bears. This is particularly amazing given how close the bears often come.

GETTING IN

Each year, more than 2,500 people apply to visit McNeil River and nearby Mikfik Creek; only 250 or so permits are granted (including standby permits). **Non-transferable permits** are required for all visitors between June 7 and August 25. Only 10 of these are available per day, and a $25 per person non-refundable application fee is required. The ADF&G (907/267-2182, www.wc.adfg.state.ak.us/mcneil) can provide you with details and a downloadable application form. Forms must be postmarked or emailed no later than March 1. The best time to find bears at McNeil is mid-July-early August, when the chum salmon are running, but it's also the time that most people apply to visit. Second choice is as close to peak as possible on the earlier side; later the excitement tapers off.

Because of McNeil's immense popularity, a lottery system is used to decide who gets the available time slots. Winners are given a four-day period at McNeil, and pay (in addition to the application) $350 per person ($150 for Alaskan residents) to visit the sanctuary. As a backup, many people also apply for a **standby permit** to get into McNeil in case they're not among the lucky applicants for the regular permits. Only three of these are available each day. A separate standby lottery is held, and those chosen pay $175 ($75 for Alaskan residents)

---

to the ground in 2006 and will not reopen until 2008 at the earliest.

Several places in King Salmon offer lodging, including **King Ko Inn** (907/246-3377 or 866/234-3474, www.kingko.com, summer only, $195 s or $210 d) with comfortable modern cabins (some with kitchenettes).

Antlers Inn (907/246-8525 or 888/735-8525) has five rooms for $140 s or $160 d, and three suites with full kitchens for $220 s or $240 d. The in-town location can be a bit noisy, but they're open all year.

A mile out of town is **King Salmon Inn** (907/246-3444, www.kingsalmoninn.com). Simple but clean rooms with two twin beds

are $125 s or $180 d, including transport from King Salmon. Most clients are fishermen who get multi-night packages that include room, meals, and boat rental.

Visit www.southwestalaska.com for links to a multitude of fishing lodges in the region, including two near King Salmon: **Bear Trail Lodge** (907/246-2327, www.beartraillodge.com) and **Rainbow Bend Charter Adventures** (907/246-3750 or 888/575-4249, www.bristolbayfishing.com).

Camping

A short distance from the Brooks Lodge, the 60-person campground at **Brooks Camp** (June-

and wait for slots to open up when regular permit holders decide to stay in camp rather than going out that day (typically when the weather is bad). People who visit on a standby basis usually get to spend at least one day at the falls, but bears are also visible around the campground and along the nearby beach.

SEEING THE BEARS

People come from around the world to see and photograph bears within McNeil River State Game Sanctuary. Visitors actually have the chance to view bears at two seasonal locations. In June, several dozen bears (primarily females with cubs) can be found feeding on a small run of sockeye salmon in **Mikfik Creek.** This area provides a great opportunity to see bears in a lush and intimate setting – they're all around you. Also, the weather is generally better than later in the summer.

The big show takes place on the nearby **McNeil River** between early July and mid-August, when a major run of chum salmon head up this much larger river. The activity peaks around July 15, when dozens of bears (including many large males) come to a low waterfall – McNeil Falls – where the fish are easier to catch. Visitors have opportunities to see and photograph bears 75-200 feet away, though the bears may occasionally come within 30 feet. Be sure to

bring plenty of film! A note to professional photographers: Because so many people have photographed bears at McNeil for so long, the market for bear pics from here is flooded. Try somewhere else if you want a shot that stands out from the crowd.

PRACTICALITIES

Visitors to McNeil overnight in a camping area and hike two miles to the viewing areas overlooking McNeil Falls (in June they head to areas along Mikfik Creek where you're more likely to see females with cubs than at McNeil). The campground has a cabin for food storage and cooking, a sauna, outhouses, and staff cabins, but no other developments or services.

ADF&G employees carry shotguns and stay with the visitors at all times when they are away from the campground. Visitors need to be in good physical condition for the hike to the falls, and if the weather is bad (a common situation) it's easy to get cold while sitting in the rain and wind for hours. Hip boots are essential, along with heavy-duty raingear, wind-resistant clothes, and gloves. People typically remain at McNeil Falls for a 6-8 hour period.

Quite a few air taxis provide transport to McNeil from Homer (the primary departure point), King Salmon, Kodiak, or Anchorage.

mid-Sept., $8 pp/night) has potable water. It's extremely popular and the spaces fill fast. Reservations are required far ahead of your visit; contact the **National Recreation Reservation Service** (877/444-6777, www.recreation.gov). The campground often gets booked for the month of July within a few hours after reservations open in early January!

Leave your kitchen sink at home for this trip; you'll have to carry it a quarter-mile from the floatplane dock to the campground, and the bear-proof caches don't have room for a sink anyway. (The Park Service provides carts to make transportation easier.) This is the only developed campground in Katmai, and backcoun-

try camping is not allowed within five miles of Brooks Camp, so don't come here without a reservation unless you're willing to hike. No-shows sometimes create openings at the campground even when it was officially full, but it's pretty risky to arrive in Brooks Camp without a place reserved. Campers can buy meals at Brooks Lodge or take showers there for $5. Katmai experiences weather similar to that of the rest of the Aleutian arc—cool, wet, and wildly windy; so come prepared to get wet!

Food

Brooks Lodge (907/243-5448 or 800/544-0551, www.katmailand.com) serves filling buffet meals and is open to both guests and the general public: $12 for breakfast, $18 for lunch, and $28 for dinner. The bar serves mixed drinks.

King Ko Inn (907/246-3377 or 866/234-3474, www.kingko.com, mid-April–mid-Oct., entrées run $15–35) in King Salmon has dependably good food three times a day in the summer, with fresh seafood, pizzas, burgers, and other faves. Big bar serves up live music some summer weekends.

Across the way is **Eddie's Fireplace Inn** (907/246-3435), with lower prices and great burgers. They're open three meals a day, year-round. Get groceries, sporting goods, and even espresso at **Alaska Commercial Company** (907/246-6109) in King Salmon.

Information and Services

The very helpful **King Salmon Visitor Center** (907/246-4250, daily 8 A.M.–5 P.M. June–Sept., Mon.–Sat. 8 A.M.–5 P.M. the rest of the year) is at King Salmon airport. Stop here for details on Katmai National Park, Aniakchak National Monument, Alaska Peninsula National Wildlife Refuge, and Bacherof National Wildlife Refuge. There's a big selection of books and cards too. Need cash? The Wells Fargo in King Salmon has an ATM.

The Park Service's **Brooks Camp Visitor Center** inside the park is open daily June–mid-September. All visitors must check in here upon arrival to learn about bear safety and to get a park orientation. Rangers lead free afternoon **cultural and nature walks,** plus evening slide shows at Brooks Camp daily throughout the summer, plus guided hikes up Dumpling Mountain. Check the bulletin boards at the visitor center, campground, and lodge for today's events.

For more on Katmai, contact the National Park Service in King Salmon (907/246-3305, www.nps.gov/katm). You can also pick up a map of the park and a copy of the informative park paper, *The Novarupta,* at the Alaska Public Lands Information Center in Anchorage.

Getting There

Getting to Katmai isn't cheap. First, fly from Anchorage to King Salmon on **Alaska**

Airlines (800/426-0333, www.alaskaair.com) by jet or by turboprop from **PenAir** (907/246-3373 or 800/448-4226, www.penair.com). From King Salmon it will cost another $164 round-trip to get out to Brooks Camp. **Katmai Air** (907/246-3079 or 800/544-0551, www.katmailand.com) has scheduled service. **Egli Air Haul** (907/246-3554, www.egliair.com) and **Branch River Air Service** (907/248-3539, www.branchriverair.com) have daily flights, along with flightseeing and trips to nearby McNeil River. One warning: The weather in King Salmon is often bad, so flight cancellations are not uncommon, and it's easy to get stuck here.

ANIAKCHAK NATIONAL MONUMENT

This remote and rarely visited park covers over 600,000 acres, and is approximately 400 miles southwest of Anchorage on the Alaska Peninsula. The park centers around the six-mile-wide **Aniakchak Caldera,** which last erupted in 1931. Located in the volcanically active Aleutian Range, the crater contains lava flows, cinder cones, and explosion pits. Dominating the crater is 3,350-foot-high Vent Mountain, with a volcanic cone that occasionally sends up plumes of smoke. On the northwest inner edge is a large eruption crater covered with patterned lava that presents an otherworldly appearance from the air. **Surprise Lake,** on the northeast side of the caldera, is the source of the Aniakchak River, which cascades through a 1,500-foot gorge cut in the caldera wall. The river is a wild whitewater trip for the experienced.

Getting There

Aniakchak Monument is infamous for bad weather, and it's an expensive flight from Homer, King Salmon, or Kodiak (the closest towns of any size). There are no developed facilities, but floatplanes can land in Surprise Lake, and the northern portion of the park is smooth enough for wheeled landings. For additional information, contact the Aniakchak National Monument office in King Salmon (907/246-4286, www.nps.gov/ania).

NATIONAL WILDLIFE REFUGES

Much of the land on the lower Alaska Peninsula and out the Aleutian Island chain lies within four national wildlife refuges. These are rarely visited by human travelers, but provide vital habitat for many species of animals.

The **Alaska Maritime National Wildlife Refuge** covers 3.5 million acres, encompassing 2,500 islands that stretch from Forrester Island in southern Southeast all the way out the Aleutians, and on scattered places up the mainland to Barrow. Headquarters is in Homer (907/235-6961, http://alaskamaritime.fws.gov).

The **Alaska Peninsula National Wildlife Refuge** covers 3.5 million acres on the peninsula, and includes a chain of volcanoes dominated by 8,400-foot Mt. Veniaminof. This massive volcano has a base almost 30 miles across, larger than any active volcano on record. And the summit crater contains the most extensive crater glacier in North America. The refuge is based in King Salmon (907/246-3339, http://alaskapeninsula.fws.gov).

Also based in King Salmon is **Becharof National Wildlife Refuge** (907/246-3339, http://becharof.fws.gov), sandwiched between Katmai National Park and Preserve and Alaska Peninsula National Wildlife Refuge. The refuge is dominated by Becharof Lake, the second largest lake in Alaska. The lake is surrounded by low rolling hills, tundra wetlands, volcanic peaks and to the east, and the 477,000 acre Becharof Wilderness. Some 10,000 caribou migrate through the refuge each spring and fall, and other wildlife—from seabirds to salmon—abound.

Izembek National Wildlife Refuge spans the tip of the Alaska Peninsula, and protects the watershed of Izembek Lagoon, a State Game Refuge containing one of the largest eelgrass beds in the world. The state and federal refuges act as an international crossroad to many thousands of migrating waterfowl and shorebirds, including the world's entire population of Pacific brant and emperor geese. For migrating shorebirds, this is the last stop before their unbelievable over-water flights to wintering areas as far away as South America, Polynesia, and New Zealand. The refuge is based in Cold Bay (907/532-2445, http://izembek.fws.gov).

The Aleutian Islands

From the tip of the Alaska Peninsula, an arc of 200 islands curves more than a thousand miles southwest to Attu Island, separating the North Pacific Ocean from the Bering Sea. The Aleutian Islands are part of the circum-Pacific "Ring of Fire," one of the most geologically unsettled regions on earth. The titanic tectonic forces clash as the Pacific plate pushes under the North American plate at the deep Aleutian Trench, making the earth rumble, quake, and spew. Of the 79 named Aleutian Islands, only 8 are occupied by humans. The 14 large and 65 smaller islands (plus countless tiny islets) are all windswept northern Pacific outposts. The meeting of the mild Japanese Current with the icy Bering Sea causes a climate of much fog, rain, and wind, but little sun. Compounding this is a meteorological

phenomenon known as the "Aleutian low," a low-pressure atmospheric valley that funnels a number of intense storms east into North America. In short—it's not the greatest place to get a tan.

High peaks drop abruptly to the sea. There is no permafrost, but the constant strong winds inhibit tree growth; only tundra and brushy vegetation survive. Frequent storms blow through (Unalaska experiences almost 250 rainy days a year), but because of the warm currents the sea never freezes. Given these harsh climatic conditions, it's perhaps surprising that, before the arrival of the Russians, every island was inhabited by Aleut peoples. On the other hand, given the abundance of the ocean, the Aleut were skillful hunters who lived in balance with the fish,

SOUTHWEST ALASKA

marine mammals, and birds of their islands. The Russians enslaved and slaughtered the Aleut, and their numbers plummeted from around 25,000 in 1741 to 2,000 a century later. The Russians also hunted the sea otters and fur seals of the islands to near extinction, and the single-minded exploitation of the islands' resources continues even today. Get the latest on the status of sea lions at www.stellersealions.noaa.gov, and on sea otters at www.ry.fws.gov/fisheries/mmm.

Getting There

PenAir (907/243-2323 or 800/448-4226, www.penair.com) provides daily non-stop flights connecting Anchorage with Aniak, Cold Bay, Dillingham, King Salmon, McGrath, Sand Point, Unalakleet, and Unalaska/Dutch Harbor, plus service several times a week to St. George and St. Paul Islands. The airline also has connecting service smaller villages, including, Atka, Akutan, Chignik Lagoon, Cold Bay, Egegik, False Pass, King Cove, Nelson Lagoon, Nikolski, and Port Moller. (Alaska Airlines no longer flies their jets to Unalaska, but the PenAir flights may be labeled "Alaska Air" on your ticket.) Try to get a seat on the right side of the plane when you fly out of Anchorage; the flight passes near the dramatic and volcanic summits of Mt. Iliamna and Mt. Redoubt.

Flights to Unalaska/Dutch Harbor are on a 30-passenger Saab, which has a bathroom onboard, but many of the other flights are in a claustrophobic 17-passenger Metroliner which lacks a bathroom—a challenge for anyone traveling with children on the longer flights. Before you board a PenAir flight, be sure to ask which plane you will be flying.

The state ferry *Tustemena* (907/465-3941 or 800/642-0066, www.ferryalaska.com) heads out twice a month (April–Oct.) to Dutch Harbor, by way of Homer, Kodiak, Chignik, Sand Point, King Cove, Cold Bay, and Akutan. The trip takes three and a half days one-way and can be very rough, so bring lots of Dramamine and an iron stomach.

HISTORY
The Japanese Challenge

During the spring of 1942, Japan was sweeping triumphantly across the Pacific to the gates of Australia and Hawaii. However, the strength of the U.S. aircraft carriers—none of which had been lost at Pearl Harbor—worried Fleet Admiral Isoroku Yamamoto, commander-in-chief of the Japanese navy. He knew that time was on the side of the United States. To win, he would have to draw the American carriers into a great naval battle where his superior forces could crush them and end the war. His target was Midway, a tiny island west of the Hawaiian chain, where the United States had recently built a base. But to first split the American forces, Yamamoto ordered a diversionary thrust at the Aleutians. In June 1942, Japanese carrier-based planes struck twice at Dutch Harbor, a large new U.S. naval base in Unalaska Bay, but inflicted only slight damage; the base continued to function. Meanwhile, at Midway, the United States had broken the Japanese naval code, and Yamamoto's plans were falling apart. Their own strength divided, one Japanese carrier after another sank before American momentum. As a face-saving move, the retiring Japanese occupied undefended Attu and Kiska at the west end of the Aleutians in the hope that bases on these islands would shield northern Japan and drive a wedge between the United States and Russia.

The Struggle for the Islands

In August 1942, the U.S. Navy occupied Adak Island and built an airfield from which to attack nearby Attu and Kiska. In January 1943, the Navy leapfrogged to Amchitka Island, right next door to Kiska, to provide an advance base. Continuous bombing and a naval blockade weakened Japanese resistance and on May 11, 1943, 16,000 U.S. troops landed on Attu. Of these, 549 Americans were killed before the 2,650 Japanese troops entrenched in the mountains were overcome. On May 29 about 800 remaining Japanese staged a banzai charge. At first they overran the American lines, but their thrust was finally quelled by reserve forces. Only 28 Japanese prisoners were taken, and the 6,000 Japanese on Kiska seemed to face a similar fate.

Late in July, however, Japanese destroyers slipped through the U.S. blockade in dense fog and evacuated their soldiers. On August 15 some 34,000 U.S. and Canadian troops landed, unopposed, on Kiska. Though there was no one to attack and rout, incredibly, they suffered a shocking 99 dead and 74 wounded through landing mishaps, "friendly fire," and other accidents. The Japanese had also booby-trapped all the structures. With their masterful evacuation, the Japanese had ended the Aleutian campaign.

UNALASKA/DUTCH HARBOR

Located about 800 miles southwest of Anchorage, Unalaska Bay cuts into the north side of mountainous Unalaska Island, creating the finest and most sheltered ice-free harbor in the Aleutians. On a clear day you can see the sometimes-smoking 6,680-foot cone of **Makushin Volcano** rising to the west. The city of Unalaska spreads across both Unalaska Island and the much smaller Amaknak Island. A 500-foot bridge officially named *Bridge from the Other Side* links the two islands.

Although often called Dutch Harbor, this name actually refers to the protected harbor rather than the town itself. Longtime Unalaskans take umbrage at the suggestion that they live in Dutch Harbor; to them it's sort of like saying "Frisco" instead of San Francisco. That doesn't stop most folks—especially the transient fishermen and cannery workers—from calling it Dutch Harbor, or simply Dutch. The folks who live in Unalaska take pride in their small city, but many others just view it as a place to get rich quick and get out. This is perhaps best symbolized by a T-shirt seen around town: On the front is a hand filled with hundred dollar bills, and below the picture it simply says, Dutch Harbor.

Dutch Harbor today is an extremely busy place, often ranking as the nation's number-one port in both pounds of seafood caught and total dollar value. At any given time you're

likely to see a dozen or more cargo ships waiting to load fish, surimi, or crab destined for Japan, Korea, the Lower 48, or elsewhere. Most impressive of all is the huge container crane at the American President Lines dock where truck-size loads are dropped onto ships. Crab pots and nets line the roads, and seven different seafood processing plants are scattered around the harbors, processing pollock, crab, salmon, halibut, cod, herring roe, and other seafood. Most of the catch is processed during the hectic winter fishing season, November–April. Despite this rowdy make-a-million-bucks present, Unalaska/Dutch Harbor is filled with history, and visitors will find a number of places worth exploring.

History

When the first Russians "discovered" Unalaska in 1759, it was already home to more than 1,000 Aleut people scattered in 24 settlements. Over the next century the Russians decimated the Aleut, enslaving many of them to harvest fur seals and sea otters. The first permanent Russian settlement of Unalaska began in 1772, and Captain Cook spent three weeks here six years later. Under the Russians, Unalaska quickly became the main trading center in the Aleutians. After America took over in 1867, the focus gradually shifted, and it became an important coal and supply station for the Nome gold rush.

In the 1940s, the U.S. Navy appropriated Dutch Harbor. After the city was bombed by the Japanese in June 1942, all the Aleuts were shipped off to relocation camps in Southeast Alaska. Ten percent of them died in these refugee camps (generally abandoned canneries) due in part to unsanitary conditions and overcrowding. Once World War II ended, they returned to a vastly different place filled with military facilities. Many of their homes had been ransacked.

The boom in bottom fishing for pollock led to rapid growth in Unalaska/Dutch Harbor, and the population now tops 4,200—plus another 2,500 transient workers. Boom times continue in the Aleutians, with lots of blue-collar

UNALASKA/ DUTCH HARBOR

To Ulakta Head

ALASKA SHIP SUPPLY

Mt Ballyhoo ▲ 1,634ft

Amaknak

Island

AIRPORT

FERRY AND CRUISE SHIP DOCK

The Spit

Unalaska

Bay

ALEUTIAN WWII VISITOR CENTER

Dutch

Harbor

AIRPORT BEACH RD

Dutch Harbor

SITKA SPRUCE PARK

MALL/EAGLE MARKET

GRAND ALEUTIAN HOTEL

Margaret Bay

EAST POINT LOOP RD

EAST POINT DR

MUSEUM OF THE ALEUTIANS

ACC STORE

UNISEA INN

Iliuliuk Bay

To Summer Bay

BISHOP'S HOUSE

CHURCH OF THE HOLY ASCENSION

BAYVIEW AVE

Haystack Hill ▲

Unalaska

VISITOR CENTER

JESSE LEE HOME

BRIDGE FROM THE OTHER SIDE

AGNES BEACH RD

POST OFFICE

BROADWAY

PTARMIGAN RD

CAPTAIN'S BAY RD

Captain's Bay

Unalaska Lake

0   0.25 mi

0   0.25 km

Inset map

Cape Cheerful

Unalaska Bay

Table Top Mtn ▲

Amaknak Island

Split Top Mtn ▲

Hog I

☾ HISTORICAL SIGHTS

▲ Mt Coxcomb

Dutch Harbor

○ Unalaska

MAP AREA

▲ Pyramid Peak

Unalaska Island

0   2 mi

0   2 km

jobs paying relatively high wages. The island also sees a handful of cruise ships each summer, but this is a long ways from anywhere else and the Gulf of Alaska can get mighty rough.

(Historical Sights

The most interesting attraction in Unalaska is the beautiful **Russian Orthodox Church of the Holy Ascension** (907/581-6404). Built 1824–1827 and restored in the 1990s, this is the oldest Russian church still standing in Alaska, and a National Historic Landmark. Out front is a small graveyard, and not far away is the **Bishop's House,** built in 1882. Another historic site is the **Jesse Lee Home** near the cemetery. It was constructed by Methodist missionaries in 1890.

The excellent **Museum of the Aleutians** (907/581-5150, www.aleutians.org, $5) is a spacious modern facility with the only archaeological collection in the Aleutians. On exhibit are artifacts from original Native cultures, the Russian era, and World War II, plus changing exhibits. Hours are Tuesday–Sunday 9 A.M.–

5 P.M. June–September, and Monday–Saturday 9 A.M.–5 P.M. the rest of the year.

Located next to the airport, the fascinating **Aleutian World War II Visitor Center** (907/581-9944, www.nps.gov/aleu, Thur.–Sun. 1–6 P.M. year-round, $4 adults, $2 seniors) is housed in the aerology building, constructed in 1943 as a weather-monitoring station for pilots defending the islands from the Japanese. Inside are historical photos and artifacts from the war, a WWII-era radio room, plus exhibits on the Aleutian campaign and the evacuation and internment of Aleut people. Step into the old-fashioned theater to watch documentaries and old newsreels from the war in the Aleutians. The facility is a partnership between the National Park Service and the Ounalashka Corporation (which operates it).

Not far from the airport is **Sitka Spruce Park,** where you'll find four scraggly stolid spruce trees planted by Russian settlers in 1805. At their base lies a plethora of stunted, struggling, younger spruce. These, plus a couple of other clusters of trees around town, make up the

Russian Orthodox Church of the Holy Ascension

only "forest" in this otherwise treeless country. The park is a National Historic Landmark.

Exploring the Country

The countryside around Unalaska is pockmarked with all sorts of evidence from World War II, including underground bunkers, gun emplacements, buildings of all types, and various flotsam and jetsam from the military. The best places to find these are on the northeast end of Amaknak Island near Ulakta Head, and in the Summer Bay area on Unalaska Island.

A popular hiking place is 1,634-foot tall **Mt. Ballyhoo,** just northeast of the airport on Amaknak Island. The easiest way to the top is to drive or mountain bike up the steep and very rough dirt road (4WD recommended, unless you have a rental car that needs a workout) that ends at Ulakta Head. This area is packed with decaying military structures of all sorts, but the open country is very pretty in late summer, with flowers galore, plus Arctic ground squirrels and bald eagles. (Red foxes are the only other wild mammal found on these islands, though some of the fishermen could fall into the "wild mammal" category.)

Climb up the ridge from the end of the road for more dramatic vistas out to sea and back to the mountain-rimmed harbors. The west side of Amaknak Island consists of a harrowing series of cliffs that plummet to the sea 1,500 feet below, so stay away from the edge. In the winter months Mt. Ballyhoo is a popular walk-up, ski-down summit.

For a good view of town, climb **Haystack Hill** on the south side of Iliuliuk River (filled with spawning pink salmon in late summer). More panoramic vistas (and military bunkers) are atop the 421-foot Bunker Hill. A road up this hill veers west of the bridge.

Get to **Summer Bay** by heading northeast out of town on Summer Bay Rd. past the dump, a good place to see eagles. Five miles out is a lagoon where you can swim on a sunny day or practice your long-jumping form on the tall sand dunes. Nice place for a picnic. Continue out the progressively rougher road past bunkers, Quonset huts, and a gun emplacement that guarded Iliuliuk Bay. Keep your eyes open for the two horses—the only ones on Unalaska—that graze here.

Entertainment

Given the nature of the population—especially the young, transient, and sometimes-wealthy fishermen—it should come as no surprise that bars are the main attraction in Unalaska. (There are only half as many churches as places with liquor licenses.) But times are changing and the town's infamous Elbow Room—where fights were once a nightly affair—was torn down in 2006. Look for live music at **Unisea Sports Bar,** a bright, glitzy place.

Recreation

Sportfishing is increasingly popular out of Unalaska, and several charter fishing operators take you out in search of the monster halibut. The world's largest sport-caught halibut—a 459-pound fish—was caught nearby in 1996; contact the information center for a list of charter boats. The Grand Aleutian Hotel specializes in sportfishing vacations.

Accommodations and Camping

Owned by UniSea, one of America's largest seafood processors, the elaborate 112-room **C Grand Aleutian Hotel** (907/581-1325 or 866/581-3844, www.grandaleutian.com, $159 s or $179 d) is *the* place to stay if you've got the bucks to go in style. Two restaurants and a lounge are on the premises, and wireless Internet is available in the lobby. Same owners and contact information for the **UniSea Inn** ($99 s or $109 d), where the 42 clean rooms have TVs, phones, and private baths.

Contact Ounalashka Corporation office (907/581-1276, www.ounalashka.com, $6/day) for camping permits, but wind and rain make this an uncomfortable proposition.

Food

Amelia's Restaurant (907/581-2800) opens at 5 A.M. for hearty breakfast—served all day—lunches, and dinners. Best place for burgers? Try the **Airport Restaurant** (907/581-6007), which also serves pizzas and Asian food. **Nicky's Place** (907/581-1570) in downtown Unalaska sells books, music, and posters, along with the best espresso coffee in town. The walls are lined with works by local artists. **UniSea Inn** (907/581-1325) has fresh seafood specials nightly.

By far the fanciest local eating places—and the best spots for fresh fish—are inside the Grand Aleutian Hotel. Downstairs find **Margaret Bay Cafe** with reasonably priced breakfast and lunches, including an all-you-can-eat soup, salad, and dessert bar. Upstairs is the fine-dining **Chart Room,** with a reasonable lunch buffet on weekdays, a Wednesday-night seafood buffet, and a Sunday brunch. There's an impressive wine selection; not at all what you might expect in this blue-collar fishing town.

Get groceries at **Alaska Commercial Co.** (ACC) or **Eagle Quality Centers** (907/581-4040). Both have in-store delis and bakeries.

Information and Services

The **Unalaska/Port of Dutch Harbor Convention and Visitors Bureau** (on Broadway at 5th St., 907/581-2612 or 877/581-2612, www .unalaska.info, Mon.–Fri. 9 A.M.–5 P.M.) is in the old World War II Army chapel in Unalaska.

Take a shower—and they throw in a free swim—at the fine **Community Center** (907/581-1297), which also houses an indoor track, weight room, and basketball court. Get fast cash from ATMs inside the Eagle store and Key Bank.

Getting There

Unalaska has not traditionally been a place for tourists, and most everyone comes here to make money, not to vacation. The high costs of transportation and accommodations will continue to keep most tourists away, though a few cruise ships visit during the summer. If you decide on a quick visit by air, try to schedule it around a period of good weather. On a clear day the countryside is stunning, but much more common are the rainy and windy periods when the place doesn't look so great and you start to wonder why you spent so much cash to get here. Besides, you may find yourself stuck

for days waiting for the weather to lift enough for planes to land.

The state ferry *Tustemena* (907/465-3941 or 800/642-0066, www.ferryalaska.com) heads out once a month (April–Oct.) from Homer to Dutch Harbor. The trip takes three and a half days one-way and can be somewhat rough, so bring lots of Dramamine. The ferry docks near the airport on Amaknak Island.

The other way to reach Unalaska is by air from Anchorage on **PenAir** (907/243-2323 or 800/448-4226, www.penair.com). These three-hour flights are in a 30-passenger turboprop plane. Alaska Airlines no longer flies their jets to Unalaska, but the PenAir flights are labeled "Alaska Air" on your ticket (the companies codeshare). It is best to book your flight through Alaska Air since their agents are better able to handle complex bookings involving other airlines or mileage tickets. Because of the limited service and high demand, flights to Unalaska often fill far in advance, and mileage ticket seats are almost impossible to obtain. Book at least two months ahead to reserve your flight.

Try to get a seat on the right side of the plane when you fly out of Anchorage. The flight passes near the dramatic and volcanic summits of Mt. Iliamna and Mt. Redoubt. PenAir also offers frequent service between Unalaska and the villages of Atka, Akutan, and Nikolski.

Getting Around

The settlements of Dutch Harbor and Unalaska are spread over two islands, and the distances mean some sort of transport is needed. Mountain bikes offer the most enjoyable way to explore the many dirt roads leading into the hills. They are not, however, nearly as much fun in the rain.

Most folks don't have cars in Unalaska, so there's a thriving **taxi** business. The companies all cruise around town, so it's very easy to get a ride to the airport or other places. Expect to pay $5–10 for most points.

Car rentals are high and gas is expensive; get the specifics at **BC Vehicle Rental** (907/581-6777) or **North Port Rentals** (907/581-3880, www.northportrentals.net). Unlimited miles, but there are only 38 miles of roads to drive anyway!

OTHER ALEUTIAN ISLANDS

The main tourist attraction for Alaska's far-flung Aleutians is probably birds; the islands get quite a few Asian species.

Akutan (pop. 400), a small island 35 miles northeast of Dutch Harbor, is a minor fishing center, with a general store, restaurant, and hotel, but not much else.

Tiny Aleut villages exist at **Atka** (on Atka Island; pop. 100) and **Nikolski** (on Umnak Island; pop. 35). Despite its fragile geological situation and frequent earthquakes, the remote volcanic island of Atka was used by the United States for underground nuclear testing until as late as 1971. In its first public action, Greenpeace sent a protest vessel into the area, and the resulting controversy led to cancellation of the tests.

Adak

This 28-mile-long island is midway out the Aleutian chain, 500 miles west of Dutch Harbor. **PenAir** (907/246-3373 or 800/448-4226, www.penair.com) provides twice-weekly service to the island from Anchorage, and cruise ships visit once or twice a summer. There's a general store with expensive supplies. Contact the city (907/592-4243, www.adakisland.com) for additional details. Anyone planning on exploring the island should drop by the Alaska Maritime National Wildlife Refuge's summer office to see a video on avoiding the unexploded ordinance on parts of the Adak. Get details from the U.S. Fish & Wildlife

Service (year-round 907/235-6961, in summer 907/592-2406). A massive $800-million floating X-Band radar station—part of a questionably effective missile defense system—was moved to Adak in 2006.

The Navy had a major base on Adak from 1943 to 2000, when they left following the end of the Cold War. Suddenly Alaska's sixth-largest city became a virtual ghost town, with just 100 or so year-round residents. The now-abandoned city would make a great setting for a post-apocalypse movie, with the incessant wind blowing through empty houses, schools, and businesses. Amazingly the Olympic-size swimming pool remains open.

Attu and Shemya

At the far western end of the Aleutians lies the surprisingly beautiful island of Attu, less than 200 miles from Siberia. The Aleut villagers of Attu were deported to Japan in 1942 by the Japanese, and more than 2,500 Japanese and Americans died in battles here. After the war, the U.S. government refused to allow the Aleuts to resettle on their island, and today the only inhabitants are the staff of the Coast Guard Loran station. Bird-watchers visit Attu to look for Asian species that have strayed into the Aleutians, and this is also the only place in America where the white-tailed eagle breeds. Visit www.attu.com for info on the island's birds. Access is by charter flight only.

Minuscule Shemya Island—so small that the airport covers half of its four-mile length—is 40 miles east of Attu, near the end of the Aleutians. The Missile Defense Agency is upgrading an early-warning radar base here, and a security clearance is required to visit.

Pribilof Islands

The remote, volcanic Pribilofs sit in the middle of the Bering Sea 250 miles north of the Aleutians, 300 miles west of the mainland, and a thousand miles from Anchorage. The two main islands—**St. Paul** (pop. 760; world's largest Aleut community) and **St. George** (pop. 150)—host what may be the largest concentration of mammals and seabirds anywhere on earth. Although both islands have abundant wildlife of all sorts, St. Paul is best known for its fur seal colonies, and St. George for its seabird rookeries. Tiny Walrus and Otter Islands also support thousands of seals and birds.

St. Paul is the largest of the islands: 14 miles long and eight miles wide, with hills reaching 500 feet in elevation. St. George has a sheer wall rising from the sea to almost 1,000 feet, with millions of waterfowl breeding in its nooks and crannies. There are no trees on either island, but the rolling tundra becomes a dense rainbow of flowers in mid-July. The weather is similar to that of the Aleutians—cool, damp, foggy, and windy; summer temperatures average 47°F, with an occasional 60°F day in July. Useful websites for information on the Pribilofs are www.southwestalaska.com and www.beringsea.com.

© DON PITCHER

St. Peter and Paul Church, St. Paul Island

SOUTHWEST ALASKA

HISTORY

Soon after Russian fur finder Gerassim Pribylov discovered the uninhabited islands in June 1786—and named them for himself—his fur company brought Aleut slaves to harvest the seals. Accounts vary, one claiming that the Russians slaughtered the seals here nearly to extinction; the other that in 1867 the population had regenerated to record numbers and that it was the Americans who trimmed their skins by the millions (these fur seal rookeries were a prime reason the U.S. government bought Alaska from the Russians). In either case, by 1911 the seal population had dwindled to fewer than 150,000 animals (10 percent of what it had been). That same year, the United States, Russia, England, and Japan signed a treaty banning ocean hunting and limiting the number allowed to be taken on land. But it wasn't until 1985 that commercial seal harvesting was finally halted, in large part because of pressure from environmental groups. The Aleut people were not given full control of their islands until 1983.

Today, the economy of St. Paul struggles along with limited seafood processing and tourism. Steller sea lions and fur seals have declined in recent years, and there is growing concern among biologists over the health of the Bering Sea ecosystem. This is still a remarkable place for anyone who loves wildlife, with outstanding birding opportunities throughout the summer and many unusual species. A large herd of reindeer are present on St. Paul Island.

◖ ST. PAUL ISLAND

Each summer thousands of northern fur seals return to the Pribilofs (the majority to St. Paul) to breed and give birth. The "beachmasters" are first to arrive at the haul-out sites and rookeries (late May), with the females coming ashore in June to give birth. At 90–130 pounds, the females are far smaller than the largest males, which can reach 600 pounds. Harbor seals, sea otters, Steller sea lions, and long-tusked walruses round out this brawling, bawling, and caterwauling marine mammalian gumbo. Nowhere else in North America, and arguably the world, is wildlife so easily seen in such numbers. If you're set on doing something really wild (and expensive) during your trip north, this would be it.

This fascinating island is approximately 17 miles long and 8 miles across. The old **St. Peter and Paul Church** is a focal point of life on St. Paul, with a lavishly ornate interior. It's right in the heart of this rough-edged town where the streets are gravel and foxes are common sights.

There's only one place to stay, the **King Eider Hotel** (907/546-2477), where $125 s or d gets you a room with a bath down the hall at the airport. The sitting area contains a guest computer and TV. It's two miles from here to town, but most visitors don't spend much time at the hotel since the tours are out all day.

The adjacent **Airport Inn** serves three meals a day: $10 breakfast, $14 lunch, and $18 dinner. There is also a small AC store with limited and expensive supplies, a tavern, two taxi companies, and vehicles from **North Star Truck Rental** (907/546-2420). Camping is not allowed on the island.

The vast majority of visitors to St. Paul arrive on **St. Paul Island Tours** (907/278-2318 or 877/424-5637, www.alaskabirding.com). These trips include round-trip air transportation from Anchorage, lodging, transport around the island, and a guide with a good knowledge of birds, wildlife, history, and cultural traditions. Meals are extra, or you can bring your own food and use the microwaves and fridges at the hotel. These trips start at $1,406 per person for three days and two nights, up to $2,420 for eight days and seven nights. Be sure to schedule a buffer of several days since foggy weather sometimes prevents flights from landing for up to a week, and bring heavy raingear and good rubber boots. The tours are offered from mid-May through August.

PenAir (907/243-2323 or 800/448-4226, www.penair.com) flies from Anchorage to St. Paul Sundays, Mondays, Wednesdays, and Fridays. Most are on a comfortable 30-passenger Saab turboprop, but it's still a long four-hour flight, much of it over open water. It can be harrowing, and planes are sometimes unable to land, forcing them to return.

ST. GEORGE ISLAND

In addition to the sea mammals, over 220 species of birds have been identified on the Pribilofs, including millions of murres and thousands of puffins, cormorants, kittiwakes, and fulmars. The late birder and artist Rodger Tory Peterson called one of St. George's rookeries "probably the greatest single bird cliff anywhere in North America." (Note, however, that only a dozen or so bird species actually breed on the islands; the rest are migrants.) Bird-watchers interested in adding to their life list may want to come early (mid-May–early June) for accidental Asian species that sometimes wander over from Siberia. Don't forget your bird book and binoculars!

St. George the Martyr Russian Orthodox Church is the most distinctive local structure, though the very simple **St. George Tanaq Hotel** (907/859-2255, www.stgeorge tanaq.com) is also a National Historic Landmark. Lodging here costs $169 per person (!) with a shared bath. Reserve ahead to be certain of a space, since there are only nine rooms. No restaurants on the island, but you can buy food locally and cook it at the hotel kitchen. **St. George Island Canteen** has limited groceries at bush prices; better to bring your own from Anchorage. Camping is not allowed on St. George.

PenAir (907/243-2323 or 800/448-4226, www.penair.com) flies from Anchorage to St. George on Tuesdays, Thursdays, and Saturdays. The four-hour flights over open water are on a claustrophobic 17-passenger Metroliner with no bathroom onboard. Fortunately, the plane often refuels in Dillingham, giving passengers a break (if you're lucky). Local taxis are available to take you into town.

WESTERN AND ARCTIC ALASKA

This is Alaska's true outback: far, far, from the reach of civilization. The scattered settlements—Dillingham, Bethel, and Nome—are really more like pinpricks on the map. The vast distances between the towns make them difficult and expensive to reach, but also exotic and fascinating to visit.

Bristol Bay, on the southern end of the Bering Sea, is considered the world's most productive red salmon fishery. Dillingham, the main port town, is home to hundreds of salmon fishing boats and a multitude of sportfishing lodges. It's also the gateway to remote Wood-Tikchik State Park, America's largest state park. Also nearby are the Walrus Islands, with an extraordinary walrus haul-out on Round Island. The village of Bethel occupies a low-lying, lake-filled delta where the Kuskokwim and Yukon Rivers spread

and finally empty into the Bering Sea. Yup'ik villages are scattered across the stark, treeless plain. Farther north is Nome, a gold rush town with an abundance of history and a network of roads across the beautiful rolling country.

The extremes of the Arctic make it hard to imagine how life survives. The too-brief summers can be gloriously beautiful, with a sun that never sets and luxuriant vegetation stretching in all directions, but winter brings a cold so bitter that even stepping outside for a few moments without proper protective clothing can be life-threatening. Visitors need to be well prepared before venturing away from the settlements. This is not a landscape to take lightly. (Note: Prudhoe Bay and the Dalton Highway are covered in the *Interior Alaska* chapter since most of the access is via buses or planes from Fairbanks.)

© DON PITCHER

HIGHLIGHTS

(Wood-Tikchik State Park: Sprawled across 1.6 million acres, the largest state park in America encompasses a series of eight spectacular lakes backed by the rugged Wood River Mountains (page 464).

(Walrus Islands State Game Sanctuary: Accessible by a three-hour boat ride from Togiak, this island is where hundreds of photogenic but ungainly walruses haul out. The remote location, often-stormy weather, and restrictions on visitation mean that only a few hardy people make it to this unique island (page 465).

(Nome Backroads: Fanning out in three directions from Nome are three wonderful dirt roads that take visitors to Native villages, a hot springs, and even the rusting hulk of "The Last Train to Nowhere" (page 472).

(Gates of the Arctic National Park: Covering more than eight million acres of wild mountain lands in the Brooks Range, this very remote park is accessible by bush plane from surrounding villages. Hikers are on their own in a vast expanse of craggy ridges and glacially carved valleys (page 479).

(Arctic National Wildlife Refuge: Home to 150,000 caribou, this refuge covers eight million acres of North Slope wilderness threatened by oil development. Raft trips are the main access method for visitors (page 480).

(Inupiat Heritage Center: Located in the north slope town of Barrow, this living-

LOOK FOR **(** TO FIND RECOMMENDED SIGHTS, ACTIVITIES, DINING, AND LODGING.

history museum provides a great introduction to Eskimo traditions. While in Barrow, dip your toes in the Arctic Ocean, look for polar bears, or taste an enchilada at Pepe's North of the Border (page 482).

PLANNING YOUR TIME

Getting into the bush is half the fun of any trip to Western and Arctic Alaska. This is a vast landscape where developments are few and access is almost entirely by air. Many visitors to Barrow arrive by Alaska Air jet for a one-day or overnight tour, but in most other areas visitors stay longer to soak up a bit of this grand country. It's quite expensive to get into the bush and costs for air travel, food, and lodging can mount rapidly, so make sure you bring sufficient cash.

The town of Dillingham sits at heart of the Bristol Bay region (www.visitbristolbay.com), best known for the millions of sockeye salmon caught commercially. Many fishing lodges are sprinkled across the headwaters of major rivers that flow into the bay, and **Wood-Tikchik State Park**—the largest state park in America—encompasses a series of eight spectacular lakes (each over 20 miles long) backed by the rugged slopes of the Wood River Mountains. West of here, and a three-hour boat ride from

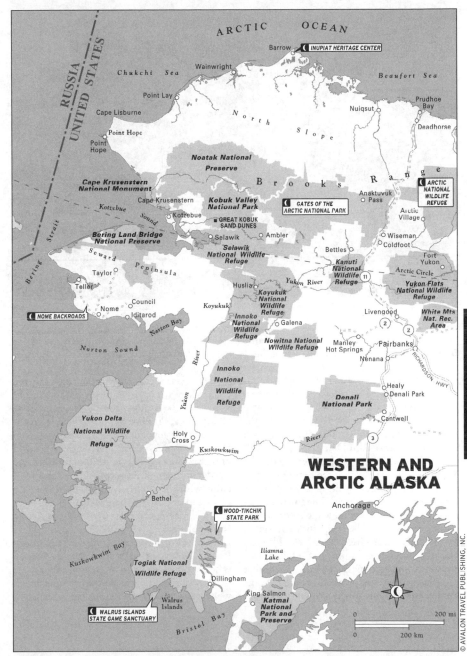

ARCTIC OCEAN

Barrow ◖ INUPIAT HERITAGE CENTER

Chukchi Sea   Wainwright   Beaufort Sea

Point Lay   Nuiqsut   Prudhoe Bay

Cape Lisburne   North   Deadhorse

Point Hope   Slope

Point Hope

RUSSIA
UNITED STATES

Noatak National Preserve

Cape Krusenstern National Monument   B r o o k s   R a n g e   ◖ ARCTIC NATIONAL WILDLIFE REFUGE

Cape Krusenstern   *Kobuk Valley National Park*   Anaktuvuk Pass

Kotzebue   ◖ GATES OF THE ARCTIC NATIONAL PARK   Arctic Village

Kotzebue Sound   ■ GREAT KOBUK SAND DUNES   Wiseman

Bering Land Bridge National Preserve   Selawik   Ambler   Coldfoot

Seward   *Selawik National Wildlife Refuge*   Bettles   Fort Yukon

Peninsula   *Kanuti National Wildlife Refuge*   Arctic Circle

Taylor   Yukon River   (11)   *Yukon Flats National Wildlife Refuge*

Teller   Huslia

Bering Strait   Council   Koyukuk   *Koyukuk National Wildlife Refuge*   Livengood   *White Mts Nat. Rec. Area*

◖ NOME BACKROADS   Nome   Iditarod   *Innoko National Wildlife Refuge*   Galena   (2)   (2)

Norton Bay   *Nowitna National Wildlife Refuge*   Manley Hot Springs   Fairbanks

Norton Sound   Yukon River   Nenana   RICHARDSON HWY

Innoko National Wildlife Refuge   Healy   Denali Park

Denali National Park

Yukon Delta National Wildlife Refuge   Holy Cross   Cantwell

Kuskokwim   River   (3)

WESTERN AND ARCTIC ALASKA

Bethel   Anchorage

◖ WOOD-TIKCHIK STATE PARK

Iliamna Lake

Togiak National Wildlife Refuge   Dillingham

Walrus Islands   King Salmon

◖ WALRUS ISLANDS STATE GAME SANCTUARY   *Katmai National Park and Preserve*

Kuskokwim Bay   Bristol Bay

0   200 mi
0   200 km

WESTERN ALASKA

WESTERN ALASKA

© DON PITCHER

Native children playing in the village of Bethel.

Togiak, are the **Walrus Islands State Game Sanctuary** and Round Island, where hundreds of these photogenic but ungainly masses of blubber haul out. Only a few hardy individuals (humans that is) are allowed to visit the island at a time.

The Yup'ik village of Bethel sits at the mouth of the mighty Kuskokwim River, with 20-million-acre Yukon Delta National Wildlife Refuge on all sides. Farther north, the Seward Peninsula juts into the Bering Sea, positioning the old gold mining town of Nome just 190 miles from Siberia. The town is a fascinating mix of Native and white cultural heritages, and serves as the endpoint each March for Alaska's "Last Great Race," the Iditarod Sled Dog Race. Gold mining still takes place around Nome, and massive dredges and other equipment are strewn across the tundra. Nome **backroads** fan out in three directions from

town, leading through magnificent country to small villages, a hot springs, and even the rusting hulk of "The Last Train to Nowhere."

Arctic Alaska is the real forbidden quarter, a place where winter rules much of the year but also where the summer sun never sets. Massive oil deposits at Prudhoe Bay drive the state's economy, and the town of Kotzebue serves as a hub for northwestern Alaska. The North Slope town of Barrow draws visitors to the **Inupiat Heritage Center** for a great intro to Eskimo traditions, along with the chance to dip toes in the Arctic Ocean or taste an enchilada at Pepe's North of the Border. Spectacular **Gates of the Arctic National Park** covers more than eight million acres of wild mountain lands in the Brooks Range, while **Arctic National Wildlife Refuge** is home to 150,000 caribou, several major rivers that attract adventurers, and the potential for oil, which attracts oil companies and politicians.

Dillingham and Vicinity

Dillingham (pop. 2,400) is the regional center for Bristol Bay, Alaska's largest sockeye salmon fishery. A large portion of the world's *wild* salmon catch comes from this enormous bay on the southern end of the Bering Sea. During the peak of the season, set nets line Dillingham beaches while gillnetters catch fish just offshore, and the town's four canneries run full blast. You won't, however, see the big fishing boats found elsewhere in Alaska, since commercial boats are limited to a maximum of 32 feet in length throughout Bristol Bay.

HISTORY

Dillingham's origins came from the first Russian fur traders who established a fort (Alexandrovski Redoubt) on the other side of Nushagak Bay in 1822. After the Americans took over, canneries were established in the area to process the enormous runs of red (sockeye) salmon up the Nushagak and Wood Rivers. When an influenza epidemic decimated the Native villages around Nushagak Bay in the winter of 1918–1919, many of the survivors moved to Dillingham. The result is a place composed of Yup'iks, Aleuts, Russians, and Americans. The local radio station, KDLG, still has Yup'ik-language broadcasts. Today, the town is almost wholly dependent upon the rich salmon fisheries of Bristol Bay, with a mix of commercial fishing and dozens of sport fishing lodges. Proposed gold mines and offshore oil development could also be on the horizon.

SIGHTS

Although there are many sportfishing lodges in the area, Dillingham is not much of a tourist town; most people come here to work. For a one-stop visit to town, head to Seward and D streets, where you'll find the **Sam Fox Museum** (907/842-5610, Mon.–Fri. 10 A.M.– 5 P.M.), which also houses a small visitor center (907/842-5115, www.dillinghamak.com). The city library (907/842- 5610, www.ci.dillingham.ak.us) is next door, with computers for Internet access.

The main attractions for visitors—if they aren't fishermen—are Wood-Tikchik State Park and Walrus Islands State Game Sanctuary. **Togiak National Wildlife Refuge** begins just three miles west of Dillingham and covers 4.3 million acres. It is a vital staging area for migrating waterfowl, especially brant, emperor geese, common eiders, and Steller's eiders. Stop by the refuge office in Dillingham (907/842-1063 or 800/817-2538, http://togiak.fws.gov) before heading out.

An enjoyable 24-mile dirt road leads out of Dillingham to the village of **Aleknagik** (pop. 200) where the state has a boat ramp on Lake Aleknagik. Wood Tikchik Park begins at the upper end of this lake.

Dillingham's main event is the **Beaver Round-Up,** a five-day March party that features a championship dog sled race, dances, and the locally heralded Miss Dillingham pageant. The **4th of July Salmon Bake** is another fun event.

ACCOMMODATIONS AND FOOD

Add an 8 percent tax to all these lodging rates. **Bristol Inn** (104 Main St., 907/842-2240 or 800/764-9704, www.alaskaoutdoors.com/bristolinn) charges $151 s or $166 d; kitchenettes are $158 s or $180 d. A continental breakfast and airport shuttle are provided.

Catering to outdoor enthusiasts, **The Bunk House B&B** (907/842- or 888/848-2715, www.dillinghamservices.com, $130 s or $170 d) has a house three miles out of town with bunks, a full kitchen, and continental breakfasts. It's especially popular with groups.

Two miles out of town atop Kleetuk Hill, **Hillside Haven** (907/842-3523, www.hillsidehavenalaska.com, $140 s or $210 d) has vistas in all directions, and the large home has two nicely furnished guest rooms. Rates include a full breakfast and dinner at **Café Hillside** (dinner entrées $13–25). The café is open for homemade lunches and dinners most

WESTERN ALASKA

days, with nightly specials. The Sunday brunch buffet ($17) is also popular.

Dillingham's most distinctive lodging place, **Thai Inn** (907/842-7378, www.thai-inn.com, $120–140 s or $130–150 d) is a huge downtown hilltop home. Several rooms are decorated with hand-carved Thai pieces, giving it a decidedly un-Alaskan look. All rooms have private baths, fridges, microwaves, and Wi-Fi. Breakfast is self-serve.

Beaver Creek B&B (907/842-7335 or 866/252-7335, www.dillinghamalaska.com, $145 s or $160 d) has a half-dozen houses and cabins in the area. All rooms include access to full kitchens, laundry facilities, free transport around town, and make-it-yourself breakfasts. Call well ahead for mid-summer reservations.

No camping in Dillingham, and much of the land out the road is in Native corporation or private hands. Showers are available at the boat harbor.

Besides the above-mentioned café Hillside, food options are limited and you may end up just eating at whichever place (if any) is open. Try **Juan Ricardos' of Dillingham** (907/842-1205), with Mexican food and surprisingly good pizzas, or **Twin Dragon** (907/842-2172) for Chinese and American food at the airport. Get groceries ($8/gallon milk!) at **N&N Market** (907/842-5283) or the larger **Alaska Commercial Company** (907/842-5444).

GETTING THERE

The airport is a bit over two miles from Dillingham; get into town ($10 per person) on **Abba Joy's Taxi** (907/842-4555) or **Nushagak Cab Company** (907/842-4403). A car is useful if you plan to spend any time in the Dillingham area, or want to head up the road to Aleknagik; rent one from **D & J Rentals** (907/842-2222).

Alaska Airlines (800/426-0333, www.alaskaair.com), **PenAir** (907/243-2323 or 800/448-4226, www.penair.com), and **Frontier Flying Service** (907/450-7200 or 800/478-6779, www.frontierflying.com) have daily flights between Anchorage and Dillingham all year. PenAir also services many surrounding villages and towns.

Local air taxis include **Arctic Circle Air**

(907/842-3870 or 888/214-2364, www.arctic-circle-air.com), **Bay Air** (907/842-2570, www.bayair-alaska.com), **Fresh Water Adventures** (907/842-5060, www.freshwateradventure.com), **Renew Air Taxi** (907/842-3440 or 888/684-0177, www.renewairtaxi.com, **Shannon's Air Taxi** (907/842-2735), **Tikchik AirVentures** (907/842-5841, www.tikchikairventures.com), and **Tucker Aviation** (907/842-1023). The dozens of regional fishing lodges keep them busy all summer.

WOOD-TIKCHIK STATE PARK

This 1.6-million-acre state facility—the largest state park in the country—is 300 miles southwest of Anchorage, and a half-hour floatplane flight from Dillingham. The park preserves a vast system of rivers and lakes, including two long chains of interconnected waterways. There are eight different lakes at least 20 miles long, plus countless smaller ponds. These lakes offer some of the most awesome sportfishing to be found: trophy salmon, trout, Arctic char, northern pike.

The east side of Wood-Tikchik is almost flat, wooded terrain, but to the west the rugged Wood River Mountains rise, some topping 5,000 feet. Canoeists or kayakers may want to float down such rivers as the Nuyakuk or Tikchik, where the unsurpassed scenery is untouched by development. You could easily spend several weeks exploring this area, but be forewarned that there's lots of big open water and storms can blow up. Also come prepared to battle the mosquitoes and other flying menaces.

Practicalities

For complete details on this remote park, contact Wood-Tikchik State Park headquarters in Anchorage (907/269-8698, www.alaskastateparks.org, year-round) or the Dillingham office (907/842-2375, late May–late Sept.).

Access is primarily by floatplane from Dillingham, but it's also possible to drive the 24 miles from Dillingham to the village of Aleknagik on Aleknagik Lake, and then boat through a long series of connected lakes. There are no trails or other developed facilities within the park itself, but camping and hiking opportunities abound if you have the right gear and a boat to get around. **Tikchik State Park Tours** (907/243-1416 or 888/345-2445, www.tikchik.com) leads kayaking trips within the park on Tikchik, Chaukaktuli, and Chikuminuk lakes, along with Tikchik River and Salmon River float trips. They also rent kayaks for do-it-yourselfers.

Most visitors to Wood-Tikchik stay at local fishing and hunting lodges, including **Bearclaw Fishing Lodge** (907/842-4060 or 866/429-2327, www.bearclawlodge.com) and **Tikchik Narrows Lodge** (907/596-3511 or 360/379-2842, www.tikchiklodge.com); the latter is recommended.

◖ WALRUS ISLANDS STATE GAME SANCTUARY

The Walrus Islands are a cluster of seven small rocky points of land in northern Bristol Bay. One of them—Round Island—is famous as a haul-out spot for thousands of walrus during the summer; only the bulls come ashore here. The walrus masses form what author Tom Kizzia called "a writhing mat of wrinkled, rust-colored leather" on the rocky beach where they rest. There are also hundreds of thousands of nesting seabirds-black-legged kittiwakes, common murres, cormorants, and parakeet auklets—as well as tufted and horned puffins. Also on the island are inquisitive red foxes. Steller sea lions come ashore on one beach.

Practicalities

Contact the Alaska Department of Fish & Game (907/842-1013, www.state.ak.us/adfg) for an information packet and permit application. You can apply as early as January 1, and it's a good idea to get your application in early to be sure of a place at the peak time (mid-June through July). To keep human impacts to a minimum, only 12 permits ($50 pp) are issued for each five-day period, so you won't have a lot of neighbors, other than the birds and bulls. Two of the 12 permits

are held open for those who apply within 10 days before a given time slot, so you might be able to get in at the last minute. Access to Round Island is difficult and equally expensive.

Two companies offer boat access to Round Island, with the permit included in the price, but you'll first need to fly to Dillingham from Anchorage (around $450 round-trip). **Frontier Flying Service** (907/450-7200 or 800/478-6779, www.frontierflying.com) flies from Anchorage directly to Togiak (an interesting Native village), where Paul Markoff of **Togiak Outfitters** (907/493-5043, www.togiakoutfitters.com) provides transportation to the islands (three hours each way) for $630 per person round-trip. He operates a fast 22-foot boat, but the service is weather and tide dependant, and it's 30 miles of open ocean. He can also assist with transportation and lodging in Togiak.

Terry Johnson of **Walrus Islands Expeditions** (907/235-9349, www.alaskawalrusisland.com) has a variety of cruises, the most popular of which is a three-day, two-night trip that includes a berth in the boat, meals, and guide for $1,395 per person. Camper drop-offs are available for $300 round-trip, or you can choose a one-day trip for $495. He operates out of Eagle Bay, so you'll need to add in a $425 per person floatplane flight from Dillingham. Johnson's boat is slower, but is also larger (40 ft.) and more stable so he can operate in most conditions.

You'll have to bring all your own camping gear, food, and supplies. The weather can be pretty wild—60-knot winds and pelting rain—so don't skimp on your tent and raingear. Be sure to take long tent stakes—and some extras—to hold everything down. Also bring enough food to last a week longer than you'd expected, since the weather can occasionally close in for long periods, making it impossible to leave. Trails lead from the camping area to outstanding cliffs where you can look down on the walrus or across to nesting seabirds. Fish & Game has two research technicians on the island who will answer your questions; they aren't guides, however.

Bethel

Flying to Bethel (pop. 5,000) from Anchorage hammers home an appreciation of how vast this country is. The Alaska Range and Kuskokwim Mountains serve up a seemingly impenetrable set of summits for over 300 miles. Then, it terminates abruptly in a range of hills that flattens into an enormous coastal plain. Far below, the land is pockmarked with thousands of ponds of all sizes, and the Kuskokwim River meanders its way toward the sea, past oxbows and brush-lined shores. The mixed Native and immigrant town of Bethel sprawls along the wide Kuskokwim River some 80 miles from its mouth.

Bethel is one of the largest settlements in the Alaskan bush. It serves as a supply center, as well as a transportation and communication hub, for dozens of outlying villages. You're likely to meet many people fluent in both English and Yup'ik (the nightly TV news is in both languages) along with a surprising number of recent emigrants from Eastern Europe and Korea. The country here is essentially flat tundra with willows along the river banks and thin black spruce forests farther upriver. In the summer, the Kuskokwim provides boat access to villages all along the river; when winter comes, it becomes an ice road for settlements hundreds of miles upriver. This is certainly one of the most unique roads in America. Each spring all commerce shuts down for a couple of weeks, when the river is too thin to drive on and the ice has not yet floated away in the big breakup.

Bethel is built on permafrost, so all buildings are constructed on stilts to prevent heat from thawing the ground and causing them to sink into a quagmire. Permafrost makes it very difficult to lay water lines, so water is trucked to holding tanks outside each home and business. This means you won't have a lot of water to waste on showers, and in some places the water is nearly undrinkable (this depends upon the source). This undrinkable water might partly explain the high sales of soda pop at local grocery stores, and makes a good excuse for the abundance of vodka in a town where alcohol cannot be legally sold.

SIGHTS

A trading post was established along the Kuskokwim River in the 1870s, and was followed a decade later by a Moravian Church mission. The town of Bethel—named for the scriptural directive "Arise, go to Bethel, and dwell there"—grew up around this mission and trading post. The old **Moravian Church,** built around 1885, is the most interesting and photogenic local structure.

The **Yupik Cultural Center** (907/543-1819), in the same building as the University of Alaska's Kuskokwim campus, contains a fascinating collection of old Yup'ik clothing and tools, along with photographic exhibits. There are seal-gut parkas, dolls, baskets, and beautiful carved ivory pieces.

Other than this, the primary sights are the town itself and the wild country that reaches for an eternity in all directions from Bethel. The **Yukon-Kuskokwin Delta Regional Hospital** is that strange yellow building you pass on the way into town from the airport. It looks like the old drawings of space stations once planned for Mars.

Hang around the Alaska Commercial Co. store for that most Bethel of all Bethel attractions, the legion of local taxi cabs—all waiting outside with their engines running while the Slavic, Albanian, and Korean drivers smoke cigarettes and talk. Imagine it as a scene from an old Western, except that the horses tied up out front have been replaced by taxis and the cowboys speak with an Eastern European or Asian accent.

Bethel lacks a visitor center, but for info try the **Bethel Chamber of Commerce** (907/543-2911, www.bethelakchamber.org) or the **Delta Discovery** website (www.delta discovery.com).

YUKON DELTA NATIONAL WILDLIFE REFUGE

The town of Bethel is encircled by this 20 million-acre wildlife refuge, largest in America. The refuge covers the widely spreading mouths of both the Yukon and Kuskokwim Rivers (The Y-K Delta), plus nearby Nunivak Island. Nearly all this land is a potholed mélange of tundra marshes, lakes, and streams. Yukon Delta National Wildlife Refuge is a vital area for waterfowl. The numbers are staggering: More than two million ducks, 750,000 geese and swans, plus another 100 million shorebirds nest here each summer. Most outsiders come to the refuge to see the birds and other animals; most Yup'ik people come here to hunt and fish as they have for time immemorial.

Access to the refuge is by boat or floatplane. Hiking is difficult on this marshy terrain. The **visitor center** at refuge headquarters in Bethel (907/543-3151, http://yukondelta.fws.gov) has wildlife displays and photographs. It occasionally offers guided bird-watching tours in the summer.

Kuskokwim Wilderness Adventures (907/543-3900, www.kuskofish.com) guides camping, rafting, and dog mushing trips in the Bethel area.

EVENTS

Bethel's primary winter event is the **Kuskokwim-300 Sled Dog Race** (907/543-3300, www.k300.org) held each January. It's a three-day mad dash up the frozen ice that attracts some of the fastest teams in the nation and even a few international entries. The **Cama'i Festival** (907/543-1977, www.bethelarts.com) in April is a three-day Native dance event with performers from all over Alaska and even Russia. This is a great time to buy Native crafts.

SHOPPING

Adjacent to the Moravian church, the **Moravian Book Store** (907/543-2474) sells books, postcards from all the surrounding villages, church pamphlets, locally made jewelry, and a dose of the religious radio station. Ask around and you might find someone to sew one of the beautiful and distinctive parkas worn by Native women, or to knit a garment out of musk ox wool, but be ready to part with a large amount of cash for either of these one-of-a-kind items. The fin-

est Alaskan baskets come from the village of Hooper Bay, 100 miles northwest of Bethel.

ACCOMMODATIONS

Pacifica Guest House (907/543-4305) has comfortable rooms for $90 s or $100 d with shared baths, and suites for $135 s or $145 d s with private baths.

Bethel's largest lodging place is **Long House Bethel Inn** (907/543-4612 or 866/543-4613, www.longhousebethelinn.com, $139–159 s or d). The coffee shop here has Internet access.

Lakeside Lodge B&B (907/543-5275, www.lakesidelodgebnb.com, $100 s or $125 d) is a quiet edge-of-town place where the three guest rooms have bunk beds. A full breakfast is included.

Bentley's Porterhouse B&B (907/543-3552, $95–140 s or $121–164 d) has 35 attractive rooms spread over six buildings. The less expensive rooms have shared baths, or you can pay a bit more for a private bath. A full breakfast and Wi-Fi are included.

Brown Slough B&B (907/543-4334 or 888/543-4334, www.bethelhotel.com) has two large and comfortable across-the-street homes along the slough. One of these is a beautiful two-story log structure. Most of the eight guest rooms share baths, and are $110 s or d, but one room has its own bath ($130 s or d). All include a continental breakfast and Wi-Fi.

FOOD

Find good pizza, calzones, and Greek specialties (including gyros, shish kebab, and baklava) at **Dimitri's Restaurant** (907/543-3434). **Front St. Café** (907/543-3408) is probably the best overall dining choice in Bethel, with an ethnic mélange of Chinese, American, pizzas, and even Mexican food under one roof. Located at Pacifica Guest House, **V.I.P. Restaurant** (907/543-4777) serves Korean, Japanese, and American meals three times a day. Out at the airport, **Arctic Sun Cafe** (907/543-4566) serves breakfast and lunch, while the adjacent **Brother's Pizza & Subs** (907/543-3553) opens in the evening.

Get groceries and supplies from **Alaska**

Commercial Company (907/543-2661) or **Swanson's** (907/543-3221).

Bethel is a "damp" town where booze cannot be sold, but can be brought in for "personal use." This creates a situation ripe for bootlegging. More than a few locals import booze—especially vodka—to sell for a high markup ($50 a fifth!) to others desperate for a drink. A few years back a man was caught with 108 bottles in his possession, but he managed to convince a jury that they were for the wedding of a long-lost daughter.

GETTING THERE AND AROUND

Bethel serves as the transportation hub for much of Western Alaska, and has the third-busiest flight service station in the state. **Alaska**

Airlines (800/426-0333, www.alaskaair.com) and **Frontier Flying Service** (907/450-7200 or 800/478-6779, www.frontierflying.com) both have daily year-round service between Anchorage and Bethel.

Several air-taxi companies offer scheduled flights or charters from Bethel to other bush villages: **Grant Aviation** (907/543-2000 or 888/359-4726, www.flygrant.com), **Arctic Circle Air** (907/543-5906 or 800/478-2928, www.arctic-circle-air.com), **JP Air Service** (907/543-3279), and **Yukon Aviation** (907/543-3280, www.yukonaviation.com).

Rent cars (starting around $95/day) from **Payless Car Rental** (907/543-3058 or 800/729-5377). Oh yes—if you want a cab, just look around; one is bound to be within a couple hundred feet of any place in town.

Nome and Vicinity

If you make only one long flight to see bush Alaska, make it to fascinating Nome (pop. 3,500, of whom nearly 1,900 are Native). The town sits on the Seward Peninsula on the edge of Norton Sound facing the Bering Sea, only 190 miles east of Siberia, and 2,300 miles north of Seattle. Flying time is 90 minutes from Anchorage.

Nome was named when a cartographer marked its unnamed location on a map as "? Name," and a second mapmaker misread it as "C. [for Cape] Nome." Lying 150 miles south of the Arctic Circle, Nome is on roughly the same latitude as Fairbanks, and shares similar hours of daylight, as well as warmer temperatures than its Arctic coast cousins, Kotzebue and Barrow—though the mercury rests around 0°F in January, and soars to a sizzling 60°F in the long days of July! Local motels advertise: "Visit picturesque Nome this summer. Three days—no nights."

Like other bush Alaska settlements, Nome is far from pretty, with piles of junk strewn about the yards and more than a few drunks stumbling from the town's eight saloons. But it

has more of a small-city feeling than Bethel or Kotzebue, with historic buildings, paved streets (some of them), and a real downtown. Although there are almost no trees in Nome, each winter the "Nome National Forest" sprouts as locals plant their former Christmas trees in the offshore pack ice. (People cut the trees near Teller each fall before the road closes for the winter.)

SIGHTS

Start out at the helpful **Nome Visitor Center** (daily 9 A.M.–9 P.M. late May–mid-Sept., Mon.–Fri. 9 A.M.–6 P.M. the rest of the year) on Front Street in the center of town, run by the Nome Convention and Visitors Bureau (907/443-6624 or 800/478-1901, www.nomechamber.org). The knowledgeable staff will point you in the right direction, and the scrapbooks, photo albums, and amazingly detailed handouts provide an excellent introduction to the area. Pick up the walking-tour brochure, mostly focusing on historical attractions, such as the nearby dredges.

Step across the street to **city hall,** with its Victorian exterior. During the Iditarod Race, the

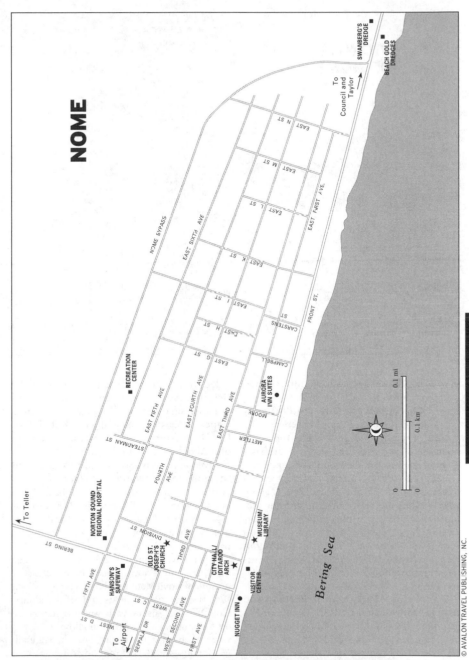

NOME

SWANBERG'S DREDGE

BEACH GOLD DREDGES

To Council and Taylor

EAST N ST

EAST M ST

EAST L ST

EAST FIRST AVE

EAST K ST

EAST' SIXTH AVE

NOME BYPASS

EAST I ST

FRONT ST.

EAST H ST

CARSTENS ST

RECREATION CENTER

EAST G ST

CAMPBELL

EAST FIFTH AVE

EAST FOURTH AVE

AURORA INN SUITES

STEADMAN ST

EAST THIRD AVE

MOORE

METTLER

FOURTH AVE

NORTON SOUND REGIONAL HOSPITAL

To Teller

BERING ST

DIVISION ST

THIRD AVE

MUSEUM/ LIBRARY

OLD ST. JOSEPH'S CHURCH

FIFTH AVE

HANSON'S SAFEWAY

CITY HALL/ IDITAROD ARCH

C ST

WEST D ST

SEPPALA DR

WEST SECOND AVE

WEST FIRST AVE

To Airport

NUGGET INN

VISITOR CENTER

Bering Sea

0.1 mi

0.1 km

0

0

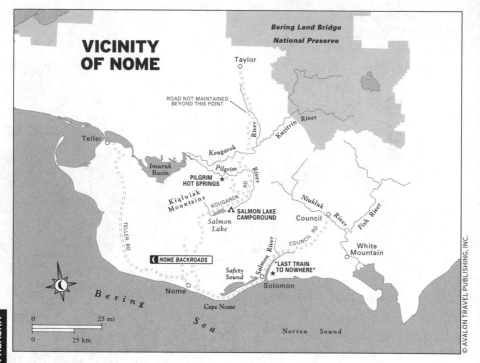

VICINITY OF NOME

Bering Land Bridge National Preserve

ROAD NOT MAINTAINED BEYOND THIS POINT

Taylor

Teller

Kougarok

Pilgrim

Inuruk Basin

PILGRIM HOT SPRINGS

Kigluaik Mountains

KOUGAROK RD

SALMON LAKE CAMPGROUND

Salmon Lake

TELLER RD

NOME BACKROADS

Kuzitrin River

River

River

Niukluk

Council

Fish River

COUNCIL RD

White Mountain

Salmon River

"LAST TRAIN TO NOWHERE"

Safety Sound

Nome

Solomon

Bering Sea

Cape Nome

Norton Sound

0   25 mi
0   25 km

© AVALON TRAVEL PUBLISHING, INC.

WESTERN ALASKA

massive **buried wooden arch** out front is moved over Front Street to mark the finish line.

The **Carrie McLain Museum** (907/443-6630, www.nomealaska.org/museum, daily 9 A.M.–5:30 P.M. June–early Sept., Tues.–Sat. noon–6 P.M. the rest of the year) is in the basement of the library, a few doors east on Front Street. It houses a fascinating collection of historical photos from the gold rush era, along with exhibits on Native culture, sled dog racing, and the discovery of gold in 1898, the arrival of Wyatt Earp, and the rush of 40,000 miners to Nome in 1900. The **Kegoayah Kozga Library** (907/443-6628) houses an interesting rare books section, plus computers you can use to check your email.

The National Park Service's **Bering Land Bridge Information Center** (179 Front St., 907/443-2522 or 800/471-2352, www.nps.gov/bela) is open Monday–Friday 8 A.M.–5 P.M. all year. Step inside to view the exhibits and

videos or to talk with the staff about nearby Bering Land Bridge National Preserve and other national parks in the vicinity, including Cape Krusenstern, Noatak, and Kobuk Valley. Guided tundra hikes to nearby areas are offered occasionally in the summer.

Over on Division Street at 3rd Avenue is **Old St. Joseph's Catholic Church** (Mon.–Fri. 10 A.M.–2 P.M. in the summer) built in 1901, but closed in 1945. The building has been lovingly restored and is now used for local events. Take your photo at "America's largest gold pan," next to the church.

If you have a car or bike (or want a nice day hike), take the 4.5-mile road to the 1,062-foot summit of **Anvil Mountain** behind Nome. World War II gun emplacements and an abandoned Cold War–era distant early warning station are on top, and on a clear day you'll be treated to views of the city, the Bering Sea, the Kigluaik Mountains, and the surrounding tundra.

NOME HISTORY

In 1898, the "three lucky Swedes," Jafet Lindberg, Erik Lindblom, and John Brynteson, discovered fabulous deposits of gold in Anvil Creek above present-day Nome. Word reached Dawson the next spring, and by fall, 10,000 stampeders had arrived and set up tents on the beach, only to have them blown away by a fierce September storm that prompted a migration inland. There, more gold was found; in fact, placer deposits were carried by most streams that emptied into the Bering Sea. By 1900, 20,000 prospectors crowded the coast, fully a third of the white population in Alaska at the time. For a time it was the territory's largest city. A railroad had been built to Anvil Creek, which produced several dozen million-dollar claims. Some became rich, but many men who had bought one-way passage to the gold fields found themselves destitute, and the Army had to be brought in to get them home before the winter of 1901. Judge James Wickersham brought law and order to Nome in 1902, after the first judge was convicted of corruption. Several devastating fires and storms have destroyed most of Nome's historic downtown buildings, but a few of the original buildings survive.

In 1925, a diphtheria epidemic required emergency delivery of serum from Nenana 650 miles overland by dog sled. Through the heroic efforts of mushers and dogs, the serum arrived in time to save many lives. This event is commemorated today in the famous Iditarod Sled Dog Race from Anchorage to Nome. The race takes place every March and turns Nome into a late winter carnival.

During World War II, Nome was a major transfer point for lend-lease aircraft being sent to Russia from the United States. The planes were flown up to Alaska from the Lower 48 states, transferred to Russian pilots in Fairbanks, and then flown on to Nome and the Soviet Union. Almost 8,000 planes came through Nome between 1942 and 1945, most making it to the front for use in the war against Germany.

Today, Nome survives on small-scale gold mining, tourism, and as a regional center for the Seward Peninsula. Many visitors try their luck at panning for gold along the beaches here. The Native people maintain subsistence fishing and hunting traditions, along with the herding of some 30,000 reindeer. The antlers are sold for medicinal use (aphrodisiacs) in Asia, and the meat is available in local stores. Nome is a good place to buy ivory and other artwork in the various gift shops, along with imported crafts from Russia. Of course, the Iditarod Race focuses international attention on Nome every March.

Gold Fever

Gold dredges were once sprinkled all across the Seward Peninsula, and the last of these operated until 1995, when low gold prices and rising costs forced the last one to shut down. With a little exploration, you're sure to find some of the more than 100 old dredges that remain in the surrounding country. A number of these are within walking distance of Nome, but don't climb on them since they're unsafe. Closest is the **Swanberg Dredge** just east of town. Nearby is a small park with old mining equipment, including a steam shovel. Far more impressive is **Dredge No. 5** a couple of miles north of town off the Teller Road. Offshore to the north of town is an enormous 14-story-tall dredge; it was the largest ever built.

Across the road from the Swanberg Dredge is a public beach where anyone can try a hand at panning for gold. The beach attracts an annual gathering of ambitious recreational miners who operate dredges throughout the summer months. It's hard work that involves a dry-suited diver operating a suction dredge atop a raft several hundred feet offshore. They're a pretty tightlipped group, but must be finding something since many return each summer.

(NOME BACKROADS

The real treat in Nome is the opportunity to explore this expansive, far-as-the-eye-can-see landscape. Over 250 miles of gravel roads fan out from town, taking you across the subarctic countryside around Seward Peninsula. Wildlife—including musk ox, red foxes, wolves, moose, reindeer, and even a few grizzlies—can be seen, and the fishing is good for salmon, pike, grayling, whitefish, and Dolly Varden. Anglers will want to pick up the free *Nome Roadside Fishing Guide* from the visitor center before heading out.

Bird-watchers come from all over the nation to track down unusual bird species in the Nome area, including some that wander across the Bering Strait from Russia. The visitor center posts unusual sightings, and has a bird checklist and brochure listing companies offering bird-watching trips. Also available at the visitor center is a brochure describing hiking routes.

In midsummer, the roads are lined with verdant tundra plants and a massive display of 200 species of flowers. Some have likened it to driving through Denali National Park, but without anyone else there. The roads lead to the tiny settlements of Teller, Council, and Taylor, taking you past remnants from the gold rush—dredges, miners' cabins, and even an old train.

Air taxis from Nome provide flights to Bering Land Bridge National Preserve, where you will find popular Serpentine Hot Springs. (See *The Arctic* section for details.)

Kougarok Road

Also known as the Taylor Road, this exceptionally scenic route leads north along Nome River into the beautiful **Kigluaik Mountains,** a great place to explore on foot. The road parallels part of the historic Wild Goose Pipeline, built of metal hoops and redwood slats between 1905 and 1909 to carry water to Nome gold mines. The pipeline was never completed, but is still intact in places. There's a free Bureau of Land Management campground and picnic area at **Salmon Lake,** 40 miles out, and a hike-in shelter cabin in the Mosquito Pass area. Contact the BLM office in Nome (907/443-2177) for

the access route. A side trip to the old Catholic church and orphanage at **Pilgrim Hot Springs** is another option. The orphanage opened after the 1918 influenza epidemic killed many Eskimo parents in the area. The springs are not open to the public. Kougarok Road is not maintained beyond the Kougarok River bridge (Mile 85), though a trail continues to the village of Taylor.

Council Road

This gravel road heads east from Nome, following the shoreline of the Bering Sea for the first 30 miles, before turning northeast. Eskimo fishing and hunting camps are all along this route. Bird-watchers flock to Safety Sound, a great place to watch for unusual species of ducks, swans, geese, and shorebirds.

At Mile 33, the road passes a favorite photographic stop, the rusting hulk of the **"Last Train to Nowhere."** The train consists of three locomotive engines and several cars from the Council City and Solomon River Railroad, begun in 1881. The engines originally served on the New York Elevated Railroad Company before they were shipped north in 1903, and are the only such engines still in existence. The railroad was originally envisioned as part of a system that would connect Nome's gold fields with the Lower 48, but the vision died because of financial problems and wild storms that destroyed the tracks along the Bering Sea in 1907. At its maximum, the tracks only extended a distance of 35 miles.

The road ends at the Niukluk River (good fishing) near **Council,** 72 miles from Nome. It is possible to drive across the river at a fording point, but don't do so without help from locals. An alternative would be to have someone take you across by boat. One unusual aspect of the country around Council is the presence of trees, a real treat after all the open tundra elsewhere on the Seward Peninsula. The settlement of Council still has remnants of log cabins from the gold rush era when the town was home to 10,000 people. Now it's a summer home area for folks from Nome. Simple cabins are available at **Camp Bendelben** (907/443-2880).

©DON PITCHER

the Last Train to Nowhere

Teller Road

It's a beautiful two-hour drive on this 73-mile gravel road that leads from Nome to the Eskimo village of **Teller** (pop. 250). Along the way, you're likely to see reindeer herded by locals, along with musk ox and unusual bird species. Two stores in Teller have limited supplies.

ENTERTAINMENT AND EVENTS

Nome is a hard-drinking town with four liquor stores and six bars, including the surprisingly capacious **Board of Trade** (on Front St., 907/443-2611). There's live music here most summer nights and during the Iditarod. The Board of Trade opened as the Dexter Saloon in 1901 under the proprietorship of gunslinger Wyatt Earp. Selling liquor and running gambling tables helped make Earp a very rich man; by the time he left Nome later that year, he had pocketed $80,000 in profits. Today, the gambling comes in the form of pull tabs and nightly bingo games.

Residents from outlying villages (all of which are dry) come to Nome to drink, and do a very thorough job of it, as you will quickly see. Things can get pretty bad sometimes as the alcohol pours and the drunks get drunker. It could be worse though—in the town's early days three-foot-thick urine glaciers were reported outside some saloons.

Nome's main attraction is the famous **Iditarod Trail Sled Dog Race** (www.iditarod.com). Beginning in Anchorage on the first Saturday in March, the race covers 1,049 miles to the finish point in Nome. It generally takes 10–12 days for the first team to reach Nome. Reserve far ahead to be sure of a motel room for the hectic finish. Everyone comes out to cheer the winning mushers and also-rans. The race ends under the burled arch that stands along Front Street.

Other March events include the **Iditarod Basketball Tournament.** With over 50 different high school boys' and girls' teams, this is said to be the largest in the nation. And, of course, there's the infamous **Bering Sea Ice**

Golf Classic. The golf classic is played on the frozen sea off Nome, a place with hazards not common to most courses. It uses orange golf balls and green-dyed ice for the "greens." Another goofball event is the annual **Summer Solstice Polar Bear Swim** in the Bering Sea—assuming the ice is out! If you aren't so foolhardy, there's always the indoor swimming pool at the high school. The Nome Convention and Visitors Bureau (907/443-6624 or 800/478-1901, www.nomealaska.org) has details on all these (and other) events.

SHOPPING

Check out Nome's gift shops for Eskimo dolls, carved ivory and soapstone, grass baskets, mukluks, and sealskin slippers. Good places to start are **Arctic Trading Post** (907/443-2686), **Maruskiya's Gift Shop** (907/443-2955), and **Chukotka-Alaska** (907/443-4128 or 800/416-4128). The last two also sell handicrafts from Provideniya, Russia, just across the Bering Strait from Nome.

Get camping gear and other outdoor supplies from **Nome Outfitters** (235 E. 1st Ave., 907/443-2880 or 800/680-6663).

ACCOMMODATIONS

Nome's best-known hotel, **Nugget Inn** (907/443-2323 or 877/443-2323) has small older rooms but the exterior and lobby are full of character. You'll feel as though you just stepped back a century. Be sure to check out the "doll house" out front; it was originally built during the gold rush. Call for current rates.

Aurora Inn & Suites (907/443-3838 or 800/354-4606, www.aurorainnome.com) has the finest lodging in Nome, with 56 bright and spacious rooms ($140 d), kitchenettes ($150–185 d), and apartments ($195–240 d). **Extra Dry Creek B&B** (907/443-7615, $115 s or $125 d) has a studio apartment unit with kitchen, bath, laundry, and Wi-Fi, including breakfast ingredients.

Mai's Guest House (907/443-4113, $60 s or $70 d) is a good budget option where the four rooms all have private baths.

At **Bering Sea B&B** (907/443-2936, $100 s or 120 d) two guest rooms share a bath, and a continental breakfast is included. **Bed for a Night** (907/443-3841, $90 s or $135 d) rents out a room with private bath and kitchen access.

During the Iditarod each March many locals open their homes for out-of-towners. The Convention and Visitors Bureau (907/443-6624 or 800/478-1901) keeps a list.

CAMPING

Anyone can camp for free on the beach on the east side of Nome, but you'll need to get water from the visitor center and take showers at the recreation center. The abundant beach driftwood makes for great campfires. There's also a free BLM campground at **Salmon Lake,** 40 miles out the Kougarok Road. Located in the mountains, it's worth the drive if you can afford a rental vehicle. Good fishing for grayling, whitefish, and Dolly Varden, too. It is also possible to camp on open tundra along the road system fanning out from Nome, but check first with the visitor center for a map of public lands since much of this is Native-owned.

FOOD

Eat at the popular **Fat Freddie's** (behind the Nugget Inn on Front St., 907/443-5899), for breakfast or a big lunch. The food is reasonable, but nothing special. They're also open evenings with steaks, fried chicken, and halibut.

Despite the name, **Milano's Pizzeria** (110 W. Front St., 907/443-2924) is not owned by an Italian. Like many other bush Alaska restaurants, it is run by Korean-Americans. To add to the confusion, it also has a sushi bar! A small cheese pizza is $11.

Airport Pizza (907/443-7992 or 877/749-9270, www.airportpizza.com) serves pizzas by the slice or pie, and is locally famous for fly-out pizzas shipped via air taxis to remote villages. The same owners also run a drive-through espresso spot across from Hanson's.

Find south-of-the-border fare at **Que Onda Mexican Restaurant** (907/443-3986). A Subway is the only fast food chain in town.

Get groceries in town from **Hanson's Safeway** (4th and Bering, 907/443-5454) or

Alaska Commercial Company (on the north edge of Nome, 907/443-2243). **Arctic Trading Post** (907/443-2686), across from the visitor center, serves espresso and also has regional books for sale.

INFORMATION AND SERVICES

Find an ATM in the Wells Fargo on Front Street. The **Recreation Center** (907/443-5432, daily, $5) is three miles east of town next to the high school, and includes a swimming pool, racquetball courts, weight room, sauna, and even a bowling alley. The **Kegoayah Kozga Library** (223 Front St., 907/443-6628, www.nome alaska.org/library) provides free Internet access. (Nome's visitor centers are described in *Sights*.)

For emergencies, head to **Norton Sound Regional Hospital** (at Bering and 5th, 907/443-3311, www.nortonsoundhealth.org).

GETTING THERE AND AROUND

Alaska Airlines (907/443-2288 or 800/426-0333, www.alaskaair.com) has daily jet service into Nome from Anchorage and Kotzebue. **Frontier Flying Service** (907/450-7200 or 800/478-6779, www.frontierflying.com) has daily flights between Fairbanks and Nome, plus service to surrounding villages and St. Lawrence Island. Other companies offering bush flights from Nome include **Bering Air** (907/443-5464 or 800/478-5422, www.beringair.com) and **Hageland Aviation** (907/443-7595 or 866/239-0119, www.hageland.com). The Nome airport is 1.5 miles from town, or a $5 per person taxi ride from **Checker Cab** (907/443-5211).

Rent pickups, vans, or SUVs from **Stampede Ventures** (907/443-5252 or 800/354-4606, www.aurorainnome.com, $95/day and up) or **Alaska Cab Garage** (907/443-2939, $85/day). Stampede has newer vehicles. Reserve ahead to be sure of finding a vehicle when you arrive. Gas prices in Nome are frequently twice those in Anchorage or the Lower 48.

Tours

Most visitors to Nome arrive as part of a see-the-

Arctic package from **Alaska Airlines Vacations** (800/468-2248, www.alaskair.com). Tour options include a day trip to Nome for $410, or an overnight trip to Nome for $530 s or $920 d. Both of these options also include local tours and round-trip air transportation from Anchorage.

For amusing and personalized tours of the Nome area, contact Richard Beneville of **Nome Discovery Tours** (907/443-2814, www.nomechamber.org/discoverytours). His background as an actor, dancer, and singer in New York may seem a bit out of place, but he's been in Alaska for many years and has deep knowledge of Nome and its fascinating history. Half-day tours of town are $60 per person, but you're much better off with a six-hour tour that also gets you out onto the tundra for $120. Full-day slice-of-life trips to Teller (highly recommended), Pilgrim Hot Springs, or Council are $170. No credit cards.

ST. LAWRENCE ISLAND

This hundred-mile-long island is about 160 miles southwest of Nome and just 36 miles from the Chukotsk Peninsula in Siberia. On a clear day, residents can see across the Bering Sea to the mountains of Siberia. The village of **Gambell** (pop. 550) is the primary settlement, and is home to Siberian Eskimos who have lived here for centuries. Most people speak Siberian Yup'ik as their primary language (though they also know English) and depend upon subsistence hunting of bowhead and gray whales, seal, walrus, fish, birds, and even polar bears. The bones of whales are scattered around the village.

Because of its location, St. Lawrence Island is a good place to find unusual bird species, including Asian stragglers. Beautifully carved ivory and other crafts are available locally, but visitors should absolutely refuse to buy any Eskimo artifacts. Many of these priceless cultural relics have been looted from ancient village sites around the island by selfish locals who pillage their own ancestors' graves for cash. Shame on them and on anyone who buys these items.

Bering Air (907/443-5464 or 800/478-5422, www.beringair.com) and **Frontier**

Flying Service (907/450-7200 or 800/478-6779, www.frontierflying.com) both have daily service to St. Lawrence from Nome.

There is a well-stocked general store in Gambell, thanks to daily flights from Nome. **Sivuqaq Native Corporation** (907/985-5826) sets up local tours and lodging. Limited lodging is also available in the island's other village, **Savoonga** (pop. 630), where walrus-hide *umiak* boats are still used. There are no cars on St. Lawrence Island; folks get around by foot or four-wheeler.

The Arctic

In Arctic Alaska, settlements are far, far apart, and the land predominates. Geographically, it is a relatively simple area. The rugged Brooks Range parallels the Arctic Circle in a long arc across the state, descending on its northern margin to the treeless tundra of the North Slope. On the tundra are thousands of lakes and ponds, creating a vital nesting area for ducks, geese, swans, and shorebirds. Polar bear, grizzly bear, arctic fox, musk ox, and other mammals are found in the Arctic, and vast herds of caribou make this their summer home, notably within the Arctic National Wildlife Refuge, which holds down the far northeast corner, bordered by the Arctic Ocean and Yukon Territory.

The Brooks Range encompasses both Noatak National Preserve and Gates of the Arctic National Park and Preserve, while other large public lands border the southern margins of these mountains: Kobuk Valley National Park, Cape Krusenstern National Preserve, and Selawik National Wildlife Refuge. Only one road connects the Arctic with the outside world: The **Dalton Highway,** which parallels the Trans-Alaska Pipeline from Livengood (north of Fairbanks) all the way to Deadhorse/Prudhoe Bay. It's almost 500 miles by car from Fairbanks to the Beaufort Sea/Arctic Ocean. (This route and the developments at **Prudhoe Bay** are detailed in the *Interior Alaska* chapter.)

The People

Only two towns of any size are found in Arctic Alaska: Kotzebue and Barrow. Both are predominately Inupiat Eskimo in population. Several national parks surround Kotzebue, and more parks and refuges encompass the Brooks Range, offering exciting possibilities for hikers and river runners in search of adventure. At the top of the continent on the Arctic Ocean lies Barrow, famous as the summertime land of the midnight sun, but also as the land where the sun does not rise for two straight months in winter. Prudhoe Bay, the source of Alaska's oil wealth, is also here, providing a temporary home for several thousand oilfield employees.

The Eskimo people who have made the Arctic their home for centuries have seen their culture undergo massive changes since their initial contact with whites 200 years ago. Christian missionaries brought new religions, attempted to obliterate all traces of their "pagan" beliefs, and forced them to take Anglicized names. Other newcomers decimated the whales, seals, walrus, and other animals that were food for the Eskimos, and brought deadly diseases for which they had no immunity. Entire villages were killed by measles and influenza. In addition, the American culture of materialism and self-accomplishment contrasted sharply with traditions that emphasized getting along and working together. But perhaps the worst scourge whites brought was alcohol. Even today, alcohol is a major factor in Alaska's high rate of suicide, drowning, and accidental deaths, particularly in the Arctic, where life is so challenging already. Visitors need to treat local people with sensitivity and respect, realizing that this is their land, not yours. If you show a genuine interest in people and their culture you'll be rewarded with a far deeper understanding of their world. For an excellent introduction to the culture from an Eskimo perspective, see

WESTERN ALASKA

The Epic of Qayaq: The Longest Story Ever Told by My People by Lela Kiana Oman.

KOTZEBUE

The state's largest Native settlement, Kotzebue (pop. 3,000) serves as a commercial hub for northwestern Alaska. The town covers a three-mile-long sandy spit at the tip of Baldwin Peninsula that has been occupied by Inupiat Eskimos for the last six centuries. Originally called Kikiktagruk (Almost An Island), today's name comes from Otto von Kotzebue, a Russian sailor who happened upon the village in 1816. Surrounding Kotzebue are the shallow waters of Kotzebue Sound, and nearby are the mouths of the Noatak, Kobuk, and Selawik rivers.

The Natives of Kotzebue lead a traditional lifestyle (with all the amenities, including snowmobiles and VCRs). It has the feeling of a large village, with a single paved road, rolling tundra, and open water. There are no trees, though the brush gets over your head in places. Just 30 miles north of the Arctic Circle, Kotzebue experiences endless sunlight for 36 days starting on June 3, but then suffers through an almost equal period of darkness around the winter solstice.

Sights

Stroll around to absorb a bit of Kotzebue's Native flavor. An interesting **cemetery** occupies several blocks in the center of town, and includes colorfully decorated graves. Unfortunately, too many of these are from young people killed from suicide or alcohol-related accidents. Another cemetery occupies a hill overlooking town, and the same road continues out a couple of miles over the tundra to the town's water source. Walk south of Kotzebue past the airport to find a **fish camp** where several dozen structures are used for the drying and smoking of fish, seal, and walrus meat.

The National Park Service's Visitors Information Center (907/442-3890 or 800/478-7252, www.nps.gov/noaa, daily 9 A.M.–6 P.M. late May–Aug.) for Kobuk Valley National Park, Cape Krusenstern National Monument, and Noatak National Preserve is at 154 2nd Avenue. Drop by to learn about the parks through displays, videos, and occasional programs.

Red Dog Mine

Kotzebue's economy is dependent upon the giant Red Dog Mine (907/426-2170, www.teckcominco.com), largest zinc mine in the world and the employer of nearly 400 workers (many of them Native). Located 100 miles north of town, Red Dog is owned by Teck Cominco, but the land belongs to the Northwest Alaska Native Association (NANA); both profit handsomely from the venture. The ore concentrate is trucked 45 miles from the mine to a port on the Chukchi Sea, where it is stored in an enormous warehouse (the largest building north of the Arctic Circle). Although mining takes place year-round, ore can only be shipped during the three-month summer, when the sea is ice-free.

Accommodations and Food

Stay at the modern **Nullagvik Hotel** (907/442-3331, www.nullagvik.com), where rooms are $189 d. Also here is a seasonal restaurant, the **Arctic Tern.**

Bayside Restaurant (907/442-3600) has decent Chinese food, along with sandwiches, steak, and halibut; it's probably your best choice.

Expensive groceries are available from **Alaska Commercial** (907/442-3285). Kotzebue is a "damp" town that doesn't allow alcohol sales, so bring your own from Anchorage.

No camping in Kotzebue, but you may be able to pitch a tent south of town past the airport along the beach. Many local people have summertime fish camps here, so ask around to make sure you aren't on someone's private space.

Services

Native arts and crafts—especially carved ivory pieces and Eskimo dolls—are sold in the Nullagvik Hotel. The city of Kotzebue website (www.cityofkotzebue.com) has local info and links. An ATM is located at the Wells Fargo building (907/442-3258). **Maniilaq Health Center** (907/442-3321, www.maniilaq.org) is a surprisingly large and modern hospital with physicians on staff.

Getting There

Alaska Airlines (800/426-0333, www.alaska air.com) has daily jet service to Kotzebue from Anchorage and Nome, while **Frontier Flying Service** (907/450-7200 or 800/478-6779, www.frontierflying.com) flies from Fairbanks to Kotzebue daily.

Scheduled flights to surrounding communities and air charters are available from **Bering Air** (907/442-3943 or 800/478-5422, www.beringair.com) and **Hageland Aviation** (907/442-2936 or 866/239-0119, www .hageland.com). You can also book air charters with **Arctic Air Guides** (907/442-3030) or **Northwestern Aviation** (907/442-3525).

ARCTIC PARKS AND REFUGES

Four little-known national parks are found within a 100-mile radius of Kotzebue: Bering Land Bridge National Preserve, Cape Krusenstern National Monument, Kobuk Valley National Park, and Noatak National Preserve. Noatak and Kobuk abut Gates of the Arctic National Park, and the three combine to create a massive 16 million-acre wilderness, with another 2 million acres of wild country within Selawik National Wildlife Refuge, immediately south of Kobuk Valley.

In addition to the Arctic National Wildlife Refuge, three other national wildlife refuges are at least partly inside the Arctic Circle. These include Selawik, Yukon Flats, and Kanuti National Wildlife Refuges. For details, contact the U.S. Fish & Wildlife Service in Anchorage (907/786-3542, http://alaska.fws.gov).

Bering Land Bridge

The 2.8 million-acre Bering Land Bridge National Preserve covers the northern Seward Peninsula 90 miles north of Nome and 50 miles south of Kotzebue. The area is considered a remnant of the land bridge that connected Siberia with Alaska during the last ice age. It served as a migratory corridor for people as well as animals, and the preserve has many archaeological sites, some of which date back 10,000 years or more.

Bering Land Bridge is vast; there are no roads that lead directly into it, and summer access is by small plane or boat. The preserve contains no trails and very few developed facilities, although six shelter cabins are available, along with a bunkhouse-style cabin at **Serpentine Hot Springs**. Next to the cabin is a bathhouse where you can soak in the mineral-laden waters. Unimproved trails lead up nearby ridges and to distinctive granite spires called tors. Other attractions include interesting lava flows near Imuruk Lake and volcanic craters. Get additional information from the Park Service office in Nome (907/443-2522 or 800/471-2352, www.nps.gov/bela).

Cape Krusenstern

The 660,000-acre Cape Krusenstern National Monument is northwest of Kotzebue, with access by boat or air charter. It contains significant archaeological sites on a series of 114 beach ridges that were formed over a period of 6,000 years. There are no developed facilities or trails within the national monument, but hikers enjoy the chance to look for a wide variety of waterfowl along with grizzlies, Dall sheep, and caribou. Park headquarters is in Kotzebue (907/442-3890 or 800/478-7252, www.nps.gov/cakr).

Kobuk Valley National Park

The 1.7 million-acre Kobuk Valley National Park lies on the south side of the Baird Mountains 80 miles east of Kotzebue. The park is best known for the **Great Kobuk Sand Dunes** that cover 25 square miles near the Kobuk River, with some reaching to 250 feet in height. The dunes are a one-hour hike from the river, but the route can be obscure in places so be sure to get directions from the Park Service in Kotzebue (907/442-3890 or 800/478-7252, www.nps.gov/kova) before heading out.

You can fly directly to the dunes from Ambler via **Ambler Air Service** (907/445-2121), or from Kotzebue with **Arctic Air Guides** (907/442-3030) or **Northwestern Aviation** (907/442-3525).

Two smaller areas of dunes dot the park, and the mountain passes are traversed by massive herds of caribou each spring and fall. In addition to the dunes, Kobuk Valley National Park offers pristine mountains and rivers, making it a destination for kayakers and canoeists. Most arrive by floatplane, flying from Bettles or Ambler into Walker Lake within Gates of the Arctic National Park. The 125-mile float trip to the village of Kobuk generally takes six days, or you can continue downriver all the way to Kiana. Contact the Park Service for more on running the river, and for a list of outfitters offering guided float trips.

There are no developed facilities within Kobuk Valley National Park itself, though several Native villages dot the banks of the wide, slow-moving, and clear Kobuk River. *The Alaska River Guide* by Karen Jettmar provides details on floating its more challenging upper reaches.

Noatak National Preserve

The 6.6 million-acre Noatak National Preserve covers the enormous Noatak River drainage northeast of Kotzebue. Gates of the Arctic National Park is immediately east of Noatak National Preserve. Its northern edge is the crest of the DeLong Mountains, while to the south lie the Baird Mountains and Kobuk Valley National Park.

There are no developed trails or other facilities within the preserve. Most visitors float the river in kayaks or rafts, with the put-in point on the upper reaches. Fly in from Bettles and get picked up in the village of Noatak, approximately 350 miles away. Expect to take at least two weeks for this extraordinary and memorable trip. Contact the Park Service in Kotzebue (907/442-3890 or 800/478-7252, www.nps.gov/noat) for additional information. Karen Jettmar's *The Alaska River Guide* has details on floating the Noatak River.

◖ Gates of the Arctic National Park

The central section of the Brooks Range is included within Gates of the Arctic National Park and Preserve, an 8.4 million-acre slice of majestic mountainous terrain. The park is famous for its deeply glaciated valleys, rugged summits—including the much-photographed **Arrigetch Peaks**—and abundant wildlife.

Park headquarters is in Fairbanks (4175 Geist Rd., 907/457-5752, www.nps.gov/gaar). Field offices include the **Arctic Visitor Center** in Coldfoot (907/678-5209, daily summers only), **Bettles Ranger Station** (907/692-5495), and **Anaktuvuk Pass Ranger Station** (907/661-3520).

There are no roads or established trails within Gates of the Arctic, and the remote location and extreme climate of the Brooks Range require travelers to have strong wilderness skills. Before visiting the park, you will need to attend a backcountry orientation program at one of these ranger stations or at park headquarters. A small museum (907/661-3413) in Anaktuvuk Pass has exhibits on Native traditions and handicrafts.

Lodging facilities can be found on the park margins in Anaktuvuk Pass, Bettles, Coldfoot, and Wiseman.

Northern Alaska Tour Company (907/474-8600 or 800/474-1986, www.northernalaska.com) leads grueling 13-hour tours from Fairbanks: van to Coldfoot, fly to Anaktuvuk Pass for a tour, and then fly back to Fairbanks. The cost is $400 per person.

Access to Gates is primarily by air out of Fairbanks, Bettles, Anaktuvuk Pass, or Coldfoot. **Brooks Range Aviation** (907/692-5444 or 800/692-5443, www.brooksrange.com) has air charter service from Bettles, and **Coyote Air Service** (907/678-5995 or 800/252-0603, www.flycoyote.com) flies out of Coldfoot.

Bettles

The settlement of Bettles lies 35 miles north of the Arctic Circle, and is renowned as a winter destination for viewing the northern lights, with the most cloud-free skies of any Alaskan town. A Park Service ranger station here is open daily in the summer, and weekdays the rest of the year.

Built in 1948, the eight-room **Bettles Lodge** (907/692-5111 or 800/770-5111, www.bettleslodge.com, $165–180 d) is open year-round with guest rooms, a restaurant, lounge, gift

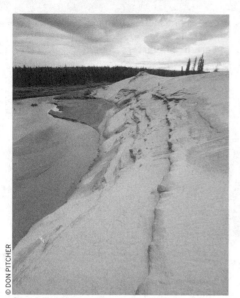
© DON PITCHER

Great Kobuk Sand Dunes

shop, and even wireless Internet. Wintertime dogsledding package trips are also available.

Spirit Lights Lodge/Bettles Trading Post (907/692-5252 or 888/692-2857, www.spiritlightslodge.com) is a comfortable lodge with a general store, café (open for breakfast daily plus lunch and dinner sometimes) that serves healthy meals, a gift shop selling local Native artwork, two suites ($100 s or $125 d) with kitchenettes and private baths, and several cabins ($75 s or $100 d) with microwaves, fridges, and shared bathhouses.

Everts Air Alaska (907/450-2350, www.evertsair.com) and **Wright Air Service** 9907/474-0502, www.wrightair.net) provide scheduled flights between Fairbanks and Bettles. Tom Holly of **Sourdough Outfitters** (907/692-5556, www.sourdoughoutfitters.com) offers wintertime dog mushing expeditions out of Bettles.

◖ Arctic National Wildlife Refuge

It doesn't get any wilder or more remote than this. The Arctic National Wildlife Refuge (ANWR; pronounced ANN-war) covers almost 20 million acres in the far northeastern part of Alaska, a landscape of flat and marshy coastal tundra, rolling hills, and tall, glaciated peaks topping 8,000 feet. Other than a few summertime travelers in search of the ultimate wilderness experience, this treeless country has almost no human presence. There has, however, been intense pressure from the oil companies and their allies (including virtually all Alaskan politicians from both parties) to "unlock" this wilderness. The oil wealth that lies beneath ANWR is undoubtedly great, but the loss of this last great wilderness would be greater. As of this writing, conservationists and their Democratic allies in the Senate have been able to block development schemes, but there is no guarantee that the oil companies won't finally win out. The battle has pitched Native people against each other—the Inupiat-owned Arctic Slope Regional Corporation is a big proponent of development (it stands to gain many millions of dollars in oil revenue)—but the Gwich'in people are adamantly opposed, fearing that development would destroy the vital caribou herds upon which they depend.

The main reason people come to ANWR—other than to experience the stunning beauty of this place—is the wildlife. During the long and fierce winter, only the hardiest animals venture out of their dens, but in summer, the refuge erupts with life. (The ubiquitous mosquitoes are the best example of this; bring headnets and insect repellents.) Best-known are the annual migrations of the 150,000-strong **Porcupine caribou herd**—they are the reason the reserve was established—but also here are millions of nesting ducks, geese, swans, loons, and other birds. Large mammals include musk ox, wolves, polar and grizzly bears, moose, and Dall sheep. Several major rivers drain ANWR on both sides of the Phillip Smith Mountains that split the refuge. The Sheenjek, Kongakut, Hulahula, and Wind Rivers are favorites of experienced kayakers and rafters.

Access to ANWR is by floatplane out of the surrounding settlements of Fort Yukon, Kaktovik, and Deadhorse. There are no developed facilities or trails within the refuge.

SAVING ANWR

An ongoing battle between developers and conservationists is whether to allow exploration and drilling for black gold within the 1.5 million-acre **Arctic National Wildlife Refuge** (ANWR). In a political compromise in 1980, the Alaska National Interest Lands Conservation Act called for a federal study to determine if oil and gas could be safely recovered within ANWR. Oil companies are concerned about the day when the North Slope reserves finally run dry, and claim that the pipeline's many years of operation have proven oil development and environmental protection to be compatible on the North Slope. Also, improved technology has greatly refined development techniques, which further safeguard the wilderness. A poll of Alaskans would come down strongly in favor of opening the wildlife refuge to development, and only a handful of elected state politicians dare stand up to

the oil companies, which can pour many thousands of dollars into their (or an opponent's) campaigns. Oil money doesn't talk in Alaska politics – it yells.

Conservationists – along with a number of vocal Inupiat people from the tiny settlement of Arctic Village – have taken a strong stand against the development of ANWR, noting that any such development could imperil the 150,000-strong Porcupine caribou herd, a vital food source in their subsistence culture. In addition, they argue that this refuge is one of the few places on earth that protect a complete spectrum of Arctic ecosystems. The battle to open ANWR to drilling flares up annually, and President Bush is a vocal proponent of its development. As of this writing, he and other drilling proponents had not succeeded. I for one am hoping that ANWR remains one of America's last great wildernesses.

Several companies offer expensive 10-day wilderness treks into ANWR down the Kongakut or Hulahula Rivers; recommended are **Alaska Discovery** (510/594-6000 or 800/586-1911, www.akdiscovery.com) and **Chilkat Guides** (907/766-2491 or 888/292-7789, www.raftalaska.com).

For more on this magnificent wild place, contact the U.S. Fish & Wildlife Service in Fairbanks (907/456-0250 or 800/362-4546, http://arctic.fws.gov). And email your members of Congress to help protect ANWR from development!

Selawik National Wildlife Refuge

This large wetland covers more than two million acres along the Selawik River and its tributaries, and provides important habitat for caribou and other animals. The refuge is used by local people for subsistence hunting, fishing, and trapping, and sees only a handful of visitors. Selawik River—a National Wild and Scenic River—is a Class I float trip from the headwaters to the village of Selawik. The War-

ing Mountains lie on the northern border of the refuge, and the Selawik Hills border the southern margin, providing hiking opportunities. Contact the refuge office in Kotzebue (907/442-3799 or 800/492-8848, http://selawik.fws.gov) for details.

BARROW

Located 350 miles north of the Arctic Circle, at 71° latitude, and 800 miles northeast of Nome, the small city of Barrow (pop. 4,400) is filled with paradoxes. Barrow has an $80 million high school with room for 2,000 students, plus a swimming pool, indoor track, and weight room. The grade school's indoor playground is useful in the winter, when typical temperatures often drop below -30°F outside, and the town also has a first-rate hospital. Despite this, all the streets are unpaved, and yards are cluttered with old snowmachines, barking sled dogs, four-wheelers, skin boats, polar bear hides, and racks hung with dead ducks, caribou, and seal meat.

Barrow's population is predominantly Inupiat Eskimo, and many people still speak their native tongue, but the taxi drivers are Filipinos, and many restaurants are owned by Koreans. One Native woman I met sews gorgeous traditional Eskimo parkas and has dead eider ducks on her front porch, but she also spends a month or two lying on the beach in Hawaii each year!

Barrow receives 84 days of uninterrupted sunlight in summer, 67 days of darkness in winter. It sits on the edge of the Arctic Ocean, which remains virtually frozen 10 months of the year—an amazing sight in itself. Wintertime temperatures plummet far below zero, and the wind chill can push them as low as -80°F! Even in the summer, the weather is often chilly, wet, and windy. By mid-August it can be downright cold; be sure to bring warm clothes no matter when you visit. The dirt roads and wind also make for dusty (or muddy) conditions much of the summer.

Most visitors to Barrow arrive as part of a summertime package tour, some staying just a few hours, and others overnight. Few independent travelers visit the town since the cost of airfare alone is often higher than the tour price. Even fewer visitors get to see the events that are so important to Barrow—the whale hunts during the spring and the fall bowhead migrations. When a whale is brought in, the entire community comes out to help. Many assist in the butchering process, and the whale's fatty meat is shared. Afterward, the carcasses are dragged far out along Point Barrow to keep polar bears from wandering into town.

History

This stretch of coast was first mapped in 1826 by Captain Beech of the British Navy, who named it after Sir John Barrow, an English nobleman who encouraged and outfitted numerous Northwest Passage and polar expeditions. Whalers began arriving in the 1870s, and many of their ships became trapped in the ice; relief expeditions helped survey the North Slope. The first plane reached Barrow in 1926, and famous bush pilot Wiley Post and humorist Will Rogers crashed and died there in 1935. Today, Barrow is the seat of the vast 88,000-square-mile North Slope Borough, and has profited greatly from the oil pipeline—as can be seen in the modern buildings, services, and high wages.

One of the early white settlers was Charles D. Brower, who established a trading post at Barrow in 1884, and later married two Native women. Their 14 children became important leaders in Barrow, and the big Brower family is still a vital part of the community. One part of town is even called Browerville.

☾ Inupiat Heritage Center

The Inupiat Heritage Center (907/852-4594, www.nps.gov/inup, Mon.–Fri. 8:30 A.M.–5 P.M. year-round, $5 adults, $2 ages 14–17, free for children and seniors) is a great place to learn about Inupiat Eskimo culture, particularly as it relates to whaling. Run by Ilisagvik College in coordination with the National Park Service, the heritage center houses artifacts, carved ivory, masks, dolls, sealskin boots, and a skin-covered boat. Fascinating dance and blanket-toss performances take place each afternoon 1–3:30 P.M. in the summer, and are $15; get tickets at Top of the World Hotel.

Surprisingly, this facility is affiliated with the New Bedford Whaling National Historical Park in New Bedford, Massachusetts. More than 2,000 whaling voyages left New Bedford for Arctic waters during the late 19th and early 20th century, and many Inupiat Eskimo people participated in these commercial whaling ventures. In the winter, the center hosts today's whaling crews as they prepare their skin boats for the hunt.

A shop here sells Inupiat Eskimo baleen baskets, ivory carvings, and jewelry. Other places to find them include gift shops at the Top of the World Hotel and King Eider Inn, and the North Slope Borough Office. The heritage center building also houses the **Barrow Public Library,** where you can check your email.

Sights

Other than the Inupiat Heritage Center, Barrow's main attraction is simply the place and its people. Located on the Arctic Ocean (technically the town is on the Chukchi Sea; the Beaufort Sea lies just east of Point Barrow), it

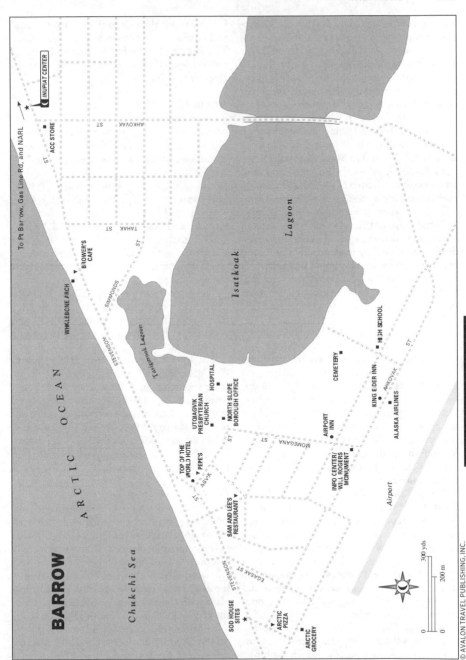

BARROW

Chukchi Sea

ARCTIC OCEAN

To Pt Barrow, Gas Line Rd, and NARL

INUPIAT CENTER

ACC STORE

AHKOVAK ST

BROWER'S CAFE

WHALEBONE ARCH

TAHAK ST

SIMMONDS

STEVENSON

Tasigrook Lagoon

Isatkoak Lagoon

HOSPITAL

UTQIAGVIK PRESBYTERIAN CHURCH

NORTH SLOPE BOROUGH OFFICE

TOP OF THE WORLD HOTEL

PEPE'S

AGVIK

ST

MOMEGANA ST

ST

AIRPORT INN

INFO CENTER/ WILL ROGERS MONUMENT

SAM AND LEE'S RESTAURANT

CEMETERY

KING EIDER INN

HIGH SCHOOL

AHKOVAK

ALASKA AIRLINES

ST

Airport

STEVENSON

EGASAK ST

SOD HOUSE SITES

ARCTIC PIZZA

ARCTIC GROCERY

300 yds

200 m

0

0

© AVALON TRAVEL PUBLISHING, INC.

has long been occupied by the Inupiat. The remains of old whale-bone-and-sod houses are visible on the shore at the west end of town, and are fascinating to explore—but do not disturb any artifacts. Walk the eroding shoreline to the east past skin-covered wooden boats and a pair of arched whalebones at Brower's Cafe. More bones, along with a "milepost" sign, can be found outside historic **Utqiagvik Presbyterian Church,** established in 1898, and rebuilt after a fire in 1909. The **North Slope Borough Office** has a big bowhead whale skull out front, and an impressive collection of artifacts—including parkas and carved walrus tusks—inside. It also sells carved ivory, garments, and other items.

Wander around Barrow and you're bound to find something of interest. There's always a dead animal hanging in somebody's yard, and the sophisticated above-ground piping system is distinctively Arctic. (Barrow's gas comes from nearby fields and is very cheap, but water must be desalinated from brackish ponds.)

East of town is a mostly inactive Distant Early Warning (D.E.W.) site and the old Naval Arctic Research Lab (N.A.R.L.), now occupied by Ilisagvik community college. More significant is the massive new **Barrow Arctic Science Consortium** (www .arcticscience.org) facility, where researchers are studying global climate change and how the rapid warming of the Arctic will affect the ecosystem. But don't tell Alaska's senators anything about global warming—they still view it as a fantasy despite all evidence to the contrary in Alaska.

Next to the airport, the **Barrow Visitor Center** is staffed daily 9 A.M.–5 P.M. mid-May–mid-September. For local information at other times, contact the **City of Barrow** (907/852-5211, www.cityofbarrow.org). Outside the visitor center stands a monument to **Wiley Post and Will Rogers,** who died nearby in 1935. Another monument is at the actual crash site, 16 miles away and accessible only by foot or four-wheeler.

Gas Line Road extends 10 miles into the tundra from Barrow, providing good access for folks who want to wander or watch for birds.

Barrow's excellent indoor **swimming pool** and recreation center are at the high school. The **Samuel Simmonds Memorial Hospital** (907/852-4611, www.arcticslope.org) provides emergency care.

Accommodations

Barrow has several places to stay. Largest and best-known is the **Top of the World Hotel** (907/852-3900 or 800/478-8520) where standard motel rooms run a budget-busting $170 s or $190 d.

Barrow's newest and nicest place, **(King Eider Inn** (907/852-4700 or 888/303-4337, www.kingeider.net), is right across from the airport, with standard rooms for $180 s or $205 d, kitchenettes for $190 s or $215 d, and a luxury suite for $285 s or 300 d. Guests appreciate the sauna, Wi-Fi, and computer for checking email.

The **Airport Inn** (907/852-2525 or 800/375-2527, $115 s or d), has clean and comfortable rooms with microwave, fridges, Wi-Fi, and continental breakfasts. Some units include kitchenettes.

The least expensive option is **Narl Hotel** (907/852-7800, $75 s or $90 d), where dorm-style rooms in an Atco trailer have shared baths. This is primarily used by construction workers and scientists, and is three miles out of town, so you'll need to pay $10 for a taxi ride. Eat next door at Ilsigavik College cafeteria, with lots of grub for the buck. Narl is often full in the summer months.

Food

For the most expensive Mexican food you could ever imagine, eat at **(Pepe's North of the Border** (907/852-8200)—a taco-enchilada combination plate is $17, and worth it! Or just order a bean burrito for $5 and fill up on chips and salsa. In business since 1978, Pepe's is run by Fran Tate, who has filled this big, fun place with the trappings of Mexico. And yes, the chefs really are from south of the border.

Another unexpected find in Barrow is **Osaka Sushi Bar** (907/852-4100), directly across from the Top of the World Hotel.

Sam & Lee's Restaurant (907/852-5555) has a filling lunchtime buffet, and is open until 2 A.M. Also try **Brower's Cafe** (907/852-3456) on the other side of town in Browerville. Outside you'll see two arched whalebones and several skin boats.

Arctic Pizza (907/852-4222) bakes surprisingly good pizzas for fair prices, and serves up prime rib on Sunday nights, plus a mix of Italian, American, and Mexican food at other times. There's a big-screen TV for watching sports, and an upstairs with windows facing the Arctic Ocean.

For do-it-yourself meals, head to the **Alaska Commercial Store** (907/852-6711), where you'll find everything from ice cream to sofas. (And yes, they do sell refrigerators, even at the top of the world.) The AC also has a deli with espresso coffee and an ATM. But hold onto your wallet: Food prices are sky-high. Many of these items arrive by air—which explains the high prices—but anything that won't spoil comes in aboard the barges that arrive during the brief ice-free period each August.

Getting There and Around

Alaska Airlines (800/426-0333, www.alaska air.com) has daily jet service between Barrow and Fairbanks, and **Frontier Flying Service** (907/450-7200 or 800/478-6779, www.frontierflying.com) flies smaller planes over the same route. Both Frontier Flying and **Hageland Aviation** (907/442-2936 or 866/239-0119, www.hageland.com) have scheduled flights out of Barrow to Prudhoe Bay and a number of Arctic villages.

Alaska Airlines offers excursions from Fairbanks that include a tour and an overnight in Barrow at Top of the World Hotel for $585 s or $970 d. Add $100 for the same trip from Anchorage. If you're really in a hurry—and have tons of cash—take a 12-hour quick trip from Fairbanks to Barrow and back with a tour of the town for $435 ($535 from Anchorage).

Northern Alaska Tour Company (907/474-8600 or 800/474-1986, www.northernalaska .com) has a package that duplicates the Alaska Air tours, and also offer a day-trip from Fairbanks to Barrow in a twin-engine Piper Chieftain for $600. The flight is lower and more scenic, and stops in Coldfoot for fuel, providing a taste of bush Alaska.

Tundra Tours (907/852-3900 or 800/478-8520) leads all-day tours that begin with a very informative bus tour around town and out to the end of the road near Point Barrow; the point itself is several more miles away. Following a lunch break, the tour shifts to the Inupiat Heritage Center for an introduction to the culture through dancing, drumming, and singing, followed by demonstrations of how traditional items are made and the opportunity to buy pieces from local artisans. The indoor blanket toss is always a highlight, but get your photos fast since they generally do just a couple of tosses. The cost is $85 per person, or combine a night's lodging at Top of the World Hotel with a day tour for $235 d or $320 d. (Transportation to Barrow, of course, is extra.)

Alaskan Arctic Adventures (907/367-3800, www.ukpik.com) leads van tours to Point Barrow.

Taxis are also available ($5 around town or $10 to NARL), or rent used cars and pickups from **UIC Car Rentals** (907/852-2700, www.ukpik.com). The **King Eider Inn** (907/852-4700 or 888/303-4337, www.kingeider.net) has vehicle rentals for their guests.

WESTERN ALASKA

BACKGROUND

The Land

The major physical features of western North America continue unbroken into that giant head of land that is Alaska. The Great Plains of the U.S. Midwest extend to become the Mackenzie Lowlands and the North Slope, while the Rocky Mountains form an inland spine from deep in Mexico to the Brooks Range. West of the Rockies, a high plateau runs from British Columbia north through the interiors of Yukon and Alaska, then west to the delta of the Yukon River, where it dips into the Bering Sea.

To the west of this plateau, two parallel chains and an intervening depression can be traced all the way from Mexico to Alaska. The Sierra Nevada of California become in turn the Cascades of Oregon and Washington, the Coast Mountains of British Columbia, the St. Elias and Wrangell Mountains, the Alaska Range, and finally the Aleutian Range, which then sinks into the Pacific just short of Asia. Closer to the ocean, California's Coast Range becomes the Olympic Mountains of Washington. Farther north, a string of islands from Vancouver to the Queen Charlottes and the Alexander Archipelago runs into the St. Elias Mountains, where the two chains unite into a jagged, ice-capped knot. In Alaska they divide again as the Chugach and Kenai Mountains swing southwest toward Kodiak Island. Between these parallel chains is a 3,000-mile-long depression starting with California's Central Valley, then continuing with Puget Sound, the Inside Passage, the Susitna Basin in Southcentral Alaska, Cook Inlet, and Southwest Alaska's Shelikof Strait. Only four low-level breaks occur in the coastal mountains: the valleys of the Columbia, Fraser, Skeena, and Stikine Rivers. Most of the places described in this book are within or near this mighty barrier, which contains the highest peaks, the largest glaciers, and most of the active volcanoes in North America.

GEOLOGY
Plate Tectonics

Briefly, the huge Pacific plate (the ocean floor) is drifting slowly northeast. It collides with the North American plate, on which the continent rests, along an arc that stretches from the western Aleutians in the Gulf of Alaska to the Inside Passage—defining one section of the famous Pacific "Ring of Fire." This meeting of plates jams the ocean floor under the continental landmass and gives rise to violent geologic forces: upthrusting mountains, extensive and large earthquakes, volcanic

LAND OF SUPERLATIVES

Alaska boasts more superlative statistics than any other state in the country (itself a superlative). Consider: Alaska's total land area – 591,000 square miles (375 million acres) – is more than twice that of the next-largest state, Texas. A little more than four Alaskas could be jammed into the continental United States, while almost 300 Delawares could be jigsaw-puzzled into the 49th state. Mt. McKinley (also known as Denali), at 20,306 feet, is the highest point in North America; the Aleutian Trench, plunging to 25,000 feet below sea level, is one of the Pacific's deepest ocean troughs. Sitka, with more than 4,700 square miles within its boundaries, has the largest area of any North American city, and the North Slope Borough, at 88,000 square miles (slightly larger than Idaho), is the largest municipally governed entity in the world. Alaska's 45,000-mile coastline is longer than the rest of the country's combined. Though only 3 percent of the state is covered in glaciers and icefields (debunking the "frozen wasteland" myth – the most common misconception about Alaska), it still has more than 100 times more glacial area than the rest of North America. With all of 635,000 people, Alaska ranks third to last among the states in population, behind only Wyoming and Vermont. If Manhattan had the same population density, 17 people would live there. And if all the Manhattanites were transplanted to Alaska, they'd each have 125 acres.

rumblings and eruptions, and movement along fault lines.

Somewhere in the mists of early geologic time, a particularly persistent and powerful collision between the two plates caused the Brooks Range to rise; erosion has whittled its highest peaks to 8,000 feet, half their original height. Later, a similar episode thrust the Alaska Range into shape. The Pacific plate even today continues to nose under the continental plate in the vicinity of Yakutat (near where Southeast meets Southcentral). The force of it pushes Mt. Logan—Canada's highest peak—slowly upward. Learn more about the geological forces that shape Alaska at the University of Alaska Fairbanks **Geophysical Institute** website (www.gi.alaska.edu).

Earthquakes

One of the world's most seismically active regions, Alaska has withstood some of the most violent earthquakes and largest tidal waves ever recorded. In the last century, more than 80 Alaskan earthquakes have registered higher than 7 on the Richter scale. The most destructive occurred at 5:35 P.M. on Good Friday, March 27, 1964, when the most powerful earthquake ever recorded in North America rocked Southcentral Alaska. This 9.2 magnitude quake (80 times bigger than the famous 1906 San Francisco earthquake, which is estimated at around 7.8) had a devastating impact on the region, flattening 75 homes and businesses in Anchorage, creating tsunamis that wiped out nearly every coastal village in Southcentral Alaska, and wreaking havoc all the way to California. The quake and its tsunamis killed 131 people. It was the second strongest in the 20th century; only a 9.5 magnitude 1960 quake in Chile was larger.

Anyone who spends more than a few months in Southwest or Southcentral Alaska will probably feel at least one earthquake, and residents of the Aleutian Islands barely take notice of anything with a magnitude less than 6. The **U.S. Geological Survey's** website (http://neic.usgs.gov/neis/states/alaska) provides detailed information on Alaskan earthquakes, including this week's activity.

Tsunamis

An earthquake deep below the ocean floor in the Gulf of Alaska or the open Pacific is especially dangerous to the coasts of Alaska and Hawaii, along with the west coast of Canada and the United States. The activity

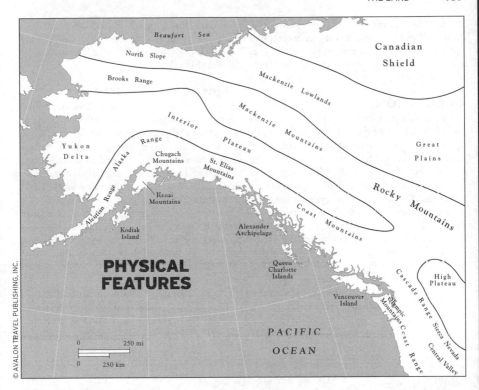

creates enormous tidal waves (tsunamis), which, though only 3–5 feet high in open ocean, can travel at speeds exceeding 500 miles an hour. Contrary to popular fears, a tsunami does not slam into the coast with 20 or 30 feet of water, washing away everything in its path like a flash flood. Instead, the water slowly inundates the land to a depth of four or five feet. Then, after a brief and chilling calm, the wave is sucked back out to sea in one vast undertow. Most of the destruction caused by the great Good Friday earthquake was of this nature, attested to by hair-raising pictures that you'll see in places like Valdez, Seward, and Kodiak. If you hear a tsunami warning, get to higher ground immediately. The **West Coast & Alaska Tsunami Warning Center** (www.wcatwc.gov) is based in Palmer, and its website provides information on recent and historical tsunamis.

Volcanoes

Like its earthquakes, Alaska's major volcanoes are located along the Aleutian chain. In fact, 57 active volcanoes stretch along this arc, and most have been active in the last 300 years. The largest recorded eruption occurred when Novarupta blew its top in 1912 (see *Katmai National Park* in the *Southwest Alaska* chapter), the most cataclysmic natural disaster since Krakatoa cracked 30 years earlier.

In the summer of 1992, Mt. Spurr, an active volcano 78 miles west of Anchorage, erupted with dramatic effects. It threw a cloud of ash nearly 50,000 feet into the air, coating Anchorage with an eighth-inch-thick layer of ash and closing Anchorage International Airport for 20 hours. If a mere eighth of an inch doesn't sound like much, imagine living inside a fireplace that hasn't been cleaned lately and you'll get an idea of how it felt. The University of Alaska Fairbanks' **Alaska Volcano Observatory** keeps track of volcanic activity, and its website (www.avo.alaska.edu) has details on current and historic eruptions.

GLACIATION

A glacier forms in areas of high precipitation and elevation where the snow is allowed to pile up to great depths, compacting the bottom layers into solid ice. The great weight above the bottom ice (along with the force of gravity) pushes it slowly downward like a giant frozen river, scooping out huge valleys and shearing off entire mountainsides. When the rate of advance is balanced by melt-off, the face of the glacier remains more or less stationary. If the glacier flows more quickly than its face melts, it advances; if it melts faster than it flows, the glacier recedes. All air bubbles are squeezed out of the glacier by this tremendous pressure, which makes glacial ice extremely dense. It's so compact that the higher frequencies of light cannot escape or penetrate it, which explains the dark-blue tinge. And because of its density, it also melts at fantastically slow rates; a small chunk or two will keep a beer in a cooler chilled for a day or two.

Signs of the Glaciers

As you travel up the coast or hike in the national parks of the Interior, you'll soon start to recognize and identify glacial landforms. While rivers typically erode V-shaped valleys, glaciers gouge out distinctly U-shaped **glacial troughs.** Valleys and ridges branching from the main valley are sliced off to create **hanging valleys** and **truncated spurs.** A side valley that once carried a tributary glacier may be left as a **hanging trough;** from these hanging valleys and troughs waterfalls often tumble. Alpine glaciers scoop out the headwalls of their accumulation basins to form **cirques.** Bare, jagged ridges between cirques are known as **arêtes.**

As a glacier moves down a valley it bulldozes a load of rock, sand, and gravel—known as **glacial till**—ahead of it, or carries it on top. Glacial till that has been dumped is called a

Margerie Glacier, Glacier Bay National Park

© DON PITCHER

moraine. **Lateral moraines** are pushed to the sides of glaciers, while a **terminal moraine** is deposited at the farthest point of the face's advance. A **medial moraine** is formed when two glaciers unite. These ribbonlike strips of rubble can be followed back to the point where the lateral moraines converge between the glaciers.

When looking at a glaciated landscape, watch for gouges and scrape marks on the bedrock, which indicate the direction of glacial flow. Watch, too, for *erratics,* huge boulders carried long distances and deposited by the glacier, which often differ from the surrounding rock. Glacial runoff is often suffused with finely powdered till or *glacial flour,* which gives it a distinctive milky-white color; the abundance of this silt in glacial streams creates a twisting, braided course. With a little practice, you'll soon learn to recognize glacial features at a glance. Learn more about glaciers and ongoing Alaska research at the **U.S. Geological Survey's** glacier and snow website (http://ak.water.usgs.gov/glaciology).

Permafrost

To picture permafrost, imagine a veneer of mud atop a slab of ice. In the colder places of the Lower 48, soil ecologists measure how much surface soil freezes in winter. In Alaska, they measure how much surface soil thaws in summer. True permafrost is ground that has stayed frozen for more than two years. To create and maintain permafrost, the annual average temperature must remain below freezing. The topsoil above the permafrost that thaws in the summer is known as the **active layer.** With the proper conditions, permafrost will penetrate downward until it meets heat from the earth's mantle. In the Arctic, permafrost begins a few feet below the surface and can extend 2,000–5,000 feet deep. This is known as **continuous permafrost,** which almost completely underlies the ground above the Arctic Circle. **Discontinuous permafrost,** with permafrost in scattered patches, covers extensive parts of Alaska, particularly boggy areas covered by black spruce forests.

Frozen ground is no problem—until you need to dig in it. Russian engineers were the first to encounter industrial-scale problems with permafrost during the construction of the Trans-Siberian Railroad. In Alaska, gold mining, especially in deep-placer operations, often required up to two years of thawing hundreds of feet of permafrost before dredging could proceed. Today, houses frequently undermine their own permafrost foundations: Heat from the house thaws the ground, causing it—and the house above it—to sink. Similarly, road-building clears the insulating vegetation layer and focuses heat on the frozen layer, causing severe "frost heaving," the roller-coaster effect common to roads in Interior Alaska. In the 1970s, pipeline engineers had to contend with the possibility that the 145°F oil flowing through the pipe would have similarly detrimental effects on the permafrost, with potentially disastrous financial and ecological consequences. That's why more than half of the Trans-Alaska Pipeline is aboveground, supported by a specially designed and elaborate system of heat-reducing pipes and radiators. Today, there is increasing concern that warming global temperatures could have a devastating impact in the Arctic, causing permafrost to melt and greatly altering the ecosystem.

CLIMATE

Granted, over the course of a year, in any given location, Alaska's weather can be extreme and unpredictable. Because of the harshness of the winters, comfortable travel to many popular destinations is difficult from early October to late April. Contrary to popular perception, however, the weather can also be quite pleasant. Alaska's spring, summer, and fall are not unlike these seasons in Minnesota. It's cool, it's warm; it's wet and dry; sometimes it's windy, sometimes it's muggy, sometimes it's foggy. Maybe it's the worst weather in the world outside, but you're snuggling with your girlfriend in your large new tent after the most exciting raft ride of your life. Maybe it's the crispest, clearest day of your trip, but your camera got soaked in the river and your boyfriend ran off with the raft company bus driver. The weather, here as everywhere, has as much to do with the internal climate as the external. Be happy in the sun. Try to stay happy in the rain. Just keep happy. You're in Alaska. For the latest outdoor forecast, visit the **National Weather Service's** Alaska website (www.arh.noaa.gov).

Extremes and Trends

It hit 100°F in the state once, in Fort Yukon in 1915. Fairbanks regularly breaks 90°F in July. It gets cold in Fort Yukon too, dropping as low as -78°F (Alaska's record low is -82°F, recorded in aptly named Coldfoot in 1989). *Any* wind at all at that temperature would make you feel even colder, if that's possible. Thompson Pass near Valdez gets quite a bit of snow, holding the records for the most in 24 hours (5 ft.), a month (25 ft.), and a year (81 ft.). But Barrow, at the tip of the proverbial "frozen wasteland," got just three inches of snow in 1936–1937. An average of almost 13 feet of rain falls in Ketchikan every year—what they call "liquid sunshine." But again, one year Barrow squeaked by with only an inch.

Though Alaska retains the reputation of the Great Frozen North, a distinct warming trend has had a noticeable effect on the state. Temperatures warmed abruptly in the summer of 1977 and have remained unusually warm ever since, throughout all the seasons. For example, meteorologists report that in the Interior, only on rare occasions over the past 20 years has the mercury dropped much below -40°F. Also, the temperature of the permafrost has risen several degrees. For the latest research, visit the website of the University of Alaska Fairbanks' **International Arctic Research Center** (www.iarc.uaf.edu).

Climatic Zones

It's possible to generalize about Alaskan weather and distinguish three climatic zones: coastal maritime, Interior, and Arctic. The main factor affecting the southern coasts is the warm Japanese Current, which causes temperatures to be much milder than the norm at those latitudes. This current also brings continuous rain as the humid Pacific air is forced up over

the coastal mountains. For example, it rains in Juneau two out of three days. However, these mountains shield the Interior plateaus from the maritime air streams, so yearly precipitation there is low—a mere 15 inches. The Interior experiences great temperature extremes, from biting cold in winter to summer heat waves. The mountains also protect the coastal areas from cold—and hot!—Interior air masses. The Arctic Zone is characterized by cool, cloudy, and windy summers (averaging 50°F) and cold, windy winters—though not as cold as in the Interior.

Based at the University of Alaska Fairbanks, the **Alaska Climate Research Center** (http://climate.gi.alaska.edu) has detailed information on the state's climate, along with current weather conditions.

THE LIGHT AND THE DARK

If you plan to be in Alaska from late May to late July, you can leave the flashlight at home. If you camped at the North Pole for a week on either side of summer solstice, the sun would barely appear to move in the sky, frying you to a crisp from the same spot overhead, as if stuck in space. The Arctic Circle, at 67° latitude, is usually defined as the line above which the sun doesn't set on June 21, nor rise on December 21.

Barrow lies at 71° latitude, 4° and roughly 270 miles north of the Arctic Circle. Here the sun doesn't dip below the horizon for 84 days, from May 10 to August 2. (You'll definitely see, and probably buy, the famous postcard with the time-lapse photograph showing the sun tracing a very mild curve: "going down" in the north-northwest, hovering above the horizon, and "coming up" in the north-northeast.)

Fairbanks, 140 miles south of the Circle, has 22 hours of direct sunlight on summer solstice, with the sky (if it's clear) going from a bright orange-blue to a sunset purple to a sunrise pink and back to bright orange-blue. Even Ketchikan, at around 55° latitude, and probably the southernmost point on most Alaskan itineraries, enjoys more than 18 hours of daylight, with the starless dusk a paler shade of twilight. Similarly, in December Ketchikan receives six hours

THE PINEAL GLAND

Most Alaskan life-forms pack a year's worth of living into five months of light, then hibernate through seven months of dark and cold. This is not only a cliché; it's also a fact based on physiology – the physiology of the pineal gland, to be specific. This gland (shaped like a *pine* cone) sits on a short stem in the oldest and most mysterious section of the human brain. It's a lonely gland – a unique, asymmetrical neuro-nub, surrounded by large masses of advanced symmetrical tissue. Until recently, it was among the most obscure structures on the human neurological frontier; in fact, only a couple of decades ago it wasn't even considered a gland but was known only as the pineal "body."

This is somewhat surprising, since its function in other vertebrates has been understood for a hundred years. In fish, reptiles, and birds, the pineal "eye" sits on a long stalk close to the brain's outer frontal section, right between the two regular eyes, where a third eye would be. However, it's not connected to the eyes or any other sensory pathways. Rather, the pineal gland is a simple, efficient photoreceptor, which senses and interprets the relative duration, intensity, and polarizing angles of light in the environment – making it the primary organ responsible for regulating internal circadian and seasonal rhythms. It tells fish how to navigate, birds when to migrate, and mammals when to sleep and reproduce.

How it works in other mammals is the key to understanding the gland's function in humans. Our gland produces a single (that we know of) hormone: melatonin. Melatonin circulates through the body and triggers two known reactions: drowsiness and reduced sex drive. What inhibits melatonin production? Light! The more sunlight – the higher its intensity and the steeper its angle – the less drowsiness and the stronger sex drive we feel. This helps explain many interesting general phenomena, such as why we sleep less deeply when it's not dark, the physiology of "spring fever," and why sex is better during the day. It also explains specific northern occurrences, such as why over two-thirds of Alaskan babies are conceived between May and September (as opposed to November and February as is commonly believed), and why you can do with a lot less sleep in Alaska in the summer.

of pale daylight and Fairbanks only three, but at Barrow you wouldn't see the sun at all for nine weeks.

Why?

The explanation for the "midnight sun" lies in the tilted angle of the Earth's axis. Because the planet rotates off-center, the Arctic Circle leans toward the sun in summer, so a complete 24-hour rotation makes little difference in the angle at which the sun's rays strike the North Country. However, the rays do have to travel farther, and they strike Alaska at a lower angle, which you'll notice: The sun never gets nearly as high in the sky here as you're probably used to. Because of the low angle, the rays are diffused over a larger area, thus losing some intensity, which accounts for the cooler air temperatures. And since the sun seems to move across the sky at a low angle, it takes longer to "set" and "rise." In addition, the atmosphere refracts (bends) the sunbeams more dramatically closer to the poles, which causes the low light to linger even after the sun is down. This soft, slanting light is often magical, with sharp shadows, muted colors, and silky silhouettes— a photographer's dream.

Northern Lights

The continual light is a trippy novelty if you're traveling around Alaska for just a few weeks, but when you're there all summer, to paraphrase the commercial, "D-A-R-K spells relief." Stars? What a concept! Headlights? Oy vey! From early August on, though, you start losing daylight quickly, to the tune of an hour a week in Fairbanks. Temperatures drop, berries and rose hips ripen, mushrooms sprout, and there's the possibility of experiencing one of life's all-time great thrills: God's light show, the aurora borealis.

The far-flung Eskimo had a variety of mythical explanations for the lights. Many believed that they represented the spirits of ancestors or animals, while others relegated the lights to malevolent forces. Prospectors preferred to think of them as vapors from rich ore deposits. The Japanese, however, have attributed the most romance to them: A marriage consummated under the lights will be especially fulfilling. Scientists have lately raised some controversy over particular aspects of the aurora, such as that the lights never dip below 40 miles above the earth (though many northerners swear they've seen the lights dancing along the ground); whether or not the lights manifest an electric sound is still a matter of some dissension, and even the experts who believe it don't know why. But these days everyone agrees that the sun, again, is responsible for the show.

When the solar surface sparks, the energy propels a wave of ionized particles (known as the "solar wind") through space. When these anxious ions encounter the gases in the Earth's atmosphere, a madcap night of oxygen-nitrogen couples dancing begins. The sun's particles and the Earth's gases pair off, with the fastest ions grabbing the highest gases. The ensuing friction causes a red or yellow afterglow. The slower ions infiltrate the lower regions, and those encounters glow green and violet. The waving, shimmering, writhing ribbons of color cannot fail to excite your own ions and gases. For detailed information on northern lights and predictions of upcoming aurora activity, visit the website of the University of Alaska's **Geophysical Institute** (www.gedds. alaska.edu/auroraforecast). Other excellent websites include www.pfrr.alaska.edu/aurora and the kid-friendly www.alaskascience.com/ aurora.htm. A number of lodges in the Fairbanks area have geared their winter season for people who come to view and photograph the northern lights, especially Chena Hot Springs Resort. Many Fairbanks hotels will provide aurora wake-up calls upon request.

Flora

VEGETATION ZONES

The vegetation of the Alaska Interior falls into four main categories: rainforest, boreal forest, taiga, and tundra. The lush coastal **rainforests** of Southeast Alaska are dominated by hemlock, spruce, and cedar. The Sitka spruce, Alaska's state tree, rivals California redwoods in height, age, beauty—and commercial value, of course. Sparser forests stretch across Southcentral Alaska, with spruce continuing through northern Kodiak Island but not farther west than the adjacent mainland. Dense thickets of alder and willow grow in the higher, subalpine areas near the coast.

The **boreal forest** of the Interior lowlands consists primarily of scattered open stands of white spruce, paper birch, alpine fir, lodgepole pine, and balsam poplar (cottonwood). **Taiga,** the transition zone between boreal forest and tundra, is characterized by sparse and stunted black spruce, dwarf shrubbery (mostly the ubiquitous willow), and swampy areas known as "muskegs."

The lower-elevation **tundra,** also known as the "moist tundra," starts at tree line, around 2,500 feet. There you find undergrowth similar to that of the taiga, without the trees. The higher-elevation alpine tundra consists of grasses, clinging mosses and lichens, and an abundance of tiny, psychedelically bright wildflowers, including the unforgettable forget-me-not (state flower), with gaze-catching petals of light blue.

TREE LINE

There are actually two tree lines in Alaska: One (the tree line) is determined by elevation, the other by latitude. Generally, tree line descends in elevation as the latitude ascends. Although alder and poplar do survive in isolated stands near the Brooks Range, the Arctic region on the North Slope is mostly treeless tundra. Dwarf willow, alder, grasses, and moss give the tundra here the appearance of a shag carpet. This tundra belt continues along the shores of the Bering Sea to the Alaska Peninsula and Aleutian Islands. Southward, the Arctic vegetation is gradually replaced by Pacific coastal varieties.

FLOWERS

While you're hiking, an excellent book to have along is *Field Guide to Alaskan Wildflowers* by Verna E. Pratt. The photographs are good, the descriptions are usable, and the flowers are conveniently arranged by color.

Fireweed is a wildflower you'll come to know intimately during your travels in the North. It enjoys sunlight and grows profusely in open areas along roads and rivers. Given

© DON PITCHER

Indian paintbrush, Glacier Bay National Park

proper conditions, tall fireweed can grow to seven feet high. Its long stalk of pink flowers blossoms from bottom to top; sourdoughs claim they can predict the arrival and severity of winter by the speed with which fireweed finishes blooming.

In Southcentral and Interior Alaska, **prickly rose** is a common sight. The plant grows stems up to four feet high, with sharp stickers. The flowers have five pink petals; the bright-red rose hips ripen in mid-August and contain highly concentrated vitamin C. Pop 'em in your mouth, suck off the slightly tart flesh, spit out the pips, and climb a mountain.

Three kinds of **primrose,** also a pinkish red, are another common sight on the tundra. Other red wildflowers of the tundra include **purple mountain saxifrage, moss campion,** and large, bright-pink **poppies.**

White flowers include the **narcissus-flowered anemone,** similar to a **buttercup,** which also grows on the tundra. **Mountain avens** are easily recognizable—they look like white roses. A half dozen different kinds of white **saxifrage** are widespread throughout the state. Be careful of the local **water hemlock,** which is deadly poisonous. Similar is the **yarrow,** a medicinal herb with a disk of small white flowers and lacelike leaves. As soon as you identify **Labrador tea,** you'll notice it everywhere in the forest and taiga. **Cotton grass** looks exactly like its name. **Daisies** and **fleabane** complete this group of plants with white flowers.

Larkspur looks similar to fireweed, only it's a dark purple. It grows on a long stalk and a dwarf bush. **Monkshood** is a beautiful dark-blue flower of the buttercup family; **harebells** and **bluebells** are easily identified around Denali. Three kinds of **violets** grow in the boreal forest. Light-purple **lupine** flowers grow in 20-inch clusters. **Asters,** resembling purple daisies, bloom all over the Interior.

BERRIES

Berries are the only fruits that grow naturally in Alaska, and luckily the many varieties are abundant, several are edible, a few even taste good, and only one is poisonous. If you're into berry collecting, get to know poisonous **baneberry** immediately. A member of the crowfoot family, it grows mostly in the Southeast and central Interior. The white berries look like black-eyed peas; they ripen to a scarlet red. **Juniper berries** grow throughout Alaska, but the **bog blueberries, Alaska blueberries,** and **huckleberries** are much tastier. Blueberries also grow on poorly drained, shady alpine slopes and are generally the first to ripen. **Salmonberries** turn a dark salmon-red in late summer, and are quite similar to raspberries.

Bunchberries and **elderberries** are good tasting but have been known to upset a stomach or two. **Bog cranberries** are best after the first frost, especially when they're a deep purple—deliciously tart. **High-bush cranberries** are common but are best just before they're completely ripe. **Wild strawberries** are even better, if you can get to them before the birds and rodents. The several kinds of **bearberries** (blue and red) are tasteless except to bears, and the **soapberry** will remind you of getting caught saying a dirty word as a kid. Pick up *Alaska Wild Berry Guide and Cookbook,* for the complete lowdown on Alaska's berries.

MUSHROOMS

Approximately 500 species of mushrooms are found in Alaska, thrusting up from the fecund forests from Ketchikan to Katmai and the rich tundra from Kantishna to Kotzebue. Most of the mushrooms are harmless to humans, and often edible; a handful are poisonous, such as varieties of **amanita** (especially the *muscaria,* or fly agaric) and **poison pax.** But if you learn to identify such common species as **hedgehogs** and **shaggy manes,** you'll enjoy happy hunting, mostly in July and August. For more information, see *Alaska's Mushrooms* by Harriette Parker.

FRANKENSTEIN CABBAGES

In 1941, the managers of the Alaska Railroad offered a $25 prize to the grower of the largest cabbage in the state, and since then cabbage growers have been competing. Usually, the largest cabbages at the Tanana Valley State Fair (in Fairbanks in mid-August) weigh in at 65–70 pounds, but the state record-holding cabbage is a 105-pounder, grown near Wasilla in 2000. It's an American, but not a world, record. Ten-pound celery, three-pound beets, two-pound turnips, and one-pound carrots are also blue-ribbon earners. Find them and more at the Alaska State Fair in Palmer at the end of August.

Fauna

If any aspect of Alaska embodies the image of the "last frontier," it's the state's animal kingdom. For millennia, Native hunters, with their small-scale weapons and limited needs, had little impact on wildlife populations. Eskimo and Aleut villages subsisted comfortably on fish, small mammals, and one or two whales a year; the interior Athabascan bands did well on a handful of moose and caribou. This all changed in the mid-1700s with the coming of the Russians and Americans. Sea otters, fur seals, and gray whales were quickly hunted to the verge of extinction. By the 1850s, the Alaskan musk ox had been annihilated. Wolves, in part because they preyed on the same game as humans, were ruthlessly hunted.

Conservation measures have nurtured their numbers and today Alaska boasts one of the largest concentrations of animal populations remaining on earth. For example, there are nearly twice as many caribou in Alaska as there are people. There's a moose and a Sitka black-tailed deer for every three people. If 80,000 sheep strikes you as an impressive number, consider 40,000 grizzly bears. Bald and golden eagles are commonplace, and while the magnificent trumpeter swan was believed near extinction in the Lower 48, it was thriving in Alaska. Marine mammals, from orcas to the recovering otters, are common (though they have recently experienced major declines in the Aleutians and western Alaska), and Alaskan waters also contain fish and other sea creatures in unimaginable quantities.

Wildlife-Viewing

Alaska's wildlife is a major draw for both visitors and residents. The state's vast stretches of wilderness contain abundant mammals, birds, and fish, including some of the largest and most magnificent animals in the world. Land mammals such as brown (grizzly) and black bears, caribou, moose, Dall sheep, wolves, and musk ox are the main attractions, but the state also has incomparable populations of birds, including such favorites as bald eagles, puffins, loons, and sandhill cranes. Marine mammals include seals, Steller sea lions, and sea otters, along with beluga whales, orca (killer) whales, humpback whales, gray whales, and others.

The *Alaska Wildlife Viewing Guide* by Michelle Sydeman and Annabel Lund, is a useful introduction to finding wild animals. Visit the Alaska Department of Fish & Game's website (www.wildlifeviewing.alaska.gov) for details on dozens of species of Alaskan animals in their "Wildlife Notebook" series, and for descriptions of places to see wildlife (click on "Viewing Trails"). The state also produces regional wildlife viewing guides, along with pamphlets covering various Alaskan towns and areas. Pick up copies in visitor centers around the state or find them on the above website.

In Alaska, wildlife may be encountered up close almost anywhere outdoors. Many animals are well prepared to defend their territories against intruders (you), and even the smallest can bite. Never attempt to feed or touch wildlife. It is seldom good for it, you, or those who follow. Any animal that appears unafraid or "tame" can be quite unpredictable, so keep your distance. One thing you don't have to worry about is snakes; there are none in Alaska. Surprisingly, however, there *are* frogs, even above the Arctic Circle.

LAND MAMMALS
Brown Bears

The brown bear (also called grizzly) is the symbol of the wild country, and a measure of its wildness. Grizzlies once roamed all over North

© DON PITCHER

brown bear

BEAR PRINTS

black bear

grizzly bear   polar bear   brown bear

America. In 1800, there were over 100,000 of them; today, around a thousand survive in the Lower 48. Ironically, the grizzly is the state animal of California, where it is now extinct. Things are very different in Alaska, where 40,000 of these magnificent creatures still inhabit the land.

Denali National Park offers some of the most accessible bear-viewing in the state. The estimated 200 Denali grizzlies are still wild, mostly in their natural state. This is especially important for the continued education of the cubs, who are taught how to dig roots, find berries, catch ground squirrels, and take moose calves. However, Denali grizzlies are not afraid of people, and are extremely curious; some have tasted canned beans, veggie burgers, and Oreo cookies. While no one has been killed by a grizzly at Denali, maulings have occurred, usually because of the foolishness of novice hikers and photographers or as a result of improper food storage. Take care, but don't be afraid to go hiking.

The natural grizzly diet is 80 percent vegetarian. They eat berries, willows, and roots, as well as preying on anything they can take: from ground squirrels to caribou, from foxes to small black bears. And they're challenged by nothing, except humans with high-powered weapons. Grizzlies are racehorse-fast and have surprising endurance; they need about 50 square miles for home territory and travel several miles a night. During the day they like to eat, sleep in the sun—often on snow patches—and entertain tourists on the shuttle buses.

Grizzlies are solitary creatures. Full-grown boars and sows are seen together only during mating season, in early summer. The gestation period is a little over five months, and the sows give birth in December to one to three cubs. The cubs are hairless, weigh one pound each, and remain blind for a week. They stay with the mother for over two and a half years—two full summers. They're then chased away sometime before July of the third summer, when the sow is ready to mate again.

Contrary to popular belief, bears do not hibernate. They do sleep deeply in dens during the winter, sometimes for weeks. But they often get hungry, lonely, or restless, and step outside to forage for frozen roots, berries, and meat. Sometimes a bear will stay out all winter; that's the one that the Natives fear the most: the winter bear. Its fur tends to build up a thick layer of ice, rendering it nearly impenetrable, almost bulletproof. And of course, sows give birth in the deep winter, which they're certainly awake for.

Grizzlies and brown bears were once thought to be different species, but now are considered the same. Their basic difference is size, which is due to habitat. Grizzlies themselves are the world's largest land omnivores, growing to heights of 6–7 feet and weighing in at 500–600 pounds. However, they're the smaller of the two, because they live in the Interior and feed mostly on vegetation. Brown bears are coastal, and with a rich source of fish protein, they have achieved near mythical sizes. Kodiak brown bears retain a reputation for being the largest, reaching heights of over 10 feet and weights of up to 1,400 pounds. On Admiralty Island in Southeast Alaska the brown bears are a bit smaller, but population densities are the highest anywhere: around one bear per square mile!

Hiking in bear country requires special precautions (see *Coexisting with Bears* in the *Interior* chapter). A number of areas offer outstanding brown-bear-viewing around Alaska. Read *Bear-Viewing* in the *Southwest Alaska* chapter for details on seeing these wonderful animals. The most famous places are McNeil River, Katmai National Park, Pack Creek, and Kodiak Island.

Black Bears

Black bears are found in most forested parts of Alaska, though not on certain Southeast Alaskan islands. They are distinguished from grizzlies and brown bears by their size (much smaller), the shape of their face (much narrower), and the lack of a shoulder hump. Black bears are actually more dangerous to people than grizzlies: There have been more attacks and maulings in Alaska by black bears than by brown. Two places on Tongass National Forest offer a fine opportunity to watch black bears as they catch salmon: Anan Creek Bear Observatory near Wrangell and Fish Creek Wildlife Observation Site near Hyder.

Polar Bears

Polar bears dwell in northern and western Alaska, spending their lives wandering on pack ice (extensive areas of drifting ice) or along the coast. In winter, they wander south on the ice, sometimes even reaching the Kuskokwim River delta, but in the summer they are found out in the Chukchi Sea and Arctic Ocean. Visitors to Alaska are highly unlikely to see a polar bear in the wild; your best bet would probably be near Kaktovik, on the edge of Arctic National Wildlife Refuge (but even there only infrequently in the summer) or the dump near Barrow. The Alaska Zoo in Anchorage has a polar bear. The best place to see and photograph polar bears in the wild is around Churchill in Manitoba, Canada. Learn more about these endangered bears at the U.S. Fish & Wildlife Service website (http://alaska.fws.gov/fisheries/mmm).

Moose

The moose is the largest member of the deer family, and Alaska has the largest moose. A bull moose in his prime gets to be about seven feet tall and weighs around 1,200 pounds, all from eating willow stems—about 30 pounds a day of them. They also eat aspen and birch, but willow is the staple of choice. The antlers, which are bone, are shed and renewed every year. Full-size antlers can weigh up to 70 pounds—that's mostly in September during the rut, or mating time. Bulls of near-equal rank and size butt their heads together to vie for dominance. You want to be real careful of bulls then. Touchy. The cows have one or two calves, rarely three, in May, and that's when you want to be real careful of the cows, too. The calves stay with the cow exactly a year; then she chases away the yearlings. Sometimes at the start of the summer season you'll spot a huge pregnant cow with a frisky yearling on her heels, and you've never seen a more hassled-looking expression on an animal's face. But that's family life.

Moose don't cover too much territory—about 30 miles a year, mostly in the forest, which provides natural defense against predators. The word *moose* comes from the Massachusetts Algonquian dialect and means "muncher of little twigs." By the way, the little flap of hair under the moose's chin is known as the "moostache." (Just kidding, it's really called the "dewlap.")

Harsh winters are deadly to moose. Deep snow and bitter cold can cause one in three moose in central Alaska to perish. Annually, hundreds of moose make their last stand along the snowless railroad tracks between Seward and Fairbanks and are killed by trains that don't stop for them. Other hundreds starve to death. Those hit by cars along roadways are butchered and distributed to the local people.

If Alaska moose are the world's largest, Kenai Peninsula moose are Alaska's largest. A Kenai moose holds the Alaskan record: at 10–11 years old, his antlers were just under 75 inches wide, he weighed 1,500–1,600 pounds, and he gave his life for Guinness.

Kenai National Wildlife Refuge was specifically established to protect moose, and these massive animals are common sights along Kenai Peninsula roads at dusk. Other places to watch for moose are within the Anchorage bowl and in the Matanuska-Susitna Valley northeast of Anchorage. Drive with care, since moose can suddenly step onto the road without warning, and their massive bulk means that a collision could be fatal to both the moose and people in the vehicle.

Moose can be very aggressive, particularly in the winter months when food is scarce. A number of people have been killed by moose attacks, even in Anchorage. Always give moose a wide berth, especially if you're walking, on a bike or skis, or with a dog. If a moose appears ready to attack, quickly hide behind a tree, car, or other obstruction. Pepper spray may be effective if all else fails, or you can try to outrun a moose if you have no other options; they generally don't run far. If the moose knocks you down, curl up in a ball, protect your head with your hands, hold still, and say a few thousand Hail Marys.

Caribou

Caribou are travelin' fools. They're extremely flighty animals—restless, tireless, fast, and graceful. Run and eat, run and eat, is pretty much all they do—oh yeah, and reproduce. Reindeer, although of the same species, are smaller and often domesticated. Caribou are peaceful critters and they'll outrun and outdistance their predators, mostly wolves, rather than fight. They like to travel in groups, unlike moose, which are loners. And they cover 10 times as much territory. Their herding and migrating imperatives are similar to those of the plains bison; they gather in large numbers and think nothing of running 50 miles, almost on a lark.

Caribou are extremely well adapted to their winter environment. They have huge nasal passages and respiratory systems in order to breathe the bitterly cold winter air. Thick fur covers almost every inch of their bodies; the fur itself is protected by large, hollow, oily guard hairs. This tends to make caribou look much larger than they really are; a good-sized bull weighs 400–500 pounds, a cow about half that. Caribou have the richest milk in the animal kingdom: 20 percent fat. They've also got huge prancing hooves, immortalized in the Santa Claus myth, which are excellent for running, swimming, disco dancing, and pawing at the snow to uncover the moss and lichens on which they subsist all through the harsh Arctic winter. The word *caribou* comes from the Maine Algonquian dialect and means "scraping hooves."

The caribou is the only member of the deer family whose females grow antlers. Babies are on their feet and nursing within an hour of birth, and at one week they can run 20 miles. If they can't, they'll most likely die, since the herd won't wait. But this helps to keep the herd healthy, controls population growth, and provides food for the carnivores.

Alaskan Natives are among the caribou's natural predators. Historically, Natives ate the meat raw, roasted, and stewed. They ate all the organs, even the half-digested greens from the stomach. The little gobs of fat from behind the eyes were considered a delicacy. They used almost exclusively caribou hide for clothes, rugs, blankets, and tents. The leg skins were used to make mukluks; the long strands of stringy sinew provided sewing thread.

Nearly a million caribou roam across Alaska, with the largest herds in the Arctic, including within Arctic National Wildlife Refuge.

Caribou are commonly seen within Denali National Park and Preserve and along Interior and Southcentral Alaskan roads, including the Glenn Highway near Eureka, the Alaska Highway east of Tok, the Denali Highway, the Dalton Highway, and the Richardson Highway near Paxson.

Dall Sheep

Named for William H. Dall, one of the first men to survey the lower Yukon (1866), Dall sheep are sometimes called Alaska bighorn sheep, because the Rocky Mountain bighorn is a closely related species. Distinguished by their brilliant white color, the rams grow large, curved horns, formed from a specialized skin structure made up of a compacted mass of hair and oil. The horns aren't shed; instead the sheep add another ring to them yearly, so the longer the horns, the older the ram, and the more dominant within the herd. The rams can weigh as much as 175 pounds; the ewes have small spiked horns and average 120 pounds.

Their habitat is the high alpine tundra, and they subsist on grasses, mosses, lichens, and flowers. Their bird's-eye view provides an excellent defense. They're also magnificent mountain climbers. Roughly 70,000 Dall sheep reside in the Chugach, Kenai, Alaska, and Wrangell mountain ranges in Alaska. During summer, the rams migrate high into the ranges, leaving the prime lower grazing grounds for the ewes and lambs. It's natural that they migrate, the same way it's natural that they have predators. Their alpine tundra habitat is very fragile, and it can take decades to regenerate after overgrazing. Migration and predation thus keep the flock healthy, control population growth, and guarantee the survival of the habitat.

Dall sheep inhabit mountain hillsides throughout much of Alaska. They are frequently seen on rocky slopes in Denali National Park, near Atigun Pass on the Dalton Highway, near Cooper Landing on the Kenai Peninsula, and along Turnagain Arm 20 miles south of Anchorage.

Dall sheep on Marmot Rock, Denali National Park

Wolves

Wolves have traditionally been one of the most misunderstood, misrepresented, and maligned mammals, in both fact and fable. We've come a long way from the days when it was believed that wolves were innately evil, with the visage of the devil himself, eating their hapless prey—or little girls in red hoods—alive. But it wasn't until the mid-1940s, when wildlife biologist Adolph Murie began a long-term and systematic study of the wolves in Mt. McKinley National Park, that all the misconceptions comprising the accepted lore about wolves began to change.

For three years Murie tramped mainly on the plains below Polychrome Pass and became extremely intimate with several wolf families. (His book, *The Wolves of Mount McKinley*, published in 1944, is still considered a classic natural history text.) Though Murie concluded that a delicate balance is established between predator and prey to their mutual advantage, declining Dall sheep populations, political pressure, and, indeed, tradition forced the park service to kill wolves, which were considered, against Murie's conclusions, to be the cause of the sheep decline. Typically, though, the wolf population was in just as dire straits as the sheep, and for several years no wolves were killed in the feds' traps *because of their scarcity.*

Since then, many researchers and writers have come to incisive conclusions about the wolf. It's been determined that their social systems—within the pack and with the prey—are amazingly complex and sophisticated. The alpha male and female are the central players in the pack, surrounded by four to seven pups, yearlings, and other adults. The dominant female receives a long, involved courtship from the dominant male (though he might not necessarily be the biological father of the pups). Territories can be as small as 200 square miles and as large as 800 square miles, depending on a host of influences.

Perhaps the most complex and fascinating aspect of wolf activity is the hunt. Barry Lopez, author of the brilliant *Of Wolves and Men*, argues persuasively that the individual prey is as responsible as the wolf for its own killing, in effect "giving itself to the wolf in ritual suicide." Lopez maintains that the eye contact between the wolf and its prey "is probably a complex exchange of information regarding the appropriateness of a chase and a kill." Lopez calls this the "conversation of death."

With the advent of radio collaring and tracking from airplanes, the movements of individual wolves and packs have continually surprised wildlife biologists. Wolves often travel 5–10 miles an hour for hours at a time. In a matter of days, an individual cut loose from a pack can wind up 500 miles away. Thus wolves are able to select and populate suitable habitats quickly.

Alaska's 7,500–10,000 wolves are thriving, even though roughly 15 percent of them are harvested yearly by trappers. They can be found all the way from the Southeastern panhandle to the Arctic slope, but are most common in Interior Alaska. Denali National Park offers travelers the best chance to see a wolf from the road system, but wolves may also be seen in other parts of the Alaska Range, in Brooks Range foothills, and in Wrangell–St. Elias National Park.

Captive wolves can be seen at the Alaska Zoo (www.alaskazoo.com) in Anchorage. A nonprofit organization, Wolf Song of Alaska (www.wolfsongalaska.org), has an education center in downtown Anchorage.

Elk

Elk—a relatively common sight in the western Lower 48—were also prevalent in Alaska 10,000 years ago but disappeared during the last ice age. In the mid-1920s, Alaskans decided that elk would be an attractive addition to the territory's big-game species, and a handful of Roosevelt elk were imported from Washington state. After a few years of island-hopping, the cervids (deer) were finally transplanted to their permanent home, Afognak Island off the north coast of Kodiak, and from there they apparently swam to Raspberry Island and Kodiak. Though the country was rugged—wet, windy, and choked with alder—the elk thrived in their new home, and some grew to 1,000 pounds. Within only

© CCN PITCHER

bison on Kodiak

20 years (1950), 27 bulls were culled from the herd by resident hunters. Hunting continued up until the late 1960s, when a series of severe winters decimated the herds. Ten years of protection and mild winters allowed the herds to regenerate; today 1,200 elk live on Afognak and Raspberry Islands, with a second small population on Etolin Island near Petersburg.

Musk Ox

The musk ox is a stocky, long-haired animal with a slight shoulder hump and a very short tail. Despite their name, musk oxen have no musk glands and are not oxen. The largest member of the sheep family, this shaggy, prehistoric-looking creature was abundant in the North Country until it was hunted into extinction by the mid-1800s. In the 1930s, several dozen musk ox were transplanted from Greenland to Nunivak Island in the Bering Sea. Like the elk on Afognak, the musk ox on Nunivak thrived, and the resident Natives used the soft underwool to establish a small cottage industry knitting sweaters, scarves, and caps. And

that's what it would have remained, a small cottage industry, if it hadn't been for Dr. John J. Teal, Jr., a student of Arctic explorer Vilhjalmur Stefansson. Stefansson recognized the potential of musk ox wool and inspired Teal to experiment with domesticating them. After spending 10 years with musk ox on his farm in Vermont, Teal concluded that they were amiable, hardy, and easy to domesticate. So in 1964, he started the Musk Ox Project at the University of Alaska in Fairbanks.

In 1984, the project moved to a farm in the Matanuska Valley, where musk ox are bred to produce *qiviut* (KEE-vee-ute), the soft underwool, which is renowned in Alaska for its insulation (eight times warmer by weight than sheep wool) and tactile (softer than the finest cashmere) properties. The *qiviut* is collected from the animals in the spring. The raw wool is sent to a mill in Rhode Island and then sold to Oomingmak (the Native word for musk ox, meaning "bearded one"; www.qiviut.com), a co-op consisting of 200 members in villages spread throughout western Alaska. Here the *qiviut* is knitted into garments, which are sold at retail outlets in Anchorage and at the farm near Palmer.

Today, wild musk ox can be found on the Seward Peninsula near Nome, on Nunivak and Nelson islands, the Yukon-Kuskokwim Delta, on the north slope near Prudhoe Bay, and in Arctic National Wildlife Refuge. The best places to see them up close are the Musk-Ox Farm in Palmer (www.muskoxfarm.org) and the Large Animal Research Station (www.uaf.edu/lars) at the University of Alaska in Fairbanks.

Lynx

Alaska's only native cat, the lynx is the northern version of the bobcat. Weighing around 20–30 pounds, these extremely secretive animals prey primarily on snowshoe hare, a species that undergoes an 8–11 year cycle of abundance. Lynx numbers fluctuate with those of hares, but lag one or two years behind. When a hare population crashes, lynx numbers soon decline, and they sometimes travel up to 400 miles in search of food. Although snowshoe hares are an important prey for lynx, when they are scarce lynx hunt grouse, ptarmigan, squirrels, and rodents, and may even take larger animals such as caribou or Dall sheep.

Lynx are sometimes seen during long periods of summer daylight, especially in years when they are abundant. Lynx have large, broad feet that function as snowshoes for winter hunting and traveling.

Mountain Goats

These members of the antelope family number between 13,000 and 15,000 in Alaska. They have snow-white coats, shaggy heads, and black, spiked horns up to a foot long, and weigh in at 150–300 pounds. They mostly inhabit the coastal ranges and eastern Alaska Range and are frequently seen high on cliffs so precipitous that they would probably scare even Dall sheep.

Sitka Black-Tailed Deer

These small deer are found throughout Southeast Alaska, in Prince William Sound, and on Kodiak and Afognak Islands. Visitors to all these areas may occasionally see deer, but some of the largest populations are on Kodiak Island. The deer population averages more than 300,000 individuals, but fluctuates widely, depending upon the severity of the winter. They're the second-most-prevalent game animal in Alaska behind caribou. They prefer a forest environment, but also roam high into the mountains for young shrubs and ripe berries in the late summer months. Males weigh 120 pounds, females 80 pounds.

Rodents

Ground Squirrels and Marmots are true hibernators: Unlike other mammals such as brown, grizzly, and polar bears, they sleep for six months straight, in a deep coma. This separation between life and death is one of the thinnest lines in the animal world. A ground squirrel's heart slows to about six beats a minute, and its body temperature lowers to just above freezing, around 38°F. (In fact, a zoologist at the University of Alaska Fairbanks has found that the core temperature of the arctic ground squirrel, the northernmost hibernator, can drop to as low as 26°F—six degrees below freezing! Of course, the squirrels don't "freeze" but "supercool.")

The hibernating squirrel takes a breath every couple of minutes. It uses up half its body weight, since it isn't eating. If you stuck a needle in a hibernating ground squirrel's paw, it would take the animal about 10 minutes to begin to feel it.

Ground squirrels provide a large part of the grizzly and wolf diet, and of scavenger birds' as well, since they're a common type of roadkill.

Marmots, similar to woodchucks, are sometimes mistaken for wolverines. They live in large rock outcroppings for protection and have a piercing whistle, which warns of approaching predators or other possible danger. Look for marmots around Polychrome Pass at Denali Park; ask the driver where exactly.

Alaska has a number of other members of the rodent family: shrews, mice, voles, lemmings, and porcupines. Long-tailed and least weasels occupy a wide habitat in the taiga and tundra.

Martens are another member of the weasel family, similar to, though much more aggressive than, mink; the pine marten is one of Alaska's most valuable fur-bearers. Wolverines are in attendance, though you'd be very lucky to see one. Red fox are common in the Interior and Southcentral, and you're likely to see one at Denali Park; the white Arctic fox is a gorgeous animal, though you'll only see one in pictures.

MARINE MAMMALS

Marine mammals are found all along the Alaskan coast, from Ketchikan in the Southeast to Barrow on the Arctic Ocean. Sea otters are frequently found in harbors, bays, and inlets, particularly around kelp beds. Good places to look for whales, seals, sea otters, sea lions, porpoises, and other marine mammals are the Inside Passage, Prince William Sound, Kodiak Island, Kachemak Bay, and Kenai Fjords. The Pribilof Islands serve as rearing and resting areas for thousands of northern fur seals, harbor seals, Steller sea lions, and walruses in the summer. Only Native Alaskans have the legal right to hunt marine mammals.

An Endangered Ecosystem?

In the last several decades, scientists have watched with increasing alarm as marine mammal populations plummeted in the North Pacific and Bering Sea, particularly around the Aleutian Islands. Environmentalists blamed overfishing of pollock, while anglers pointed the finger at long-term changes in ocean currents and temperatures. But recent evidence points in a different direction—whaling. After World War II, Japanese and Russian whalers developed lethal ways to hunt bowhead, sperm, and humpback whales, killing at least a half-million of them before commercial whaling ended in the 1970s. These giant whales formed an important part of the diet for killer whales, and without this, the orcas turned to other food sources. As top predator in the ocean, killer whales apparently worked their way across the food chain, attacking fur and harbor seals in the 1970s, Steller sea lions in the 1980s and '90s, and most recently an animal with very little meat, sea otters. If this is indeed the cause for the decline of these marine mammals, there is little that can be done to halt the damage. Overfishing (or in this case overwhaling) can have disastrous consequences for the oceans, and for animals and humans that depend upon the fish.

Sea Otters

A marine member of the weasel family, the sea otter had one characteristic that would seal its doom: a long, wide, beautiful pelt, that's one of the warmest, most luxurious, and durable furs in existence. Otter fur catalyzed the Russian *promyshleniki* to begin overrunning the Aleutians in the mid- to late-18th century, sealing the doom of the Aleuts as well as the otters. In 1803, Aleksandr Baranov (Alexander Baranov) shipped 15,000 pelts back to eastern Russia. Up until the 1840s, otter hunting was the primary industry in the Pacific, and when the Americans bought Alaska in 1867, nearly a million otters had been killed in the northern Pacific.

During the extreme lawless period in the last quarter of the 19th century, the otters were annihilated. In 1906, schooners cruised the north Pacific for months without taking a single pelt. In 1910, a crack crew of 40 Aleut hunters managed to harvest 16 otters. In 1911, otters were added to the International Fur Seal Treaty, giving them complete protection from everybody. Small, isolated populations of otters had managed to survive in the western Aleutians, and their numbers have increased over the past century to roughly 100,000 today. Approximately 90 percent of the world's sea otter population can be found in coastal Alaska. The otters are doing fine in Southeast Alaska, but in the Aleutians they have declined precipitously over the last decade, partly because of predation from killer whales, and are now listed as an threatened species. For more on the current situation, visit the Fish & Wildlife Service's website (http://alaska.fws.gov/fisheries/mmm).

Steller Sea Lions

George Wilhelm Steller was the naturalist aboard Vitus Bering's 1742 exploration of

Alaska, and the first white man to step on Alaskan soil. Two marine mammals ended up with his name: the Steller's sea cow, a cold-water relative of the manatee; and the Steller sea lion. The sea cow was driven to extinction just 26 years later, a casualty of its not being afraid of humans and the tasty flavor of its flesh. Today, the sea lion in much of Alaska is equally endangered.

Steller sea lions are pinnipeds—marine mammals with flippers, not feet. Males can weigh up to 2,000 pounds; females peak at 600 pounds. Sea lions eat several kinds of fish, but mostly pollock. They range across the North Pacific from northern Japan and Siberia all the way to California. These playful but powerful animals were abundant in western Alaskan waters until quite recently. In the 1960s, for example, an estimated 177,000 sea lions lived in the Gulf of Alaska and along the Aleutians. Commercial hunting was halted in the mid-1970s, but the population continued to drop by more than 80 percent. By 2000, a mere 34,000 survived. The western Alaska population was officially listed as endangered in 1997, while sea lion populations in Southeast Alaska and farther south to California are considered threatened.

Researchers are unsure why Steller sea lions are disappearing at such an alarming rate, and there are a multitude of possible causes—including overfishing, toxic chemicals, and predation by sharks and killer whales. Most likely is some combination of factors, but if something isn't done, the Southwest Alaska population could be headed for extinction. Learn more about these fascinating animals—including the latest research—at the National Marine Fisheries Service's website (www.fakr.noaa.gov/protectedresources).

Whales

The largest summer marine visitors to Alaska are the whales. Each spring **gray whales** are seen migrating north from Baja California; in the fall they return south. Also in the spring **humpback whales** move north from Hawaii. The humpback is easily distinguished by its humplike dorsal fin, large flippers, and huge

humpback whale and calf

© DON PITCHER

tail, which shows as it dives. These 50-foot-long creatures often breach (jump) or beat the surface of the water with their tails, as if trying to send messages. Smaller (30 ft.) **minke whales** are also common.

The **killer whale** (orca), which is not actually a whale but the largest of the dolphins (up to 24 ft. long), travels in groups hunting fish and marine mammals. Its six-foot-high, triangular dorsal fin and its black-and-white piebald pattern make it easily identifiable.

Whales can be spotted all along Alaska's thousands of miles of shoreline, but commercial whale-watching ventures are only found in Southeast Alaska, Prince William Sound, and the Kenai Peninsula. Larger towns in these areas all have charter boat operators that lead trips combining whale-watching with other activities such as fishing, sea kayaking, photography, glacier viewing, or bird-watching. The Inside Passage's protected waterways are favorite haunts of humpback and killer whales during the summer months, particularly around Admiralty Island, within Glacier Bay National Park and Preserve,

and near Sitka. Look for beluga whales in Turnagain Arm along the Seward Highway south of Anchorage. Boat tours of Prince William Sound depart from both Valdez and Whittier, providing a good opportunity to see occasional killer, minke, and humpback whales. Kenai Fjords National Park and Resurrection Bay—both accessible by boat tour from Seward—are popular places to spot killer whales and humpbacks, along with sea otters, seals, sea lions, and colonies of puffins. There's also a fair chance of seeing whales on the Kachemak Bay wildlife boat trips that depart from Homer.

For more information on whales in Alaska, visit the National Marine Fisheries Service's web site (www.fakr.noaa.gov/protectedresources).

Fur Seals

The Alaska species of fur seal *(Callorhinus ursinus)* is a kind of "seal bear," as its Latin name suggests. The bulls grow up to seven feet long and can weigh 400 pounds. Tens of thousands of these caterwauling creatures return to the Pribilof Islands yearly to breed. The dominant bulls

© DON PITCHER

northern fur seals, St. Paul Island

arrive after eight months at sea in early June, and the noisy fight for the prime beach real estate often results in bloody bulls. The cows show up a couple of weeks later—small (80 lbs.), submissive, and steeling themselves for a bloody bounce on the beach. A big stud bull might accumulate 60–70 cows in his harem, and it's exactly as debilitatingly profligate a scene as it sounds. The bulls don't eat, living only off their own fat all summer, and look like skid row derelicts by mid-August when they take off to the North Pacific to eat, sleep, and regain their strength.

The gestation period is one year, and the cows return to the same rookery to give birth. The pups swim away in late October and return after a couple of years as "bachelors." Between two and seven years old, they play in the sand and surf, until the young males have grown big and bad enough to have their way with the cows. For more information on fur seals, visit the National Marine Fisheries Service's website (www.fakr.noaa.gov/protectedresources).

Walrus

What the Pribilofs are to the fur seal, Round Island in northern Bristol Bay is to the Pacific walrus. (See the *Western and Arctic Alaska* chapter for details on Round Island.) Except here, it's a boys-only beach club; the females and babies remain in the northern Bering and Chukchi Seas, where they feed at the relatively shallow bottoms. Thousands of these giant 3,000-pound bulls cram themselves onto narrow beaches at the bottom of steep cliffs around the 1- by 2-mile island. It's an amazing sight, with the scrappy bulls ready to fight at the slightest affront; most of them are scarred from a multitude of old attacks, and broken or missing tusks are common. On the beach, walruses are ungainly, akin to Subaru-sized slugs. But in the water, these big fat fatties are slo-mo smooth. As with other marine mammals in the Bering Sea, walrus populations have declined in recent years, though they have not suffered the precipitous declines of Steller sea lions and otters. Learn more about these fascinating animals at the U.S. Fish & Wildlife Service's website (http://alaska.fws.gov/fisheries/mmm).

BIRDS AND INSECTS

More than 400 species of birds can be found within Alaska, from tiny rufous hummingbirds to the nation's national emblem, the bald eagle. Because of Alaska's proximity to Siberia, many unusual species are sometimes seen, making islands in the Aleutians and within the Bering Sea of great interest to serious birders.

One of the rarest is the bristle-thighed curlew, with a population of a mere 5,000 worldwide—and its only breeding grounds are in Alaska. Eight of the curlews were banded in the Yukon Delta Wildlife Refuge in 1988, and one was subsequently seen on Caysan Island in the South Pacific, over 2,000 miles away. Many Asian species, such as the greenshank and the Siberian ruby-throat, only foray into the Americas as far as western Alaska.

Bird-Watching

Nome, the Pribilofs, and the Aleutians are popular destinations for birders looking to add to their life list. Excellent places to see nesting colonies of seabirds such as **puffins** and **kittiwakes** include Glacier Bay National Park and Preserve, Kachemak Bay near Homer, Kenai Fjords National Park near Seward, Fort Abercrombie State Park on Kodiak Island, Prince William Sound, the Pribilof Islands, and St. Lawrence Island.

Located on the edge of Fairbanks, **Creamer's Field** is a good place to view sandhill cranes, ducks, and geese during the spring and fall migrations. Also at Creamer's Field is the **Alaska Bird Observatory** (www.alaskabird. org), which conducts songbird research, and offers educational programs and birding reports for the area. For additional information, contact the Alaska State office of the **Audubon Society** (907/276-7034, www.audubon.org/chapter/ak) or call the regional birding hotlines for the Anchorage area (907/338-2473), Interior Alaska (907/451-9213), and the Homer area (907/235-7337).

Eagles

As many eagles are found in Alaska as in the rest of the United States combined. **Bald**

© DON PITCHER

horned puffin, St. Paul Island

eagles are common sights along the coasts, but with their unmistakable white heads, seven-foot wingspans, and dive-bombing, salmon-snatching performances, the thrill of watching them is not quickly lost.

The highest concentrations of bald eagles can be found on Admiralty Island, in Prince William Sound, and along the Copper River Delta near Cordova. Admiralty has the largest nesting population of bald eagles in the world, and is a great place to find them during the summer months. Over the winter you'll find upward of 3,000 eagles at the famous **Chilkat Bald Eagle Preserve,** along with several hundred of them on the Homer Spit (where they are fed). In spring, a good place to look for eagles is the Stikine River near Wrangell.

Golden eagles, found throughout the Interior, come without the distinctive "baldness" but are no less magnificent for their size. Plentiful around Denali Park, golden eagles perched on the tundra, standing more than three feet tall, have been mistaken for everything from grizzly cubs to adolescent hikers.

The **white-tailed eagle** is an Asian raptor; Attu Island in the western Aleutians is its only North American habitat.

Trumpeter Swans

The world's largest waterfowl, these swans boast wingspans as wide as eagles (7 ft.) and can weigh up to 40 pounds! They're pure white, and so have figured prominently over the centuries in legends, drama, music, and metaphor. They fly as fast as 60 mph and as high as 10,000 feet on their migrations from Alaska to the Pacific Northwest for the winter (though a group of 500 overwinter in Alaska). They live to be 30 years old and have a hornlike call, which accounts for their common name.

In 1933, trumpeter populations hit an all-time low of 33 individuals in the Lower 48—having been hunted for their meat, down, and quills. But several thousand swans were seen by Alaskan bush plane biologists in the early 1950s, and by the early 1970s, trumpeters were removed from the Endangered Species list.

Today, of the nearly 12,000 swans in North America, about 10,000 spend their summers in Alaska, 2,000 of them in the Copper River delta. (A great place to see them is on the road from Cordova to the Million Dollar Bridge.)

Geese

The **Aleutian Canada goose** has made a remarkable comeback from the edge of extinction over the past several decades. Smaller than Canada geese, Aleutian geese were common throughout the islands up until the 20th century, when decades of fox farming nearly wiped out the geese. Only a few hundred were left alive by the late 1960s, on one fox-free island. Feral foxes were removed from a number of other Aleutians and the geese were reintroduced; by 1990, their numbers had regenerated to the point (7,000) where they were removed from the ranks of the endangered and upgraded to "threatened."

Emperor geese are a distinctive black-throated bird, and nearly the entire population of 70,000 nest in Southwest Alaska, from the Aleutians to Kodiak.

Snow geese, on the other hand, are plentiful.

Huge flocks totaling up to 100,000 birds migrate roughly 5,000 miles each year from central California through Alaska to their nesting grounds on Wrangel Island (in Russia).

Ptarmigan

The **willow ptarmigan** is the state bird, and one of the most popular targets of small-game hunters. Ptarmigan—willow, rock, and white-tailed—are similar to pheasant, quail, and partridge in the Lower 48. They reproduce in large quantities, molt from winter white to summer brown, and have a poor sense of self-preservation. The various Alaskan place-names containing "Chicken" usually refer to ptarmigan, which the namers had difficulty spelling.

Mosquitoes

The mosquito, contrary to popular belief, is not Alaska's state bird. But skeeters are nearly as much a symbol of the Great North as glaciers, totem poles, and the aurora borealis. Mosquito eggs hatch in water, so the boggy, muskegy, marshy forests and tundra, plus all the ponds, lakes, creeks, sloughs, and braided rivers of Alaska, provide the ideal habitat for these bothersome creatures. Alaska hosts around three dozen varieties of mosquitoes.

Mosquitoes hibernate in the winter and emerge starting in March and April. Peak season is in late June and early July. The males don't alight or bite, but they do buzz around people's eyes, noses, and ears, which can be as, if not more, annoying than the bites. The males live 6–8 weeks, feeding on plant juices; their sole purpose in life is to fertilize the eggs the females produce. They also feed birds and larger insects.

The females live long lives, producing batches of eggs, up to 500 at a time. To nourish the eggs they feed on the blood of mammals, using a piercing and sucking mouth tube. The tube also injects an anticoagulant, which causes the itch and swelling from a bite. No Alaskan mosquitoes carry the diseases that tropical mosquitoes are known to, such as malaria, yellow fever, encephalitis, and elephantiasis.

Mosquitoes are most active at dawn and dusk. Windy conditions and low temperatures depress mosquito feeding and breeding. Mosquitoes are attracted to dark colors, carbon dioxide, warmth, and moisture. Mosquito repellent containing DEET (diethylmetatoluamide) is the most effective. A headnet helps keep mosquitoes and other buggy critters away from your face, and is a wise investment for anyone heading into remote parts of Interior Alaska or Kodiak Island. If you wear light-colored, heavy clothing (the stinger can pierce light materials), camp in high and dry places that are apt to be breezy, and rub repellent on all exposed skin, you should be able to weather mosquito season without too much difficulty.

FISH

Get someone going on fishing in Alaska and you won't be able to shut him or her up or get a word in edgewise for the whole afternoon, guaranteed. The fisheries program in Alaska is extensive, because commercial, sport, and recreational fishing are important to almost every state resident. Commercial fishing is Alaska's second-largest industry, and Alaska accounts for more than half of the nation's total seafood production. Sportfishing has always been popular, but is playing a more important role in Alaska's economy as tourism increases. Below is a brief survey of the most popular fish in Alaska's three million lakes, 3,000 rivers, and 45,000 miles of coastline.

Salmon

Five kinds of salmon—king, red, pink, silver, and chum—all return to the same bend in the same little creek where they hatched, to spawn and die, ending one of the most remarkable life cycles and feats of migration and single-minded endurance of any living creature. You'll be steeped in salmon lore if only by osmosis by the end of your trip, and you'll get more than your fill of this most delicious and pretty fish.

The **kings** (also known as chinooks) are the world's largest salmon, and the world's largest kings spawn in Alaskan waters. The average size for a king is 40–50 pounds. The world sportfish record is 97 pounds, and a few 100-pounders have been caught in commercial nets. Kings generally spend five or six years in saltwater before returning to fresh to spawn: The more years spent in the ocean, the larger the fish. They run mostly between mid-May and mid-July.

Reds (sockeye) are the best-tasting salmon and the mainstay of the commercial fishing industry. They average 6–10 pounds and run in June and July.

Pinks (humpback) are the most plentiful, with massive runs of more than 150 million fish between late June and early September. They're smallish, 3–4 pounds, with soft flesh and a mild taste; they're mostly canned (or caught by tourists).

Silvers (coho) seem to be the most legendary of the salmon, for their speed, agility, and sixth sense. Their spawning growth rate is no less than fantastic, more than doubling their weight in the last 90 days of their lives. Silvers grow 7–10 pounds and run late, from late July all the way to November.

Chum (dog) are the least valued of the five Pacific salmon, even though they average 10–20 pounds, are extremely feisty, and are the most far-ranging, running way above the Arctic Circle. They're known as dog salmon because they've traditionally sustained working huskies, but chums remain popular with a hard-core group of sport anglers, who consider them terribly underrated. Surprisingly, they make some of the finest smoked fish.

Halibut

Halibut are Alaska's favorite monster fish and can grow so huge and strong that many anglers have an unsurpassed religious experience while catching one. "Chicken halibut" are the common 25–40 pounders, but 100- and 200-pounders are frequent sights in some ports; even 300-pounders are occasionally reeled in. The state-record halibut was a 464-pounder, more than eight feet long, caught near Dutch Harbor in 1996. Even though halibut are huge and require 80-pound test line with 20-ounce lead sinkers, they're not the fiercest fighting fish, and just about anyone can catch one on a good day's charter from Homer, Seward, Kodiak, Whittier, Sitka, or Dutch Harbor. It has a very white flesh, with a fine texture—many Alaskans regard it as the most flavorful (and least fishy-tasting) fish.

Smelt

The fattiest fish in northern waters is the Pacific Coast eulachon, also known as smelt, hooligans, and candlefish (legend claims that the dried fish are so fatty they can be wicked and lit like candles). These silver and white fish are roughly as long and slender as pencils, and run in monumental numbers for three weeks in early summer from Northern California to the Pribilofs. A traditional source of oil, the females are dumped into pits or vats by the ton and left to rot for two weeks. Then freshwater is added and the whole mess is boiled, during which the oil rises to the surface. After skimming, straining, filtering, and sterilizing, roughly 20 gallons of oil (reminiscent of cod-liver oil) can be processed from a ton of female smelt. The early males, in addition, are good tasting whether cooked, smoked, dried, or salted.

History

PREHISTORY

The Athabascan Indians of Canada have a legend that tells how, in the misty past, one of their ancestors helped a giant in Siberia slay a rival. The defeated giant fell into the sea, forming a bridge to North America. The forefathers of the Athabascans then crossed this bridge, bringing the caribou with them. Eventually the giant's body decomposed, but parts of his skeleton were left sticking above the ocean to form the Aleutian Islands.

In less fanciful terms, what probably happened was that low ocean levels—up to 450 feet below the present—offered the nomadic peoples of northeastern Asia a 50-mile-long, 600-mile-wide land "bridge" over the Bering Sea. There is considerable controversy over exactly when humans crossed this isthmus, but it was certainly used at least 12,000 years ago, and perhaps considerably earlier.

One of the earliest records of humans in the Americas is a caribou bone with a serrated edge found at Old Crow in northern Yukon. Almost certainly used as a tool, the bone has been placed at 27,000 years old by carbon dating. The interior lowlands of Alaska and the Yukon Valley, which were never glaciated, provided an ice-free migration route. As the climate warmed and the great ice sheets receded toward the Rocky Mountains and Canadian Shield, a corridor opened down the middle of the Great Plains, allowing movement farther south. (Recent scientific evidence suggests that ancient peoples also sailed or paddled along the coast from Asia to North America.)

The Athabascans

The Athabascans and other paleo-Indians were the first Native groups to cross the Bering land bridge. Their language is spoken today from Interior Alaska to the American Southwest (among Navajos and Apaches). Way back when (anywhere from 40,000 to 12,000 years ago), these Natives of the Interior followed the mastodon, mammoth, and caribou herds that supplied them with most of their necessities. Agriculture was unknown to them, but they did fashion crude implements from the raw copper found in the region. Eventually, certain tribes found their way to the coast. The Athabascan-related Tlingits, for example, migrated down the Nass River near Prince Rupert and then spread north through Southeast Alaska. The rich environment provided them with abundant fish and shellfish, as well as with the great cedar logs from which they fashioned community houses, totem poles, and long dugout canoes.

The Eskimo

Eskimos (Inuit) arrived from Asia some 4,500 years ago, migrating by boat along the coast of Alaska. Within 500 years their culture had spread across Arctic Canada and all the way to Greenland. Their language, which in Alaska is divided into the Inupiak dialect in the north and the Yup'ik and Alutiiq dialects in the south, is unrelated to any other in North America except that of the Aleuts.

Like the Tlingits, the Eskimos lived near the coast, along the migratory routes of the marine mammals they hunted in kayaks and umiaks. They also relied upon caribou, birds, and fish. Their homes were partly underground and constructed of driftwood, antlers, whale bones, and sod. (The well-known snow-and-ice igloo was exclusive to Canadian Natives.) In the summer, skin tents were used at fish camps. The Eskimo did not use dogsleds until the coming of the white people.

The Aleut

Marine mammals and fish provided the Eskimo-related Aleuts with food, clothing, and household materials. The Aleut were famous for their tightly woven baskets. Before the arrival of the Russians in the 1740s, 25,000 Aleut inhabited almost all of the Aleutian Islands, but by the year 1800 only about 2,000 survived. The ruthless Russian fur traders murdered and

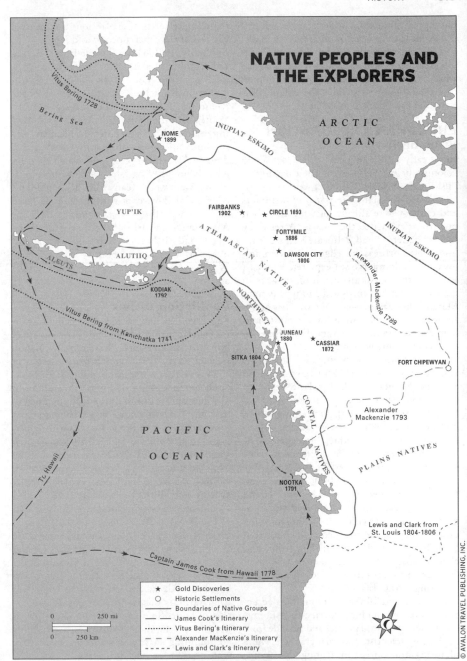

NATIVE PEOPLES AND THE EXPLORERS

Vitus Bering 1728

Bering Sea

ARCTIC OCEAN

NOME ★ 1899

INUPIAT ESKIMO

INUPIAT ESKIMO

YUP'IK

FAIRBANKS 1902 ★   ★ CIRCLE 1893

ATHABASCAN NATIVES

FORTYMILE ★ 1886

ALUTIIQ

★ DAWSON CITY 1806

ALEUTS

Alexander Mackenzie 1789

KODIAK 1792

Vitus Bering from Kamchatka 1741

NORTHWEST

JUNEAU 1880   ★ CASSIAR 1872

SITKA 1804

FORT CHIPEWYAN

Alexander Mackenzie 1793

PACIFIC OCEAN

COASTAL NATIVES

PLAINS NATIVES

To Hawaii

NOOTKA 1791

Lewis and Clark from St. Louis 1804-1806

Captain James Cook from Hawaii 1778

★	Gold Discoveries
○	Historic Settlements
——	Boundaries of Native Groups
– –	James Cook's Itinerary
······	Vitus Bering's Itinerary
– – –	Alexander MacKenzie's Itinerary
- - -	Lewis and Clark's Itinerary

0   250 mi

0   250 km

© AVALON TRAVEL PUBLISHING, INC.

kidnapped the men, enslaved or abandoned the women, and passed on their genes and diseases so successfully that today only 1,000 full-blooded Aleuts remain. The rest intermarried with the Russians, and scattered groups of their descendants are now found in the eastern Aleutians and the Pribilofs to the north.

EUROPEAN EXPLORATION
Vitus Bering

In the early 1700s, long before the New World colonists began manifesting their destiny by pushing the American frontier west to the Pacific coast, Russian *promyshleniki* (explorers and traders) were already busy pushing their own frontier east to the Pacific. After these land conquerors had delineated Russia's inhospitable northeastern edges, they were followed by indomitable sea explorers who cast off from the coasts in search of answers to questions that had intrigued Europeans since Marco Polo's *Travels*—mainly, whether or not Asia was joined with America, the mysterious land to the east that was vaguely outlined on then-contemporary maps.

Danish-born Vitus Bering, a sailor in the Russian navy for nearly 20 years, set out in 1725 for Kamchatka Peninsula, Siberia, on orders from Peter the Great. It took him and his crew three years, dragging rigging, cable, and anchors 2,000 miles over trackless wilderness and suffering innumerable deprivations to reach the coast, where their real journey into the uncharted waters of the North Pacific would begin. Bering built his first boat, *Gabriel,* and sailed past St. Lawrence Island (south of present-day Nome) and the Diomedes, but fog prevented him from glimpsing North America. He returned and wintered in Kamchatka, sailed again in the spring, and charted most of the Kamchatka coast, but foul weather and short provisions again precluded exploring farther east.

Over the next 10 years, Bering shuttled between Moscow and his beloved coast, submitting patiently to royal politics and ridicule from the leading scientists and cartographers, while planning and outfitting (though not commanding) a series of expeditions that charted the rest of the Siberian coast and Japan.

Finally, in 1741, at the age of 60, Bering undertook his remarkable voyage to America. Commanding the *St. Peter,* he sailed southeast from Kamchatka, came up south of the Aleutians, passed Kodiak, and sighted Mt. St. Elias on the mainland. By that time Bering, along with 31 members of his crew, was in the final throes of terminal scurvy. He died in December 1741 and was buried on what is now Bering Island, the westernmost of the Aleutians. Meanwhile, his lieutenant, Alexis Chirikov, commanding the *St. Paul,* had reached all the way to the site of Sitka. After much hardship, survivors from both ships made it back to Siberia—with a load of sea otter pelts. This bounty from the New World prompted a rush of Russian hunters and traders to Alaska.

Conflicting Claims

Reports of Russian advances alarmed the Spanish, who considered the entire west coast of North America theirs. Juan Perez and Bruno Hecata were ordered north from Mexico in 1774 and 1775. Spanish explorer Juan Francisco Quadra sailed as far north as Sitka in 1775 and 1779, but in the end, Spain failed to back up its claim with any permanent settlement north of San Francisco. It was Englishmen James Cook (in 1776–1780) and George Vancouver (in 1791–1792) who first carefully explored and charted this northern coast. In 1778, Cook landed on Vancouver Island, then sailed north all the way to what is now called Cook Inlet in Southcentral Alaska, in search of the Northwest Passage from the Atlantic. He continued to the Aleutians and entered the Bering Sea and the Arctic Ocean. A decade and a half later, Vancouver, aboard his ship HMS *Discovery,* charted the coast from California to Southeast Alaska and claimed the region for England. His was the first extensive exploration of Puget Sound and circumnavigation of Vancouver Island; his maps and charts of this confounding coast were so accurate that they were used for another 100 years.

Exploration by Land

Meanwhile, explorers were reaching the Pacific overland from bases in eastern Canada and the United States. In 1789 a Northwest Company trader, Alexander Mackenzie, paddled down the Mackenzie River to the Arctic Ocean. Four years later, in 1793, he became the first person to cross the entire continent by land, reaching the Pacific at Bella Coola, British Columbia. Other employees of the same aggressive Montreal-based company explored farther south. In 1808, Simon Fraser followed the Fraser River, stopping near the present site of the city of Vancouver; in 1810–1811 David Thompson traveled from the headwaters of the North Saskatchewan River to the mouth of the Columbia, near present-day Portland. In 1803, after the United States purchased 827,000 square miles of territory west of the Mississippi River from France, President Thomas Jefferson ordered a military fact-finding mission into the area. Led by Lewis and Clark, a group of explorers paddled up the Missouri River to its headwaters and crossed to the Columbia, which they followed to the Pacific (1804–1806), helping to open vast expanses of western North America. American fur traders followed close behind. (The Alaskan interior, however, was not properly explored until the gold rush at the end of the 19th century.)

The Fur Trade

The excesses of the *promyshleniki,* who had massacred and enslaved the Aleut, prompted the czar in 1789 to create the Russian America Company, headed by Grigori Shelikov, a fur trader and merchant who in 1784 had established the first permanent settlement in Alaska at Three Saints Bay on Kodiak Island. Alexander Baranof, a salesman in Siberia, was the first director of the company; he moved the settlement up to present-day Kodiak town, and for the next 20 years, Baranov *was* the law. One of the most powerful men in Alaskan history, he enslaved the remaining Aleuts, warred with the Panhandle Indians, initiated trade with the English, Spanish, and Americans, and sent his trading vessels as far away as Hawaii, Japan, and Mexico. Exhausting the resources of Kodiak and its neighborhood, he moved the company to Sitka, where, according to Merle Colby in his classic 1939 WPA *Guide to Alaska,* "from his wooden 'castle' on the hill surmounting the harbor he made Sitka the most brilliant capital in the new world. Yankee sailors, thrashing around the Horn, beating their way up the California coast, anchored at last in Sitka harbor and found the city an American Paris, its streets crowded with adventurers from half the world away, its nights gay with balls illuminated by brilliant uniforms and the evening dresses of Russian ladies." Except for the Tlingit Indians, who fought bitterly against Russian imperialism, Baranov's rule, extending from Bristol Bay in western Alaska to Fort Ross, California, was complete. His one last dream, of returning to Russia, was never fulfilled—on the voyage back to the homeland, Baranov died at the age of 72.

THE 19TH CENTURY
Political Units Form

In 1824 and 1825, Russia signed agreements with the United States and Britain, fixing the southern limit of Russian America at 54° 40' north latitude, near present-day Ketchikan. But the vast territory south of this line was left up for grabs. The American claim to the Oregon Territory around the Columbia River was based on its discovery by Robert Gray in 1792, and on the first overland exploration by Lewis and Clark. Britain based its claim to the region on its effective occupation of the land by the Northwest Company, which in 1821 merged with the Hudson's Bay Company. As American settlers began to inhabit the area, feelings ran high—President Polk was elected in 1846 on the slogan, "Fifty-four Forty or Fight," referring to the proposed northern boundary between American and British territory in the Pacific Northwest. War between Britain and the United States was averted when both agreed to draw the boundary line to the Pacific along the 49th parallel, which remains to this day the Canadian/American border. Vancouver Island went to Britain, and the new Canadian nation purchased all the territorial holdings of the Hudson's Bay Company (Rupert's Land) in 1870. In 1871, British Columbia joined the Canadian Confederation on a promise from the leaders of the infant country of a railroad to extend there from the east.

The Russians Bail Out

The year 1863 was a one for the Russian America Company. Back in the motherland, Russia's feudal society was breaking down, threatening the aristocracy's privileged status. In Alaska, competition from English and American whalers and traders was intensifying. Food was scarce and supply ships from California were unreliable and infrequent. Worst, perhaps, was the dwindled numbers of fur seals and sea otters, hunted nearly to extinction over the past century. In addition, bad relations with Britain in the aftermath of the Crimean War (1853–1856) prompted Czar Alexander the First to fear losing his far-flung Alaskan possessions to the British by force. Finally, the czar did not renew the company's charter, and the Russian America Company officially closed up shop.

Meanwhile, American technology was performing miracles. Western Union had laid two cables under the Atlantic Ocean from the United States to Europe, but neither had yet worked. So they figured, let's go the other way around the world: They proposed laying a cable overland through British Columbia, along the Yukon River, across the Bering Strait into Siberia, then east and south into Europe. In 1865, the Western Union Telegraph Expedition to Alaska, led by William Dall, surveyed the interior of Alaska for the first time, revealing its vast land and resources. This stimulated considerable interest in frontier-minded Washington, D.C. In addition, Czar Alexander's Alaska salesman, Baron Edward de Stoeckl, was spending $200,000 of his own money to make a positive impression on influential politicians and journalists.

Secretary of State William H. Seward purchased Alaska on March 30, 1867, for the all-time bargain-basement price of $7.2 million—*two cents* an acre. The American flag was hoisted over Sitka on October 18, 1867. According to Ernest Gruening, first U.S. senator to Alaska, "a year later when the House of Representatives was called upon to pay the bill, skeptical congressmen scornfully labeled Alaska 'Icebergia,' 'Walrussia,' 'Seward's Icebox,' and '[President] Johnson's Polar Bear Garden.' If American forces had not already raised the Stars and Stripes in Sitka, the House might have refused to pick up the tab." (Stoeckl, meanwhile, reimbursed himself the $200,000 he'd invested and sent the other $7 million home to Alexander.) Subsequently, Alaska faded into official oblivion for the next 15 years—universally regarded as a frozen wasteland and a colossal waste of money.

Organic Act of 1884

This act organized Alaska for the first time, providing a territorial governor and law enforcement (though not a local legislature or representation in Washington). President Chester Arthur appointed federal district court judges, U.S. attorneys, and marshals. From 1884 to 1900, only one U.S. judge, attorney, and marshal managed the whole territory, all residing in the capital, Sitka. The first three appointees to the court in Sitka were removed in disgrace amidst charges of "incompetence, wickedness, unfairness, and drunkenness." A succession of scandals dogged other federal appointees—and that was only in Sitka; the vast Interior had no law at all until 1900, when Congress divided the territory into three legal districts, with courts at Sitka, Nome, and Eagle.

William H. Dall wrote of Alaska at that time as a place where "no man could make a legal will, own a homestead or transfer it, or so much as cut wood for his fire without defying a Congressional prohibition; where polygamy and slavery and the lynching of witches prevailed, with no legal authority to stay or punish criminals." Kipling's line, "There's never law of God or man runs north of 53," also refers to the young territory of Alaska. In contrast, Colby in his WPA guide commented that the gold-rush stampeders, "although technically without civil authority, created their own form of self-government. The miners organized 'miners meetings' to enforce order, settle boundary disputes, and administer rough and ready justice. Too often this form of government failed to cope with [serious problems]... yet the profound instinct of the American people for self-government and their tradition of democracy made local self-government effective until the creation of the Alaska Legislature in 1912."

Gold!

Alaska's gold rush changed everything. After the California stampede of 1849, the search moved north. In 1858 there was a rush up the Fraser River to the Cariboo gold fields. In 1872, gold was found in British Columbia's Cassiar region. Strikes in Alaska and the Yukon followed one another in quick succession: at Juneau (1880), Fortymile (1886), Circle (1893), Dawson City (1896), Nome (1899), Fairbanks (1902), and Iditarod (1908).

A mobile group of men and women followed these discoveries on riverboats, dogsleds, and foot, creating instant outposts of civilization near the gold strikes. Gold also caused the Canadian and American governments to take a serious look at their northernmost possessions for the first time; the beginnings of Alaska's administrative infrastructure dates from those times. Still, in 1896, when Siwash George Carmack and his two Athabascan brothers-in-law discovered gold where Bonanza Creek flowed into the Klondike River in Yukon Territory, this vast northern wilderness could barely be called "settled." Only a handful of tiny non-Native villages existed along the Yukon River from Ogilvie and Fortymile in western Yukon to Circle and Fort Yukon in eastern Alaska, and a single unoccupied cabin sat on a beach

PANNING FOR GOLD

Panning for gold is not only great fun, it's also a good way to get involved in the history of Alaska. Besides, there's the chance you'll find a nugget that will become a lifelong souvenir. You might even strike it rich! The amount of equipment required is minimal: an 18-inch plastic gravity-trap gold pan (buy one at any local surplus or sporting-goods store for a couple of dollars), tweezers and an eyedropper to pick out the gold flakes, and a small vial to hold them. Ordinary rubber gloves will protect your hands from icy creek water. An automobile oil dipstick bent at one end is handy for poking into crevices, and a small garden trowel helps dig out the dirt under rocks. Look for a gravel bar where the creek takes a turn, for larger rocks forming eddies during high water, for crevices in the bedrock, or for exposed tree roots growing near the waterline. These are places where gold will lodge. Try your luck on any of the old gold-rush creeks; tourist offices can often suggest likely areas. Stay away from commercial mining operations and always ask permission if you're on someone's claim.

The principle behind panning is that gold, twice as heavy as lead, will settle to the bottom of your pan. Fill the pan half full of pay dirt you've scooped up from a likely spot and cover it with water. Hit the rim of the pan seven or eight times, or shake it back and forth. Break up lumps of dirt or clay with your hands and discard any rocks after rinsing them in the pan. Shake the pan again, moving it in a circular motion. Dip the front edge of the pan into the stream and carefully wash off excess sand and gravel until only a small amount of black sand remains. If you see gold specks too small to remove with tweezers, take the black sand out and let it dry. Later dump it on a clean sheet of paper and gently blow away the sand. The gold will remain. That's the basic procedure, though there are many ways to do it. It does take practice; ask a friendly sourdough for advice. Also, many spiked gold-panning facilities are found along the roads in Alaska – commercial, but good places to refine your technique.

at the mouth of the Skagway River at the terminus of the Inside Passage.

But by the end of 1897, perhaps 20,000 stampeders had skirted the lone cabin on their way to the headwaters of the Yukon and the sure fortunes in gold that awaited them on the Klondike. The two trails from Skagway over the coastal mountains and on to the interior rivers proved to be the most "civilized" and successful routes to Dawson. But the fortune-frenzied hordes proceeded north, uninformed, aiming at Dawson from every direction on the compass. They suffered every conceivable hardship and misery, from which death (often by suicide) was sometimes the only relief. And those who finally burst through the barrier and landed at the Klondike and Dawson were already two years too late to partake of the "ready" gold.

But the North had been conquered by whites. And by the time the gold rush had spread to Nome, Fairbanks, Kantishna, Hatcher Pass, and Hope, Alaska could finally be called settled (if not civilized).

The consequences of this Anglo invasion were devastating for the people who had lived in this harsh land for thousands of years. Epidemics of measles, influenza, and pneumonia swept through the Native communities, particularly in 1900 and 1918, sometimes killing every person in a village. Rescuers found entire families who had frozen to death because they did not have enough strength to keep the fire going. The impact of these deaths, combined with the sudden arrival of whites who introduced alcohol, depleted game and other food sources, and then brought Christianity as a replacement for indigenous beliefs, was profound. The consequences still ripple across Alaska, most notably in the form of rampant alcoholism, which is a factor in many Native accidents and suicides.

THE 20TH CENTURY

In the first decade of the 20th century, the sprawling wilderness was starting to be tamed. The military set up shop at Valdez and Eagle to maintain law and order, telegraph cables were laid across the Interior, the Northwest Passage had been found, railroads were begun at several locations, vast copper deposits were being mined, and thousands of independent pioneer-types were surviving on their own wits and the country's resources. Footpaths widened into wagon trails. Mail deliveries were regularized. Limited self-government was initiated: The capital moved to Juneau from Sitka in 1905; Alaska's first congressional delegate arrived in Washington in 1906; and a territorial legislature convened in 1912. A year later, the first men stood atop the south peak of Mt. McKinley, and the surrounding area was set aside as a national park in 1917. At that time, Alaska's white and Native populations had reached equivalency, at around 35,000 each. Judge James Wickersham introduced the first statehood bill to the U.S. Congress in 1916, but Alaska drifted along in federal obscurity until the Japanese bombed Pearl Harbor.

War

It's been said that war is good for one thing: the rapid expansion of communications and mobility technology. Alaska proves that rule. In the early 1940s, military bases were established at Anchorage, Whittier, Fairbanks, Nome, Sitka, Delta, Kodiak, Dutch Harbor, and the tip of the Aleutians, which brought an immediate influx of military and support personnel and services. In addition, in 1942 alone, thousands of miles of road were punched through the trackless wilderness, finally connecting Alaska to the rest of the world: the 1,440-mile Alaska Highway from Dawson Creek, B.C., to Delta, Alaska; the 50 miles of the Klondike Highway from Whitehorse to Carcross; the 151-mile Haines Highway; and the 328-mile Glenn Highway from Tok to Anchorage, among others. At the war's peak, 150,000 troops were stationed in the territory; all told, the U.S. government spent almost a billion dollars there during the war. (For a description of the actual fighting, see *War in the Aleutians* in the *Southwest Alaska* chapter.) After the war, as after the gold rush, Alaska's population increased dramatically, with servicemen remaining or returning. The number of residents nearly doubled between 1940 and 1950.

Statehood

The 1950s brought a boom in construction, logging, fishing, and bureaucracy to Alaska. The decade also saw the discovery of a large oil reserve off the western Kenai Peninsula in the Cook Inlet. The population continued to grow, yet Alaskans still felt like residents of a second-class colony of the United States and repeatedly asked for statehood status throughout the decade. Finally, on July 7, 1958, Congress voted to admit Alaska into the Union as the 49th state. President Dwight D. Eisenhower signed the official proclamation on January 3, 1959—43 years after Judge James Wickersham had first introduced the idea.

In the 92 years between Alaska's becoming a U.S. territory and its becoming a state, much of the land was split up into Navy petroleum reserves, Bureau of Land Management parcels, national wildlife refuges, power projects, and the like, to be administered by separate federal agencies, including national park, forest, and military services. By the time Alaska gained its statehood in 1959, only 0.003 percent of the land was privately owned—mostly homesteads and mining operations—and just 0.01 percent had been set aside for Native reservations, administered by the Bureau of Indian Affairs. The Statehood Act allowed Alaska to choose 104 million acres, but the issue of Native land ownership was not considered, and it would take oil discoveries in the late 1960s to force a redress for that injustice.

A little over five years after statehood, the Good Friday earthquake struck Southcentral Alaska; at 9.2 on the Richter scale, it remains the largest earthquake ever recorded in North America. But Alaskans quickly recovered and rebuilt with the plucky determination and optimism that still characterize the young state.

Oil Changes Everything

Alaska entered the big time, experiencing its most recent boom, in 1968, when Atlantic Richfield discovered a 10 billion-barrel oil reserve at Prudhoe Bay. The following year, Alaska auctioned off leases to almost half a million acres of oil-rich country on the North Slope for $900 million, 10 times more money than all its previous leases combined. A consortium of oil company leaseholders immediately began planning the Trans-Alaska Pipeline to carry the crude from Prudhoe Bay to Valdez. But conservationists, worried about its environmental impact, and Native groups, concerned about land-use compensation, filed suit, delaying construction for four years.

This impasse was resolved in 1971, when Congress passed the Alaska Native Claims Settlement Act (ANCSA), the most extensive compensation to any Native people in the history of the United States. It gave Alaska's aboriginal groups title to 44 million acres of traditional-use lands, plus a billion dollars to be divided among all American citizens with at least 25 percent Athabascan, Eskimo, or Aleut blood. The act also created a dozen regional Native corporations, a "13th Corporation" for Alaskan Natives in the Lower 48, plus more than 200 village and urban Native corporations.

The pipeline was built in 1974–1977. Again, after years of uncertainty, Alaska boomed, both in revenues and population. Since then, the state's economic fortunes have risen and fallen with the volatile price of oil. (See *The Wrangells and Prince William Sound* chapter for more on one of Alaska's most infamous incidents, the 1989 grounding of the *Exxon Valdez*, which poured 11 million barrels of crude into the pristine waters of Prince William Sound.)

Preserving the Wild Places

The ANCSA of 1971 had designated 80 million acres to be withdrawn from the public domain and set aside as national parks, wildlife refuges, and other preserves by 1978. In the mid- to late 1970s, in the wake of the completion of the pipeline, this was the raging land issue, generally divided between fiercely independent Alaskans who protested the further "locking-up" of their lands by Washington bureaucrats, and conservationists who lobbied to preserve Alaska's wildlife and wilderness.

When Congress failed to act, President Jimmy Carter took a bold move that forever changed the way Alaskan lands are managed; he withdrew 114 million acres of Alaskan lands as national monuments on December 1, 1978. The withdrawal still rankles the state's right-wing politicians who regard it as a criminal act that should be prosecuted.

Two years later, with the anti-environment Ronald Reagan waiting to take over the reins of power, Carter signed into law one of the most significant pieces of environmental legislation ever enacted, the Alaska National Interest Lands Conservation Act (ANILCA). The act set aside 106 million acres of federal property as "public-interest lands," to be managed by the National Park and National Forest services, the Fish and Wildlife Service, and other agencies. These "d2 lands" (from section 17:d-2 of ANCSA) included the expansion of Mt. McKinley National Park (renamed Denali); the expansion of Glacier Bay and Katmai national monuments, which became national parks; and the creation of Gates of the Arctic, Kobuk Valley, Wrangell–St. Elias, Kenai Fjords, and Lake Clark National Parks, plus the designation of numerous national monuments and preserves, scenic and wild rivers, and new wildlife refuges.

INTO A NEW CENTURY

The late 1990s were hard on Alaska, as oil prices dropped, pulp mills closed down, logging declined, and commercial fishing suffered from low prices and a market flooded with cheap farmed salmon from Chile, Norway, and British Columbia. But the first several years of the 21st century brought a reversal, with sky-high oil prices, a big push to develop a natural gas pipeline across the state, increased tourism, higher prices for Alaska's wild salmon, and major political upheavals as FBI investigations threatened the oil industry's stranglehold on state government. In 2006, voters did the unthinkable by voting to tax and regulate the cruise ship industry while simultaneously throwing out an incumbent governor (and former U.S. Senator), Frank Murkowski. Now if the voters could only follow up by evicting the daughter he appointed to fill his Senate seat . . .

Who Owns Alaska?

The vast majority of Alaska's 375 million acres is publicly owned, with less than one percent in private hands. Some 60 percent of this land is under federal management, with most of the rest in state or Native corporation hands. Get complete details on Alaska's public lands from Alaska Public Lands Information Centers (www.nps.gov/aplic/center) in Anchorage (907/271-2737), Ketchikan, Tok, and Fairbanks.

NATIONAL PARK SERVICE

In the federal scheme of things, the National Park Service gets all the glory. The national parks are the country's scenic showcases, and visitors come by the millions, usually to look, occasionally to experience. Denali National Park and Preserve—home to North America's highest mountain—is Alaska's most famous and overloved park, attracting well over a million tourists each year. Other well-known Alaskan national parks—Glacier Bay National Park and Preserve, Katmai National Park and Preserve, Kenai Fjords National Park, Klondike Gold Rush National Historical Park, Sitka National Historical Park, and Wrangell–St. Elias National Park and Preserve—are high on the list for travelers, and offer both visitor centers and various park activities. The other eight national parks and preserves (Aniakchak, Bering Land Bridge, Cape Krusenstern, Gates of the Arctic, Kobuk Valley, Lake Clark, Noatak, and Yukon-Charley Rivers) are so inaccessible that those with any facilities at all are prohibitively expensive for the average traveler, and the others are really no more than a name and a set of boundaries on the map.

People accustomed to national parks in the Lower 48 are surprised to find that very few trails run through Alaska's 15 parks. Most of the 54 million acres of national parkland are unforested and in the moist alpine tundra, where trails are not only unnecessary but largely detrimental to the ecology: As soon as the insulating ground cover is removed, the melting permafrost turns the trail into a muddy, impassable quagmire. Even in Denali, the only trails are around the park entrance and hotel area. Some parks (such as Denali, Glacier Bay, and Katmai) require backpacking permits; in the rest you're on your own. Several of the more accessible parks (Denali, Kenai Fjords, Klondike Gold Rush, Katmai, and Glacier Bay) have designated camping areas, but in the others you can pitch your tent on any level patch. For details on national parks in Alaska, request brochures from the National Park Service in Anchorage (907/271-2737, www.nps.gov/alaska).

FOREST SERVICE

In Alaska, the U.S. Forest Service manages the nation's two largest national forests: Tongass National Forest in Southeast Alaska, and Chugach National Forest in Southcentral Alaska. These forests cover 23 million acres of land, much of which is forested, but also comprising high mountains, glaciers, lakes, large rivers, and wild coastlines. Two national monuments within the Tongass—Admiralty Island and Misty Fiords—are popular with travelers, and 19 wilderness areas cover 5.7 million acres in the Tongass.

Both Tongass and Chugach are popular recreation destinations, with hundreds of miles of hiking trails and a number of campgrounds (free–$18) and visitor centers. Also within these forests are more than 180 wilderness cabins ($35–45/night), a few of which are reachable by road or trail, with the others accessible only by floatplane or boat. You must reserve them well in advance through ReserveUSA (518/885-3639 or 877/444-6777,

www.reserveusa.com). Brochures describing the cabins are available from Forest Service offices or from Alaska Public Lands Information Centers in Anchorage, Fairbanks, Tok, and Ketchikan.

For additional information, contact Tongass National Forest (907/586-7928, www.fs.fed.us/r10/tongass) and Chugach National Forest (907/271-3992, www.fs.fed.us/r10/chugach).

FISH & WILDLIFE SERVICE

The Fish & Wildlife Service manages 16 different refuges covering more than 75 million acres in Alaska. Most of these are in remote regions that see little visitation (other than local subsistence hunters and fishermen), but they provide vital habitat for birds and other animals. The best-known Alaskan refuges are Arctic National Wildlife Refuge on the North Slope, Kenai National Wildlife Refuge on the Kenai Peninsula, and Kodiak National Wildlife Refuge on Kodiak Island. Kenai sees the most tourists and has a visitor center, hiking trails, canoe routes, and campgrounds. Kodiak has a visitor center, plus a number of public-use cabins available for rent. A large new visitor center in Homer provides a great introduction to the Alaska Maritime National Wildlife Refuge, which sprawls across 2,500 Alaskan islands. The nation's largest refuge (20 million acres) is Yukon Delta National Wildlife Refuge in Western Alaska. For details on all 16 refuges, contact the F&WS (907/786-3909, http://alaska.fws.gov).

BUREAU OF LAND MANAGEMENT

Alaska's largest land-management agency (over 90 million acres) is the Bureau of Land Management (907/271-5960, www.ak.blm.gov). Most BLM land is undeveloped, but three popular recreation sites—White Mountains National Recreation Area, Chena River State Recreation Area, and Steese Natural Conservation Area—feature a handful of hiking trails, campgrounds, and public cabins in the vicinity of Fairbanks.

STATE LANDS
State Parks

The State of Alaska owns 89 million acres—almost a quarter of the state—and manages this land for a variety of purposes, from mineral and oil development to state forests. The state manages more than 110 state parks and recreation areas spread over three million acres. Located in Western Alaska, Wood-Tikchik State Park is the largest state park in America, encompassing 1.5 million acres. More accessible—it's the most popular state park in Alaska—is Chugach State Park which covers nearly a half-million acres bordering on Anchorage. Most of these state parks and recreation sites have trails and campgrounds. Camping fees are typically $10–15 per night, with some parks charging a $5 day-use fee. A number of state parks have public-use cabins for $45–65 per night.

For additional state park information call 907/269-8400 to request brochures and a statewide park map, or browse over to www.alaskastateparks.org. You can also use this website to check cabin availability; reservations are made at Department of Natural Resources public information offices in Anchorage or Fairbanks or state park offices.

Fish & Game

The Alaska Department of Fish & Game manages more than 30 state refuges, critical habitat areas, and wildlife sanctuaries, including the world-famous bear-viewing area at McNeil River and the Walrus Islands near Dillingham. It also jointly manages (with the Forest Service) the Pack Creek brown bear–viewing area on Admiralty Island. Also popular is Creamer's Field Migratory Waterfowl Refuge in Fairbanks. The agency issues sportfishing and hunting permits. For details on all its activities, contact the ADF&G (907/465-4180, www.state.ak.us/adfg).

NATIVE LANDS

Today, the 12 regional Native corporations and more than 200 village and urban corporations created in 1971 by the ANCSA own some 37 million acres in Alaska. Much of this is closed to public access except with special permits; fees are commonly charged.

The ANCSA attempted to bring Natives into the mainstream of society, and has succeeded in some ways, while failing in others. Surprisingly, the corporations created by the act have become primary forces in logging, mining, and other developments around the state, in sharp contrast to the preserve-the-land policies that might have been anticipated. In parts of Southeast and Southcentral Alaska the Native lands have been nearly all logged over; I know of one place where they logged almost within spitting distance of a Native cemetery and historic clan house. (Of course, these developments are driven by money, since corporations need profits to survive and to pay dividends to their Native shareholders.)

Economy and Government

COST OF LIVING

No doubt about it—this place is expensive. Alaska ranks near the top in cost of living for all the states. Numerous factors conspire to keep prices high. Most consumer goods must be imported from the Lower 48, and the transportation costs are tacked on along the way. In addition, the transportation and shipping rates within Alaska are similarly high, further inflating the cost of goods and services. In more remote regions especially, lack of competition, coupled with steady demand, ensures top-dollar prices. And let's not forget how long and cold and dark Alaskan winters are: the cost of heat and utilities is a hardship. Alaska ranks first in per capita energy consumption in the United States.

Visitors to Anchorage and Fairbanks will be pleased to find that prices are not totally out of line with the Lower 48. Typical food prices in these two largest cities are around 25 percent higher than those in Portland, Oregon. Both cities have large discount-chain stores that help keep prices more reasonable. The big chains have also spread to Wasilla, Juneau, and Ketchikan, driving down prices in those areas (and squeezing local businesses).

Beyond these exceptions, the prices in the North are much higher than Outside, and are generally the worst in the most remote bush communities. Food costs in places such as Galena or Fort Yukon are more than twice those in Anchorage. Even in Homer—which is on the road system—food is 40 percent more expensive than in Anchorage. These financial realities apply to residents much more than to short-term visitors: If you're well prepared and you provision yourself adequately in the major commercial centers, any time spent in the bush shouldn't be too painful to the pocketbook.

MONEY FOR NOTHIN'

In 1976, with oil wealth about to come gushing out of the south end of the pipeline, voters approved a constitutional amendment calling for a percentage of all oil and mineral revenues to be placed in a **Permanent Fund** (www .apfc.org). Money from this account can only be used for investment, not for state operating expenses, which explains why during recent Alaskan recessions, when hundreds of state workers were laid off and state funds were severely cut back, billions of surplus dollars sat untouched in the fund. It's the only one of its kind in the country: The only state fund that pays dividends to residents, and the largest pool of public money in the country. In 2006 it totaled more than $35 *billion!*

A portion of the interest and capital gains income from these assets are distributed to all Alaska residents—even children—in a yearly Permanent Fund Dividend check sent out each October. In 1982, the first year of the dividend, each Alaskan received $1,000, but it didn't reach that level again until the stock market boom of the late 1990s—when it topped out at nearly $2,000. The 2006 payout was around $1,100 per person. All this sudden cash doesn't go unnoticed by local businesses, especially car dealers, furniture stores, and airlines, who put out a plethora of special deals as soon as the money hits the banks.

MAKING A LIVING
Employment

Anyone thinking of moving to Alaska to get rich is in for a rude awakening. For a number of years after the oil boom, Alaskans earned the most per capita of any state, but now Alaska ranks 33rd for income—and near the top for cost of living. The state's unemployment figures are usually several percentage points above the national average, even during the peak summer season.

Despite this, you can still come to Alaska and make a decent living; after all, most Alaskans came from somewhere else (only a third of Alaskans were born in the state—the second-lowest such percentage in the country). But the opportunities, it should be stressed,

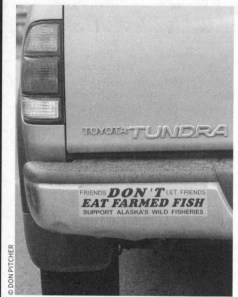

Cordova bumper sticker

herring, and others. Alaska produces almost all of the U.S. canned-salmon stock (200 million pounds), and eight Alaskan ports are among the country's top 50 producers, with Dutch Harbor/Unalaska almost always in the top three, and Kodiak not far behind.

Alaska's fisheries are probably the most carefully managed in America, with healthy stocks of wild salmon and halibut. Fish farming is illegal in Alaska, but farmed salmon from other areas have lowered demand and prices for wild salmon, forcing many Alaskan fishermen out of business. (See *Alaska Salmon* in the *Essentials* chapter for details on the controversy.)

Learn more about Alaska's seafood industry (and get some good salmon and halibut recipes) from the **Alaska Seafood Marketing Institute** in Juneau (907/465-5560 or 800/478-2903, and www.alaskaseafood.org).

Agriculture

The percentage of Alaska's land used for farming is as minuscule as the percentage of Alaska's total economy that is accounted for by agriculture. Of the state's 375 million acres (17 million of it suitable for farming), only 910,000 acres are considered cultivable; of those, only 31,000 acres are occupied by crops. The Matanuska Valley (Palmer/Wasilla) and the Tanana Valley (Fairbanks/Delta) contain almost 90 percent of Alaska's usable farmland. Hay, potatoes, barley, and oats are the state's top ag products.

In addition to legal crops, Alaska is famous for marijuana, and that crop is widely regarded as the state's biggest money-maker. Cannabis-growing operations (most are now indoor operations) are especially big in the Matanuska Valley, where the potent Matanuska Thunder gains the favor of potheads everywhere. A measure to legalize pot failed in 2004, but medical marijuana was approved by the voters several years earlier.

Gold and Minerals

From 1880 to 1980, 30 million ounces of gold were taken from Alaska. Today, the Fort Knox Mine near Fairbanks is Alaska's biggest gold

are limited. For example, almost a third of the people collecting a paycheck in Alaska work for federal, state, or local government. And the industry that accounts for 87 percent of state revenues (oil and gas) accounts for just 3 percent of employment. The real growth of late has come at the bottom end, in service jobs and retail sales, where your income would probably leave you officially listed at poverty status. So if a job as a Wal-Mart stocker is your dream, hop on the next flight to Anchorage.

For employment information, visit the **Alaska Department of Labor's** website (www.labor.state.ak.us). Here you'll find details on jobs in all sectors, including seasonal cannery work, state positions, and relocation information. The site's **Job Bank** provides an up-to-date listing of openings around the state.

Fishing

Alaska's fisheries account for over half of America's commercial fish production. Three-quarters of the value is in groundfish (pollock and cod) and salmon, the rest in shellfish, halibut,

© DON PITCHER

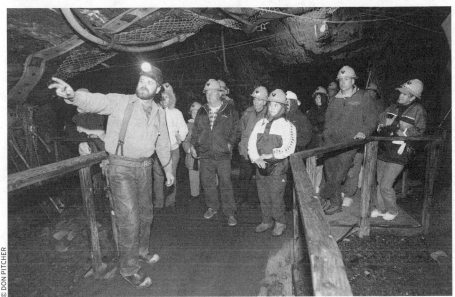

© DON PITCHER

former gold miner with tourists at AJ Mine-Gastineau Mill in Juneau

producer, extracting 1,000 ounces of gold per day. Another major gold mine is scheduled to open near Delta Junction in 2005, and other large hard-rock mines are near Galena and McGrath, while small placer mines are common across Alaska.

Zinc is the state's most valuable mineral, mined at the enormous Red Dog Mine, 90 miles north of Kotzebue. The largest zinc mine in the world, it produces 575,000 tons of zinc and 100 million tons of lead a year. Coal is mined at Usibelli, near Denali National Park, and deposits of jade, molybdenum, chromite, nickel, platinum, and uranium are known, though the cost of mining in remote Alaska limits these ventures.

Oil and Gas

Everything that moves in Alaska is lubricated with oil, primarily North Slope crude. Without oil, the Alaskan economy would stiffen, shatter, and disappear into thin air. Oil and gas revenues account for 87 percent of the state's tax revenue. Alaska is so addicted to oil revenue

that when the price of a barrel of oil drops by $1, the budget must be adjusted by $150 million. Though the industry accounts for just 3 percent of the total workforce, the average annual salary for these workers is $100,000. Few elected officials would dare speak out against the oil companies; they all know who pays the tab when election bills come in, and don't want that cash going to their opponents.

At more than 350 million barrels of oil a year, Alaska accounts for around 17 percent of the nation's oil production, second only to Texas. Peak production was in 1988, when 738 million barrels of Prudhoe crude flowed through the pipeline. The Prudhoe Bay oilfield, largest in North America and 18th in the world, had produced 14 billion barrels by 2003, but production continues to decline.

Enormous quantities of natural gas lie beneath the North Slope, and proposals have been made to build a gas pipeline paralleling the existing oil line, or to develop a gas-to-liquids technology so that the gas can be sent down the existing oil pipeline. Higher gas prices and increased demand may finally lead to its development within the next decade. In addition to the North Slope, both oil and gas are produced from offshore wells in Cook Inlet. The natural gas is used in Anchorage and Kenai, and at a fertilizer plant near Kenai.

Tourism

Tourism is Alaska's third-largest industry, behind petroleum production and commercial fishing. It's also the second-largest employer, accounting for thousands of seasonal jobs. More than a million visitors travel to Alaska each year, 90 percent of them arriving May–September from the continental United States and Canada. Approximately half of all visitors (including business travelers) travel independently; the rest come up on cruise ships and package tours.

Native Corporations

Native corporations are major players in Alaska's economy, and they also have large investments (we're talking billions of dollars) spread all over the nation. The most financially successful of the regional corporations, **Arctic Slope Regional Corporation** (www.asrc.com), had profits in 2001 topping $1 billion for its 9,000 shareholders. Other top companies include **Cook Inlet Regional Corporation (CIRI)** (www.ciri.com), **Chugach Alaska Corporation** (www.chugach-ak.com), **Doyon, Limited** (www.doyon.com), and **NANA Regional Corporation** (www.nana.com). Doyon, with more than 12 million acres, is the largest corporate landholder in the nation.

All of these companies are involved in tourism ventures around Alaska, but CIRI and NANA especially have major investments in tour companies, hotels, and other facilities. Another company that travelers to Southeast Alaska will certainly contact is the Juneau-based village **Goldbelt Corporation** (www.goldbelt.com) which runs the Mt. Roberts Tram, Glacier Bay

National Park concessions, tour boats and buses, kayak trips, a hotel, and various other operations. If you travel in the North, you'll probably spend time in a Native-owned facility or on one of their tour boats or buses.

GOVERNMENT

Like Delaware, Wyoming, Vermont, and North Dakota, Alaska has only one representative to the U.S. Congress, along with two senators. There are 20 state senators elected to four-year terms and 40 state representatives elected to two-year terms. They meet in the capitol in Juneau January–April. Local government is a mishmash: 16 first- and second-class boroughs, first- and second-class unincorporated villages, and tribal governments.

Alaskan politics start on the conservative end of the spectrum, and head from there to I'll-pull-my-gun-out-to-show-you-how-right-wing-I-am. As of 2007, Republicans have the governorship (Sarah Palin), a majority in both houses, and all three congressional seats. After being elected governor in 2002, Frank Murkowski appointed Lisa Murkowski, a relatively inexperienced legislator who happened to be his daughter to take over his seat in the U.S. Senate. She was elected in 2004, but her dad, Frank Murkowski, was thrown out of office after coming in third in the 2006 Republican primary, garnering just 20 percent of the voters in his party. The winner in 2006, Sarah Palin, ran on a reform platform that has the oil companies concerned that their power could be on the wane.

Senator Ted Stevens and Representative Don Young have enormous political clout, and are so entrenched in power that only death will loosen their grip, and even that could be in doubt, since Stevens's son is also a politician. Stevens in particular is considered a king of pork-barrel politics, and his largess makes Alaska the highest recipient of federal spending of any state, more than $11,540 per resident in 2005! Oink.

The People

In 2002, Alaska's population was 644,000. Of this, roughly 16 percent were of Native descent. The non-Native population is predominately white, with a small percentage of black, Hispanic, Asian, and Pacific Islanders. The Hispanic and Asian populations are growing rapidly in Alaska, and visitors to bush towns are often surprised to find that many of the restaurants are owned by Korean-Americans, while the cab drivers may be from the former Yugoslavia and the cannery workers came from the Philippines or Mexico. Of course, the cruise ships that ply Inside Passage waters are staffed by workers from all over the globe. Anchorage has by far the most diverse population; by 2010 more than a third of its residents will be Hispanic, Asian, black, or Native.

Joe Average
According to statistics, the "typical" Alaskan is a 32-year-old white male; I think I know him: He's single, has a college degree, lives in Anchorage, works for Federal Express, and hunts caribou with his buddies each fall, and is likely to be seen at Chilkoot Charlie's most Friday nights! The state has the second-highest percentage of kids under 18 of any state; only Utah (not surprisingly) is higher.

In Anchorage and the other large Alaskan cities, the ratio of men to women is almost equal, but the state as a whole has one of the highest male-to-female ratios in the nation: 104 males to 100 females (compared with 95 males to 100 females Outside). Of course, you should also know the old and all-too-accurate adage: Alaska, where the odds are good, but the goods are odd.

Alaska is the largest state but the third-least-populous (behind Wyoming and Vermont), resulting in the lowest population density—1.0 per square mile (compare this to Wyoming, which has the second smallest at 4.7, or New Jersey, which is the most crowded at 1,042). It's also second to last in the number of people born in-state (34 percent); Florida is last at 31 percent. Alaska takes last place in its percentage of farm workers (0.1 percent).

ALASKAN NATIVES
Southeast Natives
One of Alaska's only Indian reservations is at Metlakatla, near Ketchikan. A group of nearly 1,000 **Tsimshian** Natives relocated here in 1887 from their traditional homeland, slightly south near Prince Rupert, as a result of disagreements between William Duncan, the tribe's missionary, and his church superiors (see *Metlakatla* in the *Southeast Alaska* chapter for the complete story). These Natives are thus the only ones not included in the ANCSA. Similarly, about 800 **Haida** natives live on southern Prince of Wales Island at the southeastern tip of Alaska, and the northern extent of the Haida homeland.

The **Tlingit** (KLINK-it) Indians are the traditional dwellers of Southeast Alaska, related

statue commemorating The First Unknown Family, Golden Heart Park in Fairbanks

© DON PITCHER

CAPSULE ALASKAN GLOSSARY

A type of pidgin called "Chinook" evolved in the Pacific Northwest in the 18th century. The language first developed in interactions between the large, powerful Chinook tribe (hence the name "Chinook") of the Columbia River, which did business with white traders, and the Nootka tribe, which held a monopoly on the shells from which the shell money of the Pacific was manufactured. After Europeans arrived, Chinook adopted words from English and French; it became indispensable to traders in Alaska during the entire 19th century. Of the 500 words in the Chinook vocabulary, a few are still used today.

Some of the Alaskan words below have been borrowed from the Native tongues; the rest derive from the colorful frontier slang of explorers, traders, trappers, prospectors, fishermen, roughnecks, and travel writers.

akutak – Yup'ik Native word for Native ice cream: a combination of whipped berries, seal oil, and snow

Alaskan malamute – a particular breed of working dog used to pull sleds

Alcan – nickname for the Alaska Highway

Arctic Circle – an imaginary line, roughly corresponding to 67° north latitude, which the sun remains entirely above on summer solstice and entirely below on winter solstice

Aurora – goddess of dawn

aurora borealis – the scientific term for the northern lights

baidarka – an Aleut kayak covered with animal skins

baleen – also known as whalebone, these stiff, flexible whale's "teeth" are woven into baskets by Eskimo men

banya – Russian in origin, a small sauna in which rocks surround a wood stove, and are sprinkled with water for a steam bath; common on Kodiak Island and along the Bering Sea

barabara – traditional Aleut or Eskimo shelter, made of driftwood and a sod roof

blanket toss – originally a means of spotting game on the tundra, this Native event, where 6-8 people use a large blanket to toss the "spotter" high in the air and catch him; now part of most festivals and is demonstrated for tourists in Barrow and Kotzebue

break-up – the period in late April or early May when the river ice suddenly fractures and begins to flow downstream; a particularly muddy, slushy time of year

bunny boot – see vapor-barrier boots

bush – Borrowed from Africa and Australia, this term generally designates remote areas off the road system, particularly in Interior, Western, and Arctic Alaska

cabin fever – Alaska-size claustrophobia due to the extreme cold and dark of winter

cache – pronounced "cash," a log hut built on tin-wrapped stilts used to store food and supplies beyond the reach of animals

Chain, The – nickname for the Aleutian Islands

cheechako – meaning "just arrived," used to describe newcomers and visitors, especially those who haven't spent a winter in Alaska or received a dividend check; some sourdoughs view anyone not born in the state as a cheechako

chinook – a strong warm wind originating in Prince William Sound; can be particularly destructive in hillside sections of Anchorage

chum – a kind of salmon; also known as dog salmon, after its primary consumers

d2 – from the section of that name in the Alaska Native Claims Settlement Act; refers to the national-interest lands set aside for national parks and forests, wildlife refuges, preserves, and wild and scenic rivers

Eskimo – from French Canadian *Esquimau*, a word derived originally from northern Algonquin *askimowew*, which means "eater of raw fish"

fish wheel – an ingenious mechanism that uses the current of a river or stream for power to scoop fish into a tank

freeze-up – the time of year, mostly in Northwest and Arctic regions, during which bodies of water are frozen and seaports are icebound

gussuk – derogatory Eskimo term for white person

honey bucket – in much of bush Alaska, the local sewage system: a five-gallon plastic bucket used as a toilet. The untreated waste is often dumped into rivers in the summer or onto river ice in winter (for natural "flushing" when the ice breaks up in the spring). Because of the obvious health hazards – not to mention the smell – the state has been trying to bring sewage-treatment facilities to small villages.

hootch – shortened version of the Chinook word "hootchenoo," meaning home-distilled spirits

husky – The generic term for a sled dog. A toy poodle hooked up to a sled is technically a husky – for the brief moment before it's eaten by a large **Siberian husky.** Like the malamute, the Siberian husky is a singular breed famous for strength and intelligence.

icefog – caused by an inversion in which warm air traps cold air near the surface, which keeps getting colder and colder... until the water vapor in the air freezes, creating floating ice crystals; Fairbanks is notorious for its wintertime icefog

iceworm – originally a joke by sourdoughs on cheechakos, the joke was ultimately on the sourdoughs – iceworms actually exist, and you can see specimens in the museum in Juneau and at the Portage Glacier visitor center

Iditarod – Famous 1,000-mile dogsled race from Anchorage to Nome; takes place in February. One explanation of the name comes from the term "rod," a measurement of work accomplished in the gold fields; thus the word is actually a sentence: "I did a rod." Another holds that the name evolved from the name of an Ingalik Indian village reported as "Khadilotden." It was then reported by the USGS as "Haidilatna," and finally anglicized as Iditarod.

igloo – Alaskan Natives' shelters are never igloos made of ice (see *barabara*), except in extreme emergencies

Inside Passage – another name for Southeast Alaska; it refers to the many protected waterways of this island archipelago

Inupiak – a northern Eskimo dialect used by Inupiat peoples

iron dog – snowmobile

iron ranger – collection boxes at state and federal campgrounds

kuspuk – parka worn by Eskimo women, often with a small backpack-like pouch for carrying babies

liquid sunshine – Ketchikan's euphemism for rain

Lower 48 – an Alaskan term used to refer to the contiguous continental United States

moose nuggets – small, round, brown moose droppings, bravely made into jewelry by enterprising (usually bankrupt) local artisans

mukluk – boot made by Eskimo women, with tough sealskin soles, reindeer-hide uppers, fur and yarn trim, sewn together with caribou sinew

muktuk – an Eskimo delicacy of the rubbery outer layer of whale skin and fat; very chewy, served raw or pickled

mush – popularized by Sgt. Preston of the Yukon, this command means "Let's go!" to anxious dog teams everywhere; originally a Chinook term adapted from the French *marchons*

muskeg – swampy areas covered by moss and scrub

Native – the preferred term for Alaska's original inhabitants

no-see-ums – tiny biting flies that plague Alaska after mosquito season

nunatak – lonely rock peak jutting out above icefields

Outside – anywhere other than Alaska, primarily used in reference to the Lower 48

Panhandle – nickname for Southeast Alaska

permafrost – permanently frozen ground, with a layer of topsoil that thaws during the summer

petroglyphs – stone-age carvings on rock faces

poke – a miner's moosehide bag full of gold dust and nuggets

continued on next page

CAPSULE ALASKAN GLOSSARY (continued)

potlatch – A Native party to celebrate any occasion. Often the hosts would give away all their possessions to their guests. This exercise in the detachment from all worldly goods was also an exercise in gaining more, as the event conferred upon the guests the obligation to host a bigger potlatch with better gifts.

promyshleniki – early Russian explorers and traders

pushky – from Russian, the colloquial term for cow parsnip, a common plant that can cause caustic skin burns, particularly on a sunny day; most commonly used on Kodiak Island and in Southcentral Alaska

qiviut – underwool of musk ox, supposedly eight times lighter, warmer, and more expensive than wool

ruff – fur edge on a parka hood, often of wolf guard hairs

salt chuck – a narrow constriction at the end of a lagoon, where the direction of the water flow depends on the tides (out at low, in at high); mainly used in Southeast Alaska

shit icicle – the pile of excrement that gathers in bush outhouses each winter in the form of an inverted icicle; when it gets too close to the top, someone has the unpleasant job of knocking it down

skookum – Chinook, meaning "strong" or "worthy"

skookum **house** – jail

Slope – The gently sloping tundra around Prudhoe Bay; also known as the North Slope; Slope workers are almost always employed by the oil companies

snowmachine – snowmobile

solstice – first day of summer (June 21) or winter (December 21)

sourdough – a mixture of flour, water, sugar, and yeast, allowed to ferment before being used to make bread or hotcakes; an old-timer

squaw candy – dried or smoked salmon

surimi – processed seafood product manufactured from bottom fish (usually pollock) in Kodiak, Unalaska, and other Alaskan ports; used in "crab" salads and cocktails, as well as in less expensive sushi

taiga – from Russian word meaning "land of little sticks," which describes the transition zone between the boreal forest and treeless tundra

Taku wind – sudden gusts of up to 100 mph that sweep down on Juneau from the nearby icefields

termination dust – the first snowfall that coats mountaintops at the end of summer, a sign that Alaska's many seasonal workers are about to be terminated

tree line – the elevation (in Alaska, 2,500 feet) and latitude (generally following the Arctic Circle) above which no trees grow

tundra – from another Russian word, meaning "vast treeless plain"; used to describe nearly 30 percent of Alaska's land area

ulu – a shell-shaped Eskimo knife that tourists buy in record numbers and airlines disallow in hand luggage

umiak – an open skin-covered Eskimo boat used in the hunting of whales and other sea mammals

visqueen – thin clear plastic sheeting

XtraTufs – high-top rubber boots ubiquitous on Southeast Alaskan feet

Yup'ik – dialect of the Bering Coast Eskimo

---

to the Interior Athabascans. Blessed with an incredible abundance of food, fuel, furs, and tools, the Tlingits evolved a sophisticated and complex society, religion, and artistry. The primary social unit was the community house, which typically sheltered 50–100 people. Huge trunks of cedar and spruce provided the house posts, often carved and painted with the clan's

totemic symbols; slaves were put in the post holes to cushion the connection between totem and earth. One had to stoop to pass through the single door; no windows punctuated the long structure. Ten or so of these clan houses made up a village, and a number of neighboring villages made up a tribe. But these distinctions held little importance to the Tlingits, who felt connected genetically only to members of the same clan.

All marriages occurred between clans; marrying within the clan was considered incestuous. Descent was matrilineal: Children belonged to the mother's clan, and a man's heirs were his sisters' children. Therefore the pivotal male relationship was between uncle and nephews. At the age of 10, boys went to live with an uncle, who taught them the ways of the world. The uncle arranged the boy's marriage to a girl of another clan, who remained with her mother until the wedding. The dowry price was usually a number of blankets; the Tlingits were famous for their weaving and embroidery. Feasts known as "potlatch" honored the dead while feting the living. The Tlingits knew how to party. Often the potlatch continued for days or even weeks, during which the host fed, clothed, and entertained a neighboring, usually wealthier, clan, then "gave away" the clan's most valuable possessions to them. It was understood that the hosted clan would reciprocate eventually, with an even greater degree of festivity and generosity.

The Tlingits had an intensely animistic belief system, in which everything, from glaciers to fish hooks, had a spirit. Tlingit shamans were virtually omnipotent, alternately controlling and beseeching *yek,* or karma, on behalf of the tribe. They also professed a complete understanding of the afterlife, "on authority of men who died and came back." Tlingit arts were expressed by men who carved totems for house posts, through the potlatch and other important events, and by women who wove exquisite blankets. Unlike the Aleut, the Tlingits were fierce warriors who were never completely conquered by invading Russians, going head-to-head and hand-to-hand every inch of the way, until they settled into an uneasy coexistence.

Athabascans

Nomadic hunters and migrants, the Athabascans are related to the Tlingit of Southeast Alaska and the Navajo and Apache of the American Southwest. They subsisted on salmon and the Interior's mammals, mostly caribou and moose. They passed the cruel winters in tiny villages of no more than six houses, with a *kashim,* or community center, as the focal point. They ice-fished and trapped in the dark, using dogsleds as transportation. Their arts were expressed primarily in beautifully embroidered clothing and beadwork. The men remained constantly occupied with survival tasks—finding food, building houses, maintaining gear. When the first white explorers and traders arrived in the early 19th century, the Athabascans immediately began to trade with them, learning the new cultures and in turn educating the newcomers in local customs and skills, not the least of which was dogsledding.

A tiny separate group of Native people, the **Eyaks** are found on the coast of Alaska between Cordova and Yakutat, and have distinct links to both the Athabascans to the north and Tlingits to the east.

Aleuts

As the Athabascans were almost entirely land-based people, the Aleuts were almost entirely dependent on the sea. Clinging to the edge of tiny, treeless, windswept Aleutian Islands, they lived in small dwellings made of sealskin-covered frames, with fireplaces in the middle and steam baths attached on the sides. They made sea otter skins into clothing and processed walrus and seal intestines into parkas. Their kayaks (called *bidarka*) were made of marine mammal skins stretched over a wooden or whalebone frame. Basketry was their highest artistic achievement, and their dances were distinctly martial, with masks, rattles, and knives.

When the Russians invaded the Aleutians in the mid-1700s like furies from hell, around 25,000 Aleuts inhabited almost all the Aleutian Islands and the southern portion of the Alaska Peninsula. Within 50 years, over half had died through violence, starvation, or disease. Most of the rest became slaves and were dispersed around the New World to hunt the sea otter and fight for the Russians. In fact, Aleuts traveled as far south as Catalina Island off the Southern California coast, wiping out the Gabrielino Indians there, along with the entire otter population, in 1810. Many of the women served as concubines to the Russian overlords, further diluting the Aleut lineage. Today, most Aleuts carry only half or a quarter Aleut blood; only 1,000 are considered full-blooded.

Eskimo

The term Eskimo comes from the French-Canadian *Esquimau,* which in turn is derived from the Algonquin *askimowew,* which means "eaters of raw fish." Although the term is not at all derogatory, the Natives of these regions often prefer to use more specific titles: the **Yup'ik** peoples of Southwest Alaska, the **Inupiat** peoples of the Arctic and circumpolar region, and the **Alutiiq** peoples of Kodiak Island, the Alaska Peninsula, and parts of Kenai Peninsula and Prince William Sound. In addition, remote St. Lawrence Island contains **Siberian Yup'ik** peoples. All four groups speak distinct dialects of the same basic language.

In traditional Eskimo culture there was a strong sense of community; their society was mostly leaderless, with every able member responsible for contributing to the struggle for survival. The borderline between personal and communal property was fuzzy at best, and theft did not exist. Everything was shared, including (claim some anthropologists) wives. All justice was determined by what was deemed best for the community. Marriages, too, were so determined.

A boy entered adulthood after his first kill, and the event was celebrated by a large feast. A girl was considered grown as soon as she began menstruating, which was accompanied by a two-week ritual. The man-child selected a bride, paid a minimal price, and unceremoniously set up house in a hut similar to the Aleuts'—a bone-and-brush framework covered with moss and grass. "Igloos" made of snow and ice were used only as temporary shelters on the trail (and mostly by central Canadian Natives). Fuel was derived from whale oil and driftwood. They ate meat almost exclusively: fish, whale, walrus, caribou, birds. Also like their relatives the Aleut, they used skin and hides for clothing and boating. Masks are the most visible form of Eskimo art, but their aesthetic touch marks almost everything they make.

The Russians had little impact on the remote Eskimo, but their introduction to Western ways by the Boston whalers around the 1850s was swift and brutal. Many Eskimos quickly succumbed to whiskey, and Native men were shanghaied while unconscious to labor on the white whalers' ships. They learned about prostitution (renting the women) and slavery (selling them). They learned how to use firearms and casually kill each other, usually in a drunken fit. They acquired syphilis, white sugar, canned food, and money.

An encounter between the Eskimo of St. Lawrence Island and a single whaling vessel in 1880, described by Colby in his classic *Guide to Alaska* (1939), sums up the scene: "The master sent members of his crew ashore with bottles of grain alcohol, [for which] the Natives traded ivory, whalebone, and furs. The officers and crew selected a harem from the young women of the village, and paid them in alcohol. When the whaling vessel left, the entire village of 450 Natives was dead-drunk and beggared, for they had even cut up their skin boats to trade for liquor. Around them were plenty of hair seal and walrus, but by the time the village had sobered and collected weapons the game was gone. Only about twenty-five villagers survived."

The whaling years ended just before the gold rush began. But the ruin of the Eskimo culture was almost total. Gradually, with the help of missionaries and legislators, the Eskimo in the late 19th century turned to reindeer herding, which began to provide income, food, and skins. Today, an estimated 34,000 Eskimo live in Alaska, having doubled their number over the past 50 years. The Eskimo people live in an arc stretching from Siberia to Greenland.

NATIVE ARTS AND CRAFTS

Not unlike most other aboriginal cultures, Native Alaskan arts and crafts were intricately intertwined with animism, religious ceremony, and utility. Each group worked with its abundant natural resources to produce all the necessities of a lifestyle in which subsistence, religion, and artistic expression were inseparable.

Alaskan tourism and Native crafts have gone

hand in hand since the first Russian stepped ashore. When John Muir arrived in Wrangell by steamer in 1890, he wrote, "There was a grand rush on shore to buy curiosities and see totem poles. The shops were jammed and mobbed, high prices paid for shabby stuff manufactured expressly for tourist trade. Silver bracelets hammered out of dollars and half dollars by Indian smiths are the most popular articles, then baskets, yellow cedar toy canoes, paddles, etc. Most people who travel look only at what they are directed to look at. Great is the power of the guidebook-maker, however ignorant."

A similar advice holds today, especially in the shops selling made-in-China Alaskan trinkets or carved-in-Bali totem poles and masks. When buying Native handicrafts from anyone other than the artist, always look for the **Silver Hand** logo that identifies the work as an authentic Native piece. Get details from the Alaska State Council on the Arts (907/269-6610 or 888/278-7424, www.eed.state.ak/akca). Good places to buy Native crafts are the various museum gift shops or directly from the artisans, if you visit remote villages.

Ivory

The Inupiat Eskimo of northern coastal Alaska are renowned for their use of ivory, harvested (only) by Natives from the tusks and teeth of walruses, as well as ivory from woolly mammoths and giant mastodons uncovered by miners or erosion. The ivory is carved, also known as "scrimshawed," and made into various implements. Today you'll see ivory jewelry, *ulu* handles, cribbage boards, and the like. The use of ivory for handicrafts is severely restricted by federal regulations established to protect the walrus. Native carvers can carve on ivory obtained from walrus killed for subsistence food, and non-Natives can legally carve on fossilized ivory (darker-colored ivory that was buried in the ground). But don't make the mistake of buying an ivory piece and then taking it through Canada, unless you have a written permit from the Convention on Trade in Endangered Species (www.cites.org). Avoid border confiscations and other legal problems by mailing your pieces home. You won't have any problems carrying them onboard an aircraft, unless your plane lands outside the United States.

Baskets

All Alaskan Native groups used available resources to fashion baskets for storage, carrying, and cooking. Birch-bark baskets, often lashed with spruce roots, were made by the forest Athabascans. The coastal Haida, Tlingit, and Tsimshian Indians used the bark of big cedar trees. They also made entire baskets of spruce roots, occasionally weaving in maidenhead ferns for decoration. The Yup'ik and Aleut Natives of Western Alaska are known for small, delicate baskets fashioned from coastal rye grass. They also process baleen, the long strips of cartilage-like teeth that hang from the upper jaw of whales, and weave the strips into baskets.

The finest examples of the different baskets are displayed in the largest Alaskan museums; commercial baskets sell for anywhere from $30 for simple birch-bark trays to several thousand dollars for large baleen baskets.

Masks

Each Native culture had its traditional mask-making technology and its complex ceremonial uses for masks. Eskimo mask art and ritual were among the most highly developed in the world. Masks, like totems, represented the individual animals and birds that were worshipped, and each mask was believed to embody the spirit, or *inua*, of the animal. The masks of the Athabascans were worn by dancers, accompanied by a tribal choir, to dramatize the tribe's relationship to animal spirits, as well as to entertain guests at feasts. Some believe Aleut masks symbolized the faces of ancient inhabitants of the western Alaska archipelago, though these people were only distantly related to the Aleut, if at all.

The use of masks has declined in Alaskan Native cultures, and the art of mask-making isn't as prevalent today as it's said to have been before contact with the Western world. But you will see commercial masks in Native galleries and gift shops around the North; these bear a close resemblance to those of long ago.

Totems

Totem poles were the largest and most dramatic of the Native arts and social images, though today, totemic images are reproduced in every medium and size. Typical totemic characterizations include highly stylized wolves, whales, bears, ravens, eagles, and beavers, as well as mythological monsters, human ancestors, and religious spirits. These images are a common sight in gift shops all over Alaska. A further description of totem poles is found in the *Ketchikan* section of the *Southeast Alaska* chapter.

Other Pieces

Fur parkas are the quintessential Eskimo garment, and are available in remote villages and at shops in Anchorage and Fairbanks. The finest of these are custom-made and cost a small fortune; ask locally for the best seamstresses. Beautifully crafted **dolls** are a hallmark of Eskimo artists who typically use furs and other local materials. Other distinctively Alaskan items include **dance fans, beadwork,** and handcrafted silver or jade **jewelry.**

ESSENTIALS

Getting There and Around

BY AIR

Anchorage is the hub for air travel into Alaska, though there are nonstop flights into Fairbanks, Juneau, and Ketchikan from the Lower 48 states, plus a few international flights directly into Fairbanks. Six domestic carriers fly into and out of Anchorage International Airport: **Alaska Airlines** (800/426-0333, www.alaskaair.com), **American** (800/433-7300, www.aa.com), **Continental** (800/523-3273, www.continental.com), **Delta** (800/221-1212, www.delta.com), **Frontier** (800/432-1359, www.frontierairlines.com), **Northwest** (800/225-2525, www.nwa.com),

and **United** (800/241-6522, www.ual.com). International carriers with flights to Anchorage include **Air Canada** (888/247-2262, www.aircanada.com), **Japan Airlines** (800/525-3663, www.jal.com), **Korean Air** (800/438-5000, www.koreanair.com), **China Airlines** (800/227-5118, www.china-airlines.com), and **Condor Airlines** (800/524-6975, www.condor.com), and **Magadan Airlines** (907/248-2994). See the *Anchorage and Vicinity* chapter for details on which carriers fly where.

The state's flagship carrier, Seattle-based Alaska Airlines, has jet service to all the larger

© DON PITCHER

cities and towns in Alaska, as well as throughout the United States and all the way to Mexico.

Regional Airlines

Alaska Airlines serves most larger towns around the state, including such far-flung places as Barrow, Nome, Bethel, Kodiak, and Dillingham. **Era Aviation** (907/266-8394 or 800/866-8394, www.flyera.com) has daily service from Anchorage to Cordova, Homer, Kenai, Kodiak, and Valdez. **PenAir** (907/243-2323 or 800/448-4226, www.penair.com) flies from Anchorage to Aniak, Cold Bay, Dillingham, Dutch Harbor, Iliamna, King Salmon, McGrath, Pribilof Islands, Sand Point, and Unalakleet. **Frontier Flying Service** (907/450-7200 or 800/478-6779, www.frontierflying.com) has hubs in both Anchorage and Fairbanks, with service between the two cities several times a day, plus flights to Aniak, Barrow, Bethel, Dillingham, and many bush villages from Allakaket to Wainwright. **Arctic Circle Air** (907/842-3870 or 888/214-2364, www.arctic-circle-air.com) serves Cordova, Iliamna, King Salmon, and Yakutat. **Grant Aviation** (907/243-3592 or 888/359-4726, www.flygrant.com) connects Anchorage with Homer and Kenai, and **Hageland Aviation** (907/245-0119 or 866/239-0119, www.hageland.com) flies to Unalakleet.

BY BUSH PLANE

Flying in a real live Alaska bush plane is a spectacular way to see the state, and it's also the only practical way to access the vast majority of Alaska's roadless areas. You will never forget your first flight over Alaska, whether it's a floatplane heading to Misty Fiords National Monument or a tiny Super Cub taking you to a remote Arctic camp. These airlines have regularly scheduled, though expensive, flights to towns and attractions that either have no public ground transportation or simply can't be reached overland—which accounts for over three-quarters of the state. For many people who live in Alaska's bush, these planes provide a lifeline of mail, food, and supplies. The planes seat 2–12 passengers, and they fly no

matter how many passengers are along, for the regular fare (if the weather's cooperating).

But if you're heading to a really remote cabin, fjord, river, glacier, or park, that's when you'll encounter the famous Alaskan bush pilots, with their equally famous charter rates, which can make Alaska Airlines's fares look like the bargain of the century. Still, you'll have quite a ride—landing on tiny lakes with pontoons, on snow or ice with skis, on gravel bars with big fat tires; and loaded to the gills with people, equipment, extra fuel, tools, mail, supplies, and anything else under the sun. Make sure you agree on all the details beforehand—charges, drop-off and pickup times and locations, emergency and alternative procedures, and tidal considerations. Never be in much of a hurry; time is told differently up here, and many variables come into play, especially weather. If you're well prepared for complications, and have a flexible schedule and a loose attitude, one of these bush hops will no doubt be among your most memorable experiences in Alaska, worth every penny and minute that you spend.

As far as what you can expect to pay, most flightseeing operations have preset itineraries and prices. Some companies flying out of the larger towns also have set rates to some of the more popular destinations. However, for most drop-off trips, you pay for the ride according to engine hours, both coming and going. So if your destination is a spot that's an hour from the airstrip, you pay for four hours of engine time (an hour out and an hour back, twice).

Safety in the Air

Before you head out into the wild blue yonder, there are a few things you should know. Alaska has far more than its share of fatal airplane crashes every year, generally three to four times the national average for small planes. These have happened to even the best pilots flying for even the most conscientious companies, but certain operators cut corners in safety and allow their pilots to fly under risky weather conditions. You can't avoid all risks, of course, but you can improve your odds by taking a few precautions on your own.

First and foremost, you should choose your pilot and/or flight service with care. Just because someone has a pilot's license and is flying in Alaska doesn't mean that he or she is a seasoned bush pilot. You're well within your rights to ask about the pilot's qualifications, and about time spent flying *in Alaska*. The oft-repeated saying is, "There are old pilots and there are bold pilots, but there are no old bold pilots." Given a choice, you want an "old" one—not so much in chronological years, but one that's been flying in and out of the bush for a good long time. Ask locally about the air safety record of the various companies. Also ask which companies have the contracts with the Forest Service or other Federal agencies, since they tend to be ones that aren't allowed to take chances. You can also search the Internet for accident statistics for a specific company at the **National Transportation Safety Board's** website (www.ntsb.gov).

Even if you're just going on a 30-minute flightseeing tour, wear clothing appropriate for the ground conditions. Unplanned stops because of weather or mechanical problems aren't unusual. Warm, comfortable hiking clothes, raingear, and lightweight boots or sturdy shoes make reasonable bush plane apparel.

Weather is a major limiting factor in aviation. Small planes don't operate on airline-type schedules, with arrivals and departures down to the minute. Leave yourself plenty of leeway when scheduling trips, and don't pressure your pilot to get you back to the airstrip so you won't miss your bus, boat, train, dogsled ride, or salmon bake. More than one crash has been the result of subtle or not-so-subtle pressure by clients to fly when it was against the pilot's better judgment. Never pressure a pilot to fly, and always try to act as a second pair of eyes to look for any signs of danger, such as other aircraft in the vicinity.

Before taking off, your pilot should brief all passengers on the location of safety and survival equipment and airsickness bags, how to exit during an emergency landing (or crash), and the location and function of the Emergency Locator Transmitter (ELT) and survival kit. Ear protection may also be supplied, as most small planes are quite noisy. Just in case, buy a set of foam earplugs at a sporting goods store before you go to the airport. They cost under a buck, weigh nothing, and are perfectly adequate for aircraft noise levels.

You'll probably be asked how much you weigh (don't be coy here—lives are at stake!) and told where you should sit. Weight and balance are critical in little planes, so don't whine about not getting to sit up front if you're told otherwise. Many companies place severe restrictions on how much gear they carry, charging excess baggage fees over a certain limit (sometimes less than 50 lbs.).

Gear stowage can be a challenge in small planes, especially when transporting people who are heading out on long expeditions. Don't even think of showing up at the airfield with hard-sided luggage. Internal-frame backpacks, duffel bags, and other soft, easily compressed and stowed items are much easier to handle. Don't strap sleeping bags and other gear onto the outside of a pack. Lots of small items are much easier to arrange and find homes for than a few bulky things. Also, if you're carrying a canister of red pepper spray to deter bears, tell the pilot beforehand and follow directions for stowage. Pilots don't want the stuff inside the cabin (imagine what might happen if it went off in this enclosed space!), but they'll store it in a float if the plane is so equipped, or you may be able to strap it to a strut with duct tape.

Whenever you fly, leave a flight route, destination, expected departure and arrival times, and a contact number for the flight service with a reliable friend. Then relax and enjoy the scenery. Flying in Alaska is a tremendous experience, one that relatively few people get to enjoy, and, in spite of all the cautionary notes listed above, is still a generally safe and reliable way to get to and see the wilderness.

FERRY SERVICE

Ferries plying the Inside Passage from Bellingham to Skagway cruise up an inland waterway and through fjords far wilder than Norway's,

© DON PITCHER

Alaska Marine Highway System ferry *Matanuska,* Lynn Canal

surpassing even a trip down the coast of Chile to Punta Arenas. One difference is that the North American journey is cheaper and more easily arranged than its South American or Scandinavian counterparts. Another difference is the variety of services, routes, and destinations for this 1,000-mile historic cruise. Ferries operated by the **Alaska Marine Highway** (907/465-3941 or 800/642-0066, www.ferryalaska.com) are the core of Inside Passage travel.

There are two primary state ferry networks: one from Bellingham, Washington, or Prince Rupert, British Columbia, and throughout Southeast Alaska; the other through Southcentral Alaska from Cordova all the way to Dutch Harbor in the Aleutians. In addition, a ferry sails between Whittier and Juneau twice monthly in the summer, linking the two regions together.

British Columbia Ferries (250/386-3431 or 888/223-3779, www.bcferries.com) sails Canada's Inside Passage from Port Hardy at the northern tip of Vancouver Island to Prince Rupert on the B.C. mainland's north coast.

Alaska Marine Highway

One of the first actions of the newly created Alaska State government in 1959 was to establish a state ferry system. Originally it consisted of just a single boat, but after passage of a 1960 state bond, three new ships were built and more have been added over the years. The newest additions are two high-speed ferries (high-speed when they are operating, which can be half the time): the *Fairweather* in Southeast Alaska and the *Chenega,* for Prince William Sound. All state ferries carry both passengers and vehicles, and offer food service. The larger ferries also have cabins, showers, storage lockers, gift shops, pay phones, and cocktail lounges.

Ferries generally stop for one or two hours in the larger towns, but less than an hour in the smaller villages. You can usually go ashore while the vessel is in port. Most ferry terminals open only an hour or two before ship arrivals, closing upon their departure. A baggage cart transports luggage from the terminal to the ship if you want to save your back a bit. There is a limit of 100 pounds of luggage per person, but this is only enforced if you are way over and the ship is full.

Life Onboard

The ferries have a relaxed and slow-paced atmosphere; it's impossible to be in a hurry here! Many travelers think of the ferry as a floating motel—a place to dry off, wash up, rest up, sleep, and meet other travelers while at the same time moving on to new sights and new adventures. Ferry food is reasonably priced and quite good, but many budget travelers stock up on groceries before they board. The hot water is free in the cafeteria if you're trying to save bucks by bringing along Cup-O-Noodles and instant oatmeal.

Most ferries have Forest Service or Fish & Wildlife Service interpreters on board in the summer, showing videos, giving talks, and answering questions about trails and campgrounds. Feature movies are shown on the video monitors every day.

Staterooms or Solarium?

Staterooms offer privacy, as well as a chance to get away from the hectic crowding of midsummer. These cabins have two or four bunk beds, and some also include private baths; other folks use the baths and showers down the hall.

If you don't mind hearing others snoring or talking nearby, you can save a bundle and make new friends with fellow voyagers. There's generally space to stretch out a sleeping bag in the recliner lounge (an inside area with airline-type seats), as well as in the solarium—a covered and heated area high atop the ship's rear deck. The solarium has several dozen deck chairs to sit and sleep on, and can get so popular that at some embarkation points, there's a mad dash to grab a place. To be assured of a deck chair, get in line five hours ahead of time if you're coming aboard in Bellingham in midsummer. When the weather is good you're also likely to see the rapid development of a tent city on the rear deck, often held down with duct tape (sold in gift shops on board).

Getting Tickets

The ferries operate year-round. Get schedules and make reservations by calling 907/465-3941 or 800/642-0066, or online at www.ferryalaska.com. Reservations for the summer can be made as early as December, and travelers taking a vehicle should book as early as possible to be sure of a space. Before you get ready to board, it's always a good idea to call the local ferry terminal to make sure the ferry is on schedule; often they are running behind, and the too-frequent breakdowns can totally change departure times.

Although there is usually space for walk-on passengers, it's a smart idea to make advance reservations for ferries out of Bellingham, especially or cabins. Reservations are required for anyone with a vehicle, and are generally available six months in advance. The ferry system charges an extra fee to carry bicycles, canoes, kayaks, and inflatable boats.

CRUISE SHIPS

For many people (particularly retirees), cruise ships offer the luxury way to see Alaska. A multitude of ships ply the Inside Passage and Gulf of Alaska waters, carrying over 900,000 people each summer—half of all travelers to the state. Cruises make it easy for travelers to explore the Inside Passage while enjoying good food and cozy accommodations.

Cruise ship tourism has proven to be a mixed blessing for Alaska. True, it does bring in millions of dollars to the state, and towns such as Skagway are almost totally given over to cruise ships, but the ships also dump hundreds of thousands of gallons of wastewater into Alaska's pristine waterways, pollute the air, and cause major disruptions in local communities. In 2006, Alaskan voters were angry enough to slap a $50 head tax and various restrictions on the industry.

The Ships

Most ships depart from Vancouver, British Columbia, but some cruises also leave from Seattle or San Francisco. The largest vessel can hold more than 3,000 passengers, and some offer impressive buffets, luxurious atrium lobbies, private stateroom verandas, health spas, and lounges with live music and casinos. Not all ships are large and glitzy, however. The smallest "expedition" ships may hold just a few dozen passengers. On these, the emphasis is on education and ecotourism. Many of the smaller ships also have professional naturalists on board and act as "mother ships" for short sea kayaking or hiking trips. Not surprisingly, expedition ships are considerably more expensive than the giant cruise liners.

Big Ships

Any good travel agent—and many online travel sites—can set up an Alaska cruise, or you can book your own by contacting the companies directly. A good overall place to begin an exploration of cruise ship travel is the website of the **Cruise Lines International Association** (www.cruising.org). It has links to all the major players, plus general information. Other useful websites include www.cruisecritic.com, www.cruisereviews.com, www.cruise-chat.com, www.cruisemates.com, and www.alaskacruisingreport.com.

The large ships that visit Alaska are operated by **Carnival Cruise Lines** (888/227-6482, www.carnival.com), **Celebrity Cruises** (800/647-2251, www.celebritycruises.com), **Holland America Line** (206/281-3535 or 877/724-5425, www.hollandamerica.com), **Princess Cruises** (800/776-6237, www.princess.com), **Norwegian Cruise Lines** (800/327-7030, www.ncl.com), **Regent Seven Seas** (877/505-5370, www.rssc.com), and **Royal Caribbean International** (866/562-7625, www.royalcaribbean.com).

Smaller Cruise Ships

You don't have to join these mega-ships to see Alaska by sea. A number of companies offer smaller ships (less than 100 passengers) for a more intimate look at the state. Of course, these are also considerably more expensive than ships that pack folks into every nook and cranny. Companies with small cruise ships include **Cruise West** (206/441-4757 or 888/851-8133, www.cruisewest.com), **Clipper Cruise Line** (314/655-6700 or

800/456-8100, www.intravac.com), **Lindblad Expeditions** (212/765-7740 or 800/397-3348, www.expeditions.com), and **Magestic America Line** (800/434-1232, www.magestic americaline.com).

Even smaller boats provide the ultimate in luxury for groups of 6–8 people. Good expedition companies include **Alaska Sea Adventures** (907/772-4700 or 888/772-8588, www.yachtalaska.com), **Alaska Yacht Adventures** (907/789-1978 or 800/725-3913, www.alaskayachtcharters.com), **American Safari Cruises** (888/862-8881, www.amsafari.com), **Alaska on the Home Shore** (360/592-2375 or 800/287-7063, www.homeshore.com), **Discovery Voyages** (800/324-7602, www.discovery voyages.com), and **Piragis International Expeditions** (218/365-6745 or 800/223-6565, www.piragis.com).

Costs and Itineraries

Prices for cruises have dropped in recent years as more and larger ships have moved into the Alaskan market. The bargain deals are typically early or late in the summer season, and can be amazingly cheap at times. Cruises typically last 7–12 days, and are either taken as a round-trip tour of the Inside Passage or a one-way cruise that encompasses both the Inside Passage and towns along the Gulf of Alaska. It is also possible to add in a land tour, either as part of a hurried seven-day ship-and-bus package or as an add-on to the cruise. The add-on option often includes time in Southcentral and Interior Alaska, and might start with a trip through the Inside Passage followed by a bus tour from Skagway to Fairbanks, and a train trip to Denali National Park and then on to Anchorage where you fly home. Many other cruise options exist; contact the individual companies for details.

TRAIN

Except for the White Pass & Yukon Route excursion between Skagway and Fraser, and the kids' choo-choos around Pioneer Park in Fairbanks and Alaska Live Steamers in Wasilla, Alaska's only train is the **Alaska**

Railroad (907/265-2494 or 800/544-0552, www.akrr.com). The railroad runs 470 miles between Seward and Fairbanks, with a seven-mile spur between Portage and Whittier, and is the only state-owned railroad in America. The train—historic and a bit exotic—is also much roomier and slower than the tour buses but is about the same price (and occasionally even on time). Dining service is available, and helpful tour guides are on board in the summer months. In addition, some of the trains will make flag stops to pick up hikers or people living in the Alaskan bush.

Two daily expresses (mid-May –mid-Sept.), one northbound and one southbound, run between Anchorage and Fairbanks for $185 one-way. Anchorage to Denali costs $129, Fairbanks to Denali $56. The train also connects Seward with Anchorage ($62) and Anchorage with Whittier ($55) daily in the summer. The railroad also has luxurious double deck cars ($85 extra to Denali), and a variety of package tours that combine train rides with boat trips and other activities. In addition, Princess Tours and Holland America Tours/Gray Line hook double-decker superdome coaches to the end of the express trains in the summer.

REGIONAL BUSES

There is no regular bus service between the Lower 48 and Alaska, but you *can* get there from here. **Greyhound Canada** (604/482-8747 or 800/661-8747, www.greyhound.ca) covers much of Canada, reaching north to Whitehorse in the Yukon. From there, you'll need to hop aboard an **Alaska Direct Bus Line** (907/277-6652 or 800/770-6652, www.alaskadirectbusline.com) van to Anchorage, Fairbanks, or Skagway. Service is three times a week in the summer, and twice weekly the rest of the year. Reservations required.

Alaska/Yukon Trails (907/479-2277 or 888/600-6001, www.alaskashuttle.com) has year-round service between Anchorage and Fairbanks, and once-a-week summertime service connecting Fairbanks with Whitehorse, Yukon.

Several other companies have van service in Southcentral and Interior Alaska: **Denali Overland Transportation** (907/733-2384 or 800/651-5221, www.denalioverland.com), **Alaska Park Connection** (907/245-0200 or 800/266-8625, www.alaskacoach.com), **Seward Bus Lines** (907/563-0800, www.sewardbuslines.net), and **Homer Stage Line** (907/868-3914, www.homerstageline.com).

Green Tortoise

This is more than just a bus ride—it's a vacation and a cultural experience in itself. The ancient buses have foam mattresses, a lounge area with seats and tables, and communal meals. One of the best things about these trips is the people—alternative travel attracts good company. This is a friendly, unprivate way to travel, though not inexpensive.

Green Tortoise (415/956-7500 or 800/867-8647, www.greentortoise.com) has several trips each summer to Alaska, and each bus holds 32 passengers and 2 drivers. Book no later than March to ensure a space. Some trips leave from San Francisco and wind up in Anchorage, others start and end in Anchorage.

Despite the casual approach, Green Tortoise buses are reliable and have a good safety record. The company also runs bus trips all over the country, and even to Central America.

CARS

Getting to Alaska by car is the most flexible means of mobility. You can start anywhere, and once there, you can go anywhere there's a road, anytime you feel like it, stopping along the way for however long you decide. The roads in the North Country are especially fun, and you have some of them almost to yourself. On a few roads you'll rarely see another car. It's very open, unconfined, uninhibiting—a large part of the spell of the North.

One essential for Alaskan drivers of all types is *The Milepost,* a fat annual book that's packed with mile-by-mile descriptions for virtually every road within or to Alaska (including, of course, the Alcan). The book is sold everywhere in Alaska—even Costco—

ALASKA HIGHWAYS

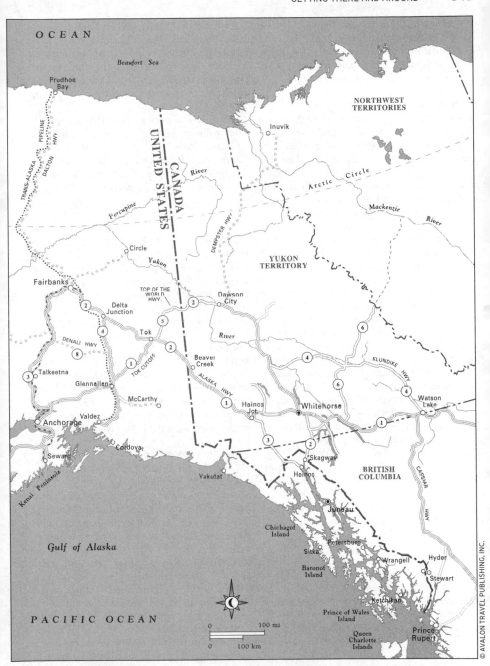

and is easy to find in Lower 48 bookstores, or online at www.themilepost.com. Warning: Don't believe everything you read in *The Milepost;* much of the text is paid ads for specific businesses—watch for the small notice.

The Alaska Highway

You can drive all the way up and back, or put the car on the ferry one way. The Alaska Highway (nicknamed the **Alcan**) has been dramatically upgraded from the early days when you had to carry extra fuel and four spare tires, when you had to protect your headlights and windshield with chicken wire, and when facilities were spaced 250 miles apart. Today, the entire road is paved, gas stations are about every 50 miles, and roadhouses and hotels are numerous. Still, this road passes through 1,442 miles of somewhat inhospitable wilderness. Frost heaves and potholes are not uncommon. Mechanics are few and far between and parts are even scarcer. Gas prices are no laughing matter, especially on the Canadian side where they're typically almost double those in the Lower 48 states. If you're coming from anywhere east of Idaho or Alberta, you can hit Mile 0 of the Alaska Highway through Edmonton without having to backtrack east at all. But if you're heading north from the West Coast, or through the Canadian Rockies, you'll probably wind up in Prince George and have to head east a bit to Dawson Creek (the starting point).

You can also head west out of Prince George on the Yellowhead and take the **Cassiar Highway** north from Meziadin Junction to just west of Watson Lake in Yukon Territory. This 458-mile paved road is scenically stunning, but services are a little less frequent than on the Alaska Highway.

Go Prepared

A few common-sense preparations can eliminate all but the most unexpected problems. A credit card (preferably Visa or MasterCard) is essential, especially if you don't want to worry about changing money on either side of the border. You can expect to get hit hard by gas prices along the Alcan and in the more remote stretches within Alaska. But along the main Interior and Southcentral Alaska thoroughfares, prices are often only a few cents higher than Outside. Finally, by driving the whole way in one direction and putting the car on the ferry in the other, you can take different routes up and back.

A reliable car is a must. Get the car carefully serviced before setting out; when you ask your mechanic, "Will it make it to Alaska?" you won't be kidding. If you get stuck somewhere, there might not be another mechanic for 100 miles. And tow trucks have been known to charge $5 *a mile.* Since you'll be tempted to drive hundreds of miles off the beaten track, the best investment you can make in your car is five good tires. Bring a pressure gauge and check the tires frequently. A few spare hoses (and hose tape) and belts take up little room and can come in very handy. Spare gas and oil filters are also useful, because of the amount of dust on the gravel roads in the dry months. Water is an absolute necessity; carry at least a five-gallon jug. Also, if you have a mobile phone it may prove useful, not only for keeping in touch with friends at home, but also for emergencies. Service is good in the major cities and most towns, but can be spotty or nonexistent elsewhere. Take tools and jumper cables even if you don't know how to use them. Someone usually comes along who doesn't have tools but knows what to do.

Winter Travel

During the winter months, travelers to Alaska need to take special precautions. Always call ahead for road and avalanche conditions (see *Safety in Avalanche Country* in the *Anchorage and Vicinity* chapter) before heading out. Studded snow tires and proper antifreeze levels are a necessity, but you should also have on hand a number of emergency supplies including tire chains, a shovel and bag of sand in case you get stuck, a first-aid kit, booster cables, signal flares, flashlight, lighter and candle, transistor radio, nonperishable foods (granola bars, canned nuts, or dried fruit), a jug of water, an ice scraper, winter clothes, blankets, and a sleeping bag. The most valuable tool may well be a **mobile phone** to call for help—assuming you're in an area with reception.

If you become stranded in a blizzard, stay in your car. You're more likely to be found, and the vehicle provides shelter from the weather. Run the engine and heater sparingly, occasionally opening a downwind window for ventilation. Don't run the engine if the tailpipe is blocked by snow, or you may risk carbon monoxide poisoning.

Road Updates

For current road conditions, construction delays, and more, contact the **Alaska Department of Transportation** online at http://511.alaska. gov, or dial 511 toll-free anywhere in Alaska or 866/282-7577 outside Alaska

Car Rentals

An increasingly popular way to see Alaska is by flying into the state and renting a car. This provides travelers with flexibility, and the costs have dropped in recent years. Rental cars are available in all the larger towns, but they are generally cheapest out of Anchorage, where most of the major car rental companies have airport booths. Rates start around $45/day or $300/week for an economy car with unlimited mileage. For long rentals, it's always best to get a car away from the airport where the taxes are higher. In the peak summer season you should reserve up to two months in advance to get the best rates, and to be assured of finding any car at all when you arrive.

If you plan to rent a car for an extended period, it's probably worth your while to check travel websites such as www.travelocity.com to see which company offers the best rates. When reserving a car, be sure to mention if you have an AAA card or are a member of Costco; you can often save substantially on the rates. Also be sure to ask about driving restrictions, since most car rental companies prohibit their use on gravel roads such as the one to McCarthy.

RV and Camper Rentals

Recreational vehicles are among the most despised sights on Alaskan roads, but they seem to proliferate like rabbits as soon as the snow melts each spring. Motor homes are infamous for cruising slowly down the Seward Highway south of Anchorage, wagging a tail of impatient cars for a mile or more behind. Many "snowbirds" drive up to Alaska for the summer in their RVs, fleeing to Arizona for the winters. Other folks fly into Anchorage, Fairbanks, or Whitehorse and rent one of these land yachts.

Despite these criticisms, RVs can be a decent choice if the gas price is not out of sight and if you can cram enough folks inside to cut your costs. But for just two people they are a profligate and environmentally disastrous investment. See the *Anchorage and Vicinity* chapter for RV and camper rental companies.

PACKAGE TOURS

A 7- to 21-day whirlwind around Alaska is available from dozens of tour packagers. All will book you onto one of a variety of cruise ships up the Inside Passage, reserve your hotel rooms, roll you between them on motorcoaches and railcars, and offer options for local and overnight side trips. Many are escorted by tour guides, and some even include all meals in the price. Many people choose this route for convenience, comfort, and security, though they certainly pay for what they get. The companies change, and their offerings also vary from year to year, so your best bet is to work through a travel agent who specializes in Alaska tours.

The two largest Alaska tour companies are **Holland America Tours/Gray Line of Alaska** (907/277-5581 or 800/544-2206, www.graylineofalaska.com) and **Princess Tours** (206/336-6000 or 800/835-8907, www.princess.com). Both of these are also major players in the cruise travel industry, and many cruise ship travelers simply add on a land segment to their voyage. **Cruise West** (888/851-8133, www.cruisewest.com) also sets up a wide variety of trips that include small-ship cruises and tours. A few other tour options include **Alaska Airlines Vacations** (800/468-2248, www.alaskaair.com), **Alaska Bound** (231/439-3000 or 888/252-7527, www.alaskabound.com), **Alaska Travel**

Baranof Wind tour boat at Margerie Glacier, Glacier Bay National Park

© DON PITCHER

Adventures (907/783-2928 or 800/334-8730, www.alaskaadventures.com), **Knightly Tours** (206/938-8567 or 800/426-2123, www.knightlytours.com), and **Tauck Tours** (800/788-7885, www.tauck.com).

Specialty Tours

For adventure travel tours, contact **CampAlaska Tours** (907/376-9438 or 800/376-9438, www.campalaska.com), **Get Up and Go Alaska Tours** (907/245-0795 or 888/868-4147, www.getupandgotours.com), **Adventure Alaska Tours** (907/782-3730 or 800/365-7057, www.adventurealaskatours.com), or **Denali Treking Company** (907/733-2566, www.alaskahiking.com). **Joseph Van Os Photo Safaris** (206/463-5383, www.photosafaris.com) leads photo trips around Alaska, with an emphasis on wildlife.

Birdwatchers should point their spotting scopes toward **Wilderness Birding Adventures** (907/694-7442, www.wildernessbirding.com) for extended trips to remote parts of the state, **St. Paul Island Tours** (907/278-2318 or 877/424-5637, www.alaskabirding.com) for trips to the Pribilofs. **Alaska Birding Tours** (907/262-5218 or 800/725-3327, www.alaskabirdingtours.com) guides trips on the Kenai Peninsula. Other recommended companies include **Victor Emanuel Nature Tours** (800/328-8368, www.ventbird.com) and **Wings Birding Tours** (520/320-9868 or 888/293-6443, www.wingsbirds.com).

For bicycle tours around Alaska, check out **Alaskabike** (907/245-2175, www.alaskabike.com) or **Backroads** (510/527-1555 or 800/462-2848, www.backroads.com).

ALASKA PASS

The Alaska Pass (206/463-6777 or 800/248-7598, www.alaskapass.com) is a good option if you plan to travel using a combination of ferries, trains, and buses. Passes are available for varying lengths of time, and you can either buy one that allows travel every day (not a good idea if you want to do something more than sit on a bus or ferry) or one that lets you travel a certain number of days out of the total. The latter cost $700 ($350 for kids) for a 12-day pass that includes eight travel days; or $850 ($425 for kids) for a 21-day pass that includes 12 travel days.

BICYCLE

Inveterate cyclists have a love affair with bike riding that makes the relationship between car and driver look like a one-night stand. If you're indifferent to or can overcome the hardships (hills, trucks, rain and wind, bugs, time, security considerations, and sore muscles), the advantages of bikes are unassailable. They're free to operate, nonpolluting, easy to maintain, and great exercise. They also slow down the world and attract the immediate friendly and curious attention of the locals.

Almost all of the bus companies, ferries, and railways will carry your bike as accompanied baggage for a nominal amount, although a few want you to have it in a box. Most airlines also accept bicycles as luggage, as long as they're boxed before check-in (you will pay an extra charge). Before you buy a ticket, compare prices, then ask each airline about taking a bicycle.

Alaska can be just as hard on bikes as on cars, however, if not harder. Fifteen-speed mountain bikes are recommended to better handle the rough roads. Know how to fix your own bike, and take along a good repair kit, as bicycle shops are few and far between. At the minimum, you should have spare tubes and tires, a patch kit, a pump, extra cables, a spare chain, and a chain tool. Carry your gear in saddlebag panniers lined with plastic bags. Fenders are nice in wet weather. Warm, waterproof clothing is essential, particularly rain pants, poncho, rain hat, wool shirt, wool socks, and waterproof shoes. Bicycling gloves, shorts, and clear goggles are also necessary. You could buy everything you need in Anchorage.

Short-distance bicycles are available for rent in every major town and are an excellent way to see the local sights, especially in fair weather.

Cycling Information Sources

The Anchorage-based **Arctic Bicycle Club** (907/566-0177, www.arcticbike.org) organizes road races, mountain bike races, and tours, and its website is an excellent source for anyone interested in cycling in Alaska. Useful books are *Alaska Bicycle Touring Guide* by Pete Praetorius and Alys Culhane and *Mountain Bike Alaska: 49 Trails in the 49th State* by Richard Larson. A few companies offer guided cycling trips around Alaska.

Tips for Travelers

VISAS AND OFFICIALDOM

Immigration officials are trained to be suspicious, particularly in this post–September 11 world. Expect heightened security measures at all border crossings, and even when boarding state ferries. Get a passport for each member of your family; you'll probably need it. Never argue or get angry with an official—it doesn't help, and they have the law on their side. The best approach is just to be as polite as possible.

Entry into the U.S.

All international travelers (including Canadians) now need a passport to enter the U.S. As of 2008, even U.S. citizens crossing the border from Canada into Alaska will need a passport. Most Western Europeans and Commonwealth residents can usually obtain a six-month travel visa easily from American consulates, and citizens of some countries can get visas at the border. You must have an onward or return ticket. No vaccinations are required, and you can bring an unlimited amount of money (over US$5,000 must be registered). Be aware that you might wind up crossing a Canadian–U.S. border four times in each direction (Lower 48 into British Columbia or Alberta, back into Southeast Alaska, then into Yukon, then back into mainland Alaska). If you're an overseas visitor, make sure you understand the requirements for *re-entering* the United States. Regulations seem to be in a constant state of flux, so get the latest border info from **U.S. Customs and Border Protection** by downloading their *Know Before You Go* publication from www.customs.gov.

Entry into Canada

No visa is required of visitors from Western Europe, most Commonwealth countries, or the United States. Americans can enter Canada by showing a birth certificate, passport (highly recommended), or voter-registration card, along with a driver's license or other form of photo identification. For children, bring a passport, birth certificate, baptismal certificate, or immigration document. Everyone else must have a passport. Travelers under 18 must be accompanied by or have written permission from a parent or guardian to enter Canada. Handguns and automatic weapons are not allowed into Canada, even if you're simply driving through to Alaska or the Lower 48. A U.S. driver's license is acceptable in Canada, but international licenses are required for residents of other countries. Get details at the **Canada Border Services Agency** website (www.cbsa-asfc.gc.ca).

TIME ZONES

Alaska is divided into two time zones, but nearly all of the state—from Southeast to the western tip of the mainland—is on Alaska time, one hour earlier than Pacific time or four hours earlier than the East Coast. The western Aleutians are on Hawaii time, two hours behind Pacific time. British Columbia and the Yukon are on Pacific time. So when you go from Prince Rupert to Ketchikan, Dawson to Eagle, or Beaver Creek to Tok you gain an hour; from Skagway to Whitehorse you lose an hour.

CONDUCT AND CUSTOMS

As you explore, remember that Northerners are fiercely independent people who value their privacy. They can also be overwhelmingly hospitable if you treat them with respect. Never put up your tent in or near a village without first asking permission. When visiting a Native village or any small, isolated community,

look people straight in the eye and be the first to say hello. Remember, you are the intruder, so you should be the one to make the effort to put them at ease.

Under no circumstances should you walk into a small settlement, fish camp, or other personal area and immediately start photographing people. This is rude and may well get folks angry. Most people are happy to pose for a photo if you simply take the time to talk, and express a genuine interest in them and their lives. But if they say no, just move on. There may also be times when it is best simply to leave before tempers flare, particularly when people have been drinking heavily (an all-too-common experience in some villages), or when their politics stray to the don't-tread-on-me fringe.

ACCESSIBLE ALASKA

Because of the undeveloped character of Alaska, much of the state is not readily accessible to those with disabilities. This is particularly true in parts of bush Alaska, where even having a flush toilet may be a luxury, and climbing into small aircraft is a major challenge. Despite this, many towns and cities—particularly those that see an influx of elderly cruise ship passengers each summer—have made great strides in recent years. Even in remote areas, some Forest Service and State of Alaska cabins have wheelchair ramps, out-sized outhouses, and fishing platforms. In addition, quite a few trails around Alaska have been built for wheelchairs, including popular ones in Ketchikan, Juneau, and Anchorage. Hotels, buses, trains, cruise ships, tour boats, and ferries throughout the state all have some sort of accommodation for travelers in wheelchairs or with limited mobility.

A good place for travelers with disabilities is **Access Alaska** (907/248-4777 or 800/770-4488, www.accessalaska.org), a nonprofit independent-living center in Anchorage that can assist travelers with specific needs, including wheelchair-accessible hotels and restaurants, along with accessible horseback rides and river trips. Other independent-living centers are in

Fairbanks (907/479-7940 or 800/770-7940) and Juneau (907/586-4920).

In Anchorage, **Hertz** (800/654-3131, www.hertz.com) has rental cars with hand controls, **Alaska Cab** (907/563-5353) offers lift-equipped van service, and **JBR Transportation** (907/441-7714), rents a lift-equipped van.

Alaska Welcomes You (907/349-6301 or 800/349-6301, www.accessiblealaska.com) is a travel agency that specializes in setting up cruises, tours, and other trips for seniors, families with young kids, and travelers with special needs. They also have a database listing accessible facilities, accommodations, attractions, and tours around the state.

TRAVELING WITH CHILDREN

Long a destination for seniors and couples, Alaska is increasingly popular with families, and even the cruise lines have gotten into the act with all sorts of kid-friendly activities and childcare onboard the larger vessels. The small adventure cruise ships are primarily the domain of couples, and children can get in the way or become bored. They're welcome on all state ferries, but parents need to keep a close watch due to the onboard hazards. Fortunately, the leisurely pace, engaging scenery, good food, naturalist talks, and free movies make the traveling easier.

Anyone traveling with kids today should consider bringing a portable DVD player (or laptop computer) with a stock of movies or games for those times when Mom and Dad want the kids to just quiet down. And don't forget the headphones so you don't need to hear *Finding Nemo* for the 347th time.

Most attractions and activities have lower rates for children, and some also offer one-size-fits-all family rates. Be sure to get your children into the great outdoors since that's really what Alaska is all about. The long bus ride into Denali National Park can be challenging for little ones, but the chance to see bears, moose, and wolves makes the trip worthwhile for everyone. Of special interest is the Park Service's **Junior Ranger Program,** in which children attend a nature program, hike a trail, or complete other activities. They're rewarded with an official Junior Ranger patch and are sworn in. It's always a big hit, but your kids may later try to arrest you if you get too close to a ground squirrel.

Be sure to set aside time for a special kid-friendly place such as the Anchorage Zoo, the kiddie train rides at Pioneer Park in Fairbanks, the Alaska SeaLife Center in Seward, the Mt. Roberts Tram in Juneau, or the one place all children love—H2Oasis Indoor Water Park in Anchorage.

Many tours are open to children, but the more hazardous ones (including helicopter flights, sea kayaking, whitewater rafting, and ziplines) impose age restrictions. Children are accepted in most Alaskan lodging places, but will not do well in certain wilderness lodges or bed and breakfasts.

TRAVELING WITH PETS

In general, travelers visiting Alaska should leave their pets at home. Dogs may good hiking companions, but if not kept under control they could bring a bear charging in your direction. Most hotels do not allow pets, and even those that do typically tack on an extra charge for the privilege. Folks driving up the Alaska Highway—particularly RVers—frequently bring along a small dog or cat, but a current rabies certificate is required when crossing into Canada.

GAY AND LESBIAN TRAVELERS

Openly gay individuals may feel uncomfortable in politically conservative Alaska, so discretion may be wise, especially in rural areas such as Glennallen where Rush Limbaugh is regarded as a liberal. Anchorage is—not surprisingly—the primary center for gays and lesbians in Alaska. The nonprofit group Identity Inc. runs a **Gay and Lesbian Community Center** (2110 E. Northern Lights Blvd., 907/929-4528, www.identityinc.org), and also produces a monthly magazine, promotes the PrideFest event (www.anchoragepride.com) each June, and operates a help line. Two Anchorage bars—**Mad Myrna's** (530 E. 5th Ave., 907/276-9762, www.alaska.net/~madmyrna)

and **The Raven** (708 E. 4th Ave., 907/276-9672)—are favorite meeting places. **Out North Contemporary Art House** (1325 Primrose St., 907/279-8200, www.outnorth.org) sometimes presents plays with a gay and lesbian slant, and several Anchorage B&Bs promote themselves for gay travelers and couples.

SENIORS

Alaska is a very popular summer destination for seniors traveling by cruise ship or RV, and for a surprising number of retirees who move to the state. Alaska Marine Highway ferries offer half-price senior discounts on certain smaller vessels in the summer, and onboard most wintertime sailings. Most museums and some restaurants have discounted rates for those over 65, and visitors to national parks can get a Golden Age Passport that allows entry to all parks for a one-time charge of $10.

Travelers over 55 should consider joining an **Elderhostel** (www.elderhostel.org) educational adventure, with dozens to choose from in Alaska. The **American Association of Retired Persons** (www.aarp.org) also has discounted Alaskan trips and other benefits.

WILDERNESS SAFETY TIPS

Dealing with bears is discussed in *Coexisting with Bears* in the *Interior* chapter. The most important part of enjoying—and surviving—the backcountry is to be prepared. Know where you're going; get maps, camping information, weather, and trail conditions from a ranger before setting out. Don't hike alone. Two are better than one, and three are better than two; if one gets hurt, one person can stay with the injured party and one can go for help. Bring more than enough food, so hunger won't cause you to continue when weather conditions say stop. Tell someone where you're going and when you'll be back.

Always carry the **essentials:** map, compass, water bottle, first-aid kit, flashlight, matches (or lighter) and fire starter (Vaseline and cotton balls work great), knife, extra clothing (a full set, in case you fall in a stream), rain gear, extra food, and sunglasses—especially if you're hiking on snow. Many travelers now also carry along a GPS unit to stay oriented. Cell phones are popular, but often don't work in remote areas. Satellite phones are the ultimate safety toy, but are a pricey addition to your trip.

Check your ego at the trailhead; stop for the night when the weather gets bad, even if it's 2 P.M., or head back, and don't press on when you're exhausted—tired hikers are sloppy hikers, and even a small injury can be disastrous in the woods.

Hypothermia

Anyone who spends much time in the outdoors will discover the dangers of exposure to cold, wet, and windy conditions. Even at temperatures well above freezing, hypothermia—the reduction of the body's inner core temperature—can prove fatal.

In the early stages, hypothermia causes uncontrollable shivering, followed by a loss of coordination, slurred speech, and then a rapid descent into unconsciousness and death. Always travel prepared for sudden changes in the weather. Wear clothing that insulates well and that holds its heat when wet. Wool and polypro are far better than cotton, and clothes should be worn in layers to provide better trapping of heat and a chance to adjust to conditions more easily. Always carry a wool hat, since your head loses more heat than any other part of your body. Bring a waterproof shell to cut the wind. Put on rain gear *before* it starts raining; head back or set up camp when the weather looks threatening; eat candy bars, keep active, or snuggle with a friend in a down bag to generate warmth.

If someone in your party begins to show signs of hypothermia, don't take any chances, even if the person denies needing help. Get the victim out of the wind, strip off his clothes, and put him in a dry sleeping bag on an insulating pad. Skin-to-skin contact is the best way to warm a hypothermic person, and that means you'll also need to strip and climb in the sleeping bag. If you weren't friends before, this should heat up the relationship! Do not give the victim alcohol or hot drinks, and do not try to warm the person too quickly since it could lead to heart failure. Once the victim has recovered, get medical help as soon as possible. Actually, you're far better off keeping close tabs on everyone in the group and seeking shelter *before* exhaustion and hypothermia set in.

Frostbite

Frostbite is a less serious but quite painful problem for the cold-weather hiker; it is caused by direct exposure or by heat loss because of wet socks and boots. Frostbitten areas will look white or gray and feel hard on the surface, softer underneath. The best way to warm the area is with other skin: Put your hand under your arm, your feet on your friend's belly. Don't rub it with snow or warm it near a fire. In cases of severe frostbite, in which the skin is white, quite hard, and numb, immerse the frozen area in water warmed to 99–104°F until it's thawed. Avoid refreezing the frostbitten area. If you're a long way from medical assistance and the frostbite is extensive, it's better to keep the area frozen and get out of the woods for help; thawing is very painful, and it would be nearly impossible to walk on a thawed foot.

Beaver Fever

Although lakes and streams in Alaska may appear clean, you could be risking a debilitating sickness by drinking the water without treating it first. The protozoan *Giardia lambia* is found throughout the state, spread by both humans and animals (including beaver). The disease is curable with drugs, but it's always best to carry safe drinking water on any trip, or to boil any water taken from creeks or lakes. Bringing water to a full boil for one minute is sufficient to kill *Giardia* and other harmful organisms.

Another option—most folks choose this one—is to use a water filter (available in camping stores). Note, however, that these may not filter out other organisms such as *Campylobactor jejuni*, bacteria that are just 0.2 microns in size. Chlorine and iodine are not always reliable, taste foul, and can be unhealthy.

CRIME

Alaska has a surprisingly high violent-crime rate; the most recent figures put the state at 10th in the nation in terms of violent crimes, with 588 such crimes per 100,000 residents. Part of this is due to simple demographics, since Alaska has the second-highest percentage of young people in the nation, but it is also a reflection of the impact of alcohol abuse. Alaska has a rape rate two-and-a-half times the national average, and the child sexual assault rate is a shocking six times the national average.

The good news is that crime has dropped in recent years, especially in Anchorage, where many of the worst incidents have taken place. In general you're quite safe traveling in Alaska, though you should take the standard precautions, such as not leaving belongings in an unlocked vehicle and not walking around certain Anchorage neighborhoods after dark. Also, it's wise to avoid situations where people have been drinking heavily, even in bush Alaska. To be honest, after 25 years in the North, my one personal experience with crime took place when gear was stolen from me in Prince Rupert, British Columbia! I'm not saying crime doesn't exist, but many Alaskan towns (particularly those off the road system) are so safe that folks leave their doors unlocked and their keys in the car.

Information and Services

MONEY

Unless otherwise stated, all prices in this handbook are in U.S. dollars. Tipping (usually 15 percent of the bill) is expected at most sit-down eating places fancier than snack bars or take-away counters. Tourism employees, fishing guides, and others providing personal service often depend on tips for their real income.

I travel almost exclusively using credit cards and an automated teller machine (ATM) card, but some people still prefer traveler's checks. The major **credit cards**—especially Visa and MasterCard—are accepted almost everywhere in the larger towns. This is probably the easiest way to travel, especially if you can get airline mileage credit at the same time. Note, however, that credit cards may not be accepted by businesses in bush Alaska, so call ahead if you aren't traveling with cash or traveler's checks.

You'll find **ATMs** in all the larger towns and increasingly in even the more remote settlements. For locations, head to www .mastercard.com and www.visa.com/atms.

Traveler's checks from American Express, Bank of America, or Visa are accepted in most businesses; but don't arrive with traveler's checks in non-U.S. currency since they're only accepted at a few banks. In some remote villages, even traveler's checks may not be accepted.

Some Canadian and U.S. cash will make your first few hours in the neighboring country less of a hassle. Note that there are no exchange facilities at the borders; Canadians take U.S. dollars at a poor rate, while Alaskan businesses often refuse Canadian dollars (they do, however, take the coins at an equal value with U.S. ones!). Most Wells Fargo offices in Anchorage (and some other cities) will exchange Canadian dollars, Japanese yen, and euros for U.S. dollars.

COMMUNICATIONS AND MEDIA
Newspapers

Alaska's unofficial state newspaper is the *Anchorage Daily News.* The paper does a good job of covering world and regional news,

and has a reputation for balanced reporting. Its website (www.adn.com) contains current stories, classified ads, upcoming events, weather, and video clips. It also produces a thick and free *Alaska Visitors Guide* that can be found in the larger visitor centers or online at www.alaska.com.

The state's other two large-circulation daily papers are the *Fairbanks Daily News-Miner* (www.newsminer.com) and the *Juneau Empire* (www.juneauempire.com).

The *Anchorage Press* (www.anchorage press.com) is a free weekly newspaper available from racks all around Anchorage. The paper takes a rough-edged anti-establishment stance and the articles tend to focus on local scandals that the *Anchorage Daily News* avoids. Its night-life coverage is also strong. Weekly newspapers come out in most of the state's mid-sized towns.

Alaska Magazine

This magazine is available at grocery checkouts and magazine racks across Alaska, and in many Lower 48 magazine shops. Like the *Milepost* and *Juneau Empire, Alaska Magazine* (907/272-6070, www.alaskamagazine.com) is owned by a Georgia-based media conglomerate, Morris Communications. The magazine has gone downhill since it was bought by Morris, but still offers glossy articles about the state. Don't expect any muckraking journalism here; the magazine is geared to Outsiders looking for taste-of-Alaska stories.

Radio

Commercial radio stations are in all the larger towns, and the state is blessed to have the **Alaska Public Radio Network** (www.aprn. org), one of the finest public radio networks in America. Anchorage's **KSKA** (91.1 FM, www.kska.org) is the flagship station, but many Alaskan towns have their own versions, from Ketchikan's KRBD (www.krbd.org) to Barrow's KBRW (www.kbrw.org). Anchorage's noncommercial **KNBA** (FM 90.3, www.knba. org) is one of the only Native-owned radio stations in the nation, and broadcasts some of the best music programming in Alaska. Two other great ones are **KBBI** (890 AM, www.kbbi.org) in Homer and **KTNA** (88.5 FM, www.ktna. org) in Talkeetna.

Post Offices

Post offices are generally open Monday–Friday 9 A.M.–5 P.M., though a few open their doors on Saturdays. Anchorage's airport post office is open 24 hours a day year-round. When post offices are closed, their outer doors usually remain open, so you can go in to buy stamps from the machines. Many grocery store checkout counters also sell books of stamps at no markup.

To receive mail on the road (does anyone really do this in this era of email?), have it addressed to yourself c/o General Delivery. Convenient general delivery addresses are: Juneau, AK 99801; Fairbanks, AK 99701; Anchorage, AK 99501. General delivery mail is held 10 days.

Phones and Email

Telephone service is excellent to all the major towns and cities in Alaska, though you may experience a delay in some remote areas, and the wilderness lodges often depend upon radio or satellite phones. Cellular phone coverage is variable, and not all systems work even when services exist, so contact your carrier for a coverage map ahead of your trip.

Alaska is surprisingly well wired, and even the most remote towns now have some sort of online connection. Nearly every library in Alaska (except Ketchikan) has at least one computer where you can check your email or surf the Web for free, though you may need to wait in line or sign up ahead of time. In addition, nearly all towns now have commercial businesses where you can rent computers by the hour for the same purpose. Wireless Internet (Wi-Fi) is becoming the norm for Alaskan hotels and bed and breakfasts, along with many local businesses. Expect to even see it on state ferries in the near future. Visit www.free-hot-spot.com or www.jiwire.com for updated listings around the state.

MAPS AND TOURIST INFORMATION

Readers of this book willing to expend a little energy will certainly be able to set up a travel itinerary that covers their own interests, but if you want to leave the arranging to others, you may want to contact one of the many itinerary planners who specialize in Alaska. These could be as close as your local travel agent, or one of the online information sources such as www.alaska.com or www.alaskaone.com. For a human touch from those in the know, try **Viking Travel** (907/772-3818 or 800/327-2571, www.alaskaferry.com), **Alaska Tours** (907/277-3000, www.alaskatours.com), **Alaska Ferry Adventures** (907/235-7099 or 800/382-9229, www.akmhs.com), or **Homer Travel & Tours** (907/235-7751 or 800/478-7751, www.alaskahomertravel.com).

Hundreds of adventure-travel package operators offer everything from helicopter skiing on icefields and scuba diving off Kodiak Island to ice-climbing on Mt. McKinley and parasailing over Turnagain Arm. The best compilation of guides and outfitters appears in the annual *Alaska State Vacation Planner.*

A great starting point when planning a trip to Alaska is the official *Alaska State Vacation Planner,* produced annually through a joint partnership between the state and private businesses. It's distributed by the Alaska Travel Industry Association (907/929-2200 or 800/862-5275, www.travelalaska.com). Find state chambers of commerce at www.alaskachamber.com.

Members of the American Automobile Association (AAA, www.aaa.com) should request an Alaska *TourBook* and *CampBook,* plus detailed maps. Overseas visitors who belong to an affiliated club in their home country can obtain this material free by showing their membership card at an AAA office in any large city.

Recreation

EXPLORING THE LAND
Hiking and Camping

Hiking and camping are the preferred outdoor recreations for the majority of Alaskans and visitors. These pastimes are available to practically anybody, from three-month-old infants to 93-year-old great-grannies. Here, you don't have to be in particularly good shape, you don't need a big bank balance, and you don't have to have the latest high-tech equipment. Most public land is open to free camping, though there are restrictions in the more populous areas.

For the size of the Alaskan outdoors, there are very few trails, but it's easy just to pick a direction, especially in the vast taiga and tundra, and go. Also, the perpetual daylight during hiking season allows for additional deviation from normal hiking-camping cycles, providing further freedom. And the definite possibility of encountering a variety and abundance of wildlife is an incalculable bonus. The few trails that do exist are covered in their respective travel chapters. For more information about hiking, contact the **Alaska Public Lands Information Centers** (www.nps.gov/aplic) in Anchorage, Fairbanks, Ketchikan, and Tok.

Mountaineering

A number of organizations guide mountaineering expeditions in Alaska. For specific destinations, visit the Park Service or Forest Service websites for a list of permitted guides. Good wilderness guiding companies include **Alaska Mountaineering School** (907/733-1016, www.climbalaska. org), **Alaska Mountain Guides & Climbing**

PHOTOGRAPHY

Hand in hand with hiking and camping goes photography – of the gorgeous scenery, the fauna and flora, and the special light. Professional photographers can have a literal field day in Alaska, because the ideal light conditions – at dawn and sunset everywhere else – continue throughout the long days of low light and long angles in the boreal region. Casual photographers are satisfied with automatic point-and-shoot, disposable, and cheap digital cameras, though none of these do justice to the grandness of Alaska.

A good starting setup would include a 28-105 zoom and a 100-300 zoom; longer and more expensive lenses (400 or 500 mm) are needed for serious wildlife work. A flash helps to fill in shadow areas on sunny days. A tripod is highly recommended, though some professional lenses have image stabilization to make it easier to hand-hold lenses at slower shutter speeds.

In the last few years digital photography has become the norm, with film relegated to an even smaller number of photographers at both the amateur and professional levels. If you're one of the holdouts, bring plenty since the type you want (especially slide films) may not be available. ISO 200 is fine for most purposes, but you may need higher speed (ISO 400) for low light situations.

Digital photographers need to plan ahead, especially for trips into backcountry areas where extra batteries and backup storage devices are vital. Small laptop computers are perfect for storing your images, checking for any problems, and sending emails while on the road.

A couple of caveats are in order. A common cause of wildlife incidents is foolish photographers either getting too close or having a false sense of security behind the camera. Your backcountry common sense should remain intact with or without a camera in front of you. Besides, there are times and places to not use a camera – mostly in order not to separate you from a given experience, but also in Native villages without permission. In addition, many museums prohibit the use of flash or tripods, and Russian Orthodox churches don't allow cameras or video.

© DON PITCHER

Mountain bikes are a fun way to explore Alaska's backroads.

School (907/766-3366 or 800/766-3396, www.alaskamountainguides.com), **Alaska Discovery** (510/594-6000 or 800/586-1911, www.akdiscovery.com), and **N.O.L.S.** (907/745-4047, www.nols.edu). A good online source for info on Alaska climbing opportunities is www.akclimber.com.

Mountain Biking

The most popular mountain biking trails are in the Anchorage area, and include many miles of paths (both paved and unpaved) along the shore and within a couple of city parks. Paved biking paths can also be found paralleling portions of the Seward Highway south of Anchorage, and in Fairbanks, Homer, Valdez, Juneau, and other cities. Many Forest Service trails are open to mountain biking, but some of these are muddy and challenging to ride. Especially popular is the Resurrection Pass Trail on the Kenai Peninsula.

The Anchorage-based **Arctic Bicycle Club** (907/566-0177, www.arcticbike.org) organizes road races, mountain bike races, and tours. Its website is an excellent source for anyone interested in cycling in Alaska, with links to bike shops and references to helpful books. (Bike tours are described near the end of this chapter in *Specialty Tours*.)

Flightseeing

Even if you don't go backpacking while you're in Alaska, treat yourself at least once to a small plane or helicopter ride over some spectacular country. The flight from Talkeetna to Denali National Park is always a highlight—particularly with a landing on the Ruth Glacier. Flights over Glacier Bay from Juneau, Haines, or Skagway will leave you hyperventilating for two days. And you won't believe how grand Columbia Glacier really is on the flight over it from Anchorage or Valdez. (For more tips on flightseeing—including safety precautions—see *By Air* earlier in this chapter.)

Birding

The **National Audubon Society** (www.audubon.org/chapter/ak) has chapters in

Anchorage (907/338-2473 birding hotline, www.anchorageaudubon.org), Juneau (www.juneau-audubon-society.org), and Fairbanks (www.arcticaudubon.org; hotline 907/451-9213). In Homer, visit www.birdinghomeralaska.org or call 907/235-7337 for unusual Kachemak Bay birds. All these websites provide details on local birding hot spots across the state. In Fairbanks, the **Alaska Bird Observatory** (907/451-7059, www.alaskabird.org) conducts research on migratory birds and has banding demonstrations. Their website features links to most other Alaska birding organizations and online sites.

FISHING

Alaska is world famous for its fish and fishing. More than half of America's commercial seafood production comes from the state, and sportfishing is a favorite activity of both Alaskan residents and visitors. Fishing options are equally vast in Alaska, where undeveloped areas stretch for hundreds of miles, and the population is clustered onto a tiny portion of the land. The state is speckled with more than a million lakes—including some of the largest in the nation—along with 34,000 miles of pristine coastline and 42 wild and scenic rivers.

The **Alaska Department of Fish and Game's** website (www.state.ak.us/adfg) has details on sportfishing, including descriptions of the various species, fishing regulations, news, and an abundance of other fish facts.

The *Anchorage Daily News* (www.adn.com) puts out an excellent free fishing guide describing the best spots in Southcentral Alaska, along with fishing tips and trends. It's available in visitor centers, or the website provides a weekly fishing forecast in the summer.

Alaska Fishing by Rene Limeres and Gunnar Pedersen is a comprehensive guide to fishing in Alaska, with detailed information on the when, where, and how to catch fish, along with natural history and other details. Locals, as always, are the best advice-givers about fishing technique, spots, and regulations, and might even share some secrets.

© DON PITCHER

Kenai River anglers, near Cooper Landing

Popular Alaskan Fish

Salmon are the primary attraction for many sport anglers, and all five species of Pacific salmon are found in Alaska. Steelhead and rainbow trout, which are also salmonid, are famous for their beautiful coloration and fighting spirit. Rainbows are found in many streams and lakes around the state; the larger steelhead are the sea-run form.

Dolly Varden (also known as Arctic char) are a sea-run trout that flourish in many Alaska rivers. Arctic grayling occur in lakes and streams across the state, particularly in Interior Alaska and the Alaska Peninsula. The fish have a large and distinctive saillike dorsal fin, and put up a big fight when hooked. Other important freshwater fish species include lake trout, brook trout (an introduced species), northern pike, sheefish, and whitefish.

Pacific halibut is a large flatfish that is commonly caught in saltwater, particularly in Southeast and Southcentral Alaska. Halibut sometimes reach the proverbial barn-door size, and it isn't uncommon to see ones that weigh in excess of 200 pounds. Many Alaskans consider halibut the best-tasting fish in the state. In addition to salmon caught in saltwater, other popular ocean-caught sport fish include rockfish and lingcod.

Catching 'Em

Fishing is not only great fun, but the way to bag some super meals. All you need are a breakdown or retractable rod, a variety of hooks, flies, spinners, spoons, sinkers, line (4- to 8-lb. for freshwater, 12- to 30-lb. for saltwater—depending on what you're after), and a reel. All but the rod will fit in a small plastic case. For bait, get a small bottle of salmon eggs for freshwater, shrimp for saltwater. Have a filet knife to clean the fish. While fishing, watch for protected areas with deadfalls or rocks where fish like to hide. You'll have the best luck in the early morning or late evening, or on cloudy days when the sun leaks out to shimmer on the water. So as not to attract bears, keep your catch on a stringer well downstream.

Fishing Regulations

Fishing licenses are required. In Alaska, 1-day nonresident sportfishing licenses cost $20, 3-day $35, and 14-day $80. If you plan to catch king salmon, all these fees increase substantially. The Alaskan license is valid in national parks.

Fishing licenses are sold in most outdoor stores and by charter fishing operators. Ask for brochures outlining local fishing regulations when you buy your license. Check open and closed seasons, bag limits, and the like, to avoid trouble with the law. For the whole thing—spelled out in minute bureaucratic detail—request a copy of the regulations booklet from the **Alaska Department of Fish and Game** (907/465-4180, www.sf.adfg.state.ak.us).

Fishing Derbies

Many Alaskan towns have salmon or halibut fishing derbies in the summer. If one is going on when you visit, it may be worth your while to buy a derby ticket before heading out on the water. The prize money gets into the thousands of dollars for some of these, and more than a few anglers tell of the big one that would have made them rich if they'd only bought a derby ticket first. Some of the biggest fishing derbies are in Seward, Homer, and Juneau.

Guided Fishing

Local knowledge is one of the best ways to be assured of a successful Alaska fishing trip. By using a charter or guide service, you're likely to have a more productive sportfishing trip. Fishing guides can be found in most Alaskan communities, some offering float trips accessible by car and others going to more remote fly-in destinations. Charter fishing boats are available at coastal locations, particularly in Southeast and Southcentral Alaska and along the Kenai Peninsula.

Particularly important charter boat fishing towns include Homer, Seward, Kodiak, Valdez, Cordova, Juneau, Sitka, and Ketchikan. Charter boat trips typically last either a half-day or all day. Remote fishing lodges are widespread throughout the state, offering top-quality sportfishing with all of the amenities; find them in the *Alaska State Vacation Planner*, or online at www.travelalaska.com. Note that it's common to tip fishing guides, particularly if they're especially helpful or if you land a big one. There's no standard amount, but a 10 percent tip would certainly be appreciated.

For information on fishing charters, available from every seaport in the state, check the local chamber of commerce websites or pick up brochures when you get into town.

ON THE WATER
Boating

Alaska's waters offer an endless range of boating opportunities, and in many coastal towns (particularly in Southeast) there are almost as many boats as cars. Boats are also important in inland parts of Alaska, particularly along major waterways such as the Yukon and Kuskokwim Rivers, where they provide a vital means of traversing undeveloped country. Skiff rentals are available in the larger coastal towns for those who want to head out on their own to explore

ALASKA SALMON

Five species of wild Pacific salmon are found in Alaskan waters. All are anadromous – spending time in both fresh and salt water – and all five species also have at least two common names, making them confusing to newcomers. The yearly return of adult salmon is a major event for wildlife in many parts of Alaska, as quiet little streams suddenly erupt in a frenzy of life and death. Commercial fishermen search out the migrating schools in the ocean as they prepare to head up rivers and creeks to spawn. Anglers line the riverbanks, hoping to catch a big king or coho. Bears pace the creeks, ready to pounce on salmon in the shallow water. Foxes, eagles, ravens, gulls, and magpies wait for the salmon to weaken or die before feeding on them. Mergansers and smaller birds such as dippers eat the eggs, as do such fish as Dolly Varden and rainbow trout. Crab and halibut move into the areas near creek mouths, eating salmon carcasses that wash downstream.

Female salmon spawn in creeks and rivers during late summer throughout much of Alaska, digging holes ("redds") in the gravel with their tails before laying hundreds of small red eggs. The males fight for position to fertilize the eggs as soon as they are laid. Shortly after spawning, the salmon die, and their carcasses create a stench that permeates late-summer evenings. But these carcasses also add important nutrients to the system, nutrients that are used by the plankton that form the basis of the food chain. The plankton in turn are eaten by the young salmon fry that emerge from the eggs, thus helping to complete this never-ending cycle of life and death.

King (Chinook) Salmon

The largest of all Pacific salmon, the king commonly exceeds 30 pounds (the sport-caught record is 97 lbs.), and is the most highly prized and one of the best-tasting sport fish in Alaska. The most famous place to catch kings is the Kenai River in Southcentral Alaska, but some of the finest kings head up the Copper River near Cordova.

Sockeye (Red) Salmon

Much smaller (6-10 lbs.), and difficult to catch on spinning rods, sockeye are considered the best-tasting salmon. They turn bright red with an olive-green head when ready to spawn. Sockeye are the most important fish in the Bristol Bay and Kodiak areas, but for sport anglers, the most famous sockeye river is the Kenai, where "combat fishing" reigns in mid-summer.

Coho (Silver) Salmon

The silvery cohos generally weigh 7-10 pounds and are a beautiful and powerful fish that can be caught in both fresh and saltwater. They are another favorite of anglers, and have a more delicate flavor.

Chum (Dog) Salmon

Chum are also quite large (5-15 lbs.) but are not considered as tasty as kings, sockeye, or coho. Spawning time turns them into grotesque monsters with huge dog-like teeth. The name dog salmon may also refer to their use as food for dogsled teams in central Alaska. Chum are a very important food source in villages along the Yukon River.

Pink (Humpback) Salmon

The smallest (3-4 lbs.) and most abundant salmon in Alaska are the pinks. "Humpie" runs sometimes turn creeks into a seething mass of spawning fish. They are considered a "trash fish" by many Alaskans, but are fine to eat when caught in saltwater before they have started to change. Once they reach freshwater, however, they develop prominently humped backs and grotesque jaws. Pinks are the major commercial fish in Southeast and Prince William Sound, and are the mainstay of many canneries.

CATCHING SALMON
When salmon move from the ocean into their spawning streams, their bodies undergo rapid changes that reduce the quality of the meat. The freshest and brightest salmon are found in the ocean or lower reaches of the rivers, rather than farther upstream. If you want to try your luck at fishing, purchase a 14-day nonresident fishing license for $50, or a 3-day nonresident license for $20. Licenses are available in sporting goods stores throughout Alaska. Before heading out, pick up a copy of the latest fishing regulations, or visit the Alaska Department of Fish & Game website (www.state.ak.us/adfg).

Many travelers carry a small collapsible fishing pole to save on space. These work well with trout and smaller salmon, but may not survive an encounter with a 10-pound silver, and certainly won't handle a 35-pound king.

WILD OR FARMED?
Alaska is world renowned for its wild salmon, and careful management ensures that the fish will still be there for future generations. Unfortunately, fishermen are not faring so well. Many struggle to make their boat payments, while others have simply given up on their life work, and are now back in school learning a new trade or flipping burgers to make ends meet. In the last decade, the price of salmon has dropped by more than 50 percent, and the worldwide market share of wild-caught salmon went from 99 percent in 1980 to less than 40 percent today.

The reason for this abrupt change is the rise of salmon farming, primarily in Chile, Norway,

the United Kingdom, and British Columbia. The state of Alaska prohibits salmon aquaculture to protect both its wild fish stocks and the 10 percent of state jobs coming from fishing. Unfortunately, the British Columbia government was considerably less far-sighted, and more than 120 fish farms dot their waters, along with another nine in the state of Washington.

Pen-raised fish are cheap, available year-round, and of a consistent quality, making them perfect for corporations feeding a global market. But they have had a disastrous impact on both commercial fishermen and the environment. Farmed salmon are more susceptible to diseases such as sea lice (which can then spread to wild fish), the huge concentrations of fish pollute local areas with waste, and they are a non-native species: Atlantic salmon. This last becomes a real problem when they escape, and hundreds of thousands of them have done so over the years, competing with the five species of wild Pacific salmon, spawning in the region's streams, and showing up in fishing nets across Alaska. Nobody knows what impact this will have on the wild Pacific salmon.

And what about the fish? Pen-raised fish are fed pellets of fishmeal, fish oil, and vitamins, plus antibiotics, not to mention the coloring added to their diet to make their meat pink instead of gray. Wild salmon taste far better, are not dyed, and have more of the omega-3 fatty acids that help protect your health. So the next time you see salmon at your local grocery store, ask if it's farmed Atlantic salmon or wild Pacific salmon. The farmed version will be cheaper, but what is the real price?

Learn more about Alaska's wild salmon and other fish from the **Alaska Seafood Marketing Institute** (907/465-5560 or 800/478-2903, www.alaskaseafood.org). For details on commercial fishing in Alaska, head to www.alaskareport.com.

or fish. Dozens of companies offer boat tours or charter boat fishing trips throughout the state, in vessels ranging from 13-foot aluminum skiffs to luxury motor yachts offering multi-day ecotours.

River Rafting

White-water rafting trips are offered by numerous adventure-travel outfitters around the state. Several of the more reasonable, short, and accessible trips include floats down the Sixmile Creek south of Anchorage, Nenana River at Denali, Kenai River at Sterling, Susitna River near Talkeetna, Mendenhall River near Juneau, Sheridan River near Cordova, and the Lowe River outside of Valdez. A large number of float-trip companies and wilderness outfitters offer overnight, several day, and up to three-week-long trips, particularly within Wrangell–St. Elias National Park. Check the list in the state's *Alaska Vacation Planner* (www.travelalaska.com) for names and addresses. Those looking to do it by themselves should buy Karen Jettmar's excellent *Alaska River Guide*.

Sea Kayaking

Sea kayaks are quiet and fairly stable, providing an outstanding way to explore hidden Alaskan coves or to watch wildlife. Because of this, kayaking has increased in popularity in recent years, both for independent travelers who rent a kayak and for those who choose a package trip with a professional guiding company.

Kayaks originated as skin-covered boats crafted by the Eskimos of Alaska and Siberia, but today's versions are built from more modern materials. Most sea kayaks have a hard outer shell of plastic or fiberglass, but folding kayaks (made with wooden or aluminum supports and waterproof covers) are also available. The latter can be folded into relatively compact packages, making them useful for travelers heading into remote areas accessible only by floatplane.

Companies offering sea kayak rentals and tours are in Southeast Alaska (Glacier Bay, Gustavus, Haines, Juneau, Ketchikan, Petersburg, Sitka, Skagway, and Wrangell), Kenai Peninsula (Homer, Seldovia, and Seward), Prince William

Sound (Cordova, Valdez, and Whittier), Southwest Alaska (Kodiak, King Salmon, and Unalaska), and Western Alaska (Dillingham).

Canoeing

Canoeing is a common activity on lakes and rivers in Alaska. Two canoe routes (Swanson River Route and Swan Lake Route) connect lakes within the Kenai National Wildlife Refuge, and another route links lakes across Admiralty Island National Monument. The Yukon River is a popular float trip, with many people starting in either Whitehorse or Dawson City and floating to the town of Eagle (or beyond). The country around Fairbanks is also very popular with canoeists who enjoy the relatively gentle Chena River. Canoe rentals are available in all these areas.

Sailing

Alaska has a small but active community of sailing enthusiasts, with sailboats in coastal towns from Ketchikan to Kodiak. Resurrection Bay near Seward generally offers the state's

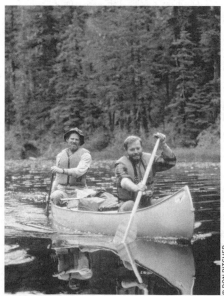

© DON PITCHER

canoeing on one of Admiralty Island's lakes

top wind conditions, and companies there offer day trips, sailing lessons, and bareboat charters. Other popular sailing areas (they have relatively dependable winds) are around Prince William Sound and in Kachemak Bay near Homer.

Surfing

Surprisingly, surfing is growing in popularity in Alaska. It will never be a particularly common sight, but many coastal towns—including Yakutat, Kodiak, Sitka, Homer, and Unalaska—have a few hard-core souls who head out when conditions are right. The state's best-known area is Yakutat in Southeast Alaska, where miles of uncrowded black-sand beaches attract surfers. Surfing supplies can be found in Yakutat and Kodiak.

Hot Springs

Alaska is a thermally active region, a fact attested to by its more than 100 hot spring sites, of which roughly a dozen are accessible and developed. Accessible, in Alaska, is a relative term: Possibly the most accessible hot spring

in the state is at Chena, 60 miles east of Fairbanks on a paved road. Also accessible near Fairbanks is Manley Hot Springs, over 150 hard dirt-road miles. Circle Hot Springs, a similar distance from Fairbanks, is no longer open to the public. Other popular hot springs are in Southeast: White Sulphur and Tenakee on Chichagof Island west of Juneau, Chief Shakes near Wrangell, and Baranof on Baranof Island. Contact the Alaska Department of Natural Resources for its map of thermally active areas in Alaska.

WINTER SPORTS
Skiing and Snowboarding

Downhill ski and snowboard areas are near Anchorage (Alyeska Resort, Hilltop Ski Area, and Alpenglow), Juneau (Eaglecrest), and Fairbanks (Moose Mountain and Skiland). The largest of these is Alyeska (907/754-1111 or 800/880-3880, www.alyeskaresort.com), with 500 skiable acres, 60 trails, a 60-passenger aerial tram, eight chair lifts, and two pony lifts.

Cross-country skiing (both classic and

© DON PITCHER

snowboarding at Alyeska Resort

FESTIVALS AND EVENTS

The biggest events in Alaska revolve around the sun and snow. A number of Alaskans, especially those who live in the Interior and the north, believe that the purpose of summer solstice is to compress all the partying encouraged by the light and heat of summer into a single 24-hour period. Fairbanks has at least three "Midnight Sun" activities on solstice. The summer is also the time for town and citywide celebrations, such as Golden Days in Fairbanks, Little Norway Festival in Petersburg, and Colony Days in Palmer. There are fishing derbies in the waters off the coastal towns and athletic competitions, such as triathlons and mountain races, everywhere.

The most famous winter festivals are Anchorage's Fur Rendezvous and the Iditarod. Every town has some sort of winter carnival that frequently includes dog mushing, a snow sports competition, and accompanying arts and crafts fairs.

Typically, the major public holidays are also a cause for celebration, including Memorial Day (last Monday in May), July 4th (Independence Day), Labor Day (last Mon. in Sept.), Thanksgiving Day (last Thurs. in Nov.), Christmas, and New Year's Eve. The happiest days of the year, though, are in mid-October when the big Permanent Fund dividend checks show up in the mailboxes of state residents.

January
Kodiak − Russian Orthodox Starring Ceremony; Bethel − Kuskokwim 300; Seward − Polar Bear Jump Off; Anchorage Folk Festival

February
Anchorage − Fur Rendezvous; Cordova − Iceworm Festival; Fairbanks − Yukon Quest Sled Dog Race; Wrangell − Tent City Festival

March
Anchorage, Nome, and Wasilla − Iditarod Trail Sled Dog Race; Dillingham − Beaver Roundup Festival; Fairbanks − World Ice Art Championships and Winter Carnival; Kodiak − Pillar Mountain Golf Classic; Nome − Bering Sea Ice Golf Classic

April
Bethel − Camai Dance Festival; Girdwood − Alyeska Spring Carnival; Juneau − Alaska Folk Festival; Valdez − World Free Skiing Championship

skate) is very popular in Alaska, particularly in Anchorage where many miles of lighted and groomed trails are available throughout the winter. Anchorage may well have the finest cross-country skiing of any American city, and a number of the nation's best Olympic skiers come from here. The city's main cross-country ski areas are in Kincaid Park, Hillside Ski Area, and the Tony Knowles Coastal Trail. Additional groomed ski trails are around Fairbanks, Homer, Juneau, Palmer, Eagle River, Seward, and Valdez. The **Nordic Skiing Association of Anchorage** (907/276-7609, www.anchorage nordicski.com) is Alaska's largest cross-country association, and its website has links to the state's other Nordic skiing groups.

Dog Mushing
Dogsledding has a rich history in Alaska, and sled dog races are a major winter staple across much of the state. The most famous are the **Iditarod Trail Sled Dog Race** from Anchorage to Nome in March and the **Yukon Quest International Sled Dog Race** between Fairbanks and Whitehorse in February. A number of companies offer wintertime dogsled tours, some of which are timed to coincide with the Iditarod or Yukon Quest.

During the summer months, visitors can ride on wheeled sleds behind teams of dogs, providing a chance to get the feel of the real thing. These very popular rides—some led by Iditarod mushers—are offered in Girdwood, Fairbanks, Seward, Wasilla, and Denali. In addition, summertime dogsled tours take place on glaciers near Juneau, Skagway, and Seward. Tourists are flown up to the glacier by helicopter, and given a chance to ride along as the dogs

May
Cordova – Copper River Delta Shorebird Festival; Haines – Great Alaska Craftbeer & Homebrew Festival; Homer – Kachemak Bay Shorebird Festival; Kodiak – Crab Festival; Nome – Memorial Day Polar Bear Swim; Petersburg – Little Norway Festival

June
Anchorage – Mayor's Midnight Sun Marathon, Elmendorf Open House and Air Show, and Taste of Anchorage; Fairbanks – Midnight Sun Baseball Game and Yukon 800 Boat Race; Haines – Kluane to Chilkat International Bike Relay; Palmer – Colony Days; Sitka – Summer Music Festival

July
Kodiak – Bear Country Music Festival; Delta Junction – Deltana Fair; Eagle River – Bear Paw Festival; Fairbanks – Golden Days, World Eskimo-Indian Olympics; Girdwood – Girdwood Forest Fair; Homer – KBBI Concert on the Lawn; Seward – Mt. Marathon Race; Talkeetna – Moose Dropping Festival

August
Fairbanks – Tanana Valley Fair; Haines – Southeast Alaska State Fair; Ketchikan – Blueberry Arts Festival; Ninilchik – Kenai Peninsula State Fair; Palmer – Alaska State Fair; Seward – Silver Salmon Derby; Talkeetna – Bluegrass Festival; Valdez – Gold Rush Days

September
Kodiak – State Fair and Rodeo; Kenai, Valdez, Whittier, Wrangell – Silver Salmon Derby

October
Anchorage – Alaska Federation of Natives Convention; Sitka – Alaska Day Festival

November
Anchorage – Great Alaska Shootout; Fairbanks – Athabascan Fiddling Festival; Haines – Alaska Bald Eagle Festival; Sitka – Whalefest

December
Kodiak – Harbor Stars Boat Parade; Talkeetna – Winterfest

head across the ice and snow. It's a unique—but very expensive—experience.

Snowmobiling

Snowmobiling—or snowmachining as it's called in Alaska—is both a bush necessity in the winter and a favorite of the motorhead crowd in urban centers. The **Alaska State Snowmobile Association** (www.aksnow .org) has additional info on their website. Rentals and tours are available in Anchorage and Fairbanks.

SPECTATOR SPORTS

The **Alaska Baseball League** consists of six semi-professional teams: Mat-Su Miners, Kenai Peninsula Oilers, Fairbanks Goldpanners, Anchorage Bucs, Anchorage Glacier Pilots, and Athletes in Action. The teams include talented college players from throughout the country who come to Alaska to play in June and July. Alaska Baseball League teams play each other, along with Outside teams from the West Coast and Hawaii, with the top teams ending up at the National Baseball Congress World Series in Wichita, Kansas. Alaskan teams have won these world series many times, and quite a few famous players have spent a summer on Alaska turf, including Mark McGwire, Tom Seaver, Graig Nettles, and Dave Winfield.

Hockey is very big in Alaska, especially in Anchorage and Fairbanks where overachiever dads push their kids onto the ice by age four. The **Alaska Aces** play professional hockey in the minor-league West Coast Hockey League, and both the University of Alaska Anchorage (UAA) and the University of Alaska

Fairbanks (UAF) have nationally competitive hockey teams.

In bush Alaska, no sport is bigger than basketball, and any visitor who can play well stands a good chance of immediately being accepted by locals. There's intense competition among high school teams at the state level, and both UAA and UAF have their own basketball squads. The state's biggest basketball event is the **Great Alaska Shootout** (www.goseawolves.com/shootout) held in Anchorage each November, and featuring seven top college teams and the lowly UAA Seawolves. This one gets national media attention because it's so early in the season.

Accommodations

HOTELS AND MOTELS

Within these pages you'll find hotels and motels in all price ranges. Prices are high in Alaska, so come prepared with a high limit on your credit card. In the major package-tour stops and off-the-beaten-track places with limited lodging, what's available is often booked way in advance. Unless you've made reservations, don't count on getting any rooms, especially the good cheap ones, at most Alaskan destinations. Fortunately, bed-and-breakfasts often offer a cheaper alternative. A good overall source for Alaskan lodging places is the official *Alaska State Vacation Planner*.

Throughout this book I have typically listed only two prices for most lodging places: **single, or s (one person),** and **double, or d (two people).** Prices listed are the midsummer rates—which are the highest of the year. These prices do not include local taxes, which can sometimes reach 10 percent. Prices, of course, are not set in stone and will certainly head up over time. Always ask to see the room before deciding to stay at one of the less expensive motels, since places that I consider more than adequate may be beneath your standards.

If in doubt about where to stay, you may want to choose somewhere that gets the American Automobile Association seal of approval. The annual **AAA TourBook** (www.aaa.com) for Alaska (free to AAA members) is a helpful guide to the better hotels and motels, offering current prices and relatively accurate ratings.

Online sources are useful tools if you want to learn more about lodging options, but keep in mind that not all these user comments are accurate; sometimes one person's experience can completely skew the "ratings." **Trip Advisor** (www.tripadvisor.com) is especially helpful, and **Yahoo Travel** (www.travel.yahoo.com) can also prove useful.

The best hotel rates can often be found online through such sites as Travelocity (www.travelocity.com) and Priceline (www.priceline.com). Using Priceline, I once booked a room at the Anchorage Sheraton for $35 when the official price was $159! Of course, this was early May, when rooms are more plentiful. But even in mid-summer you can get rooms in Anchorage for half off the going rate.

BED-AND-BREAKFASTS

Bed-and-breakfasts are popular all across Alaska, and are a great way to spend time with local residents in showcase homes, save a little money on accommodations, and get breakfast thrown in for the price of a night.

The Internet is the best place to get fast B&B information. Start with the **Bed & Breakfast Association of Alaska** (www.alaskabba.com), or one of the regional groups such as **Anchorage Alaska B&B Association** (www.anchorage-bnb.com), **Alaska's Mat-Su Bed & Breakfast Association** (www.alaskabnbhosts.com), **Fairbanks Association of B&Bs** (www.ptialaska.net/~fabb), **B&B Association of Alaska INNside**

PACK THE ESSENTIALS

The following items assume that your trip to Alaska takes place in the summer months. If you plan to travel before May or after September, additional winter supplies will certainly be needed. Even if you aren't planning to do much camping or backpacking, it's always smart to carry a sleeping bag – unless your idea of roughing it is staying at local bed-and-breakfasts. In general, plan on cool and wet weather for your trip, but also throw in a pair of short pants for those warm Fairbanks days.

Even if you arrive in Alaska without the correct gear, almost anything you need is available in the larger towns, and in Anchorage the prices are really not much higher than in Lower 48 cities. In addition, the larger cities typically have at least one place that rents outdoor gear such as tents and stoves.

In addition to the items listed below, travelers to Southeast Alaska and other rainy parts of the state should bring rubber boots and heavy-duty raingear. A cell phone can be especially useful if you want to stay in contact with friends and family while traveling, but coverage varies, so check with your phone company for specifics, and make sure your service plan doesn't hit you with stiff fees for calls from or within Alaska.

Clothing Essentials
- light, water-resistant coat (Gore-Tex works well)
- sweater or windblock jacket
- lightweight gloves
- long johns
- walking shoes
- hiking boots
- hiking socks
- liner socks
- rain pants
- warm cap
- swimsuit
- sunglasses

Camping Essentials
- 50 feet of line
- camp stove and fuel bottle
- compass
- cooking pot
- day pack
- first-aid kit
- fishing tackle
- insect repellent
- internal-frame backpack
- jackknife or Leatherman (a better option)
- padlock
- plastic bags
- plate, cup, spoon, and fork
- sewing kit
- sleeping bag
- small towel
- sunscreen
- tent and ground cloth
- Thermarest pad
- water bottle
- water filter
- waterproof matches and lighter

Passage Chapter (www.accommodations-alaska.com), and **Kenai Peninsula B&B Association** (www.kenaipeninsulabba.com). Local **chamber of commerce** websites also have links to local B&Bs; find a complete listing of these at www.alaskachamber.com.

HOSTELS

Hostels offer the least expensive *indoor* lodging options in Alaska, with bunk accommodations for $20–30 per person. They're a good choice for single travelers on a budget, or anyone who wants to meet fellow travelers. Although occasionally called "youth hostels," these really are not just for high school and college folks—you'll meet adventurous people of all ages.

At last count Alaska had more than 30 places offering hostel-type accommodations, in all the major towns, along with such surprising places as Girdwood, Slana, McCarthy, and Ninilchik. Reservations are a good idea, particularly in mid-summer.

Hostellers stay in dormitory-style rooms (separate for men and women), and have access to showers, a communal kitchen, and laundry facilities. You should bring your own sleeping bag or linen (though these can be rented), and a variety of restrictions may put a crimp in things, including that the hostels generally close during the day, that no alcohol is allowed, and that many have a curfew. A room or two are typically saved for couples or small families. The **Alaska Hostel Association's** website (www.alaskahostelassociation.org) has a complete listing.

FISHING AND HUNTING LODGES

Alaska is world famous for its many wilderness fishing and hunting lodges, most of which offer multi-night packages. These can be booked through your travel agent or directly with the lodge. A few of the better-known lodges are described briefly in this book, but see the *Alaska State Vacation Planner* (www.travelalaska.com) for a more complete listing, or check the ads in *Alaska Magazine.*

HOME SWAPS

Several companies list Alaskan homeowners who are interested in a trade. If you live in Hawaii or California and want to see Fairbanks in mid-winter, your home will be a hot property. If you live in North Dakota, good luck. Companies worth investigating include **Home Exchange** (310/798-3864 or 800/877-8723, www.homeexchange.com), **Home Link** (813/975-9825 or 800/638-3841, www.swapnow.com), and **Intervac** (800/756-4663, www.intervacus.com).

CAMPING

Tent camping is cheap (or free) in most parts of Alaska, and public showers are available in nearly every town. Any self-supporting dome tent will do: they're lightweight, and a cinch to erect, they don't need to be staked into the often rocky or frozen ground, and you can sit up in them during those long inclement stretches. For peace of mind and dryness of body in those wild and woolly nights in Southeast and Southcentral, make sure the tent is as waterproof as it can be. (Even so, bring a sponge.) A Thermarest inflatable pad will put a wonderful cushion of air between you and the ground; on top of it you can sleep on gravel, rocks, dead porcupines .... If you plan to camp for extended periods or in ultra-windy places such as Southwest Alaska, get a tent that will hold up to the weather. These cost more, and are available from better outdoor stores.

In Alaska, camping is allowed on most state lands and within the national forests (except close to towns). Some national parks require a backcountry-use permit. Camping on public property within city limits, however, is prohibited.

Campgrounds and RV Parks

Generally, two distinct types of campgrounds are available. State and federal government-operated campgrounds all offer a basic outdoor experience with a minimum of facilities, usually just pit toilets and water from pumps. Private RV park/campgrounds typically offer hot showers, washers and driers, dump stations, and plug-ins. The nicest even have Wi-Fi and cable TV.

Government campgrounds are usually cheaper (rarely more than $15 nightly) than the commercial variety (typically $25–35). The showers (around $5) at the commercial sites are generally open to noncampers, and are sometimes the only place in town to rinse off. Useful RV websites are www.campgrounds-alaska.com, www.alaskacampgrounds.net, and www.karo-ent.com.

PUBLIC CABINS

For indoor sleeping in the great outdoors, check into the many wonderful Forest Service cabins in Southeast and Southcentral Alaska. At $35–45 a night, you get bunks for 4–6 people, a woodstove, firewood, a table, and an outhouse. Of the more than 180 cabins in the Tongass and Chugach National Forests, however, only a few are accessible by road or trail; the rest require flying or boating in. These cabins are very popular, and reservations are accepted up to six months in advance. Reservations for some of the most-used cabins, especially during hunting and fishing season, are determined by lottery. All Forest Service cabin reservations are made through **ReserveUSA** (518/885-3639

or 877/444-6777, www.reserveusa.com). No extra charge for cabin reservations. This website has complete details on the cabins, including photos and access info.

Other public-use cabins are available through the Alaska Division of State Parks (various parks), the Bureau of Land Management (near Fairbanks), the National Park Service (Kenai Fjords National Park and Yukon-Charley Rivers) and the U.S. Fish & Wildlife Service (Kodiak National Wildlife Refuge). They're described in appropriate sections of this book.

LIGHTHOUSES

Alaska has more than a dozen lighthouses, 10 of which are still active. Preservation groups are working to open these to the public in one form or another, including three near Juneau: Sentinel Island Lighthouse, Point Retreat Lighthouse, and Five Fingers Lighthouse. In addition, Cape Decision Lighthouse near Wrangell is being renovated, along with the very remote Cape St. Elias Lighthouse southeast of Cordova on Kayak Island. The Coast Guard in Juneau (907/463-2267) has additional information on Alaskan lighthouses, or visit www.unc.edu/~rowlett/lighthouse/ak.htm.

Food and Drink

RESTAURANTS

Alaskan restaurants vary greatly in quality, but are much improved in recent years. True, many of the coffee shops, roadhouses, and cafés still serve pretty standard fare, and sometimes it seems they use the same menu, the same ingredients, the same grill and fryolator, and the same short-order cooks. But you'll also find a few surprises along the way, and all the larger towns have standout eateries. Anchorage—perhaps because it is home to almost half of all Alaskans—has the best selection of menu options and some of the finest restaurants in Alaska. It also has a great diversity of restaurants: bustling brewpubs, steakhouses, Thai

food, fine restaurants serving gourmet Italian or seafood, and cheap taco joints. You'll also find fine meals in Juneau, Fairbanks, Haines, Homer, Ketchikan, Seward, Sitka, and Skagway, to mention but a few.

Seafood is the primary Alaskan specialty, particularly salmon, halibut, and crab. You'll find good seafood restaurants in all the coastal towns, and surprisingly even in Interior Alaska. Of course, nearly all of the larger Alaskan towns now also have at least one café or drive-through stand selling lattes and mochas. Unfortunately, in Alaska—as in the rest of the nation—the real dining-out kings are McDonald's, Burger King, Taco Bell, Domino's, and all the other fast-food outlets that are turning regional differences into a bland mediocrity of frozen burgers and whipped-shortening "milk shakes." No wonder Alaskans are becoming increasingly obese!

Standard Alaskan breakfasts and lunches cost $8–10, but dinner prices show a greater range, from $8 burgers to steak, prime rib, chicken, or seafood entrées for $18–25.

Salmon Bakes

Splurge on these once or twice. The salmon—always wild Alaskan fish—is usually fresh, thick, and delicious, and it comes with the requisite macaroni, potato, and infernal three-bean salads, carrot and celery sticks, black olives for every finger, and sourdough rolls. Blueberry cake often tops off the meal. Different bakes have different takes on second helpings, and soft drinks or lemonade are usually included, but beer and wine are extra. The one at Pioneer Park in Fairbanks is Alaska's best; the two places in Juneau are a close second, and the one at Tok is right up there.

ALCOHOL

Alcohol is readily available in the larger Alaskan cities, along with most small towns on the road network or along the Inside Passage. Because of alcoholism problems in Native communities, many of the remote bush villages have banned its sale or importation. "Dry" communities prohibit alcohol, while "damp" towns allow limited amounts for personal use only. Before flying out to any remote village, be sure to ask about the local rules.

unloading King salmon from the tender San Juan, Juneau

In the last few years breweries and brewpubs have begun to spread across Alaska, and several excellent ones are found in Anchorage. Other towns where you can buy locally made beers include Haines, Homer, Kodiak, and Wasilla. The state's most famous microbrewery is the Alaskan Brewing Company in Juneau, which produces a number of award-winning beers available both on draught and in six-packs throughout the Pacific Northwest.

RESOURCES

Suggested Reading

An excellent place to find Alaskan books is through the **Alaska Natural History Association** (907/274-8440, www.alaskanha. org). You can order several hundred nature books, maps, calendars, guides, and other titles online or through their print catalog. Another fine source for Alaskan titles is the Anchorage-based **Cook Inlet Book Company** (907/258-4544 or 800/240-4148, www.cookinlet.com).

A number of the books listed below are out of print, but you can find many of them in regional libraries, or check the Web for special orders or rare book auctions. Amazon.com, barnesandnoble.com, and other online sites will also search used bookstores for out-of-print titles. Two recommended sources for rare and out-of-print Alaskan books are Anchorage's **Title Wave Books** (907/278-9283 or 888/598-9283, www.wavebooks.com) and Juneau's **The Observatory** (907/586-9676, www.observatorybooks.com).

ART AND LITERATURE

Bancroft-Hunt, Norman. *People of the Totem: The Indians of the Pacific Northwest*. New York: Peter Bedrick Books, 1989. A beautifully illustrated history of the art of Tlingit and other Northwest peoples. Out of print.

Bodett, Tom. *As Far As You Can Go Without a Passport*. New York: Perseus Publishing, 1986. A collection of wry, bring-a-smile-to-your-face Alaska tales. Bodett's other books include *The End of the Road* and *Small Comforts*. Out of print.

Jans, Nick. *The Last Light Breaking*. Anchorage: Alaska Northwest Books, www.gacpc.com, 1993. A beautifully written collection of essays about life in the Eskimo village of Ambler.

Jans, Nick. *A Place Beyond*. Anchorage: Alaska Northwest Books, www.gacpc.com, 1996. Another fine collection of stories by one of Alaska's most observant writers.

Kizzia, Tom. *The Wake of the Unseen Object*. Lincoln, NE: University of Nebraska Press, www.nebraskapress.unl.edu, 1998. A lovingly written journey through the wild heart of today's Alaskan Bush. Filled with insights into the clashing cultures of Native and white America.

Krakauer, Jon. *Into the Wild*. New York: Random House, www.randomhouse.com, 1997. Now a Hollywood movie, this is the tale of Chris McCandless, a foolish young man whose 1992 death in the bush north of Denali certainly does not merit the attention it received. The book is loved by many Outsiders, but viewed with disdain by most Alaskans.

London, Jack. *The Call of the Wild*. This gripping tale of a sled dog's experience along the gold rush trail was Jack London's most successful rendering of the spirit of the North. Reprint editions are available from several publishers.

Lopez, Barry. *Arctic Dreams.* New York: Random House, www.randomhouse.com, 2001. A wonderful exploration of the Arctic, with a mixture of scientific information and environmental thinking. Get this book!

Lopez, Barry. *Of Wolves and Men.* New York: Scribner, www.galegroup.com/scribners, 1982. An excellent discussion of the hunter/hunted dynamic.

Marshall, Robert. *Alaska Wilderness: Exploring the Central Brooks Range.* Berkeley: University of California Press, www.uscpress.edu, 1983. A thrilling account of the author's exploration of the Central Brooks Range.

McGinniss, Joe. *Going to Extremes.* New York: Plume, 1989. One man's journey to Alaska leads him to a series of characters as diverse as the state itself. This reissue of a 1980 book, though quite dated, is still popular with travelers.

McPhee, John. *Coming into the Country.* New York: Noonday Press, 2003. Even though it was actually written in the 1970s, this remains perhaps the best portrayal of Alaskan lifestyles ever written. It's the book you'll see folks reading on the long ferry ride north.

Muir, John. *Stikeen.* Berkeley: Heyday Books, www.heydaybooks.com, 1990. Originally published almost a century ago, this classic short dog story offers a vastly different take on Glacier Bay than that seen by the cruise ship tourists.

Schooler, Lynn. *Blue Bear: A True Story of Friendship, Tragedy and Survival in the Alaskan Wilderness.* New York: Harper-Collins Publishers, www.harpercollins.com, 2002. This beautifully crafted memoir chronicles Lynn's life and how it was changed by Michio Hoshino, the renowned wildlife photographer killed by a grizzly in 1996.

Service, Robert. *Collected Poems.* New York: Putnam Publishing, www.penguinputnam.com, 1989. No one has ever better captured the flavor of northern life than the poet Robert Service.

Stewart, Hilary. *Looking at Indian Art of the Northwest Coast.* Seattle; University of Washington Press, www.washington.edu/uwpress, 2003. A concise analysis of the art forms of this powerful culture.

Stewart, Hilary. *Looking at Totem Poles.* Seattle: University of Washington Press, www.washington.edu/uwpress, 2003. Details on the history and art of more than 100 totem poles in Alaska and British Columbia.

Walker, Spike. *Working on the Edge.* New York: St. Martin's Press, www.stmartins.com, 2003. Harrowing tales from the edge of the abyss—working the king-crab boats of the Bering Sea in the boom years of the 1970s and early '80s, when the financial stakes were almost as high as the risks to life. Read it before you even consider working on a crab boat!

DESCRIPTION AND TRAVEL

Alaska Almanac. Anchorage: Alaska Northwest Books, www.gacpc.com; published annually. A rich source of useful information about the state, all in one compact volume.

Alaska Atlas & Gazetteer. Freeport, ME: DeLorme Mapping, www.delorme.com, 2004. This large book of up-to-date topographic maps is a wise investment if you plan to explore the more remote parts of Alaska. Very easy to use,

Alaska Wilderness Guide. Augusta, GA: Morris Communications, www.morris.com, 2001. A good source for general information on all of Alaska's villages and cities, as well as its many wild places.

Colby, Merle. *A Guide to Alaska.* New York: MacMillan, 1939. Written over half a century ago, this Federal Writers' Project guide to Alaska has never been surpassed. Out of print, but can be found in a good library.

Hempstead, Andrew. *Moon Western Canada.* Emeryville, CA: Avalon Travel Publishing, www.moon.com, 2007. Like this book, Andrew Hempstead's titles are part of the Moon Handbooks series. He provides excellent advice for travelers in British Columbia and the Yukon, Alaska's neighbors to the east.

Howard, Jim. *Guide to Sea Kayaking in Southeast Alaska: The Best Trips and Tours from Misty Fjords to Glacier Bay.* Old Saybrook, CT: Globe Pequot Press, www.globepequot.com, 1999. This book describes 41 Southeast Alaska kayak trips.

Jettmar, Karen. *Alaska's Glacier Bay.* Anchorage: Alaska Northwest Books, www.gacpc.com, 1997. A good little sourcebook for park information.

Jettmar, Karen. *The Alaska River Guide.* Anchorage: Alaska Northwest Books, www.gacpc.com, 1998. Filled with vital information for anyone planning to float the more than 100 rivers in Alaska.

Kelley, Mark. *Glacier Bay National Park Alaska.* Juneau: Mark Kelley Photography, www.markkelley.com, 2000. A beautiful coffee table book by Southeast Alaska's foremost photographer.

Larson, Richard. *Mountain Bike Alaska— 49 Trails in the 49th State.* Anchorage: Glacier House Publications, 1991. An outdated but reasonably complete look at mountain biking in Alaska.

The Milepost. Augusta, GA: Morris Communications, www.themilepost.com; published annually. For motorists, this publication—in existence for more than 60 years—is the best guidebook to Alaska. The highway maps and description make it a must if you're driving north. Although the information is accurate and comprehensive, specific listings of hotels, bars, and restaurants are limited to advertisers, and the ads don't exactly tell the whole story.

Moore, Terris. *Mt. McKinley: The Pioneer Climbs.* Seattle: The Mountaineers, www.mountaineers .org, 1981. An exciting history of the challenge to climb North America's highest mountain.

Nienhueser, Helen, and John Wolfe Jr. *55 Ways to the Wilderness in Southcentral Alaska.* Seattle: The Mountaineers, www.mountaineers .org, 2002. A compact trail guide, complete with maps, photos, and descriptions of the best the region has to offer.

Praetorius, Pete and Alys Culhane. *Alaska Bicycle Touring Guide.* Juneau: Denali Press, 1992. The best source for cyclists planning a trip around Alaska and the Yukon.

Quick, Daniel L. *Kenai Canoe Trails.* Anchorage: Todd Publications, 1997. A very helpful guide to canoe routes within Kenai National Wildlife Refuge.

Romano-Lax, Andromeda. *How to Rent a Public Cabin in Southcentral Alaska.* Berkeley: Wilderness Press, www.wildernesspress.com, 2003. An enjoyable and detailed guide to dozens of Forest Service and state park cabins.

Shepherd, Shane and Owen Wozniak. *50 Hikes in Alaska's Chugach State Park.* Seattle: The Mountaineers, www.mountaineers.org, 2001. An informative guide to hiking in the second-largest state park in America.

Skillman, Don. *Adventure Kayaking: Trips in Glacier Bay.* Berkeley: Wilderness Press, www.wildernesspress.com, 1998. A helpful guide to sea kayaking around Glacier Bay.

Wayburn, Peggy. *Adventuring in Alaska.* San Francisco: Sierra Club Books, www.sierraclub .org/books, 1998. A guide to the remote wilderness regions of Alaska and how to get there.

HISTORY

Adney, Tappan. *Klondike Stampede.* Vancouver: University of British Columbia Press, www.ubcpress.ubc.ca, 1995. The best and most readable book on Alaska's gold rush.

Berton, Pierre. *The Klondike Fever.* New York: Carroll & Graf, www.carrollandgraf.com, 2003. Originally published in 1958, this remains the definitive account of the gold rush.

Chevigny, Hector. *Lord of Alaska.* Portland, OR: Binford & Mort, 1971. Biography of Alexander Baranof, manager of the Russian American Company from 1791 to 1817. Out of print.

Cohen, Stan. *The Forgotten War.* Missoula, MT: Pictorial Histories Publishing Co., 1993. A pictorial history of World War II in Alaska and northwestern Canada.

Greiner, James. *Wager with the Wind: The Don Sheldon Story.* New York: St. Martin's Press, www.stmartins.com, 1982. The true story of one of the state's most famous bush pilots.

Heller, Herbert L. *Sourdough Sagas.* Cleveland: World Publishing Co., 1967. Colorful tales of mishap and adventure among Alaska's prospecting pioneers. Out of print.

Morgan, Murray. *One Man's Gold Rush: A Klondike Album.* Seattle: University of Washington Press, www.washington.edu/uwpress, 1995. A feast of gold-rush photography.

Muir, John. *Travels in Alaska.* Written in 1915, this is Muir's classic narration of his experiences on the Stikine River and at Glacier Bay during 1879, 1880, and 1890. Several publishers offer reprints.

Neufeld, David and Frank Norris. *Chilkoot Trail, Heritage Route to the Klondike.* Whitehorse, Yukon: Lost Moose Publishing, 1996. A fascinating book about the gold rush, filled with black-and-white photos.

Okun, S.B. *The Russian-American Company.* Cambridge: Harvard University Press, 1951. This translation from the Russian gives a different view of Alaska in the period up to 1867. Out of print.

Oman, Lela Kiana. *The Epic of Qayaq: The Longest Story Ever Told by My People.* Seattle: University of Washington Press, www.washington.edu/uwpress, 1995. The story of the Inupiat people of the Kobuk Valley as told in stories passed down though the generations. Beautifully illustrated. The author is a respected elder in Nome.

Sherwood, Morgan B. *Exploration of Alaska, 1865–1900.* Fairbanks: University of Alaska Press, www.uaf.edu/uapress, 1992. This reprint of the 1965 book details the opening of the Interior.

Wilson, Graham and Clelie Rich (editors). *The Klondike Gold Rush: Photographs from 1896–1899.* Whitehorse, Yukon: Wolf Creek Books, 2003. An excellent collection of historical photos from the Klondike gold rush.

NATURAL HISTORY

Hulten, Eric. *Flora of Alaska and Neighboring Territories.* Stanford: Stanford University Press, www.sup.org, 1968. A huge manual of the vascular plants—highly technical, but easy to consult.

Matsen, Brad. *Ray Troll's Shocking Fish Tales.* Anchorage: Alaska Northwest Books, www.gacpc.com, 1993. Illustrated by Ray Troll, outrageous fish artist par excellence, this book offers a mix of scientific and philosophic ramblings about creatures of the sea. Great fun.

Murie, Adolph. *A Naturalist in Alaska.* Tucson: University of Arizona Press, www.uapress.arizona.edu, 1990. This reprint of a 1961 classic still offers excellent insight into the fauna of Alaska.

Murie, Adolph. *The Wolves of Mount McKinley.* Seattle: University of Washington Press, www.washington.edu/uwpress, 1985. Another Murie classic, originally published in 1944.

O'Clair, Rita M., Robert H. Armstrong, and

Richard Carstensen. *The Nature of Southeast Alaska.* Anchorage: Alaska Northwest Books, www.gacpc.com, 2003. See the world through the naturalists' eyes in this beautifully illustrated guide to the lives of animals and plants in Southeast Alaska.

Sydeman, Michelle and Annabel Lund. *Alaska Wildlife Viewing Guide.* Old Saybrook, CT: Globe Pequot Press, www.globcpequot .com, 1996. A small, helpful guide to the state's animals.

Walker, Tom. *River of Bears.* Stillwater, Minnesota: Voyageur Press, 1993. The story of McNeil River and the bears that have made it a favorite of photographers. Photos by Larry Aumiller, the Fish and Game employee who guides hundreds of visitors here each summer. Out of print.

Wynne, Kate. *Guide to Marine Mammals of Alaska.* Fairbanks: University of Alaska, 1997. An outstanding, easy-to-use guide to the whales, seals, porpoises, sea lions, and other sea mammals around Alaska. Perfect for anyone riding the ferry boats or heading out on a wildlife tour. Out of print.

Internet Resources

The Internet is a great source of information on Alaska. The following is a tiny sample; a quick Google search will turn up a multitude of additional websites for your area of interest.

Alaska.com
www.alaska.com
This website is a great resource, with tons of links. It's operated by the *Anchorage Daily News,* whose website (www.adn.com) has current Alaska news, fishing info, and much more, including a trivia page with all sorts of useless factoids.

Alaska Chambers of Commerce
www.alaskachamber.com
Links to all Alaskan chambers of commerce are featured here.

Alaska Climate Research Center
http://climate.gi.alaska.edu
This site includes climatic data, current weather conditions, and Alaskan forecasts.

Alaska Department of Fish and Game
www.wildlife.alaska.gov
The Alaska Department of Fish & Game's site is a good starting place for details on sport fishing and wildlife viewing around Alaska.

Alaska Department of Natural Resources
www.alaskastateparks.org
Find details on Alaska's state parks and recreation areas on this useful site.

Alaska Ecotourism
www.alaskaecotourism.org
Operated by the Alaska Wilderness Recreation and Tourism Association, this site provides links to more than 300 wilderness travel businesses.

Alaska Marine Highway
www.ferryalaska.com
Visit this website for current Alaska Marine Highway ferry schedules and fares.

Alaska Road Traveler Information Service
http://511.alaska.gov
Especially useful for winter travel in Alaska, this site has details on road conditions, ferry arrival times, highway construction updates, and more. Get the same info by dialing 511 toll-free anywhere in Alaska.

Alaska Travel Industry Association
www.travelalaska.com
This is the homepage of the Alaska Travel

Industry Association, which distributes the official Alaska State Vacation Planner.

Alaska Wilderness Recreation & Tourism Organization
www.awrta.org
Find a complete listing of Alaskan environmental groups here, with links to their homepages.

Bureau of Land Management
www.ak.blm.gov
Alaska's largest land management agency, the Bureau of Land Management has over 90 million acres in the state, including popular recreation areas near Fairbanks.

Community Advocacy
www.dced.state.ak.us/dca
The Alaska Community Database offers trivia on 350 cities and towns around the state. Maps and photos are also featured.

Don Pitcher
www.donpitcher.com and www.explorealaska.info
Don Pitcher's websites provide links to all the homepages found in this book. You can quickly connect to websites for hundreds of chambers of commerce offices, regional sights, governmental agencies, lodging places, restaurants, campgrounds, adventure travel companies, and much more. Or you can just see the author's latest photos.

Geophysical Institute
www.gedds.alaska.edu/auroraforecast
Head here for the current northern lights activity in Alaska, with predictions up to four weeks out.

National Park Service
www.nps.gov/aplic and www.nps.gov/akso
Four Alaska Public Lands Information Centers are scattered around the state; this is their homepage, which offers an overview of federal lands in Alaska. The National Park Service's Alaska homepage has details on Denali, Glacier Bay, Wrangell–St. Elias, Katmai, and 11 other national parks in Alaska.

National Weather Service
www.arh.noaa.gov
The National Weather Service site features up-to-date forecasts for Alaska.

ReserveUSA
www.reserveusa.com
A private company, ReserveUSA, books all Forest Service cabins in Alaska, plus a handful of campgrounds around the state.

State Of Alaska
www.state.ak.us
This is the State of Alaska homepage, with links to state agencies and tourism sites.

U.S. Fish & Wildlife Service
http://alaska.fws.gov
Head here for details on the U.S. Fish & Wildlife Service, which manages 16 refuges across the state, including Kodiak National Wildlife Refuge and Arctic National Wildlife Refuge.

U.S. Forest Service
www.fs.fed.us/r10
The U.S. Forest Service homepage for Alaska covers the nation's two largest national forests: Tongass and Chugach.

U.S. Geological Survey
www.usgs.gov
The U.S. Geological Survey website has downloadable topographic maps for Alaska and elsewhere.

U.S. Government Official Web Portal
www.firstgov.com
The federal government's primary Web portal offers links to all of its various agencies.

Index

CANOEING/KAYAKING

HIKING

WILDLIFE-VIEWING

XYZ

Acknowledgments

Now in its ninth edition, *Moon Alaska* began more than two decades ago as a little guide for backpackers, but has grown into a comprehensive source for travelers heading to the Great Land. It would be impossible to thank all the people who helped me with this update, but the following individuals deserve commendation.

A heartfelt thank you goes to the following people who opened doors to their hometowns, provided services, or reviewed my manuscript: Jim Collins at Allen Marine Tours, Pam Foreman at the Kodiak Island Convention & Visitors Bureau, Kori Goertz at the White Pass & Yukon Route, Karan Hautman at the Fairbanks Convention & Visitors Bureau, Lorraine Jallen at the Mat-Su Convention & Visitors Bureau, Sheila Keefe at the Talkeetna Visitor Center, Joy Landaluce at The Evelyn Cottage in Cordova, Neal J. Laugman at the Healy Chamber of Commerce, Wilma Leslie at Alaska Waters in Wrangell, John Michener at the Sitka Convention and Visitors Bureau, Martin Moe at the Cordova Chamber of Commerce, Kathryn "Ryn" Schneider at Alaska Island Hostel, Steve Webber at Adventure Bound Alaska in Juneau, Patti Mackey and Leslie Chapel at the Ketchikan Visitors Bureau, Shelley A. McCool at the Westmark Fairbanks Hotel, Kyan Reeve at the New York Hotel in Ketchikan, Jason Wettstein at the Alaska SeaLife Center in Seward, Kristin L. Wilkinson at the Skagway Convention and Visitors Bureau, Rick Winther at the Alaska Salmon Bake in Fairbanks, and Joanne Wiita at Alaska Cruises in Juneau.

Thanks also to the following people for their emailed comments: Audie Bakewell, Susan Boero, Brigid Dodge, Dennis E. Hojna, Mindy Hunter, Valerie Jensen, Hugh Kavanagh, Mike Mathews, Margaret McCann, Mark J. Novitski, Virginia Richardson, Joan C. Risley, Linda Sikorowski, and Gaia Thurston-Shaine. I wish to especially thank Elizabeth Dahl for her assistance in Juneau—from transportation to lodging to editing and Eric Pullman for his help with the Fairbanks update.

This book was shepherded through the production process by my editor, Sabrina Young. Thanks to her and the rest of the gang at Avalon Travel Publishing for getting this book into your hands.

I offer a very special thanks to my sweet wife, Karen Shemet, and our two live-wire children, Aziza and Rio, for keeping my priorities straight and adding a bit of levity.

www.moon.com

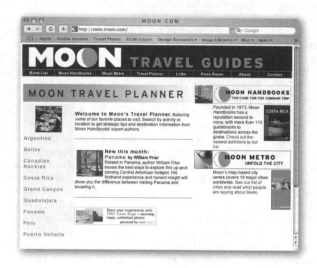

For helpful advice on planning a trip, visit www.moon.com for the **TRAVEL PLANNER** and get access to useful travel strategies and valuable information about great places to visit. When you travel with Moon, expect an experience that is uncommon and truly unique.

HANDBOOKS | METRO | OUTDOORS | LIVING ABROAD

MAP SYMBOLS

▭▭▭ Expressway	🄲 Highlight	✗ Airfield	🏌 Golf Course
▭▭▭ Primary Road	○ City/Town	✗ Airport	🅿 Parking Area
▭▭▭ Secondary Road	◉ State Capital	▲ Mountain	⛩ Archaeological Site
▬ ▬ ▬ Unpaved Road	⊛ National Capital	✛ Unique Natural Feature	⛪ Church
- - - - Trail	★ Point of Interest		⛽ Gas Station
·········· Ferry	• Accommodation	🗻 Waterfall	Glacier
▬-▬-▬ Railroad	▼ Restaurant/Bar	♠ Park	Mangrove
▭▭▭ Pedestrian Walkway	■ Other Location	� Trailhead	Reef
▥▥▥ Stairs	Λ Campground	⛷ Skiing Area	Swamp

CONVERSION TABLES

°C = (°F – 32) / 1.8
°F = (°C x 1.8) + 32
1 inch = 2.54 centimeters (cm)
1 foot = 0.304 meters (m)
1 yard = 0.914 meters
1 mile = 1.6093 kilometers (km)
1 km = 0.6214 miles
1 fathom = 1.8288 m
1 chain = 20.1168 m
1 furlong = 201.168 m
1 acre = 0.4047 hectares
1 sq km = 100 hectares
1 sq mile = 2.59 square km
1 ounce = 28.35 grams
1 pound = 0.4536 kilograms
1 short ton = 0.90718 metric ton
1 short ton = 2,000 pounds
1 long ton = 1.016 metric tons
1 long ton = 2,240 pounds
1 metric ton = 1,000 kilograms
1 quart = 0.94635 liters
1 US gallon = 3.7854 liters
1 Imperial gallon = 4.5459 liters
1 nautical mile = 1.852 km

Clock face with 24-hour conversion markings.

Thermometer with Fahrenheit and Celsius scales. WATER BOILS at 100°C / 212°F. WATER FREEZES at 0°C / 32°F.

Ruler showing INCH (0–4) and CM (0–10) scales.

MOON ALASKA

Avalon Travel Publishing
An Imprint of
Avalon Publishing Group, Inc.

AVALON
publishing group incorporated

1400 65th Street, Suite 250
Emeryville, CA 94608, USA
www.moon.com

Editor: Sabrina Young
Series Manager: Kathryn Ettinger
Acquisitions Manager: Rebecca K. Browning
Copy Editor: Kate McKinley
Graphics Coordinator: Elizabeth Jang
Production Coordinator: Tabitha Lahr
Map Editor: Albert Angulo
Cartographers: Aaron Dorden, Kat Bennett
Proofreader: Valerie Sellers Blanton
Indexer: Emily Lunceford

ISBN-10: 1-56691-929-0
ISBN-13: 1-56691-929-6
ISSN: 1547-0261

Printing History
1st Edition – 1983
9th Edition – April 2007
5 4 3 2 1

Text © 2007 by Don Pitcher
Maps © 2007 by Avalon Travel Publishing, Inc.
All rights reserved.

Some photos and illustrations are used by permission
and are the property of the original copyright owners.

Front cover photo: Bald eagle on a windy day, Homer,
Alaska © Don Pitcher
Title page photo: Eldred Rock Lighthouse, Lynn Canal
south of Haines, Alaska © Don Pitcher

Printed in USA by Malloy

KEEPING CURRENT

If you have a favorite gem you'd like to see included in the next edition, or see anything
that needs updating, clarification, or correction, please drop us a line. Send your
comments via email to feedback@moon.com, or use the address above.